RPG
A Programming Language for Today

Doris Cable

Ventura College

Wm. C. Brown Publishers

Dubuque, Iowa • Melbourne, Australia • Oxford, England

Book Team

Editor *Earl McPeek*
Developmental Editor *Linda M. Meehan*
Publishing Services Coordinator (Production) *Julie A. Kennedy*
Publishing Services Coordinator (Design) *Barbara J. Hodgson*

Wm. C. Brown Publishers
A Division of Wm. C. Brown Communications, Inc.

Vice President and General Manager *George Bergquist*
National Sales Manager *Vincent R. Di Blasi*
Assistant Vice President, Editor-in-Chief *Edward G. Jaffe*
Marketing Manager *Elizabeth Robbins*
Advertising Manager *Amy Schmitz*

Managing Editor, Production *Colleen A. Yonda*
Manager of Visuals and Design *Faye M. Schilling*
Publishing Services Manager *Karen J. Slaght*
Permissions/Records Manager *Connie Allendorf*

Wm. C. Brown Communications, Inc.

Chairman Emeritus *Wm. C. Brown*
Chairman and Chief Executive Officer *Mark C. Falb*
President and Chief Operating Officer *G. Franklin Lewis*
Corporate Vice President, Operations *Beverly Kolz*
Corporate Vice President, President of WCB Manufacturing *Roger Meyer*

Cover and section images by COMSTOCK Inc./Michael Stuckey

Copyediting and Production by *Lachina Publishing Services, Inc.*

Copyright © 1993 by Doris Cable. All rights reserved

Library of Congress Catalog Card Number: 92–70065

ISBN 0–697–11475–9

Forms reprinted by permission from International Business Machines Corporation.

No part of this publication may be reproduced, stored in a retrieval system, or transmitted, in any form or by any means, electronic, mechanical, photocopying, recording, or otherwise, without the prior written permission of the publisher.

Printed in the United States of America by Wm. C. Brown Communications, Inc., 2460 Kerper Boulevard, Dubuque, IA 52001

10 9 8 7 6 5 4 3 2 1

Contents

Preface vii

Introduction to RPG and Programming ix

SECTION 1
RPG II

1
Input and Output Processing 3

Program Processing Steps 4
RPG Coding Formats 6
Common Entries on Coding Forms 8
The Control Specifications Form (Header Format or H Specification) 8
The File Description Specifications Form (F Specification) 9
Defining the Input File 9 / File Type/File Designation Entries 10 / File Format 10 / Record Length 10 / Device 10 / Defining the Output File 11
The Input Specifications Form (I Specification) 11
Form Type/Filename Entries 11 / Sequence Number Option Entries (Columns 15–16) 12 / Record Identifying Indicator Entry (Columns 19–20) 12 / From–To Entries 13 / Field Location Entries (Columns 44–47 and 48–51) 13 / Field Name Entries (Columns 53–58) 13
The Output Specifications Form (O Specification) 14
Filename Entry (Columns 7–14) 14 / Type Entry (Column 15) 14 / Space Entry (Columns 17–18) 14 / Output Indicators (Columns 24–25, 27–28, or 30–31) 14 / Field Name (Columns 32–37) 14 / End Position (Columns 40–43) 15
The RPG Fixed Logic Cycle 15
Incorporating Comments Within a Program 17
Why Document? 17 / How Much Documentation Is Enough? 18 / How Do You Put Comments into an RPG Program? 18 / Conventions for Professional Program Documentation 19
Compiling a Program 20
Summary 23
Review Questions 24
Exercises 24
DEBUGGING EXERCISES 25
PROGRAMMING PROJECT 28

2
Arithmetic Operations and Report Formatting 29

General Rules for Coding Calculation Specifications 29
Addition 30 / Subtraction 31 / Multiplication 31 / Division 32 / Division Remainders 32 / Rounding a Result Field (Half-adjusting) 33 / Defining a Constant 34 / Calculating Cumulative Totals 35 / Summary of Arithmetic Functions in RPG 35
Sample Program Using Arithmetic Calculations 36
Input Data 36 / Output Data 36 / File Description Specifications 37 / Input Specifications 37 / Calculation Specifications 38 / Output Specifications 40 / Field Editing (Edit Codes) 42 / Other Edit Codes 44 / Editing Dollar Signs 44 / Printing Total Lines 45
Summary 46
Review Questions 47
Exercises 47
DEBUGGING EXERCISES 48
PROGRAMMING PROJECT 52

3
Computer Logic and Processing Multiple Record Types 54

Fundamental Logic Concepts (Compare) 54
Using Indicators in RPG 55
The Compare Operation 56
Comparing Alphabetic or Alphanumeric Data Fields 56 / Comparing Alphabetic or Alphanumeric Fields of Different Lengths 57 / Comparing Numeric Data Fields 57 / Comparing Numeric Fields of Different Lengths 59 / Collating Sequence for Comparing 61 / Comparing Literal Values 61 / Summary of the Compare Operation 62
Processing Multiple Record Types 62
Use of Input Indicators 62 / Field Record Relation Indicators 64 / Calculation Specifications 66
Branching Within Calculations 67
Using the GOTO Operation 67 / Using Subroutines 68 / GOTOs Revisited 69
Summary 70
Review Questions 71
Exercises 71
DEBUGGING EXERCISES 72
PROGRAMMING PROJECT 77

4
Control Breaks (The RPG Cycle) 79

Sample Program Using Level Breaks 79
Sequence of Input Data 79 / Level Break Totals 80 / Control Level Indicators 80
The Effect of the RPG Cycle on Level Breaks 85
Summary Reports 87
Summarized Output Files 87
Multiple Output Files 89
Summary 90
Review Questions 91
Exercises 91
DEBUGGING EXERCISES 92
PROGRAMMING PROJECT 96

5
Multiple Level Breaks 98

Sample Program Using Multiple Level Breaks 98
- *Input Specifications 98 / Calculation Specifications 100 / Output Specifications 103*

The RPG Cycle Revisited 103
- *Group Indication 104 / Zeroing Out a Total Field 107*

Standards for Report Formatting 110
- *Report Headings 110 / Report Totals 112*

Sample Program Defining Report Headings 112
- *Report Identification 112 / Report Title 112 / Page Number 113 / System Date and Edit Codes 113 / System Time and Edit Words 114 / Summary of Report Formatting 115*

Summary 115
Review Questions 116
Exercises 116
DEBUGGING EXERCISES 117
PROGRAMMING PROJECT 122

6
Exception Output Processing 124

Sample Program Using Exception Output Processing 125
- *File Description and Input Specifications 125 / Calculation Specifications (Program Loops) 126 / Output Specifications 128*

Page Overflow 128
- *Fetch Overflow 129 / Sample Program 130 / Internal Control (Line Counting) 134*

Moving Data (MOVE and MOVEL) 135
- *Moving Fields of Different Lengths with MOVE 136 / Moving Fields of Different Lengths with MOVEL 136 / Alphanumeric/Numeric MOVE or MOVEL 138 / Moving Literal Values 138 / Initializing a Field to Blanks 139*

Summary 140
Review Questions 141
Exercises 141
DEBUGGING EXERCISES 142
PROGRAMMING PROJECT 146

7
Table Processing 148

Types of Table Applications 148
Benefits of Table Processing 149
Extension Specifications 151
Table File Formats 151
Types of Tables (Internal and External) 151
Internal (Compile Time) Table Entries 151
Sample Program 1 Using Internal or Compile Time Tables 152
- *File Extension Specifications 152 / Record Layout 154 / Compiling Table Information 155 / Calculation Specifications for Processing Table Data 156*

External (Pre-Execution Time) Table Entries 156
Sample Program 2 Using an External or Pre-Execution Time Table 158
- *File Description Specifications 160 / Extension Specifications 161 / Record Layout 161 / Input Specifications 161 / Calculation Specifications 162 / Output Specifications 162 / Table Data File Maintenance 162*

The Time at Which Table Data Is Available 163
Avoiding Common Errors 163
Alternating Tables 164
Sample Program 3 Using Alternating Table Data 164
- *Input Specifications 164 / Calculation Specifications 164 / Output Specifications 166 / Multiple Tables 166 / Printing a Table 166*

Summary 167
Review Questions 168
Exercises 168
DEBUGGING EXERCISES 169
PROGRAMMING PROJECT 174

8
Array Processing 176

Rules for Constructing Arrays 176
Examples of Arrays 177
Extension Specifications for Arrays 177
How an Array Is Loaded 177
- *Compile Time Arrays 177 / Pre-Execution Time Arrays 179 / Execution Time Arrays 180*

Array Processing 181
- *Accessing an Entire Array 181 / Accessing Individual Elements of an Array 181*

Sample Program 1 Using Three Types of Array 182
- *The Compile Time Array 183 / Printing the Entire Array 184 / Pre-Execution Time Array 184 / Execution Time Array 184*

Sample Program 2 Showing Other Uses of Arrays 190
- *Compile Time Array 191 / Execution Time Arrays 191 / Calculation Specifications 192 / Using an Array Index 193 / Computed Index Using Exception Output 193 / Accessing an Array by Index (Looping) 193*

Sample Program 3 Using LOKUP with an Array 197
- *Special Operations for Array Data 201*

Sample Program 4 Using XFOOT 203
Sample Program 5 Using MOVEA 205
Summary 208
Review Questions 209
Exercises 209
DEBUGGING EXERCISES 210
PROGRAMMING PROJECT 215

9
Processing Multiple Sequential Files 217

Types of Files 217
- *Master Files 218 / Transaction Files 218 / Table Files 218 / History Files 219 / Backup Files 219*

Tape Media 220
- *Sequential File Processing 220 / Record Blocking 221 / Processing a Master File 223*

Method for Updating Sequential Files 223
- *Transaction Types 224 / Matching Record Logic 224*

Sample Program Using Sequential File Processing 225
- *Record Layouts 225 / File Description Specifications 226 / Input Specifications 227 / Sequence Checking 228 / Matching Record Indicator (MR) 228 / Output Specifications 229*

Packed Decimal Data 231
- *Reading and Writing Numeric Fields in Packed Decimal Format 232*

Summary 233
Review Questions 234

Exercises 234
DEBUGGING EXERCISES 235
PROGRAMMING PROJECT 240

10
Multiple File Processing (Indexed Files) 242

Direct Access Storage Devices (DASDs) 242
Disk Access Concepts 243 / File Organization on DASDs 244

Sample Program 1 Creating an Indexed File 246
File Formats 246 / File Description Specifications 247 / Input Specifications 247 / Output Specifications 248 / Inquiry Programs 249

Sample Program 2 Using Inquiry Programs 250
Chaining to an Indexed File 250 / Printed Output from an Indexed File 251 / File Maintenance (Data Updating) 252 / Reorganizing a File 253

Sample Program 3 Updating an Indexed File 253

Sample Program 4 Demonstrating Sequential Retrieval from an Indexed File 258

Record Address Files 258
Summary 261
Review Questions 262
Exercises 262
DEBUGGING EXERCISES 263
PROGRAMMING PROJECT 267

11
Additional Subjects 269

Line Counter Specifications 269
Binary Data 270
Editing Data Operations 272
Move Zone 272 / Test Zone 272 / Test Numeric 273
Reversing a Sign 274
Testing the Value of a Bit 274
Special Indicators 276
Halt Indicators 276 / External Switches 276
Indicators—A Review 279
Record Identification Indicators 279 / Field Record Relationship Indicators 279 / Resulting Indicators 279 / Overflow Indicators 279 / Level Break Indicators 279 / Matching Record Indicators 279 / Last Record Indicator 280 / Halt Indicators 280 / External Indicators (Switches) 280 / Even More Indicators 280
External Subroutines 280
Look-Ahead Feature 282
FORCE Operation 283
READ Operation 284
Debugging Methods 284
DSPLY Operation 286
Accessing Multiple Indexed Files 287
Naming Conventions 289
Program and File Names 289 / Field Names 290
Summary 290
Review Questions 291
DEBUGGING EXERCISES 292

SECTION II
RPG III/RPG 400

An Introduction to RPG III/RPG 400 299

12
Overview of RPG III/400 File Concepts 301

Introduction to RPG III/400 File Concepts 301
Benefits of Externally Defined Files 302
Programmer Productivity 302 / Standardized Naming Conventions 302 / File Changes Made Easier 303 / Automatic Documentation 303
The Data Description Specification (DDS) 303
Using Externally Defined Files 305
File Description Specifications 305 / Input Specifications 306
Explanation of Physical/Logical Files 306
Physical Files 306 / Logical Files 306 / Unique Keys in a File 308 / Multiple Indexes 309
File Format Names for Data File Descriptions 309
File Format Names for Display File Descriptions 311
File Members 311
Summary of File Organization 313
Redefinition of Fields 313
Data Structures 314
Summary 316
Review Questions 317
DEBUGGING EXERCISES 318
PROGRAMMING PROJECT 321

13
Calculation Enhancements in RPG III/400 323

Reserved Words for RPG III/400 324
Arithmetic Operations in RPG III/400 324
Structured Programming Concepts for RPG III/400 325
Structured Selection (If...Then...Else) 325 / Structured Iteration (DO Loops) 330 / Difference Between a Do While and a Do Until 332 / Use of Indicators with DOxxx 333 / Compare and Branch Operation (CABxx) 334 / Case Structure (CASxx) 334 / New Methods for Using Indicators (Setting Flags) 336 / Calling a Program from Within an RPG III/400 Program 336 / Defining Field Attributes in RPG III/400 338
Summary 340
Review Questions 341
DEBUGGING EXERCISES 342
PROGRAMMING PROJECT 347

14
File Management Techniques in RPG III/400 349

Full Functional File Processing 349
Reading a Sequential File Using SETLL and READ Operations 350
Defining a File Key in RPG III/400 (KLIST and KFLD) 351
New Methods for Accessing Files and Retrieving Records 353
Using SETLL and READ Operations (with a Key) 353 / Using SETGT and READP Operations 354 / Using SETLL and READE Operations 355 / Differences Between CHAIN and READ Operations 355
Creating Your Own Processing Cycle 356
Exception Output Labels 356

Level Breaks in RPG III/400   358
Use of Multiple Indexes   362
   *Renaming Formats   364 /
   Renaming Fields   365*
Dynamic Open and Close of Files
(OPEN/CLOSE)   365
Updating a File Using Exception
Updating   365
Updating Records in a File (UPDAT
Operation)   367
Adding Records to a File (Write
Operation)   367
Deleting Records from a File
(DELET Operation)   368
Summary   369
Review Questions   370
DEBUGGING EXERCISES   371
PROGRAMMING PROJECT   376

15
On-Line Inquiries Using RPG III/400   378

Differences Between Batch and
On-Line Processing   378
Planning the Format for the
Screen   379
On-Line Processing Concepts   380
Describing Display Files   380
Creating the Screen Design   381
   *DDS—Data Description
   Specifications   381 /
   SDA—Screen Design Aid   381 /
   SQL—Structured Query Language
   381*
Coding the Data Description
Specification   381
Programming for Interactive
Applications   383
Accessing the Screen File in the
RPG Program (EXFMT)   384
How to Use Debug in RPG
III/400   388
Summary   389
Review Questions   390
DEBUGGING EXERCISES   391
PROGRAMMING PROJECT   397

16
On-Line Updates Using RPG III/400   400

Creating the Screen Design   400
On-Screen Data Editing   404
Coding the Data Description
Specification   404
   *Key Words (DDS)   405 /
   Command Keys (Function Keys)
   410*
Sample Program Showing
Programming for On-Line File
Update   412
   *Describing the Screen Format
   414 / Accessing the Screen File
   in the RPG Program   416*
Defining Multiple Screen Formats
425
WRITE/READ Operations   429
Summary   432
Review Questions   433
DEBUGGING EXERCISES   434
PROGRAMMING PROJECT   443

17
Using Subfiles in RPG III/400   446

Sample Inquiry Program Using
Subfiles   447
   *Defining a Subfile in the DDS
   448 / Subfile Key Words   448 /
   Describing the Subfile in RPG
   III/400   450 / Loading the
   Subfile with Data   451 / Clearing
   the Subfile   452 / Displaying the
   Subfile   454 / File Updates Using
   Subfiles (READC)   456*
Managing Subfiles   458
   *Subfile Key Words   458 /
   Determining Subfile Size and
   Subfile Page Size   459*
Accessing Specific Records in a
Subfile   459
Using Multiple Subfiles   460
Exiting to Other Screens or
Programs   461
Summary   464
Review Questions   465
DEBUGGING EXERCISES   466
PROGRAMMING PROJECT   472

18
Programming Efficiencies in RPG III/400   475

File Sequence   475
   *Physical Files (Sorted)   476 /
   Logical Files (Permanent or
   Temporary)   476 / Joined Files
   477 / Open Query File
   (OPNQRYF)   479 / Array Sorts
   479 / Summarized Data   480*
File Design   480
Special Data Structures   483
   *Data Areas   483 / Multiple
   Occurrence Data Structure   484 /
   File Information Data Structure
   (INFDS)   485 / Program Status
   Data Structure   485*
Structured Programming Methods
488
Tools for the Superprogrammer
491
Summary   493
Review Questions   494
PROGRAMMING PROJECT   495

Appendix A   Chart of Collating
Sequences   497

Appendix B   Summary of
Calculation Operation Codes   498

Appendix C   Card Processing
Anomalies   500

Appendix D   Physical File
Descriptions for Files Available
on Diskette   502

Index   505

Preface

This book is a text and learning guide for students for whom RPG will be a first introduction to programming languages. It is also a guide for the experienced programmer who wishes to add a useful tool to his or her knowledge base. The book will guide the reader through the differences between RPG II and RPG III. Finally, the book provides exercises and projects together with sample data to provide a sound basis for learning the language.

RPG II is available on a wide variety of minicomputers as well as mainframes and even personal computers. The fundamental concepts presented in this book apply equally to all forms of RPG, regardless of the hardware on which it will be run. The specific orientation will be toward RPG as it is run on IBM minicomputer hardware, but in general RPG II differs very little when used on different computer hardware.

The material on RPG III, however, is hardware-specific. RPG III, in its most complete form, is available only on the IBM System/38 and on the IBM AS/400. Some of the basic tools of RPG III, however, are available on the IBM System/36 and other hardware.

This book does not attempt to be all things to all people. It is not a general overview of computer programming languages. It is specific to the RPG language and its uses in a business environment.

OBJECTIVES FOR THIS BOOK ■

This book was written to help the student learn RPG II, RPG III, and RPG/400. All three versions of the language are based on similar concepts and methods. Combining discussion of the three versions of RPG into one text makes it possible to demonstrate their differences and similarities.

The book is divided into two sections. The first section (Chapters 1–11) covers all the fundamental concepts of RPG II and is intended for the first-time programming student. It assumes no prior background in programming.

The second section (Chapters 12–18) is dedicated entirely to RPG III/400 and assumes a knowledge of the fundamentals of RPG II coding. It offers a modern approach to programming with the use of externally defined files and structured programming methods. This is one of the few texts available today that provides complete coverage of RPG III/400.

Besides the usual textbook rules of programming in RPG, there are many unwritten conventions used on a day-to-day basis by professional RPG programmers. These conventions are not required by any computer hardware or by any compiler. They are standards that are generally used across industry that make the programmer's job easier and are only learned on the job. They represent methods that programmers have discovered (sometimes the hard way) to be easier to implement, more user friendly, or more universally understood. These programming standards and conventions are included in this book so that the student can enter the working world with more than just the programming theory found in the manuals.

OVERVIEW ■

This book is intended for the first-time programming student. The fundamental concepts are described in detail using a building-block approach. Each chapter presents a different type of problem that can be solved using the programming technique introduced in that chapter. Each chapter reinforces skills learned in earlier chapters. The student will be able to write a complete RPG program after completion of the first chapter. On completing the first section of the book, the student will be able to code programs proficiently in RPG II.

Each chapter begins with an outline listing the main topics to be covered in the chapter. At the end of each chapter, all new information is reviewed in a chapter summary. This summary lists new RPG rules, terms, and features. Students will find the summary useful when studying for tests.

Following the summary in each chapter are review questions. These questions relate to the chapter material and include fill-in answers which can provide a good basis to promote class discussion. These review questions also allow the student to review and study the concepts learned.

Program Debugging Exercises at the end of each chapter provide a means for the student to discover typical programming errors. Students are asked to find the errors, give possible explanations for their occurrence, and offer a solution. These projects may be assigned for outside study and are excellent for class discussion. Students who complete these exercises should be able to avoid making the same types of errors in their own programs. Program debugging is a skill that students will find useful in their future programming careers.

Provided at the end of each chapter is a programming project that allows the student to obtain "hands-on" experience with solving typical programming problems. These projects include such business applications as sales reports, employee lists, and inventory reports. Additional projects are provided in the Instructor's Manual.

Students are given an overview of the project, the input format, processing specifications, and the output format. The data for each program is included in Appendix D and is available on diskette. The appendixes also contain additional information concerning RPG programming.

SUPPLEMENTS ■

Adopters of *RPG: A Programming Language for Today* receive an Instructor's Manual that will provide insights into the material covered in each chapter. The manual contains chapter outlines, teaching tips, more detailed descriptions of some of the more difficult concepts, answers to the Review Questions, and solutions to the Debugging Exercises and Programming Projects.

A test bank will be provided containing approximately 25 questions per chapter. These test questions are also available in computerized format, on Wm. C. Brown's TestPak 3.0. TestPak is a computerized testing service that provides you with a call-in/mail-in testing program and the complete test item file on diskette for use with your IBM PC. In addition to random test generation, TestPak allows for new questions to be added, or existing questions to be edited. TestPak 3.0 is available free to adopters of *RPG: A Programming Language for Today*.

All data needed for the programming assignments is available on an IBM 3.5- or 5.25-inch diskette. The data can easily be uploaded to your computer. This allows students to spend less time entering data and more time learning programming.

This text can be used for a single-semester class in RPG to give students a good overview of a programming language as it is used in business. Using this approach, all 18 chapters could be covered.

It is also possible to use the first 11 chapters in a first-semester class and use the second section of the book for advanced students in a second semester. This would allow time to cover each chapter thoroughly and to ensure a complete understanding of the material.

It is hoped that this text will provide a solid foundation for programmers and will prepare them for the next generation of minicomputers using RPG, the language for today and tomorrow.

ACKNOWLEDGMENTS

I would like to thank the following reviewers who offered many helpful suggestions and comments: Barbara E. Koedel, Atlantic Community College; Thomas J. Abromovich, Retired from Black Hawk College, Moline, IL; Robert S. Landrum, Jones Junior College; P. Gapen, Laramie County Community College; Russell K. Lake, Parkland College–Champaign, IL; Steve Backe; Willard H. Keeling, Blue Ridge Community College; Thomas N. Latimer, Lansing Community College/Precision Computer Systems; William C. Fink, Lewis and Clark College; Rod B. Southworth, Laramie County Community College; and Catherine D. Stoughton, CIS Instructor, Laramie County Community College.

Introduction to RPG and Programming

The data processing industry is relatively young and in many ways is still searching for guidelines and standards. Hardware has gone (and continues to go) through many changes in type and architecture. At the same time, software is experiencing similar changes and continues to evolve into something more accessible for the user.

PROGRAMMING LANGUAGES ■

Many programming languages, such as COBOL, FORTRAN, PL/1, and RPG, have been around for many years. Newer languages, such as fourth-generation languages, have been developed to make the programmer's job easier. These are all known as high-level languages because they are designed to be easy for the programmer to use (unlike low-level languages, such as assembly or machine languages, which are understood better by the computer). Most high-level languages share fundamental features such as the ability to read files, do computations, and write reports. They are nearly all compiled languages, which means that a programmer must first write the program and then compile (convert) it on the computer into machine language.

OVERVIEW OF THE RPG LANGUAGE ■

Of the many programming languages used on computers today, RPG (for Report Program Generator) is unique. Although it originated as a mere report writer in the 1960s, it has grown up to become a powerful full-service language for use in business applications. It is more widely used than any other language on minicomputers today. Interestingly, RPG is programmed in English worldwide.

RPG is defined as a problem-oriented language. Multitudes of fourth-generation languages have been developed in recent years to achieve exactly what RPG has been doing all along—solving the problems of business with a minimum of programming effort or expertise.

A Brief Glance Backward

In the early days of computers (circa 1950–1968) all business computers were large mainframes. (Minicomputers and personal computers had not yet been invented.) Programming languages were complicated, difficult to learn and to use. Often management needed only a report printed—perhaps just a listing of some file. In the languages available at that time, however, there was no such thing as a simple program.

At last, in the 1960s, IBM decided to create a language that could quickly meet the need for these simple reports. RPG was that language. It could read a data file, keep a few running totals, and write a nicely formatted report. This early version of RPG was simple to learn and easy to use,

FIGURE I.1 A Programmer at Work

but it had many limitations. It could not handle arrays of data, or make decisions, or update files. It could merely read and print. It did serve its purpose, but it was not a serious language.

Some people still think of RPG as this type of limited tool. On some mainframes, RPG remains in its original form doing only simple report writing.

RPG II—Enter the Minicomputer

In 1969 IBM announced the first of its minicomputers for the business world—the System/3. Minicomputers had been around since 1964 for engineering uses, but none had been available for business applications. The System/3 was the right machine for small businesses that could not afford roomsful of expensive programmers. IBM, therefore, decided to introduce an easy language on the System/3. It would be a programming tool that anyone could learn and use quickly. That language was an updated version of RPG called RPG II.

Along with RPG II came many improvements over the original version of RPG. It became possible to make decisions, to control the actions of the program, to update files, and to use data arrays. RPG II could perform every function needed in the business environment at that time (using batch processing) and could do it faster, easier, and cheaper than any language of its time. Small businesses could have all the advantages of a large computer at far less cost.

Before long, other computer vendors realized that they would need to make versions of RPG II available for their customers if they were to compete with IBM. RPG II had become the standard of the minicomputer industry for business applications.

On-Line Interactive Processing

By the mid-1970s, management was asking for more than RPG II could provide. They didn't like to wait for reports, and they didn't want mountains of paper on their desks. They wanted on-line, interactive, instant, available data on their terminals. Most languages had been designed long before terminals had become commonplace. No language made this type of programming easy.

As a temporary solution to this problem, IBM designed a utility called CCP which could be used in conjunction with RPG II to facilitate the writing of interactive application programs.

Everyone knew that this was not a complete answer to the problem, but they also knew that the System/3 was rapidly becoming obsolete. IBM then developed the System/34 and later the System/36 as further solutions. These machines used RPG II with an on-line capability—a big improvement over CCP.

RPG III—A Truly On-Line Language

In 1979, with the System/38, IBM introduced RPG III, a language that was specifically intended to be used for programming interactive on-line applications. RPG III is a fully functional language, providing all the benefits of a completely modern structured programming language for use in the business environment. It continues to support all of the functions of RPG II with none of the aggravations of a limited language. RPG III is a language designed for communicating with terminals. It combines the best of the more modern languages (such as PASCAL) with the ease of use of a fourth-generation programming tool. Like PASCAL, it encourages the use of completely structured programming methods.

RPG III is native to the IBM System/38 architecture for which it was designed. This means that it cannot be readily adapted for use on other computers. Versions of RPG III are now available for other minicomputers (such as the IBM System/36), but there are certain limitations. The greatest benefits of RPG III can only be realized on the IBM System/38 and AS/400.

The Future

With the announcement of IBM's AS/400 model in 1988, the functions of the System/36 and the System/38 are molded into a single framework. The language used on the AS/400 is RPG/400. RPG/400 is really RPG III with some additional operations and enhancements. With IBM's commitment to integrating the AS/400 into its planned system architecture for the 1990s, it is probable that RPG II, RPG III, and RPG/400 will share a united future in the 1990s and well into the twenty-first century.

OVERVIEW OF PROGRAMMING ■

Programming consists of planning and designing the program, documenting the plan, writing the source code, compiling the code into object form, testing the program until it is free of errors, saving the final copy of the program, and finally documenting the program for future users or programmers.

Before a programmer begins writing a program, it is necessary to determine what the program is to do. The first step is to develop a plan. This may be done by a systems analyst or a programmer/analyst. It consists of discussing the project with the user (or manager) and finding out what is needed.

The second step will consist of documenting these findings by means of flowcharts, written narrative, and sample report formats so that the user can see what to expect. If all of this is acceptable, the programmer can then begin coding in the language available. Some typical documentation is shown in Figures I.2(a), I.2(b), I.2(c), and I.2(d).

Coding the Program

The language in which programmers usually write their instructions for the computer is called a source language, or source code. It consists of words and phrases that are recognizable as human language (rather than binary symbols that have meaning only to the computer). The programmer must code with great attention to detail and accuracy to ensure that the final product will be free of errors. The programmer will write the entire program in this source language before submitting it to the computer to be compiled, or translated into machine language.

Program coding today is normally entered on a terminal using a special utility program called a text editor utility or source entry utility. Figure I.3 shows what a source program might look like on a display screen using a common utility.

FIGURE I.2(a) Flowchart

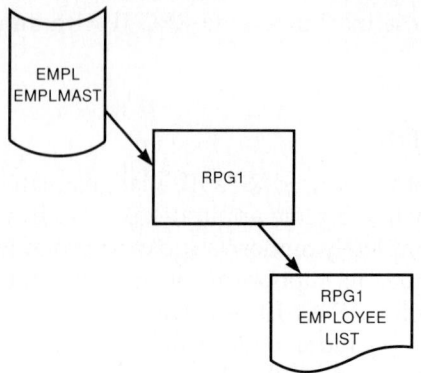

FIGURE I.2(b) Record Layout

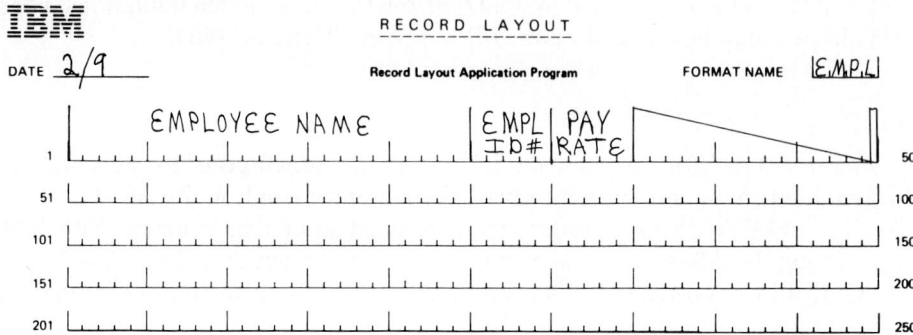

FIGURE I.2(c) Program Narrative

Program Narrative

Input: This program uses the following input files.

    EMPLMAST   Employee Master List
                           File Length 128

    EMPL   Employee Time Transactions
                           File Length 50

Process:

    EMPL records are in sequence by department. Each EMPL record is read and the employee number compared with the EMPLMAST file to determine if it is a valid employee transaction. If the employee number is invalid, the hours in the record will not be added to the totals. The invalid employee number will be printed on the report with the message "Invalid Employee Number." Processing will continue with the next record.

    If the employee number is valid, the record will be printed on the report showing department, employee name, regular hours, overtime hours, double-time hours, holiday hours, sick time hours, and a total of all hours. Total hours are computed from the hours in the input record by adding all the hour fields together.

    Each type of hours is accumulated (i.e., all regular hours, all overtime hours, etc.) and a total is printed for each department. This total will be printed at the end of each group of records for a department after advancing one line.

    A grand total for all departments will be printed at the end of the report.

FIGURE I.2(d) Printer Spacing Chart

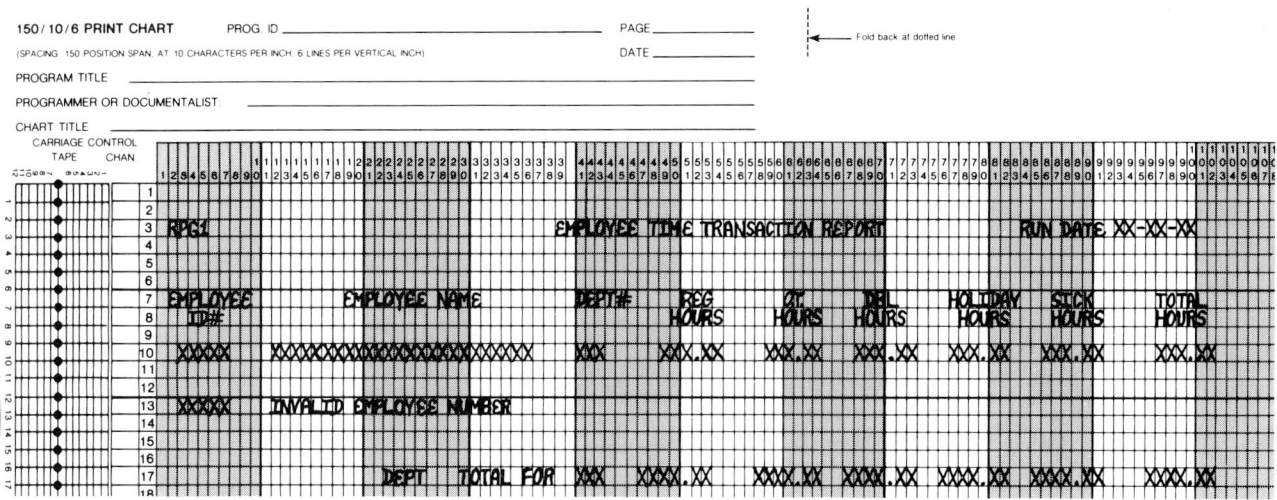

Program Compilation

After the RPG program has been completely entered and all obvious errors have been corrected, it must then be translated from the RPG source language into machine-language instructions which can be understood by the computer.

This translation is accomplished by the use of an RPG compiler. The compiler is itself a program supplied by the computer manufacturer. Figure I.4 shows the steps that occur to convert source language into compiled machine language.

To convert the RPG source program into machine language, the compiler is read into the main memory of the computer. The compiler usually resides on disk when not in use. Next, the source code is read into main memory. The compiler then goes to work translating the source code into object code (machine language). A source listing is produced at the same time. This source listing

FIGURE I.3 Display Screen Showing Source Program

Introduction   **xiii**

FIGURE I.4 Compilation Flowchart

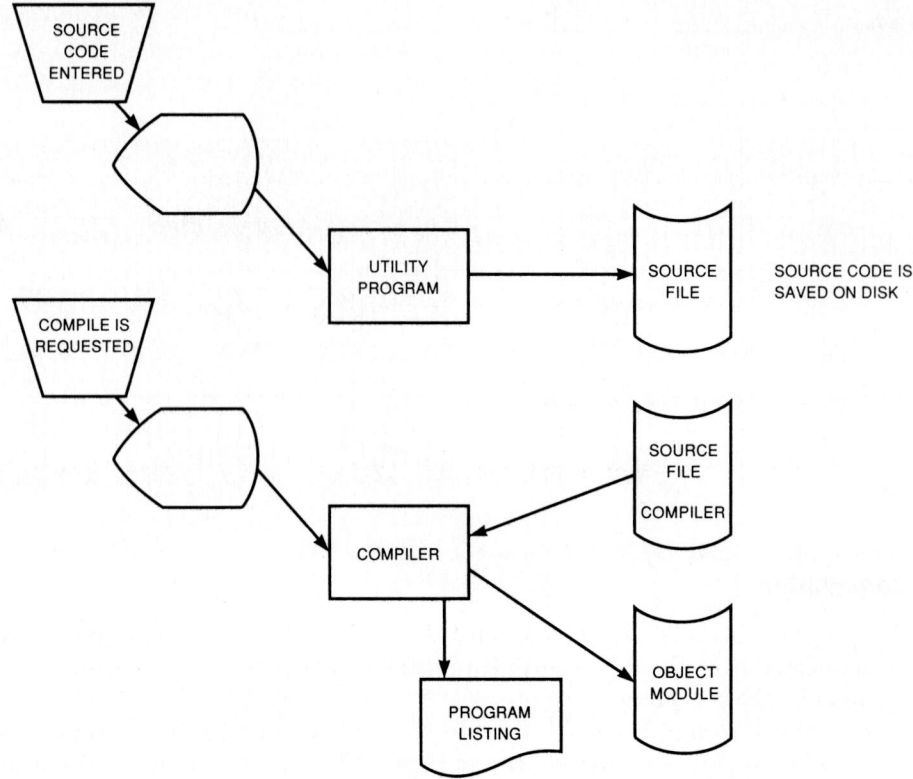

will show every line of code as it was coded by the programmer. The source listing will also note any errors and show them at the bottom of the listing. Note that the compiler will find only syntax errors or errors in spelling of key words or placement of the fields. It is not capable of finding errors in logic. If the errors are too severe to permit compilation, then it will say so and no object code will be produced at all. If all goes well, the source listing will state that, and the object code (an object module) will be created.

Once the object module is created, it should be saved on disk and the program will be ready for testing. The source code should probably also be saved on disk so that changes can be made later if needed.

In learning environments, it is often useful to do a test run immediately after the compiler has finished. This is referred to as a "load and go" method. Figure I.5 shows a source listing of an RPG program with its accompanying error messages.

Program Testing

Once the program is compiled successfully, it must be tested to determine whether it will produce the desired results. Acceptance by the compiler does not necessarily mean the output will be correct. Steps in testing are as follows:

1. *Preparing Test Data.* When a program is to be tested, it should be tested with data which was prepared for testing the various routines within the program. Test data should contain every possible combination of bad and good data to be sure all functions of the program are exercised. It is better to find the problems before the program goes into "live" productive use than to wait and let the errors be found by users, bosses, or instructors. Program testing should be extensive and thorough. The preparation of good test data is a difficult and tedious task, but it is an important part of programming.

2. *Desk Checking.* Sometimes problems are not easy to find. Sometimes the most careful programmer will find an obscure bug or error in the program that refuses to allow the program to perform correctly. The only solution to this dilemma is for the programmer to sit down with a listing of the program and "think" some data through the program line by line. This process, called "playing computer," is slow, but it is one of the best ways to discover what has gone wrong with the program.
3. *Program Debugging.* Programs containing bugs (or errors) should never be released into a production environment. Nothing will give computers a bad name faster than invalid data showing up on someone's report or screen. Unexpected program failures greatly reduce the credibility of the data processing department. It is the responsibility of every programmer to make certain that no program is released until it has been completely and thoroughly tested and found to be absolutely bug free.

FIGURE I.5 Source Listing

```
SEQUENCE         1         2         3         4         5         6         7
NUMBER   67890123456789012345678901234567890123456789012345678901234


    100   F* TITLE: SALES ANALYSIS REPORT
    200   F* DATE:  3/11            AUTHOR: D.CABLE
    300   F* DESCRIPTION:  PRINT REPORT OF ALL SALES FOR MONTH
    400   F***********************************************************
    500   F* MODIFICATIONS:
    600   F* NO.     DATE      INIT       DESCRIPTION
    700   F*        XX/XX/XX   XXX        XXXXXXXXXXXXXXXXXXXXXXXXXXXX
    800   F***********************************************************

NAME OF PROGRAM WILL BE ILL05 IN LIBRARY CABLE

          H
* 1019              ALL DECIMAL DATA ERRORS IGNORED
    900   FSALEMASTIP   F      512            DISK
   1000   FREPORT   O   F      132            PRINTER
   1100   F***********************************************************

   1200   ISALEMASTAA   01
   1300   I                                     1    2 SACMPY
   1400   I                                     3   50SALOC
   1500   I                                     6    6 SATYPE
   1600   I                                     7   21 SAPNO
   1700   I                                    22  230SAMTH
   1800   I                                    24  280SAQTY
   1900   I                                    29  352SAPRC

   2000   C                   TIME        TYME     60

   2100   OPRINT   H   101       1P
* 6001  6001-********   .
* 6035             6035-******

   2200   O                                 6 *ILL005*
   2300   O                                75 *P.C. SOLUTIONS*
   2400   O                               124 *PAGE*
   2500   O                   PAGE        132
   2600   O       H   2           1P
* 6001  6001-********   .
* 6035             6035-******

   2700   O                                 8 *RUN DATE*
   2800   O                   UDATE Y      17
   2900   O                   TYME         26 *  :  :  *
   3000   O                                60 *MONTHLY SALES ANALYSIS*
   3100   O       H   2           1P
* 6001  6001-********   .
* 6035             6035-******
```

FIGURE I.5 *Continued*

```
SEQUENCE      1         2         3         4         5         6         7
NUMBER    67890123456789012345678901234567890123456789012345678901234

   3200  O                                    10 'COMPANY'
   3300  O                                    20 'LOCATION'
   3400  O                                    26 'MONTH'
   3500  O                                    33 'QUANT'
   3600  O                                    42 'TOTAL SALES'
   3700  O         O   1     01
* 6001  6001-********  .
* 6035              6035-******
   3800  O                       SACMPY    12
   3900  O                       SALOC     20
   4000  O                       SAMTH     25
   4100  O                       SAQTY K   32
   4200  O                       SAPRC K   42
* * * * * E N D   O F   S O U R C E * * * *


* 7086     900   RPG PROVIDES BLOCK/UNBLOCK SUPPORT FOR FILE SALEMAST.
* 7064    1000   REPORT FILE NOT REFERENCED FOR OUTPUT
```

CROSS-REFERENCE LISTING

```
        FILE/RCD       DEV/RCD      REFERENCES (D=DEFINED)

        PRINT          **UNDEF**    2100
    02  REPORT         PRINTER      1000D
    01  SALEMAST       DISK          900D 1200


        FIELD          ATTR         REFERENCES (M=MODIFIED D=DEFINED)

        PAGE           P(4,0)       2500
        SACMPY         A(2)         1300D 3800
        SALOC          P(3,0)       1400D 3900
        SAMTH          P(2,0)       1700D 4000
* 7031  SAPNO          A(15)        1600D
        SAPRC          P(7,2)       1900D 4200
        SAQTY          P(5,0)       1800D 4100
* 7031  SATYPE         A(1)         1500D
        TYME           P(6,0)       2000D 2900
        UDATE          P(6,0)       2800

        INDICATOR   REFERENCES (M=MODIFIED D=DEFINED)

        LR           900D
        01          1200M 3700
        1P          2100  2600  3100
```

MESSAGES

```
  MSGID     SEV   NUMBER   TEXT

* QRG1019   00      1      IGNDECERR(*YES) SPECIFIED ON COMMAND. NO DECIMAL DATA ERRORS
* QRG6001   40      4      FILE/RECORD NAME NOT VALID, NOT DEFINED, IGNORED, OR MISSING.
                           VALID TYPE FOUND
* QRG6035   20      4      SPACE OR SKIP MUST BE SPECIFIED ONLY FOR PROGRAM DESCRIBED FI
                           ASSUMED.
* QRG7031   00      2      NAME OR INDICATOR NOT REFERENCED.
* QRG7064   40      1      PROGRAM FILE NOT REFERENCED. FILE IGNORED
* QRG7086   00      1      RPG WILL HANDLE BLOCKING FUNCTION FOR THE FILE. INFDS CONTENT
                           ARE TRANSFERRED.
```

FIGURE I.5 *Continued*

```
MESSAGE SUMMARY

TOTAL    00    10    20    30    40    50
  13      4     0     4     0     5     0

  42 RECORDS READ FROM SOURCE FILE
  SOURCE RECORDS INCLUDE   33 SPECIFICATIONS,    0 TABLE RECORDS, AND    9 COMMENTS

  QRG0008 COMPILE TERMINATED.  SEVERITY 40 ERRORS FOUND IN PROGRAM

* * * * * E N D   O F   C O M P I L A T I O N * * * * *
* QRG1020              ERROR OCCURRED CREATING OR UPDATING DATA AREA RETURNCODE. COMPIL
```

Documentation

Documentation is the process of recording all information related to a given program (or system of programs) in such a way that users, managers, other programmers, or data processing auditors will be able to quickly understand exactly what it is that your program is supposed to be doing. At a minimum it should include:

1. Record layout forms
2. Printer (or screen) layouts
3. A program narrative describing the routines used in the program
4. A flowchart and/or pseudocode outline of the program logic
5. The final copy of the source listing (produced at final compilation time)
6. Sample reports (or screens)
7. User instruction manual

Documentation is an often-neglected part of a programmer's job but a crucial one if a company is to continue to function successfully over a period of time.

CONCLUSION ■

RPG is a programming language that can serve as an excellent introduction to programming. It is a language that is best suited for business applications and is widely used on mid-range computers. RPG has been used as a business programming language since the early 1960s and is predicted to remain popular with mid-range users for many years to come.

This text presents an introduction to both RPG II and RPG III. It explains the fundamentals of programming along with standard conventions practiced in a business programming environment.

Section I

RPG II

Chapter 1

Input and Output Processing

What you will learn in Chapter 1

Program Processing Steps
RPG Coding Formats
Common Entries on Coding Forms
The Control Specifications Form
(Header Format or
H Specification)
The File Description Specifications
Form (F Specification)
   Defining the Input File
   File Type/File Designation Entries
   File Format
   Record Length
   Device
   Defining the Output File
The Input Specifications Form
(I Specification)

Form Type/Filename Entries
Sequence Number Option Entries
(Columns 15–16)
Record Identifying Indicator Entry
(Columns 19–20)
From–To Entries
Field Location Entries (Columns
44–47 and 48–51)
Field Name Entries (Columns
53–58)
The Output Specifications Form
(O Specification)
Filename Entry (Columns 7–14)
Type Entry (Column 15)
Space Entry (Columns 17–18)

Output Indicators (Columns
24–25, 27–28, or 30–31)
Field Name (Columns 32–37)
End Position (Columns 40–43)
The RPG Fixed Logic Cycle
Incorporating Comments Within a
Program
   Why Document?
   How Much Documentation Is
     Enough?
   How Do You Put Comments into
     an RPG Program?
   Conventions for Professional
     Program Documentation
Compiling a Program

When a business problem needs to be solved on a computer, a program is needed to process the data. One of the first requirements of any program is that some input data must be read. After all the processing is complete, some output data will be produced in the form of a printed report or a display on a computer screen. The computer program must deal with each of the following aspects:

1. The input and output files must be defined.
2. The input format must be described in detail.
3. The output report (or screen) format must be described in detail.

The programmer must know something about both the input and the output file(s) before starting to write (or code) the program. (In RPG, program instructions can be written on specification forms, a process called coding. Specification forms are described and illustrated later in the chapter.) There should be some documentation describing the input file, defining its record length, and identifying the characteristics of each field of data. If documentation does not exist, the programmer must somehow find this information and create the missing documentation. Figure 1.1 shows the record format for the input file which will be used in our first sample program.

FIGURE 1.1 Sample Input File

```
JONES, SAM        123 OUT STREET        MIDWAY, CA.
ADAMS, JAMES      5942 CILLEY ROAD      CABOT, TEXAS
SMITH, SUSAN      98624 GREEN ST.       SKOVILLE, NY
```

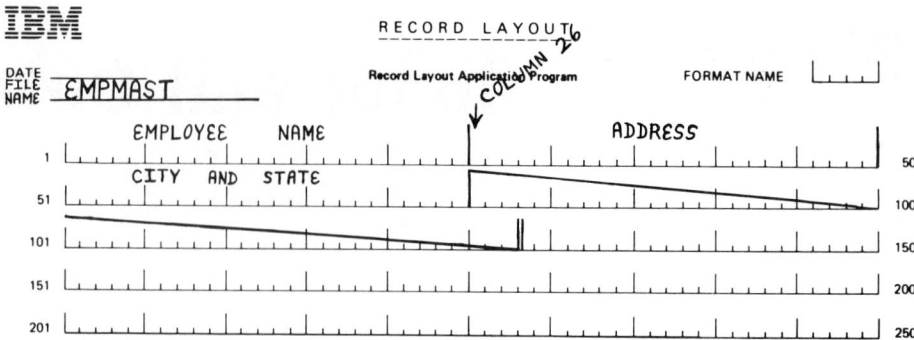

Before starting to write a program, it is a good idea to draw up a sample report on a Printer Spacing Chart. This serves two purposes. First, the sample report should be shown to the user for review and approval. If the user requests changes, it is much easier to make changes on a Printer Spacing Chart than to change a completed program. Second, the Printer Spacing Chart gives the programmer a perfect blueprint from which to complete the coding. It is far easier to code a program when you know exactly what the finished product should look like. (The same, of course, applies to screen formats.)

Figure 1.2 shows the printout requirements for the printed report which will be produced from our first sample program. The finished report will be a list of the names and addresses of all the employees in the file.

PROGRAM PROCESSING STEPS ■

To process the data, the RPG program must read the input record and write the output report. The following steps must take place:

FIGURE 1.2 Printer Spacing Chart

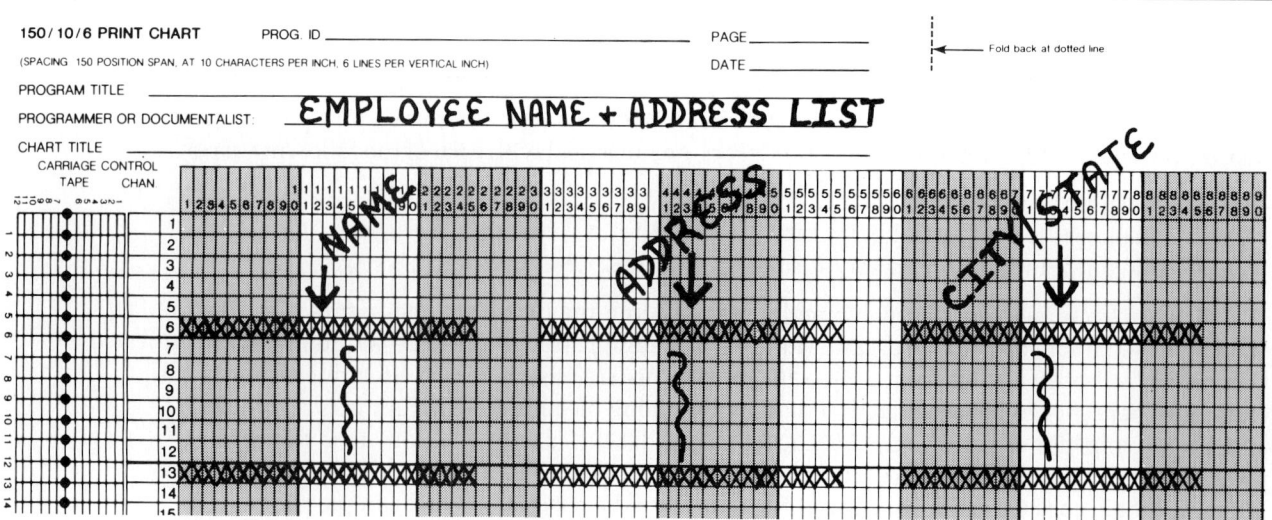

4   *RPG: A Programming Language for Today*

Step 1: A record is read into an input area in main memory (Figure 1.3).
Step 2: The data from the input record is moved to an input area in main memory (Figure 1.4).
Step 3: The data is moved from the input area to an output area in main memory (Figure 1.5).
Step 4: The data in the output area is printed on the report (Figure 1.6).

In the four steps in the above example, the data in the original record will be placed in main memory by instructions in the program. The input data is stored temporarily in main memory, from which it then is moved to the desired output positions on the report.

FIGURE 1.3 Input Record Layout

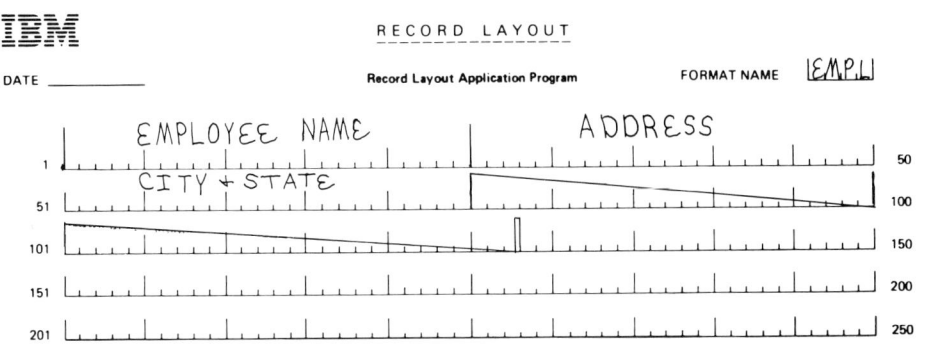

FIGURE 1.4 Data in Main Memory

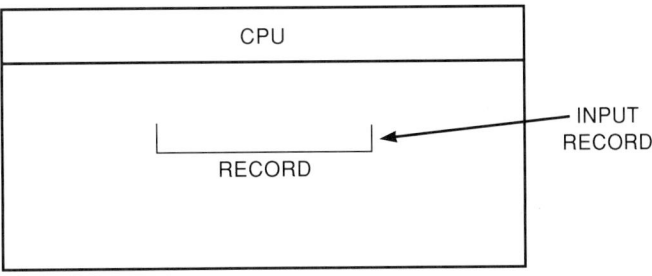

FIGURE 1.5 Data in Output Area

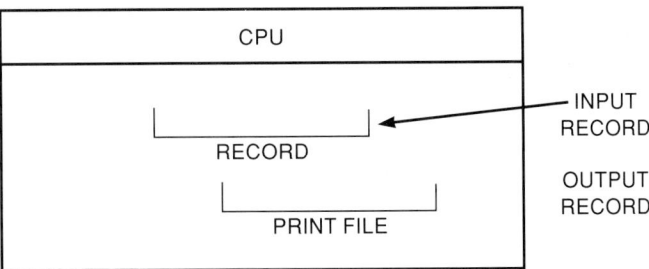

Chapter 1 Input and Output Processing

FIGURE 1.6 Data Printed on the Report

```
JONES, SAM          123 OUT STREET       MIDWAY, CA.
ADAMS, JAMES        5942 CILLEY ROAD     CABOT, TEXAS
SMITH, SUSAN        98624 GREEN ST.      SKOVILLE, N.Y.
```

RPG CODING FORMATS ■

RPG uses special coding formats for each function. This is one of the unique aspects of RPG and can be considered an advantage. A fixed coding format can be an advantage because it can serve to remind the programmer to include each necessary function.

Some of the RPG coding formats commonly used are:

    Control Specifications (Heading Format)   (H)
    File Description Specifications   (F)
    Input Specifications   (I)
    Output Specifications   (O)

Other RPG coding formats will be discussed in future chapters.

As shown in the specifications in Figures 1.7(a), 1.7(b), and 1.7(c), the RPG source program may be written on special forms. The programmer may write the program on these coding forms before entering the specifications into the computer using a source editor utility or some such text editor utility.

FIGURE 1.7(a) RPG Control and File Description Specifications Form

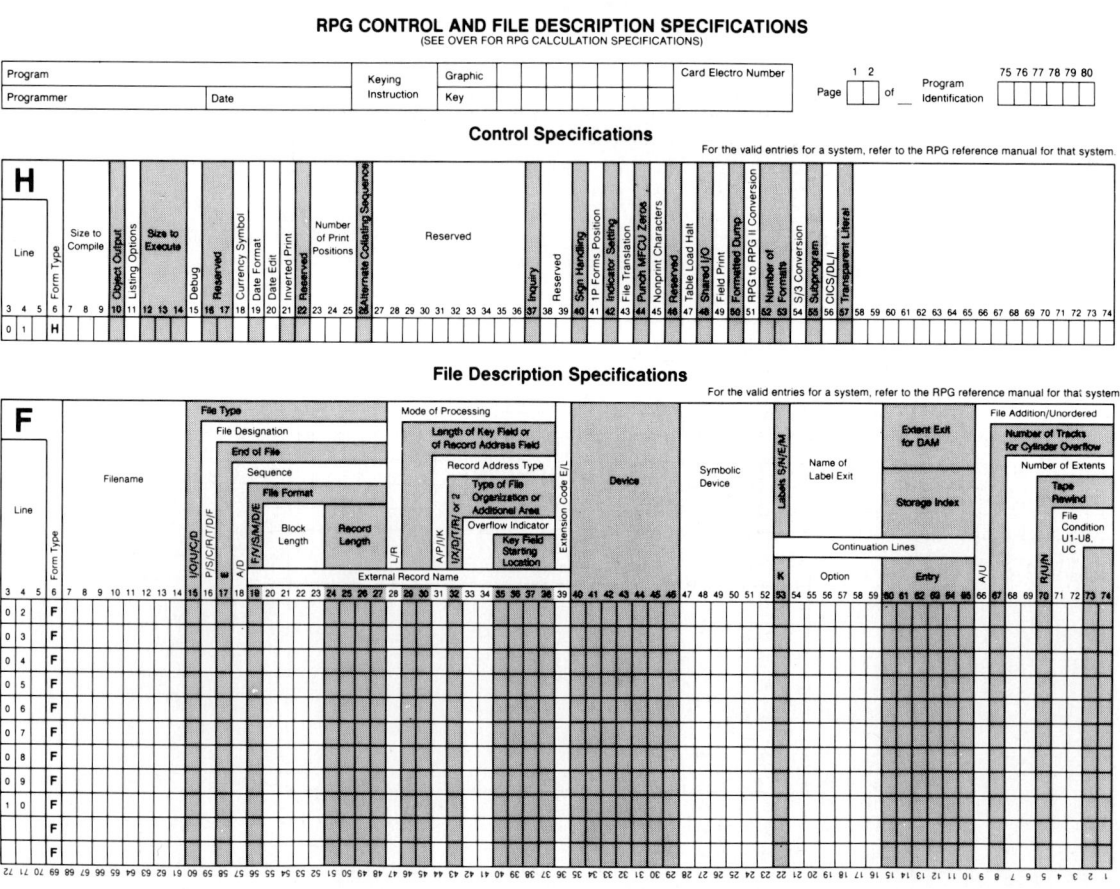

FIGURE 1.7(b) RPG Input Specifications Form

IBM © Copyright International Business Machines Corporation 1984, 1990
IBM is a registered trademark of International Business Machines Corporation, Armonk, NY

RPG INPUT SPECIFICATIONS

(SEE OVER FOR RPG EXTENSION AND LINE COUNTER SPECIFICATIONS)

GX09-1033-03 UM/050*

Printed in U.S.A.

Program | Programmer | Date | Keying Instruction | Graphic | Key | Card Electro Number | Page 1 2 of | Program Identification 75 76 77 78 79 80

I | Line | Form Type | Filename or Record Name | Data Structure Name | O R | A N D | Sequence | Number (1/N),E | Option O,U,S,I | Record Identifying Indicator, **, or DS | Subfield Initialization Value | Named Constant Value | External Field Name | Record Identification Codes 1 2 3 | Position | Not (N) | C/Z/D | Character | Stacker Select | P/B/L/R/C | Field Location | From | To | Data Structure | Occurs n Times | Length | Decimal Positions | RPG Field Name | Constant Name | Control Level (L1-L9) | Matching Fields or Chaining Fields | Field Record Relation | Field Indicators | Plus | Minus | Zero or Blank

Lines: 01, 02, 03, 04, 05, 06, 07, 08, 09, 10, 11, 12, 13, 14, 15, 16, 17, 18, 19, 20 (Form Type I)

*Number of sheets per pad may vary slightly.

FIGURE 1.7(c) RPG Output Specifications Form

RPG OUTPUT SPECIFICATIONS

Program | Programmer | Date | Keying Instruction | Graphic | Key | Card Electro Number | Page 1 2 of | Program Identification 75 76 77 78 79 80

O | Line | Form Type | Filename or Record Name | O R | A N D | Type (H/D/T/E) | Fetch (F) | Stkr # | Space Before After | Skip Before After | D E L / A D D | Output Indicators | And | And | Not | Field Name or EXCPT Name | *AUTO | Edit Codes | B/A/C/1-9/R | End Position in Output Record | P/B/L/R | Constant or Edit Word 1–24

Commas	Zero Balances to Print	No Sign	CR	–
Yes	Yes	1	A	J
Yes	No	2	B	K
No	Yes	3	C	L
No	No	4	D	M

X = Remove Plus Sign
Y = Date Field Edit
Z = Zero Suppress
5 – 9 = User Defined

Lines: 01, 02, 03, 04, 05, 06, 07, 08, 09, 10, 11, 12, 13, 14, 15, 16, 17, 18, 19, 20 (Form Type O)

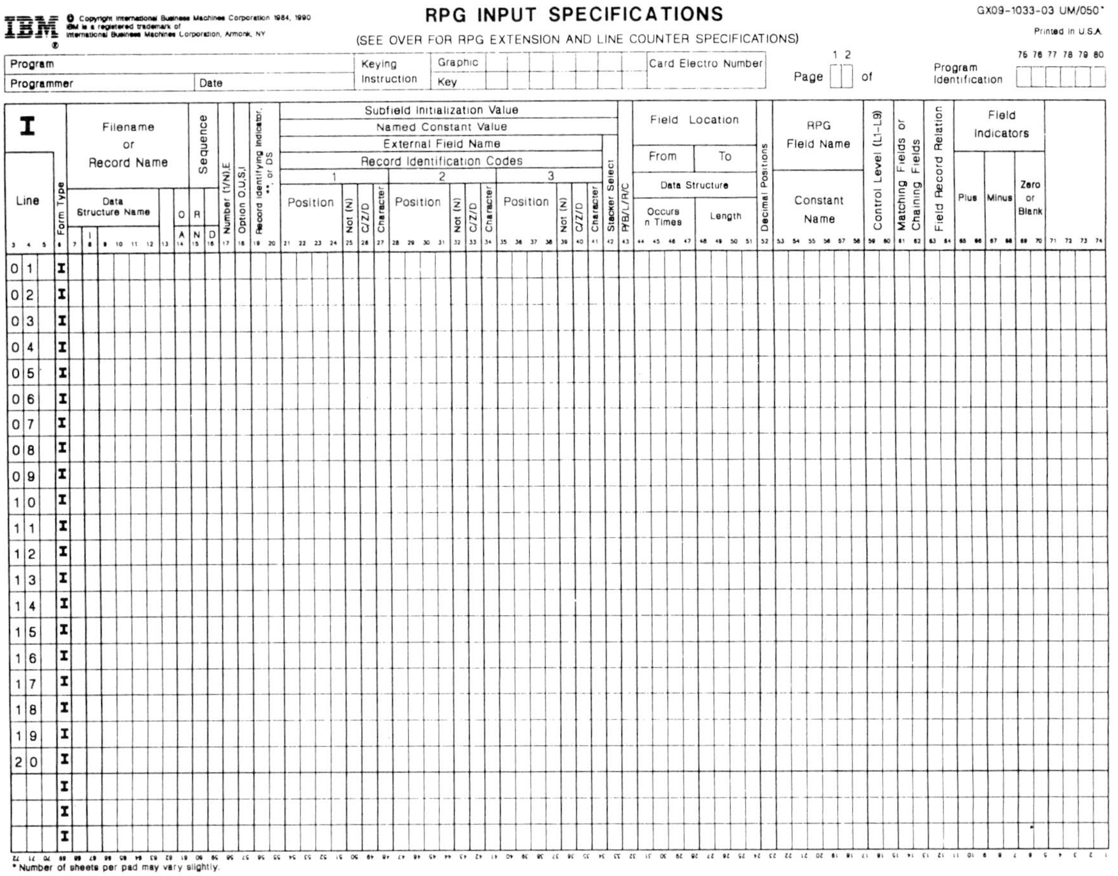

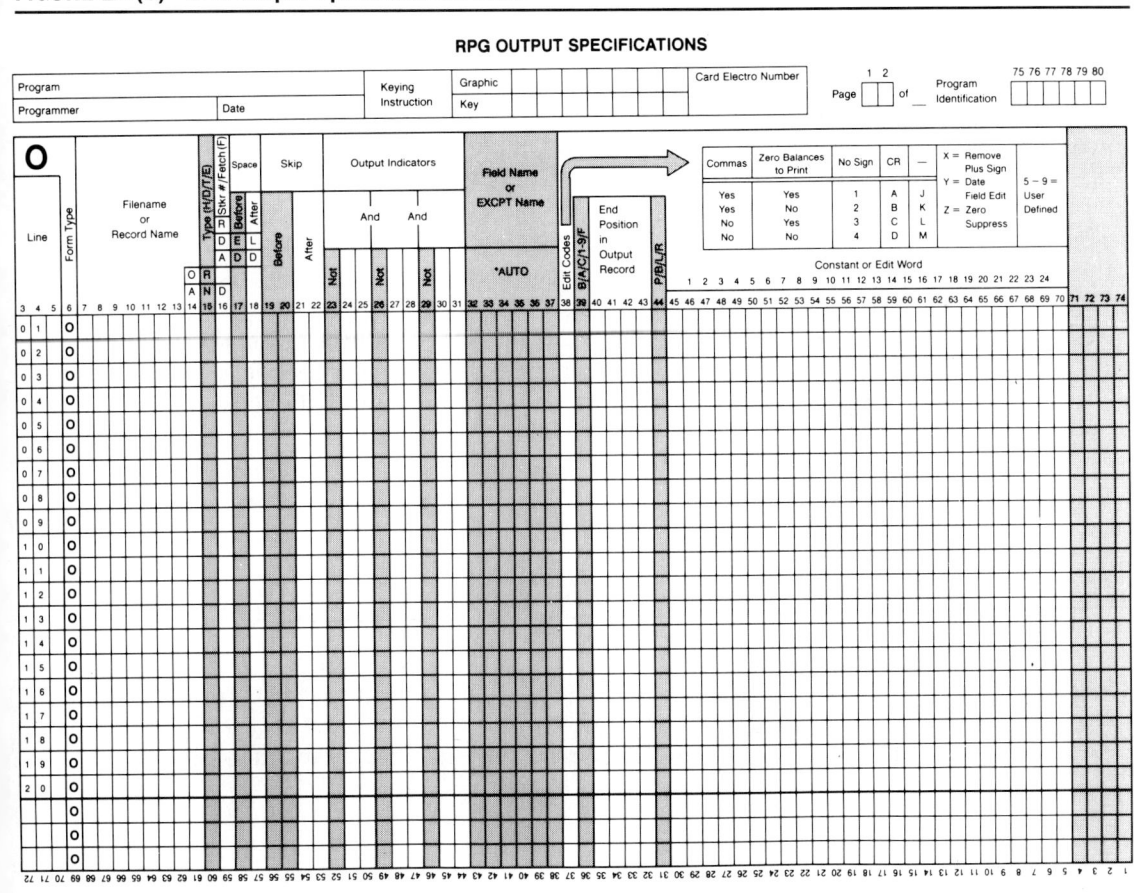

Each specification type must appear in the completed program in a prescribed sequence: The Control Specifications (H) will always be the first record, the File Description Specifications (F) must be next, the Input Specifications (I) next, and the Output Specifications (O) last.

Figure 1.8 shows the coding for a sample program which we will now define in detail. The objective of the sample program is to print a report that lists all the employees in the employee file. The report will show employee name, street address, and city and state.

COMMON ENTRIES ON CODING FORMS ■

All RPG specifications have certain common fields. These fields are used primarily for identification. The entries for Program, Programmer, and Date at the upper left of the forms are optional. These entries are useful for identification on the written forms but are not entered into the computer. The section labeled Keying Instruction may be useful if someone other than the programmer will be entering the program into the computer. In these boxes the programmer can identify characters that are easy to confuse, such as the letter *O* and the number zero, the letter *Z* and the number 2, or the letter *I* and the number 1.

The Page Number boxes at the upper right of the forms are essentially obsolete, a leftover from the days when programs were keypunched onto cards. RPG originated in the days when cards were the standard medium for inputting to computers. Imagine, for a moment, what it would be like to keypunch a complete program of, say, 1500 cards and then accidentally spill them all over the floor. That was the reason for the decision to include a page (and also a line) number on each card. Using the technology of today, you do not need to key the page or line numbers into your programs. Your text editor utility might still provide a space for these numbers (in columns 1–5) but you may ignore them as you enter your program into the computer. These sequence numbers can be useful on the handwritten document to keep your ideas in order, however.

The boxes labeled Program Identification are another relic from the days of punched cards. It was once necessary to enter the name of the program in columns 75–80 of every line in your program. This served the same purpose as the page and line numbers. If the cards for several programs were dumped on the floor, it was easy to sort them by name. Today, you need to enter the program name only on the first record of the program. RPG uses this to identify the program to the compiler (although some compilers do not require it).

Though RPG no longer requires the program name in every record, you will need to give your program a name. The program name should be no more than six characters long (although some computers will accept up to ten characters). In the example, in Figure 1.8, the name of the program in the upper right corner of the form is CDPRNT. Note that the name contains only alphabetic characters. It is acceptable to use numbers or some special characters for the program name, but the *first* character must always be a non-numeric character. Allowable special characters are $, #, and @. No other special characters are permitted. Thus, we might use program names such as PAY001, P01234, C23, AL#01, or even $MA001A. There can never be embedded blanks in the program name.

As you begin coding the program itself, you may notice on the left side of the form that each line is pre-numbered. The numbers on the coding sheets identify each line of source code. You may enter these numbers as you enter each line of code if you wish, but they are not needed in the computer.

Column 6 is the first entry that the RPG compiler needs. Column 6 is required because it identifies which specification you are coding.

THE CONTROL SPECIFICATIONS FORM (HEADER FORMAT OR H SPECIFICATION) ■

Although the Control Specifications (or Header Format) can contain several possible entries, it is the simplest to code. Most of its information is no longer needed for modern computers. Your best source of information for the requirements of your specific computer will be the manuals for that

FIGURE 1.8 File Description Entries for the Sample Program

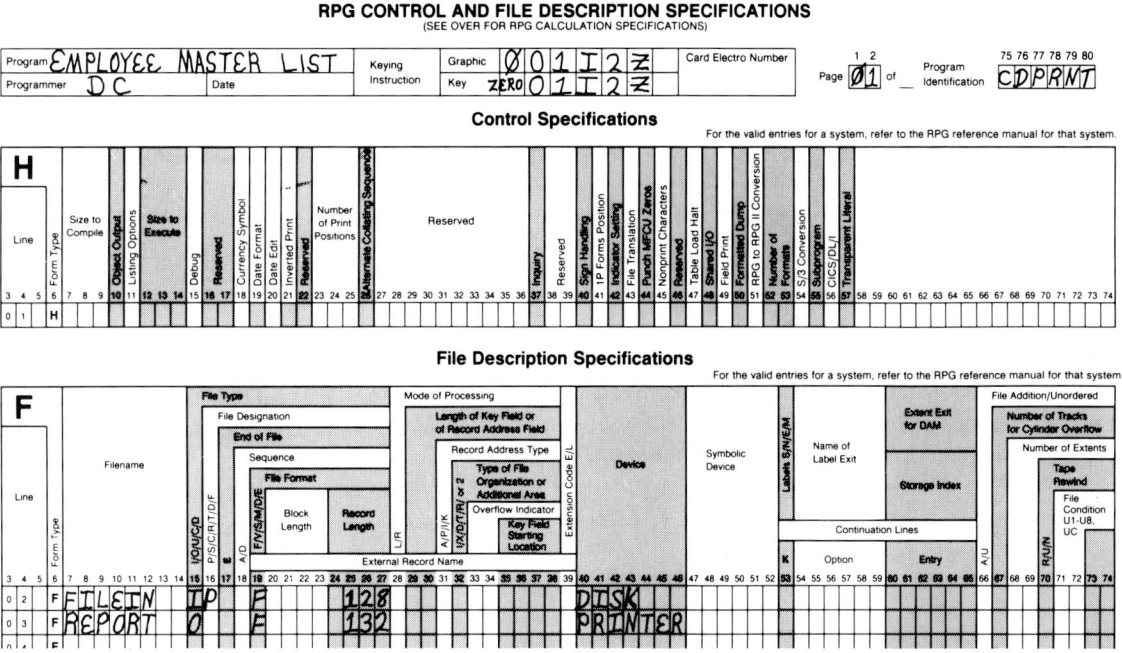

machine. RPG requires only the H in column 6 and a program name in columns 75–80. Some computers do not require the H specification at all. Check this with your instructor.

THE FILE DESCRIPTION SPECIFICATIONS FORM (F SPECIFICATION) ■

The File Description Specifications usually appear on the same coding form with the Control Specifications. The file description entries define the size and media for every file used in your program. In the sample program we will be using one input file and one output file. The printer output is treated as a file by the computer.

Defining the Input File

In your first program, you will start with a single input file. An input file could consist of any type of media, such as diskette, disk, tape, etc. In the example in Figure 1.8, the program will read an input file from disk. Note that column 6 must have its form type, F. The entry F is preprinted on the form, and you will need to enter it into your program.

The next entry (in columns 7–14) is the filename. This entry gives a name to the file which will be processed as input. In the example we use the name FILEIN but could just as well have named it MICKEY, since the compiler will allow you to name your file anything you wish. Using the name it already has on disk or tape can make it easier to remember what the program is supposed to do.

The filename used may be any name chosen by the programmer, but there are certain rules to follow. Filenames used on the File Description Specifications are created according to the following rules:

1. The filename may be 1–8 characters in length. (Note: Some compilers permit only the first seven.)
2. The name may consist of any alphabetic or numeric characters. Some special characters are also permitted, such as the dollar sign ($), the "at" symbol (@), or the pound sign (#). Embedded blanks within the filename are not permitted (a blank between two characters is not allowed).
3. The filename must begin with a non-numeric character.

Chapter 1 Input and Output Processing   9

File Type/File Designation Entries

Columns 15 and 16 specify the file type and the file designation. The entry in column 15 is an *I*, indicating that the file called FILEIN is an input file. The *P* in column 16 indicates that the file being described is the primary file in this program. Of course, this sample program has only one input file, so it must be the primary file, but in programs having more than one file as input the program must be told which one to read first as the primary file. We will discuss secondary files in future chapters.

File Format

We now must specify the attributes of the file FILEIN, and define such matters as the record format. Note from Figure 1.8 that the value *F* is entered under File Format. This means that these records are fixed in length. Each input record will contain the same number of characters as every other record in the file. All records you will deal with in RPG will be of fixed length, so you will always enter the letter *F* in column 19.

Note that we have skipped a few columns on the form. These columns will be discussed in future chapters, but they will not be needed for this program.

Record Length

Since the file has already been created for us we must ask someone else what the record looks like. When we know what the record looks like, we can define the record. The record for this example was defined in Figure 1.1(b).

In columns 24–27 the length of each record should be entered, with the last digit in column 27. In this example, the records will have a length of 128 characters. Card files would always have a length of 80 (or 96 for special cases), but tape or disk files may have varying lengths.

Block length (columns 20–23) will be discussed in a future chapter. Note, however, that the block length and record length are defined as four-position fields. These fields are right-justified, meaning they are entered in the rightmost columns for that field. Note also that entering leading zeros is not necessary. Since this field consists of four positions, you also know that a record could not be longer than 9999 characters.

Device

After the characteristics of the file have been described, you must make an entry to specify the type of device from which the file will be read. The entry in columns 40–46 is left-justified (it begins in column 40). The program will be reading this file from disk. Therefore we will make the entry DISK. However, there are many other input devices which might have been used, as follows:

READ01	IBM 2501 (80-column) card reader
READ05	IBM 3505 or 3504 (80-column) card reader
CARD	IBM card device
MFCU1	IBM 5425 (96-column) card device
TAPE	IBM tape drive
SEQ	IBM sequential devices
DISK	IBM disk drives
DISC	Hewlett-Packard disk drives

A complete list of the possible devices would be very long. Determine what hardware you will be using and determine the requirements for that particular piece of equipment.

We have now completed the description of the input file for this program.

Defining the Output File

The output file will be defined similarly to the input file with just a few differences.

In the example in Figure 1.8, the output file is given the name REPORT. Again, we could have given this file any name we chose, but it is a good idea to use a descriptive name so that you (and other programmers) will know immediately what file you are describing. In some systems it is useful to use a default name which the system will automatically recognize as a printer file. RPG, however, will recognize any name you would like to use in columns 7–14.

In column 15 we will enter the letter O to indicate that this is an output file. Column 16 will remain blank since there is only one type of output file.

The letter F is again entered in column 19 to indicate that this is a fixed format report.

Record length for the printer file is usually 132 since most standard printers today print 132 characters across the page. However, it is possible that the printer you will use could have a maximum of 80, 120, or 144 characters. It is also possible that under special circumstances (such as compressed print) you might use a longer file length for your printer file. For right now, however, let us pretend that the world contains only printers that use 132 characters.

The entry under Device for the printed report is the word PRINTER. This designation must always be entered in columns 40–46 on the File Description Specifications form for printer output.

This completes the File Description Specifications that the RPG compiler needs concerning the input and output files we will be using in this program. Fields on the File Description Specifications form which we have not discussed here will be explained in future chapters.

THE INPUT SPECIFICATIONS FORM (I SPECIFICATION) ■

Within each file (defined in the File Description Specifications above) are individual records. These records must now be described in detail. The fields within these records must also be defined so that the RPG compiler will be able to generate instructions to recognize and process each field separately as needed. As shown in Figure 1.9, the first type of entry to be made on the Input Specifications form will define which file we are about to describe in detail.

Form Type/Filename Entries

The form type (column 6) in Figure 1.9 shows the value I. This identifies the form as an Input Specifications form. As indicated earlier, each record which is part of the RPG source program must have an identification value in column 6.

The first entry to be entered by the programmer is the name of the file in which the records exist. In this example, the name of the file is FILEIN, which is the name we gave the file in the File Description Specifications. It is important to call the file by exactly the same name in both the File Description Specifications and the Input Specifications.

This relationship between the File Description Specifications (which define the file) and the Input Specifications (which define the fields) is illustrated in Figures 1.10(a) and 1.10(b). These

FIGURE 1.9 Input Specification Entries for the Sample Program

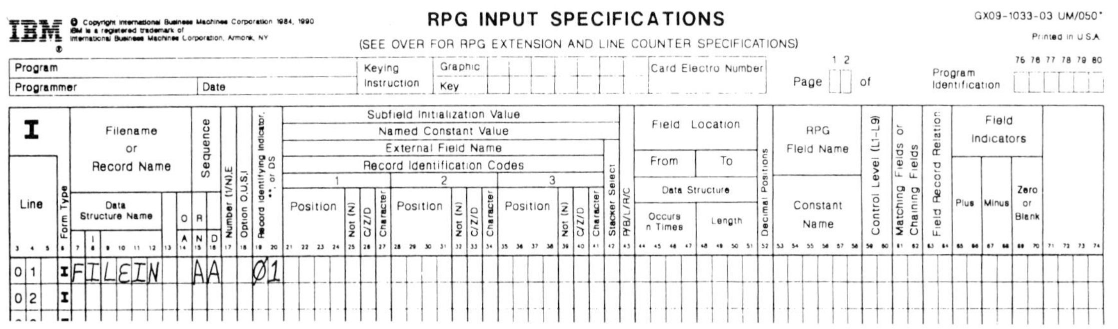

FIGURE 1.10(a) File Description Specifications

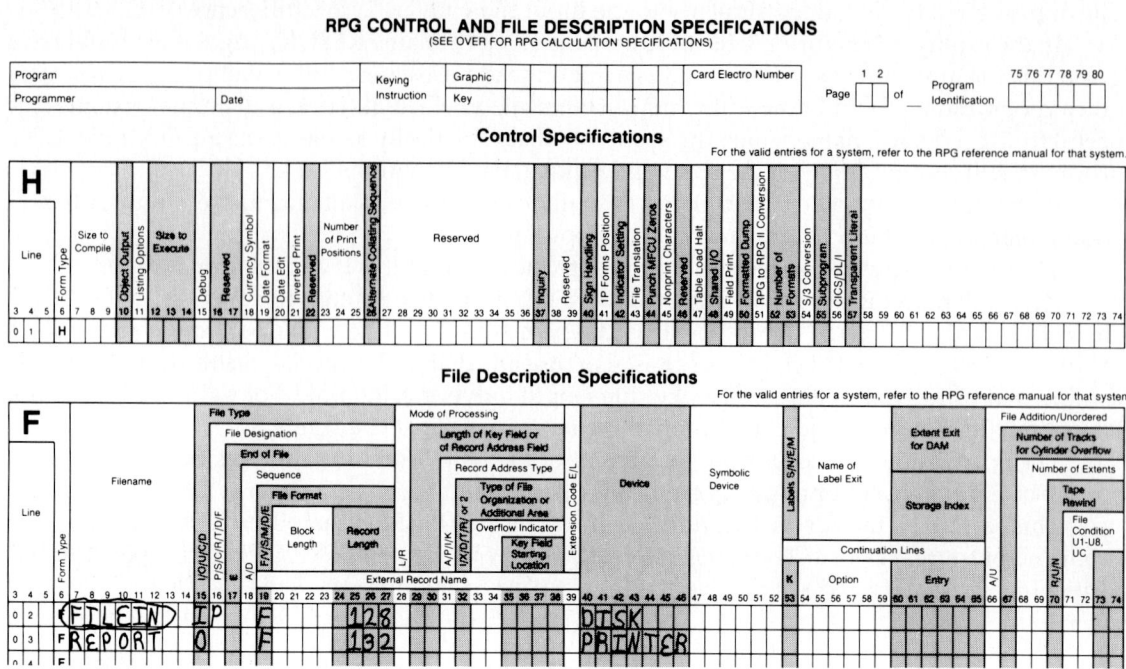

FIGURE 1.10(b) Input Specifications

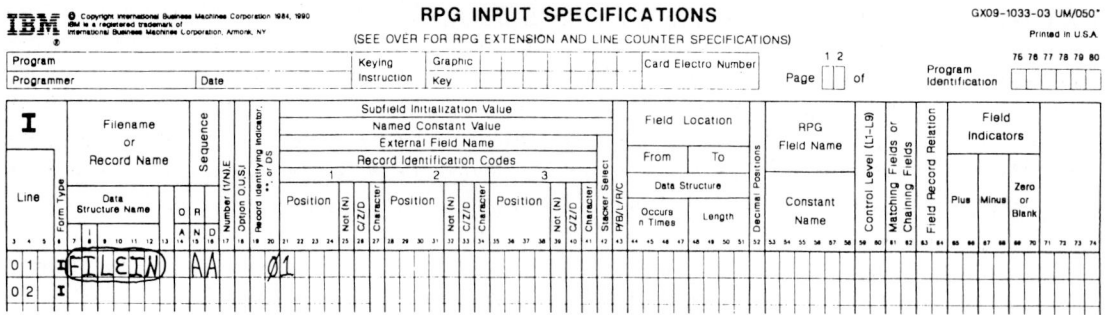

filenames must be identical so that the RPG compiler can relate the file described on the File Description Specifications to the records defined on the Input Specifications.

Sequence Number Option Entries (Columns 15–16)

The entry following the filename entry on the Input Specifications form is the sequence entry (columns 15–16). This entry is used if there is a required sequence of the records in the input file. Since no particular sequence will be checked for this example, we will simply enter AA to satisfy this requirement. This means that no sequence checking will take place. We could have used any two letters of the alphabet. Sometimes NS is used to represent no sequence.

Record Identifying Indicator Entry (Columns 19–20)

The entry in columns 19–20 represents an input function. Briefly, this indicator will identify for the program that a record is being read. We have used the indicator 01 as the indicator for this example but any number between 01 and 99 could have been used. Indicators will be discussed at length in future chapters.

This indicator will be turned *on* every time a record is read. This notifies the program that it has work to do. When an indicator is used in the Input Specifications in this manner, it is called a record identifying indicator. This indicator can be used later in the program to cause actions to be taken whenever a record is read.

The second type of entry on the Input Specifications form defines the fields within each record in the file. Column 6 will require the character I because this is still an Input Specification. Note that the field definition is entered on a separate line from the filename entry.

From–To Entries

Look back at Figure 1.1 for the Record Layout. The records contain three fields—the name field, the address field, and the city/state field. The name field is in columns 1–25, the address in columns 26–50, and the city/state in columns 51–75. There is no data in columns 76–128. To define this in RPG, we will express those facts exactly on the Input Specifications form. Figure 1.11 shows the completed Input Specification.

Field Location Entries (Columns 44–47 and 48–51)

In columns 44–47 on the Input Specifications form, the beginning position for the first field in the record is entered. This is a 1, because the name field begins in column 1. It will be right-justified in columns 44–47 and may be preceded by zeros or blanks. The ending position for the first field in the record is entered in columns 48–51. This entry is 25 because the name field ends in column 25. It will also be right-justified.

Field Name Entries (Columns 53–58)

The field name entry gives a symbolic name to each field within the record. Field names should be no longer than six characters. The rules for forming field names are similar to those for filenames. They must begin with an alphabetic character followed by either alphabetic or numeric or special characters such as @, #, or $. For example, a valid field name for the name field might be NAME, NAME01, NAME##, or FLD001. It is a good idea to use descriptive names for your field names whenever possible. It is also important that no two fields are called by the same name within the same program.

One line will be used to describe each field in the file. In the example in Figure 1.11 we need three of these lines to describe the name, address, and city/state fields. No entry will be required to describe the blank positions in columns 76–128 since these positions will not be used in this program. It is not necessary to describe fields that will not be used in the program.

FIGURE 1.11 Input Specifications

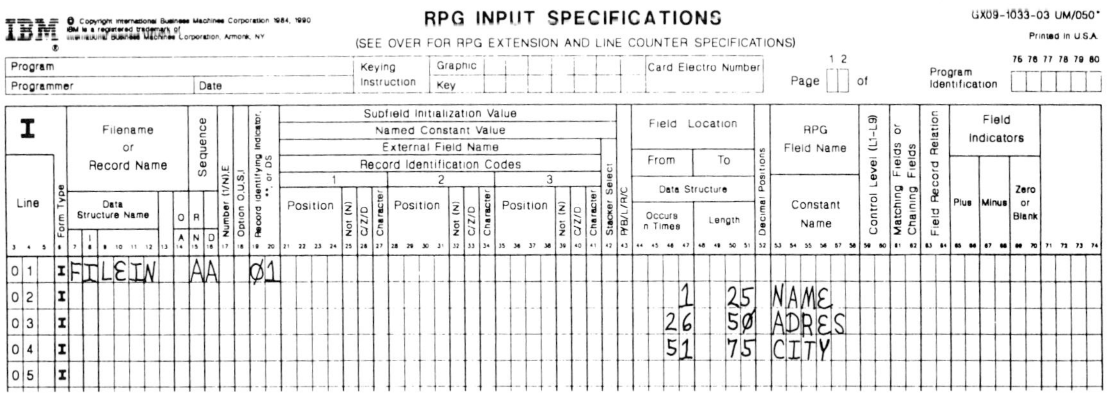

THE OUTPUT SPECIFICATIONS FORM (O SPECIFICATION) ∎

Like the format of the input records, the format of the output files also must be defined. The Output Specifications form is used to define the output files.

As with the other forms, column 6 must contain an entry defining which coding specification this is. We will enter the alphabetic character O to let the compiler know that this is an output specification.

There are two formats which will be coded on the Output Specifications form. The first format defines the output file, and the second format details the fields and their placement on the printed report. Figure 1.12 shows the Output Specifications for both formats. The first format will define which output file we are going to describe.

Filename Entry (Columns 7–14)

In the example in Figure 1.12, the first entry (in columns 7–14) is the filename, REPORT. This must be identical to the filename specified on the File Description Specifications form so that the compiler will recognize that we are talking about the same file.

Type Entry (Column 15)

The value entered in the Type field (column 15) is D. This indicates that the output line to be defined for the REPORT file is a detail line. This means that one line will be printed on the report for each record which is read from the input device.

Space Entry (Columns 17–18)

When printing a report, the spacing of the lines on the report should be considered—that is, the number of lines which will be advanced between the lines of print. Columns 17 and 18 are used for these specifications. Column 17 specifies the number of spaces to leave *before* a line is printed and column 18 the number of spaces *after* a line is printed. It is not necessary to specify both unless you have some special requirements, but it is a good idea to use at least one of them. We usually want to space at least one line (single spacing) after each line is printed so that the lines will not print one on top of the other. Entering the number 1 in column 18 tells the printer to advance one line after each line of print. Some computers automatically advance one space (default to 1) if the programmer forgot to make this entry, but it is a better practice to leave nothing to chance.

Output Indicators (Columns 24–25, 27–28, or 30–31)

The function of an output indicator is to control the moment at which an output record is to be written. In the example in Figure 1.12, the value 01 is entered in columns 24–25. This means that indicator 01 must be *on* before the line will be printed. As discussed above in the input section, this indicator will be *on* each time a record is read. Since we used indicator 01 as the input indicator, it is necessary to use 01 as the output indicator as well. In summary, the action of the READ causes indicator 01 to turn *on*, and then the printer will recognize that it is time to print a line.

The second of the output formats will define each field to be printed on the report. Column 6 will require the character O because this is still an output format.

Field Name (Columns 32–37)

In the example in Figure 1.12, the Field Name section is used to specify the name of the field to be printed on the report. The names which are placed in columns 32–37 must have been previously defined within the program. In this example, the fields were defined on the Input Specifications. Thus, the name field (NAME), the address field (ADRES), and the city/state field (CITY) will be printed on the report. The field names on the coding specification must be left-justified in the Field Name column. That is, the name of each field will begin in column 32.

FIGURE 1.12 Output Specifications

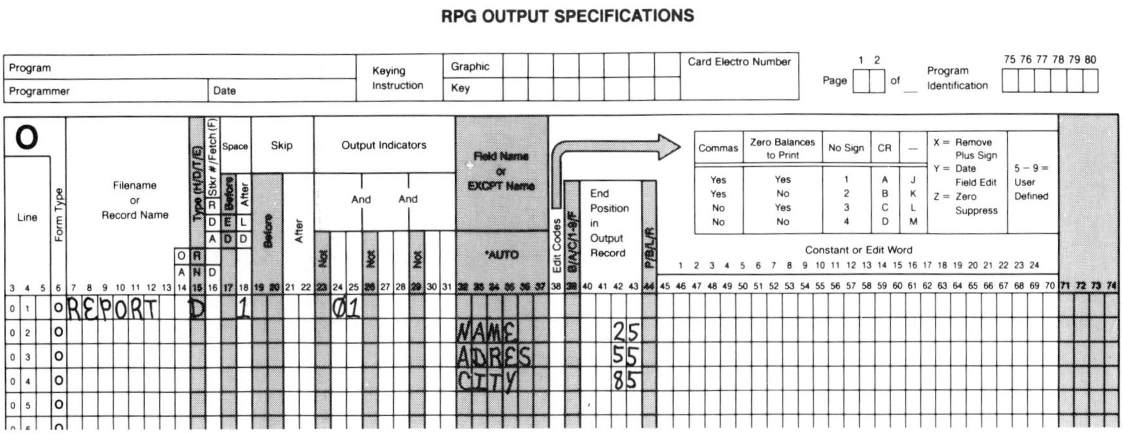

End Position (Columns 40–43)

Columns 40–43 are used to indicate the ending position of the data in each field in the output record or print line. It is not necessary to enter the beginning position for each field on the Output Specifications. The program already knows the size of the field—it now just wants to know where on the printed page you would like it to print out. Referring back to the Printer Spacing Chart shown in Figure 1.2, the ending column on the report for the name field is 25 so the name will print in columns 1–25 on the report. It is only a coincidence that this is the same as the input columns. Since we would like to see some spacing on the report between the name and the address, we will enter the address ending position as column 55. This will allow sufficient room to print the address and leave some spaces between the name and address. As the example shows, the programmer defines the spacing on the printout and the report will then be pleasing to the eye as well as easy to read. Note that this entry needs to be right-justified (as are all numeric entries) and could be preceded with either zeros or blanks. Note also that it is not necessary to define the spaces between the output fields on the printout.

We have now completed a simple program. Once you have learned the rules, supplying the entries is not complicated. You have defined the file description, the inputs, and the outputs. Figures 1.13(a), 1.13(b), and 1.13(c) show the completed program code.

When you have finished entering this sample source program into the computer and compiled it (producing an object module), you will be able to run a report containing a listing of all the names and addresses in the file.

THE RPG FIXED LOGIC CYCLE ■

Every programming language has a cycle. What that means, in simple terms, is that a program has a beginning, a middle, and an end. Most languages make hard work of this, leaving it up to the programmer to tell the computer when to open a file, read a record from the file, do the processing, print a line, go back and read another record, and so on until there are no more records, then close the file and end the program.

This cycle is necessary to the functioning of any program. In RPG this cycle is built in. Once you have defined the files (input and output) and defined what you want printed out, RPG will *automatically* handle the tasks of opening the files, reading the records, printing the lines, reading the next record, looking for the end of the file, closing files, and ending the program.

This automatic handling of input and output data is called a *fixed logic cycle*. The programmer must be aware that this cycle exists. It is important to understand what is happening in your program. In future chapters you will find good reasons for knowing exactly what your program is doing.

FIGURE 1.13(a) Complete Program Code: File Description Specifications

FIGURE 1.13(b) Input Specifications

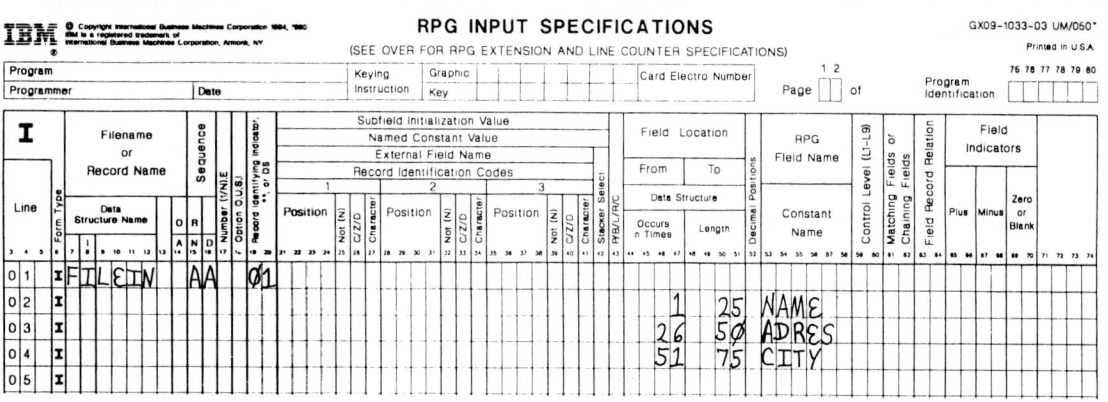

FIGURE 1.13(c) Output Specifications

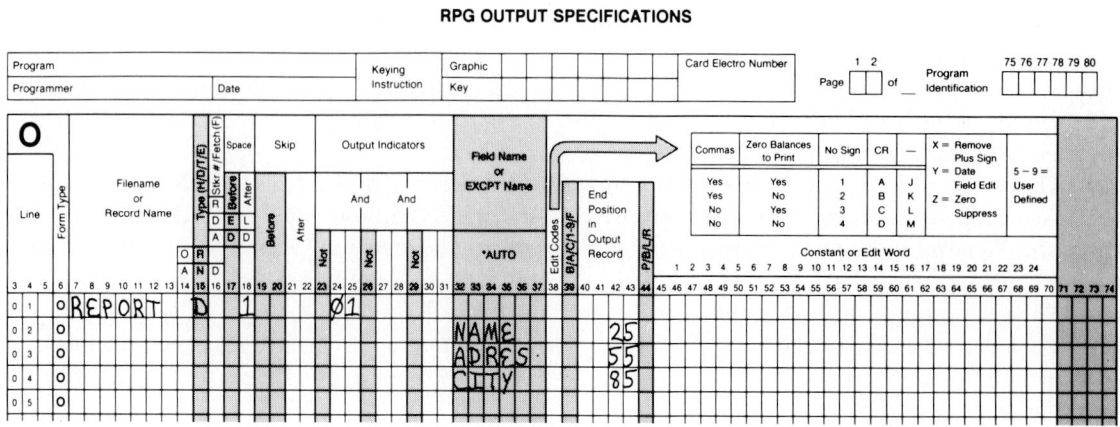

FIGURE 1.14 Simplified RPG Fixed Logic Cycle

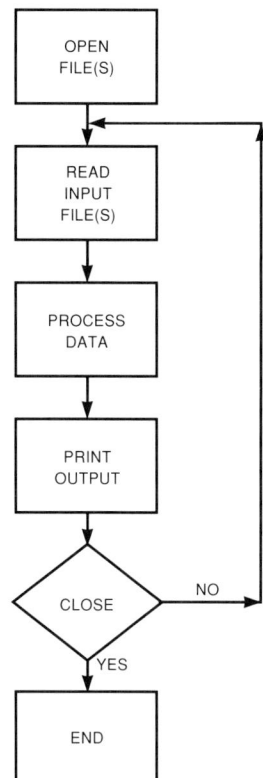

When RPG executes your file specifications, it automatically OPENS the file(s) you have defined. That means it is ready to read the first record. RPG then READS the record and executes whatever instructions you have given it. In the example above, we have told the program to print a line. It prints the line and *automatically* returns to the beginning of the program to perform the next READ. The program will continue to do this as long as there are records in the file to be read. When it comes to the end of the file, the program will automatically close the file and end the program.

Figure 1.14 shows a simplified version of the RPG cycle. In later chapters this will be expanded to include some of the other features of RPG.

INCORPORATING COMMENTS WITHIN A PROGRAM ■

Much has been written about the need for good, detailed documentation in programs. Our discussion here would not be complete without some explanation of this controversial subject, addressing the following questions:

1. Why should anyone do documentation for programs?
2. How much documentation should be done in any program?
3. How do you put comments in an RPG program?
4. What are the conventions for professional program documentation?

Why Document?

Program documentation exists in many forms—flowcharts (or pseudocode), file descriptions, printer layout charts, program narratives, operational instructions, user manuals—but these materials are often lost, misplaced, or allowed to become obsolete. Hence there is good reason to incorporate comments in the program itself. Although the coding might be perfectly clear at the moment of writing, the program can look completely foreign even to the same programmer a few months later. Even when the project appears to be so simple that its objectives must be completely obvious to everyone, it is a wise programmer who makes it a compulsive habit to enter a few lines of explanation with *every* program, no matter how trivial that program might seem at the time.

How Much Documentation Is Enough?

There is a fine line between too much and too little documentation in any program. A long dissertation on the detailed structure of your program is of little value if no one is likely to take the time to read it.

Programmers will find a few short notes much more helpful in figuring out what you had in mind. *Do not* write notes on the obvious, such as "This program prints a report." *Do* write notes about subjects that are not clear in the program, such as "This is the Customer Master File" or "Code A is for adds and Code D is for deletions."

How Do You Put Comments into an RPG Program?

Comments are coded with the form type in column 6 (as usual) and an asterisk in column 7 and then any comments you wish to enter (free form) in columns 8 through 74. (See Figures 1.15a and 1.15b.)

Note that comments can be entered for any specification type. Comments may be scattered throughout the program to document any activity needing clarification. Comments can take any format you like, since RPG is not concerned with any line containing an asterisk in column 7. RPG

FIGURE 1.15(a) Input Specifications with Comments

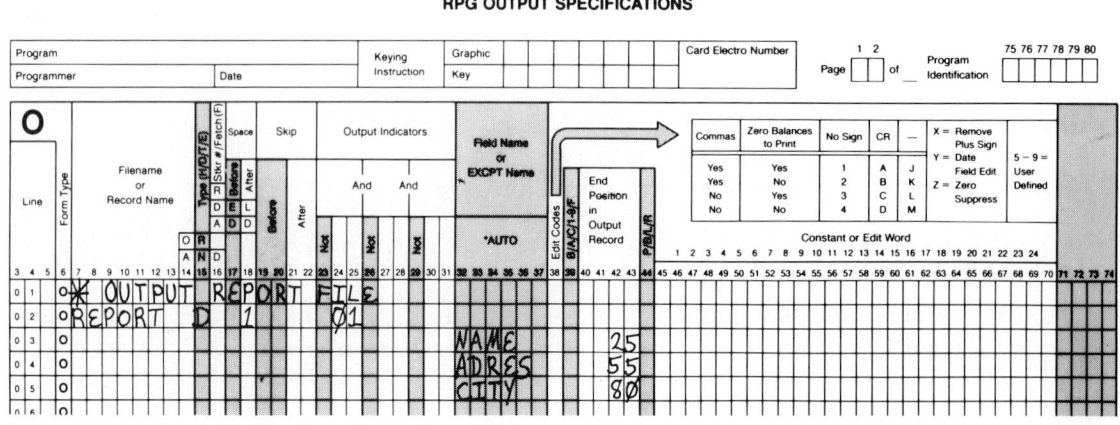

FIGURE 1.15(b) Output Specifications with Comments

18   *RPG: A Programming Language for Today*

does not compile these comments into the object module, so you may use as many as you like without worrying about degrading the efficiency of your finished product.

Conventions for Professional Program Documentation

Every company will have its own standards and conventions for documentation (or if not, it should have), but some minimum documentation is necessary for all programs. There should be at least the following:

> Program title
> Program description (a brief outline)
> Author (programmer name)
> Date written
> Modifications (if any); should include a brief note about the reason for the change, the programmer name, and the date of the change.

These comment lines should appear at the beginning of every program as a means of controlling changes as well as providing information for future programmers. Figure 1.16 shows a sample of what these heading comments might look like.

Some programmers like to place a reference list of all the indicators used in a program near the front of their program using an Indicator Summary form. (This was done in the early days of RPG, when the compiler did not provide a list of indicators at the end of each compile.) Although the practice is sometimes still followed in existing programs and may provide good insight into the functions being performed, it is better to describe each indicator on a comment line close to where the function is being performed. Figures 1.17(a) and 1.17(b) show an example of indicator documentation using both methods.

Now that you know about comments, let us look at our original program in Figures 1.18(a), 1.18(b), and 1.18(c) with some comments entered into it.

FIGURE 1.16 Program Heading Comments

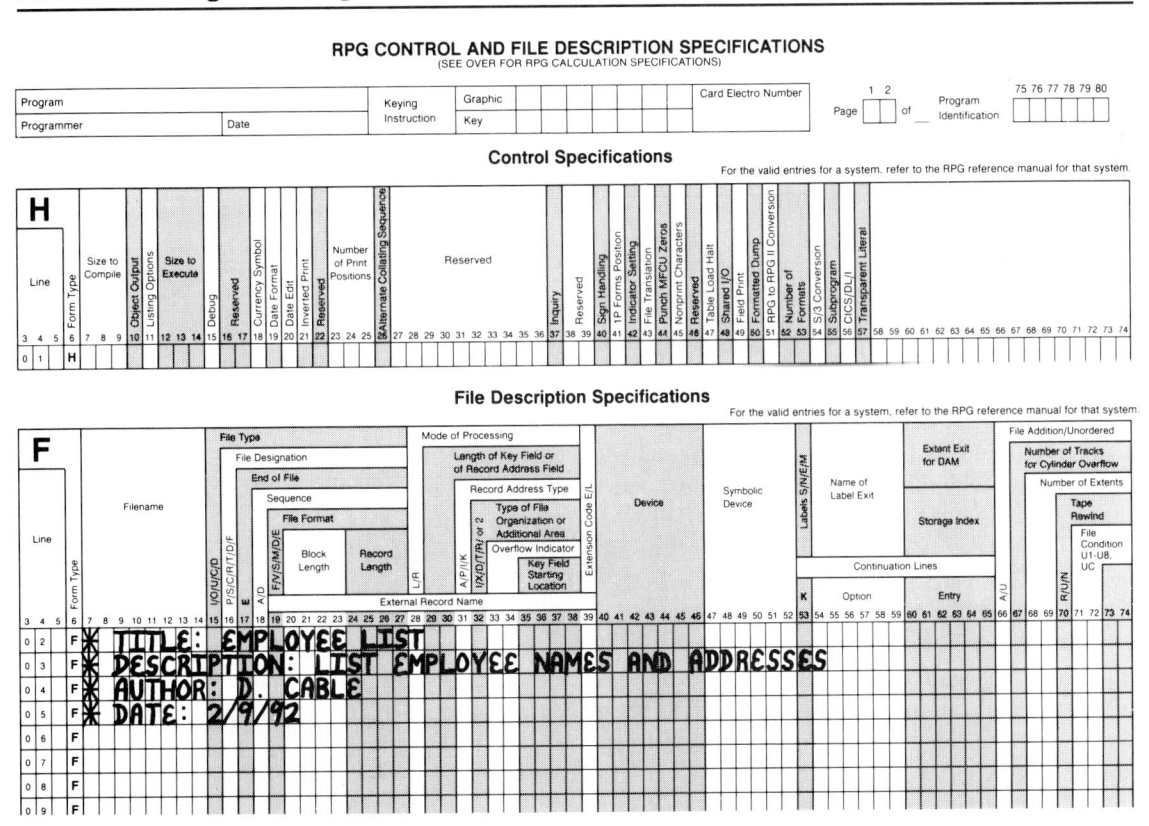

[RPG Control and File Description Specifications form showing:]

```
F* TITLE: EMPLOYEE LIST
F* DESCRIPTION: LIST EMPLOYEE NAMES AND ADDRESSES
F* AUTHOR: D. CABLE
F* DATE: 2/9/92
```

FIGURE 1.17(a) Indicator Documentation

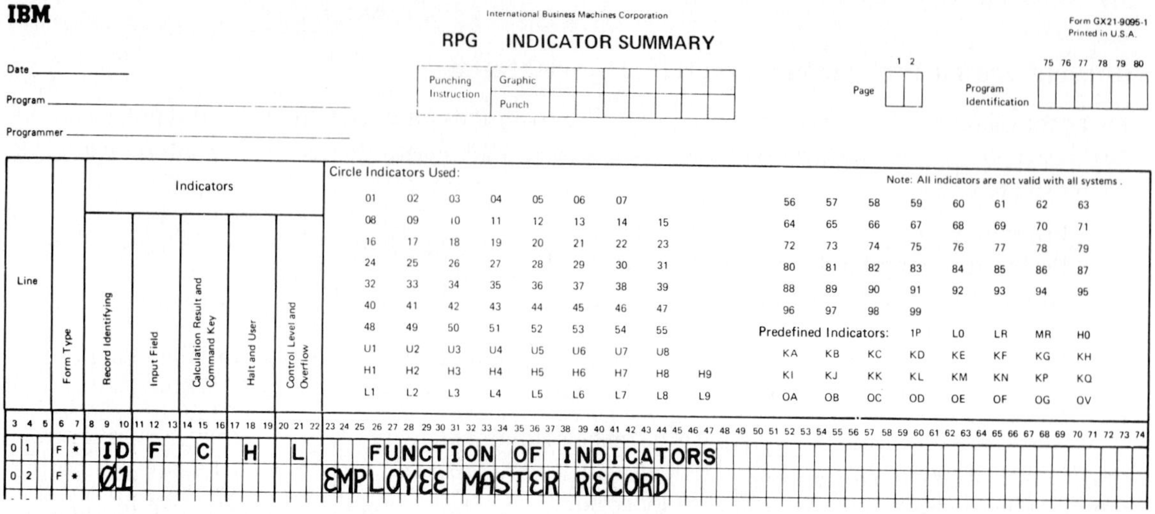

FIGURE 1.17(b) Input Specifications

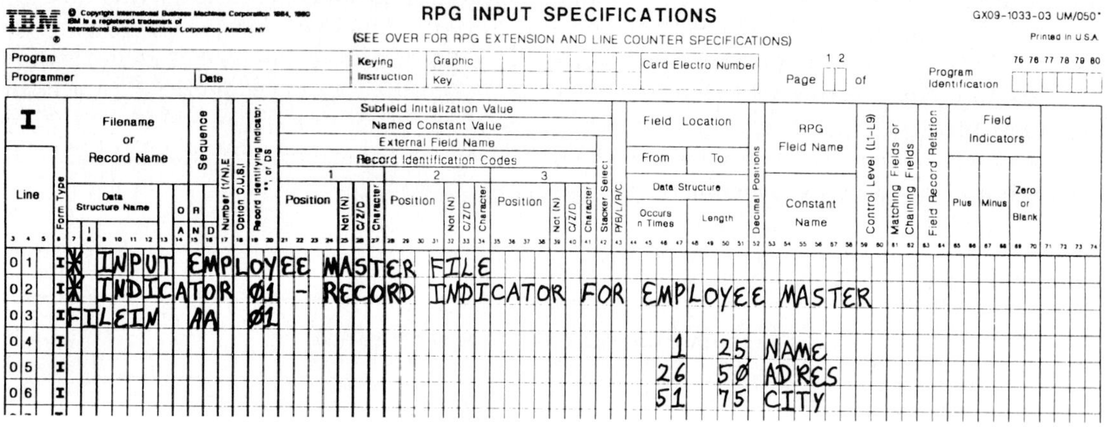

COMPILING A PROGRAM ■

Now that the sample program has been entered into the computer in source form, it is ready to be compiled into an object module before it can be executed.

The compiler will provide a listing of the program in its final form, and will then add its evaluation of the program. Some of the information you can expect to see at the end of the source listing are a list of all fields used (in alphabetic sequence), a list of all indicators used (in alphanumeric sequence), a list of all coding errors with a brief description of the error, the location of the defective line(s) of code that caused the error (when RPG can determine that), and whether that error was sufficiently serious to prevent a successful compilation of the program. Finally, the list will state whether the program did (or did not) compile.

Some compilers will give the line numbers (location) for each instance where a field or indicator was used in the program and whether the field was changed.

Since no two compilers are alike, you will need to ask your instructor how to go about doing your compiles. Then when you receive your first source listings you will be able to determine what information is available. Figure 1.19 shows a complete source listing of the sample program, which was compiled on an IBM System 38. RPG programs are simple to write. The programmer needs only to define the input fields and the output fields. The RPG fixed logic cycle will take care of nearly all the rest. Although the program described in this chapter is simple, it represents nearly all the fundamentals a programmer needs to know to build a program. Of course there is much more for the student to learn in the forthcoming chapters, but the basics are now behind us.

FIGURE 1.18(a)   Complete Program with Comments: File Description Specifications

```
F* TITLE: EMPLOYEE LIST
F* DESCRIPTION: LIST EMPLOYEE NAMES AND ADDRESSES
F* AUTHOR: D. CABLE
F* DATE: 2/9/92
FFILEIN  IP  F    128          DISK
FREPORT  O   F    132          PRINTER
```

FIGURE 1.18(b)   Complete Program with Comments: Input Specifications

```
I* INPUT EMPLOYEE MASTER FILE
I* INDICATOR 01 - RECORD INDICATOR FOR EMPLOYEE MASTER
IFILEIN  AA  01
I                              1   25 NAME
I                             26   50 ADRES
I                             51   75 CITY
```

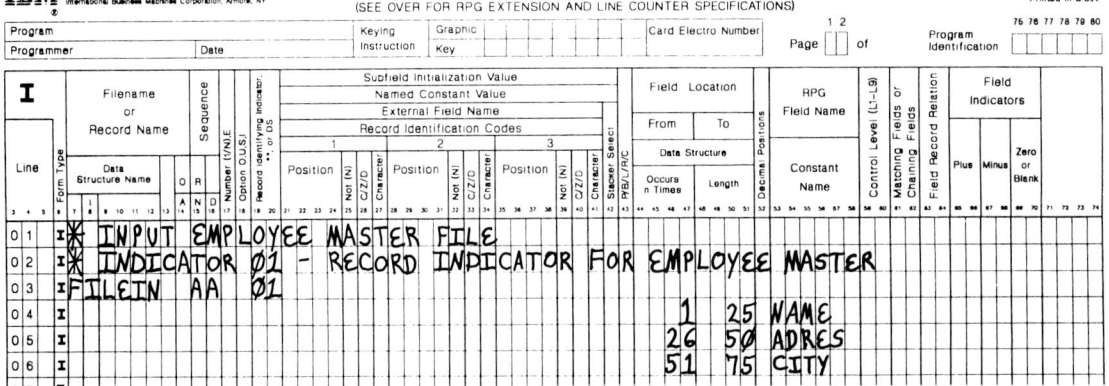

FIGURE 1.18(c)   Complete Program with Comments: Output Specifications

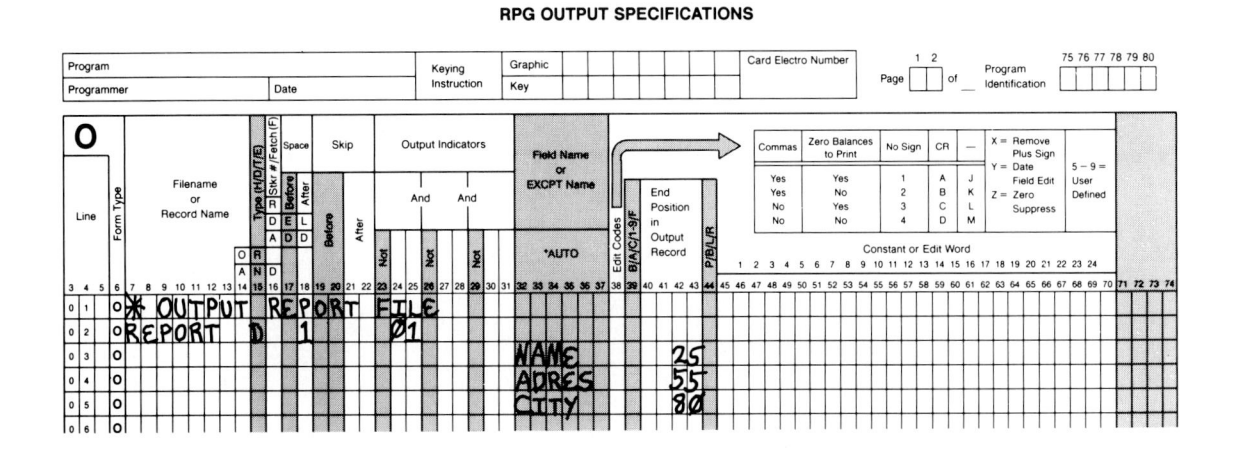

```
O* OUTPUT REPORT FILE
OREPORT   D  1     01
O                       NAME       25
O                       ADRES      55
O                       CITY       80
```

FIGURE 1.19 Compiled Program

```
      200   F* PROGRAM TO LIST EMPLOYEE NAMES AND ADDRESSES
      300   F* DATE WRITTEN: 2/9/91
      400   F* AUTHOR: D.CABLE
      500   F*
      600   FFILEIN   IP  F      128           DISK
      700   FREPORT   O   F      132           PRINTER


      800   I* INPUT EMPLOYEE MASTER FILE
      900   I* INDICATOR 01 - RECORD INDICATOR FOR EMPLOYEE MASTER
     1000   IFILEIN   AA   01
     1100   I                                   1   25 NAME
     1200   I                                  26   50 ADRES
     1300   I                                  51   75 CITY


     1400   O* OUTPUT REPORT FILE
     1500   OREPORT   D   1       01
     1600   O                             NAME     25
     1700   O                             ADRES    55
     1800   O                             CITY     80
*  6103       1801    OVERFLOW INDICATOR OA ASSIGNED TO FILE REPORT
 * * * *  E N D   O F   S O U R C E * * * *


*  7086        600    RPG PROVIDES BLOCK/UNBLOCK SUPPORT FOR FILE FILEIN.



         CROSS-REFERENCE LISTING



         FILE/RCD      DEV/RCD      REFERENCES (D=DEFINED)

    01   FILEIN        DISK         600D 1000
    02   REPORT        PRINTER      700D 1500   1801

         FIELD         ATTR         REFERENCES (M=MODIFIED D=DEFINED)

         ADRES         A(25)        1200D 1700
         CITY          A(25)        1300D 1800
         NAME          A(25)        1100D 1600


         INDICATOR   REFERENCES (M=MODIFIED D=DEFINED)

         LR          600D
         OA          700D 1801
         01          1000M 1500



    MESSAGES

    MSGID      SEV   NUMBER   TEXT

*   QRG1019    00    1        IGNDECERR(*YES) SPECIFIED ON COMMAND. NO DECIMAL DATA ERROR
*   QRG6103    00    1        NO OVERFLOW INDICATOR SPECIFIED. OVERFLOW INDICATOR ASSIGN
                              TO 6 GENERATED
*   QRG7086    00    1        RPG WILL HANDLE BLOCKING FUNCTION FOR THE FILE. INFDS CONT
                              ARE TRANSFERRED.
```

FIGURE 1.19 *Continued*

```
MESSAGE SUMMARY

TOTAL     00      10      20      30      40      50
  3        3       0       0       0       0       0

   18 RECORDS READ FROM SOURCE FILE
SOURCE RECORDS INCLUDE    11 SPECIFICATIONS,     0 TABLE RECORDS, AND      7 COMMENTS

PRM HAS BEEN CALLED

QRG0003 PROGRAM ILL119 PLACED IN LIB CABLE.  00 HIGHEST SEVERITY FOUND

* * * * * E N D   O F   C O M P I L A T I O N * * * * *
* QRG1020              ERROR OCCURRED CREATING OR UPDATING DATA AREA RETURNCODE. COMP
```

SUMMARY ■

In your introduction to the programming language RPG, you have already learned a great deal about the language. You have seen how to create a complete program to read in data records and to print the information contained in those records in a simple report format.

RPG requires a special coding format for entering the program into the computer. You have learned to use the File Description Specifications, the Input Specifications, and the Output Specifications formats. You have learned the essentials for coding these forms in order to read records and print reports.

Besides describing the input records, you have learned what an input indicator is and what it does. You know how to describe the printed report to meet your requirements (or the requirements of a systems analyst or your boss) and you have learned how to do line spacing for your report.

You have been introduced to the RPG fixed logic cycle so you can understand how a program works and how it can read one input record after another with no apparent help from the programmer. You have learned the importance of putting comments in your program code and how those comments are coded.

Although you have only started to learn about RPG, you are already well on your way to becoming an RPG programmer.

REVIEW QUESTIONS

1. Explain the difference between a source program and an object program.

2. Explain the function of a compiler.

3. Explain the function of coding forms and how they are used.

4. List the four most commonly used RPG coding forms.

5. Give the rules for creating a filename.

6. What is the maximum number of characters allowed in a filename? In a field name?

7. List some of the valid names for input devices. For output devices.

8. When specifying the positions a field will occupy on a printed report, does the programmer specify the beginning position or the ending position for the output field?

9. How are the lines advanced on a printed output?

10. What will happen if you attempt to compile a program with the coding form types in the wrong sequence?

EXERCISES

1. On a File Description Specifications form, enter the coding which will read data from disk. The filename is TIMEDATA.

2. On the same File Description Specifications form, enter the coding to define a printer output file.

3. On an Input Specifications form, make the appropriate entries to define the input record for the file TIMEDATA. The fields in the record are:

Column 1–3	Department Number
Column 4–6	Employee Number
Column 7	Shift Worked
Column 8–12	Total Hours Worked

4. On an Output Specifications form, make the appropriate entries to describe a report which prints the data from the file TIMEDATA.

DEBUGGING EXERCISES

Instructions

The following RPG programs contain an error or errors. Some of these errors are indicated by the RPG compiler on the program listing. A list of syntax errors is given at the end of the program listing. Other types of errors may occur which will not be shown. These are called logic errors.

Study each program and its syntax errors. Locate each error (including logic errors) and on a separate coding form make the correct entry for the line(s) in error.

Explain each error and how it should be corrected.

```
       100   F* TITLE: DEBUG PROJECT 1-A
       200   F* DATE:  2/28/91         AUTHOR: D.CABLE
       300   F* DESCRIPTION:  PRINT REPORT
       400   F*************************************************
       500   F* MODIFICATIONS:
       600   F* NO.      DATE      INIT      DESCRIPTION
       700   F*          XX/XX/XX  XXX       XXXXXXXXXXXXXXXXXXXXXXXXXXXXX
       800   F*************************************************

NAME OF PROGRAM WILL BE PJ001A IN LIBRARY CABLE

              H
* 1019               ALL DECIMAL DATA ERRORS IGNORED
       900   FPJMASTFLIP    F     80           DISK
      1000   FREPORT   O    F    132           PRINT
* 2013                                  2013-******

      1100   F*************************************************

      1200   IPJMASTFLAA
* 4137                 4137-**

      1300   I                                      1   6 ID#
      1400   I                                      7  10 CODE
      1500   I                                     11  21 DESCRP
      1600   I                                     22  25 DESC2

      1700   OREPORT   D  1        01
* 6035                 6035-******
      1800   O                          IDNO      12
      1900   O                          CODE01    20
      2000   O                          DESC      40
* * * * * E N D   O F   S O U R C E * * * * *


* 7086      900   RPG PROVIDES BLOCK/UNBLOCK SUPPORT FOR FILE PJMASTFL.
* 7086     1000   RPG PROVIDES BLOCK/UNBLOCK SUPPORT FOR FILE REPORT.



CROSS-REFERENCE LISTING
```

Chapter 1 Input and Output Processing

```
            FILE/RCD      DEV/RCD      REFERENCES (D=DEFINED)

        01  PJMASTFL      DISK          900D 1200
        02  REPORT        DISK         1000D 1700


            FIELD         ATTR         REFERENCES (M=MODIFIED D=DEFINED)

*  7031    CODE          A(4)         1400D
*  7030    CODE01        A(4)         1900
*  7030    DESC          A(4)         2000
*  7031    DESCRP        A(11)        1500D
*  7031    DESC2         A(4)         1600D
*  7031    ID#           A(6)         1300D
*  7030    IDNO          A(4)         1800


            INDICATOR   REFERENCES (M=MODIFIED D=DEFINED)

            LR           900D
*  7030    01           1700


    MESSAGES

      MSGID      SEV   NUMBER   TEXT

*  QRG1019     00      1       IGNDECERR(*YES) SPECIFIED ON COMMAND. NO DECIMAL DATA ERR
*  QRG2013     10      1       DEVICE (POSITIONS 40-46) NOT PRINTER, CARD, DISK, WORKSTN
*  QRG4137     00      1       RECORD IDENTIFICATION INDICATOR (POSITIONS 19-20) BLANK
*  QRG6035     20      1       SPACE OR SKIP MUST BE SPECIFIED ONLY FOR PROGRAM DESCRIBE
                               ASSUMED.
*  QRG7030     30      4       FIELD OR INDICATOR NOT DEFINED.
*  QRG7031     00      4       NAME OR INDICATOR NOT REFERENCED.
*  QRG7086     00      2       RPG WILL HANDLE BLOCKING FUNCTION FOR THE FILE. INFDS CON
                               ARE TRANSFERRED.


    MESSAGE SUMMARY

      TOTAL    00     10     20     30     40     50
       14       8      1      1      4      0      0

      20 RECORDS READ FROM SOURCE FILE
      SOURCE RECORDS INCLUDE     11 SPECIFICATIONS,     0 TABLE RECORDS, AND     9 COMMENTS

    QRG0008 COMPILE TERMINATED. SEVERITY 30 ERRORS FOUND IN PROGRAM

      * * * * * E N D   O F   C O M P I L A T I O N * * * * *
    *  QRG1020              ERROR OCCURRED CREATING OR UPDATING DATA AREA RETURNCODE. CON
```

```
       100  F* TITLE: DEBUG PROJECT 1-B
       200  F* DATE: 2/28/91           AUTHOR: D.CABLE
       300  F* DESCRIPTION:  PRINT REPORT
       400  F*********************************************************
       500  F* MODIFICATIONS:
       600  F* NO.     DATE       INIT      DESCRIPTION
       700  F*        XX/XX/XX    XXX       XXXXXXXXXXXXXXXXXXXXXXXXXXXXXX
       800  F*********************************************************

    NAME OF PROGRAM WILL BE PJ001B IN LIBRARY CABLE

              H
*  1019              ALL DECIMAL DATA ERRORS IGNORED
       900  FINPUT    IP  F         90              DISK
      1000  FREPORT   O   F        132              PRINT
*  2013                                             2013-*******

      1100  F*********************************************************
```

```
     1200 IINPUT    AA  01
     1300 I                                    1   3 DEPT
     1400 I                                    4   5 EMP#
     1500 I                                   21  21 CODE


     1600 OREPORTT D 1    01
* 6001 6001-********  .
* 6035          6035-******

     1700 O                         DEPT      2
     1800 O                         CODE     20
     1900 O                         EMP#     40
* * * * * E N D   O F   S O U R C E * * * * *



* 7086      900   RPG PROVIDES BLOCK/UNBLOCK SUPPORT FOR FILE INPUT.
* 7064     1000   REPORT FILE NOT REFERENCED FOR OUTPUT

    CROSS-REFERENCE LISTING



         FILE/RCD     DEV/RCD      REFERENCES (D=DEFINED)

     01  INPUT        DISK          900D 1200
     02  REPORT       DISK         1000D
         REPORTT      **UNDEF**    1600



         FIELD       ATTR       REFERENCES (M=MODIFIED D=DEFINED)

         CODE        A(1)       1500D 1800
         DEPT        A(3)       1300D 1700
         EMP#        A(2)       1400D 1900



         INDICATOR   REFERENCES (M=MODIFIED D=DEFINED)

         LR           900D
         01          1200M 1600



    MESSAGES

    MSGID      SEV   NUMBER    TEXT

 *  QRG1019    00      1       IGNDECERR(*YES) SPECIFIED ON COMMAND. NO DECIMAL DATA ERRORS
 *  QRG2013    10      1       DEVICE (POSITIONS 40-46) NOT PRINTER, CARD, DISK, WORKSTN,
 *  QRG6001    40      1       FILE/RECORD NAME NOT VALID, NOT DEFINED, IGNORED, OR MISSING
                               VALID TYPE FOUND
 *  QRG6035    20      1       SPACE OR SKIP MUST BE SPECIFIED ONLY FOR PROGRAM DESCRIBED F
                               ASSUMED.
 *  QRG7064    40      1       PROGRAM FILE NOT REFERENCED. FILE IGNORED
 *  QRG7086    00      1       RPG WILL HANDLE BLOCKING FUNCTION FOR THE FILE. INFDS CONTEN
                               ARE TRANSFERRED.



    MESSAGE SUMMARY

    TOTAL     00     10     20     30     40     50
       6       2      1      1      0      2      0

    19 RECORDS READ FROM SOURCE FILE
    SOURCE RECORDS INCLUDE   10 SPECIFICATIONS,    0 TABLE RECORDS, AND     9 COMMENTS

    QRG0008 COMPILE TERMINATED. SEVERITY 40 ERRORS FOUND IN PROGRAM

    * * * * * E N D   O F   C O M P I L A T I O N * * * * *
 *  QRG1020              ERROR OCCURRED CREATING OR UPDATING DATA AREA RETURNCODE. COMPI
```

Chapter 1 Input and Output Processing

PROGRAMMING PROJECT

Project Overview

A report is to be printed listing names and categories for all customers. Write the RPG program to produce this listing. Sample data for this project can be found in Appendix D.

Input Format

The input data for the project is found in a file called CUSTMAST in the sample data. The Record Layout for this file is shown in Figure 1.20.

Output Format (Printer Spacing Chart)

The output format for the project is a report. No report headings are needed for this project. The report will show the customer number, name, and category for each customer in the file. The Printer Spacing Chart for this report is shown in Figure 1.21.

An example of the finished report is shown in Figure 1.22.

FIGURE 1.20 Programming Project: Record Layout

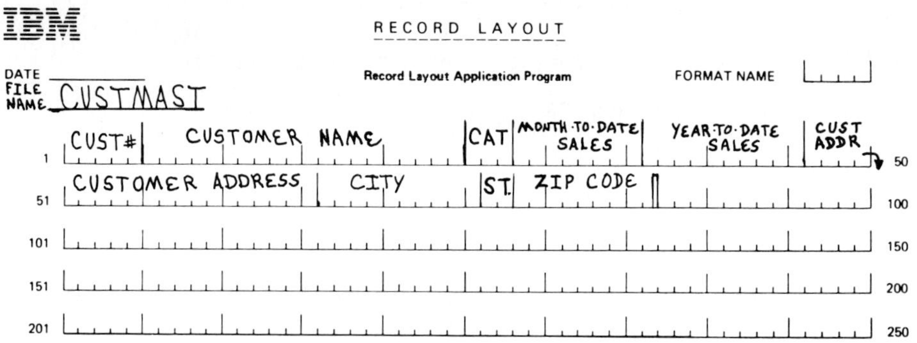

IBM — RECORD LAYOUT

FILE NAME: CUSTMAST

Line 1 (positions 1–50): CUST# | CUSTOMER NAME | CAT | MONTH-TO-DATE SALES | YEAR-TO-DATE SALES | CUST ADDR

Line 2 (positions 51–100): CUSTOMER ADDRESS | CITY | ST | ZIP CODE

FIGURE 1.21 Programming Project: Printer Spacing Chart

150/10/6 PRINT CHART

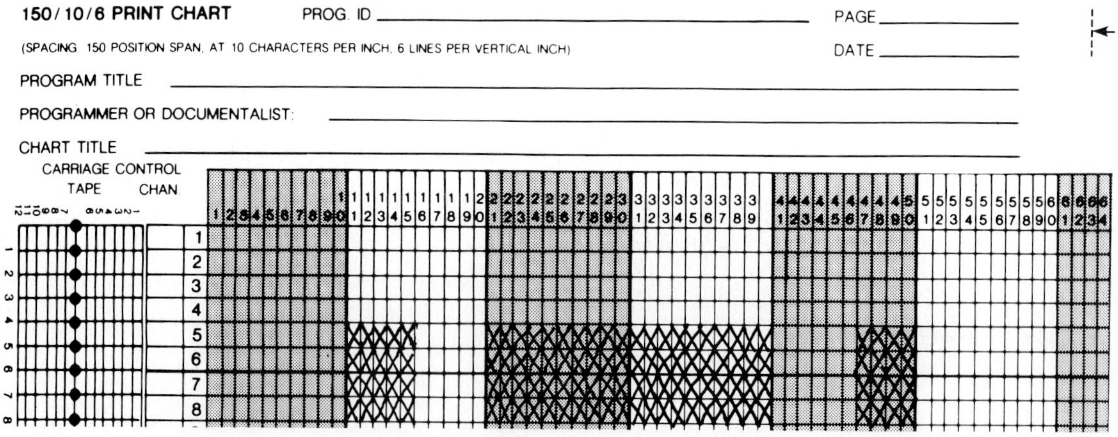

FIGURE 1.22 Programming Project: Finished Report

```
01023     VPMI INDUSTRIES         050         00045     FRESH FOODS MARKET     VX
02345     BULLFROG INC.           060         00059     METHOD MARKETS         VX
04568     FIRST CITY BANK         090         00078     OPEN MARKETS           VX
06892     DOLLAR INC              100         00128     OPEN MARKETS           VX
09871     BOOKS INC.              050         00025
00032     SAMS PLACE              VX          00026
```

RPG: A Programming Language for Today

Chapter 2

Arithmetic Operations and Report Formatting

What you will learn in Chapter 2

General Rules for Coding Calculation Specifications
Addition
Subtraction
Multiplication
Division
Division Remainders
Rounding a Result Field (Half-adjusting)

Defining a Constant
Calculating Cumulative Totals
Summary of Arithmetic Functions in RPG
Sample Program Using Arithmetic Calculations
Input Data
Output Data
File Description Specifications

Input Specifications
Calculation Specifications
Output Specifications
Field Editing (Edit Codes)
Other Edit Codes
Editing Dollar Signs
Printing Total Lines

A programming language for business applications must be capable of performing the arithmetic functions of addition, subtraction, multiplication, and division. In this chapter you will learn how to perform all of these functions using the Calculation Specifications form.

GENERAL RULES FOR CODING CALCULATION SPECIFICATIONS ■

Any fundamental arithmetic calculation can be performed in RPG. It is possible to add, subtract, multiply, or divide using the normal rules of arithmetic. Figure 2.1 shows a blank RPG Calculation Specifications form which is used for performing arithmetic functions.

On the Calculation Specifications form, the fields to be calculated are entered in factor 1 (columns 18–27) and factor 2 (columns 33–42). The operation to be performed is entered in the operation columns (28–32). A result field name is entered in columns 43–48. Valid operation code entries for performing arithmetic are:

ADD — adds factor 1 to factor 2
SUB — subtracts factor 2 from factor 1
MULT — multiplies factor 1 by factor 2
DIV — divides factor 1 by factor 2

These operation codes are special words or reserved words in RPG and must always be spelled the same way. That may appear obvious, but not all operation codes and special words are quite so simple to remember. Reserved words must *never* be used as field names in a program.

FIGURE 2.1 RPG Calculation Specifications Form

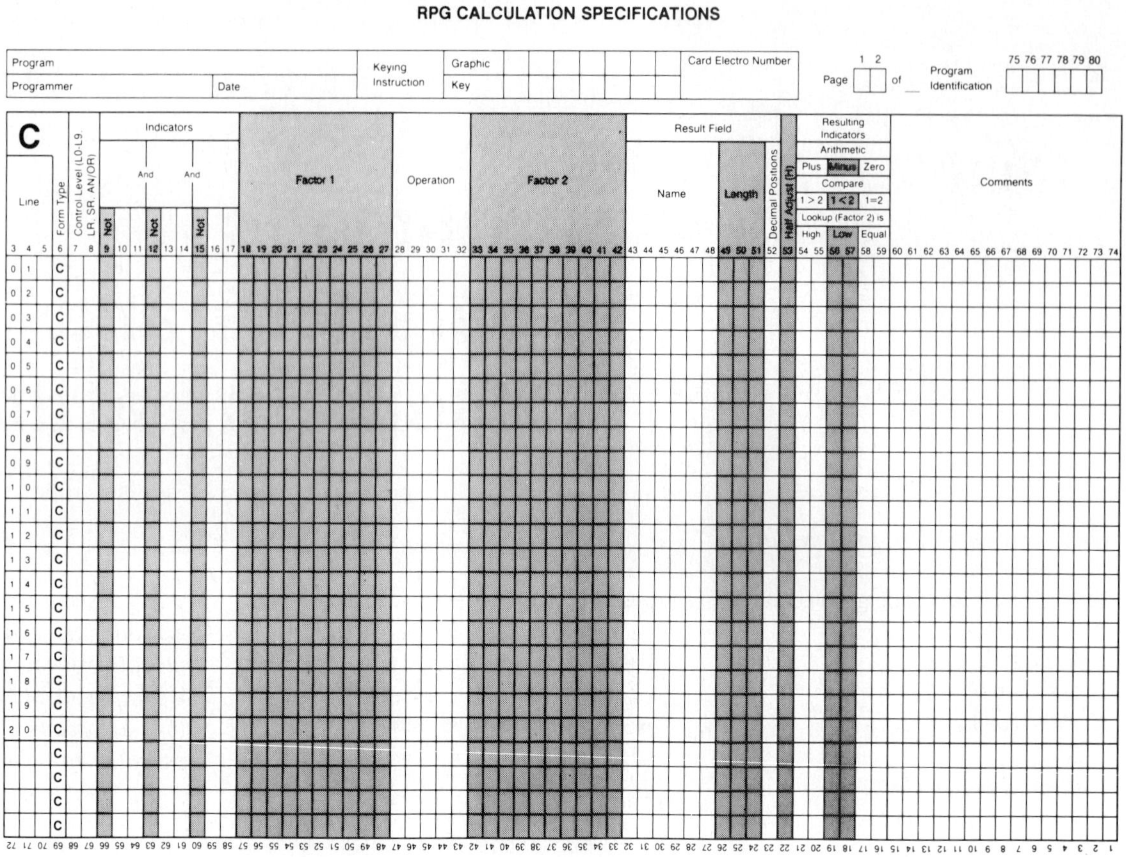

The result field may contain a new name invented by the programmer. When this is a new field that has not been defined anywhere else in the program, it is necessary to define the length of the result field, entering the number in columns 49–51. It is also necessary to enter the number of decimal positions in column 52. (Enter the digit 0 for zero decimal positions.) Once a field has been defined in a program, it is not necessary to define it again in any other lines of code.

At the beginning of the RPG cycle, before any input records have been read, RPG automatically assigns the value of zero to all numeric fields and moves blanks to all alphabetic fields. This means that at the beginning of calculations, all result fields will contain zeros. It is then up to the programmer to determine what value will be in each field.

Addition

One field can be added to another by placing one variable (or literal) field in factor 1 and the other in factor 2. The operation code for addition is ADD. As is true of any addition, it does not matter which field name is placed in factor 1 and which in factor 2 (2 can be added to 4 or 4 can be added to 2 with the same result). The result of the addition will be found in the field defined in the result field. Figure 2.2 shows an example of a Calculation Specification for performing an addition operation.

It is important that the result field be sufficiently large to contain the final total. For example, if a three-position field is being added to a four-position field, the result field should be defined as a five-position field to ensure that it can contain the largest possible combination to be added (e.g., 999 and 9999 would give the result 10998). If the result field is not defined with a sufficient number of positions to contain the result, the high-order position(s) will be dropped. For example, if the result field were defined as four positions and the answer should have been 10998, the first position would be lost and the answer would show as 0998, which is obviously wrong. This is referred to as truncation and should be avoided.

FIGURE 2.2 Calculation Specifications for an Addition Operation

RPG CALCULATION SPECIFICATIONS

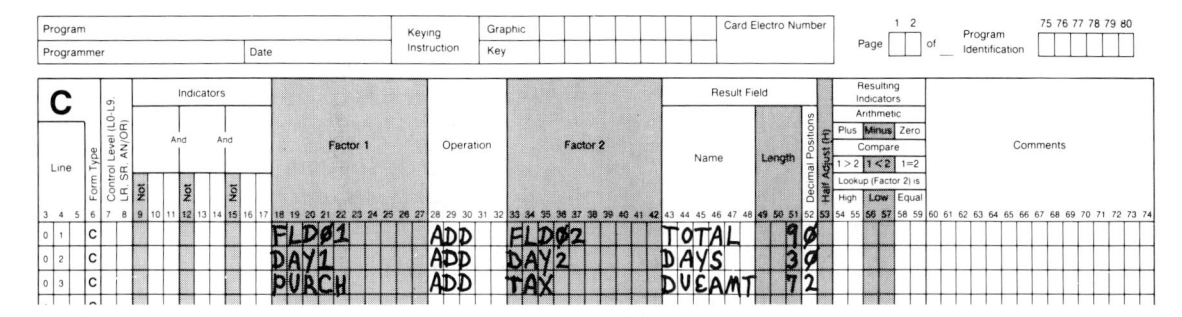

Line	Form Type	Control Level	Indicators (And/Not)	Factor 1	Operation	Factor 2	Result Field Name	Length	Decimal Positions	Resulting Indicators	Comments
01	C			FLD01	ADD	FLD02	TOTAL	9	0		
02	C			DAY1	ADD	DAY2	DAYS	3	0		
03	C			PURCH	ADD	TAX	DUEAMT	7	2		

Subtraction

The operation code for subtraction is SUB. One field can be subtracted from another by putting one number in factor 1 and the other in factor 2. In subtraction, however, care must be taken as to which number is placed in which factor. The number to be subtracted from (the subtrahend) must be placed in factor 1 and the number to subtract (the minuend) must be placed in factor 2. Figure 2.3 shows an example of a Calculation Specification for performing a subtraction operation.

Multiplication

Multiplication is accomplished using the MULT operation code. As is true of addition, it does not matter which field is placed in factor 1 and which in factor 2. When performing any multiplication operation, whether manually or with a computer, the maximum size of the result can be determined by adding the number of digits in the multiplier to the number of digits in the multiplicand. For example, if a four-digit number is multiplied by a two-digit number, the maximum size of the result will be six digits. The programmer must be aware of this and define the result field accordingly. It would be wise to define the result field as a six-position field even though the programmer might feel that the result would not normally ever reach six digits. It is a good idea to provide for the largest possible total rather than practice a false thrift and allow only for the normal result. Figure 2.4 shows an example of a Calculation Specification for performing a multiplication operation.

Occasionally, the programmer has prior knowledge of the data and can make good judgment decisions on result field sizes. For example, if the multiplier is a 10-position field with 8 decimal positions (most of which are unused in actual practice) and the multiplicand is a 12-position field with 9 decimal positions, it would be foolish (and impossible in RPG II) to define the result field as a 22-position field with 17 decimal positions. The wise programmer would sensibly drop the non-significant decimal positions. By defining the result field as a 6-position field with 1 decimal position, the extra decimal positions would simply be dropped.

The important point to learn here is the application of common sense to ensure that a valid answer will be derived from the incoming data.

FIGURE 2.3 Calculation Specifications for a Subtraction Operation

RPG CALCULATION SPECIFICATIONS

Line	Form Type	Control Level	Indicators (And/Not)	Factor 1	Operation	Factor 2	Result Field Name	Length	Decimal Positions	Resulting Indicators	Comments
01	C			FLD02	SUB	FLD01	TOTFLD	5	0		
02	C			INVAMT	SUB	DISCNT	AMTDUE	7	2		
03	C			TOTHRS	SUB	OTHRS	REGHRS	3	1		

Chapter 2 Arithmetic Operations and Report Formatting

FIGURE 2.4 Calculation Specifications for a Multiplication Operation

RPG CALCULATION SPECIFICATIONS

Line	Factor 1	Operation	Factor 2	Result Field Name	Length
01	HOURS	MULT	RATE	PAYAMT	72
02	DAYS	MULT	HOURS	TOTHRS	41
03	QTY	MULT	PRICE	TOTDUE	72

Division

When division is to be performed in an RPG program, the DIV operation is specified on the Calculation Specifications form. In the example in Figure 2.5, the year-to-date sales field (YTDSAL in factor 1) is to be divided by the month field (MONTH in factor 2) to determine average monthly sales (AVGSAL in the result field). The year-to-date sales field forms the dividend, the month field forms the divisor, and the answer (or quotient) shows the average sales. The remainder after the DIV operation is complete happens to be zero in this example.

The key to remembering which field is the divisor and which the dividend is to remember that factor 1 is *divided by* factor 2.

To determine how large to define the result field, look at the size of the dividend and make the length of the quotient (result) exactly the same. This will always be the maximum size needed for the result field. (This assumes that you are dividing by a number greater than or equal to 1; dividing a number by a decimal may result in a quotient with more positions than the dividend.)

The programmer must take care that the program will *never* attempt to divide by zero. Besides the fact that such an attempt would be a mathematical impossibility, many computer systems will come to a complete halt if such a condition is encountered. At the very least, incorrect results will be produced if the program is allowed to continue. Some good methods for error detection will be described in future chapters, but for the moment it is necessary only that the student be aware that such dangers exist and to try to ensure that the input data or data definitions are sufficiently error-free that such an event could never occur.

Division Remainders

Our final concern with division is the remainder. Certainly, many division computations will produce a remainder. The user may want the remainder to be simply dropped as was done in multiplication on the unnecessary decimal positions. This is often the case in the business world.

FIGURE 2.5 Calculation Specifications for a Division Operation (No Remainder)

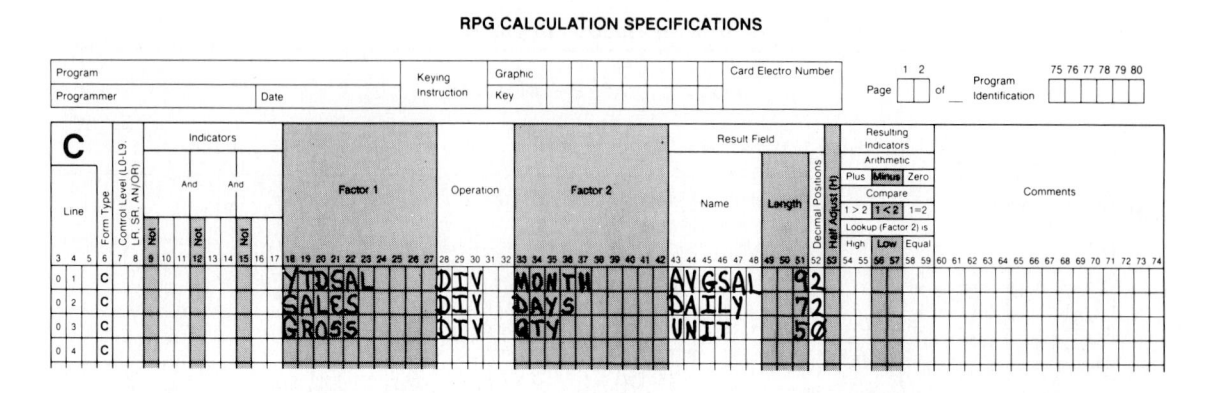

RPG CALCULATION SPECIFICATIONS

Line	Factor 1	Operation	Factor 2	Result Field Name	Length
01	YTDSAL	DIV	MONTH	AVGSAL	92
02	SALES	DIV	DAYS	DAILY	72
03	GROSS	DIV	QTY	UNIT	50
04					

RPG: A Programming Language for Today

FIGURE 2.6 Calculation Specifications for a Division Operation (with Remainder)

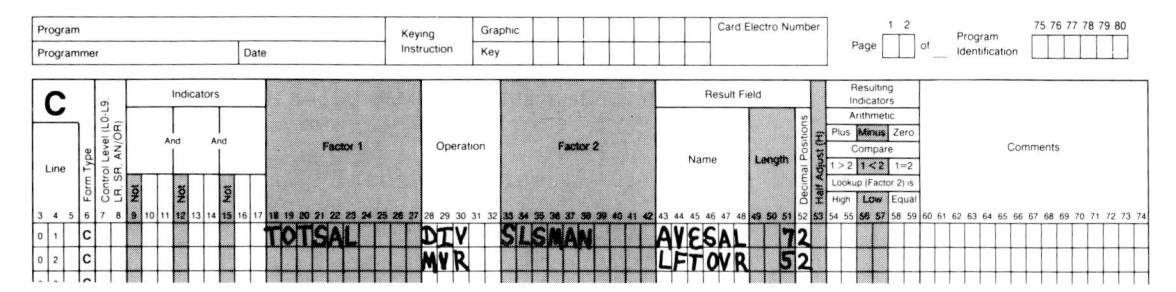

```
Line  C  Factor 1    Operation  Factor 2    Result Field  Length  Dec
01    C  TOTSAL      DIV        SLSMAN      AVESAL        7   2
02    C              MVR                    LFTOVR        5   2
```

For example, checks are not made out for fractions of pennies and some management reporting shows only the dollar figures, dropping the pennies completely. In some environments, however, the remainder is needed, and the programmer must have a method for retrieving that figure.

RPG provides that capability using the MVR (move remainder) operation code. Immediately after the division calculation has been performed, the remainder is available and can be used by the program. The programmer must move that remainder immediately (using the MVR command) into a field where it will be saved (to be printed or used in other calculations). Factors 1 and 2 are left blank and the remainder will be placed in the result field. In the example in Figure 2.6, TOTSAL is divided by SLSMAN with a result of AVESAL. On the very next line, using the MVR (move remainder) operation code, the remainder is moved into the result field, which in this example is called LFTOVR. It is defined as a five-position field with two decimal positions. LFTOVR can now be printed on the report along with all the other information.

The important point to remember is that the MVR operation must *directly* follow the DIV operation on the very next line of code.

Rounding a Result Field (Half-adjusting)

In programs for business applications involving decimal positions, it is often desirable to round off (half-adjust) the result field to the nearest useful decimal position. For example, if an answer came out to 6.2222, it might be desirable to round the answer to $6.22 so the amount could be paid in dollars and cents. If the answer had come out to 6.2269, the amount would commonly be rounded upward to the next penny and paid as $6.23. It is common practice to round upward any digit equal to or greater than 5 and to simply drop anything less than 5.

To do rounding in RPG, it is necessary only to enter the letter *H* (for half-adjust) in column 53 on the Calculation Specifications. See the example in Figures 2.7(a) and 2.7(b).

Half-adjust may be used for any arithmetic operation, but if MVR is being used with a division operation it is not possible (nor would it be desirable) to use the half-adjust function for that calculation. Half-adjust can be used only if the number of decimal positions in the result will be greater than the number of decimal positions specified for the result field.

FIGURE 2.7(a) Rounding: Input Specifications

```
Line  I   Filename       Position          Field Location   Field
01    I   INPUT    AA  01
02    I                                    24  28 3 RATE
03    I                                    29  32 2 HOURS
```

Chapter 2 Arithmetic Operations and Report Formatting   33

FIGURE 2.7(b) Rounding: Calculation Specifications

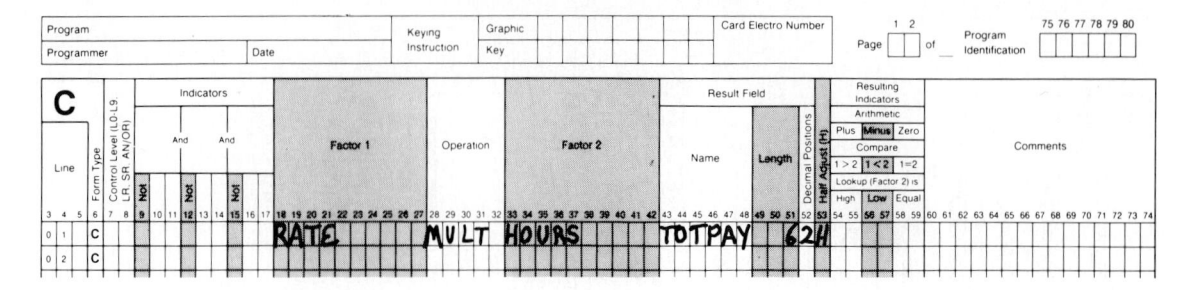

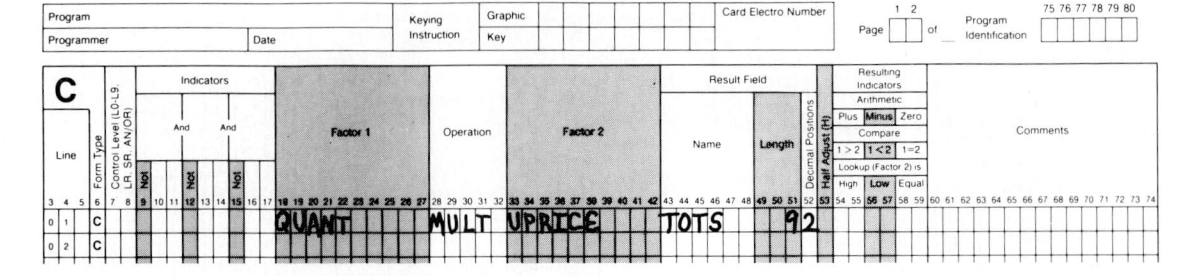

Line	C	Factor 1	Operation	Factor 2	Result Field Name	Length	Decimal Positions	Half Adjust
01	C	RATE	MULT	HOURS	TOTPAY	6	2	H
02	C							

One constraint of RPG is that a numeric field can never have more than 15 positions, including the decimal portion of the field. Defining a dollar value field as a 15-position field (with two decimals) would allow that field to contain $9,999,999,999,999.99, which seems quite sufficient for any business application. Figures 2.8(a) and 2.8(b) show an example of a calculation resulting in a very large number.

Defining a Constant

It is possible to define numeric data explicitly within a program when that data is a known quantity. Instead of reading a field of input data from somewhere else (such as a disk file), it is sometimes more efficient to define a data value within the program calculations. For example, in calculating a sales tax total, the programmer will already know the percentage amount that must be used. If the sales tax is always 6% of the sales amount, there is no need to enter .06 in every input record. Such data can be defined in the program as a constant.

To enter a constant value, the programmer can enter the value needed for the computation in factor 1 or factor 2 of the Calculation Specifications. Figure 2.9 shows some examples of the use of

FIGURE 2.8(a) Data for a Large-Size Result

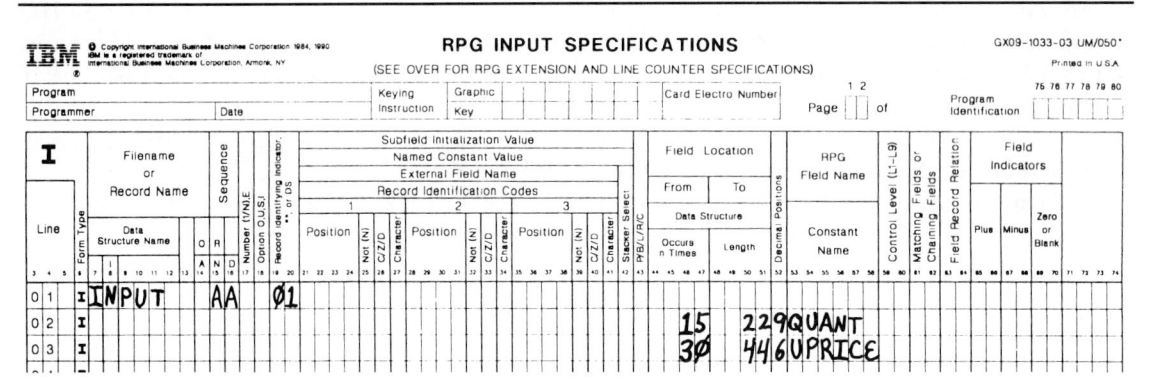

Line	I	Filename or Record Name	Sequence		Field Location From	To	RPG Field Name
01	I	INPUT	AA	01			
02	I					15	229 QUANT
03	I					30	446 UPRICE

FIGURE 2.8(b) Input Specifications

Line	C	Factor 1	Operation	Factor 2	Result Field Name	Length	Decimal Positions
01	C	QUANT	MULT	UPRICE	TOTS	9	2
02	C						

34   *RPG: A Programming Language for Today*

FIGURE 2.9 Examples of Constants

```
RPG CALCULATION SPECIFICATIONS
Line  Form  Factor 1   Operation  Factor 2   Result    Length  Dec
                                              Field
01  C       PURCH      MULT       .06        TAXAMT    62  H
02  C       AMT        MULT       100        TOTAL     72
03  C       2.75       ADD        SALE       TOTSAL    92
04  C       TOTAL      MULT       -1         NEGTOT    50
05  C       YEARS      DIV        12         MONTH     72
```

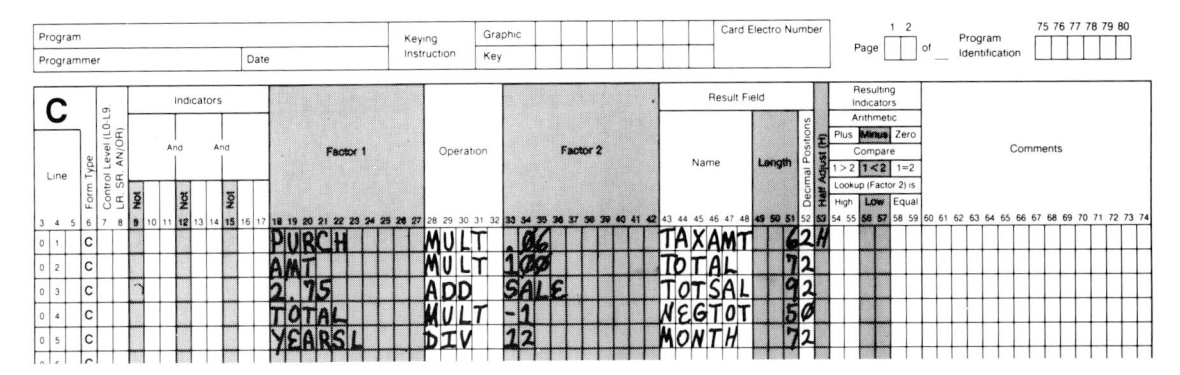

constants in coding. The numeric value is entered exactly as needed for the calculation. When RPG finds a numeric value in factor 1 or factor 2, it recognizes the value as a constant. The value entered for 6% is .06 (including the decimal point). A negative value may be entered by preceding it with a dash.

Calculating Cumulative Totals

Calculating single totals, as shown in the previous examples, is not sufficient for providing reports that will require a cumulative total for a string of numbers. Just as an adding machine provides a grand total for a string of entered numbers, a computer report is expected to provide a final total for a column of numbers.

The method for doing this involves the same operation codes already discussed in this chapter. It is usually done using the ADD function. The addition will be done each time an input record is read. The input figure will be added to the total field, producing a new total field. This is shown in Figure 2.10.

The input field HOURS in factor 1 is added to TOTHRS in factor 2, giving the result TOTHRS. On the first time through the program, TOTHRS contains zero. If the first input record contains 2.0 hours, 2.0 is added to zero, giving a total of 2.0 hours in the field TOTHRS. On the second time through the program, the hours in the second record will be added to the total in TOTHRS. If the second record contains 3.0 hours, 3.0 will be added to the total of 2.0 which is already waiting in the total field (TOTHRS), and the result will be 5.0 hours.

This will continue for each record until all records have been added to the cumulative total. This total can then be printed as a final total at the end of the report.

Summary of Arithmetic Functions in RPG

All the necessary arithmetic functions of RPG II have now been covered. Computations more complicated than these must be handled by the programmer. However, in the world of business, these basic functions will adequately fulfill most demands.

FIGURE 2.10 Cumulative Addition

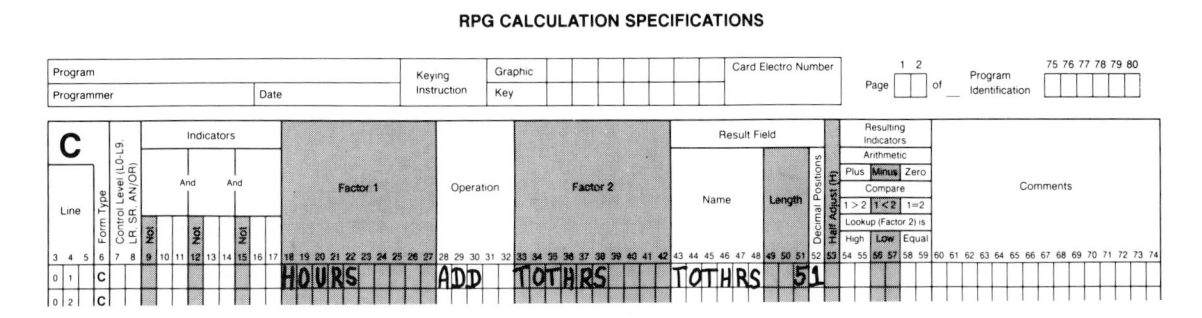

```
RPG CALCULATION SPECIFICATIONS
01  C       HOURS      ADD        TOTHRS     TOTHRS    51
02  C
```

Chapter 2 Arithmetic Operations and Report Formatting

FIGURE 2.11 ACME Enterprises Report

```
                    ACME ENTERPRISES
     EMPL#          NAME              REG      O.T.     D.T.     TOTAL
                                      HRS      HRS      HRS      HRS

       123      JONES, SAM            8.0       .5                8.5
      3682      PARRISH, DOTTI        8.0      4.0       .5      12.5
      3999      RILEY, MITZI          8.0      2.0              10.0
      5107      VOLKMANN, JODY        7.0                         7.0
      8667      WEBER, HEATHER        8.0      1.5                9.5

                                     39.0      8.0       .5      47.5
```

It is possible to do any arithmetic calculations in RPG by using the operation codes ADD, SUB, MULT, or DIV. The rules for each of these functions are the same as in arithmetic done in the conventional manner. Totals produced may be printed or used in further arithmetic calculations.

SAMPLE PROGRAM USING ARITHMETIC CALCULATIONS ■

Figure 2.11 is a report summarizing payroll data for each of five employees of Acme Enterprises, adding overtime hours and double-time hours to regular hours to give final total hours. Included for each employee are number and name, regular hours, overtime hours, double-time hours, and total hours worked. Total hours in each category are printed at the bottom of the report.

RPG can easily perform all the functions needed to generate this report using the Calculation Specifications. The sample program demonstrating this is similar to the program described in Chapter 1, but some fields have been added to the input record. The input Record Layout for this project is shown in Figure 2.12.

Input Data

The input record is similar to the employee input record in Chapter 1 (employee number, name, address, and city/state). The new fields are regular hours, overtime hours, and double-time hours. These fields will contain numeric values (for example, 8.0 for eight hours of regular time or 0.5 for a half hour of overtime). (There is no actual decimal point in the input data. It is an assumed decimal point upon which the programmer and analyst have agreed. It is shown only as a vertical dotted line on the input format.) The fields for the hours worked consist of three columns (or positions) each, two for the whole number (hours) and one for tenths of an hour.

Output Data

The output from the sample program will be a report listing employee number and name, as it was in Chapter 1. Here the similarity ends, however, because neither the address nor the city/state will

FIGURE 2.12 Input Record Layout

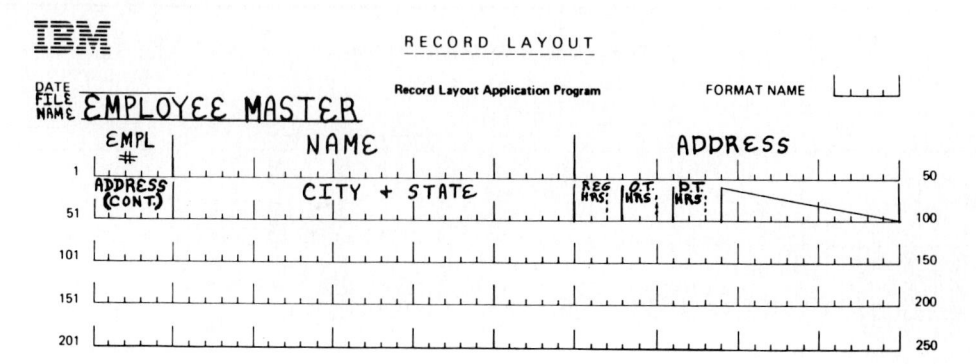

FIGURE 2.13 Printer Spacing Chart

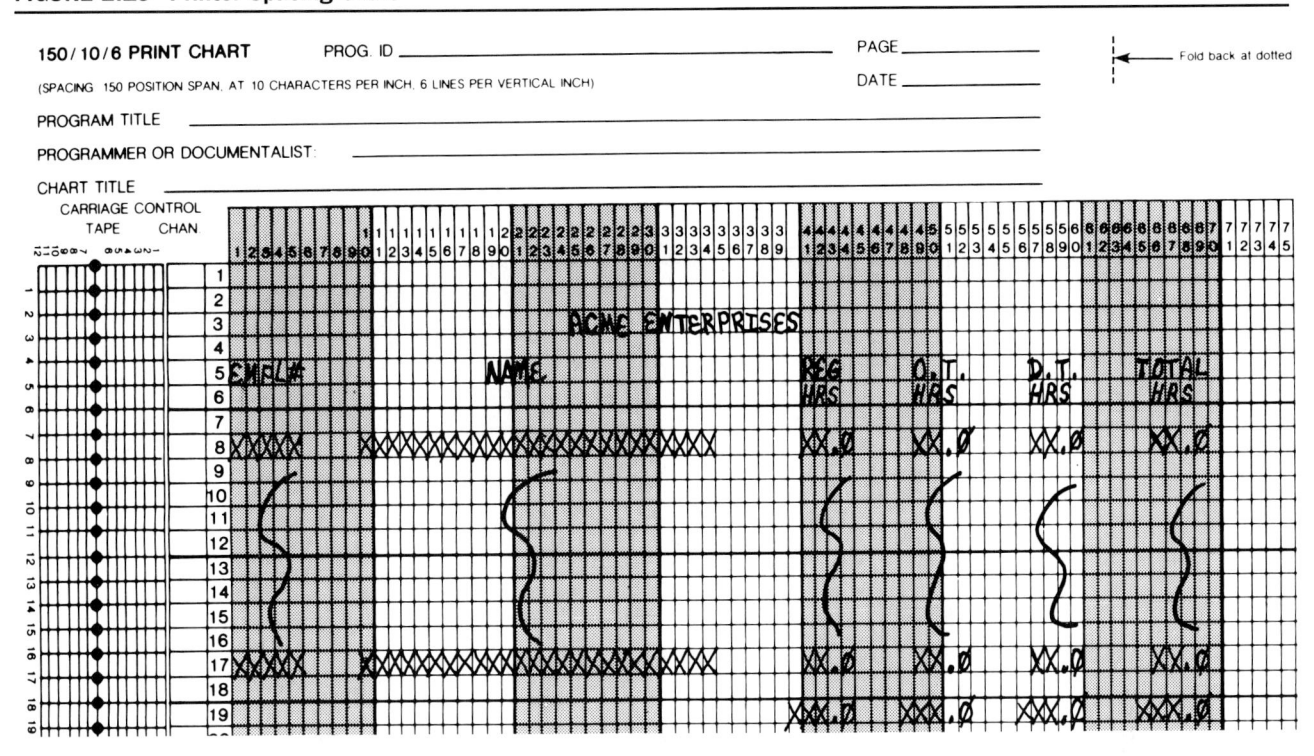

be used. RPG does not object to this omission. It will print out whatever it is told to print out and omit whatever it is told to omit.

Figure 2.13 shows a Printer Spacing Chart for the output report. Unlike the report in Chapter 1, this prints three lines of heading before it prints the main body of the report.

Let us now look at the coding for this program.

File Description Specifications

Exactly as in the program in Chapter 1, the File Description Specifications show the file PAYMAST as an input file with a length of 128 which is being read from disk (Figure 2.14).

The output file is defined as a PRINTER file named REPORT with a length of 132. The only new entry on this line is the OF entry in columns 33–34. This is an overflow indicator, a kind of flag used in the Output Specifications to notify RPG that the report being printed has completely filled up one page and is ready to overflow to a new page. (Other acceptable indicators which could have been used are OA, OB, OC, OD, OE, OG, or OV. These would be used if you were printing more than one report in the same program.) The programmer can then use this indicator to take some action in the program, such as printing totals or page headings or skipping to a new page.

Input Specifications

The input file, PAYMAST, must be defined on the Input Specifications. We will use record identifying indicator 01, just as in Chapter 1. When a record is read from this file, indicator 01 will be turned *on* to indicate that a record has been read and is ready for processing. Figure 2.15 shows the Input Specifications.

Just as in Chapter 1, it is necessary to describe each field in the file. The only new feature shown here is the use of column 52 of the Input Specifications form. If column 52 is blank, it means that the field is *alphabetic* and can never have arithmetic functions performed on it. A number entered in column 52 identifies the field as *numeric* and specifies the number of decimal positions contained in that field. This means that arithmetic calculations can be performed using this field, and it also means that the field can be edited on the output report.

Chapter 2 Arithmetic Operations and Report Formatting **37**

FIGURE 2.14 File Description Specifications

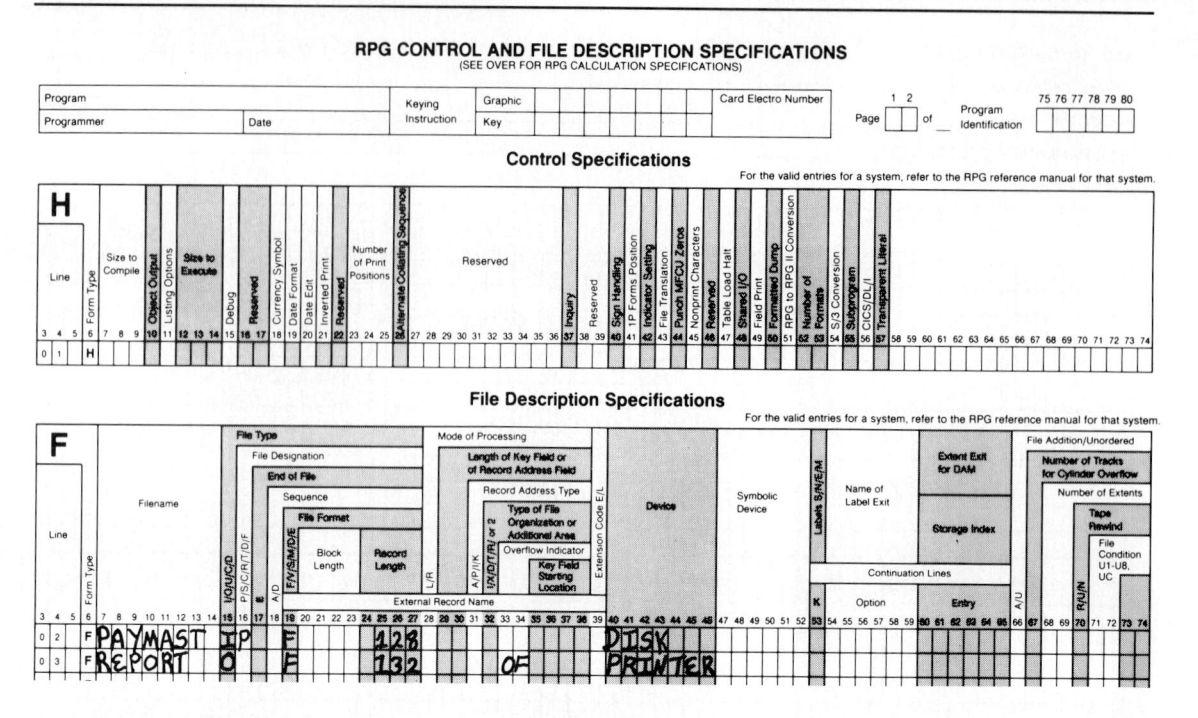

The employee number (EMPL#) field is defined as columns 1 through 5. The zero in column 52 of the Input Specifications defines the EMPL# field as a numeric field having no decimal positions (i.e., it is a whole number). The fields NAME, ADDRES, and CITY have blanks in column 52, defining them as alphabetic fields. The fields REGHRS, OTHRS, and DTHRS have been defined as numeric fields with one decimal position each.

Calculation Specifications

Whenever calculations are to be performed within an RPG program, the Calculation Specifications form is used. Calculations for the sample program are shown in Figure 2.16. The entry C is always recorded under Form Type (column 6) of the Calculation Specifications.

Each line of the Calculation Specifications performs one calculation in the program. First, the regular hours worked and the overtime hours worked are to be added together. Next, that total is to be added to the double-time hours. The programmer simply tells the computer to do each calculation in the sequence in which it should occur.

FIGURE 2.15 Input Specifications

38   RPG: A Programming Language for Today

FIGURE 2.16 Calculation Specifications

[Figure: RPG Calculation Specifications form showing two lines:
Line 01: Factor 1 = REGHRS, Operation = ADD, Factor 2 = OTHRS, Result Field = TOTHRS, Length = 3, Decimal Positions = 1
Line 02: Factor 1 = TOTHRS, Operation = ADD, Factor 2 = DTHRS, Result Field = TOTHRS]

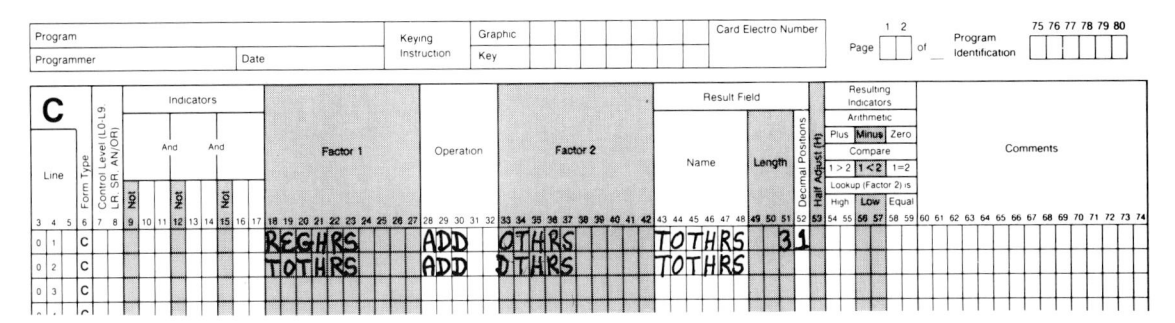

Columns 9–17 are reserved for indicators. For the moment, we can assume that indicators are not needed in this program, because only one file is being read and the program will be processing every record in that file. In effect, the calculations will be defaulting to an indicator 01. This means that every time a record is read, indicator 01 is turned *on* and these calculations will be performed.

In the operation columns (28–32) of the Calculation Specifications the operation code for addition, ADD, is entered. The name of the first field to be added (REGHRS) goes in factor 1, and the name of the second (OTHRS) in factor 2. These field names are listed exactly as on the Input Specifications form. The name of the result field will be specified in the result field of the Calculation Specifications. Since this field was not specified on the Input Specifications, the programmer can assign any name to it. Of course, the name follows the same rules as those required for field names on the Input Specifications.

In the sample program the result field is named TOTHRS. Since the size and characteristics of TOTHRS have not been defined on the Input Specifications (or anywhere else), they need to be defined on the Calculation Specifications. First, the length of the field TOTHRS is entered as 3 in columns 49–51, meaning that TOTHRS has a length of 3 positions. Next, to define TOTHRS as a numeric field, a number must be entered in column 52 of the Calculation Specifications. This number specifies the number of decimal positions. Since TOTHRS needs to have one decimal position, the number 1 is entered in column 52.

Once TOTHRS has been defined, it will never need to be defined again within this program. Once a field has been defined, it may not be redefined with different attributes within the same program. Although a field can be defined several times (always with exactly the same definition), it is safer to define it only once.

This completes the first line of the calculations. Note that except for the length field, which is a numeric field and must be right-justified, all names are left-justified in their respective fields on the form. Note also that it is not necessary to enter leading zeros in the length field, although leading zeros are permissible.

As shown in Figure 2.16, the second line of calculations is similar to the first. The total (TOTHRS) is entered in factor 1, the operation code ADD is entered, and the double-time hours (DTHRS) are entered in factor 2. The result field will contain the total of this calculation (TOTHRS). This time, TOTHRS need not be defined because it was defined on the first line of calculations and one definition is sufficient. RPG would accept it if the field had been defined again on the second line, but both definitions must be exactly the same. For this reason, it is better to define TOTHRS only once since it is easy to make an error on the second line and cause yourself unnecessary problems.

The double-time hours have now been added to the total that was created in the first line of calculations. All decimal points are understood. That is, decimal points are not keyed into any of the numeric fields, but the computer will "understand" where they are to go.

Entering Comments on Calculation Lines

Space is provided to enter comments on the calculation line in columns 60–74. RPG ignores these comments completely. Since the area provided is small, however, it is usually better to use a complete line for comments (entering an asterisk in column 7) as explained earlier.

FIGURE 2.17 Calculation of Final Totals

RPG CALCULATION SPECIFICATIONS

Line	Form Type	Factor 1	Operation	Factor 2	Result Field Name	Length	Dec
01	C	REGHRS	ADD	FINREG	FINREG	5	1
02	C	OTHRS	ADD	FINOT	FINOT	5	1
03	C	DTHRS	ADD	FINDT	FINDT	5	1
04	C	TOTHRS	ADD	FINTOT	FINTOT	5	1

Calculating Final Totals

The next calculation that needs to be made for each record is the calculation of final totals. Since in the sample program a total is needed for each of the four columns (REGHRS, OTHRS, DTHRS, and TOTHRS), four separate calculations will be needed to accumulate the final totals for each. FINREG, FINOT, FINDT, and FINTOT will contain the final totals for the report. They are defined with a length of five positions to allow for a larger cumulative total. Figure 2.17 shows this coding.

Output Specifications

In addition to the data to be printed on the report, headings also need to be printed. The report needs a title, and the columns should have headings so the reader will know what the columns mean. To print headings, it is necessary to learn how to code heading lines on the Output Specifications. In the sample program (Figure 2.18) these specifications are shown.

On the Output Specifications, column 6 will contain the letter O. The filename (in columns 7–15) for the output report is REPORT (as specified on the File Specifications).

The entry in column 15 may be H (for header), D (detail), or T (Total). Although an H is appropriate for headings and will work effectively, using D is equally acceptable. RPG really makes no differentiation between headings and detail.

Line Spacing for Heading Lines

As described in Chapter 1, columns 17–22 control the spacing and page overflow for the report. Columns 17 and 18 control spacing. Every time a line is printed on a report, it is usually necessary to advance at least one line to the next line. The number of lines to advance *before* printing a line is specified in column 17. The number of lines to advance *after* printing a line is specified in column 18. As shown in the Printer Spacing Chart for this sample program (Figure 2.13), one line is left blank between the main heading and the start of the column heads to make the report easier to read. This means that two lines should be advanced after printing the heading, so a 2 is entered in column 18.

FIGURE 2.18 Output Specifications for Report Headings

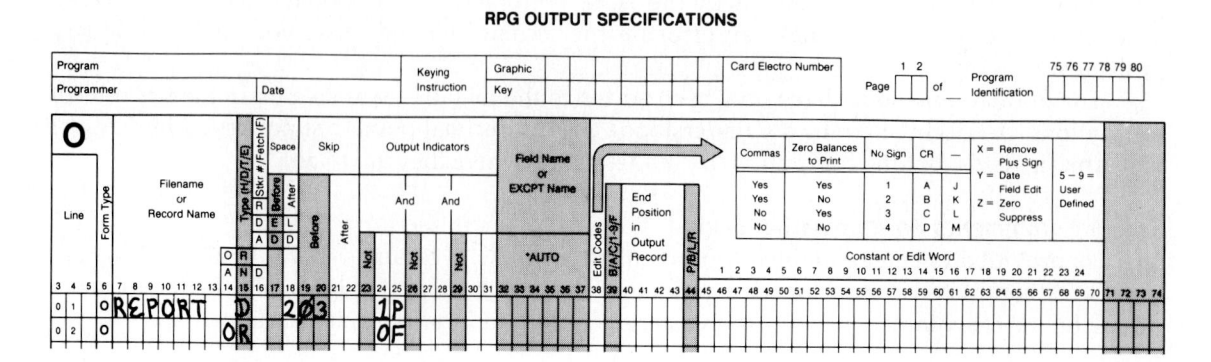

RPG OUTPUT SPECIFICATIONS

Line	Form Type	Filename or Record Name	Type	Space Before	Space After	Skip Before	Skip After	Output Indicators	Field Name or EXCPT Name	End Position in Output Record
01	O	REPORT	D	2	03			1P	*AUTO	
02	O	OR						OF		

Page Overflow (Starting a New Page)

Columns 19–22 on the Output Specifications form control skipping to a new page on a report. When this sample report is printed, it should skip to the top of a new page, print the headings, and then begin printing the report. When the end of a page is reached, it should skip to a new page, print the headings again, and then continue printing the report. This is accomplished by specifying (in columns 19–22) the line numbers on which these heading lines should print.

In the sample program, the Printer Spacing Chart in Figure 2.13 shows the heading printed on the third line of each page. Therefore, the Output Specifications form will need an 03 in columns 19–20 to tell the program to skip to the third line of each page *before* printing the first heading line. Another programmer might have chosen to start on line 1 or line 2, both equally good choices. This shows that the programmer can have complete control over the way a report can look.

Output Indicators (Indicator 1P)

In columns 23–31 the output indicators are defined. In the example, the indicator 1P, denoting page 1, has been entered. This means that the heading will print on the first page of the report every time it is run. What about page 2 or page 3? If a heading is expected on those pages, it is necessary to tell the program that. The way to do this is to use the overflow indicator explained under File Description Specifications (Figure 2.14). This indicator will be available whenever an end-of-page overflow has been reached and can now be used on the Output Specifications to cause a heading to print. This is done by a second line of code specifying that the headings should also print when the indicator OF is encountered. Notice that the word OR was entered in columns 14–15 and the letters OF in the indicator column (columns 24–25). This means that these headings should also be printed if the indicator OF (overflow to a new page) is found.

Heading Content (Literal Data)

Now the heading itself can be defined.

REPORT TITLE. As shown in Figure 2.11, the report title is positioned in the center of the page. The end position for the title needs to be defined. The program title should end in column 40, so the ending position 40 will be entered in columns 40–43. Leading zeros are not necessary in columns 40–43, although entering them would have been equally correct. In columns 45–70, any fixed or literal information to be printed on the report can be entered—in this case, the program title ACME ENTERPRISES. 'ACME ENTERPRISES' is entered on the Output Specifications within quotation marks. (Note that IBM computers use single quotation marks to define a literal. Many other computers require double quotation marks.) Anything entered within the quotation marks will print on the report exactly as stated. The quotation marks will *not* be printed on the report—they are only needed by the program to define the literal. Figure 2.19 shows these entries.

To center the heading, it was necessary to make the ending position 40. This is why a report format is designed on a Printer Spacing Chart before coding begins. It is helpful to consult the Printer Spacing Chart to determine in which position the literals or fields will need to end.

FIGURE 2.19 The Report Title

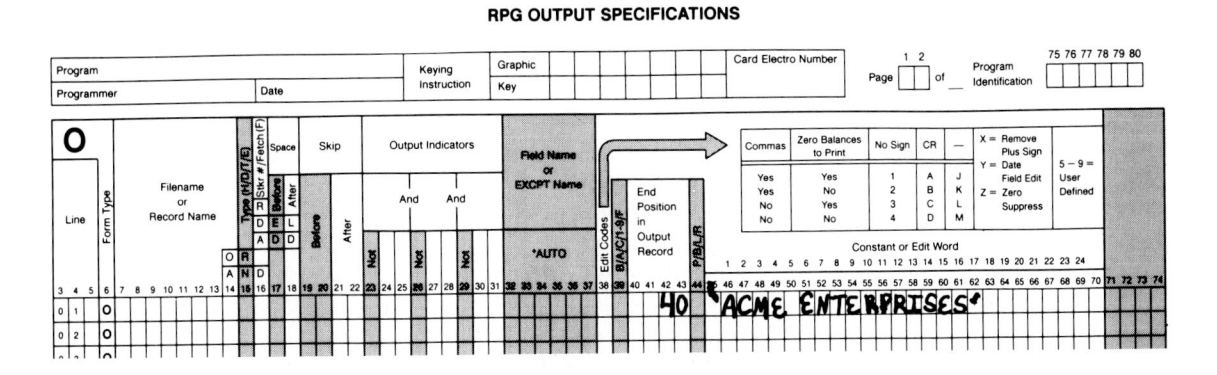

FIGURE 2.20 Heading Lines for Column Headings

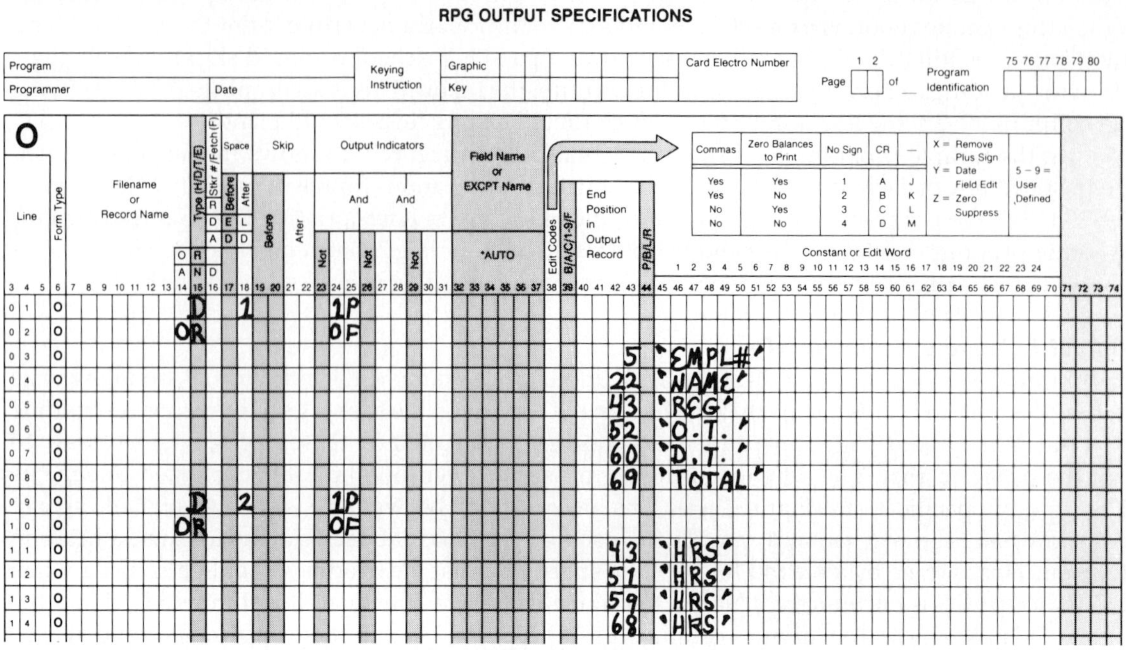

COLUMN HEADINGS. In the example in Figure 2.20, it can be seen that the second and third heading lines to be printed on the report are identified by the value D in column 15 and that each of the lines will be written on the report when either the first page indicator (1P) or the overflow (OF) are *on*.

Note that it was not necessary to repeat the filename (REPORT) on each of these lines because RPG assumes that every line following the filename (REPORT) will continue to apply to that same filename (until it finds some different name). The printer will space once after the second line is printed and twice after the third line is printed. Each column of the report will be headed with a suitable title such as NAME over the column containing the employee name, and so on.

Each column heading is given an ending position indicating where it will appear on the report. Note that the ending positions must lie somewhere between positions 1 and 132 (the width of the page on which the report will be printed). Keep in mind that the first word in the heading must fit on the page. For example, a five-position field must end no farther left than position 5.

Report Detail

The body of the report can now be defined. Column 15 contains a *D* to indicate that this event will occur when detail input records are read. Column 18 contains a 1 because this report should advance one line after printing each line, and once again the indicator 01 will be used to cause each detail line to print (just as was done in Chapter 1). Figure 2.21 shows the detail coding for the body of the report. Each field on the report is defined with an ending position which should align it under its proper heading.

Field Editing (Edit Codes)

Most business reports need some editing to make them more readable. That is, reports are easier to read if the numeric fields have decimal points, if commas and sometimes dollar signs are printed, and if leading zeros are omitted. This is made easy in RPG through the use of edit codes.

Column 38 on the Output Specifications form provides a variety of editing options for each numeric field. For example, the edit code Z entered in column 38 after the EMPL# field tells RPG to omit the leading zeros in employee numbers. This will not change the original data; it simply makes the report look better.

The edit code K entered in column 38 after the fields for regular hours, overtime hours, double-time hours, and total hours tells RPG to print a decimal point to show where the fractions of hours occur. The leading zeros will also be suppressed to make the report more readable.

FIGURE 2.21 Detail Coding

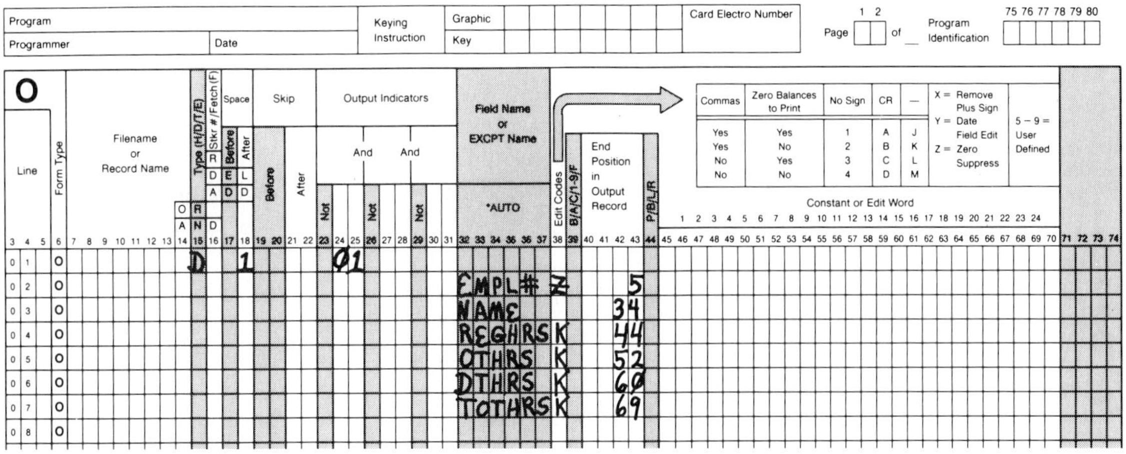

Figure 2.22 summarizes the effect on various data of using the edit code K on a numeric field containing two decimal positions. Note the following:

1. If the entire number is zero, the field printed will be blank.
2. When there are non-significant leading zeros, they are suppressed, the commas are also suppressed, and the number will print correctly.
3. When the number has fewer leading zeros, the zeros are suppressed and the comma and decimal point will print correctly.
4. When all digits are significant, they will all print showing the decimal point and appropriate comma(s).
5. If the number is a negative number, a minus sign will print after the number.
6. When only two positions are significant, all leading zeros are suppressed and the decimal point will print as expected.
7. When only one position is significant, all leading zeros are suppressed up to the decimal point. The decimal point will print and the leading zero after the decimal point will continue to be printed.

Note that even when all the data is positive, as it is in the sample program, use of edit code K will leave a space for a minus sign after the number. Be sure to take this into account when planning the print format. For example, when indicating that a field should end in position 120 (with an edit code of K), position 120 is reserved for the sign and the field itself will appear to end in position 119. It is also important to ensure that the next field will not overlay the minus sign inadvertently. This is one of the good reasons for always drawing up a Printer Spacing Chart before beginning to code the Output Specifications.

FIGURE 2.22 Summary of Edit Codes

Commas	Zero Balances to Print	No Sign	CR	—
Yes	Yes	1	A	J
Yes	No	2	B	K
No	Yes	3	C	L
No	No	4	D	M

X = Remove Plus Sign
Y = Date Field Edit
Z = Zero Suppress
5 – 9 = User Defined

Constant or Edit Word

Chapter 2 Arithmetic Operations and Report Formatting

Other Edit Codes

Besides the edit codes Z and K, there are several other edit codes that may be used to alter the way a numeric field is printed. Any of these codes may be entered in column 38 on the Output Specifications to change the editing of a field.

The codes follow these rules:

Code 1: Commas and zero balances will print. No sign will be printed.
Code 2: Commas will print. Zero balances will *not* print. No sign will be printed.
Code 3: Commas will *not* print. Zero balances will print. No sign will be printed.
Code 4: Neither commas nor zero balances will print. No sign will be printed.
Code A: Commas and zero balances will print. A CR symbol will be printed for negative numbers.
Code B: Commas will print. Zero balances will *not* print. A CR symbol will be printed for negative numbers.
Code C: Commas will *not* print. Zero balances will print. A CR symbol will be printed for negative numbers.
Code D: Neither commas nor zero balances will print. A CR symbol will be printed for negative numbers.
Code J: Commas and zero balances will print. A – (minus sign) will be printed for negative numbers.
Code K: Commas will print. Zero balances will *not* print. A – (minus sign) will be printed for negative numbers.
Code L: Commas will *not* print. Zero balances will print. A – (minus sign) will be printed for negative numbers.
Code M: Neither commas nor zero balances will print. A – (minus sign) will be printed for negative numbers.
Code X: Removes the plus sign (so you need not allow room for it in the field).
Code Y: Puts the slashes (/) in a six-position date field so that it prints in the format 01/01/92.
Code Z: Suppresses leading zeros.

Figure 2.23 shows the various edit codes that may be used. This chart appears in the upper right corner of every Output Specifications form as a handy reference. Some of these codes are more commonly used than others but they are all available to the programmer to meet any requirement.

Editing Dollar Signs

In many business applications fields often represent dollar values. Sometimes it is desired to print a dollar sign in front of a field. If there is sufficient space on the report, it is useful to print a floating dollar sign—that is, a dollar sign just in front of the first significant character in the edited output field. To do this, all that is required is placing the symbol within single quotation marks (double quotation marks on a non-IBM computer) in columns 45–47 of the Output Specifications following the field. This is illustrated in Figure 2.24.

When this method is used, the floating dollar sign is printed to the left of the leftmost significant digit in the field. In some applications, it is desirable to print a fixed dollar sign which will always appear in the same position regardless of the size of the value in the field. To do this,

FIGURE 2.23 Effect of Edit Code K

INPUT FIELD (2 DECIMALS)	PRINTED RESULT
000000000	
000034100	341.00
000682501	6,825.01
040003120	400,031.20
140003120	1,400,031.20
004388125 (NEGATIVE)	43,881.25-
000000001	.01

FIGURE 2.24 Output Specifications for a Floating Dollar Sign Edit

[RPG Output Specifications form showing line 01 with field AMOUNT, edit code K, end position 100, and constant '$']

the dollar sign should be specified as a literal on a coding line by itself (not attached to any field) with the ending position defined as the position where it is desired to print the dollar sign. See example in Figure 2.25.

Printing Total Lines

In the sample program, it was decided to print a line of totals at the end of the report. This was specified as illustrated in Figure 2.26.

When a total line is to be printed (i.e., a line to be printed only at a specified time other than detail time) the letter T is entered in column 15 (the type field). It is not necessary to repeat the filename REPORT. The number 2 has been entered in column 17 to indicate that the program should advance two lines before printing the total line. The indicator in columns 24–25 tells the program when this total line should be printed. The indicator used is LR, which means last record. What this tells RPG is to print the final total after all the records in this file have been read and the indicator LR is *on*.

As in the previous examples, the field specifications for the total line are placed on the next coding line from the entries to define the type of record to be printed. It is helpful to print a literal such as "TOTAL FOR ALL EMPLOYEES" on the line on which the totals are printed. It is also useful to edit each field in the same way that the detail lines were edited. It is also important that the total fields have the same ending positions as the corresponding detail fields. This is not absolutely required, but it makes for a more readable report. Thus in the example the total for regular hours appears exactly beneath the detail regular hours, and so on.

This completes the sample program.

Arithmetic in RPG is as simple as stating the arithmetic problem. The program executes the arithmetic functions step by step exactly as written. RPG can do addition, subtraction, multiplication, and division. It can round result fields and it can save the remainders in division. It can perform calculations on numeric fields up to 15 positions in length (including decimal positions). Literal numeric fields can be included in calculations.

FIGURE 2.25 Output Specifications for a Fixed Dollar Sign Edit

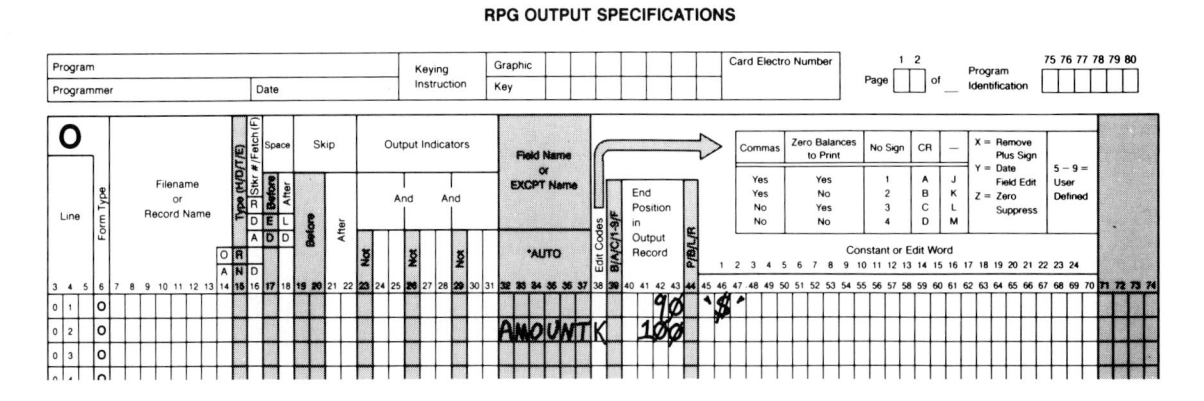

[RPG Output Specifications form showing line 01 with end position 90 and constant '$', line 02 with field AMOUNT, edit code K, end position 100]

FIGURE 2.26 Printing a Total Line

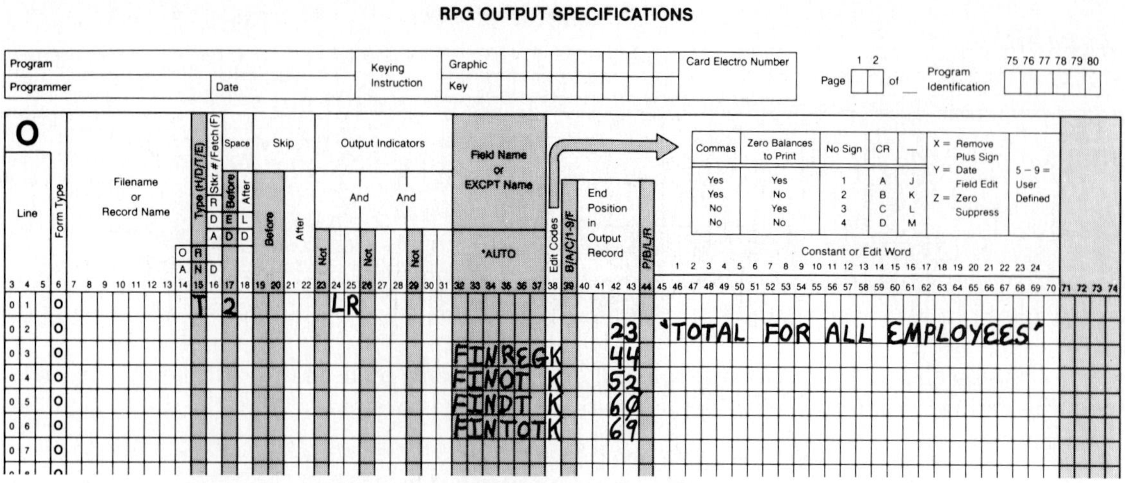

[RPG Output Specifications form showing:
- Line 01: O, T 2, LR
- Line 02: O, 23, 'TOTAL FOR ALL EMPLOYEES'
- Line 03: O, FINREGK, 44
- Line 04: O, FINOT K, 52
- Line 05: O, FINDT K, 60
- Line 06: O, FINTOTK, 69
- Line 07: O]

Report formatting can be done with the use of defined constants for headings or titles of any kind. Numeric fields can be easily edited to display dollar signs, commas, decimal points, minus signs, etc., on the output report.

SUMMARY ■

In this chapter, you have learned how to do all types of arithmetic computations.

You have learned how to use the Calculation Specifications to perform the arithmetic functions needed for most business applications. You have learned how to perform addition, subtraction, multiplication, and division. You have also learned how to determine the field length for the result fields created by your calculations.

You know how to round (half-adjust) a result field to the number of decimal positions needed. You know how to save the remainder created from a division operation to be printed or saved for future calculations.

Besides all the simple calculations, you have learned how to compute a cumulative total which can be printed at the end of the report. Along with this, you know how to use the LR (last record) indicator.

You learned how to print report headings and column titles not only on the first page, using the first page indicator (1P), but also on subsequent pages using page overflow techniques.

You learned how to suppress leading (non-significant) zeros in a numeric field on a report and you learned the use of other valuable edit codes which make a report more readable.

Although you have completed only two chapters, you already are capable of writing a useful program that will do any type of calculation, keep cumulative totals, and print reports that display all the results of these computations.

REVIEW QUESTIONS

1. Explain how a field is defined on the Input Specifications as numeric or alphabetic.
2. Describe the coding of the ADD operation.
3. Why is it necessary to place an entry in the length field (columns 49–51) on the Calculation Specifications for arithmetic operations?
4. Why is it important to place an entry in the decimal position (column 52) on the Calculation Specifications for arithmetic operations?
5. In what way does the coding for the SUB operation differ from the coding for the ADD operation?
6. What is the maximum length permitted in RPG II for a numeric field?
7. Describe how cumulative totals are developed.
8. Explain what "half-adjusting" a result field means.
9. When coding for a multiplication (MULT) operation, which field should be entered in factor 1, the multiplier or the multiplicand? Which field should be entered in factor 2?
10. What must a programmer *never* do when coding the statement for division?
11. Describe the coding for finding the remainder when a division operation is performed.
12. Explain how to determine optimal field lengths for result fields when performing calculations.
13. Explain the use of constants in performing calculations.
14. Explain the use of comments on the Calculation Specifications.
15. What function is performed by the 1P indicator on the Output Specifications?
16. Explain the function of the page overflow.
17. Explain how literals are defined when printing reports.
18. How are preceding zeros suppressed for numeric fields on reports?
19. Explain the methods for editing a numeric field for printing on a report.
20. How does the compiler recognize heading lines, detail lines, and total lines?

EXERCISES

1. On a Calculation Specifications form, enter the coding which will add a constant of 20.00 to a field named PRICE giving a result field named TOTPRC. TOTPRC is a five-position field including two decimal positions. This calculation is to be performed only when indicator 20 is *on*.
2. On a Calculation Specifications form, enter the coding which will subtract a field named TAX from a field named GROSS giving a result field named NETPRC. NETPRC is a six-position field including two decimal positions. This calculation is to be performed only when indicator 35 is *off*.
3. On a Calculation Specifications form, enter the coding which will multiply a field named NETPRC by a field named RATE giving a result field named TOTAL. NETPRC is a six-position field and RATE is a four-position field. Both contain two decimal positions. The result field should be half-adjusted (rounded) to two decimal positions.
4. On a Calculation Specifications form, enter the coding to divide a field named SCORES by a field named TOTNUM giving a result field named AVERAG. All fields have zero decimal positions. Make the entry for moving any remainder to a field named REM.

DEBUGGING EXERCISES

Instructions

The following RPG programs contain an error or errors. Some of these errors are indicated by the RPG compiler on the program listing. A list of syntax errors is given at the end of the program listing. Other types of errors may occur which will not be shown. These are called logic errors.

Study each program and its syntax errors. Locate each error (including logic errors) and on a separate coding form make the correct entry for the line(s) in error.

Explain each error and how it should be corrected.

```
       100   F* TITLE: DEBUG PROJECT 2-A
       200   F* DATE:   2/28/91         AUTHOR: D.CABLE
       300   F* DESCRIPTION:  CALCULATE PRICES
       400   F***************************************************
       500   F* MODIFICATIONS:
       600   F* NO.      DATE       INIT       DESCRIPTION
       700   F*          XX/XX/XX   XXX        XXXXXXXXXXXXXXXXXXXXXXXXXXXXX
       800   F***************************************************

NAME OF PROGRAM WILL BE PJ002A IN LIBRARY CABLE

              H
* 1019                   ALL DECIMAL DATA ERRORS IGNORED
       900   FFILEIN  IP  F       120          DISK
      1000   FREPORT  O   F       132          PRINT
* 2013                                    2013-******

      1100   F***************************************************

      1200   IFILEIN   AA   01
      1300   I                              1  10 PNNUM
      1400   I                             11  11 CODE
      1500   I                             12  170QUANT
      1600   I                             18  230PRICE

      1700   OREPORT  H   101    1P
* 6035                  6035-******

      1800   O        OR         OF
* 6036                 6036-**

      1900   O                                  12 'PART#'
      2000   O                                  15 'CD'
      2100   O                                  21 'QTY'
      2200   O                                  30 'PRICE'
      2300   O                                  40 'TOTAL'
      2400   O        D   1      01
* 6035                  6035-******

      2500   O                       PNNUM      12
      2600   O                       CODE       14
      2700   O                       QUANTZ     21
      2800   O                       PRICE Z    30
      2900   O                       TOTPRCZ    40
      3000   O        T   1      LR
* 6035                  6035-******

      3100   O                                  15 'TOTAL'
      3200   O                       COUNT      15
```

48 *RPG: A Programming Language for Today*

```
  SEQUENCE        1         2         3         4         5         6         7
  NUMBER    678901234567890123456789012345678901234567890123456789012345678901234
      3300  O                        FINTOTZ    40
  * * * * *  E N D   O F   S O U R C E * * * * *
```

* 7086   900   RPG PROVIDES BLOCK/UNBLOCK SUPPORT FOR FILE FILEIN.
* 7086   1000   RPG PROVIDES BLOCK/UNBLOCK SUPPORT FOR FILE REPORT.

CROSS-REFERENCE LISTING

```
          FILE/RCD     DEV/RCD      REFERENCES (D=DEFINED)
     01   FILEIN       DISK           900D  1200
     02   REPORT       DISK          1000D  1700   2400   3000


          FIELD        ATTR         REFERENCES (M=MODIFIED D=DEFINED)
          CODE         A(1)          1400D  2600
* 7030    COUNT        A(4)          3200
* 7030    FINTOT       P(5,0)        3300
          PNNUM        A(10)         1300D  2500
          PRICE        P(6,0)        1600D  2800
* 7031    QUANT        P(6,0)        1500D
* 7030    QUANTZ       A(4)          2700
* 7030    TOTPRC       P(5,0)        2900


          INDICATOR    REFERENCES (M=MODIFIED D=DEFINED)
          LR            900D  3000
* 7030    OF
          01           1200M  2400
          1P           1700
```

MESSAGES

```
  MSGID     SEV  NUMBER  TEXT
* QRG1019   00     1     IGNDECERR(*YES) SPECIFIED ON COMMAND. NO DECIMAL DATA ERRORS
* QRG2013   10     1     DEVICE (POSITIONS 40-46) NOT PRINTER, CARD, DISK, WORKSTN, S
* QRG6035   20     3     SPACE OR SKIP MUST BE SPECIFIED ONLY FOR PROGRAM DESCRIBED F
                         ASSUMED.
* QRG6036   20     1     OVERFLOW INDICATOR USED NOT ASSIGNED TO THIS FILE. INDICATOR
* QRG7030   30     5     FIELD OR INDICATOR NOT DEFINED.
* QRG7031   00     1     NAME OR INDICATOR NOT REFERENCED.
* QRG7086   00     2     RPG WILL HANDLE BLOCKING FUNCTION FOR THE FILE. INFDS CONTENT
                         ARE TRANSFERRED.
```

MESSAGE SUMMARY

```
TOTAL   00    10    20    30    40    50
  14     4     1     4     5     0     0

   33 RECORDS READ FROM SOURCE FILE
   SOURCE RECORDS INCLUDE    24 SPECIFICATIONS,     0 TABLE RECORDS, AND    9 COMMENTS

QRG0008 COMPILE TERMINATED. SEVERITY 30 ERRORS FOUND IN PROGRAM
   * * * * *  E N D   O F   C O M P I L A T I O N * * * * *
* QRG1020            ERROR OCCURRED CREATING OR UPDATING DATA AREA RETURNCODE. COMPIL
```

```
100  F* TITLE: DEBUG PROJECT 2-B
200  F* DATE:  2/28/91         AUTHOR: D.CABLE
300  F* DESCRIPTION:  CALCULATE EMPLOYEE EARNINGS
400  F*********************************************************
500  F* MODIFICATIONS:
600  F* NO.     DATE       INIT      DESCRIPTION
700  F*         XX/XX/XX   XXX       XXXXXXXXXXXXXXXXXXXXXXXXXXXX
800  F*********************************************************
```

NAME OF PROGRAM WILL BE PJ002B IN LIBRARY CABLE

```
              H
* 1019                ALL DECIMAL DATA ERRORS IGNORED
       900  FEMPRCD   IP  F       120            DISK
      1000  FREPORT   O   F       132      OF    PRINTER
      1100  F*********************************************************

      1200  IEMPRCD   AA   01
      1300  I                                        1   1 RCDTYP
      1400  I                                        2   6 EMP#
      1500  I                                        7  22 NAME
      1600  I                                       23 262RATE
      1700  I                                       27 302HOURS

      1800  C          RATE      MPY  HOURS       TOTPAY    32
* 5014                            5014-*****.
* 5024                                              5024-**********

      1900  C          HOURS     ADD THOURS       TOTPAY    32
* 5014                            5014-*****         .    .    ..
* 5031                                              5031-******.   ..
* 5038                                                    5038-***  ..
* 5048                                                         5048-*.
* 5051                                                         5051-**

      2000  C          COUNT     SUB '1'          COUNT     70
* 5167                            5167-**********


      2100  OREPORT   H   203      1P
      2200  O         OR           OF
      2300  O                                     30 'EMPLOYEE EARNINGS'
      2400  O         H   2        1P
      2500  O         OR           OF
      2600  O                                      5 'EMP#'
      2700  O                                     21 'RATE'
      2800  O                                     30 'HOURS'
      2900  O                                     40 'EARNINGS'
      3000  O         D   1        01
      3100  O                              EMP#    6
      3200  O                              RATE   21
      3300  O                              HOURS  30
      3400  O                              TOTPAY 40
      3500  O         T   1        01
      3600  O                                     15 'TOTAL HOURS'
      3700  O                              THOURS 30
* * * * * E N D   O F   S O U R C E * * * * *


* 7086     900   RPG PROVIDES BLOCK/UNBLOCK SUPPORT FOR FILE EMPRCD.
```

CROSS-REFERENCE LISTING

```
          FILE/RCD    DEV/RCD      REFERENCES (D=DEFINED)
      01  EMPRCD      DISK         900D 1200
      02  REPORT      PRINTER      1000D 2100  2400  3000  3500
```

```
           FIELD       ATTR         REFERENCES (M=MODIFIED D=DEFINED)
* 7030     COUNT       A(4)         2000
           EMP#        A(5)         1400D 3100
           HOURS       P(4,2)       1700D 1900 3300
* 7031     NAME        A(16)        1500D
           OTPAY                    1800D
           OUNT        P(7,0)       2000D
           RATE        P(4,2)       1600D 1800 3200
* 7031     RCDTYP      A(1)         1300D
* 7030     THOURS      A(4)         1900 3700
* 7030     TOTPAY      A(4)         3400


           INDICATOR   REFERENCES (M=MODIFIED D=DEFINED)

           LR          900D
           OF          1000D 2200 2500
           01          1200M 3000 3500
           1P          2100  2400


MESSAGES

   MSGID       SEV   NUMBER   TEXT

* QRG1019      00      1      IGNDECERR(*YES) SPECIFIED ON COMMAND. NO DECIMAL DATA ERRORS
* QRG5014      30      2      OPERATION CODE ENTRY (POSITIONS 28-32) NOT VALID. SPECIFICAT
* QRG5024      30      1      FACTOR 2 ENTRY (POSITIONS 33-42) NOT VALID SYNTACTICALLY. IF
                              OTHERWISE BLANK ASSUMED.
* QRG5031      30      1      SYNTAX OF RESULT FIELD NAME (POS 43-48) NOT VALID. IF ENTRY
                              BLANK ASSUMED.
* QRG5038      20      1      RESULT FIELD LENGTH (POSITIONS 49-51) NOT VALID. 4 ASSUMED
* QRG5048      10      1      HALF ADJUST ENTRY (POSITION 53) MUST BE H OR BLANK. H ASSUME
* QRG5051      10      1      RESULTING INDICATORS (POSITIONS 54-59) NOT VALID. BLANK ASSU
* QRG5167      30      1      FACTOR 2 LITERAL (POSITIONS 33-42) NOT VALID. SPEC IGNORED I
                              ENTRY ASSUMED BLANK
* QRG7030      30      3      FIELD OR INDICATOR NOT DEFINED.
* QRG7031      00      2      NAME OR INDICATOR NOT REFERENCED.
* QRG7086      00      1      RPG WILL HANDLE BLOCKING FUNCTION FOR THE FILE. INFDS CONTEN
                              ARE TRANSFERRED.


MESSAGE SUMMARY

   TOTAL     00     10     20     30     40     50
     15      4      2      1      8      0      0

   37 RECORDS READ FROM SOURCE FILE
   SOURCE RECORDS INCLUDE   28 SPECIFICATIONS,   0 TABLE RECORDS, AND   9 COMMENTS

QRG0008 COMPILE TERMINATED. SEVERITY 30 ERRORS FOUND IN PROGRAM

* * * * * E N D   O F   C O M P I L A T I O N * * * * *
* QRG1020               ERROR OCCURRED CREATING OR UPDATING DATA AREA RETURNCODE. COMPI
```

PROGRAMMING PROJECT

Project Overview

A report is to be printed listing customer number, month-to-date sales, and year-to-date sales figures for each customer. Write the RPG program to produce this listing. Sample data for this project can be found in Appendix D.

Input Format

The input data for the project is found in a file called CUSTMAST in the sample data. The Record Layout for this file is shown in Figure 2.27.

Output Format (Printer Spacing Chart)

The output format for the project is a report with standard headings. The report will show the customer number, name, month-to-date sales, and year-to-date sales for each customer. A final total is printed at the end of the report for total month-to-date and year-to-date figures. The Printer Spacing Chart for this report is shown in Figure 2.28.

An example of the finished report is shown in Figure 2.29.

FIGURE 2.27 Programming Project: Record Layout

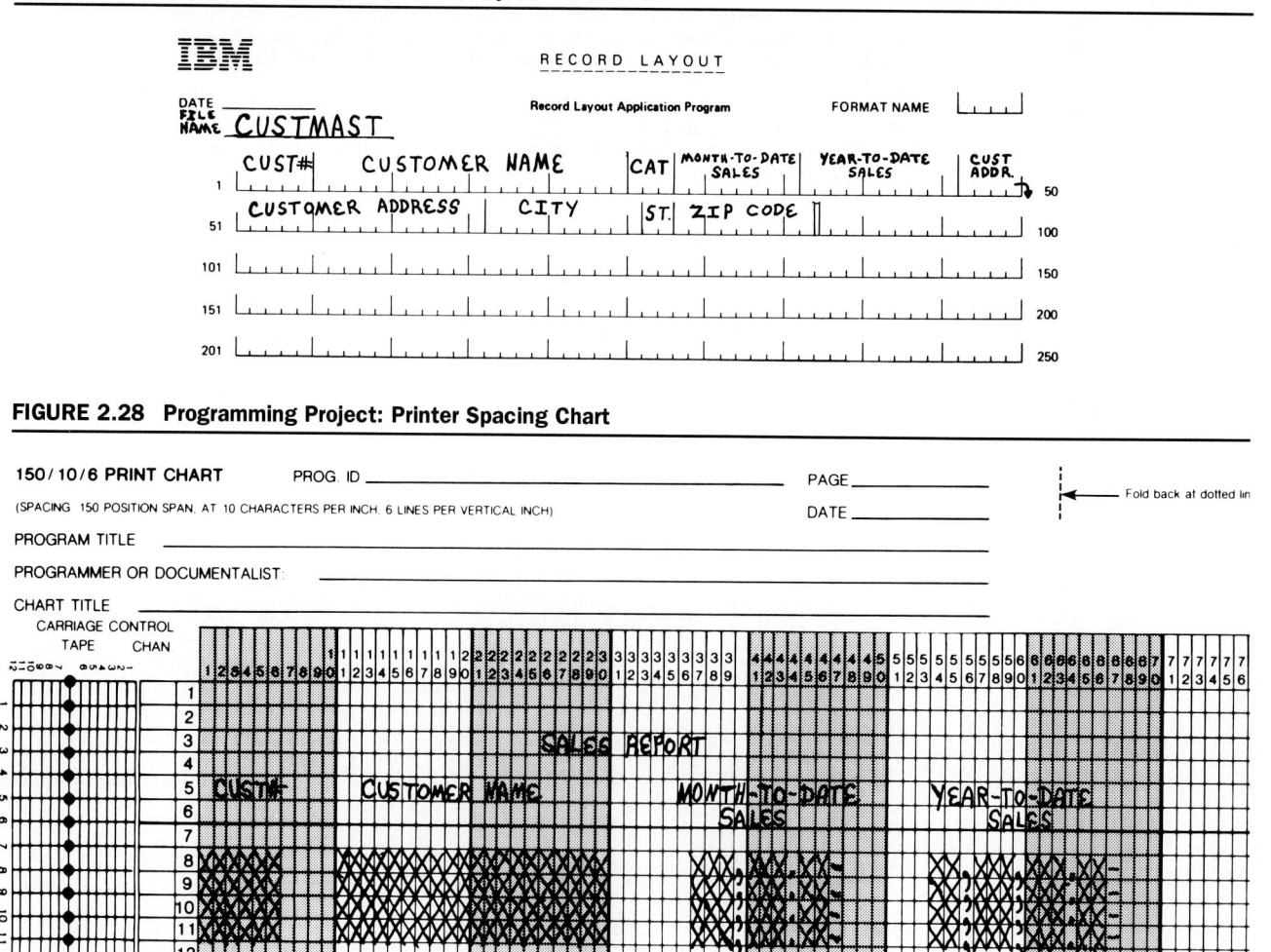

FIGURE 2.28 Programming Project: Printer Spacing Chart

FIGURE 2.29 Programming Project: Finished Report

```
                        SALES REPORT
    CUST#    CUSTOMER NAME      MONTH-TO-DATE     YEAR-TO-DATE
                                    SALES             SALES

    01023    VPMI INDUSTRIES       10,680.00         56,805.00
    02345    BULLFROG INC.             35.80          5,865.41
    04568    FIRST CITY BANK       90,051.80         90,051.80
    06892    DOLLAR INC             8,650.18        886,650.18
    09871    BOOKS INC.             4,590.80          9,561.72
    00032    SAMS PLACE                18.93             18.93
    00045    FRESH FOODS MARKET       320.00            960.00
    00059    METHOD MARKETS           205.00          3,500.00
    00078    OPEN MARKETS             375.00          3,985.62
    00128    OPEN MARKETS             985.00          9,356.01
    00025
    00026

                                  115,912.51      1,066,754.67
```

Chapter 3

Computer Logic and Processing Multiple Record Types

What you will learn in Chapter 3

Fundamental Logic Concepts (Compare)
Using Indicators In RPG
The Compare Operation
    Comparing Alphabetic or Alphanumeric Data Fields
    Comparing Alphabetic or Alphanumeric Fields of Different Lengths

Comparing Numeric Data Fields
Comparing Numeric Fields of Different Lengths
Collating Sequence for Comparing
Comparing Literal Values
Summary of the Compare Operation
Processing Multiple Record Types

Use of Input Indicators
Field Record Relation Indicators
Calculation Specifications
Branching Within Calculations
    Using the GOTO Operation
    Using Subroutines
    GOTOs Revisited

In addition to having the ability to do arithmetic functions, computers also can perform logical operations. This means that the computer can compare the values in two fields and determine whether one of the fields is greater than, less than, or equal to the other. A programmer can then use this determination to control other actions performed in the program.

This capability makes computers appear to be making almost human judgments. In fact, however, a programmer has made all of the real decisions and judgments and the program simply carries them out.

FUNDAMENTAL LOGIC CONCEPTS (COMPARE) ∎

Let us look at a flowchart illustrating the concept behind the logic (or compare) function. Note in Figure 3.1 the points at which a yes or no decision changes the path. If a customer's purchases are within a specified credit limit, no special action is taken. If the purchases exceed the credit limit, however, a message is printed on the report. In RPG, such a decision is accomplished with the use of the compare function and resulting indicators. Let us look first at indicators, what they are and how they work.

FIGURE 3.1 Credit Limit Flowchart

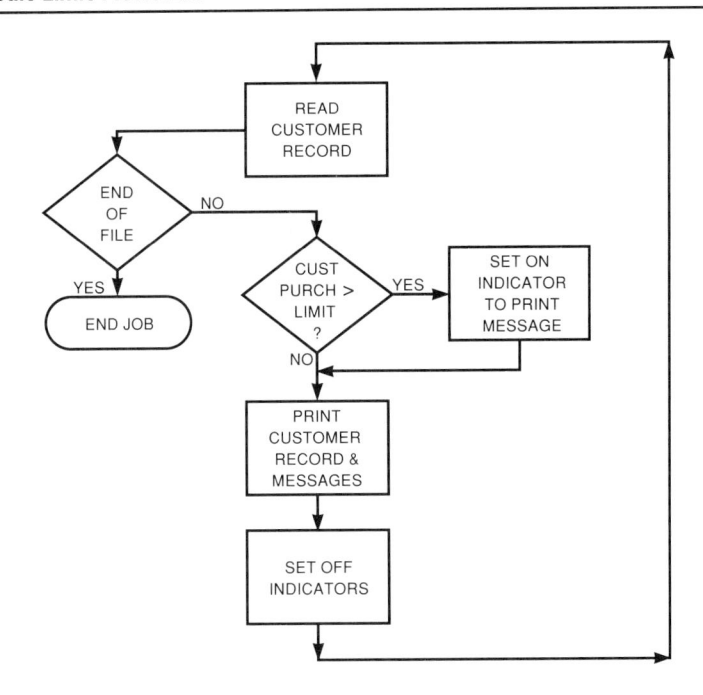

USING INDICATORS IN RPG ■

In RPG, many actions are accomplished with the use of indicators. In other languages these are referred to as flags. When the compare statement is executed (operation code COMP), RPG will set some indicators on or off (columns 54–59 on the Calculation Specifications form). These indicators represent greater than, less than, or equal to conditions. See the example in Figure 3.2. The entry in columns 54–55 will turn on an indicator if the result of a COMP operation shows that the value contained in the field in factor 1 is greater than the value of the field in factor 2. In the example in Figure 3.2, we have chosen 20 as the indicator, although any two-digit number may be used. Once an indicator has been set *on*, the programmer can cause some action to take place; if the indicator is set *off*, that action will not take place or some alternative action can be performed.

The next step is to decide what should be done if the indicator is found to be *on*. For example, the programmer may want a message to print only if the indicator is *on*. Following the Output Specifications in Figure 3.3, a line will be printed on the report only if indicator 20 is *on*. Indicators in columns 23–31 on the Output Specifications form will handle this decision (see Figure 3.3). Notice that the form allows room for three indicators. Sometimes it may be necessary for two or more indicators to be *on* to allow a field or message to be printed. Notice also that the form allows for a *not on* condition. This gives the programmer complete flexibility to define the conditions.

FIGURE 3.2 Calculation Specifications for Comparing Fields

Chapter 3 Computer Logic and Processing Multiple Record Types

FIGURE 3.3 Output Specifications for Result of Comparison

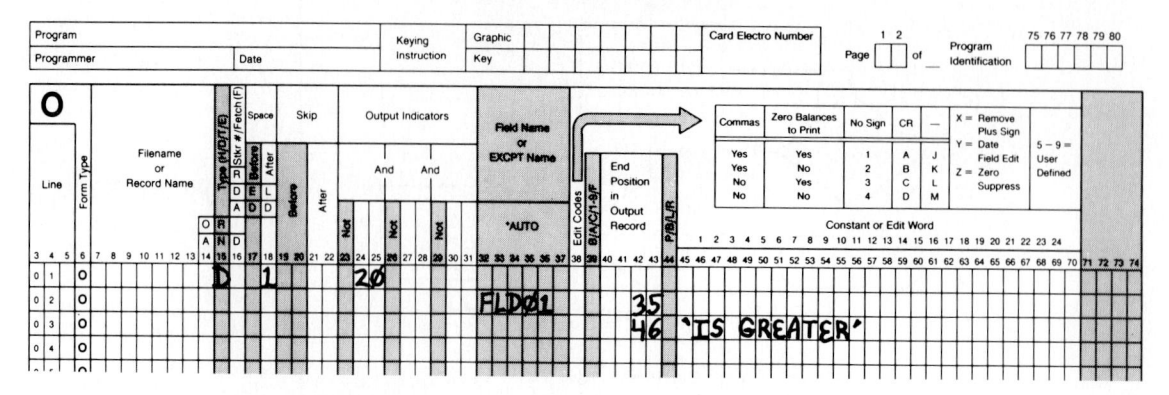

THE COMPARE OPERATION ■

Several rules govern the use of comparisons and indicators:

1. An alphabetic (or alphanumeric) field can be compared only to another alphabetic (or alphanumeric) field or literal.
2. A numeric field can be compared only to another numeric field or literal.
3. Resulting indicators will be set on or off based on the results of the comparison. (They do not randomly flip-flop back and forth.) The programmer can depend on their being set *on* when a condition is true and set *off* when a condition is not true.
4. Fields of different lengths can be compared.

Comparing Alphabetic or Alphanumeric Data Fields

Fields containing alphabetic data (or a combination of alphabetic and numeric data) are referred to as alphanumeric (or alphameric) fields. No arithmetic can be performed on these fields, but they can be used for comparing data. The example in Figure 3.4 illustrates the comparison of the following alphabetic data.

Input Data

PART A — VALUE IS "NUTS"
PART B — VALUE IS "BOLT"

The rules for comparison of alphabetic or alphanumeric data are the same. We will refer to these fields as alphanumeric even if they contain alphabetic data.

Alphanumeric fields often contain data (such as names or descriptions) that need to be compared. Alphanumeric fields are normally left-justified, meaning that they begin in the first position of the field and progress from left to right. This is not a requirement of RPG or of the compare

FIGURE 3.4 Comparison of Alphanumeric Data

56   RPG: A Programming Language for Today

operation, but is done for consistency in data format. Alphanumeric compares always begin with the leftmost character. In the example, comparing a value called NUTS with a value called BOLT, the comparison will begin with the first character of each factor. The first character of factor 1 is compared with the first character of factor 2. If they are equal, it will progress to the second character and continue comparing until it finds which comes later in the alphabet (i.e., greater than) or until it reaches the end of the field. In an alphanumeric comparison, values increase as one moves from *A* to *Z*.

In the example, *N* will be compared with *B* and will be determined to be greater. Indicator 30 will be set on and no further comparisons will be necessary. Blanks are considered by the computer to be real characters and will always be assigned the least value. Blanks are always considered less than the letter *A* or even the number zero.

Comparing Alphabetic or Alphanumeric Fields of Different Lengths

It is not necessary for two alphanumeric fields to contain the same number of characters for comparison. If a field that is 15 positions long is to be compared with a field 5 positions long, RPG will begin by comparing the leftmost characters in both fields and progress from left to right. When the comparison reaches position 6, it will pad the 5-position field with blanks. Thus, it is really comparing two 15-position fields, but the second field contains blanks from the sixth position on. An example follows.

FIELDA (LENGTH 15)	VALUE IS "APPLE—ROME"
FIELDB (LENGTH 5)	VALUE IS "APPLE"

Figure 3.5 shows the Calculation Specifications form for this input data.

Comparing Numeric Data Fields

Numeric fields are always right-justified. This means that the values are positioned at the right of the field and preceded with zeros. They are positioned so the decimal points will line up. Thus, a field that had been defined with three decimal positions would always contain three decimal positions, even when those decimal positions contain zeros. Even if the data entry operator did not enter leading zeros before the number, the computer would fill in the zeros to make the field a pure numeric field. The computer would not be able to perform arithmetic on a field containing blanks since a blank is considered an alphanumeric field.

When RPG performs comparing functions on a numeric field, it cannot do it from left to right as it did with the alphanumeric fields. It is necessary to compare the number by its value. It will compare the two numbers exactly as a human would do it (exactly as a programmer would want RPG to do it) by lining up the decimal points and comparing one value to the other. Thus, it is possible to compare a field having no decimal positions with a field containing three decimal positions. RPG will line up the decimal points, pad some zeros to the right where the decimal positions would be, and compare value against value as shown below and in Figure 3.6.

NUM01 (LENGTH 5 (3 DECIMALS))	DATA IS 50.255	VALUE IS 50.255
NUM02 (LENGTH 6 (0 DECIMALS))	DATA IS 000500	VALUE IS 500.000

FIGURE 3.5 Comparison of Alphanumeric Data

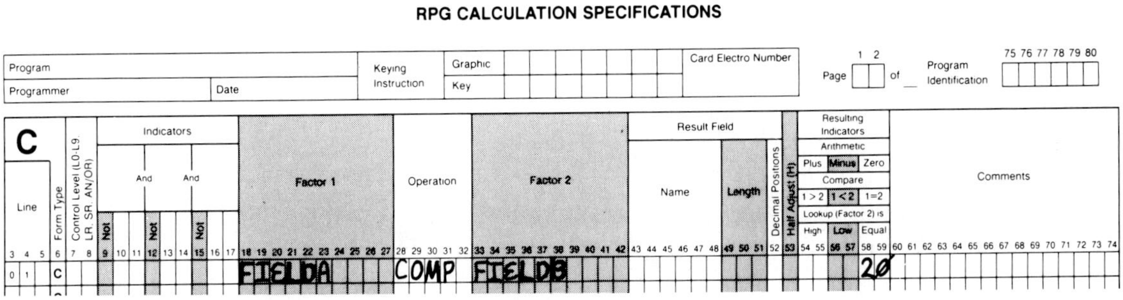
RPG CALCULATION SPECIFICATIONS

Line	Form Type	Control Level	Indicators	Factor 1	Operation	Factor 2	Result Field Name	Length	Decimal Positions	Half Adjust	Resulting Indicators (High / Low / Equal)	Comments
01	C			FIELDA	COMP	FIELDB					20	

FIGURE 3.6 Comparison of Numeric Data

RPG CALCULATION SPECIFICATIONS

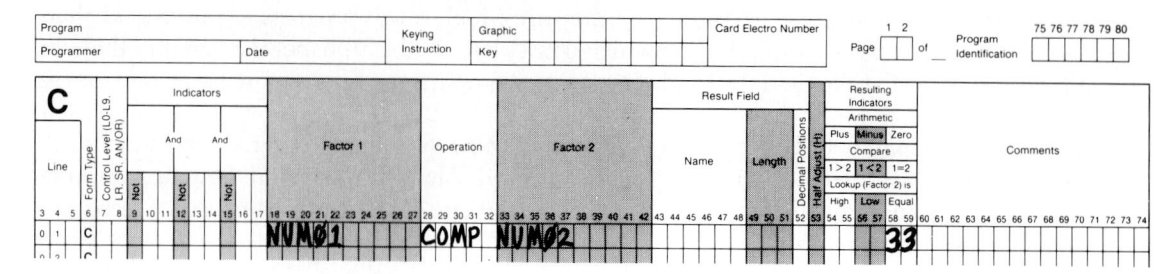

[Calculation spec form showing: Factor 1 = NUM01, Operation = COMP, Factor 2 = NUM02, Resulting Indicators: High/Low/Equal = 33]

Sample Program 1

For the first sample program we will write a program to provide a report of customer purchases showing a message for customers who have exceeded their credit limit.

The flowchart in Figure 3.1 shows the steps to be completed to determine whether or not a message is to be printed for a customer. The flowchart directs us to print a message line on a report if the customer balance is equal to or greater than the customer credit limit. This can be accomplished with the use of indicators. In this case, the indicator 20 has been chosen. If the customer balance (CSTBAL) is less than the credit limit (LIMIT) of $900.00, indicator 20 will remain *off*. If the customer balance is $900.00 or greater, indicator 20 will be set *on*. The fields in factors 1 and 2 are numeric, so this will be a numeric comparison.

In the example in Figures 3.7(a) and 3.7(b), the message line will be printed only if the indicator 20 is found to be *on* (i.e., the condition has been met and this customer is over the credit limit).

Sample Program 2

For the second sample program we will write a program, similar to the first example, to provide a report of customer purchases showing the amount by which the credit limit has been exceeded.

FIGURE 3.7(a) Comparison of Numeric Data

RPG CALCULATION SPECIFICATIONS

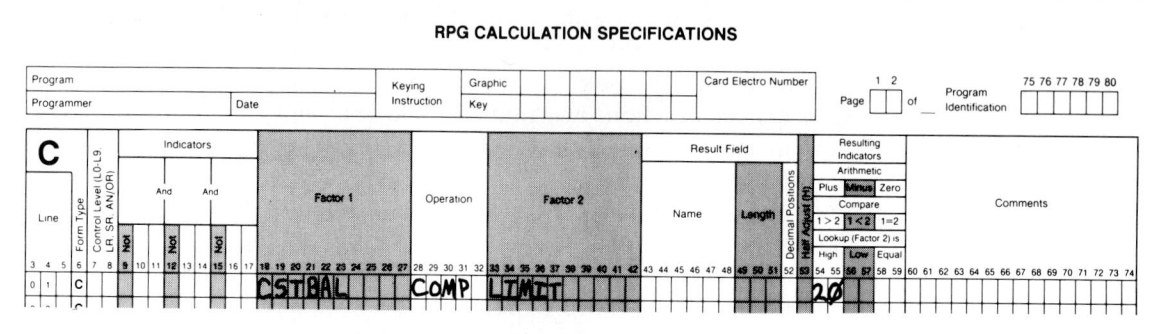

[Calculation spec form showing: Factor 1 = CSTBAL, Operation = COMP, Factor 2 = LIMIT, Resulting Indicator = 20]

FIGURE 3.7(b) Output Specifications for Results of Comparison

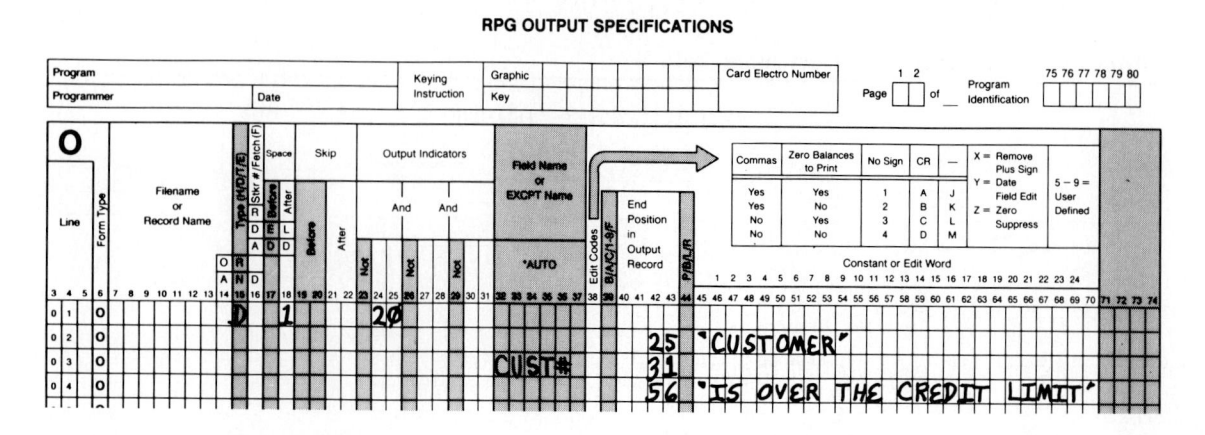

RPG OUTPUT SPECIFICATIONS

[Output spec form showing:
- Line 01: Type D, Space 1, Output Indicator 20
- Line 02: End Position 25, Constant "CUSTOMER"
- Line 03: Field Name CUST#, End Position 31
- Line 04: End Position 56, Constant "IS OVER THE CREDIT LIMIT"]

58 *RPG: A Programming Language for Today*

FIGURE 3.8(a) Calculation Specifications for Comparison of Numeric Data

RPG CALCULATION SPECIFICATIONS

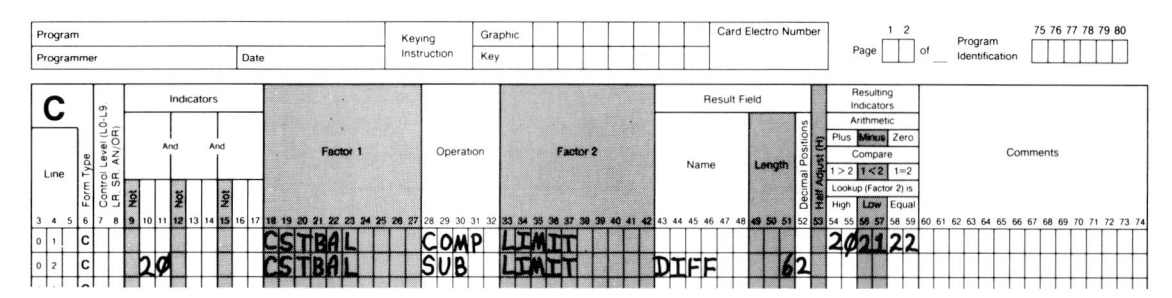

Line	Form Type	Control Level	Indicators	Factor 1	Operation	Factor 2	Result Field Name	Length	Decimal Positions	Resulting Indicators 1>2 1<2 1=2	Comments
01	C			CSTBAL	COMP	LIMIT				20 21 22	
02	C		20	CSTBAL	SUB	LIMIT	DIFF	62			

FIGURE 3.8(b) Output Specifications for Results of Comparison

RPG OUTPUT SPECIFICATIONS

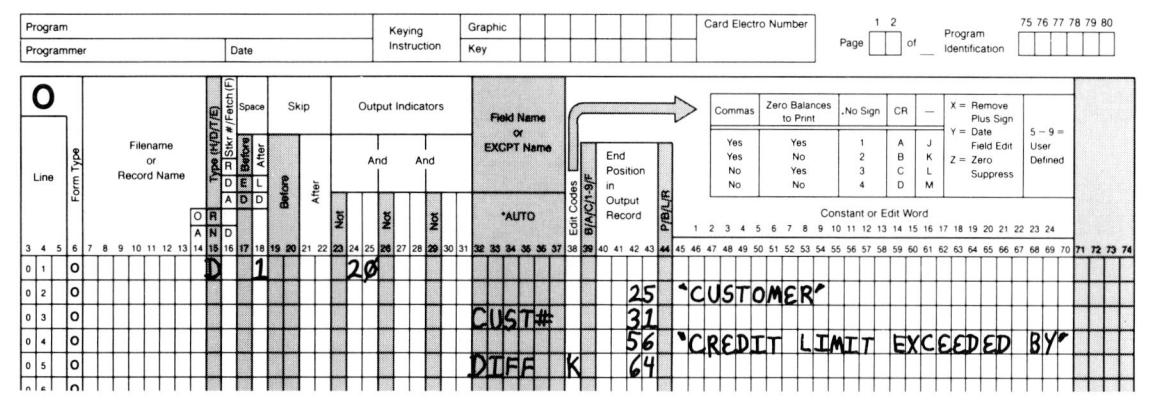

Line	Form Type	Filename or Record Name	Type	Space Before/After	Skip Before/After	Output Indicators And And	Field Name or EXCPT Name	Edit Codes	End Position in Output Record	B/A/C/1-9/F	Constant or Edit Word
01	O		D	1		20					
02	O								25		'CUSTOMER'
03	O						CUST#		31		
04	O								56		'CREDIT LIMIT EXCEEDED BY'
05	O						DIFF	K	64		

In the first example, a message was printed when indicator 20 was *on*. Indicators can also be used to trigger calculations. To print the amount by which a purchase has exceeded the credit limit, for example, the coding would look like that in Figures 3.8(a) and 3.8(b). On the first line in Figure 3.8(a), the comparison is specified, setting *on* indicator 20 if factor 1 is greater than the limit, setting *on* indicator 21 if factor 1 is less than the limit, or setting *on* indicator 22 if factor 1 exactly equals the limit. Only one of these indicators will be set on for any one transaction, since of course no balance could ever exceed, equal, and not exceed the limit at the same time.

On the second line of the calculations, the programmer can tell the program to take alternative action. In the example, if indicator 20 is *on*, the program will subtract the limit from the customer balance amount to provide the amount by which the limit has been exceeded. This calculation would not be done if the purchases were under the limit.

By entering indicator 20 in columns 10–11 on the second line, the program has been directed to perform this calculation *only* if the limit has been exceeded. Otherwise, this line of code will be bypassed.

The Output Specifications can now show not only the message that the limit has been exceeded but also the amount by which it has been exceeded. If indicator 21 or 22 were set *on*, no action would need to be taken for this problem. They could have been omitted entirely or they might have been used for some other types of calculations elsewhere in the program.

Comparing Numeric Fields of Different Lengths

It is possible to compare two numeric fields of different lengths and different decimal positions. RPG makes this possible because numeric fields are always lined up by the decimal point and the two *values* are compared. RPG automatically provides the extra zeros needed at either end of the field so the two fields will appear to the computer as being the same length. The programmer need do nothing special in the coding to effect this. The examples in Figures 3.9(a), 3.9(b), 3.9(c), and 3.9(d) show a comparison of a field of four positions with two decimal positions (03.20) with a field

FIGURE 3.9(a) Comparison of Numeric Data

NUMERIC COMPARISON

03.20 COMPARED TO 00003.200 *WILL* BE EQUAL
(COMPARES BY *VALUE*)

FIGURE 3.9(b) Input Specifications

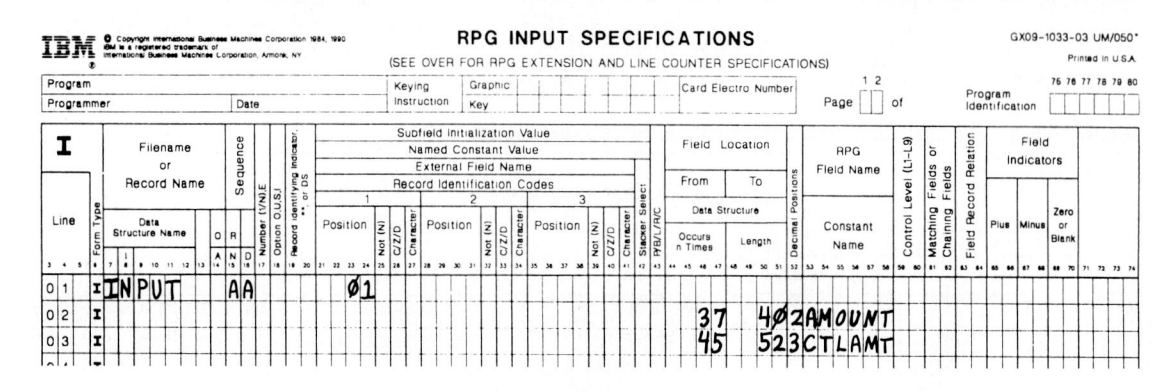

```
I INPUT   AA  01
I                          37 402AMOUNT
I                          45 523CTLAMT
```

FIGURE 3.9(c) Calculation Specifications for Comparison

```
C         AMOUNT  COMP CTLAMT              303132
```

FIGURE 3.9(d) Output Specifications for Results of Comparison

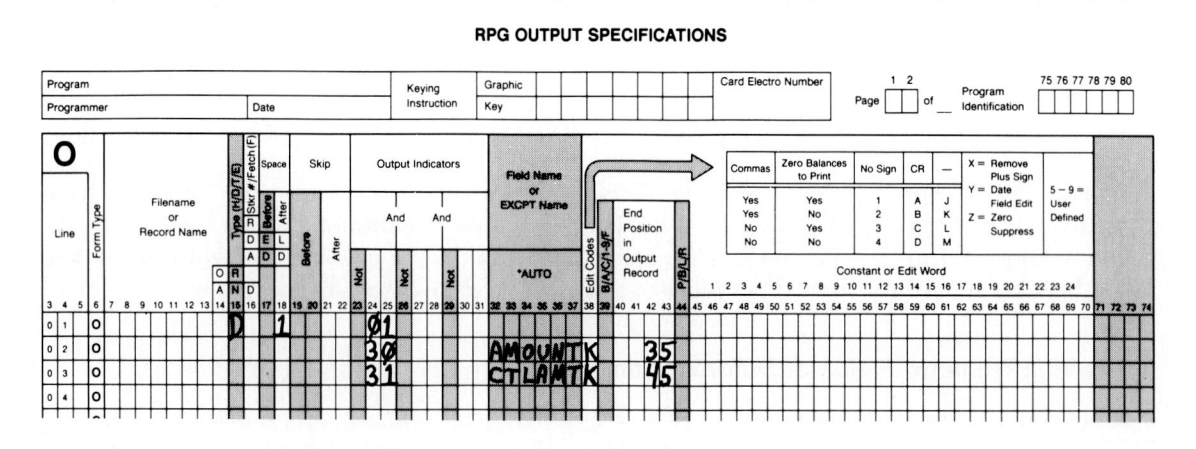

```
O    D 1        01
O               30    AMOUNTK   35
O               31    CTLAMTK   45
```

60 *RPG: A Programming Language for Today*

of eight positions with three decimal positions (00003.200); the values are compared and the indicators are set according to the *values* contained in the fields. Note that RPG considers a negative value as less than a positive value.

In brief, RPG compares two numeric fields just as the programmer would on paper, and it sets on the appropriate indicator(s) for the programmer to use.

Notice that it is possible, in the Output Specifications (see Figure 3.9d), to use the indicator on the detail lines to condition the printing of an individual field.

Collating Sequence for Comparing

The term collating sequence involves the question, "Which character will be considered smaller by the computer and which will be considered larger?" When comparing numbers this is fairly obvious: the number 1 will be considered smaller than the number 2, and so on. When comparing purely alphabetic characters, the letter *A* has a lower value than the letter *B*, and so on. The question really arises when special characters are being compared and it is necessary to determine which takes precedence over the other. The key to this question is yet another question: "What computer is being used?"

Generally speaking, there are two kinds of computers in the world: those using ASCII and those using EBCDIC coding patterns. Appendix A shows the collating sequence for each of these types of computer. Note that a blank has the lowest value in either collating sequence. Keep in mind that a blank will always precede a zero (or be considered less than a zero).

A program that works in a certain fashion on an EBCDIC computer may work just fine on an ASCII machine until it does a compare and the different collating sequence causes it to execute in an unpredictable manner. It may be a bit early to point out such differences, but it is important for the programmer to be aware that these differences exist and to see to it that the correct logic is used for the computer on which the programs are being compiled and run.

Comparing Literal Values

Not only can two input *fields* be compared, but it is also possible to compare a field to a *literal*. A literal is a data element defined by the programmer within the program. It is data whose value is given by the characters themselves. A literal will not change unless the programmer wishes to change it. A literal can be any value the programmer would like to enter.

Figure 3.10 shows how a field can be compared to an alphanumeric literal. In the example, the program compares a field (called MONTH) to a literal (JULY) for an alphabetic compare. Notice in Figure 3.10 that JULY is enclosed in quotation marks. (An IBM computer uses single quotation marks for this purpose but most other computers use double quotation marks.) The quotation marks define this field as an alphanumeric literal. If the quotation marks had been omitted, RPG would have interpreted JULY as simply a field name.

It is also possible to compare a field to a specific numeric amount. In the sample program earlier in this chapter two fields, customer balance and credit limit, were compared (see Figure 3.7). An alternate approach would be to replace the credit limit field with a numeric literal of 900.00, on

FIGURE 3.10   Comparison to an Alphanumeric Literal

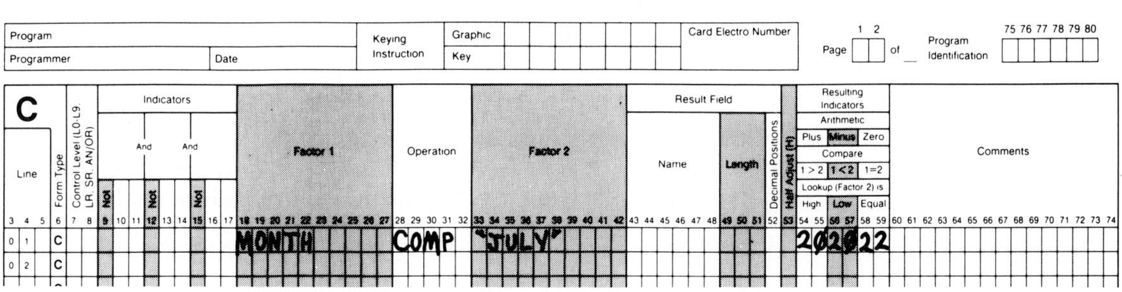

FIGURE 3.11 Comparison to a Numeric Constant

RPG CALCULATION SPECIFICATIONS

Line	Form Type	Control Level	Indicators	Factor 1	Operation	Factor 2	Result Field Name	Length	Decimal Positions	Half Adjust (H)	Resulting Indicators (Plus/High/1>2, Minus/Low/1<2, Zero/Equal/1=2)	Comments
01	C			CUSAMT	COMP	9ØØ.ØØ					2Ø 21 22	
02	C		21	CUSAMT	ADD	TOTAMT	TOTAMT	7	2			
03	C		2Ø	CUSAMT	MULT	-.Ø2	PCT	6	2	H		NEGATIVE
04	C											

the assumption that the limit would never need to be changed. This coding is shown on line 1 of the Calculation Specifications form in Figure 3.11.

Note that when a numeric literal is used, there is no need for quotation marks, since there could never be a field name that begins with a number. It is acceptable to put a decimal point in a numeric literal even though the value to which the literal is being compared would not contain an actual decimal point. The decimal point is there to indicate where the decimal point should be. It would also be acceptable to precede the number with a dash to indicate a negative amount as shown on line three of Figure 3.11. It should be added that in today's environment of rising costs and fluctuating rates, using a literal dollar figure may not be a wise practice.

Summary of the Compare Operation

The compare operation logically compares the values in the field or literal in factor 1 to the values in the field or literal in factor 2. The operation causes resulting indicators to be conditioned (set on or off). These indicators can then be used to achieve the desired results in the program.

PROCESSING MULTIPLE RECORD TYPES ■

Each of the files shown in previous examples has contained only one type of input record. A file, however, can contain many more than one type of record. For example, it is possible for a transaction file to contain one record describing the name of the salesperson and numerous records describing the transactions themselves, which may be of several different types, such as debits and credits.

Each record type must have some kind of identifier (a field containing a code of some kind) so that the program can recognize which type of record is being processed. Figure 3.12 is an example of a data file containing multiple record types.

The report that displays this data may need to be formatted differently for each record type. Figure 3.13 shows a Printer Spacing Chart for a report that obtains its input from several record types.

Use of Input Indicators

For a sample exercise in processing multiple record types, three types of input records will be input to the program. Figure 3.14 shows the coding used on the Input Specifications form to describe the record types. A record identifying indicator is entered in columns 19–20 to indicate each type of record. The indicator 01 will identify the record describing the salesperson, the indicator 02 will identify a detail debit transaction, the indicator 03 will identify a detail credit transaction, and the indicator 99 will identify all other record types. Note that the filename INPUT does not have to be

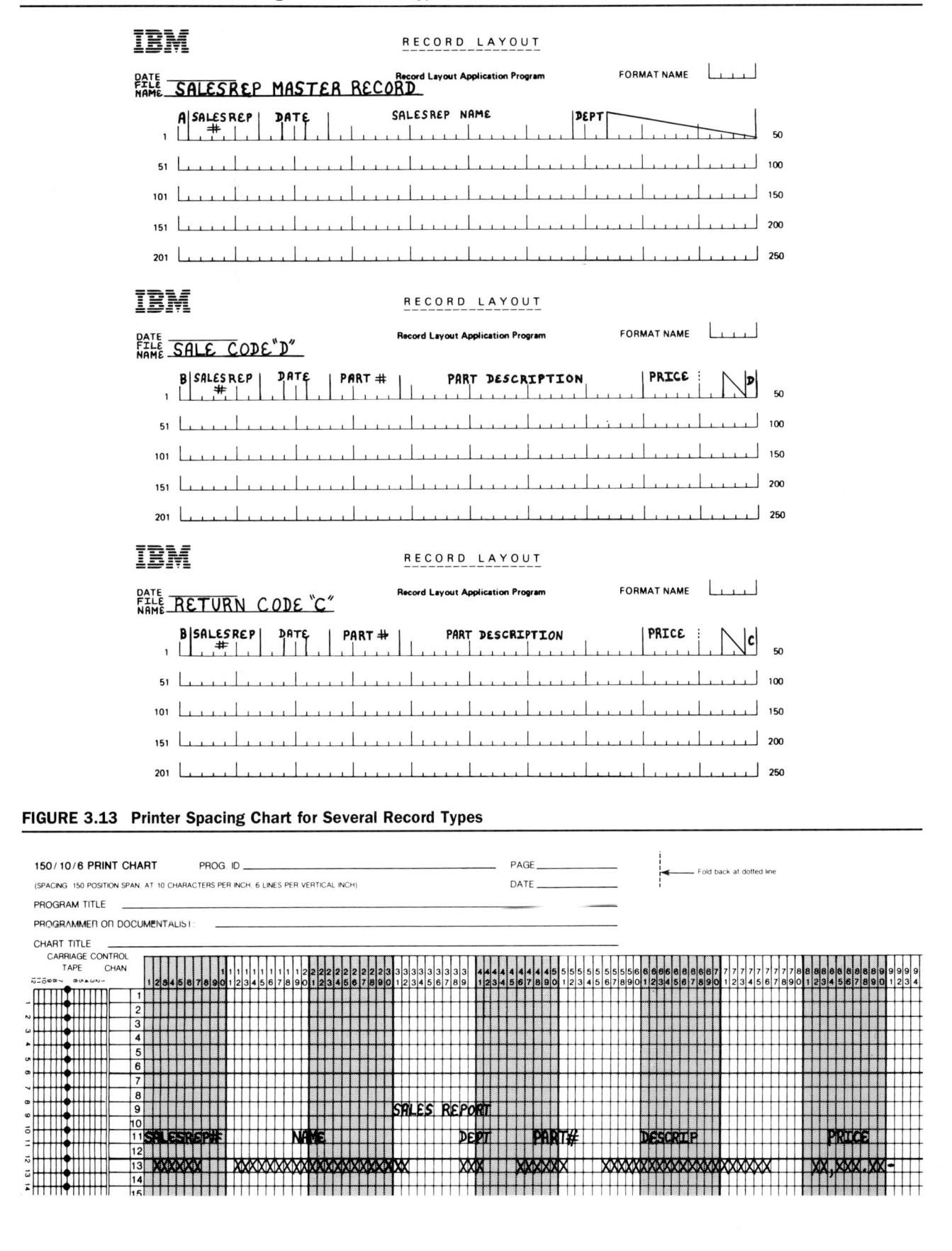

FIGURE 3.12 Data File Containing Several Record Types

IBM Record Layout
FILE NAME: SALESREP MASTER RECORD
Fields: A | SALESREP # | DATE | SALESREP NAME | DEPT

IBM Record Layout
FILE NAME: SALE CODE "D"
Fields: B | SALESREP # | DATE | PART # | PART DESCRIPTION | PRICE | D

IBM Record Layout
FILE NAME: RETURN CODE "C"
Fields: B | SALESREP # | DATE | PART # | PART DESCRIPTION | PRICE | C

FIGURE 3.13 Printer Spacing Chart for Several Record Types

150/10/6 PRINT CHART

Line 9: SALES REPORT
Line 11: SALESREP#   NAME   DEPT   PART#   DESCRIP   PRICE
Line 13: XXXXXX   XXXXXXXXXXXXXXXXXX   XXX   XXXXXX   XXXXXXXXXXXXXXXXXX   XX,XXX.XX-

63

FIGURE 3.14 Input Specifications for Multiple Record Types

Line	Filename or Record Name		Record Identification Codes 1			2			3		
			Position		Character	Position		Character	Position		Character
01	I INPUT	AA	01		1	CA					
02	I	OR	02		1	CB	50		CD		
03	I	OR	03		1	CB	50		CC		
04	I	OR	99								

repeated after line 1. It is necessary only to enter the word OR in columns 14–15 to notify RPG that this is a further description of the data to be expected from this input file.

Columns 21–41 on the Input Specifications form are reserved for record identification codes. The data file in Figure 3.12 is the source of these codes. Columns 21–24 specify the column to be evaluated. Since the code in the data file is in column 1, the numeral 1 is entered in this field. (Note that this is right-justified and that leading zeros need not be included.)

The entry in column 26 is used to specify which type of value is to be checked. The possible types are character (C), digit only (D), and zone only (Z). An entry of C means that the entire character will be examined for a valid match. C is selected for this specification because the code for this record is an alphabetic character. The alternatives will be discussed later.

Column 27 of the Input Specifications form picks up the code given in column 1 of the input record—A for salesperson, B for sale or return transaction. When an input record is read and the character A is found in column 1, the indicator 01 will be turned *on*.

Since transactions can be either debits or credits in this example, a further definition is required. The second set of criteria is defined in columns 28–34. Since the debit/credit code appears in the data in column 50, a 50 will be entered in columns 28–31. (Again the entry is right-justified.) Entering a C in column 33 indicates a full character compare; column 34 shows D for a debit transaction and C for a credit.

All three transaction types have now been defined, but there is still one more line of code needed before continuing with the actual field names. Though not required by RPG, this line of code is a good safeguard against the possibility that a record might happen to be processed that did *not* contain either code A or code B in column 1. It is also necessary to protect against the possibility that a record code B might contain an invalid code in column 50 (i.e., neither a D nor a C).

Line 4 contains only the word OR and the indicator 99. This tells RPG to set on indicator 99 any time an invalid record is read. This allows the programmer to use indicator 99 to print an error message, to alert someone that invalid data is being processed, or to ignore the record entirely.

If the programmer fails to code this protective line to catch errors, the program will fail whenever invalid data is found, because the program has not been told what to do in case the criteria on lines 1, 2, or 3 are not met. Even if the programmer believes that faulty data will *never* reach this program, it is wise to include the default line of code just in case it does.

An alternate method for coding line 4 is shown in Figure 3.15. This method uses the *not* condition and specifies that if column 1 is not A and not B indicator 98 will be set on. A fifth line of code is needed if column 1 is code B and column 50 is not D and not C. This fifth line will set on indicator 99. This takes care of all possible combinations of errors and allows for a more specific error message.

Field Record Relation Indicators

Now that each record type has been defined, it is time to code the actual description of each of the records. This is done in the same manner as in earlier chapters, defining the length, position, and characteristics of each field on the Input Specifications form.

FIGURE 3.15 Input Specifications for Multiple Record Types with *Not* Conditions

Line	Form Type	Filename or Record Name / Data Structure Name	Sequence	Number (1/N)/E	Option O,U,S,I	Record identifying indicator, **, or DS	Record Identification Codes 1: Position / Not (N) / C/Z/D / Character	Record Identification Codes 2: Position / Not (N) / C/Z/D / Character	Record Identification Codes 3: Position / Not (N) / C/Z/D / Character
01	I	INPUT	AA		01	1 CA		
02	I		OR		02	1 CB	50 CD	
03	I		OR		03	1 CB	50 CC	
04	I		OR		98	1NCA	1NCB	
05	I		OR		99	1 CB	50NCD	50NCC
06	I							

Figure 3.16 shows one method that could be used to code the Input Specifications for multiple record types. The alternate method shown in Figure 3.17 uses field record relation indicators. With this method, indicators are entered in columns 63–64. When describing fields that appear only in the salesperson record, the salesperson record indicator (indicator 01) is entered in columns 63–64 after each field. When describing fields that appear only in the transaction record for debits, the transaction record indicator for debits (indicator 02) is entered in columns 63–64 after each field. When describing fields that appear only in the transaction record for credits, the transaction record indicator for credits (indicator 03) is entered in columns 63–64 after each field.

When the fields are the same in all three records (columns 2–7 contain the salesperson number and columns 8–13 contain the date in all three records), they do not need to be repeated for each record type. They can be entered once and the field record relation indicator is left blank.

FIGURE 3.16 Input Specification for Multiple Record Types

Line	Form Type	Filename or Record Name	Sequence	Rec ind	Rec ID Codes Pos 1	C1	Pos 2	C2	From	To	Decimal	Field Name
01	I	INPUT	AA	01	1 CA						
02	I								2	7	0	SLSREP
03	I								8	13	0	DATE
04	I								14	34		NAME
05	I								35	37		DEPT
06	I		BB	02	1 CB	50	CD					
07	I								2	7	0	SLSREP
08	I								8	13	0	DATE
09	I								14	19		PART#
10	I								20	40		DESC
11	I								41	47	2	PRICE
12	I		CC	03	1 CB	50	CC					
13	I								2	7	0	SLSREP
14	I								8	13	0	DATE
15	I								14	19		PART#
16	I								20	40		DESC
17	I								41	47	2	PRICE
18	I		ZZ	99								
19	I											
20	I											

Chapter 3   Computer Logic and Processing Multiple Record Types

FIGURE 3.17 Alternate Method Using Field Record Relationship Indicators

Line	Form Type	Filename or Record Name / Data Structure Name	Sequence	Number (1/N)/E	Option O.U.S.| Record Identifying Indicator or **	Position	Not (N)	C/Z/D	Character	Position	Not (N)	C/Z/D	Character	Position	Not (N)	C/Z/D	Character	Stacker Select P/B/L/R/C	From	To	Decimal Positions	Field Name / Constant / Data Structure Occurs n Times / Length	Control Level (L1-L9)	Matching Fields or Chaining Fields	Field Record Relation	Plus	Minus	Zero or Blank
01	I	INPUT	AA		01	1	CA																					
02	I		OR		02	1	CB				50	CD																
03	I		OR		03	1	CB				50	CC																
04	I																		2	7	0	SLSREP						
05	I																		8	13	0	DATE						
06	I																		14	34		NAME			01			
07	I																		35	37		DEPT			01			
08	I																		14	19		PART2			02			
09	I																		20	40		DESC2			02			
10	I																		41	47	2	PRICE2			02			
11	I																		14	19		PART3			03			
12	I																		20	40		DESC3			03			
13	I																		41	47	2	PRICE3			03			
14	I		ZZ		99																							

Calculation Specifications

When processing multiple record types, it becomes necessary to determine which record is being processed. It would not be a good idea to try to calculate the total of the debit or credit amounts if the record being processed at that moment was the salesperson record containing no dollar amount information at all. This is the reason for using indicators in the Calculation Specifications. Indicators inform RPG what it should be calculating and when to calculate it.

Figure 3.18 shows the calculation coding needed to compute totals for the sample program. To compute total dollars, the debit amounts need to be added to the total and the credit amounts subtracted. Salesperson records should not affect the total at all, but it might be a good idea to make a record count of all the salesperson records to ensure that all of the salespersons have been processed.

The first line of calculations will add the debit amount to the field called TOTSAL. Indicator 02 in columns 10–11 ensures that this line will be processed only when indicator 02 is on. The second line (indicator 03 in columns 10–11) will subtract the credit amounts from the field called TOTSAL. The third line will handle the record count, adding 1 to a COUNT field whenever a salesperson record is processed. The indicators control what is to happen for each calculation line.

FIGURE 3.18 Calculation Specifications to Compute Totals

Line	Form Type	Control Level (L0-L9, LR, SR, AN/OR)	Indicators Not	And Not	And Not	Factor 1	Operation	Factor 2	Result Field Name	Length	Decimal Positions	Half Adjust (H)	Resulting Indicators Arithmetic Plus 1>2 / High	Minus 1<2 / Low	Zero 1=2 / Equal	Comments
01	C		02			PRICE2	ADD	TOTSAL	TOTSAL	82						
02	C		03			TOTSAL	SUB	PRICE3	TOTSAL							
03	C		01			COUNT	ADD	1	COUNT	40						
04	C															

BRANCHING WITHIN CALCULATIONS

The Input Specifications for the sample program include an indicator 99 to provide for any erroneous input data. If an invalid input record did appear while calculations were taking place, the program would go through each step one by one, trying to determine if there was anything for it to do. If the program were very large, a search through the calculations triggered by an invalid record could waste time and serve no good purpose. To avoid this, the GOTO operation can be used to cause erroneous records to skip past all the calculations.

Using the GOTO Operation

A GOTO (branching) command must be given a destination. It is necessary to give it the label of the place in the calculations to which it should go. In Figure 3.19, the line has been conditioned with an indicator 99, GOTO has been entered as the operation code, and the label of the destination has been entered in factor 2. No entries are necessary in factors 1 or the result field for this operation. The label can be the name of any label in the program, but it is necessary that the label really exist in the program.

The destination line will contain the label name in factor 1 and the operation code TAG. This TAG line performs no calculation function. It is simply a place to which the program can branch. It is a destination.

Every GOTO line *must* have a corresponding TAG line. Several GOTO lines could reference the same TAG line. The TAG line can be placed anywhere in the Calculation Specifications, so a GOTO could cause a program to leap backwards to an earlier calculation line or forward (as in the example) to a line later in the program. RPG will allow the programmer to have complete control over the sequence of events within the calculations.

A danger to watch out for, however, is the never-ending loop. When a GOTO is used to jump back to an earlier line of code there is a danger that the program might just keep going around and around in circles repeating the same lines of code over and over. It is very important to be sure that the program will not get into this kind of looping problem.

In the example in Figure 3.19, when indicator 99 is on the program is instructed to skip all calculations to a TAG called ENDJOB. The names chosen for TAG labels are entirely up to the programmer and must abide by the same rules for field names as any other field in RPG. Some programmers like to number their labels (for example, TAG001) to make them easier to find in the program. The important rule is to use the GOTO operation wisely.

FIGURE 3.19 GOTO Operations in Calculations

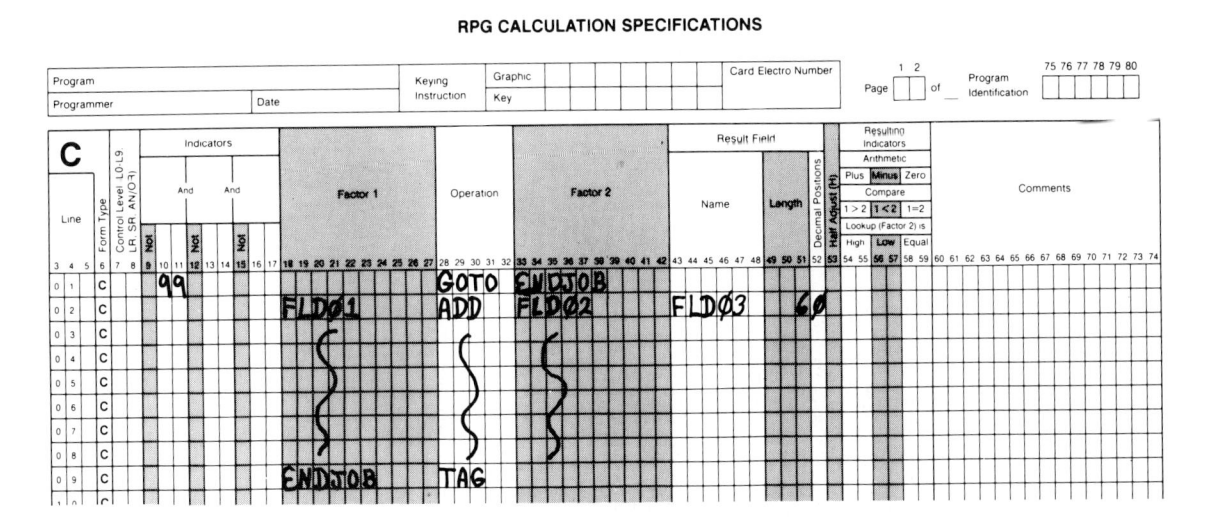

Using Subroutines

Now that the GOTO (branch) function has been described, it is time to learn a more structured approach to managing the logical sequence of events within a program. Although the GOTO is a legitimate operation in RPG, it permits a programmer to create very unstructured programs. It is possible to write a sequence of code that takes the program in continuous loops or into very inefficient routings through an otherwise simple sequence of steps. A more structured approach to performing a branch in RPG uses internal subroutines.

In any language, a subroutine is a set of codes to perform a single function which can be called upon from any place within the logic of the program. Some examples of subroutines might be a routine for editing the date, one for converting a calendar date (MM/DD/YY) into a Julian date (YYDDD), or one for moving last names in front of first names. It is useful if the subroutine can be isolated from the main body of the program and simply retrieved whenever it is needed.

Figure 3.20 shows the coding for a subroutine. In the Calculation Specifications form, the subroutine itself is isolated from the body of the calculations, placed at the very end of the calculations. Each line of a subroutine is identified by SR in columns 7–8. The subroutine must begin with BEGSR (begin subroutine) and it must end with ENDSR (end subroutine). The begin subroutine operation must have a name in factor 1. This subroutine name can be any name chosen by the programmer. The name could be an informative one such as DATERT or JULIAN, or it could be a numbered label such as SUB001 or SUB002. In a very large program, it can be very difficult to locate a label like DATERT somewhere within 70 pages of code. Labeling each subroutine by number is probably a better idea.

This is how a subroutine is coded, but it is necessary to know how it works. In the main body of the calculations the program advances line by line through the code. Rather than using a GOTO to perform some separate section of code, the EXSR (execute subroutine) operation is entered. This causes the program to branch to the subroutine itself, perform every line within the subroutine, and return to the line *immediately following* the EXSR from which it has just branched! Figure 3.21 shows the coding for the EXSR operation.

RPG does not permit entry into the center of a subroutine from somewhere outside the subroutine. It is also not permitted to GOTO somewhere else outside the subroutine when executing statements within a subroutine. This ensures that a subroutine is a self-contained unit without confusing influences from the outside. A subroutine has only one entry point and one exit point.

It is, however, possible to exit from within one subroutine to another, and when the second subroutine has been completed, control returns to the statement in the first subroutine from which it was called. It will then complete the remaining instructions and return to the original main portion of the program from which it started. There are no limits on how many levels deep a program may go in using subroutines.

FIGURE 3.20 Subroutine in Calculations

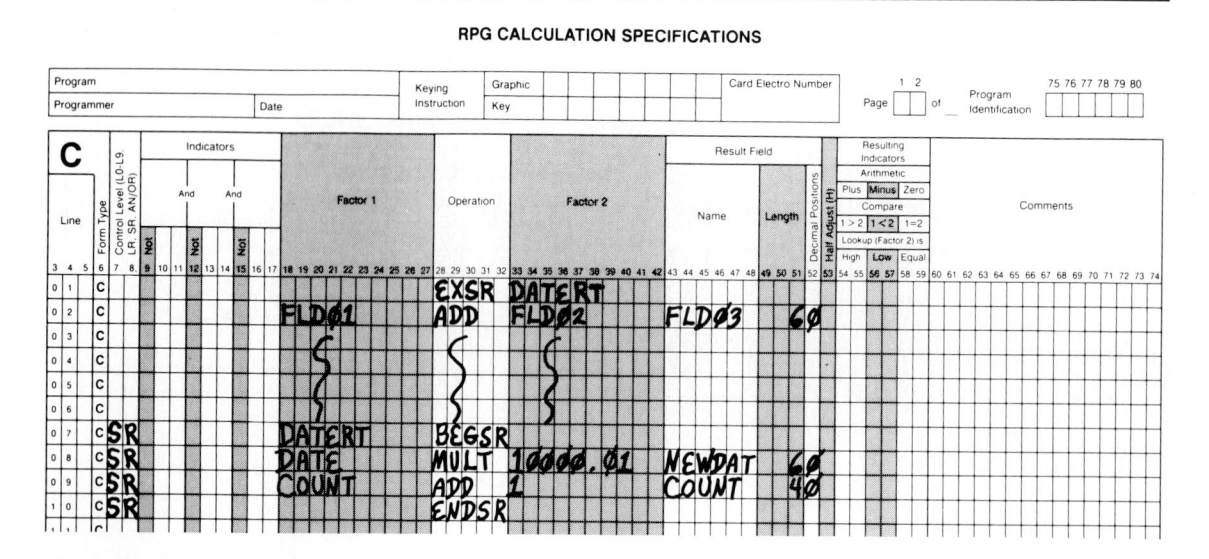

FIGURE 3.21 EXSR Operation

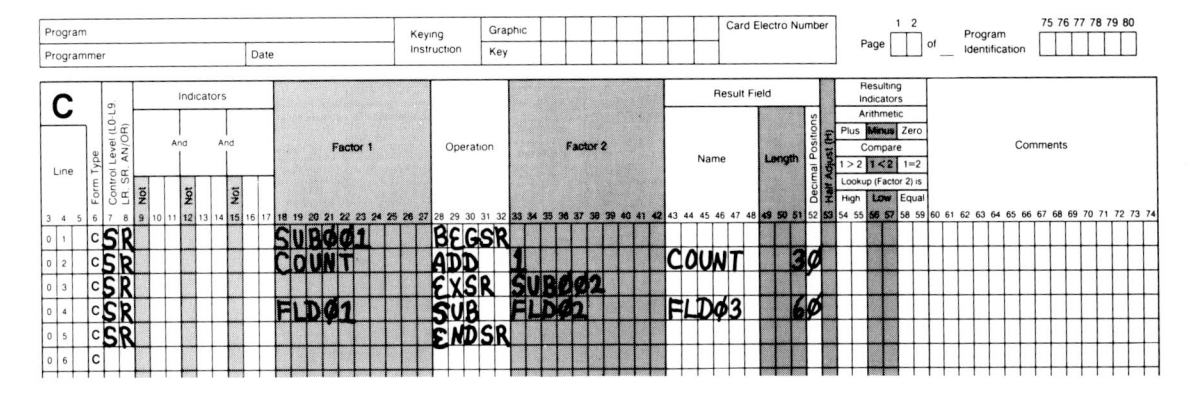

```
RPG CALCULATION SPECIFICATIONS

Line  Form  Control  Indicators   Factor 1   Operation   Factor 2   Result Field            Resulting    Comments
      Type  Level    And  And                                       Name    Length  Dec Pos Indicators
01    C     SR                    SUB001     BEGSR
02    C     SR                    COUNT      ADD         1          COUNT   3  0
03    C     SR                               EXSR        SUB002
04    C     SR                    FLD01      SUB         FLD02      FLD03   6  0
05    C     SR                               ENDSR
06    C
```

If the programmer needs to exit from a subroutine, it is possible to skip to the end of the subroutine by using a GOTO. This can be done by adding a TAG statement just before the end of the subroutine. The TAG statement is not necessary, however, because it is also possible to enter a label in factor 1 of the ENDSR statement and use it as though it were a TAG (see Figure 3.22).

The programmer is now assured that the program logic will progress in a straightforward and logical manner. Use of subroutines avoids the circuitous loops that can often result when GOTO statements are used. It makes the logic easier to read. If there is faulty logic in the program, it will be easier to detect.

A truly structured program should consist of a main body of the program which calls a series of subroutines one by one until the end of calculations is reached. This type of coding is far easier to read and maintain than a program of loops and GOTOs.

GOTOs Revisited

The rules for when to use a GOTO and when to use a subroutine are as follows:

> *Never* use an unconditional GOTO. There should always be an indicator to condition the GOTO.
> *Always* try to use a subroutine to cause the program to return to the place from which it came and perform the next instruction.
> *Use* GOTOs sparingly. They are useful when the program needs to be forced to skip coding lines (an error in the data, for example).

FIGURE 3.22 Subroutine with Label on ENDSR

```
RPG CALCULATION SPECIFICATIONS

Line  Form  Control  Indicators   Factor 1   Operation   Factor 2   Result Field            Resulting    Comments
      Type  Level    And  And                                       Name    Length  Dec Pos Indicators
01    C     SR                    SUB002     BEGSR
02    C     SR                    FLD01      COMP        FLD02                              20 21 22
03    C     SR    20                         GOTO        END002
04    C     SR                    FLD3       ADD         FLD4       FLD5
05    C     SR                    END002     ENDSR
06    C
```

Chapter 3 Computer Logic and Processing Multiple Record Types

SUMMARY ■

In this chapter, you have learned all about logic as it applies to computers, and you have learned that an input file can contain more than one type of record.

You have learned that RPG allows you to compare two fields to determine whether they are exactly equal or whether the first is greater than or less than the second.

You have learned the rules controlling these compare functions. You know that an alpha-numeric field cannot be compared to a numeric field. You have learned the rules for doing alpha-numeric and for numeric compares.

You have learned the use of literals in comparing fields.

You have learned the use of indicators in completing the compare functions.

You have learned how to use various record formats as input and how to define them in your program.

You have also learned all about field record relation indicators with multiple record types used as input.

And finally, you have learned about GOTO statements—when to use and when not to use them.

This completes the third chapter and also the three basic functions of a computer. Computers can do only three things: input/output (Chapter 1); arithmetic (Chapter 2); and logic (Chapter 3).

All that remains is to learn how to use these three fundamental concepts to perform all the wonderful things for which computers are famous.

REVIEW QUESTIONS

1. Explain the meaning of computer logic.
2. Explain how logic (comparing) is done in RPG.
3. What is the meaning of the three results possible when two fields are compared?
4. What are the three indicators that can result from a comparison of two fields?
5. Explain how the comparison of two alphanumeric fields is carried out.
6. Explain how the comparison of two numeric fields is carried out.
7. What is the meaning of the term *literal*?
8. How are literals compared to data fields?
9. What are the rules for entering numeric literals in a comparison statement? For entering alphanumeric literals?
10. Explain the use of input indicators.
11. When is it necessary or useful to define multiple record types?
12. How many record identification codes can be tested on one line of the input statement?
13. How can additional codes be tested?
14. Explain field record relation indicators.
15. When multiple record types are used in a file, what special action will need to be taken in the Calculation Specifications to ensure that an operation is performed on the right record type?
16. What is the operation code used in RPG to perform a branch or jump function in the calculations?
17. When the branching function is used, how is the line coded to which the logic will branch?
18. Explain why a branch function is a less desirable method of coding than using internal subroutines.
19. Every subroutine must begin with the _____ operation and end with the _____ operation.
20. A subroutine is executed when the _____ statement is performed.

EXERCISES

1. On a Calculation Specifications form, enter the coding which will compare the value in an alphabetic field called MONEY to another field called TWENTY. Set on indicator 22 if the two fields are found to be equal.
2. On a Calculation Specifications form, enter the coding which will compare the value in a numeric field called DAVE with another field called SECOND. Set on indicator 35 if the first field is greater than the second.
3. On a Calculation Specifications form, enter the coding which will compare the value in a numeric field called AMOUNT with a numeric literal representing 2000.50. Set on indicator 61 if the first field is less than the literal.
4. On a Calculation Specifications form, enter the coding which will compare a numeric literal of negative 25.00 with the value in a numeric field called BALANC. Set on indicator 68 if the first field is greater than or equal to the literal.
5. On an Input Specifications form, enter the coding needed to define a file (80 columns in length) containing two record types. A record type of *H* or *G* is found in column 80 of each record.
6. On a Calculation Specifications form, enter the two lines of code needed to branch from one place in the calculations to another using the label AGAIN.
7. On a Calculation Specifications form, enter the three lines of code needed to perform a subroutine named SUBR01.
8. Give the results of the following alphabetic comparisons:

Factor 1	Factor 2	Result > < =
a. SMITH, J.	SMITHSON, J.	_____
b. TABLE LAMPS	TABLE LAMPS	_____
c. 30-3398-65	30-3398-66	_____

9. Give the results of the following numeric comparisons:

Factor 1	Factor 2	Result > < =
a. 500.00	500.00	_____
b. .2354	.235	_____
c. 000.358	.000358	_____
d. 3.1	003.095	_____

DEBUGGING EXERCISES

Instructions

The following RPG programs contain an error or errors. Some of these errors are indicated by the RPG compiler on the program listing. A list of syntax errors is given at the end of the program listing. Other types of errors may occur which will not be shown. These are called logic errors.

Study each program and its syntax errors. Locate each error (including logic errors) and on a separate coding form make the correct entry for the line(s) in error.

Explain each error and how it should be corrected.

```
100  F* TITLE: DEBUG PROJECT 3-A
200  F* DATE:  2/28/91      AUTHOR: D.CABLE
300  F* DESCRIPTION: PRINT STUDENT REPORT
400  F***************************************************
500  F* MODIFICATIONS:
600  F* NO.     DATE       INIT     DESCRIPTION
700  F*         XX/XX/XX   XXX      XXXXXXXXXXXXXXXXXXXXXXXXXXXXX
800  F***************************************************

NAME OF PROGRAM WILL BE PJ003A IN LIBRARY CABLE

              H
* 1019                ALL DECIMAL DATA ERRORS IGNORED
900  FGRADES   IP  F      120           DISK
1000 FREPORT   O   F      132       OF  PRINTER
1100 F***************************************************

1200 IGRADES   AA  01
1300 I                                  1  10 ID#
1400 I                                 11  26 NAME
1500 I                                 27  29 CLASS
1600 I                                 30  320POINTS

1700 C         COUNT    ADD 1       COUNT   40
1800 C         POINTS   COMP 95              35 35
1900 C         POINTS   COMP 85              36
2000 C         POINTS   COMP 750             37

2100 OREPORT  H  203     1P
2200 O        OR         OF
2300 O                              30 'STUDENT GRADE REPORT'
2400 O        H  2       1P
2500 O        OR         OF
2600 O                               5 'ID#'
2700 O                              15 'NAME'
2800 O                              31 'POINTS'
2900 O                              40 'GRADE'
3000 O        D  1       01
3100 O                      ID#     10
3200 O                      NAME    26
3300 O                      POINTSZ 30
3400 O                   35         40 'A'
3500 O                   36         40 'B'
3600 O                   37         40 'C'
3700 O                   N35N36N37  40 'D'
3800 O        T  1       LR
3900 O                              15 'TOTAL STUDENTS'
4000 O                      COUNT Z 20
```

```
SEQUENCE       1         2         3         4         5         6         7
NUMBER   678901234567890123456789012345678901234567890123456789012345678901234
```

* * * * * E N D O F S O U R C E * * * * *

* 7086   900   RPG PROVIDES BLOCK/UNBLOCK SUPPORT FOR FILE GRADES.

CROSS-REFERENCE LISTING


```
        FILE/RCD    DEV/RCD      REFERENCES (D=DEFINED)
   01   GRADES      DISK          900D 1200
   02   REPORT      PRINTER      1000D 2100  2400  3000  3800


        FIELD       ATTR         REFERENCES (M=MODIFIED D=DEFINED)
* 7031  CLASS       A(3)         1500D
        COUNT       P(4,0)       1700  1700D 4000
        ID#         A(10)        1300D 3100
        NAME        A(16)        1400D 3200
        POINTS      P(3,0)       1600D 1800  1900  2000  3300
        1           LITERAL 1700
        750         LITERAL 2000
        85          LITERAL 1900
        95          LITERAL 1800


        INDICATOR   REFERENCES (M=MODIFIED D=DEFINED)
        LR           900D 3800
        OF          1000D 2200  2500
        01          1200M 3000
        1P          2100  2400
        35          1800M 1800M 3400  3700
        36          1900M 3500  3700
        37          2000M 3600  3700
```

MESSAGES

```
MSGID       SEV  NUMBER   TEXT
* QRG1019    00    1      IGNDECERR(*YES) SPECIFIED ON COMMAND. NO DECIMAL DATA ERRORS
* QRG7031    00    1      NAME OR INDICATOR NOT REFERENCED.
* QRG7086    00    1      RPG WILL HANDLE BLOCKING FUNCTION FOR THE FILE. INFDS CONTEN
                          ARE TRANSFERRED.
```


MESSAGE SUMMARY

```
TOTAL    00   10   20   30   40   50
  3       3    0    0    0    0    0
```

40 RECORDS READ FROM SOURCE FILE
SOURCE RECORDS INCLUDE   31 SPECIFICATIONS,   0 TABLE RECORDS, AND   9 COMMENTS

PRM HAS BEEN CALLED

QRG0003 PROGRAM PJ003A PLACED IN LIB CABLE. 00 HIGHEST SEVERITY FOUND

* * * * * E N D O F C O M P I L A T I O N * * * * *

```
100  F* TITLE: DEBUG PROJECT 3-B
200  F* DATE:  3/7           AUTHOR: D.CABLE
300  F* DESCRIPTION: CALCULATE EMPLOYEE EARNINGS
400  F***********************************************************
500  F* MODIFICATIONS:
600  F* NO.    DATE      INIT     DESCRIPTION
700  F*        XX/XX/XX  XXX      XXXXXXXXXXXXXXXXXXXXXXXXXXXXX
800  F***********************************************************
```

NAME OF PROGRAM WILL BE PJ003B IN LIBRARY CABLE

```
              H
* 1019                    ALL DECIMAL DATA ERRORS IGNORED
     900  FPARTS    IP  F      120            DISK
    1000  FREPORT   O   F      132      OF    PRINTER
    1100  F***********************************************************

    1200  IPARTS    AA  01
    1300  I                                       1   10  PARTNO
    1400  I                                      11   26  DESCR
    1500  I                                      27   27  TYPE
    1600  I                                      28   322UPRC
    1700  I                                      33   37  QTY


    1800  C            CNT       ADD   1        CNT     40
    1900  C            TYPE      COMP  'A'                      65
    2000  C            TUPE      COMP  'B'                      66
    2100  C            TYPE      COMP  C                        67
    2200  C     65     QTY       MULT  UPRC      EXPRC   72
* 5014                           5014-****
    2300  C     66     UPRC      MULT  .0100     RATE    72
    2400  C     66     QTY       MULT  RATE      EXPRC
    2500  C     67     QTY       MULT  0         EXPRC
* 5006       5006-*.
* 5007       5007-**

    2600  C            FINVAL    ADD   EXPRC     FINVAL  92
* 5008              5008-**********.
* 5014              5014-****


    2700  OREPORT   H   203      1P
    2800  O         OR           OF
    2900  O                                30 'TOTAL INVENTORY VALUE'
    3000  O         H   2        1P
    3100  O         OR           OF
    3200  O                                11 'PART NUMBER'
    3300  O                                25 'PART DESCR'
    3400  O                                35 'UNIT PRICE'
    3500  O                                40 'QUANTITY'
    3600  O                                50 'TOTAL VALUE'
    3700  O         D   1        01
    3800  O                         PARTNO    10
    3900  O                         DESCR     30
    4000  O                         UPRC   K  33
    4100  O                         QTY    Z  38
    4200  O                         EXPRC  K  48
    4300  O         T   1        LR
    4400  O                                15 'TOTAL VALUE'
    4500  O                         FINVAL K  48
* * * * * E N D   O F   S O U R C E * * * * *
```

```
* 7086        900    RPG PROVIDES BLOCK/UNBLOCK SUPPORT FOR FILE PARTS.
* 7044       2400    QTY MUST BE NUMERIC FIELD FOR THIS OPERATION
* 7044       2500    QTY MUST BE NUMERIC FIELD FOR THIS OPERATION
* 7059       4100    EDITING SPECIFIED BUT FIELD NAME QTY NOT NUMERIC
```

CROSS-REFERENCE LISTING

```
        FILE/RCD    DEV/RCD     REFERENCES (D=DEFINED)
   01   PARTS       DISK        900D  1200
   02   REPORT      PRINTER     1000D 2700  3000  3700  4300


        FIELD       ATTR        REFERENCES (M=MODIFIED D=DEFINED)
* 7030  C           A(1)        2100
        CNT         P(4,0)      1800  1800D
        DESCR       A(16)       1400D 3900
* 7030  EXPRC       P(5,0)      2200D 2400M 2500M 2600  4200
* 7030  FINVAL      P(5,0)      2600D 4500
        PARTNO      A(10)       1300D 3800
        PRC                     2200
        QTY         A(5)        1700D 2200  2400  2500  4100
        RATE        P(7,2)      2300D 2400
* 7030  TUPE        A(1)        2000
        TYPE        A(1)        1500D 1900  2100
        UPRC        P(5,2)      1600D 2300  4000
        .0100       LITERAL     2300
        'A'         LITERAL     1900
        'B'         LITERAL     2000
        0           LITERAL     2500
        1           LITERAL     1800


        INDICATOR   REFERENCES (M=MODIFIED D=DEFINED)
        LR          900D  4300
        OF          1000D 2800  3100
        01          1200M 3700
        1P          2700  3000
        65          1900M 2200
        66          2000M 2300  2400
* 7031  67          2100M
```

MESSAGES

```
  MSGID      SEV  NUMBER  TEXT
* QRG1019    00   1       IGNDECERR(*YES) SPECIFIED ON COMMAND. NO DECIMAL DATA ERRORS
* QRG5006    10   1       POSITIONS 9, 12, AND 15 MUST BE N OR BLANK. N ASSUMED
* QRG5007    10   1       CONDITIONING INDICATOR ENTRY (POSITIONS 10-11, 13-14, OR 16-1
* QRG5008    30   1       FACTOR 1 FIELD NAME (POSITIONS 18-27) NOT VALID SYNTACTICALLY
                         ENTRY ASSUMED BLANK IF NOT NEEDED.
* QRG5014    30   2       OPERATION CODE ENTRY (POSITIONS 28-32) NOT VALID. SPECIFICATI
* QRG7030    30   4       FIELD OR INDICATOR NOT DEFINED.
* QRG7031    00   1       NAME OR INDICATOR NOT REFERENCED.
* QRG7044    30   2       FIELD NOT VALID FOR SPECIFIED OPERATION. FIELD MUST BE NUMERI
* QRG7059    20   1       EDIT MUST BE SPECIFIED ONLY WITH NUMERIC FIELD. EDITING IGNOR
* QRG7086    00   1       RPG WILL HANDLE BLOCKING FUNCTION FOR THE FILE. INFDS CONTENT
                         ARE TRANSFERRED.
```

```
MESSAGE SUMMARY

TOTAL      00      10      20      30      40      50
  15        3       2       1       9       0       0
       45 RECORDS READ FROM SOURCE FILE
       SOURCE RECORDS INCLUDE    36 SPECIFICATIONS,    0 TABLE RECORDS, AND    9 COMMENTS

   QRG0008 COMPILE TERMINATED. SEVERITY 30 ERRORS FOUND IN PROGRAM

   * * * * * E N D   O F   C O M P I L A T I O N * * * * *
 * QRG1020              ERROR OCCURRED CREATING OR UPDATING DATA AREA RETURNCODE. COMPIL
```

PROGRAMMING PROJECT

Project Overview

A report is to be printed listing inventory transactions. A receipt into inventory is coded as an *R*. A shipment out of inventory is coded as an *S*. An adjustment to inventory is coded as an *A*. For each transaction on the report, print the appropriate description of the transaction. For example, the word "Receipt" would be printed after a line for a receipt transaction. If the type is not *A* or *R* or *S*, then the words "invalid type" should be printed on the report. Write the RPG program to produce this listing. Sample data for this project can be found in Appendix D.

Input Format

The input data for the project is found in a file called INVTRAN in the sample data. The Record Layout for this file is shown in Figure 3.23.

Output Format (Printer Spacing Chart)

The output format for the project is a report with standard headings. The report will show the part number, the quantity, and the literal which describes the transaction. A final total of all quantities is printed at the end of the report. The Printer Spacing Chart for this report is shown in Figure 3.24.

An example of the finished report is shown in Figure 3.25.

FIGURE 3.23 Programming Project: Record Layout

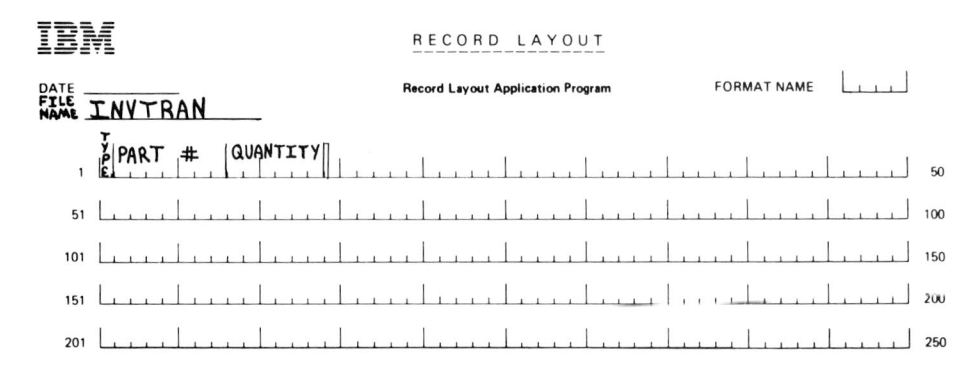

FIGURE 3.24 Programming Project: Printer Spacing Chart

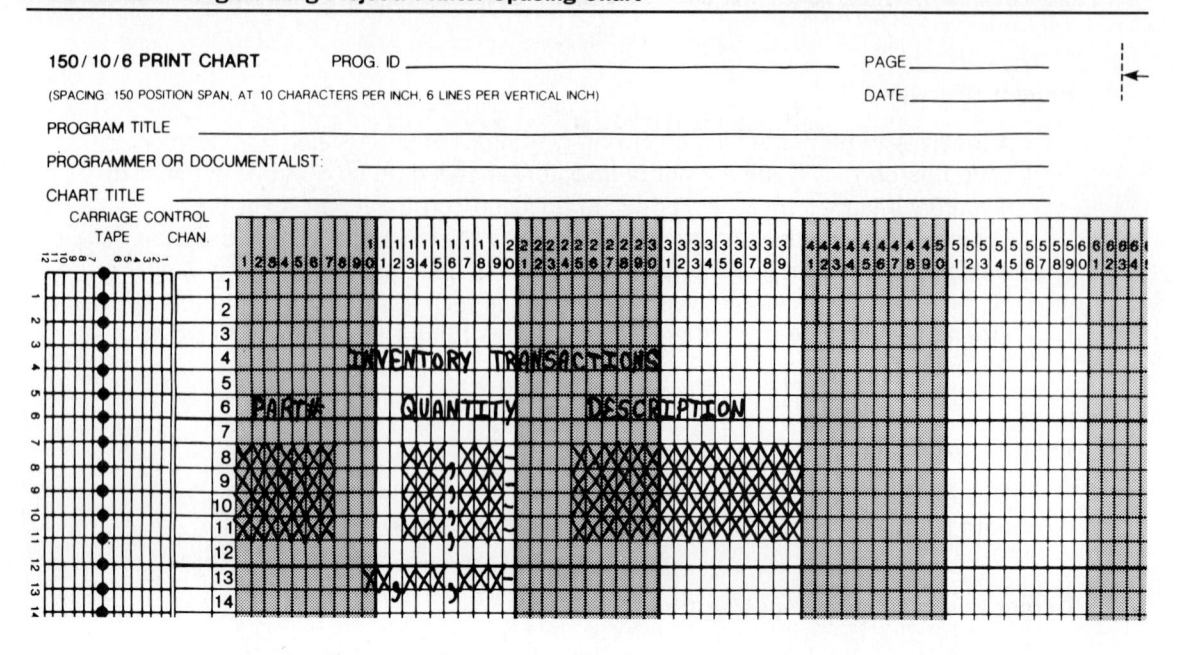

FIGURE 3.25 Programming Project: Final Report

```
              INVENTORY TRANSACTIONS

       PART#        QUANTITY      DESCRIPTION
       0000123         1,000      RECEIPT
       0000698                    SHIPMENT
       0000698         1,000      SHIPMENT
       0000798            23      ADJUSTMENT
       0001234           500      INVALID TYPE
       0001234           900      ADJUSTMENT
       0009875           25-      INVALID TYPE
       0009903           100      INVALID TYPE

                       3,498
```

RPG: A Programming Language for Today

Chapter 4

Control Breaks (The RPG Cycle)

What you will learn in Chapter 4

Sample Program Using Level Breaks
    Sequence of Input Data
    Level Break Totals
    Control Level Indicators
The Effect of the RPG Cycle on
    Level Breaks

Summary Reports
Summarized Output Files
Multiple Output Files

Business reports usually present accumulations of data with totals that have been calculated in the program. Although a list of data with a final total at the end of the report can be useful, it is often desirable to print subtotals at the end of groups of data within the body of the report. In RPG, these subtotals are achieved through the use of control breaks or level breaks. A level break is the point in a file where one group of records ends and a new group of records begins. The grouping is determined by some key field in the record. Figure 4.1 shows a typical business report listing customer purchases with a control break between customers. The report shows a total for each customer.

SAMPLE PROGRAM USING LEVEL BREAKS ■

To create a report of all the customer purchases for the example shown in Figure 4.1, a program will be needed to read the customer file and print a report totaling up all the purchases for each customer, record by record. The report will print a line showing the total amount for each customer. A level break will tell RPG when to print the customer totals.

Sequence of Input Data

Before such a report can be developed, we must ensure that the input data is in a sequence that will produce the desired report. For example, to print a list of all customers in alphabetical order, it would be necessary to sort the customer file in sequence by the field called NAME before printing the report. In the example in Figure 4.1, the report is in sequence by customer number. It was necessary to sort the customer file in sequence by customer number so that each customer's transactions would be gathered into one group on the page.

FIGURE 4.1 Report Showing Customer Purchases

```
                    SALES BY CUSTOMER
    CUST#    QUANT      PRICE      TOTAL
    02513       8       49.55     396.40
    02513       5      200.00   1,000.00
    02513      20       45.08     901.60

         CUSTOMER TOTAL         2,298.00  * CUST PURCH OVER $1000.00

    10508       1       39.95      39.95
    10508       1      205.50     205.50

         CUSTOMER TOTAL           245.45  *

    55008      10      100.00   1,000.00
    55008       3       25.00      75.00

         CUSTOMER TOTAL         1,075.00  * CUST PURCH OVER $1000.00
```

One method for putting a file into a desired sequence is called sorting, although other methods are also used. A program could be written in RPG, or any other language, to accomplish this sort function, but it is usually easier and more productive to use a sort utility, which is already available on most computers. The sort utility requires only that the programmer enter the parameters for the sort. This means that the programmer must tell the sort utility what fields need to be sorted and in what sequence. For the example in Figure 4.1, the programmer would have asked for a sort by customer number in ascending sequence.

For this sample program, assume that the input file has already been sorted into the sequence needed. This makes it possible to begin programming the report showing the correct totals for each customer. Figure 4.2 shows the input file containing the three customers' transactions.

In this example, customer number 2513 has made three purchases, customer number 10508 has made two purchases, and customer number 55008 has made two purchases. To obtain a total for each of these customers, it will be necessary for the program to recognize the moment the end of a group of records has been reached.

Level Break Totals

Chapter 3 described how comparing is performed in RPG. It would be possible in this program for RPG to compare each customer number to the customer number preceding it and determine when to print a total. In fact, that would be the method used in many other programming languages. RPG has a much easier and more efficient method for causing this level break to occur. RPG does the hard part; the programmer needs only to tell RPG where the level break is to be taken and what to print (or calculate) when it happens.

Control Level Indicators

RPG identifies level breaks by means of level indicators. Level indicators are somewhat like other indicators but with some special characteristics. They always start with the letter L and are never used for any other purpose than for managing level breaks. Level indicators are automatically set

FIGURE 4.2 Input File

```
             INPUT DATA FOR SALES BY CUSTOMER
      STORE    DEPT     CUST #    QUANT     PRICE
       01      230      2513        8       49.55
       01      230      2513        5      200.00
       01      235      2513       20       45.08
       01      235     10508        1       39.95
       01      235     10508        1     1205.50
       01      235     55008       10      100.00
       01      235     55008        3       25.00
```

FIGURE 4.3 Customer File Layout

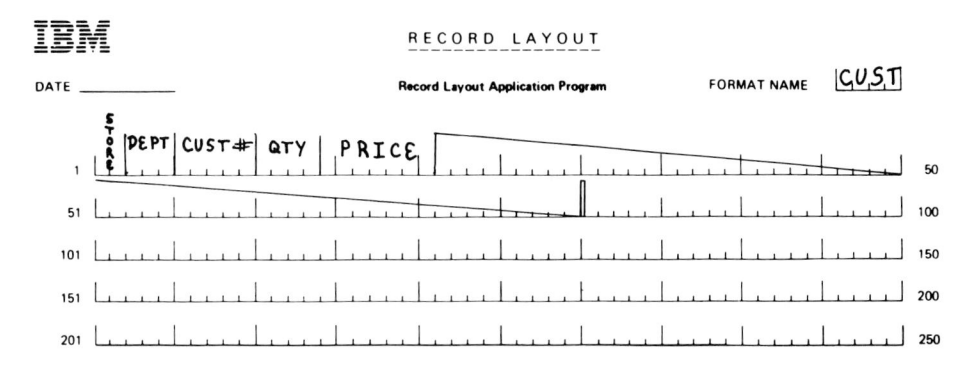

```
IBM                           RECORD LAYOUT
DATE _____         Record Layout Application Program    FORMAT NAME  CUST

    S|DEPT|CUST#|QTY| PRICE |                                    |
  1 T|    |     |   |       |                                    | 50
 51  |____|_____|___|_____|_____| 100
101  |____|_____|___|_____|_____| 150
151  |____|_____|___|_____|_____| 200
201  |____|_____|___|_____|_____| 250
```

on by RPG when a level break is encountered. RPG provides ten level indicators, L0–L9. For this chapter, only the L1 indicator will be used. The remaining indicators will be discussed in later chapters.

The sample program will use the input data shown in Figure 4.2. The format of the file is shown in Figure 4.3.

File Description Specifications
The File Description Specifications form will be coded exactly as it was in earlier examples with an input file and a printer file.

Input Specifications
To create the report for the example, a level break is to occur when all records for each customer have finished processing. That is, a level break will occur whenever a customer number is found that differs from that of the record preceding it. The Input Specification is coded with a level indicator for the field for which the level break should occur.

Figures 4.4(a) and 4.4(b) show the coding for the File Description and Input Specifications. The entries are similar to those in previous sample programs. The only new entry is the level indicator L1 in columns 59–60 of the Input Specifications, after the field named CUST. This identifies the field that will be the control field for the input record. Indicator L1 will be turned on automatically when a level break occurs.

FIGURE 4.4(a) File Description for Customer Purchases

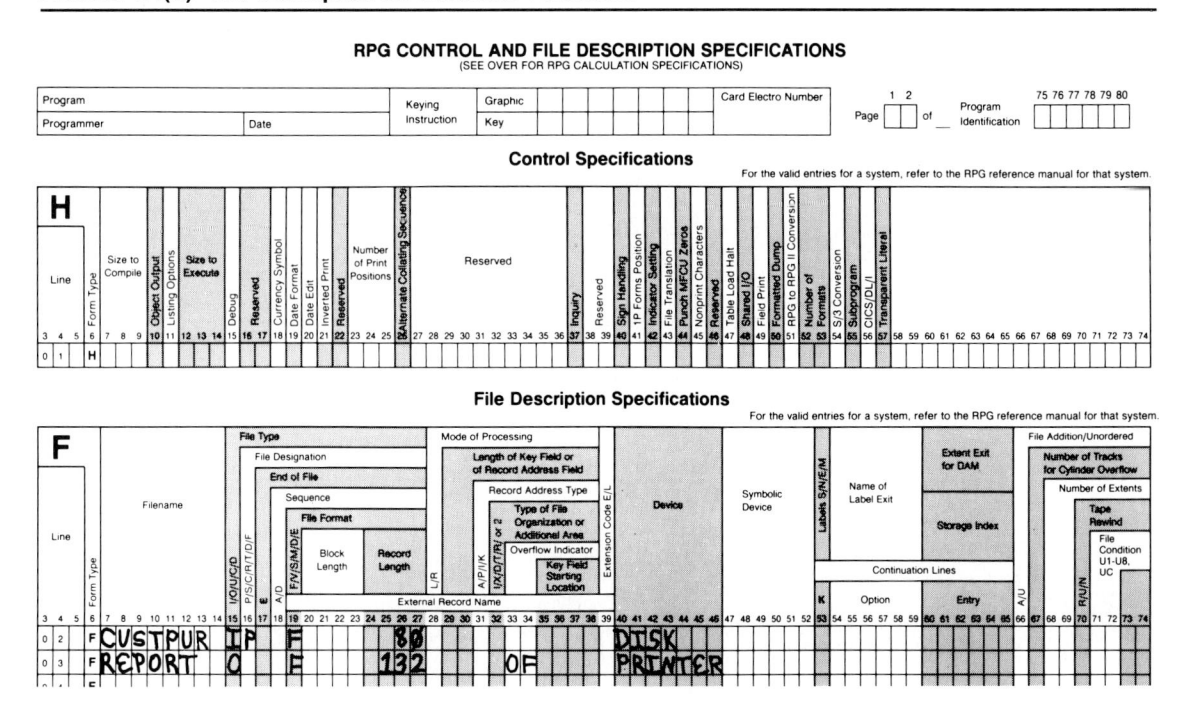

Line	Form Type	Filename	File Type	File Designation	End of File	Sequence	File Format	Block Length	Record Length	Mode of Processing	Device
02	F	CUSTPUR	I	P			F		80		DISK
03	F	REPORT	O				F		132	OF	PRINTER

Chapter 4 Control Breaks (The RPG Cycle) 81

FIGURE 4.4(b) Input Specifications for Customer Purchases

(RPG Input Specifications form)

Line	Form Type	Filename or Record Name	Sequence	Number	Option	Record identifying indicator	Position	Not	C/Z/D	Character	Position	Position	Field Location From	To	Decimal Positions	RPG Field Name	Control Level	Matching Fields	Field Record Relation	Field Indicators (Plus/Minus/Zero)
01	I	CUSTPUR	AA			01	80		CS											
02	I												1	2		STORE				
03	I												3	5		DEPT				
04	I												6	10		CUST	L1			
05	I												11	14	0	QUANT				
06	I												15	21		PRICE				
07	I					ZZ	99													

Calculation Specifications

To print a total of all purchases made by each customer, we need to compute a cumulative total of each purchase as each input record is read. This is done as shown in Figure 4.5 by adding each input amount to a total field. This is similar to the examples in previous chapters where a final total was accumulated. The difference here is that the accumulation will be printed at level break time instead of last record (LR) time.

At the end of each group of records (L1 total time), it would also be useful to compare the total purchases to an arbitrary credit limit for all customers. Any customer total equal to or greater than $1000.00 will cause a message to print on the report.

This comparison will need to take place only after all purchases for a customer have been computed. This occurs at level 1 (L1) time. Figure 4.6 shows this calculation. The L1 is entered in columns 7–8 to show that this calculation will occur only at L1 *total* time.

FIGURE 4.5 Calculation Specifications for Customer Purchases

(RPG Calculation Specifications form)

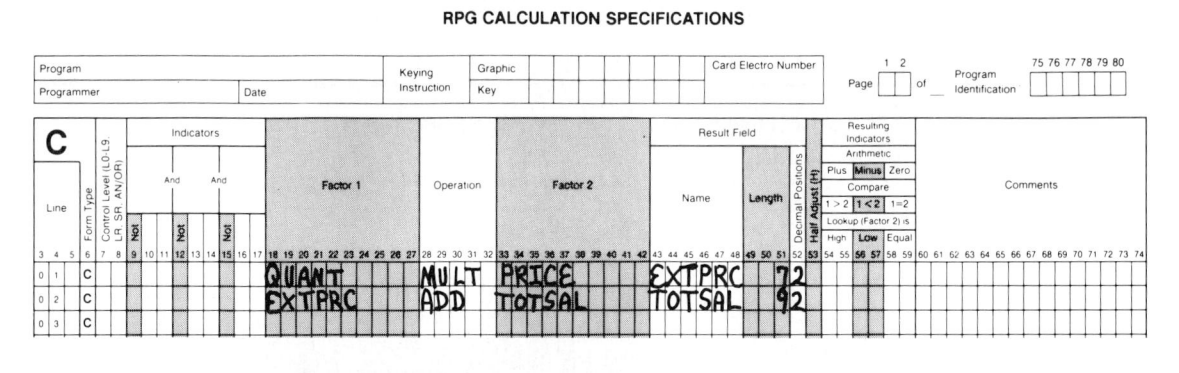

Line	Form Type	Control Level	Indicators And/And/And	Factor 1	Operation	Factor 2	Result Field Name	Length	Decimal Positions	Half Adjust	Resulting Indicators (Plus/Minus/Zero, 1>2 1<2 1=2)	Comments
01	C			QUANT	MULT	PRICE	EXTPRC	72				
02	C			EXTPRC	ADD	TOTSAL	TOTSAL	92				
03	C											

FIGURE 4.6 Calculation Specifications for Level Break Comparison

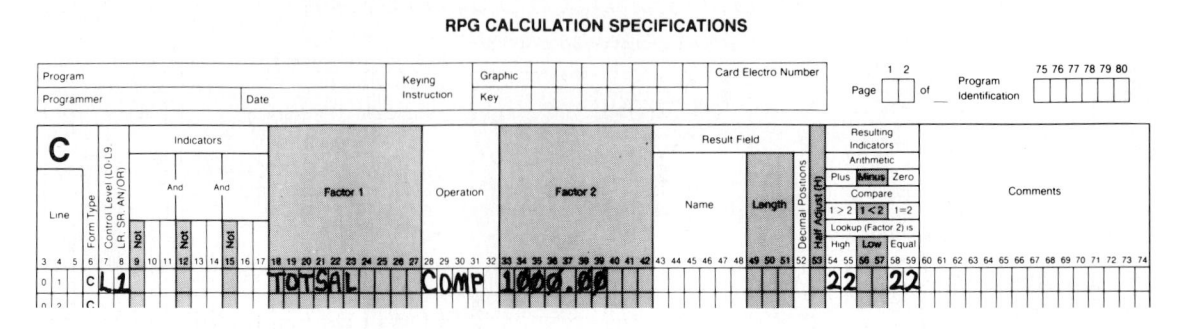

(RPG Calculation Specifications form)

Line	Form Type	Control Level	Indicators	Factor 1	Operation	Factor 2	Result Field Name	Length	Decimal Positions	Half Adjust	Resulting Indicators	Comments
01	C	L1		TOTSAL	COMP	1000.00					22 22	

FIGURE 4.7 Output Specifications for Customer Purchases

Line	Form Type	Filename or Record Name	Type (H/D/T/E)	Stkr # Fetch (F)	Space Before	Space After	Skip Before	Skip After	Output Indicators			Field Name or EXCPT Name	Edit Codes	End Position in Output Record	Constant or Edit Word
01	O	REPORT	D		2	01			1P						
02	O	OR							OF						
03	O													40	'SALES BY CUSTOMER'
04	O		D		2				1P						
05	O	OR							OF						
06	O													6	'CUST#'
07	O													15	'QUANT'
08	O													25	'PRICE'
09	O													35	'TOTAL'
10	O		D		1				01						
11	O											CUST		6	
12	O											QUANT	K	15	
13	O											PRICE	K	25	
14	O											EXTPRCK		35	
15	O														

Output Specifications

The coding for the Output Specifications to print detail lines and intermediate totals is no different from that for the programs in previous chapters. The headings and the detail lines will be coded exactly the same way, as shown in Figure 4.7.

The new entries cover the level break total lines. As shown in Figure 4.8, the total specifications must be entered after the detail specifications. RPG would give an error message if the total time outputs were coded first. The letter T is entered in column 15 to show that this will be a total time output. More will be said about total time later in this chapter.

To make the total easier to find on the report, it is a good idea to space a line or two before and after the total line. For this reason a 1 is entered in column 17 to space one line before and a 2 is entered in column 18 to space two lines after the total line is printed.

Indicator L1 is entered in columns 24–25 to let RPG know that these totals should be printed when the L1 indicator is turned on. The next line shows the constant CUSTOMER TOTAL, which is to be printed on the total line ending in column 20. This title is not a necessity, but it is a help for the person who must read the report to know what total is being printed. The customer total

FIGURE 4.8 Output Specifications for L1

Line	Form Type	Filename or Record Name	Type (H/D/T/E)	Space Before	Space After	Output Indicators			Field Name or EXCPT Name	Edit Codes	End Position in Output Record	Constant or Edit Word
01	O		T	1	2	L1						
02	O										20	'CUSTOMER TOTAL'
03	O								TOTSALK B		35	
04	O										37	
05	O					22					62	'* CUST PURCH OVER $1000.00'
06	O											
07	O											

FIGURE 4.9 RPG Fixed Logic Chart

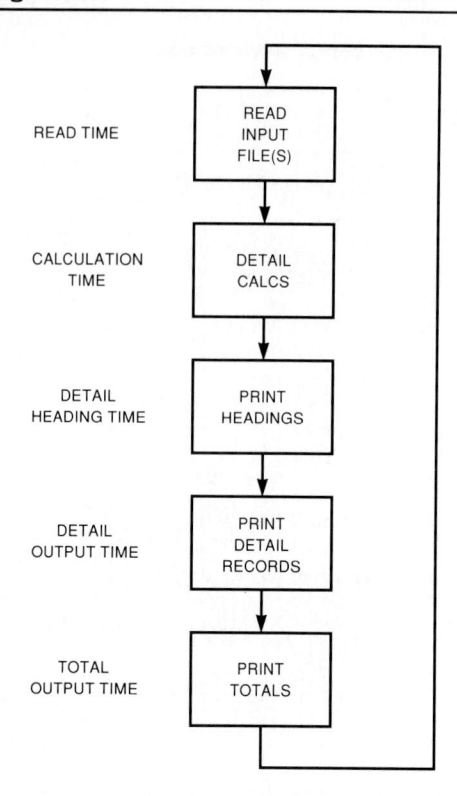

```
READ TIME              ┌──────────┐
                       │  READ    │◄─────┐
                       │  INPUT   │      │
                       │  FILE(S) │      │
                       └────┬─────┘      │
                            ▼            │
CALCULATION            ┌──────────┐      │
TIME                   │  DETAIL  │      │
                       │  CALCS   │      │
                       └────┬─────┘      │
                            ▼            │
DETAIL                 ┌──────────┐      │
HEADING TIME           │  PRINT   │      │
                       │ HEADINGS │      │
                       └────┬─────┘      │
                            ▼            │
DETAIL                 ┌──────────┐      │
OUTPUT TIME            │  PRINT   │      │
                       │  DETAIL  │      │
                       │  RECORDS │      │
                       └────┬─────┘      │
                            ▼            │
TOTAL                  ┌──────────┐      │
OUTPUT TIME            │  PRINT   │      │
                       │  TOTALS  │──────┘
                       └──────────┘
```

amount will be printed ending in column 35, following the words CUSTOMER TOTAL. This field is edited with a K so it will contain commas and a decimal point.

Clearing a Field After Printing (Blank After)

A new feature in this example is the *B* in column 39. This is a very important entry. It is this code that can make all the difference in whether or not the resulting totals will be correct. This *B*, representing Blank After, instructs the program to reset the value of the field TOTSAL to zero after the customer total has been printed so that the totals for one customer do not continue to accumulate into the totals for the *next* customer. Resetting to zero could be handled within the Calculation Specifications in other ways which will be discussed in later chapters, but entering *B* in column 39 is certainly the simplest method. Finally, a constant * (asterisk) will be printed following the customer total to make it easier for the user to see that it is a total.

Detail Time and Total Time

Printing a report using level breaks requires that the programmer be aware that events in an RPG program occur at specific times. The chart in Figure 4.9 explains some of the events in a program and the times at which they occur.

An input record is read at *read* time. A line is printed on a report at *detail* output time. A computed total amount should only be printed at *total* output time. It is important to understand exactly how the times affect the accuracy of the program.

When printing an output report, RPG recognizes three times: heading time, detail time, and total time. Heading time is the time at which headings are printed, and this is the only time at which the 1P indicator is turned on. When a line needs to be printed at 1P time, the letter *H* is coded in column 15 on the Output Specifications. See the example in Figure 4.10.

Headings can be printed at either *H* or *D* time. Detail lines, however, must always be coded as *D* to show that they are to be output at detail time.

Total fields to be printed on a report must always be coded as *T* on the Output Specifications because these totals are available (with a correct figure) only at total time. Requesting a total at the wrong time will produce inaccurate results. The example in Figure 4.11 shows sample coding for detail lines and for total lines.

FIGURE 4.10 Output Specifications for Report Headings

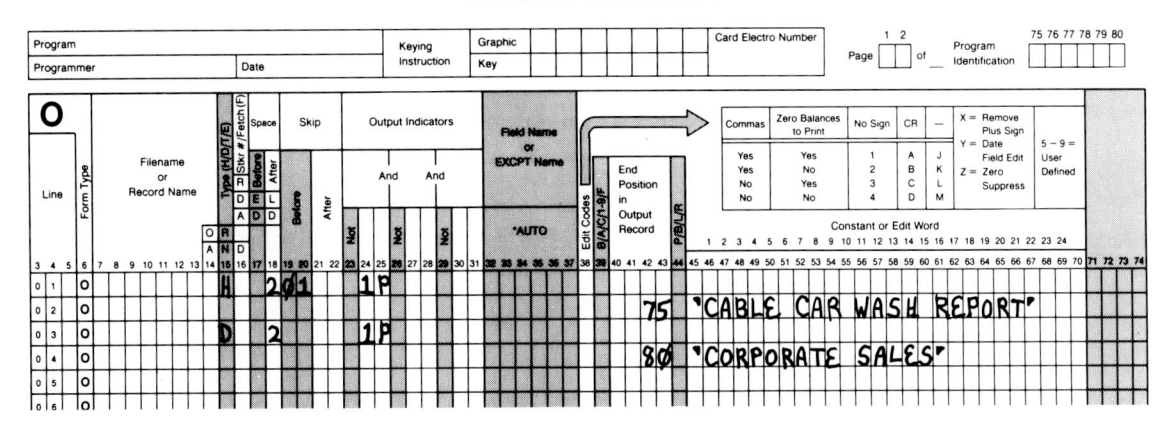

[RPG Output Specifications form showing:
- Line 01: H, Space 2/01, Output indicator 1P, "CABLE CAR WASH REPORT" ending position 75
- Line 03: D, Space 2, Output indicator 1P, "CORPORATE SALES" ending position 80]

FIGURE 4.11 Output Specifications for Detail and Total Lines

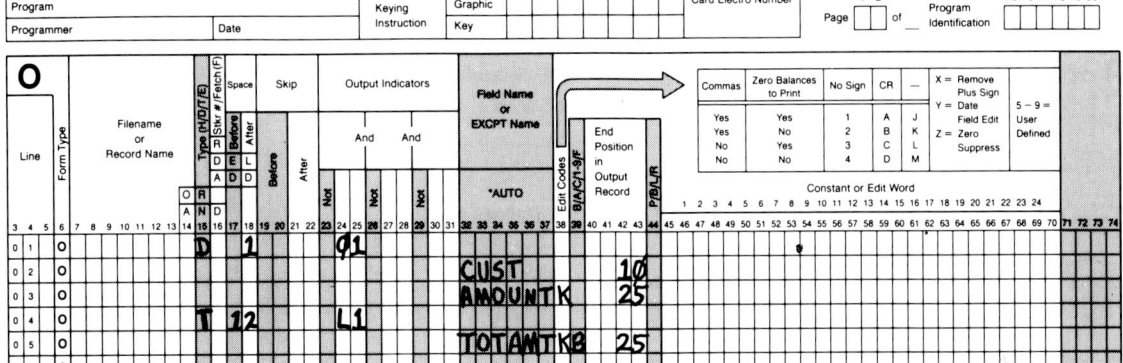

[RPG Output Specifications form showing:
- Line 01: D, Space 1, Output indicator 01
- Line 02: CUST, end position 10
- Line 03: AMOUNTK, end position 25
- Line 04: T, Space 12, Output indicator L1
- Line 05: TOTAMTKB, end position 25]

THE EFFECT OF THE RPG CYCLE ON LEVEL BREAKS ■

In Chapter 1, the RPG fixed logic cycle was discussed. Now is a good time to review the RPG cycle to describe its effect on level breaks. It is extremely important to understand the RPG cycle and to recognize when each event will occur.

Figure 4.12 shows the fixed logic cycle for RPG. Each process occurring in an RPG program happens in a given sequence. This flowchart is a kind of road map to the route the data is taking through the program. Awareness of these steps enables the programmer to code the program so that it will execute correctly.

The very first thing an RPG program does is to obtain and open all the files that are specified in the File Description Specifications. The indicator 1P is set on, all other indicators are set off, and any numeric fields used within the program are set to zero. These events are performed *automatically* by RPG and never need to be managed by the programmer. It is important for the programmer to be aware that all of these events have taken place.

If the program uses 1P for printing the heading on the first page of the report, this is the time at which the heading will be printed. At this stage of the cycle the first record in the file has not yet been read and therefore no data is yet available to be printed. After printing the headings, RPG will set the 1P indicator off automatically and begin processing records.

Now it is time to read a record. If no record is read (because the end of the file has been reached), the LR indicator will be set on. LR will cause *all other* level indicators to be turned on.

Total time calculations will be executed. That means that any Calculation Specifications having L1 or LR in columns 7–8 will be executed at that time. Then all total time output will be

FIGURE 4.12 RPG Fixed Logic Cycle

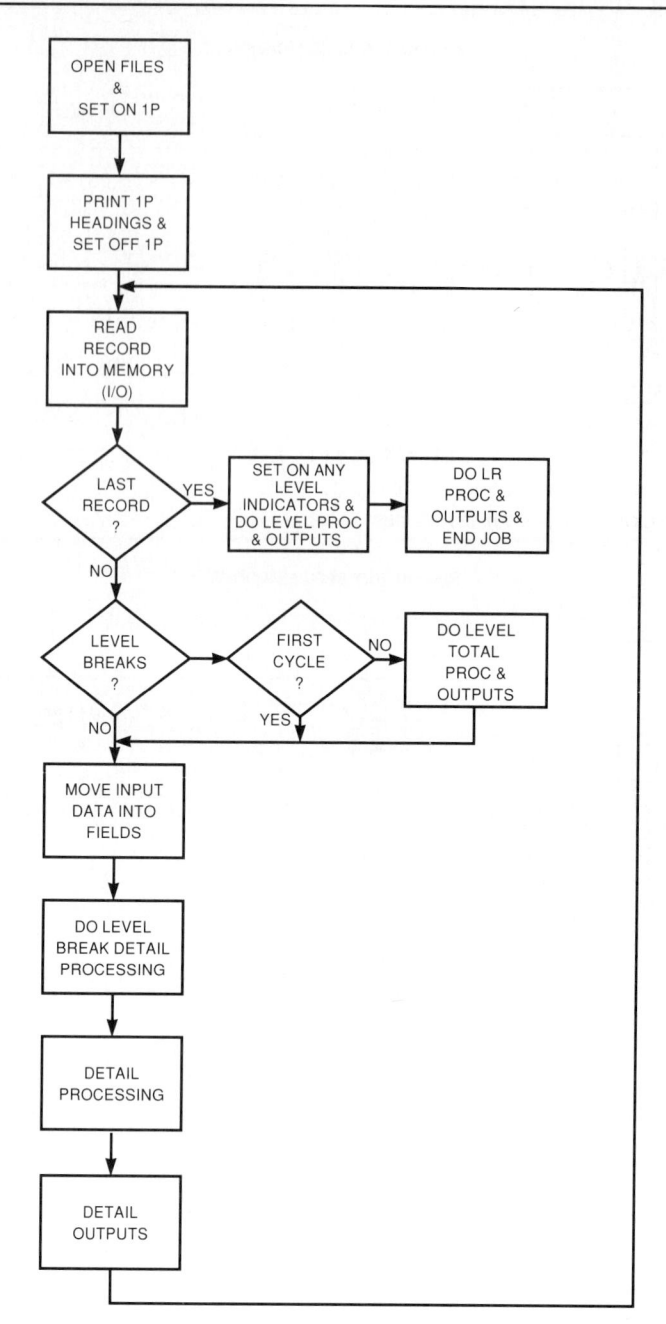

```
          ┌─────────────┐
          │ OPEN FILES  │
          │     &       │
          │ SET ON 1P   │
          └──────┬──────┘
                 ↓
          ┌─────────────┐
          │  PRINT 1P   │
          │ HEADINGS &  │
          │ SET OFF 1P  │
          └──────┬──────┘
                 ↓  ←──────────────────────────────────────────┐
          ┌─────────────┐                                       │
          │    READ     │                                       │
          │   RECORD    │                                       │
          │ INTO MEMORY │                                       │
          │    (I/O)    │                                       │
          └──────┬──────┘                                       │
                 ↓                                              │
            ╱ LAST ╲      ┌──────────────┐   ┌──────────┐       │
           ╱ RECORD ╲ YES │  SET ON ANY  │   │  DO LR   │       │
           ╲    ?   ╱────→│    LEVEL     │──→│  PROC &  │       │
            ╲     ╱       │  INDICATORS &│   │ OUTPUTS &│       │
             ╲ ╱          │ DO LEVEL PROC│   │ END JOB  │       │
             NO↓          │   & OUTPUTS  │   └──────────┘       │
                          └──────────────┘                      │
            ╱ LEVEL╲         ╱ FIRST ╲  NO  ┌──────────┐        │
           ╱ BREAKS ╲ YES   ╱  CYCLE  ╲────→│ DO LEVEL │        │
           ╲    ?   ╱─────→ ╲    ?   ╱      │  TOTAL   │        │
            ╲     ╱          ╲     ╱        │  PROC &  │        │
             ╲ ╱              ╲ ╱           │ OUTPUTS  │        │
             NO↓              YES↓          └────┬─────┘        │
                 ←──────────────┴────────────────┘              │
          ┌─────────────┐                                       │
          │ MOVE INPUT  │                                       │
          │  DATA INTO  │                                       │
          │   FIELDS    │                                       │
          └──────┬──────┘                                       │
                 ↓                                              │
          ┌─────────────┐                                       │
          │  DO LEVEL   │                                       │
          │ BREAK DETAIL│                                       │
          │ PROCESSING  │                                       │
          └──────┬──────┘                                       │
                 ↓                                              │
          ┌─────────────┐                                       │
          │   DETAIL    │                                       │
          │ PROCESSING  │                                       │
          └──────┬──────┘                                       │
                 ↓                                              │
          ┌─────────────┐                                       │
          │   DETAIL    │                                       │
          │   OUTPUTS   │                                       │
          └──────┬──────┘                                       │
                 └───────────────────────────────────────────────┘
```

performed. That means that the totals for level 1 will print and then the final (LR time) totals will print and the program will end.

If, however, a record is read, the record identifying indicator will be turned on, the record will be placed in an input area in main memory, and processing can begin. Before processing can begin, however, it will be necessary to determine whether a control break has occurred. If the current record has a different control field from the record that preceded it, the level indicator will be turned on.

On the first cycle through the program, before any records have been processed, it would not be useful to print level break totals or to do level break processing. For that reason, the level break total processing is not done on the first cycle, even though the first record read must look to RPG as though it should have caused a level break.

Before processing can proceed, it will also be necessary to determine whether a page overflow has been encountered. If an end of page has occurred, then RPG will print the page headings controlled by the overflow indicator before processing any other calculations.

FIGURE 4.13 Summary Report

```
         ILL413                    SALES BY CUSTOMER
         CUST#                          TOTAL
         02513                         2,298.00    * CUST PURCH OVER $1000.00

         10508                           245.45    *

         55008                         1,075.00    * CUST PURCH OVER $1000.00
```

Now the program can begin performing the detail Calculation Specifications as they were coded. The detail lines will be printed as expected. At the end of this processing, the program is ready to go around again and read the next record and go through all the testing again.

Although this may appear difficult to follow at first, it should become a permanent part of your programming knowledge. This cycle works the way you would want a program to work. RPG is checking all the things that you would check intuitively when preparing a report by hand.

It is useful to think of a program as a never-ending cycle, constantly returning to read a record and process it until at last it finds no more records.

SUMMARY REPORTS ■

In the example report shown in Figure 4.1, a detail line was printed for each transaction and a total was printed at the end of each customer's transactions. In a large company this could produce a very lengthy report, and management might decide they did not need to see every individual transaction. They might request a report that showed only the customer totals. Figure 4.13 shows what such a report might look like.

In this summary report, only one line is printed for each customer, a line showing only the total amount of all purchases for that customer. The detail information is not shown. This total line is printed only when the customer number in the transaction file changes. Notice that the totals are the same as the totals derived in the detail report in Figure 4.1. The only difference in the reports is that the detail is missing from the summary report.

Programming such a summary report uses coding quite similar to the coding for the detail report. It is still necessary to read every record in the input file. It is still necessary to do all the calculations. The L1 indicator still controls the level break.

The only difference is that the detail records are not printed. It is useful to print some information on the total line to identify each customer (customer number) but the rest of the coding remains the same. The customer number is still available at total time from the last record that was read. Figure 4.14 shows the coding for the Output Specifications for such a report.

SUMMARIZED OUTPUT FILES ■

Until now, the only types of output files discussed have been printed reports. RPG can produce any type of output file, such as screen displays or disk files as well as printed output. Any type of file that can be used as an input file (disk, tape, diskette, etc.) can also be used as an output file.

Sometimes there is a need to create another file in a format different from that of the input file. It is sometimes useful to summarize a data file, such as a transaction file, keeping only the summarized totals for each group of transactions. This has various benefits. Computer storage space might be too limited to keep large detail files for long periods. It might be useful to retain only the summarized total information for several years for statistical analysis. It might be useful to create a summary file to take to another computer at another location. There are many such reasons for summarizing a file, but our interest here is how to do it.

FIGURE 4.14 Output Specifications for Summary Report

The method for outputting a file is the same method used for outputting a printed report. Using the data from the sample program, the format required for an output file is shown in Figure 4.15.

The File Description Specifications (Figure 4.16) will require a filename as input files and output reports do. This file will be defined as an output file by entering an O in column 15. The record length for the output summary file is defined as 21 characters since it does not need to be as long as the detail transaction file. Of course, this will vary depending on the layout for the particular file. The device name will be the device on which the output file will eventually reside. In this example, the output device will be disk.

The rest of the program will be the same as the programs that produce reports. The calculations can be the same as they were for the program which produced a detail or summary report. The only difference will be that the Output Specifications will be coded to define the output record format and the current date will be added to the record. Figure 4.17 shows the Output Specifications for outputting to a file instead of to a printed report.

The Output Specifications for the summary file carry the filename CUSTSUMM to define which output file is being described. The letter T is entered in column 15 to instruct the program to create a record in the output file only when a total has been created. No records will be created at detail time, so there is no need for detail time output. The indicator in columns 24–25 is L1 because a summary record needs to be created each time a level break is found. No entries are made in columns 17–22 because these entries are used only for printed reports.

FIGURE 4.15 Record Layout

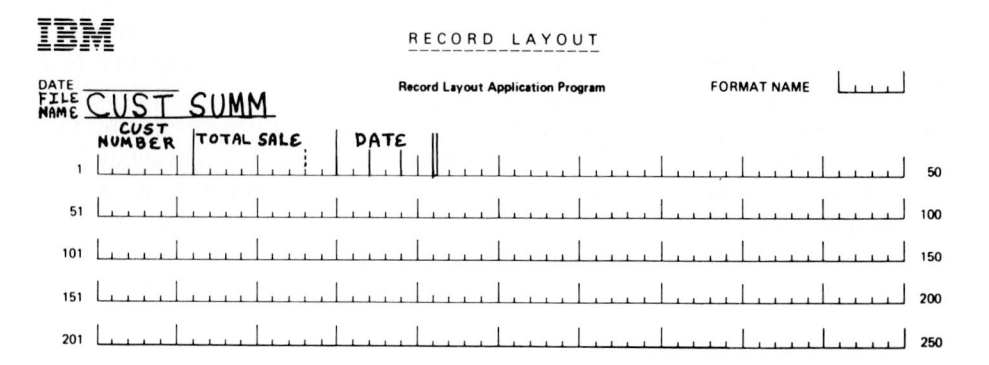

88   *RPG: A Programming Language for Today*

FIGURE 4.16 File Description Specifications

[RPG Control and File Description Specifications form with entries:]
- 02 F CUSTPUR IP F 80 DISK
- 03 F CUSTSUMMO F 21 DISK

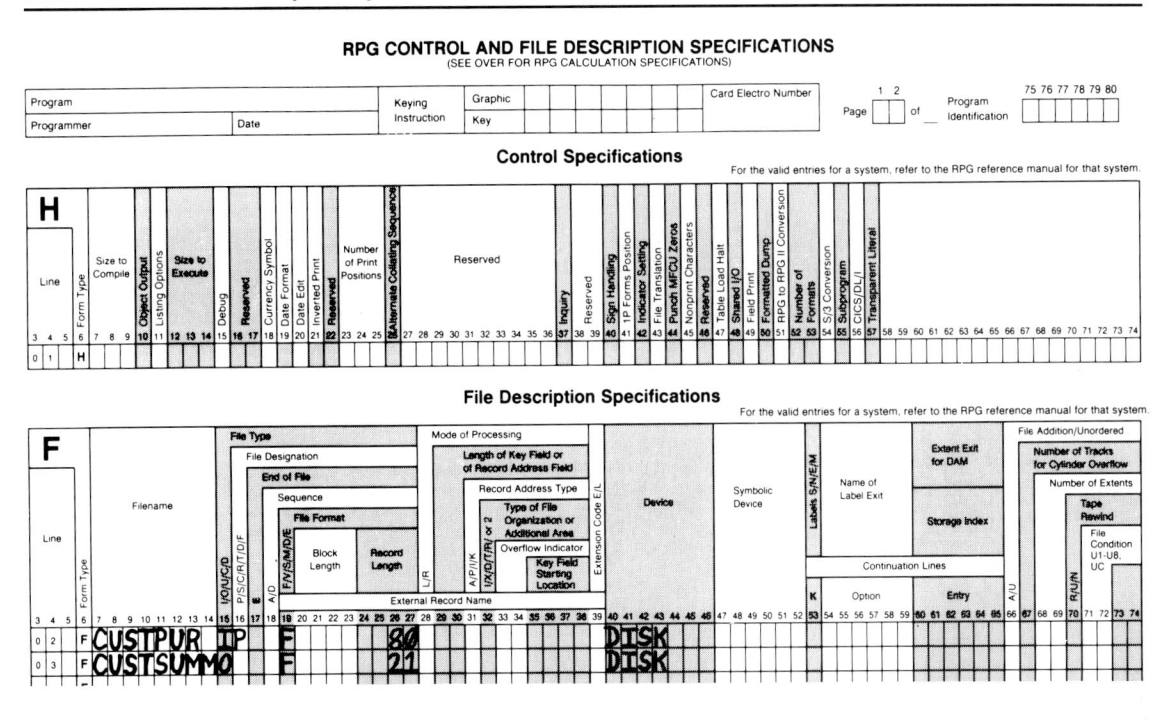

FIGURE 4.17 Output Specifications for Outputting to a File

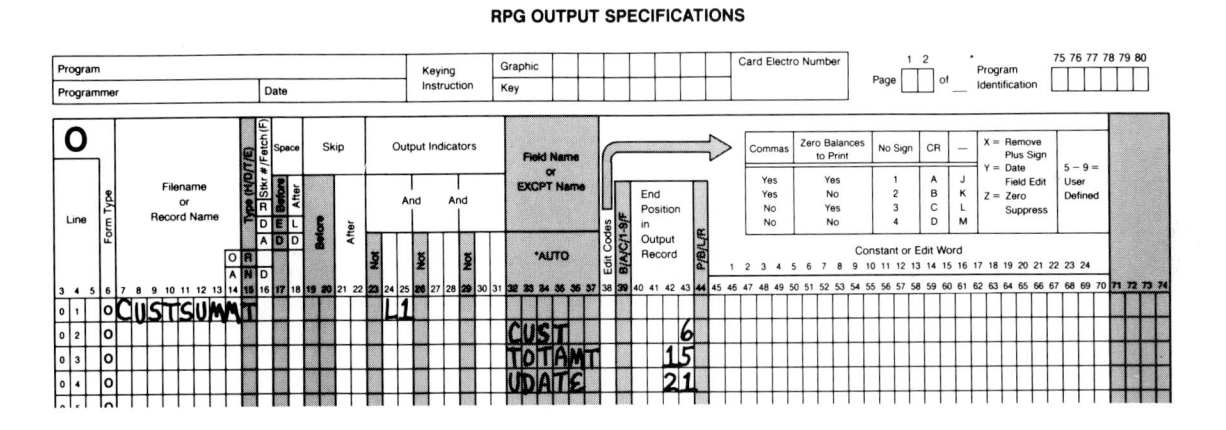

[RPG Output Specifications form with entries:]
- 01 O CUSTSUMM L1
- 02 O CUST 6
- 03 O TOTAMT 15
- 04 O UDATE 21

The remaining Output Specifications show that only the customer number, the total amount, and the current date are needed in the output file. The customer number will be output in columns 1–6 and the customer total in columns 7–15. The current date (UDATE) will be output in columns 16–21. No edit codes will be entered because these fields will be going to a disk file and not to a printed report.

MULTIPLE OUTPUT FILES ■

In Figure 4.18 the Output Specifications are defined for outputting both a summary report and a summary file. Although it is not necessary to print a report for every program where a summary file is required, it is a useful method for proving that the program did what it was supposed to do and that the totals in the output file are correct.

When outputting more than one file from a program, perhaps the most important entry to look at carefully will be the entry in column 39 on the line for the total amount. Remember that

Chapter 4 Control Breaks (The RPG Cycle) **89**

FIGURE 4.18 Output Specifications for a Summary Report and Summary File

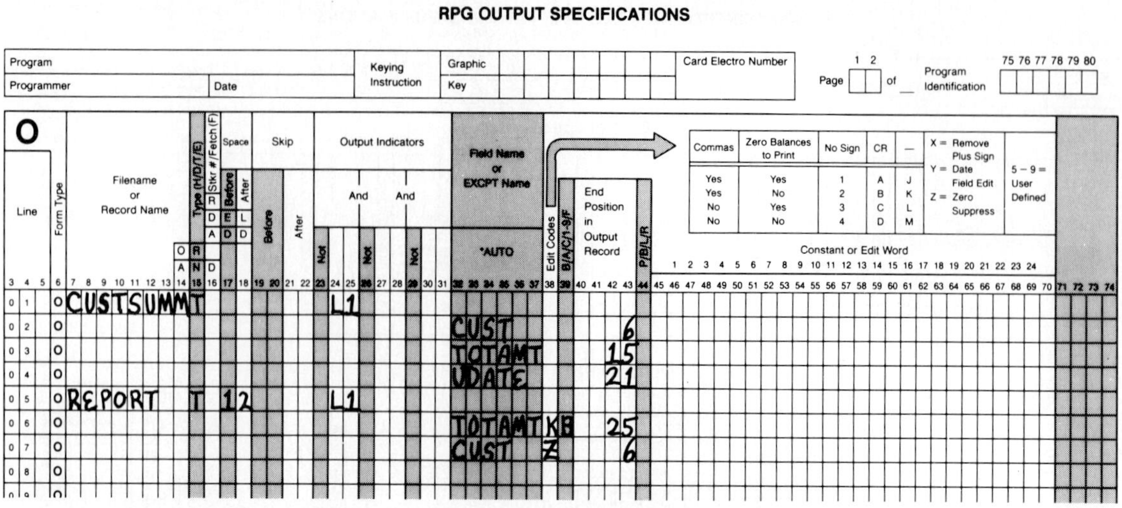
RPG OUTPUT SPECIFICATIONS

```
0 1 O CUSTSUMM T      L1
0 2 O                        CUST        6
0 3 O                        TOTAMT     15
0 4 O                        UDATE      21
0 5 O REPORT   T  12  L1
0 6 O                        TOTAMT KB  25
0 7 O                        CUST   Z    6
```

entering a *B* (for Blank After) in this column tells RPG to reset the value of the field to zero. The total field for the summary file *does not* have a *B* in column 39 but the total field (which is the same for both files) on the report *does*. Since the summary file record will be produced *before* the report, it is important that the total is *not* zeroed out until *after* the report line has been printed. If *B* had been entered for the summary file, then the contents of the field for the report would have been zero—which is obviously not correct!

It makes no difference which output file appears first on the Output Specifications, the disk file or the report, but it is extremely important that particular attention be paid to the location of the *B* for blanking after the totals.

Now that the value and uses of level breaks have been explained, it will be possible to understand the use of an L0 level break. L0 really occurs at no specific level break. It is useful if there are calculations which should occur only at total time. It is used to indicate a total calculation that is to be performed on every program cycle. Level zero is always *on* at every total time.

SUMMARY ▪

In this chapter, you have learned how to print intermediate totals for groups of related detail data on your reports. Your reports can now begin to take on a more professional appearance.

Reports nearly always need to be totaled in a variety of ways and with the knowledge you now have, you can begin to produce these.

You have learned how to do summarization on reports and how to clear out totals on reports using the "blank after."

You can also produce summary files which might be useful for other programs. You also know how to output multiple files or reports from one program.

REVIEW QUESTIONS

1. Intermediate totals may be printed on reports using a function of RPG called a _____ .

2. Why is the sequence of the data important in printing a report using level breaks?

3. Level breaks are defined on the Input Specifications by using the special indicators _____ .

4. What are the level break indicators?

5. When may level break indicators be used in the Calculation Specifications?

6. Explain the RPG fixed logic cycle as it applies to level breaks.

7. When a level break occurs within the RPG fixed logic cycle, at what point are the total routines processed?

8. How are level breaks used on the Output Specifications?

9. When totals are processed within the RPG fixed logic cycle, what values are found in the input fields?

10. When is it important to zero or clear out the values in a field?

11. Why is it important that a total field be printed on a report before the field is cleared?

12. A field may be zeroed or cleared by entering the letter _____ in column _____ of the _____ Specifications.

13. Besides printed reports, program output can consist of files such as _____ , _____ , or _____ .

14. When multiple outputs are created in a program, it is important that totals are not cleared _____ the time they are needed.

EXERCISES

1. On an Input Specifications form, enter the coding which will cause a level break to be taken. The field is department# (DEPT#).

2. On a Calculation Specifications form, enter the coding that will cause two fields (TOT1 and TOT2) to be added together at level 1 total time.

3. On an Output Specifications form, enter the coding to print a total field (TOTAMT) at level break time.

4. On an Output Specifications form, enter the coding to clear a total field after it has been printed. The field name is TOTAMT.

DEBUGGING EXERCISES

Instructions

The following RPG programs contain an error or errors. Some of these errors are indicated by the RPG compiler on the program listing. A list of syntax errors is given at the end of the program listing. Other types of errors may occur which will not be shown. These are called logic errors.

Study each program and its syntax errors. Locate each error (including logic errors) and on a separate coding form make the correct entry for the line(s) in error.

Explain each error and how it should be corrected.

```
 100    F* TITLE: DEBUG PROJECT 4-A
 200    F* DATE:   3/7            AUTHOR: D.CABLE
 300    F* DESCRIPTION:  PRINT ACCOUNTS PAYABLE REPORT
 400    F*****************************************************
 500    F* MODIFICATIONS:
 600    F* NO.      DATE      INIT     DESCRIPTION
 700    F*          XX/XX/XX  XXX      XXXXXXXXXXXXXXXXXXXXXXXXXXXXXXX
 800    F*****************************************************

NAME OF PROGRAM WILL BE PJ004A IN LIBRARY CABLE

              H
 * 1019              ALL DECIMAL DATA ERRORS IGNORED
  900    FAPOPEN  IP  F     128           DISK
 1000    FREPORT  O   F     132    OF     PRINTER
 1100    F*****************************************************

 1200    IAPOPEN   AA  01
 1300    I                                     1   60VENDOR
 1400    I                                     7   12 INV#
 1500    I                                    13   180INVDAT
 1600    I                                    19   230INQTY
 1700    I                                    24   302INPRC
 1800    I                                    31   31 INCODE

 1900    C            CNT      ADD  1         CNT     40
 2000    C            INQTY    MULT INPRC     TPRC    72
 2100    C            TPRC     MULT .02       DISCNT  72
 2200    C            TPRC     SUB  DISCNT    PAYPRC  72
 2300    C            PAYPRC   ADD  TOTAMT    TOTAMT  72
 2400    CL1          TOTAMT   ADD  FINAMT    FINAMT  92

 2500    OREPORT  H  203      1P
 2600    O        OR           OF
 2700    O                                6 'PJ004A'
 2800    O                         UDATE Y  50
 2900    O                                30 'OPEN ACCOUNTS PAYABLE'
 3000    O        H  2        1P
 3100    O        OR           OF
 3200    O                                5 'VEND#'
 3300    O                                15 'INV# '
 3400    O                                24 'INV DATE'
 3500    O                                40 'QUANTITY'
 3600    O                                50 'TOTAL INVOICE'
 3700    O        D  1        01
 3800    O                         VENDOR   6
 3900    O                         INV#    15
 4000    O                         INVDATY 24
```

```
SEQUENCE       1         2         3         4         5         6         7
NUMBER    67890123456789012345678901234567890123456789012345678901234
   4100  O                       INPRC K   33
   4200  O                       INQTY Z   38
   4300  O                       TOTAMTK   48
   4400  O       T 1     LR
   4500  O                                 15 'TOTAL AMOUNT DUE'
   4600  O                       FINAMTK   48
* * * * * E N D   O F   S O U R C E * * * *
```

* 7086   900   RPG PROVIDES BLOCK/UNBLOCK SUPPORT FOR FILE APOPEN.
* 8003   4500   FIELD LENGTH 0016 GREATER THAN RECORD LENGTH 0015

CROSS-REFERENCE LISTING

```
        FILE/RCD    DEV/RCD    REFERENCES (D=DEFINED)
   01   APOPEN      DISK       900D  1200
   02   REPORT      PRINTER    1000D 2500  3000  3700  4400


        FIELD       ATTR       REFERENCES (M=MODIFIED D=DEFINED)
        CNT         P(4,0)     1900  1900D
        DISCNT      P(7,2)     2100D 2200
        FINAMT      P(9,2)     2400  2400D 4600
* 7031  INCODE      A(1)       1800D
        INPRC       P(7,2)     1700D 2000  4100
        INQTY       P(5,0)     1600D 2000  4200
        INV#        A(6)       1400D 3900
        INVDAT      P(6,0)     1500D 4000
        PAYPRC      P(7,2)     2200D 2300
        TOTAMT      P(7,2)     2300  2300D 2400  4300
        TPRC        P(7,2)     2000D 2100  2200
        UDATE       P(6,0)     2800
        VENDOR      P(6,0)     1300D 3800
        .02         LITERAL    2100
        1           LITERAL    1900


        INDICATOR   REFERENCES (M=MODIFIED D=DEFINED)
        LR          900D  4400
* 7030  L1          2400
        OF          1000D 2600  3100
        01          1200M 3700
        1P          2500  3000
```

MESSAGES

```
  MSGID    SEV  NUMBER  TEXT
* QRG1019  00   1       IGNDECERR(*YES) SPECIFIED ON COMMAND. NO DECIMAL DATA ERRORS
* QRG7030  30   1       FIELD OR INDICATOR NOT DEFINED.
* QRG7031  00   1       NAME OR INDICATOR NOT REFERENCED.
* QRG7086  00   1       RPG WILL HANDLE BLOCKING FUNCTION FOR THE FILE. INFDS CONTEN
                        ARE TRANSFERRED.
* QRG8003  30   1       END POSITION (POSITIONS 40-43) NOT LARGE ENOUGH. SPECIFICATI
```

MESSAGE SUMMARY

TOTAL	00	10	20	30	40	50
5	3	0	0	2	0	0

46 RECORDS READ FROM SOURCE FILE
SOURCE RECORDS INCLUDE   37 SPECIFICATIONS,   0 TABLE RECORDS, AND   9 COMMENTS

QRG0008 COMPILE TERMINATED. SEVERITY 30 ERRORS FOUND IN PROGRAM

* * * * * E N D O F C O M P I L A T I O N * * * * *
* QRG1020   ERROR OCCURRED CREATING OR UPDATING DATA AREA RETURNCODE. COMPII

```
  100  F* TITLE: DEBUG PROJECT 4-B
  200  F* DATE:  3/7            AUTHOR: D.CABLE
  300  F* DESCRIPTION:  PRINT TOTAL SALES PER CUSTOMER
  400  F*********************************************************************
  500  F* MODIFICATIONS:
  600  F* NO.    DATE      INIT      DESCRIPTION
  700  F*       XX/XX/XX   XXX       XXXXXXXXXXXXXXXXXXXXXXXXXXXXXXXX
  800  F*********************************************************************

NAME OF PROGRAM WILL BE PJ004B IN LIBRARY CABLE

             H
* 1019              ALL DECIMAL DATA ERRORS IGNORED
  900  FSALESIN IP  F      512              DISK
 1000  FREPORT   O  F      132         OF   PRINTER
 1100  F*********************************************************************


 1200  ISALESIN AA  01
 1300  I                                          1   50CUST   L1
 1400  I                                          6   11 INVOIC
 1500  I                                         12   170INDATE
 1600  I                                         18   242AMOUNT
 1700  I                                         25   282DISC


 1800  C            AMOUNT    SUB  DISC      TAMT     72
 1900  C            TAMT      ADD  L1AMT     L1AMT    72
 2000  CL1          L1AMT     ADD  L1AMT     L1AMT    72


 2100  OREPORT  H  203        1P
 2200  O        OR            OF
 2300  O                                       6 'PJ004B'
 2400  O                            UDATE Y   50
 2500  O                                      30 'CUSTOMER SALES TOTALS'
 2600  O        H    2        1P
 2700  O        OR            OF
 2800  O                                       5 'CUST#'
 2900  O                                      15 'INVOICES'
 3000  O                                      23 'INV DATE'
 3100  O                                      33 'AMOUNT'
 3200  O                                      42 'DISC'
 3300  O                                      52 'TOTAL AMOUNT'
 3400  O        D    1        01
 3500  O                            CUST#      5
 3600  O                            INVOIC    12
 3700  O                            INDATEY   24
 3800  O                            AMOUNTZ   33
 3900  O                            DISC  K   42
 4000  O                            TAMT  K   51
```

RPG: A Programming Language for Today

```
SEQUENCE       1         2         3         4         5         6         7
NUMBER    67890123456789012345678901234567890123456789012345678901234567890123 4

  4100  O        T  1           LR
  4200  O                                             15 'TOTAL VALUE'
  4300  O                             L1AMT K    51
* * * * * E N D   O F   S O U R C E * * * * *


* 7086        900   RPG PROVIDES BLOCK/UNBLOCK SUPPORT FOR FILE SALESIN.



    CROSS-REFERENCE LISTING



           FILE/RCD     DEV/RCD      REFERENCES (D=DEFINED)
      02   REPORT       PRINTER      1000D 2100   2600    3400   4100
      01   SALESIN      DISK          900D 1200


           FIELD        ATTR         REFERENCES (M=MODIFIED D=DEFINED)
           AMOUNT       P(7,2)       1600D 1800   3800
* 7031     CUST         P(5,0)       1300D
* 7030     CUST#        A(4)         3500
           DISC         P(4,2)       1700D 1800   3900
           INDATE       P(6,0)       1500D 3700
           INVOIC       A(6)         1400D 3600
           L1AMT        P(7,2)       1900  1900D  2000    2000   2000D  4300
           TAMT         P(7,2)       1800D 1900   4000
           UDATE        P(6,0)       2400


           INDICATOR    REFERENCES (M=MODIFIED D=DEFINED)
           LR            900D 4100
           L1           1300M 2000
           OF           1000D 2200   2700
           01           1200M 3400
           1P           2100  2600


  MESSAGES

  MSGID       SEV   NUMBER    TEXT
* QRG1019     00      1       IGNDECERR(*YES) SPECIFIED ON COMMAND. NO DECIMAL DATA ERRORS
* QRG7030     30      1       FIELD OR INDICATOR NOT DEFINED.
* QRG7031     00      1       NAME OR INDICATOR NOT REFERENCED.
* QRG7086     00      1       RPG WILL HANDLE BLOCKING FUNCTION FOR THE FILE. INFDS CONTEN
                              ARE TRANSFERRED.


  MESSAGE SUMMARY

  TOTAL     00    10    20    30    40    50
    4        3     0     0     1     0     0

     43 RECORDS READ FROM SOURCE FILE
     SOURCE RECORDS INCLUDE   34 SPECIFICATIONS,    0 TABLE RECORDS, AND    9 COMMENTS

  QRG0008 COMPILE TERMINATED. SEVERITY 30 ERRORS FOUND IN PROGRAM
     * * * * * E N D   O F   C O M P I L A T I O N * * * * *
   * QRG1020             ERROR OCCURRED CREATING OR UPDATING DATA AREA RETURNCODE. COMPI
```

Chapter 4 Control Breaks (The RPG Cycle)

PROGRAMMING PROJECT

Project Overview

A report is to be printed listing the open accounts payable (bills to be paid). Each invoice record will be printed. A total amount owed will be printed for each vendor. Write the RPG program to produce this listing. Sample data for this project can be found in Appendix D.

Input Format

The input data for the project is found in a file called APOPEN in the sample data. The Record Layout for this file is shown in Figure 4.19.

Processing

The net amount due is computed by subtracting the discount amount from the amount of the invoice.

Output Format (Printer Spacing Chart)

The output format for the project is a report with standard headings. The report will show the vendor number, vendor name, invoice number, due date, quantity, and dollar amount due. A total dollar amount is printed for each vendor. A final total of the entire amount due is printed at the end of the report. This is a detail printed report. The Printer Spacing Chart for this report is shown in Figure 4.20.

An example of the finished report is shown in Figure 4.21.

FIGURE 4.19 Programming Project: Record Layout

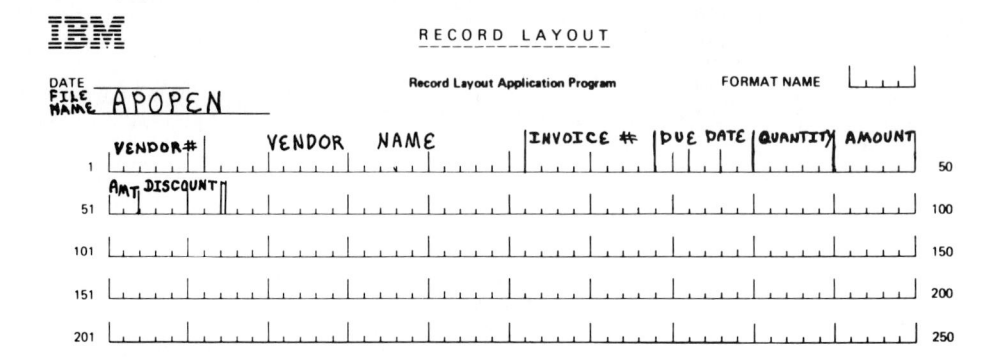

FIGURE 4.20 Programming Project: Printer Spacing Chart

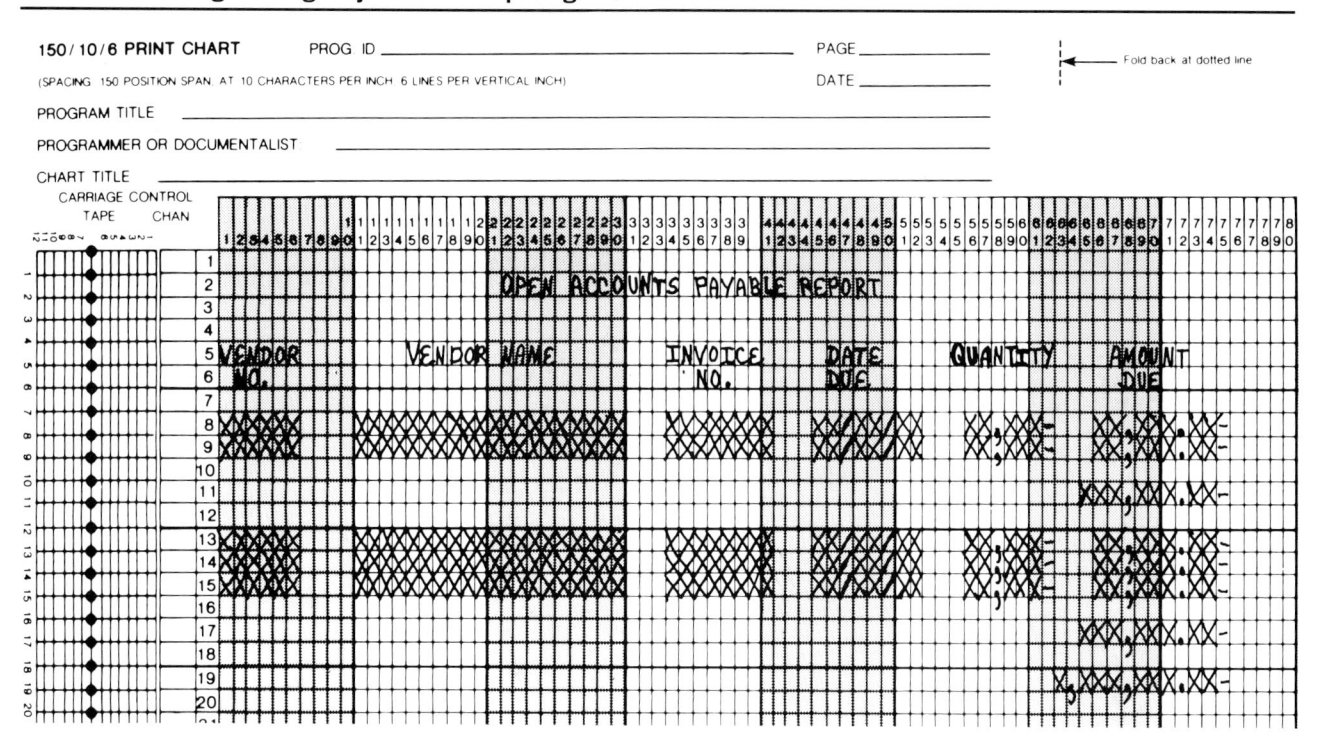

FIGURE 4.21 Programming Project: Final Report

```
                    OPEN ACCOUNTS PAYABLE REPORT

        VENDOR      VENDOR NAME        INVOICE     DATE      QUANTITY    AMOUNT
                                       NO.         DUE                   DUE

        059         VERONICA SUPPLIES  12345000    3/21/92        1      5,000.00
        059         VERONICA SUPPLIES  89700000    3/28/92       50        475.00
                                                                         5,475.00

        159         OLIVE DISTRIBUTORS 65650000    3/19/92      500        713.00
        159         OLIVE DISTRIBUTORS 88800000    2/28/92      500      6,500.00
                                                                         7,213.00

        8520        LOTUS SUPPLIES     64970000    3/15/92       65      7,644.75
                                                                         7,644.75


                                                                        20,332.75
```

Chapter 5

Multiple Level Breaks

What you will learn in Chapter 5

Sample Program Using Multiple
  Level Breaks
  Input Specifications
  Calculation Specifications
  Output Specifications
The RPG Cycle Revisited
  Group Indication

Zeroing Out a Total Field
Standards for Report Formatting
  Report Headings
  Report Totals
Sample Program Defining Report
  Headings
  Report Identification

Report Title
Page Number
System Date and Edit Codes
System Time and Edit Words
Summary of Report Formatting

Previous chapters have covered arithmetic calculations and level breaks. In the real world of business, many levels of control may be required; reports having six or seven levels or even more are not uncommon. Figure 5.1 shows a typical business report with three level break totals and a final total.

SAMPLE PROGRAM USING MULTIPLE LEVEL BREAKS ■

This report can be produced by using multiple level breaks to provide sales totals for each customer, for each sales representative, and for each region. Management is always interested in the total amount of sales made in a particular region and in the share of the total achieved by each sales representative. Management also wants to know which customers are buying the largest amount of the product. Instead of printing three separate reports to show these three pieces of information, it is often better to consolidate the three totals into one report. Using the data file described in Figure 5.2, a program can be written to produce this useful report. Assuming that the input data is already in the correct sequence, the coding for this project can be started.

Input Specifications

Chapter 4 described how to create a single level break by entering the indicator L1 in columns 59–60 on the Input Specifications form following the field on which the level break should occur. In RPG, it is possible to specify as many as nine level breaks. This means that a report may have as many as nine level breaks as well as the last record (LR) indicator.

FIGURE 5.1 Sales Report

```
                         SALES REPORT
   REGION    SALES  CUSTOMER    PART#        DATE     AMOUNT
              REP#                                    SOLD
     020      035    280000     012345      3/28/9     40.82
                                                       40.82 *

     020      035    180000     009438      3/21/9     46.74
                                                       46.74 *

                                                       87.56 **

     020      050    490000     007183      3/21/9     38.44
     020      050    490000     004152      3/21/9     54.14
                                                       92.58 *

     020      050    268000     004259      3/21/9     36.44
                                                       36.44 *

                                                      129.02 **

                                                      216.58 ***

     030      001    160000     005857      3/21/9     29.38
                                                       29.38 *

     030      001    248000     005444      3/21/9     80.70
     030      001    248000     008784      3/21/9     76.26
                                                      156.96 *

                                                      186.34 **

     030      050    180000     003178      3/21/9     40.61
                                                       40.61 *

                                                       40.61 **

                                                      226.95 ***

                                                      443.53 ****
```

To create a report having multiple level totals, it is a simple matter to define more levels on the Input Specifications. Producing the report described in Figure 5.1 requires levels L1, L2, and L3 and of course a final total for the entire report as well. The sequence in which L1, L2, and L3 are entered depends on the sequence in which the totals will be desired. For this example we will print all the sales detail first for every customer and then for every salesperson, and then show the total for the entire region to which that salesperson is assigned.

Sales region will be the most important total and should be assigned L3. The intermediate total, salespeople, should be assigned L2. The customer field will be least important and should be assigned L1, the lowest level break. Figure 5.3 shows the coding for three level breaks. These are referred to as *major*, *intermediate*, and *minor* level breaks.

FIGURE 5.2 Record Layout

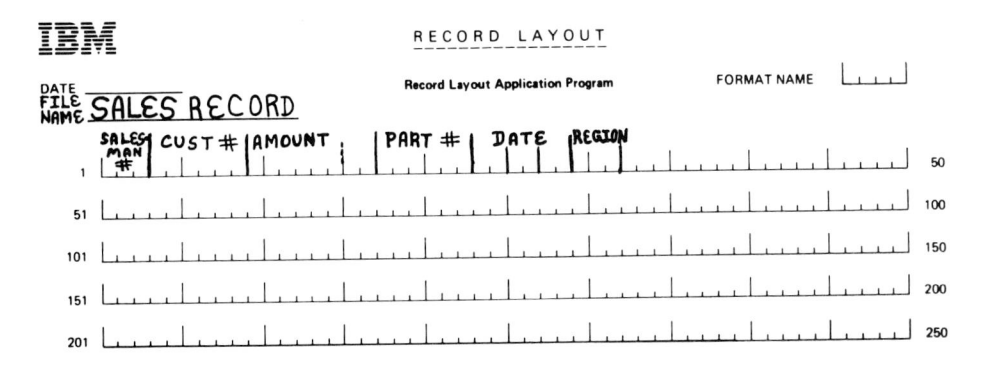

IBM

RECORD LAYOUT

Record Layout Application Program

DATE
FILE NAME: SALES RECORD

FORMAT NAME

Fields: SALES MAN #, CUST #, AMOUNT, PART #, DATE, REGION

Chapter 5 Multiple Level Breaks

FIGURE 5.3 Input Specifications for Three Level Breaks

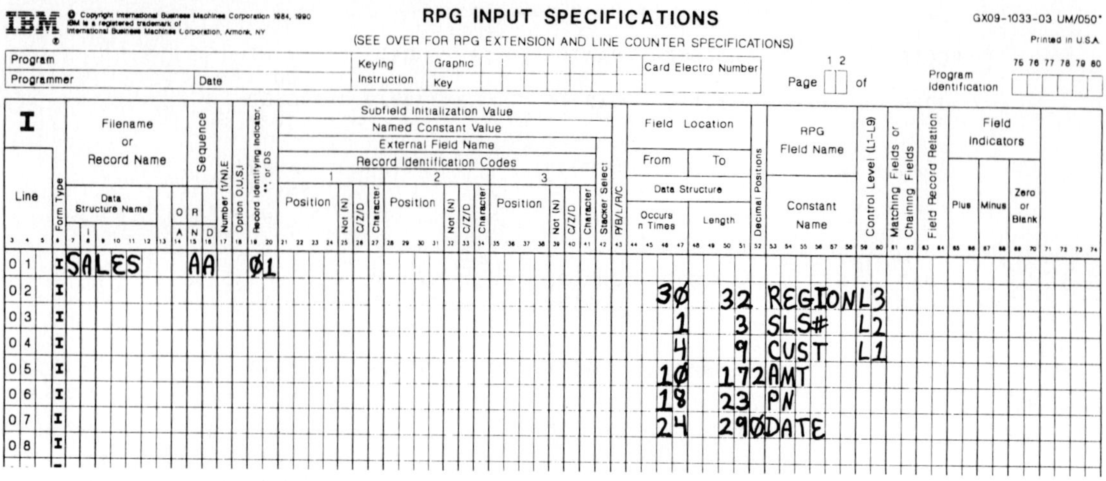

RPG INPUT SPECIFICATIONS

Line	Form Type	Filename or Record Name	Sequence	Record Identifying Indicator	From	To	Decimal Positions	RPG Field Name	Control Level (L1–L9)
01	I	SALES	AA	Ø1					
02	I				3Ø	32		REGION	L3
03	I				1	3		SLS#	L2
04	I				4	9		CUST	L1
05	I				1Ø	17	2	AMT	
06	I				18	23		PN	
07	I				24	29	Ø	DATE	
08	I								

Figure 5.4 shows another method for coding the Input Specifications. This shows the same fields with level breaks, but they are in a different sequence on the coding sheet. RPG will treat either version of the program exactly the same. The sequence of the lines on the Input Specifications has no effect on the manner in which the level breaks will be taken. The level break sequence is controlled entirely by the level indicators.

Calculation Specifications

It will be necessary to develop cumulative totals for each of the level totals: customer, salesperson, region, and final total. This is done for each total as was done in previous chapters, developing each total individually. See the calculation example in Figure 5.5.

Methods for Developing Cumulative Totals (Level Breaks)

There are two methods for calculating multiple cumulative totals in an RPG program. Each of the two methods for accumulating totals is valid and each has certain advantages and disadvantages.

The first and probably simplest method for accumulating totals is to code each total field separately, defining a separate total for each level type. That is, a line would be coded for developing the customer totals, another line for developing the salesperson totals, and a third line for the region totals. Each of these totals is computed at detail time. Each is independent of all the other totals. Figure 5.6 shows this coding.

FIGURE 5.4 Another Method for Coding Three Level Breaks

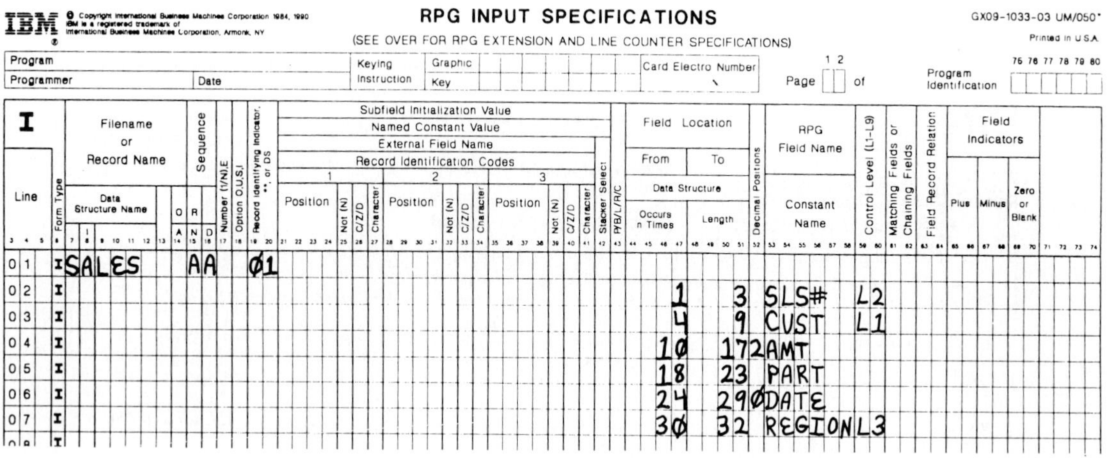

RPG INPUT SPECIFICATIONS

Line	Form Type	Filename or Record Name	Sequence	Record Identifying Indicator	From	To	Decimal Positions	RPG Field Name	Control Level (L1–L9)
01	I	SALES	AA	Ø1					
02	I				1	3		SLS#	L2
03	I				4	9		CUST	L1
04	I				1Ø	17	2	AMT	
05	I				18	23		PART	
06	I				24	29	Ø	DATE	
07	I				3Ø	32		REGION	L3
08	I								

FIGURE 5.5 Calculation Specification for Accumulating Level 1 Total

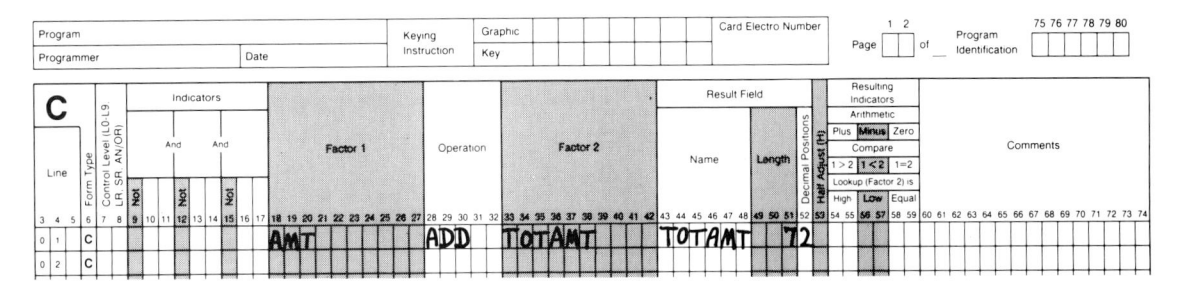

RPG CALCULATION SPECIFICATIONS

```
01 C        AMT      ADD  TOTAMT    TOTAMT   72
02 C
```

The second method for developing multiple level totals uses the first-level total to create the second-level total, uses the second to create the third, and so on. This is not as difficult as it sounds. The level 1 total is computed at detail time, exactly as it was in the first method.

The level 2 total is computed at L1 *total* time. The L1 indicator is entered in columns 7–8 to control the time at which this calculation will occur. With the L1 indicator in columns 7–8, this calculation can only occur at *total* time for level 1. Each time the level 1 total is completed, that total can be added to the next total for the salesperson. Instead of adding each detail line to the salesperson total, only the total for that customer will be added. Thus, the result field from the first-level calculation will be used as factor 1 to be added to the total for the next level.

The level 3 total is developed in the same manner, by entering L2 in columns 7–8 to cause that calculation to be done only when the level 2 total calculations have been completed for each salesperson. This method is called *rolling totals* from one level into the next. Figure 5.7 shows how this would be coded.

Level Total Method Summary

The first method (the independent method) for computing totals is certainly simpler and more straightforward than the second method. Since each total level is completely independent of every other total level, it might be simpler to make changes to the program at some future time if someone wanted to change the report. In some ways this method might be easier to read and analyze.

The disadvantage of the first method is that it involves more work for the computer. This might not be important for a small program which was being run only occasionally. However, if a very large program involving thousands of computations on many fields were being run constantly during the day by many users, the programmer might want to try to improve its efficiency by using method 2. Method 2 (the dependent method) would be much more efficient for the computer since it would be calculating the level break totals *only* at a level break time. The amount of time saved might never be visible to the user, but a programmer should be aware of different methods of coding to achieve a variety of goals.

FIGURE 5.6 Independent Totals

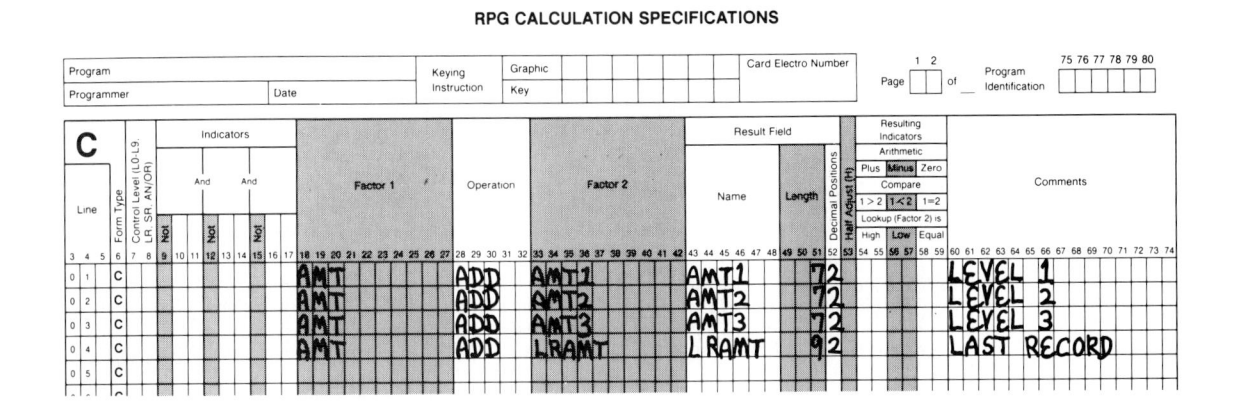

RPG CALCULATION SPECIFICATIONS

```
01 C        AMT      ADD  AMT1      AMT1     72          LEVEL 1
02 C        AMT      ADD  AMT2      AMT2     72          LEVEL 2
03 C        AMT      ADD  AMT3      AMT3     72          LEVEL 3
04 C        AMT      ADD  LRAMT     LRAMT    92          LAST RECORD
05 C
```

Chapter 5 *Multiple Level Breaks*   **101**

FIGURE 5.7 Dependent (Rolling) Totals

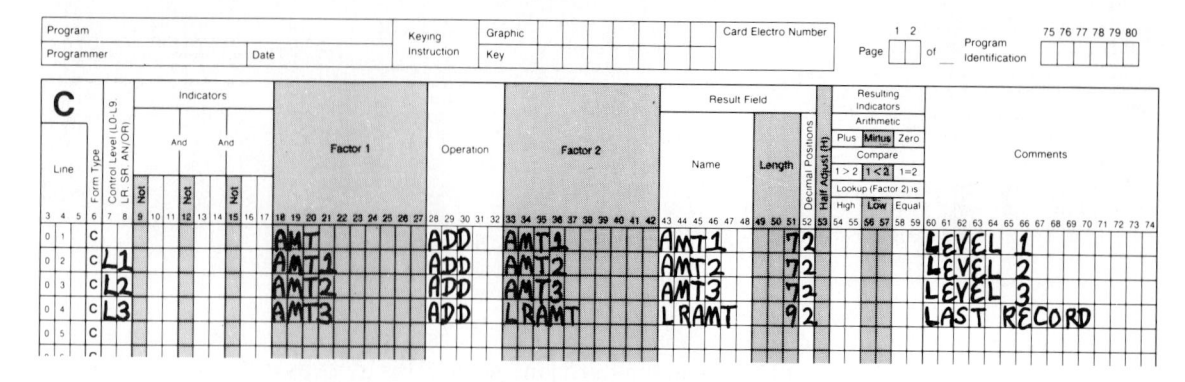

Line	Form Type	Control Level	Indicators (And/And)	Factor 1	Operation	Factor 2	Result Field Name	Length	Dec	Comments
01	C			AMT	ADD	AMT1	AMT1	7	2	LEVEL 1
02	C	L1		AMT1	ADD	AMT2	AMT2	7	2	LEVEL 2
03	C	L2		AMT2	ADD	AMT3	AMT3	7	2	LEVEL 3
04	C	L3		AMT3	ADD	LRAMT	LRAMT	9	2	LAST RECORD
05	C									

The real advantage of the dependent method is that the final total proves the validity of all the intermediate totals because each total is completely dependent on the previous total. If the final total is correct, then it proves that all the other intermediate totals must also be correct. This can be very reassuring from an audit standpoint.

Which method should you use? By all means try to learn and understand both methods. Programmers often inherit old programs that need repairs or changes. Both methods will show up in old programs. The choice of method to adopt as a personal standard may be guided by personal preference or the standards of the organization. Since programming is the most costly item in the data processing budget, the most important factor is no longer the efficiency of a program in the computer. The important factors are program reliability, timeliness, and the ease of program coding and maintenance. For this reason, it is important that the program be coded correctly and quickly.

FIGURE 5.8 Output Specifications for Detail Report

Line	Form Type	Filename or Record Name	Type	Space Before/After	Skip Before/After	Output Indicators (And/And)	Field Name or EXCPT Name	Edit Codes	End Position in Output Record	Constant or Edit Word
01	O	REPORT	H	201		1P				"SALES REPORT"
02	O	OR				OF				
03	O									
04	O		H	2		1P				
05	O	OR				OF				
06	O								6	"REGION"
07	O								15	"SALES"
08	O								24	"CUSTOMER"
09	O								31	"PART#"
10	O								37	"DATE"
11	O								45	"AMOUNT"
12	O		D	1		01				
13	O						REGION		5	
14	O						SLS#		12	
15	O						CUST		23	
16	O						PART		32	
17	O						DATE	Y	38	
18	O						AMT	M	46	

102 RPG: A Programming Language for Today

FIGURE 5.9 Output Specifications for Total Lines

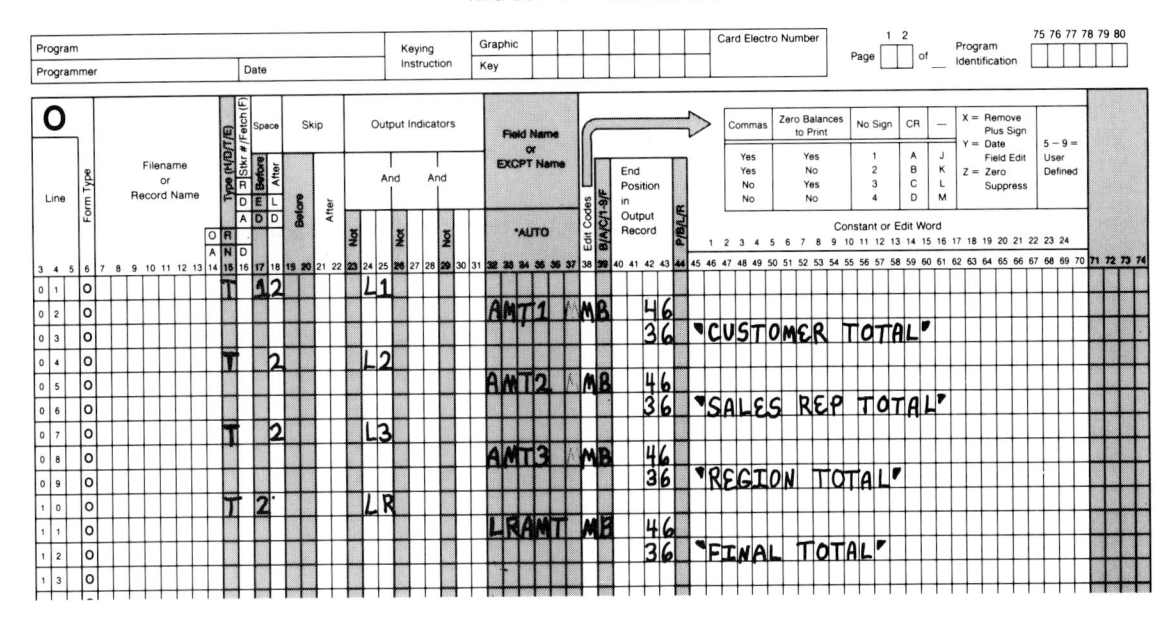

[RPG Output Specifications form showing total lines coded as:
- Line 01: T, 12, L1
- Line 02: AMT1, M B, 46
- Line 03: 36, "CUSTOMER TOTAL"
- Line 04: T, 2, L2
- Line 05: AMT2, M B, 46
- Line 06: 36, "SALES REP TOTAL"
- Line 07: T, 2, L3
- Line 08: AMT3, M B, 46
- Line 09: 36, "REGION TOTAL"
- Line 10: T, 2, LR
- Line 11: LRAMT, M B, 46
- Line 12: 36, "FINAL TOTAL"]

Output Specifications

The coding for the Output Specifications for the sample program showing multiple level breaks contains no big surprises. It is similar to the program coding in earlier chapters. In the example in Figure 5.8, the headings and detail lines are coded as in previous examples.

Notice that edit code Y has been used with the date field to cause a slash (/) to print. This edits the date, automatically inserting the slashes between month, day, and year. Edit code M has been used to edit the amount. This puts the decimal point between the dollars and cents and inserts commas as needed.

Figure 5.9 shows how the Output Specifications are coded to cause the total lines to print. The total lines are coded as *T* lines and the indicator is entered for each level as needed: L1 for level 1 totals, L2 for level 2 totals, and so on. Level 1 totals must precede level 2 totals on the Output Specifications form because the level 1 totals should appear on the output report before the level 2 totals.

RPG will always take care of all preceding-level totals automatically. When LR is turned on after all records have been read, it will automatically set on L1, L2, L3, etc. The programmer does not need to take any special action to cause this to happen. A higher-level indicator will *always* set on all the level indicators below it automatically so that all the lower-level totals will print first.

THE RPG CYCLE REVISITED ■

Before attempting to understand the function of group indication in RPG, it would be a good idea to review the RPG fixed logic cycle chart once again. See Figure 5.10.

Level break time occurs between the time a record is read into main memory and the time when the fields from that record are moved into an input area in memory. RPG will check at that moment to determine whether the record that was just processed (and perhaps printed) had a different control field from the record just read in. If the control fields differ, RPG will then execute the level *total* commands and print the *total* lines on the report.

FIGURE 5.10 RPG Fixed Logic Cycle

- (A) OPEN FILES & SET ON 1P
- (B) PRINT HEADINGS & SET OFF 1P

LEVEL INDICATORS ARE SET OFF

- (C) READ INPUT RECORD
- (D) LAST RECORD? — YES → SET ON ALL LEVEL INDICATORS & DO TOTAL CALCS & OUTPUTS → DO LR CALCS & OUTPUTS & END JOB

IF LR ON THEN L1-L9 WILL BE SET ON

- (E) LEVEL BREAKS? — YES → FIRST CYCLE? — NO → DO TOTAL CALCS & OUTPUTS; YES ↓

A HIGHER LEVEL WILL SET ON ALL LOWER LEVELS

- (F) MOVE INPUT DATA TO INPUT FIELDS
- (G) DO LEVEL BREAK DETAIL PROCESSING

LEVEL INDICATORS REMAIN ON

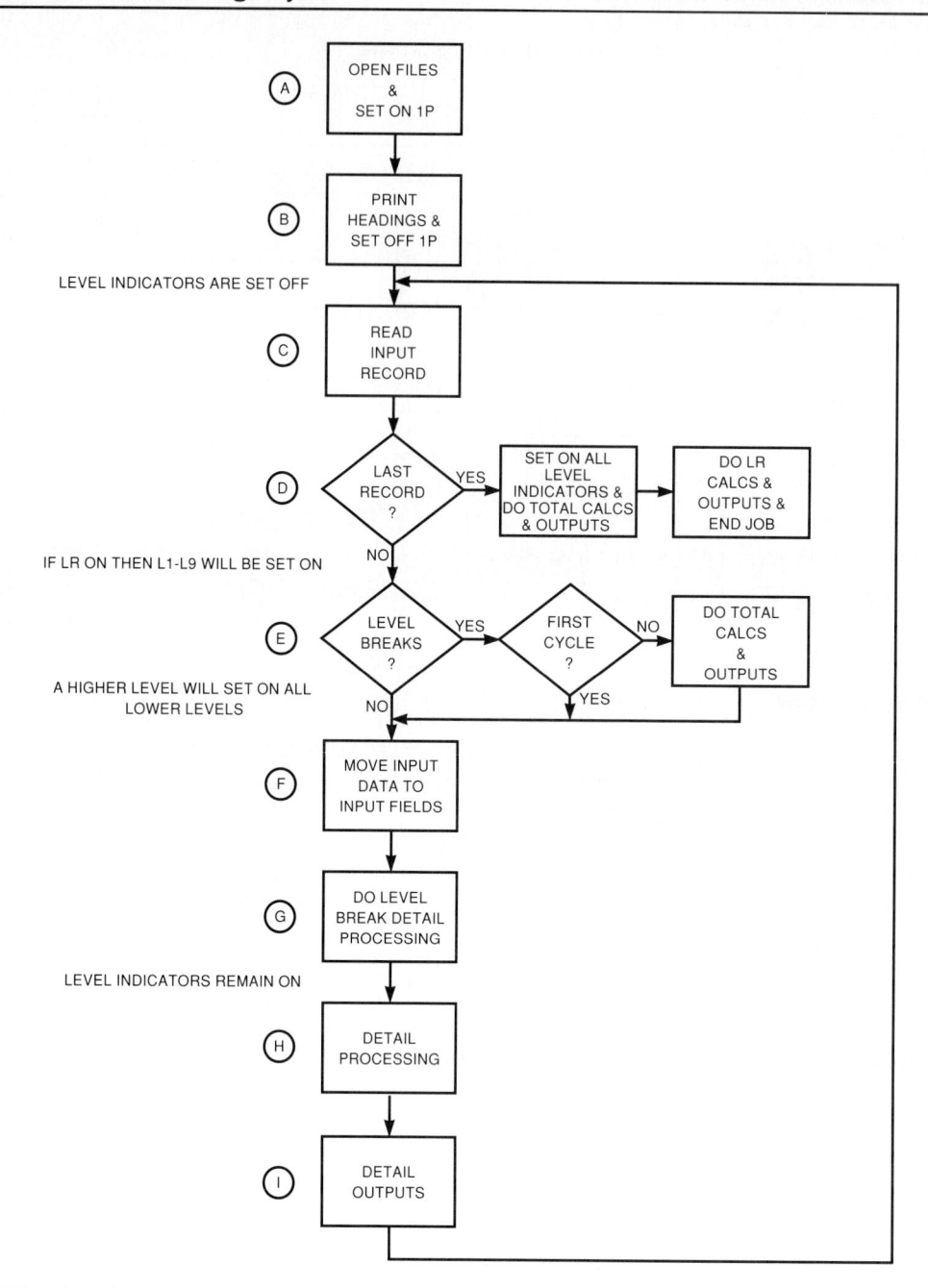

- (H) DETAIL PROCESSING
- (I) DETAIL OUTPUTS

   The detail record that has just been read into memory has not yet been processed. *After* all the necessary totals have been handled, RPG will move to the next step (step F) to move the input data into fields. The level break indicators are *still on!* Figures 5.11(a) and 5.11(b) show the values contained in the fields during each step of the cycle.
   One of the important concepts underlying the RPG language is the timing of events. Once this timing is understood, it is much easier to write an RPG program that will work the first time through (or very soon after that). The concept that detail time occurs *after* total time is difficult to accept, but it allows the programmer to have control over the data in some very useful ways.

Group Indication

   One of the best ways to take advantage of the RPG cycle is to use it for group indication. The clearest way to explain group indication is to display a report that does not use it and then show how that report could be improved using group indication.

FIGURE 5.11(a) Values Contained in the Fields: Sample Data

```
                    SAMPLE DATA
     VENDOR#     VENDOR NAME       AMOUNT
      0123       ACME PLUMBING      250.00
      6528       JONES GROCERS     1200.00
      6528       JONES GROCERS       10.50
```

FIGURE 5.11(b) Field Content During the RPG Cycle

FIELD CONTENT WHEN SECOND RECORD IS READ

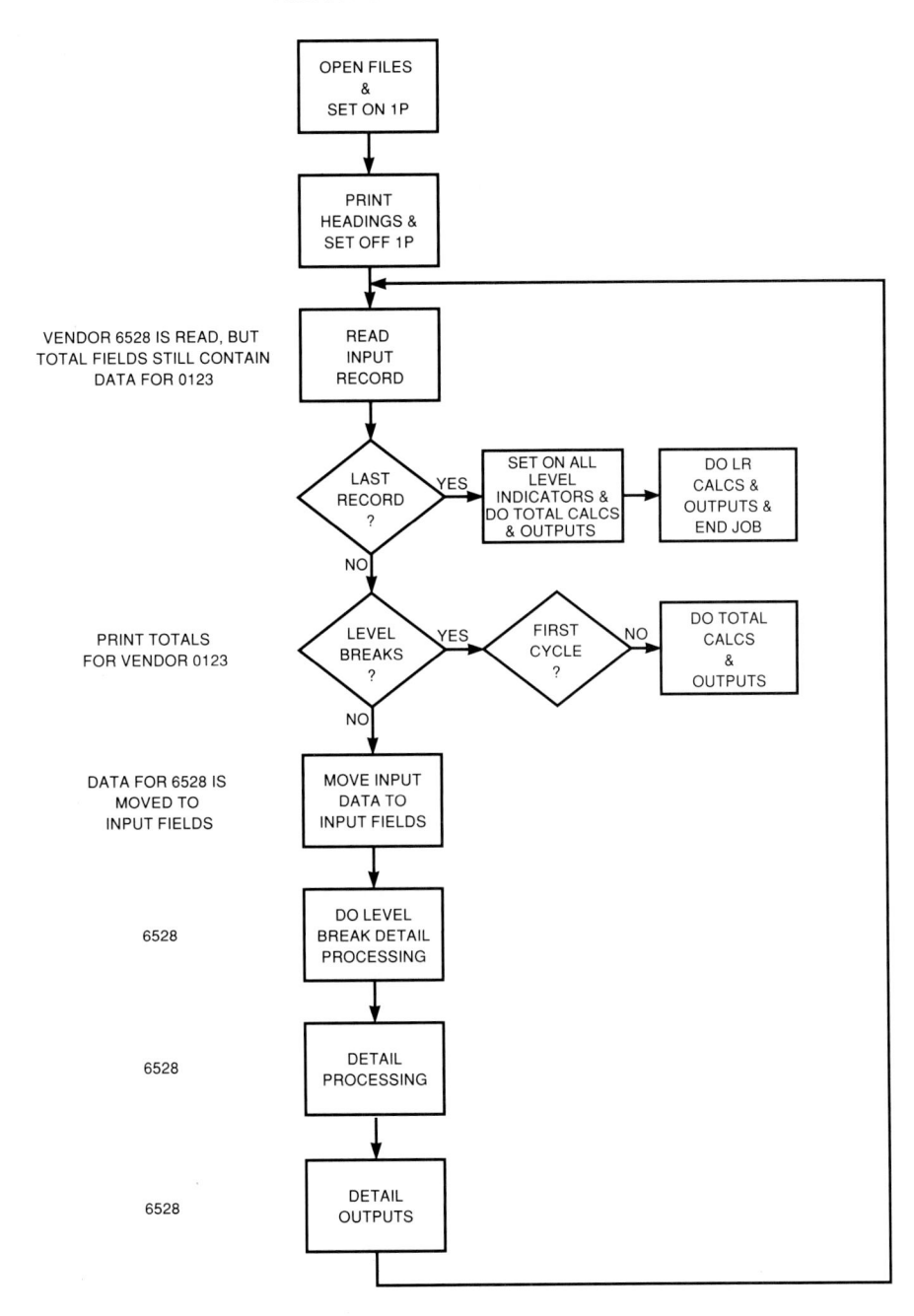

```
                          ┌──────────────┐
                          │ OPEN FILES   │
                          │      &       │
                          │ SET ON 1P    │
                          └──────┬───────┘
                                 ▼
                          ┌──────────────┐
                          │   PRINT      │
                          │ HEADINGS &   │
                          │ SET OFF 1P   │
                          └──────┬───────┘
                                 ▼  ◄──────────────────────────────┐
VENDOR 6528 IS READ, BUT  ┌──────────────┐                         │
TOTAL FIELDS STILL CONTAIN│    READ      │                         │
    DATA FOR 0123         │   INPUT      │                         │
                          │   RECORD     │                         │
                          └──────┬───────┘                         │
                                 ▼                                 │
                              ╱     ╲        ┌───────────┐  ┌───────────┐
                             ╱ LAST  ╲  YES  │ SET ON ALL│  │  DO LR    │
                            ╱ RECORD  ╲─────▶│  LEVEL    │─▶│  CALCS &  │
                            ╲    ?    ╱      │INDICATORS&│  │ OUTPUTS & │
                             ╲       ╱       │DO TOTAL CALCS│ END JOB  │
                              ╲ NO  ╱        │ & OUTPUTS │  └───────────┘
                                 ▼                              
PRINT TOTALS                  ╱     ╲         ╱     ╲     ┌───────────┐
FOR VENDOR 0123              ╱ LEVEL ╲  YES  ╱ FIRST ╲ NO │ DO TOTAL  │
                            ╱ BREAKS ╲─────▶╱ CYCLE  ╲──▶│  CALCS    │
                            ╲    ?    ╱     ╲    ?    ╱   │    &      │
                             ╲       ╱       ╲       ╱    │ OUTPUTS   │
                              ╲ NO  ╱                     └───────────┘
                                 ▼
DATA FOR 6528 IS          ┌──────────────┐
MOVED TO                  │ MOVE INPUT   │
INPUT FIELDS              │  DATA TO     │
                          │ INPUT FIELDS │
                          └──────┬───────┘
                                 ▼
     6528                 ┌──────────────┐
                          │  DO LEVEL    │
                          │ BREAK DETAIL │
                          │ PROCESSING   │
                          └──────┬───────┘
                                 ▼
     6528                 ┌──────────────┐
                          │   DETAIL     │
                          │ PROCESSING   │
                          └──────┬───────┘
                                 ▼
     6528                 ┌──────────────┐
                          │   DETAIL     │
                          │   OUTPUTS    │
                          └──────┬───────┘
                                 └─────────────────────────────────┘
```

The reports used as examples thus far have displayed every field of data on every detail line of the report. For example, the report in Figure 5.1 listed every line of detail data repeating the sales region, the salesperson number, and the customer number over and over even though once would have been quite sufficient.

A better-looking report would be one that printed the region, salesperson number, and customer just once, at the beginning of a group, as illustrated in Figure 5.12. Reducing the clutter by using group indication makes the report much easier to read, a particularly important consideration for reports containing more information than the sample.

The coding to achieve this group indication is possible because of the RPG cycle described above. When the level break indicator is set on, it is *total* time for the preceding group of records. Totals are printed and then the next detail record (the one that caused the break) is ready to be processed. Remember that the level indicator(s) are still *on*.

Because the cycle is at *detail* time, the level indicator can be used to condition events to happen at *detail* time. This is why the level indicator can be used at detail time for controlling the printing, as shown in Figure 5.13. By entering the level indicator on the *detail* line for these fields, the fields will print *only* on the first line of a group.

It is possible to use this same logic to control calculations which are needed only at the beginning of a group of records. An example of this is the need to zero out a total field *after* it has been printed but *before* the next detail group starts processing.

FIGURE 5.12 Group Indication Report

```
                              SALES REPORT

     REGION    SALES  CUSTOMER    PART#        DATE     AMOUNT
               REP#                                     SOLD
       020     035     280000    012345       3/28/9     40.82
                                                         40.82 *

                       180000    009438       3/21/9     46.74
                                                         46.74 *

                                                         87.56 **

               050     490000    007183       3/21/9     38.44
                                 004152       3/21/9     54.14
                                                         92.58 *

                       268000    004259       3/21/9     36.44
                                                         36.44 *

                                                        129.02 **

                                                        216.58 ***

       030     001     160000    005857       3/21/9     29.38
                                                         29.38 *

                       248000    005444       3/21/9     80.70
                                 008784       3/21/9     76.26
                                                        156.96 *

                                                        186.34 **

               050     180000    003178       3/21/9     40.61
                                                         40.61 *

                                                         40.61 **

                                                        226.95 ***

                                                        443.53 ****
```

FIGURE 5.13 Output Specifications for Group Indication

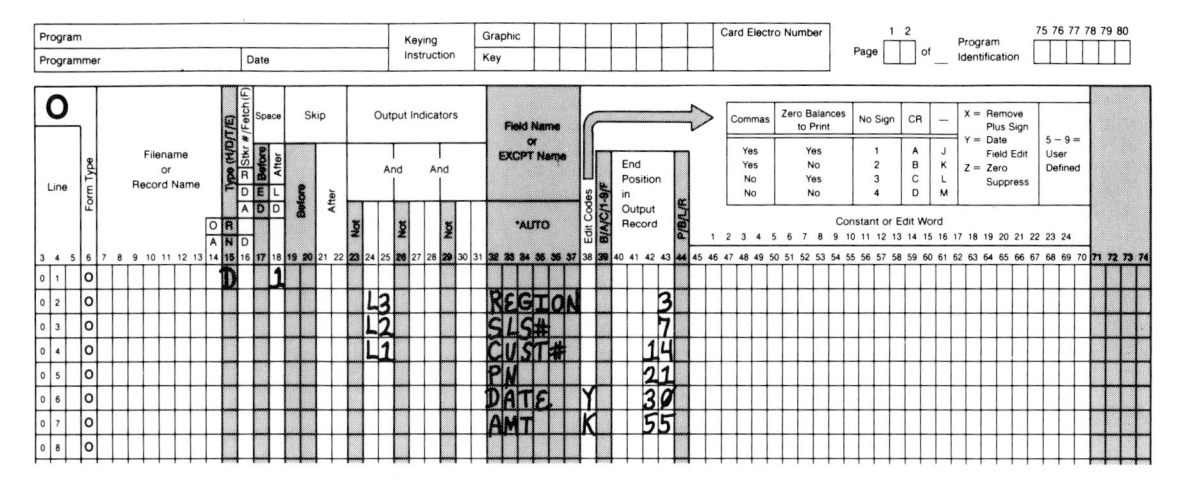

Zeroing Out a Total Field

There are a number of methods that can be used to return a field to zero. All work equally well.

1. Use the Blank After code in column 39 of the Output Specifications form (see Figure 5.14).
2. Using the Calculation Specifications, subtract the number from itself giving zero as the result (see Figure 5.15).
3. Using the Calculation Specifications, multiply the number by zero (see Figure 5.16).
4. Using the Calculation Specifications, use the Z-ADD operation code to zero the field (see Figure 5.17). A Z-ADD operation code will first move zeros into the field and then add to the field whatever value is designated by the programmer. In the example the programmer is adding zero to the field. This will force the field to contain zeros. Notice that factor 1 requires no entry for the Z-ADD operation.
5. Using the Calculation Specifications, use the Z-SUB operation code to zero the field (see Figure 5.18). The Z-SUB works exactly the same as the Z-ADD operation except that a value is subtracted. When using Z-SUB zero, the effect will still be zero.

FIGURE 5.14 Zeroing a Field with a Blank After

Chapter 5 Multiple Level Breaks

FIGURE 5.15 Zeroing a Field by SUB

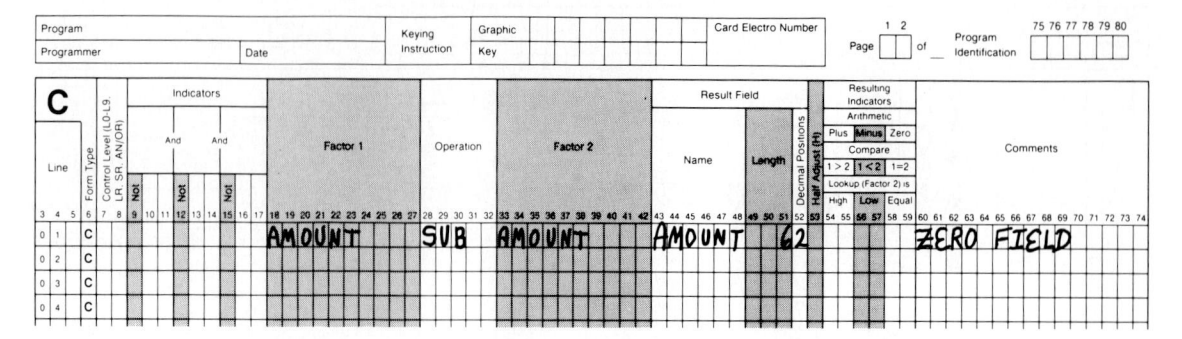

Factor 1: AMOUNT | Operation: SUB | Factor 2: AMOUNT | Result: AMOUNT | Length: 62 | Comments: ZERO FIELD

FIGURE 5.16 Zeroing a Field by a MULT

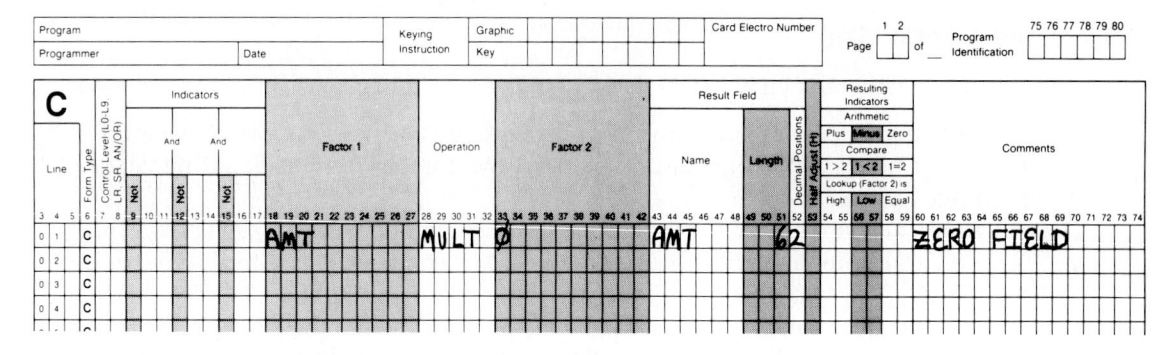

Factor 1: AMT | Operation: MULT | Factor 2: 0 | Result: AMT | Length: 62 | Comments: ZERO FIELD

FIGURE 5.17 Zeroing a Field Using a Z-ADD

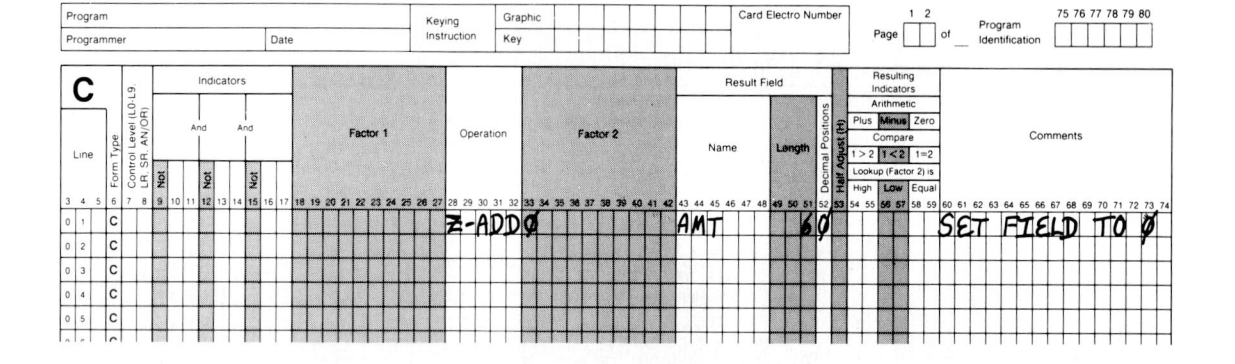

Operation: Z-ADD | Factor 2: 0 | Result: AMT | Length: 60 | Comments: SET FIELD TO 0

FIGURE 5.18 Zeroing a Field Using a Z-SUB

RPG CALCULATION SPECIFICATIONS

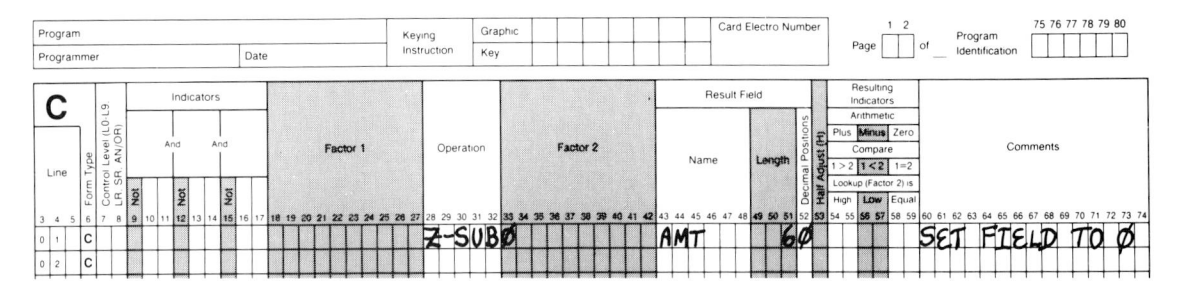

Line	Form Type	Control Level	Indicators	Factor 1	Operation	Factor 2	Result Field Name	Length	Decimal Positions	Resulting Indicators	Comments
0 1	C				Z-SUB 0		AMT	6 0			SET FIELD TO 0
0 2	C										

Of the above methods, the Z-ADD is the most often used because it provides a clear statement of what is being done. Structured programming methods recommend that a program should be easily maintainable by future programmers. The Z-ADD operation provides readability and standardization.

The important thing to recognize is the need to get the totals printed *before* clearing them out and setting them to zero. *After* the totals have been printed, the fields can be set to zero to be ready for the next set of calculations.

With the Blank After method this problem is taken care of by RPG because it is being done in the Output Specifications. But it is not always possible to use this method for clearing out a field. Suppose there is a field that will not be printed on the report—for example, an interim total being used to develop the final totals on the report. Suppose this total needs to be cleared out at total time.

When a field must be cleared out after totals have been completed, it is necessary to clear it out *after* the total has been completely processed and *before* data from the next group of records is started. That moment occurs at *detail* level time (review the RPG cycle chart in Figure 5.10). This is done by putting the coding instructions to clear totals somewhere early in the Calculation Specifications with the level indicator in columns 9–17 (detail time), as shown in Figure 5.19. Figure 5.20 emphasizes when totals should be cleared.

FIGURE 5.19 Clearing a Field Before Detail Calculations

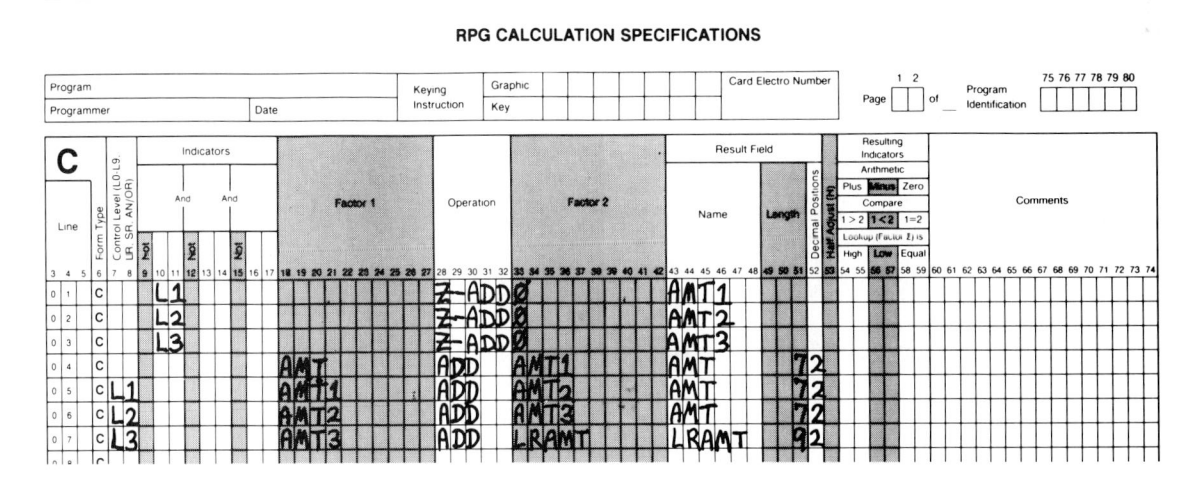

RPG CALCULATION SPECIFICATIONS

Line	Form Type	Control Level	Indicators	Factor 1	Operation	Factor 2	Result Field Name	Length	Decimal Positions	Resulting Indicators	Comments
0 1	C	L1			Z-ADD 0		AMT1				
0 2	C	L2			Z-ADD 0		AMT2				
0 3	C	L3			Z-ADD 0		AMT3				
0 4	C			AMT	ADD	AMT1	AMT	7 2			
0 5	C	L1		AMT1	ADD	AMT2	AMT	7 2			
0 6	C	L2		AMT2	ADD	AMT3	AMT	7 2			
0 7	C	L3		AMT3	ADD	LRAMT	LRAMT	9 2			

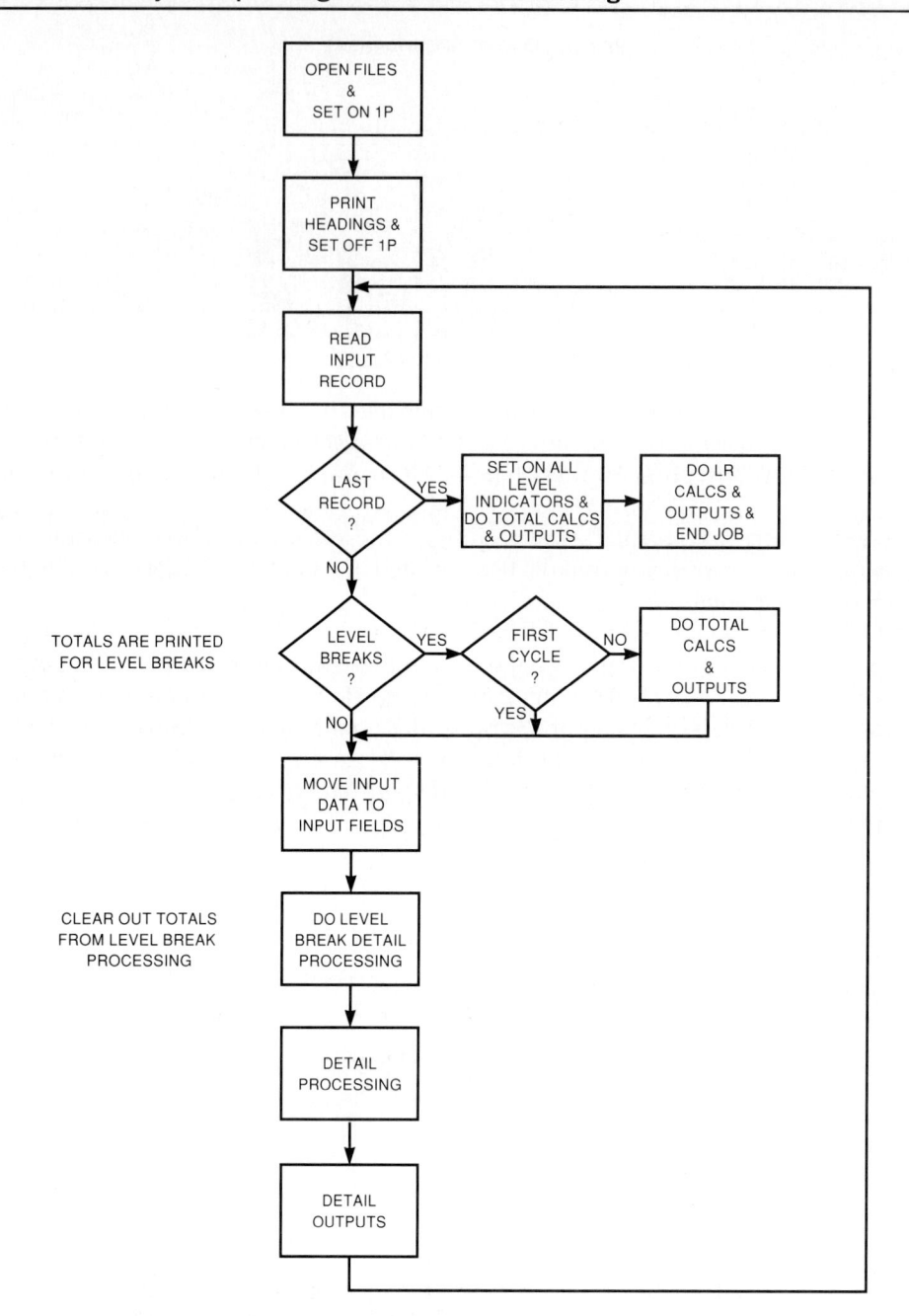

FIGURE 5.20 RPG Cycle Emphasizing When Totals Need Clearing

```
                    ┌──────────────┐
                    │  OPEN FILES  │
                    │      &       │
                    │  SET ON 1P   │
                    └──────┬───────┘
                           ▼
                    ┌──────────────┐
                    │    PRINT     │
                    │  HEADINGS &  │
                    │  SET OFF 1P  │
                    └──────┬───────┘
                           ▼ ◄────────────────────────────────────┐
                    ┌──────────────┐                              │
                    │     READ     │                              │
                    │    INPUT     │                              │
                    │   RECORD     │                              │
                    └──────┬───────┘                              │
                           ▼            ┌─────────────┐   ┌────────────┐
                         ╱    ╲   YES   │ SET ON ALL  │   │   DO LR    │
                        ╱ LAST ╲────────│   LEVEL     │──▶│  CALCS &   │
                        ╲RECORD╱        │ INDICATORS &│   │  OUTPUTS & │
                         ╲  ? ╱         │DO TOTAL CALCS│   │  END JOB   │
                          ╲ ╱           │  & OUTPUTS  │   └────────────┘
                           │NO          └─────────────┘
                           ▼
                         ╱    ╲                    ╱    ╲          ┌────────┐
TOTALS ARE PRINTED      ╱ LEVEL╲   YES            ╱FIRST ╲   NO    │DO TOTAL│
FOR LEVEL BREAKS        ╲BREAKS╱──────────────────╲CYCLE ╱────────▶│ CALCS  │
                         ╲  ? ╱                    ╲  ? ╱          │   &    │
                          ╲ ╱                       ╲ ╱            │OUTPUTS │
                           │NO                       │YES          └────┬───┘
                           ▼                         │                  │
                    ┌──────────────┐                 │                  │
                    │  MOVE INPUT  │◄────────────────┴──────────────────┘
                    │   DATA TO    │
                    │ INPUT FIELDS │
                    └──────┬───────┘
CLEAR OUT TOTALS           ▼
FROM LEVEL BREAK    ┌──────────────┐
PROCESSING          │   DO LEVEL   │
                    │ BREAK DETAIL │
                    │  PROCESSING  │
                    └──────┬───────┘
                           ▼
                    ┌──────────────┐
                    │    DETAIL    │
                    │  PROCESSING  │
                    └──────┬───────┘
                           ▼
                    ┌──────────────┐
                    │    DETAIL    │
                    │   OUTPUTS    │
                    └──────┬───────┘
                           └──────────────────────────────────────┘
```

STANDARDS FOR REPORT FORMATTING ■

There are some new conventions to be learned before continuing further. Before creating this report it will be useful to discuss report headings and report totals.

Report Headings

In earlier chapters report headings have not been a concern, but now it is time to talk about refinements to make a report look more professional.

Nearly all business reports have some form of heading. Some headings are too long and wordy. Some are too brief, giving the user little idea of what the report contains. As a professional,

FIGURE 5.21 Printer Spacing Chart

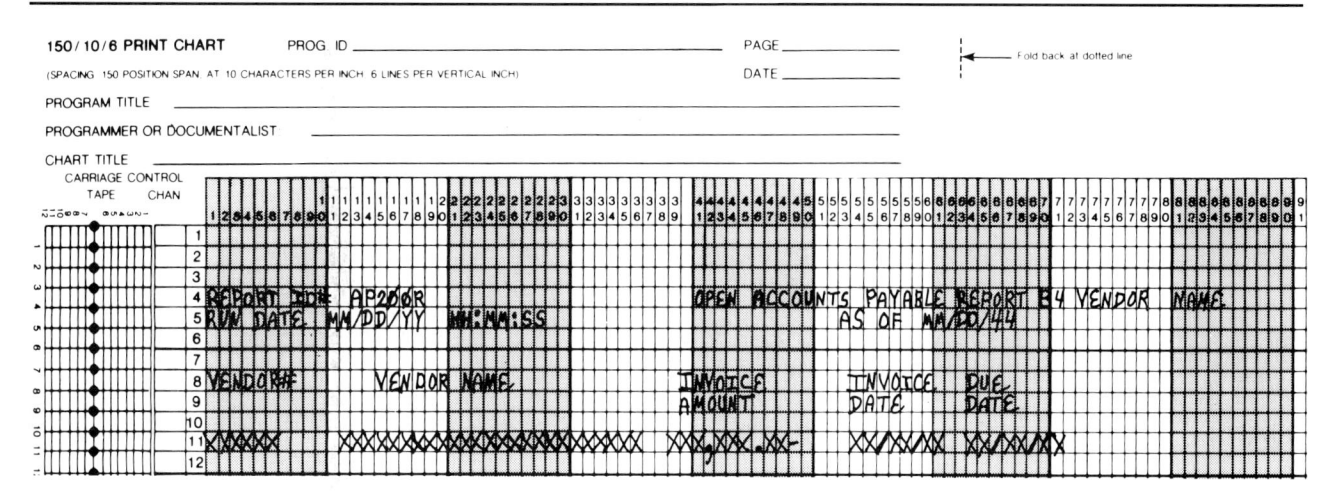

you will want to create headings that indicate clearly what the user will find in the report. Sometimes a systems analyst will have written up the proper wording on the Printer Spacing Chart, as shown in Figure 5.21.

However, the luxury of an in-house systems analyst may not always be available and the heading format may often be left up to the programmer. Several questions come to mind:

1. What information should a heading contain?
2. How is this information identified in RPG?
3. What, if any, standards exist?

The following information should be included in a report heading:

1. *Every* report should have a report identification name. This name is always the same as the program name. This name will normally be printed in the upper left corner of every page of the report. This identification name is of critical importance to computer users, operators, data control personnel, programmers, and analysts. This name identifies each report and is used by operators or data control people to check or balance the report or to distribute the report to the appropriate user. The identification name makes it easier for users to request additional copies or to request modifications to the program. Last, but not least, the report identification name assists the programmer or analyst in finding which program to fix or modify if a user needs something corrected or changed.
2. *Every* report should have a title centered on the top line of every page. The title should be meaningful. A title such as "Employee List" does not give the user a clear idea of what the report contains. A better choice would be "Active Employees by Department," "Active Employees by Hire Date," or "Retired Employees by Date of Termination."
3. *Every* report should have page numbers. Page numbers are usually shown in the upper right corner of the report.
4. *Every* report should have two dates: the date the report was run on the computer *and* the date represented by the data. Both dates are usually shown in the format month/day/year (although the format day/month/year is favored in many countries outside the United States). The RUN date and the AS OF date are not necessarily the same. The report could cover the month of December (AS OF December 31) but it might be run on January 5. It is poor programming to show only the run date and let the user guess what period is covered by the data. It is equally bad form to omit the run date. Both dates are important.

5. *Every* report should also show the time the report was run. This information can prove valuable when trying to trace some error in processing or in determining which is the correct version of a report that was run more than once on the same day.
6. *Every* report should have a heading for each column shown in the body of the report. These headings should be brief but they should *clearly* define what is contained in each column. For example, the column heading "DATE" does not give the user enough information. Instead, use two heading lines and say something like:

>   ORDER   DUE   SHIP
>   DATE   DATE   DATE

Much more could be said about heading formats. The above guidelines are generally accepted throughout the industry as standard practice, but much is up to the preferences of the user, the programming manager, or the individual programmer.

Report Totals

Even when the user does not specify the need for a final total, it is a good idea to provide a total at the end of every report. This gives operators and data control personnel a means of determining whether a report is complete and correct. It ensures that two versions of the same report are (or are not) the same. Auditors usually expect some kind of control total on reports. If the report being produced contains no useful control totals, a record count or hash total can be shown. When nothing of this nature exists on the report, it is useful to at least print the words "END OF REPORT" on the last page.

SAMPLE PROGRAM DEFINING REPORT HEADINGS ■

Report Identification

Figure 5.22 shows the coding for the Output Specifications to print headings for this report. So that a program identification name will be printed in the upper left-hand corner of every page of the report, the name of this sample program, PAY001, is entered as constant information in columns 45–52 within quotation marks. It is also necessary to define the ending position for the program name. To print the program name ending in column 6, a 6 is entered in columns 40–43.

Report Title

The report title is usually centered at the top of each page of the report. This is done by specifying the ending position in columns 40–43 and defining the constant information in columns 45–70 within quotation marks.

FIGURE 5.22 Program Name and Title

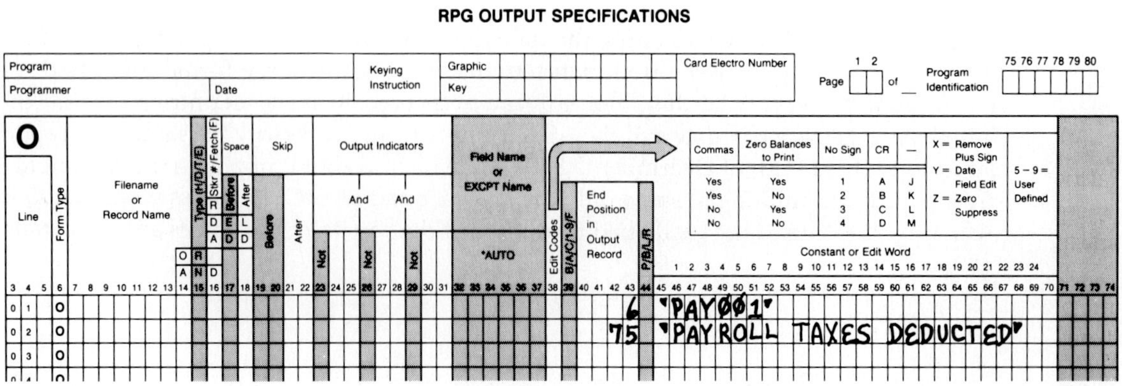

FIGURE 5.23 Coding for Page Numbering

[RPG Output Specifications form showing:]
- Line 01: Field Name "PAGE#" as constant in quotes, end position 124
- Line 02: Field name PAGE, end position 130

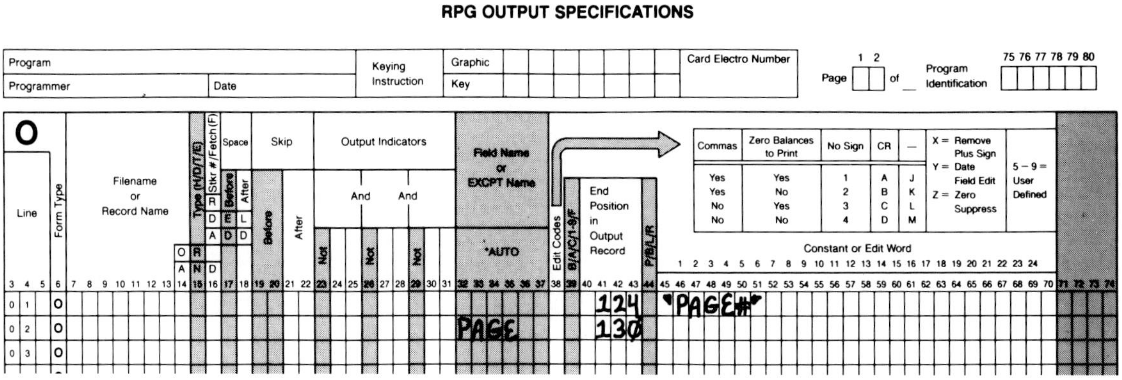

Page Number

Figure 5.23 shows the coding for page numbering. To print the page number in the upper right corner of the report, specify column 124 as the ending position and then place the words "PAGE#" within quotation marks in columns 45–51. The second entry specifies a field name of PAGE. This is a special reserved field name. The field PAGE automatically keeps a page count of each page printed. This page count is always available to the programmer to be printed or used in the program whenever needed. When the first page is printed, the value in PAGE is 1. It is incremented by one each time a new page is printed. The PAGE field is a four-digit numeric field, unless it has been defined differently in the Calculation Specifications, so you must leave enough room for it to print on the output line. It is possible to do calculations using the field PAGE (for example, zeroing out the page number at the end of a level break and starting the page numbering over for a new group), but in this example there is no need to do so.

System Date and Edit Codes

It is important to know the date on which a report was run. The computer always knows what the current date is and RPG can retrieve that date, using the reserved word UDATE to give the current date to the program. The date should print in columns 8–17 so the special word UDATE will be entered in the column marked Field Name. UDATE always contains the date the computer believes to be the current date. The UDATE is passed to the program as a six-position numeric field, usually in the format MMDDYY. This depends on the particular system so it may be necessary to check with the systems programmer to determine the format. The date should print in positions 6–17 on the report, so the program needs to be told that this field should end in position 17 (columns 40–43). Figure 5.24 shows the format for system date.

Printing the date in the format MMDDYY without punctuation would make it difficult to read. Inserting slashes to make it easier to read can be done with an edit code. The edit code for dates is a Y entered in column 38 of the Output Specifications.

FIGURE 5.24 Format for System Date

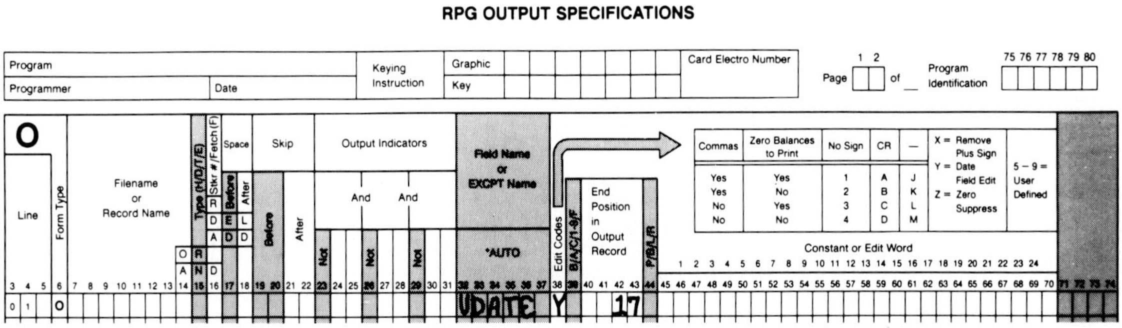

[RPG Output Specifications form showing:]
- Line 01: Field Name UDATE, Edit Code Y, end position 17

System Time and Edit Words

It is often useful to know the time of day at which a report was run. The computer always knows what the current time is and RPG can retrieve that time, using the operation code TIME in the calculations. The result field will contain the time and the programmer may assign any name to the field, defined as six positions in length. Figures 5.25(a) and 5.25(b) show this coding.

Note that the field name TYME is not a reserved word. The programmer may use any field name for this purpose. A length of 6 is entered for the field TYME, because this is a programmer-assigned field name. It is also necessary to enter 0 in the decimal positions field because it is a numeric field.

The time of day should be printed in columns 19–28. The field name TYME is entered on the Output Specifications in the column headed Field Name and the ending position 28 is assigned. This will cause the time of day to print. Computers are usually set for a 24-hour clock so that users will know whether a report was run in the morning or the afternoon. A report run at 1:00 in the afternoon would show a time of 13:00:00. Providing for the insertion of colons to separate hours, minutes, and seconds is handled through the use of edit words. An edit *word* is similar to an edit *code* but it is more flexible, since it allows the programmer to use any character(s) needed to produce the desired results on the report.

Edit words may be used only with numeric fields. The edit word is entered in columns 45–70 of the Output Specifications, on the same line as the field name (columns 32–37). It is enclosed in quotation marks and must provide the right number of spaces to accommodate the field being edited. Figure 5.26 shows several examples of edit words.

FIGURE 5.25(a) System Time: Calculation Specifications

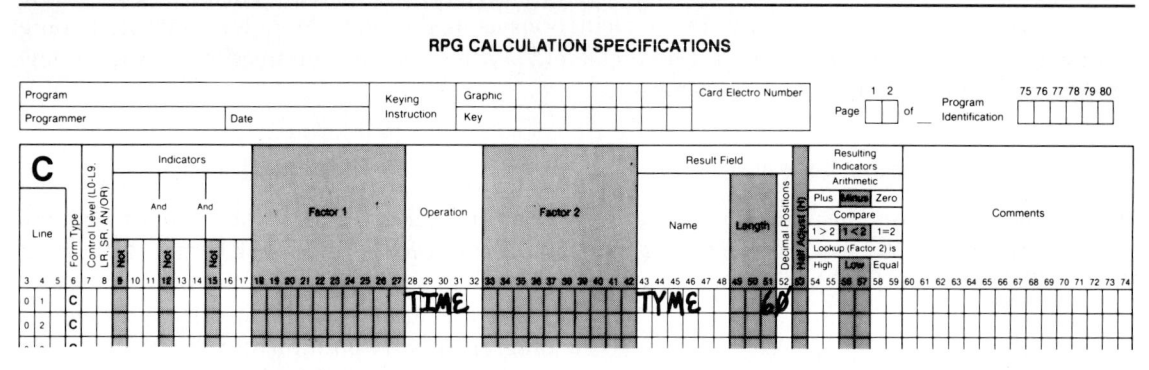

FIGURE 5.25(b) System Time: Output Calculations

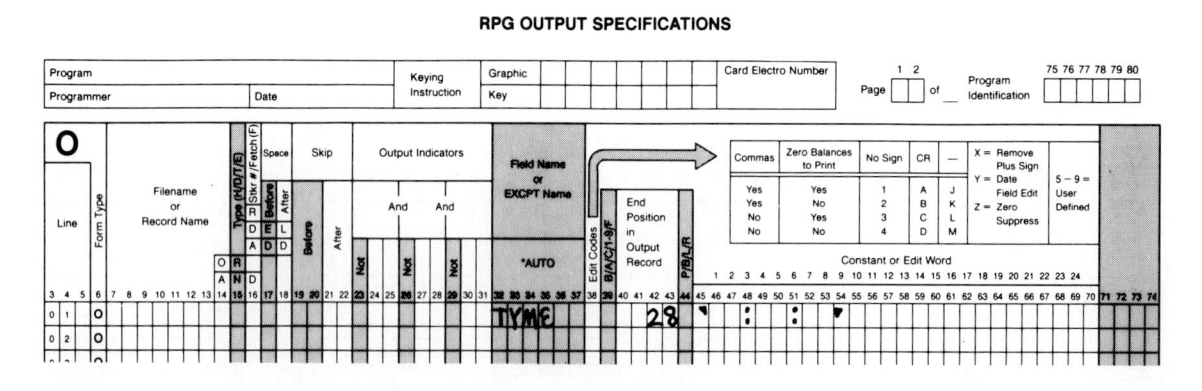

FIGURE 5.26 Examples of Edit Words

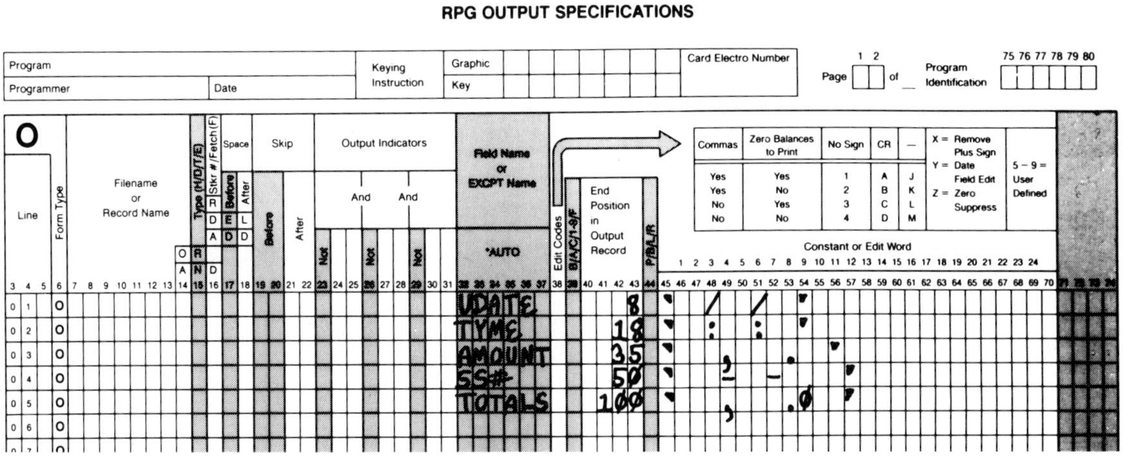

[RPG Output Specifications form showing edit word examples:
- UPDATE, field 8
- TYME, field 18
- AMOUNT, field 35
- SS#, field 50
- TOTALS, field 100]

FIGURE 5.27 Personnel Report Format

```
PAY001                              PAYROLL TAXES DEDUCTED
RUN DATE  3/08/92 10:40:00              AS OF 12/31/92

DIV  DEPT       NAME              EARNINGS           TAX AMOUNT

050  001  KEVIN BEHR              89,545.00          22,386.25
070  002  KRYSTLE CLEAR           65,482.00          16,370.50
070  003  MERRIDEE DANCER         96,587.00          24,146.75
070  004  ASTRID LEON-TERRA       86,056.00          21,514.00
080  004  OWEN MOHR                   65.00              16.25
080  004  ANDY GAIN
```

Edit words may *not* be used on the same line where an edit code is used. It is important to allow sufficient space on the report to accommodate the field together with all the edit characters being inserted. Care must be taken to count the exact number of spaces in the field and to ensure that the same number of spaces is provided in the edit word.

Summary of Report Formatting

The sample program in Figure 5.27 shows what the report might look like. Although these standards will vary from one organization to another, a professional programmer will do well to adopt personal standards and modify them as needed for individual requirements.

SUMMARY ∎

In this chapter, you have learned how to print intermediate totals for multiple levels of related detail data on your reports. Your reports are now beginning to be somewhat complex and to look truly professional.

You have learned that there is more than one way to develop cumulative totals to be used for level break totals.

You have learned how to do group indication on reports to make your reports easier to read.

You have learned a variety of methods for setting a field back to zero using calculations.

You have gained a better insight into the RPG fixed logic cycle.

You have learned about standards for putting report headings on your report so that they will contain all the necessary information. You have learned how RPG will do page numbering for you automatically and you know how to retrieve the system date and time to be printed on your reports.

REVIEW QUESTIONS ■

1. What are uses of multiple control breaks?

2. How many level break indicators may be defined in a program?

3. Explain the sort sequence used for producing multiple control breaks in a program.

4. Which level break total will print first on a report?

5. Explain the difference between a group printed report and one that uses group indication.

6. What is the difference between entering level break indicators at detail time or at total time?

7. When level totals are developed independently of each other they are referred to as _____ totals.

8. When level totals are rolled over into the next level total these are referred to as _____ totals.

9. Discuss the benefits of using each of the preceding two methods for developing multiple level totals in RPG.

10. What are some methods for zeroing or clearing out the value contained in a field?

11. The reserved word with which RPG automatically provides a page number is _____ .

12. The reserved word used in RPG to obtain the system date is _____ .

13. Is there a reserved word in RPG to describe time of day? Explain how time of day is obtained.

14. A good standard report heading should include the following items: _____ , _____ , _____ , _____ , _____ , _____ , and _____ .

15. When are edit words used instead of edit codes?

EXERCISES ■

1. On an Input Specifications form, enter the coding which will cause four level breaks to be taken. The fields are company number, group number, department number, and employee number (CMP#, GRP#, DEPT#, and EMPL#). Company number is the major sequence and employee number is the minor sequence.

2. On a Calculation Specifications form, enter the coding which will "roll over" totals in a field named TOTLV1 from level 1 to level 2 in a field named TOTLV2 (employee totals into department totals).

3. On an Output Specifications form, enter the coding which will cause the department number to print only for the first line of a group of records on a report using group indication.

4. On a Calculation Specifications form, enter the coding to define the time of day.

5. On a Calculation Specifications form, enter the coding to zero out the totals in the field TOTAMT. (Use two different methods for clearing out this field.)

DEBUGGING EXERCISES

Instructions

The following RPG programs contain an error or errors. Some of these errors are indicated by the RPG compiler on the program listing. A list of syntax errors is given at the end of the program listing. Other types of errors may occur which will not be shown. These are called logic errors.

Study each program and its syntax errors. Locate each error (including logic errors) and on a separate coding form make the correct entry for the line(s) in error.

Explain each error and how it should be corrected.

```
     100  F* TITLE: DEBUG PROJECT 5-A
     200  F* DATE:   3/7           AUTHOR: D.CABLE
     300  F* DESCRIPTION:  PRINT TOTAL SALES BY REGION
     400  F***********************************************
     500  F* MODIFICATIONS:
     600  F* NO.       DATE     INIT     DESCRIPTION
     700  F*        XX/XX/XX    XXX      XXXXXXXXXXXXXXXXXXXXXXXXXXXXX
     800  F***********************************************

NAME OF PROGRAM WILL BE PJ005A IN LIBRARY CABLE

              H
* 1019              ALL DECIMAL DATA ERRORS IGNORED
     900  FSALESIN IP  F      80              DISK
    1000  FREPORT   O  F     132       OF     PRINTER
    1100  F***********************************************

    1200  ISALESIN AA  01
    1300  I                                      1   2 SLSDIV      L3
    1400  I                                      3   5 SLSRGN      L2
    1500  I                                      6   9 SLSREP      L1
    1600  I                                     10  15 SLSDAT
    1700  I                                     16  22 SLSTOT
    1800  I                                     23  23 SLSTYP

    1900  C           SLSTYP    COMP 'I'                      33
    2000  C     33    SLSTOT    ADD  L1TOT   L1TOT   72
    2100  C     N33   SLSTOT    SUB  L1TOT   L1TOT   72
    2200  CL1         L1TOT     ADD  L2AMT   L2AMT   82
    2300  CL2         L2AMT     ADD  L3AMT   L3AMT   82
    2400  C           CNT       ADD  1       CNT     40
* 5002 5002-**
    2500  CL3         L3AMT     ADD  LRAMT   LRAMT   92

    2600  OREPORT   H  103           1P
    2700  O         OR                OF
    2800  O                                         6 'PJ005A'
    2900  O                                UDATE Y 50
    3000  O                                        30 'MONTH-TO-DATE SALES'
    3100  O         H    2           1P
    3200  O         OR                OF
    3300  O                                        25 'BY REGION'
    3400  O         H    2           1P
    3500  O         OR                OF
    3600  O                                         3 'DIV'
    3700  O                                         7 'REG#'
    3800  O                                        14 'SALES REP'
```

Chapter 5 Multiple Level Breaks

```
SEQUENCE        1         2         3         4         5         6         7
NUMBER    67890123456789012345678901234567890123456789012345678901234

  3900   O                                        24 'SALES DATE'
  4000   O                                        34 'SALES AMOUNT'
  4100   O         D  1      01
  4200   O                        SLSDIV      3
  4300   O                        SLSRGN      7
  4400   O                        SLSREPY    12
  4500   O                        SLSDATY    23
  4600   O                        SLSTOTK    34
  4700   O         T  2      L1
  4800   O                                        15 'SALES REP TOTAL'
  4900   O                        L1TOT  K   48
  5000   O         T  2      L2
  5100   O                                        15 'REGION TOTAL'
  5200   O                        L2TOT  K   48
  5300   O         T  2      L3
  5400   O                                        15 'DIVISION TOTAL   '
  5500   O                        L3TOT  K   48
  5600   O         T  1      LR
  5700   O                                        15 'GRAND TOTAL VALUE'
  5800   O                        LRTOT  K   48
* * * * * E N D   O F   S O U R C E * * * * *
```

```
*  7086      900    RPG PROVIDES BLOCK/UNBLOCK SUPPORT FOR FILE SALESIN.
*  7059     4400    EDITING SPECIFIED BUT FIELD NAME SLSREP NOT NUMERIC
*  8003     5400    FIELD LENGTH 0016 GREATER THAN RECORD LENGTH 0015
*  8003     5700    FIELD LENGTH 0017 GREATER THAN RECORD LENGTH 0015
```

CROSS-REFERENCE LISTING

```
         FILE/RCD   DEV/RCD    REFERENCES (D=DEFINED)
    02   REPORT     PRINTER    1000D  2600   3100   3400   4100   4700   5000
                               5300   5600
    01   SALESIN    DISK        900D  1200

         FIELD      ATTR       REFERENCES (M=MODIFIED D=DEFINED)
         CNT        P(4,0)     2400   2400D
         LRAMT      P(9,2)     2500   2500D
* 7030   LRTOT      P(5,0)     5800
         L1TOT      P(7,2)     2000   2000D  2100   2100D  2200   4900
         L2AMT      P(8,2)     2200   2200D  2300
* 7030   L2TOT      P(5,0)     5200
         L3AMT      P(8,2)     2300   2300D  2500
* 7030   L3TOT      P(5,0)     5500
         SLSDAT     P(6,0)     1600D  4500
         SLSDIV     A(2)       1300D  4200
         SLSREP     A(4)       1500D  4400
         SLSRGN     A(3)       1400D  4300
         SLSTOT     P(7,2)     1700D  2000   2100   4600
         SLSTYP     A(1)       1800D  1900
         UDATE      P(6,0)     2900
         'I'        LITERAL    1900
         1          LITERAL    2400
```

```
         INDICATOR   REFERENCES (M=MODIFIED D=DEFINED)

         LR           900D 5600
* 7030   L1          1500  2200  4700
* 7030   L2          1400  2300  2400  5000
* 7030   L3          1300  2500  5300
         OF          1000D 2700  3200  3500
         01          1200M 4100
         1P          2600  3100  3400
         33          1900M 2000  2100


MESSAGES

MSGID     SEV   NUMBER   TEXT

* QRG1019  00      1     IGNDECERR(*YES) SPECIFIED ON COMMAND. NO DECIMAL DATA ERRORS
* QRG5002  10      1     SPEC WITHOUT CONTROL LEVEL (POSITIONS 7-8) ENTRY FOLLOWS ONE
                         PRECEDING CONTROL LEVEL ASSUMED.
* QRG7030  30      6     FIELD OR INDICATOR NOT DEFINED.
* QRG7059  20      1     EDIT MUST BE SPECIFIED ONLY WITH NUMERIC FIELD. EDITING IGNOR
* QRG7086  00      1     RPG WILL HANDLE BLOCKING FUNCTION FOR THE FILE. INFDS CONTENT
                         ARE TRANSFERRED.
* QRG8003  30      2     END POSITION (POSITIONS 40-43) NOT LARGE ENOUGH. SPECIFICATIO


MESSAGE SUMMARY

TOTAL   00    10    20    30    40    50
  12     2     1     1     8     0     0

 58 RECORDS READ FROM SOURCE FILE
SOURCE RECORDS INCLUDE   49 SPECIFICATIONS,    0 TABLE RECORDS, AND    9 COMMENTS

QRG0008 COMPILE TERMINATED. SEVERITY 30 ERRORS FOUND IN PROGRAM

* * * * * E N D   O F   C O M P I L A T I O N * * * * *
* QRG1020              ERROR OCCURRED CREATING OR UPDATING DATA AREA RETURNCODE. COMPIL
```

```
    100  F* TITLE: DEBUG PROJECT 5-B
    200  F* DATE:   4/7         AUTHOR: D.CABLE
    300  F* DESCRIPTION:  PRINT TOTAL EMPLOYEE COUNT BY YEAR
    400  F***********************************************************
    500  F* MODIFICATIONS:
    600  F* NO.    DATE      INIT      DESCRIPTION
    700  F*      XX/XX/XX    XXX       XXXXXXXXXXXXXXXXXXXXXXXXXXXXXXXX
    800  F***********************************************************

NAME OF PROGRAM WILL BE PJ005B IN LIBRARY CABLE

              H
* 1019                   ALL DECIMAL DATA ERRORS IGNORED
    900  FEMPMAST IP  F       120              DISK
   1000  FREPORT   O  F       132       OF     PRINTER
   1100  F***********************************************************

   1200  IEMPMAST AA   01
   1300  I                                        1    2 EMPDIV   L4
   1400  I                                        3    4 EMPDPT   L3
   1500  I                                        5   60EMPHMO
   1600  I                                        7   80EMPHDA
   1700  I                                        9  100EMPHYR   L2
   1800  I                                       11   13 EMPNO
   1900  I                                       14   29 EMPNAM
   2000  I                                       30   30 EMPTYP
```

```
        2100  C              EMPTYP    COMP *A*                              75
        2200  C      23      1         ADD  EMPCNT    EMPCNT   40
        2300  CL1            L1TOT     ADD  L2TOT     L2TOT    52
        2400  CL2            L2TOT     ADD  L3TOT     L3TOT    52
        2500  CL3            L3TOT     ADD  LRTOT     LRTOT    52


        2600  OREPORT   H    103       1P
        2700  O         OR             OF
        2800  O                                        6 *PJ005B*
        2900  O                              UDATE Y  50
        3000  O                                       30 *EMPLOYEE COUNT BY YEAR*
        3100  O         H    2         1P
        3200  O         OR             OF
        3300  O                                        3 *DIV*
        3400  O                                        8 *DEPT*
        3500  O                                       14 *EMP#*
        3600  O                                       24 *EMPLOYEE NAME*
        3700  O                                       42 *HIRE DATE*
        3800  O         D    1         01
        3900  O                              EMPDIV    3
        4000  O                              EMPDPT    8
        4100  O                              EMPNO  Z 14
        4200  O                              EMPNAM   34
        4300  O                              EMPMO    38
        4400  O                              EMPDA    40
        4500  O                              EMPYR    42
        4600  O         T    2         L1
        4700  O                                       15 *TOTAL FOR YEAR*
        4800  O                              L1TOT KB 48
        4900  O         T    2         L2
        5000  O                                       15 *TOTAL FOR DEPT*
        5100  O                              L2TOT KB 48
        5200  O         T    2         L3
        5300  O                                       15 *TOTAL FOR DIVISION*
        5400  O                              L3TOT KB 48
        5500  O         T    1         LR
        5600  O                                       15 *TOTAL EMPLOYEES*
        5700  O                              LRTOT K  48
    * * * * * E N D   O F   S O U R C E * * * * *



*  7086       900    RPG PROVIDES BLOCK/UNBLOCK SUPPORT FOR FILE EMPMAST.
*  7059      4100    EDITING SPECIFIED BUT FIELD NAME EMPNO NOT NUMERIC
*  8003      5300    FIELD LENGTH 0018 GREATER THAN RECORD LENGTH 0015



    CROSS-REFERENCE LISTING



            FILE/RCD    DEV/RCD      REFERENCES (D=DEFINED)

        01  EMPMAST     DISK          900D 1200
        02  REPORT      PRINTER      1000D 2600  3100  3800  4600  4900  5200
                                     5500


            FIELD       ATTR         REFERENCES (M=MODIFIED D=DEFINED)

            EMPCNT      P(4,0)       2200  2200D
*  7030     EMPDA       A(4)         4400
            EMPDIV      A(2)         1300D 3900
            EMPDPT      A(2)         1400D 4000
*  7031     EMPHDA      P(2,0)       1600D
*  7031     EMPHMO      P(2,0)       1500D
*  7031     EMPHYR      P(2,0)       1700D
*  7030     EMPMO       A(4)         4300
            EMPNAM      A(16)        1900D 4200
```

```
           EMPNO        A(3)     1800D 4100
           EMPTYP       A(1)     2000D 2100
* 7030     EMPYR        A(4)     4500
           LRTOT        P(5,2)   2500  2500D 5700
* 7030     L1TOT        P(5,0)   2300  4800M
           L2TOT        P(5,2)   2300  2300D 2400  5100M
           L3TOT        P(5,2)   2400  2400D 2500  5400M
           UDATE        P(6,0)   2900
           'A'          LITERAL  2100
           1            LITERAL  2200


           INDICATOR  REFERENCES (M=MODIFIED D=DEFINED)

           LR           900D  5500
* 7030     L1           2300  4600
* 7030     L2           1700  2400  4900
* 7030     L3           1400  2500  5200
* 7030     L4           1300
           OF           1000D 2700  3200
           01           1200M 3800
           1P           2600  3100
* 7030     23           2200
* 7031     75           2100M


   MESSAGES

   MSGID     SEV  NUMBER  TEXT

*  QRG1019   00    1      IGNDECERR(*YES) SPECIFIED ON COMMAND. NO DECIMAL DATA ERRORS
*  QRG7030   30    9      FIELD OR INDICATOR NOT DEFINED.
*  QRG7031   00    4      NAME OR INDICATOR NOT REFERENCED.
*  QRG7059   20    1      EDIT MUST BE SPECIFIED ONLY WITH NUMERIC FIELD. EDITING IGNO
*  QRG7086   00    1      RPG WILL HANDLE BLOCKING FUNCTION FOR THE FILE. INFDS CONTEN
                          ARE TRANSFERRED.
*  QRG8003   30    1      END POSITION (POSITIONS 40-43) NOT LARGE ENOUGH. SPECIFICATI


   MESSAGE SUMMARY

   TOTAL     00    10    20    30    40    50
    17       6      0     1    10     0     0

    57 RECORDS READ FROM SOURCE FILE
    SOURCE RECORDS INCLUDE   48 SPECIFICATIONS,    0 TABLE RECORDS, AND    9 COMMENTS

   QRG0008 COMPILE TERMINATED. SEVERITY 30 ERRORS FOUND IN PROGRAM

   * * * * * E N D  O F  C O M P I L A T I O N * * * * *
*  QRG1020            ERROR OCCURRED CREATING OR UPDATING DATA AREA RETURNCODE. COMPI
```

PROGRAMMING PROJECT

Project Overview

A report is to be printed listing the sales made for one day by each sales representative. Each sale will be printed in detail with level breaks for each sales representative at each store location. Write the RPG program to produce this listing. Sample data for this project can be found in Appendix D.

Input Format

The input data for the project is found in a file called SALES in the sample data. The Record Layout for this file is shown in Figure 5.28.

Output Format (Printer Spacing Chart)

The output format for the project is a report with standard headings. The report will show the store location number, sales representative number, date of sale, item sold, quantity, unit price, and extended price. A total dollar amount is printed for each sales representative and for a total for the entire store. A final total of the entire daily sales is printed at the end of the report. This is a detail printed report. The Printer Spacing Chart for this report is shown in Figure 5.29.

An example of the finished report is shown in Figure 5.30.

FIGURE 5.28 Programming Project: Record Layout

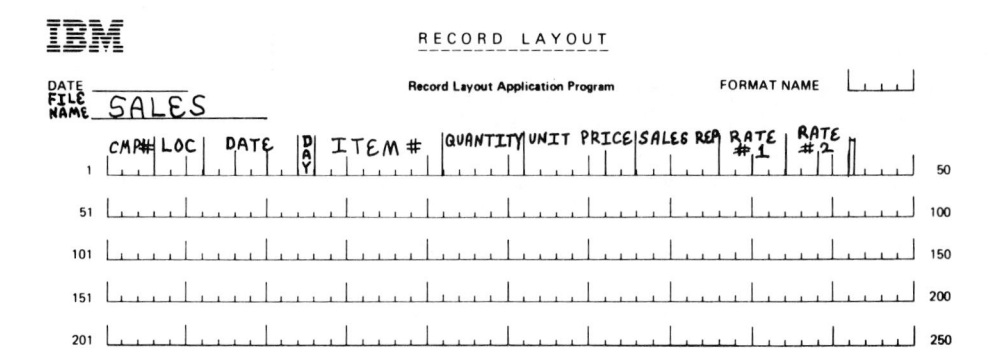

[Record Layout form: File Name SALES, with fields: CMP#, LOC, DATE, DAY, ITEM #, QUANTITY, UNIT PRICE, SALES REP, RATE #1, RATE #2]

FIGURE 5.29 Programming Project: Printer Spacing Chart

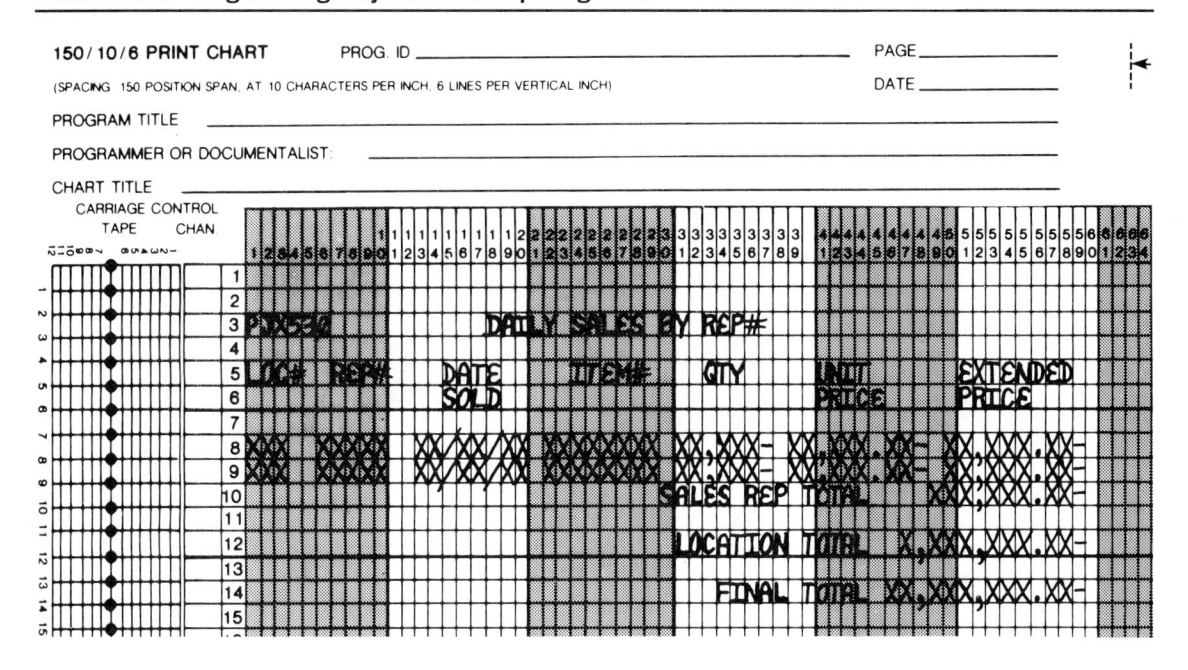

FIGURE 5.30 Programming Project: Final Report

```
PJX530              DAILY SALES BY REP#

LOC#   REP#    DATE     ITEM#    QTY      UNIT       EXTENDED
               SOLD                       PRICE      PRICE

  1      1    5/01/91   123230     1      250.00        250.00
                                 SALES REP TOTAL        250.00

                                 LOCATION TOTAL         250.00

  2      1    3/21/91      689     1    2,500.00      2,500.00
                                 SALES REP TOTAL      2,500.00

  2     65    5/01/91   461390    25      985.00     24,625.00
  2     65    3/21/91      999     2       50.00        100.00
                                 SALES REP TOTAL     24,725.00

                                 LOCATION TOTAL      27,225.00

  5     23    5/01/91   659821    20       50.00      1,000.00
  5     23    3/21/91      879     8       16.00        128.00
                                 SALES REP TOTAL      1,128.00

  5     79    5/01/91   798293    28      203.33      5,693.24
  5     79    3/21/91      688     1    8,000.00      8,000.00
                                 SALES REP TOTAL     13,693.24

                                 LOCATION TOTAL      14,821.24

  1      1    4/28/91    75391     1       23.25         23.25
                                 SALES REP TOTAL         23.25

                                 LOCATION TOTAL          23.25

  2      5    4/29/91   123569     1      883.00        883.00
                                 SALES REP TOTAL        883.00

                                 LOCATION TOTAL         883.00

  6      6    4/28/91   123987     1      789.00        789.00
                                 SALES REP TOTAL        789.00

                                 LOCATION TOTAL         789.00

                                 FINAL TOTAL         43,991.49
```

Chapter 6

Exception Output Processing

What you will learn in Chapter 6

Sample Program Using Exception Output Processing
File Description and Input Specifications
Calculation Specifications (Program Loops)
Output Specifications

Page Overflow
Fetch Overflow
Sample Program
Internal Control (Line Counting)
Moving Data (MOVE and MOVEL)
Moving Fields of Different Lengths with MOVE

Moving Fields of Different Lengths with MOVEL
Alphanumeric/Numeric MOVE or MOVEL
Moving Literal Values
Initializing a Field to Blanks

Previous chapters have explained the RPG fixed logic cycle and how input and output processing is handled automatically within the RPG program. To review:

    An input record is read.
    Total calculations are completed.
    Totals are output (either to print or to another file).
    Detail calculations are processed.
    Detail output is produced.
    The cycle repeats itself until all records have been read.

All of these functions occur with no special commands from the programmer. Although the fixed logic cycle is a key advantage of RPG and saves the programmer much effort, there are times when it is useful (even necessary) for the programmer to take control of the sequence of events in a program so that outputs are produced at some alternate time. This chapter outlines a method that allows the programmer to take control of the output timing.

Common reasons for taking control of the output timing include the following:

1. The need to print the same information more than once for a single input record (for example, printing three address labels for each customer record in the file).
2. The need to print error messages before printing a detail or total line.
3. The need to print a page of summary totals as a second report *after* a report has finished printing all its detail and total lines.
4. The need to output a summary file at a level which is different from any of the levels being used on the output report.

5. The need to print detail or total lines based on exceptional criteria—for example, printing a line only if the department number is 100, the total dollar amount is greater than zero, and the ZIP Code is west of the Mississippi.

Since it would be difficult to accomplish any of these tasks using the normal fixed logic cycle, RPG uses exception output processing to handle such requirements.

SAMPLE PROGRAM USING EXCEPTION OUTPUT PROCESSING ■

This sample program requires exception output processing because three address labels are to be printed for each customer. Exception output processing is done in the calculation section of the program. Since the normal cycle will not be used, it is necessary to code the program to execute its output lines or records exactly at the moment needed. The operation for forcing a line to be printed (or an output record produced) is the operation code EXCPT.

In coding exception output processing on the Calculation Specifications, no entries are used in factors 1 or 2 or the result field. The EXCPT operation by itself causes an output record to be produced, as shown in Figure 6.1. Controlling *when* the output record will be written and *what* output record will be written is handled through the use of indicators.

This program will use a name and address file similar to that used in earlier chapters. Figure 6.2 shows the Record Layout for the customer master file.

File Description and Input Specifications

The File Description and Input Specifications for the customer master file are similar to those used in earlier chapters. They are shown in Figures 6.3(a) and 6.3(b).

FIGURE 6.1 EXCPT Calculation Specifications

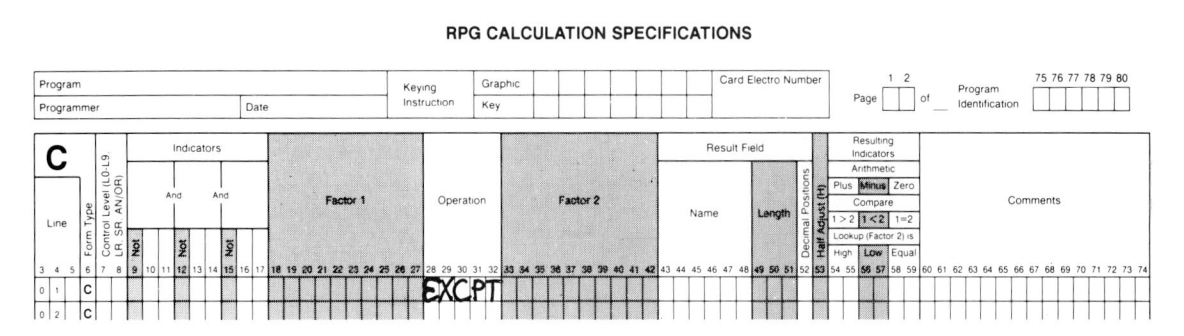

FIGURE 6.2 Record Layout for Customer Master File

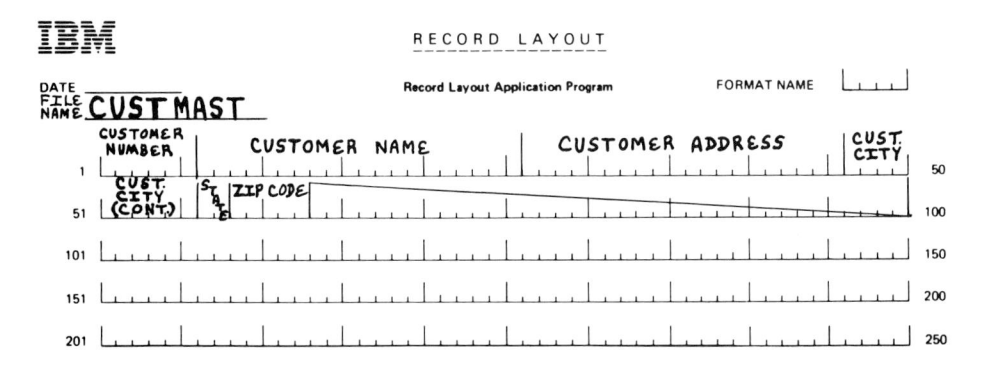

FIGURE 6.3(a) Customer Master File: File Description Specifications

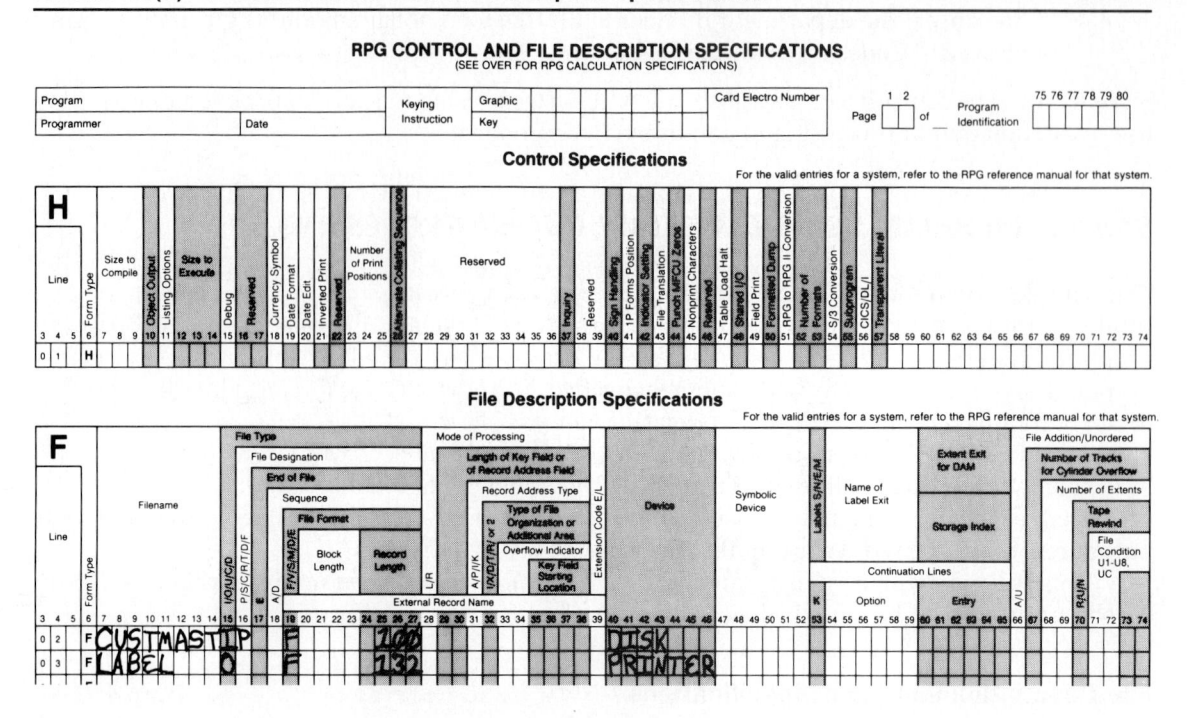

Line	Filename								
02	F CUSTMAST	IP		F		100		DISK	
03	F LABEL	O		F		132		PRINTER	

FIGURE 6.3(b) Customer Master File: Input Specifications

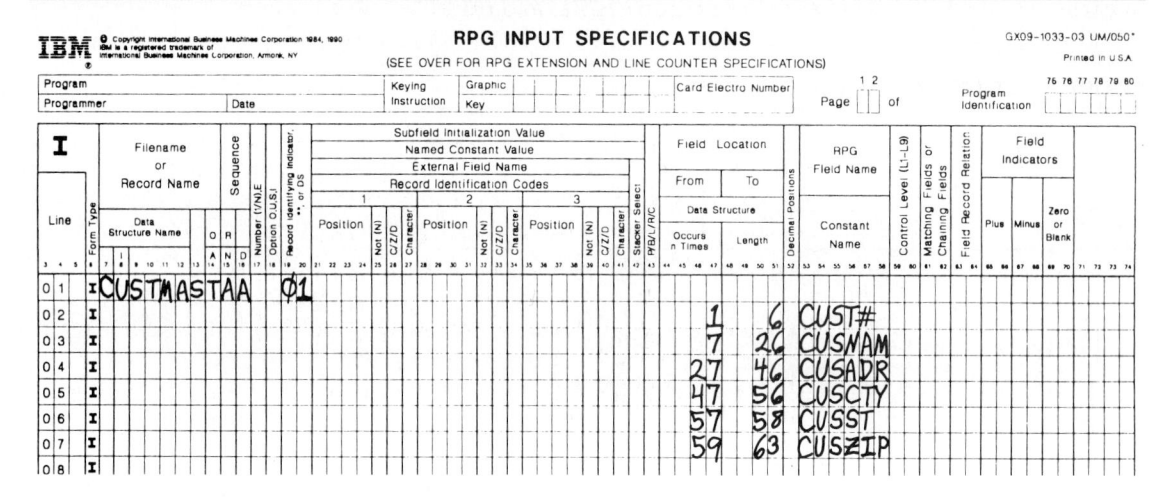

Line	Filename				From	To	Field Name
01	I CUSTMAST	AA		01			
02	I				1	6	CUST#
03	I				7	26	CUSNAM
04	I				27	46	CUSADR
05	I				47	56	CUSCTY
06	I				57	58	CUSST
07	I				59	63	CUSZIP
08	I						

Calculation Specifications (Program Loops)

To produce three copies of a label for every customer in the file, a structure called a loop is employed. Loops are a necessary part of most programs. In fact, the fixed logic cycle of RPG is itself a loop, repeating the same steps over and over.

A loop is constructed by causing a series of program instructions to be repeated over and over. This is achieved in RPG through the use of the GOTO operation. The GOTO instructs the logic of the program to return to an earlier line in the calculations and repeat the same series of instructions. The programmer must use indicators that condition the GOTO so the loop will occur a specific number of times and then continue with the rest of the processing. Proper conditioning of a loop with indicators prevents the disaster of a never-ending loop.

For the sample program, the loop will be repeated three times. Each time the loop is repeated, a customer label will be printed. Figures 6.4(a) and 6.4(b) show an example of a loop that repeats three times and executes exception output each time through the loop.

The first entry on the Calculation Specifications is the TAG entry. This is the beginning of the loop. The next entry adds 1 to the field called NUMBER. Next a compare (COMP operation) is done to determine if three labels have been printed yet. If the NUMBER field is less than or equal to 3, indicator 33 will be turned *on*. If indicator 33 is *on* a label should be printed for this customer. The next entry is the EXCPT, which will cause a label to be printed. This exception line is conditioned with the indicator 33. On the next entry, if the indicator 33 is on, control of the program will GOTO the beginning of the loop to repeat. For the first, second, and third passes through the loop, a label will be printed each time because the entry is conditioned with the indicator 33, and indicator 33 is *on*. After the third pass, the NUMBER field will be greater than 3 and indicator 33 will be turned off. If indicator 33 is off, the program will drop through to the next line of code, which sets the value of the NUMBER field back to zero.

The program will continue to read the next record in the file and take that record through the loop three times.

FIGURE 6.4(a) Example of a Loop: Calculation Specifications

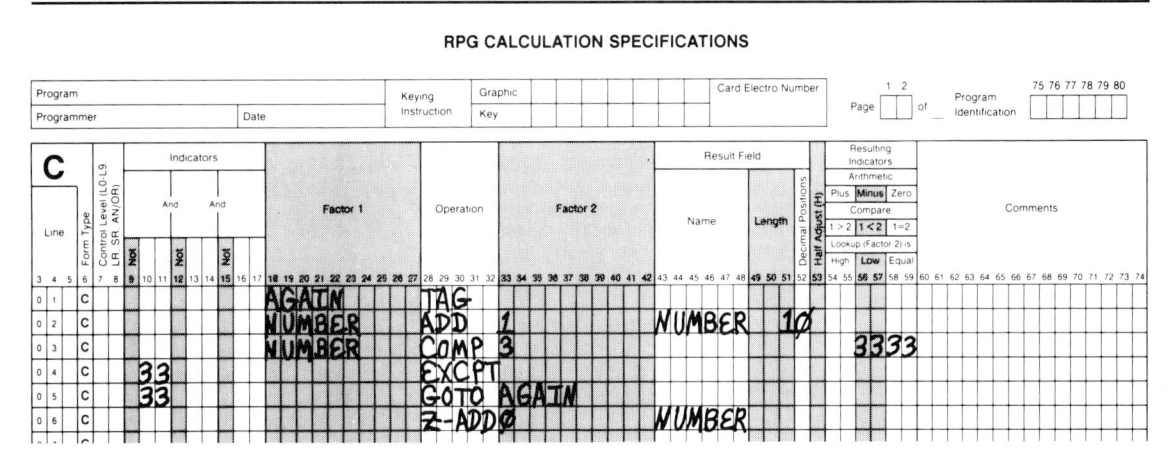

```
RPG CALCULATION SPECIFICATIONS

Line  Ind  Factor 1   Operation  Factor 2   Result Field  Len  Resulting Indicators
01  C              AGAIN      TAG
02  C              NUMBER     ADD        1          NUMBER        10
03  C              NUMBER     COMP       3                              33 33
04  C    33                   EXCPT
05  C    33                   GOTO       AGAIN
06  C                         Z-ADD      0          NUMBER
```

FIGURE 6.4(b) Output Specifications Using Exception Output

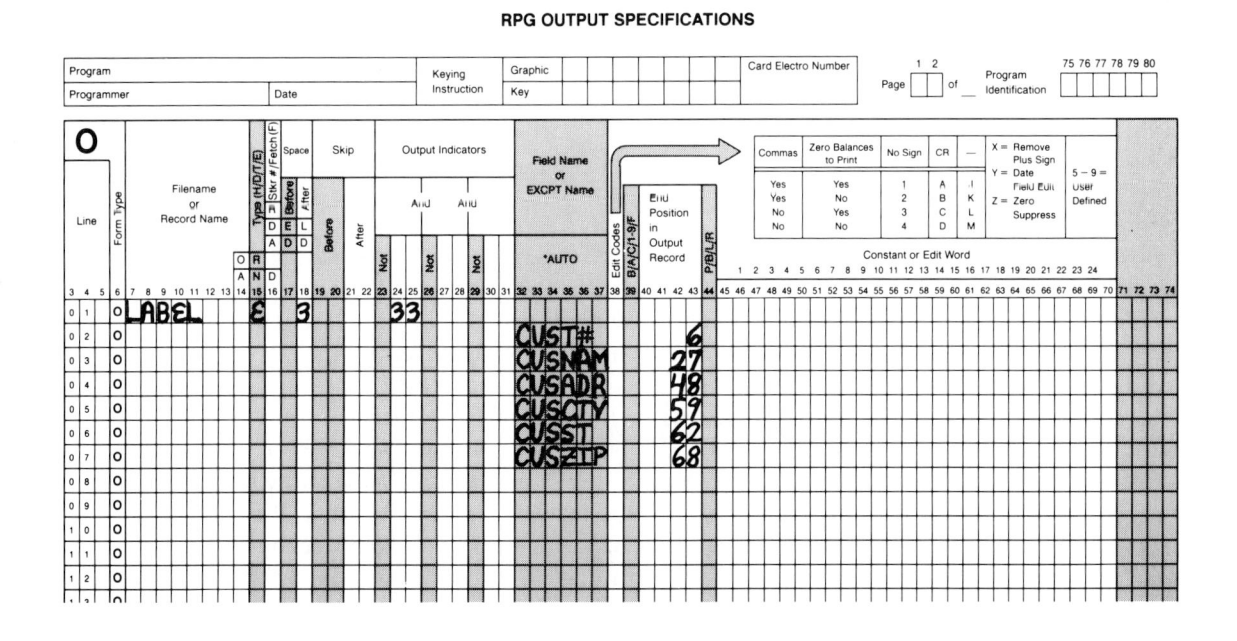

```
RPG OUTPUT SPECIFICATIONS

Line  Filename     Type  Output Indicators  EXCPT Name  End Pos
01  O  LABEL        E    3         33
02  O                                        CUST#       6
03  O                                        CUSNAM     27
04  O                                        CUSADR     48
05  O                                        CUSCTY     59
06  O                                        CUSST      62
07  O                                        CUSZIP     68
```

Chapter 6 Exception Output Processing

FIGURE 6.5 Printed Labels

```
6523    ACME ENTERPRISES       695 AERO CIRCLE      PORT CITY    NJ 06501

6523    ACME ENTERPRISES       695 AERO CIRCLE      PORT CITY    NJ 06501

6523    ACME ENTERPRISES       695 AERO CIRCLE      PORT CITY    NJ 06501

7871    VENTURA SERVICES       921 TELEPORT WAY     SPACE CITY   NY 04088

7871    VENTURA SERVICES       921 TELEPORT WAY     SPACE CITY   NY 04088

7871    VENTURA SERVICES       921 TELEPORT WAY     SPACE CITY   NY 04088

8899    INFO-FUTURES INC.      4652 OJAI BLVD       FILLMORE     CA 99200

8899    INFO-FUTURES INC.      4652 OJAI BLVD       FILLMORE     CA 99200

8899    INFO-FUTURES INC.      4652 OJAI BLVD       FILLMORE     CA 99200

9100    COOPER BARRELS CO.     456 SANTA CLARA ST   SAN JOSE     CA 95501

9100    COOPER BARRELS CO.     456 SANTA CLARA ST   SAN JOSE     CA 95501

9100    COOPER BARRELS CO.     456 SANTA CLARA ST   SAN JOSE     CA 95501
```

Output Specifications

The Output Specifications for printing the labels are quite similar to those in earlier program examples using the fixed logic cycle. The only difference is the letter *E* in position 15. This indicates that the line is to be printed at *exception* time instead of at detail or total time. Instead of being conditioned to output using the input indicator 01, the line is conditioned to output if indicator 33 is on. Although it would not have been wrong in this instance to use indicator 01 (because the program is a simple one), it is somewhat better form to use the same indicator used to condition the exception in the calculations. In a complex program with many outputs being conditioned by multiple indicators, it could become very confusing to decide which line is being output at what time. By conditioning the output with the same indicator as that used for the exception calculation, much confusion can be avoided.

Figure 6.5 shows the printed labels.

PAGE OVERFLOW ■

Earlier chapters explained the methods for controlling the printing of report headings or other elements when the end of a page was reached. By entering OF (or some valid overflow indicator) in the File Description Specifications and Output Specifications forms, it was possible to print headings on each new page. This is shown in Figures 6.6(a) and 6.6(b).

Although this nearly automatic handling of page overflow works very well for many reports, there are times when it is not sufficient. Before suggesting alternate methods for handling page overflow, we should study the sequence of events that occurs when the overflow indicator is used.

According to the flowchart in Figure 6.7, the headings will be printed after RPG has completed printing all the total lines. If there had been nine levels of totals to be printed, and an overflow had been detected, RPG would have printed all nine total lines before printing the next heading line. This might cause totals to continue to print to the end of the page, through the perforation and for several lines onto the next page before skipping to a new page. This is not what the programmer had in mind.

Some examples of times when the normal page overflow will not work are:

1. When printing several levels of totals that may occur at the bottom of a page.
2. When using exception output (which causes lines to be printed at unscheduled times).
3. When a page overflow is needed at a time other than the normal time.

To get around these types of problems, RPG uses a feature called fetch overflow.

Fetch Overflow

Fetch overflow is simple to use: Enter the letter *F* in column 16 of the Output Specifications for the heading lines that need to be printed at overflow time.

RPG will test to see whether the overflow indicator has been turned on. This test will be made at detail time and at exception time as well as at total time.

A review of the flowchart in Figure 6.8 shows the time at which fetch overflow will cause headings to be printed. It is important to use fetch overflow any time exception output is used.

FIGURE 6.6(a) Overflow Indicator: File Description Specifications

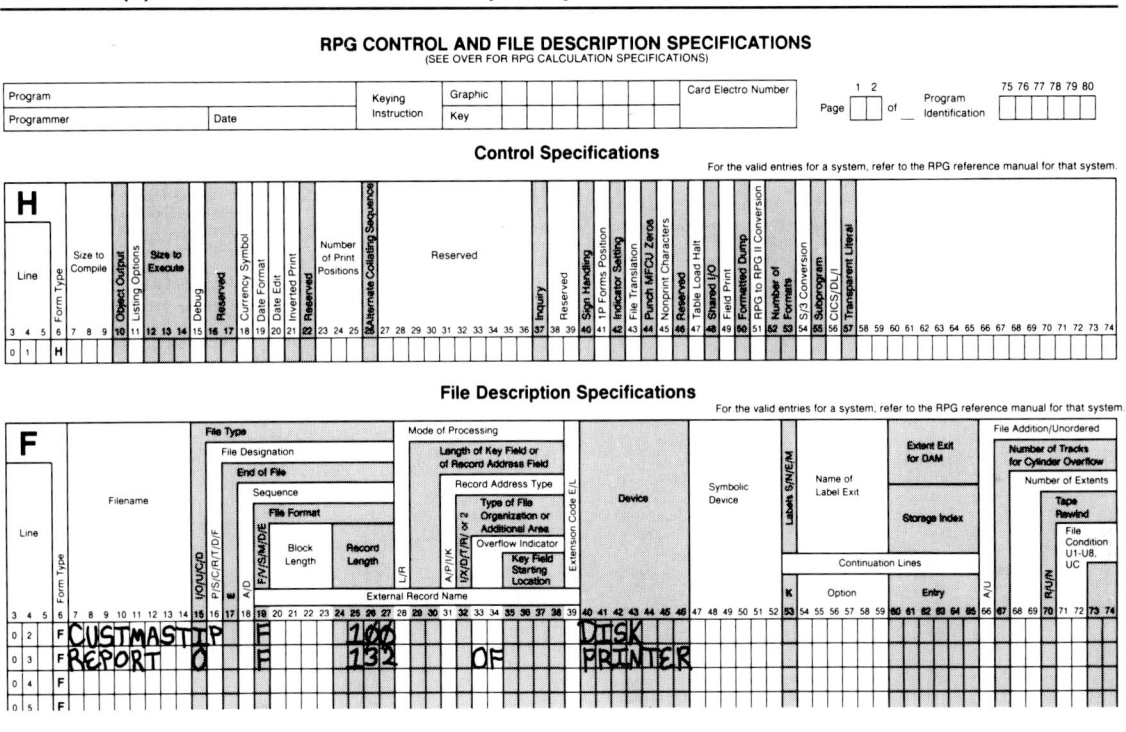

FIGURE 6.6(b) Output Specifications

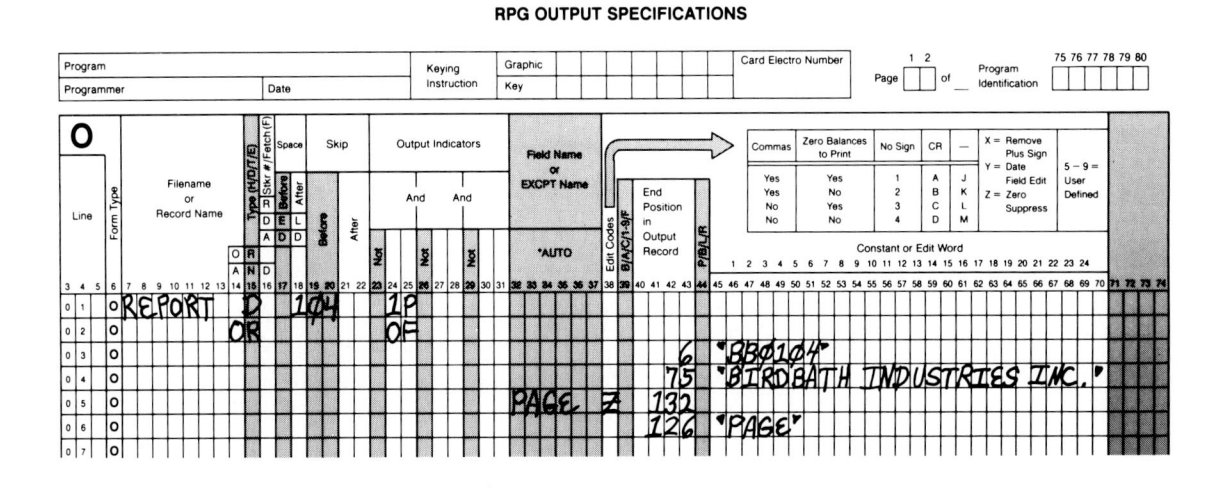

FIGURE 6.7 RPG Logic Cycle for Page Overflow

```
        ┌─────────────┐
        │ OPEN FILES  │
        │     &       │
        │ SET ON 1P   │
        └──────┬──────┘
               ▼
        ┌─────────────┐
        │   PRINT     │
        │ HEADINGS &  │
        │ SET OFF 1P  │
        └──────┬──────┘
               ▼  ◄─────────────────────────────────────────┐
        ┌─────────────┐                                     │
        │    READ     │                                     │
        │   INPUT     │                                     │
        │   RECORD    │                                     │
        └──────┬──────┘                                     │
               ▼                                            │
          ╱ LAST ╲   YES   ┌───────────┐   ┌───────────┐    │
         ╱ RECORD ╲──────► │ SET ON ALL│──►│  DO LR    │    │
         ╲   ?    ╱        │  LEVEL    │   │  CALCS &  │    │
          ╲     ╱          │INDICATORS&│   │  OUTPUTS &│    │
            │ NO           │DO TOTAL   │   │  END JOB  │    │
            ▼              │CALCS &    │   └───────────┘    │
                           │OUTPUTS    │                    │
                           └───────────┘                    │
          ╱ LEVEL╲   YES   ╱ FIRST ╲  NO   ┌───────────┐    │
         ╱ BREAKS ╲──────►╱  CYCLE  ╲─────►│ DO TOTAL  │    │
         ╲   ?    ╱       ╲    ?   ╱       │  CALCS    │    │
          ╲     ╱          ╲     ╱         │    &      │    │
            │ NO             │ YES         │  OUTPUTS  │    │
            ▼                │             └─────┬─────┘    │
                             └───────┬───────────┘          │
                                     ▼                      │
          ╱ PAGE ╲    YES   ┌───────────┐                   │
         ╱OVERFLOW╲───────► │ DO PAGE   │                   │
         ╲   ?    ╱         │ OVERFLOW  │                   │
          ╲     ╱           │ HEADINGS  │                   │
            │ NO            └─────┬─────┘                   │
            ▼◄───────────────────┘                          │
        ┌─────────────┐                                     │
        │ MOVE INPUT  │                                     │
        │   DATA TO   │                                     │
        │INPUT FIELDS │                                     │
        └──────┬──────┘                                     │
               ▼                                            │
        ┌─────────────┐                                     │
        │  DO LEVEL   │                                     │
        │BREAK DETAIL │                                     │
        │ PROCESSING  │                                     │
        └──────┬──────┘                                     │
               ▼                                            │
        ┌─────────────┐                                     │
        │   DETAIL    │                                     │
        │ PROCESSING  │                                     │
        └──────┬──────┘                                     │
               ▼                                            │
        ┌─────────────┐                                     │
        │   DETAIL    │                                     │
        │   OUTPUTS   │                                     │
        └──────┬──────┘                                     │
               └─────────────────────────────────────────────┘
```

Sample Program

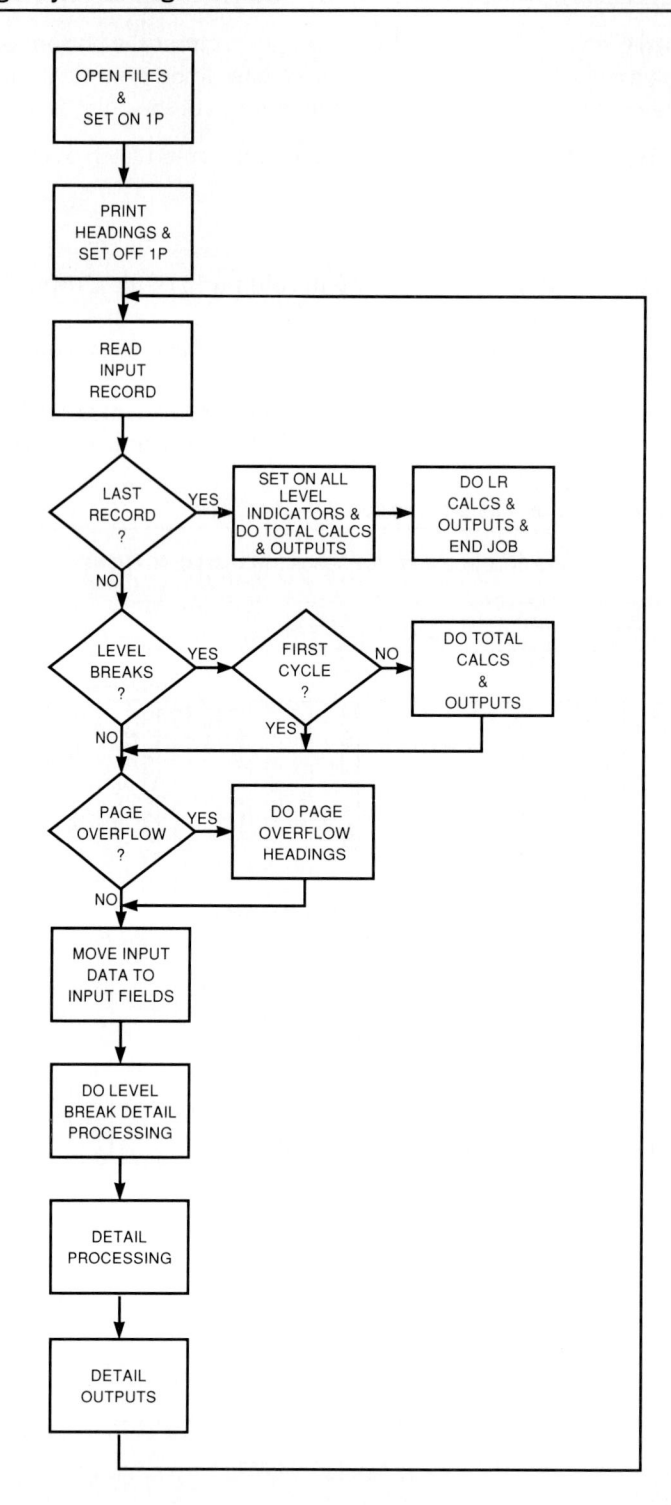

The sample program in Figure 6.9 is used to show payments due on loans. A line will be printed showing payments due on each loan for the entire period of the loan. For example, if the borrower took out a loan of $3,000 to be paid back over a period of 12 months, the program would compute an amount of $250 for each payment. Because the number of lines will vary for each borrower, this program must use exception output and fetch overflow.

FIGURE 6.8 RPG Logic Cycle for Page Overflow Using Fetch Overflow

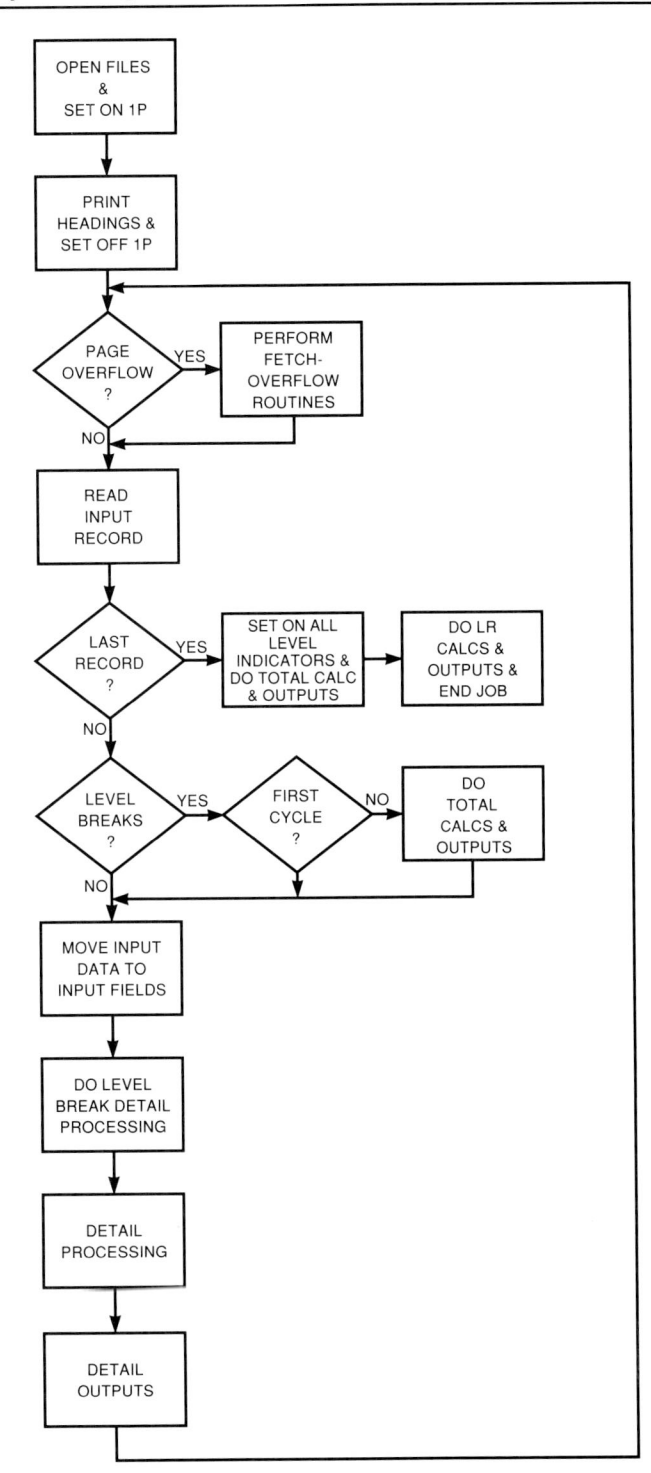

```
         ┌──────────────┐
         │  OPEN FILES  │
         │      &       │
         │  SET ON 1P   │
         └──────┬───────┘
                ▼
         ┌──────────────┐
         │    PRINT     │
         │  HEADINGS &  │◄─────────────────────────────┐
         │ SET OFF 1P   │                              │
         └──────┬───────┘                              │
                ▼                                      │
         ┌──────────┐  YES  ┌──────────────┐           │
         │   PAGE   ├──────►│   PERFORM    │           │
         │ OVERFLOW │       │    FETCH-    │           │
         │    ?     │       │   OVERFLOW   │           │
         └────┬─────┘       │   ROUTINES   │           │
           NO │             └──────┬───────┘           │
              │◄───────────────────┘                   │
              ▼                                        │
         ┌──────────────┐                              │
         │    READ      │                              │
         │    INPUT     │                              │
         │   RECORD     │                              │
         └──────┬───────┘                              │
                ▼                                      │
         ┌──────────┐  YES ┌──────────────┐  ┌───────┐ │
         │   LAST   ├─────►│  SET ON ALL  │  │ DO LR │ │
         │  RECORD  │      │    LEVEL     │  │CALCS &│ │
         │    ?     │      │ INDICATORS & ├─►│OUTPUTS│ │
         └────┬─────┘      │DO TOTAL CALC │  │& END  │ │
           NO │            │  & OUTPUTS   │  │  JOB  │ │
              ▼            └──────────────┘  └───────┘ │
         ┌──────────┐  YES ┌──────────┐ NO ┌────────┐  │
         │  LEVEL   ├─────►│  FIRST   ├───►│   DO   │  │
         │  BREAKS  │      │  CYCLE   │    │ TOTAL  │  │
         │    ?     │      │    ?     │    │CALCS & │  │
         └────┬─────┘      └─────┬────┘    │OUTPUTS │  │
           NO │                  │         └───┬────┘  │
              │◄─────────────────┴─────────────┘       │
              ▼                                        │
         ┌──────────────┐                              │
         │  MOVE INPUT  │                              │
         │   DATA TO    │                              │
         │ INPUT FIELDS │                              │
         └──────┬───────┘                              │
                ▼                                      │
         ┌──────────────┐                              │
         │  DO LEVEL    │                              │
         │ BREAK DETAIL │                              │
         │ PROCESSING   │                              │
         └──────┬───────┘                              │
                ▼                                      │
         ┌──────────────┐                              │
         │    DETAIL    │                              │
         │  PROCESSING  │                              │
         └──────┬───────┘                              │
                ▼                                      │
         ┌──────────────┐                              │
         │    DETAIL    │                              │
         │   OUTPUTS    ├──────────────────────────────┘
         └──────────────┘
```

In the calculations, the total amount of the loan is divided by the number of months, giving the amount of each payment. A small remainder may exist and this will become the final payment. (In the real world of finance, these calculations would be much more complex.)

It is necessary to set up a loop to determine the due dates. The loop will control the total number of lines printed for each customer. This will be the number of months for which the loan was incurred. There may also be one more line printed to show a final payment due if there is a remainder. Each line of the month field is incremented by 1 until it reaches 12 to allow the program to print the correct number of the month for each payment.

FIGURE 6.9 Sample Report

```
ACCT#     MONTH     PAYMENT DUE
10304      01         250.00
           02         250.00
           03         250.00
           04         250.00
           05         250.00
           06         250.00
           07         250.00
           08         250.00
           09         250.00
           10         250.00
           11         250.00
           12         250.00
                       .00  FINAL BALANCE
```

To simplify the example, the year is omitted and all loans are assumed to be due on the first of the month. The input record will contain the beginning month as well as the total number of months for which the loan will run. Figures 6.10(a), 6.10(b), 6.10(c), and 6.10(d) show the Specifications forms for this program. Note the entry *F* in column 16 in Figure 6.10(d) to indicate fetch overflow.

The value of the field called MONTH is incremented by 1 each time a line is printed. For example, if the field initially contained 03, the first payment date would be 03/01 (the first of March). The next time through the loop MONTH would contain 04. MONTH is compared to 12 each time, and when it is greater than 12 it is reset to 01 using the Z-ADD operation.

The loop is controlled by the field called TERM, which contains the number of months for the loan. This field will begin with the total number of months. Each time the loop is performed, the program will subtract 1 from TERM. TERM is compared to zero each time through the loop; once TERM equals zero, all lines have been printed.

At that time control of the program will end the loop and perform a final compare of the remainder field. If the remainder is not equal to zero, the month field will be incremented by 1 and a line will be printed for the amount of the remainder.

FIGURE 6.10(a) Program Using Fetch Overflow: File Description Specifications

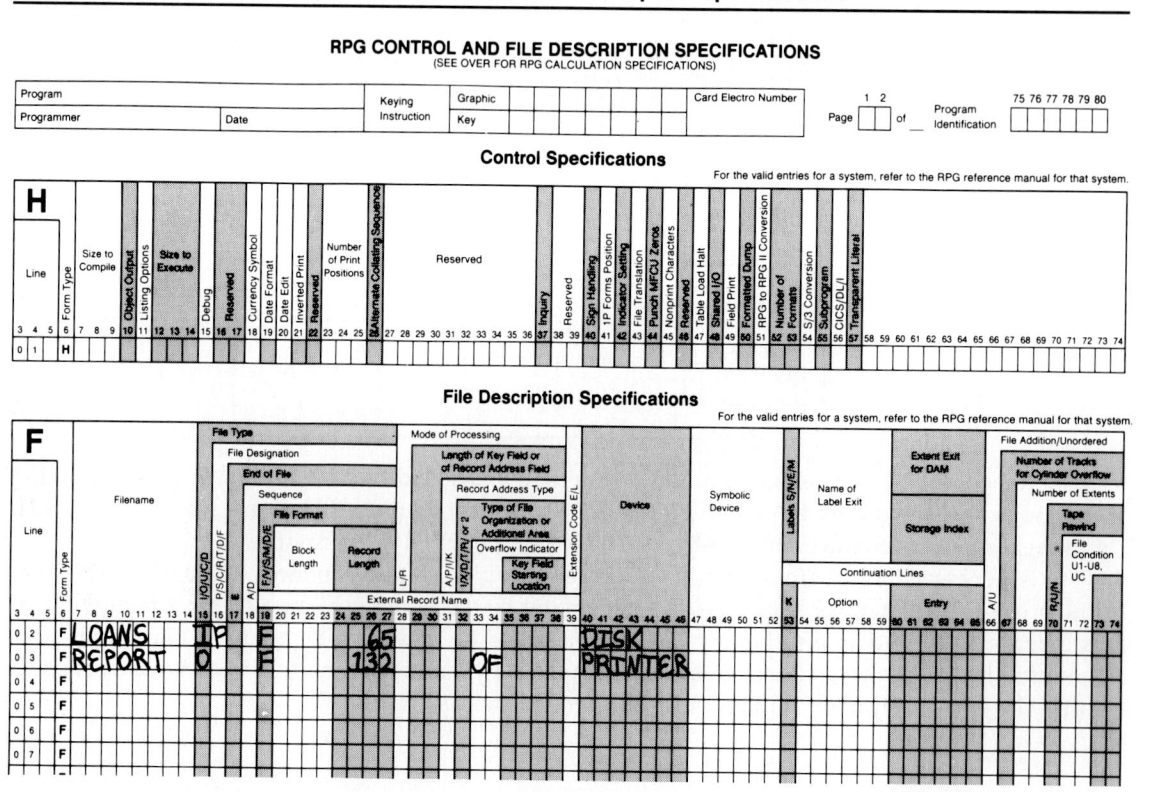

FIGURE 6.10(b) Input Specifications

RPG INPUT SPECIFICATIONS

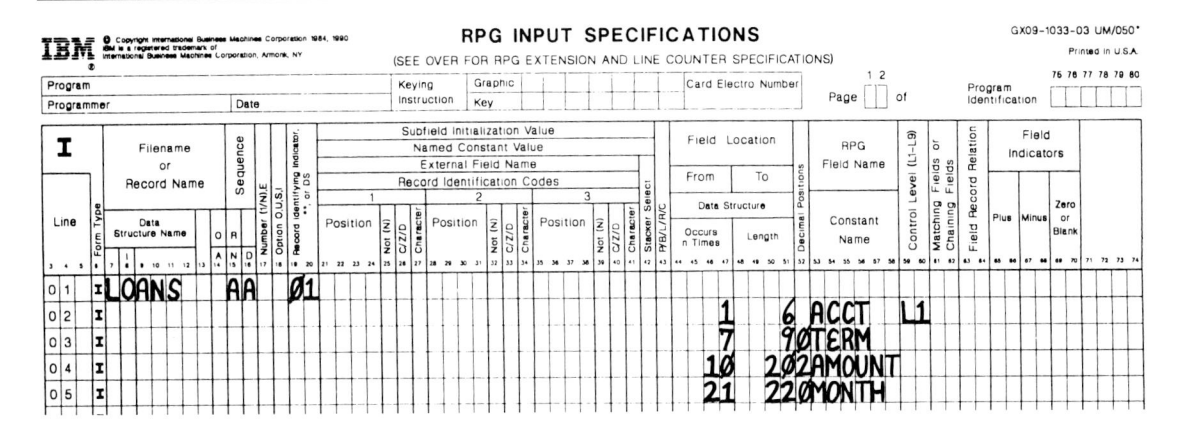

Line	Form Type	Filename or Record Name	Sequence	Number (1/N1)	Option O,U,S,I	Record Identifying Indicator or ** or DS	Position	Not (N)	C/Z/D	Character	Position	Not (N)	C/Z/D	Character	Position	Not (N)	C/Z/D	Character	Stacker Select	P/B/L/A/C	From	To	Decimal Positions	Field Name	Control Level (L1-L9)	Matching Fields or Chaining Fields	Field Record Relation	Plus	Minus	Zero or Blank
01	I	LOANS	AA			01																								
02	I																			1	6		ACCT	L1					
03	I																			7	9	0	TERM						
04	I																			10	20	2	AMOUNT						
05	I																			21	22	0	MONTH						

FIGURE 6.10(c) Calculation Specifications

RPG CALCULATION SPECIFICATIONS

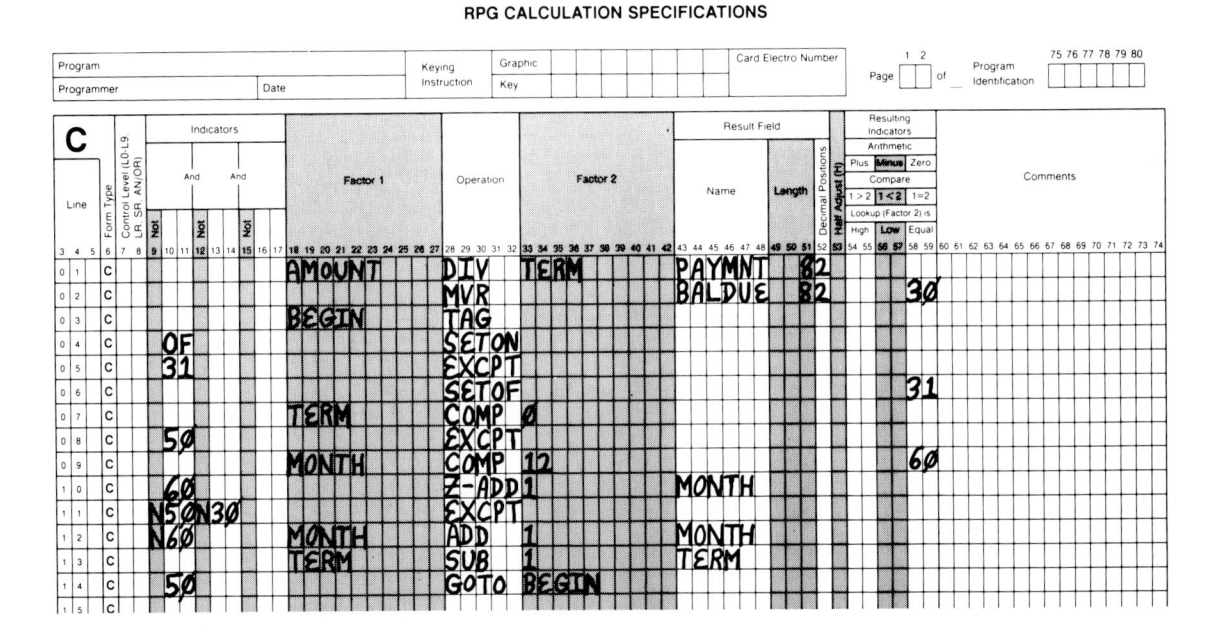

Line	Form Type	Control Level (L0-L9, LR, SR, AN/OR)	Ind Not	Ind And Not	Ind And Not	Factor 1	Operation	Factor 2	Result Field Name	Length	Decimal Positions	Half Adjust (H)	Plus (High)	Minus (Low)	Zero (Equal)	Comments
01	C					AMOUNT	DIV	TERM	PAYMNT	8	2					
02	C						MVR		BALDUE	8	2				30	
03	C					BEGIN	TAG									
04	C		OF				SETON									
05	C		31				EXCPT									
06	C						SETOF								31	
07	C					TERM	COMP	0								
08	C		50				EXCPT									
09	C					MONTH	COMP	12							60	
10	C		60				Z-ADD	1	MONTH							
11	C		N50	N30			EXCPT									
12	C		N60			MONTH	ADD	1	MONTH							
13	C					TERM	SUB	1	TERM							
14	C		50				GOTO	BEGIN								
15	C															

FIGURE 6.10(d) Output Specifications Using Fetch Overflow

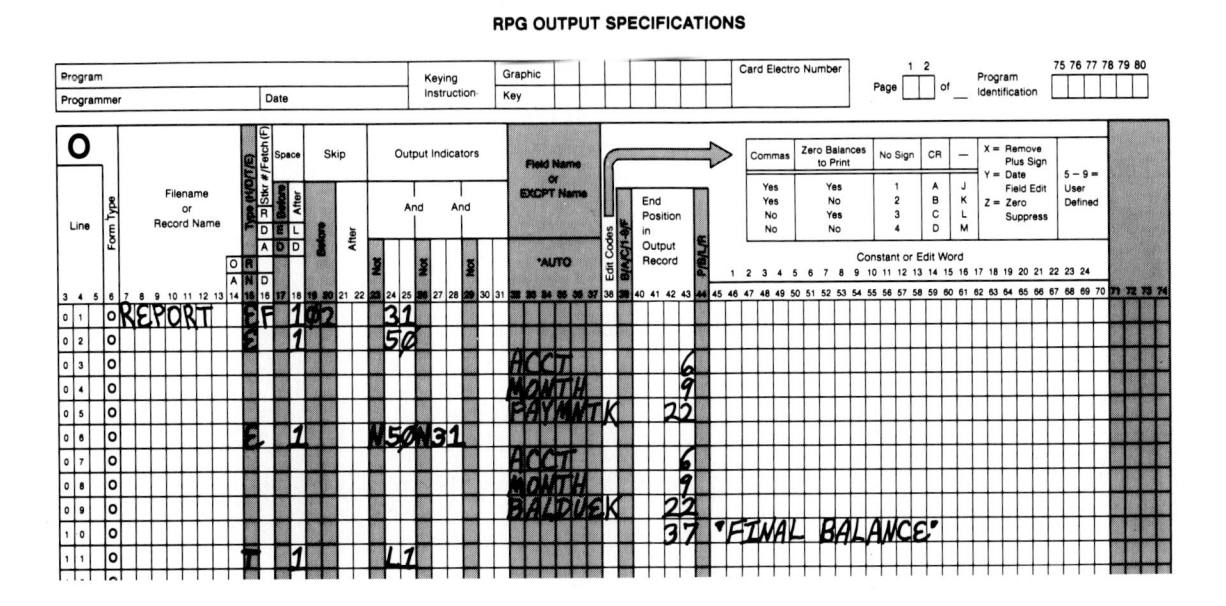

RPG OUTPUT SPECIFICATIONS

Line	Form Type	Filename or Record Name	Type (H/D/T/E)	Stkr #/Fetch (F)	Space Before	Space After	Skip Before	Skip After	Output Indicators	And	And	Field Name or EXCPT Name	Edit Codes	B/A/C/D	P/B/L/R	End Position in Output Record	Constant or Edit Word
01	O	REPORT	D	F	1	02			31								
02	O					1			50								
03	O											ACCT				6	
04	O											MONTH				9	
05	O											PAYMNT	K			22	
06	O		E		1				N50	N31							
07	O											ACCT				6	
08	O											MONTH				9	
09	O											BALDUE	K			22	
10	O															37	'FINAL BALANCE'
11	O		T		1				L1								

Internal Control (Line Counting)

Although RPG provides the ease of using automatic control of the page overflow, some programmers prefer to handle the overflow problem themselves. Programmers often encounter unusual problems, such as the need to print nonstandard-size forms (3-1/2-inch-wide checks or inventory tags, for example) or the need to print varying numbers of lines of print (for example, invoices that might have from 1 to 200 lines and require one or several invoice forms per customer). Some printers can accommodate various "lines per inch" of print, and this can also present programming problems.

It is usually simpler in these unusual situations to manage the overflow and headings within the calculations. The sample code in Figures 6.11 and 6.12 demonstrates the line-counting method for controlling page overflow.

Exception output processing can be used to control the overflow by counting the number of lines printed. A counter is set up (initialized to zero) and 1 is added to it every time a line is printed. In this example, this data is placed in a field called COUNT. The COUNT field is compared to some desired number of lines per page. When the desired number of lines has been reached, the overflow indicator is turned on and headings are printed (and any other desired functions are performed). The COUNT field is then reset to zero to prepare for the next page. Note that the field COUNT is not a reserved word and any field name may be assigned.

Conventional computer paper (printing at 6 lines per inch) will hold approximately 66 lines of print. Allowing for some white space at top and bottom of the report, a good line count per page might be 60, but this will vary depending on the needs of the users or the whim of the programmer.

Note that the headings for the first page in this example will print because indicator 45 is off when the first record is read. For all other pages, the headings will be controlled entirely by the line count.

FIGURE 6.11 Line Counting Method for Controlling the Page Overflow: Calculation Specifications

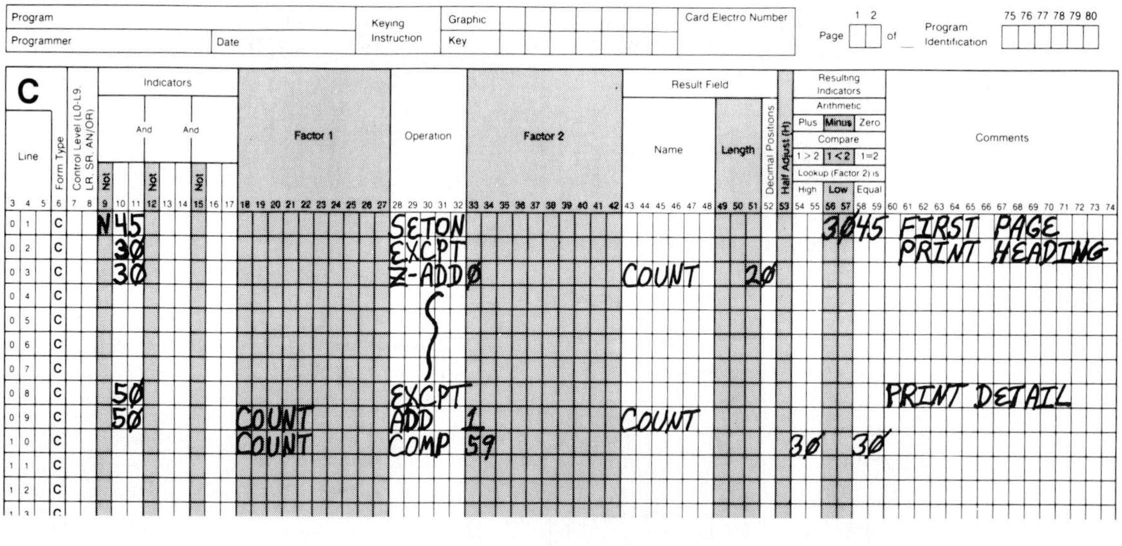

```
Line  Indicators           Factor 1   Operation  Factor 2   Result    Length   Comments
                                                            Field
01  C  N45                             SETON                                    3045 FIRST PAGE
02  C  30                              EXCPT                                         PRINT HEADING
03  C  30                              Z-ADD   0   COUNT     20
04  C
05  C
06  C
07  C
08  C                                  EXCPT                                         PRINT DETAIL
09  C  50                              ADD     1   COUNT
10  C         COUNT                    COMP    59                      30 30
11  C
12  C
13  C
```

FIGURE 6.12 Output Specifications

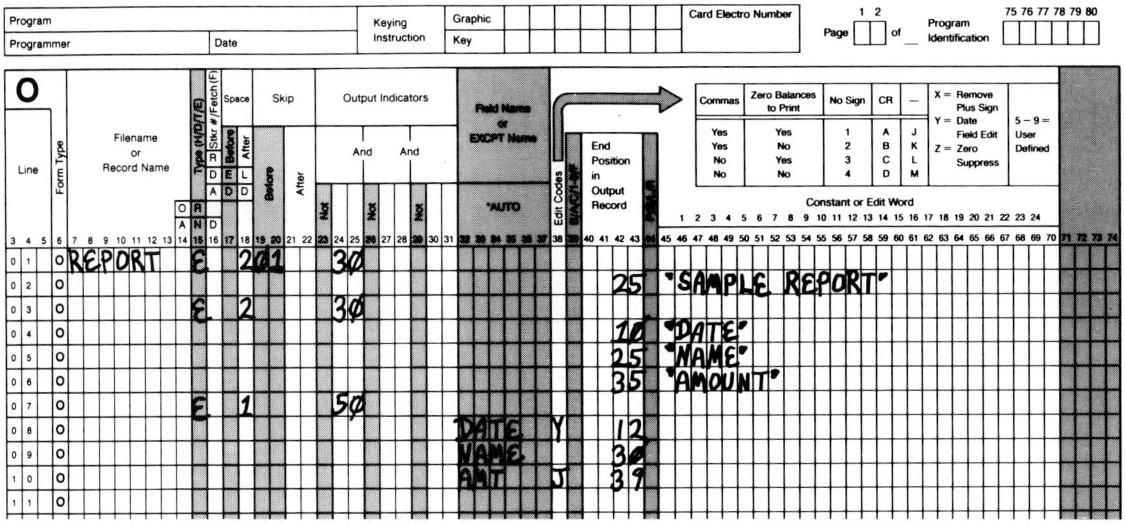

RPG OUTPUT SPECIFICATIONS

Line	Form Type	Filename or Record Name	Type (H/D/T/E)	Space / Skip	Output Indicators	Field Name or EXCPT Name	Edit Codes	End Position in Output Record	Constant or Edit Word
01	O	REPORT	E	2Ø1	3Ø				
02	O							25	'SAMPLE REPORT'
03	O		E	2	3Ø				
04	O							10	'DATE'
05	O							25	'NAME'
06	O							35	'AMOUNT'
07	O		E	1	5Ø				
08	O					DATE	Y	12	
09	O					NAME		3Ø	
10	O					AMT	J	39	
11	O								

MOVING DATA (MOVE AND MOVEL) ▪

In earlier sample programs, it was necessary to reset fields to zero using the Z-ADD operation. This operation is used when the field is a numeric field. If the field is alphanumeric, however, the problem requires a different solution.

Sometimes it is necessary to force a specific value into a data field. This is done in RPG with the MOVE or MOVEL operation codes. The example in Figure 6.13 shows that both operations are coded in a similar manner. Factor 1 remains blank, and MOVE or MOVEL is specified in the operation field. Factor 2 contains the field name for the data to be moved, and the result field contains the name of the field to which the data is being moved.

Although the operation is called MOVE, RPG does not really move the data. It is *copied* from one field into another. After the MOVE operation has been completed, there will be two copies of the data.

The MOVE and MOVEL operations cause the new data to *replace* whatever is contained in the result field. Thus, if the field OUTDAT originally contained the date 060190, after the move it might contain the date 071592. The old date would be overlaid or replaced by the new date. The number of characters moved by the MOVE or MOVEL operations depends on the lengths of the fields specified in factor 2 and the result field.

The MOVE operation moves data beginning at the rightmost column of the "from" field (factor 2) into the rightmost column of the result field. The MOVEL operation moves data beginning at the leftmost column of the "from" field (factor 2) into the leftmost column of the result field.

When both the "from" and "to" fields contain the same number of characters, it makes no difference whether a MOVE or MOVEL operation is used. All the characters in the "from" field will be copied into the result field in either case.

It is only when the programmer wishes to manipulate the contents of a field in some manner that it becomes useful to use fields of different lengths and to manage that data using MOVE or MOVEL. Generally, the use of this technique will be dictated by the nature of the problem.

FIGURE 6.13 MOVE and MOVEL

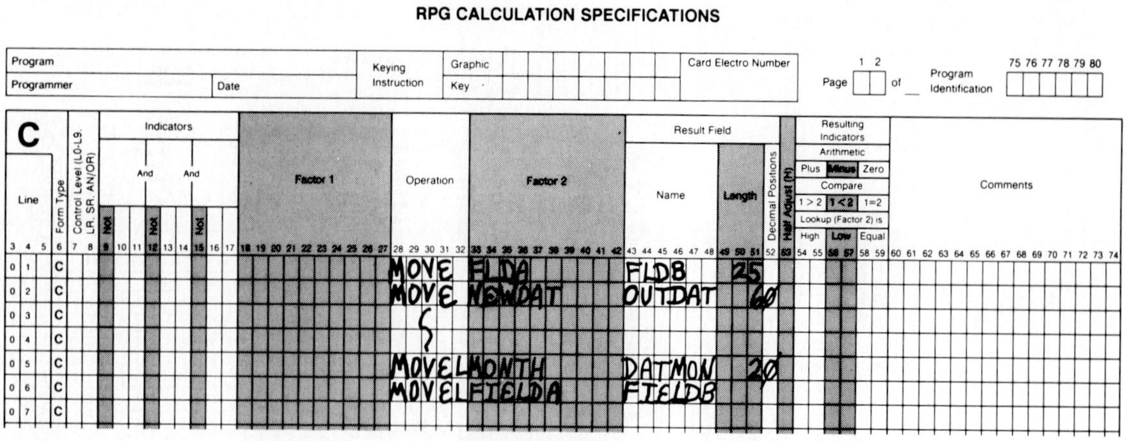

RPG CALCULATION SPECIFICATIONS

Line	Form Type	Control Level	Indicators (And/And/Not)	Factor 1	Operation	Factor 2	Result Field Name	Length	Decimal Positions	Half Adjust (H)	Resulting Indicators	Comments
01	C				MOVE	FLDA	FLDB	25				
02	C				MOVE	NEWDAT	OUTDAT	60				
03	C											
04	C											
05	C				MOVEL	MONTH	DATMON	20				
06	C				MOVEL	FIELDA	FIELDB					
07	C											

Moving Fields of Different Lengths with MOVE

Using the MOVE operation code, data is copied beginning from the rightmost column of the "from" field into the rightmost column of the result field. If factor 2 is longer than the result field, the leftmost positions of factor 2 will not appear in the result field. Figure 6.14 shows the results of this type of move.

If the result field is longer than the field in factor 2, the leftmost positions of the result field will not be changed. Figure 6.15 shows the results of this type of move. Notice that the unchanged portion of the result field *might not* contain blanks. If the result field already contains some data, that data will remain and only the rightmost positions are replaced with the data from factor 2. This can be very useful, but it could cause problems if the programmer had expected automatic blanking.

Moving Fields of Different Lengths with MOVEL

Using the MOVEL operation code, data is copied beginning from the leftmost column of the "from" field into the leftmost column of the result field. If factor 2 is longer than the result field, the rightmost positions of factor 2 will not appear in the result field. Figure 6.16 shows the results of this type of move.

FIGURE 6.14 Examples of MOVE of Long to Short Fields

MOVE OPERATION		
"From" Field	Result Field Before	Result Field After
0 3 0 2 9 0		9 0
0 1 0 6 9 3		9 3
0 4 0 8 9 5	8 8	9 5

FIGURE 6.15 Examples of MOVE of Short to Long Fields

MOVE OPERATION		
"From" Field	Result Field Before	After
9 0	0 3 0 2 8 6	0 3 0 2 9 0
9 3	0 1 0 6 9 9	0 1 0 6 9 3
9 5		9 5

FIGURE 6.16 Examples of MOVEL of Long to Short Fields

MOVEL OPERATION		
"From" Field	Result Field Before	After
M E D I C A L	0 0 3	M E D
C O N S T R U C T	0 0 5	C O N
L A W Y E R	0 1 4	L A W
T E C H N I C A L	3 8 1	T E C

FIGURE 6.17 Examples of MOVEL of Short to Long Fields

MOVEL OPERATION		
"From" Field	Result Field Before	After
0 1	1 2 0 1 9 1	0 1 0 1 9 1
0 1	0 3 0 4 9 6	0 1 0 4 9 6
0 1		0 1

If the result field is longer than the field in factor 2, the rightmost positions of the result field will not be changed. Figure 6.17 shows the results of this type of move. As was the case for the MOVE operation, if the result field had already contained some data, that data will remain and only the leftmost positions are replaced with the data from factor 2.

Alphanumeric/Numeric MOVE or MOVEL

The MOVE and MOVEL operations permit the movement of data from alphanumeric to alphanumeric field, numeric to numeric field, numeric to alphanumeric field, or even alphanumeric to numeric field.

Care must be taken when specifying numeric result fields so that the accuracy of the sign (positive or negative) is retained. Although RPG attempts to retain the integrity of the sign for numeric fields when moving from numeric to numeric fields even when field lengths differ, it is usually a better programming practice to use Z-ADD for transferring numeric data from one numeric field to another.

When moving from numeric to numeric fields, there is always a danger of moving fewer than the required number of positions to the resulting numeric field. For example, when moving a four-position numeric field to a six-position numeric field, one could overlook the fact that a six-position numeric field will contain four digits preceded by two blanks. Although some computers will automatically put the two leading zeros in for numeric fields, there are some computers that will allow the leading blanks to remain and wait until a calculation is being performed to let the programmer know that disaster is imminent. This is another good reason for using the Z-ADD for numeric fields.

If alphabetic data is encountered when attempting arithmetic functions on the numeric result field, there is a good possibility that the computer will not be able to handle it and the program will terminate with a halt, a failure, or a system dump. Even if the program were able to do the calculations, the results would be meaningless.

Sometimes the programmer will have some prior knowledge that the input field will always contain valid numeric data. If the input field were defined as alphanumeric and the program needed to perform calculations on this field, the only way to transform the field in this case would be to use the MOVE operation.

Moving Literal Values

It is possible to move a literal into a field. This can be very useful for moving some fixed data into a field. In previous chapters, the Z-ADD operation was used to initialize a field to zero (or to some other constant). To move an alphanumeric constant (such as blank characters) into a field, the MOVE or MOVEL operation is used. Figure 6.18 shows an example of this operation.

When moving alphanumeric literals, factor 2 will contain the literal. An alphanumeric literal is enclosed in quotation marks (single quotation marks for IBM computers and conventional quotation marks for other computers, as explained in earlier chapters). This limits the size of the literal to a maximum of eight characters, although a longer literal could be created by using more than one operation, as shown in Figure 6.19.

Numeric literals may also be moved to a field, but it is usually a safer practice to use a Z-ADD operation to ensure that the field is properly zero-filled and signed.

FIGURE 6.18 Moving Alphabetic Literals Including Blanks

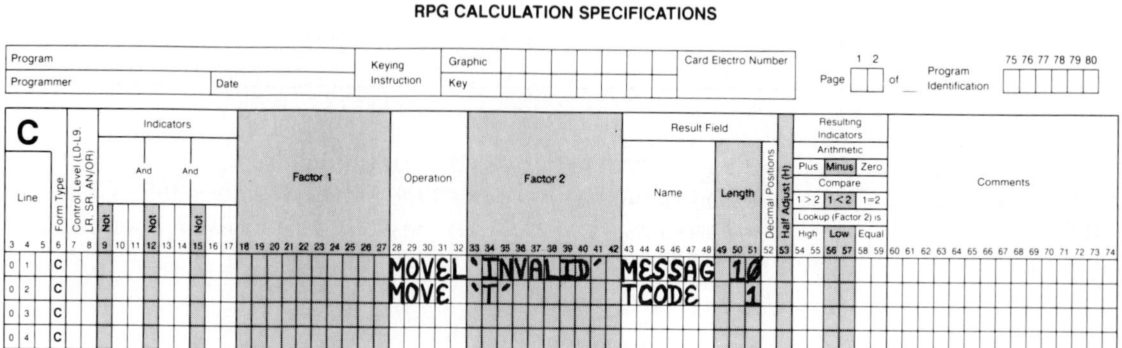

FIGURE 6.19 Moving a Long Literal

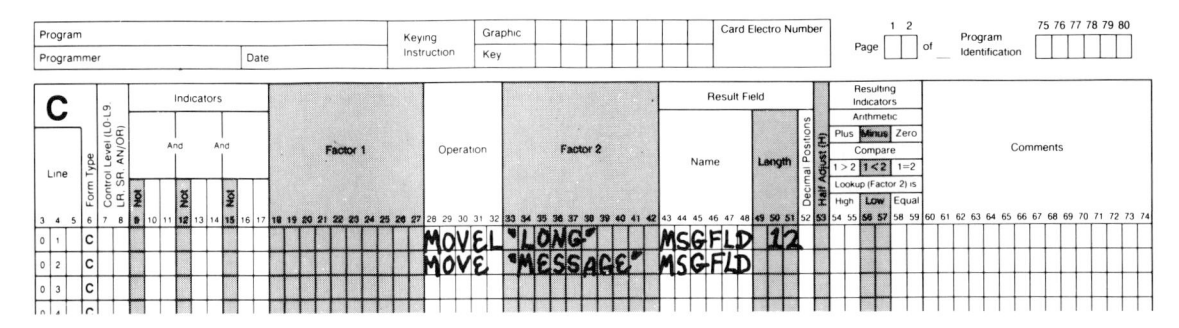

```
     MOVEL 'LONG'     MSGFLD 12
     MOVE  'MESSAGE'  MSGFLD
```

Initializing a Field to Blanks

It is useful to move blanks to a field for a variety of reasons. When the field is large (for example, a description field of 30 positions), however, moving a literal of blanks into it won't work. Of course, RPG will initialize the field at the beginning of the program, but once data is moved into the field it will remain there until something else is moved into it.

The ideal method to avoid repeating unwanted data line after line on a report is as follows:

1. Move one or more blanks into a field, defined with the length of the field that will need to be blanked out later. (In the above problem the length would be 30.)
2. When the program requires that the description field be cleared out, perform a MOVE to move the field from step 1 into the description field.
3. Never move any data of any kind (other than the blanks) into the initial field.

Figure 6.20 shows the coding for providing such a "blank bucket" for any program.

Because the initial field is never used for anything other than blanks, it will always safely contain blanks that may be used throughout the program to clear any alphabetic field of any length (up to 30 positions).

FIGURE 6.20 Moving Blanks

```
           MOVE  ' '       BLANKS 30
           ...
        30 MOVE  PNNUM     PART#  20
       N30 MOVE  BLANKS    PART#
       N30 MOVE  BLANKS    DESCR  30
```

Chapter 6 Exception Output Processing

SUMMARY ■

Earlier chapters covered functions that are performed automatically, such as the fixed logic cycle and the automatic page overflow control. With the material in this chapter, the programmer can begin to take over any of these operations and force them to be performed when needed.

In this chapter you have learned that although the fixed logic cycle is a very useful feature for printing simple reports, a complex report or format may require human skill and logic to create a program that produces a customized product.

You have learned that the use of exception output processing and page overflow control puts the programmer back in control. Exception output means that lines can be forced to print during calculation time on an as-needed basis. Control of the page overflow means that overflow, headings, and totals can be forced to occur at the precise time they are needed instead of by some predetermined cycle.

You have learned the MOVE and MOVEL operation codes, which give the programmer the power to reformat and restructure data, clear out fields, and manipulate fields to produce desired results.

Most of the basic functions of RPG have now been covered. You should be able to produce a program for any type of report needed.

REVIEW QUESTIONS

1. Define exception output.
2. The operation code used to produce output at exception time is the _____ code.
3. What entry is needed on the Output Specifications to define exception output?
4. What are some good applications for the exception output operation?
5. What happens to the RPG fixed logic cycle when exception output is used?
6. What kinds of problems are encountered in using page overflow with a report for which exception output is used?
7. Explain the use of the MOVE operation.
8. After a MOVE operation has been performed, what will be found in the original field from which the data was moved?
9. When a field of 10 positions is moved into a field of 5 positions using the MOVE operation, what will be contained in the resulting field?
10. When a field of 10 positions is moved into a field of 5 positions using the MOVEL operation, what will be contained in the resulting field?
11. What is the danger in performing moves to numeric data?
12. Is it possible to perform a MOVE or MOVEL operation on literal data?
13. When the MOVE operation is performed, the value of the originating field is moved to the _____ position of the receiving field.
14. When the MOVEL operation is performed, the value of the originating field is moved to the _____ position of the receiving field.
15. Why is there no need in RPG for a "move right" operation?

EXERCISES

1. On a Calculation Specifications form, enter the coding that will cause four identical sets of labels to be printed sequentially using exception processing.
2. On an Output Specifications form, enter the coding that will be needed to complete the exception processing for question 1.
3. On a Calculation Specifications form, enter the coding to move data from a 5-position field (FLD1) to another 5-position field (FLD2).
4. On a Calculation Specifications form, enter the coding to move a 5-position literal (TOTAL) to the rightmost position of a 10-position field named TOTAL.
5. What will be the contents of the result field after the MOVE operation has been executed? (FLD1 is a 25-position field containing the words THIS IS A TEST.)

Result Field (25 positions) (before MOVE)	Result Field (25 positions) (after MOVE)
a. THIS IS NOT A TEST	_____
b.	_____
c. THIS IS A xxxx TO xxxx	_____
d. TEST TIME	_____

6. What will be the contents of the result field after the MOVEL operation has been executed? (FLD1 is a 25-position field containing the words THIS IS A TEST.)

Result Field (before MOVEL)	Result Field (after MOVEL)
a. THIS IS NOT A TEST	_____
b.	_____
c. THIS IS A xxxx TO xxxx	_____
d. TEST TIME	_____

DEBUGGING EXERCISES

Instructions

The following RPG programs contain an error or errors. Some of these errors are indicated by the RPG compiler on the program listing. A list of syntax errors is given at the end of the program listing. Other types of errors may occur which will not be shown. These are called logic errors.

Study each program and its syntax errors. Locate each error (including logic errors) and on a separate coding form make the correct entry for the line(s) in error.

Explain each error and how it should be corrected.

```
         100    F* TITLE: DEBUG PROJECT 6-A
         200    F* DATE:  4/7           AUTHOR: D.CABLE
         300    F* DESCRIPTION: PRINT EMPLOYEE NAME/ADDR 3 TIMES-EXCEPTION OUTPUT
         400    F*************************************************************
         500    F* MODIFICATIONS:
         600    F* NO.       DATE      INIT       DESCRIPTION
         700    F*           XX/XX/XX  XXX        XXXXXXXXXXXXXXXXXXXXXXXXXXXXX
         800    F*************************************************************

NAME OF PROGRAM WILL BE PJ006A IN LIBRARY CABLE

                H
* 1019                    ALL DECIMAL DATA ERRORS IGNORED
         900    FEMPMAST IP  F      120           DISK
        1000    FREPORT  O   F      132     OF    PRINTER
        1100    F*************************************************************

        1200    IEMPMAST AA   01
        1300    I                                              1   2 EMPDIV
        1400    I                                              3   4 EMPDPT
        1500    I                                              5  60EMPHMO
        1600    I                                              7  80EMPHDA
        1700    I                                              9 100EMPHYR
        1800    I                                             11  13 EMPNO    L1
        1900    I                                             14  29 EMPNAM
        2000    I                                             30  30 EMPTYP
        2100    I                                             31  46 EMPADR
        2200    I                                             47  57 EMPCTY

        2300    C                    Z-ADD0     CNT     40
        2400    C           EMPTYP   COMP  'A'                    75
        2500    C* PRINT THREE TIMES
        2600    C                    CNT  COMP  3                 33
        2700    C   N33 75           EXCPT
        2800    C           CNT      ADD   1     CNT
        2900    C                    GOTO  AGAIN

        3000    O        E   1       33
* 6001 6001-********  .
* 6035                6035-******
        3100    O                          EMPNO      5
        3200    O                          EMPNAM    30
        3300    O        E   1       33
* 6001 6001-********  .
* 6035                6035-******
        3400    O                          EMPADR    35
```

```
        SEQUENCE    1         2         3         4         5         6         7
        NUMBER      67890123456789012345678901234567890123456789012345678901234567890

          3500  O           E  1      33
* 6001  6001-********  .
* 6035              6035-******

          3600  O                              EMPCTY    35
    * * * * * E N D   O F   S O U R C E * * * * *



* 7086       900    RPG PROVIDES BLOCK/UNBLOCK SUPPORT FOR FILE EMPMAST.
* 7064      1000    REPORT FILE NOT REFERENCED FOR OUTPUT
* 7043      2900    AGAIN NOT LABEL OF TAG OR ENDSR




        CROSS-REFERENCE LISTING



              FILE/RCD      DEV/RCD       REFERENCES (D=DEFINED)

          01  EMPMAST       DISK          900D  1200
          02  REPORT        PRINTER       1000D



              FIELD         ATTR          REFERENCES (M=MODIFIED D=DEFINED)

* 7030    AGAIN         A(4)          2900
          CNT           P(4,0)        2300D  2600   2800   2800M
          EMPADR        A(16)         2100D  3400
          EMPCTY        A(11)         2200D  3600
* 7031    EMPDIV        A(2)          1300D
* 7031    EMPDPT        A(2)          1400D
* 7031    EMPHDA        P(2,0)        1600D
* 7031    EMPHMO        P(2,0)        1500D
* 7031    EMPHYR        P(2,0)        1700D
          EMPNAM        A(16)         1900D  3200
          EMPNO         A(3)          1800D  3100
          EMPTYP        A(1)          2000D  2400
          'A'           LITERAL       2400
          0             LITERAL       2300
          1             LITERAL       2800
          3             LITERAL       2600


              INDICATOR     REFERENCES (M=MODIFIED D=DEFINED)

              LR            900D

* 7030    L1            1800
* 7031    OF            1000D
* 7031    01            1200M
          33            2600M  2700   3000   3300   3500
          75            2400M  2700



        MESSAGES

        MSGID       SEV    NUMBER     TEXT

* QRG1019     00      1        IGNDECERR(*YES) SPECIFIED ON COMMAND. NO DECIMAL DATA ERRORS
* QRG6001     40      3        FILE/RECORD NAME NOT VALID, NOT DEFINED, IGNORED, OR MISSING
                               VALID TYPE FOUND
* QRG6035     20      3        SPACE OR SKIP MUST BE SPECIFIED ONLY FOR PROGRAM DESCRIBED F
                               ASSUMED.
```

* QRG7030	30	2	FIELD OR INDICATOR NOT DEFINED.	
* QRG7031	00	7	NAME OR INDICATOR NOT REFERENCED.	
* QRG7043	30	1	FACTOR 2 (POSITIONS 33-42) OR RESULT FIELD (POSITIONS 43-48) NOT TAG OR ENDSR. LINE IGNORED	
* QRG7064	40	1	PROGRAM FILE NOT REFERENCED. FILE IGNORED	
* QRG7086	00	1	RPG WILL HANDLE BLOCKING FUNCTION FOR THE FILE. INFDS CONTENT ARE TRANSFERRED.	

MESSAGE SUMMARY

TOTAL	00	10	20	30	40	50
19	9	0	3	3	4	0

36 RECORDS READ FROM SOURCE FILE
SOURCE RECORDS INCLUDE   26 SPECIFICATIONS,   0 TABLE RECORDS, AND   10 COMMENTS

QRG0008 COMPILE TERMINATED. SEVERITY 40 ERRORS FOUND IN PROGRAM

* * * * * E N D   O F   C O M P I L A T I O N * * * * *
* QRG1020   ERROR OCCURRED CREATING OR UPDATING DATA AREA RETURNCODE. COMPIL

```
       100   F* TITLE: DEBUG PROJECT 6-3
       200   F* DATE:  4/7          AUTHOR: D.CABLE
       300   F* DESCRIPTION: INVENTORY VALUE REPORT - EXCEPTION OUTPUT
       400   F****************************************************
       500   F* MODIFICATIONS:
       600   F* NO.     DATE      INIT      DESCRIPTION
       700   F*         XX/XX/XX  XXX       XXXXXXXXXXXXXXXXXXXXXXXXXXXXXX
       800   F****************************************************

       NAME OF PROGRAM WILL BE PJ006B IN LIBRARY CABLE

             H
* 1019              ALL DECIMAL DATA ERRORS IGNORED
       900   FPARTS   IP  F      120            DISK
      1000   FREPORT  O   F      132       OF   PRINTER
      1100   F****************************************************

      1200   IPARTS    AA  01
      1300   I                                      1  10 PARTNO
      1400   I                                     11  26 DESCR
      1500   I                                     27  27 CLAS
      1600   I                                     28  322UPRC
      1700   I                                     33  370QTY

      1800   C                          SETON                         55
      1900   C             CNT          ADD  1         CNT     40
      2000   C                          CLAS COMP 'A'                    65
      2100   C                          CLAS COMP 'B'                    66
      2200   C                          CLAS COMP 'C'                    67
      2300   C   N65N66N67              SETON                         55
      2400   C   55                     EXCPT
      2500   C             FINVAL       ADD  EXPRC    FINVAL 102

      2600   OREPORT   H  203      1P
      2700   O         OR           OF
      2800   O                                         6 'PJ006B'
      2900   O                                UDATE Y 50
      3000   O                                        30 'TOTAL INVENTORY VALUE'
      3100   O         H  2        1P
      3200   O         OR           OF
      3300   O                                        11 'PART NUMBER'
      3400   O                                        25 'PART DESCR'
      3500   O                                        35 'UNIT PRICE'
      3600   O                                        40 'QUANTITY'
      3700   O                                        50 'TOTAL VALUE'
      3800   O         E  1        01
      3900   O                                PARTNO 10
      4000   O                                DESCR  30
```

```
SEQUENCE       1         2         3         4         5         6         7
NUMBER    67890123456789012345678901234567890123456789012345678901234567890123 4
    4100 O                              UPRC   K  33
    4200 O                              QTY    Z  38
    4300 O                              EXPRC  K  48
    4400 O           E  2     55
    4500 O                                         55 'TYPE CODE IS IN ERROR'
    4600 O           T  2     LR
    4700 O                                         15 'TOTAL VALUE'
    4800 O                              FINVALK   48
* * * * * E N D   O F   S O U R C E * * * * *


* 7086       900    RPG PROVIDES BLOCK/UNBLOCK SUPPORT FOR FILE PARTS.


    CROSS-REFERENCE LISTING

          FILE/RCD      DEV/RCD       REFERENCES (D=DEFINED)

      01  PARTS         DISK          900D 1200
      02  REPORT        PRINTER       1000D 2600  3100  3800  4400  4600



          FIELD         ATTR          REFERENCES (M=MODIFIED D=DEFINED)

          CLAS          A(1)          1500D 2000  2100  2200
          CNT           P(4,0)        1900  1900D
          DESCR         A(16)         1400D 4000
* 7030    EXPRC         P(5,0)        2500  4300
          FINVAL        P(10,2)       2500  2500D 4800
          PARTNO        A(10)         1300D 3900
          QTY           P(5,0)        1700D 4200
          UDATE         P(6,0)        2900
          UPRC          P(5,2)        1600D 4100
          'A'           LITERAL       2000
          'B'           LITERAL       2100
          'C'           LITERAL       2200
          1             LITERAL       1900


          INDICATOR     REFERENCES (M=MODIFIED D=DEFINED)

          LR            900D  4600
          OF            1000D 2700  3200
          01            1200M 3800
          1P            2600  3100
          55            1800M 2300M 2400  4400
          65            2000M 2300
          66            2100M 2300
          67            2200M 2300

MESSAGES

  MSGID      SEV   NUMBER    TEXT

* QRG1019    00    1         IGNDECERR(*YES) SPECIFIED ON COMMAND. NO DECIMAL DATA ERROR
* QRG7030    30    1         FIELD OR INDICATOR NOT DEFINED.
* QRG7086    00    1         RPG WILL HANDLE BLOCKING FUNCTION FOR THE FILE. INFDS CONTE
                             ARE TRANSFERRED.

MESSAGE SUMMARY

  TOTAL      00    10    20    30    40    50
    3        2     0     0     1     0     0

    48 RECORDS READ FROM SOURCE FILE
  SOURCE RECORDS INCLUDE   39 SPECIFICATIONS,   0 TABLE RECORDS, AND   9 COMMENTS


  QRG0008 COMPILE TERMINATED. SEVERITY 30 ERRORS FOUND IN PROGRAM

  * * * * * E N D   O F   C O M P I L A T I O N * * * * *
  * QRG1020              ERROR OCCURRED CREATING OR UPDATING DATA AREA RETURNCODE. COMP
```

PROGRAMMING PROJECT

Project Overview

A report is to be printed listing the payment dates which will be due on a loan. The original loan information is read and a payment schedule projected into the future for one year. Payments are due on the first of each month and all loans begin on January 1. Write the RPG program to produce this listing. Sample data for this project can be found in Appendix D.

Input Format

The input data for the project is found in a file called LOANS in the sample data. The Record Layout for this file is shown in Figure 6.21.

Processing

A record is read and the amount of the loan is divided by 12 (rounding the result if necessary). A line is printed showing the date and amount of the first payment. A line is printed for each month showing the amount due for each month. Each line is printed at exception time.

Output Format (Printer Spacing Chart)

The output format for the project is a report with standard headings. The report will show the loan number and the total amount of the loan on the first line, followed by the due date and the amount of each payment. The Printer Spacing Chart for this report is shown in Figure 6.22.

An example of the finished report is shown in Figure 6.23.

FIGURE 6.21 Programming Project: Record Layout

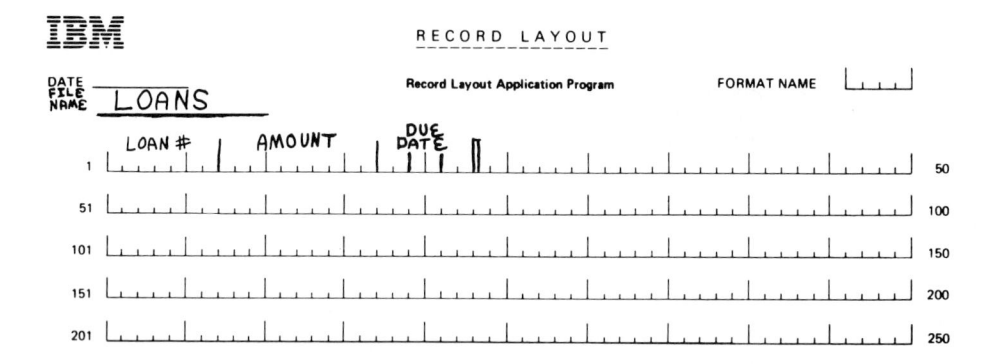

FIGURE 6.22 Programming Project: Printer Spacing Chart

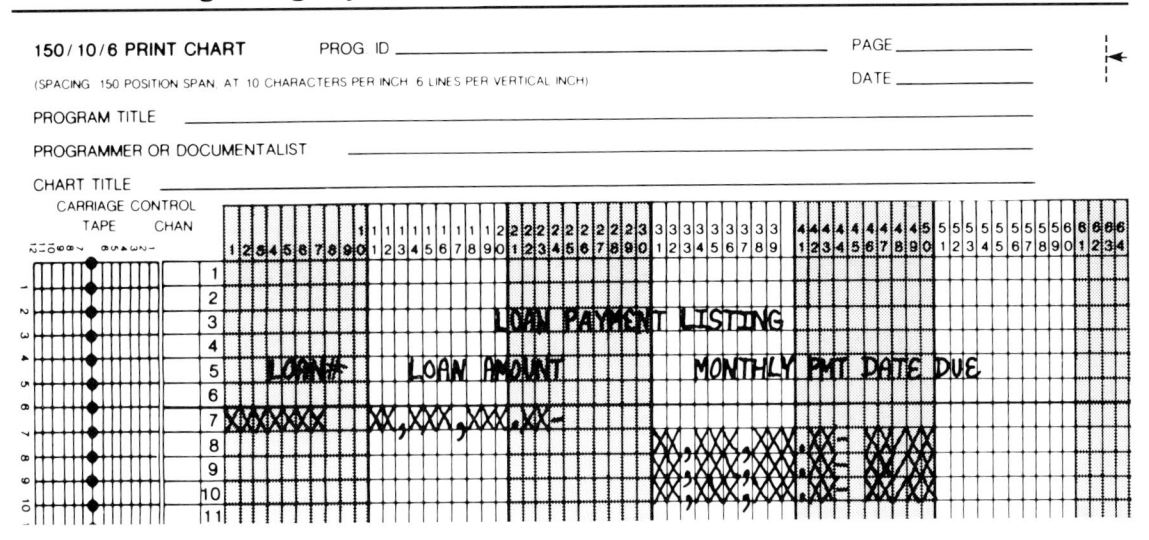

FIGURE 6.23 Programming Project: Final Report

```
                    LOAN PAYMENT LISTING
        LOAN#    LOAN AMOUNT    MONTHLY PMT  DATE DUE
        62589    10,528.98
                                   877.42    01/01
                                   877.42    02/01
                                   877.42    03/01
                                   877.42    04/01
                                   877.42    05/01
                                   877.42    06/01
                                   877.42    07/01
                                   877.42    08/01
                                   877.42    09/01
                                   877.42    10/01
                                   877.42    11/01
                                   877.42    12/01
        62378    35,872.18
                                 2,989.35    01/01
                                 2,989.35    02/01
                                 2,989.35    03/01
                                 2,989.35    04/01
                                 2,989.35    05/01
                                 2,989.35    06/01
                                 2,989.35    07/01
                                 2,989.35    08/01
                                 2,989.35    09/01
                                 2,989.35    10/01
                                 2,989.35    11/01
                                 2,989.35    12/01
        69875   128,585.00
                                10,715.42    01/01
                                10,715.42    02/01
                                10,715.42    03/01
                                10,715.42    04/01
                                10,715.42    05/01
                                10,715.42    06/01
                                10,715.42    07/01
                                10,715.42    08/01
                                10,715.42    09/01
                                10,715.42    10/01
                                10,715.42    11/01
                                10,715.42    12/01
```

Chapter 7

Table Processing

What you will learn in Chapter 7

Types of Table Applications
Benefits of Table Processing
Extension Specifications
Table File Formats
Types of Tables (Internal and External)
Internal (Compile Time) Table Entries
Sample Program 1 Using Internal or Compile Time Tables
   File Extension Specifications
   Record Layout
   Compiling Table Information
   Calculation Specifications for Processing Table Data

External (Pre-Execution Time) Table Entries
Sample Program 2 Using an External or Pre-Execution Time Table
   File Description Specifications
   Extension Specifications
   Record Layout
   Input Specifications
   Calculation Specifications
   Output Specifications
   Table Data File Maintenance

The Time at Which Table Data Is Available
Avoiding Common Errors
Alternating Tables
Sample Program 3 Using Alternating Table Data
   Input Specifications
   Calculation Specifications
   Output Specifications
Multiple Tables
Printing a Table

A table is a collection of data laid out in rows and columns. In computer programming, a table is a collection of similar or related data stored in consecutive locations in computer main memory for rapid access and simplicity of programming. Tables can be used in many business applications where a series of similar data needs to be analyzed, compared, or referenced.

TYPES OF TABLE APPLICATIONS ■

Three types of table applications are generally used in business programming: the simple table, the cross-reference table, and the range cross-reference table.

    The simple table contains a group of valid elements that can be accessed to verify the validity of a data field in an input file. It is also known as an argument table.

    The cross-reference table contains a group of valid elements with accompanying functions. The table is accessed by a search element, and when the correct data is found the program can retrieve the corresponding function. It is also known as a related table.

The range cross-reference table contains a group of valid elements with a range of values and accompanying functions. The table is accessed by a search element, and when the correct range has been found, the program can retrieve the corresponding function. This is another type of related table.

BENEFITS OF TABLE PROCESSING ■

Tables are particularly beneficial in computer processing because programs using tables run more efficiently (execute faster) than programs performing the same computations without tables. Previous chapters described the method for obtaining input data as retrieving each record from an external device, such as disk or tape. Retrieving an input record from an external device is relatively slow because the record must first be copied into computer main memory before any processing can be done. Tables, however, are stored in computer main memory while a program is executing, so the program can have immediate access to each element. This benefit alone would recommend the use of tables, but there are even more reasons why tables are preferred for many types of processing.

Tables make coding easier when there is a need to refer one element to another. For example, if a program needed to print the word DECEMBER when the input record contained month 12, a routine relating the two-digit month field to some alphabetic field would be needed, either in the program or on an input record (as shown in Figure 7.1).

If the alphabetic field containing the month name were on an alternate input record, the program would be slowed by the need to access this second record. If the month field were included in the first record type, then a data entry person would have to key that field into every record, and the extra data would take up extra space on the auxiliary storage device. In this example, the month data would not take up much space on disk, nor would it take much longer to key, but some programs have very long, complex sets of data that take up considerable space and are difficult to key. Using tables in such programs reduces the need for repetitive, time-consuming data entry and, consequently, reduces the risk that keying errors will be introduced.

In the example relating a numeric month to an alphabetic description it would be possible to solve the problem within the program itself by performing compares, setting up 12 indicators and either moving a literal description into an output field or coding the alphabetic description directly on the Output Specifications. These options are shown in Figures 7.2(a) and 7.2(b).

FIGURE 7.1 Input Data Related to a Table List

```
              TABLE OF MONTHS

        01    JANUARY
        02    FEBRUARY
        03    MARCH
        04    APRIL
        05    MAY
        06    JUNE
        07    JULY
        08    AUGUST
        09    SEPTEMBER
        10    OCTOBER
        11    NOVEMBER
        12    DECEMBER
```

FIGURE 7.2(a) Moving a Literal Description into an Output Field

RPG CALCULATION SPECIFICATIONS

Line	Factor 1	Operation	Factor 2	Result Field Name	Length	Resulting Indicators
01	MTHIN	COMP	01			01
02	01	MOVEL	'JANUARY'	MONTH	10	
03	MTHIN	COMP	02			02
04	02	MOVEL	'FEBRUARY'	MONTH		
...		ETC.				

FIGURE 7.2(b) Coding an Alphabetic Description Directly in the Output Specifications

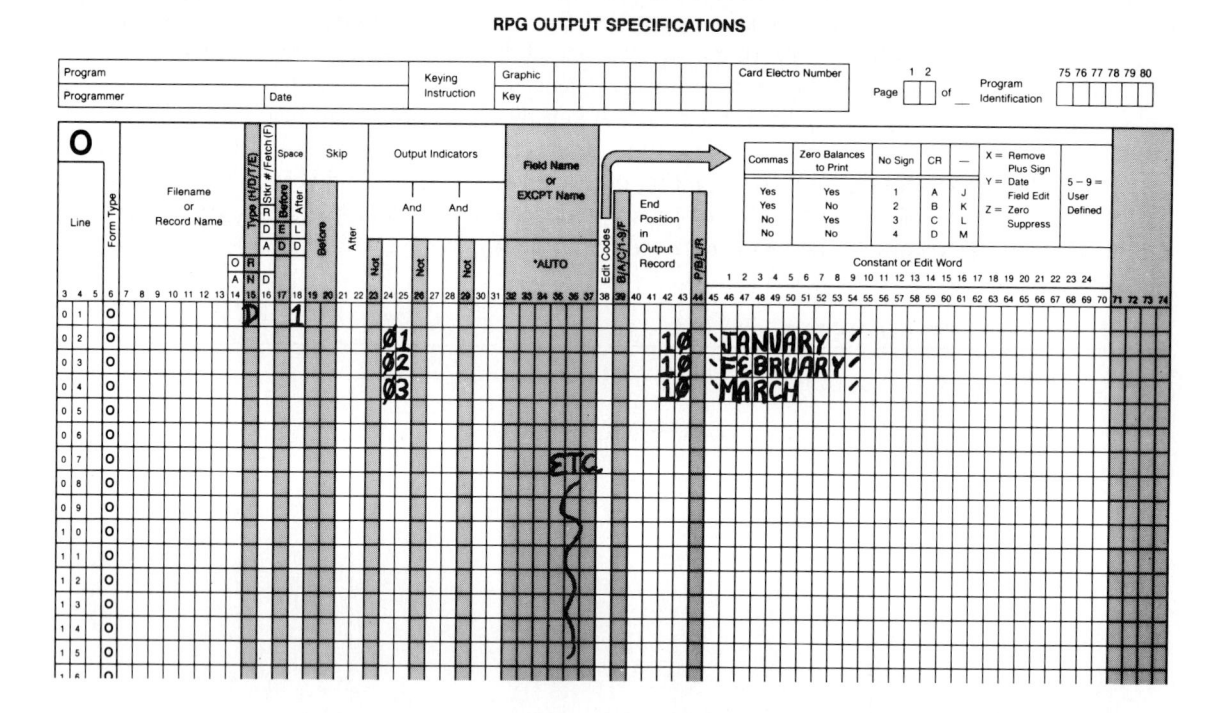

RPG OUTPUT SPECIFICATIONS

Line	Type	Space Before	Output Indicators	Field Name	End Position	Constant or Edit Word
01	D	1				
02			01		10	'JANUARY'
03			02		10	'FEBRUARY'
04			03		10	'MARCH'
...			ETC.			

Although either method would work, they both appear cumbersome and would certainly not be practical for a data file consisting of 2000 elements with very long descriptions, or for data that needed to be changed daily.

Table processing is an alternate solution that is used in nearly all programming languages and produces a more efficient program. The program is easier to code, reduces external storage requirements, and produces more accurate results.

EXTENSION SPECIFICATIONS ■

In RPG, tables are defined on the Extension Specifications. This is a new specification form that has not been used for previous projects. It is required only when RPG needs more information about a file than is contained on the File Description Specifications. Table files are one of several kinds of files which must be described on the Extension Specifications. The Extension Specifications form is shown in Figure 7.3.

The Extension Specifications form, when used, must always follow the File Description Specifications and precede the Input Specifications.

TABLE FILE FORMATS ■

The table format consists of two fields, the argument field and the function field. The argument field contains the key or identifying code that will be used to search for the correct data or description. The argument field is required for all tables. The function field is not required for simple tables. It is used only when a function accompanies the argument—that is, it is used with cross-reference tables. The function field contains the description that is related to the argument.

TYPES OF TABLES (INTERNAL AND EXTERNAL) ■

There are two types of tables: internal and external. They are also called compile time tables (internal) and pre-execution time tables (external). Compile time tables are contained completely within the program itself. Pre-execution time tables are loaded from an independent file, external to the program.

The data from a table is loaded in its entirety as the first step in the execution of an RPG program, even before the first input record has been read.

INTERNAL (COMPILE TIME) TABLE ENTRIES ■

Internal tables are useful for lists that never change, such as the months of the year, the days of the week, or a table of error messages, or for seldom-changing tables, such as predefined job titles or store locations.

FIGURE 7.3 Extension Specifications Form

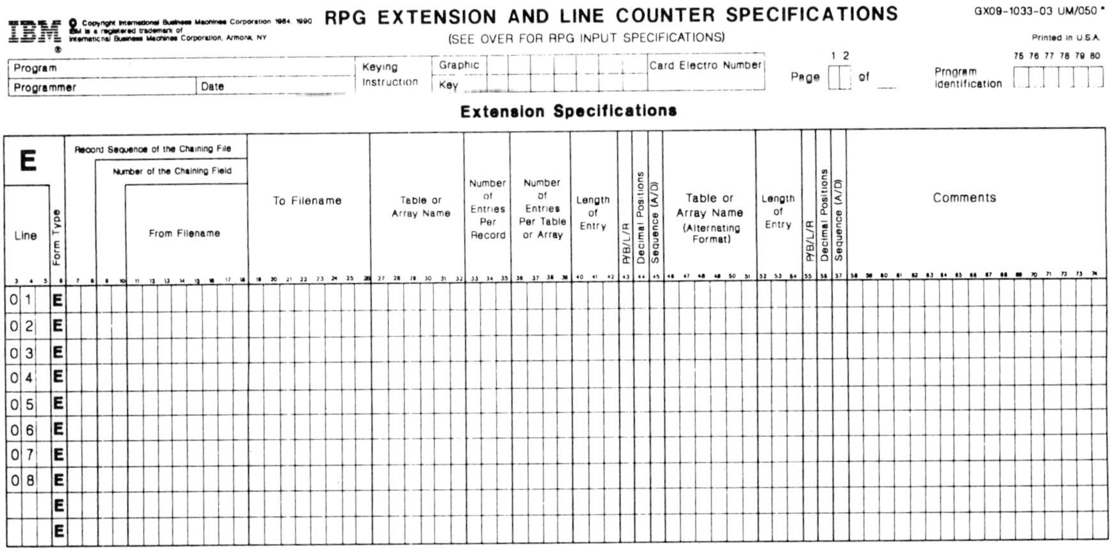

These somewhat permanent tables can be entered as an integral part of a program and compiled as an internal table. These tables do not require File Description Specifications because they are not external files. Internal or compile time tables are described in the Extension Specifications, but no filename is entered. The program then looks for the table internally at the end of the program and compiles the table data as part of the object program. The tables become part of the program itself at the time it is compiled.

SAMPLE PROGRAM 1 USING INTERNAL OR COMPILE TIME TABLES ■

To demonstrate the use of internal tables, a report will be designed that will print the day of the week in front of the keyed input data for each employee. The report will list the total hours for each employee for each day worked. Figures 7.4(a) and 7.4(b) show the format of the input data file and a sample of the report.

The File Description Specifications are shown in Figure 7.5. Notice that no table file needs to be defined.

File Extension Specifications

To define the format of the table data for the sample program, entries will be made on the Extension Specifications, as shown in Figure 7.6. As noted earlier, when the Extension Specifications form is used, it must follow the File Description Specifications and precede the Input Specifications. The table format is defined in terms of its two fields, the argument and the function.

FIGURE 7.4(a) Input Data for Employee Time Report

```
              INPUT DATA FILE
                    DAY      HOURS
          EMPL#    WORKED    WORKED
          0325       1         8.0
          0325       2         4.0
          0325       3          .5
          0325       4         8.0
          0325       5         8.0
          0528       1         4.0
          0528       2         8.0
          0528       3         8.0
          0528       4         8.0
          0528       5         8.0
          0528       6         4.0
```

FIGURE 7.4(b) Sample Employee Time Report

```
          EMPL#   DAY        HOURS

          0325 MONDAY         8.0
          0325 TUESDAY        4.0
          0325 WEDNESDAY       .5
          0325 THURSDAY       8.0
          0325 FRIDAY         8.0
                             28.5 *

          0528 MONDAY         4.0
          0528 TUESDAY        8.0
          0528 WEDNESDAY      8.0
          0528 THURSDAY       8.0
          0528 FRIDAY         8.0
          0528 SATURDAY       4.0
                             40.0 *
```

FIGURE 7.5 File Description Specifications Using Internal Table

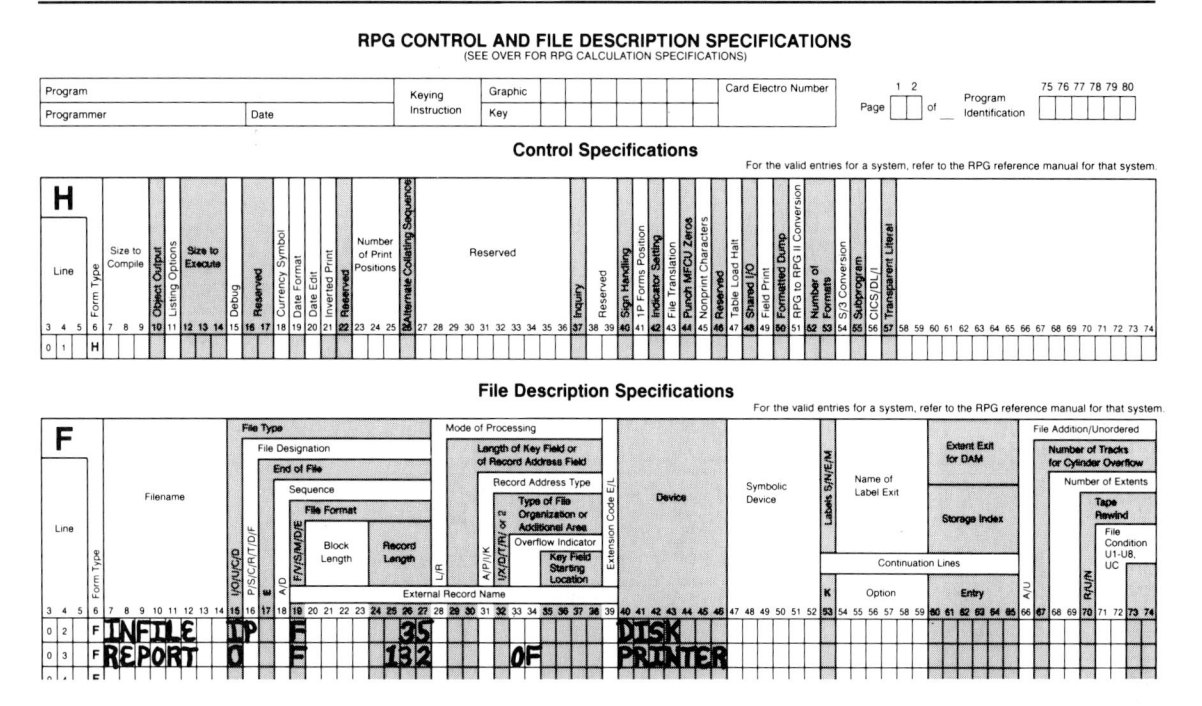

(RPG Control and File Description Specifications form)

```
F INFILE  IP  F    35        DISK
F REPORT  O   F   132     OF PRINTER
```

Defining the Argument

The name of the argument field, which must always begin with the letters TAB, is entered in columns 27–32. In the example, the argument field name is TABDAY, referring to the numeric day code which will be the argument of the table. The number of entries per record field (columns 33–35) will be 4 for this example—it is possible to enter more than one entry per record. (This is explained further in the Record Layout Section on page 154.) This entry is right-justified.

The number of entries per table field (columns 36–39) indicates the total number of argument/function sets which will be included. For example, in defining a table of months, this entry would be 12 (12 sets of arguments/functions). It is necessary for RPG to know the total number of items in each table, because all the records in a table must be read into memory at once. This entry can present some difficulty to the programmer. The table of months is obviously a total of 12 records, but for a table of descriptions that may vary from day to day this can be a problem. This entry must *not* be less than the total table. When the total number is not known, the programmer must determine a reasonable maximum and ensure that dummy records are entered into the table file to compensate for the difference. For this example, there will be a total of seven entries in the table because there are seven days in a week.

The length of entry field specifies the length of the field. In the example, the day code is one position long, so 1 will be entered in columns 40–42 (right-justified).

FIGURE 7.6 Extension Specifications for Internal Table

(RPG Extension and Line Counter Specifications form)

```
E            TABDAY  4  7  1  0ATABWEK 9    DAYS OF WEEK
```

Chapter 7 Table Processing

Column 44 defines field type (alphanumeric or numeric) using the same method used on the Input Specifications. For our example, a zero is entered to define the field as numeric with no decimal positions.

The sequence field defines whether the table file is sequenced in ascending or descending order. Table files must be in some logical sequence by which the program can locate a matching input record. Although RPG permits either an ascending or a descending sequence it is probable that most programs would use the ascending sequence. For this example, an *A* is entered in column 45 for ascending sequence.

Defining the Function

The name of the function field must also begin with the letters TAB. This field name is entered in columns 46–51 (right-justified). In the example, the function field is TABWEK, referring to the description portion of the table. Since this field will not exceed nine characters (WEDNESDAY will be the longest name needed), the numeral 9 is entered in columns 52–54 (right-justified).

Column 56 defines whether a field is alphanumeric or numeric. For this example, column 56 remains blank to define the field as an alphanumeric field. The function field is seldom in any special sequence, so the sequence field (column 57) is usually blank.

Comment Field

The comment field, like all comments, is an optional entry. The comment is entered in columns 58–74. This permits a brief description of table files.

Record Layout

Figure 7.7 shows the Record Layout for this table file. Notice that all seven table entries are defined in two records. RPG can accept more than one table entry per table record. There is no particular benefit to be gained from this type of format, and file maintenance may be simplified by retaining one table set per record. For our example, however, there will be four table entries per record. Since there are only seven entries in the table, the second record will contain only three entries.

FIGURE 7.7 Table File Record Layout

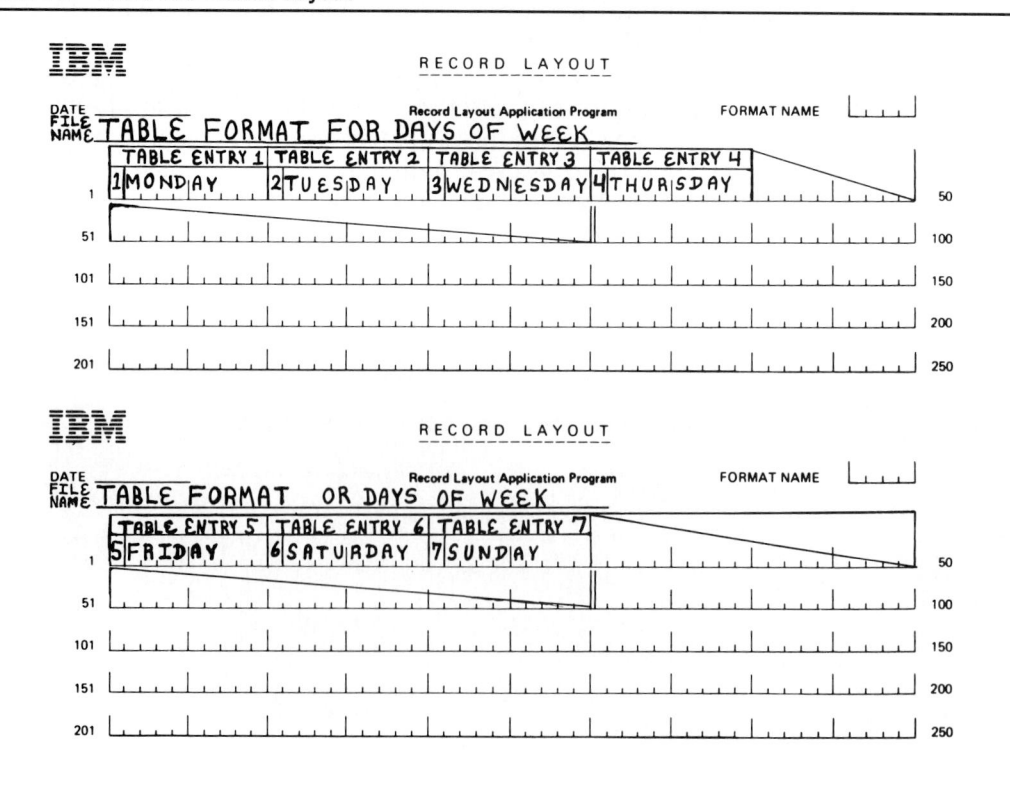

FIGURE 7.8(a)   Input Specifications

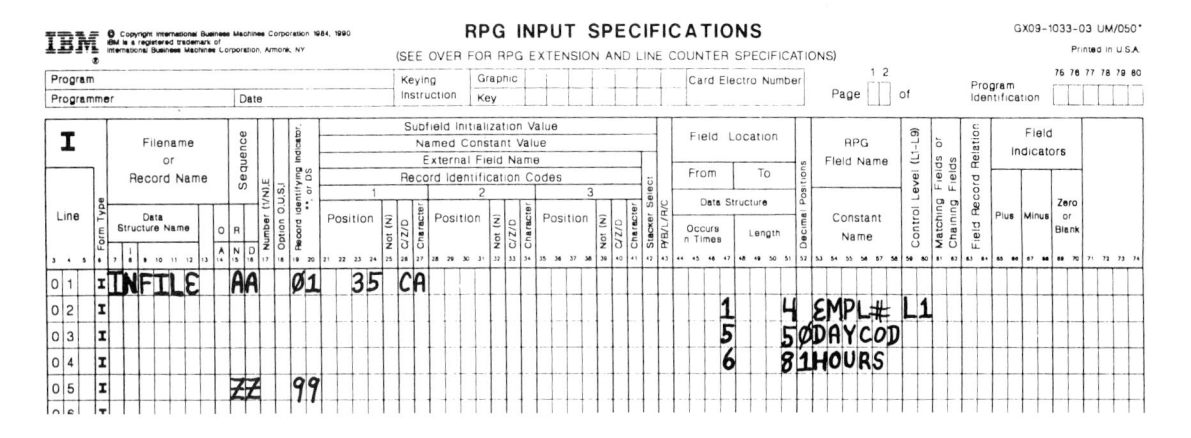

[RPG Input Specifications form with the following entries:]

Line	Filename	Sequence	Number	Option	Record ID	Position	C/Z/D	Character	From	To	Decimal Positions	Field Name	Control Level	Indicators
01	INFILE	AA	01			35	C	A						
02									1	4		EMPL#	L1	
03									5	5	0	DAYCOD		
04									6	8	1	HOURS		
05		ZZ	99											

FIGURE 7.8(b)   Output Specifications for Internal Table

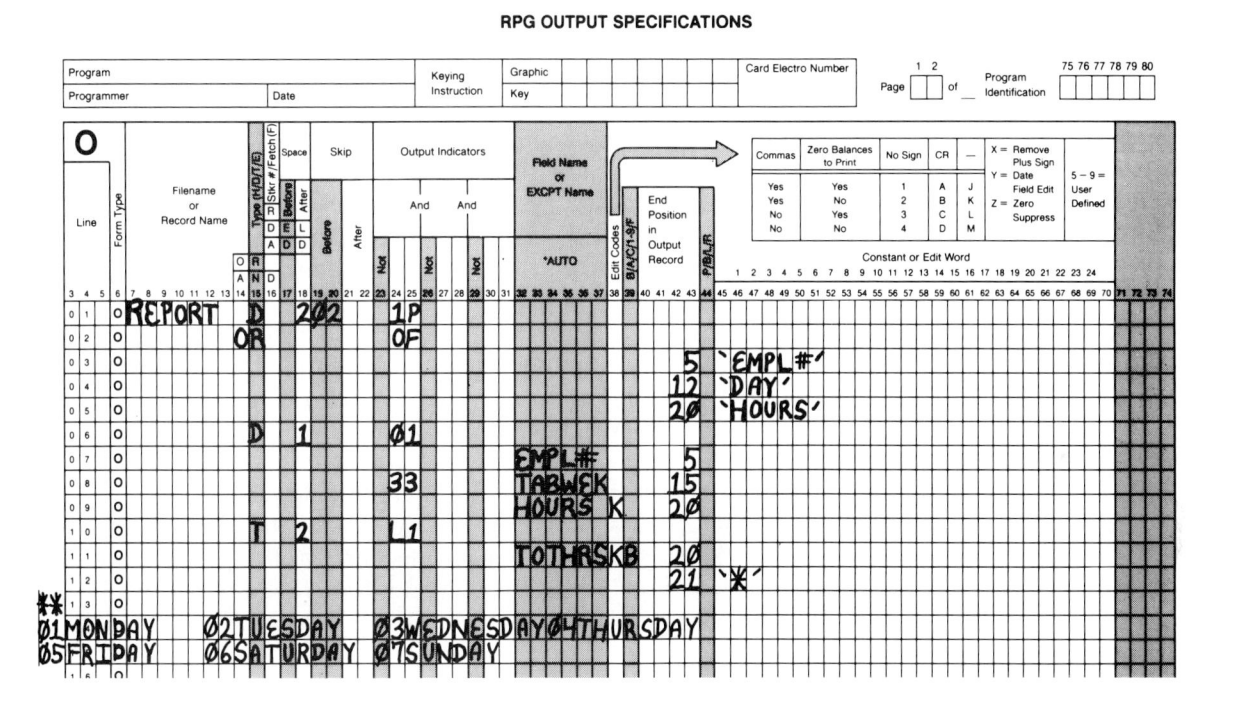

[RPG Output Specifications form with the following entries:]

Line	Filename	Type	D/Add	Before/After	Skip	Output Indicators	Field Name / EXCPT Name	Edit Codes	End Position	P/B/L/R
01	REPORT	D		202		1P				
02		OR				OF				
03							'EMPL#'		5	
04							'DAY'		12	
05							'HOURS'		20	
06		D	1			01				
07							EMPL#		5	
08						33	TABWEK		15	
09							HOURS	K	20	
10		T	2			L1				
11							TOTHRS	KB	20	
12							'*'		21	

```
**
01MONDAY   02TUESDAY   03WEDNESDAY04THURSDAY
05FRIDAY   06SATURDAY  07SUNDAY
```

Compiling Table Information

In this project, the table information will be compiled with the program itself. Therefore, the table data will need to be entered *with* the program. It is entered immediately after the last of the Output Specifications, as shown in Figures 7.8(a) and 7.8(b), as additional information. The table data is separated from the Output Specifications by a record containing two asterisks in columns 1–2.

Notice that the table information begins in column 1, not in column 6 where normal RPG specifications would start. Although the coding form provides no columns for entries in columns 1–2, it will be possible to key into these columns on the computer. The table consists of the argument field followed by the function field with no intervening spaces.

The table consists of seven entries, one for each day of the week. This agrees with the entry on the Extension Specifications which defined seven entries. For tables that will never change, this is an excellent way to ensure that the table becomes a permanent part of the program. However, this is not a good method if the table is expected to change often because the program would need to be recompiled every time the table changed.

Chapter 7   Table Processing

FIGURE 7.9 Processing the Table LOKUP Routine

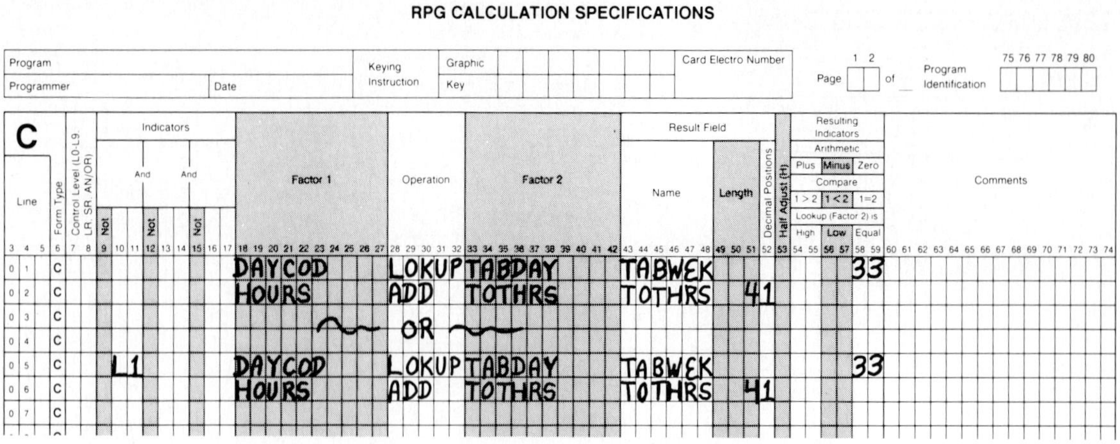

RPG CALCULATION SPECIFICATIONS

Line	Factor 1	Operation	Factor 2	Result Field Name	Length	Resulting Indicators (High/Low/Equal)
01	DAYCOD	LOKUP	TABDAY	TABWEK		33
02	HOURS	ADD	TOTHRS	TOTHRS	41	
03		OR				
04						
05 (L1)	DAYCOD	LOKUP	TABDAY	TABWEK		33
06	HOURS	ADD	TOTHRS	TOTHRS	41	
07						

Calculation Specifications for Processing Table Data

To search a table, a LOKUP instruction is used in calculations. When a record is read (indicator 01 is on) and the calculations are executed, a LOKUP operation can compare the key field from the input record to the argument field in the table file to seek a description. The program will compare the key field to each entry in the table and will continue to repeat this operation until a match has been found or until the end of the table has been reached. When a match is found, RPG will turn on an indicator and stop searching the table file. If no match is found in the entire table search, the indicator will be turned off. Figure 7.9 shows the Calculation Specifications for processing the LOKUP routine for this example.

In this example, the key from the input record (DAYCOD) is entered in factor 1. The operation LOKUP is entered in the operation field. The name of the argument field (TABDAY) from the table file is entered in factor 2. The result field (if a matching record is found in the table file) will be the description contained in the function field (TABWEK) from the table record file.

Indicator 33 will be turned on if (and only if) an equal condition is found between the key field and the argument field. If the entire table is searched and an equal condition is not found, then indicator 33 will not be turned on and no new description will be moved into the result field.

In this example, indicator 33 will be turned on if a match has been found. (Indicator 33 can then be used to condition other calculations or output.) The data contained in the function field is then available and can be printed on the report. Figure 7.10 shows the entire program for sample 1.

EXTERNAL (PRE-EXECUTION TIME) TABLE ENTRIES ■

When external or pre-execution time tables are used, the table file is in fact a true file residing on disk. It becomes a table file in nature only when it is read into main memory by the program. This is probably the better method for storing table files, particularly if the file is subject to frequent changes. Although they reside outside the program, external tables are automatically loaded before any other processing begins (thus the name pre-execution time).

Some examples of table files that should be maintained externally are tables containing product descriptions that could change daily or weekly, commission rate tables that fluctuate from month to month, and tax tables, which may change only annually but are of a critical nature and are best updated by a knowledgeable accountant or payroll manager rather than a data entry clerk or programmer.

FIGURE 7.10 Entire Program for Sample Program 1

RPG CONTROL AND FILE DESCRIPTION SPECIFICATIONS

Control Specifications:
```
01 H
```

File Description Specifications:
```
02 F INFILE  IP  F   35      DISK
03 F REPORT  O   F  132  OF  PRINTER
04 F
```

RPG EXTENSION AND LINE COUNTER SPECIFICATIONS

Extension Specifications:
```
01 E         TABDAY  4  7  1 DATABWEK  9  DAYS OF WEEK
02 E
```

RPG INPUT SPECIFICATIONS

```
01 I INFILE  AA  01  35 CA
02 I                            1  4 EMPL# L1
03 I                            5  50DAYCOD
04 I                            6  81HOURS
05 I
```

FIGURE 7.10 *Continued*

[RPG Calculation Specifications form]

Line	Form Type	Factor 1	Operation	Factor 2	Result Field Name	Length	Dec	Resulting Indicators
01	C	DAYCOD	LOKUP	TABDAY	TABWEK			33
02	C	HOURS	ADD	TOTHRS	TOTHRS	41		
03	C							

[RPG Output Specifications form]

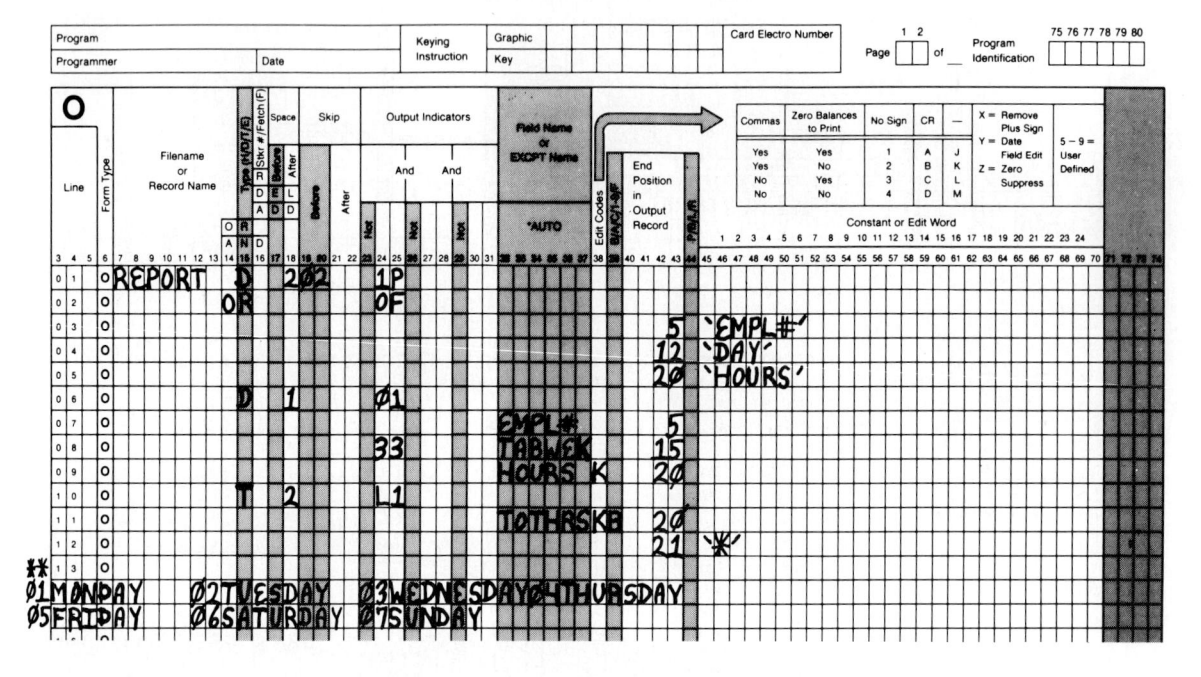

Line	Form Type	Filename/Record Name	Type	Space Before/After	Skip Before/After	Output Indicators	Field Name or EXCPT Name	Edit Codes	End Position	Constant or Edit Word
01	O	REPORT	D	2 02	1P					
02	O		OR		0F					
03	O								5	'EMPL#'
04	O								12	'DAY'
05	O								20	'HOURS'
06	O		D	1	01					
07	O						EMPL#		5	
08	O					33	TABWEK		15	
09	O						HOURS K		20	
10	O		T	2	L1					
11	O						TOTHRS KB		20	
12	O								21	'*'
13	O									

```
**  01MONDAY   02TUESDAY  03WEDNESDAY04THURSDAY
    05FRIDAY   06SATURDAY 07SUNDAY
```

SAMPLE PROGRAM 2 USING AN EXTERNAL OR PRE-EXECUTION TIME TABLE ■

The sample program to illustrate the function of external (pre-execution time) tables will use an input file containing descriptions of parts in a lamp factory. The part numbers are four positions long and represent a list of part descriptions. The list of descriptions and their related codes is shown in Figure 7.11.

The report to be printed will list all the inventoried parts in alphabetic sequence by description showing quantity on hand. The Record Layout, Printer Spacing Chart, and sample report are shown in Figures 7.12(a), 7.12(b), and 7.12(c).

The Record Layout in this example does not contain a description, but imagine for a moment what would happen if it did. Each data entry person would have as many as 20 additional characters to key into every record. Not only would that increase the workload for data entry, it would almost guarantee keying errors in the description field, since handwritten input documents might be written differently and operators might interpret descriptions in various ways. For example, BROWN LAMP BASES might be keyed as LAMP BASES—BROWN in one instance or BASES, BROWN or BROWN BASES. None of these interpretations is technically wrong, but when the report is printed, the inventory of BROWN LAMP BASES will appear to be a collection of unrelated items.

FIGURE 7.11 Product Codes and Descriptions

```
                PART# TABLE

      0401      LAMP BASES-BROWN
      0405      LAMP BASES-BRONZE
      0502      LAMP BASES-WOOD
      2388      LAMP SHADES-PLAIN
      2450      LAMP SHADES-PLEATED
```

FIGURE 7.12(a) Record Layout for Parts Data

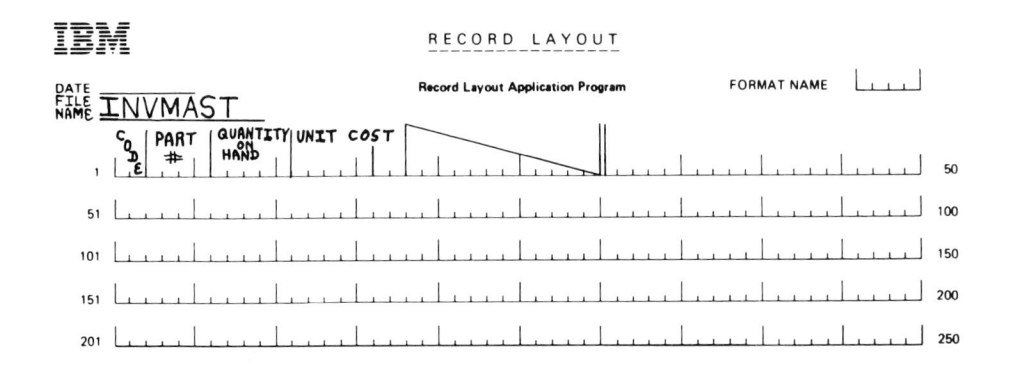

IBM RECORD LAYOUT

DATE
FILE NAME: INVMAST
Record Layout Application Program   FORMAT NAME

Fields: CODE | PART # | QUANTITY ON HAND | UNIT COST

FIGURE 7.12(b) Printer Spacing Chart for Parts List

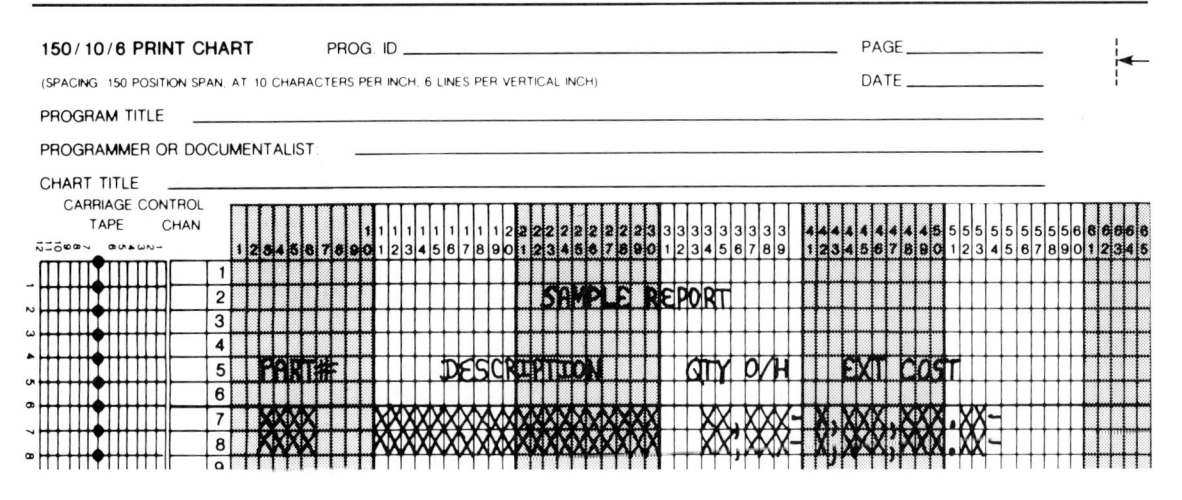

150/10/6 PRINT CHART   PROG. ID _____   PAGE _____
(SPACING 150 POSITION SPAN, AT 10 CHARACTERS PER INCH, 6 LINES PER VERTICAL INCH)   DATE _____
PROGRAM TITLE _____
PROGRAMMER OR DOCUMENTALIST: _____
CHART TITLE _____

Line 2: SAMPLE REPORT
Line 5: PART#   DESCRIPTION   QTY O/H   EXT COST
Line 7: XXXX   XXXXXXXXXXXXXXX   XX,XXX-   X,XXX,XXX.XX-
Line 8: XXXX   XXXXXXXXXXXXXXX   XX,XXX-   X,XXX,XXX.XX-

FIGURE 7.12(c) Sample Parts List Report

```
      PART#   DESCRIPTION           QTY ON HAND   TOTAL COST

      0401    LAMP BASES-BROWN              33        495.00
      0401    LAMP BASES-BROWN               1         15.00
      0405    LAMP BASES-BRONZE             20        500.00
      0405    LAMP BASES-BRONZE              1         25.00
      0502    LAMP BASES-WOOD               50      1,012.50
      0502    LAMP BASES-WOOD              100      1,500.00
      0905    INVALID PART NUMBER          100      6,500.00
      2388    LAMP SHADES-PLAIN          1,000      1,000.00
      2450    LAMP SHADES-PLEATED          233        582.50
```

To avoid these problems, it is much better to key a description only once (wrong or right, it will be consistent within every report). The description can then be accessed from a short part number or identification code. Data entry may still make keying errors, but using the short number reduces the risk of error and rules out differing interpretations.

The description record will provide a table containing a part number and description. The part number that is keyed in the input data will then be used by the program to search the table file until it finds its corresponding description. This description can then be printed on the report. If the part number is never found in the table file, an error message, such as "INVALID PART NUMBER" or "PART NUMBER NOT FOUND," can be printed on the report.

File Description Specifications

To describe an external table file there must be a File Description Specifications entry. A table file, however, is treated as neither a primary nor a secondary file. The table file itself will look like any data file. It may reside on disk, tape, or any other external storage device. It is the manner in which the file is treated within the program that transforms it into a table file. Figure 7.13 shows the File Description Specifications for the sample program.

The filename for this table is DESCFIL. In column 15 an *I* is entered defining it as an input file. In column 16 a *T* is entered to notify RPG that this is a table file. This entry is the important difference in the processing method for table files.

The rest of the entries for the table file on the File Description Specifications are the same as for any other input file. The file format, record length, and device are defined as in earlier sample programs.

The only new entry on the File Description Specifications, besides the *T* in column 16, is an *E* entered in column 39. This entry notifies RPG that more information about this table file will be contained on another line of code. This additional information will be entered on the Extension Specifications.

FIGURE 7.13 File Specifications for External Table

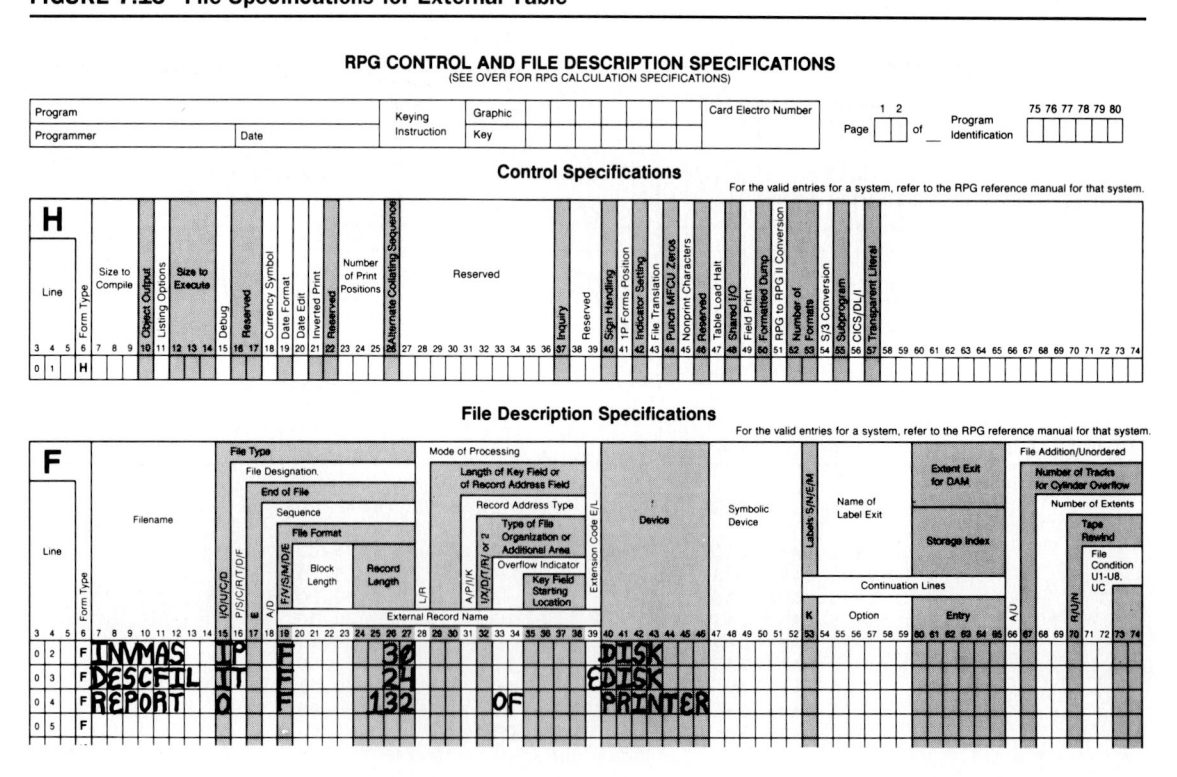

FIGURE 7.14 Extension Specifications for External Table

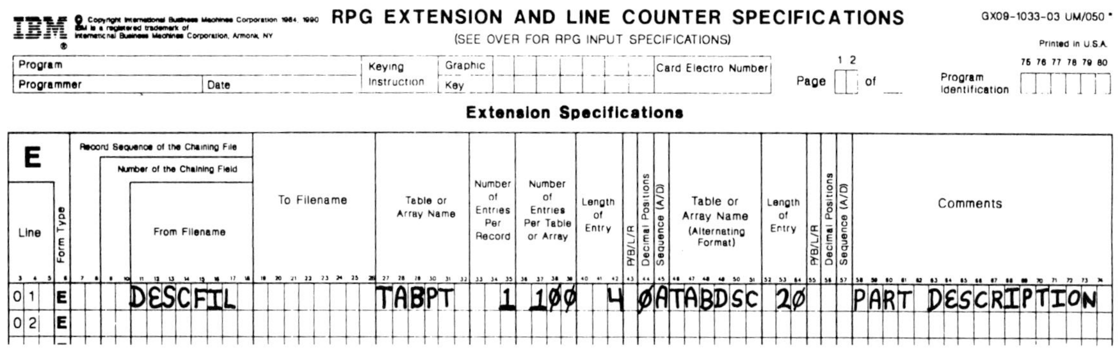

```
E  DESCFIL              TABPT    1 100 4 0ATABDSC  20  PART DESCRIPTION
E
```

Extension Specifications

As for the first sample program, the table is described in detail on the Extension Specifications, as shown in Figure 7.14.

An external table requires that the name of the table file be entered in columns 11–18, exactly as entered on the File Description Specifications. This lets RPG know which table file is being described on the Extension Specifications. This was not necessary for compile time tables since the table data was contained within the program itself.

Defining the Argument

Since the name of the argument field must begin with the letters TAB (columns 27–32 of the Extension Specifications) we have entered TABPT. This refers to the numeric part number which will be the argument of the table.

The number of entries per record field (columns 33–35) will be 1 for this example because there will be one entry per record in the table file. The number of entries per table field (columns 36–39) will be 100, the number of different lamps available. The length of entry field (in columns 40–42) will be 4 because the part number is four positions long.

Since this is a numeric field, a zero is entered to define the field as a numeric with no decimal positions (column 44). Although the sequence will default to ascending without an entry in column 45, it is better to define it as *A* so future programmers will not be in doubt about your intentions.

Defining the Function

In this example, the function field is TABDSC and refers to the description portion of the table. The function field will occupy a length of 20, entered in columns 52–54. Column 56 remains blank, defining the function field as an alphanumeric field.

Comment Field

It is often a help to enter a brief note to identify what the table is used for. Columns 58–74 of the Extension Specifications are reserved for this purpose. When longer comments are needed, you would use a complete comment line (asterisk in column 7) as explained in earlier chapters.

Record Layout

The Record Layout for the table file for the sample project is shown in Figure 7.15. Columns 1–4 contain the part number and columns 5–24 contain the description.

Input Specifications

The Input Specifications follow the same rules as those for input files in earlier chapters and are shown in Figure 7.16.

FIGURE 7.15 Record Layout for a Table File

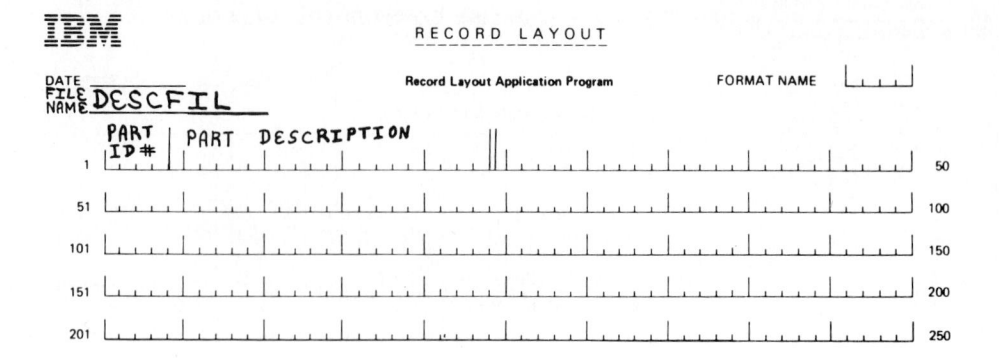

```
IBM                           RECORD LAYOUT
DATE
FILE NAME  DESCFIL            Record Layout Application Program    FORMAT NAME

        PART | PART DESCRIPTION
        ID #
    1   |_____| 50
   51   |_____| 100
  101   |_____| 150
  151   |_____| 200
  201   |_____| 250
```

Calculation Specifications

In the example shown in Figure 7.17, the name of the part number (the key) from the input record (PARTNO) is entered in factor 1. The operation LOKUP is entered in the operation field. The name of the argument field from the table file is entered in factor 2.

Indicator 54 will be turned on if (and only if) an equal condition is found between the key field and the argument field. If the entire table is searched and an equal condition is not found, indicator 54 will not be turned on and no new description will be moved into the result field. If a matching record is found in the table file, the result field will be the description contained in the function field from the table record file TABDSC.

Output Specifications

The indicator from the LOKUP operation can be used to control the output that will be printed. If the record has been found in the table file (in the example, indicator 54 is on), the description will be printed on the report. If the record was not found in the table file (indicator 54 is off) a message should be printed to show that the part was not found. Perhaps a keying error was made in the input data or possibly a new record should be added to the table file. Figure 7.18 shows the Output Specifications. In this example, the message "INVALID PART NUMBER" will print in the description field when indicator 54 is off.

Table Data File Maintenance

Unless a table file contains some unchanging data such as the months of the year, it will need to have changes made to it occasionally. Adding, changing, or deleting records from a table file, or any kind of file, is called file maintenance. This maintenance to an external table is performed as for any other regular file. New records must be added, existing table records can be changed, and old records can be removed entirely.

FIGURE 7.16 Input Specifications

162   RPG: A Programming Language for Today

FIGURE 7.17 Calculation Specifications for Table LOKUP Project

RPG CALCULATION SPECIFICATIONS

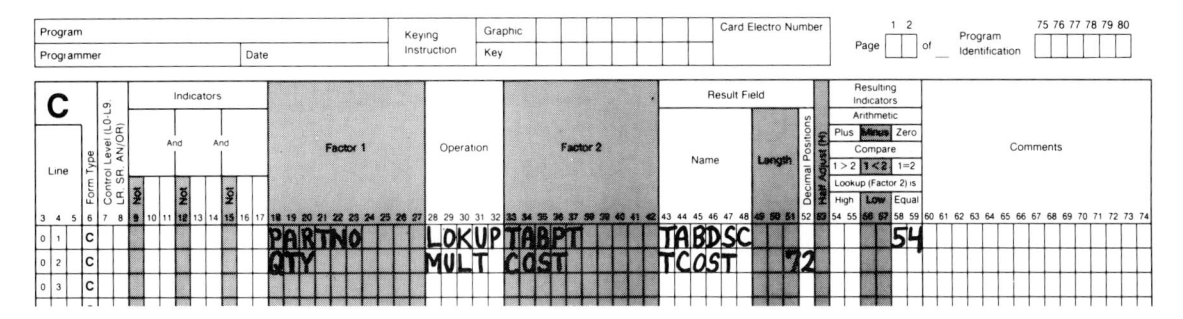

```
C 01  PARTNO  LOKUP TABPT  TABDSC        54
C 02  QTY     MULT  COST   TCOST   72
C 03
```

FIGURE 7.18 Output Specifications for External Table Project

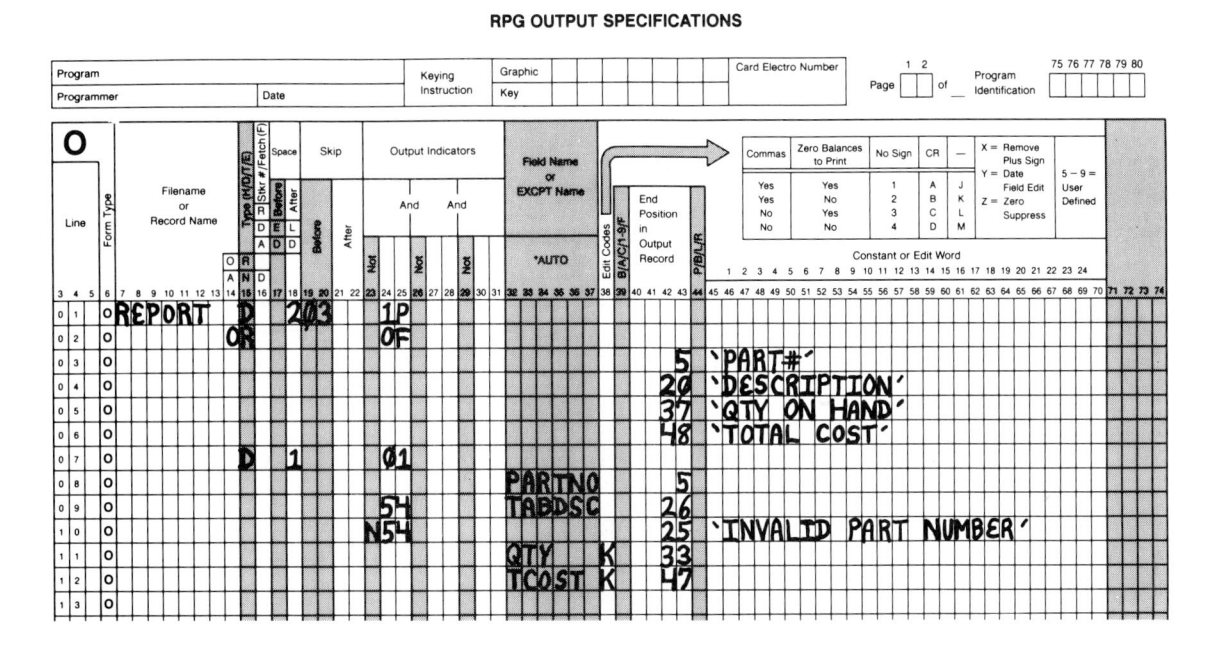

RPG OUTPUT SPECIFICATIONS

```
O 01  REPORT  D  203   1P
O 02       OR            OF
O 03                              5 'PART#'
O 04                             20 'DESCRIPTION'
O 05                             37 'QTY ON HAND'
O 06                             48 'TOTAL COST'
O 07          D  1     01
O 08                            PARTNO    5
O 09                     54     TABDSC   26
O 10                    N54                 25 'INVALID PART NUMBER'
O 11                            QTY   K   33
O 12                            TCOST K   47
O 13
```

THE TIME AT WHICH TABLE DATA IS AVAILABLE ∎

The program will always read table files *first* before reading any other input files. Regular input files are read into main memory one record at a time, but table files are read into main memory in their entirety. The whole table file needs to reside in memory before the program can begin processing its first input record. For this reason, tables should never be so large that they will not fit into the available memory comfortably. When a table file is too large to fit into main memory, the computer operating system may manage to perform the processing but the efficiency benefits may be lost.

While the program is executing, the table(s) defined on the File Description and Extension Specifications is (are) stored in main memory.

AVOIDING COMMON ERRORS ∎

An error programmers commonly make is inadvertently omitting the result field on the LOKUP operation on the Calculation Specifications. RPG permits the result field to be blank—in such a case, it assumes that the programmer did not want to retrieve data from the function field and only

Chapter 7 Table Processing **163**

needed to know whether a table record had been found (whether the indicator was on or off). Since the description field is often needed for some further processing, it is a good habit to enter the result field whether it is needed or not.

Another common error is entering the indicator in the wrong position of the Calculation Specifications. This could mean that the indicator was turned on when the argument was either less than or greater than the table record. This would give very different results—probably not the results the programmer had in mind.

ALTERNATING TABLES ■

In sample programs 1 and 2 above, a single table was used to describe and locate related table information. It is possible to use two tables to accomplish the same results. Perhaps the data for the argument portion of the information exists in a file. Using the same example as before, the part number file might exist in a master file but, for some reason, there is no description in the master file format. It would be possible to create another file consisting of the descriptions *only*. The two tables would be defined in RPG to obtain the same results as those obtained in sample program 1. The same input file and output report will be used in sample program 3 to demonstrate that a two-table search can operate exactly the same as a single-table search.

SAMPLE PROGRAM 3 USING ALTERNATING TABLE DATA ■

Sometimes it is useful to define two tables and to use these tables as if they were related. Figure 7.19 shows the report that will be printed in this example.

In the File Description Specifications, the input file will be defined as before, but instead of one table file there will be two. Both will be defined exactly as any table file would be defined. The first will be named PART and the second, DESCRIP. They will be used together to search and retrieve the description for each part in the input file. Figures 7.20(a) and 7.20(b) show the Record Layout for the two table files.

The Extension Specifications are similar to the earlier example, but there will be no entries in the function description for either of the table files. The function is really being described in the second table. Figure 7.21 shows the Extension Specifications for the two table files, which will be acting together.

Input Specifications

The Input Specifications are the same as for sample program 1.

Calculation Specifications

Figure 7.22 shows the method to be used in processing two table files which are acting together as if they were a single table with a function entry. The first table contains the argument and the second table contains the function. The name of the search field is entered in factor 1 for the LOKUP

FIGURE 7.19 Sample Report

PART#	DESCRIPTION	QTY ON HAND	TOTAL COST
0401	LAMP BASES-BROWN	33	495.00
0401	LAMP BASES-BROWN	1	15.00
0405	LAMP BASES-BRONZE	20	500.00
0405	LAMP BASES-BRONZE	1	25.00
0502	LAMP BASES-WOOD	50	1,012.50
0502	LAMP BASES-WOOD	100	1,500.00
0905	INVALID PART NUMBER	100	6,500.00
2388	LAMP SHADES-PLAIN	1,000	1,000.00
2450	LAMP SHADES-PLEATED	233	582.50

FIGURE 7.20(a) Record Layout for Table File

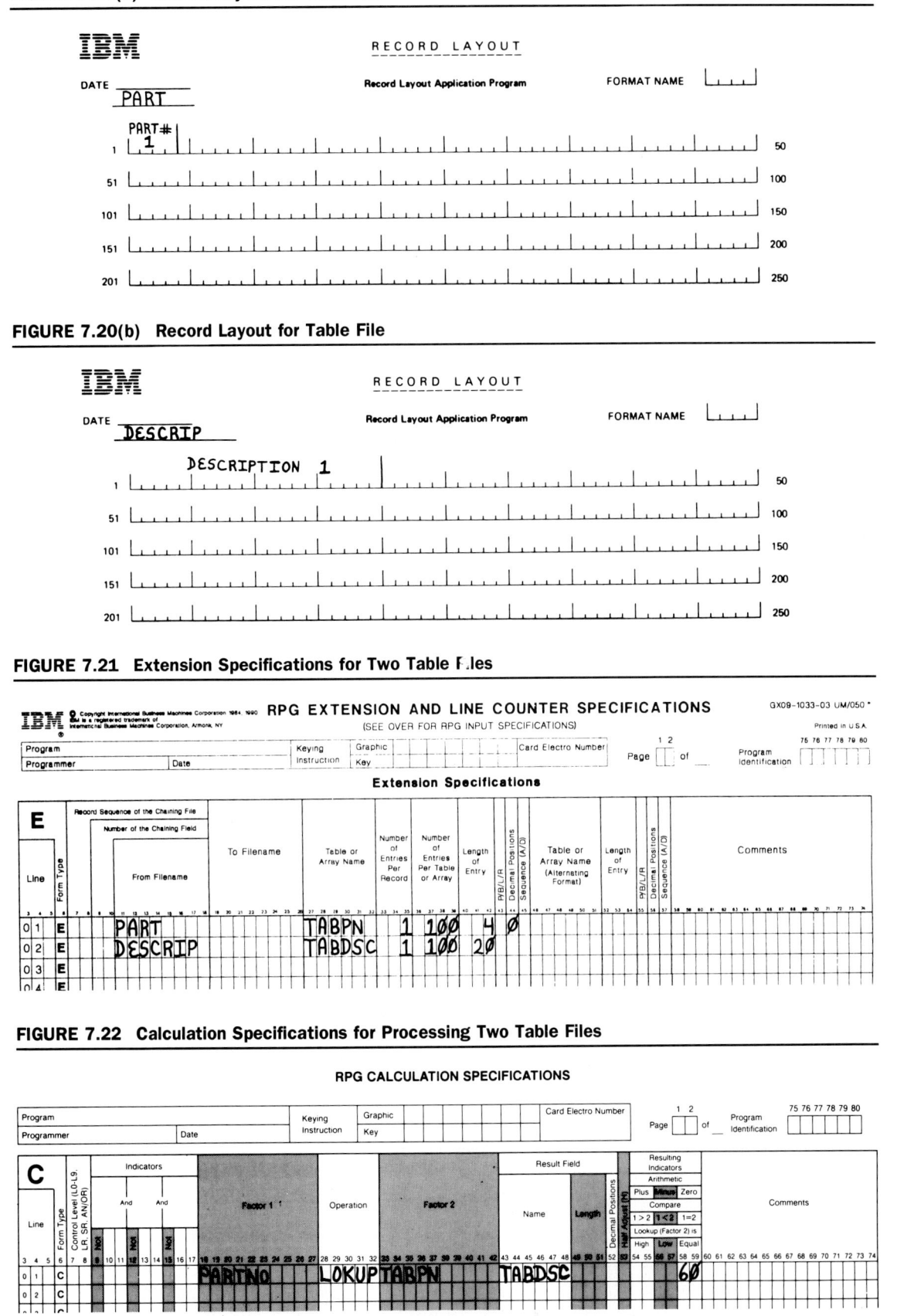

IBM RECORD LAYOUT
DATE: PART
PART# 1

FIGURE 7.20(b) Record Layout for Table File

IBM RECORD LAYOUT
DATE: DESCRIP
DESCRIPTION 1

FIGURE 7.21 Extension Specifications for Two Table Files

RPG EXTENSION AND LINE COUNTER SPECIFICATIONS

Line	Form Type	From Filename	To Filename	Table or Array Name	Number of Entries Per Record	Number of Entries Per Table or Array	Length of Entry	Decimal Positions	Sequence (A/D)
01	E	PART		TABPN	1	100	4	0	
02	E	DESCRIP		TABDSC	1	100	20		
03	E								
04	E								

FIGURE 7.22 Calculation Specifications for Processing Two Table Files

RPG CALCULATION SPECIFICATIONS

Line	Form Type	Factor 1	Operation	Factor 2	Result Field	Equal
01	C	PARTNO	LOKUP	TABPN	TABDSC	60
02	C					

operation and the name of the table argument for the first table is entered in factor 2. An indicator is specified in columns 58–59 just as it was in the earlier examples. The new concept shown here is that the result field will contain the name of the argument field for the second table.

RPG will search the first table for a matching argument. When it finds a match in the first table, it will then return the corresponding element of the second table as its function.

Output Specifications

The Output Specifications will be similar to those used in sample program 2.

Although the coding for a two-table search is no more difficult than for a single-table search, it is not a popular method for handling tables. There is an inherent danger that the data in the two tables might become unrelated or nonsynchronous. It is far safer to keep both sets of data in a single file.

MULTIPLE TABLES ■

There may be a need for more than one table in the same program. These can be either external or internal table files.

External table files must be defined in a separate File Description and Extension entry for each table. For internal tables, a separate Extension Specifications entry is needed for each table. At the end of the program, the tables themselves must be separated by a record containing two asterisks in columns 1–2. It is of critical importance that the table data at the end of the program appear in the *exact* sequence as the table Extension Specifications. See Figures 7.23(a) and 7.23(b) for an example of multiple internal table definitions.

PRINTING A TABLE ■

It is sometimes useful to see a printout of an entire table file, either to verify its accuracy or to use as information on a report. Although this can be done in the conventional manner by reading the table file and then causing it to print, there is an even easier method. By entering the name of the printer file on the Extension Specifications in columns 19–26, the entire contents of the table file will print at LR (last record) time (see Figure 7.24).

This can be a quick method for the programmer to use to verify a table file. Keep in mind that the table is output in the exact format as the table input records. For this reason, the table printout might be difficult for users to read if there is more than one table entry per record or if there is no space between the argument and function fields.

FIGURE 7.23(a) Extension Specifications for Multiple Internal Tables

Line	Form Type	From Filename	To Filename	Table or Array Name	Number of Entries Per Record	Number of Entries Per Table or Array	Length of Entry	P/B/L/R	Decimal Positions	Sequence (A/D)	Table or Array Name (Alternating Format)	Length of Entry	P/B/L/R	Decimal Positions	Sequence (A/D)	Comments
01	E			TAB1	1	4	4	Ø			ATABDSC	20				PART#
02	E			TAB2	1	7	1	Ø			ATABWK	10				DAY OF WEEK
03	E															

FIGURE 7.23(b) Output Specifications for Multiple Internal Tables

```
*
01LAMP BASES-BROWN
02LAMP BASES-BRONZE
03LAMP BASES-SILVER
04LAMP BASES-WOOD
*
1MONDAY
2TUESDAY
3WEDNESDAY
4THURSDAY
5FRIDAY
6SATURDAY
7SUNDAY
```

FIGURE 7.24 Extension Specifications for Printing a Table File

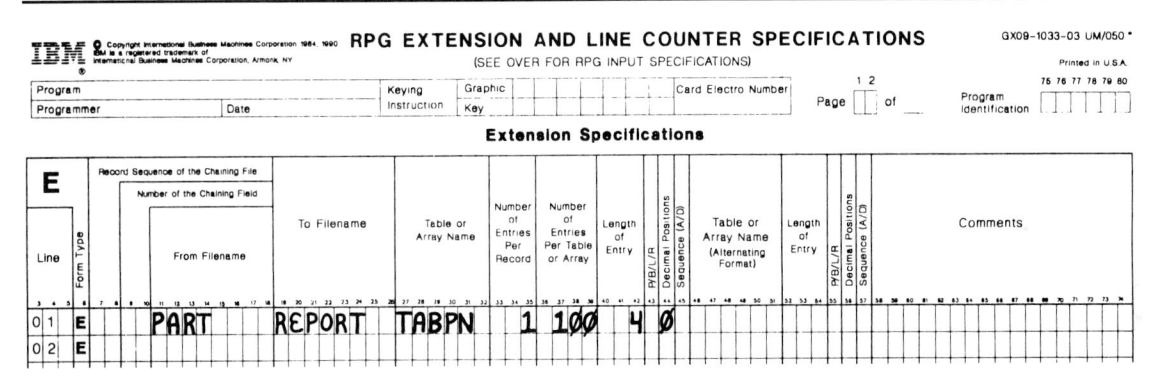

Line	Form Type	From Filename	To Filename	Table or Array Name	Number of Entries Per Record	Number of Entries Per Table or Array	Length of Entry	P/B/L/R	Decimal Positions	Sequence (A/D)	Table or Array Name (Alternating Format)	Length of Entry	P/B/L/R	Decimal Positions	Sequence (A/D)	Comments
01	E	PART	REPORT	TABPN	1	100	4	0								
02	E															

SUMMARY ■

This chapter has introduced the use of tables. You have learned that tables are one of the most efficient methods for relating a fixed description or calculation factor to a code or input key.

In this chapter you have learned the benefits to be gained by placing a table of fixed information directly into main memory rather than accessing it repeatedly from a direct access device. In addition to greater efficiency, other benefits gained from the use of tables are greater accuracy, reduced data entry, and smaller storage requirements.

The three types of table applications were discussed: simple, cross-reference, and range cross-reference. The Extension Specification was introduced, and the use of the LOKUP operation in calculations was defined. The relative merits of external versus internal tables were discussed. Methods for maintaining a semipermanent table within the program were described.

Finally, you have learned that a program can have more than one table file and these can be either internal or external or a combination of both.

REVIEW QUESTIONS ■

1. Define *table processing*.
2. The RPG form on which a table can be described is the _____ Specifications.
3. The three characters with which the name of a table must begin are _____ .
4. List some of the benefits or advantages to be gained from the use of tables in an RPG program.
5. A table consists of a(n) _____ and a(n) _____ . Explain the difference between the two.
6. When searching the contents of a table, the _____ operation is used.
7. The two times at which a table can be introduced into a program are at _____ time or at _____ time.
8. An internal table is referred to as a _____ time table.
9. An external table is referred to as a _____ time table.
10. Internal tables are separated from each other by _____ .

EXERCISES ■

1. On an Extension Specifications form, enter the coding to define an internal table.
2. On a File Description Specifications form, enter the coding to define a table named RATES.
3. On an Extension Specifications form, enter the coding to further define the table named RATES.
4. On an Extension Specifications form, enter the coding to describe a table which has an argument and a function. The name of the argument is TABIN. The name of the function is DESC.
5. On a Calculation Specifications form, make the entry to search the table TABIN. The name of the search key field is CUSTIN.

DEBUGGING EXERCISES

Instructions

The following RPG programs contain an error or errors. Some of these errors are indicated by the RPG compiler on the program listing. A list of syntax errors is given at the end of the program listing. Other types of errors may occur which will not be shown. These are called logic errors.

Study each program and its syntax errors. Locate each error (including logic errors) and on a separate coding form make the correct entry for the line(s) in error.

Explain each error and how it should be corrected.

```
     100   F* TITLE: DEBUG PROJECT 7-A
     200   F* DATE:   4/14           AUTHOR: D.CABLE
     300   F* DESCRIPTION: PHYSICAL INVENTORY  (TABLES)
     400   F************************************************
     500   F* MODIFICATIONS:
     600   F* NO.       DATE      INIT      DESCRIPTION
     700   F*         XX/XX/XX    XXX    XXXXXXXXXXXXXXXXXXXXXXXXXXXXX
     800   F************************************************

NAME OF PROGRAM WILL BE PJ007A IN LIBRARY CABLE

              H
* 1019                 ALL DECIMAL DATA ERRORS IGNORED
     900   FPHYSINV IP  F      120          DISK
    1000   FREPORT   O  F      132    OF    PRINTER
    1100   F************************************************

    1200   E                TABCL    1    5  4  ATABDES 15  CLASS TABLE

    1300   IPHYSINV AA  01
    1400   I                                      1   3 WHSE
    1500   I                                      4  10 PTNO
    1600   I                                     11  26 DESCR
    1700   I                                     27  31 QTY
    1800   I                                     32  34 PGNO
    1900   I                                     35  37 BIN
    2000   I                                     38  41 CLAS

    2100   C           CNT       ADD  1       CNT     40
    2200   C           CLAS      LOKUPTABCL
* 5053                                             5053-******

    2300   OREPORT  H   203          1P
    2400   O        OR              OF
    2500   O                                        6 'PJ007A'
    2600   O                        UDATE Y        50
    2700   O                                       30 'PHYSICAL INVENTORY'
    2800   O                                       36 'COUNT'
    2900   O        H   2            1P
    3000   O        OR              OF
    3100   O                                       11 'WAREHOUSE'
    3200   O                                       25 'PART#'
    3300   O                                       32 'DESCRIP'
    3400   O                                       45 'QUANTITY'
    3500   O                                       53 'PAGE#'
    3600   O                                       58 'BIN'
```

Chapter 7 Table Processing

```
SEQUENCE       1         2         3         4         5         6         7
NUMBER    6789012345678901234567890123456789012345678901234567890123456789 01234
    3700 O                                              65 'CLASSIFICATION'
    3800 O        D  1     01
    3900 O                              WHSE       4
    4000 O                              PTNO      12
    4100 O                              DESCR     36
    4200 O                              QTY   Z   44
    4300 O                              PGNO      42
    4400 O                              BIN       48
    4500 O                              TABDES    65
    4600 O        T  2        LR
    4700 O                                              15 'TOTAL RECORDS'
    4800 O                              CNT   K   25
* * * * *  E N D   O F   S O U R C E * * * * *
```

* 7086   900   RPG PROVIDES BLOCK/UNBLOCK SUPPORT FOR FILE PHYSINV.
              TABLE/ARRAY ------- TABCL
              TABLE/ARRAY ------- TABDES
* 8043   1200   NO DATA PRESENT FOR TABLE/ARRAY. ZEROS/BLANKS ASSUMED

CROSS-REFERENCE LISTING

FILE/RCD   DEV/RCD   REFERENCES (D=DEFINED)

01 PHYSINV   DISK   900D 1300
02 REPORT   PRINTER   1000D 2300 2900 3800 4600

FIELD   ATTR   REFERENCES (M=MODIFIED D=DEFINED)

BIN   A(3)   1900D 4400
CLAS   A(4)   2000D 2200
CNT   P(4,0)   2100 2100D 4800
DESCR   A(16)   1600D 4100
PGNO   A(3)   1800D 4300
PTNO   A(7)   1500D 4000
QTY   P(5,0)   1700D 4200
TABCL(5)   A(4)   1200D 2200
TABDES(5)   A(15)   1200D 4500
UDATE   P(6,0)   2600
WHSE   A(3)   1400D 3900
1   LITERAL   2100

INDICATOR   REFERENCES (M=MODIFIED D=DEFINED)

LR   900D 4600
OF   1000D 2400 3000
01   1300M 3800
1P   2300 2900

MESSAGES

MSGID   SEV NUMBER TEXT

* QRG1019 00   1   IGNDECERR(*YES) SPECIFIED ON COMMAND. NO DECIMAL DATA ERRORS
* QRG5053 30   1   RESULTING INDICATORS (POSITIONS 54-59) MUST BE ENTERED FOR SI
                       LINE IGNORED
* QRG7086 00   1   RPG WILL HANDLE BLOCKING FUNCTION FOR THE FILE. INFDS CONTENT
                       ARE TRANSFERRED.
* QRG8043 10   1   NO SOURCE RECORDS PROVIDED TO INITIALIZE ARRAY/TABLE. ALPHAME
                       NUMERIC ELEMENTS ASSUMED ZERO

MESSAGE SUMMARY

```
TOTAL    00      10      20      30      40      50
  4       2       1       0       1       0       0
```

48 RECORDS READ FROM SOURCE FILE
SOURCE RECORDS INCLUDE   39 SPECIFICATIONS,   0 TABLE RECORDS, AND   9 COMMENTS

QRG0008 COMPILE TERMINATED. SEVERITY 30 ERRORS FOUND IN PROGRAM

* * * * * E N D   O F   C O M P I L A T I O N * * * * *
* QRG1020   ERROR OCCURRED CREATING OR UPDATING DATA AREA RETURNCODE. COMPIL

```
        100   F* TITLE: DEBUG PROJECT 7-B
        200   F* DATE:  4/14          AUTHOR: D.CABLE
        300   F* DESCRIPTION: SALES BY SALES REP (TABLES)
        400   F*********************************************************
        500   F* MODIFICATIONS:
        600   F* NO.      DATE      INIT      DESCRIPTION
        700   F*         XX/XX/XX    XXX      XXXXXXXXXXXXXXXXXXXXXXXXXXXXX
        800   F*********************************************************

NAME OF PROGRAM WILL BE PJ007B IN LIBRARY CABLE

              H
* 1019                ALL DECIMAL DATA ERRORS IGNORED
        900   FSALES    IP  F      50              DISK
       1000   FTABRGN   IT  F      80              DISK
* 2010                                      2010-*

       1100   FREPORT   O   F     132      OF      PRINTER
       1200   F*********************************************************

       1300   E    TABRGN         TABSL   1  20  3 ATABRGN  3  REGION TABLE
* 5194                                    5194-******

       1400   E                   TABR    1   5  3 ATABDSC 10  DESCR TABLE

       1500   ISALES    AA  01
       1600   I                                     1    3 SLSREP
       1700   I                                     4    90SLDATE
       1800   I                                    10   11 SLSTOR
       1900   I                                    12   160QTY
       2000   I                                    17   23 SLITM#
       2100   I                                    24   302SLUPRC

       2200   C                         SETOF                    2526
       2300   C            SLSREP       LOKUPTABS  TABRGN            25
* 5123                                  5123-***********.
* 5194                                             5194-******

       2400   C       25   TABRGN       LOKUPTABR  TABDSC            26
* 5194              5194-***********

       2500   C            SLQTY        MULT SLUPRC  EPRC   92
       2600   C            EPRC         ADD  TPRC    TPRC  102

       2700   OREPORT   H  203       1P
       2800   O         OR           OF
       2900   O                                  6 'PJ007B'
```

```
SEQUENCE       1         2         3         4         5         6         7
 NUMBER    67890123456789012345678901234567890123456789012345678901234

   3000   0                            UDATE Y   50
   3100   0                                      30 'SALES BY SALES REP'
   3200   0         H  2      1P
   3300   0        OR         OF
   3400   0                                       7 'REGION'
   3500   0                                      17 'SALES REP'
   3600   0                                      25 'ITEM#'
   3700   0                                      34 'QUANTITY'
   3800   0                                      45 'UNIT PRICE'
   3900   0                                      55 'TOTAL'
   4000   0         D  1      01
   4100   0                            TABDSC    10
   4200   0                            SLREP     16
   4300   0                            SLITM#    30
   4400   0                            SLQTY Z   35
   4500   0                            UPRC  K   45
   4600   0                            EPRC  K   55
   4700   0         T  2      LR
   4800   0                                      15 'DAILY RECORDS'
   4900   0                            TPRC  K   55
 * * * * * E N D   O F   S O U R C E * * * * *


* 7086       900   RPG PROVIDES BLOCK/UNBLOCK SUPPORT FOR FILE SALES.
* 7086      1000   RPG PROVIDES BLOCK/UNBLOCK SUPPORT FOR FILE TABRGN.
                   TABLE/ARRAY ------- TABR
                   TABLE/ARRAY ------- TABDSC
* 8043      1400   NO DATA PRESENT FOR TABLE/ARRAY. ZEROS/BLANKS ASSUMED



         CROSS-REFERENCE LISTING



             FILE/RCD    DEV/RCD     REFERENCES (D=DEFINED)

         03  REPORT      PRINTER     1100D 2700   3200   4000   4700
         01  SALES       DISK         900D 1500
         02  TABRGN      DISK        1000D 1300



             FIELD       ATTR        REFERENCES (M=MODIFIED D=DEFINED)

             EPRC        P(9,2)      2500D 2600   4600
* 7031       QTY         P(5,0)      1900D
* 7031       SLDATE      P(6,0)      1700D
             SLITM#      A(7)        2000D 4300
* 7030       SLQTY       P(5,0)      2500  4400
* 7030       SLREP       A(4)        4200
             SLSREP      A(3)        1600D 2300
* 7031       SLSTOR      A(2)        1800D
             SLUPRC      P(7,2)      2100D 2500
             TABDSC(5)   A(10)       1400D 2400   4100
             TABR(5)     A(3)        1400D 2400
* 7030       TABRGN      A(4)
* 7030       TABS        A(4)        2300
* 7031       TABSL(20)   A(3)        1300D
             TPRC        P(10,2)     2600  2600D 4900
             UDATE       P(6,0)      3000
* 7030       UPRC        P(5,0)      4500
```

172   *RPG: A Programming Language for Today*

```
            INDICATOR   REFERENCES (M=MODIFIED D=DEFINED)

            LR           9000 4700
            OF           11000 2800  3300
            01           1500M 4000
            1P           2700  3200
            25           2200M 2300M 2400
*  7031     26           2200M 2400M


     MESSAGES

      MSGID     SEV  NUMBER    TEXT

*  QRG1019      00     1       IGNDECERR(*YES) SPECIFIED ON COMMAND. NO DECIMAL DATA ERRORS
*  QRG2010      10     1       EXTENSION CODE (POS 39) NOT VALID. L (PGM-DESCRIBED PRINTER)
                               OR BLANK (ALL OTHER FILES) ASSUMED.
*  QRG5123      30     1       FACTOR 2 (POSITIONS 33-42) MUST BE AN ARRAY/TABLE TO BE SEAR
                               SPECIFICATION LINE IGNORED
*  QRG5194      30     3       NAME SPECIFIED PREVIOUSLY DEFINED AS FILE/RECORD FORMAT. IF
                               OTHERWISE BLANK ASSUMED.
*  QRG7030      30     5       FIELD OR INDICATOR NOT DEFINED.
*  QRG7031      00     5       NAME OR INDICATOR NOT REFERENCED.
*  QRG7086      00     2       RPG WILL HANDLE BLOCKING FUNCTION FOR THE FILE. INFDS CONTEN
                               ARE TRANSFERRED.
*  QRG8043      10     1       NO SOURCE RECORDS PROVIDED TO INITIALIZE ARRAY/TABLE. ALPHAM
                               NUMERIC ELEMENTS ASSUMED ZERO


     MESSAGE SUMMARY

     TOTAL     00     10     20     30     40     50
      19        8      2      0      9      0      0

      49 RECORDS READ FROM SOURCE FILE
     SOURCE RECORDS INCLUDE   40 SPECIFICATIONS,    0 TABLE RECORDS, AND    9 COMMENTS


     QRG0008 COMPILE TERMINATED. SEVERITY 30 ERRORS FOUND IN PROGRAM


     * * * * * E N D   O F   C O M P I L A T I O N * * * * *
*  QRG1020              ERROR OCCURRED CREATING OR UPDATING DATA AREA RETURNCODE. COMPI
```

Chapter 7 Table Processing

PROGRAMMING PROJECT

Project Overview

A report that lists inventory transactions is to be printed. These transactions contain only the part number, quantity, and a code for the type of transaction. The coding is as follows:

S	Shipment	(Item has been shipped)
R	Receipt	(Received into the warehouse)
T	Stock transfer	(Item transferred to another warehouse)
A	Adjustment	(Quantity adjusted to show correct quantity)

Write the RPG program to produce a listing of the daily transactions. Sample data for this project can be found in Appendix D.

Input Format

The input data for the project is found in a file called INVTRAN in the sample data. The Record Layout for this file is shown in Figure 7.25.

Processing

The description for the table codes will be obtained from an internal table containing four records (one for each transaction type). As each transaction record is processed, a search is made to validate the transaction code and to obtain the correct description for each type of transaction.

Output Format (Printer Spacing Chart)

The output for the project is a report with standard headings. The report will show the part number, the quantity, and the description associated with the record code. When an invalid record code is found, an error message should be printed. A final total for the entire report will also be needed. The Printer Spacing Chart for this report is shown in Figure 7.26.

An example of the finished report is shown in Figure 7.27.

FIGURE 7.25 Programming Project: Record Layout

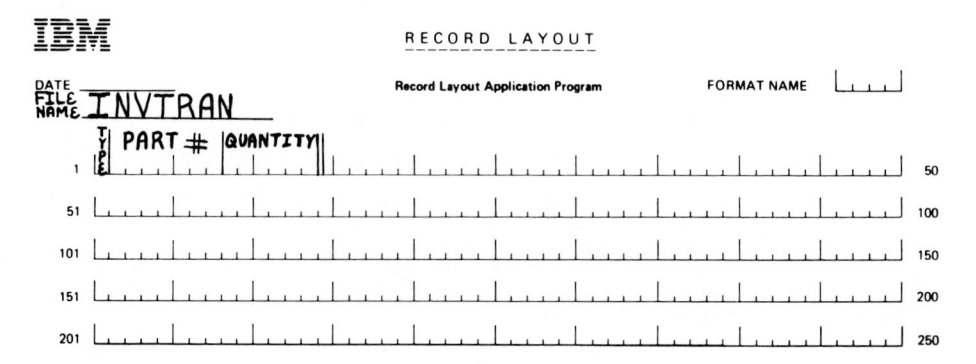

FIGURE 7.26 Programming Project: Printer Spacing Chart

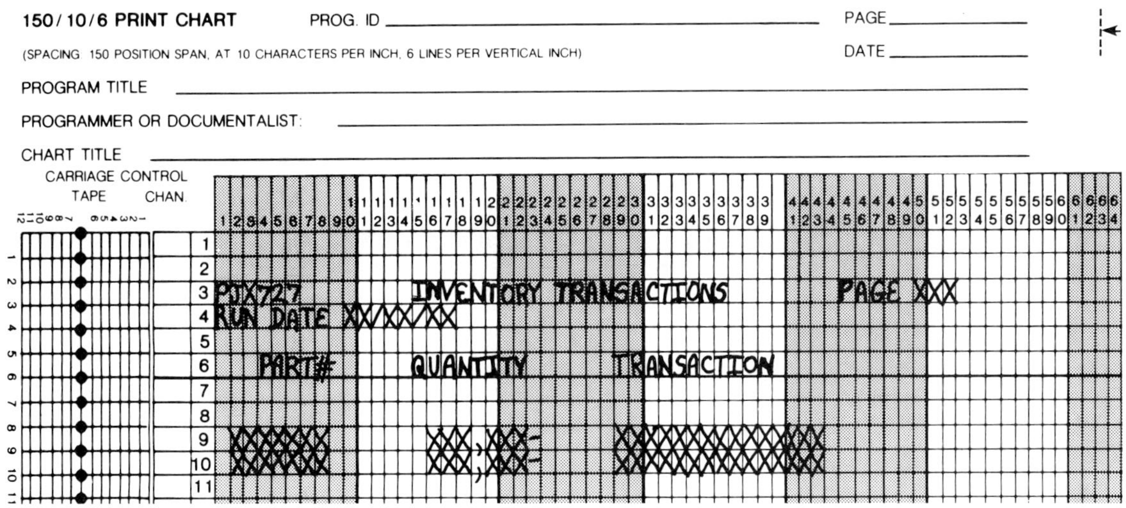

FIGURE 7.27 Programming Project: Final Report

```
PJX727         INVENTORY TRANSACTIONS         PAGE    1
RUN DATE  2/21/92

    PART#       QUANTITY        TRANSACTION

     123          1,000         RECEIPT
     698                        SHIPMENT
     698          1,000         SHIPMENT
     798             23         ADJUSTMENT
    1234            500         INVALID TRAN CODE
    1234            900         ADJUSTMENT
    9875             25-        STOCK TRANSFER
    9903            100         STOCK TRANSFER


    FINAL TOTAL    3,498
```

Chapter 8

Array Processing

What you will learn In Chapter 8

Rules for Constructing Arrays
Examples of Arrays
Extension Specifications for Arrays
How an Array Is Loaded
   Compile Time Arrays
   Pre-Execution Time Arrays
   Execution Time Arrays
Array Processing
   Accessing an Entire Array
   Accessing Individual Elements of an Array

Sample Program 1 Using Three Types of Array
   The Compile Time Array
   Printing the Entire Array
   Pre-Execution Time Array
   Execution Time Array
Sample Program 2 Showing Other Uses of Arrays
   Compile Time Array
   Execution Time Arrays
   Calculation Specifications

Using an Array Index
Computed Index Using Exception Output
Accessing an Array by Index (Looping)
Sample Program 3 Using LOKUP with an Array
   Special Operations for Array Data
Sample Program 4 Using XFOOT
Sample Program 5 Using MOVEA

An array can be defined as a series of data elements having the same characteristics. The data elements can be treated collectively as well as individually. An array is simply a one-dimensional table. The computer will treat tables and arrays very nearly the same. The coding techniques and the applications for arrays differ from those for tables, however.

Using arrays provides many of the same benefits provided by using tables. Arrays make coding easier, reduce coding errors, make the program process much faster, and improve program readability.

RULES FOR CONSTRUCTING ARRAYS ■

The elements of an array must all be of the same size and have the same attributes. An array may contain either all alphanumeric or all numeric fields. An array can contain 1–9999 data elements.

An array can be loaded at compile time or pre-execution time, or it can be created at execution time. (Remember that a table can be loaded only at compile or pre-execution time but *never* at execution time.)

An array can be used to define input data, to define fields being developed within calculations, or to define data being prepared for output. The maximum number of arrays and tables permitted in a program is 200.

EXAMPLES OF ARRAYS ■

An example of an alphanumeric array might be the days of the week: SAT SUN MON TUE WED THU FRI. Each element in this array is alphanumeric and contains three characters. The entire array would consist of seven elements.

A numeric array might contain numbers representing the months of the year: 01 02 03 04, etc. Each element is numeric, containing two positions with zero decimal positions. This array would consist of 12 elements.

EXTENSION SPECIFICATIONS FOR ARRAYS ■

All arrays are defined on the Extension Specifications form, in a manner similar to that used for defining tables. Figure 8.1 shows an example of an entry for an array on an Extension Specifications form.

Columns 27–32 contain the name of the array. This is the name by which the entire array can be accessed. The name used for the array in this example is AR. Notice that an array name *cannot* begin with TAB; those letters are reserved for tables only.

Compile time arrays always require an entry in columns 33–35 to indicate the number of elements per record. A record in this context refers to a line of data. The programmer decides on the number of elements to be entered in each record. In this example, the array contains three elements per record.

Columns 36–39 specify the number of elements in the entire array. Notice that the entire array will contain 30 entries (columns 36–39). As just stated, there will be three entries in each record.

Columns 40–42 contain the length of each element. Column 44 defines the number of decimal places for numeric array elements. In this example, each entry is five positions in length with a decimal position of two.

HOW AN ARRAY IS LOADED ■

There are three times at which an array can be loaded to be used in an RPG program—compile time, pre-execution time, or execution time. The method used to load the arrays (and the arrays themselves) are the same at each time.

Compile Time Arrays

An array may be defined and loaded with data from within the program itself. This means that the array becomes part of the program at the time the program is compiled. The initial contents of the array can be established at the end of the source program, similar to the way in which data is defined for a table (see Chapter 7).

FIGURE 8.1 Extension Specifications for an Array

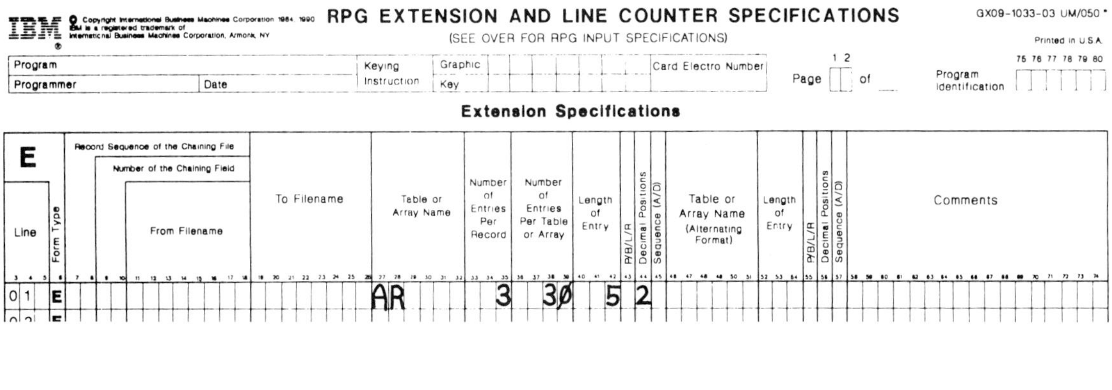

Although compile time arrays might be the easiest and quickest solution to a problem, it is usually wiser to restrict the use of this type of array to groups of items that are guaranteed to be unchanging. Any time the data contained in a compile time array must be changed, the program must be changed and recompiled. This may not present a problem until the need for the change occurs at midnight on the evening when the programmer is planning to leave for vacation, or is nowhere to be found. Some good candidates for compile time arrays might be the number of days in a month or the months of the year.

Figures 8.2(a) and 8.2(b) show the Extension Specifications and Record Layout for a compile time array for months of the year. Note that the entry length is 9 to accommodate the month with the longest name (SEPTEMBER).

FIGURE 8.2(a) Compile Time Array: Extension Specifications

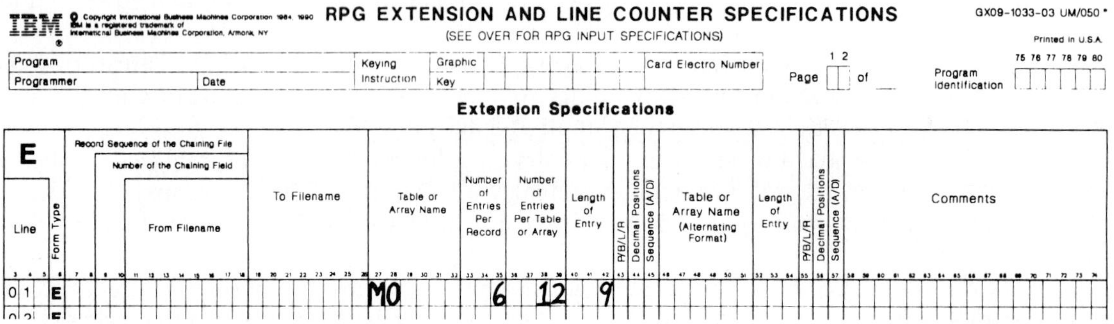

RPG Extension form showing line 01 with Table or Array Name "MO", Number of Entries Per Record = 6, Number of Entries Per Table or Array = 12, Length of Entry = 9.

FIGURE 8.2(b) Array Data

Record Layout "MONTH ARRAY":
Line 1: JANUARY   FEBRUARY MARCH   APRIL   MAY   JUNE

Record Layout "MONTH ARRAY" (continued):
Line 1: JULY   AUGUST   SEPTEMBEROCTOBER NOVEMBER DECEM
Line 51: BER

178 *RPG: A Programming Language for Today*

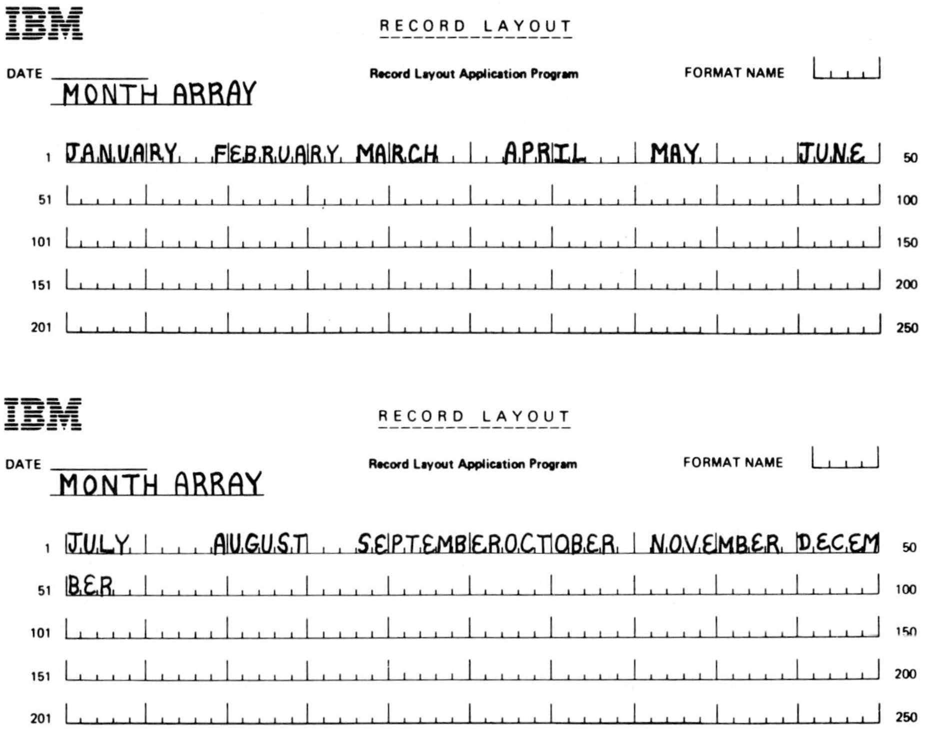

Pre-Execution Time Arrays

A pre-execution time array is stored as a data file of its own, independent of the program (or programs) that will use the array data. This permits independent maintenance of the data by an end-user and provides complete flexibility by allowing the user to enter the unpredictable changes that often occur in the business environment.

Pre-execution time arrays are useful for large volumes of data which may need to be changed occasionally. End-users can be responsible for making the necessary changes to these arrays without the assistance of a programmer. Some examples of array data which should ideally be stored as separate files are tax tables, lists of departments, and groups of standard pay rates for computing standard costs.

The programs using these arrays will treat them as though they were ordinary input files. The difference is that these files will be loaded immediately at the beginning of processing *before* the first input record is read, as whole arrays rather than as separate records.

Figures 8.3(a) and 8.3(b) show examples of the coding for a pre-execution time array.

FIGURE 8.3(a) Pre-Execution Time Array: File Description Specifications

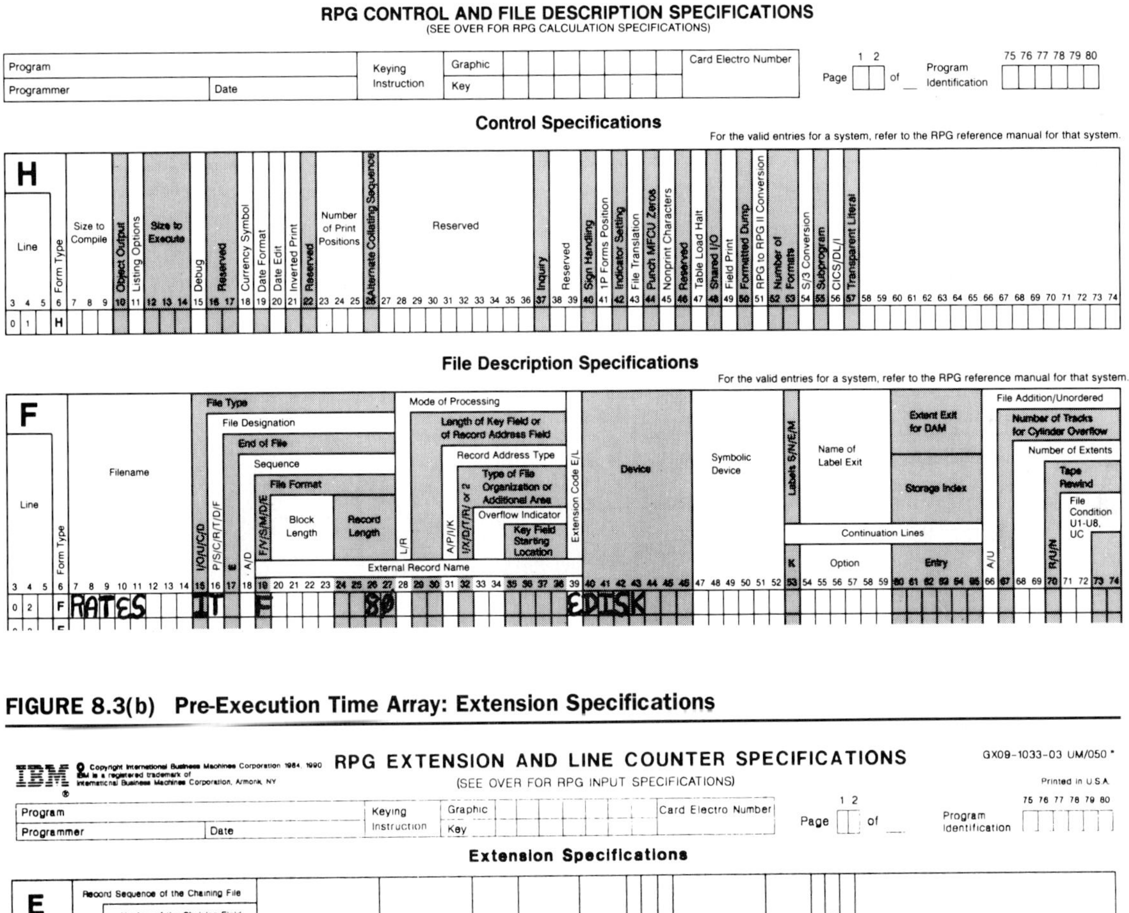

F-spec: `F RATES   IT F  80        EDISK`

FIGURE 8.3(b) Pre-Execution Time Array: Extension Specifications

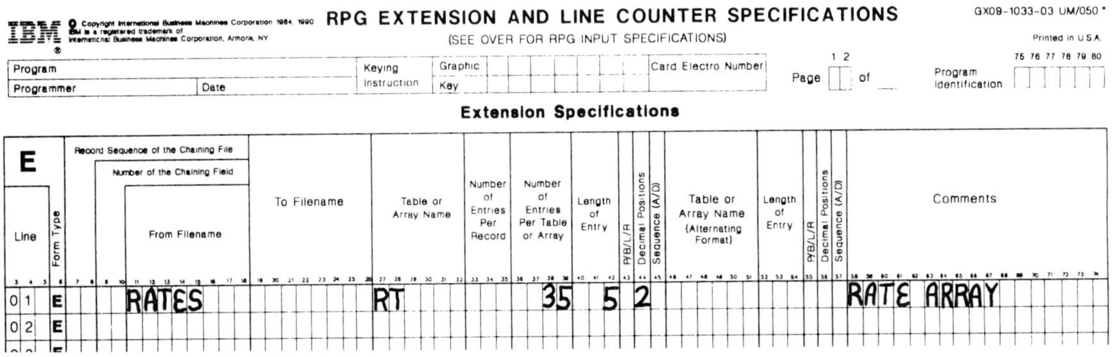

E-spec: `E   RATES       RT    35  5 2       RATE ARRAY`

Chapter 8 *Array Processing*

Execution Time Arrays

Array data which is entered as input data or which will change during the execution of a program is loaded as an execution time array. The initial contents of an execution time array will be blank for alphanumeric arrays and zero for numeric arrays. The programmer does not have to do anything to ensure this. RPG handles this as it would any type of input field. Data is placed in the array during the normal execution of a program.

An execution time array is the most flexible of the arrays and can be used for a multitude of applications in a wide variety of ways. For example, a group of totals might be accumulated in an array during the detail processing of a report and printed on a separate summary page at the end of the report. Figures 8.4(a), 8.4(b), and 8.4(c) show examples of the coding for an execution time array.

FIGURE 8.4(a) Execution Time Array: Extension Specifications

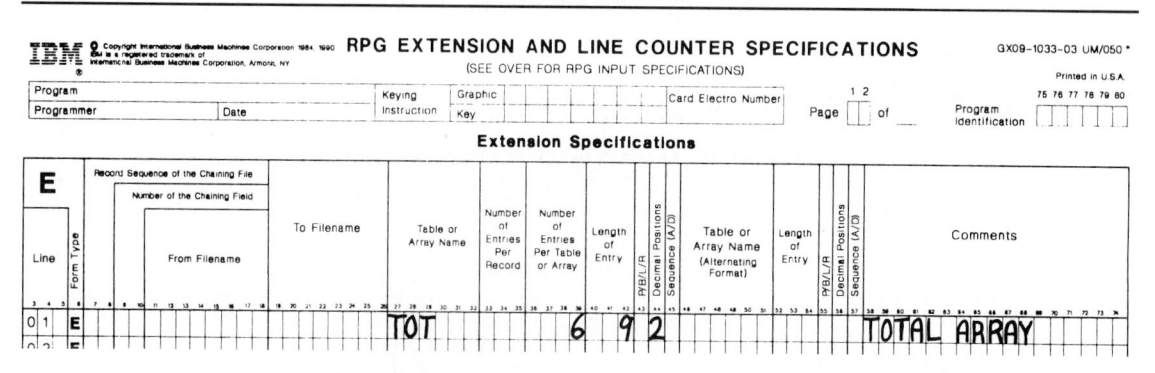

On the RPG Extension Specifications form, line 01:
- Array Name: TOT
- Number of Entries Per Record: 6
- Number of Entries Per Table or Array: 9 (shown as 6 and 92 across columns)
- Length of Entry: 2
- Comments: TOTAL ARRAY

FIGURE 8.4(b) Calculation Specifications

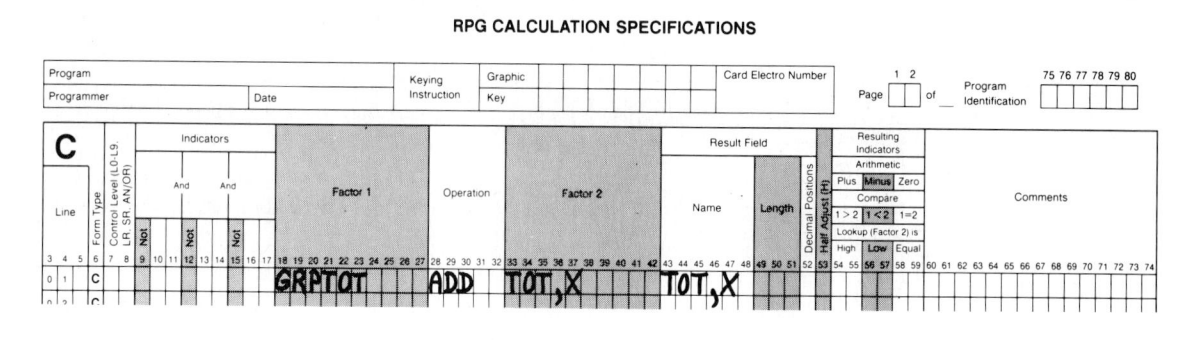

On the RPG Calculation Specifications form, line 01:
- Factor 1: GRPTOT
- Operation: ADD
- Factor 2: TOT,X
- Result Field Name: TOT,X

FIGURE 8.4(c) Output Specifications

On the RPG Input Specifications form:
Line	Filename	T	Sequence	Record ID	Field	K	End
01	SUMRPT	T	1	LR			
02					TOT,1	K	13
03					TOT,2	K	27
04					TOT,3	K	41
05					TOT,4	K	55
06					TOT,5	K	69
07					TOT,6	K	83

ARRAY PROCESSING ■

Nearly every RPG operation can be performed on an array or array element as it is performed on any other field. Array data is accessed in either of two ways. An entire array may be accessed all at once as a single unit, or the program can access each data element of the array individually.

Accessing an Entire Array

An array in RPG is given a name. This allows the programmer to refer to the entire array by name and to perform any operation on the whole array with a single line of code. This means that every element within the array is affected equally by the calculation. To add a value of .10 to every element of an array, all that is needed is one Calculation Specification adding .10 to the array itself, as shown in Figures 8.5(a) and 8.5(b). In this example, the entire array is named RT and contains 236 elements, with each element containing three positions including two decimal positions. Each element will be incremented by .10 in this operation.

Without using arrays, it would have been necessary to add .10 to each of the 236 fields. This would have required 236 separate lines of code. The saving in time and effort is obvious, not to mention the reduction of the risk of keying errors.

Any type of arithmetic operation may be performed on an entire array in this same manner. A very useful function of an array is the use of the Z-ADD or Z-SUB operation to clear out totals in every element of an array all at once.

Accessing Individual Elements of an Array

It may be necessary to perform calculations on individual elements within an array independently from calculations being performed on other elements in the same array. Since the element in the array has no name of its own, it is necessary to have a method for identifying the particular element by itself.

The location of the element within the array is identified by an index. (In any other language, including mathematics, this would be called a subscript.). Figure 8.6 shows how an index is coded in RPG. The array HRS is followed by its index (separated by a comma). The index in the example is 3, which means that the third element of the array will be multiplied by the rate of pay field, resulting in a field called TOTPAY.

Array names are usually limited to three positions or fewer to allow space for entering an index. For example, if an array were named ARRAY, there would not be enough room in the result field on the Calculation Specifications or in the field name on the Output Specifications to enter a comma and a digit. If an array contained 1000 elements, you would need to allow for the comma and four positions to code the index. This would restrict the name of the array to only one position.

RPG does *not* support multidimensional arrays or nested arrays, although there are always other methods for coaxing RPG to accomplish this. Single-dimension arrays are usually sufficient for most business applications.

FIGURE 8.5(a) Extension Specifications: Array

FIGURE 8.5(b) Calculation Specifications: Adding to an Array

Line	Form Type	Factor 1	Operation	Factor 2	Result Field	Length	Comments
01	C	RT	ADD	.10	RT		INCREASE RATES

FIGURE 8.6 Coding an Array Index

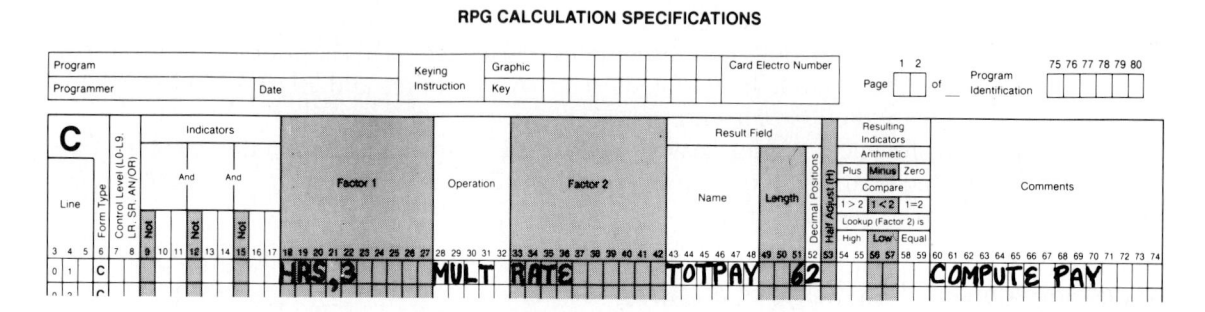

Line	Form Type	Factor 1	Operation	Factor 2	Result Field	Length	Comments
01	C	HRS,3	MULT	RATE	TOTPAY	62	COMPUTE PAY

SAMPLE PROGRAM 1 USING THREE TYPES OF ARRAY ■

The following sample program will incorporate examples of all three types of arrays with some typical applications for their use.

This program will print a list of inventory items showing the quantity on hand for each item at each of ten store locations. The store locations will print across the page so that only one line will be required for each inventory item. Store locations are represented by a nine-position field for each store heading.

A total will be printed at the end of each product group for each of the ten stores and a final total will be computed for all ten stores. Figure 8.7 shows the Printer Spacing Chart for the desired report.

FIGURE 8.7 Printer Spacing Chart for the Sample Program

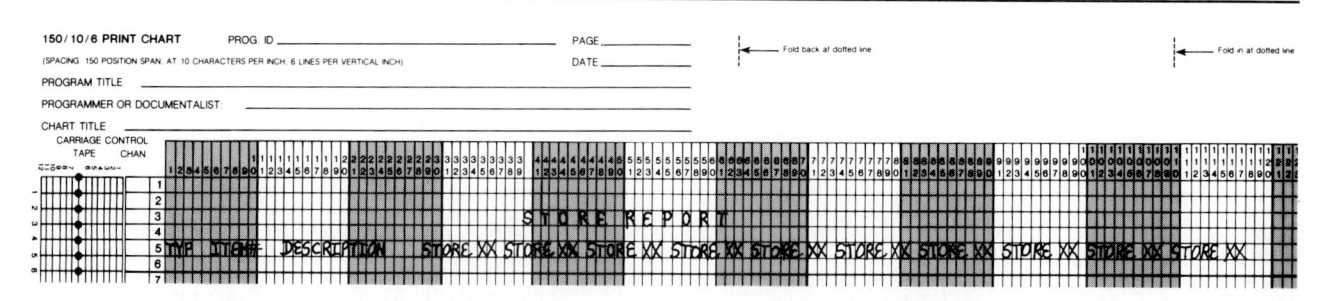

Line 3: STORE REPORT
Line 5: TYP ITEM# DESCRIPTION STORE XX STORE XX STORE XX STORE XX STORE XX STORE XX STORE XX STORE XX STORE XX STORE XX

FIGURE 8.8 Extension Specifications for the Sample Program

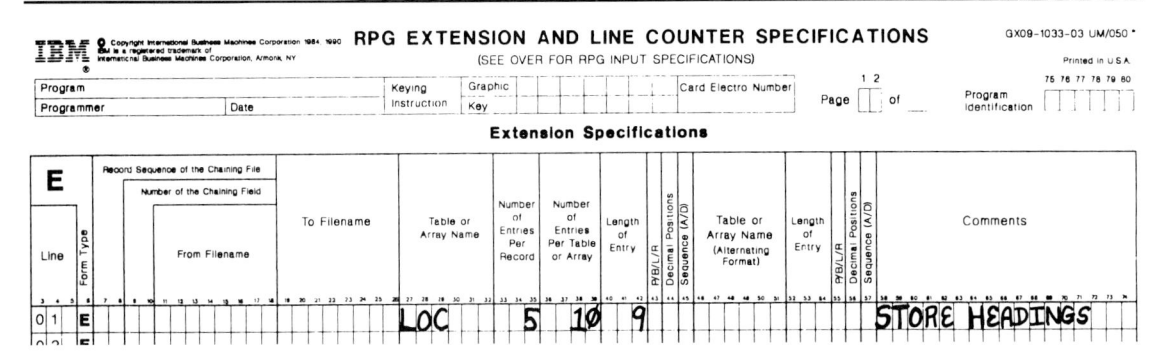

Line	Form Type	From Filename	To Filename	Table or Array Name	Number of Entries Per Record	Number of Entries Per Table or Array	Length of Entry	P/B/L/R	Decimal Positions	Sequence (A/D)	Table or Array Name (Alternating Format)	Length of Entry	P/B/L/R	Decimal Positions	Sequence (A/D)	Comments
01	E			LOC	5	10	9									STORE HEADINGS
02	E															

The Compile Time Array

Figure 8.8 shows the Extension Specifications for the sample project. No File Description Specifications are needed for a compile time array.

The compile time array has been named LOC and will contain the heading title for each of the store locations. The entire array will contain ten entries (columns 36–39) and there will be five entries in each record. Each entry is nine positions in length. The decimal position is blank since the elements are alphanumeric.

The initial contents of compile time arrays are defined at the end of the source program after all of the Output Specifications, as they were for tables in Chapter 7. Figure 8.9 shows the array data itself following some Output Specifications. The array data is separated from the Output Specifications by asterisks in columns 1–2.

The array consists of a total of ten entries (nine positions each) representing each of ten store locations. Each line of array data contains five locations.

FIGURE 8.9 Array Data

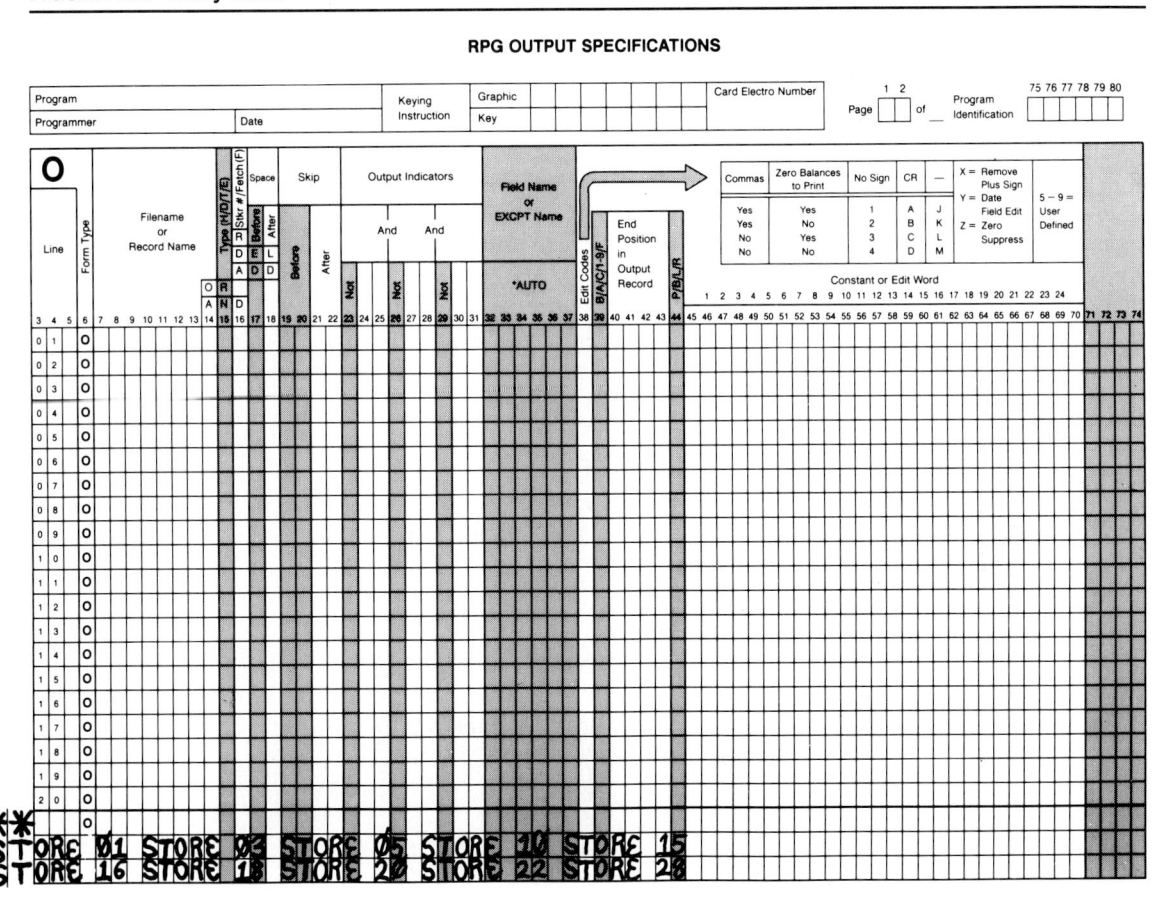

```
**
STORE 01 STORE 03 STORE 05 STORE 10 STORE 15
STORE 16 STORE 18 STORE 20 STORE 22 STORE 28
```

Chapter 8 Array Processing

FIGURE 8.10(a) Output Specifications

[RPG Output Specifications form showing coded entries:]

```
01  O  REPORT    D  203      L1
02  O     OR                 OFNL1
03  O                                     71  'STORE REPORT'
04  O            D  2        L1
05  O     OR                 OFNL1
06  O                                     24  'DESCRIPTION'
07  O                                      3  'TYP'
08  O                                     10  'ITEM#'
09  O                         LOC        117
10  O
```

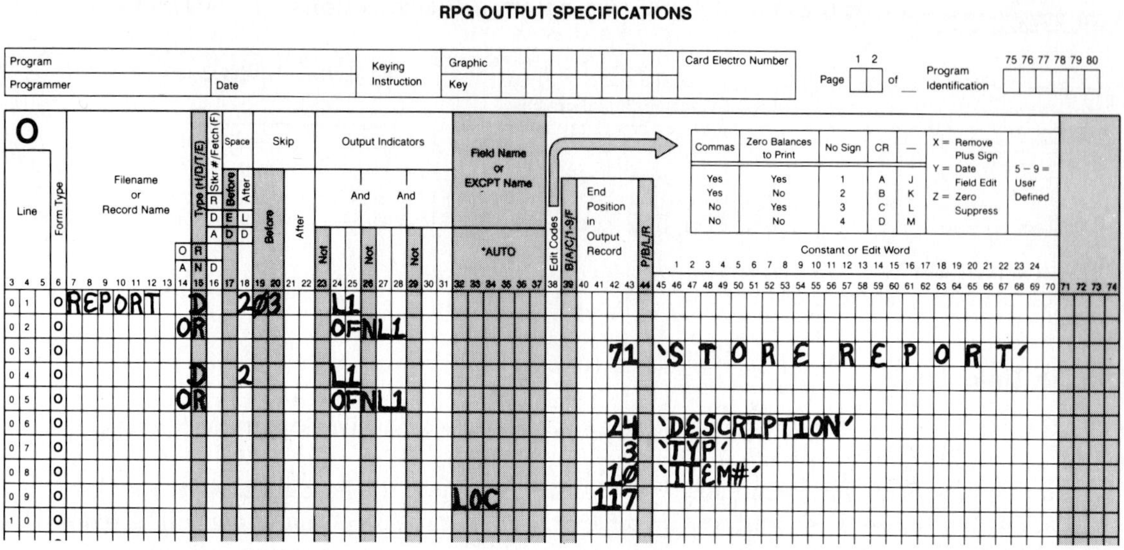

FIGURE 8.10(b) Sample Report

```
                                   STORE REPORT
TYP ITEM#  DESCRIPTION   STORE 01 STORE 03 STORE 05 STORE 10 STORE 15 STORE 16 STORE 18 STORE 20 STORE 22 STORE 28
```

Printing the Entire Array

An array can be referenced all at once by referring to it by name. This entire array can be printed in the heading of the report by referring to it by name on the Output Specifications and specifying an ending position for the last location. Figure 8.10(a) shows the coding for the Output Specifications and Figure 8.10(b) shows a printout. Notice that the location will print for all ten locations with only one line of code having been specified.

Pre-Execution Time Array

To illustrate the use of pre-execution time arrays, the sample program is continued. A pre-execution time array is loaded *before* any input is read. This array contains the valid part number. The input data can be checked against this array of valid part numbers to ensure their accuracy before processing. Figures 8.11(a), 8.11.(b), and 8.11(c) show the coding for this pre-execution time array.

Execution Time Array

The Record Layout for the input data is shown in Figure 8.12. Of course, it is convenient that the quantities on hand at each of the stores are contained in a single record. Each record contains the inventory item number, a description field, and a three-position product type code followed by each of the ten quantities.

Defining and Loading the Execution Time Array

In this example, the programmer makes use of an array to define the input file. Since the quantity fields in the input file are all of the same length and type (five positions, numeric), they can be defined as a single array. The array will consist of ten elements of five positions each.

FIGURE 8.11(a) Pre-Execution Time Array: File Specifications

Control Specifications:
- Line 01: H

File Description Specifications:
- Line 02: F PARTFILE IT F 150 EDISK

FIGURE 8.11(b) Extension Specifications

Extension Specifications:
- Line 01: E PARTFILE PN 20 20 7 0 VALID PART ARRAY

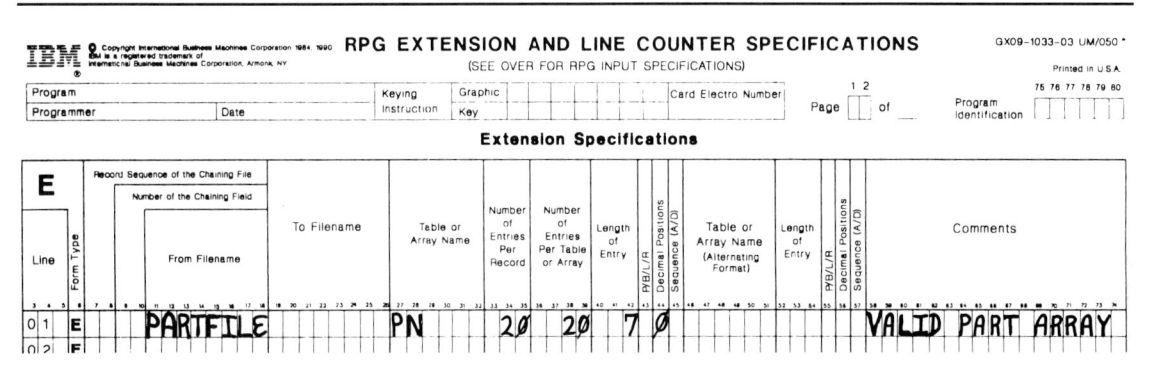

FIGURE 8.11(c) Input Specifications

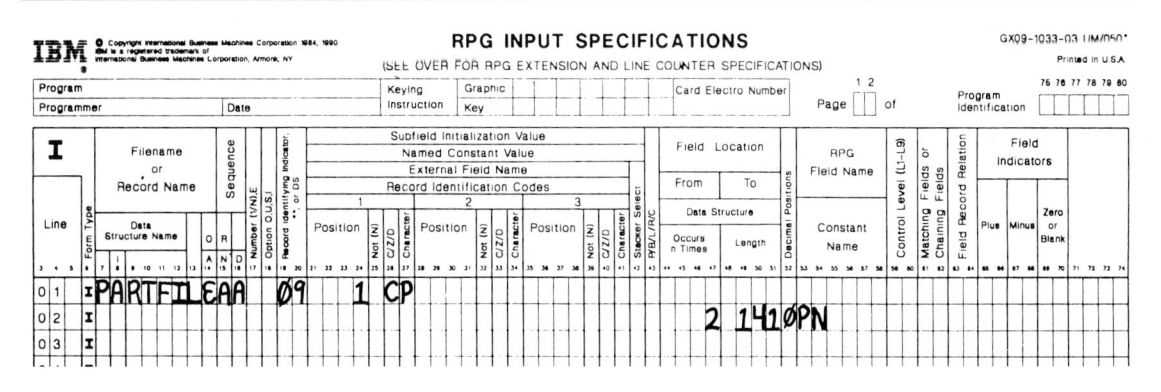

Input Specifications:
- Line 01: I PARTFILE AA 09 1 CP
- Line 02: I   2   14 0PN
- Line 03: I

FIGURE 8.12 Input Data Record Layout

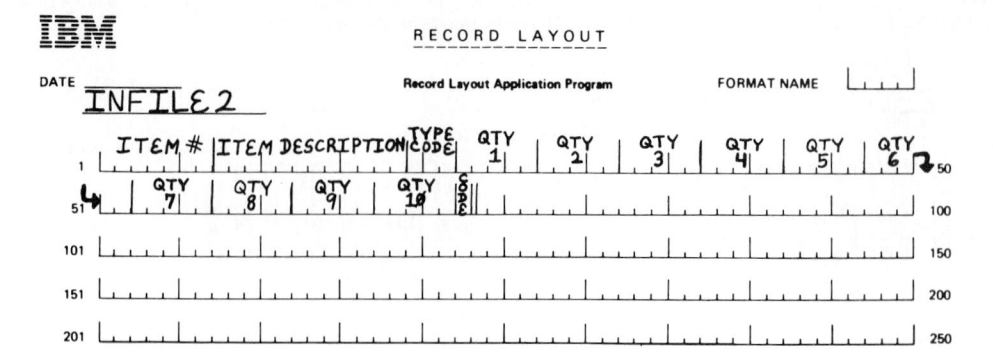

```
IBM                                    RECORD LAYOUT
DATE                          Record Layout Application Program    FORMAT NAME
   INFILE 2
           ITEM # | ITEM DESCRIPTION | TYPE | QTY | QTY | QTY | QTY | QTY | QTY
                                      CODE   1     2     3     4     5     6
  1                                                                              50
        QTY | QTY | QTY | QTY
  51     7     8     9    10                                                    100
 101                                                                            150
 151                                                                            200
 201                                                                            250
```

The characteristics of the array are defined on the Extension Specifications. Figures 8.13(a), 8.13(b), and 8.13(c) show the coding for the File Description Specifications, the Extension Specifications, and the Input Specifications for this example. Notice that the array name entered in columns 27–32 of the Extension Specifications must be the same name used on the Input Specifications to describe the location of the array in the input record. The array is described on the Input Specifications as a single field although it contains ten separate pieces of information. The name chosen for the input array for this example is QTY.

QTY is defined as a single field which is 50 positions long. It is defined as numeric (0 in column 52 of the Input Specifications). This means that each of the elements within the array is five positions, numeric, and has zero decimal positions.

On the Extension Specifications, the array name is also QTY. The array is defined in detail by further entries. The number of entries per table or array (10) is entered in columns 36–39. The length of each entry (5) is entered in columns 40–42. The number of decimal positions for each element (0) is entered in column 44. The entry for the decimal positions on the Extension Specifications must always correspond to the entry in column 52 of the Input Specifications. Notice that columns 33–35 remain blank for an execution time array.

FIGURE 8.13(a) Array Defining Input File: File Description Specifications

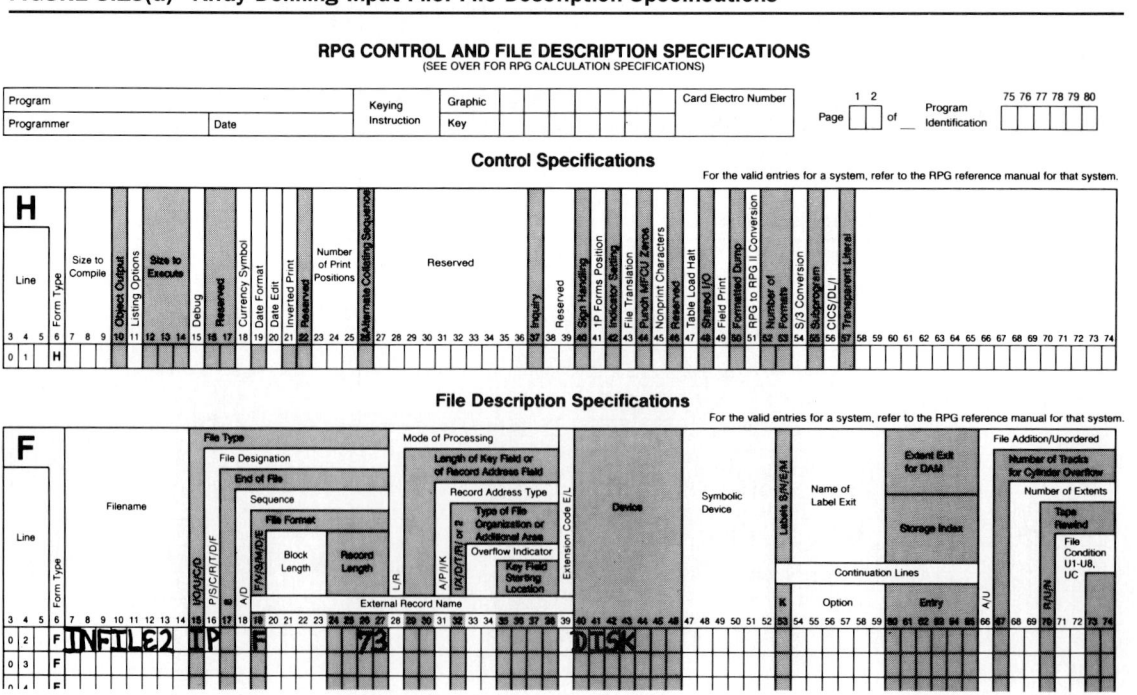

[RPG Control and File Description Specifications form with entry:
F INFILE2 IP F 73 DISK]

186 *RPG: A Programming Language for Today*

FIGURE 8.13(b) Extension Specifications

E-spec row 01: From Filename (blank), To Filename (blank), Table or Array Name = QTY, Number of Entries Per Record = 10, Length of Entry = 5, Decimal Positions = 0, Comments = QUANTITY ARRAY

FIGURE 8.13(c) Input Specifications

Line	Filename/Record	Sequence	Record Id Codes	From	To	Field Name	Control Level
01	INFILE2	AA	01 73 CI				
02				1	7	ITEM#	
03				8	19	DESC	
04				20	22	TYPE	L1
05				23	72	QTY	
06		ZZ	99				

Each time an input record is read, the array will be loaded with the quantities from that input record. This means that each element of the input array can be accessed either individually or as a group. A level break (L1) will be taken on the TYPE field so a total can be printed for each type.

Reading the first record in this project causes the input data to be loaded into the array.

Calculating the Level Totals

In calculating the level totals, the array is first checked to ensure that a valid item number has been entered. A valid item will cause indicator 24 to be turned on.

Compared to coding level totals for each of the ten quantity fields individually, coding level totals for an entire array is a very simple task. As shown in Figure 8.14(a), only one line of code is required to develop the product group totals and only one line of code is needed to compute the

FIGURE 8.14(a) Coding Level Totals for an Entire Array: Extension Specifications

Line	From Filename	To Filename	Table or Array Name	Number of Entries Per Record	Length of Entry	Decimal Positions	Comments
01			QTY	10	5	0	DETAIL QUANTITIES
02			LQT	10	5	0	LEVEL QTYS
03			FQT	10	5	0	FINAL QTYS

Chapter 8 Array Processing

FIGURE 8.14(b) Calculation Specifications

RPG CALCULATION SPECIFICATIONS

Line	Form Type			Factor 1	Operation	Factor 2	Result Field Name	Length		Resulting Indicators			Comments
01	C			ITEM#	LOKUP	PN						24 VALID ITEM#
02	C	24			LQT	ADD	QTY	LQT					
03	C	L1			FQT	ADD	LQT	FQT					

final totals. Simply add the entire array into another array. This is all defined within the program itself at execution time. As shown in Figure 8.14(b), the array QTY is added to an array called LQT giving a result of LQT.

The quantity value in the first element of the QTY array will be added to the first element of the LQT array. The second element will be added to the second element in LQT and so on until the entire array contains the correct totals for each element.

This LQT array will accumulate a total for all items until a store level is encountered, printed, and cleared. At level 1 time, the LQT totals can then be added to the final total array called FQT. All of this is accomplished with only two lines of Calculation Specifications.

Printing the Detail Amounts

The detail lines of the report can now be printed on the output report. As shown in Figure 8.15, the product group, the inventory part number, and the description will be printed exactly as expected on each line. The array data from QTY, however, will be printed individually element by element. This is defined by the index. The first element is referred to as QTY,1 and is printed ending in

FIGURE 8.15 Output Specifications for Printing Array

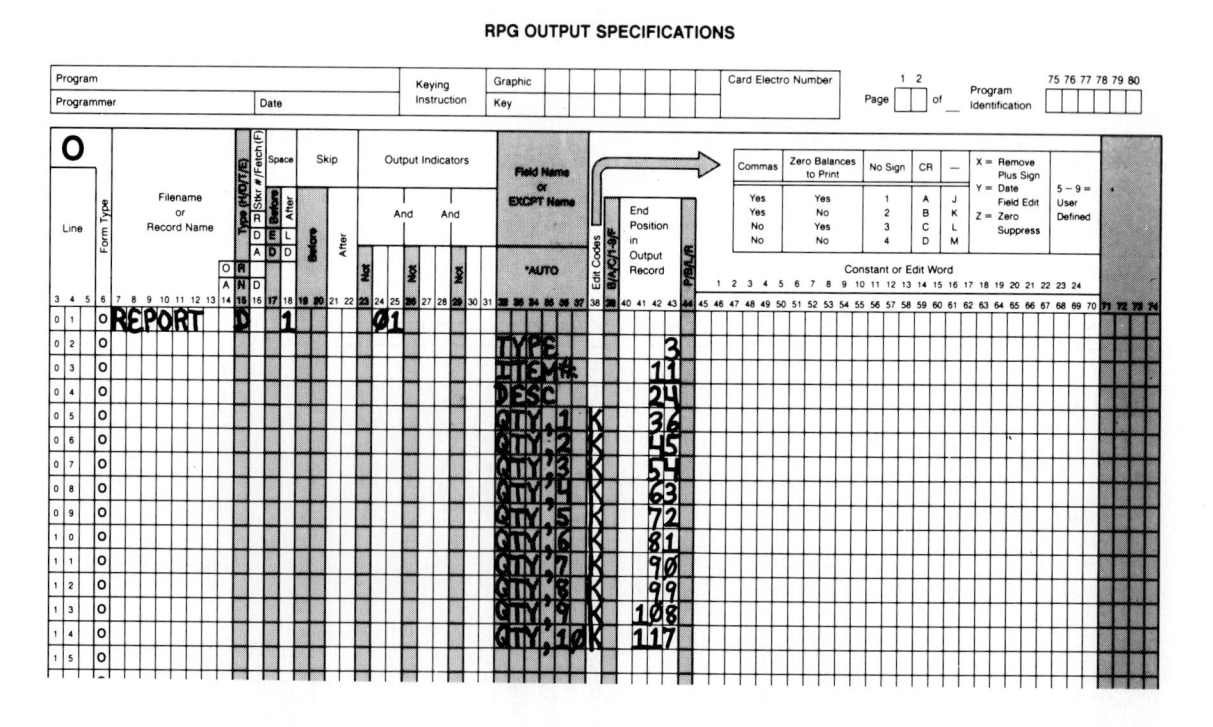

RPG OUTPUT SPECIFICATIONS

Line	Form Type	Filename or Record Name	Type			Output Indicators	Field Name or EXCPT Name		End Position in Output Record		Constant or Edit Word
01	O	REPORT	D	1		01					
02	O						TYPE		3		
03	O						ITEM#		11		
04	O						DESC		24		
05	O						QTY,1	K	36		
06	O						QTY,2	K	45		
07	O						QTY,3	K	54		
08	O						QTY,4	K	63		
09	O						QTY,5	K	72		
10	O						QTY,6	K	81		
11	O						QTY,7	K	90		
12	O						QTY,8	K	99		
13	O						QTY,9	K	108		
14	O						QTY,10	K	117		

position 36; the second element is QTY,2 and is printed next, and so on. Thus, each element will appear in its proper place on the report. Each element is edited with an edit code K as any other field is edited.

Printing the Level Totals

Level totals are printed in the same way that the detail lines were printed. Figures 8.16(a) and 8.16(b) show the completed program and finished report.

This sample program has made use of all three types of arrays: compile time, pre-execution, and execution time. A program can make use of any one or all of these types of arrays.

FIGURE 8.16(a) Completed Program

```
SEQUENCE        1         2         3         4         5         6         7
NUMBER   67890123456789012345678901234567890123456789012345678901234



       100  F* TITLE: ILLUSTRATION FOR 8.16
       200  F* DATE:   4/30           AUTHOR: D.CABLE
       300  F* DESCRIPTION:
       400  F**************************************************************

NAME OF PROGRAM WILL BE ILL816 IN LIBRARY CABLE

            H
* 1019              ALL DECIMAL DATA ERRORS IGNORED
       500  FPARTFILEIT  F      150           EDISK
       600  FINFILE2 IP  F       73           DISK
       700  FREPORT  O   F      132     OF    PRINTER
       800  F**************************************************************

       900  E               LOC      5   10  9           STORE HEADINGS
      1000  E    PARTFILE   PN      20   20  7 0         VALID PT ARRAY
      1100  E               QTY         10  5 0          INPUT QTY
      1200  E               LQT         10  5 0          1ST LEVEL QTY
      1300  E               FQT         10  5 0          FINAL TOT QTY

      1400  IINFILE2 AA  01   73 CI
      1500  I                                1   7OITEM#
      1600  I                                8  19 DESC
      1700  I                               20  22 TYPE    L1
      1800  I                               23  72OQTY
      1900  I          ZZ    99

      2000  C           ITEM#    LOKUPPN                   24VALID ITEM#?
      2100  C    24     LQT      ADD   QTY     LQT
      2200  CL1         FQT      ADD   LQT     FQT

      2300  ORCPORT   D   203   L1
      2400  O    OR               OF
      2500  O                                  71 'S T O R E   R E P O R T'
      2600  O         D   2      L1
      2700  O    OR               OF
      2800  O                                   3 'TYP'
      2900  O                                  10 'ITEM#'
      3000  O                                  24 'DESCRIPTION'
      3100  O                          LOC    117
      3200  O         D   1     01 24
      3300  O                          TYPE     3
      3400  O                          ITEM#   11
      3500  O                          DESC    24
      3600  O                          QTY,1 K 36
      3700  O                          QTY,2 K 45
      3800  O                          QTY,3 K 54
```

FIGURE 8.16(a) Continued

```
         SEQUENCE      1          2          3          4          5          6          7
         NUMBER     67890123456789012345678901234567890123456789012345678901234

           3900   O                             QTY,4   K     63
           4000   O                             QTY,5   K     72
           4100   O                             QTY,6   K     81
           4200   O                             QTY,7   K     90
           4300   O                             QTY,8   K     99
           4400   O                             QTY,9   K    108
           4500   O                             QTY,10K      117
           4600   O           D  1      01N24
           4700   O                             TYPE          3
           4800   O                             ITEM#        11
           4900   O                             DESC         24
           5000   O                                          39 'INVALID ITEM#'
           5100   O           T  2      L1
           5200   O                                          17 'TYPE TOTAL'
           5300   O                             LQT    KB   117
           5400   O           T  1      LR
           5500   O                                          18 'FINAL TOTAL'
           5600   O                             FQT    K    117
      * * * * * E N D   O F   S O U R C E * * * * *


      * 7086        500    RPG PROVIDES BLOCK/UNBLOCK SUPPORT FOR FILE PARTFILE.
      * 7086        600    RPG PROVIDES BLOCK/UNBLOCK SUPPORT FOR FILE INFILE2.
                  TABLE/ARRAY ------- LOC
           5800   STORE 01  STORE 03  STORE 05  STORE 10  STORE 15
           5900   STORE 16  STORE 18  STORE 20  STORE 22  STORE 28
```

FIGURE 8.16(b) Finished Report

```
                              S T O R E   R E P O R T

TYP  ITEM#    DESCRIPTION   STORE 01 STORE 03 STORE 05 STORE 10 STORE 15 STORE 16 STORE 18 STORE 20 STORE 22 STORE 28

 A   0000123  ONETWOTHREE       1        5       10       15                20       25        1        8        9
 A   0000234  TWOTHREEFOUR      1        1        1        1        1        1        1        1        1
 A   0000532  FIVETHREETWO  INVALID ITEM#
 A   0002020  TWENTYTWENTY     25       25       25       25                                           25      900
           TYPE TOTAL          27       31       36       41        1       21       26        2       34      909


                              S T O R E   R E P O R T

TYP  ITEM#    DESCRIPTION   STORE 01 STORE 03 STORE 05 STORE 10 STORE 15 STORE 16 STORE 18 STORE 20 STORE 22 STORE 28

 B   0006000  NEWONE        INVALID ITEM#
           TYPE TOTAL


           FINAL TOTAL          27       31       36       41        1       21       26        2       34      909
```

SAMPLE PROGRAM 2 SHOWING OTHER USES OF ARRAYS ∎

To demonstrate how flexible an array can be, sample program 2 will print a summary of the same inventory information, presenting the array vertically instead of horizontally on the report. Instead of printing the quantity fields horizontally across the page each time a record is read, the report will list each location vertically down the page, printing total quantities followed by total dollar amounts for each location. The report will summarize and print only a total for each location. Figure 8.17 shows the Printer Spacing Chart for this new version of the inventory report.

To obtain the dollar amounts, the input record has been expanded to include a second set of fields containing a unit price for each inventory item. As a further complication, the price charged for each inventory item may differ among stores. Figure 8.18 shows the revised input format.

FIGURE 8.17 Printer Spacing Chart for the Summary Report

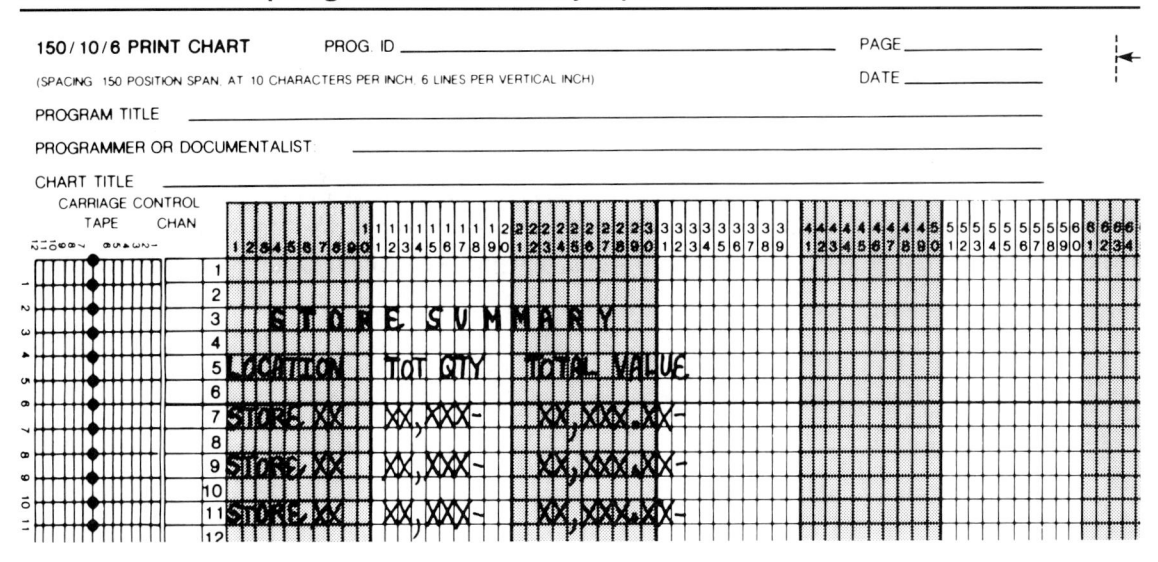

```
                    STORE SUMMARY
            LOCATION    TOT QTY    TOTAL VALUE

            STORE XX    XX,XXX     XX,XXX.XX-

            STORE XX    XX,XXX     XX,XXX.XX-

            STORE XX    XX,XXX     XX,XXX.XX-
```

FIGURE 8.18 Revised Input Specifications

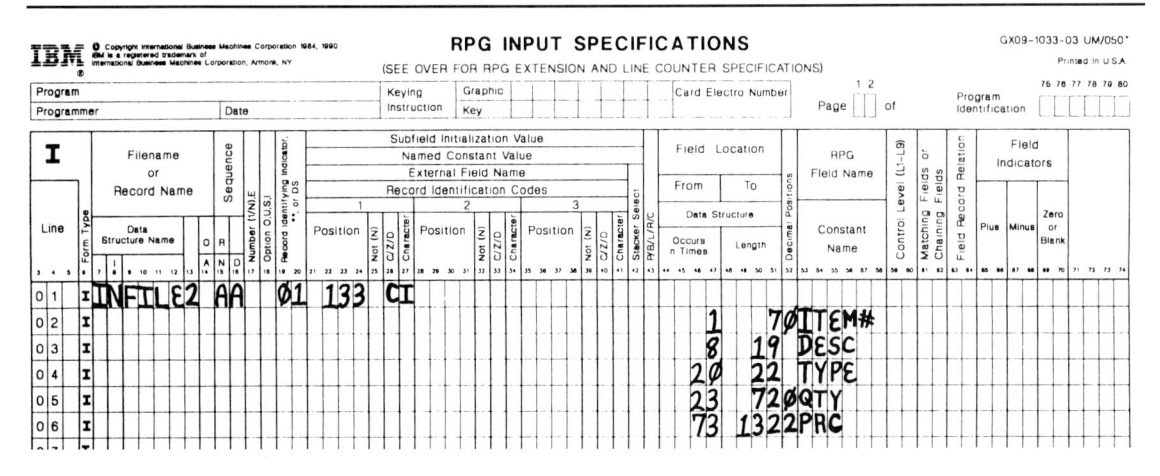

```
01  I INFILE2  AA   01 133   CI
02  I                                    1   70 ITEM#
03  I                                    8   19 DESC
04  I                                   20   22 TYPE
05  I                                   23  720 QTY
06  I                                   73 1322 PRC
```

Compile Time Array

The compile time array for the ten store locations will be the same as it was for sample program 1.

Execution Time Arrays

For this problem, there will be two arrays to define the input data (shown in Figure 8.19). One array will contain all the quantities and the second will contain all the prices.

FIGURE 8.19 Arrays Defining Input Data

```
01  E                    QTY      10  5 0          QUANTITY ARRAY
02  E                    PRC      10  6 2          UNIT PRICE ARRAY
```

Chapter 8 Array Processing

Calculation Specifications

Calculations to compute the totals for each store location will be quite brief. Since the first element in all arrays contains information related to location 1, it is reasonable that each array can be processed simultaneously using the same index to retrieve related information for location 1. Thus, QTY,1 corresponds to PRC,1 and also to LOC,1. The same would be true of location 2 and the others as well. Therefore it is a simple matter to multiply the QTY array by the PRC array, resulting in a total price array called EXT. The QTY and EXT arrays can be accumulated for a store total. Figures 8.20(a), 8.20(b), and 8.20(c) show the Extension, Input, and Calculation Specifications needed to do the computations to extend the dollar totals for each inventory item and accumulate the totals.

FIGURE 8.20(a) Extension Specifications for Arrays

Line	Table or Array Name	Number of Entries Per Record	Number of Entries Per Table or Array	Length of Entry	Decimal Positions	Comments
01	QTY		10	5	0	QUANTITY ARRAY
02	PRC		10	6	2	PRICE ARRAY
03	EXT		10	7	2	EXTENDED PRICE
04	FQT		10	6	0	TOTAL QTY/STORE
05	FEX		10	8	2	TOTAL PRICE/STORE
06	LOC	5	10	9		LOCATION

FIGURE 8.20(b) Input Specifications

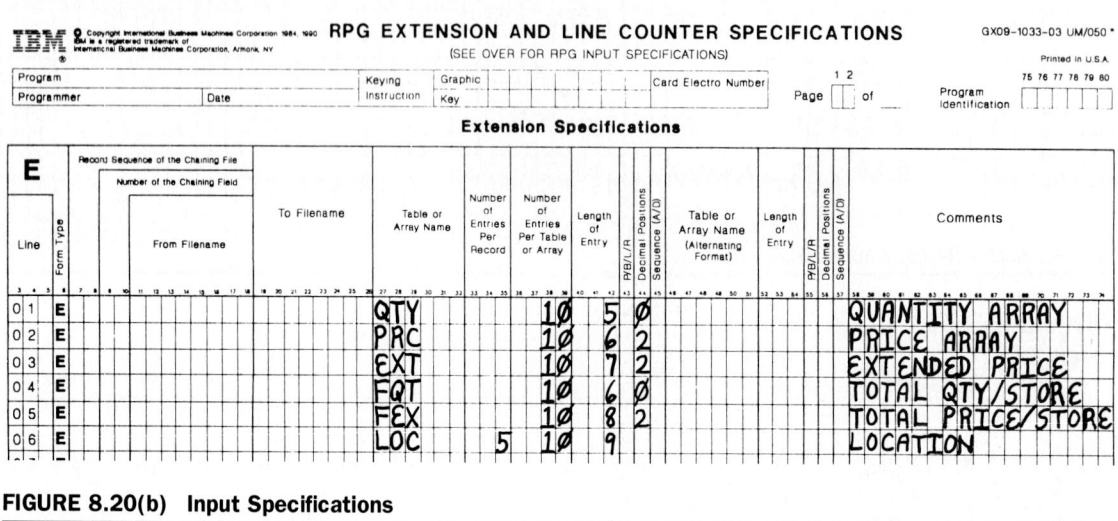

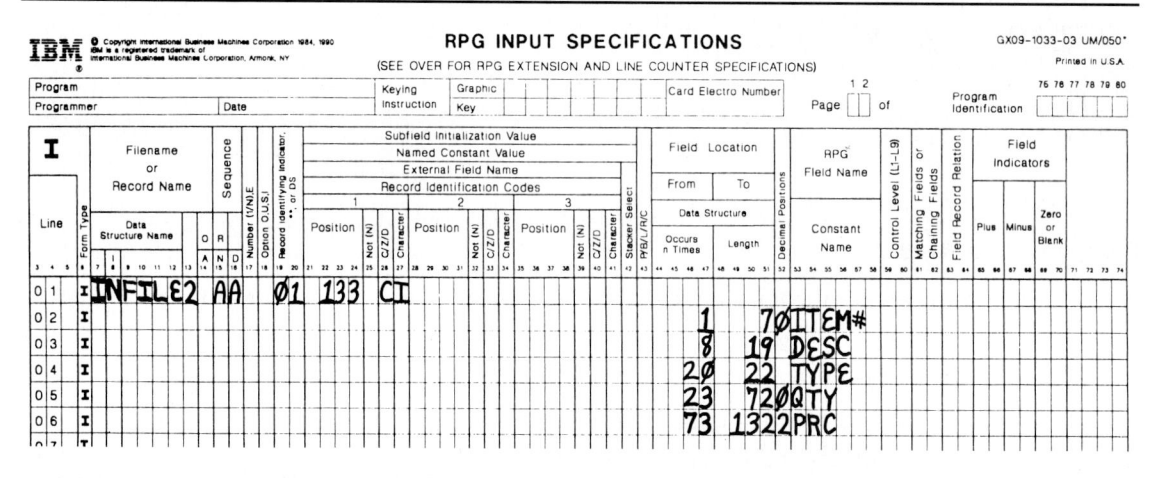

Line	Filename or Record Name	Sequence	Record Identification Codes Position	Field Location From	To	Decimal Positions	RPG Field Name
01	INFILE2	AA	01 133 C1				
02				1	7	0	ITEM#
03				8	19		DESC
04				20	22		TYPE
05				23	72	0	QTY
06				73	132	2	PRC

FIGURE 8.20(c) Calculation Specifications

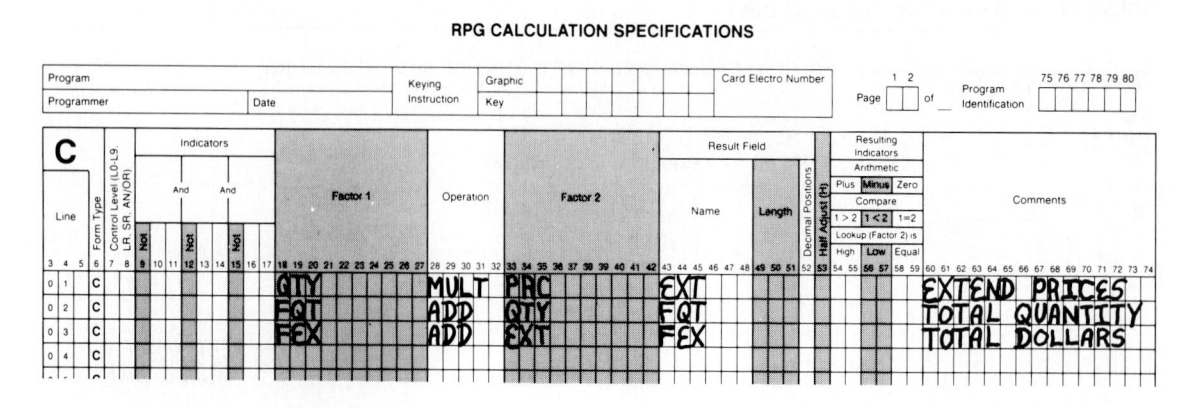

Line	Factor 1	Operation	Factor 2	Result Field Name	Comments
01	QTY	MULT	PRC	EXT	EXTEND PRICES
02	FQT	ADD	QTY	FQT	TOTAL QUANTITY
03	FEX	ADD	EXT	FEX	TOTAL DOLLARS

Using an Array Index

Instead of printing at L1 time, this report will print a line for each element of the array. Since not all the totals for each location are known until all the records have been read and calculated, this report cannot be printed until LR (last record) time. This will result in printing ten lines of information. Figures 8.21(a), 8.21(b), and 8.21(c) show what this coding would look like. The entire report is printed at LR total time showing each specific index corresponding to each store location.

Computed Index Using Exception Output

Although the above report will be accurate and fairly easy to program, there may be a better way to accomplish the same report with less effort. Coding ten lines of Output Specifications does not require much extra work, but suppose there had been 1000 store locations instead of ten. The amount of keying would be discouraging. RPG has a better method for dealing with repetitive operations such as the one just described.

Rather than specifying the exact digit for the index for each line of print it is better to produce the report using exception output. The report will be created at LR time, but the index of the array element to be printed is computed in the Calculation Specifications.

It is possible to create a field that contains the correct index for each calculation. This field is then used as the index with which to locate the array element, as shown in Figures 8.22(a) and 8.22(b). Notice that all the exception output occurs at LR time.

Accessing an Array by Index (Looping)

In order to access an array by index, the field that will hold the index is first set to 1. We will call this field X. By setting X to 1, the first element printed will be element 1. You should *not* set the index to zero or to a negative number, since the program could never find anything within the

FIGURE 8.21(a) Output Specifications for a Report Showing a Specific Index Corresponding to Each Store Location

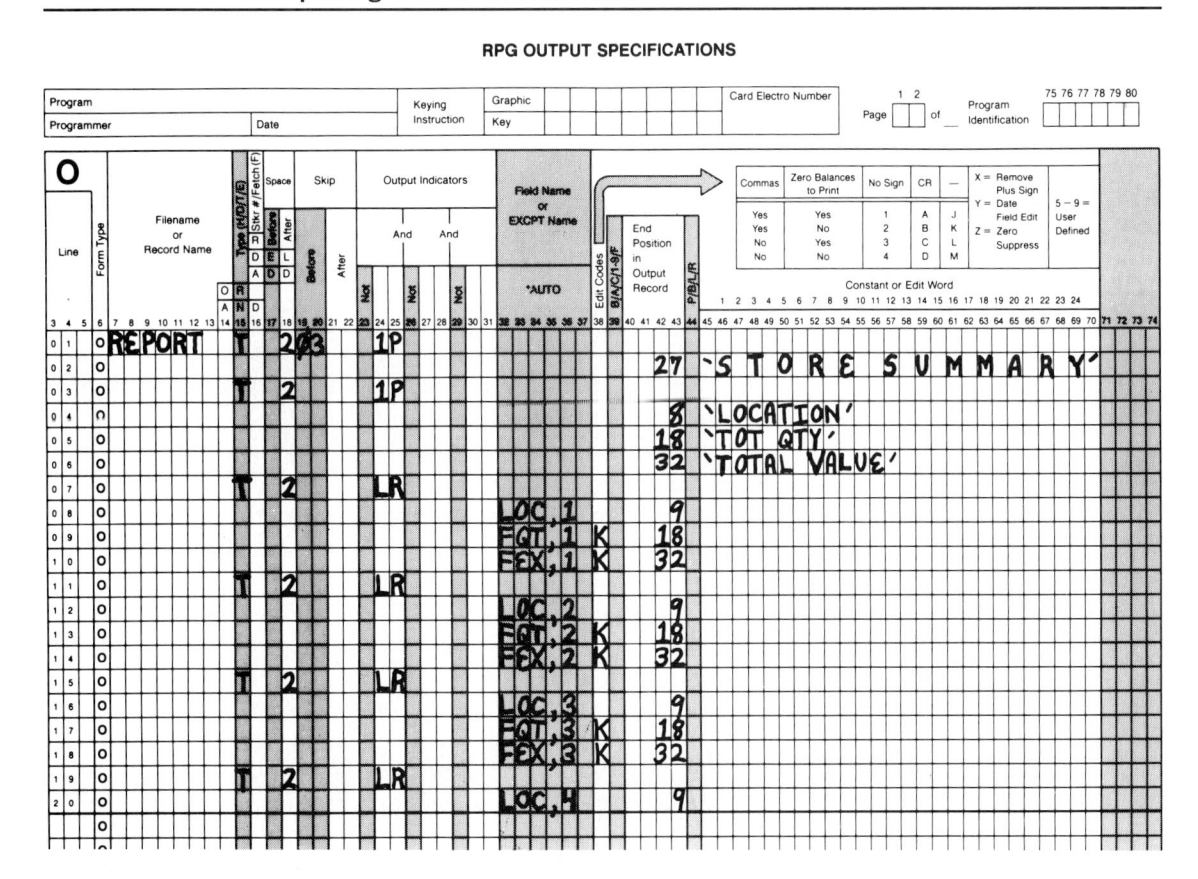

Chapter 8 Array Processing

FIGURE 8.21(b) Output Specifications

FIGURE 8.21(c) Output Specifications

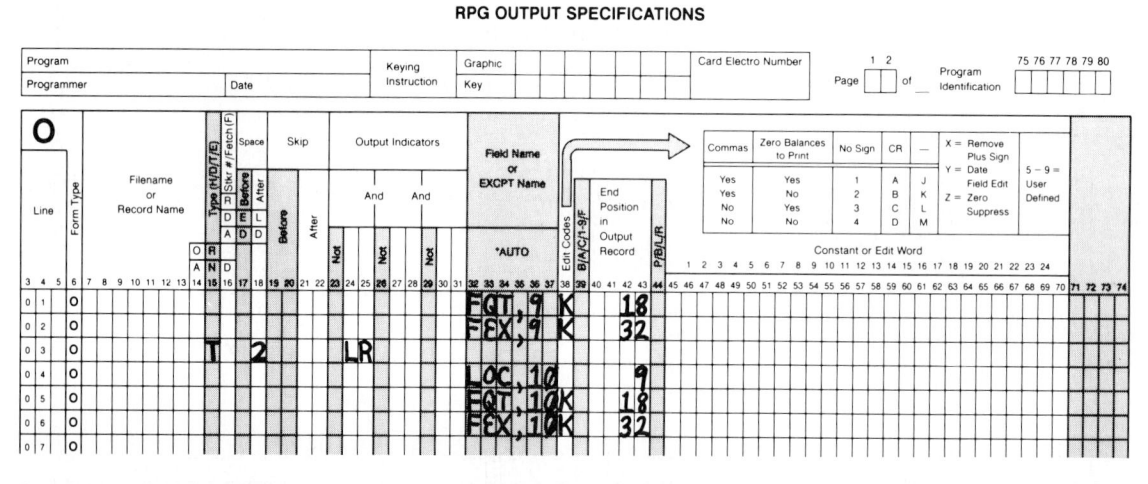

boundaries of the array. You must also ensure that an index is not greater than the largest number of entries in an array, since this would also point to a location outside the array. Either condition would cause the program to abort.

Next, the line of totals for location 1 is printed using the EXCPT operation. There is only one set of lines on the Output Specifications, and each output field is referred to by the index, X, rather than by the specific array element.

The index is next incremented by 1. The index field, X, will now contain the value 2.

At each step, X is compared to ten because there are ten elements in this array. If we tried to print something for an 11th element, the program would abort. These steps are repeated by a GOTO, which returns the program to the first step in this sequence and repeats the process until X is once again greater than ten.

FIGURE 8.22(a) Calculation Specifications for Index and Loop

RPG CALCULATION SPECIFICATIONS

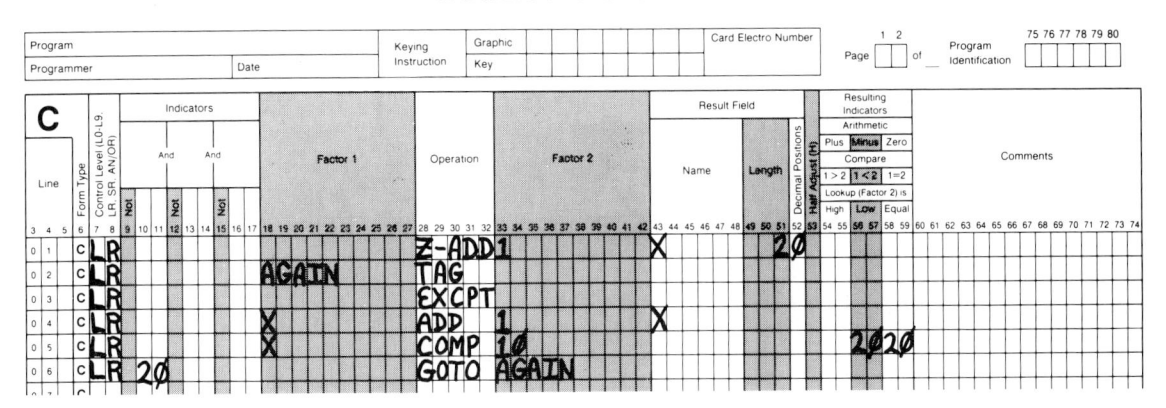

Line	Form Type	C/L	N	N	N	Factor 1	Operation	Factor 2	Result Field Name	Length	Dec	H	Hi	Lo	Eq	Comments
01	C	LR					Z-ADD	1	X	2	0					
02	C	LR				AGAIN	TAG									
03	C	LR					EXCPT									
04	C	LR				X	ADD	1	X							
05	C	LR				X	COMP	10						20	20	
06	C	LR 20					GOTO	AGAIN								

FIGURE 8.22(b) Output Specifications

RPG OUTPUT SPECIFICATIONS

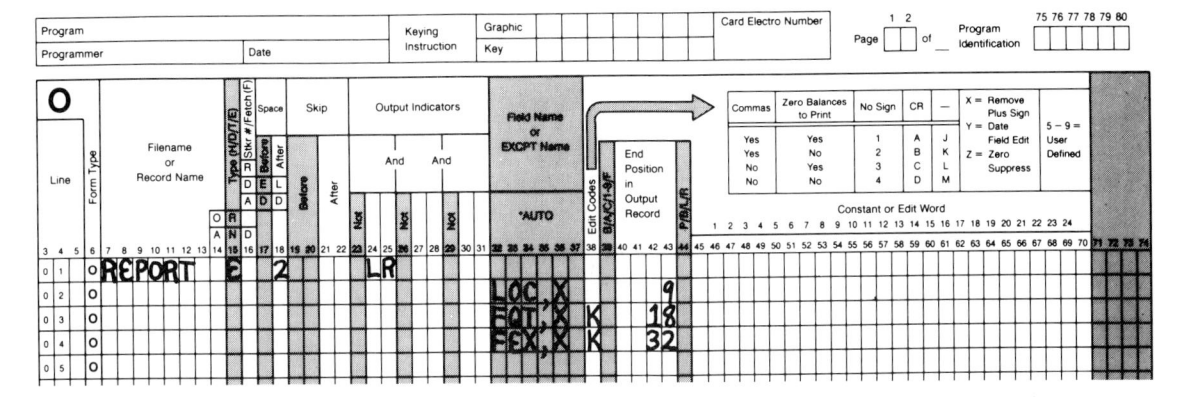

Line	Form Type	Filename or Record Name	Type	Space Before/After	Skip Before/After	Output Indicators And And	Field Name or EXCPT Name	Edit Codes	End Position in Output Record	P/B/L/R	Constant or Edit Word
01	O	REPORT	E	2		LR					
02	O						LOC,X		9		
03	O						QTY,X	K	18		
04	O						EX,X	K	32		
05	O										

A loop has been created that will cause ten lines to be printed on the report showing all ten store locations with their corresponding quantities sold and total dollars. A final total line can also be printed and the report is complete. Figures 8.23(a) and 8.23(b) show the completed program and final report, using exception output for the final totals.

FIGURE 8.23(a) Entire Sample Program for the Store Summary

```
SEQUENCE      1         2         3         4         5         6         7
NUMBER    67890123456789012345678901234567890123456789012345678901234567890123456789012345678901234


      100   F* TITLE: ILLUSTRATION FOR 8.23 (SAMPLE PROG 2)
      200   F* DATE:  5/4            AUTHOR: D.CABLE
      300   F* DESCRIPTION:
      400   F***************************************************

NAME OF PROGRAM WILL BE ILL823 IN LIBRARY CABLE

            H
* 1019              ALL DECIMAL DATA ERRORS IGNORED
      500   FINFILE3 IP  F     133               DISK
      600   FREPORT  O   F     132         OF    PRINTER
      700   F***************************************************
```

Chapter 8 Array Processing

FIGURE 8.23(a) Continued

```
 800  E                  LOC       5  10  9         STORE HEADINGS
 900  E                  QTY          10  5 0       INPUT QTY
1000  E                  PRC          10  6 2       UNIT PRICE
1100  E                  EXT          10  7 2       EXTENDED PRC
1200  E                  FQT          10  6 0       TOT QTY/STORE
1300  E                  FEX          10  7 2       TOT PRC/STORE

1400  IINFILE3 AA  01 133 CI
1500  I                                         1    7OITEM#
1600  I                                         8   19 DESC
1700  I                                        20   22 TYPE    L1
1800  I                                        23   72OQTY
1900  I                                        73  1322PRC
2000  I         ZZ   99

2100  C    01   QTY     MULT PRC   EXT              EXTEND PRICE
2200  C    01   FQT     ADD  QTY   FQT              TOT QTY
2300  C    01   FEX     ADD  EXT   FEX              TOT DOLLARS
2400  CLR              Z-ADD1      X         20
2500  CLR      AGAIN    TAG
2600  CLR               EXCPT
2700  CLR       X       ADD  1     X
2800  CLR       X       COMP 10                    2020
2900  CLR 20            GOTO AGAIN

3000  OREPORT  D  203    1P
3100  O                                 27 'S T O R E   S U M M A R Y'
3200  O        D   2     1P
3300  O                                  8 'LOCATION'
3400  O                                 18 'TOT QTY'
3500  O                                 32 'TOTAL VALUE'
3600  O        E   2     LR
3700  O                        LOC,X     9
3800  O                        FQT,X K  18
3900  O                        FEX,X K  32
* * * * E N D  O F  S O U R C E * * * *

* 7086     500   RPG PROVIDES BLOCK/UNBLOCK SUPPORT FOR FILE INFILE3.
           TABLE/ARRAY ------- LOC
      4100  STORE 01 STORE 03 STORE 05 STORE 10 STORE 15
      4200  STORE 16 STORE 18 STORE 20 STORE 22 STORE 28
```

FIGURE 8.23(b) Completed Report for the Store Summary

```
                  S T O R E   S U M M A R Y

         LOCATION    TOT QTY     TOTAL VALUE

         STORE 01      33           86.25

         STORE 03      37          129.75

         STORE 05      42          171.25

         STORE 10      67          328.99

         STORE 15      15           79.89

         STORE 16      22          220.25

         STORE 18      26          266.50

         STORE 20       2           20.50

         STORE 22      34          122.25

         STORE 28     911        1,460.00
```

SAMPLE PROGRAM 3 USING LOKUP WITH AN ARRAY ■

A search of an array can be done using LOKUP in much the same manner as with a table. There are some advantages, however, to using an array rather than a table. First, the array need not be created before execution of the program. Second, an array can return to the program the location of the array element found as a result of the search. This location can then be used to locate a corresponding element in several other arrays. This is somewhat similar to the use of alternating tables in Chapter 7, but with a good deal more certainty.

A search of an array can begin with the first element or at a specified element. If you specify an array name without an index in factor 2, the search starts with the first element of the array, and the result will be a yes or no answer. This is adequate for validating incoming data, but it provides no more benefit than a simple table provides. Figure 8.24 shows how that statement might be coded.

A better use of LOKUP in an array is shown in Figure 8.25, in which the index returns the location of the array element found.

For this sample program, we will expect that the array data will be input into the program as a part of the input file. The first four records in the input file contain a series of price codes, a series of prices, a series of costs, and a series of descriptions. The rest of the records in the file contain the daily sales data, which carries a part number, a price code, and a quantity. Figure 8.26 shows the Record Layout for these five types of records.

FIGURE 8.24 Search Array Using LOKUP

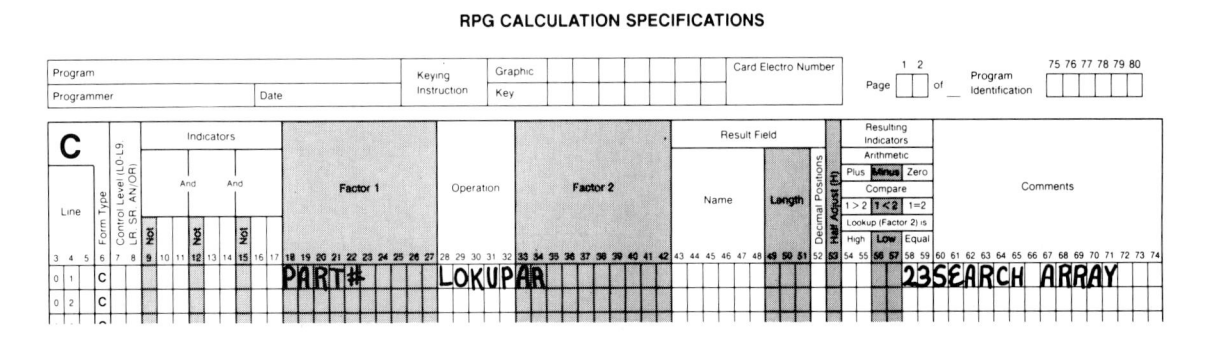

FIGURE 8.25 Search Array Using LOKUP with Index

FIGURE 8.26 Five Types of Input Records

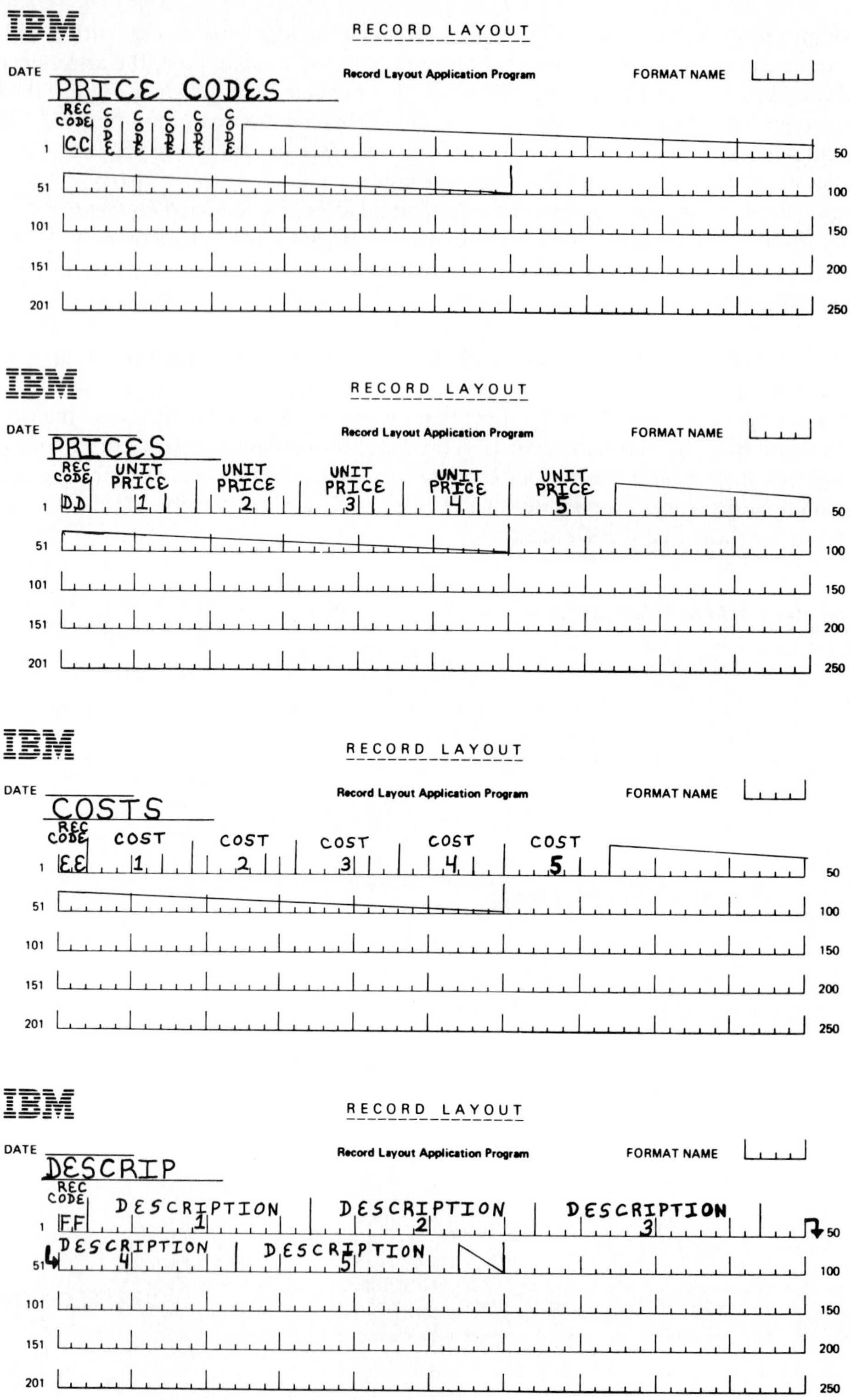

[IBM Record Layout form — PRICE CODES: REC CODE "CC", followed by fields CODE, CODE, CODE, CODE, CODE]

[IBM Record Layout form — PRICES: REC CODE "DD", followed by UNIT PRICE 1, UNIT PRICE 2, UNIT PRICE 3, UNIT PRICE 4, UNIT PRICE 5]

[IBM Record Layout form — COSTS: REC CODE "EE", followed by COST 1, COST 2, COST 3, COST 4, COST 5]

[IBM Record Layout form — DESCRIP: REC CODE "FF", followed by DESCRIPTION 1, DESCRIPTION 2, DESCRIPTION 3, DESCRIPTION 4, DESCRIPTION 5]

FIGURE 8.26 *Continued*

```
IBM                                    RECORD LAYOUT
    DATE  SALES              Record Layout Application Program    FORMAT NAME
          REC          QUANT.
          CODE ITEM #  C  SALES
                       O
                       D
                       E
      1   G,G                                                                    50
     51                                                                         100
    101                                                                         150
    151                                                                         200
    201                                                                         250
```

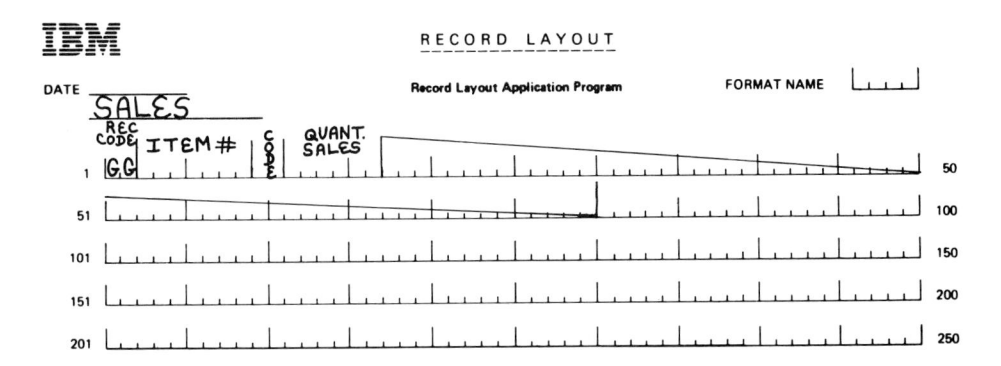

The File Description, Extension, and Input Specifications are shown in Figures 8.27(a), 8.27(b), and 8.27(c). Each record type is given a separate record indicator based on the record type code.

In the Calculation Specifications, each series of array data is loaded into an array as it is read into the program. This provides a set of four related arrays.

As the daily sales data is read, the correct price, cost, and description can be retrieved from the four sets of arrays based on the price code alone. Figure 8.28 shows the Calculation Specifications for this program. The code in the sales data is used to search for the location of the appropriate array element. If the search returns a location of 3, that index can be used to locate the third element in the price, cost, and description arrays.

Figure 8.29 shows the Output Specifications, which can list the appropriate information related to each sale made for the day.

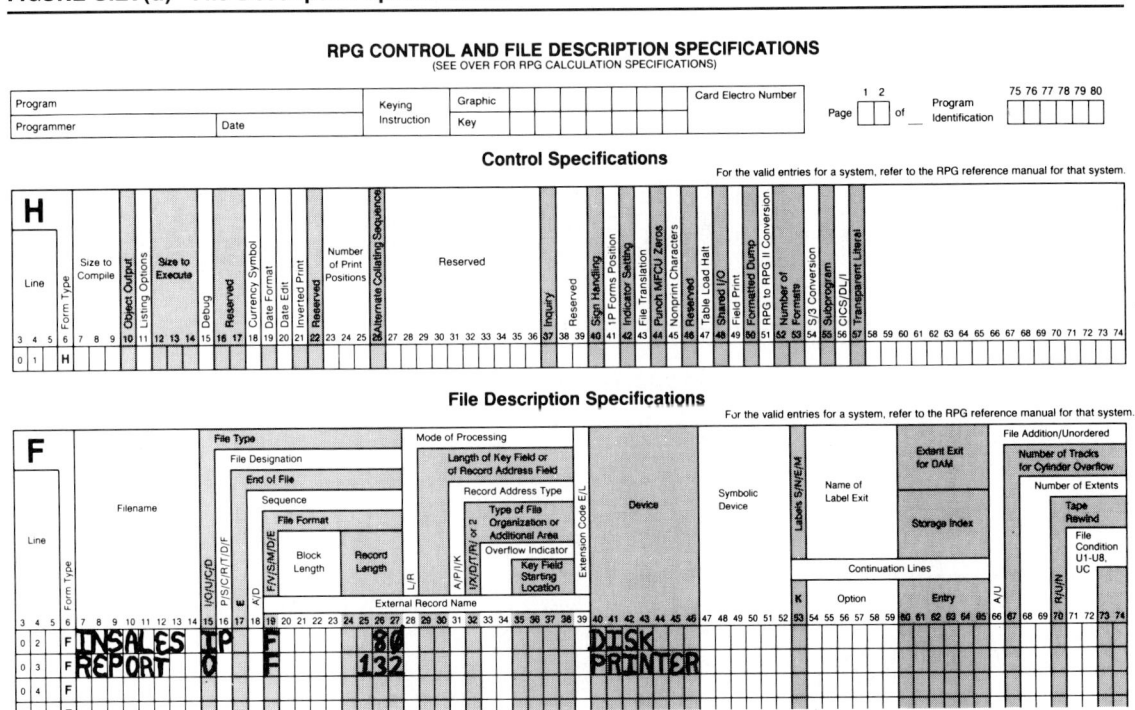

FIGURE 8.27(a) File Description Specifications

Line	Form Type	Filename	File Type	Length	Device
02	F	INSALES	IP F	80	DISK
03	F	REPORT	O F	132	PRINTER
04	F				

FIGURE 8.27(b) Extension Specifications

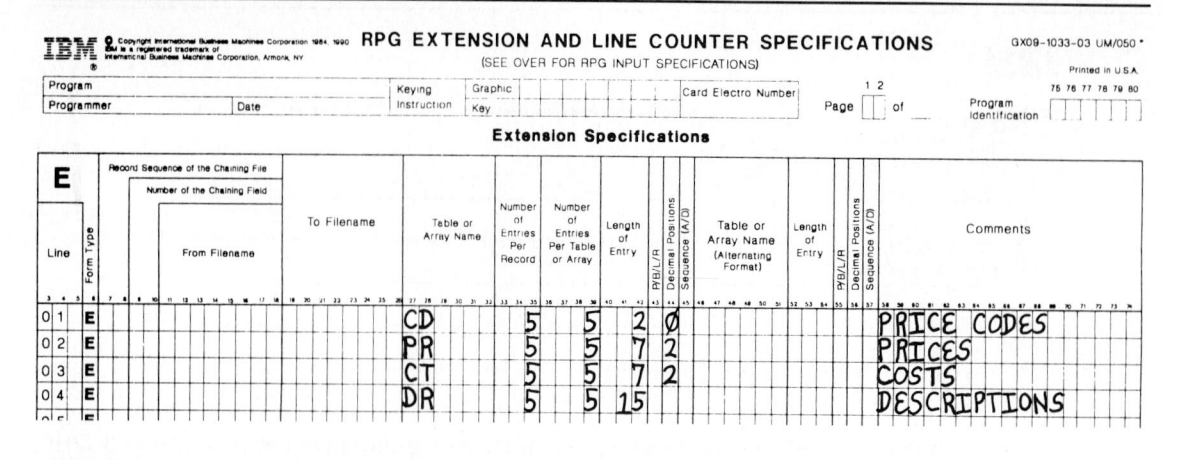

RPG EXTENSION AND LINE COUNTER SPECIFICATIONS

Line	Form Type	From Filename	To Filename	Table or Array Name	Number of Entries Per Record	Number of Entries Per Table or Array	Length of Entry	P/B/L/R	Decimal Positions	Sequence (A/D)	Table or Array Name (Alternating Format)	Length of Entry	P/B/L/R	Decimal Positions	Sequence (A/D)	Comments
01	E			CD	5	5	2		0							PRICE CODES
02	E			PR	5	5	7		2							PRICES
03	E			CT	5	5	7		2							COSTS
04	E			DR	5	5	15									DESCRIPTIONS

FIGURE 8.27(c) Input Specifications

RPG INPUT SPECIFICATIONS

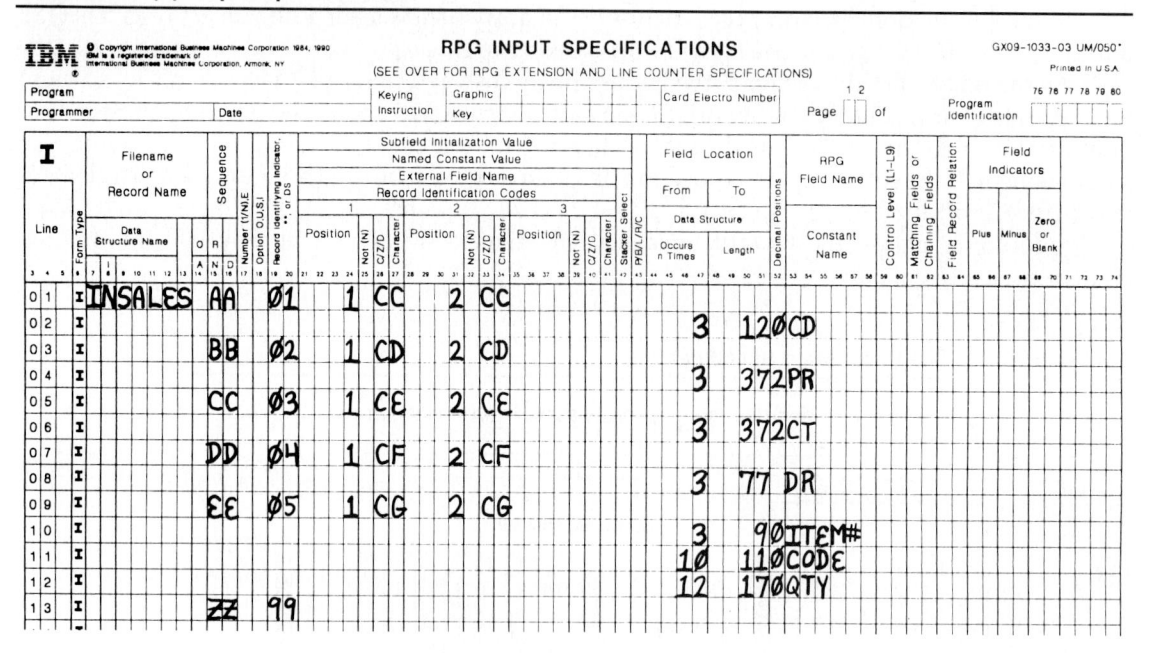

Line	Form Type	Filename or Record Name	Sequence	Number (1/N)	Option (O/U/S)	Record Identifying Indicator or ** or DS	Pos	Not	C/Z/D	Char	Pos	Not	C/Z/D	Char	Pos	Not	C/Z/D	Char	Stacker Select	From	To	Decimal Positions	Field Name	Control Level	Matching Fields	Field Record Relation	Plus	Minus	Zero or Blank
01	I	INSALES	AA	01			1		CC		2		CC															
02	I																			3	12	0	CD					
03	I		BB	02			1		CD		2		CD							3	37	2	PR					
04	I																											
05	I		CC	03			1		CE		2		CE							3	37	2	CT					
06	I																											
07	I		DD	04			1		CF		2		CF							3	77		DR					
08	I																											
09	I		EE	05			1		CG		2		CG							3	9	0	ITEM#					
10	I																			10	11	0	CODE					
11	I																			12	17	0	QTY					
12	I																											
13	I		ZZ	99																								

FIGURE 8.28 Using LOKUP to Locate Elements in an Array

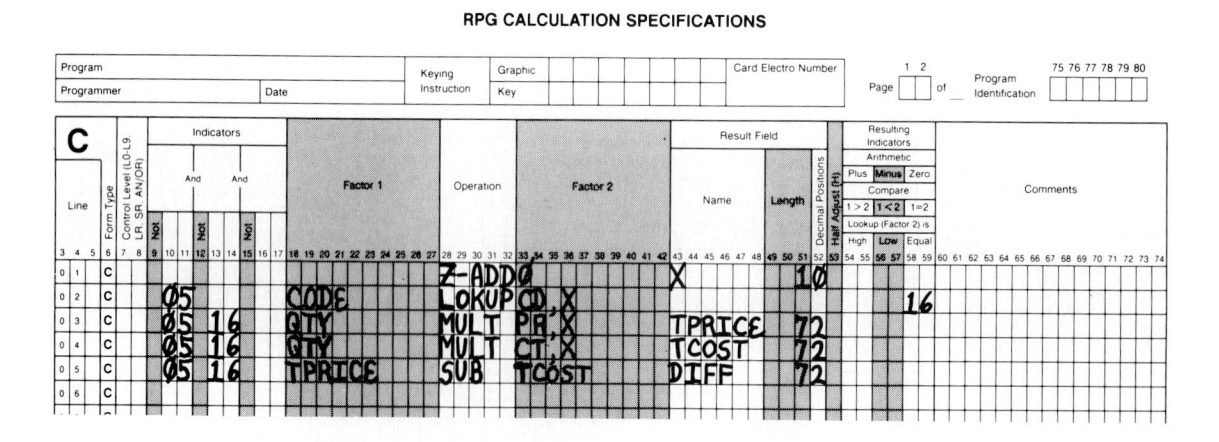

RPG CALCULATION SPECIFICATIONS

Line	Form Type	Control Level	And	And	Factor 1	Operation	Factor 2	Result Field Name	Length	Decimal Positions	Half Adjust	1>2	1<2	1=2	Comments
01	C														
02	C	05				Z-ADD	0	X	10						
03	C	05				LOKUP	CD,X							16	
04	C	05	16		QTY	MULT	PR,X	TPRICE	72						
05	C	05	16		QTY	MULT	CT,X	TCOST	72						
06	C	05	16		TPRICE	SUB	TCOST	DIFF	72						

FIGURE 8.29 Using Arrays to Print Sale Information

[RPG Output Specifications form showing:]
- Line 01: O REPORT D 2 01 1P
- Line 02: O OR OF
- Line 03: O 40 'DAILY SALES'
- Line 04: O D 2 1P
- Line 05: O OR OF
- Line 06: O 6 'ITEM#'
- Line 07: O 19 'DESCRIPTION'
- Line 08: O 31 'QUANTITY'
- Line 09: O 38 'PRICE'
- Line 10: O 48 'COST'
- Line 11: O 58 'MARGIN'
- Line 12: O D 05
- Line 13: O ITEM# 7
- Line 14: O N16 20 'INVALID CODE'
- Line 15: O 16 DR X 23
- Line 16: O 16 QTY Z 30
- Line 17: O 16 TPRICE KB 38
- Line 18: O 16 TCOST KB 48
- Line 19: O 16 DIFF KB 58

Special Operations for Array Data

There are some special operations which can be performed only on arrays. These are:

  XFOOT — Cross-foot an entire array
  MOVEA — Move array data
  SORTA — Sort array data

Cross-Footing an Array (XFOOT)

The XFOOT operation code allows an entire array to be added up algebraically to a single total. Algebraically means that positive numbers are added and negative numbers are subtracted to produce the result. This operation can save considerable programming effort—in an array containing 1000 elements, one line of calculations would replace 1000 lines. Figure 8.30 shows an example of using the XFOOT operation to total an array.

FIGURE 8.30 The XFOOT Operation

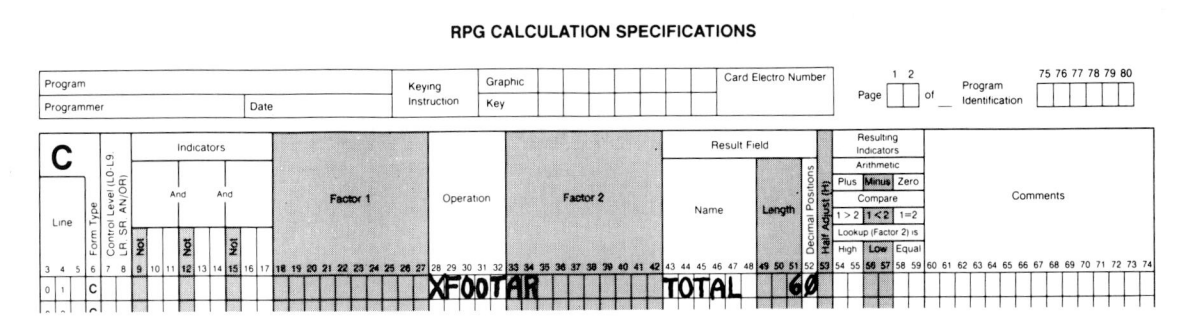

[RPG Calculation Specifications form showing:]
- Line 01: C XFOOT AR TOTAL 60

Chapter 8 Array Processing 201

Moving Array Data (MOVEA)

With the use of the MOVEA operation, the data in an entire array can be moved all at once. The data can be moved into a field or into another array using only one line on the Calculation Specifications. Conversely, a field can be moved into an array using the MOVEA operation. It is also possible to move only a portion of an array into a field by specifying a beginning array element.

The MOVEA operation may only be used on alphanumeric arrays. Figure 8.31 shows an example of using the MOVEA operation to move data from a field into an array. The MOVEA operation offers some interesting alternatives to the traditional MOVE or MOVEL.

Sorting Array Data (SORTA)

The SORTA operation can be used to sort an array of data in ascending sequence. This can be useful if the array contains data in random sequence (possibly generated from within the program itself) and a report needs to be printed which is arranged in some definite sequence. Without the SORTA operation, a second program would be needed to print the report after invoking a sort utility. Figure 8.32 shows an example of using the SORTA operation to sort an array.

FIGURE 8.31 The MOVEA Operation

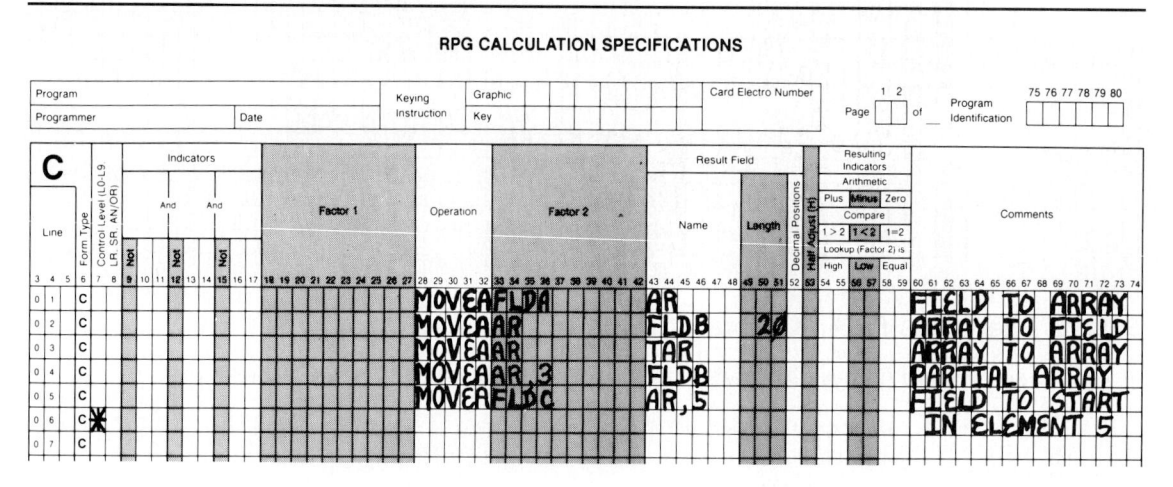

Line	Factor 1	Operation	Factor 2	Result Field	Length	Comments
01		MOVEA	FLDA	AR		FIELD TO ARRAY
02		MOVEA	AR	FLDB	20	ARRAY TO FIELD
03		MOVEA	AR	TAR		ARRAY TO ARRAY
04		MOVEA	AR,3	FLDB		PARTIAL ARRAY
05		MOVEA	FLDC	AR,5		FIELD TO START IN ELEMENT 5

FIGURE 8.32 The SORTA Operation

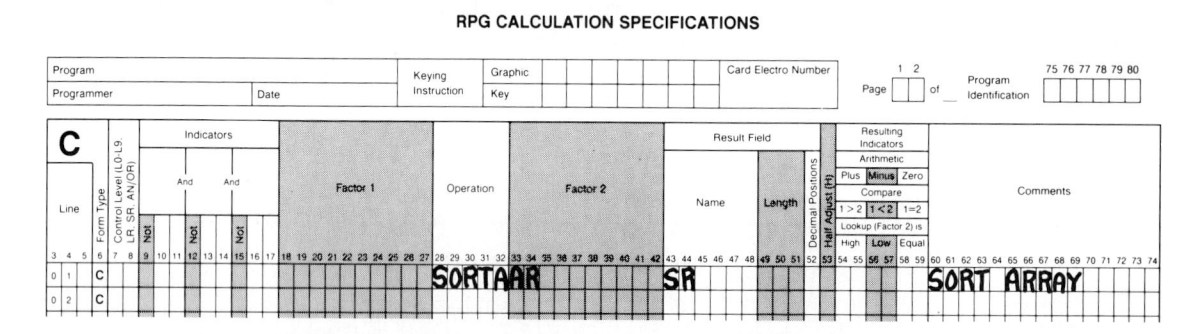

Line	Factor 1	Operation	Factor 2	Result Field	Comments
01		SORTA	AR	SR	SORT ARRAY

SAMPLE PROGRAM 4 USING XFOOT

Using the same input data used in sample program 2 we can print a report which looks very much like the report in sample program 1. This time, however, dollar figures instead of quantities will be computed and printed. A total for all locations will be accumulated and printed in the rightmost column of the report. Figure 8.33 shows the completed report generated by this program.

Since a total is needed for each line, all the dollar amounts for all the locations need to be added together. This is a simple matter when an array has been defined. The operation is XFOOT. The XFOOT operation requires no entry in factor 1 of the Calculation Specifications. The name of the array, DOL, is entered in factor 2 and a field name TOTDOL is entered in the result column. The field name TOTDOL is defined in columns 49–51 as seven positions in length with two decimal positions. Figure 8.34 shows the entire program.

RPG will automatically compute the total of all ten entries in the array DOL and place the total in the field TOTDOL.

FIGURE 8.33 Completed Report

```
                                        S T O R E   R E P O R T

TYP  ITEM#   DESCRIPTION   STORE 01 STORE 03 STORE 05 STORE 10 STORE 15 STORE 16 STORE 18 STORE 20 STORE 22 STORE 28   TOTAL

A    0000123 ONETWOTHREE     10.00    52.50   100.00   157.50            205.00   256.25    10.25    80.00    99.00    970.50
A    0000234 TWOTHREEFOUR    10.00    11.00    10.25    10.25    10.00    10.25    10.25    10.25    11.00              93.25
A    0000532 FIVETHREETWO     5.00     5.00     4.75     4.99    54.89                                                   74.63
A    0002020 TWENTYTWENTY    31.25    31.25    31.25    31.25                                        31.25 1,350.00  1,506.25
          TYPE TOTAL         56.25    99.75   146.25   203.99    64.89   215.25   266.50    20.50   122.25 1,449.00  2,644.63

TYP  ITEM#   DESCRIPTION   STORE 01 STORE 03 STORE 05 STORE 10 STORE 15 STORE 16 STORE 18 STORE 20 STORE 22 STORE 28   TOTAL

B    0006000 NEWONE          30.00    30.00    25.00   125.00    15.00     5.00                              11.00    241.00
          TYPE TOTAL         30.00    30.00    25.00   125.00    15.00     5.00                              11.00    241.00

          FINAL TOTAL        86.25   129.75   171.25   328.99    79.89   220.25   266.50    20.50   122.25 1,460.00  2,885.63
```

FIGURE 8.34 Complete Program for XFOOT

```
SEQUENCE          1         2         3         4         5         6         7
NUMBER   67890123456789012345678901234567890123456789012345678901234567890123456789012345


          100   F* TITLE: ILLUSTRATION FOR 8.34 (SAMPLE PROG 4)
          200   F* DATE:   5/4            AUTHOR: D.CABLE
          300   F* DESCRIPTION:
          400   F*********************************************************

NAME OF PROGRAM WILL BE ILL834 IN LIBRARY CABLE

                H
 * 1019                 ALL DECIMAL DATA ERRORS IGNORED
          500   FINFILE3 IP   F      133              DISK
          600   FREPORT   O   F      132     OF       PRINTER
          700   F*********************************************************


          800   E                 LOC      5   10  9           STORE HEADINGS
          900   E                 QTY         10  5 0          INPUT QTY
         1000   E                 PRC         10  6 2          UNIT PRICE
         1100   E                 EXT         10  6 2          EXTENDED PRC
         1200   E                 LEX         10  6 2          LEVEL 1
         1300   E                 FEX         10  6 2          FINAL TOTAL
```

FIGURE 8.34 *Continued*

```
1400    IINFILE3 AA   01 133 CI
1500    I                                              1   70ITEM#
1600    I                                              8   19 DESC
1700    I                                             20   22 TYPE   L1
1800    I                                             23   72 QTY
1900    I                                             73 1322PRC
2000    I            ZZ   99


2100    C    01         QTY       MULT PRC    EXT                EXTEND PRICE
2200    C    01                   XFOOTEXT    TOTAL   82
2300    C* LEVEL 1 TOTALS
2400    C    01         LEX       ADD  EXT    LEX                LEVEL 1
2500    CL1                       XFOOTLEX    L1TOT   82
2600    CL1             LEX       ADD  FEX    FEX                FINAL TOTAL
2700    CLR                       XFOOTFEX    LRTOT   82


2800    OREPORT    D   203     1P
2900    O          OR          OF
3000    O                                              71 'S T O R E   R E P O R T'
3100    O          D   2       L1
3200    O          OR          OF
3300    O                                               3 'TYP'
3400    O                                              10 'ITEM#'
3500    O                                              24 'DESCRIPTION'
3600    O                                 LOC         117
3700    O                                             127 'TOTAL'
3800    O          D   1       01
3900    O                                 TYPE          3
4000    O                                 ITEM#        11
4100    O                                 DESC         24
4200    O                                 EXT,1 K      36
4300    O                                 EXT,2 K      45
4400    O                                 EXT,3 K      54
4500    O                                 EXT,4 K      63
4600    O                                 EXT,5 K      72
4700    O                                 EXT,6 K      81
4800    O                                 EXT,7 K      90
4900    O                                 EXT,8 K      99
5000    O                                 EXT,9 K     108
5100    O                                 EXT,10K     117
5200    O                                 TOTAL K     127
5300    O          T   2       L1
5400    O                                              17 'TYPE TOTAL'
5500    O                                 LEX,1 KB     36
5600    O                                 LEX,2 KB     45
5700    O                                 LEX,3 KB     54
5800    O                                 LEX,4 KB     63
5900    O                                 LEX,5 KB     72
6000    O                                 LEX,6 KB     81
6100    O                                 LEX,7 KB     90
6200    O                                 LEX,8 KB     99
6300    O                                 LEX,9 KB    108
6400    O                                 LEX,10KB    117
6500    O                                 L1TOT KB    127
6600    O          T   1       LR
6700    O                                              18 'FINAL TOTAL'
6800    O                                 FEX,1 KB     36
6900    O                                 FEX,2 KB     45
7000    O                                 FEX,3 KB     54
7100    O                                 FEX,4 KB     63
7200    O                                 FEX,5 KB     72
7300    O                                 FEX,6 KB     81
7400    O                                 FEX,7 KB     90
7500    O                                 FEX,8 KB     99
7600    O                                 FEX,9 KB    108
```

FIGURE 8.34 *Continued*

```
     7700  O                         FEX,10K9 117
     7800  O                         LRTOT K  127
* * * * * E N D   O F   S O U R C E * * * * *

* 7086      500    RPG PROVIDES BLOCK/UNBLOCK SUPPORT FOR FILE INFILE3.
           TABLE/ARRAY ------ LOC
     8000    STORE 01 STORE 03 STORE 05 STORE 10 STORE 15
     8100    STORE 16 STORE 18 STORE 20 STORE 22 STORE 28
```

SAMPLE PROGRAM 5 USING MOVEA ■

The example for MOVEA will use the input data for an employee master file described in Figures 8.35(a), 8.35(b), and 8.35(c).

The employee name has been separated into three fields: last name, first name, and middle initial. Although this is often a useful format in which to carry data within the computer, on a report or payroll check the first name should appear first, followed by the middle initial (with no more than one space between) and last name. Since the names will vary in length, it will not be possible for the programmer to predict the location in which to begin printing the middle initial field. Figures 8.36(a) and 8.36(b) show the Extension and Calculation Specifications to perform this minor miracle.

FIGURE 8.35(a) Employee Master File: Sample Data

```
                    SAMPLE DATA FILE
          00653    SMITH         JAMES      L
          01897    ALLENFIELD    WILLIAM    B
          35210    MOBLEY        SUSAN      C
```

FIGURE 8.35(b) File Description Specification

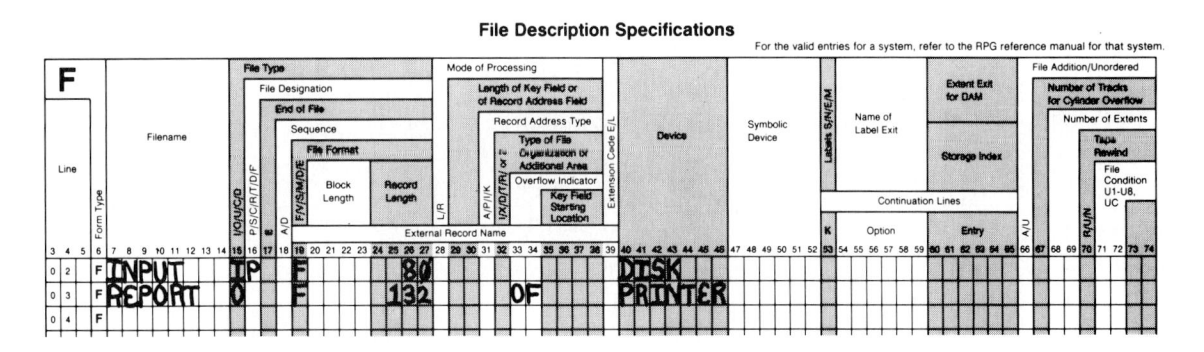

[File Description Specifications form showing:
Line 02: F INPUT IP F 80 DISK
Line 03: F REPORT O F 132 OF PRINTER
Line 04: F]

Chapter 8 Array Processing

FIGURE 8.35(c) Input Specifications

Line	Form Type	Filename or Record Name	Sequence	Number	Option	Record Identifying Indicator	Position	Not	C/Z/D	Character	Position	Not	C/Z/D	Character	Position	Not	C/Z/D	Character	Stacker Select	From	To	Decimal Positions	RPG Field Name / Constant Name	Control Level	Matching Fields	Field Record Relation	Plus	Minus	Zero or Blank
01	I	INPUT	AA	01		80			C	M																			
02	I																			1	5		EMPNO						
03	I																			6	25		LAST						
04	I																			26	35		FIRST						
05	I																			36	36		MIDDLE						

FIGURE 8.36(a) Extension Specifications for Printing Employee Name

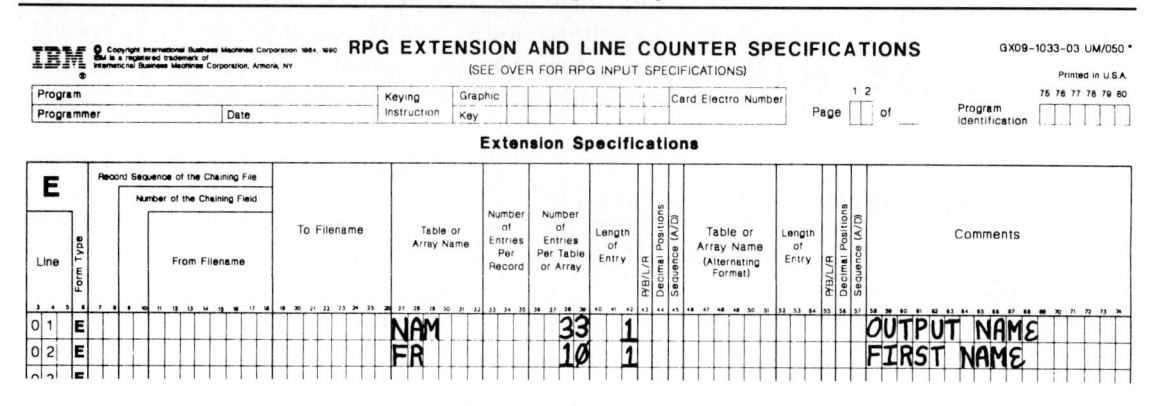

Line	Form Type	From Filename	To Filename	Table or Array Name	Number of Entries Per Record	Number of Entries Per Table or Array	Length of Entry	P/B/L/R	Decimal Positions	Sequence (A/D)	Table or Array Name (Alternating Format)	Length of Entry	P/B/L/R	Decimal Positions	Comments
01	E			NAM		33	1								OUTPUT NAME
02	E			FR		10	1								FIRST NAME

FIGURE 8.36(b) Calculation Specifications for Printing Employee Name

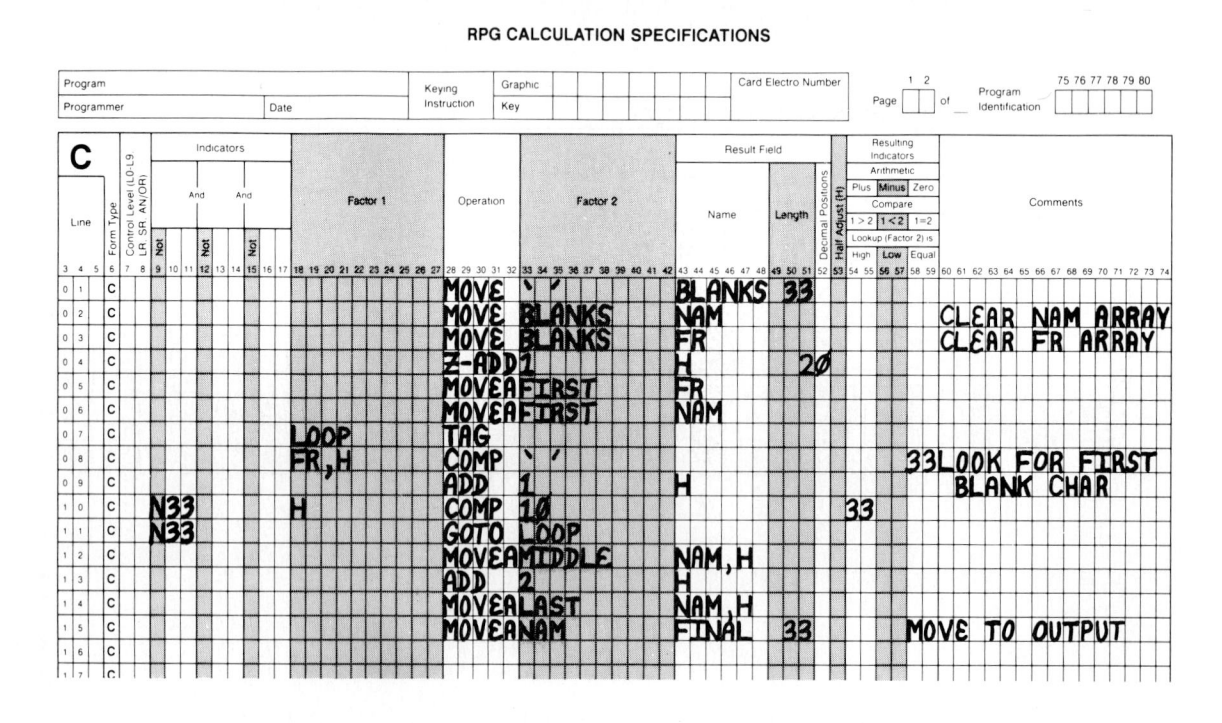

Line	Form Type	Control Level	Indicators And	Indicators And	Indicators Not	Factor 1	Operation	Factor 2	Result Field Name	Length	Decimal Positions	Half Adjust	Resulting Indicators Plus 1>2 High	Resulting Indicators Minus 1<2 Low	Resulting Indicators Zero 1=2 Equal	Comments
01	C						MOVE	' '	BLANKS	33						
02	C						MOVE	BLANKS	NAM							CLEAR NAM ARRAY
03	C						MOVE	BLANKS	FR							CLEAR FR ARRAY
04	C						Z-ADD	1	H	20						
05	C						MOVEA	FIRST	FR							
06	C						MOVEA	FIRST	NAM							
07	C					LOOP	TAG									
08	C					FR,H	COMP	' '						33		LOOK FOR FIRST
09	C						ADD	1	H							BLANK CHAR
10	C		N33			H	COMP	10							33	
11	C		N33				GOTO	LOOP								
12	C						MOVEA	MIDDLE	NAM,H							
13	C						ADD	2	H							
14	C						MOVEA	LAST	NAM,H							
15	C						MOVEA	NAM	FINAL	33						MOVE TO OUTPUT

NAM is the name of an array containing 33 elements of one position each. This array will contain the newly created format for the name field that will eventually be printed on the report. Before moving a new name into the array NAM, it is a good idea to ensure that all elements have been set to blanks. The first name field can now be moved into the first ten elements of the NAM array.

Before the final name field can be created, we must determine the exact length of the first name. To do this, the first name field is broken up into a ten-element array of one position each. This array is called FR. The ten-position field containing the first name is moved into the array FR using the MOVEA operation. Each field of the array can now be tested to determine whether it contains blanks. This is repeated until blanks are found or until all ten elements of the array have been tested. When blanks are found or ten is reached, the index is incremented by 1 (to leave a space before the middle initial) and the field containing the middle initial is then placed in the array NAM, again using the MOVEA operation. By indexing the NAM array, the MOVEA will place the field MIDDLE in the element of the array given in the index. In the example, the first blank was found at element 6 after the name JAMES. The index was incremented by 2 so NAM,H will be pointing to element 8 in the array. The middle initial will be placed in position 8.

The index is incremented again by 2. This points to element 10 of the array NAM. The field LAST is then moved to the array (using the MOVEA operation) beginning with element 10 and continuing to the end of the field. The resulting array contains the entire name correctly formatted. The array can be moved to a 33-position field which will be printed on the report. Figures 8.37(a) and 8.37(b) show the entire program for sample program 5.

FIGURE 8.37(a) Output Specifications for Sample Program 5

RPG OUTPUT SPECIFICATIONS

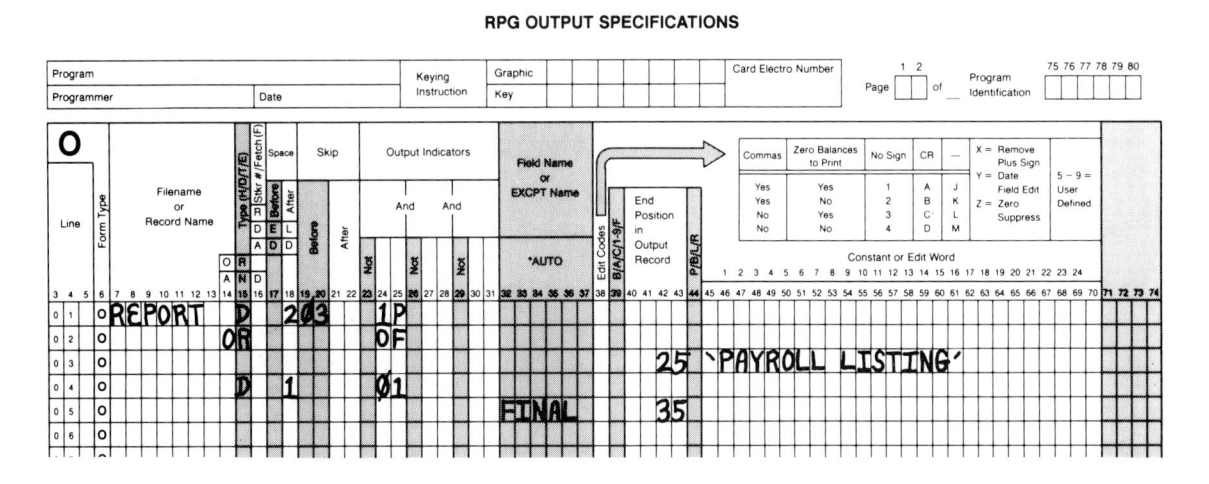

```
01 O REPORT   D  2 03   1P
02 O         OR         OF                      25 'PAYROLL LISTING'
03 O
04 O          D  1      01
05 O                       FINAL                35
06 O
```

FIGURE 8.37(b) Final Report for Sample Program 5

```
                PAYROLL LISTING

        JAMES   L SMITH
        WILLIAM B ALLENFIELD
        SUSAN   C MOBLEY
```

SUMMARY ■

In this chapter, you have learned that array processing provides some very sophisticated tools with which a programmer can perform extensive calculations with very little effort in coding.

You have learned that the benefits of array processing are much less coding to be done and fewer opportunities for mistakes. This results in more readable programs and a more structured programming method. The benefits in speed of processing and greater efficiency in operation may be more difficult to measure but are of considerable value in a busy computer.

You have learned that an array will often facilitate what might otherwise be an extremely complex project. Arrays may be loaded at compile time, execution time, or pre-execution time.

You have learned that an array consists of several fields, all of which have identical attributes. An array may be addressed as an entire unit, or each element within the array may be addressed individually. Nearly any arithmetic or logical operation can be performed on an array or array element.

You have learned that arrays can be used in a wide variety of ways to provide better methods for calculating results in RPG programs. There are so many ways to use an array that the whole process appears more complex than it really is. Arrays can be used to perform calculations on a large number of elements simultaneously. This can facilitate coding for long lists of related calculations. Arrays can be used to locate a selected item from a group of similar data. Arrays can be used to retain summary totals which can be printed at the end of a report or printed as a second report. Arrays can be used to alter the presentation of data so that the final report need not be in the same sequence as the incoming data. Arrays can be used to reformat fields or other arrays.

Finally, you have learned that the XFOOT, MOVEA, and SORTA operations enhance the use of arrays and provide the programmer with even greater flexibility.

REVIEW QUESTIONS ■

1. Define array.
2. What benefits can be gained with the use of array processing?
3. What is the maximum size for an array element?
4. What is the maximum number of array elements that may be contained in an array?
5. What is the maximum number of arrays and tables permitted in one RPG program?
6. What are the three times at which an array may be loaded?
7. The elements of an array must be all of the same _____ and have the same _____ .
8. Arrays are defined on the _____ Specifications.
9. What type of data should probably not be used in compile time arrays?
10. Describe the difference between pre-execution time arrays and execution time arrays.
11. Describe the two methods by which the data in an array can be accessed.
12. Explain indexing as it applies to array processing in an RPG program.
13. When is the data loaded in a pre-execution time array? An execution time array? A compile time array?
14. What will happen if an index is specified as zero or as greater than the size of the array?
15. Explain the benefits of using the operation LOKUP with an array.
16. What benefit is gained with the use of the XFOOT operation?
17. Explain the use of the MOVEA operation.
18. When data is moved using a MOVEA operation, what is the first character to be moved?
19. What operation is used to accomplish sorting in an RPG program?
20. What benefit is gained by doing sorting within an RPG program?

EXERCISES ■

1. On an Extension Specifications form, enter the coding that will describe a compile time array named CR.
2. On an Extension Specifications form, enter the coding that will describe a pre-execution time array named FE. Also code the File Description Specifications form to accompany this array.
3. On an Extension Specifications form, enter the coding that will describe an execution time array named AR.
4. On a Calculation Specifications form, enter the coding that will be needed to multiply an array element named QT by another array element named PR (one element at a time).
5. On an Output Specifications form, enter the coding that will be needed to print the array elements QT and PR individually.

DEBUGGING EXERCISES

Instructions

The following RPG programs contain an error or errors. Some of these errors are indicated by the RPG compiler on the program listing. A list of syntax errors is given at the end of the program listing. Other types of errors may occur which will not be shown. These are called logic errors.

Study each program and its syntax errors. Locate each error (including logic errors) and on a separate coding form make the correct entry for the line(s) in error.

Explain each error and how it should be corrected.

```
         100   F* TITLE: DEBUG PROJECT 8-A
         200   F* DATE:  4/14           AUTHOR: D.CABLE
         300   F* DESCRIPTION: AVERAGE SCORES    (ARRAYS)
         400   F*******************************************************
         500   F* MODIFICATIONS:
         600   F* NO.      DATE       INIT       DESCRIPTION
         700   F*          XX/XX/XX   XXX        XXXXXXXXXXXXXXXXXXXXXXXXXXXXXX
         800   F*******************************************************

NAME OF PROGRAM WILL BE PJ008A IN LIBRARY CABLE

               H
* 1019              ALL DECIMAL DATA ERRORS IGNORED
         900   FRESULTS IP  F     128           DISK
        1000   FREPORT  O   F     132       OF  PRINTER
        1100   F*******************************************************

        1200   E              RSQ         8   5 0             ARRAY

        1300   IRESULTS AA   01
        1400   I                                    1    5 RSID#
        1500   I                                    6   20 RSDSCR
        1600   I                                   21   27 RSCODE
        1700   I                                   28  672RSQ
* 4105                                              4105-*

        1800   C                       Z-ADD1    X         10
        1900   C                       XFOOTRSQ  TRSQ      60
        2000   C        TRSQ     DIV   5         AVTEST    50
        2100   C        COUNT    ADD   1         COUNT     50
        2200   C        AVTEST   ADD   TTEST     TTEST     70
        2300   CLR      TTEST    DIV   COUNT     FAVG      50

        2400   OREPORT  H   101   1P
        2500   O        OR               OF
        2600   O                                 6 'PJ008A'
        2700   O                          UDATE Y          50
        2800   O                                30 'AVERAGE SCORES'
        2900   O        H   2     1P
        3000   O        OR               OF
        3100   O                                 5 'ID#'
        3200   O                                25 'TEST DESCRIPTION'
        3300   O                                30 'CODES'
        3400   O                                65 'SCORES'
        3500   O                                90 'AVERAGE'
        3600   O        D   1     01
```

```
SEQUENCE         1          2          3          4          5          6          7
NUMBER    67890123456789012345678901234567890123456789012345678901234567890123456789012345
    3700  0                         RSID#     5
    3800  0                         RSDSCR   25
    3900  0                         RSCODE   30
    4000  0                         RSQ    Z 80
    4100  0                         AVTESTK  90
    4200  0        T  2    LR
    4300  0                                  15 'FINAL AVERAGE'
    4400  0                         TTEST  Z 25
* * * * * E N D   O F   S O U R C E * * * * *

* 7086       900    RPG PROVIDES BLOCK/UNBLOCK SUPPORT FOR FILE RESULTS.

   CROSS-REFERENCE LISTING

      FILE/RCD      DEV/RCD      REFERENCES (D=DEFINED)

   02 REPORT        PRINTER      1000D 2400   2900   3600   4200
   01 RESULTS       DISK          900D 1300


      FIELD         ATTR         REFERENCES (M=MODIFIED D=DEFINED)

      AVTEST        P(5,0)       2000D 2200   4100
      COUNT         P(5,0)       2100  2100D  2300
      FAVG          P(5,0)       2300D
      RSCODE        A(7)         1600D 3900
      RSDSCR        A(15)        1500D 3800
      RSID#         A(5)         1400D 3700
      RSQ(8)        P(5,0)       1200D 1700   1900   4000
      TRSQ          P(6,0)       1900D 2000
      TTEST         P(7,0)       2200  2200D  2300   4400
      UDATE         P(6,0)       2700
      X             P(1,0)       1800D
      1             LITERAL      1800  2100
      5             LITERAL      2000


      INDICATOR   REFERENCES (M=MODIFIED D=DEFINED)

      LR           900D 2300   4200
      OF          1000D 2500   3000
      01          1300M 3600
      1P          2400  2900


MESSAGES

MSGID       SEV   NUMBER    TEXT

* QRG1019   00      1       IGNDECERR(*YES) SPECIFIED ON COMMAND. NO DECIMAL DATA ERRORS
* QRG4105   20      1       DECIMAL POSITIONS ENTRY (POSITION 52) FOR AN ARRAY IS DIFFER
                            ENTRY ASSUMED
* QRG7086   00      1       RPG WILL HANDLE BLOCKING FUNCTION FOR THE FILE. INFDS CONTEN
                            ARE TRANSFERRED.


MESSAGE SUMMARY

TOTAL    00    10    20    30    40    50
  3       2     0     1     0     0     0

   44 RECORDS READ FROM SOURCE FILE
   SOURCE RECORDS INCLUDE    35 SPECIFICATIONS,    0 TABLE RECORDS, AND    9 COMMENTS

QRG0008 COMPILE TERMINATED. SEVERITY 20 ERRORS FOUND IN PROGRAM

* * * * * E N D   O F   C O M P I L A T I O N * * * * *
* QRG1020             ERROR OCCURRED CREATING OR UPDATING DATA AREA RETURNCODE. COMPIL
```

```
        100   F* TITLE: DEBUG PROJECT 8-B
        200   F* DATE:   4/14          AUTHOR: D.CABLE
        300   F* DESCRIPTION:           (ARRAYS)
        400   F*************************************************************

     NAME OF PROGRAM WILL BE PJ008B IN LIBRARY CABLE

              H
* 1019                ALL DECIMAL DATA ERRORS IGNORED
        500   FSALES    IP  F      50           DISK
        600   FREPORT   O   F     132      OF   PRINTER
        700   F*************************************************************


        800   E                   TAB1   3 1   5 3
* 3017                             3017-***

        900   E                   AR       1   5 3
       1000   E                   TR       1   4 3
       1100   E                   STR          6 3 0


       1200   ISALES    AA  01
       1300   I                                         1   3 SLSREP
       1400   I                                         4   90SLDATE
       1500   I                                        10  11 SLSTOR
       1600   I                                        12  160QTY
       1700   I                                        17  23 SLITM#
       1800   I                                        24  302SLUPRC


       1900   C           QTY     ADD  AR      AR        60
* 5054                                          5054-****

       2000   C           QTY     XFOOTAR       AR        60
* 5010              5010-**********
* 5158                                          5158-******.
* 5054                                          5054-****

       2100   C                   MOVEAQTY      QT
* 5176              5176-*****

       2200   C                   Z-ADD1        X
       2300   C           STR,X   ADD  SLSTOR   STR,X


       2400   OREPORT  H  203     1P
       2500   O          OR       OF
       2600   O                                  6 'PJ008B'
       2700   O                           UDATE Y 50
       2800   O                                 30 'SALES SUMMARY'
       2900   O        H    2     1P
       3000   O          OR       OF
       3100   O                                  7 'REGION'
       3200   O        D    1     01
       3300   O                           REGION  10
       3400   O                           AR    K 50
       3500   O        T    2     LR
       3600   O                                 15 'DAILY RECORDS'
       3700   O                           TR    K 50
* * * * * E N D   O F   S O U R C E * * * * *
```

```
* 7086        500    RPG PROVIDES BLOCK/UNBLOCK SUPPORT FOR FILE SALES.
* 7044       1900    AR MUST BE NUMERIC FIELD FOR THIS OPERATION
* 7044       1900    AR MUST BE NUMERIC FIELD FOR THIS OPERATION
* 7044       2300    SLSTOR MUST BE NUMERIC FIELD FOR THIS OPERATION
* 7059       3400    EDITING SPECIFIED BUT FIELD NAME AR NOT NUMERIC
* 7059       3700    EDITING SPECIFIED BUT FIELD NAME TR NOT NUMERIC
             TABLE/ARRAY ------- TAB1
* 8046        800    ARRAY NOT USED IN PROGRAM. ARRAY NOT CREATED
* 8043        800    NO DATA PRESENT FOR TABLE/ARRAY. ZEROS/BLANKS ASSUMED
             TABLE/ARRAY ------- AR
* 8043        900    NO DATA PRESENT FOR TABLE/ARRAY. ZEROS/BLANKS ASSUMED
             TABLE/ARRAY ------- TR
* 8043       1000    NO DATA PRESENT FOR TABLE/ARRAY. ZEROS/BLANKS ASSUMED
```

CROSS-REFERENCE LISTING

```
        FILE/RCD    DEV/RCD     REFERENCES (D=DEFINED)

   02   REPORT      PRINTER     600D  2400   2900   3200   3500
   01   SALES       DISK        500D  1200


        FIELD       ATTR        REFERENCES (M=MODIFIED D=DEFINED)

        AR(5)       A(3)         900D  1900   1900D  2000   2000D  3400
* 7030  QT          A(4)        2100M
        QTY         P(5,0)      1600D  1900   2000   2100
* 7030  REGION      A(4)        3300
* 7031  SLDATE      P(6,0)      1400D
* 7031  SLITM#      A(7)        1700D
* 7031  SLSREP      A(3)        1300D
        SLSTOR      A(2)        1500D  2300
* 7031  SLUPRC      P(7,2)      1800D
        STR(6)      P(3,0)      1100D
        STR,X                   2300   2300M
* 7031  TAB1(5)     A(3)         800D
        TR(4)       A(3)        1000D  3700
        UDATE       P(6,0)      2700
* 7030  X           P(5,0)      2200M  2300   2300
        1           LITERAL     2200


        INDICATOR   REFERENCES (M=MODIFIED D=DEFINED)

        LR           500D  3500
        OF           600D  2500   3000
        01          1200M  3200
        1P          2400   2900
```

MESSAGES

```
    MSGID      SEV   NUMBER   TEXT

*   QRG1019    00      1      IGNDECERR(*YES) SPECIFIED ON COMMAND. NO DECIMAL DATA ERRORS
*   QRG3017    10      1      NUMBER OF ENTRIES PER RECORD (POS 33-35) NOT VALID. 1 ASSUME
*   QRG5010    20      1      FACTOR 1 ENTRY (POSITIONS 18-27) MUST BE BLANK FOR SPECIFIED
*   QRG5054    20      2      RESULT FIELD ENTRY (POSITIONS 43-48) PREVIOUSLY DEFINED WITH
                              DEFINITION USED
*   QRG5158    30      1      ARRAY NAME IN RESULT FIELD (POSITIONS 43-51) NOT VALID FOR S
                              LINE IGNORED
*   QRG5176    30      1      FACTOR 2 (POSITIONS 33-42) OR RESULT FIELD (POSITIONS 43-52)
                              OPERATION. SPECIFICATION LINE IGNORED
```

* QRG7030	30	3	FIELD OR INDICATOR NOT DEFINED.
* QRG7031	00	5	NAME OR INDICATOR NOT REFERENCED.
* QRG7044	30	3	FIELD NOT VALID FOR SPECIFIED OPERATION. FIELD MUST BE NUMERI
* QRG7059	20	2	EDIT MUST BE SPECIFIED ONLY WITH NUMERIC FIELD. EDITING IGNOF
* QRG7086	00	1	RPG WILL HANDLE BLOCKING FUNCTION FOR THE FILE. INFDS CONTENT ARE TRANSFERRED.
* QRG8043	10	3	NO SOURCE RECORDS PROVIDED TO INITIALIZE ARRAY/TABLE. ALPHAME NUMERIC ELEMENTS ASSUMED ZERO
* QRG8046	20	1	COMPILE TIME ARRAY/TABLE DEFINED BUT NOT REFERENCED

MESSAGE SUMMARY

TOTAL	00	10	20	30	40	50
25	7	4	6	8	0	0

37 RECORDS READ FROM SOURCE FILE
SOURCE RECORDS INCLUDE   32 SPECIFICATIONS,   0 TABLE RECORDS, AND   5 COMMENTS

QRG0008 COMPILE TERMINATED. SEVERITY 30 ERRORS FOUND IN PROGRAM

* * * * * E N D   O F   C O M P I L A T I O N * * * * *
* QRG1020   ERROR OCCURRED CREATING OR UPDATING DATA AREA RETURNCODE. COMPIL

PROGRAMMING PROJECT

Project Overview

A report is to be printed listing sales for each day of the week. Some stores are closed on some days of the week, so it is not possible to predict what stores will produce sales on what days. Sample data for this project can be found in Appendix D.

Input Format

The input data for the project is found in a file called SALES in the sample data. The Record Layout for this file is shown in Figure 8.38.

Processing

A record is read and the sales amount is added to the appropriate day of the week in the sales array. Sales are totaled for a level break for each day and sales accumulated for a final total.

Output Format (Printer Spacing Chart)

The output for the project is a report with standard headings. At level break time, a line is printed for each day showing the day, the store number, and the total sales for that day. A final total is also printed. The Printer Spacing Chart for this report is shown in Figure 8.39.

An example of the finished report is shown in Figure 8.40.

FIGURE 8.38 Programming Project: Record Layout

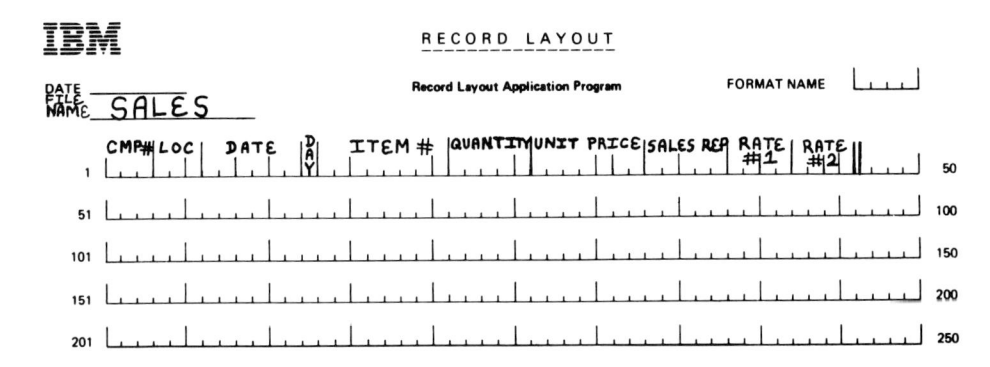

FIGURE 8.39 Programming Project: Printer Spacing Chart

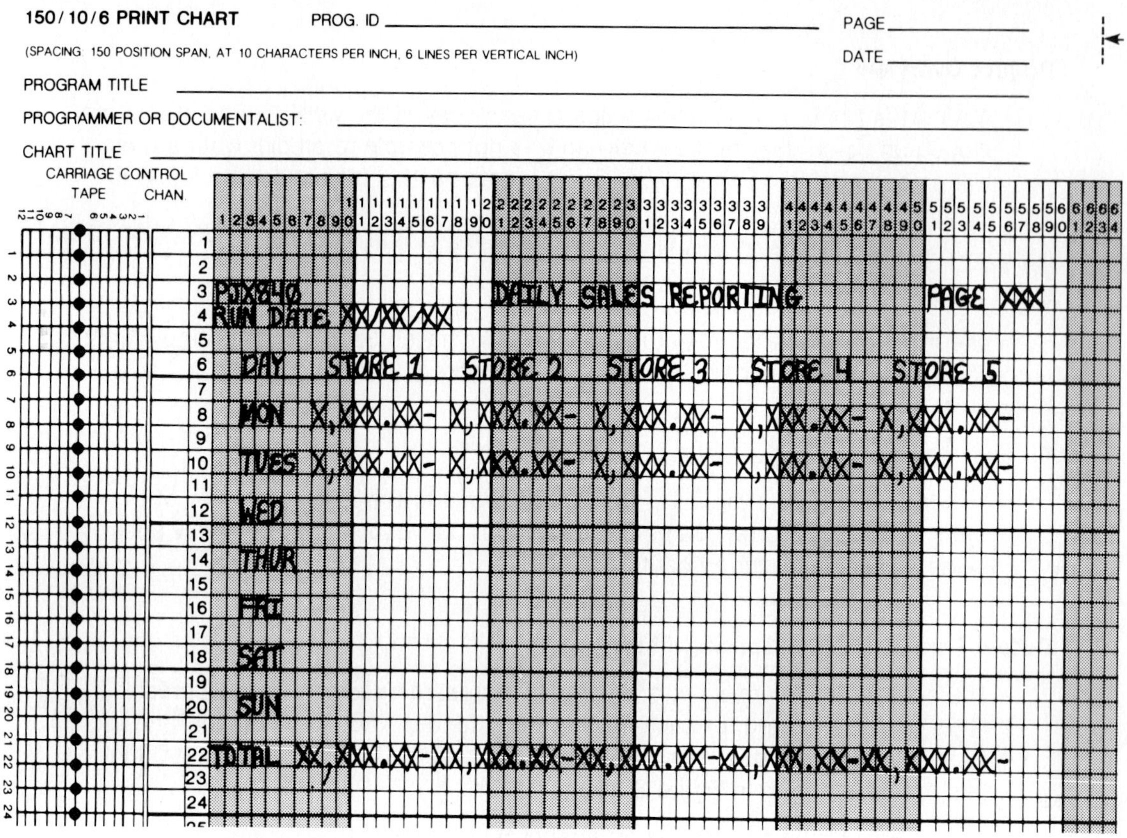

```
PJX840              DAILY SALES REPORTING              PAGE XXX
RUN DATE XX/XX/XX

DAY     STORE 1     STORE 2     STORE 3     STORE 4     STORE 5

MON    X,XXX.XX-   X,XXX.XX-   X,XXX.XX-   X,XXX.XX-   X,XXX.XX-
TUES   X,XXX.XX-   X,XXX.XX-   X,XXX.XX-   X,XXX.XX-   X,XXX.XX-
WED
THUR
FRI
SAT
SUN

TOTAL XX,XXX.XX- XX,XXX.XX- XX,XXX.XX- XX,XXX.XX- XX,XXX.XX-
```

FIGURE 8.40 Programming Project: Final Report

```
PJX840              DAILY SALES REPORT              PAGE   1
RUN DATE  2/21/92

     DAY     STORE 1     STORE 2     STORE 3     STORE 4     STORE 5

     MON      250.00
     WED                 7,225.00                            4,821.24
     THUR      23.25
     SAT                   883.00
     SUN


     TOTAL    273.25    8,108.00                             4,821.24
```

Chapter 9

Processing Multiple Sequential Files

What you will learn in Chapter 9

Types of Files
    Master Files
    Transaction Files
    Table Files
    History Files
    Backup Files
Tape Media
    Sequential File Processing
    Record Blocking

Processing a Master File
Method for Updating Sequential Files
    Transaction Types
    Matching Record Logic
Sample Program Using Sequential File Processing
    Record Layouts
    File Description Specifications

Input Specifications
Sequence Checking
Matching Record Indicator (MR)
Output Specifications
Packed Decimal Data
    Reading and Writing Numeric Fields in Packed Decimal Format

---

All the projects in earlier chapters have used only a single input file. There are many occasions when the data needed to produce a report or to complete some function on the computer is contained in two or more files. A programmer must know how to write programs that will read from more than one file.

TYPES OF FILES ■

Before discussing the use of multiple input files, it is useful to understand the different types of files that coexist on a computer system.

There are definite categories into which files can be classified. In general they are as follows:

    master files
    transaction files
    table files
    history files
    backup files

Master Files

A master file is usually a permanent file that contains data related to the current status of some aspect of a business. One example of a master file is the employee master file, which contains current information about an employee such as employee number, name, address, rate of pay, job classification, and other related data. This information must be secured so that unauthorized persons cannot change it. It is usually considered a permanent file which must always be available for processing on the computer, even though the data about individual employees might change. Other master files might be the customer master, inventory master, general ledger master, and open accounts payable master. Figure 9.1 shows an example of a customer master file.

Transaction Files

A transaction file is a dynamic file which may change from minute to minute. It contains transactions that occur during normal business activities. One example of a transaction file might be the time and attendance records that are processed each day as employees record their time on a time clock. The transaction file accepts new records each time an employee starts or stops work. At the end of the week or pay period, the transactions are totaled up and the employee will be paid for the number of hours worked. These transactions are not permanent. They are useful only for the short period during which they are processed and until the employee has been paid. After that, they are of interest only as historical information.

Some other kinds of transactions that might be entered into a temporary file of this type are sales in a retail store, invoices, receipts, and adjustments to inventory. Typically, this type of data is gathered for a specific period and then removed to some off-line storage media. Figure 9.2 shows an example of daily sales transactions.

Table Files

In Chapter 7 we discussed table files and how they are used in RPG. Conceptually, they contain reference lists of facts to which programs will refer when processing either master or transaction files. A payroll program might need a table file containing the tax rates to compute income tax for a given year. A program to convert currency values might use a table file that gives the exchange rates among currencies from various countries. Although some table files might require changes quite often, table files are usually considered permanent since they need to be available for any processing. Figure 9.3 shows an example of a table file containing sales commission rates.

FIGURE 9.1 Customer Master Data

```
                        SAMPLE DATA
                    CUSTOMER MASTER FILE

    0302    ACME PAINT          23 GREEN ST      RED BLUFF      AK    NET 30
    1508    HEAVY METAL CO      128 STEELE RD    SILVER CITY    WA    COD
    2001    LITE TRUCKING       5653 LONG HWY    DOWNHILL       CO    NET 90
   16359    ORB BALL BEARING    88 CIRCLE DR     ROUNDSTONE     CA    NET 60
```

FIGURE 9.2 Daily Sales Transactions Data

```
                            SAMPLE DATA
                       DAILY SALES TRANSACTIONS

                                              TRAN    TENDER            EXT
 STORE#  REGISTER   DATE    DRAWER   ITEM#   QUANT   TYPE    TYPE   PRICE    PRICE    TAX     TOTAL
   02       1      030999     2      60502     4      01      02    199.99   799.96   48.00   847.96
   02       1      030999     1      18301     1      01      02     48.50    48.50    -0-    48.50
   02       1      030999     2       6537     1      02      03      2.98     2.98    .18     3.16
```

FIGURE 9.3 Table File Containing Sales Commission Rates

```
                SAMPLE DATA
             COMMISSION TABLE FILE
              MGR000.10
              AST000.08
              SLS000.05
              TRN000.02
```

History Files

Businesses are most interested in current data, such as sales for the current month or year-to-date earnings for the current year. It is often useful, however, to compare current activity with previous years' activity to determine progress. Because a computer is the ideal tool for this type of analysis, most businesses want to store older data, making it available for comparisons and trend analysis reporting. This data is stored in history files, which might be exact duplicates of the format of the current data files or might be summarized versions of the data from prior periods. They may be accumulations of transaction files over some period. It is important that old data be purged from these files on some specific recurring schedule. Figure 9.4 shows an example of a file containing a summarized version of sales for past years.

Backup Files

It is absolutely necessary to create copies of all important data files and store them off-line in a safe, secure place. Backup procedures are usually performed during off hours when no users are signed on to the computer. This might be done weekly, daily, or even more often if the data is extremely important. Any data processing department that does not maintain good backup systems is in danger of experiencing serious losses in both time and money if its data is lost due to some mistake or natural disaster.

Figure 9.5 shows an example of a backup file. Notice that it is an exact copy of the customer master file shown earlier. Backup files are usually exact duplicates of important files.

FIGURE 9.4 Sales History Summary Data

```
                          SAMPLE DATA
                   SALES HISTORY SUMMARY FILE
```

ITEM#	YEAR	JAN	FEB	MAR	APR	MAY	JUNE	JUL	AUG	SEP	OCT	NOV	DEC
6537	90	1032.00	6583.00	4281.50	1385.85	6499.99	1234.00	1032.00	6500.00	2300.00	3000.00	6583.00	9382.00
6537	91	738.00		1000.00	656.00		950.00	950.00	850.00	1000.00	900.00	682.00	785.00
6537	92	425.00											
18301	90			695.00	695.00	1698.00	2100.00	2598.50	1205.00	1205.00	3500.00	6000.00	6000.00
18301	91	8050.00	1500.00	2506.00	698.00	6588.00	7000.00	7500.00	8000.00	8000.00	9000.00	9500.00	9500.00
18301	92	9000.00											
60502	90	858.00	6000.00	500.00	2588.00	7085.00	5005.00	6000.00	5005.00	4500.00	2585.00	3000.00	2100.00
60502	91	2851.00	400.00	650.00	1000.00	250.00	250.00	100.00	75.00	150.00	75.00	50.00	
60502	92	50.00											

FIGURE 9.5 Backup File for Customer Master Data

```
                     SAMPLE DATA
              CUSTOMER MASTER FILE BACKUP
       0302  Acme Paint        23 Green St.    Red Bluff    AK   Net 30
       1508  Heavy Metal Co.   128 Steele Rd.  Silver City  WA   C.O.D.
       2001  Lite Trucking     5653 Long Hwy.  Downhill     CO   Net 90
      16359  Orb Ball Bearing  88 Circle Dr.   Roundstone   CA   Net 60
```

TAPE MEDIA ■

The media for inputting information into a computer can vary from program to program. Thus far, the media we have discussed has been disk, even though details about making the best use of disk have not yet been a concern. Although disk is perhaps the most common media in use today, it is useful to understand how other media might be used to perform sequential processing. We will use tape media to illustrate the use of sequential files, although sequential files could also reside on disk.

Data which is to be processed on a computer may be input or output on a wide variety of devices. Each year new devices come into the marketplace and some of the older devices become obsolete. One device type which has been used for many years is the tape drive. Although it would be difficult to predict how long tape media will continue to be used, it is probable that some similar form of off-line storage media will be used.

Tape is a media that is transportable between dissimilar computers. This is sometimes a real necessity for moving data from one computer site to another. Tape is relatively inexpensive and a single tape can hold a large amount of data. A tape can be stored off-line (away from the computer) for long periods with little deterioration of the data. In short, tape is an excellent media for off-line storage. It is ideal for backup files and history files.

Information is stored on magnetic tape as a series of incredibly small magnetized "dots" which represent bits of information. These bits make up the bytes that comprise records and files, just as in other media. Figure 9.6 shows records as they are arranged on a tape file.

Tape media might be on a tape reel or in cartridge form. Tape drives operate in a wide variety of modes with different densities and speeds of operation, which will be discussed here only as they relate to RPG. These variations have changed as the technology has improved (faster speeds and greater density), but RPG continues to handle tape operation in the same manner, processing each record sequentially.

Sequential File Processing

Sequential processing means that records are read or written one after another. Records stored on magnetic tape are arranged sequentially. Figure 9.7 illustrates a sequential file.

FIGURE 9.6 Records in a Sequential File

| RECORD 3 | RECORD 2 | RECORD 1 |

FIGURE 9.7 Record Layout for a Sequential File

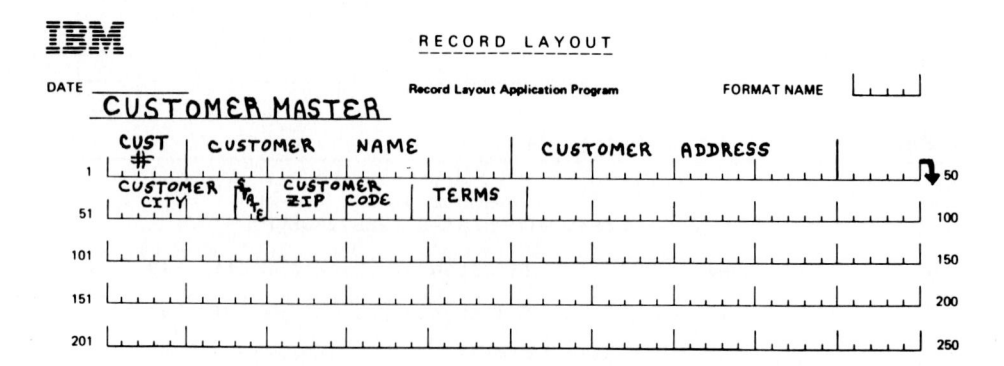

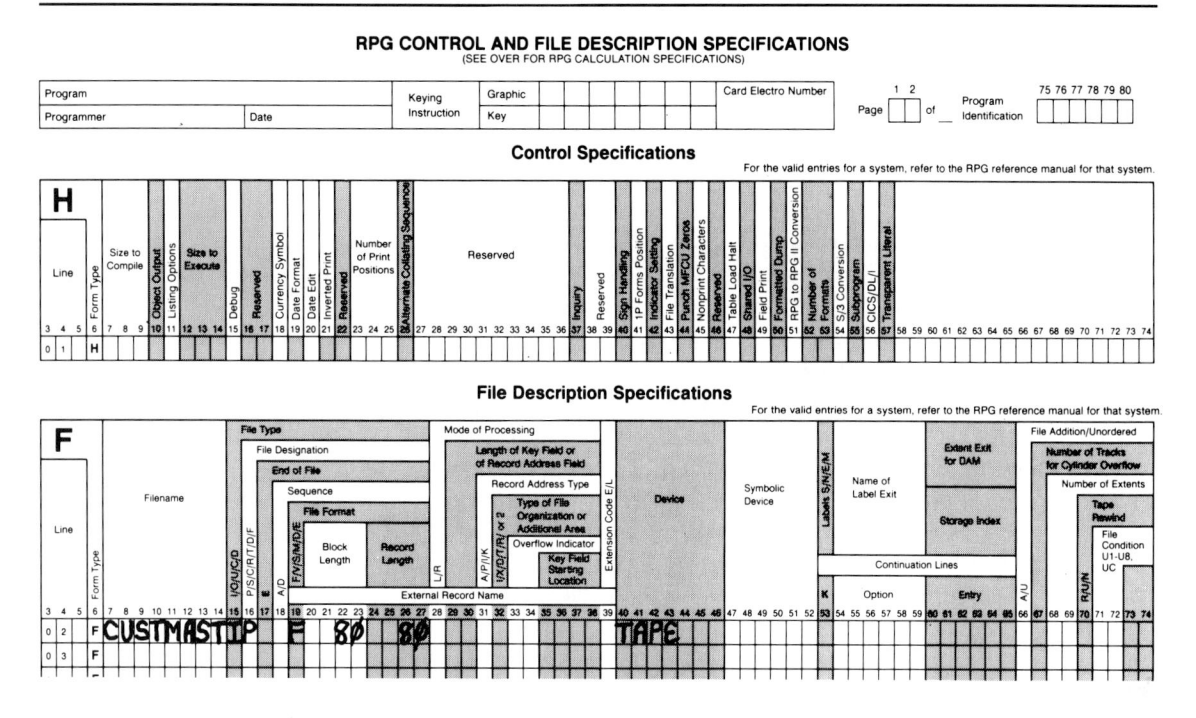

FIGURE 9.8 File Description for a Tape Input File

All the files used in earlier chapters have been arranged in this same sequential format. Figure 9.8 shows the File Description Specifications for defining an input file that is on tape.

Most of the coding on the File Description Specifications for a tape file remains the same as for disk. There are only two new items. The device name (columns 40–46) is TAPE. On some computers the correct device entry is SEQ, which would apply to any type of device for which sequential processing is used.

Columns 20–23 on the File Description Specifications is a field titled block length. In previous chapters, this field was ignored. When processing tape, however, block length is a required field.

To understand the function of block length, we must understand how a tape drive works. Since records on tape are arranged sequentially, the tape drive must be able to recognize where one record ends and the next record begins. This is done, as shown in Figure 9.9, by means of a blank space between each record where there are no magnetic bits written. This is known as an inter-record gap and it is approximately .6 inches long.

A special character called a tape mark is written at the end of the file.

Record Blocking

Tape must be moved physically across a read-write head for processing. The tape drive starts the tape moving, reads the record into main memory, and then stops at the inter-record gap. These stops slow processing in main memory. The gaps also take up space on the tape that might be needed to store more data.

FIGURE 9.9 Inter-Record Gap on Tape

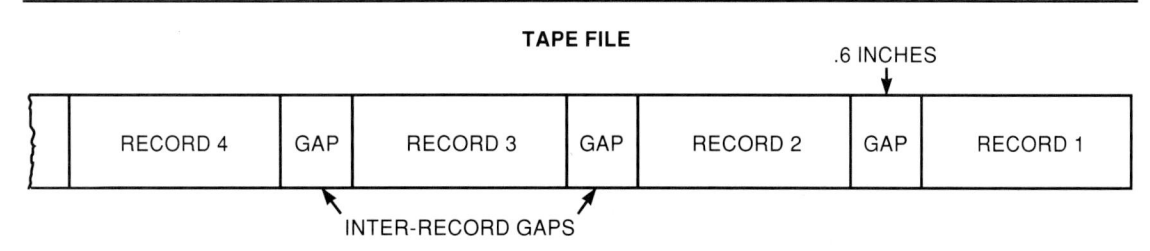

FIGURE 9.10 Tape File with Records Blocked Three Per Block

TAPE FILE
BLOCKED RECORDS
(BLOCKING FACTOR 3)

	RECORD 4	GAP	RECORD 3	RECORD 2	RECORD 1

To overcome these two problems, it is better to create a file on tape with fewer gaps. This is called blocking the records. The records are written on the tape sequentially without gaps between each record. A gap is placed after a group of records. This gap can now more correctly be called an inter-block gap. Figure 9.10 shows what a tape file might look like using a blocking factor of three records per block.

The tape drive operates exactly as it did when reading single records, except that it moves a group of records into main memory at one time, thus speeding up the processing. The program must recognize the individual records within the group in order to be processed in main memory.

In RPG, all that is needed to accomplish this is entering the blocking factor into the File Description Specifications as was shown in Figure 9.8.

If the tape file is an output file, the blocking factor may be chosen by the programmer. The more records that can be blocked together, the faster the program can run. However, the entire block of records must fit into main memory at one time. If main memory is small or if many other users will need to be on the system at the same time, it would be unreasonable to make the blocking factor very large.

When the tape file is an input file, the programmer must know what blocking factor was used by the program that wrote the file and must specify it.

The blocking factor is the number of logical records that make up the physical record on tape. If the logical records were 50 columns in length, and the programmer decided to block them in groups of ten, that would be referred to as a blocking factor of ten. The File Description Specifications would be coded as shown in Figure 9.11 with 50 entered as record length but 500 as the block length—ten records at 50 columns per record.

FIGURE 9.11 File Description Specifications for Tape Output File

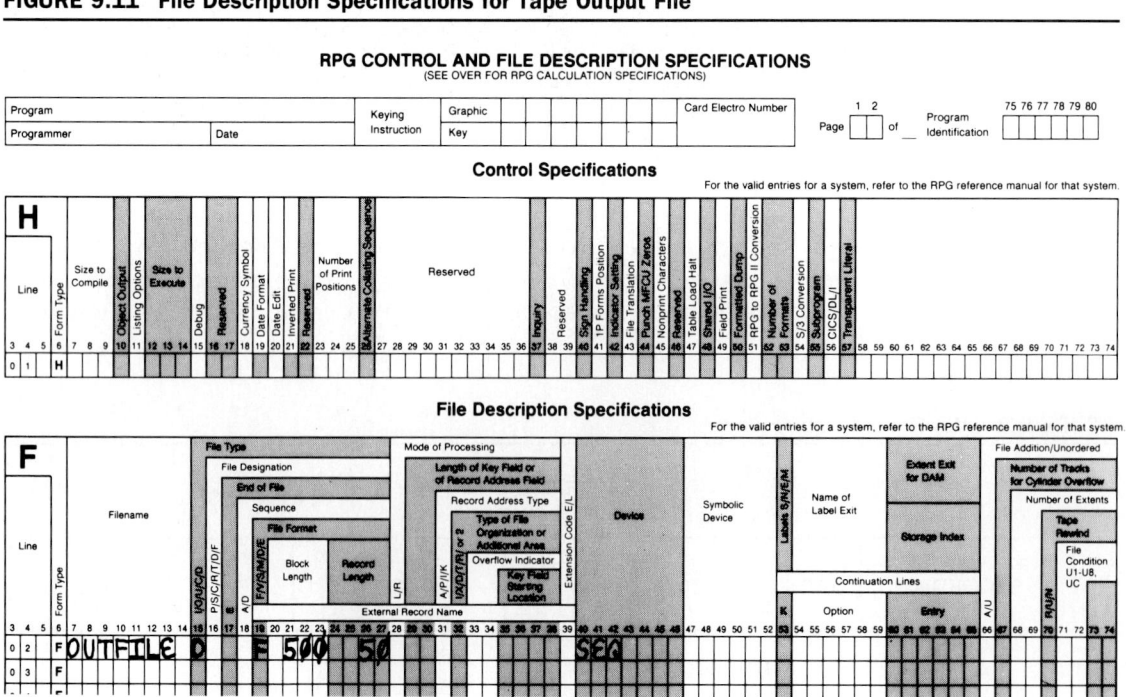

FIGURE 9.12 Employee Master File

```
                                    EMPLOYEE MASTER FILE DATA

              EMPL ID#      NAME         ADDRESS           CITY        ST    DEPT    RATE    SEX
                0123      JONES, SAM     33 SWING ST.      ROCKVILLE   TX     38     6.95     M
              ┌ 0888      ACRES, MARY    14 WIDE ST.       EL PASO     TX     29     7.50     F
   DIFFERENT  │ 0895      ACRES, MARY    12865 24TH ST.    EL PASO     TX     45    12.18     F
   EMPLOYEE  ─┤ 1462      ACRES, JOE     75 WINDING LN.    JUAREZ      MX     18     5.40     M
     ID#      └ 2944      ACRES, M.      48 EL RIO DR.     EL PASO     TX     77     5.95     M
                3827      ADAMS, W.      345 MAIN ST.      LITTLETON   TX     29     6.52     M
```

Processing a Master File

The records in a master file usually contain some key field which allows each record to be uniquely identified. This key could be an employee identification number, an inventory part number, or some such field that is unique to each record in the master file. For example, each record in an employee master file will contain some type of employee identification field. This ensures that each employee record is different from every other employee record, even if the name of the employee is the same. The key field in the employee master file shown in Figure 9.12 is the employee ID number field.

METHOD FOR UPDATING SEQUENTIAL FILES ■

We can now discuss the relationship between master files and transaction files.

A common computer application for processing more than one file involves programs which use transaction files to do updating to a master file.

Updating a file is the process of making changes to some of the data in the file, adding records to the file, or deleting old records from the file. This updating process is sometimes referred to as file maintenance. In the following sections we will discover how this type of update program is written.

To make updates to a sequential master file, the update transactions are first keyed into a transaction file. This file will contain the key field as well as the desired changed or added field(s) as shown in Figure 9.13. Without this key, it would be very difficult to relate each transaction to its proper master record. In this example, the key field represents an employee ID number and carries the heading KEY on the report.

Before updating can be done correctly for a sequential file, the records in both the master file and the transaction file must be in sequence according to the key field. As shown in Figure 9.14, the files are put into sequence according to some significant key field which occurs in both files. (These sequences are taken from the key fields shown in Figures 9.12 and 9.13.)

FIGURE 9.13 Transaction File Showing Search Key

```
                                    TRANSACTION FILE DATA

CODE   EMPL ID#   RATE    NAME          ADDRESS          CITY      ST    DEPT   COMMENT
 A       0700     4.95    SMITH, A.     75 WINDING LN.   JUAREZ    MX     77    NEW HIRE
 C       0888     8.05                                                          RATE CHG
 C       2944                           14 WIDE ST.      EL PASO   TX           ADDR CHG
 D       3827                                                                   TERMINATED
```

FIGURE 9.14 Two Sequential Files in Order

```
            MASTER FILE     TRANSACTION FILE
               0123               0700
               0888               0888
               0895               2944
               1462               3827
               2944
```

FIGURE 9.15 Files Involved in an Update Program

```
        TRANSACTION         ORIGINAL
           FILE             MASTER
                             FILE


              ┌──────────┐
              │          │    NEW
              │ COMPUTER │   MASTER
              │          │    FILE
              └──────────┘                UPDATED
                    │                     WITH ALL
                    ▼                    TRANSACTIONS
              TRANSACTION
                REPORT
```

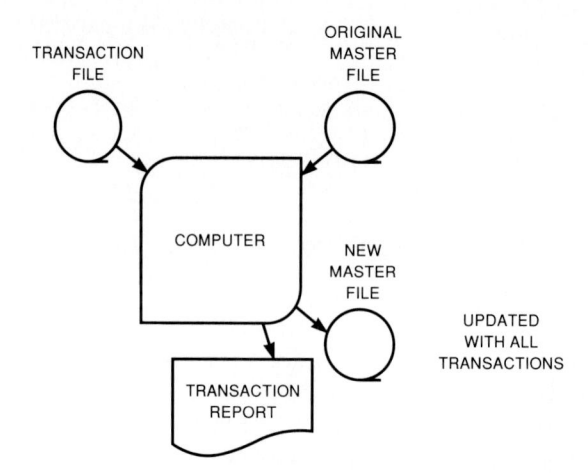

Updates to a sequential file will require an input file for the master file, an input file for the transaction file, and an output file for the new updated master file. It is usually wise to print a report from this same program to show the activity that has been performed on the master file. Figure 9.15 shows a diagram of the files involved in an update program.

In this example, a master file stored on magnetic tape will be updated by a file of transactions which have been sorted into the same sequence as the master file. The output will be a new master file and a report which might show every transaction or only those transactions for which an error was found. For example, an error might occur if a transaction was entered to make a change to an employee record for which no master record was found.

Transaction Types

Transaction records will usually contain a code to identify the type of activity to be performed. Code *C* in column 1 means it is a change, code *A* means a record is to be added, and code *D* means that the record is to be deleted from the master file.

There is nothing magical about these codes. Any set of codes would work equally well, such as 1, 2, 3, or others. *A*, *C*, and *D* are user-friendly since they are easier to remember.

Matching Record Logic

Before coding the sample program for this chapter, it is important to understand the processing which will take place.

1. A master record is read.
2. A transaction record is read.
3. The key field from the transaction record is compared with the key field from the master record to determine whether the master record is equal to, less than, or greater than the transaction record.
4. The processing is performed according to the results of the comparison.

Figure 9.16 shows some sample data with the expected results.

The first master record has no matching activity on the transaction file so no change is expected. The original master record must be written out in its original form to be stored to the new master file. Remember that the new employee master tape will replace the old one.

RPG then reads the transaction file. The first transaction record has a code *A* which means that a new record is to be added to the new employee master file. All of the new information from the transaction record is used to create a new master record.

FIGURE 9.16 Sample Data and Expected Results

```
      MASTER FILE     TRANSACTION FILE
         0123              0700
         0888              0888
         0895              2944
         1462              3827
         2944
         3827

              NEW MASTER FILE
                 0123
                 0700
                 0888
                 0895
                 1462
                 2944
```

Another transaction record is read. Since the transaction record has not yet found a matching part number, another record must be read from the master file. This time a match is found. The code in the transaction file is a C so a change will be made to the master information and the new information will be written out to the new employee master tape together with all the unchanged information in the master record.

The last transaction record has a code D (delete). A matching record is found in the old employee master file, but nothing needs to be done because of the delete code. The record will not be written on the new employee master file.

SAMPLE PROGRAM USING SEQUENTIAL FILE PROCESSING ■

An inventory master file is a very important file for many businesses and needs to be updated daily. This updating consists of adding new part masters for new products in the inventory, deleting old part masters no longer carried in stock, and making changes to part masters, such as price changes and description changes, whenever necessary. It will also be necessary to add to or subtract from the quantity on hand as products are received or shipped.

Record Layouts

For an example of how a master file can be updated using sequential file processing, we will use an inventory master file, the Record Layout for which is shown in Figure 9.17. These records are arranged on tape sequentially by the six-digit part number.

FIGURE 9.17 Record Layout for Inventory Master File

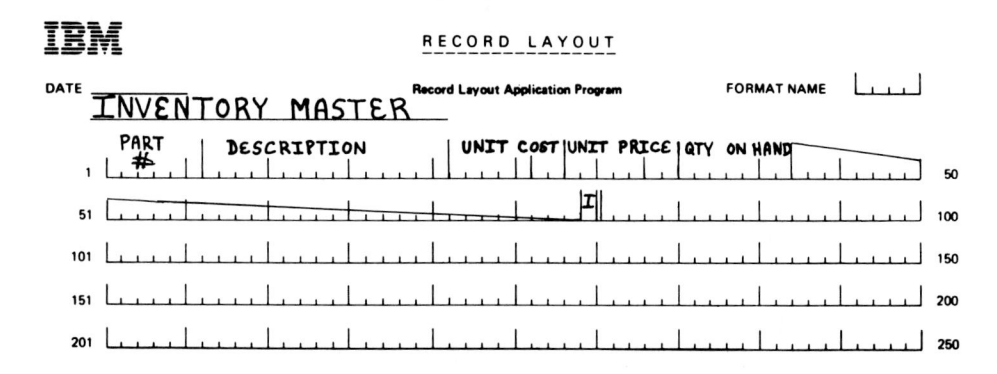

FIGURE 9.18 Record Layout for Inventory Transaction File

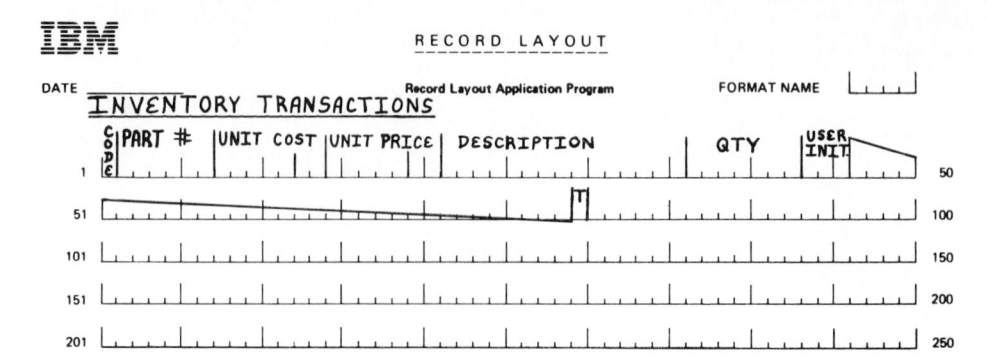

```
IBM                                    RECORD LAYOUT
DATE              Record Layout Application Program      FORMAT NAME
    INVENTORY TRANSACTIONS
    C|PART #|UNIT COST|UNIT PRICE| DESCRIPTION    | QTY  |USER|
    O                                                    |INIT|
    D                                                           50
    E                                                    
  51                                              T           100
 101                                                          150
 151                                                          200
 201                                                          250
```

The transaction record does not need to be in the same *format* as the master file but it does need to carry much of the same information. The transactions have been keyed to disk and then sorted by the six-digit part number. The format for the transaction file is shown in Figure 9.18.

File Description Specifications

The File Description Specifications coding for this program is quite similar to previous examples. Since there are two input files we must code a separate line for each. Figure 9.19 shows the coding for the two input files. There will also need to be a new output file, as shown in the flowchart in Figure 9.15, and an output printer file to show what updates have been made to the master file.

The master file is coded as a primary input file (IP in columns 15–16). It has a record length of 80 and a block length of 800, which means it contains ten records in each block (a blocking factor of ten). The device is SEQ for sequential processing.

Column 18 contains the letter *A* to notify RPG that the records are in ascending sequence. This is important when doing matching record processing of two files. If the records were in descending sequence, the letter *D* would be entered.

FIGURE 9.19 File Description Specifications for Two Input Files

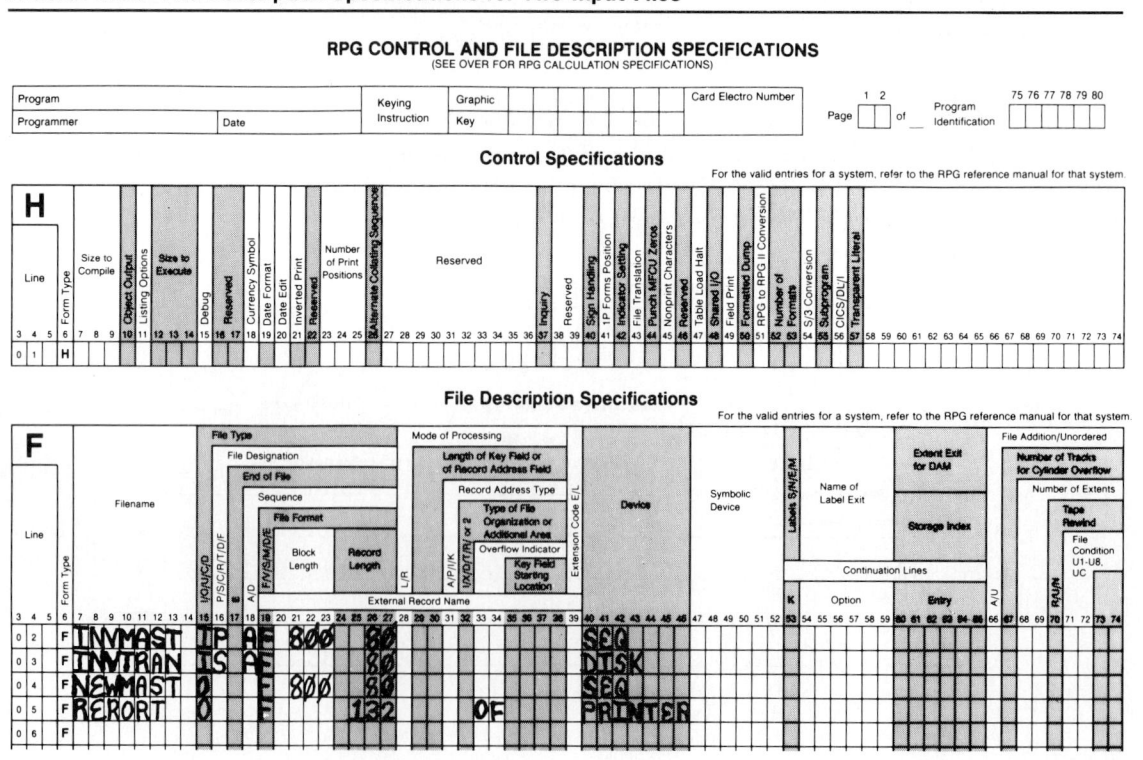

Line	Filename	Type	Block Length	Record Length	Device
02	INVMAST	IP AF	800	80	SEQ
03	INVTRAN	IS AF		80	DISK
04	NEWMAST	O	800	80	SEQ
05	REPORT	O		132	OF PRINTER
06	F				

226   RPG: A Programming Language for Today

The transaction file is coded as a secondary file (IS in columns 15–16). These records will be entered from disk for this example, so the entry in columns 40–45 for device will be DISK, which requires no blocking factor. This line also contains the letter *A* in column 18 for ascending sequence.

Only one file may be identified as the primary file. All other files are identified as secondary files. In most, if not all, sequential update programs using matching record processing, it is better to make the master file the primary file and the transaction file the secondary for accurate processing.

The output file is defined the same as any other output file except that it will need a blocking factor when it is a tape file.

Input Specifications

Both files will be described on the Input Specifications; it does not matter which is described first. In the example in Figure 9.20, the master file is described using a record identifying indicator of 01 and the transaction file is described using a record identifying indicator of 02. Each field is described as in previous examples. Column 1 contains the identifying code for each of the transaction types—add, change, or delete.

The master record has been defined twice, however, in the Input Specifications. Some of the fields are described individually and then the entire record is defined as one big field called RECORD. Although this is not a requirement for this type of processing, it will simplify the output coding.

The only new entries on the Input Specifications are the entries M1 in columns 61–62 for matching fields (following the key fields). This means that the part number field in both input records will be used as the key or controlling fields to determine whether or not the records match.

Notice that the part number field in both records *must* have the same length and attributes. It would not be of much use to compare unlike fields and expect them to match. In this example, only an M1 was used. In a more complex problem, we could have used several key fields and identified them as M1, M2, . . . M9. Thus, there could have been as many as nine controlling fields that would have to match before a transaction could be considered for an update.

FIGURE 9.20 Input Specifications

IBM — RPG INPUT SPECIFICATIONS (SEE OVER FOR RPG EXTENSION AND LINE COUNTER SPECIFICATIONS) — GX09-1033-03 UM/050

Line	Form Type	Filename or Record Name	Sequence	Record Identifying Indicator	Position	C/Z/D	Character	Field Location From	Field Location To	Decimal Positions	RPG Field Name	Matching Fields
01	I	INVMAST	AA	01	80	C	I					
02	I							1	6		PART#	M1
03	I							7	21		DESC	
04	I							22	28	2	COST	
05	I							29	35	2	PRICE	
06	I							36	42	0	QUANT	
07	I							1	80		RECORD	
08	I		ZZ	98								
09	I	INVTRAN	BB	02	80	C	T					
10	I							1	1		CODE	
11	I							2	7		PN	M1
12	I							8	14	2	TCOST	
13	I							15	21	2	TPRICE	
14	I							22	36		TDESC	
15	I							37	43		TQTY	
16	I							44	46		TINIT	
17	I		ZZ	99								
18	I											

Sequence Checking

When a matching record indicator such as M1 is used in the Input Specifications, RPG will automatically check the file to ensure that it is in sequence. If an out-of-sequence condition is found, RPG will halt and produce an error message. To avoid this, be sure that both files are in sequence before attempting to perform an update.

Matching Record Indicator (MR)

The record matching function is coded in the Calculation and Output Specifications with the use of the MR indicator. Even if several levels were defined on the Input Specifications (M1, M2, etc.), there will be only one level indicated on the Calculation and Output Specifications. When a complete match has been found for all levels, the MR indicator is turned on.

Do not make hard work out of matching record processing. It works exactly as you would want it to or exactly as if you were processing the records manually.

- RPG always reads the primary file first, so the first record in will be a master record.
- RPG will then read the secondary file.
- RPG will compare the two records to determine whether the second is a match to the first. This is automatic and requires no further coding other than the M1–M9 in the Input Specifications. If a match is found (i.e., if the key fields are equal), the MR indicator is turned on. It is then up to the programmer to use this MR indicator to perform whatever functions are desired.
- Another record will be read from both files and compared. Processing will continue until both files are exhausted.

The Calculation Specifications, shown in Figure 9.21, control the processing for each type of transaction. The first routine compares the transaction code to determine if it is a record to be added (code *A*). An equal condition turns on indicator 10. The next line compares for code *C* (for changes) and turns on indicator 11 if it is equal. A code *D* will turn on indicator 12 for transactions to be deleted. If a transaction code has set on none of these (N10, N11, or N12), the code is invalid and an error will be recorded on the report, but no updating will be done to the master file.

These routines must be done *only* for transaction records, and never for master records. It is therefore extremely important that each calculation is performed *only* when indicator 02 is on.

If the transaction is an addition or deletion, no further calculations are necessary.

If the transaction is a change, then the quantity in the transaction record will be added to the quantity in the master record to compute the new quantity on hand. (Shipment transactions are generally keyed as negative amounts since they reduce the quantity on hand.)

If the record is a transaction record (indicator 02 is on) and the transaction code is a *C* for change (indicator 11 is on) and there is a matching master record found (the MR indicator is on) then the computation for the new quantity can be made. Only one line of calculations is needed to do this, as shown in Figure 9.22. Notice that the MR indicator is used in the same way as any other indicator. It is not possible to use M1 or M2 independently. MR signifies a complete match of all the key fields.

FIGURE 9.21 Calculation Specifications

FIGURE 9.22 Computing Quantity, Based on MR Indicator

RPG CALCULATION SPECIFICATIONS

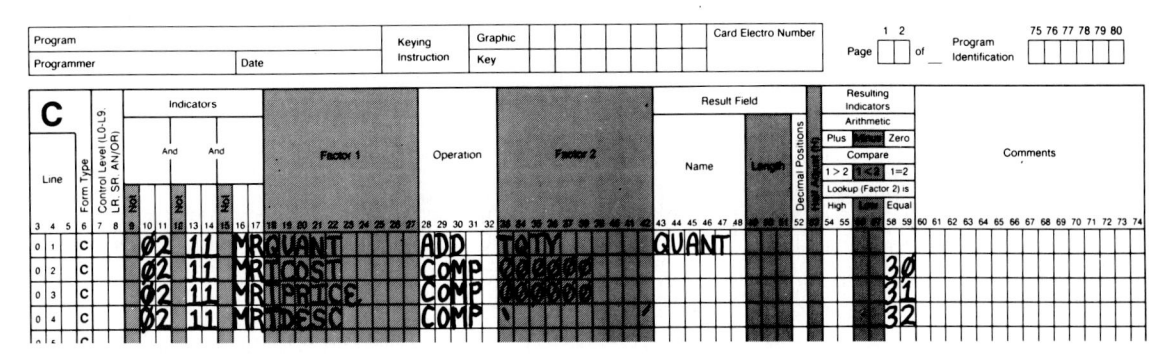

Line	Form Type	Control Level	Indicators (And/And/Not)	Factor 1	Operation	Factor 2	Result Field Name	Length	Dec Pos	Resulting Indicators
01	C	02	11	MRQUANT	ADD	TQTY	QUANT			
02	C	02	11	MRCOST	COMP	000000				30
03	C	02	11	MRPRICE	COMP	000000				31
04	C	02	11	MRDESC	COMP					32

Output Specifications

The new master file is created in the Output Specifications. There are three conditions that govern the creation of an output record.

1. A new record is created in its entirety based on an add transaction.
2. An old record is reproduced just like the original.
3. An old record is reproduced with whatever changes were found in the transaction.

The conditions under which a record is created for an add transaction are as follows:

1. Must be a transaction record (indicator 02 is on).
2. Must be a code *A* (indicator 10 is on).
3. Must *not* be a matching record (indicator MR is off).

The Output Specifications to create a record are shown in Figure 9.23. All of the output fields are obtained from the transaction record.

The conditions under which an old record is reproduced unchanged are either of the following:

1. Must be a master record (indicator 01 is on).
2. Must *not* be a matching record (indicator MR is off).

or

1. A transaction record is found (indicator 02 is on).
2. Transaction code is *A* (indicator 10 is on).
3. Has a matching master record (indicator MR is on). (It would be an error to attempt to add a new record if the key already existed. In such a case, the old record is retained and the new record ignored.)

FIGURE 9.23 Output Specifications: Creating a New Output Record

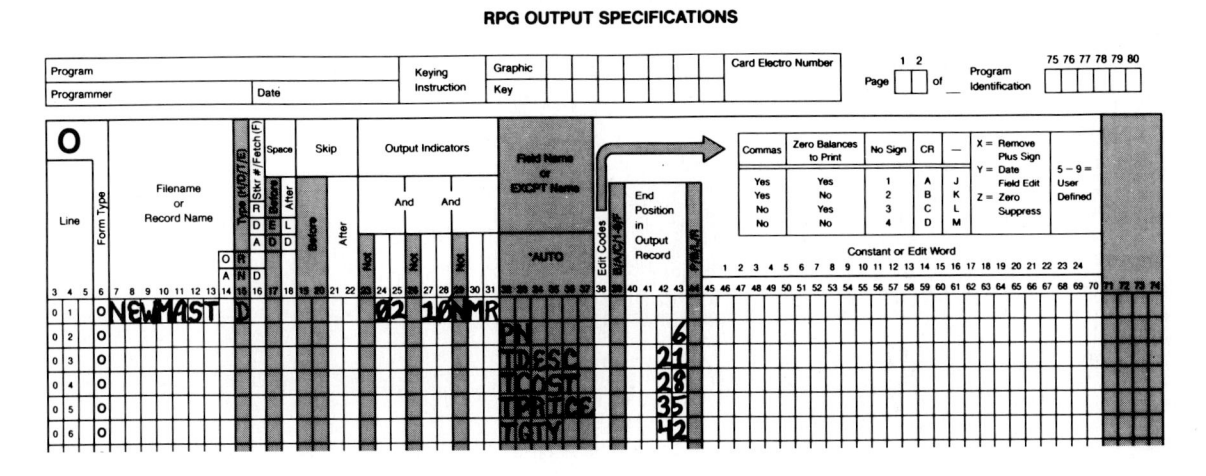

RPG OUTPUT SPECIFICATIONS

Line	Form Type	Filename or Record Name	Type	Output Indicators (And/And/Not)	Field Name or EXCPT Name	End Position in Output Record
01	O	NEWMAST	D	02 10 NMR		
02	O				TN	6
03	O				TDESC	21
04	O				TCOST	28
05	O				TPRICE	35
06	O				TQTY	42

FIGURE 9.24 Output Specifications: Reproducing an Old Record

RPG OUTPUT SPECIFICATIONS

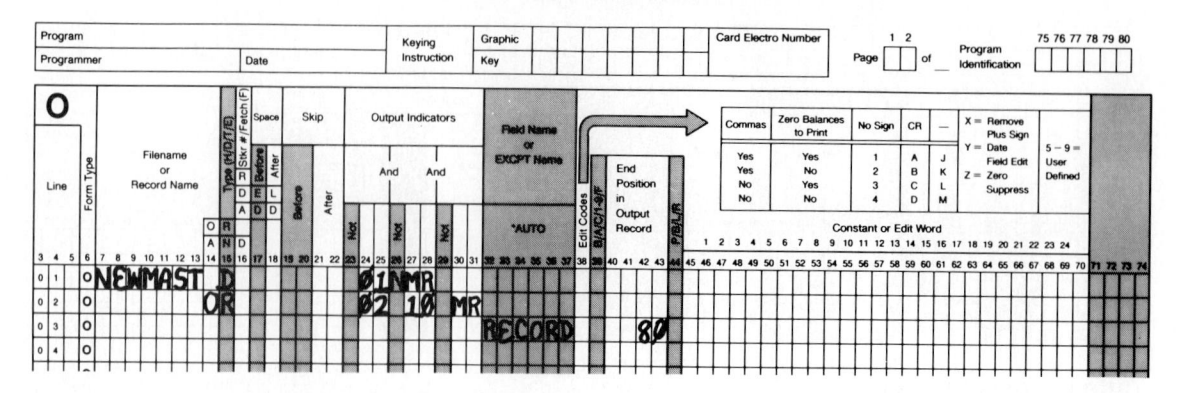

Line	Form Type	Filename or Record Name					Output Indicators			Field Name or EXCPT Name	End Position in Output Record
01	O	NEWMAST D						01		NMR	
02	O	OR						02	10	MR	
03	O									RECORD	80
04	O										

The Output Specifications to reproduce an old record are shown in Figure 9.24. Notice that an old record will be reproduced under two circumstances. Notice also that each field was not coded individually on the output. It was necessary only to define the entire record as one field. This simplifies the coding (and avoids the risk of errors).

The conditions under which an old record is changed and placed in the new file are as follows:

1. Must be a transaction record (indicator 02 is on).
2. Must be a code C (indicator 11 is on).
3. Must be a matching record (indicator MR is on).

The Output Specifications to reproduce a master record with the changes from the transaction are shown in Figure 9.25. The original master record is placed in the output area. Then the new fields are placed in the output area, replacing only the fields that need to be updated. The new fields will overlay the old fields in the same manner as sometimes happens inadvertently on output reports. When this overlay occurs the output fields are moved to the output area in the same sequence as specified on the Output Specifications.

The fields will be updated only if the fields in the transaction record are not zero or blank (indicators 30, 31, and 32). Figure 9.25 shows the Output Specifications for this.

If a record is to be deleted (indicator 12 is on) then no output record needs to be output. In this case no action will be taken.

FIGURE 9.25 Output Specifications: Creating a Changed Record

RPG OUTPUT SPECIFICATIONS

Line	Form Type	Filename or Record Name					Output Indicators			Field Name or EXCPT Name	End Position
01	O	NEWMAST D					02	11	MR		
02	O									RECORD	80
03	O									QUANT	42
04	O						N30			TCOST	28
05	O						N31			TPRICE	35
06	O						N32			TDESC	21
07	O										

FIGURE 9.26 Output Specifications: Transaction Report

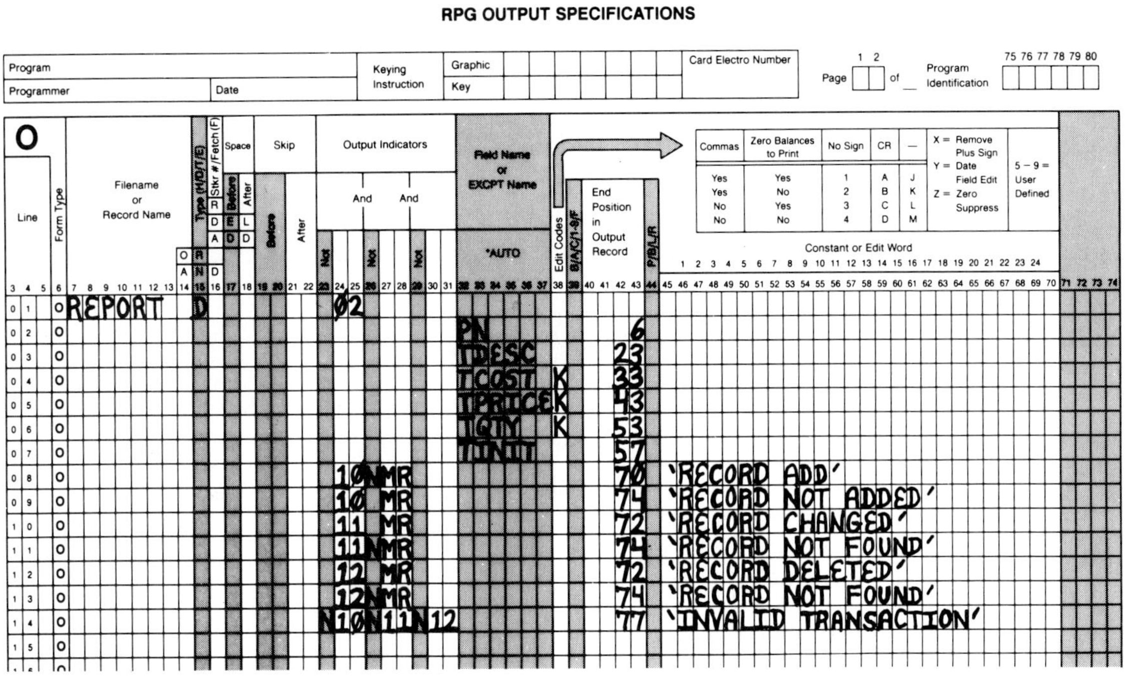

[RPG Output Specifications form showing:]

Line	Filename/Record Name	Output Indicators	Field Name/EXCPT Name	End Position	Constant or Edit Word
01	O REPORT D			02	
02	O		PN	6	
03	O		TDESC	23	
04	O		TCOST K	33	
05	O		TPRICE K	43	
06	O		TQTY K	53	
07	O		TUNIT	57	
08	O	10 MR		70	'RECORD ADD'
09	O	10 NMR		74	'RECORD NOT ADDED'
10	O	11 MR		72	'RECORD CHANGED'
11	O	11 NMR		74	'RECORD NOT FOUND'
12	O	12 MR		72	'RECORD DELETED'
13	O	12 NMR		74	'RECORD NOT FOUND'
14	O	N10 N11 N12		77	'INVALID TRANSACTION'

Figure 9.26 shows all the Output Specifications for the transaction report, giving messages for both valid and invalid transactions.

A detail line will be printed on the report only when a transaction is processed. A message is then printed after each transaction line to indicate what action has been taken. This will notify the user of any error conditions which may need correction in the system.

Error conditions are:

Add transaction with matching master	– 02	10	MR	
Change transaction with no matching master	– 02	11	NMR	
Delete transaction with no matching master	– 02	12	NMR	
Invalid transaction code	– 02	N10	N11	N12

Of course, it is always important to begin every report with the appropriate headings and total lines. These are not shown in this example but a genuine report would provide them.

PACKED DECIMAL DATA ■

All the sample data used thus far has contained numeric fields defined as *zoned decimal* fields. There are other formats in which data can be stored. Numeric fields can be stored more efficiently as *packed decimal* fields.

When data is stored in *zoned decimal* format, each digit of the number is stored in one byte of storage. This means that one digit requires *eight* bits. The byte needs four bits for the zone portion and four bits for the numeric portion of the byte. The zone portion performs no function other than informing the computer that this is not an alphabetic field. Figure 9.27 shows the format of a zoned decimal three-digit number. Notice that it requires three bytes.

Instead of wasting the zone portion of every byte, it is more thrifty to put a number in every *four* bits. This is called a *packed decimal* field.

The sign (positive or negative) is always stored in the rightmost four bits. Thus, a three-position signed field will require only two bytes in packed decimal format as shown in Figure 9.28.

Chapter 9 Processing Multiple Sequential Files

FIGURE 9.27 Zoned Decimal Data

ZONED DECIMAL DATA

129

EBCDIC

1 1 1 1	0 0 0 1	1 1 1 1	0 0 1 0	1 1 1 1	1 0 0 1
ZONE	NUMBER	ZONE	NUMBER	ZONE	NUMBER

THREE BYTES

FIGURE 9.28 Packed Decimal Data

PACKED NUMERIC DATA

129

EBCDIC

0 0 0 1	0 0 1 0	1 0 0 1	
NUMBER	NUMBER	NUMBER	SIGN

TWO BYTES

By storing two digits in every byte, storage requirements are reduced by nearly half for every field. Whenever RPG does a calculation, it automatically converts the incoming field (if it is in zoned decimal) to packed decimal format before it does the computation. If the field is already in packed decimal format, then RPG will not need to perform that function. This provides both savings in storage space and savings in program execution time.

Reading and Writing Numeric Fields in Packed Decimal Format

The coding for defining a numeric field as packed decimal format is quite simple. Figures 9.29(a) and 9.29(b) show the coding for the Input and Output Specifications.

FIGURE 9.29(a) Input Specifications: Packed Decimal Format

```
01 I INFILE   AA 01  80 C3
02 I                                    1  2 CODE
03 I                              P     3 102 AMOUNT
```

232 *RPG: A Programming Language for Today*

FIGURE 9.29(b) Output Specifications: Packed Decimal Format

```
O OUTFILE D        01
O                      CODE        2
O                      AMOUNT     10P
O
```

A field is defined as packed decimal by placing a P in column 43 on the Input Specifications line for that field. The field being read must, of course, already be in packed decimal format. The program will handle the field as it would any other numeric field and if the field were to be printed on a report, RPG would automatically unpack it for printing with no special coding required on the Output Specifications. When creating a new file (either on tape or disk) it is important to treat packed decimal fields correctly in an update program.

A field will be defined as packed decimal on an output file by placing a P in column 44 on the Output Specifications line for file updates for the field. It is extremely important that a packed input field be defined as a packed output field on file updates to prevent overlaying some other field with the data.

SUMMARY ∎

In this chapter, you have learned that multiple file processing is an important part of file handling. There are five types of files: master files, transaction files, table files, history files, and backup files.

You have learned that master files are updated by the data in transaction files. When the files are sequential, the method for accomplishing an update function is by matching the two files sequentially and updating to a new file.

This chapter uses tape media to demonstrate the use of sequential file processing. You have learned that tape files require the use of a blocking factor to make the record input more efficient.

You have learned that packed decimal data is more efficient for numeric fields if calculations are performed on them. This makes better use of the file space since nearly twice as many digits can be stored in the same amount of space on disk or tape.

REVIEW QUESTIONS ■

1. What are the five general types of files?
2. When might it be necessary to process more than one file in an RPG program?
3. What type of file is generally expected to be a permanent file that is always current and available?
4. Which type of file is a dynamic file which might change from minute to minute?
5. What type of file contains such things as rates or descriptions?
6. What is the value of history files and why is it important to keep them?
7. Explain the importance of regularly copying files to a backup media.
8. What is one of the most common media used for storing backup files?
9. Explain the meaning of sequential file processing.
10. On magnetic tape, what is written on the tape to notify the tape drive that the end of record has been found? How much space is taken up on tape by this?
11. On magnetic tape, what is written on the tape to notify the tape drive that an end of file has been found?
12. Explain the meaning of record blocking.
13. Why is it important for a programmer to know the blocking factor of a tape file which is to be read in a program?
14. Explain the difference between a physical record and a logical record on a tape file.
15. What are the three functions that might be performed when a file is being updated or maintained?
16. When sequential updating is being performed, why is it important that both the master file and the transaction file be in the same sequence by key?
17. Why must a key field be unique in the master file?
18. Why should transaction records contain a transaction code?
19. Describe the matching record process.
20. Matching record is indicated on the Input Specifications by the _____ indicators and on the Calculation Specifications by the _____ indicator.
21. A new record is added to the new master file only when the transaction code is _____ and _____ is found in the master file.
22. When a transaction record contains a code for deleting a record, _____ record will be written to the new master file.
23. A changed record will be written to the new master file only when there is a transaction record containing a code for _____ a record and a _____ record is found on the original master file.
24. Explain the difference between zoned decimal and packed decimal data.
25. A zoned decimal field of nine positions could be contained in a packed decimal format requiring only _____ positions.
26. Packed decimal fields are described on the Input Specifications by entering a _____ in column _____ and on the Output Specifications by entering a _____ in column _____ .

EXERCISES ■

1. On an Input Specifications form, enter the coding to describe two files with three matching fields.
2. On a Calculation Specifications form, enter the coding to perform matching record calculations.
3. On an Output Specifications form, enter the coding needed to print a line only when matching records have been found.

DEBUGGING EXERCISES

Instructions

The following RPG programs contain an error or errors. Some of these errors are indicated by the RPG compiler on the program listing. A list of syntax errors is given at the end of the program listing. Other types of errors may occur which will not be shown. These are called logic errors.

Study each program and its syntax errors. Locate each error (including logic errors) and on a separate coding form make the correct entry for the line(s) in error.

Explain each error and how it should be corrected.

```
 100   F* TITLE: DEBUG PROJECT 9-A
 200   F* DATE:   5/18          AUTHOR: D.CABLE
 300   F* DESCRIPTION:   (MATCHING RECORDS)
 400   F*********************************************************
 500   F* MODIFICATIONS:
 600   F* NO.        DATE      INIT      DESCRIPTION
 700   F*            XX/XX/XX  XXX       XXXXXXXXXXXXXXXXXXXXXXXXXXXXXX
 800   F*********************************************************

NAME OF PROGRAM WILL BE PJ009A IN LIBRARY CABLE

            H
* 1019           ALL DECIMAL DATA ERRORS IGNORED
 900   FMAST     IP  F      50              DISK
1000   FTRANS    IS  F      80              DISK
1100   FNEWMAST  O   F      50              DISK
1200   FREPORT   O   F     132       OF     PRINTER
1300   F*********************************************************

1400   IMAST     AA  01
1500   I                                         1   3 MGROUP
1600   I                                         4   5 MTYPE
1700   I                                         6  11 MID#   L1M1
1800   I                                        12  160MQTY
1900   I                                        17  36 MDESC
2000   I                                        37 432MPRC
2100   ITRANS    BB  03
2200   I                                         1   3 TGROUP
2300   I                                         4   5 TTYPE
2400   I                                         6  11 TID#   L1M1
2500   I                                        12  160TQTY
2600   I                                        17  36 TDESC
2700   I                                        37 432TPRC
2800   I                                        80  80 CODE
2900   I                                         1  80 RECORD

3000   C            CODE      COMP 'A'                      20    ADD
3100   C   N20      CODE      COMP 'S'                      21    SUB
3200   C   20 MR    MQTY      ADD  TQTY     NEWQTY  60
3300   C   21 MR    MQTY      SUB  TQTY     NEWQTY  60

3400   ONEWMAST  D         01NMR
3500   O                                 RECORD    80
3600   O         D          03 MR
3700   O                                 TQTY      16
3800   OREPORT   H   203    1P
3900   O             OR     OF
4000   O                                           6 'PJ009A'
```

```
SEQUENCE      1         2         3         4         5         6         7
NUMBER    67890123456789012345678901234567890123456789012345678901234

     4100 O                              UDATE Y   50
     4200 O                                       30 'TRANSACTION REPORT'
     4300 O      H  2         1P
     4400 O      OR           OF
     4500 O                                        5 'GROUP'
     4600 O                                       10 'TYPE'
     4700 O                                       25 'ID#'
     4800 O                                       34 'QUANTITY'
     4900 O                                       45 'UNIT PRICE'
     5000 O      D  1         02
     5100 O                              TGROUP    4
     5200 O                              TTYPE     9
     5300 O                              TID#     30
     5400 O                              TQTY  Z  35
     5500 O                              TPRC  K  45
    * * * * * E N D   O F   S O U R C E * * * * *
```

```
* 7086     900   RPG PROVIDES BLOCK/UNBLOCK SUPPORT FOR FILE MAST.
* 7086    1000   RPG PROVIDES BLOCK/UNBLOCK SUPPORT FOR FILE TRANS.
* 7086    1100   RPG PROVIDES BLOCK/UNBLOCK SUPPORT FOR FILE NEWMAST.
* 8002    3500   END POS OF 0080 GREATER THAN RECORD LENGTH 0050
```

CROSS-REFERENCE LISTING

```
         FILE/RCD     DEV/RCD      REFERENCES (D=DEFINED)

      01 MAST         DISK          900D 1400
      03 NEWMAST      DISK         1100D 3400  3500
      04 REPORT       PRINTER      1200D 3800  4300  5000
      02 TRANS        DISK         1000D 2100


         FIELD        ATTR         REFERENCES (M=MODIFIED D=DEFINED)

         CODE         A( 1)        2800D 3000  3100
* 7031   MDESC        A(20)        1900D
* 7031   MGROUP       A( 3)        1500D
* 7031   MID#         A( 6)        1700D
* 7031   MPRC         P( 7,2)      2000D
         MQTY         P( 5,0)      1800D 3200  3300
* 7031   MTYPE        A( 2)        1600D
         NEWQTY       P( 6,0)      3200D 3300D
         RECORD       A(80)        2900D 3500
* 7031   TDESC        A(20)        2600D
         TGROUP       A( 3)        2200D 5100
         TID#         A( 6)        2400D 5300
         TPRC         P( 7,2)      2700D 5500
         TQTY         P( 5,0)      2500D 3200  3300  3700  5400
         TTYPE        A( 2)        2300D 5200
         UDATE        P( 6,0)      4100
         'A'          LITERAL      3000
         'S'          LITERAL      3100


         INDICATOR    REFERENCES (M=MODIFIED D=DEFINED)

         LR            900D
* 7031   L1           1700M 2400M
         MR           3200  3300  3400  3600
         M1           1700M 2400M
         OF           1200D 3900  4400
         01           1400M 3400
* 7030   02           5000
         03           2100M 3600
         1P           3800  4300
         20           3000M 3100  3200
         21           3100M 3300
```

```
MESSAGES

MSGID      SEV  NUMBER   TEXT

* QRG1019   00    1      IGNDECERR(*YES) SPECIFIED ON COMMAND. NO DECIMAL DATA ERRORS
* QRG7030   30    1      FIELD OR INDICATOR NOT DEFINED.
* QRG7031   00    7      NAME OR INDICATOR NOT REFERENCED.
* QRG7086   00    3      RPG WILL HANDLE BLOCKING FUNCTION FOR THE FILE. INFDS CONTENT
                         ARE TRANSFERRED.
* QRG8002   30    1      END POSITION ENTRY (POSITIONS 40-43) LARGER THAN RECORD LENG


MESSAGE SUMMARY

TOTAL  00    10    20    30    40    50
  13   11     0     0     2     0     0

   55 RECORDS READ FROM SOURCE FILE
   SOURCE RECORDS INCLUDE   46 SPECIFICATIONS,   0 TABLE RECORDS, AND   9 COMMENTS

QRG0008 COMPILE TERMINATED. SEVERITY 30 ERRORS FOUND IN PROGRAM

* * * * *  E N D   O F   C O M P I L A T I O N * * * * *
* QRG1020              ERROR OCCURRED CREATING OR UPDATING DATA AREA RETURNCODE. COMPIL
```

```
        100   F* TITLE: DEBUG PROJECT 9-B
        200   F* DATE:  5/18         AUTHOR: D.CABLE
        300   F* DESCRIPTION:     MATCHING RECORDS
        400   F***************************************************
        500   F* MODIFICATIONS:
        600   F* NO.    DATE      INIT       DESCRIPTION
        700   F*       XX/XX/XX   XXX     XXXXXXXXXXXXXXXXXXXXXXXXXXXXXX
        800   F***************************************************
NAME OF PROGRAM WILL BE PJ009B IN LIBRARY CABLE

              H
* 1019                  ALL DECIMAL DATA ERRORS IGNORED
        900   FSALMAST  IP  F    160            DISK
       1000   FINPUT    IS  F     20            DISK
       1100   FMASTOUT  O   F    160            DISK
       1200   FREPORT   O   F    132       OF   PRINTER
       1300   F***************************************************

       1400   ISALMAST  AA   01
       1500   I                                      1    5 SALID#L1M1
       1600   I                                      6   11 SALDTE
       1700   I                                     12   13 SALCOD
       1800   I                                     14   21 SALQTY
       1900   I                                     22   28 SALAMT
       2000   I                                     29   30 TYPE   L2M2
       2100   I                                     31   50 DESCRP
       2200   I                                      1  160 RECORD
       2300   IINPUT     BB   02
       2400   I                                      1    6 DATE
       2500   I                                      7    8 TYPE   L2M2
       2600   I                                      9   14 ID#    L1M1
* 4057              MATCH FIELD LENGTH FOR M1 IS 006. IT SHOULD BE 005
* 4133                                                           4133-**

       2700   I                                     15   19 TQTY
       2800   I                                     20   20 CODE
* 4055                                                           4055-**

       2900   C              CODE      COMP '1'                  25
       3000   C    25 MR     SALQTY    ADD  TQTY   NEWQTY   60

       3100   OMASTOUT  D        01NMR
       3200   O                            RECORD  160
       3300   O         D        02 MR
       3400   O                            RECORD  160
       3500   O                            NEWQTY   21
```

Chapter 9 Processing Multiple Sequential Files

```
SEQUENCE        1         2         3         4         5         6         7
NUMBER   67890123456789012345678901234567890123456789012345678901234

  3600  O      D          02NMR
  3700  O                        ID#       6
  3800  O                        DATE     11
  3900  O                        TQTY     21
  4000  O                        TYPE     30
  4100  OREPORT H  203  1P
  4200  O    OR        OF
  4300  O                                  6 'PJ009B'
  4400  O                        UDATE Y  50
  4500  O                                 30 'SALES UPDATE'
  4600  O       H   2   1P
  4700  O    OR        OF
  4800  O                                  7 'ITEM#'
  4900  O                                 17 'TYPE'
  5000  O                                 30 'DATE'
  5100  O                                 40 'QUANTITY'
  5200  O      D   1   01
  5300  O                        SALID#    6
  5400  O                        TYPE     16
  5500  O                        SALDTEY  30
  5600  O                        SALQTYZ  37
  5700  O      D   1   02
  5800  O                        ID#       6
  5900  O                        TYPE     16
  6000  O                        DATE  Y  30
  6100  O                        TQTY  Z  37
  6200  O                        MR       50 'MASTER NOT FOUND'
* * * * * E N D  O F  S O U R C E * * * * *


* 7086     900  RPG PROVIDES BLOCK/UNBLOCK SUPPORT FOR FILE SALMAST.
* 7086    1000  RPG PROVIDES BLOCK/UNBLOCK SUPPORT FOR FILE INPUT.
* 7086    1100  RPG PROVIDES BLOCK/UNBLOCK SUPPORT FOR FILE MASTOUT.



        CROSS-REFERENCE LISTING



            FILE/RCD    DEV/RCD    REFERENCES (D=DEFINED)

       02   INPUT       DISK       1000D 2300
       03   MASTOUT     DISK       1100D 3100  3300  3600
       04   REPORT      PRINTER    1200D 4100  4600  5200  5700
       01   SALMAST     DISK        900D 1400

            FIELD       ATTR       REFERENCES (M=MODIFIED D=DEFINED)

            CODE        A(1)       2800D 2900
            DATE        P(6,0)     2400D 3800  6000
* 7031      DESCRP      A(20)      2100D
            ID#         A(6)       2600D 3700  5800
            NEWQTY      P(6,0)     3000D 3500
            RECORD      A(160)     2200D 3200  3400
* 7031      SALAMT      P(7,2)     1900D
* 7031      SALCOD      A(2)       1700D
            SALDTE      P(6,0)     1600D 5500
            SALID#      A(5)       1500D 5300
            SALQTY      P(8,0)     1800D 3000  5600
            TQTY        P(5,0)     2700D 3000  3900  6100
            TYPE        A(2)       2000D 2500D 4000  5400  5900
            UDATE       P(6,0)     4400
            '1'         LITERAL    2900
```

```
              INDICATOR   REFERENCES (M=MODIFIED D=DEFINED)
         LR          900D
* 7031   L1         1500M
* 7031   L2         2000M 2500M
         MR         3000  3100  3300  3600  6200
         M1         1500M 2600M
         M2         2000M 2500M
         OF         1200D 4200  4700
         01         1400M 3100  5200
         02         2300M 3300  3600  5700
         1P         4100  4600
         25         2900M 3000
```

MESSAGES

```
    MSGID     SEV  NUMBER  TEXT

*  QRG1019    00     1     IGNDECERR(*YES) SPECIFIED ON COMMAND. NO DECIMAL DATA ERRORS
*  QRG4055    50     1     COMPLETE SET OF MATCH FIELDS NOT DEFINED FOR ALL RECORD TYPE
                           TERMINATED.
*  QRG4057    50     1     MATCH FIELD LENGTHS NOT SAME BETWEEN RECORD TYPES. COMPILATI(
*  QRG4133    20     1     CONTROL FIELD LENGTH LARGER THAN PREVIOUSLY DEFINED CONTROL F
                           IGNORED
*  QRG7031    00     5     NAME OR INDICATOR NOT REFERENCED.
*  QRG7086    00     3     RPG WILL HANDLE BLOCKING FUNCTION FOR THE FILE. INFDS CONTEN
                           ARE TRANSFERRED.
```

MESSAGE SUMMARY

```
TOTAL   00   10   20   30   40   50
 12      9    0    1    0    0    2
```

```
   62 RECORDS READ FROM SOURCE FILE
SOURCE RECORDS INCLUDE    53 SPECIFICATIONS,    0 TABLE RECORDS, AND    9 COMMENTS

QRG0000 COMPILE TERMINATED. SEVERITY 50 ERRORS FOUND IN PROGRAM

* * * * * E N D   O F   C O M P I L A T I O N * * * * *
* QRG1020            ERROR OCCURRED CREATING OR UPDATING DATA AREA RETURNCODE. COMPIL
```

PROGRAMMING PROJECT

Project Overview

A tape file is to be read and summarized. The new summarized file is to be output to another tape. A report is also to be printed showing the summarized transactions. Sample data for this project can be found in Appendix D.

Input Format

The input data for the project is found in a file called SALES in the sample data. The records are blocked by ten. The Record Layout for this file is shown in Figure 9.30.

Processing

As each sale record is read, the amount of the sale is computed (quantity multiplied by unit price). The result is added to the appropriate array element based on the month of the sale. A new record will be created at level break time for each item number. Final totals will be accumulated for each month.

Output Format (Printer Spacing Chart)

The output for the project will be a summary tape and a report with standard headings showing the item number and the total amount of sales for each month. The layout for the output record, SALESUMM, is shown in Figure 9.31(a). A line will be printed on the report only at total time. A final total will also be printed for each month and for a year-to-date total. The Printer Spacing Chart for this report is shown in Figure 9.31(b).

An example of the finished report is shown in Figure 9.32.

FIGURE 9.30 Programming Project: Input Record Layout

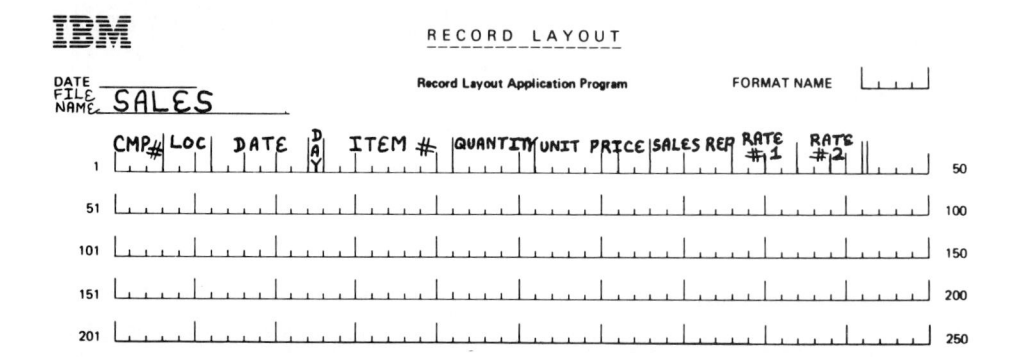

FIGURE 9.31(a) Programming Project: Output Record Layout

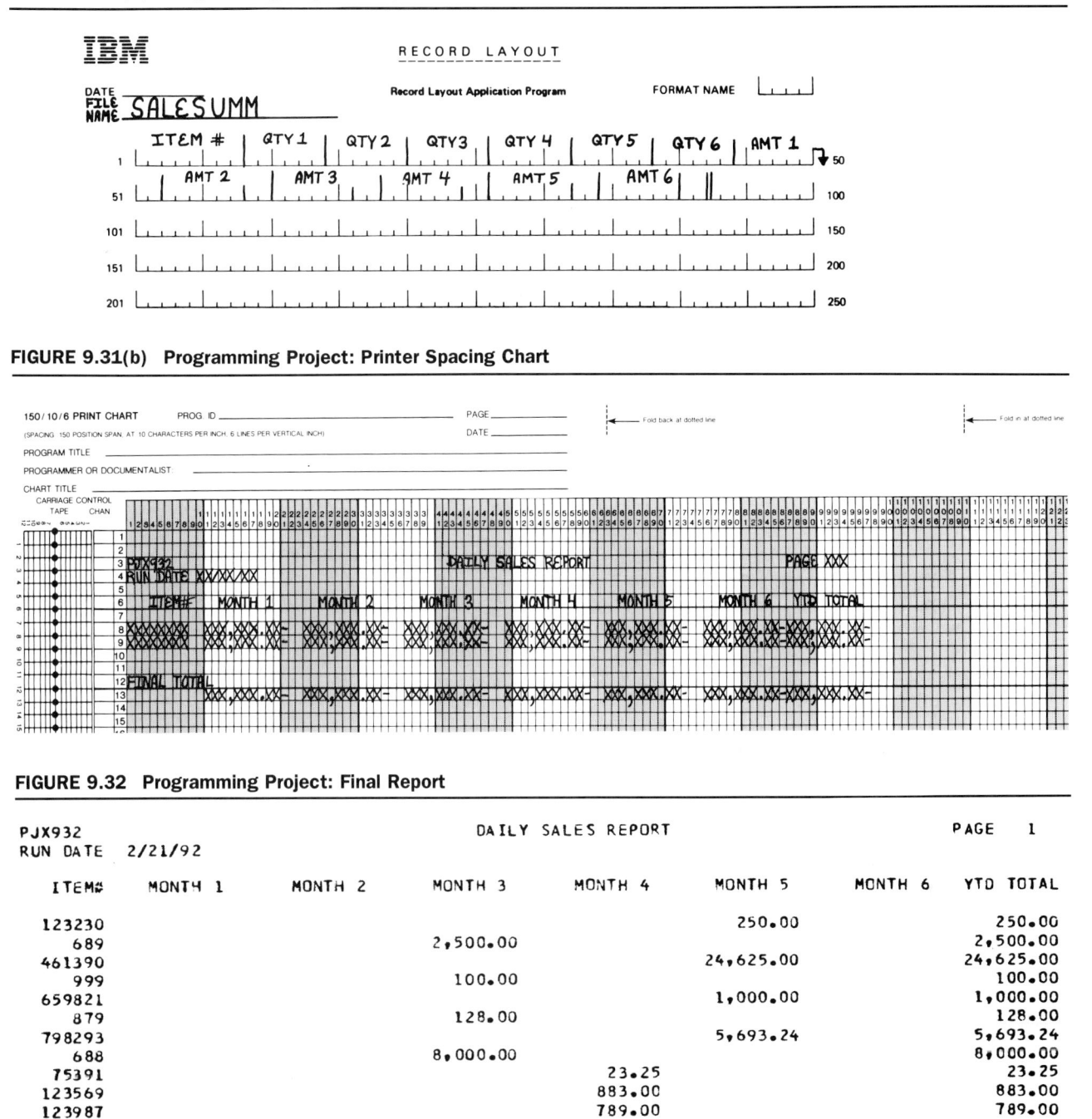

IBM

RECORD LAYOUT

DATE
FILE NAME: SALESUMM

Record Layout Application Program   FORMAT NAME

| ITEM # | QTY 1 | QTY 2 | QTY 3 | QTY 4 | QTY 5 | QTY 6 | AMT 1 |
| AMT 2 | AMT 3 | AMT 4 | AMT 5 | AMT 6 |

FIGURE 9.31(b) Programming Project: Printer Spacing Chart

```
PJX932                     DAILY SALES REPORT              PAGE XXX
RUN DATE XX/XX/XX

ITEM#    MONTH 1    MONTH 2    MONTH 3    MONTH 4    MONTH 5    MONTH 6    YTD TOTAL
XXXXXX   XX,XXX.XX- XX,XXX.XX- XX,XXX.XX- XX,XXX.XX- XX,XXX.XX- XX,XXX.XX- XXX,XXX.XX-

FINAL TOTAL
         XXX,XXX.XX- XXX,XXX.XX- XXX,XXX.XX- XXX,XXX.XX- XXX,XXX.XX- XXX,XXX.XX- XXX,XXX.XX-
```

FIGURE 9.32 Programming Project: Final Report

```
PJX932                           DAILY SALES REPORT                              PAGE   1
RUN DATE  2/21/92

   ITEM#   MONTH 1     MONTH 2     MONTH 3     MONTH 4     MONTH 5     MONTH 6    YTD TOTAL

  123230                                                     250.00                  250.00
     689                           2,500.00                                         2,500.00
  461390                                                   24,625.00               24,625.00
     999                             100.00                                           100.00
  659821                                                    1,000.00                1,000.00
     879                             128.00                                           128.00
  798293                                                    5,693.24                5,693.24
     688                           8,000.00                                         8,000.00
   75391                                         23.25                                 23.25
  123569                                        883.00                                883.00
  123987                                        789.00                                789.00

FINAL TOTAL
                                  10,728.00   1,695.25   31,568.24                 43,991.49
```

Chapter 10

Multiple File Processing (Indexed Files)

What you will learn in Chapter 10

Direct Access Storage Devices (DASDs)
 Disk Access Concepts
 File Organization on DASDs
Sample Program 1: Creating an Indexed File
 File Formats
 File Description Specifications
Input Specifications
Output Specifications
Inquiry Programs
Sample Program 2: Using Inquiry Programs
Chaining to an Indexed File
Printed Output from an Indexed File
File Maintenance (Data Updating)
Reorganizing a File
Sample Program 3: Updating an Indexed File
Sample Program 4: Demonstrating Sequential Retrieval from an Indexed File
Record Address Files

Previous chapters have provided nearly all the basic tools for coding RPG II programs using sequential files. Although sequential processing is still a viable method for producing useful computer reports, there are now many alternative methods for accessing data.

In this chapter, we will discuss concepts related to processing data in a nonsequential mode, including the RPG coding methods for accomplishing random processing.

DIRECT ACCESS STORAGE DEVICES (DASDs) ■

Perhaps the most popular media on which to store data are direct access storage devices (DASDs). These devices provide the means to access data using random access processing. Random access processing is a method by which records can be retrieved from a file nonsequentially, and applies to all types of DASDs. Some of the types of direct access storage devices are diskette, magnetic drum storage, disk storage devices, and data cell devices. Figure 10.1 is a photo of a group of disk storage devices that are used on midrange computers.

When using sequential files, such as those found on tape media, it is not possible to retrieve records randomly. Records are read sequentially beginning with the first record, then the second, and so on.

When using very dynamic files from which records need to be retrieved or updated randomly by a variety of users, it becomes necessary to provide a means to obtain any record in any sequence at any time. Modern business would be severely handicapped without this capability.

FIGURE 10.1 Photo of a DASD

Sequential files are usually found on tape media or even older types of devices that were developed before direct access storage devices became available. Although it is possible to create sequential files on DASDs, it is usually better to create what are called indexed files, which can be accessed either sequentially or randomly.

Although there are several methods for accessing records randomly from disk, the simplest and most popular for RPG users is the indexed sequential access method. Indexed sequential processing allows both sequential and random access.

Disk Access Concepts

Records are organized on direct access storage devices by location on the disk. This location is identified by an address giving either a surface/cylinder/record number or a surface/sector location.

A disk pack or disk module or diskette is made up of one or more flat disks that have two surfaces. Data is written on each surface on a series of concentric tracks, as shown in Figure 10.2.

The disk surface shown in Figure 10.2 contains 400 tracks numbered from track zero on the outer edge to track 399 on the inner edge. Data is placed onto the surface in the form of magnetic

FIGURE 10.2 Tracks on Surface of Disk

CONCENTRIC TRACKS ON ONE SURFACE OF A DISK

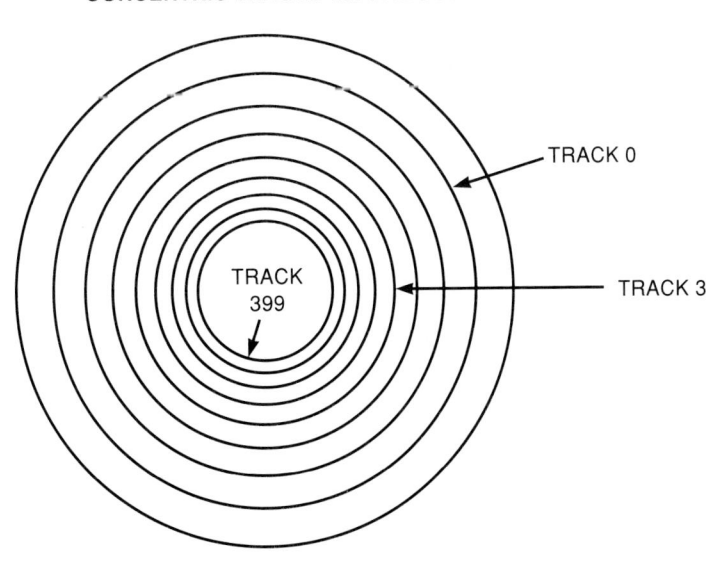

Chapter 10 Multiple File Processing (Indexed Files)   **243**

lines of force. The data is read from or written to the recording surface by a read-write head, which is carried on an access arm and positioned over the desired track on the disk surface. As the disk rotates under the read-write head, the data is read or written. Note that the read-write head never actually comes in contact with the disk surface. The read-write head rides on a tiny cushion of air to protect the data from being damaged.

Some disk packs may have more than one of these rotating disks. Large disk packs may contain as many as 20 recording surfaces. A single access arm controls the movement of the read-write heads for all 20 surfaces. For example, when the arm positions the read-write head to read track 200 on the top surface, it has also positioned the read-write heads for all other surfaces for track 200 as well. This is referred to as a cylinder. All the read-write heads are now positioned to read cylinder 200, although only one surface is read at a time. Storing a file on a single cylinder instead of consecutively on a single disk surface can minimize the number of movements of the access arm, thereby improving access time to retrieve data. Note that the number of disk surfaces per pack and the number of tracks per surface varies depending on the type of device. Figure 10.3 shows how the read-write heads may be aligned to read a cylinder.

The RPG programmer need not be concerned with the computer hardware or how it accesses the data. It helps, however, to visualize the way the data is organized on disk, particularly for files that will be accessed randomly.

File Organization on DASDs

Data resides on DASDs either as sequential files, indexed files, or direct files.

FIGURE 10.3 Read-Write Heads on Multiple Surfaces of Disk

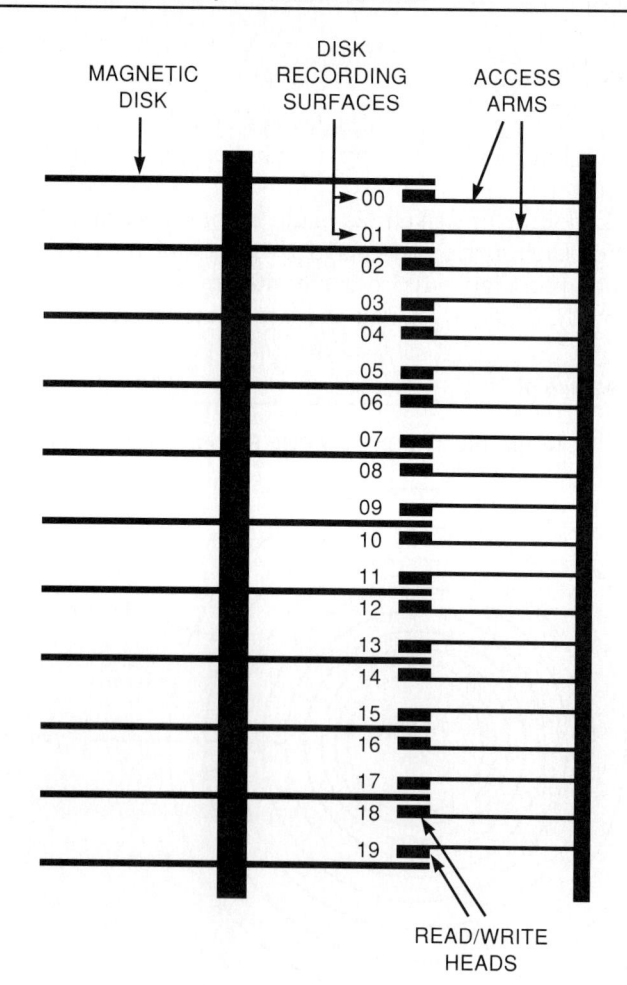

Sequential File Organization

In sequential file organization, records are stored on disk in the same sequence as they were loaded. They are accessed sequentially using the same methods used for tape or any other media that uses sequential file organization.

Updates to a sequential file are accomplished by creating a new version of the file, as discussed in earlier chapters. A sequential file may contain some key field which represents its logical sequence. However, this key is not required and is not necessarily used by the computer for determining processing sequence or access. Figure 10.4 shows the arrangement of a sequential file on disk.

Indexed File Organization

In indexed file organization, records are stored on disk in the same sequence as they are loaded, but as they are loaded an index is created. This index contains the key and a pointer to the location of the record itself with which that key is associated. Figure 10.5 shows the arrangement of an indexed file on disk.

Notice that there is an index, a prime data area where all the data is loaded, and an overflow area which initially contains nothing at all. When new records are added to the file, they will be placed in this overflow area and the index will be updated with their locations. When the overflow area becomes full, a new overflow area will be created. This can mean that portions of a file could be scattered all over a disk (or even several disks), but this is not apparent to the user or programmer. Notice also that the records are in no particular sequence. Only the index is kept in sequence.

The key field is determined by the programmer and should be a number unique to each record in the file. Each record in the file will be accessed and retrieved by that unique key. On most computers, the program will abort when an attempt is made to add a duplicate record.

The programmer indicates to RPG which field is to be used as the key. The computer performs all the hard work of keeping track of the locations of the records. The index will consist of the key field and a pointer indicating the surface/cylinder/track on which the physical record is located. For efficiency of space and processing, it is a good idea to select as a key field one that is numeric and short, although this is not a requirement.

FIGURE 10.4 Sequential File Organization

SEQUENTIAL FILE ORGANIZATION

RECORD 4	RECORD 3	RECORD 2	RECORD 1

FIGURE 10.5 Indexed File Organization

INDEXED FILE ORGANIZATION

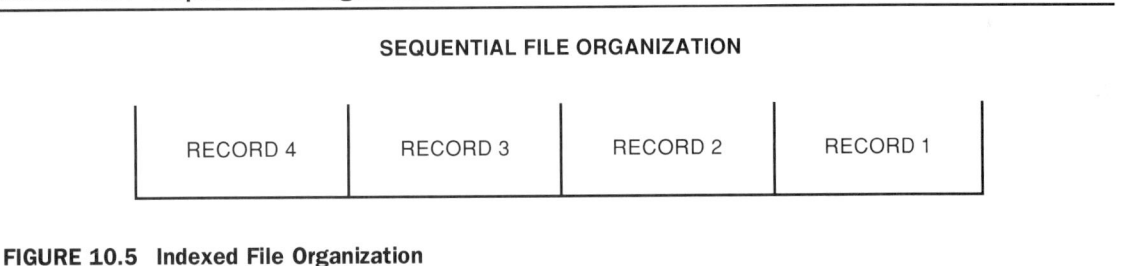

INDEX	KEY 1	KEY 2	KEY 3	KEY 4	KEY 5	KEY 6			
PRIME DATA AREA				RECORD 1		RECORD 6	RECORD 4	RECORD 3
OVERFLOW AREA									

FIGURE 10.6 Direct File Organization

DIRECT FILE ORGANIZATION

| | | RECORD 6 | | | RECORD 2 |

| | | RECORD 5 | RECORD 1 | | RECORD 7 |

| | RECORD 4 | | | RECORD 3 | |

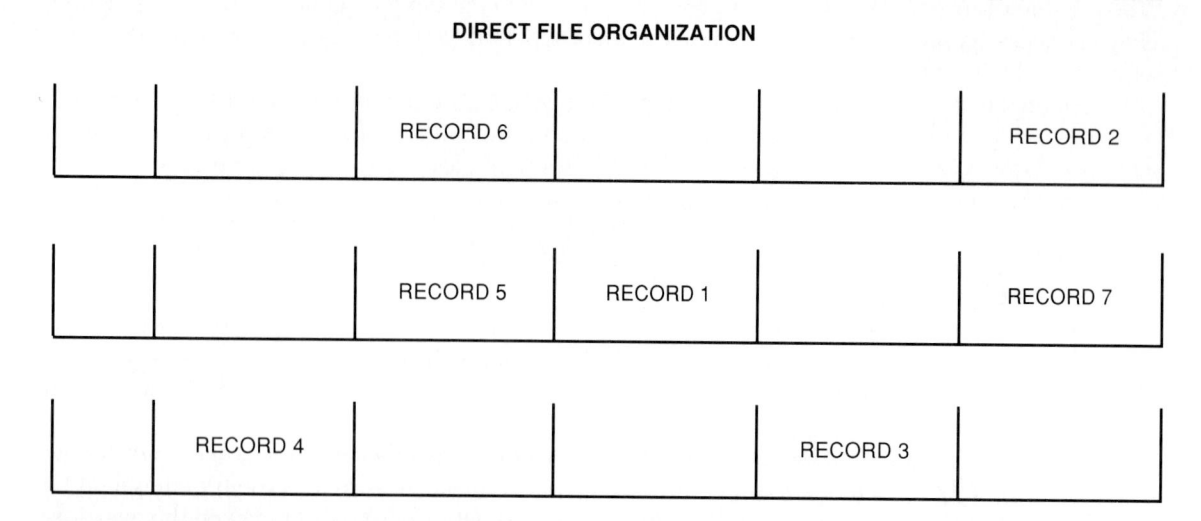

Direct File Organization

In direct file organization, records are stored on disk in a predetermined location based on computations made in the program. This method of file organization provides the fastest access time since it is not necessary to search through an index to find the location of each record. However, it requires more sophisticated programming, and a certain amount of disk space has to be reserved for later input. Figure 10.6 shows the arrangement of a direct file on disk. These records appear to be scattered randomly in the file but there is a definite position for each one and only a computer program will be able to locate them.

SAMPLE PROGRAM 1: CREATING AN INDEXED FILE ■

The sample programs in this chapter will cover the use of indexed files. For this first project, a new indexed file will be created for the customer master file.

File Formats

The input data will be entered from a sequential file. The Record Layout for the sequential file is shown in Figure 10.7.

Each record contains a unique customer number which will become the key in the indexed file when it is loaded to disk. The Record Layout for the new disk file is shown in Figure 10.8. Notice that the input record is longer than the output record. There are some blank fields in the input record that do not need to be transferred to the disk file. Some fields, such as the Zip Code field, have been reformatted.

FIGURE 10.7 Input Record Layout for a Sequential File

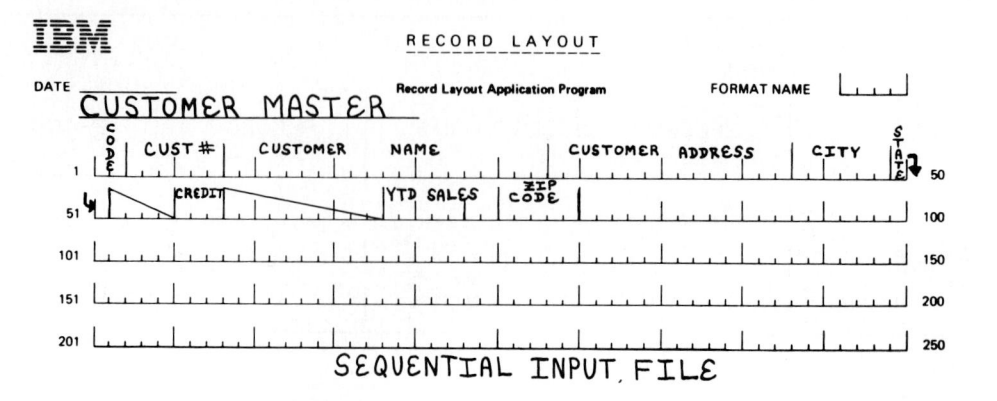

[IBM Record Layout form — CUSTOMER MASTER — fields: CODE, CUST#, CUSTOMER NAME, CUSTOMER ADDRESS, CITY, STATE, CREDIT, YTD SALES, ZIP CODE — SEQUENTIAL INPUT FILE]

246   *RPG: A Programming Language for Today*

FIGURE 10.8 Output Record Layout for Indexed File on Disk

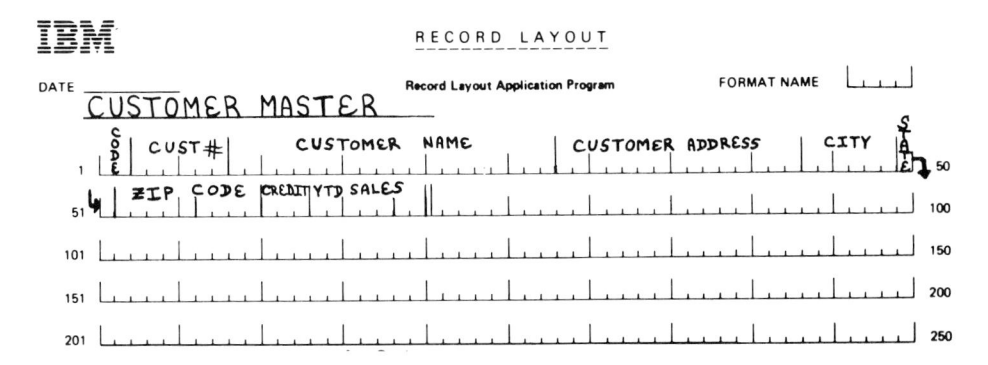

File Description Specifications

The File Description Specifications for loading the sequential file and creating an indexed file are shown in Figure 10.9. The input record is defined as any sequential file would be defined. The indexed disk file is defined as an output file with a length of 70. The block length may be entered on some computers, but other computers calculate an optimal blocking factor internally and do not require the entry of a blocking factor at all.

The length of the key is defined in columns 29–30. Although RPG allows for a key field to be as long as 99 positions, it is a good idea to use a short field as the key for greater efficiency in processing and to avoid errors in keying.

For indexed processing, an *A* is entered in column 31 to define the key as an alphanumeric key field. This means that the key field (customer number) can be either alphabetic or numeric but not packed decimal. If a packed decimal field were used as the key, column 31 would contain a *P*.

Column 32 will contain an *I* to describe the file as indexed. Columns 35–38 will contain the beginning position of the key field in the record. In this program the key field is the customer number, which is located in columns 3–8 in the disk record, so the entry in column 38 on the File Description Specifications will be a 3.

From this coding example, you can see that the key can consist of only one field. If it is desirable to have two fields considered the key, the record is designed so that the two fields are located next to each other. RPG would consider both fields as one long key, but the two fields could be treated separately in the detail coding of the program.

The device name will be DISK, as discussed earlier. The letter *A* is entered in column 66 to allow records to be added to the file.

Input Specifications

The Input Specifications are the same for this input file as for any other input file, as shown in Figure 10.10. It is important to ensure that there will be no attempt to add a duplicate key to the

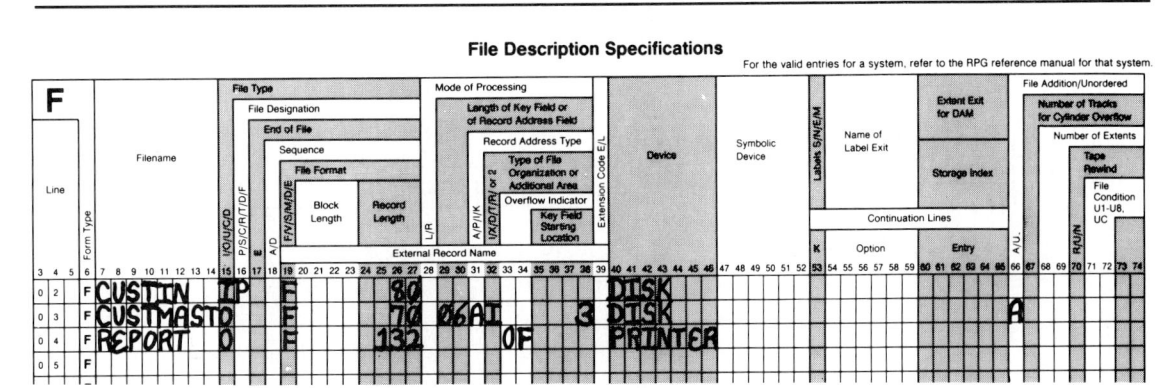

FIGURE 10.9 File Description Specifications for Sample Program

FIGURE 10.10 Input Specifications for Sample Program

Line	Filename or Record Name	Sequence	Number	Option	Record Identifying Indicator	Record Identification Codes Position 1	C/Z/D	Character	Position 2	C/Z/D	Character	Position 3	C/Z/D	Character	From	To	Decimal Positions	Field Name	Control Level
01	ICUSTIN	AA	01		1		C	C										
02	I														1	2		CODE
03	I														3	8	0	CUST#
04	I														9	28		NAME
05	I														29	43		ADDR
06	I														44	49		CITY
07	I														50	51		STATE
08	I														56	58	0	CREDIT
09	I														69	75	2	YTDSLS
10	I														76	80		ZIP
11	I		ZZ	99														

indexed file. On most computers such an attempt would cause the job to abort. The input file need not be in sequence by customer number for loading an indexed file, but to avoid problems, it is recommended that the input file be sorted to ensure that any duplicates will arrive together.

Output Specifications

At L1 time every field containing data will be copied into the output file, including the key field of customer number. The key field will be repeated in the index. Figures 10.11(a) and 10.11(b) show the Calculation and Output Specifications for loading this file.

It is a good idea to report any duplicate records encountered in the processing. It is possible that they are not really duplicates of the same customer, but simply keying errors in which two customers were given the same customer number. Some simple calculations can check for that condition and an exception report of the errors can be printed. It is a good practice always to compute the number of records loaded to the file and give that total on the report as well.

Notice that no special coding is necessary on the Output Specifications to handle the key field. This is all managed automatically by RPG when the file is described as an indexed file on the File Description Specifications.

FIGURE 10.11(a) Calculation Specifications for Sample Program

Line	Form Type	Control Level	Indicators	Factor 1	Operation	Factor 2	Result Field Name	Length	Decimal Positions	Resulting Indicators 1>2	1<2	1=2	Comments
01	C	01		CUST#	COMP	LSTCUS						28	DUPLICATE?
02	C	01			MOVE	CUST#	LSTCUS	60					
03	C	01		COUNT	ADD	1	COUNT	50					
04	C	01			SETON							30	
05	C	30			EXCPT								CREATE RCD
06	C				SETOF					28		30	

248   *RPG: A Programming Language for Today*

FIGURE 10.11(b) Output Specifications for Sample Program

Line	Form Type	Filename or Record Name	Type	Space Before	Space After	Skip Before	Skip After	Output Indicators	Field Name or EXCPT Name	Edit Codes	End Position in Output Record	Constant or Edit Word
01	O	CUSTMASTE ADD						30 N28				
02	O								CODE		2	
03	O								CUST#		8	
04	O								NAME		28	
05	O								ADDR		43	
06	O								CITY		49	
07	O								STATE		51	
08	O								ZIP		56	
09	O								CREDIT		63	
10	O								YTDSLS		70	
11	O	REPORT	D	2	02			1P				
12	O		OR					OF				
13	O										30	'CUSTOMER MASTER LOAD'
14	O		E	2				30				
15	O								CUST#	Z	6	
16	O		E	2				28				
17	O										25	'DUPLICATE RECORD FOUND'
18	O								CUST#	Z	33	
19	O		T	2				LR				
20	O								COUNT	Z		
	O										24	'RECORDS LOADED TO'
	O										38	'CUSTMAST FILE'

The entry ADD in columns 16–18 (following the E) allows records to be added to the file. Notice also that edit codes are *not* used on the Output Specifications for an output file. Only a printed report is allowed to use edit codes.

Figure 10.12 is the completed report, showing an error message for the duplicate found and a final total of records accepted.

Inquiry Programs

One reason for using random file organization is to make each record in the file immediately accessible to a user. When someone using a workstation needs to know some piece of information, it is very convenient to be able to retrieve that record immediately and view the information quickly, rather than spend time looking it up in file drawers or ledger books. By using indexed files, the user needs only to key in the customer number to obtain all the related information about a customer.

FIGURE 10.12 Completed Sample Report

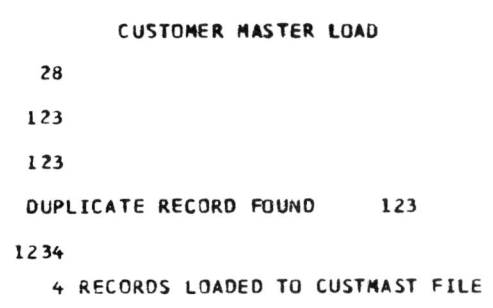

```
                    CUSTOMER MASTER LOAD
           28

          123

          123

          DUPLICATE RECORD FOUND     123

         1234
            4 RECORDS LOADED TO CUSTMAST FILE
```

Chapter 10 Multiple File Processing (Indexed Files)

SAMPLE PROGRAM 2: USING INQUIRY PROGRAMS ■

Inquiry programs are programs that will print out all the information requested about one or several selected customers. The customer numbers are keyed onto a diskette and the master file is searched for only those customers. In this example, only three customers have been requested for inquiry. The search can be completed very rapidly even if the master file is very large, because the program will not look at every record in the master file. It will retrieve only the three records demanded. Figures 10.13(a) and 10.13(b) show the diskette Record Layout for requesting this printout. Note that the record length for diskette files is always 128.

Figures 10.14(a) and 10.14(b) show the File Description and Input Specifications for the inquiry program. The transaction file containing the requested customer numbers is a simple sequential file. The customer numbers need not be sorted in any particular sequence, because the records will be randomly retrieved.

The request transaction file is defined as the primary input file (IP in columns 15–16). The device name for diskette files may be DISKET on some computers and SEQ on others. The customer master file is defined with an *I* in column 15 because it is an input file and a C in column 16 because it will be a *chained* file—a reference to the method of accessing this file, described in the next section.

Since this file will be accessed randomly, we must enter an *R* in column 28. Also defined are the length of the key, the AI in columns 31–32, and the starting column for the key (in columns 35–38). Of course, the report will be the output file.

Because the REQUEST file is the primary input, RPG will read this file first. RPG will *never* read the random file (CUSTMAST) unless told to do so by the CHAIN operation in the Calculation Specifications.

Chaining to an Indexed File

The word *chaining* may be somewhat misleading, but performing a CHAIN operation is quite simple. A key is entered by a user to request retrieval of a record. The program uses that key field to compare to a master file index and search for a particular record. If the key is not found, an indicator is set on in the greater-than position.

FIGURE 10.13(a)   Record Layout for Inquiry Request

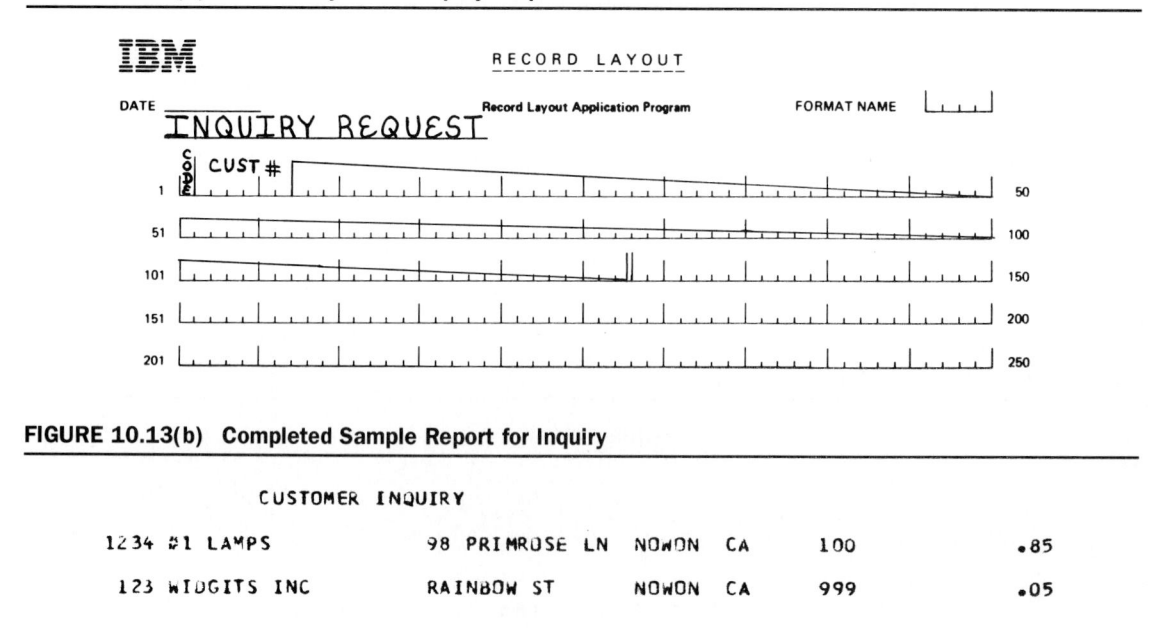

FIGURE 10.13(b)   Completed Sample Report for Inquiry

```
          CUSTOMER  INQUIRY

    1234  #1 LAMPS          98 PRIMROSE LN   NOWON   CA     100      .85

     123  WIDGITS INC       RAINBOW ST       NOWON   CA     999      .05
```

250   *RPG: A Programming Language for Today*

FIGURE 10.14(a) File Description Specifications for the Inquiry Program

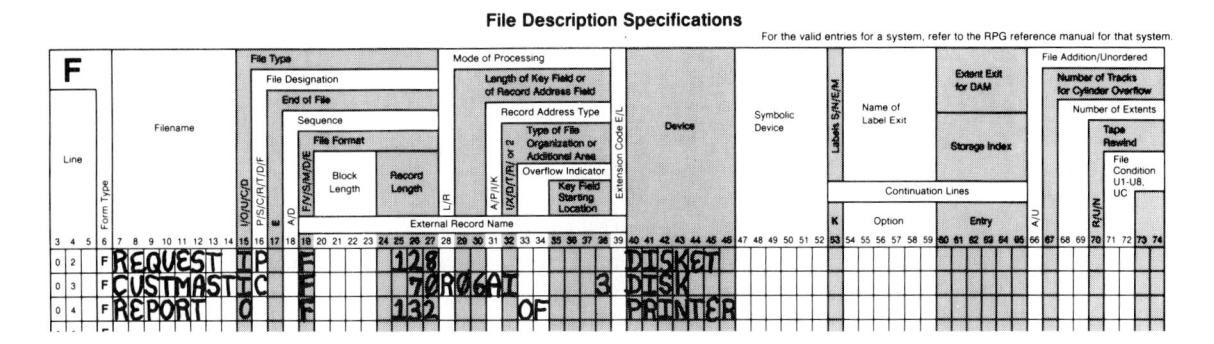

Line	Filename	File Type	File Designation	End of File	Sequence	File Format	Block Length	Record Length	Mode of Processing	Record Address Type	Type of File Organization	Overflow Indicator	Key Field Starting Location	Extension Code	Device	Symbolic Device
02	F REQUEST	IP						128							DISKETTE	
03	F CUSTMAST	IC				F		70R06AI						3	DISK	
04	F REPORT	O				F		132		OF					PRINTER	

FIGURE 10.14(b) Input Specifications for the Inquiry Program

Line	Filename or Record Name	Sequence	Number (1/N)	Option O,U,S	Record Identifying Indicator	Record Identification Codes 1	Position	Not (N)	C/Z/D	Character	Position 2	Not (N)	C/Z/D	Character	Position 3	Not (N)	C/Z/D	Character	P/B/L/R/C	From	To	Decimal Positions	RPG Field Name
01	I REQUEST	AA			01	1	CR																
02	I																			2	7	0	CUS
03	I CUSTMAST	BB			05	1	CC																
04	I																			3	8	0	CUST#
05	I																			9	28		NAME
06	I																			29	43		ADDR
07	I																			44	49		CITY
08	I																			50	51		STATE
09	I																			52	60		ZIP
10	I																			61	63	0	CREDIT
11	I																			64	70	2	YTDSLS
12	I				ZZ	99																	

The desired key field from the transaction file is entered in factor 1 on the Calculation Specifications. The operation CHAIN is entered. The name of the indexed file in which the record resides is entered in factor 2. A resulting indicator is entered in columns 54–55 to notify RPG whether the requested record was found in the master file. Figure 10.15 shows the Calculation Specifications needed for this inquiry. Notice that the CHAIN is made to a *filename* (CUSTMAST) and not to a field name.

We have used the indicator 90 to signify a successful CHAIN. Note that the indicator is entered in the greater-than position (54–55). If indicator 90 is off, the CHAIN is successful and the customer information will be printed. If indicator 90 is on (the customer was *not* found), an error message will be printed.

Printed Output from an Indexed File

The report will be written at exception time, but it could be written at detail time equally well. Figures 10.16(a) and 10.16(b) show the Output Specifications for printing the inquiry report along with the final report. Headings are printed at detail time, but the customer information is printed at exception time. Either a customer record will be retrieved and printed or an error message will be printed, based on the condition of indicator 90.

FIGURE 10.15 Calculation Specifications for Indexed Inquiry

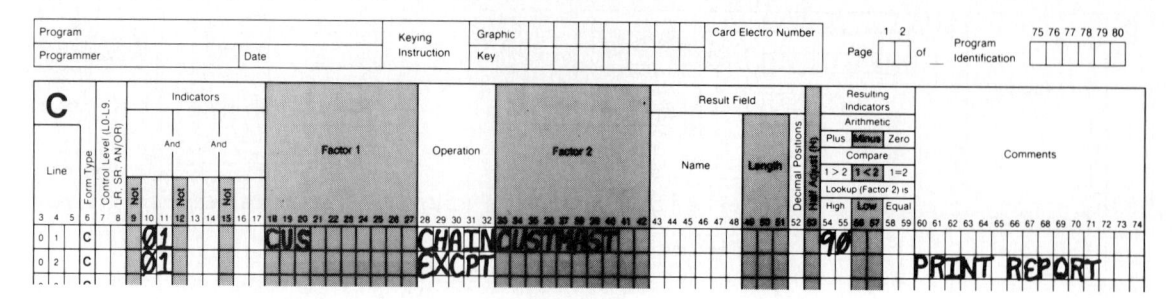

```
01 C  01    CUS    CHAIN CUSTMAST              90
02 C  01           EXCPT                                PRINT REPORT
```

FIGURE 10.16(a) Output Specifications for Inquiry Program

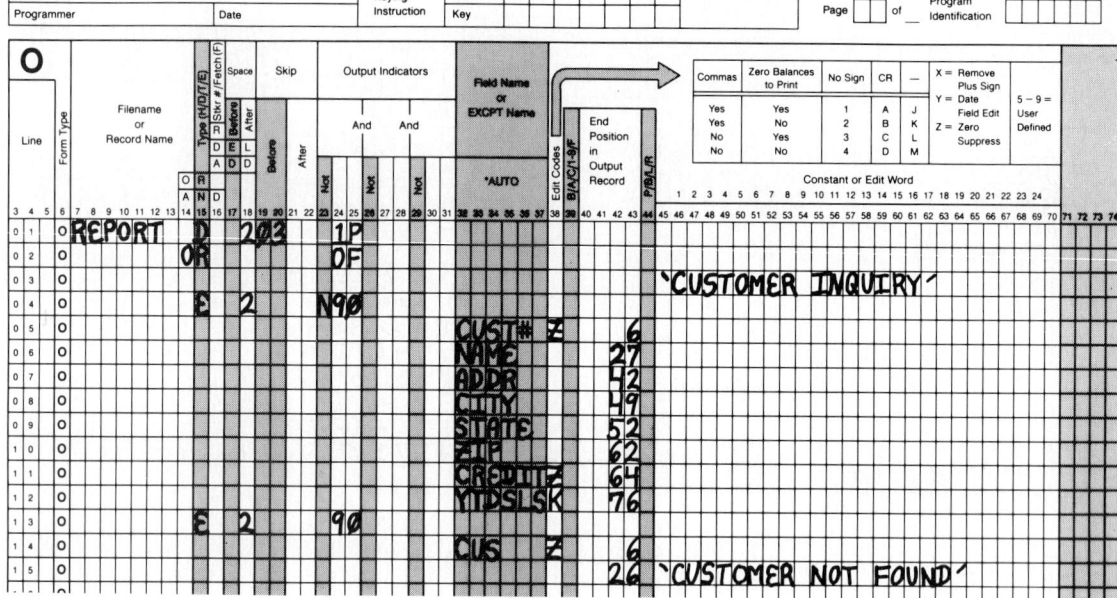

```
01 O REPORT  D  2 03        1P
02 O         OR             OF
03 O                                            'CUSTOMER INQUIRY'
04 O         E  2          N90
05 O                              CUST#  Z     6
06 O                              NAME         27
07 O                              ADDR         42
08 O                              CITY         49
09 O                              STATE        52
10 O                              ZIP          62
11 O                              CREDIT Z     64
12 O                              YTDSLS K     76
13 O         E  2           90
14 O                              CUS    Z     6
15 O                                           26  'CUSTOMER NOT FOUND'
```

FIGURE 10.16(b) Final Inquiry Report

```
            CUSTOMER INQUIRY
   1234 #1 LAMPS        98 PRIMROSE LN   NOWON  CA    100    .85
    123 WIDGITS INC     RAINBOW ST       NOWON  CA    999    .05
```

File Maintenance (Data Updating)

Once an indexed file has been created, it will need to be updated with new data on a regular basis. Several maintenance functions will need to be performed:

1. Adding records to the file
2. Making changes to existing records
3. Deleting records from the file

An indexed file is not copied over to a new version in the manner in which sequential files are maintained. An indexed file is updated in place, with adds, changes, and deletions made all in the same file.

Be sure there is a *recent* backup of the file before updating an indexed file. This is just good professional common sense. It can prevent disastrous consequences caused by new, untested programs, keying errors in the update transactions, power failures in the middle of the update, or any number of other accidents.

Adding Records to an Indexed File

When records are added to an indexed file, the records are added to the end of the file (in the overflow area). This means they will be physically out of sequence in the file. This is not a problem, however, since the key field will be added to the index and the index can then locate the record no matter where it is.

Changing a Field in an Indexed File

When changes are made to a record in an indexed file, the record is brought into main memory, the changes are made to the record in main memory (together with any editing and validation that the program may perform), and then the record is rewritten back to the original location on the direct access storage device. The key, of course, is never changed. To change a key, the entire record must be deleted and a new record added with the new key.

Deleting Records from an Indexed File

When records need to be deleted from an indexed file, a program will retrieve the record into main memory, perform any edits to ensure that the record is the correct one to be deleted, and tag it with some type of label (code or flag) to identify it as a deleted record. The record is rewritten back to the original location on the direct access storage device.

Any other programs that read this file will disregard all records that have been tagged as deleted. Some computer systems will actually remove from the index the key of any deleted records, preventing a user from changing his or her mind and reinstating a deleted record. Sometimes this is a desirable option, but the program would need to be written differently to allow for this type of capability.

Reorganizing a File

Eventually, an indexed file will become full of deleted records that waste space on disk. The added records become scattered on various tracks, causing processing to become slower. It becomes necessary to tidy up the file and get rid of the deleted records. This is usually done with a system utility (not an RPG program, although you could write one if necessary). This should be done on a regular schedule (weekly, monthly, yearly) as frequently as needed, depending on the amount of activity in the file.

SAMPLE PROGRAM 3: UPDATING AN INDEXED FILE ■

A Sample Program to update an indexed file will appear quite similar to the inquiry program described earlier. The record format for the indexed file is the same customer master file. The transaction record format is shown in Figures 10.17(a) and 10.17(b). There will be a code *A* for records to be added to the file, code *C* for changes, and code *D* for records that are to be deleted.

The File Description Specifications will be nearly the same as those used in the inquiry program. As shown in Figures 10.18(a) and 10.18(b), the name of the transaction file is TRAN, and it has a record length of 128. The most significant difference between the inquiry program and the update program is the *U* in column 15 in the specification for the master file. This means that the master file can be updated with this program. Since records will sometimes be added to this file, it is also necessary to enter an *A* in column 66. Input Specifications are the same as for any other program.

FIGURE 10.17(a) Transaction Record Layout

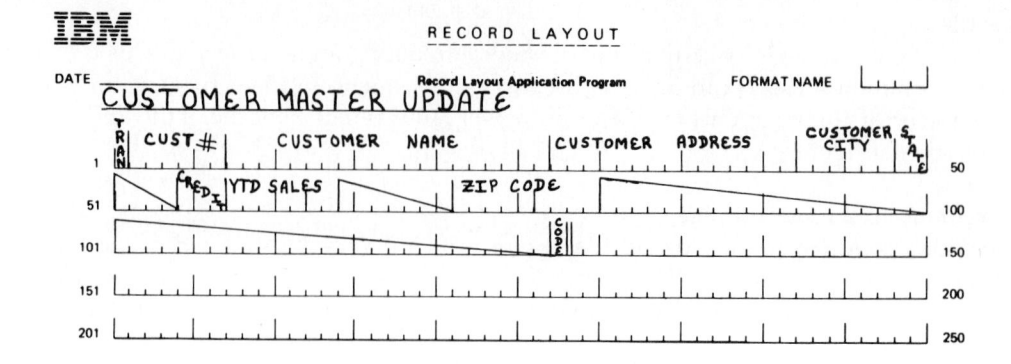

FIGURE 10.17(b) Customer Master Record Layout

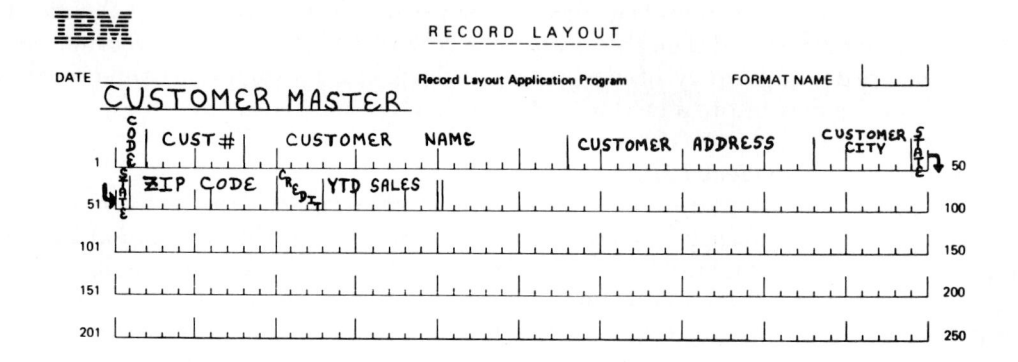

FIGURE 10.18(a) File Description Specifications for Updating an Indexed File

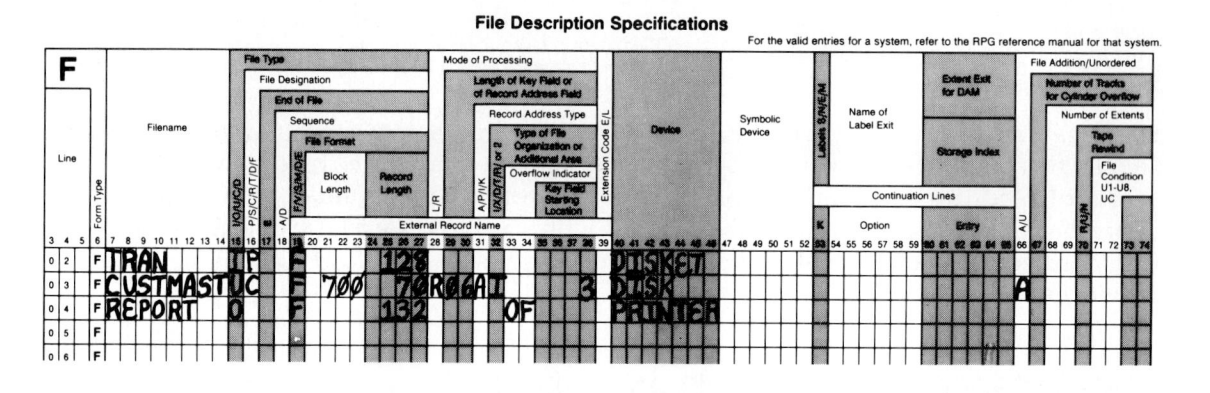

FIGURE 10.18(b) Input Specifications for Updating an Indexed File

RPG INPUT SPECIFICATIONS

Line	Form Type	Filename or Record Name	Sequence	Number	Option	Record identifying indicator	Position	Not	C/Z/D	Character	Position	Not	C/Z/D	Character	Position	Not	C/Z/D	Character	From	To	Decimal Positions	Field Name	Control Level	Matching Fields	Field Record Relation	Plus	Minus	Zero/Blank
01	I	TRAN	AA			01	1			28	CA																	
02	I																		1	1		TRNCOD						
03	I																		2	7	0	TCUS						
04	I																		8	27		TNAME						
05	I																		28	42		TADDR						
06	I																		43	48		TCITY						
07	I																		49	50		TSTATE						
08	I																		55	57	0	TCRED						
09	I																		58	64	2	TSALE						
10	I																		72	80		TZIP						
11	I			ZZ		99																						
12	I	CUSTMAST	BB			05	1			CC																		
13	I																		3	8	0	CUST#						
14	I																		9	28		NAME						
15	I																		29	43		ADDR						
16	I																		44	49		CITY						
17	I																		50	51		STATE						
18	I																		52	60		ZIP						
19	I																		61	63	0	CREDIT						
20	I																		64	70	2	YTDSLS						

The Calculation Specifications first will examine the transaction code in the transaction record to determine whether it is an add, change, or delete (or an invalid code). Indicators are set on for each record type.

Next, the CHAIN operation is used to retrieve the selected record from the master file. Figure 10.19 shows the first part of the calculations.

Finally, the program determines what action will be taken in updating the master file. Depending on the condition of the indicators, the master will be updated (or not updated) and a message will be printed. Figure 10.20 shows the actions to be taken and the condition of the indicators for each possible event.

FIGURE 10.19 First Calculation Specifications for the Update Program

RPG CALCULATION SPECIFICATIONS

Line	Form Type	Control Level	And	And	Factor 1	Operation	Factor 2	Result Field Name	Length	Decimal Positions	Half Adjust	Plus	Minus	Zero	Comments
01	C	01			TRNCOD	COMP	'A'						20		ADD
02	C	01			TRNCOD	COMP	'C'						21		CHANGE
03	C	01			TRNCOD	COMP	'D'						22		DELETE
04	C	N20	N21	N22		SETON							23		INVALID TRAN
05	C	01	N23		TCUS	CHAIN	CUSTMAST					30			

Chapter 10 Multiple File Processing (Indexed Files)

FIGURE 10.20 Condition of Indicators for an Event

TRANS TYPE	MASTER FOUND	INDICATORS	ACTION	MESSAGE TO BE PRINTED
A	yes	20 N30	none	error-master exists
A	no	20 30	update file	record added
C	yes	21 N30	update file	record changed
C	no	21 30	none	error-master not found
D	yes	22 N30	update file	record deleted
D	no	22 30	none	error-master not found
invalid code		23	none	invalid trans code

When a record is being added, every new field will be updated. When the transaction is a change, we want to change *only* the fields for which there is new input data. Each field must be tested in a change transaction to determine if it contains blanks or zeros. In the sample program we have created a fictitious field called BLANKS that will provide the fields with which to make this comparison.

The file is updated and the report is printed using the EXCPT operation. Figures 10.21(a), 10.21(b), and 10.21(c) show the complete Calculation and Output Specifications.

When a record is to be added to the file the exception output for the file needs to have ADD coded in columns 16–18 on the first specification for the output file. The fields in the transaction record are output and placed in the correct positions on the master record.

When a record is to be changed in the master file, *only* the changed fields need to be output. The changes are made in the original record, so there is no need to repeat the existing unchanged fields.

When a record is to be deleted, only the delete code needs to be output. This is treated as a change; some other program will eventually perform the reorganization of the file, doing the actual dropping of deleted records.

It is very important to ensure in the coding that a record that is to be added does not already exist. If it does, the program (in most environments) will terminate with an error message. It is not desirable to allow duplicate keys to exist in an indexed file.

It is equally important to ensure that an update is *not* executed when the requested record has not been found. If an update were made, it might be made to some other record. The results would be unpredictable.

This type of update program must be tested and retested thoroughly (on test data) to ensure that damage is not done accidentally to a valuable master file.

FIGURE 10.21(a) Update Program: Calculation Specifications

RPG CALCULATION SPECIFICATIONS

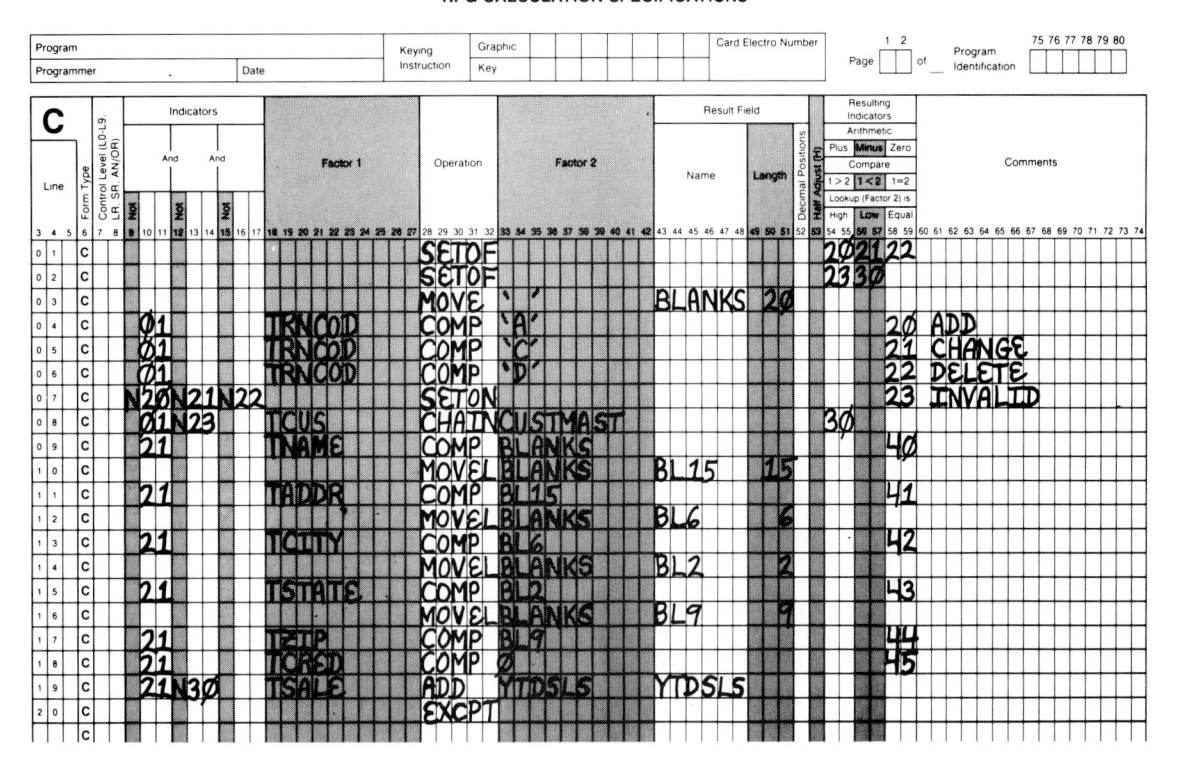

Line	Form Type	Control Level	Indicators (And/And/Not)	Factor 1	Operation	Factor 2	Result Field Name	Length	Dec	Resulting Indicators (Plus/Minus/Zero)	Comments
01	C				SETOF					202122	
02	C				SETOF					2330	
03	C				MOVE	' '	BLANKS	20			
04	C		01	TRNCOD	COMP	'A'				20	ADD
05	C		01	TRNCOD	COMP	'C'				21	CHANGE
06	C		01	TRNCOD	COMP	'D'				22	DELETE
07	C		N20N21N22		SETON					23	INVALID
08	C		01N23	TCUS	CHAIN	CUSTMAST				30	
09	C		21	TNAME	COMP	BLANKS				40	
10	C				MOVEL	BLANKS	BL15	15			
11	C		21	TADDR	COMP	BL15				41	
12	C				MOVEL	BLANKS	BL6	6			
13	C		21	TCITY	COMP	BL6				42	
14	C				MOVEL	BLANKS	BL2	2			
15	C		21	TSTATE	COMP	BL2				43	
16	C				MOVEL	BLANKS	BL9	9			
17	C		21	TZIP	COMP	BL9				44	
18	C		21	TCRED	COMP	0				45	
19	C		21N30	TSALE	ADD	YTDSLS	YTDSLS				
20	C				EXCPT						

FIGURE 10.21(b) Update Program: Output Specifications

RPG OUTPUT SPECIFICATIONS

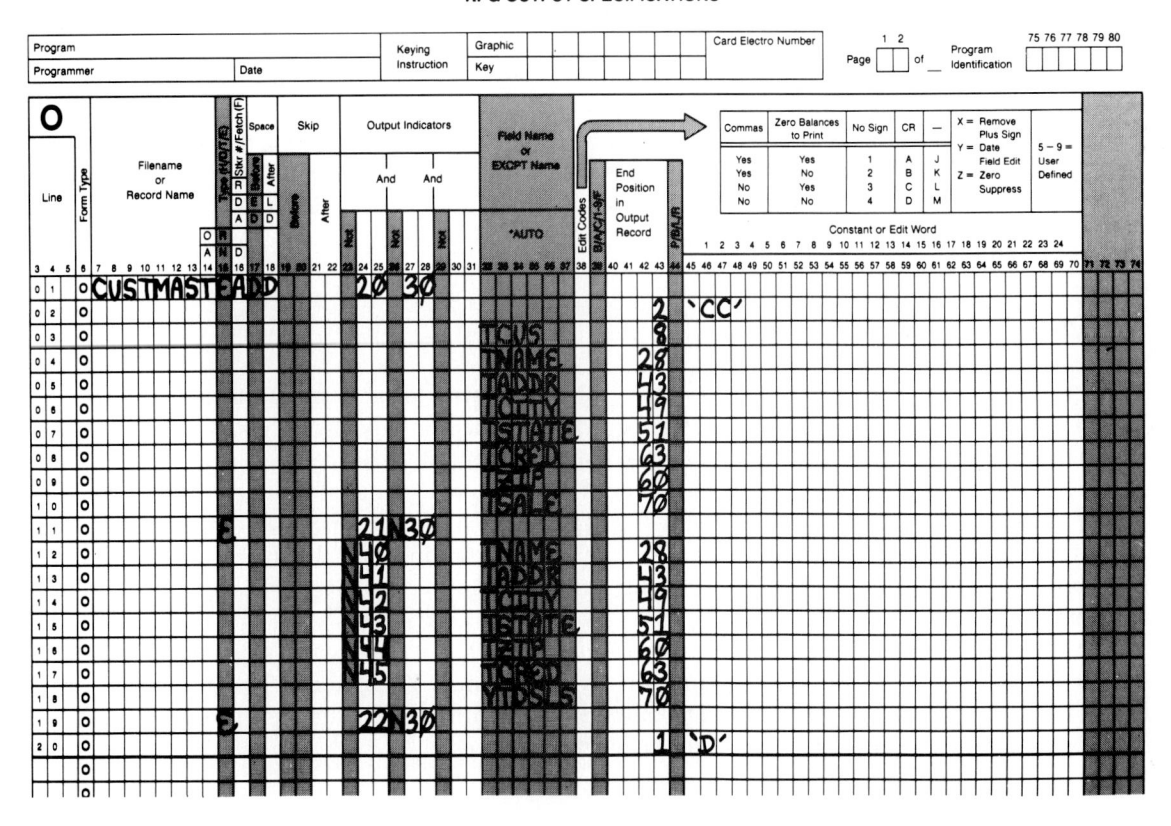

Line	Form Type	Filename or Record Name	Type	Space/Skip	Output Indicators	Field Name or EXCPT Name	End Position	Edit Codes	Constant or Edit Word
01	O	CUSTMAST	E ADD		20 30				
02	O						2		'CC'
03	O					TCUS	8		
04	O					TNAME	28		
05	O					TADDR	43		
06	O					TCITY	49		
07	O					TSTATE	51		
08	O					TCRED	63		
09	O					TZIP	60		
10	O					TSALE	70		
11	O		E		21N30				
12	O				N40	TNAME	28		
13	O				N41	TADDR	43		
14	O				N42	TCITY	49		
15	O				N43	TSTATE	51		
16	O				N44	TZIP	60		
17	O				N45	TCRED	63		
18	O					YTDSLS	70		
19	O		E		22N30				
20	O						1		'D'

FIGURE 10.21(c) Update Program: Output Specifications

```
   O  REPORT   D    202    1P
      OR              OF
                                              'CUSTOMER MASTER UPDATE'
         D    2    20N30
                                           27 'INVALID ADD - RECORD'
                                           42 'ALREADY EXISTS'
                             CUST#          6
         D    2    21 30
                             CUST#          6
                                           30 'INVALID CHANGE - RECORD'
                                           40 'NOT FOUND'
         D    2    22 30
                             CUST#          6
                                           30 'INVALID DELETE - RECORD'
                                           40 'NOT FOUND'
         D    2    23
                             CUST#          6
                                           31 'INVALID TRANSACTION CODE'
         D    2    99
                                           26 'INVALID RECORD TYPE'
```

SAMPLE PROGRAM 4: DEMONSTRATING SEQUENTIAL RETRIEVAL FROM AN INDEXED FILE ■

Records can be retrieved from an indexed file either randomly or sequentially. To produce a report in sequence by the key field of an indexed file, the file must be defined as an indexed file in the File Description Specifications.

Figures 10.22(a), 10.22(b), and 10.22(c) show a simple program to read the customer file and print a report. Even though the records are not physically in sequence, the records on the report will be in sequence because the sequence is controlled by the index.

RECORD ADDRESS FILES ■

When an indexed file is very large, it is not always desirable to print a report containing every record in the file. If some smaller group of records is needed, it is useful to print only that small group on the report. This can be done with the use of a record address file.

A record address (RA) file is nothing more than a file with which to make a selection of the range of records needed from the master file. This file is defined on the File Description and Extension Specifications. An entry of *L* must be made in column 28 on the indexed file to specify that an RA file is to be used. The entries for the sample program are shown in Figures 10.23(a) and 10.23(b).

The indexed file is defined as the primary input file. The length of the key (columns 29–30), the record address type and file organization (AI in columns 31–32), and the key field starting location (column 38) are all specified. The entry *L* in column 28 indicates that processing will be done using a record address file to define the limits.

The record address file is defined as an input file with a file designation of *R* for record address (column 16). Any filename can be used for this file. Besides the usual entries, such as record length and device, it is necessary to enter the length of the key field (columns 29–30) and an *E* in column 39. This indicates that an Extension Specification will be used.

The Extension Specifications form will contain the name of the RA file in columns 11–18. The name of the indexed file for which the limits are being established is entered in columns 19–26. This defines the relationship between the two files.

Each record in an RA file will contain only two fields. The first field contains the key value for the first requested record to be printed. The second field contains the key value for the last record to be processed from the master file.

FIGURE 10.22(a) Sequential Retrieval: File Description Specifications

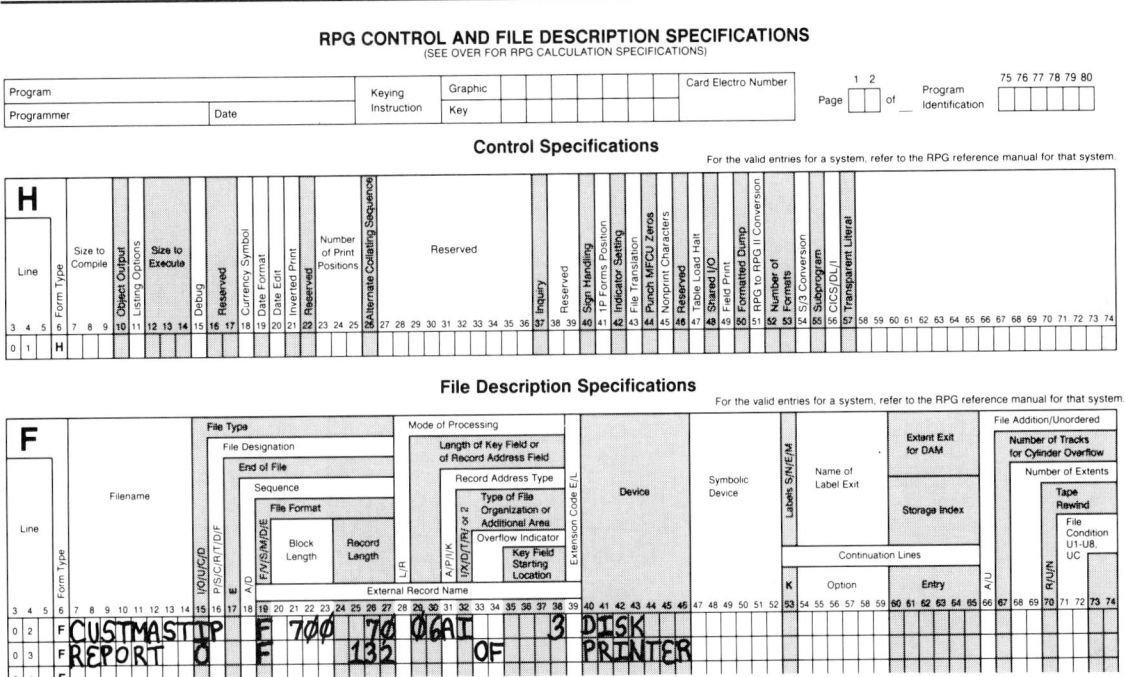

```
F CUSTMAST IP  F 700  70  06AI     3 DISK
F REPORT   O   F 132          OF     PRINTER
```

FIGURE 10.22(b) Sequential Retrieval: Input Specifications

```
I CUSTMAST AA  01   1 CC
I                                         3  80 CUST#
I                                         9  28 NAME
I                                        29  43 ADDR
I                                        44  49 CITY
I                                        50  51 STATE
I                                        52  60 ZIP
I                                        61  630CREDIT
I                                        64  702YTDSLS
I          ZZ      99
```

Chapter 10 Multiple File Processing (Indexed Files)

FIGURE 10.22(c) Sequential Retrieval: Output Specifications

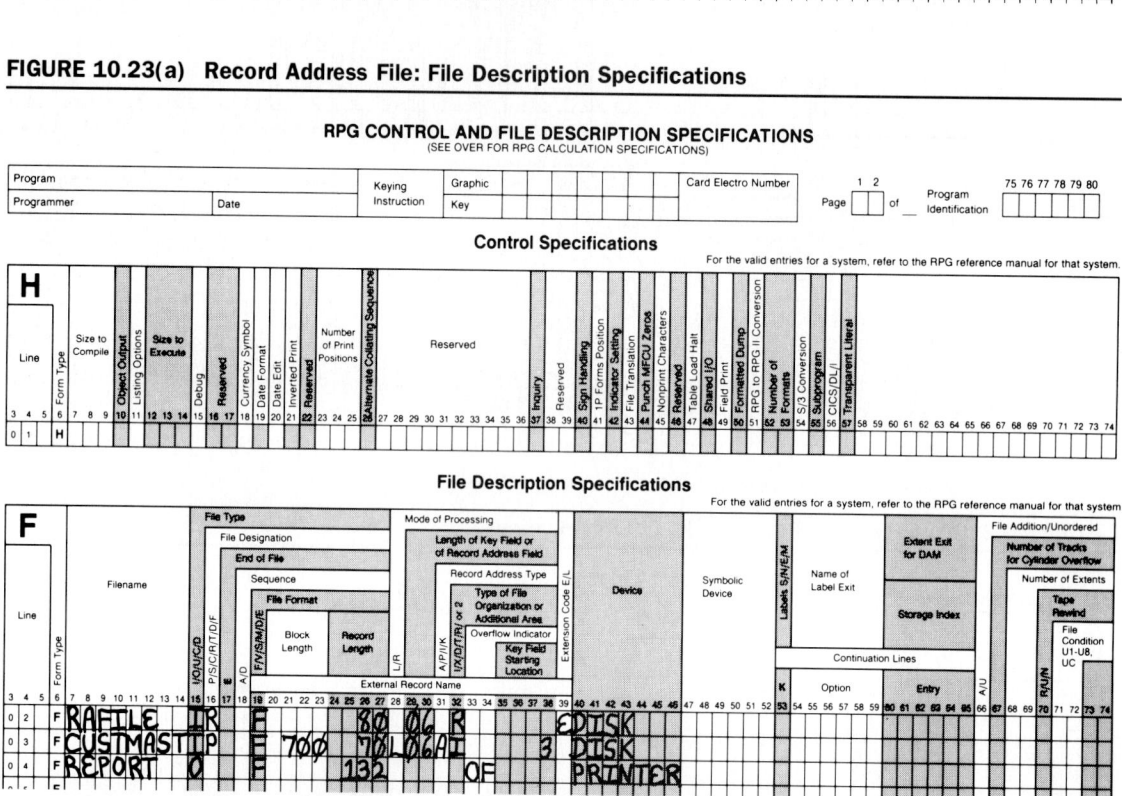

Line	Form Type	Filename or Record Name	Sequence	Number (1/N/E)	Option O/U/S	Record Identifying Indicator / ** or DS	Position	Not	C/Z/D	Character	Position	Not	C/Z/D	Character	Position	Not	C/Z/D	Character	Stacker Select	P/B/L/R/C	Field Location From	To	Decimal Positions	RPG Field Name / Constant	Control Level (L1-L9)	Matching Fields or Chaining Fields	Field Record Relation	Plus	Minus	Zero or Blank
01	I	REPORT				D 203	1P																						
02	I	OR					OF																						
03	I																					50	'CUSTOMER MASTER LIST'						
04	I					D 1	01																						
05	I																						CUST#	6					
06	I																						NAME	27					
07	I																						ADDR	43					
08	I																						CITY	50					
09	I																						STATE	53					
10	I																						ZIP	64					
11	I																						YTDSLSK	74					
12	I																												

FIGURE 10.23(a) Record Address File: File Description Specifications

Control Specifications

Line	Form Type	H entries
01	H	

File Description Specifications

Line	Form Type	Filename	I/O/U/C/D	P/S/C/R/T/D/F	F/V/S/M/D/E	A/D	Block Length	Record Length	L/R	Length of Key Field or of Record Address Field	Record Address Type A/P/I/K	Type of File Organization or Additional Area / UX/D/T/R/I or 2	Overflow Indicator	Key Field Starting Location	Extension Code E/L	Device	Symbolic Device	Labels S/N/E/M	Name of Label Exit	Extent Exit for DAM	Storage Index	Continuation Option	Continuation Entry
02	F	RAFILE	I R		F			80	06	R						DISK							
03	F	CUSTMAST	I P		F			700	70	L06AI					3	DISK							
04	F	REPORT	O					132					OF			PRINTER							

260

FIGURE 10.23(b) Record Address File: Extension Specifications

IBM Copyright International Business Machines Corporation 1984, 1990. IBM is a registered trademark of International Business Machines Corporation, Armonk, NY

RPG EXTENSION AND LINE COUNTER SPECIFICATIONS

(SEE OVER FOR RPG INPUT SPECIFICATIONS)

GX09-1033-03 UM/050 *

Printed in U.S.A.

Program | Keying Instruction | Graphic | Key | Card Electro Number | Page 1 2 of | Program Identification 75 76 77 78 79 80

Programmer | Date

Extension Specifications

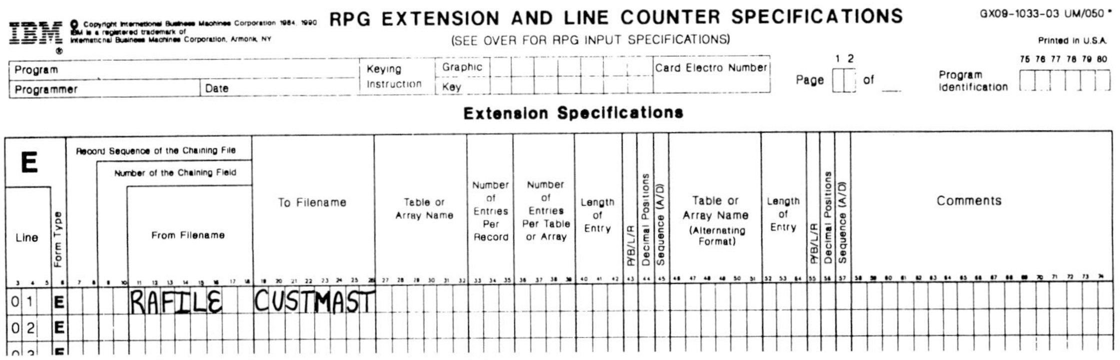

Line	Form Type	Record Sequence of the Chaining File	Number of the Chaining Field	From Filename	To Filename	Table or Array Name	Number of Entries Per Record	Number of Entries Per Table or Array	Length of Entry	P/B/L/R	Decimal Positions	Sequence (A/D)	Table or Array Name (Alternating Format)	Length of Entry	P/B/L/R	Decimal Positions	Sequence (A/D)	Comments
01	E			RAFILE	CUSTMAST													
02	E																	
03	E																	

A record address file can provide a convenient method for accessing a range of records (on a request basis) without a lot of complicated programming.

There are many uses for indexed files. Current technology almost demands the use of random access to data on an immediate basis. Indexed files not only provide instant access and ease of processing but also make it far easier for the programmer to obtain the data needed.

SUMMARY ▪

In this chapter, you have been introduced to direct access storage devices (DASDs) and how they work. You have also learned about random files and how they are processed. Although sequential files can be used on disk and are still a practical tool for batch processing, modern data retrieval methods give direct access to data using random access files. The use of indexed files is perhaps the most popular method for retrieving data quickly and easily for use in an on-line environment.

In this chapter, you have learned how key fields are used with indexed files for rapid retrieval of data. You have also learned how an indexed file is updated using the CHAIN operation. Finally, you have learned about record address (RA) files, a method for retrieving only selected portions of an indexed file.

REVIEW QUESTIONS ■

1. Explain the function of direct access storage devices (DASDs).

2. Explain the difference between sequential processing and random file processing.

3. The two methods for locating a record on disk are by _____ _____ _____ or _____ _____ .

4. Explain the meaning of *cylinder* in terms of DASDs.

5. Explain the meaning of *surface* in terms of DASDs.

6. When a file is organized by index, the records are retrieved by means of a _____ field.

7. The File Description Specifications for an indexed file will always need the length of the _____ and its beginning position.

8. Columns 31–32 on the File Description Specifications will contain _____ for an indexed file using an alphanumeric key field.

9. If records are to be added to an indexed file, the File Description Specifications will need to contain the letter _____ in column 66.

10. Indexed or direct files are the best to use for programs which are given to users for performing _____ .

11. A record is retrieved from an indexed file with the use of the _____ operation in the Calculation Specifications.

12. When this operation is performed, factor 1 will contain the key that is being requested and factor 2 will contain the _____ .

13. When this operation is performed, the resulting indicator will be placed in _____ .

14. When a record is added to an indexed file, it is placed at the _____ of the file.

15. If a program attempts to make a change to a record that does not exist on the file, what will happen?

EXERCISES ■

1. On a File Description Specifications form, enter the coding which will describe an indexed file.

2. On a Calculation Specifications form, enter the coding which will be needed to chain to a file named INPUT. The resulting indicator is 33. Enter a second line of code to add two fields together if the chain is successful.

DEBUGGING EXERCISES

Instructions

The following RPG programs contain an error or errors. Some of these errors are indicated by the RPG compiler on the program listing. A list of syntax errors is given at the end of the program listing. Other types of errors may occur which will not be shown. These are called logic errors.

Study each program and its syntax errors. Locate each error (including logic errors) and on a separate coding form make the correct entry for the line(s) in error.

Explain each error and how it should be corrected.

```
 100   F* TITLE: DEBUG PROJECT 10-A
 200   F* DATE:   5/19          AUTHOR: D.CABLE
 300   F* DESCRIPTION:          INDEXED FILES
 400   F*******************************************************

NAME OF PROGRAM WILL BE PJ010A IN LIBRARY CABLE

       H
* 1019           ALL DECIMAL DATA ERRORS IGNORED
 500   FARMAST  IF  F      50 01AI    1 DISK
 600   FPAYMENT IP  F      50           DISK
 700   FREPORT  O   F     132        OF PRINTER
 800   F*******************************************************

 900   IPAYMENT AA  01
1000   I                                    1   5 CUST#
1100   I                                    6  11 DATE
1200   I                                   12  17 INV#
1300   I                                   18  252AMTPD
1400   IARMAST   BB  02
1500   I                                    1   5 CUST#
1600   I                                    6  11 DATE
1700   I                                   12  17 INV#
1800   I                                   18  252AMTDUE

1900   C        01       CUS       CHAINARMAST                 90
2000   C        01N90    AMTDUE    SUB  AMTPD   BALDU    72

2100   OREPORT  H   203          1P
2200   O                OR       OF
2300   O                                         6 'PJ010A'
2400   O                              UDATE Y   50
2500   O                                        30 'PAYMENT REPORT'
2600   O        H   2            1P
2700   O                OR       OF
2800   O                                         7 'CUST#'
2900   O                                        16 'INV DATE'
3000   O                                        24 'INV#'
3100   O                                        34 'AMT DUE'
3200   O                                        45 'AMT PAID'
3300   O                                        55 'BAL DUE'
3400   O        D   1            01N90
3500   O                             CUST#       6
3600   O                             DATE  Y    14
3700   O                             INV#       24
3800   O                             AMTDUEK    35
3900   O                             AMTPD K    46
4000   O                             BALDU K    56
```

```
SEQUENCE       1         2         3         4         5         6         7
NUMBER    67890123456789012345678901234567890123456789012345678901234567890123456789012 34
          4100   0        D    1       01 90
          4200   0                              CUST#        6
          4300   0                              DATE    Y   14
          4400   0                              INV#        24
          4500   0                                          56 'INVOICE NOT FOUND'
          * * * * * E N D   O F   S O U R C E * * * * *
```

* 7086   600   RPG PROVIDES BLOCK/UNBLOCK SUPPORT FOR FILE PAYMENT.

CROSS-REFERENCE LISTING


```
         FILE/RCD      DEV/RCD       REFERENCES (D=DEFINED)

    01   ARMAST        DISK          500D  1400   1900
    02   PAYMENT       DISK          600D   900
    03   REPORT        PRINTER       700D  2100   2600   3400   4100


         FIELD         ATTR          REFERENCES (M=MODIFIED D=DEFINED)

         AMTDUE        P(8,2)        1800D  2000   3800
         AMTPD         P(8,2)        1300D  2000   3900
         BALDU         P(7,2)        2000D  4000
* 7030   CUS           A(1)          1900
         CUST#         A(5)          1000D  1500D  3500   4200
         DATE          P(6,0)        1100D  1600D  3600   4300
         INV#          A(6)          1200D  1700D  3700   4400
         UDATE         P(6,0)        2400


         INDICATOR     REFERENCES (M=MODIFIED D=DEFINED)

         LR            600D
         OF            700D  2200   2700
         01            900M  1900   2000   3400   4100
* 7031   02            1400M
         1P            2100  2600
         90            1900M 2000   3400   4100
```

MESSAGES


```
   MSGID      SEV   NUMBER    TEXT

*  QRG1019    00    1         IGNDECERR(*YES) SPECIFIED ON COMMAND. NO DECIMAL DATA ERRORS
*  QRG7030    30    1         FIELD OR INDICATOR NOT DEFINED.
*  QRG7031    00    1         NAME OR INDICATOR NOT REFERENCED.
*  QRG7086    00    1         RPG WILL HANDLE BLOCKING FUNCTION FOR THE FILE. INFDS CONTEN
                              ARE TRANSFERRED.

MESSAGE SUMMARY

TOTAL    00    10    20    30    40    50
   4      3     0     0     1     0     0

    45 RECORDS READ FROM SOURCE FILE
    SOURCE RECORDS INCLUDE   40 SPECIFICATIONS,    0 TABLE RECORDS, AND    5 COMMENTS

    QRG0008 COMPILE TERMINATED. SEVERITY 30 ERRORS FOUND IN PROGRAM

    * * * * * E N D   O F   C O M P I L A T I O N * * * * *
*  QRG1020                    ERROR OCCURRED CREATING OR UPDATING DATA AREA RETURNCODE. COMPI
```

```
 100  F* TITLE: DEBUG PROJECT 10-B
 200  F* DATE:  5/19              AUTHOR: D.CABLE
 300  F* DESCRIPTION:                      P (ARRAYS)
 400  F*********************************************************
```

NAME OF PROGRAM WILL BE PJ010B IN LIBRARY CABLE

```
          H
* 1019            ALL DECIMAL DATA ERRORS IGNORED
 500  FYIELDS   IP  F    30           DISK
 600  FSTATMASTUF  F   100 15AI     3 DISK
 700  FREPORT   O   F   132       OF  PRINTER
 800  F*********************************************************

 900  IYIELDS  AA  01
1000  I                                           1  15 ITEM#
1100  I                                          16  160OPER
1200  I                                          17  220WDATE
1300  I                                          25  290QTY
1400  ISTATMASTAA  02
1500  I                                           1   2 TYPE
1600  I                                           3  17 ITM#
1700  I                                          18  180OP1
1800  I                                          19  240TQTY1
1900  I                                          25  250OP2
2000  I                                          26  310TQTY2
2100  I                                          32  320OP3
2200  I                                          33  380TQTY3

2300  C                        SETOF                         252627
2400  C   01       ITEM#       CHAINSTATMAST                 90
2500  C            OPER        COMP OP1                      25
2600  C            OPER        COMP OP2                      26
2700  C            OPER        COMP OP3                      27
2800  C   N90 25   QTY         ADD  TQTY1     TQTY1
2900  C   N90 26   QTY         ADD  TQTY2     TQTY2
3000  C   N90 27   QTY         ADD  TQTY3     TQTY3
3100  C                        EXCPT

3200  OSTATMASTE            90
3300  O                          TQTY1      24
3400  O                          TQTY2      31
3500  O                          TQTY3      38
3600  OREPORT   H   203      1P
3700  O         OR            OF
3800  O                                      6 'PJ010B'
3900  O                          UDATE  Y   50
4000  O                                     30 'PRODUCT YIELDS'
4100  O         H    2       1P
4200  O         OR            OF
4300  O                                      7 'ITEM#'
4400  O                                     25 'QTY1'
4500  O                                     35 'QTY2'
4600  O                                     45 'QTY3'
4700  O         D    1       01
4800  O                          ITEM#      15
4900  O                          TQTY1      25
5000  O                          TQTY2      35
5100  O                          TQTY3      45
* * * * * END  OF  SOURCE * * * *
```

```
* 7086      500   RPG PROVIDES BLOCK/UNBLOCK SUPPORT FOR FILE YIELDS.
```

CROSS-REFERENCE LISTING

```
        FILE/RCD    DEV/RCD      REFERENCES (D=DEFINED)
    03  REPORT      PRINTER      700D 3600  4100  4700
    02  STATMAST    DISK         600D 1400  2400  3200
    01  YIELDS      DISK         500D  900


        FIELD       ATTR         REFERENCES (M=MODIFIED D=DEFINED)
        ITEM#       A(15)        1000D 2400  4800
* 7031  ITM#        A(15)        1600D
        OPER        P(1,0)       1100D 2500  2600  2700
        OP1         P(1,0)       1700D 2500
        OP2         P(1,0)       1900D 2600
        OP3         P(1,0)       2100D 2700
        QTY         P(5,0)       1300D 2800  2900  3000
        TQTY1       P(6,0)       1800D 2800  2800M 3300  4900
        TQTY2       P(6,0)       2000D 2900  2900M 3400  5000
        TQTY3       P(6,0)       2200D 3000  3000M 3500  5100
* 7031  TYPE        A(2)         1500D
        UDATE       P(6,0)       3900
* 7031  WDATE       P(6,0)       1200D


        INDICATOR   REFERENCES (M=MODIFIED D=DEFINED)

        LR          5000
        OF          700D 3700  4200
        01          900M 2400  4700
* 7031  02          1400M
        1P          3600  4100
        25          2300M 2500M 2800
        26          2300M 2600M 2900
        27          2300M 2700M 3000
        90          2400M 2800  2900  3000  3200


    MESSAGES

      MSGID    SEV  NUMBER    TEXT

    * QRG1019   00    1       IGNDECERR(*YES) SPECIFIED ON COMMAND. NO DECIMAL DATA ERRORS
    * QRG7031   00    4       NAME OR INDICATOR NOT REFERENCED.
    * QRG7086   00    1       RPG WILL HANDLE BLOCKING FUNCTION FOR THE FILE. INFDS CONTENT
                              ARE TRANSFERRED.


    MESSAGE SUMMARY

    TOTAL    00     10    20    30    40    50
      6       6     0      0     0    0     0

      51 RECORDS READ FROM SOURCE FILE
    SOURCE RECORDS INCLUDE    46 SPECIFICATIONS,    0 TABLE RECORDS, AND    5 COMMENTS

    PRM HAS BEEN CALLED

    QRG0003 PROGRAM PJ010B PLACED IN LIB CABLE. 00 HIGHEST SEVERITY FOUND

         * * * * * E N D   O F   C O M P I L A T I O N * * * *
    * QRG1020           ERROR OCCURRED CREATING OR UPDATING DATA AREA RETURNCODE. COMPIL
```

PROGRAMMING PROJECT

Project Overview

The order master file is to be read using indexed processing methods. A sequential file containing the requested order numbers is read, and the order data is retrieved from the order master file and a report printed using exception time output. Only the requested orders will be printed. Write the RPG program to produce this listing. Sample data for this project can be found in Appendix D.

Input Format

The input data for the project is found in a file called ORDMAST in the sample data. The requested order numbers are found in a file called ORDREQS. The Record Layouts for these files are shown in Figures 10.24(a) and 10.24(b).

Processing

A request record is read and the order master file is accessed using the CHAIN operation. If the record is found, a line is printed on the report. If the record is not found, an error message is printed on the report. Each line is printed at exception time.

Output Format (Printer Spacing Chart)

The output for the project is a report with standard headings. The report will show the order number, part number, order date, quantity ordered, and quantity shipped. The Printer Spacing Chart for this report is shown in Figure 10.25.

An example of the finished report is shown in Figure 10.26.

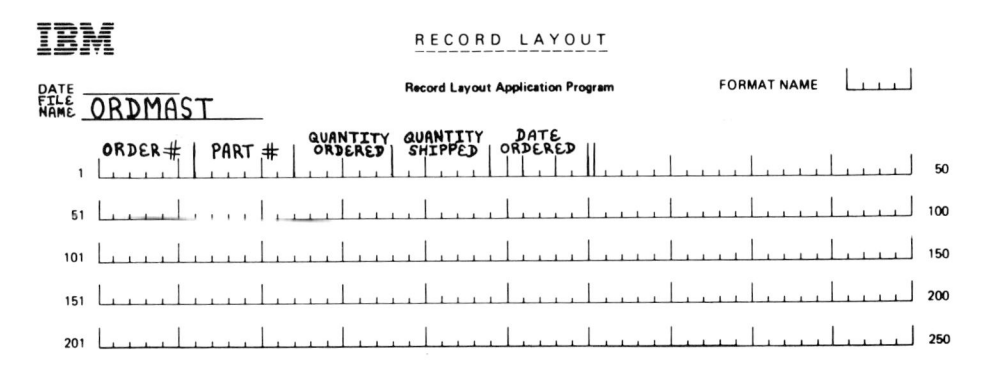

FIGURE 10.24(a) Programming Project: Record Layout

File: ORDMAST

Fields: ORDER#, PART#, QUANTITY ORDERED, QUANTITY SHIPPED, DATE ORDERED

FIGURE 10.24(b) Programming Project: Record Layout

IBM — RECORD LAYOUT

DATE _____
FILE NAME: ORDREQS
Record Layout Application Program   FORMAT NAME ____

ORDER #

FIGURE 10.25 Programming Project: Printer Spacing Chart

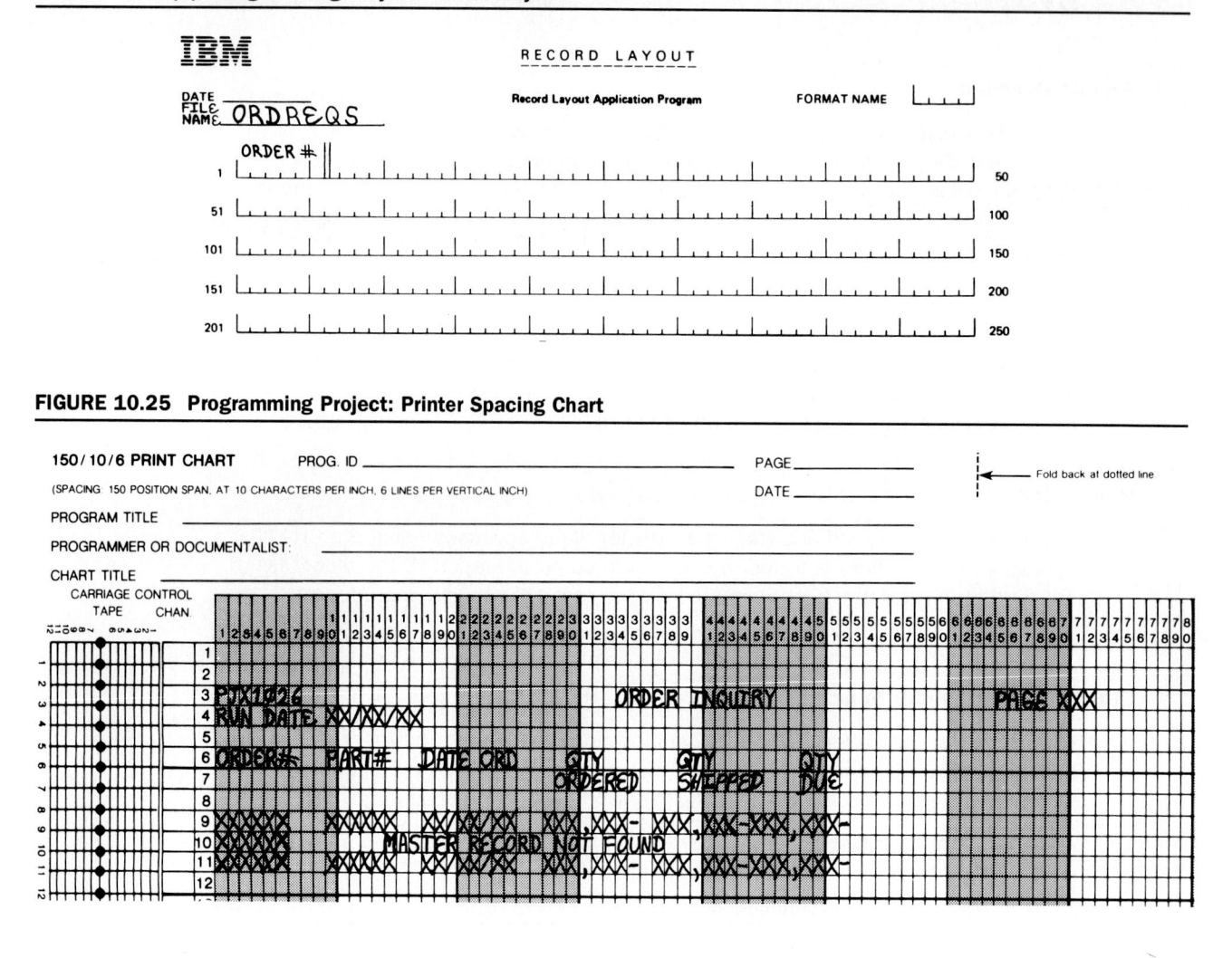

150/10/6 PRINT CHART   PROG. ID _____   PAGE _____
(SPACING: 150 POSITION SPAN, AT 10 CHARACTERS PER INCH, 6 LINES PER VERTICAL INCH)   DATE _____
PROGRAM TITLE _____
PROGRAMMER OR DOCUMENTALIST: _____
CHART TITLE _____

```
 3  PJX1026                          ORDER INQUIRY                          PAGE XXX
 4  RUN DATE XX/XX/XX
 6  ORDER#   PART#   DATE ORD   QTY       QTY       QTY
 7                              ORDERED   SHIPPED   DUE
 9  XXXXXX   XXXXXX  XX/XX/XX   XXX,XXX-  XXX,XXX-  XXX,XXX-
10  XXXXXX           MASTER RECORD NOT FOUND
11  XXXXXX   XXXXXX  XX/XX/XX   XXX,XXX-  XXX,XXX-  XXX,XXX-
```

FIGURE 10.26 Programming Project: Final Report

```
        PJX1025                   ORDER INQUIRY
        RUN DATE  3/12/92

        ORDER#   PART#   DATE ORD   QTY       QTY       QTY
                                    ORDERED   SHIPPED   DUE

        000350   165081  3/30/91    500       250       250
        128586   000051  3/15/91     20        18         2
        832500           MASTER RECORD NOT FOUND
```

Chapter 11

Additional Subjects

What you will learn in Chapter 11

Line Counter Specifications
Binary Data
Editing Data Operations
    Move Zone
    Test Zone
    Test Numeric
Reversing a Sign
Testing the Value of a Bit
Special Indicators
    Halt Indicators
    External Switches
Indicators—A Review

Record Identification Indicators
Field Record Relationship
    Indicators
Resulting Indicators
Overflow Indicators
Level Break Indicators
Matching Record Indicators
Last Record Indicator
Halt Indicators
External Indicators (Switches)
Even More Indicators
External Subroutines

Look-Ahead Feature
FORCE Operation
READ Operation
Debugging Methods
DSPLY Operation
Accessing Multiple Indexed Files
Naming Conventions
    Program and File Names
    Field Names

Previous chapters have covered all the fundamentals of RPG II, including most of the operations and processing techniques for producing useful business reports. In this chapter we will discuss some additional methods which can be useful in solving particular problems.

LINE COUNTER SPECIFICATIONS ■

Line spacing on reports is often controlled by using the line and spacing fields on the Output Specifications form. The Line Counter Specification is useful when the output will have a nonstandard format, such as a preprinted check form or invoice form requiring a variety of spacing and skipping.

    This specification is also used when the report will be output to a media such as tape or disk instead of directly to a printer. If a print file is being output to tape to be later converted to a report format on microfilm or microfiche, the skipping and spacing must be precisely defined on the Line Counter Specification because the tape device has no built-in functions to handle printer commands. Line Counter Specifications may be used for any type of printer output if desired. When a Line Counter Specification is used, an *L* is entered in column 39 of the corresponding File Description Specifications.

For the Line Counter Specifications, the form type in column 6 is an *L*. The filename in columns 7–14 must correspond to the name of the printer file specified in the File Description Specifications. Figures 11.1(a) and 11.1(b) show the entries for the File and Line Counter Specifications.

Columns 15–17 specify the total number of lines on the form. The usual form length for reports is 66 lines; RPG will default to 66 if no entry is made. For special forms an entry will be required.

The designation FL in columns 18–19 indicates form length. The entry in columns 20–22 is the line number at which form overflow will occur. Columns 23–24 show OL for overflow line. The portion of the form not shown in Figures 11.1(a) and 11.1(b) includes fields that indicate channel positions for controlling spacing on older equipment.

BINARY DATA ■

Earlier chapters have discussed two types of data: decimal data and packed-decimal data. Decimal data is simply the normal data format carrying a number in its readable form stored in one eight-bit byte. Packed-decimal data stores two characters per byte and must be unpacked for printing so that it will be readable.

A third type of data is binary data. A number in binary format can be stored in even less space. RPG can process binary data as long as the program is informed that the data is in binary format. The method is similar to that used for processing packed-decimal data.

As shown in Figures 11.2(a) and 11.2(b), a *B* is entered in column 43 of the Input Specifications to indicate that an input field will be arriving in binary format. Data which is to be output in binary format will require a *B* in column 44 of the Output Specifications.

FIGURE 11.1(a) *File Description Specifications Entry*

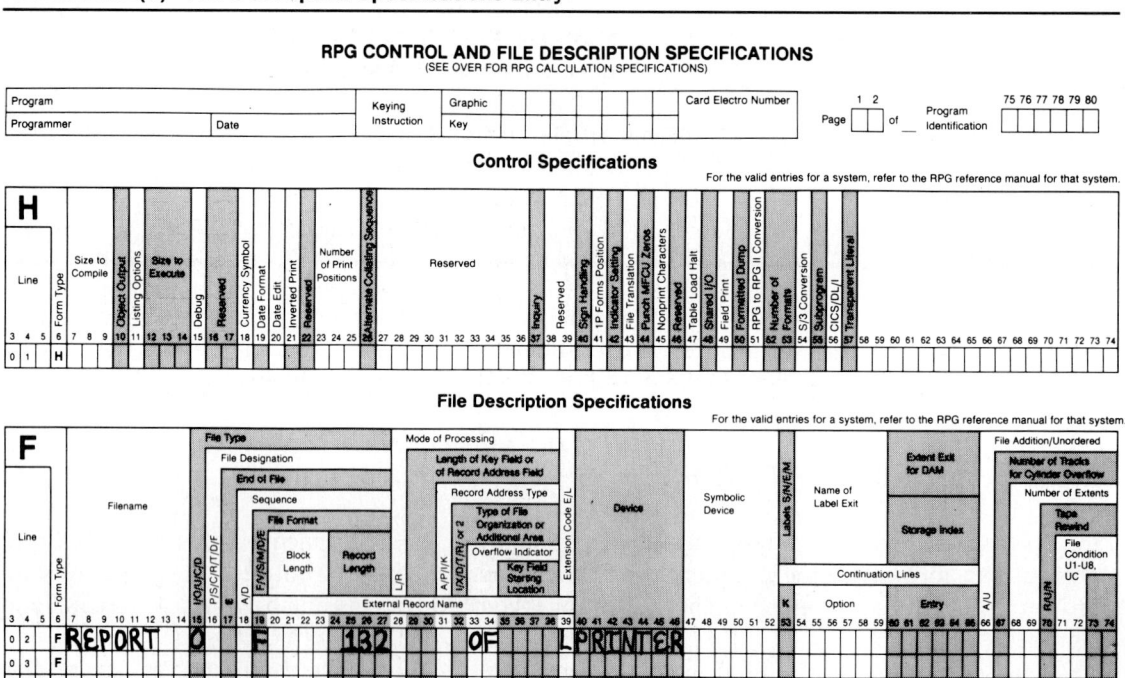

FIGURE 11.1(b)   Line Counter Specifications

Line Counter Specifications

Line	Form Type	Filename	Line Number	FL or Channel Number	OL or Channel Number	...
01	L	REPORT	066	FL	0600L	
02	L					
	L					

FIGURE 11.2(a)   Input Specifications for Binary Data

RPG INPUT SPECIFICATIONS

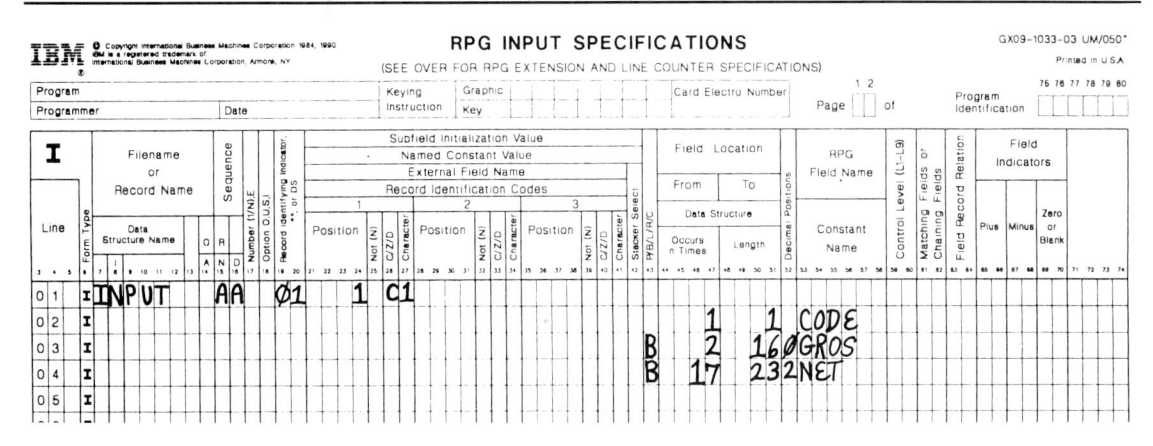

Line	Form Type	Filename or Record Name	Sequence	Number (1/N).E	Option O,U,S	Record Identifying Indicator or DS	Position	Not (N)	C/Z/D	Character	Position	Not (N)	C/Z/D	Character	Position	Not (N)	C/Z/D	Character	Stacker Select	P/B/L/R/C	Data Structure Occurs n Times	Length	From	To	Decimal Positions	RPG Field Name / Constant Name	Control Level	Matching Fields or Chaining Fields	Field Record Relation	Plus	Minus	Zero or Blank
01	I	INPUT	AA			01	1		C	1																						
02	I																						1	1		CODE						
03	I																			B			2	16	0	GROS						
04	I																			B			17	23	2	NET						
05	I																															

FIGURE 11.2(b)   Output Specifications for Binary Data

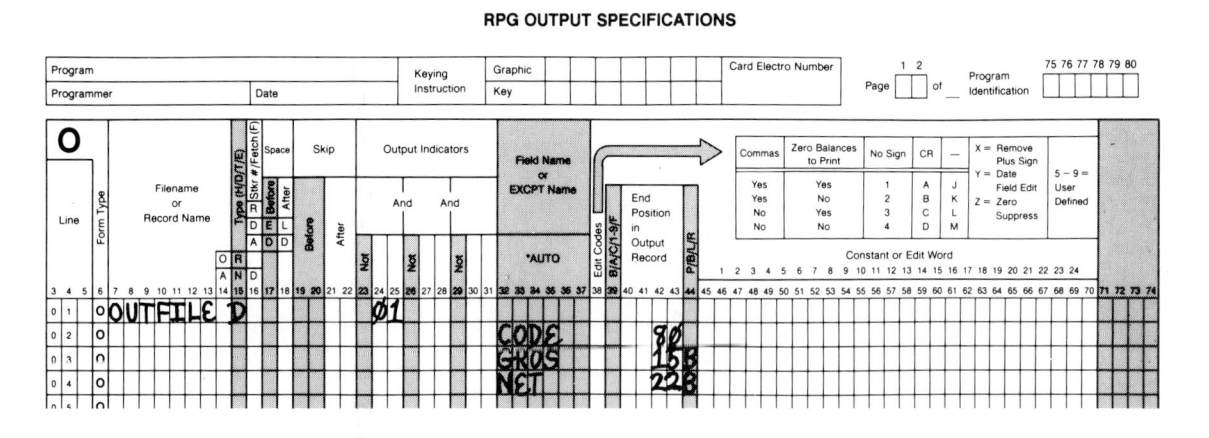

RPG OUTPUT SPECIFICATIONS

Line	Form Type	Filename or Record Name	Type (H/D/T/E)	Stkr #/Fetch (F)	Space Before	Space After	Skip Before	Skip After	Output Indicators	And	And	Field Name or EXCPT Name	*AUTO	Edit Codes B/A/C/1-9/F	End Position in Output Record	P/B/L/R	Constant or Edit Word
01	O	OUTFILE	D						01								
02	O											CODE			8		
03	O											GROS			15	B	
04	O											NET			22	B	
05	O																

EDITING DATA OPERATIONS ■

Move Zone

Data stored in a computer in the zoned-decimal format is stored in an eight-bit byte consisting of a zone portion and a digit portion. A numeric field in the zoned-decimal format will contain the sign (positive or negative) in the zone portion of the rightmost (low order) byte. Figure 11.3 shows the structure of data fields.

The move zone operations are used to move the zone portion of a field to the zone portion of another field. Although this operation is seldom used, it is sometimes useful to manipulate the signs (positive or negative) of numeric fields or to make changes to a character within an alphanumeric field.

There are four operation codes associated with moving zones:

MLLZO	Move low-to-low zone
MHHZO	Move high-to-high zone
MHLZO	Move high-to-low zone
MLHZO	Move low-to-high zone

"High" refers to the leftmost (high order) character in a field. "Low" refers to the rightmost (low order) character in a field. As was true of the MOVE operation, these operations do not remove the zone from the field from which it was taken. They are really copy instructions, copying the zone from one field and placing it in the receiving field. Figure 11.4 shows the effect move zone operations will have on some fields.

One common use of this operation is exercised when a numeric field arrives without a sign and the sign appears in a completely separate field. To simplify the arithmetic operations, it is useful to move the sign (zone) into the rightmost position (zone) of the numeric field. Figure 11.5 shows some examples of coding for move zone operations.

Test Zone

The test zone operation (TESTZ) allows testing of the zone portion of the high order (leftmost) position of an alphanumeric field. This operation turns on an indicator that is entered in columns 54–59 on the Calculation Specifications.

On a computer which uses the EBCDIC coding method, the alphabetic characters fall into three groups:

A–I	Zone will turn on the plus indicator (positions 54–55)
J–R	Zone will turn on the minus indicator (positions 56–57)
S–Z	Zone will turn on the zero indicator (positions 58–59)

FIGURE 11.3 Structure of Data Fields

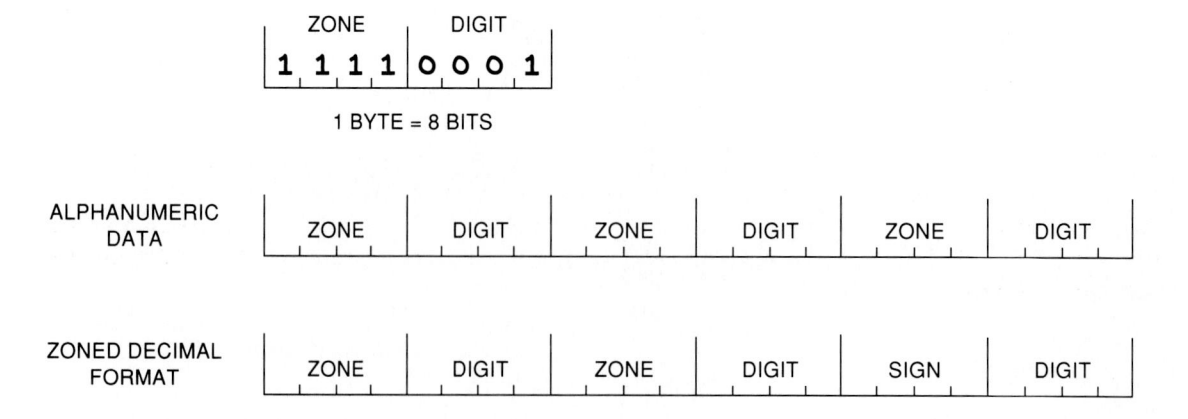

FIGURE 11.4 Effect of Move Zone Operations

MOVE HIGH TO HIGH — MHHZO

MOVE HIGH TO LOW — MHLZO

MOVE LOW TO LOW — MLLZO

MOVE LOW TO HIGH — MLHZO

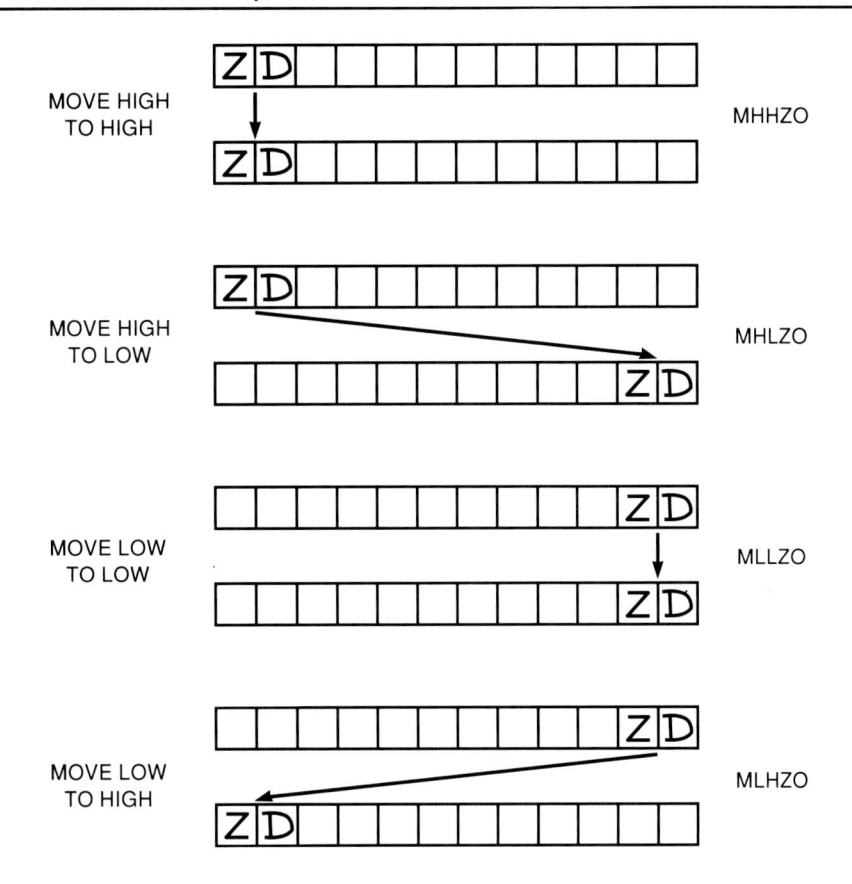

FIGURE 11.5 Coding for Move Zone Operations

```
C           MHHZO FIELDA    FIELDB
C           MHLZO FIELDA    NEWFLD
C           MLLZO FIELDA    FIELDN
C           MLHZO FIELDA    NEW
```

The TESTZ operation offers a simple way to determine whether the first character of a field falls into one of these three categories. Figure 11.6 shows how a TESTZ operation is coded.

Most special characters will give a resulting indicator of zero (positions 58–59). The exceptions are the ampersand (&), which will result in a plus indicator, and the minus sign (–), which will turn on the minus indicator.

Test Numeric

The test numeric operation is used to test an alphanumeric field for the presence (or absence) of numeric data.

Chapter 11 Additional Subjects

FIGURE 11.6 Coding a TESTZ Operation

RPG CALCULATION SPECIFICATIONS

```
01 C              TESTZ         ALPH1         505152
02 C
```

FIGURE 11.7 Coding a TESTN Operation

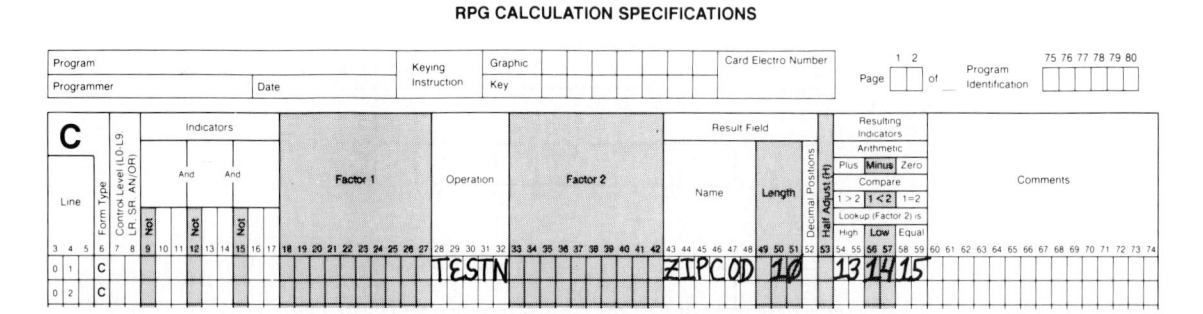

RPG CALCULATION SPECIFICATIONS

```
01 C              TESTN         ZIPCOD 10     131415
02 C
```

Before attempting to perform arithmetic operations on a field, it is important that the field contains pure numeric data. An attempt to perform arithmetic on a non-numeric field will almost guarantee that the job will come to an abrupt halt. Some computers will insert leading zeros into a numeric field, but there are occasions when it is useful to perform edits within the program itself. Since blanks are non-numeric characters, it is useful to edit for them. Figure 11.7 shows the coding for performing an edit.

If all numeric characters are found, the plus indicator will be turned on. If one or more leading blank characters are found, the minus indicator will be turned on. If the entire field contains blanks, the zero indicator will be turned on. Notice that this operation is performed on an alphanumeric field *before* moving the field into a numeric field.

REVERSING A SIGN ■

Sometimes it is required that a sign be reversed—for example, a field that has been input as a positive must become negative within the program so it can proceed into the next program as a negative, or perhaps it will just make the calculations simpler to do so. This is done by subtracting the number from zero, or by using the Z-SUB operation, or by multiplying the number by a –1. Any of these methods can use the original field name as the result field. Figure 11.8 shows an example of all three methods for reversing the sign of a field.

TESTING THE VALUE OF A BIT ■

Users of RPG usually deal with whole fields or with whole characters within a field. It is possible in an RPG program to examine the exact bits within a byte to determine the condition of each. The operation codes used for this function are: BITON, BITOF, and TESTB.

A one-position alphanumeric field (a byte) is defined to contain the set of bits to be tested. The bits within this byte are identified from left to right by the digits 0–7.

FIGURE 11.8 Three Methods of Reversing the Sign of a Field

RPG CALCULATION SPECIFICATIONS

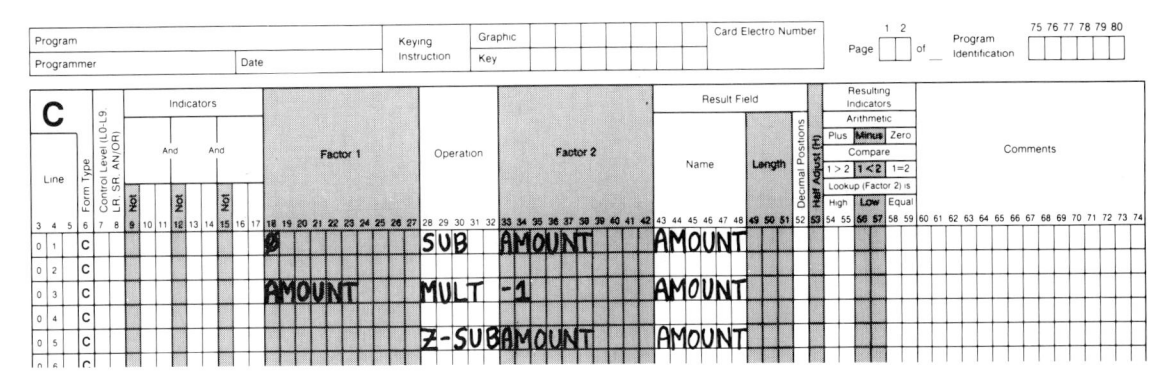

Line	Factor 1	Operation	Factor 2	Result Field	Length
01	0	SUB	AMOUNT	AMOUNT	
02					
03	AMOUNT	MULT	-1	AMOUNT	
04					
05		Z-SUB	AMOUNT	AMOUNT	

FIGURE 11.9 BITON Operation

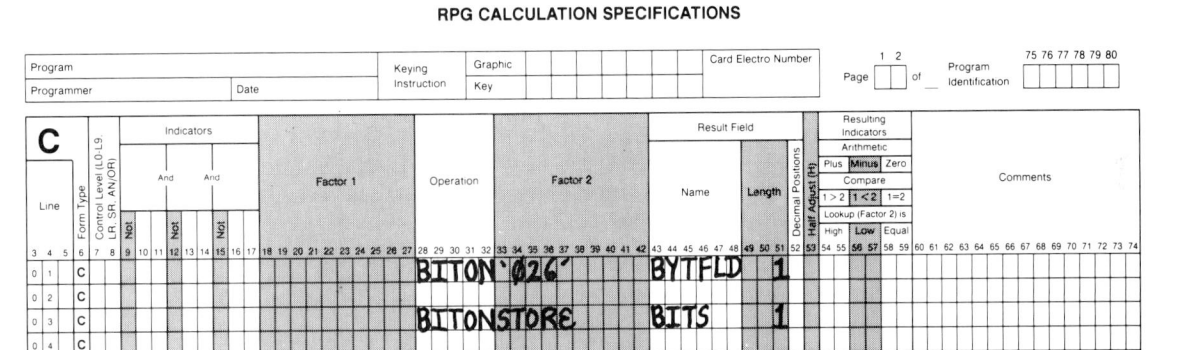

RPG CALCULATION SPECIFICATIONS

Line	Factor 1	Operation	Factor 2	Result Field	Length
01		BITON	'026'	BYTFLD	1
02					
03		BITON	STORE	BITS	1
04					
05		BITON	AR,1	BITSW	1

Bits are turned on using the operation code BITON as shown in Figure 11.9. In the first example the first, third, and seventh (0, 2, 6) bits are turned on. All others remain as they were. Note that the bits to be turned on are enclosed within single quotation marks. It is also possible to store the bits in a field or array element which is then used with the BITON operation.

Bits are turned off using the operation code BITOF, as shown in Figure 11.10. In this example the second, third, and sixth bits (1, 2, 5) are turned off. All others remain as they were.

Bits can be tested using the TESTB operation. Figure 11.11 shows how this is coded. Resulting indicators are turned on based on the condition of the bits in the field BYTFLD.

If the bits to be tested are all off, the indicator in columns 54–55 is turned on. If the bits to be tested are mixed (some are on and some are off), the indicator in columns 56–57 is turned on. If the bits to be tested are all on, the indicator in columns 58–59 is turned on.

FIGURE 11.10 BITOF Operation

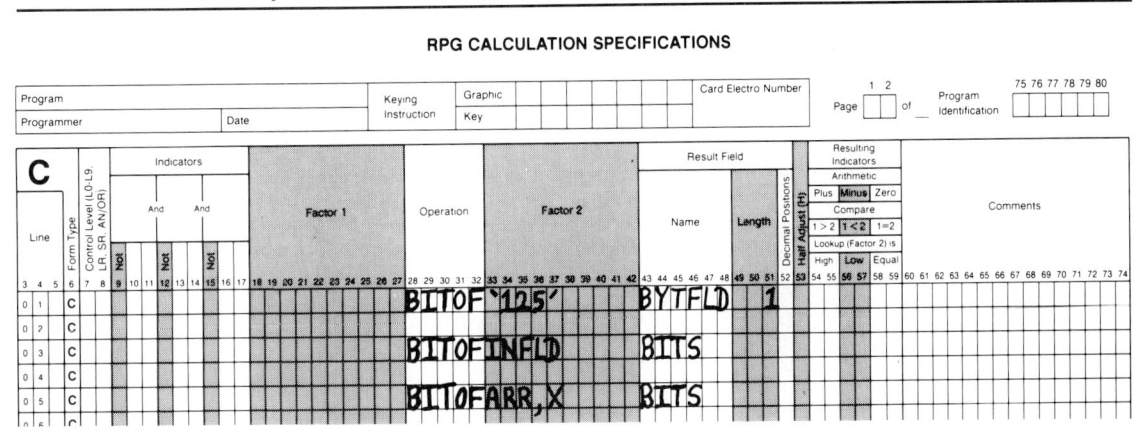

RPG CALCULATION SPECIFICATIONS

Line	Factor 1	Operation	Factor 2	Result Field	Length
01		BITOF	'125'	BYTFLD	1
02					
03		BITOF	INFLD	BITS	
04					
05		BITOF	ARR,X	BITS	

FIGURE 11.11 TESTB Operation

[RPG Calculation Specifications form showing:]
Line 01: C TESTB '125' BYTFLD 202122

SPECIAL INDICATORS ■

Halt Indicators

When an error occurs in a program, it is sometimes helpful if the program comes to a halt and lets the operator know what is wrong. This is possible in RPG with the use of halt indicators (H1–H9). Figure 11.12 shows the coding for a halt indicator.

Halt indicators were useful when punched cards were the standard input medium and computer operators were entrusted with the responsibility for the integrity of the data, but they should generally be avoided today. Operators should not be responsible for correcting data errors. There are methods by which the programmer can prevent errors (editing incoming data, for example) or by which a report can direct the user to take corrective action. So, even though halt indicators are still valid in RPG, the programmer should use them only in unusual circumstances.

External Switches

Processing can be controlled in RPG by using switches which are turned on or off externally (outside the program itself). There are many uses for this capability. For example, a single program may be used to produce a variety of reports having only minor differences. One report might be run daily and would require the heading "Daily Report." A similar report might be run at the end of the week and would need the heading "Weekly Report."

Rather than write two separate programs, it is much more practical to write one program and control the different headings with the use of external switches. These switches are sent to the program from the command language outside the program. The condition of these switches is then interpreted by the program to determine which heading to print on the report.

FIGURE 11.12 Halt Indicator

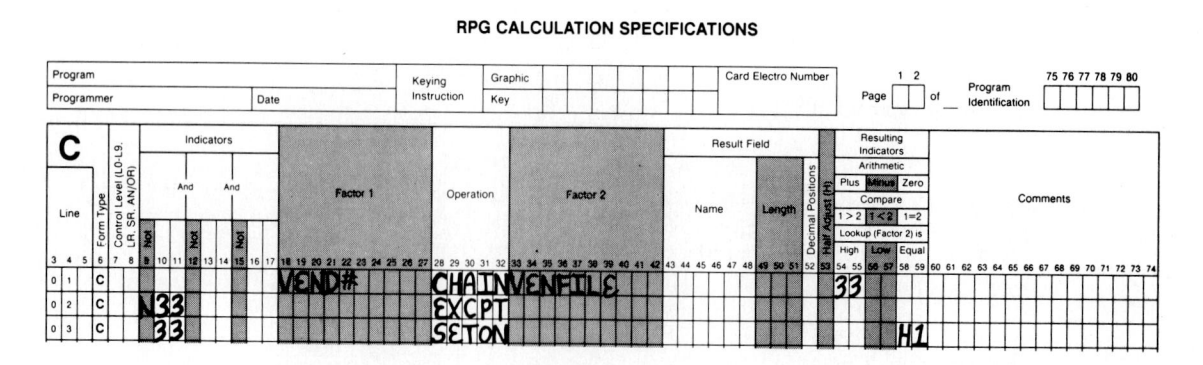

[RPG Calculation Specifications form showing:]
Line 01: C   VEND#   CHAIN VENFILE   33
Line 02: C N33   EXCPT
Line 03: C   33   SETON   H1

To make use of the external switch technique, the RPG coding to handle the external switches from inside the program needs to be discussed. Also, we will discuss command languages, but only generally and briefly since they differ from one machine to another.

RPG Coding for External Switches

The internal coding for using switches works in the same way as the coding for indicators already presented. There are eight switches available, designated U1–U8; in fact, a switch is similar to the byte used in the BITON/BITOF function. RPG designates a set of eight bits (a byte) as a place to keep some switches. These switches are all set *outside* the RPG program. The RPG program then has the option of using them or ignoring them.

External switches may be used in both the Calculation and the Output Specifications as any other indicator might be used to condition an activity in the program. In the example for controlling the headings on a report, the switches are used as shown in Figure 11.13. The headings are controlled by switch 1. Only one heading can print for any one report. In this program, the seven other switches are ignored. If U1 is on, the first heading will print. If U1 is off, the second heading will print.

More than one external switch can be used in a program. It is possible to use combinations of several switches together to achieve some desired result. The examples in Figures 11.14(a) and 11.14(b) show some combinations of switches which might be used in a program.

FIGURE 11.13 External Switches on Output Specifications

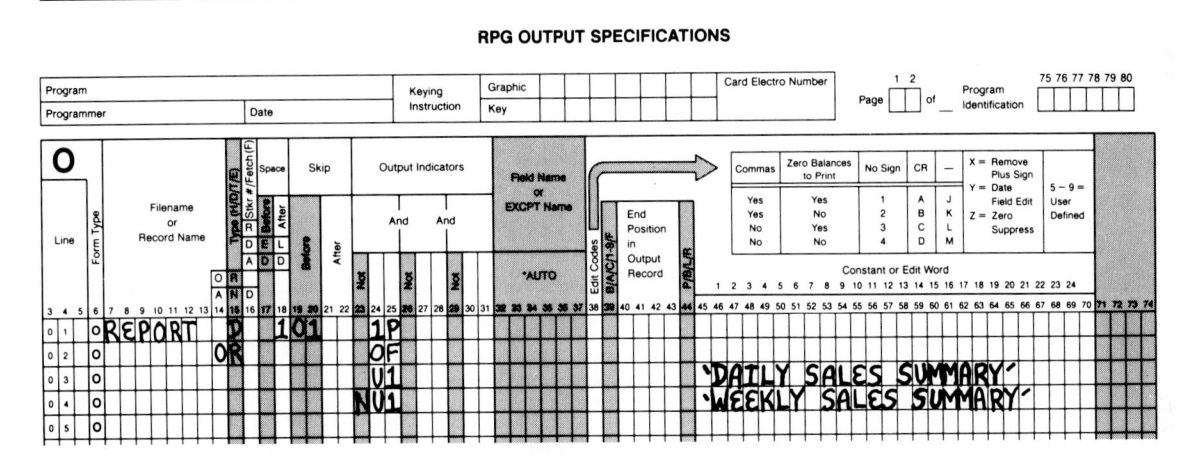

[RPG Output Specifications form showing:]
- Line 01: O REPORT D 101 1P
- Line 02: O OR OF
- Line 03: O U1 'DAILY SALES SUMMARY'
- Line 04: O NU1 'WEEKLY SALES SUMMARY'
- Line 05: O

FIGURE 11.14(a) Combinations of Switches: Calculation Specifications

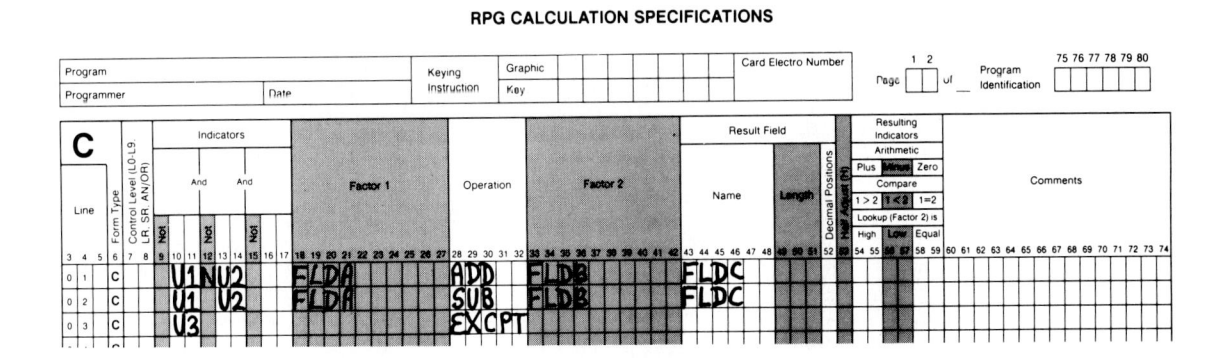

[RPG Calculation Specifications form showing:]
- Line 01: C U1NU2 FLDA ADD FLDB FLDC
- Line 02: C U1 U2 FLDA SUB FLDB FLDC
- Line 03: C U3 EXCPT

Chapter 11 Additional Subjects

FIGURE 11.14(b) Combinations of Switches: Output Specifications

External switches are used for one further function for which normal indicators cannot be used. An external switch can be used in the File Description Specifications to select files. If one of two files is used, it is not necessary to write two programs. When a switch is entered in columns 71–72 of the File Description Specifications, that file will be used only when that switch is on. Figure 11.15 shows an example of this.

Command Language for External Switches

Command languages cannot be explained in depth, since they vary with the type of computer. Examples of the format for entering an external switch in the command procedure are given in Figure 11.16. Notice that in every instance, there is a set of eight bits. Each bit may be set to 1 or 0 to indicate that a switch is set on or off. The exact format(s) for these switch commands should be obtained from the appropriate computer manuals.

FIGURE 11.15 External Switches on File Description Specifications

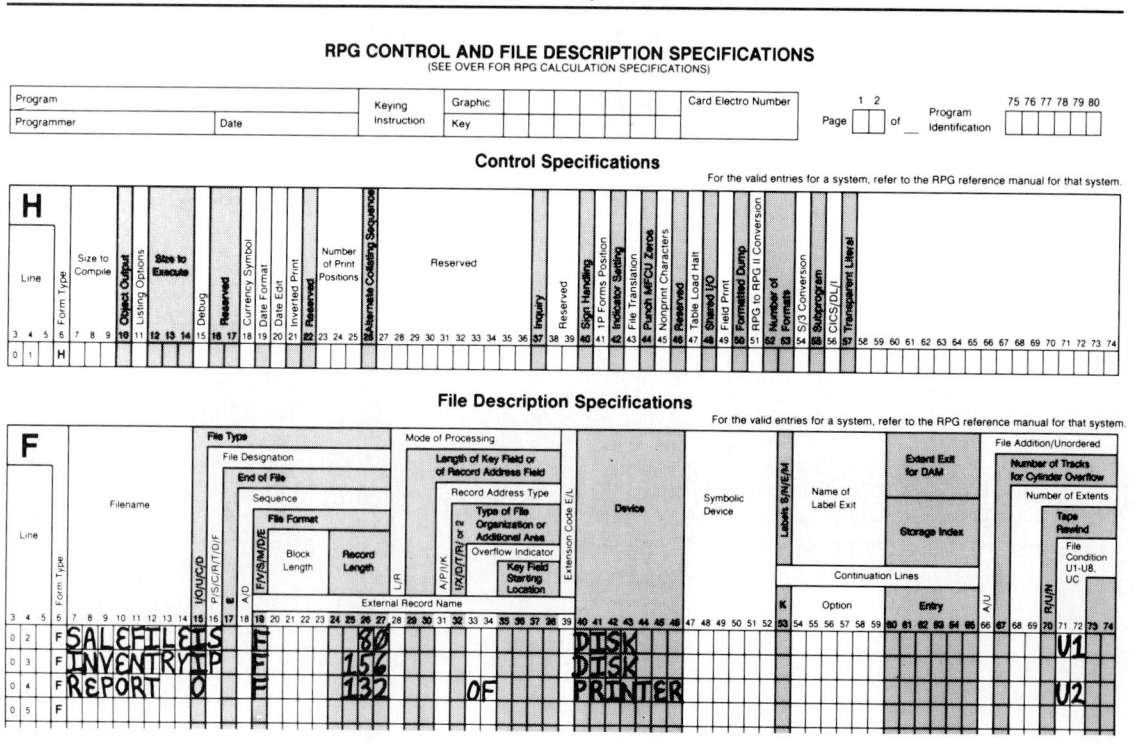

278 RPG: A Programming Language for Today

FIGURE 11.16 Formats for Entering an External Switch in the Command Procedure

```
// UPSI 1                  IBM 370 DOS          (switch 1 is on)

// SWITCH 11000000         IBM S/36             (switches 1 & 2 are on)

CHGJOB SWS(00000000)       IBM S/38 & AS/400    (all switches are off)

!USWITCH:  U1=ON,U8=OFF    HP-3000              (switch 1 is on & switch 8
                                                 is being set off)
```

INDICATORS—A REVIEW ■

Many types of indicators have been discussed in previous chapters. The following section is a review of all the types of indicators used in RPG with their common or required usage.

Record Identification Indicators

Record identification indicators are used on the Input Specifications to identify input files. Indicators within the range 01–10 are ordinarily used, although any indicator within the range 01–99 is permissible. Indicator 99 is often used as a catch-all indicator to trap erroneous input data.

Field Record Relationship Indicators

Field record relationship indicators are used on the Input Specifications to identify fields that are related to a particular record. Indicators within the range 11–19 are ordinarily used, although any indicator within the range 01–99 is permissible. These are seldom used today, but the student may encounter them in an old program.

Resulting Indicators

Resulting indicators are produced as the result of a calculation operation in the Calculation Specifications. Although any indicator within the range 01–99 is valid, the indicators 20–99 are customarily used. The range 91–99 is usually reserved for error conditions.

Overflow Indicators

Overflow indicators are specified on the File Description Specifications for print files. These indicators can control the printing of heading lines and overflow pages on reports. Indicators OA–OF and OV are valid indicators for this purpose.

Level Break Indicators

Level break indicators are used to represent the times at which a level break is to be taken in the program. These are used in the Calculation and Output Specifications. Indicators L1–L9 are used for this function.

Matching Record Indicators

M1–M9 are used to relate fields for comparison of the controlling fields on the Input Specifications. When a match is found, the MR indicator is turned on. This indicator can be used on the Calculation and Output Specifications to control an update or reporting operation.

Last Record Indicator

The last record indicator (LR) is used to indicate to RPG that the last record in a file has been read and processed.

Halt Indicators

Halt indicators are still available in RPG, although they are not as useful today as in the past. Indicators H1–H9 are used to cause a program to come to a halt.

External Indicators (Switches)

External indicators or switches are passed to an RPG program from the command language of a computer. The condition of the switch can then be analyzed to control the functions within the program. U1–U8 are available within RPG for use as external switches.

Even More Indicators

If it should happen that all of these indicators have been used up in a program and more are needed, the programmer can manufacture additional indicators by using the BITON, BITOF, and TESTB operations. This capacity provides an almost unlimited supply of indicators to be used in any desired combination to control the functions of the program.

EXTERNAL SUBROUTINES ■

It is often useful to have the ability in an RPG program to use routines that have already been written. One example of routines that might be used in many programs is date routines. Many programs need to convert a calendar date (MMDDYY) to a date in the format YYDDD where YY represents the year and DDD represents the day of the year (1–365 or 1–366). It may also be necessary to convert that date back to a calendar date after calculations have been made. Such a routine need not be re-created for each program.

The EXIT operation makes it possible to write the routine only once and then retrieve it for use in several RPG programs. This routine may be written in RPG or in any language of an equal or lower level (such as COBOL or Assembler). Figure 11.17 shows the relationship between programs that call a subroutine.

FIGURE 11.17 Relationship Between Programs Calling an External Subroutine

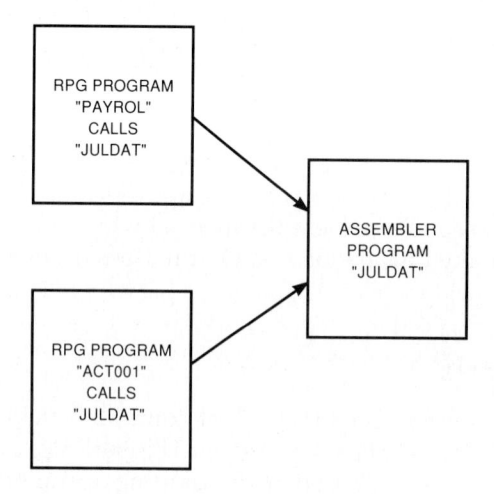

```
┌──────────────┐
│ RPG PROGRAM  │
│  "PAYROL"    │
│   CALLS      │
│  "JULDAT"    │
└──────────────┘ ──────┐
                       │    ┌──────────────┐
                       │    │  ASSEMBLER   │
                       ├───▶│   PROGRAM    │
                       │    │  "JULDAT"    │
                       │    └──────────────┘
┌──────────────┐       │
│ RPG PROGRAM  │       │
│  "ACT001"    │ ──────┘
│   CALLS      │
│  "JULDAT"    │
└──────────────┘
```

To use an external subroutine, the calling program (RPG in this example) must exit from the program to the subroutine. This means that control is transferred to the subroutine. After the subroutine has been executed, control is transferred back to the original program and processing continues from the point at which the exit took place. It is usually necessary to pass some information from the calling program to the called subroutine. After the subroutine has been completed, it is often necessary to pass some results back to the calling program. The instructions for this operation are the EXIT, the RLABL, and the ULABL. Figure 11.18 shows the coding for retrieving a prewritten external subroutine.

The EXIT operation must specify in factor 2 the name of the subroutine to be called. The RLABL operation contains the data which is being sent to the subroutine and must immediately follow the EXIT. The result field of the RLABL (columns 43–48) contains the name of the field which is to be sent. More than one RLABL entry may accompany an EXIT. It is possible to send several fields to the subroutine.

The ULABL operation must immediately follow any RLABL instructions. The ULABL instruction contains any data which is being returned from the subroutine. Some computers (such as the Hewlett-Packard) do not recognize the ULABL operation. For these computers, the returned fields are defined as additional RLABL lines.

Figure 11.19 shows how fields may be sent and returned using EXIT, RLABL, and ULABL. In this example, CALDAT is the name of the field to be sent. CALDAT has been defined earlier in the program and contains some date information. The result field for the ULABL contains the field name JULIAN. This is the name of the field containing the results of the processing that occurred in the subroutine. This field needs to be defined in the RPG calling program since it is a new field. We have defined it as a five-position numeric field. Several fields may be similarly defined to be returned from the subroutine. These additional ULABL instructions would follow the first.

Some computers use the instruction PARM instead of the RLABL and ULABL. More about this will be presented in Section II.

FIGURE 11.18 Retrieving an External Subroutine

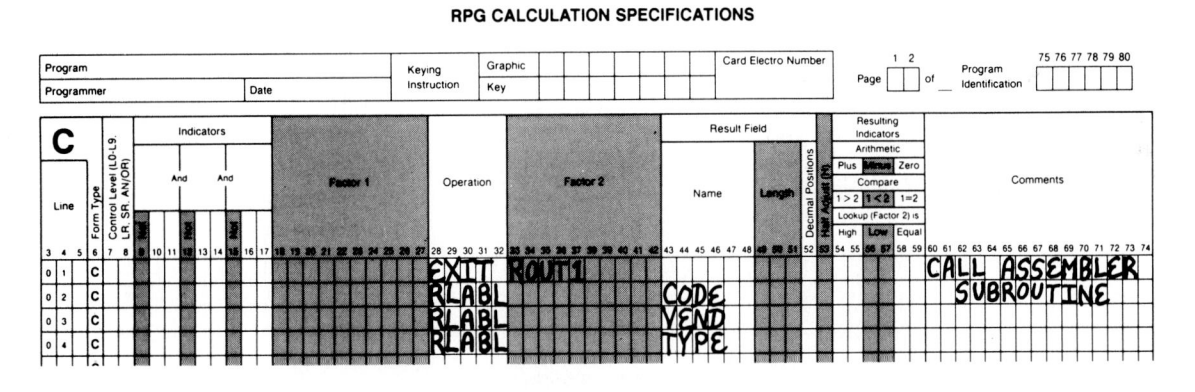

Line	Operation	Factor 2	Result Field	Comments
01	EXIT	ROUT1		CALL ASSEMBLER
02	RLABL		CODE	SUBROUTINE
03	RLABL		VEND	
04	RLABL		TYPE	

FIGURE 11.19 EXIT, RLABL, and ULABL Operations

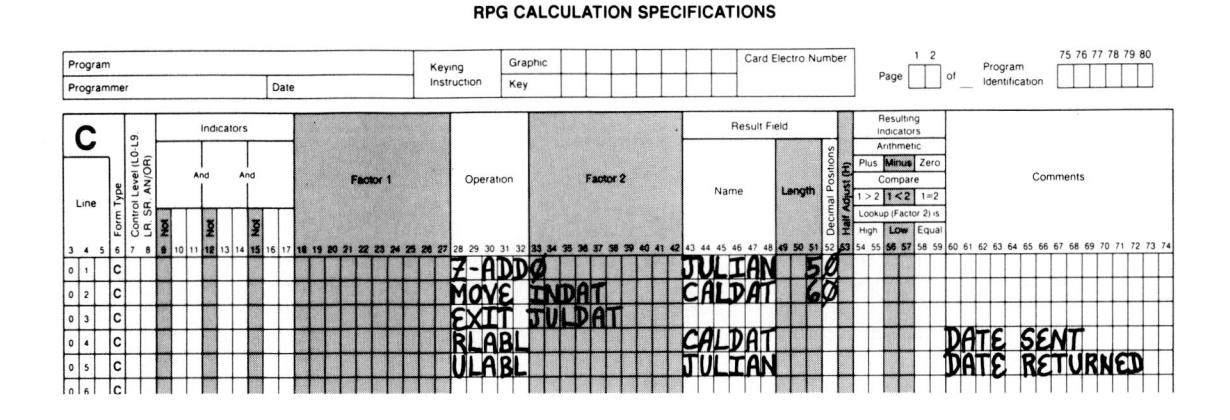

Line	Operation	Factor 2	Result Field	Length	Comments
01	Z-ADD	0	JULIAN	50	
02	MOVE	INDAT	CALDAT	60	
03	EXIT	JULDAT			
04	RLABL		CALDAT		DATE SENT
05	ULABL		JULIAN		DATE RETURNED
06					

Chapter 11 Additional Subjects   281

LOOK-AHEAD FEATURE ■

Although it is seldom used today, the look-ahead feature provides an interesting insight into the way in which data is processed on a computer. Within the normal RPG program, a record is read and processed, and the results of the process will cause some action to be taken. Sometimes, however, the programmer would like to be able to take a peek at the next record before deciding what to do with the record being processed. RPG provides this capability with the use of the look-ahead feature. Look-ahead allows the computer to look at information in the next record to be processed.

Look-ahead fields are defined on the Input Specifications as shown in Figure 11.20. After the input file has been defined, an entry is made that contains asterisks in positions 19–20. This is followed by the name of the field or fields that will be interrogated on a look-ahead basis.

Note that the field containing the SKU number is defined twice, first as a normal field (called SKU#) within the record and again (called SKUNXT) below the line designated with the two asterisks in the record identifying indicator. Fields designated as look-ahead fields cannot be altered within the program. They can, however, be compared to other fields to determine their content. Further action in the program can then continue based on the results of that comparison.

Figures 11.21(a) and 11.21(b) show the coding to demonstrate a possible use for look-ahead. In this program, the field containing the SKU number is examined to determine whether it is the last record in a group. When it is the last record of a group, a special code will be added into the field SPEC in the new file being created.

FIGURE 11.20 Look-Ahead Fields: Input Specifications

FIGURE 11.21(a) Look-Ahead Program: Calculation Specifications

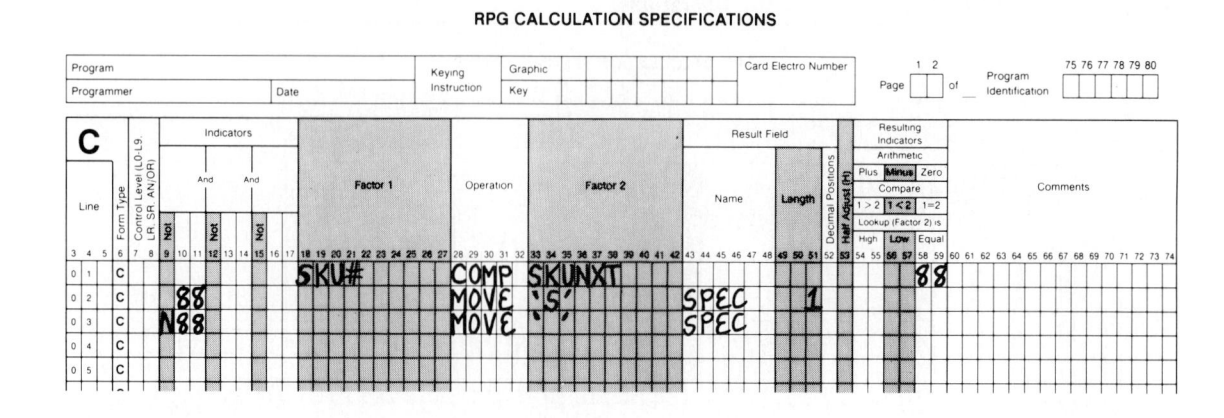

282   *RPG: A Programming Language for Today*

FIGURE 11.21(b) Look-Ahead Program: Output Specifications

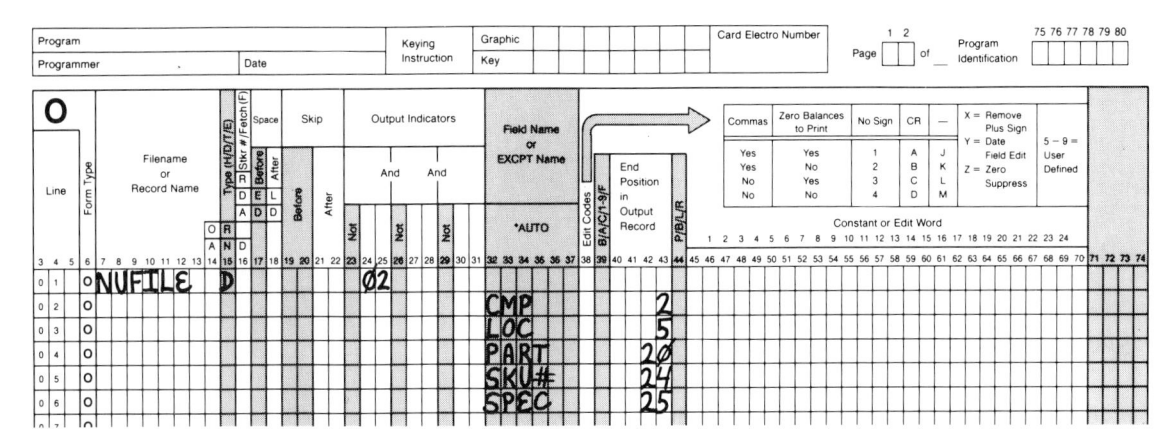

FORCE OPERATION ■

Within the RPG cycle, records are read sequentially, one after another. When multiple sequential files are processed, RPG will read the primary file first and then the secondary or secondaries. When there are multiple files, the programmer may sometimes wish to take control over the file read sequence.

The FORCE operation allows the programmer to determine which file will be read next. Figure 11.22 shows the coding for a FORCE operation.

The name of the file to be read is entered in factor 2 of the Calculation Specifications. The FORCE operation can be used with a look-ahead function to determine which input record should be processed next.

Some rules concerning the FORCE operation follow:

1. The first record processed cannot be forced. The fixed logic controls this.
2. A FORCE can only be used during *detail* calculations, never at total time.
3. A FORCE will control only one cycle—on the next cycle the control returns to the fixed logic cycle.
4. If the file for which the FORCE was issued has already reached the end of the file, normal RPG logic will determine which record will be read.

FIGURE 11.22 FORCE Operation

Chapter 11 Additional Subjects 283

READ OPERATION

It is possible for the programmer to take complete control over the time at which files are read. Although this may appear unnecessary, it is often the best method to use for retrieving the exact record requested, which is useful if multiple sequential files need to be read. It is sometimes a good idea to ensure that the next record read is the one you expected. This control is possible using demand files.

A file is designated as a demand file by entering D in the file designation (column 16) of the File Description Specifications as shown in Figure 11.23.

The file can then be accessed at any time within the Calculation Specifications using the READ operation with the filename entered in factor 2. Some sample coding is shown in Figure 11.24.

DEBUGGING METHODS

When a programmer has a problem with logic (that is, the syntax of the program is correct and the program has compiled, but the results are still not correct), there are times when all the thinking and revising in the world will not provide any insight into what is wrong. A method is needed for looking inside the program to see exactly what is in each field and which indicators are on or off line by line as the program is executing.

FIGURE 11.23 Demand File: File Description Specifications

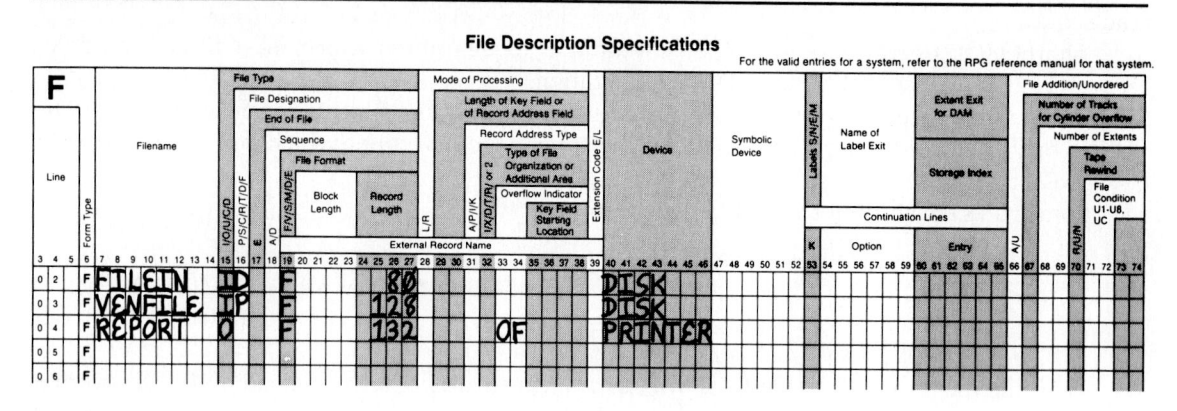

Line	Filename	File Type	File Designation	Length	Mode of Processing	Device
02	FILEIN	ID	F	80		DISK
03	VENFILE	IP	F	128		DISK
04	REPORT	O	F	132	OF	PRINTER
05						
06						

FIGURE 11.24 Accessing a Demand File with READ Operation

Line	Indicators	Factor 1	Operation	Factor 2	Result Field	Resulting Indicators	Comments
01			SETOF			65 88	
02		AGAIN	TAG				
03			READ	FILEIN		88	
04	88		GOTO	ENJOB			
05		VENDOR	COMP	SAVVEN		65	
06	65		GOTO	AGAIN			
07							
08							NORMAL PROCESSING
09							
10							
11		ENJOB	TAG				
12							

This method is called a debug function. To do a debug on a program, a 1 is entered in column 15 of the Control Specifications. This is only a temporary entry until the problem bug has been located. After the problem has been located and resolved, the temporary code is removed and the program recompiled. Next, the programmer must decide which lines of code may be causing the problem and enter the debug operation in the Calculation Specifications at the point in the program where the errors are occurring. Factor 2 should contain the name of the printer file on which the debug statements will print. Figures 11.25(a) and 11.25(b) show the format for this statement. When this statement is executed, all indicators which are found to be on will be printed. The contents of the fields specified by the debug operation can be displayed by entering the name of that field in the result field of the Calculation Specifications.

FIGURE 11.25(a) Format for Debug: Control Specifications

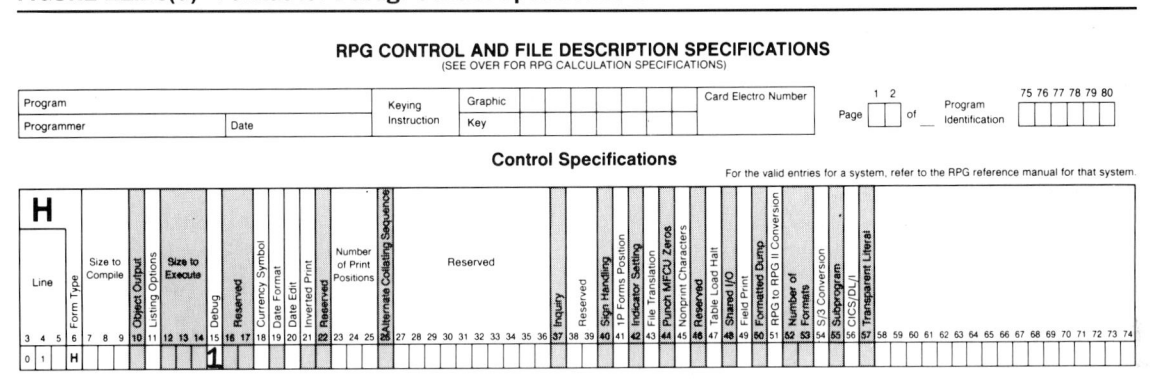

FIGURE 11.25(b) Format for Debug: Calculation Specifications

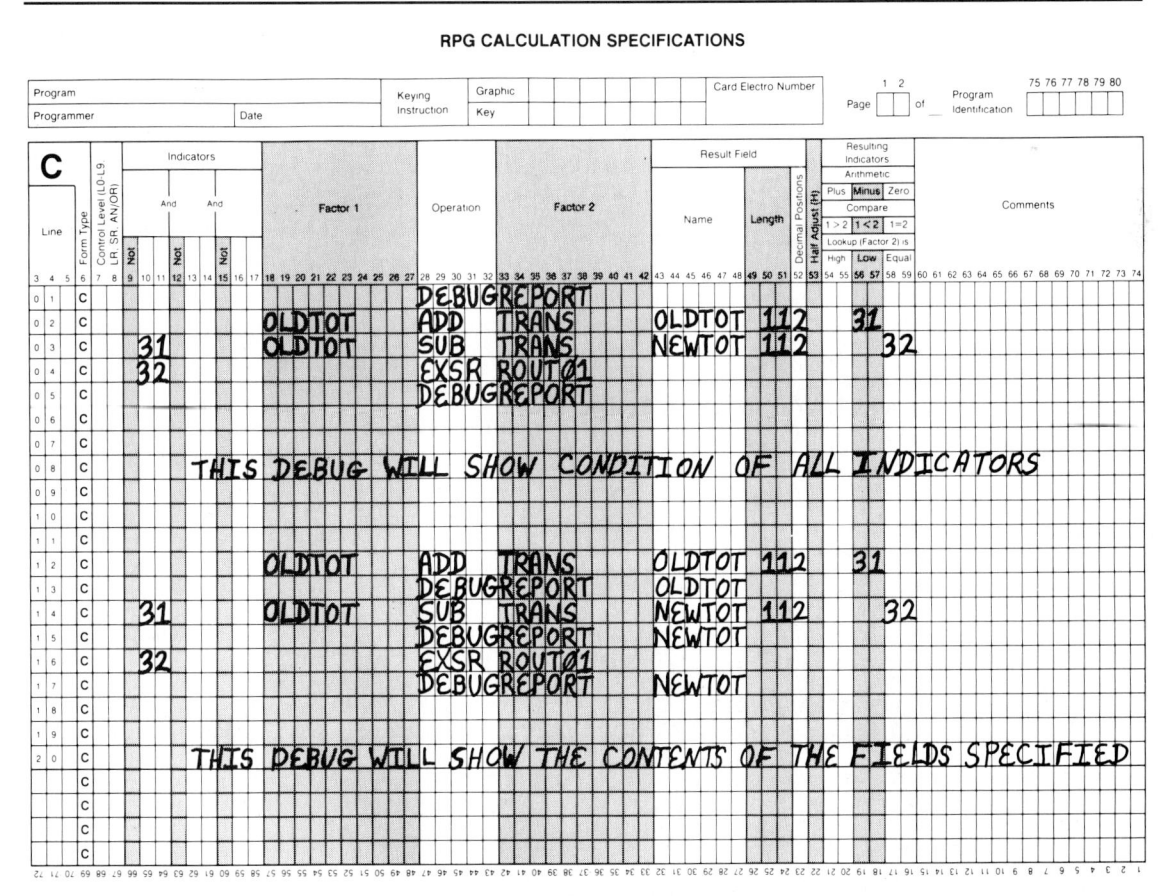

Line	Factor 1	Operation	Factor 2	Result Field Name	Length	Resulting Indicators
01			DEBUG REPORT			
02	OLDTOT	ADD	TRANS	OLDTOT	112	31
03	31 OLDTOT	SUB	TRANS	NEWTOT	112	32
04	32	EXSR	ROUT01			
05			DEBUG REPORT			
06						
07						
08	THIS DEBUG WILL SHOW CONDITION OF ALL INDICATORS					
09						
10						
11						
12	OLDTOT	ADD	TRANS	OLDTOT	112	31
13			DEBUG REPORT	OLDTOT		
14	31 OLDTOT	SUB	TRANS	NEWTOT	112	32
15			DEBUG REPORT	NEWTOT		
16	32	EXSR	ROUT01			
17			DEBUG REPORT	NEWTOT		
18						
19						
20	THIS DEBUG WILL SHOW THE CONTENTS OF THE FIELDS SPECIFIED					

FIGURE 11.26 Debug Statements: Calculation Specifications

```
RPG CALCULATION SPECIFICATIONS
  Line  Form  Control  Indicators     Factor 1    Operation   Factor 2       Result Field        Resulting
        Type  Level    And   And                                          Name      Length       Indicators
  01    C                                LINE47    DEBUG REPORT
  02    C                                AMOUNT    DIV  NUM    AVG         50
  03    C                                AVG       ADD  TOTAVG TOTAVG      60   303132
  04    C                                LINE49    DEBUG REPORT AVG
  05    C              30                LINE50    DEBUG REPORT TOTAVG
```

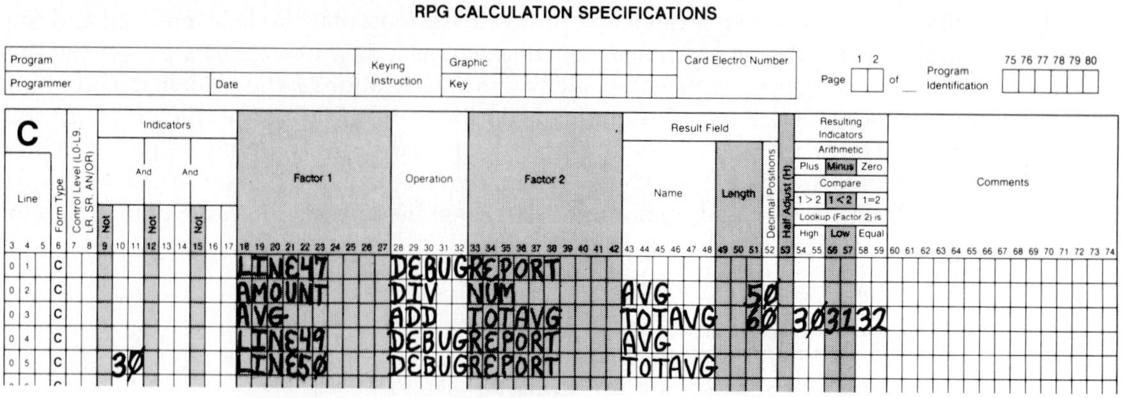

If there are many debug statements in a program, it is useful to identify the line of the program from which the debug results have been obtained. This is done by making an entry in factor 1 of the debug statement. Figure 11.26 shows a variety of debug statements.

It is also acceptable to condition the debug statement with indicators in columns 9–17. When this is done, the debug will occur only when the conditions of the indicators are met.

DSPLY OPERATION ∎

A brief message may be displayed on a system console or workstation with the use of the DSPLY operation. This instruction is not intended to provide the capability for interactive on-line programming. It is used to display a limited message, possibly to a system operator to give instructions or obtain information.

The DSPLY instruction can be used to display an informational message only, or it can display a field, table, or array element allowing that data to be changed.

Factor 1 will contain a literal, or the name of the field, table, or array element that is to be displayed on the screen. This display may be up to 125 characters in length, so a message could be placed in the field before it is displayed. The operation is DSPLY. Factor 2 contains the filename of the device on which the message is to be displayed. Figure 11.27 shows the coding for this display.

Although this coding is valid, there are many computers on which the execution of this operation would result in no message at all. The message would be displayed so rapidly that it would never be seen. To overcome this, it is necessary to force a halt to occur. This allows someone

FIGURE 11.27 Coding for DSPLY: Calculation Specifications

```
RPG CALCULATION SPECIFICATIONS
  01  C    25           MSGFLD    DSPLY SCREEN                    DISPLAY ONLY
```

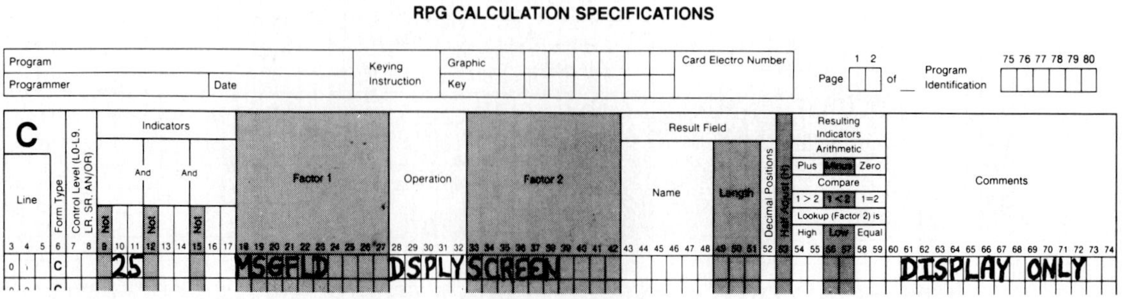

FIGURE 11.28 DSPLY with Halt: Calculation Specifications

Line	Form Type	Control Level	Indicators	Factor 1	Operation	Factor 2	Result Field Name	Length	Decimal Positions	Half Adjust	Resulting Indicators	Comments
01	C			MSGFLD	DSPLY	SCREEN	DATEIN					REQUEST A DATE
02	C											
03	C				DSPLY	SCREEN	WORDS					REQUEST A FIELD
04	C											
05	C	40		ENDOFJOB	DSPLY	SCREEN	HOLD					DISPLAY MESSAGE

time to read it and then press a return key allowing processing to continue. By making an entry in the result field, the DSPLY instruction will be forced to halt. The coding for this is shown in Figure 11.28.

Information may be entered into a displayed field. A typical use for this type of construction might be a field requesting the entry of a date. The message would be displayed (requesting entry of a date), the program would halt, an operator would enter a date, and program execution would resume using the new date.

Indicators are optional in columns 9–17. No indicators are allowed in the resulting indicator fields. Some computers do not accommodate the use of the DSPLY instruction since it is better to display messages using modern techniques. These will be discussed in future chapters.

ACCESSING MULTIPLE INDEXED FILES ■

In earlier chapters we discussed how indexed files are used. In today's business environment, it is probable that a given program will access as many as 20 indexed files (or even more) to retrieve all the information necessary to produce a report or screen. The method for accessing multiple indexed files does not differ from the methods you have already learned for an individual file.

One of the rules of modern programming is that a piece of data should occur in only one place in computer storage. That means that redundant data should not be repeated in every file in which that information might be needed. An example of a program that accesses multiple files might be an order entry program, which might need information from all of the following files:

Customer Master	(Name and address)
Part Master	(Part description and price)
Warehouse Master	(Quantity on hand & warehouse)
Location Master	(Shelf location of parts available)
Order Backlog Header	(Total order information)
Order Backlog Detail	(Item detail quantity & due dates)
Order Special Instr.	(Special handling instructions)
Shipping Instr. Mast.	(Special shipping instructions)
Packaging Instr. Mast.	(Special packaging instructions)
Order # Control	(Next order number to be assigned)

Although the programming for such a system would be very complex, the method is quite simple. Each file is accessed, one by one, as it is needed. A chain to a file is made, some piece of information is obtained, the file is updated, and the program goes on to the next set of instructions.

This coding is mentioned to make the student aware of the need to access each file, obtain the information, and store it without becoming entangled in data from some other file. It is not a safe assumption that data from a file accessed much earlier is still available after several more files have been interrogated. Other data may have been moved into the fields by some other action in the program. Figures 11.29(a), 11.29(b), and 11.29(c) show a few instructions in a program which accesses multiple files.

FIGURE 11.29(a)   Multiple Chains: File Description Specifications

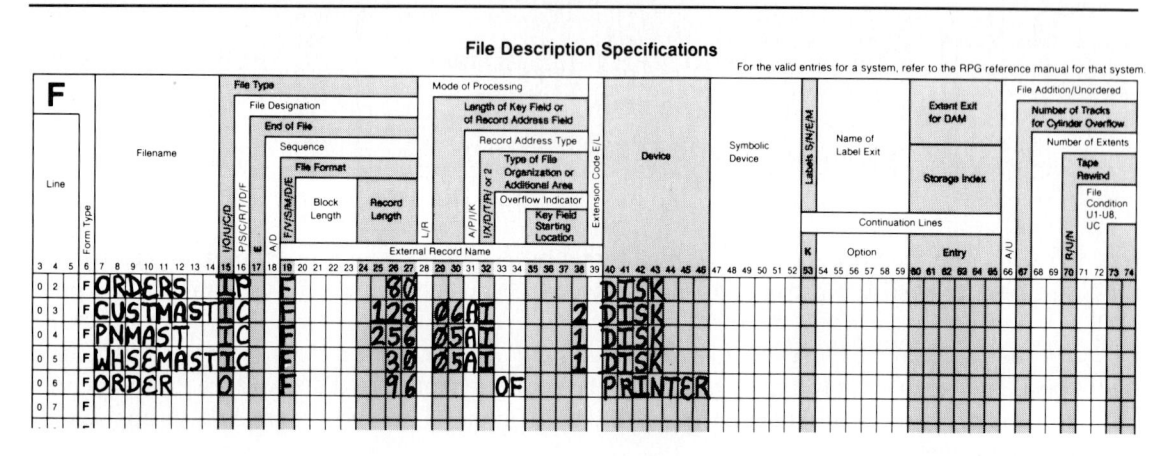

Line	Form Type	Filename	I/O/U/C/D	P/S/C/R/T/D/F	A/O	F/N/S/M/D/E	Block Length	Record Length	L/R	A/P/I/K I/X/D/T/R or 2	Length of Key Field or Record Address Field	External Record Name	Extension Code E/L	Device	Symbolic Device	Labels S/N/E/N	Name of Label Exit	Storage Index	Continuation Lines	Option	Entry	A/U	File Condition U1-U8, UC	R/U/N	Number of Extents	Tape Rewind
02	F	ORDERS	IP			F		80						DISK												
03	F	CUSTMAST	IC			F		128			06AI		2	DISK												
04	F	PNMAST	IC			F		256			05AI		1	DISK												
05	F	WHSEMAST	IC			F		30			05AI		1	DISK												
06	F	ORDER	O			F		96		OF				PRINTER												
07	F																									

FIGURE 11.29(b)   Multiple Chains: Calculation Specifications

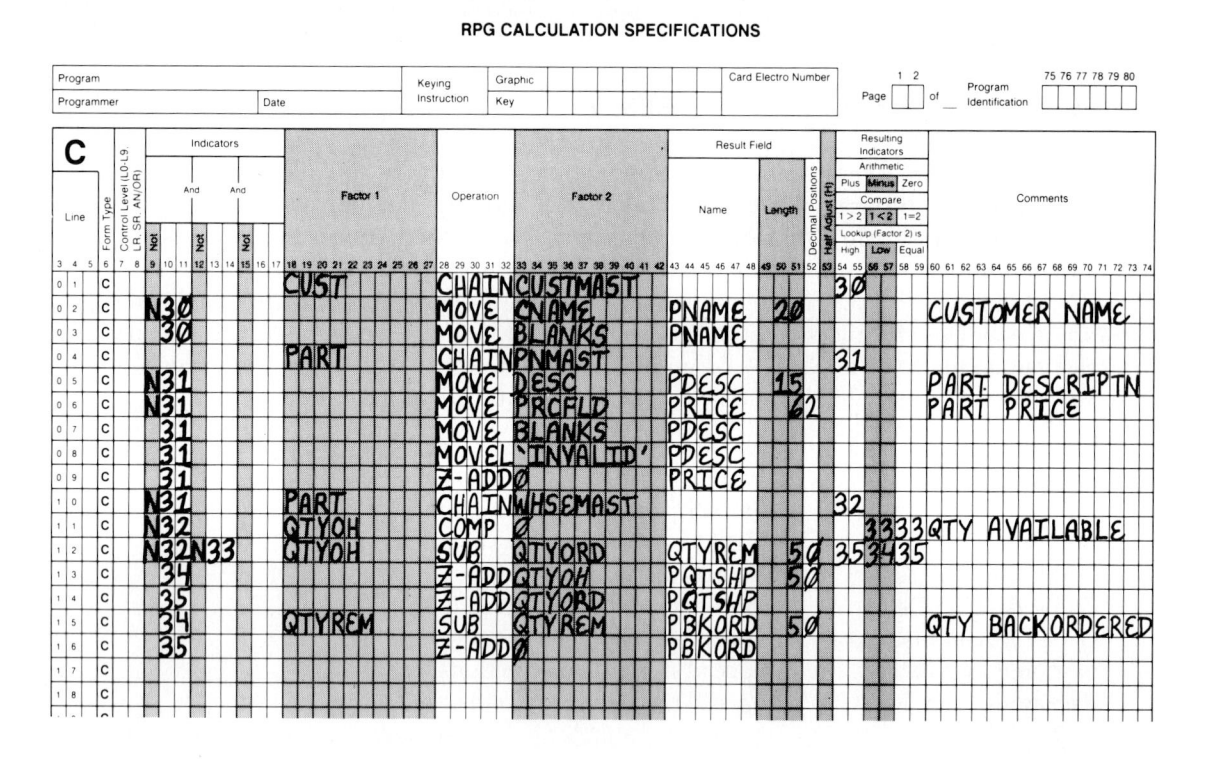

RPG CALCULATION SPECIFICATIONS

Line	Form Type	Control Level (L0-L9, LR, SR, AN/OR)	Not	Indicators And Not	And Not	Factor 1	Operation	Factor 2	Result Field Name	Length	Decimal Positions	Half Adjust (H)	Resulting Indicators Arithmetic Plus/Minus/Zero; Compare 1>2 / 1<2 / 1=2; Lookup High/Low/Equal	Comments
01	C					CUST	CHAIN	CUSTMAST					30	
02	C	N30					MOVE	CNAME	PNAME	20				CUSTOMER NAME
03	C	30					MOVE	BLANKS	PNAME					
04	C					PART	CHAIN	PNMAST					31	
05	C	N31					MOVE	DESC	PDESC	15				PART DESCRIPTN
06	C	N31					MOVE	PRCFLD	PRICE	62				PART PRICE
07	C	31					MOVE	BLANKS	PDESC					
08	C	31					MOVEL	'INVALID'	PDESC					
09	C	31					Z-ADD	0	PRICE					
10	C	N31				PART	CHAIN	WHSEMAST					32	
11	C	N32				QTYOH	COMP	0					33 33	QTY AVAILABLE
12	C	N32N33				QTYOH	SUB	QTYORD	QTYREM	50			35 34 35	
13	C	34					Z-ADD	QTYOH	PQTSHP	50				
14	C	35					Z-ADD	QTYORD	PQTSHP					
15	C	34				QTYREM	SUB	QTYREM	PBKORD	50				QTY BACKORDERED
16	C	35					Z-ADD	0	PBKORD					
17	C													
18	C													

288   *RPG: A Programming Language for Today*

FIGURE 11.29(c) Multiple Chains: Output Specifications

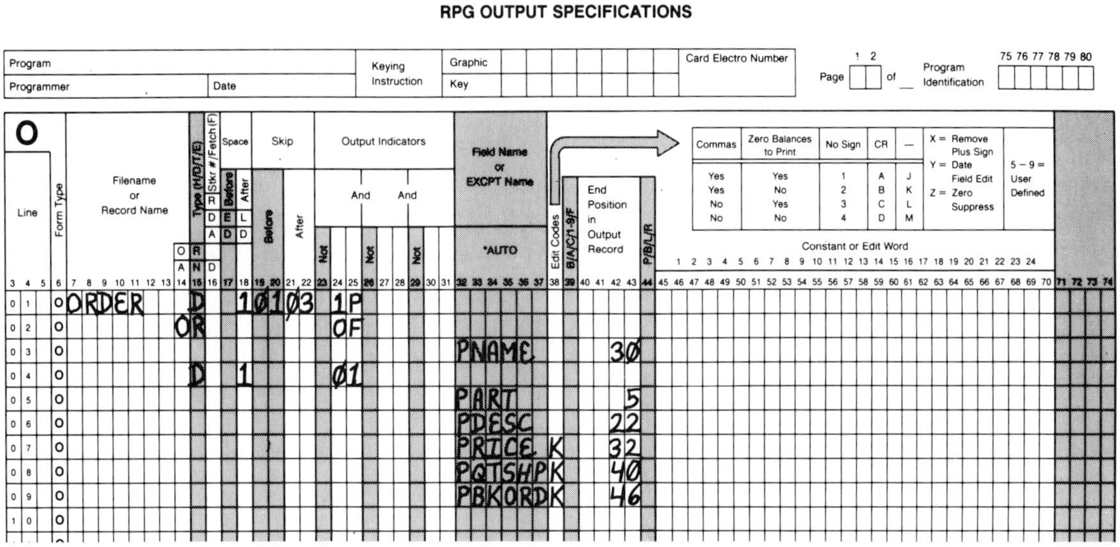

NAMING CONVENTIONS ■

Most data processing endeavors encompass a conglomeration of software packages, in-house programs written by a variety of qualified and unqualified programmers, and system commands with rules of their own. It would be useful if some standardization could be imposed to coordinate the naming conventions among all of these. Although RPG manuals do not mention naming conventions, there are some ideas which might be proposed concerning file and field names. None of these ideas is necessary to write an executable RPG program, but they could contribute much toward making the task easier when attempting to coordinate a group of related systems.

Program and File Names

A program name or a filename should originate when the file or program is created. A program name or filename should begin with some system designation. Possibly the first two characters of the name might designate the system in which it operates. For example, PO could designate a purchase order system; IN might designate an inventory system. Many packages and systems already utilize such designations.

Programs can then be numbered from 001–999. The last position of the six-digit program name for RPG programs is often *R* for RPG, but there is a system that uses this position to identify the type of program, such as *P* for print programs or *U* for update programs.

Files need some identity for master files, such as CUST for the customer master or VEND for the vendor master file. The customer master file might be named ARCUST or ARCUSTMAST to indicate that it is part of the AR (accounts receivable) system and CUST or CUSTMAST to identify it as the customer master.

Transaction or temporary files need to be identified as files that are *not* master files. This can be done by giving them the designation of the program that produced them. This provides a trail to their origins and gives them a unique designation as well. Some packages attach *T* or *FL* to the end of a filename to identify it as a file rather than a program. Thus, a transaction or temporary file produced in program AR010R would be named AR010T or AR010FL.

Chapter 11 Additional Subjects 289

Field Names

Although programmers may be less interested in standardizing field names, there have been many articles written concerning the value of such conventions. If a field name is always the same in every program, it is easier to remember its origin and function. It is also helpful if the first character (or first two characters) of a field agree with the filename. This makes it easier to recognize and less likely to be confused with a similar field from another file. This is especially true in programs that have a large number of files.

SUMMARY ∎

This chapter has provided a wide variety of information about RPG instructions not covered in previous chapters.

You have learned that Line Counter Specifications can control page overflow on reports that are output to devices other than printers. You are now able to process binary data, and to perform such editing functions as move zone, test zone, and test numeric data. Although these are seldom-used functions, there may be times when they are needed.

Indicators were reviewed extensively, and two new ones were added. The external switch is one of the most useful indicators available in any programming language. The halt indicator, though less useful, has been defined since the student may encounter it in old programs.

You have learned that external subroutines can access other programs and routines written in either RPG or languages of a lower level. The look-ahead feature can prove useful to predict the future when processing sequential files, although it is seldom used today. The FORCE and READ operations provide a method for accessing a record which would not otherwise be available at a selected moment in processing using the normal RPG cycle.

You have learned to use a debug tool to discover what the problems are in a program, an absolute necessity for the programmer who works on complex projects. The DSPLY allows a brief message to be sent to the system operator. Although the subject of chaining to files has been covered in earlier chapters, you have learned more about this subject in the context of using multiple files in one program.

Finally, you have learned about naming conventions and standardization, useful concepts which are an important but often neglected part of the RPG programming environment.

REVIEW QUESTIONS

1. When might a Line Counter Specification be useful?
2. How is binary data described on the Input and Output Specifications?
3. How can a sign be reversed in RPG?
4. Explain the use of the BITON, BITOF, and TESTB operations.
5. When should a halt indicator be used?
6. How are external switches turned on or off?
7. How are external switches identified in RPG?
8. What are some uses for external switches?
9. Explain the use of external subroutines.
10. External subroutines are accessed in the Calculation Specifications with the use of the _____ operation followed by one or more _____ .
11. Pieces of data are passed to the external subroutine by means of the _____ .
12. Explain the function of a look-ahead field.
13. Explain the debug function.
14. Explain how a message might be displayed.
15. Explain the benefits of using standardized naming conventions.

DEBUGGING EXERCISES

Instructions

The following RPG programs contain an error or errors. Some of these errors are indicated by the RPG compiler on the program listing. A list of syntax errors is given at the end of the program listing. Other types of errors may occur which will not be shown. These are called logic errors.

Study each program and its syntax errors. Locate each error (including logic errors) and on a separate coding form make the correct entry for the line(s) in error.

Explain each error and how it should be corrected.

```
         100    F* TITLE: DEBUG PROJECT 11-A
         200    F* DATE:    6/9          AUTHOR: D.CABLE
         300    F* DESCRIPTION:           MISCELLANEOUS
         400    F************************************************************

       NAME OF PROGRAM WILL BE PJ011A IN LIBRARY CABLE

                  H
* 1019                      ALL DECIMAL DATA ERRORS IGNORED
         500    FINPUT   IP  F     50              DISK
         600    FREPORT  O   F    132    OF        PRINTER
         700    F************************************************************

         800    IINPUT      AA  01
         900    I                                  1   3 SLSREP
        1000    I                                  4   9 SLDATE
        1100    I                                 10  11 SLSTOR
        1200    I                                 12  16 QTY
        1300    I                                 17  23 SLITM#
        1400    I                                 24  30 UPRC

        1500    C           SLUPRC   MLLZONEWPRC   NEWPRC    82
* 5010                      5010-********

        1600    C                    TESTZNEWPRC                       25
* 5025                               5025-*********.
* 5030                                              5030-******

        1700    C                    TESTN        SLITM#          202122
        1800    C                    BITON*026*
* 5030                                              5030-******

        1900    C                    TESTB*026*   BITS
* 5053                                              5053-******

        2000    OREPORT  H  203      1P
        2100    O        OR          OF
        2200    O                                    6 *PJ011A*
        2300    O                                UDATE Y  50
        2400    O                                   30 *SALES BY SALES REP*
        2500    O        H    2      1P
        2600    O        OR          OF
        2700    O                                   17 *SALES REP*
        2800    O                                   25 *ITEM#*
        2900    O                                   34 *QUANTITY*
        3000    O                                   45 *UNIT PRICE*
        3100    O        D    1      01
```

```
         3200   0                         SLSREP      15
         3300   0                         SLITM#      30
         3400   0                         QTY     Z   35
         3500   0                         UPRC    K   45
* * * * * E N D   O F   S O U R C E * * * * *
```

* 7086   500   RPG PROVIDES BLOCK/UNBLOCK SUPPORT FOR FILE INPUT.

CROSS-REFERENCE LISTING

```
        FILE/RCD    DEV/RCD      REFERENCES (D=DEFINED)

   01   INPUT       DISK         500D  800
   02   REPORT      PRINTER      600D 2000  2500  3100

        FIELD       ATTR         REFERENCES (M=MODIFIED D=DEFINED)

* 7030  BITS        A(4)         1900
        NEWPRC      P(8,2)       1500  1500D 1600
        QTY         P(5,0)       1200D 3400
* 7031  SLDATE      P(6,0)       1000D
        SLITM#      A(7)         1300D 1700  3300
        SLSREP      A(3)          900D 3200
* 7031  SLSTOR      A(2)         1100D
        SLUPRC                   1500
        UDATE       P(6,0)       2300
        UPRC        P(7,2)       1400D 3500
        '026'       LITERAL      1800  1900


        INDICATOR   REFERENCES (M=MODIFIED D=DEFINED)

        LR           500D
        OF           600D 2100  2600
        01           800M 3100
        1P          2000  2500
* 7031  20          1700M
* 7031  25          1600M
```

MESSAGES

```
   MSGID       SEV   NUMBER    TEXT

*  QRG1019     00     1        IGNDECERR(*YES) SPECIFIED ON COMMAND. NO DECIMAL DATA ERRORS
*  QRG5010     20     1        FACTOR 1 ENTRY (POSITIONS 18-27) MUST BE BLANK FOR SPECIFIED
*  QRG5025     20     1        FACTOR 2 ENTRY (POSITIONS 33-42) MUST BE BLANK FOR SPECIFIED
*  QRG5030     30     2        RESULT FIELD NAME (POSITIONS 43-48) MUST BE ENTERED FOR SPEC
                               IGNORED
*  QRG5053     30     1        RESULTING INDICATORS (POSITIONS 54-59) MUST BE ENTERED FOR SI
                               LINE IGNORED
*  QRG7030     30     1        FIELD OR INDICATOR NOT DEFINED.
*  QRG7031     00     4        NAME OR INDICATOR NOT REFERENCED.
*  QRG7066     00     1        RPG WILL HANDLE BLOCKING FUNCTION FOR THE FILE. INFDS CONTEN
                               ARE TRANSFERRED.
```

MESSAGE SUMMARY

```
TOTAL    00    10    20    30    40    50
  12      6     0     2     4     0     0

   35 RECORDS READ FROM SOURCE FILE
   SOURCE RECORDS INCLUDE   30 SPECIFICATIONS,    0 TABLE RECORDS, AND    5 COMMENTS
```

QRG0008 COMPILE TERMINATED. SEVERITY 30 ERRORS FOUND IN PROGRAM

```
* * * * * E N D   O F   C O M P I L A T I O N * * * * *
*  QRG1020             ERROR OCCURRED CREATING OR UPDATING DATA AREA RETURNCODE. COMPIL
```

```
         100  F* TITLE: DEBUG PROJECT 11-B
         200  F* DATE:   6/9         AUTHOR: D.CABLE
         300  F* DESCRIPTION:         MISCELLANEOUS
         400  F***********************************************************

       NAME OF PROGRAM WILL BE PJ011B IN LIBRARY CABLE

             H
* 1019                ALL DECIMAL DATA ERRORS IGNORED
         500  FINPUT   IP  F      50              DISK
         600  FVENDFILEIS  F      20              DISK
         700  FREPORT  O   F     132       OF     PRINTER
         800  F***********************************************************

         900  IINPUT    AA  01
        1000  I                                    1   3 SLSREP
        1100  I                                    4   90SLDATE
        1200  I                                   10  11 SLSTOR
        1300  I                                   12  16 0QTY
        1400  I                                   17  23 SLITM#
        1500  I                                   24  302UPRC
        1600  IVENDFILEBB  02
        1700  I                                    1  10 VND#
        1800  I                                   11  20 VNDNAM

        1900  C                    SETON                        H1
        2000  C   NH1      QTY     ADD  TOTALS    TOTALS   60
        2100  C                    DEBUGREPORT    TOTALS
* 5152                             5152-*****
        2200  C   UO       QTY     MULT UPRC      EPRC     92 33
* 5007        5007-**

        2300  C   33               FORCEVENDFILE
        2400  C                    DEBUGVENDFILE
* 5152                             5152-*****.
* 5020                             5020-********

        2500  OREPORT  H  203      1P U1
        2600  O           OR       OF
        2700  O                                    6 'PJ011B'
        2800  O                            UDATE Y 50
        2900  O                                   30 'VENDOR REPORT'
        3000  O        H    2      1P U1
        3100  O           OR       OF
        3200  O                                   17 'SALES REP'
        3300  O                                   25 'ITEM#'
        3400  O                                   34 'QUANTITY'
        3500  O                                   45 'UNIT PRICE'
        3600  O                                   55 'TOTAL'
        3700  O        D    1      01 U1
        3800  O                            SLSREP  16
        3900  O                            SLITM#  30
        4000  O                            QTY   Z 35
        4100  O                            UPRC  K 45
        4200  O                            EPRC  K 55
* * * * * E N D   O F   S O U R C E * * * * *


* 7086        500  RPG PROVIDES BLOCK/UNBLOCK SUPPORT FOR FILE INPUT.
* 7086        600  RPG PROVIDES BLOCK/UNBLOCK SUPPORT FOR FILE VENDFILE.
```

CROSS-REFERENCE LISTING

```
       FILE/RCD    DEV/RCD     REFERENCES (D=DEFINED)
   01  INPUT       DISK        500D  900
   03  REPORT      PRINTER     700D 2100  2500  3000  3700
   02  VENDFILE    DISK        600D 1600  2300  2400


       FIELD       ATTR        REFERENCES (M=MODIFIED D=DEFINED)
       EPRC        P(9,2)      2200D 4200
       QTY         P(5,0)      1300D 2000  2200  4000
* 7031 SLDATE      P(6,0)      1100D
       SLITM#      A(7)        1400D 3900
       SLSREP      A(3)        1000D 3800
* 7031 SLSTOR      A(2)        1200D
       TOTALS      P(6,0)      2000  2000D 2100M
       UDATE       P(6,0)      2800
       UPRC        P(7,2)      1500D 2200  4100
* 7031 VND#        A(10)       1700D
* 7031 VNDNAM      A(10)       1800D


       INDICATOR   REFERENCES (M=MODIFIED D=DEFINED)
       H1          1900M 2000
       LR          500D
       OF          700D  2600  3100
       U1          2500  3000  3700
       01          900M  3700
* 7031 02          1600M
       1P          2500  3000
       33          2200M 2300
```

MESSAGES

```
  MSGID    SEV  NUMBER  TEXT
* QRG1019  00   1       IGNDECERR(*YES) SPECIFIED ON COMMAND. NO DECIMAL DATA ERRORS
* QRG5007  10   1       CONDITIONING INDICATOR ENTRY (POSITIONS 10-11, 13-14, OR 16-1
* QRG5020  30   1       DEBUG OPERATION (POS 28-32) NOT VALID WITH SPECIFIED FACTOR 2
                        LINE IGNORED.
* QRG5152  00   2       DEBUG OR DUMP USED BUT NOT SPECIFIED IN CONTROL SPEC (1 IN PO
                        CODE NOT GENERATED
* QRG7031  00   5       NAME OR INDICATOR NOT REFERENCED.
* QRG7086  00   2       RPG WILL HANDLE BLOCKING FUNCTION FOR THE FILE. INFDS CONTENT
                        ARE TRANSFERRED.
```

MESSAGE SUMMARY

```
TOTAL  00  10  20  30  40  50
  12   10   1   0   1   0   0
```

42 RECORDS READ FROM SOURCE FILE
SOURCE RECORDS INCLUDE   37 SPECIFICATIONS,   0 TABLE RECORDS, AND   5 COMMENTS

QRG0008 COMPILE TERMINATED. SEVERITY 30 ERRORS FOUND IN PROGRAM

* * * * * E N D O F C O M P I L A T I O N * * * * *
* QRG1020   ERROR OCCURRED CREATING OR UPDATING DATA AREA RETURNCODE. COMPIL

Section II

RPG III/
RPG 400

An Introduction to RPG III/RPG 400

Before beginning an exploration of RPG III and RPG 400, we need to understand what RPG III/400 is, how it differs from RPG II, and why it is an important language today.

Of the many languages available for use in a business environment, few serve as well as RPG III/400. It is the first language expressly developed to make programming easy for *on-line, interactive* applications. Many of the older languages were developed long before the words *on-line* or *interactive* had even been coined. Many recent languages were developed for purposes far removed from the business scene, but RPG III/400, a relative newcomer, is almost exclusively dedicated for use in business reporting.

RPG III emerged with the IBM System/38, in approximately 1979. RPG III/400 is intended for use on mid-range computers, at first with the IBM System/38 and more recently with the AS/400.

THE HARDWARE ■

The IBM System/38 was designed to serve the needs of the mid-range business community. Although most were sold to medium-sized companies, many System/38 computers were purchased by large companies as well to support the workload of their large mainframes. Some large corporations purchased dozens of System/38s and operated them in tandem with a big network.

In 1988, IBM announced the AS/400 to replace their System 34/36/38 lines of computers. The IBM AS/400 operates very much like the System/38. RPG III on an AS/400 (referred to as RPG 400) is almost identical to RPG III on a System/38 with a few added features.

IBM has announced its commitment to the AS/400 line of computers. They plan to continue to upgrade this same mid-range computer and to encompass several other mid-range systems into its architecture in the mid-1990s. This means that the mid-range computer (whatever the name or model number) will be around for many years to come. It also means continuing support for the RPG programming language.

LANGUAGE LOOK-ALIKES ■

With the success of the IBM System/38 and RPG III, software houses quickly recognized the benefits of an improved RPG. They began writing versions of RPG approximating RPG III which would run on computers other than the System/38. These packages offer many of the improved commands of the real RPG III, and they can be used on System/36 or even non-IBM hardware. Although these versions do not offer every capability of RPG III in its native environment, they do provide the benefits of structured programming and some of the new commands which can enhance RPG coding.

STANDARDIZATION (SAA) ■

Beyond all the constraints of hardware, IBM has recently presented a standardization concept to the data processing community called SAA (system application architecture). The idea is not really new. The idea of standardization must have developed as early as the very first computer. Over the years, many independent efforts at standardization have been tried.

The idea behind SAA is that all computers within the IBM community should be able to communicate with all other computers. Giant mainframes should be able to exchange freely with tiny personal computers any data or programs necessary. Programs which can be used on one computer should be executable on another. Keyboards should be standard throughout the entire range of workstations. The list goes on, but the message is clear: standardization and compatibility throughout all IBM hardware and software systems.

FUTURE EXPECTATIONS ■

The future of RPG III/400 within the framework of SAA has not been completely defined. In the early stages RPG was rumored to have been eliminated, but IBM realized that public protest would not allow this. Others claim that RPG will change drastically in form and capability. The mid-range community is betting that RPG III/400 will stay around for a long time in its best form based on its inherent superiority over other available business languages. They are also betting on the demand of the loyal mid-range users whose numbers are quite large and are increasing with every sale of an AS/400.

WHY LEARN RPG III/RPG 400? ■

The following chapters will benefit the mid-range programmer regardless of hardware or system size or configuration. On-line, interactive programs are now the norm, and structured programming concepts have long been accepted as a better programming method. It is time that a programming language to support these concepts can be studied.

Both the System/38 and the AS/400 will accept programs written in RPG II and will process them exactly as they would have been processed on an older machine configuration. To benefit from the enhanced capabilities of the newer hardware technology, however, it is desirable to learn and take advantage of all the RPG III/400 features.

The following chapters will describe in detail programming in RPG III as it is used on an IBM System/38 or AS/400. The programming structures and commands that are covered will also be of interest to the programmer who is using look-alike RPG III software (realizing that the look-alike will contain some limitations).

Chapter 12

Overview of RPG III/400 File Concepts

What you will learn in Chapter 12

Introduction to RPG III/400 File Concepts
Benefits of Externally Defined Files
    Programmer Productivity
    Standardized Naming Conventions
    File Changes Made Easier
    Automatic Documentation
The Data Description Specification (DDS)

Using Externally Defined Files
    File Description Specifications
    Input Specifications
Explanation of Physical/Logical Files
    Physical Files
    Logical Files
    Unique Keys in a File
    Multiple Indexes

File Format Names for Data File Descriptions
File Format Names for Display File Descriptions
File Members
Summary of File Organization
Redefinition of Fields
Data Structures

Before beginning to learn about the RPG III/400 programming language as it is implemented on an IBM System/38 or AS/400, the student should understand some fundamental differences between these computers and all other types of computers. The difference lies in the way the System/38 and AS/400 store and manipulate files on direct access storage devices. Because these computers have a built-in relational-like database management system, data files can be accessed in a program in a completely new way that makes programming in RPG far more efficient.

INTRODUCTION TO RPG III/400 FILE CONCEPTS ■

On a System/38 or AS/400 computer, files are object-oriented—that is, they are stored as objects. This means that a file must be described and created on the system before any programs are written that will use this file. These files are called externally defined files, meaning they are defined outside the RPG program and can be referenced without the need for redefinition within the program. Therefore, programs written in RPG III run on these computers do not require Input Specifications.

    Any file that will be accessed in a program is designed and described to the computer before the program is coded. The programmer uses the command language CPF (control program facility) to create the file before writing the program. This means that an empty file will exist on the system before any data is actually entered into it. The name assigned to the file when it is created on disk is the same name that will be used in the RPG program to reference the file (in the File Description Specifications).

BENEFITS OF EXTERNALLY DEFINED FILES ■

Programmer Productivity

Coding in earlier versions of RPG included the tedious and time-consuming task of entering many lines of Input Specifications, where the field-by-field description of each file was defined. If a file were being updated, a field-by-field description was needed on the Output Specifications as well. Not only were these tasks uninspiring, but they also had to be repeated again and again for every program.

This has been overcome in RPG III/400 with the use of the externally defined file. This means that the file is defined only once (independent of any program); all subsequent programs may access the file from the system in the File Description Specifications. Figure 12.1 shows how this would work.

Besides reducing the amount of coding needed for every program (and therefore the risk of keying errors), there are several other benefits to be gained from the use of externally defined files.

Standardized Naming Conventions

It is often difficult to enforce standards for data definition. If there is a large programming staff, the need for standardization is of even greater importance and becomes increasingly difficult to monitor.

Some of the issues of standardization are as follows:

1. No more than one version of any file or piece of data should exist.
2. The name of a file (or field) should be the same in every program where that file or field is used.
3. The attributes of a field should be defined consistently in every program where that field is used. (Attributes are the length of the field, whether it is alphanumeric or numeric, how many decimal positions it contains, what values it may accept, etc.)
4. When a change is made to the attributes of a field (or file) in one program, the same change should be made consistently in every program.

These issues represent some of the problems which are eliminated with the use of a single definition for each file.

FIGURE 12.1 Steps in File Creation

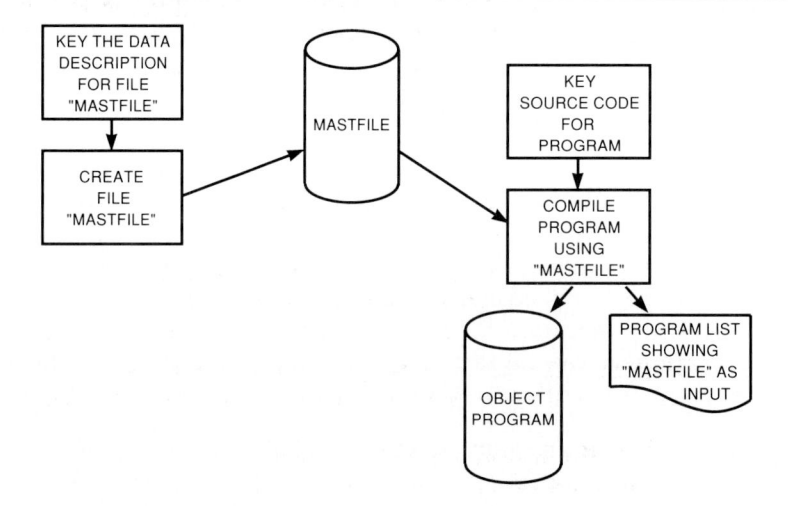

File Changes Made Easier

Another benefit of using externally defined files is the ease with which changes can be made to the structure. When a change needs to be made to a file, it is made in only one place. It is not necessary to make the change to every program which may use that file. Only the file definition needs to be changed and the programs recompiled. Programs that are not affected by the change may continue to run with no change at all.

Automatic Documentation

Everyone recognizes the difficulty of maintaining good, up-to-date documentation of file descriptions. When they exist at all, they may be out-of-date or at least suspect.

With the use of externally defined files, the documentation is self-perpetuating. To see the most recent and accurate version of the file description, the programmer can request a printout of the current data definition for that file on the system.

THE DATA DESCRIPTION SPECIFICATION (DDS) ▪

To describe externally defined files, a new specification is introduced. This form is the Data Description Specifications (DDS) form, shown in Figure 12.2. This specification is not a part of the RPG program but is used to describe the fields and characteristics of a file. The file is created *before* the development of the RPG program. The form type (in column 6) for this form is an *A*. This form is used only for describing the attributes of the records in a file.

The description of the records in an externally defined file is called a record format. The record format is assigned a unique name. The format name and the filename are limited to eight characters. The first line in Figure 12.2 contains the record format name ORD01, and an *R* is entered in column 17 to indicate that this is a record format name.

Lines 2–6 contain the field names, with the length and other attributes for each. Field names are restricted to six positions (conforming to the rules of all RPG programming). Unlike the RPG Input Specifications which specify the beginning and ending positions for each field, these data definitions give only a field length. The sequence of the field names on the form determines the beginning and ending positions of the fields in the file. By specifying length only, it is easier to make changes to the file description.

FIGURE 12.2 Data Description Specifications

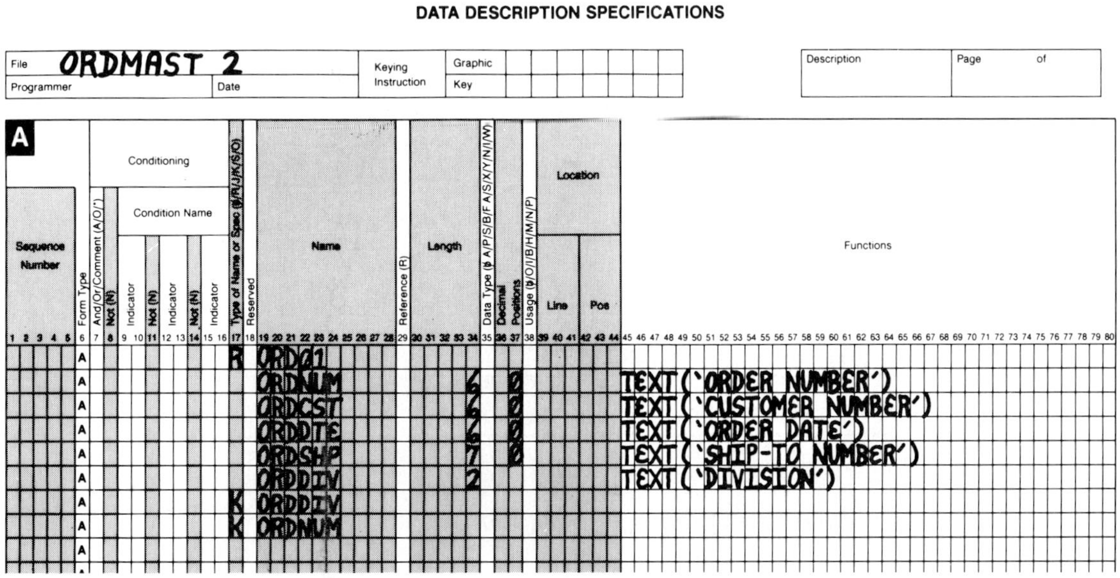
DATA DESCRIPTION SPECIFICATIONS

File ORDMAST 2 | Programmer | Date | Keying Instruction: Graphic, Key | Description | Page of

Form Type (6)	Type of Name (17)	Name (19–28)	Length (30–34)	Decimal Positions (36–37)	Functions (45–80)
A	R	ORD01			
A		ORDNUM	6	0	TEXT('ORDER NUMBER')
A		ORDCST	6	0	TEXT('CUSTOMER NUMBER')
A		ORDDTE	6	0	TEXT('ORDER DATE')
A		ORDSHP	7	0	TEXT('SHIP-TO NUMBER')
A		ORDDIV	2		TEXT('DIVISION')
A	K	ORDDIV			
A	K	ORDNUM			
A					

An entry in the decimal positions (columns 36–37) indicates a numeric field. Comments may be entered in columns 45–80 by using the keyword TEXT followed by the comment enclosed within parentheses and single quotation marks.

Lines 7 and 8 contain information about the key to the file. Although it is not a requirement that a file be keyed or indexed, it is usually advantageous to assign a key so that the file can be updated or printed according to some sequence. Unlike flat files used in RPG II (and many other languages), these database files can have more than one key field, and these fields need not be contiguous fields in the record. The *K* in column 17 indicates that this is a key field. The first key field (ORDDIV) will be the major sequence of the file and the subsequent key field(s) (ORDNUM) will be the minor sequence.

Figure 12.3 shows the Record Layout for the file described on the Data Description Specifications. While the layout is a better tool for visualizing the physical properties of the file, the DDS can be used to obtain all of the same information.

Once the file has been described in a DDS, it can be created as a physical file using a CPF system command. (CPF is the system control language used by the System/38 and the AS/400.) The programmer uses the system command CRTPF on the System/38 or AS/400 to create and name the file. The command CRTPF represents "Create Physical File." Figure 12.4 shows the command for creating a physical file named ORDMAST2:

> The command is CRTPF.
> The filename is ORDMAST2.
> The name of the library on which this file will reside when it is created is DATALIB.
> The name of the file that contains the source code DDS is QDDSSRC.
> The name of the library on which QDDSSRC resides is SRCELIB.
> The name of the member within the DDS was also ORDMAST, so this did not need to be specified. Had the name of the member in QDDSSRC been something different, it would have been entered at the end of the statement (it is usually a good idea to give both the source and the object the same name, however).

A filename of up to ten positions is permitted on the System/38 or AS/400. However, it is wiser to restrict the filename to eight characters or fewer because the RPG File Description Specifications can accommodate no more than eight positions.

An empty file is created and data can be entered into it. The data in the file can then be accessed by any program that requests that file. Figure 12.5 shows the steps that must occur when a file is to be created.

FIGURE 12.3 Record Layout for ORDMAST2

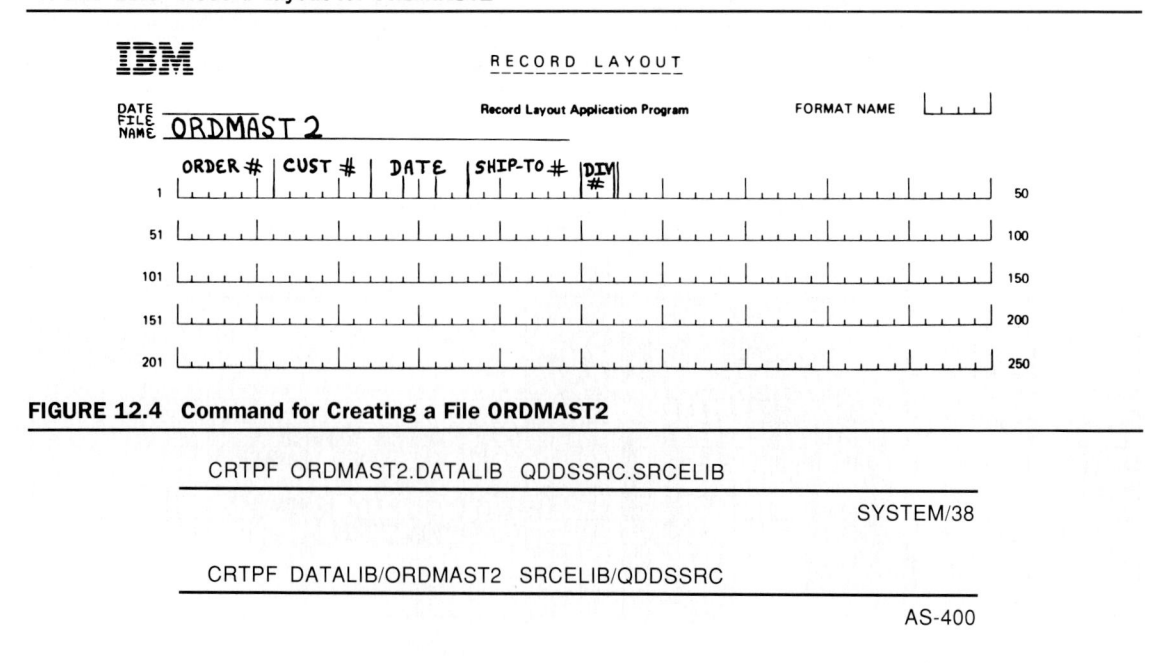

[IBM Record Layout form for ORDMAST2 showing fields: ORDER #, CUST #, DATE, SHIP-TO #, DIV #]

FIGURE 12.4 Command for Creating a File ORDMAST2

```
CRTPF  ORDMAST2.DATALIB  QDDSSRC.SRCELIB
```
SYSTEM/38

```
CRTPF  DATALIB/ORDMAST2  SRCELIB/QDDSSRC
```
AS-400

FIGURE 12.5 Steps in Creating a File

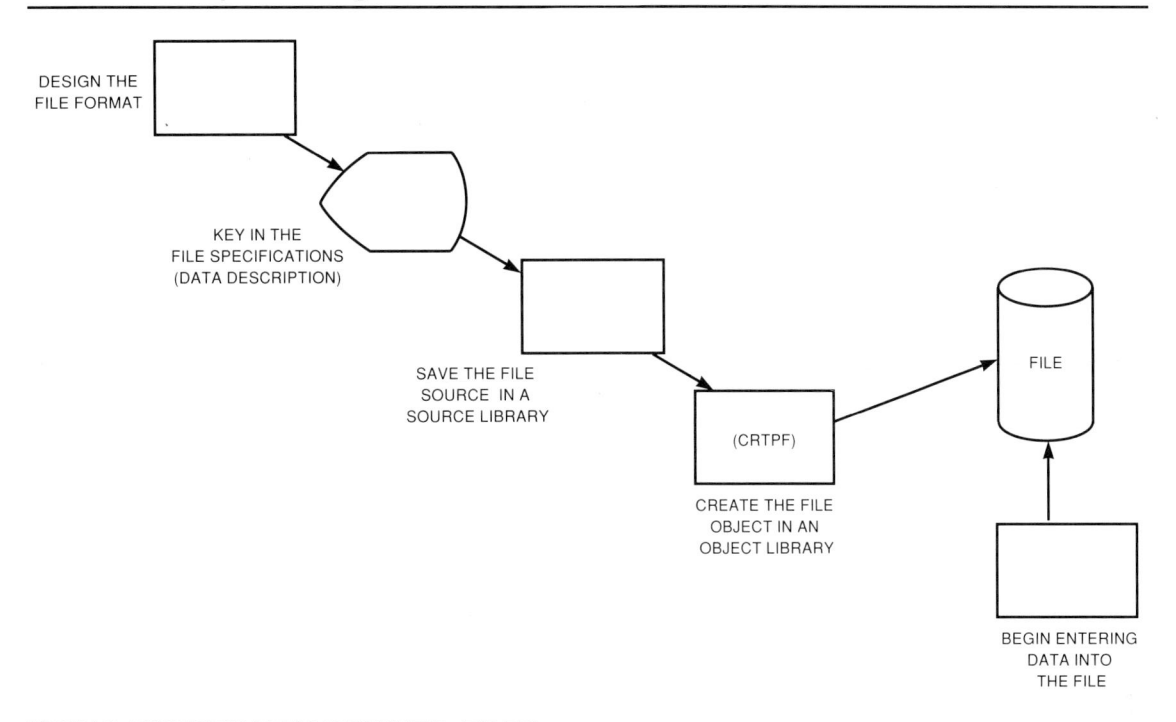

[Flowchart: DESIGN THE FILE FORMAT → KEY IN THE FILE SPECIFICATIONS (DATA DESCRIPTION) → SAVE THE FILE SOURCE IN A SOURCE LIBRARY → (CRTPF) CREATE THE FILE OBJECT IN AN OBJECT LIBRARY → FILE ← BEGIN ENTERING DATA INTO THE FILE]

USING EXTERNALLY DEFINED FILES ■

File Description Specifications

Now that the file has been created, we can begin coding a program using an externally defined file. Figure 12.6 shows the File Description Specifications for a program in which the file is externally described.

The filename must be exactly the same as the filename created with the DDS. This allows the system to find the data definition for the file and provide the information in the program.

This file will be an input primary file, so the IP is entered as in RPG II. Column 19 contains an *E* to indicate that this is an externally defined file. RPG III will accept an *F* in column 19 if the programmer insists on describing the file internally using the Input Specifications, but that would really be using RPG II methods and is unnecessary. When the file is described externally, no entries are needed in columns 20–27—the programmer does not even need to know the length of the file!

If the file is a keyed file, a *K* is entered in column 31, but even this is not required if the sequence of the file is irrelevant to the program. The programmer does not need to look up the documentation to find out what the keys are or worry about making erroneous entries in the columns that describe the keys. The device name is entered in columns 40–46 as always.

FIGURE 12.6 Externally Described File: File Description Specifications

[Form showing: Line 02 F ORDMAST2 IP E K DISK]

Chapter 12 Overview of RPG III/400 File Concepts **305**

FIGURE 12.7 Compiled Program Using an Externally Defined File

```
                  H
* 1019                      ALL DECIMAL DATA ERRORS IGNORED
          500     FORDMAST2IP    E              K          DISK
                  RECORD FORMAT(S):    FILE ORDMAST2 LIB CABLE
                                  EXTERNAL FORMAT ORDER01 RPG NAME ORDER01

          600     FREPORT   O    F        132       OF       PRINTER

A000000           INPUT  FIELDS FOR RECORD ORDER01 FILE ORDMAST2 FORMAT ORDER01
A000001                                                P    1    40ORDNUM
A000002                                                P    5    80ORDCST
A000003                                                P    9   120ORDDTE
A000004                                                P   13   160ORDSHP
A000005                                                    17   180ORDDIV
          700     OREPORT   D   202      1P
          800     O         OR           OF
          900     O                                        5  'ORD#'
         1000     O                                       12  'CUST#'
         1100     O                                       20  'DATE'
         1200     O         D    1       01
         1300     O                            ORDNUM      7
         1400     O                            ORDCST     13
         1500     O                            ORDDTEY    21
* * * * * E N D    O F   S O U R C E * * * * *
```

Input Specifications

There will be no need for *any* Input Specifications. When the program is compiled, the data definition will be retrieved from the DDS and inserted into the program in a format that looks as though it had been keyed into the program. The field names appear exactly as they were specified in the DDS. Beginning and ending positions are shown just as they would appear on a hand-entered Input Specification. Each field has the attributes that were defined in the DDS. Figure 12.7 shows a program that uses an externally defined file as it would be printed on the compiled listing. Notice that the field comments from the DDS appear beside each input field. This is just one more benefit of using an externally defined file description.

Notice also that the compiler assigns a different line numbering system to the externally defined file. The file is numbered A000001, A000002, etc., so you will know it was not keyed as part of the program. If a second file had been included it would have been numbered B000001, B000002, etc. The rest of the program uses these input fields as if they were part of the program.

EXPLANATION OF PHYSICAL/LOGICAL FILES ■

Data files on the System/38 or AS/400 are stored on disk in two different forms. They are stored as either physical files or logical files.

Physical Files

A physical file contains the actual data as it is described in the DDS for that file. If the DDS describes a file having a length of 128 that contains 14 fields, the physical file will contain records of exactly that definition (assuming data has been keyed into the file). It may contain no records or thousands of records. It may have one or several fields defined as key fields. Direct access to the file will usually be made through an access path defined by the keys.

Logical Files

A logical file contains no data. It contains *only* an access path to a physical file. The logical file obtains access to data in a physical file using key fields, which are defined in a DDS for the logical file. Figure 12.8 shows the relationship between a physical file (CUSTMAST) and several logical files.

FIGURE 12.8 Relationship Between Physical and Logical Files

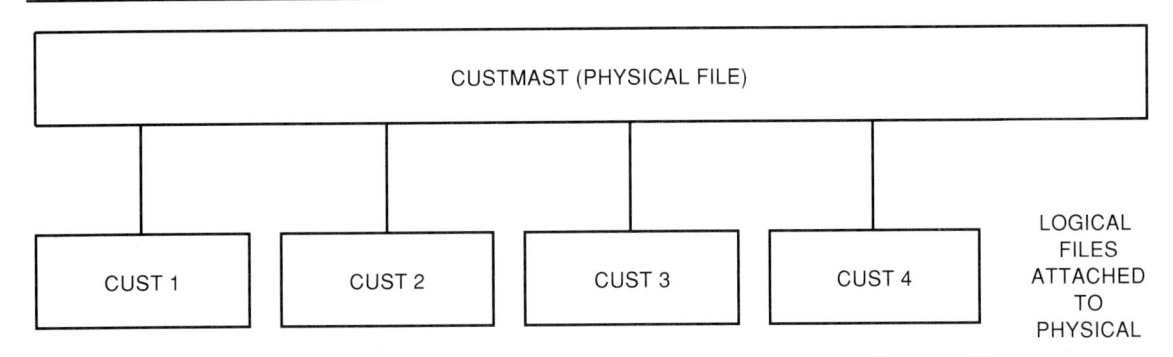

```
┌─────────────────────────────────────────────────────────────┐
│                   CUSTMAST (PHYSICAL FILE)                  │
└─────────────────────────────────────────────────────────────┘
     │             │             │             │
┌─────────┐  ┌─────────┐  ┌─────────┐  ┌─────────┐      LOGICAL
│ CUST 1  │  │ CUST 2  │  │ CUST 3  │  │ CUST 4  │       FILES
└─────────┘  └─────────┘  └─────────┘  └─────────┘     ATTACHED
                                                           TO
                                                        PHYSICAL
```

Some examples may help clarify this. A customer master file (the physical file) would probably be keyed by customer number. Sometimes a list is needed in sequence by customer name. Instead of sorting the file by name and creating a duplicate file from which to print the report, a logical file is created in which customer name is the key. This logical file contains no data of its own. It contains only pointers to the location of records in the physical file. Figure 12.9 shows how a physical file might have several logical files attached, each of which is keyed differently.

It is also possible to create a logical file that combines information from two or more physical files. This logical file will again contain no physical data. It will contain only the pointers (access paths) to the physical files that contain the real data.

Logical files take up very little space on disk and therefore can remain on disk permanently if desired. These logical files may be updated every time a change is made to the data in the physical file. This means improved processing time for a report that might otherwise require a lengthy sort every time it is run. The logical file can always be ready to produce the report quickly and in the proper sequence.

FIGURE 12.9 Logical Files Attached to a Physical File

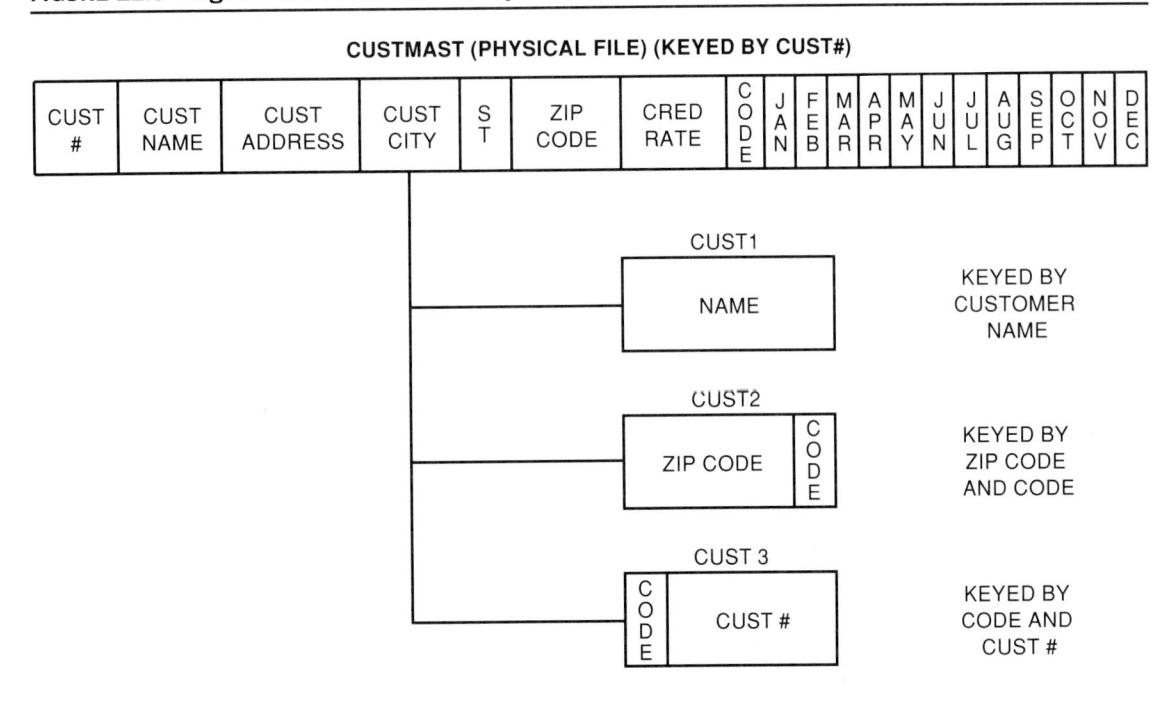

CUSTMAST (PHYSICAL FILE) (KEYED BY CUST#)

CUST #	CUST NAME	CUST ADDRESS	CUST CITY	ST	ZIP CODE	CRED RATE	CODE	JAN	FEB	MAR	APR	MAY	JUN	JUL	AUG	SEP	OCT	NOV	DEC

CUST1

NAME

KEYED BY CUSTOMER NAME

CUST2

ZIP CODE	CODE

KEYED BY ZIP CODE AND CODE

CUST 3

CODE	CUST #

KEYED BY CODE AND CUST #

Chapter 12 Overview of RPG III/400 File Concepts

All these capabilities are optional, to be used at the discretion of the programmer or manager. Each case needs to be evaluated separately to determine which is the best method to solve that particular problem.

Some of the options are as follows:

1. Sort the file, creating another temporary physical file.
2. Create a logical file that resides temporarily on disk and is deleted after the report has been printed.
3. Create a logical file that resides permanently on disk, to which updates are applied only at the time the report is to be printed.
4. Create a logical file that resides permanently on disk and is updated immediately each time an update is made to the physical file.

The time it takes to accomplish either option 1 or option 2 is about the same. Unless there is a good reason for permanently sorting a physical file, it is probably better to choose options 2, 3, or 4. Option 4 will produce the report in the shortest time but may lengthen the time required for updating the physical file on a daily basis.

If a report is run daily or more often, a permanent logical file is a good option. If a report is run very seldom (e.g., once a month, or as needed but seldom needed), a logical file that is updated only when the report is run would be the better option.

Unique Keys in a File

A physical file may have an index that is the key by which the data in the file is updated. Sometimes the physical file is a non-keyed file. In this case, a logical file is built that contains the key by which the file is updated. In either instance, the key field must be unique so that update functions are performed on the precise record to which those updates belong. This is specified in the DDS for the keyed file by using the DDS key word UNIQUE. Figure 12.10 shows the Data Description Specifications for a keyed physical file whose key must be unique.

When UNIQUE is specified in the DDS, a machine halt will occur when an attempt is made to add a record to a file that already contains a record with the same key field (or fields). Duplicate keys are not allowed in such a file.

FIGURE 12.10 Data Description Specifications for a Physical File with a Unique Key

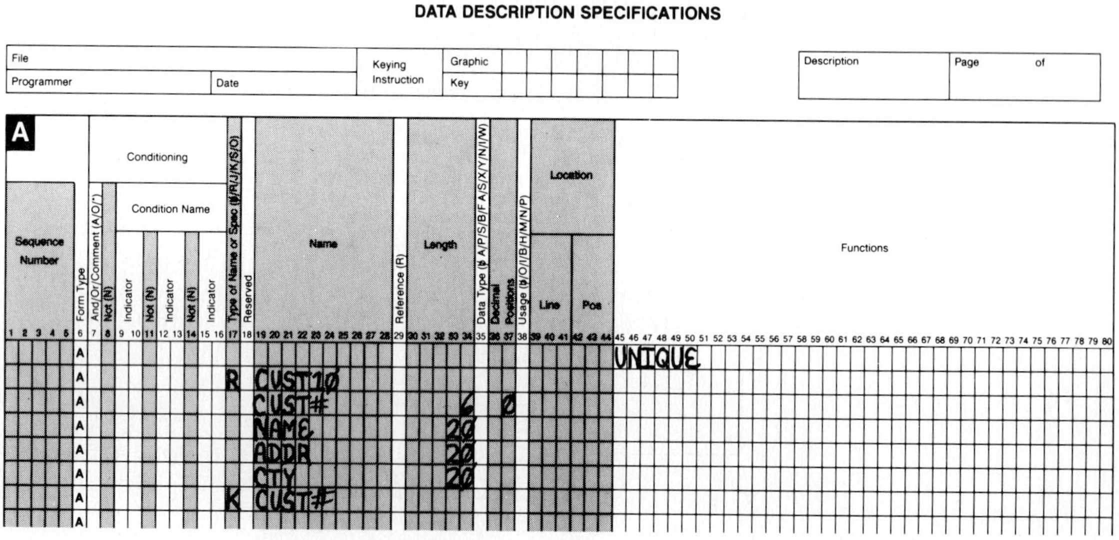

```
     A                                      UNIQUE
     A          R CUST10
     A            CUST#          6  0
     A            NAME          20
     A            ADDR          20
     A            CTY           20
     A          K CUST#
     A
```

FIGURE 12.11 Logical Files Attached to a Physical File

PHYSICAL FILE INVENTORY MASTER (NO-KEY)

D I V	L O C	PART ID#	DESCRIPTIVE PART#	VENDOR #	DESCRIPTION	QTY	PRICE	DEPT	CLASS

LOGICAL FILES KEYED BY:
UNIQUE:
   1. PART ID#
   2. DESCRIPTIVE PART#

NOT UNIQUE:
   1. DIV/LOC/VENDOR
   2. DIV/LOC/DESCRIPTION
   3. DIV/LOC/DEPT/CLASS/PART ID#
   4. DEPT/LOC/DESCRIPTIVE PART#
   5. CLASS/VENDOR
   6. DESCRIPTION

Multiple Indexes

It is often necessary to create a logical file for which there will be duplicate keys. Since this logical file might not be used for updating the physical data, there may be no need to prevent duplicate keys. In fact, a report that will be printed in some given sequence may quite often contain several records with fields that contain the same data. An example of this would be a customer master file keyed uniquely by customer number. Printing a report grouping all identical Zip Codes may require a logical file by Zip Code. This logical file would *not* have UNIQUE specified in its DDS.

Any physical file may need many different indexes with which to present reports or screen formats in a variety of sequences. Figure 12.11 shows some of the logical files that might be attached to a physical file.

Good file management should ensure that no two logical files repeat the same keys, since this is a waste of resources. Careful planning can sometimes provide one logical file format that may satisfy the needs of several programs.

FILE FORMAT NAMES FOR DATA FILE DESCRIPTIONS ■

In the DDS shown in Figure 12.12, a format name of FORM01 is shown. This is the name by which the program will address this file in the Calculation Specifications. A data file may contain only one format. Thus, when accessing a data file, the filename and format name seem to be interchangeable.

The DDS shown in Figure 12.13 is for a logical file that is to be attached to the physical file. Notice that the same format name is used although the filename must be different. Notice also that the key word PFILE is used. This key word is used to identify the physical file to which the logical file will be attached.

Figure 12.14 shows the commands for creating a physical file and its related logical file. In this example, a physical file named CUSTMSTR is being built in a library called MAINLIB. After the physical file has been created, the logical file can be built. It is called CUSTMST2, so it is easily recognizable as a relative of CUSTMSTR. Other related logical files can be given numeric increments, such as CUSTMST3, etc. Other standard naming conventions may be used to simplify work for the programmer. Neither CPF nor RPG have requirements for naming files other than the usual rule that the first position of the filename must be an alphabetic character.

FIGURE 12.12 Data Description Specifications: Format Name "FORM01"

DATA DESCRIPTION SPECIFICATIONS

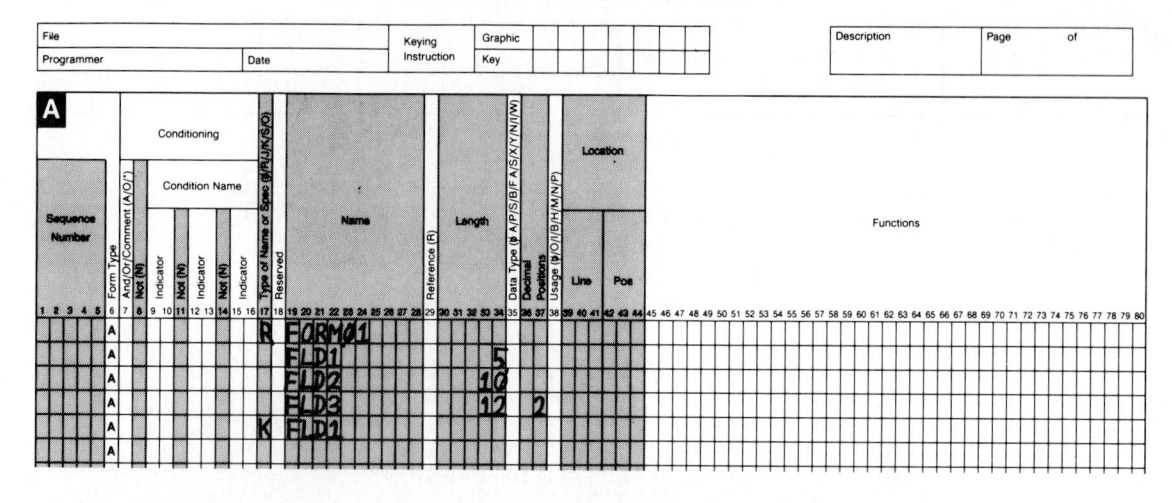

```
A R FORM01
A   FLD1     5
A   FLD2    10
A   FLD3    12  2
A K FLD1
```

FIGURE 12.13 Data Description Specifications: Logical File Showing Same Format Name

DATA DESCRIPTION SPECIFICATIONS

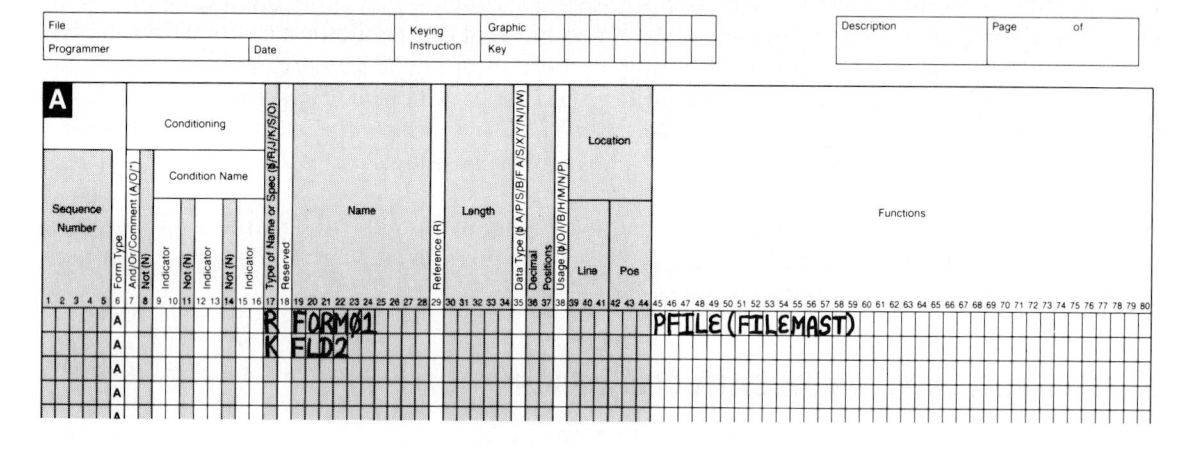

```
A R FORM01                    PFILE(FILEMAST)
A K FLD2
```

FIGURE 12.14 Commands for Creating a Physical File and Its Related Logical File

CRTPF CUSTMSTR.MAINLIB QDDSSRC.QGPL

SYSTEM/38

CRTPF MAINLIB/CUSTMSTR QGPL/QDDSSRC

AS-400

CRTLF CUSTMST2.MAINLIB QDDSSRC.QGPL

SYSTEM/38

CRTLF MAINLIB/CUSTMST2 QGPL/QDDSSRC

AS-400

FIGURE 12.15 Data Description Specifications for Multiple Formats for Screens

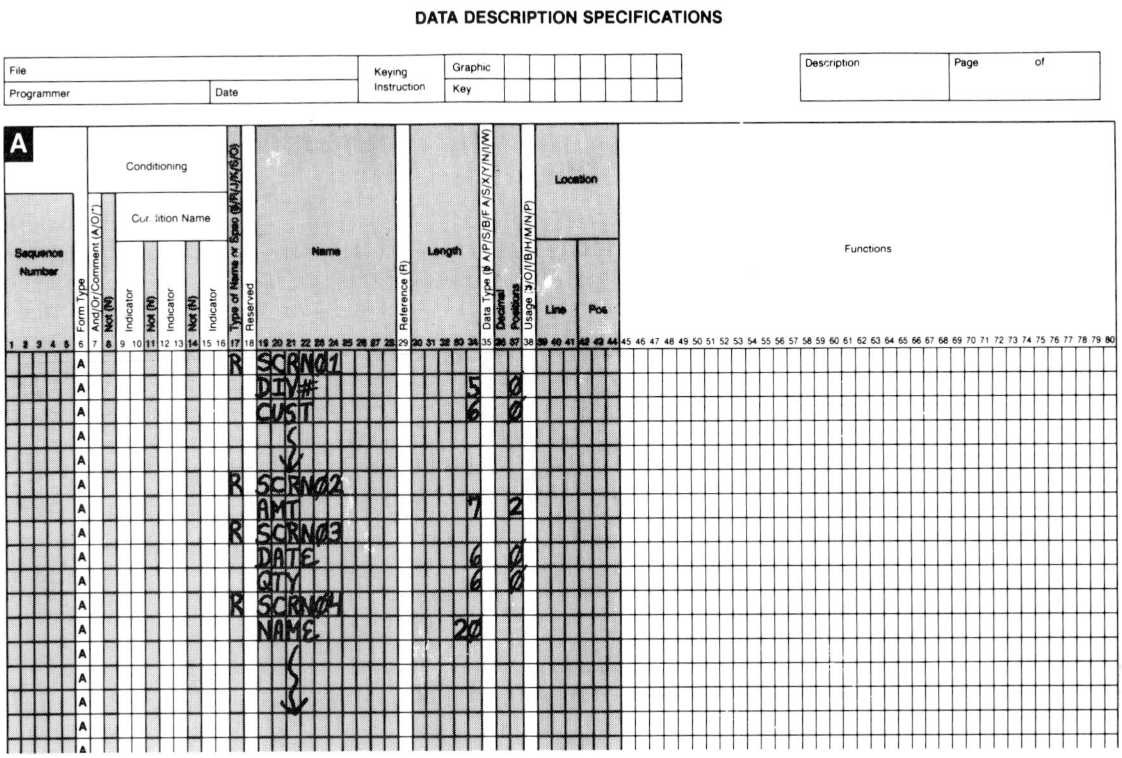

[DDS form showing multiple record formats: R SCRN01 with fields DIV# (5,0) and CUST (6,0); R SCRN02 with field AMT (7,2); R SCRN03 with fields DATE (6,0) and QTY (6,0); R SCRN04 with field NAME (20).]

FILE FORMAT NAMES FOR DISPLAY FILE DESCRIPTIONS

Later in this text, you will learn about designing programs that will display screens instead of printing reports. At that time, you will learn how to create a DDS for a display file. A display file can contain many formats because your program may need to change the format of what is being displayed on the screen.

Each format will then require a unique name. A good method might be to use part of the filename as the format name and follow that with a sequence number. The DDS for a screen display file in Figure 12.15 shows multiple formats sequentially numbered.

The DDS for a display file looks quite different from the DDS for a file. These differences will be discussed in detail in future chapters.

FILE MEMBERS

Having multiple members within a file may be a new concept to many programmers. Let us look at an example of a typical business situation. Company XYZ is composed of three divisions:

A manufacturing facility	Division 01
A retail and distribution warehouse	Division 02
An import/export enterprise	Division 03

The company is even considering purchasing several other companies, which will become Divisions 04, 05, and 06. At the central office, one computer still handles all the data processing for all divisions. Since the business at all divisions is handled in a somewhat similar manner (i.e., payroll is payroll no matter which division is being processed), they use the same programs for much of the processing. The data files, however, remain separate because Division 01 is paid on a different day from Division 02, and Division 03 is paid monthly while 01 and 02 are paid weekly. Management always worries that the data might become mixed and Division 02 might find out what is happening at Division 01. There are some peculiar codes in Division 03 data that could cause problems if it were commingled with the others. Therefore, a separate file has been created for each application for each division.

Many companies have operated in this manner in the past. Many still do today. There is nothing wrong with this approach. A certain amount of overhead is associated with each file, but that is probably negligible. Some of the real danger lurks in the timing of backup or recovery procedures. Operators could become confused, particularly if the company continues to add divisions with no upgrade in methodology.

The System/38 and AS/400 provide a better method for keeping all these separate but related files under control. The method is called file *members*.

A file can contain more than one member. In company XYZ, the payroll file could have been contained in a single file, but each division would reside in its own separate member. The data then would not be intermingled, although it could be consolidated for reporting purposes if needed.

The method for keeping the data separated is not so different from the old method but provides better self-documentation within the system. Each member is accessed by a unique name within the file. A file containing multiple members is created as shown in Figure 12.16.

The filename is ORDFILE, but the member name within that file is DIV01. Since this file will contain more than one member, it is necessary to specify the number of members allowed. This could be specified as a number if the exact number is known. Here, it has been specified as no maximum (*NOMAX), so the number can be flexible.

Figure 12.17 shows the command for adding more members to the file, ADDPFM (add physical file member). Notice that a source file is not specified in the ADDPFM command because the file has already been built. Any members added have the same format as the original file.

It is also possible to create logical files containing multiple members. The command for adding a member to a logical file is ADDLFM. One danger to be aware of when creating logical files (or adding logical members) over a physical file containing multiple members is that the logical file will default to *all members* unless the programmer specifies which member (or members) in the physical file the new logical member should be attached to. Figure 12.18 shows the relationship between a multi-member physical file and one of its logical files.

Many data processing organizations choose not to use the member concept for their applications, but a programmer should be aware that such a tool is available when multiple versions of a file might help solve a special problem.

FIGURE 12.16 Command for Creating a File Containing Multiple Members

```
CRTPF  ORDFILE.MAINLIB  QDDSSRC.SRCELIB  MBR(DIV01)  MAXMBRS(*NOMAX)
```
SYSTEM/38

```
CRTPF  MAINLIB/ORDFILE  SRCELIB/QDDSSRC  MBR(DIV01)  MAXMBRS(*NOMAX)
```
AS-400

FIGURE 12.17 Command for Adding Members to a File

```
ADDPFM  ORDFILE.MAINLIB  MBR(DIV02)
```
SYSTEM/38

```
ADDPFM  MAINLIB/ORDFILE  MBR(DIV02)
```
AS-400

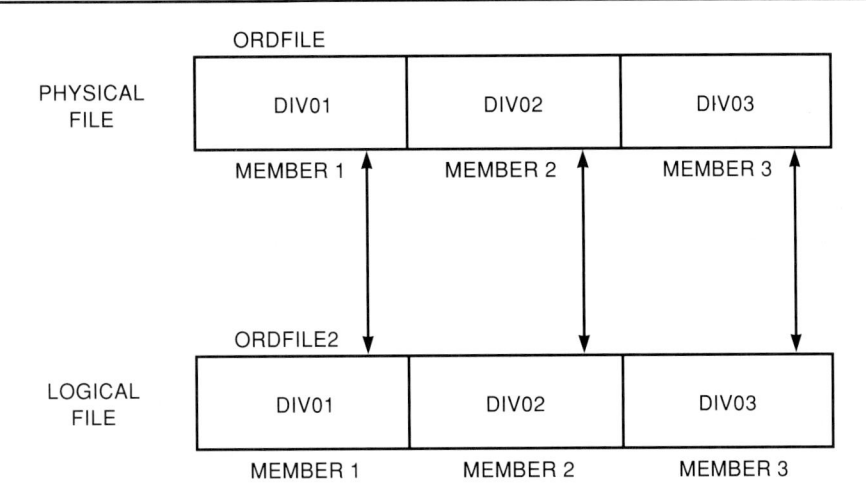

FIGURE 12.18 Relationship Between a Multi-Member Physical File and a Logical File

```
                    ORDFILE
                 ┌─────────┬─────────┬─────────┐
   PHYSICAL      │  DIV01  │  DIV02  │  DIV03  │
     FILE        └─────────┴─────────┴─────────┘
                  MEMBER 1  MEMBER 2  MEMBER 3
                      ↕         ↕         ↕
                   ORDFILE2
                 ┌─────────┬─────────┬─────────┐
   LOGICAL       │  DIV01  │  DIV02  │  DIV03  │
     FILE        └─────────┴─────────┴─────────┘
                  MEMBER 1  MEMBER 2  MEMBER 3
```

SUMMARY OF FILE ORGANIZATION ■

We have discussed the various methods by which data files can be carried on the System/38 or AS/400 disk devices. Files may continue to be handled as flat files if desired; a physical file still contains physical data, as it does on any device.

The value of a full database management system, however, is realized by creating multiple logical files. These logical files contain alternate key sequences and access paths to reach the physical data.

A physical file may contain multiple members. Any logical files built over this physical file may be attached to just one of the members or to several. Within the description of a file, a format name is specified. This name is used in the RPG calculations to access the specific format within the file.

REDEFINITION OF FIELDS ■

Now that files, members, and formats have been defined we can return to the subject of defining the fields within the record itself.

When the file is described in the DDS, each field is defined with specific attributes. This could present a problem for the programmer if those prespecified attributes do not lend themselves to easy implementation in the program in which they are used. Are externally defined files so rigid that the programmer cannot change them to fit the problem in hand? Not at all. Input Specifications can be used to redefine fields or to extend their usefulness. This means there is complete flexibility in defining the way a file is presented to a program. Figure 12.19 shows some examples of how the Input Specifications can be used to modify the description of a file.

In this example, the field in the DDS externally defining the file was entered as ORDNUM. The programmer wishes to call the field ORDER so it will not conflict with some other field in the program. The original name (ORDNUM) is entered in columns 21–26 and the new name (ORDER) is entered in columns 53–58. The program will always refer to this field as ORDER.

Since the external definition of a file can never carry a control level indicator, a programmer might want to add a program definition for level breaks in the program. In this example, the programmer has defined a level break on an externally defined field called DIV.

FIGURE 12.19 Modifying the External Description of a File Within the RPG Program

FORMAT NAME — *RENAME A FIELD*

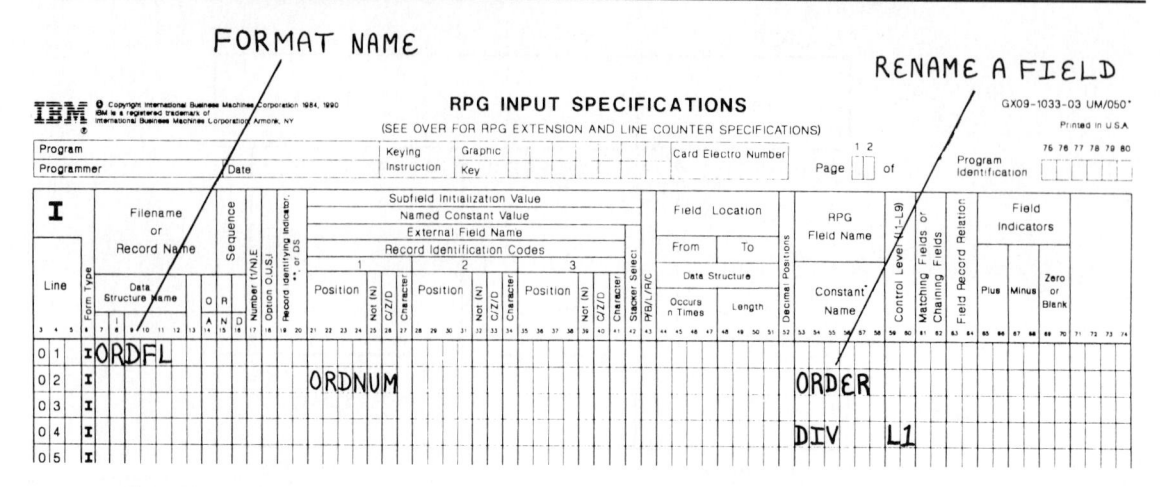

Line 01: I ORDFL
Line 02: I ... ORDNUM ... ORDER
Line 03: I
Line 04: I ... DIV L1
Line 05: I

DATA STRUCTURES ■

Fields may be redefined with the use of the data structure. For example, if a date field is externally defined as an alphabetic field six positions long in the format YYMMDD, how can it be printed easily using editing? Figure 12.20 shows the data structure that redefines the alphabetic field DATEA into three separate fields, YY, MM, and DD. Each of these field names is now available for the program to print as separate fields.

A second data structure can be created that uses the individual fields MM, DD, and YY to define a new numeric six-position field, rearranging the sequence of each two-position unit. The end product is a field (DATNUM) which contains the date in the desired format (MMDDYY) ready for printing and editing. Figure 12.21 shows this data structure.

Data structures can be defined to build data units that originated within the Calculation Specifications as well. The sample program in Figures 12.22(a) and 12.22(b) shows how a data structure is used in combination with calculations to create an output file or to redefine an input record.

The information in this chapter forms the heart and soul of RPG III/400. The externally defined file together with the power of physical/logical files forms the platform on which RPG III/400 functions.

FIGURE 12.20 Redefining a Field DATEA in a Data Structure

Line 01: I DS
Line 02: I ... 1 ... 6 DATEA
Line 03: I ... 1 ... 2 YY
Line 04: I ... 3 ... 4 MM
Line 05: I ... 5 ... 6 DD
Line 06: I

314 *RPG: A Programming Language for Today*

FIGURE 12.21 Redefining DATEA to DATNUM in a Data Structure

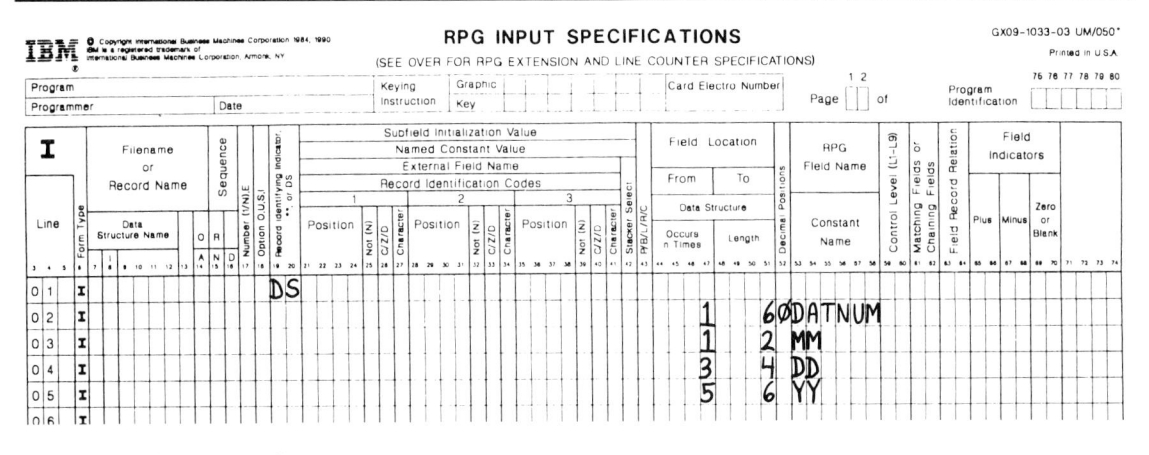

Line	Form Type	Data Structure Name				Position							From	To		RPG Field Name
01	I				DS											
02	I												1	6	0	DATNUM
03	I												1	2		MM
04	I												3	4		DD
05	I												5	6		YY
06	I															

FIGURE 12.22(a) Data Structure

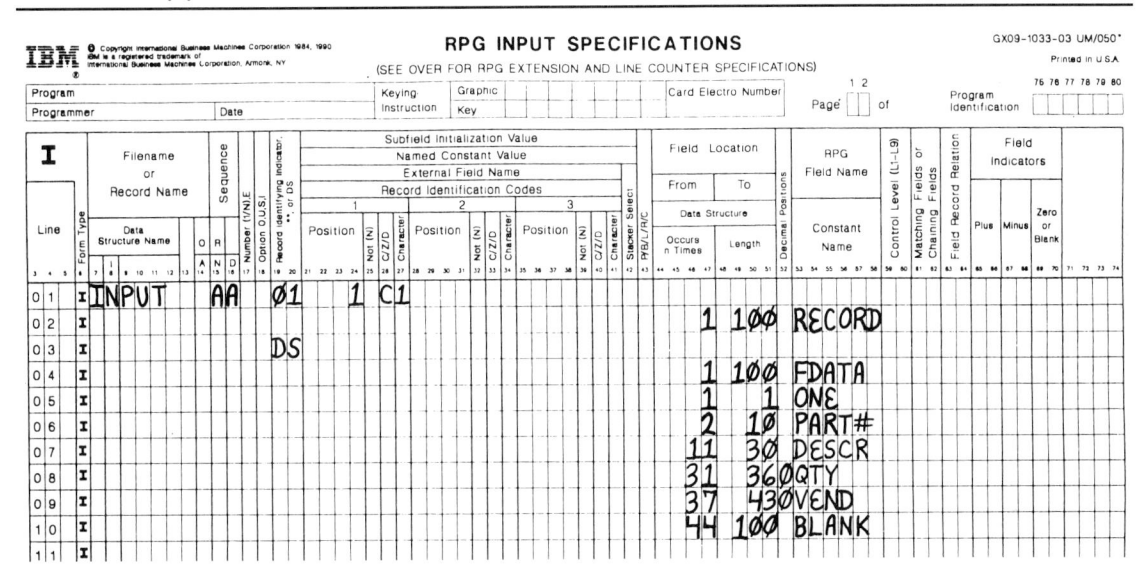

Line	Form Type	Filename or Record Name / Data Structure Name				Position 1			Position 2				From	To		RPG Field Name
01	I	INPUT	AA		01	1		C1								
02	I												1	10	0	RECORD
03	I				DS											
04	I												1	10	0	FDATA
05	I												1	1		ONE
06	I												2	10		PART#
07	I												11	30		DESCR
08	I												31	36	0	QTY
09	I												37	43	0	VEND
10	I												44	100		BLANK
11	I															

FIGURE 12.22(b) Calculation Specifications

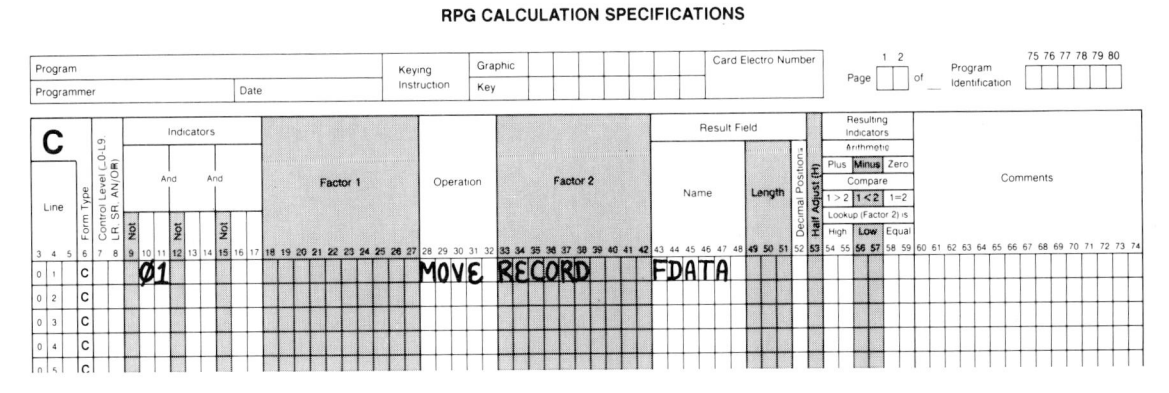

Line	Form Type	Indicators	Factor 1	Operation	Factor 2	Result Field Name	Length
01	C	01		MOVE	RECORD	FDATA	
02	C						
03	C						
04	C						
05	C						

RPG III look-alikes do not possess this power because it is intrinsic to the hardware architecture and the operating system. It cannot be readily transformed by any version of the RPG compiler.

By understanding externally defined files, and the methods for redefining and manipulating these files, the programmer has the tools to cope with any type of business-related programming.

Chapter 12 Overview of RPG III/400 File Concepts

SUMMARY ■

This chapter has presented the concepts of file structure and definition, concepts that drastically change the way programmers handle files in RPG.

In this chapter, you have learned the fundamental methods by which the IBM System/38 and the AS/400 store, access, and manipulate files on disk.

The benefits of using externally defined files in a program have been explored. The methods for describing a file using Data Description Specifications (DDS) and then creating the file have been presented, including the use of hardware-specific commands for the System/38 and AS/400.

You have learned about the relationship between physical and logical files, together with the use of the file member concept. Finally, data structures have been described briefly. These will be understood more clearly in the next chapters when applications are explored.

REVIEW QUESTIONS ■

1. What is meant by *object-oriented files*?
2. What is meant by *externally defined files*?
3. What are some of the benefits of using externally defined files?
4. How are externally defined files described?
5. How are externally defined files presented to the RPG program?
6. How are externally defined files described on the File Description Specifications?
7. Which specification will no longer be needed for describing input files?
8. Explain the difference between physical and logical files in the database environment.
9. Explain the use of multiple key fields.
10. Explain the use of keys that are not unique.
11. What is the value of using logical files?
12. Explain the function of having multiple members in a file.
13. Explain how a file is created.
14. Explain the meaning of data structures and how they can be used in a program.
15. When coding a data structure on the Input Specifications, the first entry will contain only the two letters _____ in columns 15–16.

DEBUGGING EXERCISES

Instructions

The following RPG programs contain an error or errors. Some of these errors are indicated by the RPG compiler on the program listing. A list of syntax errors is given at the end of the program listing. Other types of errors may occur which will not be shown. These are called logic errors.

Study each program and its syntax errors. Locate each error (including logic errors) and on a separate coding form make the correct entry for the line(s) in error.

Explain each error and how it should be corrected.

```
FILE NAME    -   PJ012FLA.HOLD           TYPE OF FILE -      PHYSICAL
SOURCE FILE  -   QDDSSRC.CABLE           MEMBER       -      PJ012FLA       06/25/91    7:30:14
TYPE OF DATA -   *DATA
OPTIONS      -   *SRC     *LIST
GENLVL       -   20
AUTHORITY    -   *ALL
TEXT         -   DEBUG PROJ 12A
COMPILER     -   IBM SYSTEM/38 DATA DESCRIPTION PROCESSOR

                                      DATA DESCRIPTION SOURCE

SEQNBR  *... ...1 ... ...2 ... ...3 ... ...4 ... ...5 ... ...6 ... ...7 ... ...8   DATE
   100      A*  TITLE: DEBUG PROJECT 12A
   200      A*  DATE:  6/24           AUTHOR: CABLE
   300      A*  DESCRIPTION:    XXXXXXXXXXXXXXXXXXXXXXXXXXXXXXXXXXXXXX
   400      A*************************************************************
   500      A          R PJ01201
   600      A            PJRPT#         10                TEXT('REPORT#')
   700      A            PJNAME         20                TEXT('RPT TITLE')
   800      A            PJTOT          15                TEXT('BAL TOT')
   900      A            PJPAGE          4                TEXT('PAGE#')
*                          CPD7410-*.
*                          CPD7401-*****
  1000      A            PJCYCL          2                TEXT('WHEN RUN')
  1100      A            PJDESC         40                TEXT('DESC')
  1200      A          K PJRPT#

                     * * * * *  E N D   O F   S O U R C E  * * * * *


5714SS1 R08 M00 861114              DATA DESCRIPTION                PJ012FLA.HOLD

                                      EXPANDED SOURCE
                                                                                     FIELD
SEQNBR  *... ...1 ... ...2 ... ...3 ... ...4 ... ...5 ... ...6 ... ...7 ... ...8    LEN

   500             R PJ01201
   600               PJRPT#       10A   B    TEXT('REPORT#')                          10
                                             COLHDG('PJRPT#')
   700               PJNAME       20A   B    TEXT('RPT TITLE')                        20
                                             COLHDG('PJNAME')
   800               PJTOT        15A   B    TEXT('BAL TOT')                          15
                                             COLHDG('PJTOT')
  1000               PJCYCL        2A   B    TEXT('WHEN RUN')                          2
                                             COLHDG('PJCYCL')
  1100               PJDESC       40A   B    TEXT('DESC')                             40
                                             COLHDG('PJDESC')
  1200             K PJRPT#

             * * * * *  E N D   O F   E X P A N D E D   S O U R C E  * * * * *
```

```
5714SS1 R08 M00 861114              DATA DESCRIPTION              PJ012FLA.HOLD
                                        MESSAGES

    MSGID     SEV   NUMBER   TEXT

  * CPD7401   30      1      VALUE REQUIRED FOR INDICATED FIELD
  * CPD7410   30      1      FIELD CONTAINS INVALID CHARACTER(S). DEFAULT VALUE ASSUMED.


                                     MESSAGE SUMMARY

    TOTAL   INFO(0-9)    WARNING(10-19)    ERROR(20-29)    SEVERE(30-99)
      2         0              0                0                2


  * CPF7302  40   FILE PJ012FLA NOT CREATED IN LIBRARY HOLD.
```

```
5714SS1 R08 M00 861114              DATA DESCRIPTION              PJ012FLB.HOLD

    FILE NAME -       PJ012FLB.HOLD      TYPE OF FILE -   PHYSICAL
    SOURCE FILE -     QDDSSRC.CABLE      MEMBER -         PJ012FLB      09/12/91  14:26:03
    TYPE OF DATA -    *DATA
    OPTIONS -         *SRC   *LIST
    GENLVL -          20
    AUTHORITY -       *ALL
    TEXT -            DEBUG PROJ 12B
    COMPILER -        IBM SYSTEM/38 DATA DESCRIPTION PROCESSOR

                                  DATA DESCRIPTION SOURCE

  SEQNBR  *... ... 1 ... ... 2 ... ... 3 ... ... 4 ... ... 5 ... ... 6 ... ... 7 ... ... 8
     100     A* TITLE: DEBUG PROJECT 12B
     200     A* DATE:  6/24           AUTHOR: CABLE
     300     A* DESCRIPTION:   XXXXXXXXXXXXXXXXXXXXXXXXXXXXXXXXXXXXXX
     400     A*************************************************************
     500     A          R PB01201
     600     A            PBRPT#         10                TEXT('REPORT#')
     700     A            PBNAME         20                TEXT('RPT TITLE')
     800     A            PBTOT          15                TEXT('BAL TOT')
     900     A            PBPAGE          4                TEXT('PAGE#')
    1000     A            PBCYCL          2                TEXT('WHEN RUN')
    1100     A            PBDESC         40    A           TEXT('DESC')
  *                                   CPD7416-***
    1200     A          K PBRPT#

                          *  *  *  *  *   E N D   O F   S O U R C E   *  *  *  *  *
```

```
5714SS1 R08 M00 861114                    DATA DESCRIPTION                    PJ012FLB.HOLD
                                           EXPANDED SOURCE
    SEQNBR  *... ... 1 ... ... 2 ... ... 3 ... ... 4 ... ... 5 ... ... 6 ... ... 7 ... ... 8
      500                   R PB01201
      600                     PBRPT#       10A   B    TEXT('REPORT#')
                                                     COLHDG('PBRPT#')
      700                     PBNAME       20A   B    TEXT('RPT TITLE')
                                                     COLHDG('PBNAME')
      800                     PBTOT        15A   B    TEXT('BAL TOT')
                                                     COLHDG('PBTOT')
      900                     PBPAGE        4A   B    TEXT('PAGE#')
                                                     COLHDG('PBPAGE')
     1000                     PBCYCL        2A   B    TEXT('WHEN RUN')
                                                     COLHDG('PBCYCL')
     1100                     PBDESC       40A   B    TEXT('DESC')
                                                     COLHDG('PBDESC')
     1200                   K PBRPT#

                      * * * * *   E N D   O F   E X P A N D E D   S O U R C E   * * * * *

                                              MESSAGES
        MSGID    SEV  NUMBER   TEXT
     * CPD7416   20     1      POSITIONS RESERVED FOR PHYSICAL AND LOGICAL FILES BUT NOT BLANK.


                                           MESSAGE SUMMARY
        TOTAL   INFO(0-9)    WARNING(10-19)    ERROR(20-29)    SEVERE(30-99)
          1         0              0                1                0

     * CPF7302   40    FILE PJ012FLB NOT CREATED IN LIBRARY HOLD.
```

PROGRAMMING PROJECT

Project Overview

A physical file needs to be described externally. The filename will be SALEHEAD. Code the Data Description Specification for this file, create the file using the CRTPF command, and code the RPG program that will provide a simple list of the file. The format for this file is shown below. Note that this will be a non-keyed file.

Input Format

The file SALEHEAD does not exist in the sample data provided. This file must be created by the student. You will need to key data into your file using a data entry utility (such as DFU on a System/38). The Record Layout for this file is shown in Figure 12.23.

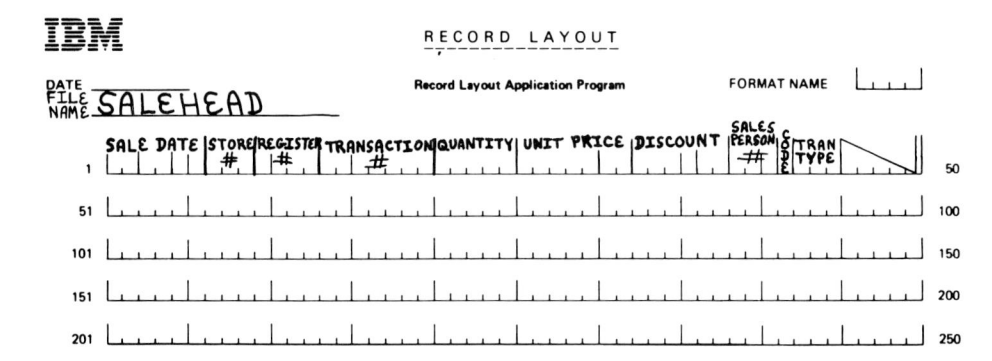

Output Format (Printer Spacing Chart)

The output format for the project is a report with standard headings. The report will show each field as it exists in the input record. The Printer Spacing Chart for this report is shown in Figure 12.24.

An example of the finished report is shown in Figure 12.25.

FIGURE 12.23 Programming Project: Record Layout

Chapter 12 Overview of RPG III/400 File Concepts

FIGURE 12.24 Programming Project: Printer Spacing Chart

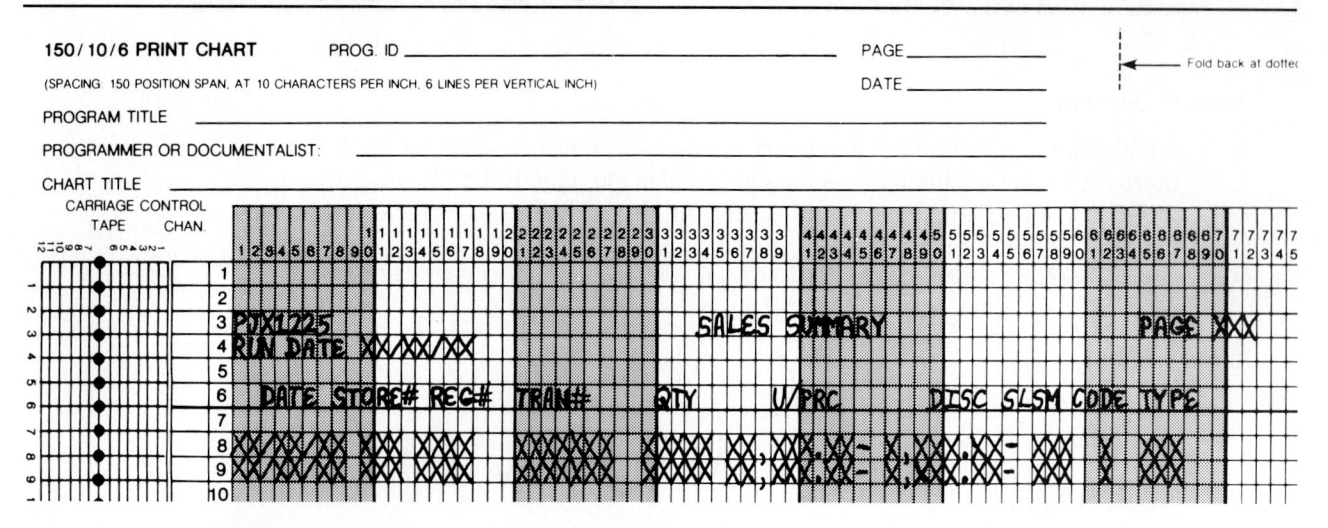

FIGURE 12.25 Programming Project: Final Report

```
PJX1225                        SALES SUMMARY                    PAGE    1
RUN DATE   3/16/92

    DATE STORE# REG#   TRAN#     QTY     U/PRC    DISC SLSM CODE TYPE
   0/00/00
   3/05/91    1    1     125       1     35.00          123   A   23
   3/25/91    1    2     665       2    285.00           35   A   88
   3/25/91    2    1    9985      35    356.55    3.57   91   B  987
```

Chapter 13

Calculation Enhancements in RPG III/400

What you will learn in Chapter 13

Reserved Words for RPG III/400
Arithmetic Operations in RPG III/400
Structured Programming Concepts for RPG III/400
    Structured Selection (If...Then...Else)
    Structured Iteration (DO Loops)

Difference Between a Do While and a Do Until
Use of Indicators with DOxxx
Compare and Branch Operation (CABxx)
Case Structure (CASxx)

New Methods for Using Indicators (Setting Flags)
Calling a Program from Within an RPG III/400 Program
Defining Field Attributes in RPG III/400

RPG III/400 enables the programmer to write programs that perform on-line interactive processing. On-line inquiries and file updates are not only possible, but also easy to code. RPG III/400 has introduced some very easy methods for presenting screens for interactive processing.

    RPG III/400 allows the programmer to take control of the program cycle to solve complex problems. It is now possible to access several files in various sequences, or to access the same file in a variety of ways. RPG III/400 allows the programmer to create a cycle (or cycles) within calculations. But it still permits the programmer to use the old RPG II cycle and methods if desired.

    RPG III/400 provides the tools with which to write structured programs. Although it is possible to write in a structured manner in some of the older business programming languages, few offer the commands necessary to make those structures an integral part of the language.

    RPG III/400 encourages the programmer to write each program almost entirely within the Calculation Specifications. Since the need for Input and Output Specifications has been reduced and in some cases eliminated, it is now possible to write an entire program using only the Calculations with just a few lines of File Specifications. This results in a much more readable program.

    The use of indicators has always been a concern in RPG II. The need for record identification, field record relationship, level break, and matching record indicators has been *eliminated* in RPG III/400. All controls are included in the Calculation Specifications without the use of indicators. This does not mean that the old methods cannot be used, just that a better method now exists for handling decisions in RPG III/400.

    Since the Calculation Specifications have become the focal point of RPG III/400 coding, many new operation codes have been added to simplify and enhance the coding. By using structured coding methods, it is possible to read and understand exactly why an event is occurring at a particular moment in the program, and it is no longer necessary to chase obscure indicators all over several pages of code.

RESERVED WORDS FOR RPG III/400

All of the reserved words used in RPG II, such as UDATE and PAGE, remain available in RPG III/400. In addition to these, several new words are available on the more modern computers such as the IBM System/36, System/38, and AS/400. Among these added reserved words are *ZERO and *BLANK. As might be expected, the value of blank characters is contained in *BLANK and the value of zeros is contained in *ZEROS. This allows the programmer to move blanks or zeros into a field when needed.

The length of the receiving field determines the number of blanks or zeros that are moved. It is not important whether the plural or singular forms of these words are used. Figure 13.1 shows how these reserved words are used.

ARITHMETIC OPERATIONS IN RPG III/400

ADD, SUB, MULT, DIV, and MVR have not changed as operation codes. However, it is no longer necessary to make an entry in factor 1 for an addition or subtraction operation when doing accumulation. Figure 13.2 shows examples of both operations in RPG III/400.

FIGURE 13.1 Use of *ZERO and *BLANK

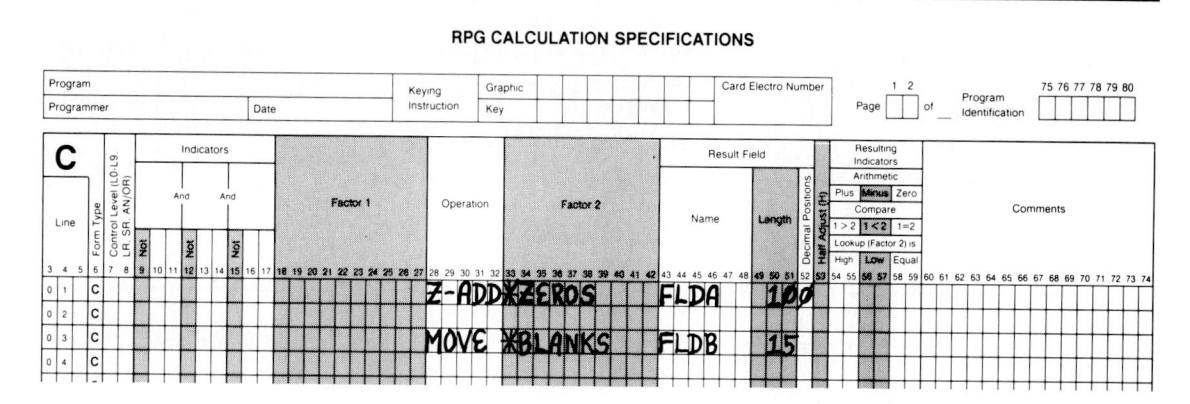

Line	Operation	Factor 2	Result Field	Length
01	Z-ADD	*ZEROS	FLDA	100
03	MOVE	*BLANKS	FLDB	15

FIGURE 13.2 ADD and SUB Operations

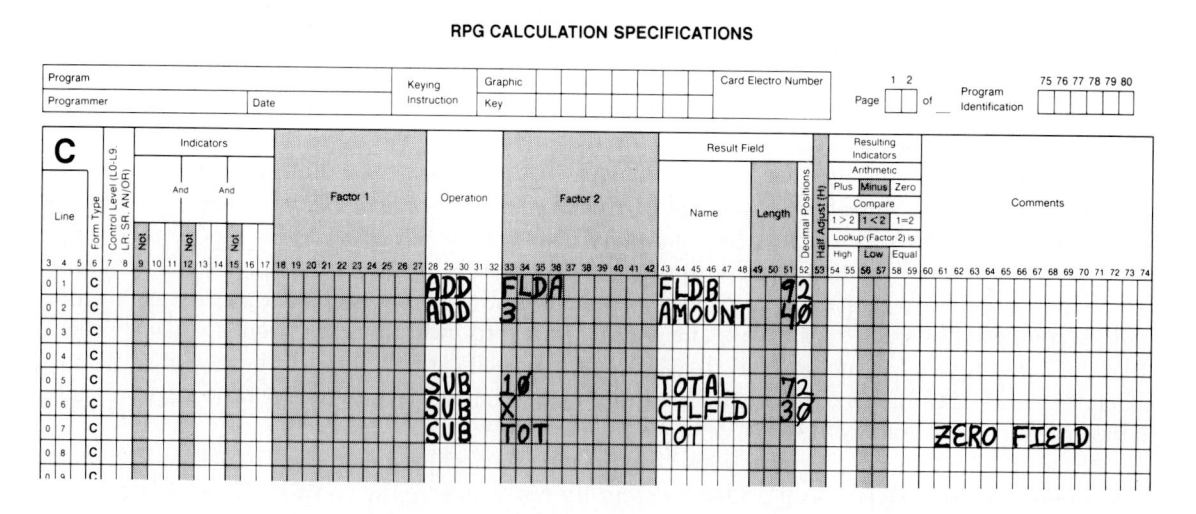

Line	Factor 1	Operation	Factor 2	Result Field	Length	Comments
01		ADD	FLDA	FLDB	72	
02		ADD	3	AMOUNT	40	
05		SUB	10	TOTAL	72	
06		SUB	X	CTLFLD	30	
07		SUB	TOT	TOT		ZERO FIELD

STRUCTURED PROGRAMMING CONCEPTS FOR RPG III/400

Many new operation codes have been added in RPG III/400. The compare operation (COMP) has been replaced with the structured programming method. There are now a multitude of codes, such as the IFxx, DOxxx, CABxx, and CASxx operations. The x's act as placeholders for letters that describe the relationship, such as equal (EQ) or greater than (GT). These operations discourage the use of indicators and provide very readable logic statements. Instead of controlling logic with resulting indicators defined several pages away, the logic is defined where it is used. This new concept brings true structured programming to the RPG language. Although many of the logic operations permit the use of indicators, it is hoped that programmers will keep indicators to an absolute minimum or omit them entirely.

RPG III/400 provides a complete set of operations to perform If...Then constructs and Do While or Do Until logic. Note that every If...Then operation and every Do Until operation will require an END instruction for the statement. Figure 13.3 shows the general outline for these logic units.

Structured Selection (If...Then...Else)

Structured selection refers to the programming structure for coding decisions that allow a program to take alternative action based on a comparison of two values. If two values satisfy a stated relationship (equal to, greater than, or less than), (THEN) some action will be taken, otherwise (ELSE) some alternative action will be taken.

Factor 1 and factor 2 of an IFxx operation must contain either a literal or a field name. The attributes of the field or literal must be alike—that is, both entries must be defined as either numeric or alphanumeric.

Figure 13.4 shows a complete IF statement. It describes a comparison between an input date (INDAT) and the current date (UDATE). If the input date is equal to the current date, then some calculations will be performed.

Both factor 1 and factor 2 are numeric six-position fields. If the two fields were not equal, the calculations within the IF statement would not be performed. Program control would pass to the calculation operation immediately following the associated END operation.

FIGURE 13.3 IF...END and DO...END

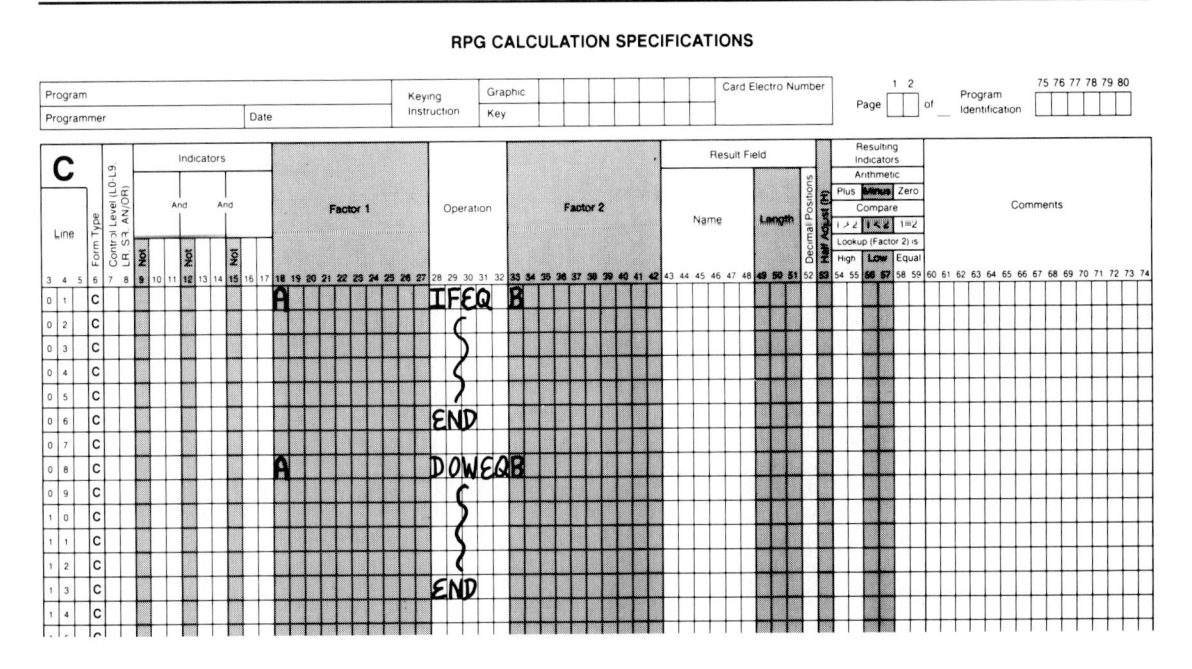

FIGURE 13.4 A Complete IF Statement

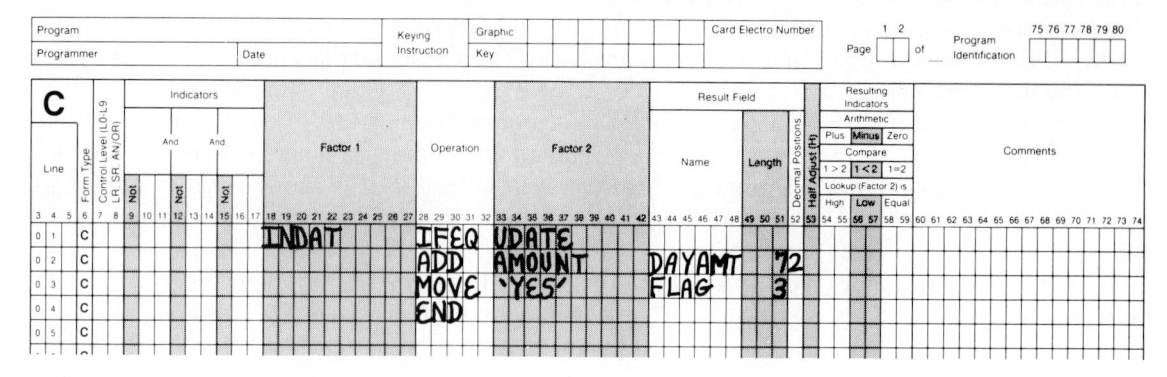

```
C           INDAT     IFEQ UDATE
C                     ADD  AMOUNT    DAYAMT  72
C                     MOVE 'YES'     FLAG     3
C                     END
```

Use of Indicators with IFxx

RPG III/400 permits the use of indicators in columns 9–17 for the IFxx statement, and in the statements within the IFxx statement. However, it is *not* good structured programming technique to use the indicators, since the readability of the program will be decreased.

IFxx Operations

A complete set of IFxx operations is available in RPG III/400.

IFEQ	If factor 1 is EQUAL to factor 2
IFNE	If factor 1 is NOT EQUAL to factor 2
IFGT	If factor 1 is GREATER THAN factor 2
IFLT	If factor 1 is LESS THAN factor 2
IFGE	If factor 1 is GREATER THAN or EQUAL to factor 2
IFLE	If factor 1 is LESS THAN or EQUAL to factor 2

All of these use the same format and function in the same manner.

Alternative Action in an IF Statement (ELSE)

It is possible to take alternative action when the IFxx statement turns out to be *not* true—i.e., if the input date in the example were *not* equal to the current date, a different calculation could be performed. This is done with the use of the ELSE operation, as shown in Figure 13.5.

No indicators have been used. There is no doubt about what set of criteria caused the alternative action to be performed. All of the logic is in one compact set of code.

FIGURE 13.5 ELSE Operation

```
C           INDAT     IFEQ UDATE
C                     ADD  AMOUNT    DAYAMT  72
C                     MOVE 'YES'     FLAG     3
C                     ELSE
C                     ADD  AMOUNT    PRIOR   72
C                     MOVE 'NO '     FLAG
C                     END
```

326   *RPG: A Programming Language for Today*

Selection with Multiple Conditions (ANDxx)

Often, two or more conditions must be met before performing a set of calculations. This might be stated: "IF this is true AND that is true THEN . . . ." It could also be stated: "IF this is untrue AND that is untrue THEN . . . ."

In the earlier example, the input date must be equal to the current date. It would be possible to specify a second condition, such as a code in the input record. This is coded using the ANDxx operation code, as shown in Figure 13.6.

The ANDxx operations may be used for all functions of the IF statement:

ANDEQ	If factor 1 is EQUAL to factor 2
ANDNE	If factor 1 is NOT EQUAL to factor 2
ANDGT	If factor 1 is GREATER THAN factor 2
ANDLT	If factor 1 is LESS THAN factor 2
ANDGE	If factor 1 is GREATER THAN or EQUAL to factor 2
ANDLE	If factor 1 is LESS THAN or EQUAL to factor 2

These may be used in any combination to complete whatever logical decisions might be needed in the program. Figure 13.7 shows examples of some very complex decisions. The intentions of the programmer in these examples are much clearer than with coding using indicators. The format follows the rules of structured programming for the selection process.

FIGURE 13.6 ANDxx Operation

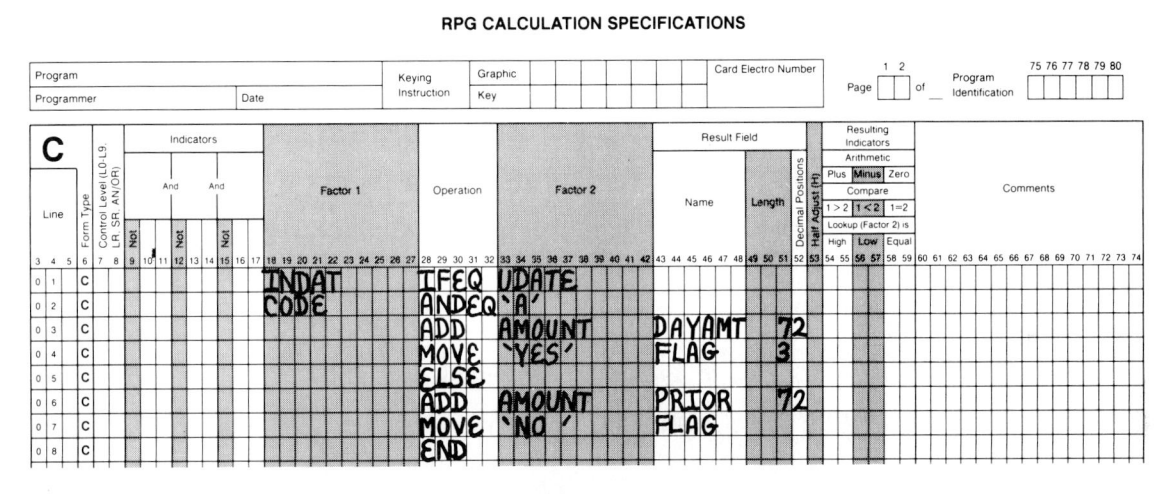

```
RPG CALCULATION SPECIFICATIONS

Line  Form   Factor 1   Operation   Factor 2   Result    Len
                                               Name
01  C        INDAT      IFEQ        UDATE
02  C        CODE       ANDEQ       'A'
03  C                   ADD         AMOUNT     DAYAMT    72
04  C                   MOVE        'YES'      FLAG      3
05  C                   ELSE
06  C                   ADD         AMOUNT     PRIOR     72
07  C                   MOVE        'NO '      FLAG
08  C                   END
```

FIGURE 13.7 Complex Decisions Using IFxx, ANDxx

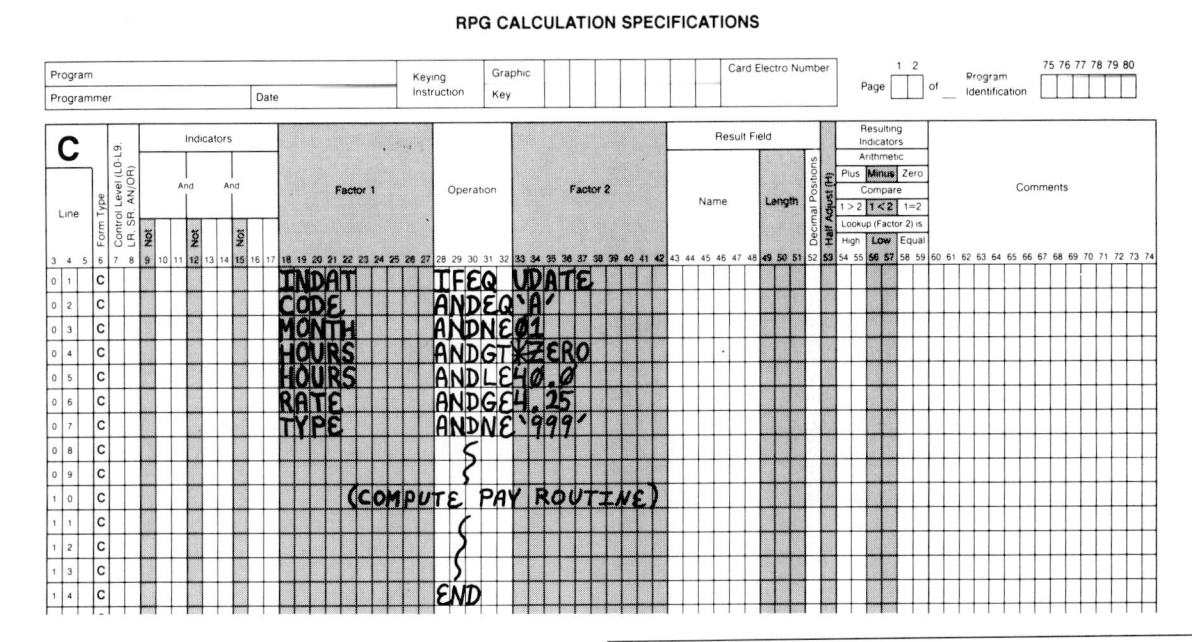

```
RPG CALCULATION SPECIFICATIONS

Line  Form   Factor 1   Operation   Factor 2
01  C        INDAT      IFEQ        UDATE
02  C        CODE       ANDEQ       'A'
03  C        MONTH      ANDNE       01
04  C        HOURS      ANDGT       ZERO
05  C        HOURS      ANDLE       40.0
06  C        RATE       ANDGE       4.25
07  C        TYPE       ANDNE       '999'
08  C
09  C
10  C                   (COMPUTE PAY ROUTINE)
11  C
12  C
13  C
14  C                   END
```

Chapter 13 Calculation Enhancements in RPG III/400

Selection with Multiple Alternative Conditions (ORxx)

It may sometimes be necessary to specify two or more alternative conditions that will satisfy the criteria of the comparison. This might be stated: "IF this is true OR that is true THEN . . . ." The CODE field for a valid input record might be either an *A* or a *B*. This is coded using the ORxx operation code, as shown in Figure 13.8.

The ORxx operations may be used for all functions of the IF statement:

OREQ	If factor 1 is EQUAL to factor 2
ORNE	If factor 1 is NOT EQUAL to factor 2
ORGT	If factor 1 is GREATER THAN factor 2
ORLT	If factor 1 is LESS THAN factor 2
ORGE	If factor 1 is GREATER THAN or EQUAL to factor 2
ORLE	If factor 1 is LESS THAN or EQUAL to factor 2

These may be used in any combination depending on the logical decisions needed in the program. OR statements are useful for defining a range of valid data. For example, any number less than 1 or greater than 999999 might be invalid data for which an error message should be printed or displayed. The IFxx statement for this is shown in Figure 13.9.

It is possible to use a combination of ANDxx statements with ORxx statements, but it must be done with care. It is difficult to determine the intentions of the programmer who coded the example in Figure 13.10.

FIGURE 13.8 ORxx Operation

```
RPG CALCULATION SPECIFICATIONS

01 C           CODE    IFEQ  'A'
02 C           CODE    OREQ  'B'
03 C           HOURS   MULT  RATEA   TOTPAY  72
04 C                   ELSE
05 C           HOURS   MULT  RATEC   TOTPAY
06 C                   END
```

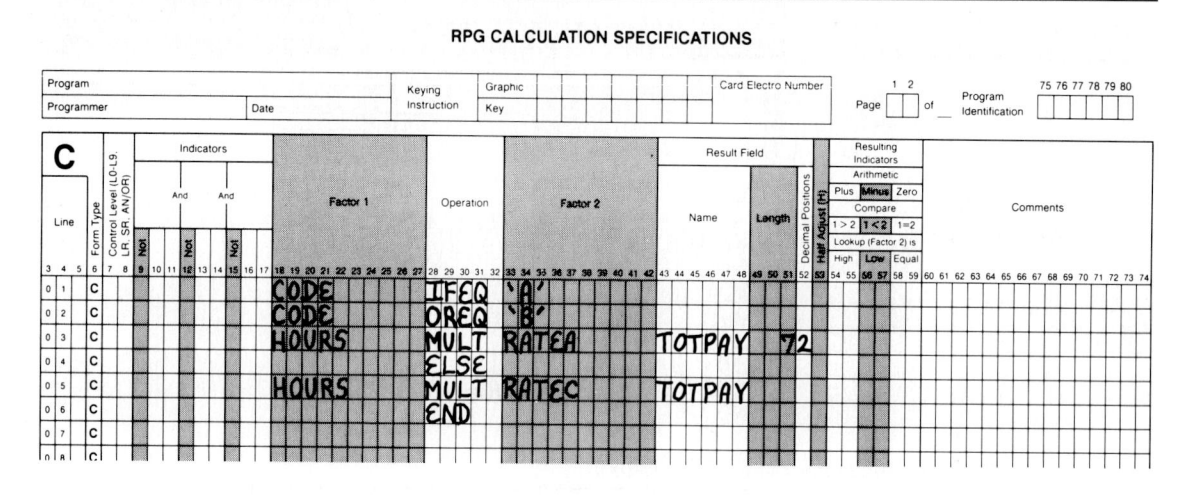

FIGURE 13.9 Complex Decisions Using IFxx, ORxx

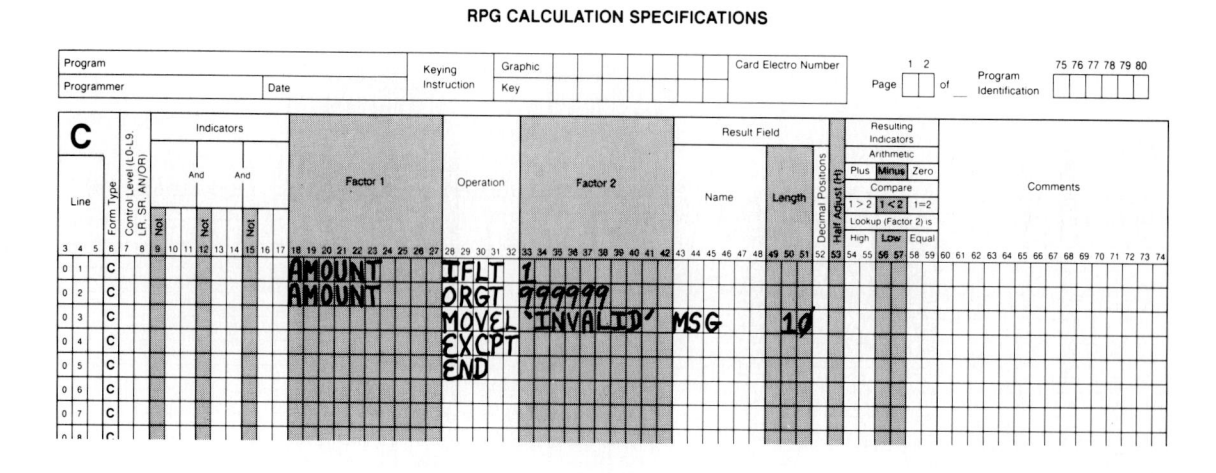

```
RPG CALCULATION SPECIFICATIONS

01 C           AMOUNT  IFLT  1
02 C           AMOUNT  ORGT  999999
03 C                   MOVEL 'INVALID' MSG   10
04 C                   EXCPT
05 C                   END
```

328 *RPG: A Programming Language for Today*

FIGURE 13.10 Combination of AND and OR

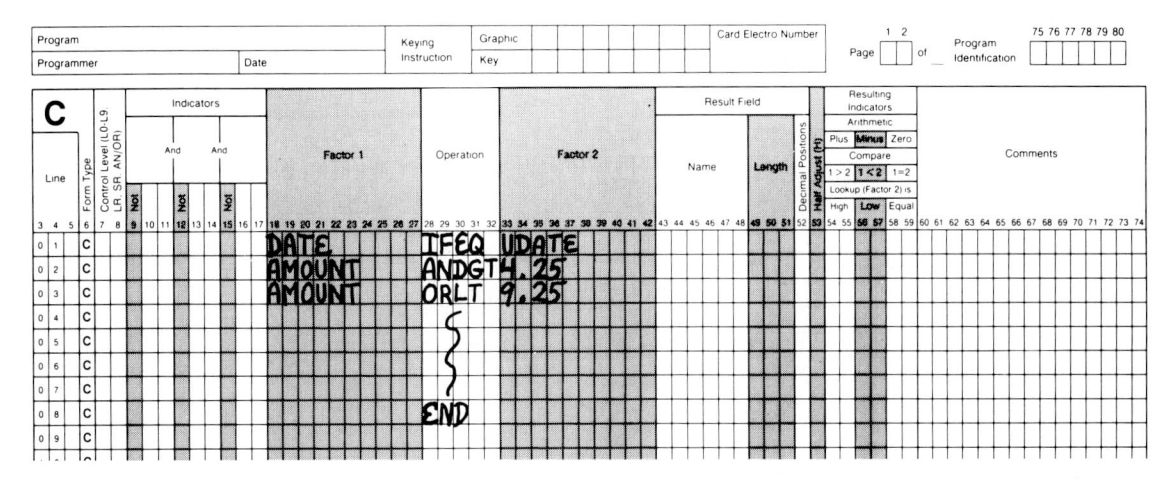

```
         Factor 1      Operation    Factor 2
01  C    DATE          IFEQ         UPDATE
02  C    AMOUNT        ANDGT        4.25
03  C    AMOUNT        ORLT         9.25
...
08  C                  END
```

Nested IFxx Statements

The term "nested IFxx statement" is used to describe an IF statement that is contained within another IF statement. A third IF statement may be contained within the second and so on. Each nested statement is dependent on the outcome of the IF statement in which it is contained. Often the execution of a set of decisions depends on the outcome of a prior set, as illustrated by the flowchart shown in Figure 13.11. Such a situation calls for the use of nested IF statements; in this case:

> If sales are over $5000.00
> If salesperson is male or female

The coding for this program is shown in Figure 13.12. Note that there are two END statements, one for each IF. (One END is sufficient when using AND or OR statements in combination with an IF.)

FIGURE 13.11 Nested IF Statements Flowchart

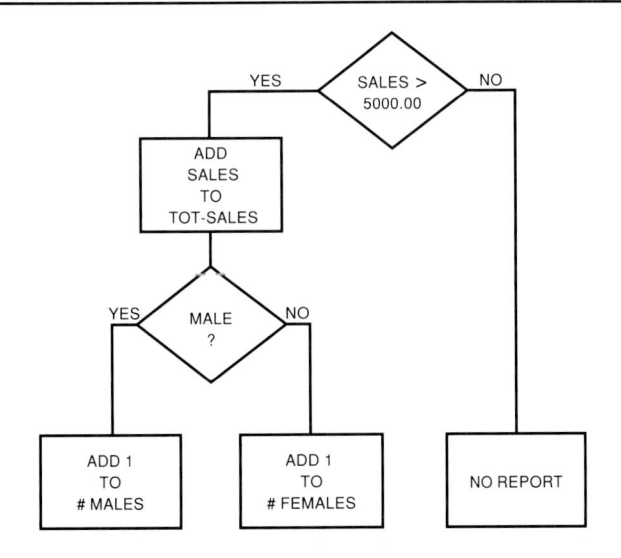

Chapter 13 Calculation Enhancements in RPG III/400

FIGURE 13.12 Coding for Problem—Second Set of Decisions Is Dependent on the Outcome of the First Set

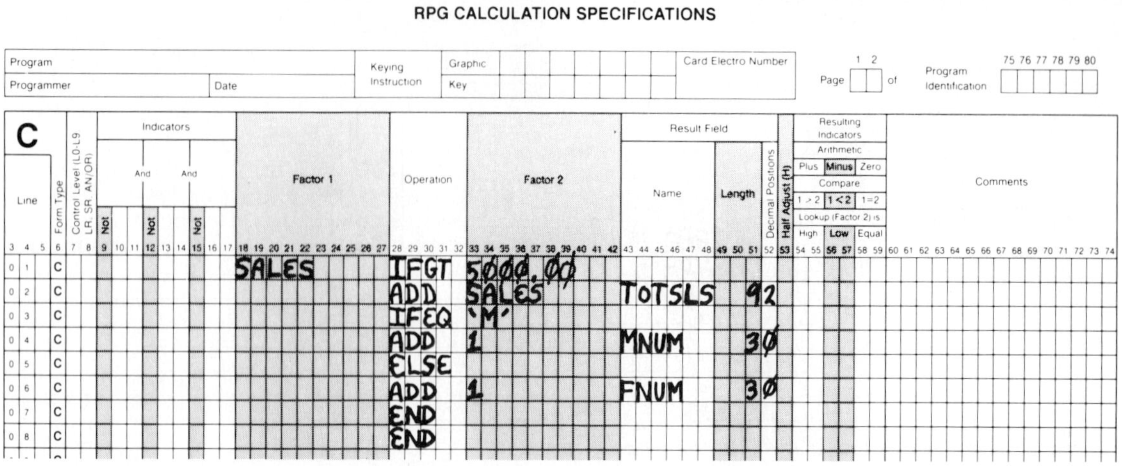

```
RPG CALCULATION SPECIFICATIONS

Line  Form  C/L  Indicators       Factor 1    Operation  Factor 2      Result Field   Len  Dec
                And  And  Not
01     C                           SALES       IFGT       5000.00
02     C                                       ADD        SALES         TOTSLS         92
03     C                                       IFEQ       'M'
04     C                                       ADD        1             MNUM           30
05     C                                       ELSE
06     C                                       ADD        1             FNUM           30
07     C                                       END
08     C                                       END
```

Figure 13.13 shows a compiled listing of a program using some nested IF statements. Along the right margin (to the left of the date) are letters and numbers entered by the compiler to help the programmer to debug a program. The beginning of the IFxx statement is defined with the letter *B*. The END of the IFxx statement is defined with the letter *E*. An ELSE statement is defined by the letter *X*. The first IFxx statement in a group of nested IFxx statements is labeled B001. The related END is E001. The second level within the nested group is labeled B002 and E002. When a third level is nested within the second level, it is labeled B003 and E003. The sequence of these labels can be of great assistance in locating where errors in logic have occurred in a program.

Although RPG III/400 places no restriction on the number of IFxx statement groups that may be nested, it is better to keep a program as simple as possible.

Structured Iteration (DO Loops)

Although the word *loop* has earned a bad reputation in computer programming, it is a structure available in every programming language and used in any program that executes a group of statements more than once.

The old fixed RPG cycle was nothing more than a predefined loop for which the programmer was never responsible. Because GOTO statements were often used indiscriminately to create loops in RPG and many other languages, structured programming prohibits the use of GOTO statements. In RPG III/400, although the GOTO instruction is still available, the use of the GOTO is discouraged. Whenever a section of several calculation lines needs to be repeated, the Do While, Do Until, or Do structure should be used instead. The Do While and Do Until operations are similar and generally follow the same rules.

The Do Loop in RPG III/400 (DOWxx and DOUxx)

Factor 1 and factor 2 of the DOxxx instruction must contain either a literal or a field name. The attributes of the fields or literals must be alike—i.e., both entries must be either numeric or alphanumeric.

The DOWxx operation code represents Do While. The DOUxx operation code represents Do Until. This means that the specifications contained between the line of code and its corresponding END statement will be performed while or until some two fields (or some field and a literal) meet the criteria specified in the xx portion of the statement. Figure 13.14 shows a complete DOWxx statement that will be executed as long as the field TOTAL remains equal to zero.

If the field is not equal to zero, the calculations within the DOWxx statement will *not* be performed. Program control will pass to the calculation operation immediately following the associated END operation.

FIGURE 13.13 Compiled Program with Nested IFs

```
     300   F* DESCRIPTION:  SHOWS HOW RPG COMPILER PRINTS BEG/END OF IFS
     400   F*************************************************************


 NAME OF PROGRAM WILL BE ILL1313 IN LIBRARY CABLE

           H
*  1019              ALL DECIMAL DATA ERRORS IGNORED
     500   FINVNEW  IP  E                 DISK
            RECORD FORMAT(S):  FILE INVNEW LIB CABLE
                     EXTERNAL FORMAT NEW01 RPG NAME NEW01

     600   FQSYSPRT O    F      132      OF       PRINTER


  A000000    INPUT  FIELDS FOR RECORD NEW01 FILE INVNEW FORMAT NEW01
  A000001                                                1    1 NEWACT
  A000002                                                2    80NEWPNO
  A000003                                                9   27 NEWDSC
  A000004                                               28   29 NEWUM
  A000005                                               30   362NEWAVG
  A000006                                               37   41 NEWBIN
  A000007                                               42   460NEWQTY
  A000008                                               47   490NEWDIV
  A000009                                               50   54 NEWSTY
  A000010                                               55   57 NEWWHS
     700   C                  SETOF                         20          2
     800   C         NEWAVG   IFGT 100.50                                  B001
     900   C                  ADD  1         COUNT   60                     001
    1000   C         NEWDIV   IFLT 20                                      B002
    1100   C                  ADD  1         DIVCNT  60                     002
    1200   C                  ELSE                                         X002
    1300   C         NEWSTY   IFGT '4000 '                                 B003
    1400   C                  EXCPT                                         003
    1500   C                  END                                          E003
    1600   C                  END                                          E002
    1700   C                  END                                          E001
    1800   C*
    1900   C         NEWWHS   IFEQ '004'                                   B001
    2000   C                  SETON                         20          2   001
    2100   C                  EXCPT                                         001
    2200   C                  END                                          E001
    2300   C***************************************************


    2400   O* PRINT THE REPORT
    2500   OQSYSPRT E  1     20
    2600   O                        NEWDIV     5
    2700   O                        NEWWHS    10
* * * * *  E N D   O F   S O U R C E  * * * * *
```

FIGURE 13.14 Complete DOWxx Statement

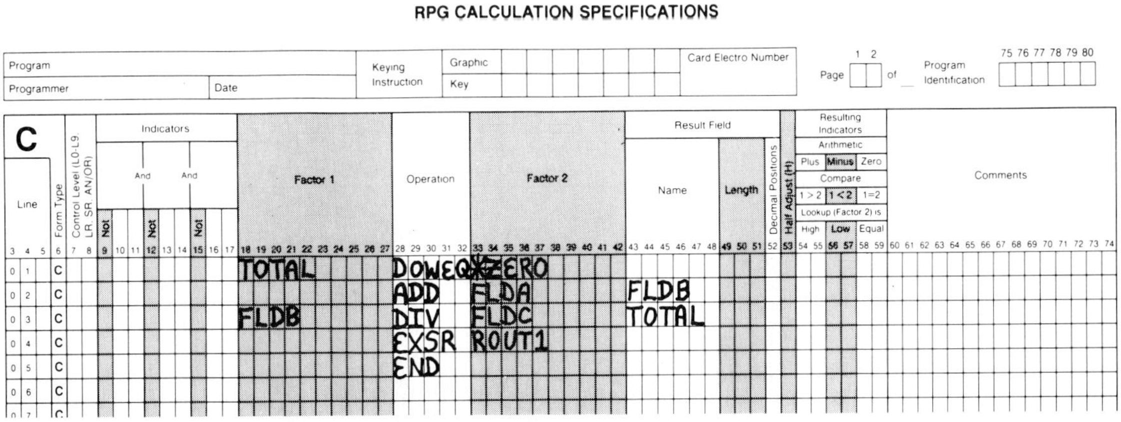

RPG CALCULATION SPECIFICATIONS
Program
Programmer
Date
Keying Instruction
Graphic
Key
Card Electro Number
Page of
Program Identification
C
Indicators
Factor 1
Operation
Factor 2
Result Field
Name
Length
Decimal Positions
Half Adjust (H)
Resulting Indicators
Arithmetic
Plus Minus Zero
Compare
1 > 2 1 < 2 1 = 2
High Low Equal
Comments
Line
Form Type
Control Level (L0-L9, LR, SR, AN/OR)
0 1 C TOTAL DOWEQZERO
0 2 C ADD FLDA FLDB
0 3 C FLDB DIV FLDC TOTAL
0 4 C EXSR ROUT1
0 5 C END
0 6 C
0 7 C

The following formats are available for the DOWxx operation (with corresponding formats for the DOUxx operation):

DOWEQ	Do while factor 1 is EQUAL to factor 2
DOWNE	Do while factor 1 is NOT EQUAL to factor 2
DOWGT	Do while factor 1 is GREATER THAN factor 2
DOWLT	Do while factor 1 is LESS THAN factor 2
DOWGE	Do while factor 1 is GREATER THAN or EQUAL to factor 2
DOWLE	Do while factor 1 is LESS THAN or EQUAL to factor 2

Difference Between a Do While and a Do Until

Although Do While and Do Until statements operate in a similar manner and appear to perform the same function, there is one very important difference between the two commands. It is possible that a DOWxx (Do While) group of instructions would *never* be executed in a program because the criteria are never met. Figure 13.15 is an example of a DOWxx group of instructions which will never be executed. Because the constant 'BAD' is forced into the field called CHECK, the DOWEQ will find the field to be unequal to 'TOT' and will therefore cause this set of instructions to be skipped.

A DOUxx (Do Until) will *always* be executed at least once in a program because a DOUxx does not make the real comparison until *after* the section of code has been executed. Figure 13.16 shows the same example but as a DOUxx group of instructions. This section of code *will* be executed at least once whenever the program is executed although the field CHECK is not equal to 'TOT.'

FIGURE 13.15 DOWxx Instructions That Will Never Be Executed

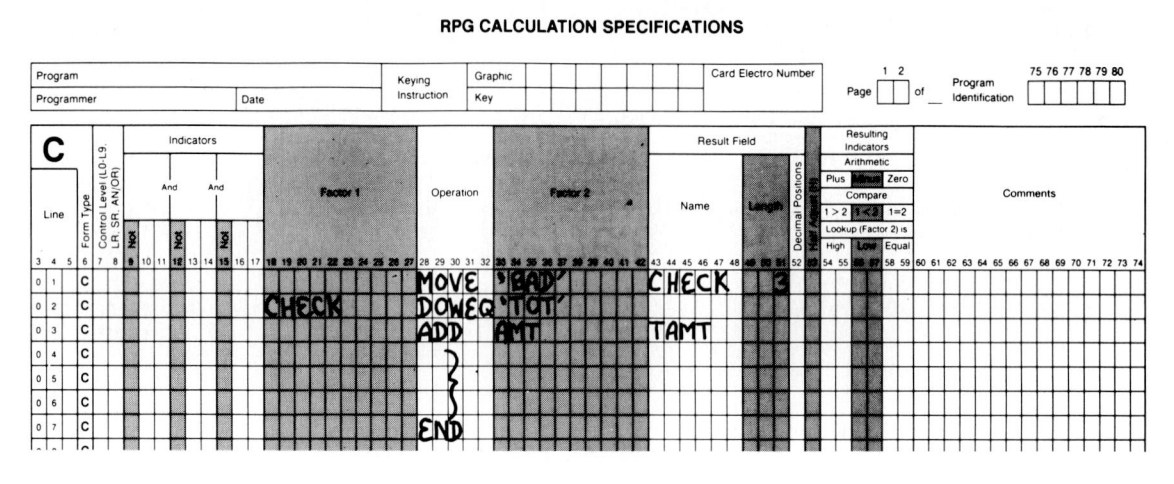

FIGURE 13.16 DOUxx Instructions That Will Be Executed Once

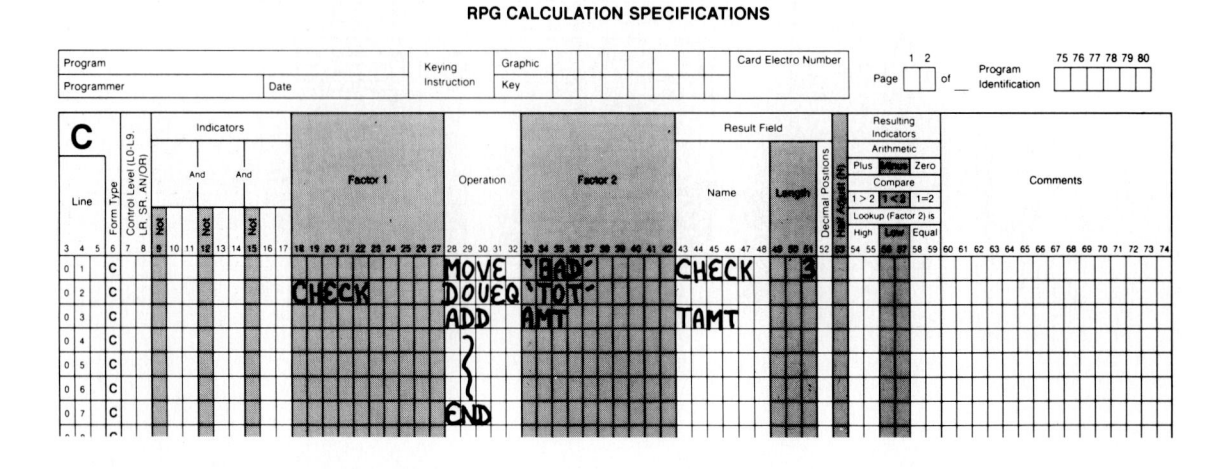

Use of Indicators with DOxxx

RPG III/400 permits the use of indicators in columns 7–17 for the DOxxx statement, and in the statements within the loop. It is *not* good structured programming technique to use them, however, since the readability of the program is decreased.

Using the DO Loop to Control the Number of Repetitions

A DO operation begins a group of operations that are to be performed some predefined number of times. A DO operation will have an associated END statement to mark the end of the group. Figure 13.17 shows a very simple DO loop that will repeat three times.

The number of times the group of statements will be performed is controlled by the starting value, the limit value, and the index field on the DO statement. The starting value is entered in factor 1. If this is blank, the starting value will begin at 1. The limit value is entered in factor 2. If this is blank, the limit value will be 1. The index field, which will contain the current index value, is entered in the result field. All of these entries can be either field names or literals. Each can be modified within the DO group of statements to affect the number of times it will process. Figure 13.18 shows an example of a complex DO group that will be repeated ten times based on the index and limit fields.

If factor 2 of the associated END statement contains an increment value, the index will be incremented by that amount. If it is blank, the index will be incremented by 1 each time the group is repeated. Figure 13.19 shows how a DO group might use this capability to increment the index by 2.

FIGURE 13.17 Simple DO Loop

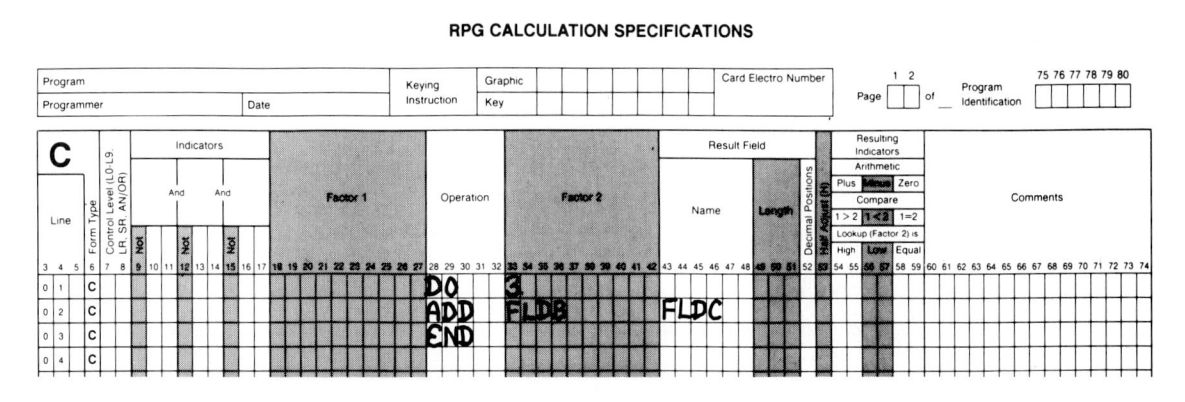

Line	Factor 1	Operation	Factor 2	Result Field
01 C		DO	3	
02 C		ADD	FLDB	FLDC
03 C		END		
04 C				

FIGURE 13.18 Complex DO Loop

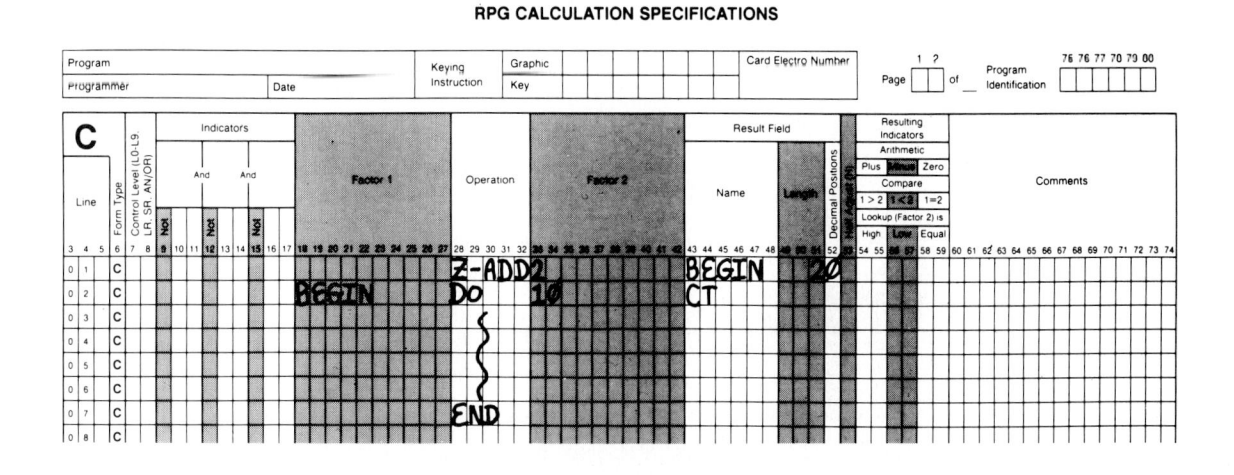

Line	Factor 1	Operation	Factor 2	Result Field	Length
01 C		Z-ADD	2	BEGIN	20
02 C	BEGIN	DO	10	CT	
03 C					
04 C					
05 C					
06 C					
07 C		END			
08 C					

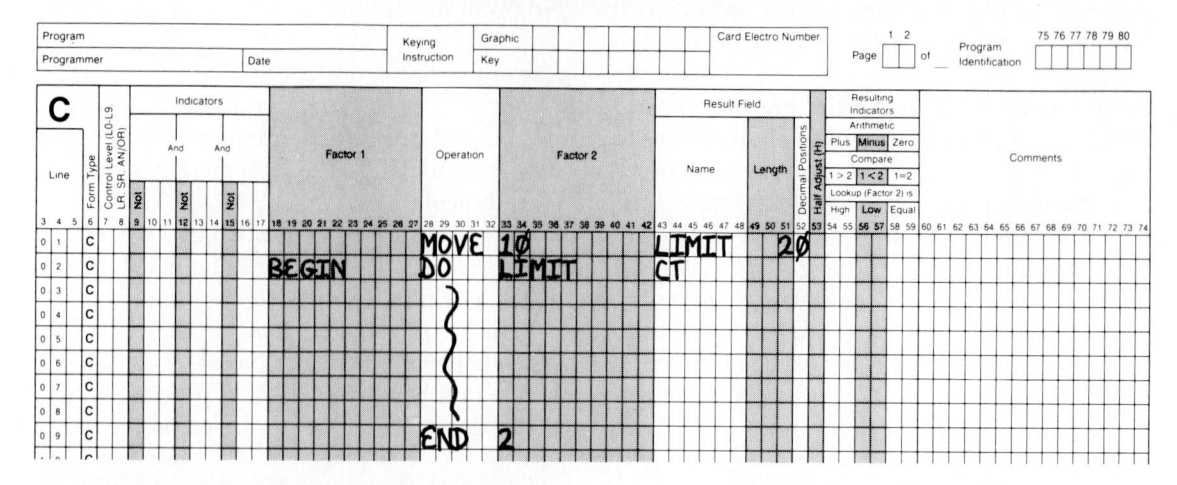

FIGURE 13.19 DO Loop with END Statement and Factor to Increment by Twos

```
       Factor 1    Operation   Factor 2   Result   Length
01  C                           MOVE  10   LIMIT
02  C              BEGIN        DO    LIMIT  CT            20
03  C
04  C
05  C
06  C
07  C
08  C
09  C                           END         2
```

Compare and Branch Operation (CABxx)

RPG III/400 provides one more instruction for comparing two fields. This is the CABxx instruction.

A field may need to be validated to ensure that it contains a specific code. In the example in Figure 13.20, column 1 must contain the code A, C, or D. Any other code would be incorrect.

The coding for this example could be done with three IFxx statements and a final statement for all invalid codes. This would require some less-structured code with GOTO statements. Although the program would work, it would contain more lines of code than necessary and would be more difficult to read.

The CABxx operation provides a more readable code, using only one line for each comparison. The operation code for this instruction is CABxx, where xx can be EQ, NE, GT, LT, GE, or LE, as was used with the IFxx and DOxxx statements. Figure 13.21 shows the coding for this project. Factors 1 and 2 contain the two fields to be compared. They may be fields, array elements, or literals. The result field contains the TAG label to which program control will branch.

The entire logic structure has been accomplished in five lines of code, and it is completely readable. Had there been 100 codes to be validated, the code would have been equally readable. When new codes are added or removed, the programmer can do so with a minimum of effort and little opportunity for error.

Case Structure (CASxx)

Although the IFxx, the DOxxx, and the CABxx instructions give a programmer all the tools necessary to create structured programs, RPG III/400 offers even more sophisticated commands with which to design better programs.

FIGURE 13.20 Record Layout for Validating a Code Example

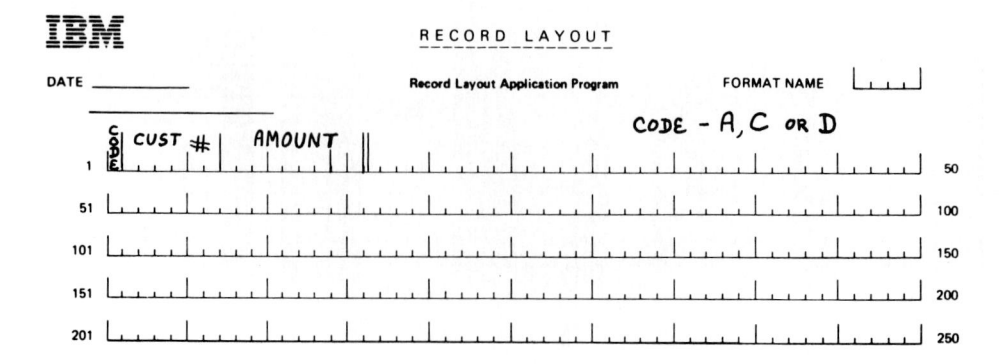

334 *RPG: A Programming Language for Today*

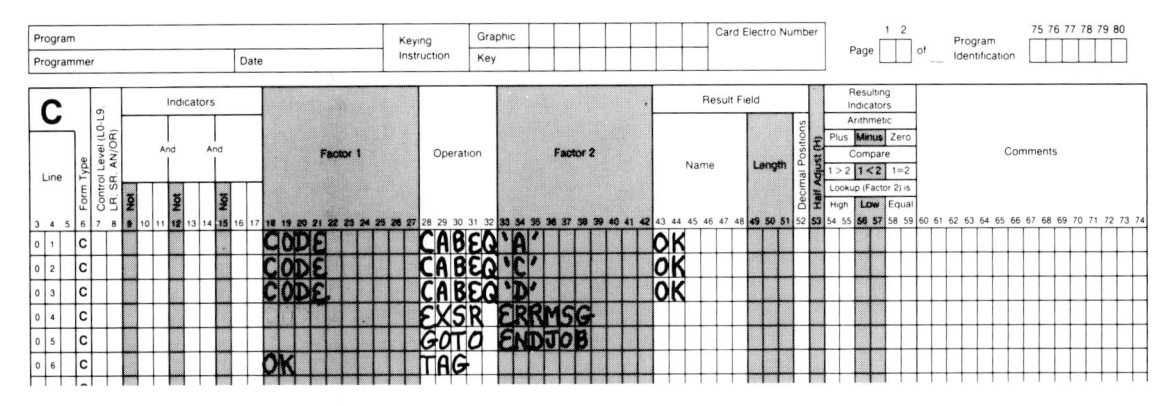

FIGURE 13.21 CABxx Operation (Compare and Branch)

```
01 C          CODE      CABEQ 'A'      OK
02 C          CODE      CABEQ 'C'      OK
03 C          CODE      CABEQ 'D'      OK
04 C                    EXSR  ERRMSG
05 C                    GOTO  ENDJOB
06 C          OK        TAG
```

The problem presented in the previous section, which was solved using the CABxx instruction, could have been structured so a series of functions would be performed for each code. The CASxx instruction refers to a CASE structure and allows control to be given to a subroutine. Figure 13.22 shows the coding for this type of structure.

In this example, ADDOK, CHGOK, and DELOK are the names of subroutines. If the CODE field is found to be *A*, then ADDOK subroutine will be executed, control will pass to the END statement, and no further testing will be done. If the CODE field is not *A*, then the second line will test for *C*, and so on. If the CODE field is not *A*, *C*, or *D*, the error routine will be executed. This could also have been coded as shown in Figure 13.23, where ERR represents the name of another subroutine.

FIGURE 13.22 CASxx Operation (Case Structure)

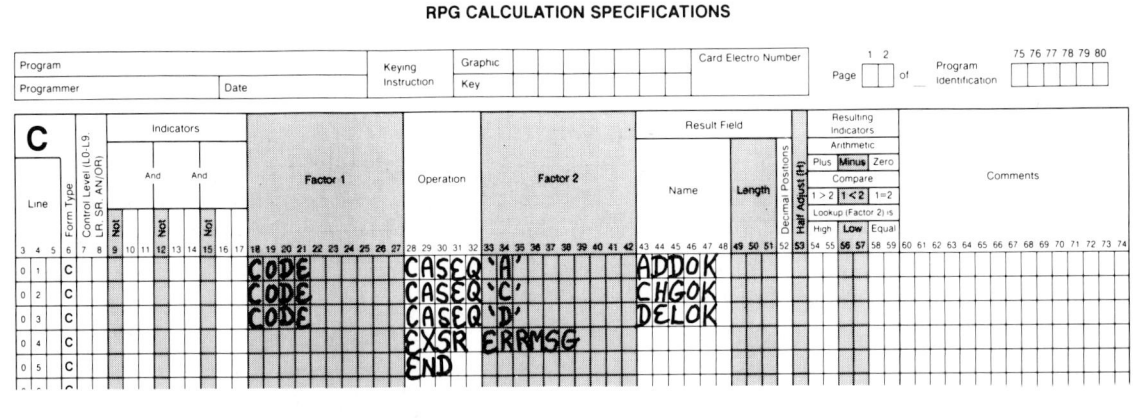

```
01 C          CODE      CASEQ 'A'      ADDOK
02 C          CODE      CASEQ 'C'      CHGOK
03 C          CODE      CASEQ 'D'      DELOK
04 C                    EXSR  ERRMSG
05 C                    END
```

FIGURE 13.23 CASxx Operation (Case Structure)

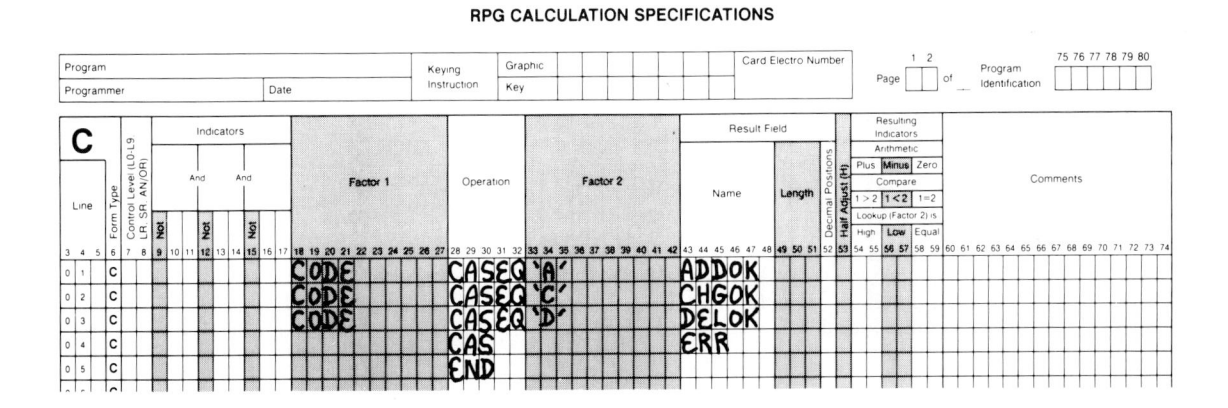

```
01 C          CODE      CASEQ 'A'      ADDOK
02 C          CODE      CASEQ 'C'      CHGOK
03 C          CODE      CASEQ 'D'      DELOK
04 C                    CAS            ERR
05 C                    END
```

New Methods for Using Indicators (Setting Flags)

Although the use of indicators is discouraged in RPG III/400, there are many times when a programmer must set up a field to be used as an indicator, or flag as it is called in other programming languages. Although this could be done by creating an actual field (for example, FLAG1 could be a one-position field which is set aside to contain a flag 1 or 0), RPG III/400 provides some specific places for storing such flags.

These flags are used exactly as indicators have been used in RPG II. Instead of entering the conditioning indicators in columns 9–17, the indicator is entered as factor 1 of an IF or DO statement. Factor 1 contains the indicator preceded by the characters *IN. Factor 2 contains either a 0 or 1 enclosed in single quotation marks. A '0' in factor 2 means that the indicator was found to be *off*. A '1' in factor 2 means that the indicator was found to be *on*. Figure 13.24 shows how this is coded.

The first line in Figure 13.24 is interpreted: "If indicator 33 is found to be on . . . ." The second line is interpreted: "If indicator 34 is *not* found to be on . . . ." In the third statement, the DO loop will be performed until indicator 35 is found to be on. By coding the indicator within an IFxx statement, the structure becomes much more readable.

Calling a Program from Within an RPG III/400 Program

It is often desirable to call a program from within another program. This is done in RPG III/400 with the use of the CALL operation code. There are many reasons to call a second or third or even more programs. Sometimes the first program allows some selection to be made. The result of user decisions in the first program can determine which will be the next program called.

Sometimes a separate program is called that is written in another language. This language may be better suited to the routines that need to be performed. The RPG program performs the simple introductory routines and then calls the second program (written in COBOL or assembly language, for example), does the computations required, and then returns to the original calling program with the answers ready to be printed. Figure 13.25 shows a diagram of several interconnected programs.

FIGURE 13.24 Using Indicators in a Structured Format

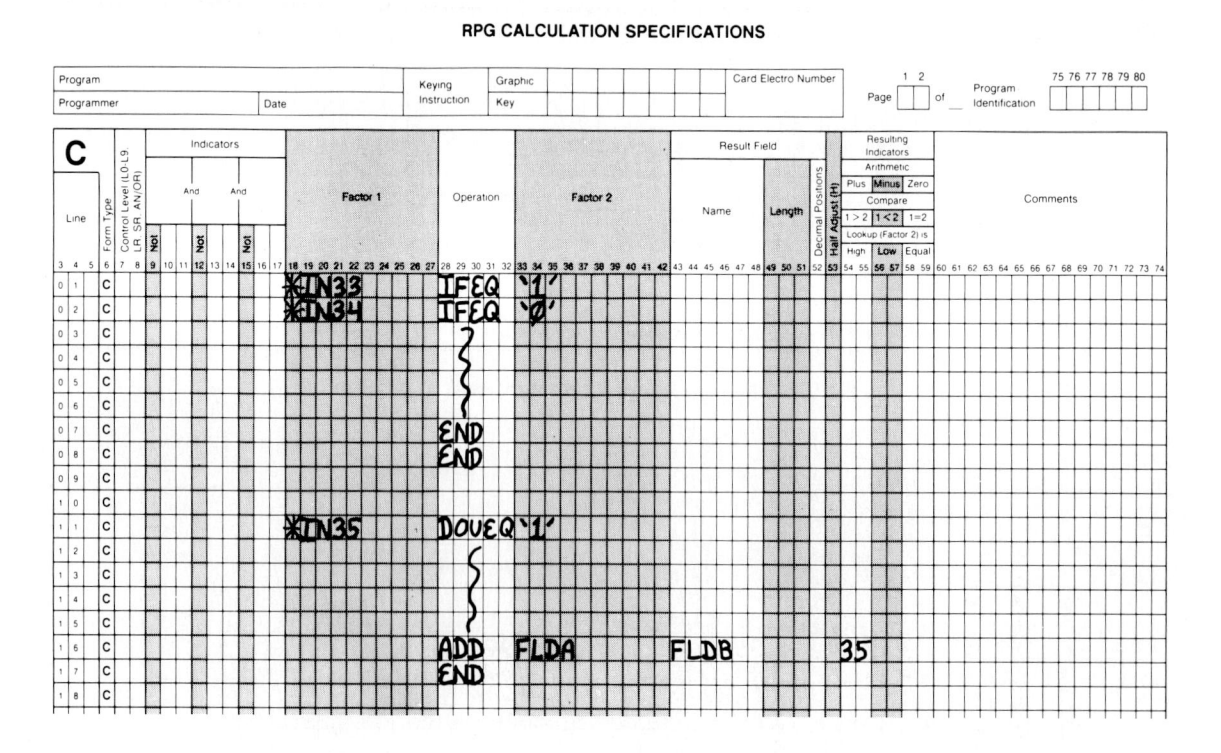

FIGURE 13.25 Interconnected Programs

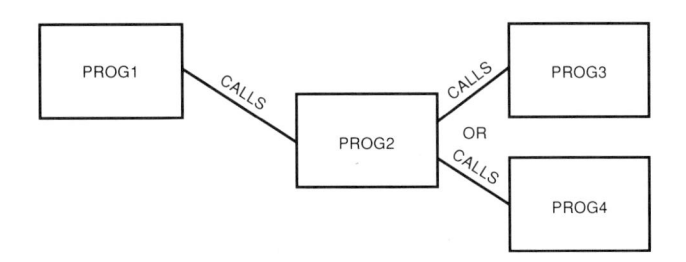

[Diagram: PROG1 CALLS PROG2, which CALLS PROG3 OR CALLS PROG4]

Passing Parameters to a Called Program

To send some data from the original (calling) program to the second (called) program, the PARM operation code is used. The PARM performs no function of its own. It must always accompany some other command, such as the CALL. Several PARM statements may accompany the CALL operation. Figure 13.26 shows the coding for calling a second program. Factor 2 contains the name of the program being called.

In this example, parameters for a date field, a customer number, and a specific literal code are being sent by the PARM code for use in the called program that will be receiving these fields. The called program will expect the parameters to arrive in some specific sequence. The called program expects the date first, the customer second, and the literal last.

Often the called program will need to send some information back to the calling program. This also is done in the parameter field. Using the same example, two more parameters could be attached to the CALL, as shown in Figure 13.27.

Besides the three parameters sent to the called program, there are now two fields being sent that are empty and carry no information. When the called program has completed, these two fields will contain some value. That value will be sent back to the calling program.

Receiving Parameters in a Called Program

If parameters are sent to a program, these PARMS will need to be announced to the called program. This is done in the Calculation Specifications with the PLIST operation. This instruction begins a list of incoming parameters. In the coding for this operation, factor 1 will contain either the reserved word *ENTRY or a tag. The PLIST instruction is followed by the parameters (PARM operations). The PARM fields must be entered in the same sequence in which the sending program listed the PARMs on the CALL statement. Figure 13.28 shows a PLIST statement followed by the same five parameters sent in the CALL example earlier. The field names in this second (called) program do not need to be the same names used in the first (calling) program, but the attributes *must* be the same.

Note that the attributes must be restated in the called program. The second program has no access to the calling program other than the data received from it.

FIGURE 13.26 Calculation Specifications: Calling a Second Program

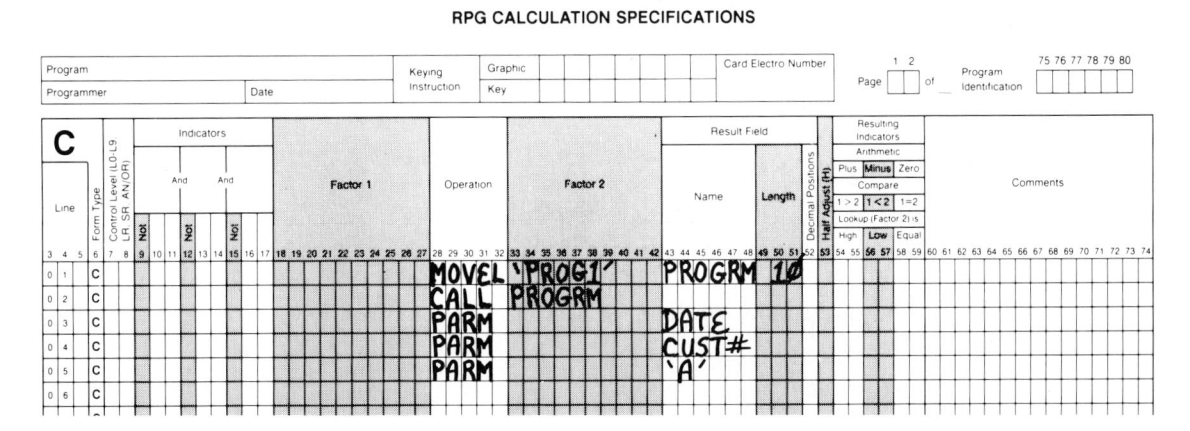

RPG CALCULATION SPECIFICATIONS

Line	Factor 1	Operation	Factor 2	Result Field	Length
01		MOVEL	'PROG1'	PROGRM	10
02		CALL	PROGRM		
03		PARM		DATE	
04		PARM		CUST#	
05		PARM		'A'	
06					

Chapter 13 Calculation Enhancements in RPG III/400

FIGURE 13.27 Sending Five Parameters to a Called Program

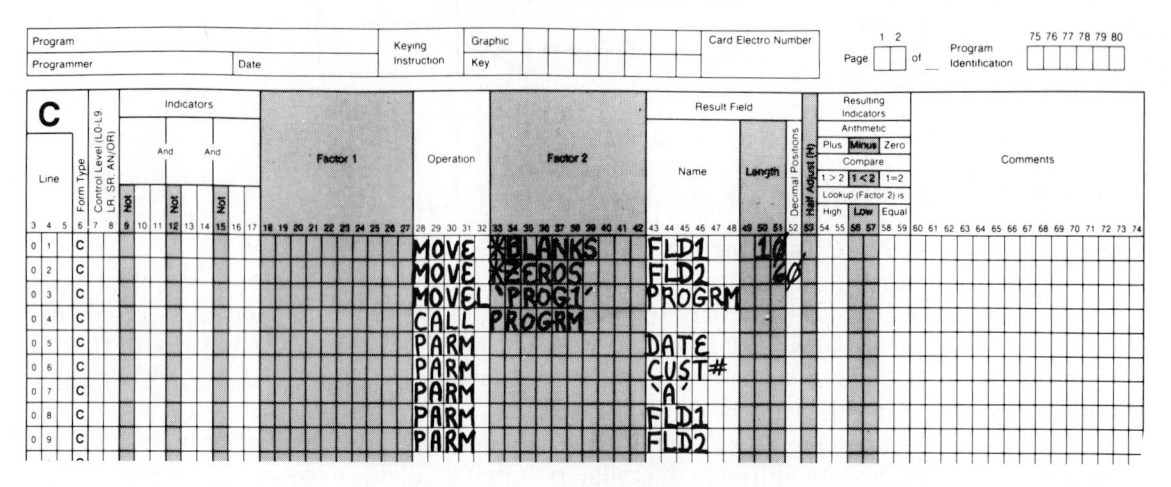

Line	Form Type	Factor 1	Operation	Factor 2	Result Field Name	Length
01	C		MOVE	*BLANKS	FLD1	10
02	C		MOVE	*ZEROS	FLD2	60
03	C		MOVEL	'PROG1'	PROGRM	
04	C		CALL	PROGRM		
05	C		PARM		DATE	
06	C		PARM		CUST#	
07	C		PARM		'A'	
08	C		PARM		FLD1	
09	C		PARM		FLD2	

FIGURE 13.28 PLIST Statement and Five Parameters in a Called Program

Line	Form Type	Factor 1	Operation	Factor 2	Result Field Name	Length
01	C	*ENTRY	PLIST			
02	C		PARM		DATEIN	60
03	C		PARM		CUSTIN	60
04	C		PARM		OPTION	1
05	C		PARM		FLD1	10
06	C		PARM		FLD2	60

Returning to a Calling Program

If there is no need to return to the original calling program, the second program can be ended in the usual way. More often, however, control returns to the original program, passing some parameters back for completion in the calling program. This is done with the RETRN operation. No other entries are necessary with the RETRN. Figure 13.29 shows a return to a calling program.

The RETRN operation returns control to the calling program exactly at the point in the Calculation Specifications where the call was made. Calculation will continue in the first program at the first statement following the PARM statements.

It is possible that a called program could call a third program, sending parameters even further. Each RETRN operation would return control back to the program which had sent the call. The third program would return to the second, and so on.

Defining Field Attributes in RPG III/400

Field attributes are usually defined externally in RPG III/400. Fields created within calculations may be defined, as always, by means of the length and decimal descriptors in columns 49–52. It is difficult to locate these descriptors in a very large program. These fields must remain concurrent with any changes that might be made to their counterparts in the input file.

FIGURE 13.29 Return to a Calling Program

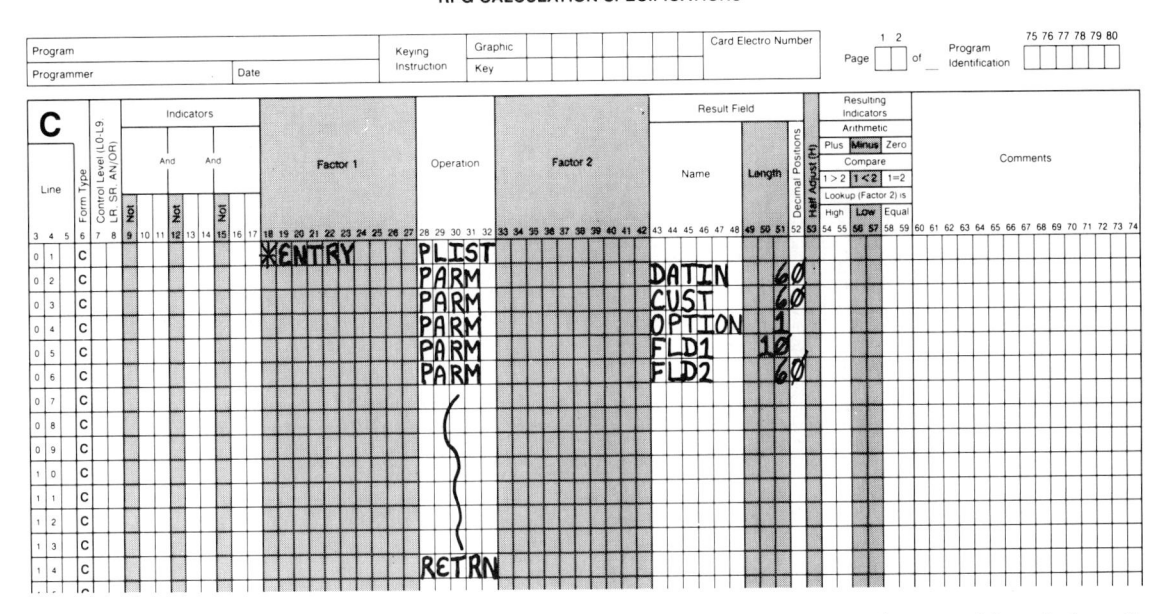

RPG CALCULATION SPECIFICATIONS

Line	Form Type	Factor 1	Operation	Factor 2	Result Field Name	Length
01	C	*ENTRY	PLIST			
02	C		PARM		DATIN	60
03	C		PARM		CUST	60
04	C		PARM		OPTION	1
05	C		PARM		FLD1	10
06	C		PARM		FLD2	60
07	C					
08	C					
09	C					
10	C					
11	C					
12	C					
13	C					
14	C		RETRN			

Figures 13.30(a) and 13.30(b) show an input field that at one time was three positions in length with no decimal positions and has been changed to an eight-position field with five decimal positions.

The calculations based on this field produce a result field that provides for no decimal positions. If the resulting quantity field must parallel the input quantity field, it is necessary to change every program to ensure that the result fields are handled correctly.

To avoid all this reprogramming, RPG III/400 provides the DEFN operation code. This allows the programmer to let RPG know that the result field should carry the same attributes as the field it emulates. Figure 13.31 shows the operation DEFN with *LIKE entered in factor 1. The field INQTY has been defined earlier in the program or in the data description for an externally defined file. The fields REVQTY, LSTQTY, and ORDQTY are defined in the DEFN operation as being "just like" INQTY.

FIGURE 13.30(a) Input Specifications for Revised Field Size

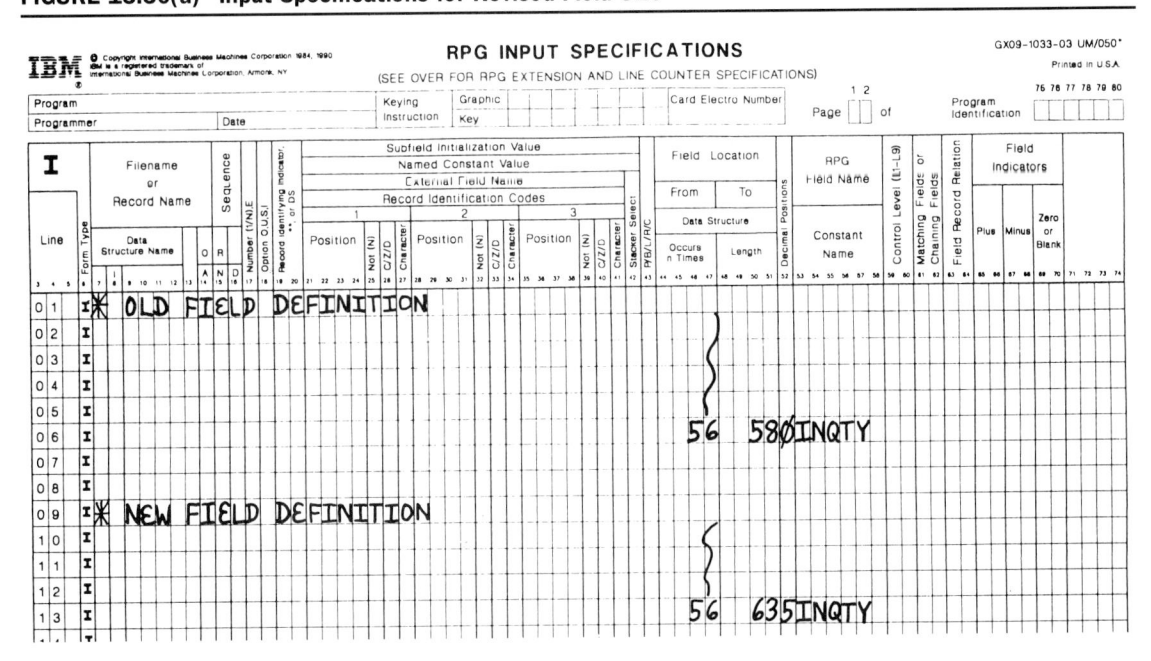

RPG INPUT SPECIFICATIONS

Line	Form Type	Filename or Record Name	Field Location From	To	RPG Field Name
01	I	* OLD FIELD DEFINITION			
02	I				
03	I				
04	I				
05	I				
06	I		56	58	INQTY
07	I				
08	I				
09	I	* NEW FIELD DEFINITION			
10	I				
11	I				
12	I				
13	I		56	635	INQTY

Chapter 13 Calculation Enhancements in RPG III/400

FIGURE 13.30(b) Calculation Specifications Showing Field Size

Line	C	Factor 1	Operation	Factor 2	Result Field Name	Length	Decimal
01	C	INQTY	MULT	.05	REVQTY	3	0H
02	C	INQTY	DIV	8	LSTQTY	3	0
03	C	INQTY	MULT	RATE	ORDQTY	3	0

FIGURE 13.31 Calculation Specifications Using DEFN Operation with *LIKE in Factor 1

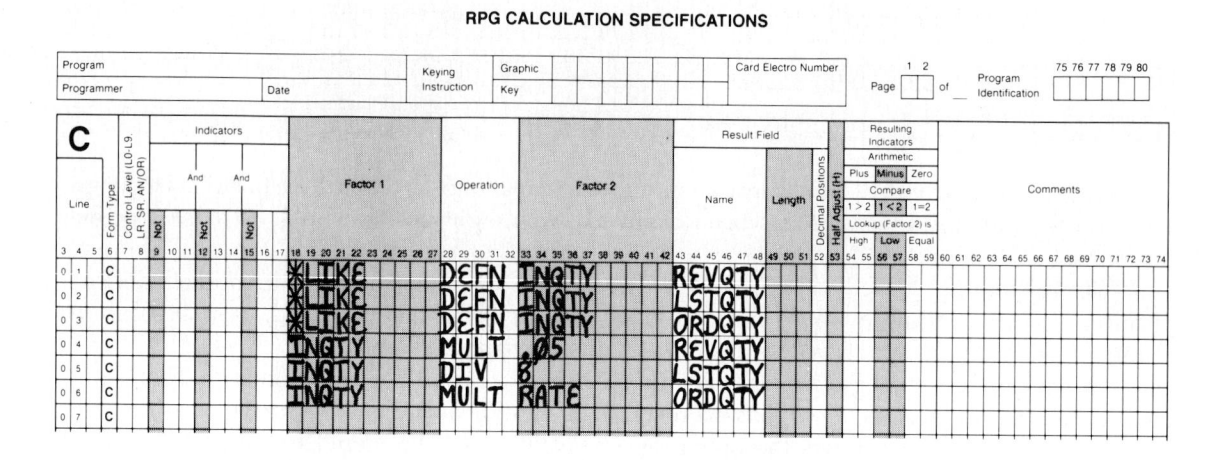

Line	C	Factor 1	Operation	Factor 2	Result Field Name
01	C	*LIKE	DEFN	INQTY	REVQTY
02	C	*LIKE	DEFN	INQTY	LSTQTY
03	C	*LIKE	DEFN	INQTY	ORDQTY
04	C	INQTY	MULT	.05	REVQTY
05	C	INQTY	DIV	8	LSTQTY
06	C	INQTY	MULT	RATE	ORDQTY

Whenever the attributes of an externally defined field are modified, the program will need only to be recompiled. All the fields that have been defined with the DEFN statement will take on the new attributes.

SUMMARY ∎

In this chapter, you have been introduced to a great number of new operations and methods which allow the programmer to take advantage of structured programming techniques not available in RPG II. Among these are the IF statements, which include all combinations of the classic AND/OR logic. This eliminates most of the need for using indicators in RPG.

You have also begun to appreciate the value of using the Do While and the Do Until structures, which provide for looping through a series of instructions until some criterion has been fulfilled. This chapter explores the uses for calling a program from within another program. This also permits passing parameters back and forth between several programs.

The DEFN operation has also been explained. This allows for a more flexible database since data attribute changes will not require extensive programming changes.

All of the subjects discussed together provide a very structured and flexible programming base from which to create any kind of programs.

REVIEW QUESTIONS ■

1. The reserved words that provide the values zero and blank in an RPG III program are _____ and _____ .

2. The factor that is no longer necessary to perform an ADD or SUB operation in RPG III/400 is _____ .

3. The IF statement in RPG III/400 has replaced the old _____ operation in RPG II.

4. An IF or DO statement will always require a(n) _____ statement following the activity being performed.

5. An IF statement may contain alternative action which is indicated by the _____ statement.

6. More than one condition may be specified with the use of the _____ and the _____ .

7. An IF statement in RPG III/400 can compare for the following conditions: _____ , _____ , _____ , _____ , _____ , and _____ .

8. A structured loop can be constructed in RPG III/400 with the use of the _____ or the _____ .

9. A CABxx statement will pass control of the program to a(n) _____ .

10. A CASxx statement will pass control of the program to a(n) _____ .

11. A second program can be called from within an RPG III/400 program with the use of the _____ operation.

12. Parameters are passed between programs with the use of the _____ operation.

13. Parameters are received in the receiving program with the use of the _____ operation followed by one or more _____ operations.

14. Field attributes can be defined within a program with the use of the _____ operation.

15. What are the benefits of defining attributes in this manner?

DEBUGGING EXERCISES

Instructions

The following RPG programs contain an error or errors. Some of these errors are indicated by the RPG compiler on the program listing. A list of syntax errors is given at the end of the program listing. Other types of errors may occur which will not be shown. These are called logic errors.

Study each program and its syntax errors. Locate each error (including logic errors) and on a separate coding form make the correct entry for the line(s) in error.

Explain each error and how it should be corrected.

```
         100   F* TITLE: DEBUG PROJECT 13-A
         200   F* DATE:   5/19           AUTHOR: D.CABLE
         300   F* DESCRIPTION:      INDEXED FILES
         400   F********************************************

       NAME OF PROGRAM WILL BE PJ013A IN LIBRARY CABLE

                     H
* 1019                     ALL DECIMAL DATA ERRORS IGNORED
         500   FPICTNFL IP   E             K        DISK
* 2120         500   DATA DESCRIPTIONS FOR FILE PICTNFL NOT FOUND
         600   FQSYSPRT O   F    132       OF       PRINTER
         700   F********************************************

         800   C           *LIKE     DEFN
* 5030                                        5030-******

         900   C                     ADD  1         LINES  20
        1000   C                     ADD  EXPRC     FINVAL 102
        1100   C           INTOT     ADD            TOTAL  92
* 5023                                        5023-********

        1200   C                     SUB  1         LINES  20
        1300   C                     MULT RATE      TOTSS  72
        1400   C                     DIV  10        NUM    72

        1500   OQSYSPRT H  203       1P
        1600   O        OR           OF
        1700   O                                    6  *PJ013A*
        1800   O                            UDATE Y 50
        1900   O                                   30 *PHYSICAL INVENTORY*
        2000   O        H   2        1P
        2100   O        OR           OF
        2200   O                                   11 *COMPANY*
        2300   O                                   25 *LOCATION*
        2400   O                                   35 *PART NUMBER*
        2500   O                                   44 *QUANT*
        2600   O                                   55 *PRICE*
        2700   O        D   1        01
        2800   O                            PARTNO  10
        2900   O                            DESCR   30
        3000   O                            INV#    24
        3100   O                            AMTDUEK 35
        3200   O                            QTY   K 45
        3300   O                            EXPRC K 56
        3400   O        D   1        LR
        3500   O                                   20 *TOTAL VALUE*
        3600   O                            FINVALK 56
       * * * * * END  OF  SOURCE * * * *
```

```
* 7064        500   PICTNFL FILE NOT REFERENCED FOR INPUT
     CROSS-REFERENCE LISTING


            FILE/RCD    DEV/RCD      REFERENCES (D=DEFINED)
       01   PICTNFL     DISK         500D
       02   QSYSPRT     PRINTER      600D  1500  2000  2700  3400


            FIELD       ATTR         REFERENCES (M=MODIFIED D=DEFINED)

            *LIKE                     800
* 7030      AMTDUE      P(5,0)       3100
* 7030      DESCR       A(4)         2900
* 7030      EXPRC       P(5,0)       1000  3300
            FINVAL      P(10,2)      1000D 3600
* 7030      INTOT       A(4)         1100
* 7030      INV#        A(4)         3000
            LINES       P(2,0)       900D  1200D
            NUM         P(7,2)       1400D
* 7030      PARTNO      A(4)         2800
* 7030      QTY         P(5,0)       3200
* 7030      RATE        P(5,0)       1300
            TOTAL       P(9,2)       1100D
            TOTSS       P(7,2)       1300D
            UDATE       P(6,0)       1800
            1           LITERAL       900  1200
            10          LITERAL      1400


            INDICATOR   REFERENCES (M=MODIFIED D=DEFINED)

            LR          500D  3400
            OF          600D  1600  2100
* 7030      01          2700
            1P          1500  2000


     MESSAGES

            MSGID   SEV   NUMBER   TEXT

*  QRG1019   00    1       IGNDECERR(*YES) SPECIFIED ON COMMAND. NO DECIMAL DATA ERRORS
*  QRG2120   40    1       EXTERNAL DESCRIPTION NOT FOUND FOR FILE SPECIFIED AS EXTERNA
                           IGNORED.
*  QRG5023   30    1       FACTOR 2 (POSITIONS 33-42) MUST BE ENTERED FOR SPECIFIED OPE
*  QRG5030   30    1       RESULT FIELD NAME (POSITIONS 43-48) MUST BE ENTERED FOR SPEC
                           IGNORED
*  QRG7030   30    9       FIELD OR INDICATOR NOT DEFINED.
*  QRG7064   40    1       PROGRAM FILE NOT REFERENCED. FILE IGNORED


     MESSAGE SUMMARY

     TOTAL   00    10    20    30    40    50
       14     1     0     0    11     2     0

       36 RECORDS READ FROM SOURCE FILE
     SOURCE RECORDS INCLUDE   31 SPECIFICATIONS,   0 TABLE RECORDS, AND   5 COMMENTS

     QRG0008 COMPILE TERMINATED. SEVERITY 40 ERRORS FOUND IN PROGRAM

     * * * * * E N D   O F   C O M P I L A T I O N * * * * *
     * QRG1020           ERROR OCCURRED CREATING OR UPDATING DATA AREA RETURNCODE. COMPI
```

```
     100  F* TITLE: DEBUG PROJECT 13-B
     200  F* DATE:   6/25         AUTHOR: D.CABLE
     300  F* DESCRIPTION:       G/L FILES
     400  F************************************************

    NAME OF PROGRAM WILL BE PJ013B IN LIBRARY CABLE

               H
* 1019              ALL DECIMAL DATA ERRORS IGNORED
     500  FSAGLRECSIP  E          K        DISK
          RECORD FORMAT(S):  FILE SAGLRECS LIB MOMS
                      EXTERNAL FORMAT SAGL10 RPG NAME SAGL10

     600  FREPORT  O  F    132        OF    PRINTER
     700  F************************************************

   A000000    INPUT  FIELDS FOR RECORD SAGL10 FILE SAGLRECS FORMAT SAGL10
   A000001                                          1   1 ACTIVE
   A000002                                          2   40STORE#
   A000003                                          5  100DTBTCH
   A000004                                         11  140REG#
   A000005                                         15  190GLACT#
   A000006                                         19  200GLSTR#
   A000007                                         21  220GLDEPT
   A000008                                      P  23  272AMOUNT
   A000009                                         28   47 NOTE20
     800  C           ACTIVE    IFEQ 'A'
     900  C                     SETON                     33
    1000  C                     EXCPT
    1100  C           GLACT#    IFNGT000
* 5014                5014-*****

    1200  C                     SETON                     34
    1300  C                     END
    1400  C           COUNT     DOWLE3
    1500  C                     ENDDO
* 5014                5014-*****

    1600  C                     SETOF                     33
    1700  C    55              EXCPT
    1800  C                     ADD  AMOUNT   TOTVAL 102
* 5177                5177-*****


    1900  OREPORT  H  203        1P
    2000  O        OR            OF
    2100  O                                    6 'PJ013B'
    2200  O                      UDATE Y      50
    2300  O                                   30 'GENERAL LEDGER'
    2400  O        H  2          1P
    2500  O        OR            OF
    2600  O                                   11 'ACCT NUMBER'
    2700  O                                   25 'STORE'
    2800  O                                   35 'DEPT'
    2900  O                                   50 'AMOUNT'
    3000  O        D  1          01
    3100  O                      GLACT#       10
    3200  O                      GLSTR#       30
    3300  O                      GLDEPT       33
    3400  O                      AMOUNTZ      48
    3500  O        D  1          LR
    3600  O                      TOTVALK      48
    3700  O                                   20 'TOTAL G/L AMOUNT'
* * * * * E N D   O F   S O U R C E * * * * *
```

```
* 7086        500     RPG PROVIDES BLOCK/UNBLOCK SUPPORT FOR FILE SAGLRECS.
* 7026       1000     NO UNNAMED EXCEPTION OUTPUT SPECIFICATIONS IN PROGRAM
* 7026       1700     NO UNNAMED EXCEPTION OUTPUT SPECIFICATIONS IN PROGRAM

     KEY FIELD INFORMATION


                      PHYSICAL     LOGICAL
            FILE/RCD  FIELD        FIELD        ATTRIBUTES


         01 SAGLRECS
               SAGL10
                      STORE#                    ZONE  3,0  SIGNED
                      DTBTCH                    ZONE  6,0  SIGNED
                      REG#                      ZONE  4,0  SIGNED
                      GLACT#                    ZONE  4,0  SIGNED
                      GLSTR#                    ZONE  2,0  SIGNED
                      GLDEPT                    ZONE  2,0  SIGNED


     CROSS-REFERENCE LISTING



            FILE/RCD   DEV/RCD    REFERENCES (D=DEFINED)

         02 REPORT     PRINTER      600D     1900    2400    3000
                                    3500
         01 SAGLRECS   DISK         500D

               SAGL10                         500D   A000000


            FIELD       ATTR      REFERENCES (M=MODIFIED D=DEFINED)

            ACTIVE      A(1)      A000001D     800
            AMOUNT      P(9,2)    A000008D    1800    3400
* 7030      COUNT       P(1,0)       1400
* 7031      DTBTCH      P(6,0)    A000003D
            GLACT#      P(4,0)    A000005D    1100    3100
            GLDEPT      P(2,0)    A000007D    3300
            GLSTR#      P(2,0)    A000006D    3200
* 7031      NOTE20      A(20)     A000009D
* 7031      REG#        P(4,0)    A000004D
* 7031      STORE#      P(3,0)    A000002D
            TOTVAL      P(10,2)   1800D       3600
            UDATE       P(6,0)    2200
            'A'         LITERAL    800
            000         LITERAL   1100
            3           LITERAL   1400


            INDICATOR  REFERENCES (M=MODIFIED D=DEFINED)

            LR            500D    3500
            OF            600D    2000    2500
* 7030      01           3000
            1P           1900     2400
* 7031      33            900M    1600M
* 7031      34           1200M
* 7030      55           1700
```

MESSAGES

MSGID	SEV	NUMBER	TEXT
* QRG1019	00	1	IGNDECERR(*YES) SPECIFIED ON COMMAND. NO DECIMAL DATA ERRORS
* QRG5014	30	2	OPERATION CODE ENTRY (POSITIONS 28-32) NOT VALID. SPECIFICAT
* QRG5177	30	1	END STATEMENT MISSING FOR DO, DOUXX, DOWXX, OR IFXX GROUP. E
* QRG7026	30	2	NO UNNAMED EXCPT OUTPUT IN PROGRAM. EXCPT CALCULATION SPECIF
* QRG7030	30	3	FIELD OR INDICATOR NOT DEFINED.
* QRG7031	00	6	NAME OR INDICATOR NOT REFERENCED.
* QRG7036	00	1	RPG WILL HANDLE BLOCKING FUNCTION FOR THE FILE. INFDS CONTEN ARE TRANSFERRED.

MESSAGE SUMMARY

TOTAL	00	10	20	30	40	50
16	8	0	0	8	0	0

37 RECORDS READ FROM SOURCE FILE

5714RG1 RPG R08M00 861114   PJ013B.CABLE   03/12/92 15:07:10 PAGE   5

SOURCE RECORDS INCLUDE   32 SPECIFICATIONS,   0 TABLE RECORDS, AND   5 COMMENTS

QRG0008 COMPILE TERMINATED. SEVERITY 30 ERRORS FOUND IN PROGRAM

* * * * * E N D O F C O M P I L A T I O N * * * * *
* QRG1020   ERROR OCCURRED CREATING OR UPDATING DATA AREA RETURNCODE. COMPI

PROGRAMMING PROJECT

Project Overview

A report is to be printed to show the value of all inventory in warehouse 01. Obsolete items should be identified. The word "obsolete" should be printed on items having the code DD in the category code field. Use only RPG III/400 coding functions in this assignment. Sample data for this project can be found in Appendix D.

Input Format

The input data for the project is found in a file called INVDETL in the sample data. The Record Layout for this file is shown in Figure 13.32.

Processing

A record is read and if the warehouse number is 01, the record should be processed and printed. All other records should be ignored.

The quantity is multiplied by the average cost to produce an extended cost. A total cost is accumulated to be printed at the end of the report. Each record must also be counted and a final total number of items in inventory printed at the end of the report.

If a category code is found to be DD, the word "obsolete" should be moved into the message field. If the code is not DD, then blanks (using the reserved word for blanks) should be moved into the message field. The message field is printed on each line.

Output Format (Printer Spacing Chart)

The output format for the project is a report with standard headings. The report will show each item, quantity, unit average cost, extended cost, and the appropriate message. The Printer Spacing Chart for this report is shown in Figure 13.33.

An example of the finished report is shown in Figure 13.34.

FIGURE 13.32 Programming Project: Record Layout

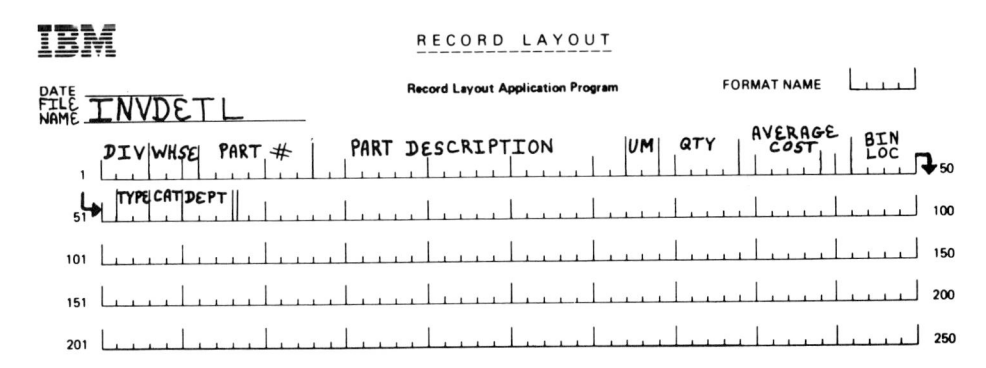

FIGURE 13.33 Programming Project: Printer Spacing Chart

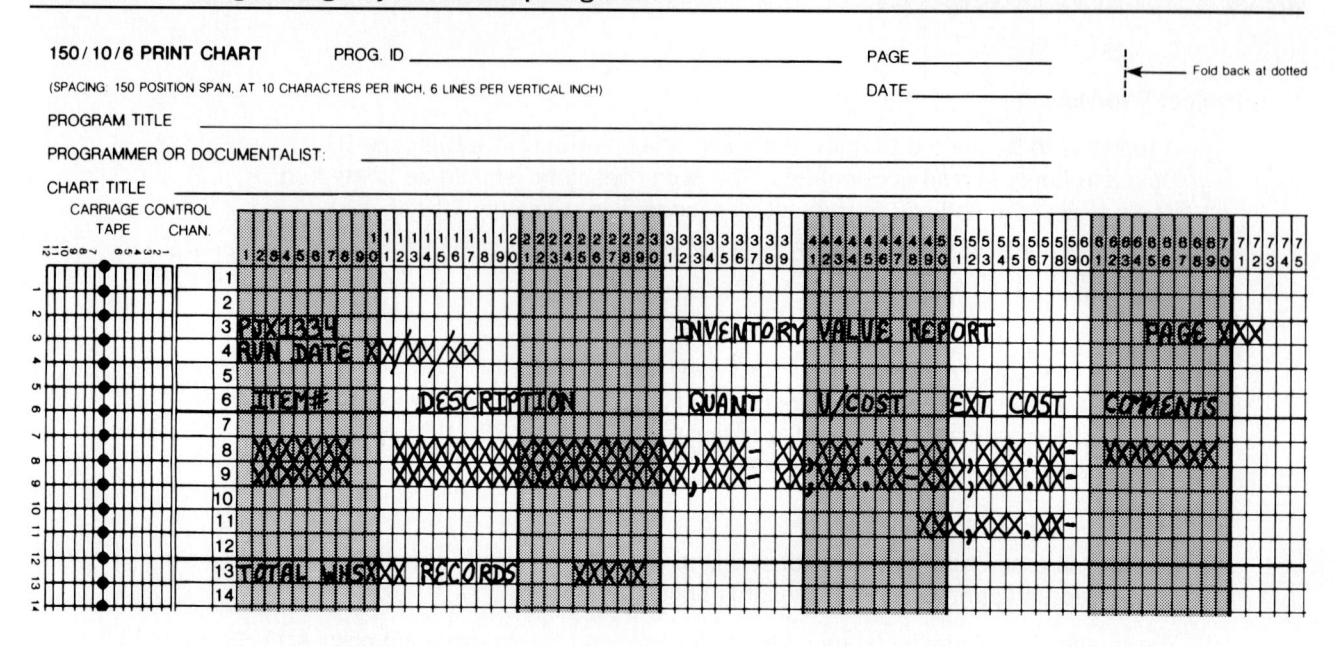

FIGURE 13.34 Programming Project: Final Report

```
PJX1334                    INVENTORY VALUE REPORT           PAGE    1
RUN DATE  3/12/92

   ITEM#     DESCRIPTION      QUANT      U/COST      EXT COST    COMMENTS
     123    STRIPED WIDGETS     283        2.50        707.50
     698    YELLOW GADGETS      300        1.25        375.00    OBSOLETE
     798    WIRE, SPECIAL     1,200    1,500.00    800,000.00
    9875    NAILS               500         .03         15.00
    9903    RIBBON, YELLOW      396         .25         99.00
     125    BOXES, SHIPPING                 .01
   98555    CUBES, SILVER                200.00                  OBSOLETE
      51    PAPER PLATES      1,000         .01         10.00

                                                    801,206.50

       TOTAL WHS 01 RECORDS            8
```

Chapter 14

File Management Techniques in RPG III/400

What you will learn in Chapter 14

Full Functional File Processing
Reading a Sequential File Using SETLL and READ Operations
Defining a File Key in RPG III/400 (KLIST and KFLD)
New Methods for Accessing Files and Retrieving Records
 Using SETLL and READ Operations (with a Key)
 Using SETGT and READP Operations

Using SETLL and READE Operations
Differences Between CHAIN and READ Operations
Creating Your Own Processing Cycle
Exception Output Labels
Level Breaks In RPG III/400
Use of Multiple Indexes
 Renaming Formats
 Renaming Fields

Dynamic Open and Close of Files (OPEN/CLOSE)
Updating a File Using Exception Updating
Updating Records in a File (UPDAT Operation)
Adding Records to a File (WRITE Operation)
Deleting Records from a File (DELET Operation)

Files can be accessed in RPG III/400 from within the Calculation Specifications. Unlike RPG II, which depends on the fixed RPG cycle to retrieve records automatically, RPG III/400 makes it possible for the programmer to take control of the file access. This provides greater flexibility in the manner and sequence in which records are read. Although it is still possible to use the old methods, the advantages of the new methods are quickly apparent.

FULL FUNCTIONAL FILE PROCESSING ■

Using the new methods for controlling the retrieval of records, it is possible to read a file sequentially with or without a key for access. To take advantage of the new operations for RPG III/400, files must be defined in the File Description Specifications as full functional (or full procedural) files by entering the letter *F* in column 16. This means that the file is neither a primary nor a secondary file. Its activity will be determined by the Calculation Specifications within the program. All the operations described in this chapter must be used with full functional files. Notice also that the file must be externally defined to be accessed in this manner. Figure 14.1 shows the File Description Specifications for a full functional file.

FIGURE 14.1 File Description Specifications for Full Functional File

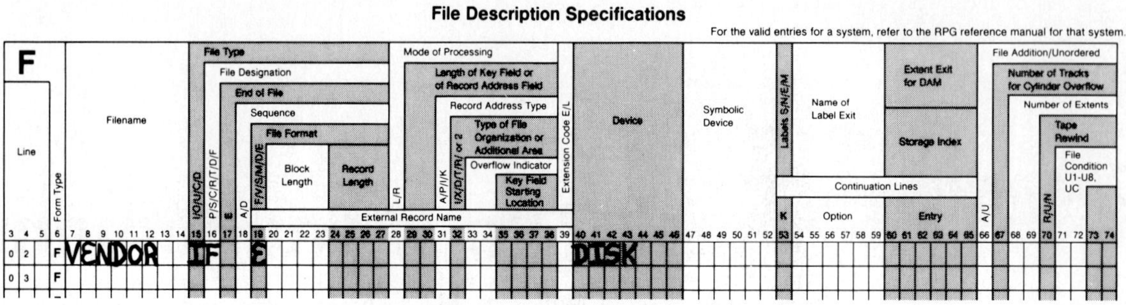

```
02 FVENDOR  IF  E                           DISK
03 F
```

READING A SEQUENTIAL FILE USING SETLL AND READ OPERATIONS ■

A file can be read sequentially from the beginning using a combination of the SETLL and the READ operations. The SETLL operation (set lower limits) sets the lower limit at which the reading will begin. Factor 1 of the SETLL operation will contain the reserved word *LOVAL, which means that the first record read will be the record with the lowest-value key (i.e., the beginning of the file). Factor 2 of the SETLL operation will contain either the filename or the name of the record format for the file for which the pointer (access path) is being set. Conditioning indicators and resulting indicators are optional for the SETLL operation. The resulting indicators reflect the status of the SETLL operation. These will be discussed in greater depth later, along with the subject of indexed file access.

The READ operation will retrieve the first record of the file for processing. For the READ operation, factor 1 remains blank. Factor 2 will contain either the filename or the name of the record format for the file that is to be read. Conditioning indicators are optional, but a resulting indicator in columns 58–59 is required for the READ operation. This indicator will be set on when the end of the file is found.

The READ operation then reads the next record found. It is up to the programmer to use the SETLL operation to control which record will be the first one read. (It is also the programmer's job to control which subsequent records will be read.) Figure 14.2 contains an example of the SETLL and READ operations as they are used to read the first record in a file.

The SETLL is required *only* to locate the first record in a series of records to be read. Once the beginning position has been located, subsequent records are retrieved by continuing to perform the READ statement. Figure 14.3 shows how this structure might be used to read a complete file.

Note that it is a safer practice to use the SETLL operation to position the first read. If a READ operation is used without a SETLL preceding it, results can be unpredictable.

If it is not necessary to read an entire file, a key can be used to begin reading the file at some predetermined midpoint. The following section describes how a specific key can be defined for a SETLL and READ.

FIGURE 14.2 SETLL and READ Operations

RPG CALCULATION SPECIFICATIONS

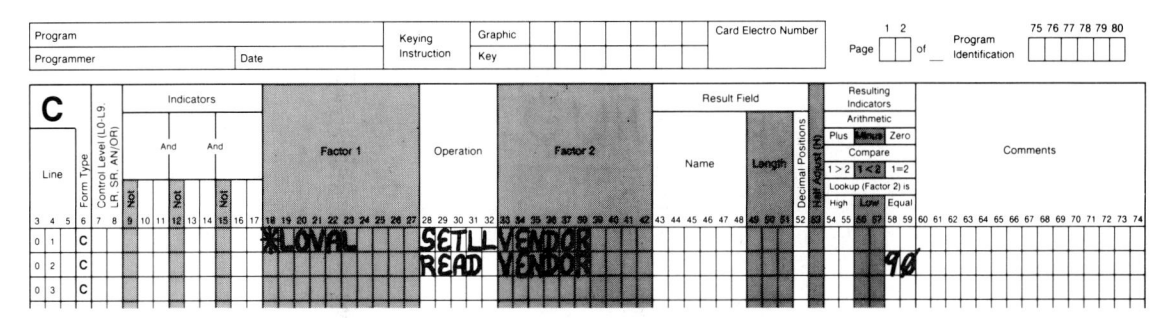

```
C  *LOVAL    SETLL VENDOR
C            READ  VENDOR                           90
C
```

FIGURE 14.3 Reading a Complete File Using SETLL and READ

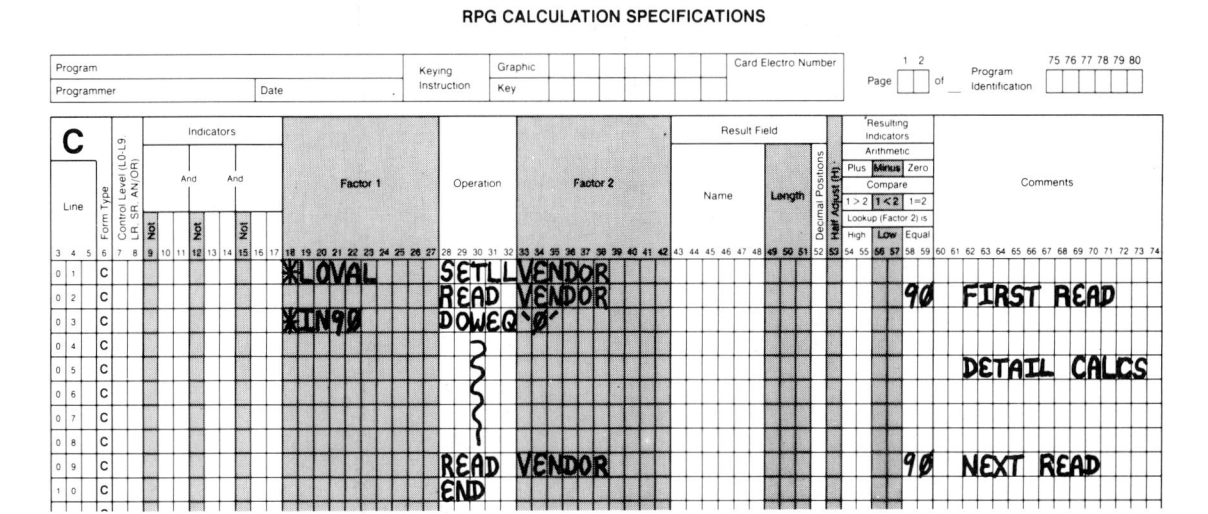

RPG CALCULATION SPECIFICATIONS

```
C  *LOVAL    SETLL VENDOR
C            READ  VENDOR                           90  FIRST READ
C  *IN90     DOWEQ '0'
C
C                                                       DETAIL CALCS
C
C
C
C            READ  VENDOR                           90  NEXT READ
C            END
```

DEFINING A FILE KEY IN RPG III/400 (KLIST AND KFLD)

The key to a file in RPG III/400 is defined within the Calculation Specifications. Unlike RPG II, which permits only a single key field for an indexed file, RPG III/400 allows the programmer to define as many key fields as needed. These key fields need not be contiguous in the record. Figures 14.4(a) and 14.4(b) show a Record Layout and DDS in which four separate fields are used as the key.

FIGURE 14.4(a) Record Layout for Vendor Master File

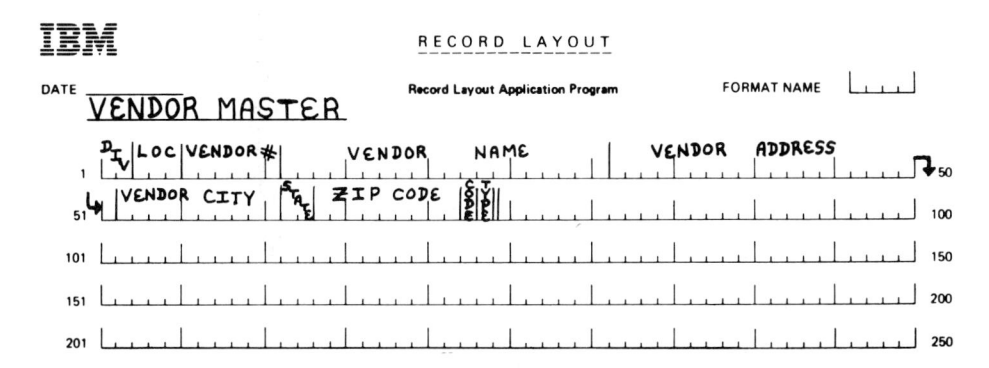

IBM RECORD LAYOUT

DATE VENDOR MASTER

```
  D
  T
  V | LOC | VENDOR # |  VENDOR NAME  |  VENDOR ADDRESS        | 50
    | VENDOR CITY | S T A T E | ZIP CODE | C O D E |          | 100
```

Chapter 14 File Management Techniques in RPG III/400   351

FIGURE 14.4(b) Data Description Specifications for Vendor Master File with Four Key Fields

DATA DESCRIPTION SPECIFICATIONS

Seq	Type	Name	R	Length	Dec	K
A	R	VEND01				
A		DIV		2		
A		LOC		3	0	
A		VENDNO		6	0	
A		VNAME		20		
A		VADDR		20		
A		VCITY		10		
A		VST		2		
A		VZIP		9	0	
A		VCODE		1		
A		VTYPE		1		
A		VCODE				K
A		VLOC				K
A		VTYPE				K
A		VENDNO				K

The operation code used to define a key in RPG III/400 is the KLIST. This is followed immediately in the Calculation Specifications by one or more KFLD operations representing each of the key fields.

Factor 1 of the KLIST statement contains the name, assigned by the programmer, to be used for accessing this key. This name will be used elsewhere in the program when it is necessary to address this file by its key.

Following the KLIST, each KFLD line contains the name of the key field in the result field entry. The name entered need not be the same name as the external name. However, the attributes of the field must be the same. The fields must also be in the same sequence in which they are defined in the key on the external definition. Figure 14.5 presents an example of a KLIST statement for the file described earlier.

FIGURE 14.5 KLIST Statement

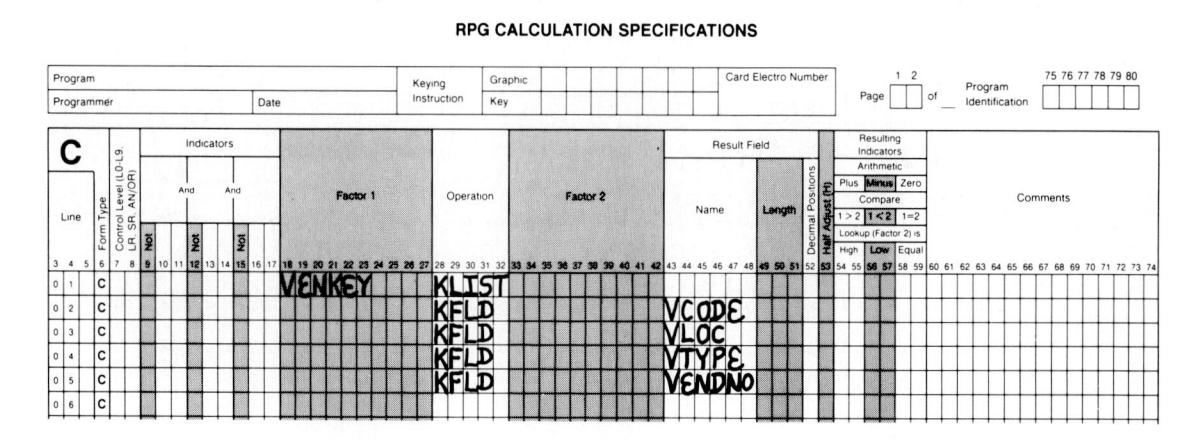

RPG CALCULATION SPECIFICATIONS

Line	Form	Factor 1	Operation	Factor 2	Result Field
01	C	VENKEY	KLIST		
02	C		KFLD		VCODE
03	C		KFLD		VLOC
04	C		KFLD		VTYPE
05	C		KFLD		VENDNO
06	C				

The KLIST statement may be placed *anywhere* within the Calculation Specifications. Programs may have several sets of KLIST groups accessing several files. All of the KLIST statements might be placed as the very first calculation statements. Some programmers like to place each KLIST near its related activity in the program. Sometimes KLIST statements are placed in a separate subroutine. They could even show up after the LR calculations. It is a good idea to be consistent in placing KLIST statements so they will be easy to find.

NEW METHODS FOR ACCESSING FILES AND RETRIEVING RECORDS ∎

Not only is it possible to read an entire keyed file sequentially beginning with the first record, it is also possible to read sections of the file starting at a selected record.

Using SETLL and READ Operations (with a Key)

Instead of using *LOVAL in factor 1 of the SETLL operation, it is possible to use a specific key to control the position from which the reading will begin. Factor 1 may contain an index value such as a field, a constant, or a key list. It could even contain a relative record number. Factor 2 will contain the name of a file or externally defined record format. The resulting indicators are optional for the SETLL statement. Figures 14.6(a) and 14.6(b) show how a keyed file might be accessed beginning somewhere within the file, based on a selected key.

The SETLL will position the file to begin reading just before the record to be retrieved. Moving the literals into the field before setting lower limits causes the reading to begin with the first record containing the requested fields. When the first record has been located, all records following it according to the key can be read. When the last record in the file has been read, the indicator will be turned on. The programmer must ensure that reading will end when the last record has been processed. In this example, reading will cease because it is controlled by the indicator specified in the DOWEQ operation.

FIGURE 14.6(a) File Description Specifications

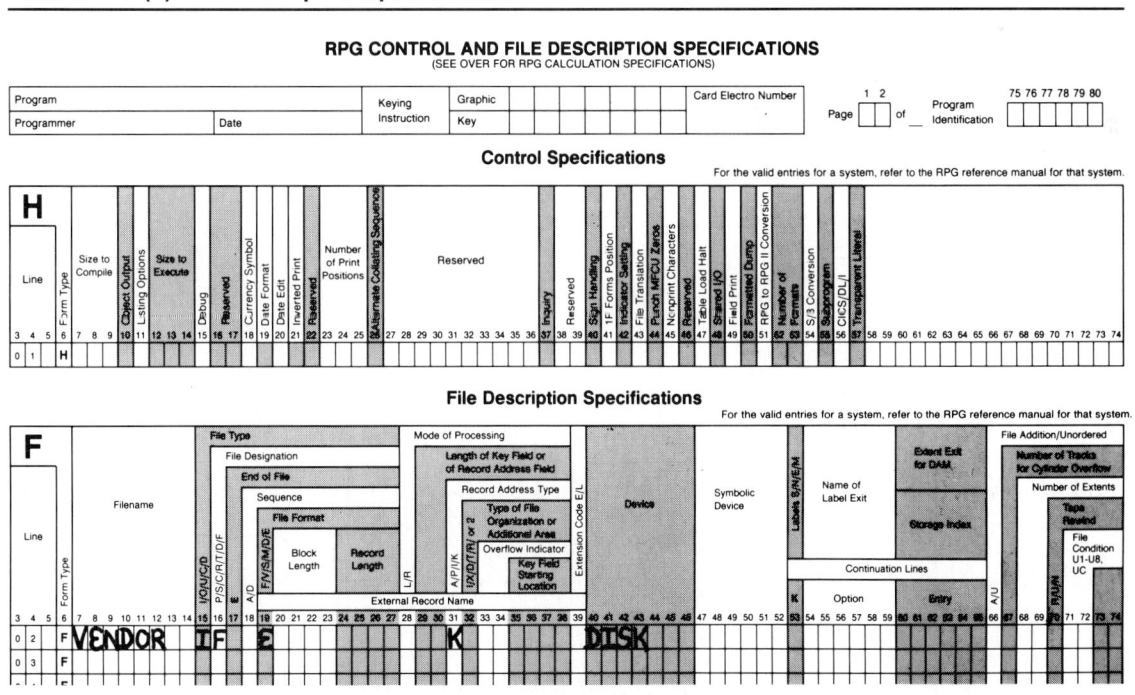

FIGURE 14.6(b) Calculation Specifications for Accessing a Key File Based on a Selected Key

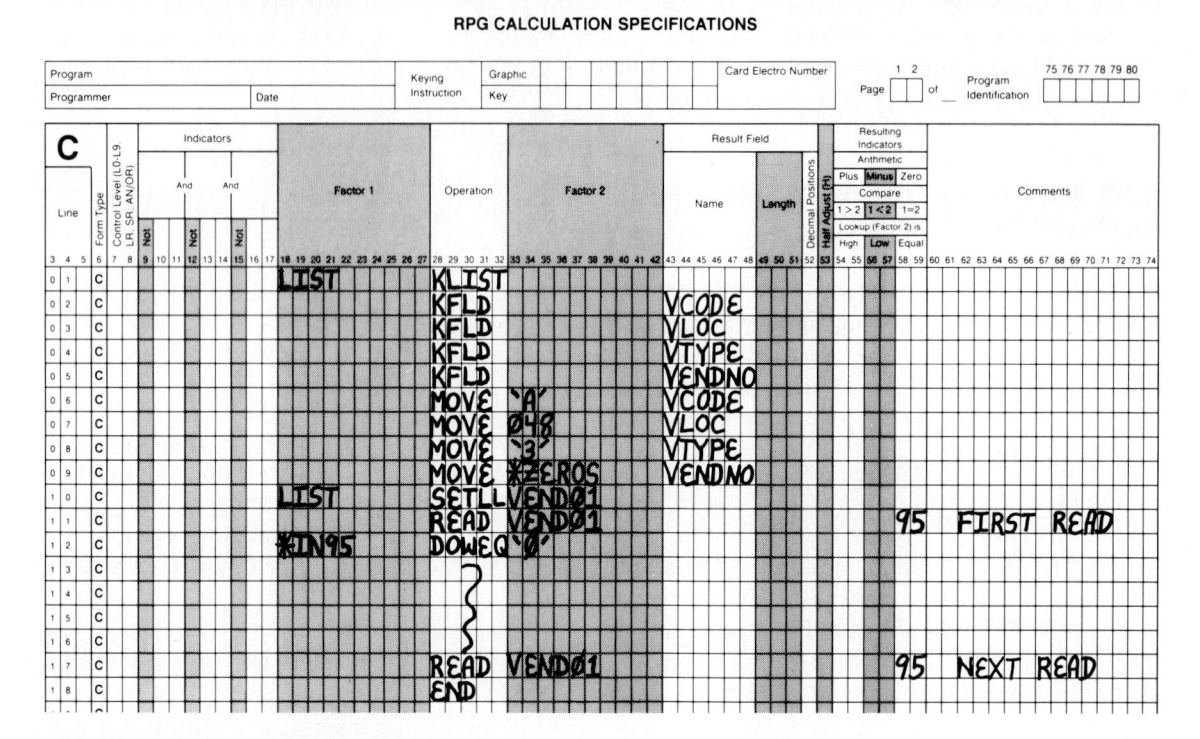

```
RPG CALCULATION SPECIFICATIONS

Line  Form  Factor 1   Operation  Factor 2    Result    Len  Resulting   Comments
                                              Field          Indicators
01    C                LIST       KLIST
02    C                           KFLD         VCODE
03    C                           KFLD         VLOC
04    C                           KFLD         VTYPE
05    C                           KFLD         VENDNO
06    C                           MOVE 'A'     VCODE
07    C                           MOVE 048     VLOC
08    C                           MOVE '3'     VTYPE
09    C                           MOVE *ZEROS  VENDNO
10    C     LIST       SETLL      VEND01
11    C                READ       VEND01                 95   FIRST READ
12    C     *IN95      DOWEQ '0'
13    C                {
14    C                {
15    C                {
16    C                {
17    C                READ       VEND01                 95   NEXT READ
18    C                END
```

Using SETGT and READP Operations

It is also possible to read the record previous to the position where processing is being done. This is done using the SETGT (set greater than) and the READP (read previous record) operation, as shown in Figure 14.7.

The SETGT operation sets the higher limit at which the READP operation will begin to search. For the READP statement, factor 1 will remain blank. Factor 2 will contain the name of a file or externally defined record format. The resulting indicator is required. The READP will read backwards through the file, retrieving the record just prior to the position read.

FIGURE 14.7 SETGT and READP Operations

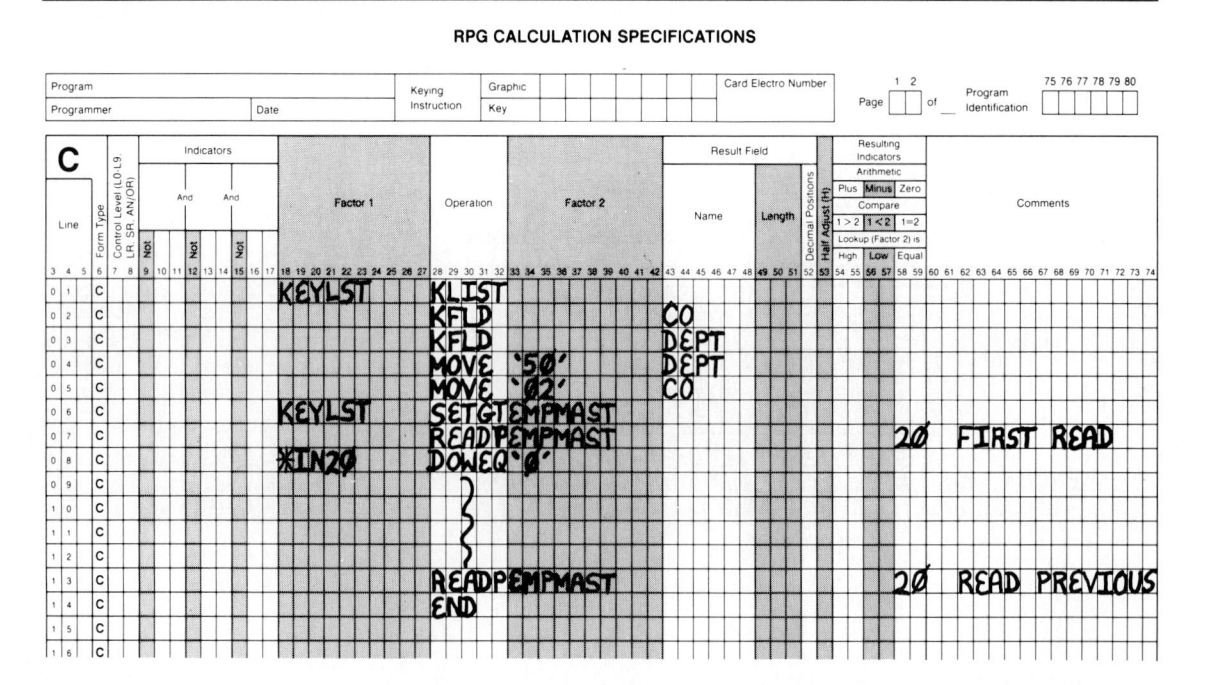

```
RPG CALCULATION SPECIFICATIONS

Line  Form  Factor 1   Operation  Factor 2    Result    Len  Resulting   Comments
                                              Field          Indicators
01    C     KEYLST     KLIST
02    C                KFLD                   CO
03    C                KFLD                   DEPT
04    C                MOVE '50'              DEPT
05    C                MOVE '02'              CO
06    C     KEYLST     SETGT      EMPMAST
07    C                READP      EMPMAST                20  FIRST READ
08    C     *IN20      DOWEQ '0'
09    C                {
10    C                {
11    C                {
12    C                {
13    C                READP      EMPMAST                20  READ PREVIOUS
14    C                END
15    C
16    C
```

354 *RPG: A Programming Language for Today*

Sometimes the last record in a file needs to be retrieved based on the key. This can be done even if the programmer has no idea what record is the last record. The reserved word *HIVAL is used to do this. This reserved word, used with the SETGT operation, will position the reading to begin at the last record in the file, as shown in Figure 14.8.

Using SETLL and READE Operations

To retrieve one particular record from a file, a combination of the SETLL and the READE (read equal) operations is used. Although this is similar to the SETLL and READ operations described earlier, it is more precise about the record retrieved. In the example in Figure 14.9, the SETLL will position the file to begin reading just before the requested record. The record will then be read by a READE statement. Factor 1 may contain a constant index, a field containing an index, or a key list name (KLIST). Factor 2 will contain a filename or the name of an externally defined record format. An indicator is required in columns 58–59. This indicator will be set on if the desired record is *not* found.

In Figure 14.9, a part number has been entered into a field variable called SEARCH. The program reads the file, beginning with the record containing a part number just *before* the value contained in the search variable. If the record retrieved is *not* the same as the key requested, then the indicator in columns 58–59 will be set on and the programmer can decide what to do next.

As was done earlier, the SETLL operation positions the lower limit at which the READE operation will begin to search. Factor 1 of the READE operation will contain the key. The resulting indicator is required.

Differences Between CHAIN and READ Operations

Each of the READx operations serves a special purpose. READ is useful for reading records forward through the file, with no need to meet any criteria. The READP operation allows the program to read backwards through the file.

The READE operation is useful to search for a particular record in the file. It is quite similar to the CHAIN function, which was used in RPG II to retrieve a specific record from an indexed file. The CHAIN function can be used in RPG III/400 in the same way that it was used in RPG II, but only for files which have a UNIQUE key.

Since RPG III/400 can handle indexed files for which the key is *not* unique, there must be a method for retrieving specific records when they are needed. This is the special function served by the READE operation.

FIGURE 14.8 SETGT and READP Operations Using *HIVAL

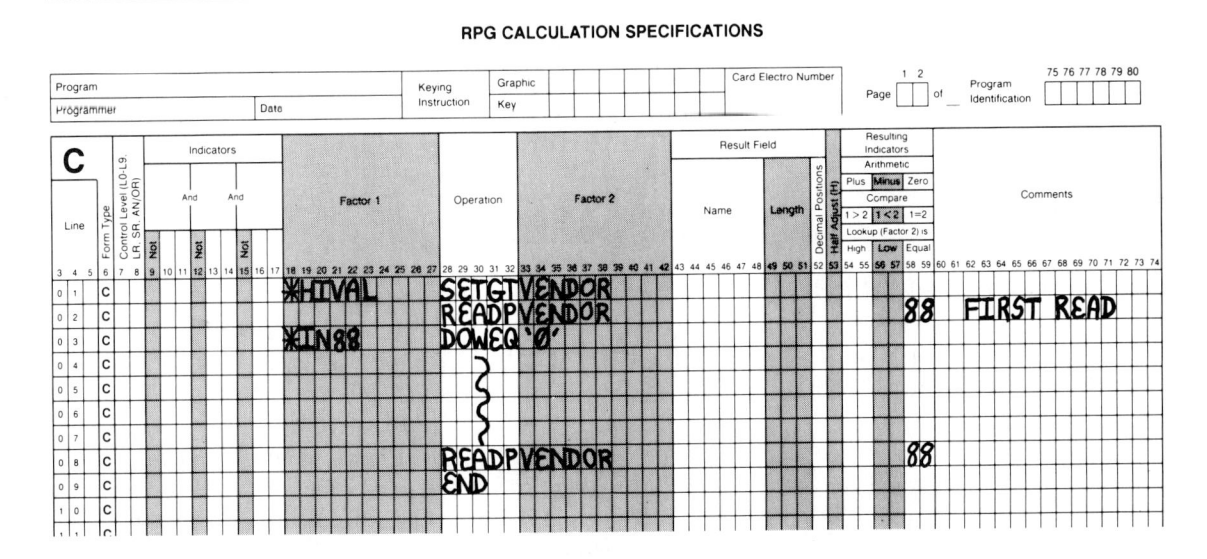

```
01 C           *HIVAL    SETGTVENDOR
02 C                     READPVENDOR                        88  FIRST READ
03 C           *IN88     DOWEQ'0'
04 C
05 C
06 C
07 C
08 C                     READPVENDOR                        88
09 C                     END
```

FIGURE 14.9 SETLL and READE, Moving a Literal into the Key Field

Line	Form Type	Factor 1	Operation	Factor 2	Result Field Name	Resulting Indicators 1<2	Comments
01	C	INVKEY	KLIST				
02	C		KFLD		COMPNY		
03	C		KFLD		LOC		
04	C		KFLD		PART#		
05	C		MOVE	'03'	COMPNY		
06	C		MOVE	099	LOC		
07	C		MOVE	SEARCH	PART#		
08	C	INVKEY	SETLL	INVMAST01			SEARCH FOR RCD
09	C	INVKEY	READE	INVMAST01		22	
10	C	*IN22	IFEQ	'1'			
11	C		EXSR	ERROR			
12	C		ELSE				
13	C		EXSR	PROCES			
14	C		END				

For example, a part master record might contain a unique key that will be the part number. A second file will contain information about each part number, such as the warehouse location, where the part is stored, and the quantity on hand at each of these locations. This file has keys that are *not* unique. When a report is needed to list a total of all the parts, their locations, and total quantity on hand, the part master file must first be read sequentially. The detail information is retrieved from the detail file for each part using the part number to locate all the detail records that have the *same* part number.

After a part master has been read, a SETLL will begin the search in the detail file at the first record containing the matching part number. The READE will read the *first* record found to be *equal* to the key. A DO loop can be created to go back and do another READE and continue reading through the detail file until a record is encountered which is *not* equal to the key. At this point the loop will end and processing will return to reading the master file for the next part number. Figure 14.10 shows what this program would look like.

CREATING YOUR OWN PROCESSING CYCLE ■

By now it should be clear that records can be retrieved from a file whenever and however they are needed. The programmer has complete control of the retrieval of records. This makes it possible to create a processing cycle independent of the automatic RPG II fixed cycle, resulting in more structured programs. Figure 14.11 shows how a program to read a file might be written.

EXCEPTION OUTPUT LABELS ■

The familiar EXCPT operation is an integral part of RPG III/400 and becomes particularly important when all processing is being done within the Calculation Specifications instead of depending on the fixed RPG cycle.

All outputs are controlled by the Calculation Specifications and are executed precisely at the time dictated by the program. Although indicators could be used to help manage this control, a better method is available in RPG III/400. Each output record or line can be assigned a label. The EXCPT operation requests the appropriate label in factor 2. This not only eliminates the need for

FIGURE 14.10 Calculation Specifications for Using READE Operation

RPG CALCULATION SPECIFICATIONS

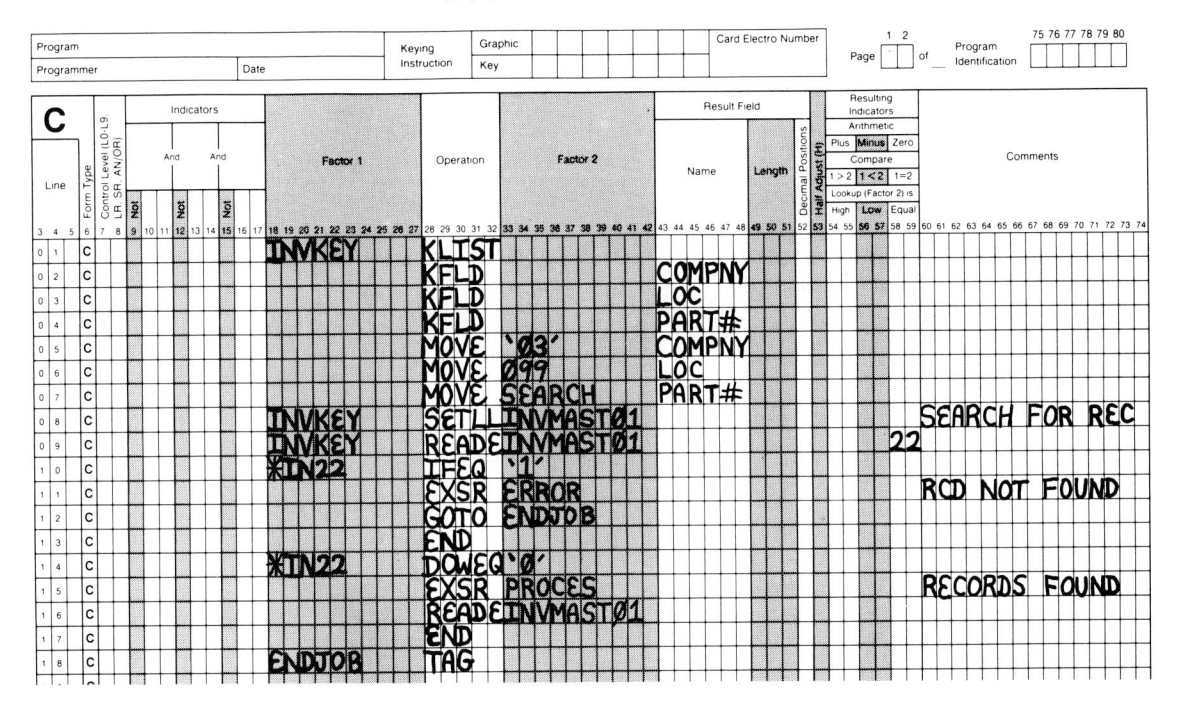

```
Line  Factor 1   Operation   Factor 2      Result     Indicators  Comments
                                           Field
01 C  INVKEY     KLIST
02 C             KFLD                      COMPNY
03 C             KFLD                      LOC
04 C             KFLD                      PART#
05 C             MOVE '03'                 COMPNY
06 C             MOVE 099                  LOC
07 C             MOVE SEARCH               PART#
08 C  INVKEY     SETLL INVMAST01                                  SEARCH FOR REC
09 C  INVKEY     READE INVMAST01                      22
10 C  *IN22      IFEQ '1'
11 C             EXSR ERROR                                       RCD NOT FOUND
12 C             GOTO ENDJOB
13 C             END
14 C  *IN22      DOWEQ '0'
15 C             EXSR PROCES                                      RECORDS FOUND
16 C             READE INVMAST01
17 C             END
18 C  ENDJOB     TAG
```

FIGURE 14.11 Sample Program for Reading an Entire File

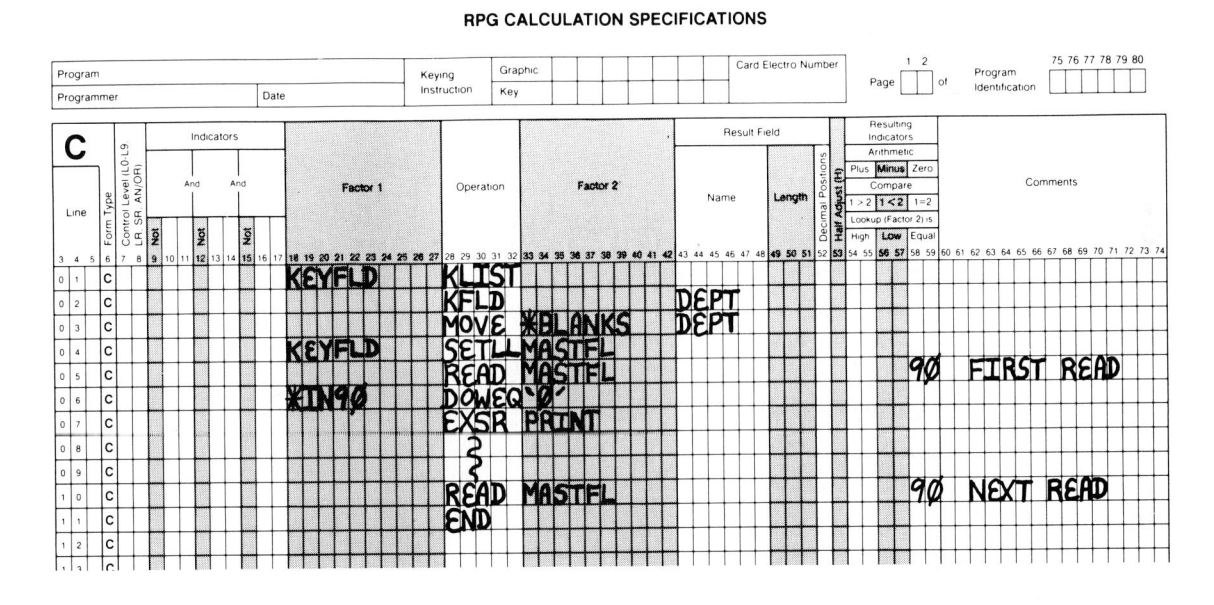

RPG CALCULATION SPECIFICATIONS

```
Line  Factor 1   Operation   Factor 2      Result     Indicators  Comments
                                           Field
01 C  KEYFLD     KLIST
02 C             KFLD                      DEPT
03 C             MOVE *BLANKS              DEPT
04 C  KEYFLD     SETLL MASTFL
05 C             READ MASTFL                          90          FIRST READ
06 C  *IN90      DOWEQ '0'
07 C             EXSR PRINT
08 C
09 C
10 C             READ MASTFL                          90          NEXT READ
11 C             END
```

indicators to control exception output time, but it also provides a more readable cue for the programmer. Further, it offers a wide variety in the number of labels that can be used. Figures 14.12(a) and 14.12(b) show an example of the coding for exception output using the label #TOTS. Any permissible field name may be used as a label for exception output. When an exception label is used, only those Output Specifications containing the same label will be written.

FIGURE 14.12(a) Coding for Exception Output Using Labels

RPG CALCULATION SPECIFICATIONS

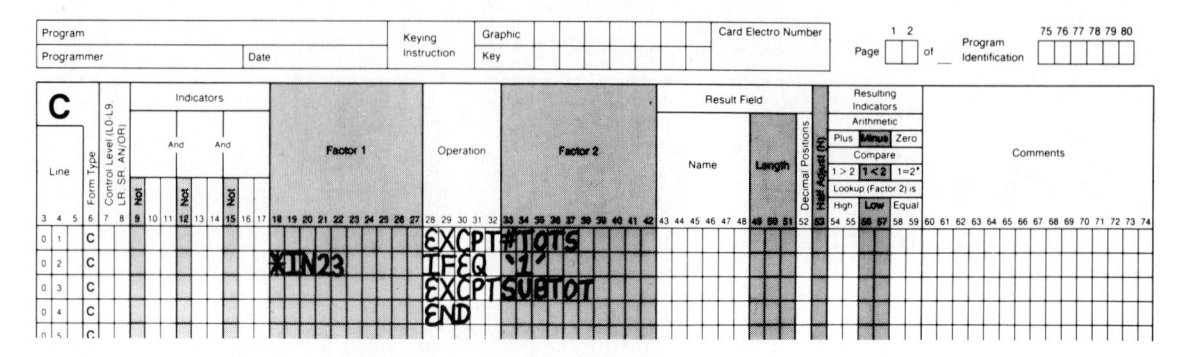

Line	Factor 1	Operation	Factor 2
01		EXCPT	#TOTS
02	*IN23	IFEQ	'1'
03		EXCPT	SUBTOT
04		END	

FIGURE 14.12(b) Output Specifications Using Labels

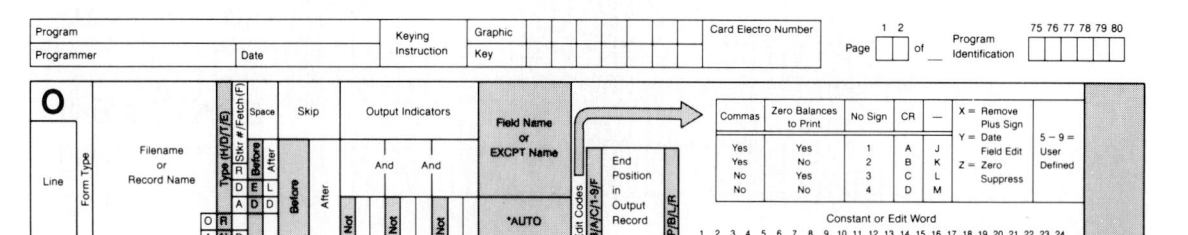

RPG OUTPUT SPECIFICATIONS

Line	Type	Before/After	Skip	Output Indicators	Field Name or EXCPT Name	End Position
01	O	E		1	#TOTS	
02	O				DEPT	5
03	O				DESC	30
04	O				AMT K	40
05	O	E		2	SUBTOT	
06	O				TOTAMT K	40

LEVEL BREAKS IN RPG III/400

With the use of full functional, externally defined files, it might appear that the capability to do automatic level breaks has been lost. Level breaks are very necessary for reporting. This function has not been lost but rather has been returned to the control of the programmer.

It would be possible, as shown in Figure 14.13, to redefine a field in the Input Specifications with a level indicator. This emulates the way level breaks were done in RPG II. This is not the preferred solution, however. The better way to handle level breaks in a structured manner is to control them within the Calculation Specifications as they are handled in most other structured languages.

Level breaks can be produced by comparing a control field to that of the previous record and causing a level break to occur when a difference is found. Using the program example from Figure 14.11, a level break has been inserted at the beginning of processing. Figure 14.14 shows this coding.

The control field (EMPDPT) is moved to a save field called LSTDPT. Notice that it is moved to a save field on the initial read so an erroneous level break is not taken before the first record is processed. Each time a record is read, the control field (EMPDPT) is compared to the previously saved control field (LSTDPT) as shown on line 1200 in the example. When they are found to be different (i.e., not equal), the subroutine for printing totals (PRTTOT) is executed. This subroutine checks for overflow and prints headings if needed. It then prints the total line (as shown on line 3000) using exception output and the label #LEVEL.

Multiple control levels can be defined in the same manner, as shown in Figure 14.15. Notice that the major control (line 1200) must be tested before the minor control (line 1900) is tested. The major level is executed in the subroutine PRTDIV. The minor level is executed in the subroutine PRTTOT. Notice that a major level break will force a minor break as shown on lines 1300 and 1400.

FIGURE 14.13 Redefining a Field with a Level Indicator

Line	Form Type	Filename or Record Name / Data Structure Name																																	From	To		Field Name	Control Level						
01	I	EMPLMAST																																												
02	I																																					DEPT	L1						

FIGURE 14.14 Program for Creating a Level Break in the Calculation Specifications

```
SEQUENCE     1         2         3         4         5         6         7
NUMBER   67890123456789012345678901234567890123456789012345678901234


    100  F* TITLE:  ILLUS FOR 14.14
    200  F* DATE:   6/24         AUTHOR: D.CABLE
    300  F* DESCRIPTION:  RPG III READ A FILE   (SINGLE LEVEL BREAK)
    400  F***********************************************************

NAME OF PROGRAM WILL BE ILL1414 IN LIBRARY CABLE

              H
* 1019             ALL DECIMAL DATA ERRORS IGNORED
    500  FEMPLMASTIF   E              K        DISK
           RECORD FORMAT(S):  FILE EMPLMAST LIB CABLE
                 EXTERNAL FORMAT EMPMAST RPG NAME EMPMAST

    600  FQSYSPRT O   F     132        OF      PRINTER
    700  F***********************************************************


    800  C* START-UP ROUTINE
A000000     INPUT  FIELDS FOR RECORD EMPMAST FILE EMPLMAST FORMAT EMPMAST
A000001                                          1     3 EMPDIV
A000002                                          4     6 EMPDPT
A000003                                          7    11 EMPL#
A000004                                         12    31 EMPNAM
A000005                                         32    49 EMPADR
A000006                                         50    63 EMPCTY
A000007                                         64    65 EMPST
A000008                                         66    74 EMPZIP
A000009                                         75    80 EMPJOB
A000010                                         81   872EMPCUR
A000011                                         88   942EMPYTD
    900  C  N10            EXSR HSKPNG
   1000  C* MAINLINE ROUTINE
   1100  C         *IN90   DOWEQ'0'
   1200  C         EMPDPT  IFGT LSTDPT
   1300  C                 EXSR PRTTOT
   1400  C                 MOVE EMPDPT    LSTDPT  3
   1500  C                 END
   1600  C                 EXSR DETAIL
   1700  C                 READ EMPLMAST              90
   1800  C                 END
   1900  C* WRAP-UP ROUTINE
   2000  C                 EXSR PRTTOT
   2100  C                 SETON                      LR
   2200  C***********************************************************
   2300  C         PRTTOT  BEGSR
   2400  C* CONTROL PRINT LINES
   2500  C                 ADD  1         LINES   20
   2600  C         LINES   IFGE 53
   2700  C                 EXCPT#HEAD
   2800  C                 Z-ADD0         LINES
   2900  C                 END
```

FIGURE 14.14 *Continued*

```
SEQUENCE      1         2         3         4         5         6         7
NUMBER     67890123456789012345678901234567890123456789012345678901234567890ial234

   3000   C                     EXCPT#LEVEL
   3100   C                     ENDSR
   3200   C********************************************************************
   3300   C           DETAIL    BEGSR
   3400   C* DETAIL CALCULATIONS
   3500   C                     ADD  1         COUNT   30
   3600   C                     ENDSR
   3700   C********************************************************************
   3800   C           HSKPNG    BEGSR
   3900   C* HOUSEKEEPING FUNCTIONS
   4000   C                     SETON                          10
   4100   C                     Z-ADD53        LINES
   4200   C           *LOVAL    SETLLEMPLMAST
   4300   C                     READ EMPLMAST                          90
   4400   C                     MOVE EMPDPT    LSTDPT  3
   4500   C                     ENDSR
   4600   C********************************************************************


   4700   O* PRINT THE REPORT
   4800   OQSYSPRT E   103           #HEAD
   4900   O                                    7 'ILL1414'
   5000   O                                   46 'EMPLOYEE SUMMARY'
   5100   O                                   68 'PAGE'
   5200   O                                    PAGE Z  72
   5300   O         E   2           #HEAD
   5400   O                                    8 'RUN DATE'
   5500   O                                    UDATE Y  17
   5600   O         E   1           #HEAD
   5700   O                                   10 'DEPT#'
   5800   O                                   19 'COUNT'
   5900   O         E   1           #LEVEL
   6000   O                                    LSTDPT  10
   6100   O                                    COUNT KB 19
* * * * * E N D  O F  S O U R C E * * * * *
```

FIGURE 14.15 **Program Defining Multiple Control Levels in the Calculation Specifications**

```
SEQUENCE      1         2         3         4         5         6         7
NUMBER     67890123456789012345678901234567890123456789012345678901234567890123456

    100   F* TITLE: ILLUS FOR 14.15
    200   F* DATE:  6/24           AUTHOR: D.CABLE
    300   F* DESCRIPTION:  RPG III READ A FILE (MULTIPLE LEVEL BREAK)
    400   F********************************************************************

NAME OF PROGRAM WILL BE ILL1415 IN LIBRARY CABLE

           H
* 1019            ALL DECIMAL DATA ERRORS IGNORED
    500   FEMPLMASTIF  E          K        DISK
          RECORD FORMAT(S):  FILE EMPLMAST LIB CABLE
                  EXTERNAL FORMAT EMPMAST RPG NAME EMPMAST

    600   FQSYSPRT O   F    132        OF       PRINTER
    700   F********************************************************************

    800   C* START-UP ROUTINE
 A000000   INPUT  FIELDS FOR RECORD EMPMAST FILE EMPLMAST FORMAT EMPMAST
 A000001                                    1    3 EMPDIV
 A000002                                    4    6 EMPDPT
 A000003                                    7   11 EMPL#
 A000004                                   12   31 EMPNAM
 A000005                                   32   49 EMPADR
 A000006                                   50   63 EMPCTY
```

FIGURE 14.15 *Continued*

```
A000007                                    64 65 EMPST
A000008                                    66 74 EMPZIP
A000009                                    75 80 EMPJOB
A000010                                    81 872EMPCUR
A000011                                    88 942EMPYTD
 900   C   N10           EXSR HSKPNG
1000   C* MAINLINE ROUTINE
1100   C               *IN90    DOWEQ'0'
1200   C               EMPDIV   IFGT LSTDIV
1300   C                        EXSR PRTTOT
1400   C                        EXSR PRTDIV
1500   C                        MOVE EMPOPT    LSTOPT  3
1600   C                        MOVE EMPDIV    LSTDIV  3
1700   C                        END
1800   C*
1900   C               EMPOPT   IFGT LSTOPT
2000   C                        EXSR PRTTOT
2100   C                        MOVE EMPOPT    LSTOPT  3
2200   C                        END
2300   C                        EXSR DETAIL
2400   C                        READ EMPLMAST                90
2500   C                        END
2600   C* WRAP-UP ROUTINE
2700   C                        EXSR PRTTOT
2800   C                        EXSR PRTDIV
2900   C                        SETON                     LR
3000   C***********************************************
3100   C               PRTDIV   BEGSR
3200   C* CONTROL PRINT LINES FOR MAJOR LEVEL
3300   C                        ADD  2         LINES  20
3400   C               LINES    IFGE 53
3500   C                        EXCPT#HEAD
3600   C                        Z-ADD0         LINES
3700   C                        END
3800   C                        EXCPT#DIV
3900   C                        ENDSR
4000   C***********************************************
4100   C               PRTTOT   BEGSR
4200   C* CONTROL PRINT LINES
4300   C                        ADD  1         LINES  20
4400   C               LINES    IFGE 53
4500   C                        EXCPT#HEAD
4600   C                        Z-ADD0         LINES
4700   C                        END
4800   C                        EXCPT#LEVEL
4900   C                        ENDSR
5000   C***********************************************
5100   C               DETAIL   BEGSR
5200   C* DETAIL CALCULATIONS
5300   C                        ADD  1         COUNT  30
5400   C                        ADD  1         DIVCNT 30
5500   C                        ADD  1         FINCNT 40
5600   C                        ENDSR
5700   C***********************************************
5800   C               HSKPNG   BEGSR
5900   C* HOUSEKEEPING FUNCTIONS
6000   C                        SETON                     10
6100   C                        Z-ADD53        LINES
6200   C               *LOVAL   SETLLEMPLMAST
6300   C                        READ EMPLMAST                90
6400   C                        MOVE EMPDIV    LSTDIV  3
6500   C                        MOVE EMPOPT    LSTOPT  3
6600   C                        ENDSR
6700   C***********************************************

6800   O* PRINT THE REPORT
6900   OQSYSPRT E  103          #HEAD
7000   O                                   7 'ILL1415'
7100   O                                  46 'EMPLOYEE SUMMARY'
7200   O                                  68 'PAGE'
```

FIGURE 14.15 *Continued*

```
7300  O                              PAGE  Z    72
7400  O       E   2                  #HEAD
7500  O                                      8  'RUN DATE'
7600  O                              UDATE Y  17
7700  O       E   1                  #HEAD
7800  O                                      4  'DIV#'
7900  O                                     10  'DEPT#'
8000  O                                     19  'COUNT'
8100  O       E   1                  #DIV

SEQUENCE       1         2         3         4         5         6         7
NUMBER    678901234567890123456789012345678901234567890123456789012345678901234

8200  O                                     35  'DIVISION TOTAL'
8300  O                              LSTDIV    4
8400  O                              DIVCNTKB 19
8500  O       E   1                  #LEVEL
8600  O                              LSTDPT   10
8700  O                              COUNT KB 19
8800  O                                     31  'DEPT TOTAL'
8900  O       T   1       LR
9000  O                                     32  'FINAL TOTAL'
9100  O                              FINCNTKB 19
* * * * * E N D   O F   S O U R C E * * * * *
```

USE OF MULTIPLE INDEXES ■

Many applications require access to more than one indexed file. It is very common to see programs accessing five or six files, retrieving different pieces of information to complete a report or to process a transaction file. Figure 14.16 shows a sample program that accesses several files. The program is no more complex than one that uses only a single file because each file is accessed in turn.

FIGURE 14.16 Program Accessing Several Files

```
SEQUENCE       1         2         3         4         5         6         7
NUMBER    678901234567890123456789012345678901234567890123456789012345678901234

       100  F* TITLE: ILLUS FOR 14.16
       200  F* DATE:  6/27         AUTHOR: D.CABLE
       300  F* DESCRIPTION:  RPG III READ MULTIPLE FILES
       400  F*******************************************************

NAME OF PROGRAM WILL BE ILL1416 IN LIBRARY CABLE

             H
* 1019              ALL DECIMAL DATA ERRORS IGNORED
       500  FEMPLMASTIF   E           K        DISK
              RECORD FORMAT(S):  FILE EMPLMAST LIB CABLE
                         EXTERNAL FORMAT EMPMAST RPG NAME EMPMAST

       600  FEMPLEARNIF   E           K        DISK
              RECORD FORMAT(S):  FILE EMPLEARN LIB CABLE
                         EXTERNAL FORMAT EARN01 RPG NAME EARN01

       700  FQSYSPRT O    F      132       OF  PRINTER
       800  F*******************************************************

       900  C* STARTUP ROUTINE
   A000000      INPUT FIELDS FOR RECORD EMPMAST FILE EMPLMAST FORMAT EMPMAST
   A000001                                           1    3 EMPDIV
   A000002                                           4    6 EMPDPT
   A000003                                           7   11 EMPL#
```

FIGURE 14.16 *Continued*

```
A000004                                        12  31 EMPNAM
A000005                                        32  49 EMPADR
A000006                                        50  63 EMPCTY
A000007                                        64  65 EMPST
A000008                                        66  74 EMPZIP
A000009                                        75  80 EMPJOB
A000010                                        81  872EMPCUR
A000011                                        88  942EMPYTD
B000000      INPUT   FIELDS FOR RECORD EARN01 FILE EMPLEARN FORMAT EARN01
B000001                                         1   3 ERNDIV
B000002                                         4   6 ERNDPT
B000003                                         7  11 ERNEMP
B000004                                        12  30 ERNNAM
B000005                                        31  342ERNHRS
B000006                                        35  392ERNRAT
B000007                                        40  450ERNDAT
1000   C   N10               EXSR HSKPNG
1100   C* MAINLINE ROUTINE
1200   C          *IN90      DOWEQ'0'
1300   C                     EXSR PRTTOT
1400   C                     EXSR DETAIL
1500   C                     READ EMPLMAST                   90
1600   C                     END
1700   C* WRAP-UP ROUTINE
1800   C                     EXSR PRTTOT
1900   C                     SETON                           LR
2000   C************************************************************
2100   C          PRTTOT     BEGSR
2200   C* CONTROL PRINT LINES
2300   C                     ADD  1         LINES    20
2400   C          LINES      IFGE 53
2500   C                     EXCPT#HEAD
2600   C                     Z-ADD0         LINES
2700   C                     END
2800   C                     ENDSR
2900   C************************************************************
3000   C          DETAIL     BEGSR
3100   C* DETAIL CALCULATIONS
3200   C                     SETOF                           91
3300   C                     ADD  1         COUNT    30
3400   C                     MOVE EMPL#     ERNEMP
3500   C          KEY2       SETLLEMPLEARN
3600   C          KEY2       READEEMPLEARN                   91
3700   C          *IN91      IFEQ '0'
3800   C                     EXCPT#DTL
3900   C                     ELSE
4000   C                     EXCPT#ERR
4100   C                     END
4200   C                     ENDSR
4300   C************************************************************
4400   C          HSKPNG     BEGSR
4500   C* HOUSEKEEPING FUNCTIONS
4600   C                     Z-ADD53        LINES
4700   C                     SETON                    10
4800   C                     MOVE 070       EMPDIV
4900   C          KEY1       SETLLEMPLMAST
5000   C                     READ EMPLMAST                   90
5100   C* KEY FOR EMPLMAST
5200   C          KEY1       KLIST
5300   C                     KFLD           EMPDIV
5400   C                     KFLD           EMPDPT
5500   C* KEY FOR EMPLEARN
5600   C          KEY2       KLIST
5700   C                     KFLD           ERNEMP
5800   C                     ENDSR
5900   C************************************************************

6000   O* PRINT THE REPORT
6100   OQSYSPRT E  103            #HEAD
6200   O                                        7 'ILL1416'
6300   O                                       46 'EMPLOYEE EARNINGS'
6400   O                                       68 'PAGE'
6500   O                                PAGE Z 72
6600   O        E    2              #HEAD
6700   O                                        8 'RUN DATE'
6800   O                                UDATE Y 17
6900   O        E    1              #HEAD
7000   O                                        4 'DIV#'
```

363

FIGURE 14.16 *Continued*

```
SEQUENCE      1         2         3         4         5         6         7
NUMBER    678901234567890123456789012345678901234567890123456789012345678901234
   7100  O                                      10 'DEPT#'
   7200  O                                      16 'EMPL#'
   7300  O                                      22 'HOURS'
   7400  O       E  1              #DTL
   7500  O                         EMPDIV    4
   7600  O                         EMPDPT    9
   7700  O                         EMPL#    16
   7800  O                         ERNHRSK  22
   7900  O       E  1              #ERR
   8000  O                         EMPDIV    4
   8100  O                         EMPDPT    9
   8200  O                         EMPL#    16
   8300  O                                      45 'NO EARNINGS RECORD'
   8400  O       T  1        LR
   8500  O                                      20 'RECORDS PROCESSED'
   8600  O                         COUNT  Z  25
* * * * * E N D   O F   S O U R C E * * * *
```

Renaming Formats

Sometimes the *same* file must be accessed by two different keys. This surprising event can be handled in RPG III/400 by defining two logical files in the program. Since the names of the two files are different, the program will treat them as though they were two completely different files.

Often the format names are the same for both logical files. To allow the program to recognize each separate file format, the format name for one of the files is redefined. Figure 14.17 shows the File Description Specifications for the two logical files that have the same format names (VEND01). The format name for the second file is redefined on a File Description Continuation Specification line. The external name of the format is entered in columns 19–28. The key word RENAME is

FIGURE 14.17 Two Logical Files with the Same Format Names: File Description Specifications

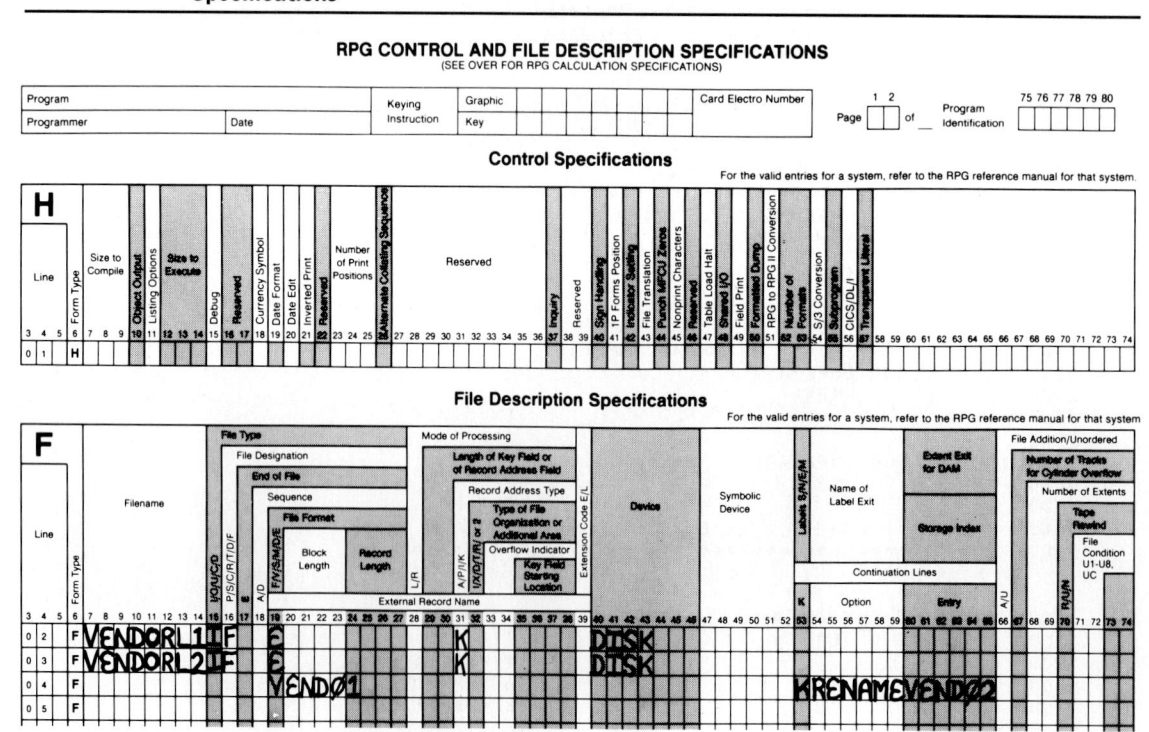

FIGURE 14.18 Renaming Fields in Input Specifications

Line		Filename or Record Name				External Field Name			Record Identification Codes									Field Location From To		RPG Field Name				Field Indicators
01	I	VENDORL2																						
02	I					VTYPE														NUTYPE				
03	I					VENDNO														NUVEND				
04	I					VCODE														NUCODE				
05	I					VLOC														NULOC				
06	I					VNAME														NUNAME				
07	I																							

entered in columns 54–59 and a new format name is entered in columns 60–65. The *K* in column 53 indicates that this is a continuation line for the File Description Specifications. The program will use the new format name for accessing the second logical file. The File Description Continuation Specification is used for many other purposes which will be discussed in later chapters.

Renaming Fields

Since the program in the example is accessing the same file through two logical versions, the field names in these externally defined files will be identical. While it is not a requirement that field names be different, identical field names could cause erroneous results in some instances. Field names can be changed in the program using a field rename capability.

The external name of the field is entered in positions 21–26. A new field name is entered in columns 53–58. The new name is the one that will be used by the program. Figure 14.18 shows the Input Specifications for renaming several fields.

DYNAMIC OPEN AND CLOSE OF FILES (OPEN/CLOSE) ∎

All versions of RPG can *automatically* open and close files. Many languages provide no such convenience. In these languages, the programmer must enter a command to open each file at the beginning of program execution and another command to close each file at completion.

RPG III/400 has the ability to use the dynamic OPEN and CLOSE commands if desired. When a file is needed for only a small fraction of the time to run the program, it is inefficient to keep it open for the entire time the program is running.

On the Calculation Specifications, factor 2 contains the name of the file to be opened or closed. The file must be a full functional file. Figure 14.19 shows an example of the OPEN and CLOSE operations.

UPDATING A FILE USING EXCEPTION UPDATING ∎

A file may be updated in the conventional manner using exception output with the EXCPT operation. When this method is used, the fields entered on the Output Specifications will be updated. Figures 14.20(a) and 14.20(b) show the coding for exception output.

It is also possible in RPG III/400 to update all fields by entering the figurative constant *ALL as the first and only field entry for the exception output.

FIGURE 14.19 OPEN and CLOSE Operations

RPG CALCULATION SPECIFICATIONS

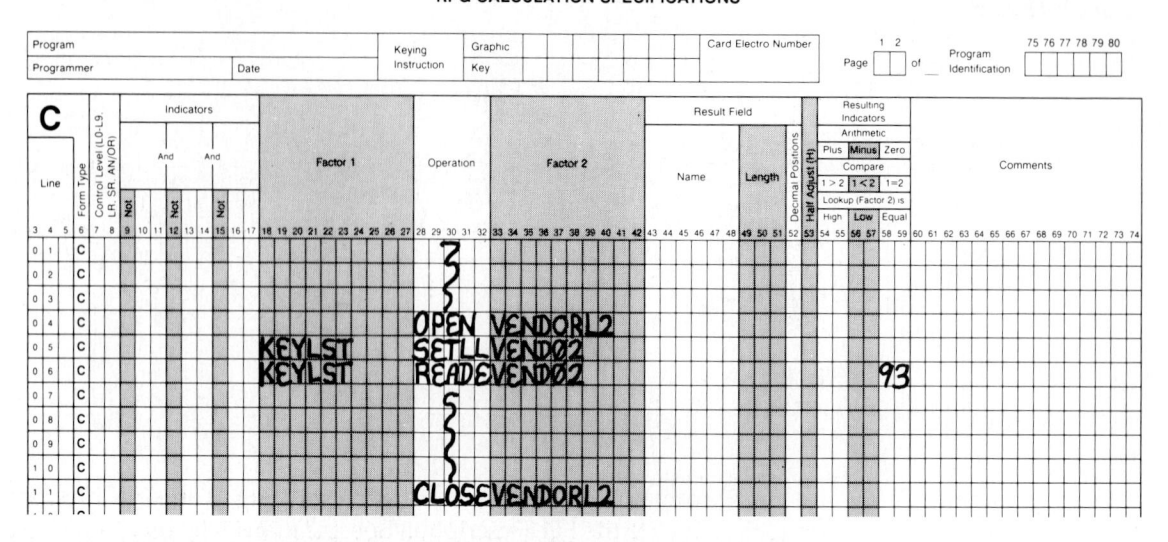

```
Line  Factor 1   Operation   Factor 2            Result Field   Resulting Indicators
01  C
02  C
03  C
04  C              OPEN     VENDORL2
05  C  KEYLST      SETLL    VEND02
06  C  KEYLST      READE    VEND02                               93
07  C
08  C
09  C
10  C
11  C              CLOSE    VENDORL2
```

FIGURE 14.20(a) Calculation Specifications to Update a File Using EXCPT

RPG CALCULATION SPECIFICATIONS

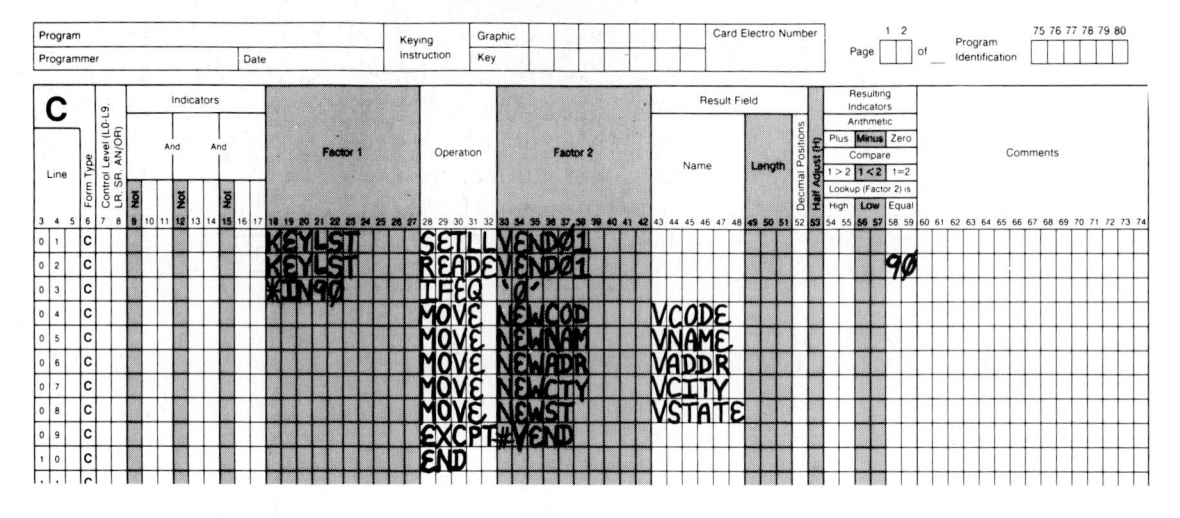

```
Line   Factor 1   Operation   Factor 2    Result Field
01  C  KEYLST     SETLL    VEND01
02  C  KEYLST     READE    VEND01                        90
03  C  *IN90      IFEQ     '0'
04  C             MOVE     NEWCOD      VCODE
05  C             MOVE     NEWNAM      VNAME
06  C             MOVE     NEWADR      VADDR
07  C             MOVE     NEWCTY      VCITY
08  C             MOVE     NEWST       VSTATE
09  C             EXCPT    #VEND
10  C             END
```

FIGURE 14.20(b) Output Specifications to Update a File Using EXCPT

RPG OUTPUT SPECIFICATIONS

```
Line  Filename/Record Name   Field Name or EXCPT Name
01  O  VENDORL1 E            #VEND
02  O                        VCODE
03  O                        VNAME
04  O                        VADDR
05  O                        VCITY
06  O                        VSTATE
07  O
```

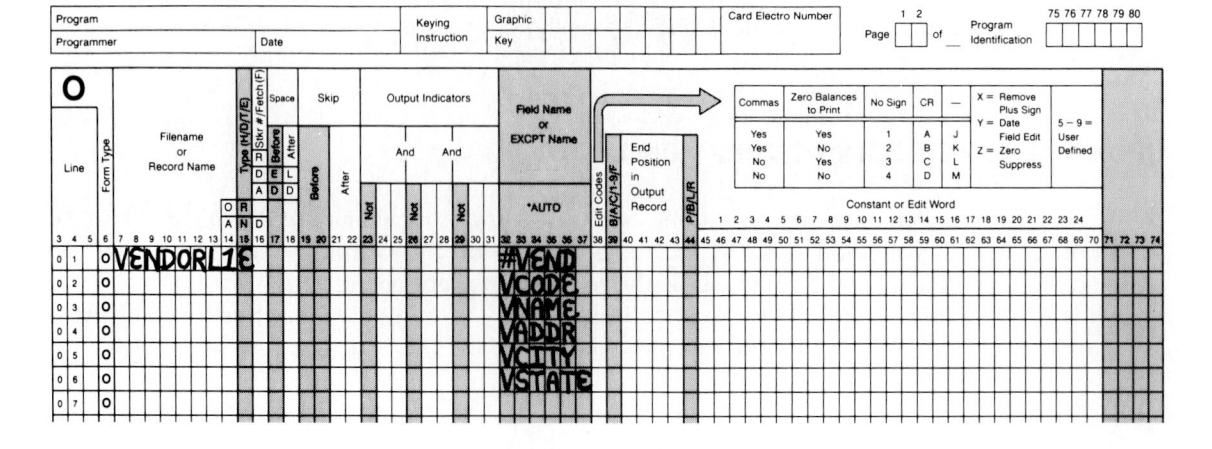

UPDATING RECORDS IN A FILE (UPDAT OPERATION)

A more structured method for updating files is available in RPG III/400. Using the operation UPDAT, changes can be made to a record within the Calculation Specifications.

The file is first searched to locate the correct record for update. This is usually done using either the SETLL and READE operations or by using the CHAIN operation. When the record has been located, the new data is moved into the fields to be changed, and this is followed by the UPDAT operation. Figure 14.21 shows the Calculation Specifications for making changes to a file. No Output Specifications are required.

This method provides a more structured, readable, and reliable file update. The new data must be moved into the fields *after* the record has been retrieved so that the new data replaces the data in the existing record. It is also important that the indicator is checked to ensure that the desired record was really found before updating.

ADDING RECORDS TO A FILE (WRITE OPERATION)

In RPG III/400, records are added to a file using a method similar to the one used for updating a file. The operation WRITE is used to add records to a file. This function is also performed entirely within the Calculation Specifications.

If the file is defined with a unique key, then the file must first be searched to ensure that the record to be added does not exist. This is usually done using either the SETLL and READE operations or by using the CHAIN operation. If a duplicate record is located, an error condition exists and some action must be taken to notify the user. If the record is *not* found, the new data is moved into the fields of the record to be added, and this is followed by the WRITE operation. Figure 14.22 shows the Calculation Specifications for adding records to a file.

The new data must be moved into the fields *after* the search for the record has been completed. If the file has unique keys, it is important that the indicator is checked to ensure that the record does *not* exist.

FIGURE 14.21 Making Changes to a File Using UPDAT Operation

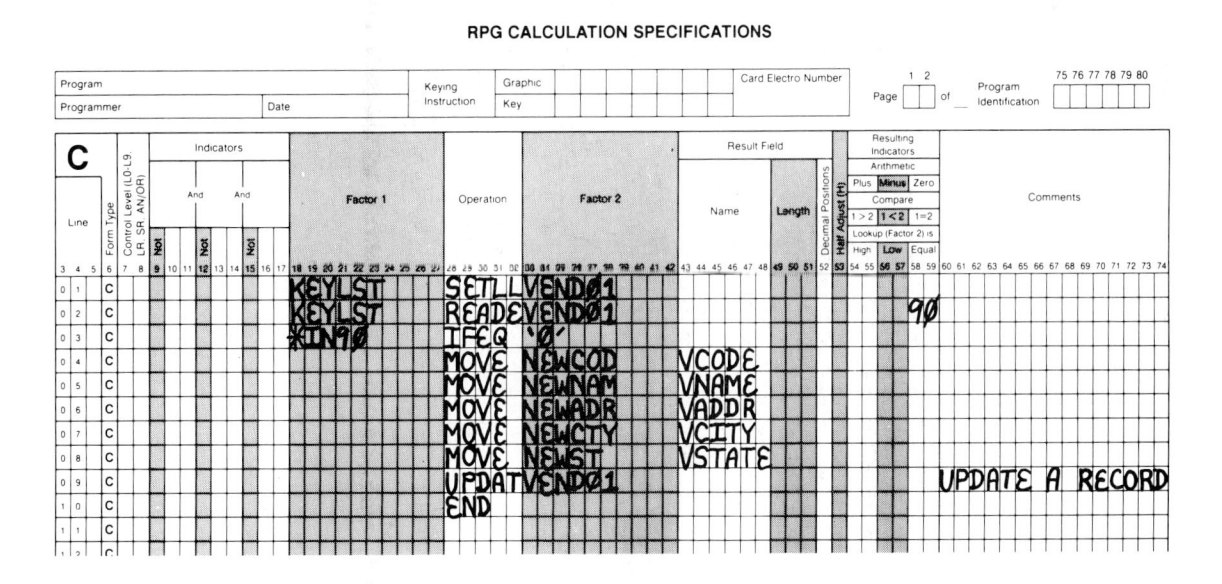

RPG CALCULATION SPECIFICATIONS

Line	Factor 1	Operation	Factor 2	Result Field	Resulting Indicators	Comments
01	KEYLST	SETLL	VEND01			
02	KEYLST	READE	VEND01		90	
03	*IN90	IFEQ	'0'			
04		MOVE	NEWCOD	VCODE		
05		MOVE	NEWNAM	VNAME		
06		MOVE	NEWADR	VADDR		
07		MOVE	NEWCTY	VCITY		
08		MOVE	NEWST	VSTATE		
09		UPDAT	VEND01			UPDATE A RECORD
10		END				

FIGURE 14.22 Adding Records to a File Using WRITE Operation

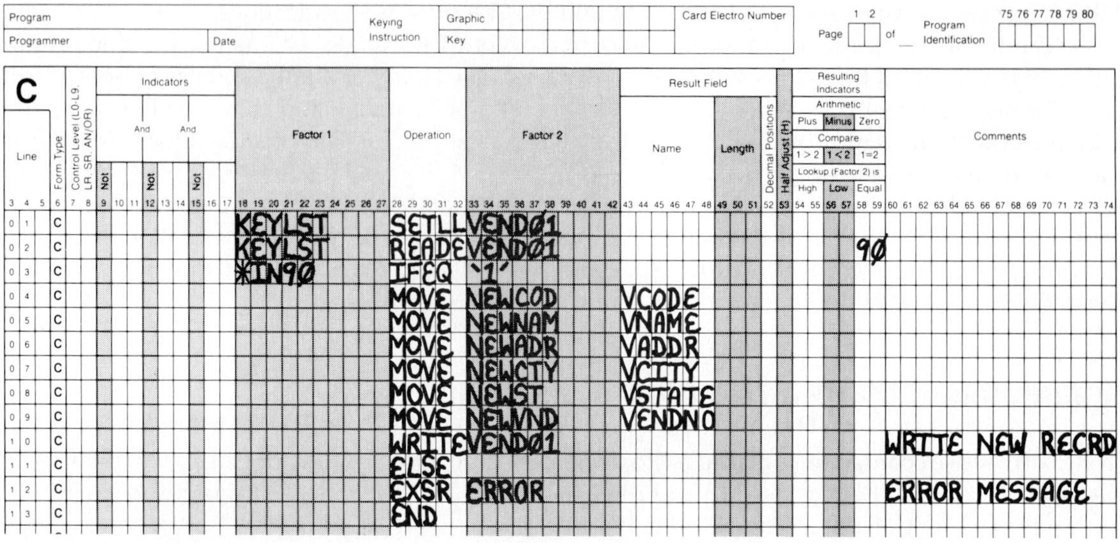

RPG CALCULATION SPECIFICATIONS

```
01 C   KEYLST    SETLL VEND01
02 C   KEYLST    READE VEND01                          90
03 C   *IN90     IFEQ  '1'
04 C             MOVE  NEWCOD    VCODE
05 C             MOVE  NEWNAM    VNAME
06 C             MOVE  NEWADR    VADDR
07 C             MOVE  NEWCTY    VCITY
08 C             MOVE  NEWST     VSTATE
09 C             MOVE  NEWVND    VENDNO
10 C             WRITE VEND01                    WRITE NEW RECRD
11 C             ELSE
12 C             EXSR  ERROR                     ERROR MESSAGE
13 C             END
```

DELETING RECORDS FROM A FILE (DELET OPERATION) ■

In RPG III/400, records are deleted from a file using nearly the same procedure as used for updating or writing records. The operation DELET is used to delete a record from a file. This function is also performed entirely within the Calculation Specifications.

The file is first searched to ensure that the record to be deleted does exist in the file. This is usually done using either the SETLL and READE operations or by using the CHAIN operation. When the record has been located, the DELET operation immediately removes the record. Figure 14.23 shows the Calculation Specifications for removing records from a file.

The programmer should be aware that the DELET operation is final. The record is removed completely and *cannot be recovered* (unless it exists on a backup version of the file). It is also important that the indicator is checked to ensure that the record deleted is the record for which the search was made.

Methods for performing batch updating of files in RPG III/400 make it easier for the programmer to write a program that is structured so that it can be more easily maintained. All of the usual precautions must be taken to ensure that updating is done accurately.

FIGURE 14.23 Removing Records from a File Using DELET Operation

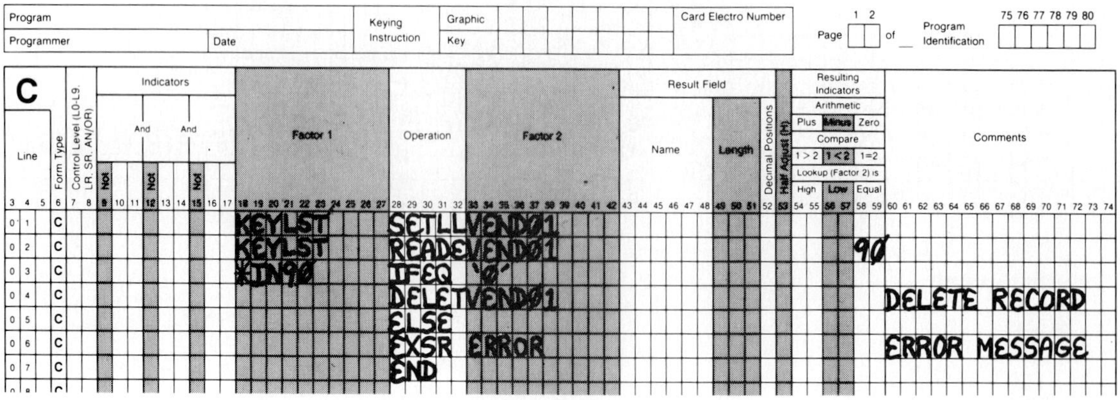

RPG CALCULATION SPECIFICATIONS

```
01 C   KEYLST    SETLL VEND01
02 C   KEYLST    READE VEND01                          90
03 C   *IN90     IFEQ  '0'
04 C             DELET VEND01                    DELETE RECORD
05 C             ELSE
06 C             EXSR  ERROR                     ERROR MESSAGE
07 C             END
```

SUMMARY ■

In this chapter, you have learned about full functional files, which give RPG III/400 the complete flexibility unavailable in RPG II. It is no longer necessary to depend on the fixed logic cycle of RPG II. Full functional files can be read and manipulated as they are in any modern business programming language using structured programming concepts. The programmer can take control of the program logic using the OPEN, SETLL, SETGT, READ, READE, READP, and CLOSE operations. With these instructions, a program cycle can be created so that a file is accessed and read as needed.

You have also learned that keyed files combine several noncontiguous fields as a single key. These keys are defined to the program by the KLIST operation followed by a series of KFLD instructions that define the fields comprising the key.

You have learned that level breaks are no longer defined in the Input Specifications but are controlled within the main logic of the program using conventional structured logic methods. Output is written using the EXCPT operation with the additional enhancement of a label with which to identify its output statements. This eliminates the need for indicators and makes the program easier to read and maintain.

You have learned that multiple indexes over the same file are possible with the same program using the renaming facility. Format names as well as individual field names on input files can be renamed.

Finally, you have learned that files can be updated using the EXCPT operation or the UPDAT operation. Records can be added to a file using the WRITE operation and can be deleted using the DELET operation.

REVIEW QUESTIONS

1. Explain the meaning of full functional files.
2. Using full functional files, a file is read using the _____ and _____ operations.
3. To begin reading a file at the beginning, the reserved word _____ can be used in factor 1 of the Calculation Specifications.
4. A _____ can be set up to control the reading of the file.
5. Keys are defined in RPG III/400 by using the operation _____ followed by one or more _____ .
6. Each key is given a title in factor _____ to define the key.
7. Where in the Calculation Specifications are keys described?
8. Records may be read in reverse sequence using the _____ operation followed by the _____ operation.
9. *HIVAL can be used to access the _____ record in a file.
10. A specific record can be accessed using either the CHAIN or the _____ operation code.
11. When exception time output is used in RPG III/400, it is not necessary to use indicators to control the time at which the exception output will occur. Describe the alternate method for identifying the exception time output.
12. Describe the structured method for creating level breaks in RPG III/400.
13. How can the same file data be accessed by different keys in the same program?
14. How can input fields be renamed within a program?
15. How are files updated in RPG III/400? Explain the use of the UPDAT, WRITE, and DELET operations.

DEBUGGING EXERCISES

Instructions

The following RPG programs contain an error or errors. Some of these errors are indicated by the RPG compiler on the program listing. A list of syntax errors is given at the end of the program listing. Other types of errors may occur which will not be shown. These are called logic errors.

Study each program and its syntax errors. Locate each error (including logic errors) and on a separate coding form make the correct entry for the line(s) in error.

Explain each error and how it should be corrected.

```
       100   F* TITLE: DEBUG PROJECT 14-A
       200   F* DATE:    5/25            AUTHOR: D.CABLE
       300   F* DESCRIPTION:       SALES TAX
       400   F***********************************************

NAME OF PROGRAM WILL BE PJ014A IN LIBRARY CABLE

             H
* 1019                ALL DECIMAL DATA ERRORS IGNORED
       500   FSALESTAXIP   E                    DISK
* 2120        500   DATA DESCRIPTIONS FOR FILE SALESTAX NOT FOUND
       600   FQSYSPRT O    F       132     OF       PRINTER
       700   F***********************************************

       800   C           *LOVAL    SETLLSALE01
* 5132                             5132-**********

       900   C           *IN90     DOWNE'0'
      1000   C                     READ SALE01                    90
* 5132                             5132-**********

      1100   C           RATE      MULT PRICE
* 5030                                       5030-******

      1200   C           PRICE     ADD  TAX       EXTPRC
      1300   C                     EXCPT
      1400   C                     END
      1500   C                     ADD  TAX       TOTTAX

      1600   OQSYSPRT H  203    1P
      1700   O         OR               OF
      1800   O                                  6  'PJ014A'
      1900   O                          UDATE Y 50
      2000   O                                 30  'SALES TAX REPORT'
      2100   O         H  2     1P
      2200   O         OR               OF
      2300   O                                 11  'ITEM NUMBER'
      2400   O                                 25  'RATE'
      2500   O                                 35  'TIME'
      2600   O                                 50  'TOTAL VALUE'
      2700   O         D  1      01
      2800   O                          ITEMNO  10
      2900   O                          PRICE   30
* 6026                                   6026-****

      3000   O                          TAX   K  33
      3100   O                          EXPRC K  48
      3200   O         D  1     LR
      3300   O                                 20  'TOTAL TAXES'
```

```
SEQUENCE       1         2         3         4         5         6         7
NUMBER     678901234567890123456789012345678901234567890123456789012345678901234
    3400  0                          TOTTAXK   48
* * * * * E N D   O F   S O U R C E * * * * *


*  7064      500    SALESTAX FILE NOT REFERENCED FOR INPUT
*  7026     1300    NO UNNAMED EXCEPTION OUTPUT SPECIFICATIONS IN PROGRAM

   TABLE OF END POSITION OFFSETS FOR FIELDS DESCRIBED USING POSITION NOTATION
   STMT NO      POS      STMT NO      POS      STMT NO      POS      STMT NO      POS
      2900      15
```

CROSS-REFERENCE LISTING

```
          FILE/RCD    DEV/RCD     REFERENCES (D=DEFINED)
      02  QSYSPRT     PRINTER     600D  1600  2100  2700  3200
      01  SALESTAX    DISK        500D


          FIELD       ATTR        REFERENCES (M=MODIFIED D=DEFINED)
          *IN90       A(1)        900
* 7030    EXPRC       P(5,0)      3100
* 7030    EXTPRC      P(5,0)      1200M
* 7030    ITEMNO      A(4)        2800
* 7030    PRICE       P(5,0)      1100  1200  2900
* 7030    RATE        A(4)        1100
* 7030    TAX         P(5,0)      1200  1500  3000
* 7030    TOTTAX      P(5,0)      1500M  3400
          UDATE       P(6,0)      1900
          *LOVAL      LITERAL     800
          '0'         LITERAL     900


          INDICATOR   REFERENCES (M=MODIFIED D=DEFINED)
          *IN         900
          LR          500D  3200
          OF          600D  1700  2200
* 7030    01          2700
          1P          1600  2100
          90          900   1000M
```

MESSAGES

```
   MSGID     SEV   NUMBER   TEXT
*  QRG1019    00     1      IGNDECERR(*YES) SPECIFIED ON COMMAND. NO DECIMAL DATA ERRORS
*  QRG2120    40     1      EXTERNAL DESCRIPTION NOT FOUND FOR FILE SPECIFIED AS EXTERNA
                            IGNORED.
*  QRG5030    30     1      RESULT FIELD NAME (POSITIONS 43-48) MUST BE ENTERED FOR SPEC
                            IGNORED
*  QRG5132    30     2      FACTOR 2 (POSITIONS 33-42) MUST CONTAIN THE NAME OF MULTIPLE
                            SPECIFICATION IGNORED.
*  QRG6026    10     1      END POSITION (POS 40-43) NOT VALID. PLUS 000 ASSUMED AND THI
                            PRECEDING FIELD.
*  QRG7026    30     1      NO UNNAMED EXCPT OUTPUT IN PROGRAM. EXCPT CALCULATION SPECIF
*  QRG7030    30     8      FIELD OR INDICATOR NOT DEFINED.
*  QRG7064    40     1      PROGRAM FILE NOT REFERENCED. FILE IGNORED
```

MESSAGE SUMMARY

TOTAL   00   10   20   30   40   50
 16   1   1   0   12   2   0

   34 RECORDS READ FROM SOURCE FILE
   SOURCE RECORDS INCLUDE   29 SPECIFICATIONS,   0 TABLE RECORDS, AND   5 COMMENTS

QRG0008 COMPILE TERMINATED. SEVERITY 40 ERRORS FOUND IN PROGRAM

* * * * * E N D   O F   C O M P I L A T I O N * * * *
* QRG1020   ERROR OCCURRED CREATING OR UPDATING DATA AREA RETURNCODE. COMPI

```
   100   F* TITLE: DEBUG PROJECT 14-B
   200   F* DATE: 6/25          AUTHOR: D.CABLE
   300   F* DESCRIPTION:    SALES REPORT
   400   F************************************************************
```

NAME OF PROGRAM WILL BE PJO14B IN LIBRARY CABLE

```
            H
* 1019              ALL DECIMAL DATA ERRORS IGNORED
   500   FPOSDTA  IF  E                    DISK
           RECORD FORMAT(S):  FILE POSDTA LIB MOMS
                        EXTERNAL FORMAT POSDTA01 RPG NAME POSDTA01

   600   FQSYSPRT O   F     132        OF       PRINTER
   700   F************************************************************

A000000   INPUT  FIELDS FOR RECORD POSDTA01 FILE POSDTA FORMAT POSDTA01
A000001                                        1    60DTBTCH
A000002                                        7    90STORE#
A000003                                       10   130REG#
A000004                                       14   140DRAWR#
A000005                                       15   200TRNXN#
A000006                                       21    21 RECTYP
A000007                                       22   240RTSEQ#
A000008                                       25   151 PSDATA
   800   C             KEY       KLIST
   900   C                       KFLD          IICMP#
  1000   C                       KFLD          IILOC#
  1100   C                       KFLD          IIITM#
  1200   C************************************************************
  1300   C                       EXCPT#HEAD
  1400   C             *LOVAL    SETLLPOSDTA01
  1500   C             *IN90     DOWNE'O'
  1600   C                       READ POSDTA01                    90
  1700   C   90                  GOTO ENDJOB
  1800   C             DATE      IFNE LSTDAT
  1900   C                       EXCPT#LEVEL
  2000   C                       MOVE DATE     LSTDAT  60
  2100   C                       END
  2200   C             IQTY      MULT IPRICE   TPRICE  90
  2300   C                       ADD  TPRICE   LPRICE  90
  2400   C                       ADD  TPRICE   FPRICE  90
  2500   C                       EXCPT#DTL
  2600   C                       END
  2700   C             ENDJOB    TAG
  2800   C                       SETON                         LR

  2900   OQSYSPRT E  203         #HEAD
  3000   O                                6 'PJO14B'
```

```
SEQUENCE      1         2         3         4         5         6         7
NUMBER    67890123456789012345678901234567890123456789012345678901234567890123 4

  3100   O                              UDATE Y   50
  3200   O                                        30 'TOTAL SALES REPORT'
  3300   O         E 2                  #HEAD
  3400   O                                        11 'DATE'
  3500   O                                        25 'STORE#'
  3600   O                                        35 'REGISTER'
  3700   O                                        43 'TRANS#'
  3800   O                                        50 'AMOUNT'
  3900   O         E 1                  #DTL
  4000   O                              DATE Y    10
  4100   O                              STORE#    30
  4200   O                              REG#      33
  4300   O                              TRNSN#K   38
  4400   O                              PRICE K   55
  4500   O         E 2                  #LEVEL
  4600   O                              TPRICEK   55
  4700   O         D 1     LR
  4800   O                                        20 'TOTAL SALES'
  4900   O                              FPRICEK   55
* * * * * E N D   O F   S O U R C E * * * * *


* 7055      1400      #LOVAL NOT VALID FOR PROCESSING BY RELATIVE RECORD NUMBER



CROSS-REFERENCE LISTING



          FILE/RCD    DEV/RCD    REFERENCES (D=DEFINED)
      01  POSDTA      DISK       500D
          POSDTA01               500D    A000000   1400    1600
      02  QSYSPRT     PRINTER    600D    2900      3300    3900    4500
                                 4700


          FIELD       ATTR       REFERENCES (M=MODIFIED D=DEFINED)
          *IN90       A(1)       1500
          #DTL        EXCPT      2500    3900
          #HEAD       EXCPT      1300    2900      3300
          #LEVEL      EXCPT      1900    4500
* 7030    DATE        P(6,0)     1800    2000      4000
* 7031    DRAWR#      P(1,0)     A000004D
* 7031    DTBTCH      P(6,0)     A000001D
          ENDJOB      TAG        1700    2700D
          FPRICE      P(9,0)     2400D   4900
* 7030    IICMP#      A(4)       900
* 7030    IIITM#      A(4)       1100
* 7030    IILOC#      A(4)       1000
* 7030    IPRICE      P(5,0)     2200
* 7030    IQTY        P(5,0)     2200
* 7031    KEY         KLIST      800D
          LPRICE      P(9,0)     2300D
          LSTDAT      P(6,0)     1800    2000D
* 7030    PRICE       P(5,0)     4400
* 7031    PSDATA      A(127)     A000008D
* 7031    RECTYP      A(1)       A000006D
          REG#        P(4,0)     A000003D  4200
* 7031    RTSEQ#      P(3,0)     A000007D
          STORE#      P(3,0)     A000002D  4100
          TPRICE      P(9,0)     2200D   2300      2400    4600
* 7030    TRNSN#      P(5,0)     4300
* 7031    TRNXN#      P(6,0)     A000005D
          UDATE       P(6,0)     3100
          *LOVAL      LITERAL    1400
          '0'         LITERAL    1500
```

```
         INDICATOR    REFERENCES  (M=MODIFIED D=DEFINED)

          *IN              1500
          LR               2800M      4700
* 7031    OF                600D
          90               1500       1600M     1700
```

MESSAGES

```
  MSGID     SEV   NUMBER   TEXT

* QRG1019   00       1     IGNDECERR(*YES) SPECIFIED ON COMMAND. NO DECIMAL DATA ERRORS
* QRG7030   30       8     FIELD OR INDICATOR NOT DEFINED.
* QRG7031   00       8     NAME OR INDICATOR NOT REFERENCED.
* QRG7055   30       1     FACTOR 1 NAME (POSITIONS 18-27) NOT VALID FOR SPECIFIED OPERA
```

MESSAGE SUMMARY

```
TOTAL    00    10    20    30    40    50
  18      9     0     0     9     0     0
```

49 RECORDS READ FROM SOURCE FILE
SOURCE RECORDS INCLUDE   43 SPECIFICATIONS,   0 TABLE RECORDS, AND   6 COMMENTS

QRG0008 COMPILE TERMINATED. SEVERITY 30 ERRORS FOUND IN PROGRAM

* * * * * E N D   O F   C O M P I L A T I O N * * * * *
* QRG1020   ERROR OCCURRED CREATING OR UPDATING DATA AREA RETURNCODE. COMPIL

PROGRAMMING PROJECT

Project Overview

A report is to be printed listing the fixed assets of a company. Using full functional file processing methods, read the entire asset file and print all items that belong to division 06. Accumulate totals for the depreciated value. Write the RPG program to produce this listing. Sample data for this project can be found in Appendix D.

Input Format

The input data for the project is found in a file called ASSETS in the sample data. The Record Layout for this file is shown in Figure 14.24.

Processing

Using the SETLL and READ operations, read the entire file using the key field (ASSET#). If the division number is 06, accumulate the total for depreciated value and print the line. Use the DOWEQ operation to control the reading of the file.

Output Format (Printer Spacing Chart)

The output format for the project is a report with standard headings. The report will show the division number, location, asset number, description, and depreciated value. A final total of value is printed at the end of the report. The Printer Spacing Chart for this report is shown in Figure 14.25.

An example of the finished report is shown in Figure 14.26.

FIGURE 14.24 Programming Project: Record Layout

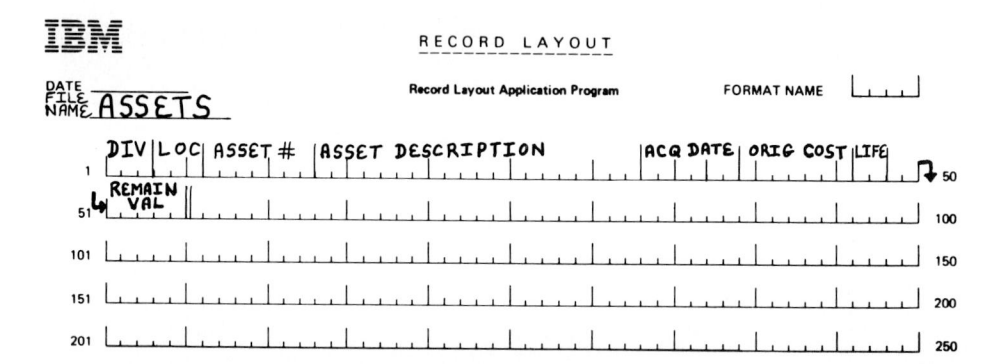

FIGURE 14.25 Programming Project: Printer Spacing Chart

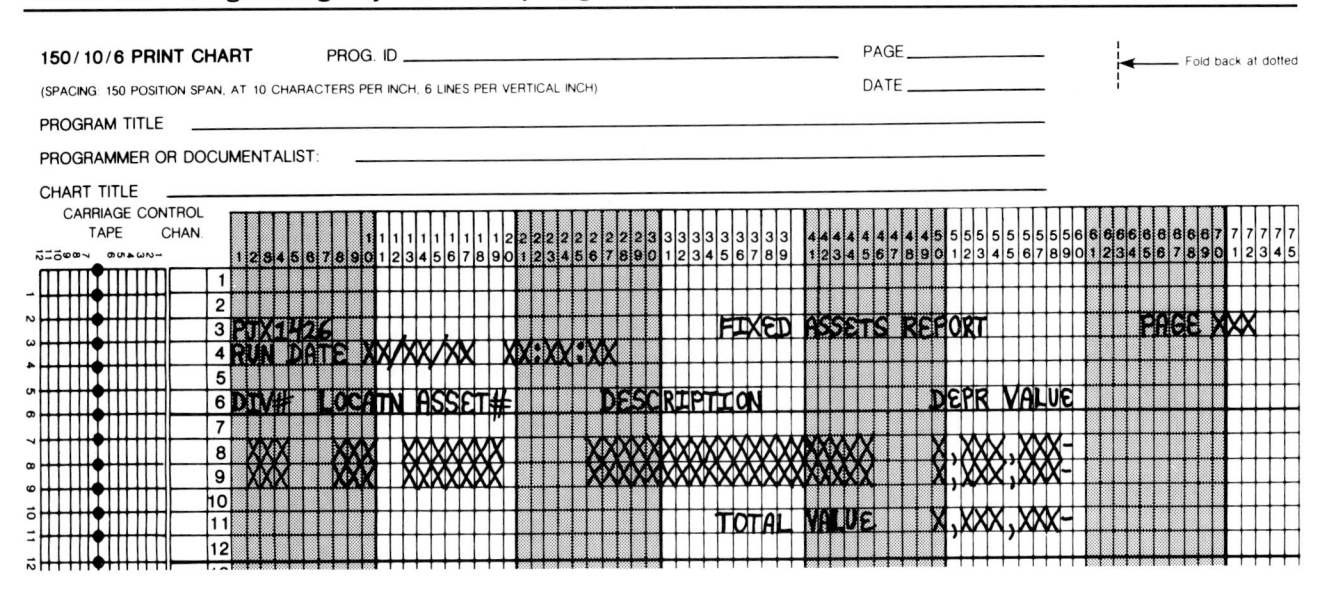

FIGURE 14.26 Programming Project: Final Report

```
PJX1426                       FIXED ASSETS REPORT        PAGE   1
RUN DATE  3/16/92 10:56:36

DIV#   LOCATN ASSET#     DESCRIPTION            DEPR VALUE
  6     099    48605     WANES-GAUGE                  100
  6     099    58421     PAPER CUTTER              45,892
  6     099    73258     CODE GENERATOR            98,521

                         TOTAL VALUE              144,513
```

Chapter 15

On-Line Inquiries Using RPG III/400

What you will learn in Chapter 15

Differences Between Batch and On-Line Processing
Planning the Format for the Screen
On-Line Processing Concepts
Describing Display Files
Creating the Screen Design

DDS—Data Description Specifications
SDA—Screen Design Aid
SQL—Structured Query Language
Coding the Data Description Specification

Programming for Interactive Applications
Accessing the Screen File in the RPG Program (EXFMT)
How to Use Debug in RPG III/400

On-line processing gives the user greater access to the information available on the computer. Using a terminal, a user can request information from the computer at any time. A user can also enter data directly into a terminal at any time. This capability permits data to be processed in a more timely manner than batch processing methods allow. And by having the data edited immediately as it is being input, erroneous data can be filtered out before it ever gets into the computer files.

DIFFERENCES BETWEEN BATCH AND ON-LINE PROCESSING ■

Programming for on-line, interactive applications can present many challenges. Some differences between batch processing and on-line interactive processing follow.

Batch Programs	*Interactive Programs*
Programs are executed in a more controlled framework within a job stream.	Programs are often executed by untrained users.
Processing usually progresses sequentially through a file and ends when the last record has been processed.	Processing may begin or end anywhere in any file (or files) selected.

Data is put through an edit program prior to processing for important reporting or for file updates.	Editing must be done as the data is being entered. Errors must be prevented from entering the system.
Processing is run on a predictable schedule. Jobs are run in a precise sequence.	Processing may be run at any time a user wishes. Jobs may be run out of sequence.
Security is controlled because access can be restricted to data processing or other selected personnel.	Anyone having access to the system is able to access the program.

Before writing a program to do on-line processing, some planning should be done to ensure that the results will be easy to use, that proper editing will be done, and that sound data processing principles are used.

PLANNING THE FORMAT FOR THE SCREEN ■

The format for the screen should be outlined on paper before any coding is done. This cuts down on time wasted revising the program later. The planning form shown in Figure 15.1 is a helpful tool for sketching the format for the screen. The most common size of screen displays 80 characters horizontally and 24 lines vertically, as shown in Figure 15.1.

Screen formatting should observe the following conventions and rules of design:

1. Every screen should have a clear, descriptive title. The title must be brief but must clearly state the function of the screen so that the user will have no doubt what function is performed.
2. The program name should be displayed, usually in the upper left corner of the screen. If several programs are executed within the system, the name of the first program should be displayed. This helps future programmers to identify which program is being used when a user has a problem or requests a modification.
3. The date, time of day, and user identification are sometimes useful to the programmer when tracking a series of events or performing routine duties.

FIGURE 15.1 Common Screen Display

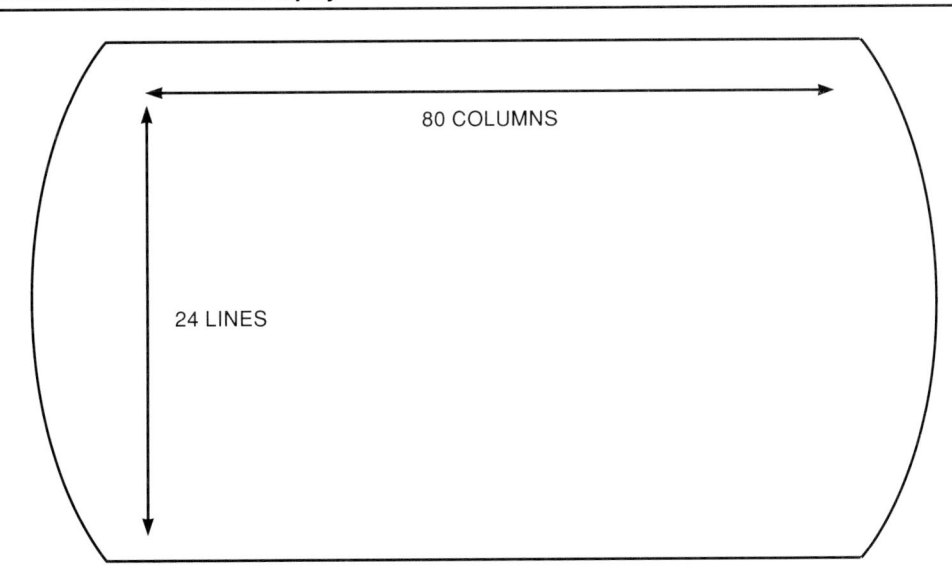

FIGURE 15.2 Screen Format That Allows User Input

```
   CF090R                    CHECK FROM OFFICE                  3/22/92
                                                               10:46:00



                   ENTER STORE NO.....

                   BEGINNING DATE.....   0/00/00

                   ENDING DATE.........  0/00/00




                              CF1-EXIT
```

4. Options to be selected or entries to be made by the user should be clearly explained on the screen by a series of prompts. These entries should never depend on the knowledge of the user or on some printed manual to explain all the codes. If the explanations become too lengthy to display on the screen, a second "help" screen should be available.
5. Function keys (or command keys) will be discussed later in this chapter. If a function key is available in a program, its use should be clearly described on the screen. These descriptions are often displayed at the bottom of the screen or in a window that can be requested using a help key. The use of function keys should be standardized within an organization.
6. There must always be some method for escaping from a screen without updating or in any way distorting the data in any files. This is necessary for the user who accidentally calls the wrong program. The escape should return the user to the previous screen from which this program was selected.

Every organization will have its own specific standards and conventions. Figure 15.2 shows an example of a screen format that allows a user to enter a request for data.

ON-LINE PROCESSING CONCEPTS ■

Two general types of on-line programs are available: inquiry and update. Inquiry programs allow a user to select (by entering key fields) a particular set of information. This data may reside in one or many files in auxiliary storage. After the user has entered the key fields for the item and pressed the ENTER or RETURN key, the program searches the files for the data and then displays all the requested information on the screen.

Update programs permit the user to make changes to the file. These changes will take the form of added records, changes to existing records, or deletions of records. These programs must be written with full editing functions to ensure that invalid data is not accepted into the file, and care must be taken to ensure that data in the master file is not altered inadvertently. Updates will be discussed in more detail in Chapter 16.

DESCRIBING DISPLAY FILES ■

When a program is written for an on-line application, a method is needed for describing the screen (or screens) that will be presented to the user. Although this can be part of the program itself, it is simpler to create the format of the screen as an independent file. The screen format is then accessed in the program as any other file is accessed.

CREATING THE SCREEN DESIGN ∎

It is not absolutely necessary to define the screen format externally. In fact, years ago the screens were always defined within the program itself. RPG III/400 has at least three methods for defining screens. Each method has certain advantages and drawbacks.

DDS—Data Description Specifications

The Data Description Specification (DDS) is a utility tool available with IBM mid-range systems. It uses the same coding form as that used for externally describing physical and logical files. There are some new requirements that must be learned for coding display formats.

The programmer should first outline the design of the screen on a layout form. Then the field and descriptive entries can be entered for the DDS format.

SDA—Screen Design Aid

The Screen Design Aid (SDA) is a utility program available with IBM mid-range systems. It allows a programmer to design and describe a screen very rapidly. It is easy to learn and to use.

The programmer is prompted to enter a series of parameters; SDA then creates the DDS. The DDS can be adjusted later by using the DDS format itself or by returning to SDA.

The SDA programming tool can be studied and learned using the manuals available in most IBM mid-range computer facilities. It is not usually available on mainframes, personal computers, or non-IBM computers, although some similar software may be available.

SQL—Structured Query Language

Structured Query Language (SQL) is a tool that allows the programmer to incorporate display (and other) files into a program without the use of external descriptions. It can be used with either COBOL or RPG and is useful on computers where externally defined files are not available.

This tool can be studied and learned using the manuals. Although it is less efficient than RPG standard screen design methods, its advantage is that it can be used on PC and mainframe computers.

After the screen format has been designed and compiled as an object on the system, the programming can be done. More than one program can access the same screen, although there is usually a need for a unique screen for each program. Just as externally defined files must first exist to be used in a program, the screen format must also exist before the program can be compiled successfully.

CODING THE DATA DESCRIPTION SPECIFICATION ∎

The rules for coding the Data Description Specification are extensive and cannot be adequately covered here. In the following examples, only the most necessary coding will be explained. For a detailed explanation, the IBM manual on DDS coding is recommended.

The Data Description Specification for a display file is similar to that for a physical or logical file, but certain rules must be followed. Figures 15.3(a), 15.3(b), and 15.3(c) show sample screens for an on-line inquiry and the DDS entries for creating those screens.

A display file will often require more than one screen format. In the example, there are two screen formats. The first format, called REQUEST, describes the screen to be displayed initially, and includes a prompt for the user to enter a request for information. This format will accept the request from the user and edit for a valid number. The second format, called ANSWER, will display the requested data. It allows the user to return to request another record or end the searching program.

The screen heading "INVENTORY INQUIRY BY PART#" is coded within single quotation marks in columns 45–80. The location of the heading on the screen is defined in columns 39–41 for

FIGURE 15.3(a) Sample Screen for On-Line Inquiry (Screen 1)

```
INV012                    INVENTORY INQUIRY BY PART#




             ENTER PART#








                                              CF-01 TO EXIT
```

FIGURE 15.3(b) Sample Screen for On-Line Inquiry (Screen 2)

```
INV012                    INVENTORY INQUIRY BY PART#



      STRIPED WIDGETS       PRICE    2.50    QTY O/H   283




    ENTER TO REQUEST ANOTHER PART              CF-01 TO EXIT
```

FIGURE 15.3(c) DDS for Creating On-Line Inquiry Screen

DATA DESCRIPTION SPECIFICATIONS

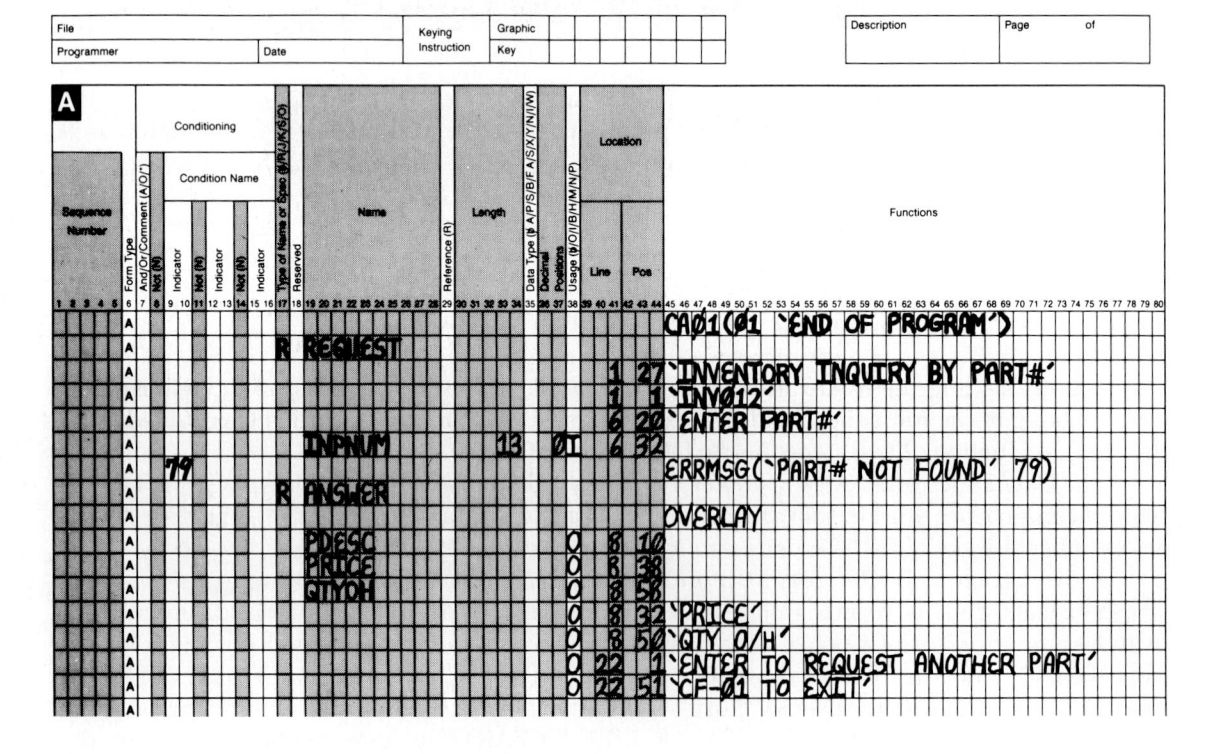

Seq	Form Type	Name	Length	Data Type	Dec	Usage	Line	Pos	Functions
	A								CA01(01 'END OF PROGRAM')
	A	R REQUEST							
	A						1	27	'INVENTORY INQUIRY BY PART#'
	A						1	1	'INV012'
	A						6	20	'ENTER PART#'
	A	INPNUM	13	0		I	6	32	
	A 79								ERRMSG('PART# NOT FOUND' 79)
	A	R ANSWER							
	A								OVERLAY
	A	PDESC				O	8	10	
	A	PRICE				O	8	38	
	A	QTYOH				O	8	58	
	A					O	8	32	'PRICE'
	A					O	8	50	'QTY O/H'
	A					O	22	1	'ENTER TO REQUEST ANOTHER PART'
	A					O	22	51	'CF-01 TO EXIT'

the line number and columns 42–44 for the position on that line where the heading should *begin*. In this example, the heading will be placed on line 1 on the screen, beginning in position 27. Notice that this differs from the convention for headings or fields used for printer files, for which the *ending* position is identified on the Output Specifications.

The program name will print on line 1 beginning in column 2. Notice that these first two heading lines can be coded in any sequence. They may appear anywhere within the description for the REQUEST format. The heading "ENTER PART#" will appear on line 6 beginning in position 20.

The field for entering the part number is named INPNUM. This is entered in columns 19–24. It may be the real name of the field as it is defined in the inventory file or a new name defined specifically for this screen. Its length of 7 positions is entered in columns 30–34. It is a numeric field (with no decimal positions), so a zero is entered in columns 36–37.

An *I* is entered in column 38 (Usage) to indicate that this field will be an input field. The data will be input by the user making the request. Input-capable fields will display on the screen as underlined fields. This cues the user that an entry can be made. The location on the screen where this field will be input is line 6. It begins in position 32, after the words instructing the user to "ENTER PART#." The field, INPNUM, must not overlay the words "ENTER PART#."

If the part number is not found in the inventory file, a message should be displayed on the screen to inform the user that the part number entered does not exist. This logic will be handled in the program and an indicator will be set on if the part number is not found. The DDS will need to recognize the indicator and display a message. There are three sets of indicators available in columns 8–16 on the DDS form, similar to those used on the Calculation Specifications. Indicator 79 is used for this example and is entered in columns 9–10. The key word ERRMSG is entered in columns 45–50 followed by the desired message enclosed within parentheses and single quotation marks. If a requested part number is not found, the error message will be displayed. The user may then enter another number.

A user must be allowed to escape or exit from the screen at any time. In this example, this is done with the use of function key or command key 1. This is coded on the DDS by entering CA01(01 'End of Program') in columns 45–80. It will be necessary to code the logic for setting on indicator 1 to notify the program to end within the Calculation Specifications. When the user presses function key 1, the program will recognize it as a request to end processing.

The format ANSWER will display the descriptive information about the requested part number after the record is retrieved from the file. The key word OVERLAY in columns 45–51 will cause the ANSWER format to be displayed at the bottom of the screen without erasing the REQUEST format.

The part description, price, and quantity-on-hand fields will print on line 8. Care must be taken that fields do not overlap. One space is required by DDS between each field displayed on a line. If fields are defined in overlapping positions, one or more of them will not be displayed on the screen and the desired results will not be achieved.

The usage for these fields is entered in column 38 on the DDS as O, which means they are output fields only. Fields defined as either O or blank in column 38 are treated as output fields. These fields are displayed on the screen but cannot be changed.

The message "Enter to Request Another Part" will appear on line 22, beginning in position 1.

A message on the screen should explain the use of the function key. This is provided in the DDS with the constant message "CF-01 to Exit." This message will print on line 22 beginning at position 51.

This completes a very simple DDS for an inquiry program screen. The logic to support this screen must be done in the RPG program. Remember that the format for the screen file must exist before attempting to compile the program that uses it.

PROGRAMMING FOR INTERACTIVE APPLICATIONS ■

File Description Specifications for an interactive program will need to include a file for the workstation. Like printed reports, which must be defined as files, the workstation using the program

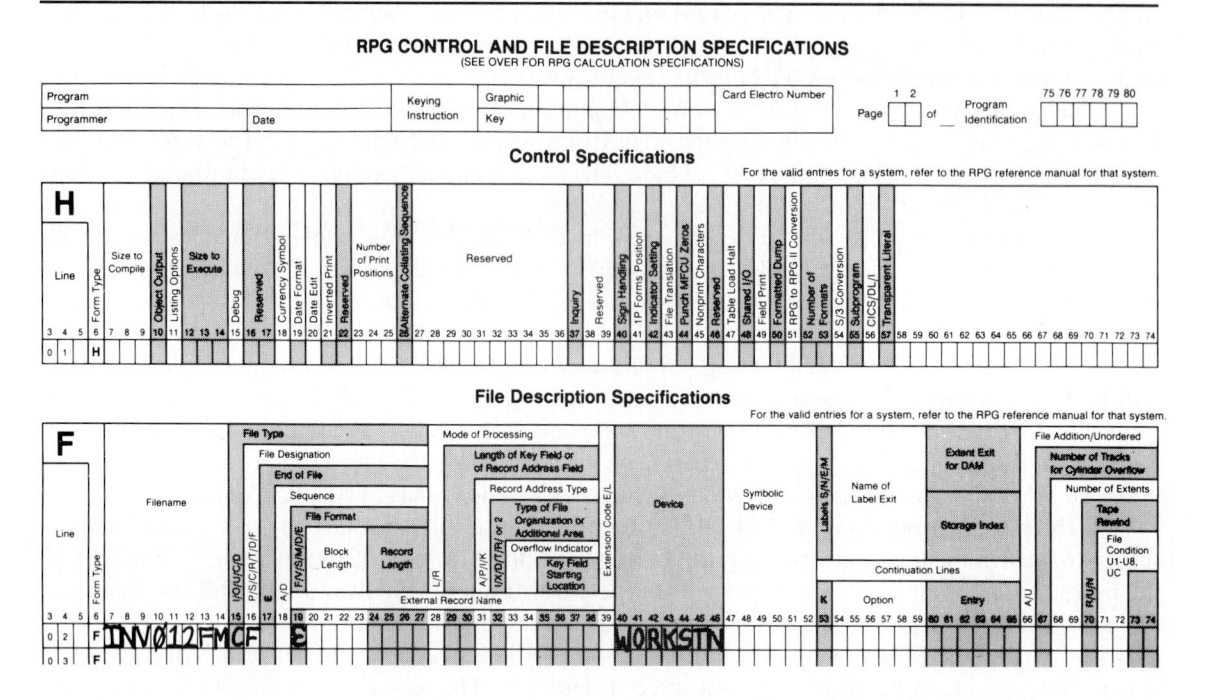

FIGURE 15.4 File Description Specification for a Workstation File

will need to be defined as well. Figure 15.4 shows the coding for a program that uses a workstation for input and for output.

Columns 15–16 contain the letters CF. The C represents a combined file. This means that the file is used for both input and output functions. The F means that the file is full functional. Column 19 contains an E because the screen format is externally defined. The device name is WORKSTN.

ACCESSING THE SCREEN FILE IN THE RPG PROGRAM (EXFMT) ∎

As shown in Figure 15.5, in the compiled program the Input Specifications are automatically retrieved from the external Screen Specifications. It will place them in the program as input descriptions just like any other externally defined file description as described in Chapter 12.

It will not be necessary to code any Output Specifications for this program. All the work will be done within the Calculation Specifications.

The calculation functions must take care of the entire processing cycle for this program. The program must remain active from the time it is called by the user until the user exits from the screen. When the program is first called, the first screen format should be displayed. This is done with the operation EXFMT (Execute Format). Factor 2 contains the name of the format to be displayed. Figure 15.6 shows the coding for displaying the format REQUEST.

The EXFMT not only writes the format to the screen, but also accepts any entries made by the user. When the format is displayed, the cursor is automatically positioned at the beginning of the input field (although it is possible for the programmer to control the cursor positioning as well).

The program stops at this point to wait for the user to take the next action. If the user decides to exit from the program at this point, the program must be ready to allow for termination of the program. This is why the next line of code tests to determine whether function key 1 has been pressed. Figure 15.7 shows the coding to handle the exit from the program.

If the user does not exit the program at this point, he or she may enter a part number and press the ENTER key. This causes RPG to read the information entered into input fields on the screen. In this example, the input field is the part number. The program must next search the inventory file for the requested part number. Figure 15.8 shows the next lines of code used to search for the correct record.

FIGURE 15.5 Compiled Program for On-line Processing (File Input Specifications)

```
SEQUENCE         1          2          3          4          5          6          7
NUMBER   67890123456789012345678901234567890123456789012345678901234


     100   F* TITLE: ILLUS FOR 15.5
     200   F* DATE:  6/24           AUTHOR: D.CABLE
     300   F* DESCRIPTION:  SCREEN EXAMPLE
     400   F************************************************************


NAME OF PROGRAM WILL BE ILL155 IN LIBRARY CABLE

           H
* 1019           ALL DECIMAL DATA ERRORS IGNORED
     500   FINVDETL IF   E           K         DISK
           RECORD FORMAT(S):  FILE INVDETL LIB CABLE
                    EXTERNAL FORMAT INVDTL01 RPG NAME INVDTL01

     600   FINV012FMCF   E                     WORKSTN
     700   F************************************************************


     800   C* START-UP ROUTINE
           RECORD FORMAT(S):  FILE INV012FM LIB CABLE
                    EXTERNAL FORMAT REQUEST RPG NAME REQUEST
                    EXTERNAL FORMAT ANSWER RPG NAME ANSWER
A000000    INPUT  FIELDS FOR RECORD INVDTL01 FILE INVDETL FORMAT INVDTL01
A000001                                         1      3 DTLDIV
A000002                                         4      6 DTLWHS
A000003                                         7     13 DTLPNO
A000004                                        14     32 DTLDSC
A000005                                        33     34 DTLUM
A000006                                        35     39 DTLQOH
A000007                                        40     46 DTLAVG
A000008                                        47     51 DTLBIN
A000009                                        52     53 DTLTYP
A000010                                        54     55 DTLCAT
A000011                                        56     58 DTLDPT
B000000    INPUT  FIELDS FOR RECORD REQUEST FILE INV012FM FORMAT REQUEST
B000001                                         1      1 *IN01
B000002                                         2      2 *IN79
B000003                                         3      9 INPNUM
C000000    INPUT  FIELDS FOR RECORD ANSWER FILE INV012FM FORMAT ANSWER
C000001                                         1      1 *IN01
```

FIGURE 15.6 Calculation Specification to Display a Screen

RPG CALCULATION SPECIFICATIONS

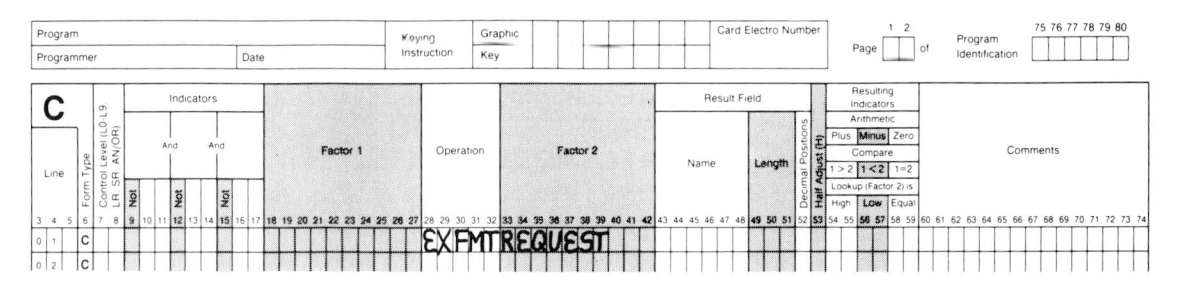

```
01 C                           EXFMT REQUEST
02 C
```

FIGURE 15.7 Coding for Exiting the Program

RPG CALCULATION SPECIFICATIONS

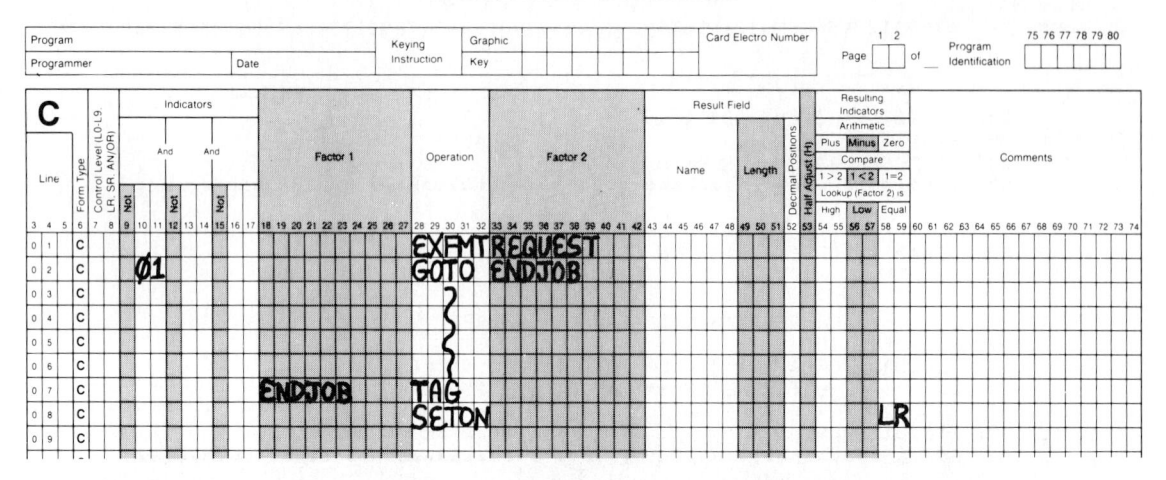

```
01  C                        EXFMT REQUEST
02  C   01                   GOTO  ENDJOB
03  C
04  C
05  C
06  C
07  C             ENDJOB     TAG
08  C                        SETON                           LR
09  C
```

FIGURE 15.8 Coding for Searching for the Correct Record

RPG CALCULATION SPECIFICATIONS

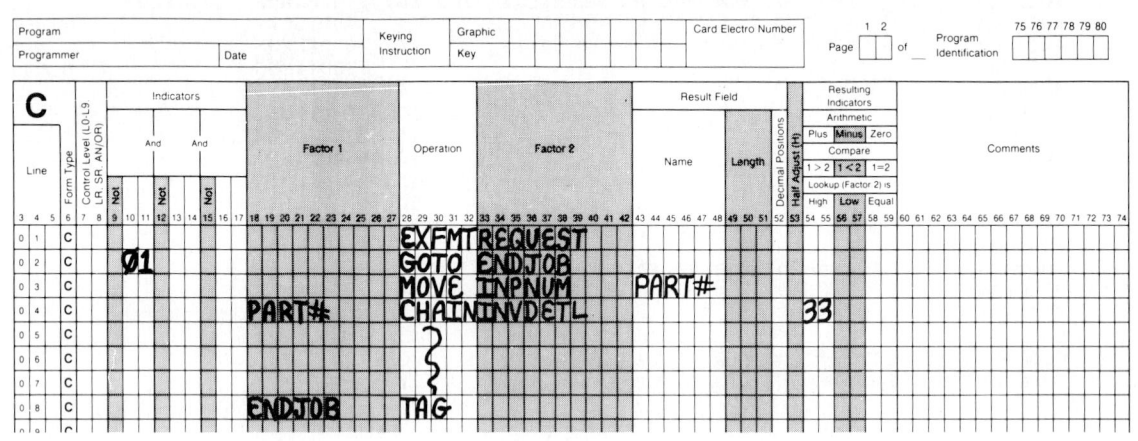

```
01  C                        EXFMT REQUEST
02  C   01                   GOTO  ENDJOB
03  C                        MOVE  INPNUM   PART#
04  C             PART#      CHAIN INVDETL              33
05  C
06  C
07  C
08  C             ENDJOB     TAG
09  C
```

If the record is *not* found, indicator 79 will be set on and an error message will be displayed on the screen. The format REQUEST must be redisplayed to cause this message to appear. The message prompts the user to enter another part number. To search for the new part number, the program must return to the beginning and repeat the same steps. It is not necessary to clear the error message since it is controlled in the DDS by the indicator.

If the record *is* found, indicator 79 will be set off and the fields from the requested inventory record will be available for display on the screen in the format ANSWER. Another EXFMT is coded for this format. Figure 15.9 shows the coding for displaying the requested information.

The REQUEST portion of the program remains on the screen. The inventory information is displayed at the bottom of the screen. When the user is ready for another transaction, the ENTER key is pressed. The program must clear the information in the output fields and return to the beginning of the program for another transaction. Figure 15.10 shows the entire program for this application.

Since the calculations are made up of a never-ending loop, the program can only be terminated when the user presses a function key to the exit program. This structure is typical of all interactive on-line programs.

FIGURE 15.9 Coding for Displaying the Requested Information

RPG CALCULATION SPECIFICATIONS

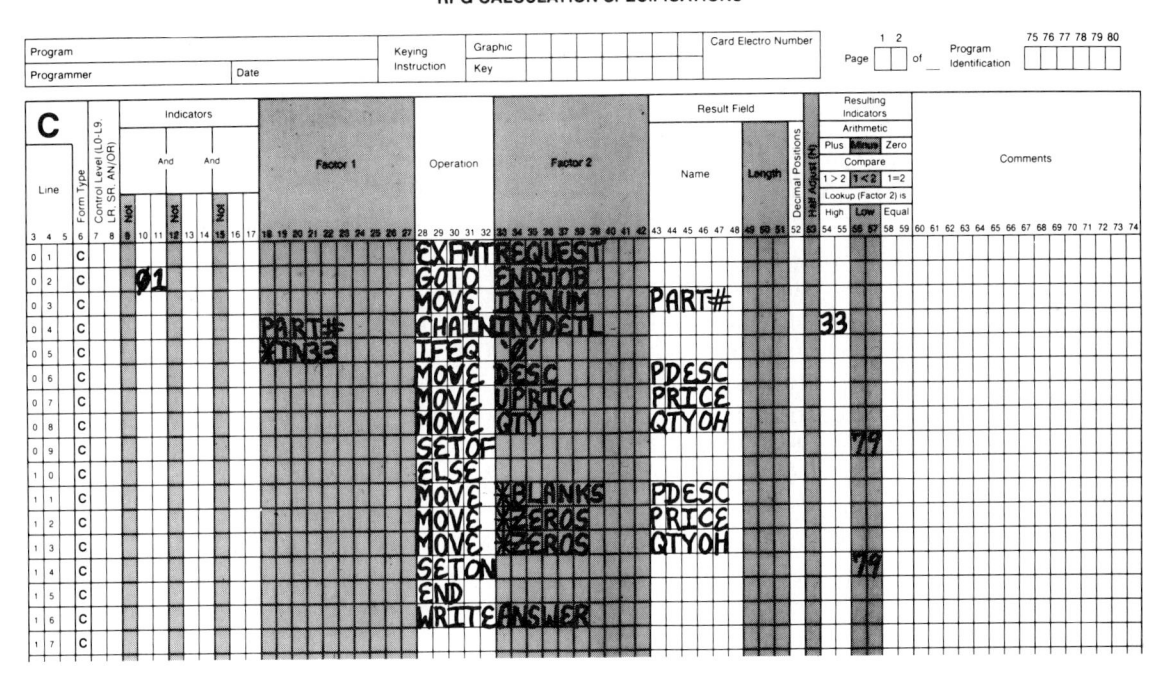

Line	Form Type	Control Level	Indicators (Not/And/Not/And/Not)	Factor 1	Operation	Factor 2	Result Field Name	Length	Dec	H	Resulting Indicators (Plus/Minus/Zero or 1>2/1<2/1=2)	Comments
01	C				EXFMT	REQUEST						
02	C	01			GOTO	ENDJOB						
03	C				MOVE	INPNUM	PART#					
04	C			PART#	CHAIN	INVDETL					33	
05	C			*IN33	IFEQ	'0'						
06	C				MOVE	DESC	PDESC					
07	C				MOVE	UPRIC	PRICE					
08	C				MOVE	QTY	QTYOH					
09	C				SETOF						79	
10	C				ELSE							
11	C				MOVE	*BLANKS	PDESC					
12	C				MOVE	*ZEROS	PRICE					
13	C				MOVE	*ZEROS	QTYOH					
14	C				SETON						79	
15	C				END							
16	C				WRITE	ANSWER						
17	C											

FIGURE 15.10 Complete Calculations for Displaying a Screen and Retrieving Data

RPG CALCULATION SPECIFICATIONS

Line	Form Type	Control Level	Indicators	Factor 1	Operation	Factor 2	Result Field Name	Length	Dec	H	Resulting Indicators	Comments
01	C			BEGIN	TAG							
02	C				EXFMT	REQUEST						
03	C	01			GOTO	ENDJOB						
04	C				MOVE	INPNUM	PART#					
05	C			PART#	CHAIN	INVDETL					33	
06	C			*IN33	IFEQ	'0'						
07	C				MOVE	DESC	PDESC					
08	C				MOVE	UPRIC	PRICE					
09	C				MOVE	QTY	QTYOH					
10	C				SETOF						79	
11	C				ELSE							
12	C				MOVE	*BLANKS	PDESC					
13	C				MOVE	*ZEROS	PRICE					
14	C				MOVE	*ZEROS	QTYOH					
15	C				SETON						79	
16	C				END							
17	C				WRITE	ANSWER						
18	C				GOTO	BEGIN						
19	C			ENDJOB	TAG							
20	C				SETON						LR	
	C											

HOW TO USE DEBUG IN RPG III/400 ∎

Program debugging is necessary in every type of environment since program errors can happen wherever coding is complex. The debug function is available for both batch and on-line programming. Problems are more difficult to discover in on-line programs, however, since there is no printed report to show where the problems are occurring. For this reason, the programmer needs to know how to use the superior debugging tool provided in the RPG III/400 environment.

The debug function in RPG III/400 improves on the one available in RPG II. No entries are required within the RPG program itself. This saves time and effort removing them. It is not even necessary to recompile the program after performing debug functions in RPG III/400, unless changes need to be made to the program.

This is all possible because the debug function is performed *outside* the program and is requested in the system command language. On the System/38, the command for performing debug functions is ENTDBG (enter debug mode). On the AS/400, the command is STRDBG (start debug mode).

The command for executing the debug function states the name of the program on which it is to be performed, with the library if needed, as shown in Figure 15.11.

In this illustration, the program name is INV100, which is located in a library named PRODLIB. The parameter UPDPROD is required and prompts the programmer to decide whether files are really to be updated. To perform a debug of a program, it is usually a good idea to use the update mode to find all errors in the program. The programmer should be using test data and should *not* be testing on real data. Some sample data should be placed in a separate file for the purpose of testing or debugging a program.

No file updates are being done in the sample program described earlier, so the reply *YES will have no effect on the results of this test.

This command (ENTDBG or STRDBG) is followed by a series of one or more break points that will display the suspect data or condition of indicators at various places within the program. Figure 15.12 shows a series of break points for determining the condition of indicator 79 and the content of the fields INPNUM and INPART.

The first break point corresponds to line number 500 of the Calculation Specifications in the program. When the program is executed and line 500 is reached in the calculations, the contents of the field INPNUM will be displayed on the screen. When two or more fields need to be examined, they must be enclosed within single quotation marks and parentheses as shown on the second break point example. To display the condition of a specific indicator, a break point is defined as shown on the third break point example. The last break point, at line 1200, will show the condition of all indicators at that moment.

FIGURE 15.11 Command to Perform the Debugging Function

```
              ENTDBG INV100.PRODLIB UPDPROD(*YES)

                               OR

              STRDBG PRODLIB/INV100 UPDPROD(*YES)
```

FIGURE 15.12 Break Points in a Debugging Function

```
              ENTDBG  INV100.PRODLIB UPDPROD(*YES)
              ADDBKP  500  INPNUM
              ADDBKP  700  ('INPNUM' 'INPART')
              ADDBKP  1000 *IN79
              ADDBKP  1200 *IN
```

This enables the programmer to see exactly what is happening behind the scenes in the program. It is a powerful analysis tool that is particularly useful in very complex programs.

The program may be run as many times as necessary until the programmer determines the cause of any errors. The break points may be altered dynamically during the running of the test to display other fields or indicators at different points in the program.

When all errors have been located and the programmer is satisfied that the corrections needed are understood, the debug function can be ended by entering the command ENDDBG.

If the ENDDBG command is *not* entered, all further execution of the program at *that* workstation under *that* session will continue to operate in debug mode. However, when the programmer signs off, the debug function will be terminated automatically.

The debugging function is a useful and necessary tool for determining the cause of problems in programs. It is particularly useful for testing interactive programs in which the sequence of actions taken by a user may be less predictable. The use of the debug command can speed up the testing phase of program development.

Programming for on-line inquiry systems is more complicated than programming for batch systems since the programmer must provide for all the possible actions that a user might take in using an application. It is more satisfying, however, because the data can be displayed interactively, providing the user with immediate access to data.

SUMMARY ■

In this chapter, you have learned that developing on-line applications is more complex than writing programs that read a file and print a report. The programmer should plan and design a display screen that will be easy to use. It should be self-sufficient, to guide the user through prompts to make the appropriate entries on the screen. The screen must be designed and defined before any programming begins. The screen is most often defined using the Data Description Specifications, although other methods are available. Other methods include a design tool available on most IBM hardware called Screen Design Aid (SDA), which allows the programmer to design the screen on-line. The DDS is produced automatically by the SDA utility. Another tool available for use on machines which do not provide separate screen definition is Structured Query Language (SQL).

After the screen has been defined, the program can be written to access the screen, obtain a request, and retrieve data from a disk. This data can then be displayed and reviewed by the user. The operation to accept a request and display data is EXFMT.

You have also learned about debugging tools. Since it is more difficult to detect the cause of problems with on-line programs, a debugging tool has been provided with RPG III/400. This is the debug command for performing the debug function. It allows for external viewing of the internal workings of a program while it is executing.

REVIEW QUESTIONS ■

1. Explain the differences between batch processing and on-line interactive processing.
2. How are display files described?
3. What are the three alternative methods for describing a display file?
4. Explain how the coding of the Data Description Specification for display files differs from the coding for physical or logical files.
5. Explain the use of command or function keys.
6. The device name on the File Description Specifications for a workstation is _____ .
7. The operation code that will cause data to be written to the screen in RPG III/400 is _____ .
8. The operation code that will cause data to be read from the screen in RPG III/400 is _____ .
9. The operation code that will cause data to be both written to and read from the screen in RPG III/400 is _____ .
10. Describe how the debug function is used in RPG III/400.

DEBUGGING EXERCISES

Instructions

The following RPG programs contain an error or errors. Some of these errors are indicated by the RPG compiler on the program listing. A list of syntax errors is given at the end of the program listing. Other types of errors may occur which will not be shown. These are called logic errors.

Study each program and its syntax errors. Locate each error (including logic errors) and on a separate coding form make the correct entry for the line(s) in error.

Explain each error and how it should be corrected.

```
       100   F* TITLE: DEBUG PROJECT 15-A
       200   F* DATE: 6/29              AUTHOR: D.CABLE
       300   F* DESCRIPTION: SCREEN EXAMPLE
       400   F*************************************************


NAME OF PROGRAM WILL BE PJ015A IN LIBRARY CABLE


             H
* 1019               ALL DECIMAL DATA ERRORS IGNORED
       500   FP0055FM CF   E                    WORKSTN
               RECORD FORMAT(S): FILE P0055FM LIB NEWMOD
                   EXTERNAL FORMAT P005501 RPG NAME P005501

       600   FIIPOMSFLIF  E           K         DISK
       700   F*************************************************
               RECORD FORMAT(S): FILE IIPOMSFL LIB MOMS
                   EXTERNAL FORMAT IIPOMS10 RPG NAME IIPOMS10


       800   E                   MSG       1   3 20


       900   C* START-UP ROUTINE
    A000000    INPUT  FIELDS FOR RECORD P005501 FILE P0055FM FORMAT P005501
    A000001                                          1    1 *IN01
    A000002                                          5    5 *IN05
    A000003                                          6    6 *IN09
    A000004                                          4    4 *IN79
    A000005                                          2    2 *IN80
    A000006                                          3    3 *IN81
    A000007                                          7    8  SCCMP#
    A000008                                          9   110SCLOC#
    A000009                                         12   180SCPONO
    A000010                                         19   272SCAMT
    B000000    INPUT  FIELDS FOR RECORD IIPOMS10 FILE IIPOMSFL FORMAT IIPOMS10
    B000001                                          1    2 IPCMP#
    B000002                                     P    3    40IPLOC#
    B000003                                     P    5    80IPPONO
    B000004                                     P    9   110IPLNNO
    B000005                                     P   12   150IPVND#
    B000006                                         16   28 IPITM#
    B000007                                     P   29   330IPUORD
    B000008                                     P   34   383IPOPRC
    B000009                                     P   39   410IPCSCT
    B000010                                     P   42   450IPPODT
    B000011                                         46   46 IPSTCD
    B000012                                     P   47   500IPDLDT
    B000013                                     P   51   550IPUTBO
    B000014                                     P   56   590IPDUED
      1000   C           KEY       KLIST
      1100   C                     KFLD           IPCMP#
```

Chapter 15 On-Line Inquiries Using RPG III/400

```
SEQUENCE        1         2         3         4         5         6         7
NUMBER    67890123456789012345678901234567890123456789012345678901234

   1200  C                    KFLD           IPLOC#
   1300  C                    KFLD           IPPONO
   1400  C* MAINLINE ROUTINE
   1500  C           BEGIN    TAG
   1600  C                    EXFMTP005501
   1700  C     01             GOTO ENDJOB
   1800  C                    MOVE SCCMP#    IPCMP#
   1900  C                    MOVE SCLOC#    IPLOC#
   2000  C           KEY      SETLLIIPOMS10
   2100  C           KEY      READEIIPOMS10                    33
   2200  C           *IN33    IFEQ '1'
   2300  C                    MOVELMSG,1     SCERR
   2400  C                    END
   2500  C           *IN33    IFEQ '0'
   2600  C           SCAMT    IFNE POAMT
   2700  C           POAMT    SUB  SCAMT     SCDIFF
   2800  C                    MOVELMSG,2     SCERR
   2900  C                    ELSE
   3000  C                    MOVELMSG,3     SCERR
   3100  C                    END
   3200  C                    GOTO BEGIN
   3300  C           ENDJOB   TAG
   3400  C**********************************************************
* 5177                   5177-*****

   C000000   OUTPUT  FIELDS FOR RECORD P005501 FILE P0055FM FORMAT P005501
   C000001                          SCCMP#    2  CHAR    2
   C000002                          SCLOC#    5  ZONE    3,0
   C000003                          SCPONO   12  ZONE    7,0
   C000004                          SCAMT    21  ZONE    9,2
   C000005                          POAMT    30  ZONE    9,2
   C000006                          SCDIFF   39  ZONE    9,2
   C000007                          SCERR    69  CHAR   30
   * * * * * E N D   O F   S O U R C E * * * *


* 7023            PROGRAM MAY LOOP. NO MEANS OF PROGRAM TERMINATION FOUND
         TABLE/ARRAY ------ MSG
   3600  P.O. NUMBER NOT FOUND
   3700  P.O. AMOUNT DOES NOT AGREE
   3800  P.O. AMOUNT IS CORRECT

   KEY FIELD INFORMATION


                    PHYSICAL   LOGICAL
         FILE/RCD   FIELD      FIELD      ATTRIBUTES


   02  IIPOMSFL
           IIPOMS10
                    IPCMP#                CHAR   2
                    IPLOC#                PACK   2,0  SIGNED
                    IPPONO                PACK   7,0  SIGNED
                    IPLNNO                PACK   4,0  SIGNED



   CROSS-REFERENCE LISTING



         FILE/RCD    DEV/RCD   REFERENCES (D=DEFINED)

   02  IIPOMSFL     DISK       6000
           IIPOMS10            6000  6000000   2000    2100
   01  P0055FM      WORKSTN    5000
           P005501             5000  A000000   1600    C000000
```

```
             FIELD       ATTR        REFERENCES (M=MODIFIED D=DEFINED)

*  7031     *IN01        A(1)        A000001
*  7031     *IN05        A(1)        A000002
*  7031     *IN09        A(1)        A000003
            *IN33        A(1)            2200          2500
*  7031     *IN79        A(1)        A000004
*  7031     *IN80        A(1)        A000005
*  7031     *IN81        A(1)        A000006
            BEGIN        TAG            1500D         3200
            ENDJOB       TAG            1700         33000
            IPCMP#       A(2)        B000001D         1100         1800M
*  7031     IPCSCT       P(5,0)      B000009D
*  7031     IPDLDT       P(6,0)      B000012D
*  7031     IPDUED       P(6,0)      B000014D
*  7031     IPITM#       A(13)       B000006D
*  7031     IPLNNO       P(4,0)      B000004D
            IPLOC#       P(2,0)      B000002D         1200         1900M
*  7031     IPOPRC       P(9,3)      B000008D
*  7031     IPPUDT       P(6,0)      B000010D
            IPPONO       P(7,0)      B000003D         1300
*  7031     IPSTCD       A(1)        B000011D
*  7031     IPUORD       P(9,0)      B000007D
*  7031     IPUTBO       P(9,0)      B000013D
*  7031     IPVND#       P(6,0)      B000005D
            KEY          KLIST          1000D         2000         2100
            MSG(3)       A(20)          8000
              MSG,1                     2300
              MSG,2                     2800
              MSG,3                     3000
            POAMT        P(9,2)         2600          2700         C000005D
            SCAMT        P(9,2)      A000010D         2600         2700         C000004D
            SCCMP#       A(2)        A000007D         1800         C000001D
            SCDIFF       P(9,2)         2700M         C000006D
            SCERR        A(30)          2300M         2800M        3000M        C000007D
            SCLOC#       P(3,0)      A000008D         1900         C000002D
            SCPONO       P(7,0)      A000009D         C000003D
            '0'          LITERAL        2500
            '1'          LITERAL        2200
            1            LITERAL        2300
            2            LITERAL        2800
            3            LITERAL        3000

            INDICATOR    REFERENCES (M=MODIFIED D=DEFINED)

            *IN          A000001       A000002       A000003      A000004      A000005      A000006
                            2200          2500
            01           A000001          1700
*  7031     05           A000002
*  7031     09           A000003
            33              2100M         2200          2500
*  7031     79           A000004
*  7031     80           A000005
*  7031     81           A000006

   MESSAGES

   MSGID     SEV    NUMBER    TEXT

*  QRG1019    00      1       IGNDECERR(*YES) SPECIFIED ON COMMAND. NO DECIMAL DATA ERRORS
*  QRG5177    30      1       END STATEMENT MISSING FOR DO, DOUXX, DOWXX, OR IFXX GROUP. E
*  QRG7023    40      1       COMPILER CANNOT DETERMINE HOW PROGRAM CAN TERMINATE. PROGRAM
*  QRG7031    00     22       NAME OR INDICATOR NOT REFERENCED.

   MESSAGE SUMMARY

   TOTAL     00      10      20      30      40      50
    25       23       0       0       1       1       0

    38 RECORDS READ FROM SOURCE FILE
    SOURCE RECORDS INCLUDE    26 SPECIFICATIONS,      3 TABLE RECORDS, AND     8 COMMENTS


   QRG0008 COMPILE TERMINATED. SEVERITY 40 ERRORS FOUND IN PROGRAM

   * * * * *  E N D   O F   C O M P I L A T I O N * * * * *
*  QRG1020             ERROR OCCURRED CREATING OR UPDATING DATA AREA RETURNCODE. COMPI
```

```
       100   F* TITLE: DEBUG PROJECT 15-9
       200   F* DATE:   6/30         AUTHOR: D.CAPLE
       300   F* DESCRIPTION:
       400   F************************************************************

          NAME OF PROGRAM WILL BE PJ0159 IN LIBRARY CABLE

                   H
* 1019                    ALL DECIMAL DATA ERRORS IGNORED
       500   FPJ012FM CF  E                         WORKSTN
* 2120       500   DATA DESCRIPTIONS FOR FILE PJ012FM NOT FOUND
       600   FIBODTLFLIF  E           K             DISK
       700   F************************************************************

       800   C* START-UP ROUTINE
             RECORD FORMAT(S):    FILE IBODTLFL LIB MOMS
                     EXTERNAL FORMAT IBODTL10 RPG NAME IBODTL10
A000000      INPUT  FIELDS FOR RECORD IBODTL10 FILE IBODTLFL FORMAT IBODTL10
A000001                                              1    2 BDCMP#
A000002                                         P    3   40BDLOC#
A000003                                         P    5   90BDORD#
A000004                                         P   10  110BDSEQ#
A000005                                         P   12  150BDODTE
A000006                                         P   16  190BDOQTY
A000007                                             20   32 BDITM#
A000008                                         P   33  373BDPRCE
A000009                                         P   38  402BDDISC
A000010                                             41   45 BDUNIT
A000011                                         P   46  500BDACT#
A000012                                         P   51  540BDSQTY
A000013                                         P   55  560BDFEET
A000014                                             57   62 BDLCTN
A000015                                             63   63 BDTAXI
A000016                                         P   64  683BDCOST
A000017                                         P   69  710BDDEPT
A000018                                             72   84 BDCATL
A000019                                         P   85  870BDPPD#
A000020                                         P   88  900BDSET#
A000021                                         P   91  942BDSHCG
A000022                                             95   96 BDRSNC
A000023                                         P   97  990BDJINV
A000024                                         P  100 1040BDSQT1
A000025                                         P  105 1090BDSQT2
A000026                                         P  110 1110BDSLC1
A000027                                         P  112 1130BDSLC2
A000028                                            114  114 BDDRPS
A000029                                         P  115 1170BDPRCG
A000030                                            118  118 BDRSTK
A000031                                         P  119 1212BDCMRT
A000032                                         P  122 1262BDMKDN


   SEQUENCE         1         2         3         4         5         6         7
   NUMBER   67890123456789012345678901234567890123456789012345678901234567890123456789012345

       900   C           KEY       KLIST
      1000   C                     KFLD           IBCMP#
      1100   C                     KFLD           IBLOC#
      1200   C* MAINLINE ROUTINE
      1300   C           BEGIN     TAG
      1400   C                     EXFMTPJ01201
* 5154                             5154-**********

      1500   C   01                GOTO ENDJOB
      1600   C                     MOVE SCCMP#    IBCMP#
      1700   C                     MOVE SCLOC#    IBLOC#
      1800   C           KEY       SETLLIBODTL10
      1900   C           KEY       READEIBODTL10                    45
      2000   C           *IN45     IFEQ '0'
```

```
         2100  C                   SCAMT     ANDGT*ZERO
         2200  C                   IBOAMT    ADD  TAMT      TAMT
         2300  C                             GOTO BEGIN
         2400  C                   ENDJOB    TAG
         2500  C                             SETON                          LR
         2600  C************************************************************
*  5177                         5177-*****
```

* * * * * E N D   O F   S O U R C E * * * * *

```
*  7064       500    PJ012FM FILE NOT REFERENCED FOR OUTPUT
*  7064       500    PJ012FM FILE NOT REFERENCED FOR INPUT
*  7089       500    RPG PROVIDES SEPARATE INDICATOR AREA FOR FILE PJ012FM.
*  7073      1800    KFLD AT SEQ NBR   1000 HAS LENGTH OF    4 BUT KEY FIELD HAS LENG
*  7072      1800    KFLD AT SEQ NBR   1100 IS CHAR BUT KEY FIELD IS PACK.
*  7073      1900    KFLD AT SEQ NBR   1000 HAS LENGTH OF    4 BUT KEY FIELD HAS LENG
*  7072      1900    KFLD AT SEQ NBR   1100 IS CHAR BUT KEY FIELD IS PACK.
```

KEY FIELD INFORMATION

```
                          PHYSICAL    LOGICAL
         FILE/RCD         FIELD       FIELD       ATTRIBUTES


    02   IBODTLFL
             IBODTL10
                          BDCMP#                  CHAR    2
                          BDLOC#                  PACK    2,0   SIGNED
                          BDORD#                  PACK    9,0   SIGNED
                          BDSEQ#                  PACK    3,0   SIGNED
```

CROSS-REFERENCE LISTING

```
         FILE/RCD        DEV/RCD      REFERENCES (D=DEFINED)

    02   IBODTLFL        DISK          6000
             IBODTL10                  6000  A000000     1800       1900
    01   PJ012FM         WORKSTN       5000

         FIELD           ATTR         REFERENCES (M=MODIFIED D=DEFINED)

         *IN45           A(1)          2000
*  7031  BDACT#          P(9,0)        A000011D
*  7031  BDCATL          A(13)         A000018D
*  7031  BDCMP#          A(2)          A000001D
*  7031  BDCMRT          P(4,2)        A000031D
*  7031  BDCOST          P(9,3)        A000016D
*  7031  BDDEPT          P(4,0)        A000017D
*  7031  BDDISC          P(4,2)        A000009D
*  7031  BDDRPS          A(1)          A000028D
*  7031  BDFEET          P(2,0)        A000013D
*  7031  BDITM#          A(13)         A000007D
*  7031  BDJINV          P(5,0)        A000023D
*  7031  BDLCTN          A(6)          A000014D
*  7031  BDLOC#          P(2,0)        A000002D
*  7031  BDMKDN          P(9,2)        A000032D
*  7031  BDODTE          P(6,0)        A000005D
*  7031  BDOQTY          P(7,0)        A000006D
*  7031  BDORD#          P(9,0)        A000003D
*  7031  BDPPD#          P(5,0)        A000019D
*  7031  BDPRCE          P(9,3)        A000008D
*  7031  BDPRCG          P(5,0)        A000029D
*  7031  BDRSNC          A(2)          A000022D
*  7031  BDRSTK          A(1)          A000030D
*  7031  BDSEQ#          P(3,0)        A000004D
*  7031  BDSET#          P(5,0)        A000020D
*  7031  BDSHCG          P(7,2)        A000021D
*  7031  BDSLC1          P(2,0)        A000026D
*  7031  BDSLC2          P(2,0)        A000027D
*  7031  BDSQTY          P(7,0)        A000012D
```

* 7031	BDSQT1	P(9,0)	A000024D			
* 7031	BDSQT2	P(9,0)	A000025D			
* 7031	BDTAXI	A(1)	A000015D			
* 7031	BDUNIT	A(5)	A000010D			
	BEGIN	TAG	1300D	2300		
	ENDJOB	TAG	1500	2400D		
* 7030	IBCMP#	A(4)	1000	1600M		
* 7030	IBLOC#	A(4)	1100	1700M		
* 7030	IBOAMT	P(5,0)	2200			
	KEY	KLIST	900D	1800	1900	
* 7030	SCAMT	A(4)	2100			
* 7030	SCCMP#	A(4)	1600			
* 7030	SCLOC#	A(4)	1700			
* 7030	TAMT	P(5,0)	2200	2200M		
	*ZERO	LITERAL	2100			
	'0'	LITERAL	2000			

INDICATOR REFERENCES (M=MODIFIED D=DEFINED)

	*IN	2000	
	LR	2500M	
* 7030	01	1500	
	45	1900M	2000

MESSAGES

MSGID	SEV	NUMBER	TEXT
* QRG1019	00	1	IGNDECERR(*YES) SPECIFIED ON COMMAND. NO DECIMAL DATA ERRORS
* QRG2120	40	1	EXTERNAL DESCRIPTION NOT FOUND FOR FILE SPECIFIED AS EXTERNAL IGNORED.
* QRG5154	30	1	RECORD FORMAT NAME IN FACTOR 2 (POSITIONS 33-42) NOT DEFINED IGNORED.
* QRG5177	30	1	END STATEMENT MISSING FOR DO, DOUXX, DOWXX, OR IFXX GROUP. EN
* QRG7030	30	8	FIELD OR INDICATOR NOT DEFINED.
* QRG7031	00	32	NAME OR INDICATOR NOT REFERENCED.
* QRG7064	40	2	PROGRAM FILE NOT REFERENCED. FILE IGNORED
* QRG7072	30	2	KFLD TYPE NOT SAME AS CORRESPONDING KEY FIELD IN FILE. SPECIF
* QRG7073	30	2	LENGTH OF KFLD NOT SAME AS CORRESPONDING KEY FIELD IN FILE. S
* QRG7089	00	1	RPG PROVIDES SEPARATE INDICATOR AREA FOR FILE.

MESSAGE SUMMARY

TOTAL	00	10	20	30	40	50
51	34	0	0	14	3	0

26 RECORDS READ FROM SOURCE FILE
SOURCE RECORDS INCLUDE   18 SPECIFICATIONS,   0 TABLE RECORDS, AND   8 COMMENTS

QRG0008 COMPILE TERMINATED. SEVERITY 40 ERRORS FOUND IN PROGRAM

* * * * * E N D O F C O M P I L A T I O N * * * * *
* QRG1020   ERROR OCCURRED CREATING OR UPDATING DATA AREA RETURNCODE. COMPIL

PROGRAMMING PROJECT

Project Overview

An inquiry is needed that will display a customer name, address, and month-to-date and year-to-date sales information.

Design and create the screen (using DDS) and write the RPG program to provide this inquiry. Sample data for this project can be found in Appendix D.

Input Format

The input data for the project is found in a file called CUSTMAST in the sample data. The name of the screen is CUSTSCR. The Record Layout for this file is shown in Figure 15.13.

Processing

A screen is displayed prompting the entry of a customer number. The program uses this customer number to retrieve the desired information from the CUSTMAST file. The customer information is then displayed on the screen. When the ENTER key is pressed, the first inquiry screen is displayed. If an invalid customer number is requested, the first prompt screen is repeated and the words "Customer# Not Found" are displayed.

Output Format (Screen Layout)

The output format for the project is a screen with standard headings. The customer screen will show the customer number, name, street address, city, and state. The month-to-date and year-to-date sales amounts will also be displayed. The Screen Layouts are shown in Figures 15.14(a) and 15.14(b).

An example of each screen is shown in Figures 15.15(a) and 15.15(b).

FIGURE 15.13 Programming Project: Record Layout

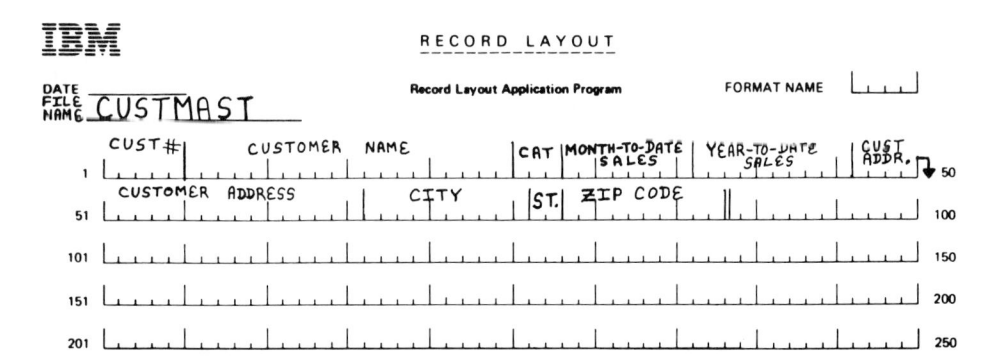

FIGURE 15.14(a) Programming Project: Screen Layout 1

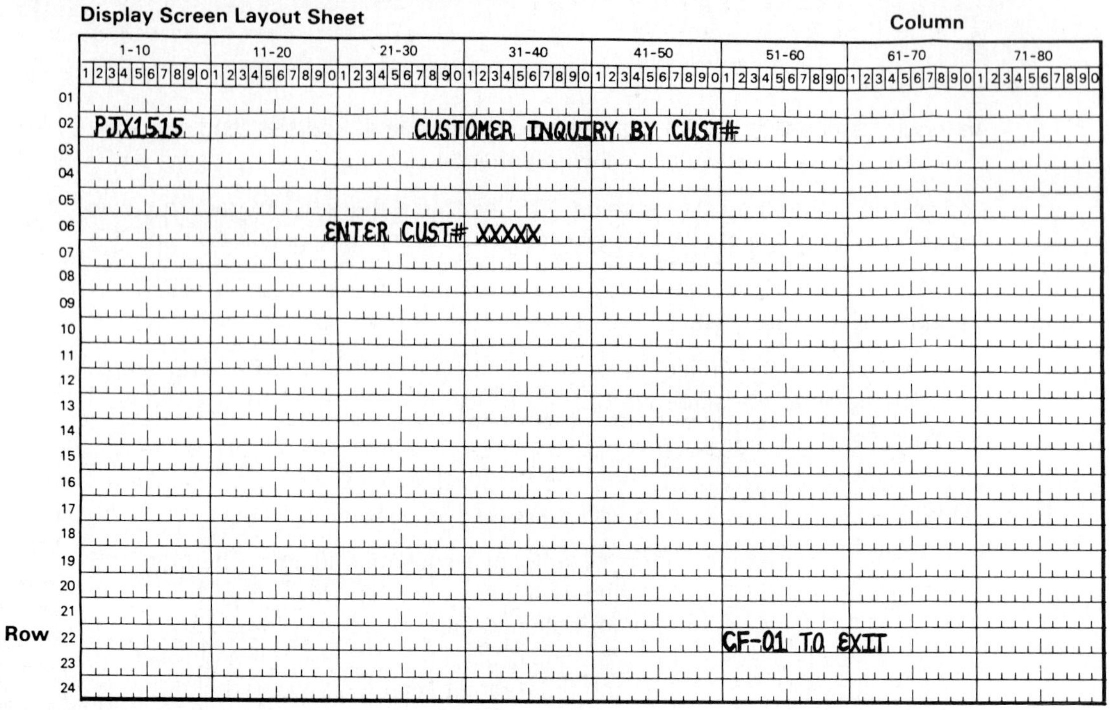

Display Screen Layout Sheet

Row 02: PJX1515   CUSTOMER INQUIRY BY CUST#
Row 06:   ENTER CUST# XXXXX
Row 22:   CF-01 TO EXIT

FIGURE 15.14(b) Programming Project: Screen Layout 2

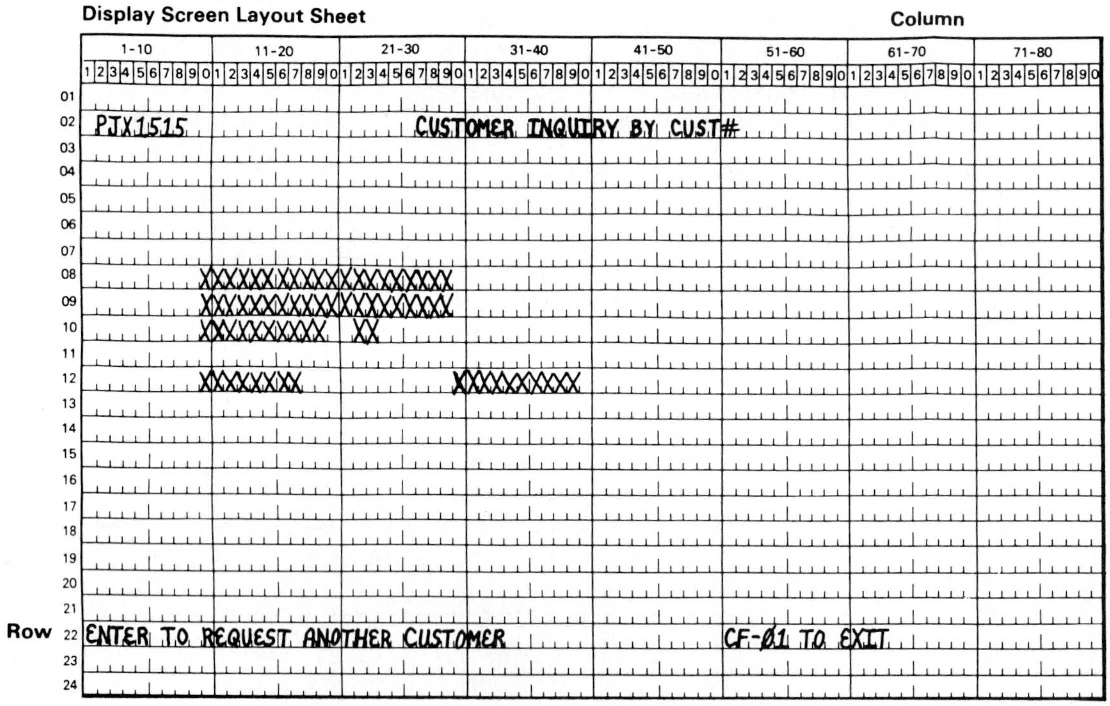

Display Screen Layout Sheet

Row 02: PJX1515   CUSTOMER INQUIRY BY CUST#
Row 08:   XXXXXXXXXXXXXXXXXXXX
Row 09:   XXXXXXXXXXXXXXXXXXXX
Row 10:   XXXXXXXXXX XX
Row 12:   XXXXXXXX   XXXXXXXX
Row 22: ENTER TO REQUEST ANOTHER CUSTOMER   CF-01 TO EXIT

FIGURE 15.15(a)   Programming Project: Sample Screen 1

```
PJX1515                    CUSTOMER INQUIRY BY CUST#



                        ENTER CUST#








                                                              CF-01 TO EXIT
```

FIGURE 15.15(b)   Programming Project: Sample Screen 2

```
PJX1515                    CUSTOMER INQUIRY BY CUST#



            SAMS PLACE
            23 PRODUCE LANE
            CENTRAL       WA
               1893                    1893




       ENTER TO REQUEST ANOTHER CUSTOMER            CF-01 TO EXIT
```

Chapter 16

On-Line Updates Using RPG III/400

What you will learn in Chapter 16

Creating the Screen Design
On-Screen Data Editing
Coding the Data Description Specification
   Key Words (DDS)
Command Keys (Function Keys)
Sample Program Showing Programming for On-Line File Update
Describing the Screen Format
Accessing the Screen File in the RPG Program
Defining Multiple Screen Formats
WRITE/READ Operations

On-line updating of data files provides the user with a means for obtaining more timely and useful data. It also requires the user to take responsibility for the accuracy of that data. While timeliness is a desirable goal, the data will not be useful if it contains many errors. Even a careful user will make keying mistakes if the program permits the entry of erroneous data. The programmer must take every precaution to ensure that invalid data cannot be entered.

Planning is crucial to the success of on-line file update applications. Stringent editing should be performed for each data element entered. Screens should be self-explanatory and easy to use. A carefully designed screen can improve the efficiency of the data entry function. Users are often the best source of ideas for creating good screen designs.

CREATING THE SCREEN DESIGN ■

If a user is transcribing data from a source document, a screen should be designed to follow the sequence of the data elements on that document. This eliminates the need to turn pages or to hunt all over a page to locate each piece of data. It is not always possible or cost-effective to redesign a source document. The programmer, therefore, should try to design a screen that will make the data entry function as simple as possible. Figures 16.1(a) and 16.1(b) show an invoice document and a screen that follows the sequence of the data to be entered from the source document.

Screen titles should clearly describe the function of the screen. Fields for entering data should have titles that define the information to be entered. For example, a field title "DATE" does not tell the user exactly what date is expected. A title of "SHIP DATE" or "ORDER DATE" is more helpful.

Field formats can be prompted on the screen by displaying an example or by displaying a default value (such as the current date) in the field. The user has the option of accepting the default value or overriding it with the correct value. The default value can act as an example to show the user the format of the date expected. The screen shown in Figure 16.2 carries a default date of December 31.

FIGURE 16.1(a) Invoice Document

```
                        VALLEY TAX
                     378 VENTURA AVENUE
                     OAKVIEW, CA  93022
                        805-649-2608
==========================================================

    DATE:  July 17, 1993                    INVOICE NO: VT0791

                   TO:  Oakview Liquor Store

               For Professional Services Rendered In:

    Bookkeeping Services Month of June 1993


                       TOTAL FEE................$ 100.00
                       RECEIVED ON ACCOUNT......$   0.00
                       AMOUNT DUE...............$ 100.00
```

FIGURE 16.1(b) Sample Screen for Invoice Data Entry

```
       ILL161                    INVOICE DATA ENTRY



          INVOICE#
          VEND#
          DUE DATE
          AMOUNT




                       CF-01 TO EXIT
```

FIGURE 16.2 Screen with Date Default

```
       ILL162                    INVOICE DATA ENTRY



          INVOICE#
          VEND#
          DUE DATE      1231
          AMOUNT




                       CF-01 TO EXIT
```

A user should not have to enter any more data than is necessary to accomplish a given task. Fewer keystrokes will result in fewer errors. Default values should be displayed whenever possible. The program should retrieve any descriptive information based on short codes or key fields. For example, a user should not be required to key the name and address fields for a customer. By entering a customer number, the user should be able to retrieve the name and address information from a master file.

When an identification number is not known to the user and is not included on the input document, the program could provide a method for looking up the number based on another key. The look-up might permit the user to enter a portion of the customer name to retrieve a customer in that range of names. Figures 16.3(a) and 16.3(b) show the original entry screen and a customer look-up screen.

One of the most frustrating events for a user is receiving an ambiguous error message. When a user has made an invalid entry, the program should display a very clear message explaining the nature of the error and some alternative action that may be taken. If an invalid code has been entered, the error message might display a list of appropriate codes from which to choose. The meaning of each code should be displayed so the user can make an informed choice. Figures 16.4(a), 16.4(b), 16.4(c), and 16.4(d) show an error condition with error message and alternative options.

FIGURE 16.3(a) Original Entry Screen

```
ILL 163B                    CUSTOMER DATA




           ENTER THE CUSTOMER # OR CUSTOMER NAME
           CUST#

           CUST NAME     SAM








                                                CF-01 TO EXIT
```

FIGURE 16.3(b) Customer Look-Up Screen

```
ILL 163B                    CUSTOMER DATA




           CUST#        00032
           CUSTOMER NAME         SAMS PLACE
           STREET ADDRESS        23 PRODUCE LANE
           CITY/STATE            CENTRAL     WA








                     CF-01 TO EXIT
```

FIGURE 16.4(a) Screen Showing Error Condition and Alternative Options

```
ILL164                   CUSTOMER DATA



     ENTER THE CUSTOMER # OR CUSTOMER NAME
     CUST#

     CUST NAME
     ENTRY CODE (A, C, OR D)




                                    CF-01 TO EXIT
```

FIGURE 16.4(b) Screen Showing Error Condition and Alternative Options

```
ILL164                   CUSTOMER DATA



     ENTER THE CUSTOMER # OR CUSTOMER NAME
     CUST#                  00032

     CUST NAME
     ENTRY CODE (A, C, OR D)
     INVALID CODE ENTERED
     ENTER CODE A FOR ADDS
           CODE C FOR CHANGES
           CODE D FOR DELETES

                                    CF-01 TO EXIT
```

FIGURE 16.4(c) Screen Showing Error Condition and Alternative Options

```
ILL164                   CUSTOMER DATA



     ENTER THE CUSTOMER # OR CUSTOMER NAME
     CUST#                  00020

     CUST NAME
     ENTRY CODE (A, C, OR D) A
     INVALID CUSTOMER # ENTERED
     ENTER ANOTHER SELECTION

                                    CF-01 TO EXIT
```

FIGURE 16.4(d) Screen Showing Error Condition and Alternative Options

```
ILL164                   CUSTOMER DATA




     CUST#          00032
     CUSTOMER NAME        SAMS PLACE
     STREET ADDRESS       23 PRODUCE LANE
     CITY/STATE           CENTRAL      WA


          CF-01 TO EXIT
```

ON-SCREEN DATA EDITING ■

Editing a screen entry permits immediate feedback to the user when an invalid entry is made. The user can then correct the entry with no loss of time. The rules for editing data are the same whether the editing occurs in a batch or in an interactive program. The following rules apply to any edit program:

1. Validate length and attributes of a field
   a. Alphabetic or numeric data only
   b. Precede with zeros if needed
   c. Must not be blank
2. Test a field for a range of values
   a. Must be positive or negative
   b. Reasonableness
3. Test a field for a specific value or set of values
4. Validate a field against a master file

The length and attributes of a display field are preset in the Data Description Specifications (DDS). The exact field length will be displayed on the screen. This restricts the size of the entry—it can be no longer than the described field. If a field must be completely filled, editing will need to be done within the program. If a field is described as a numeric field in the DDS, the user will be prevented from inadvertently entering alphabetic data. If a field is described as alphanumeric, both alphabetic and numeric data will be accepted. The programmer can edit the field to exclude numeric data or to ensure that it contains an entry.

A range of entry values can be specified within the DDS or in the program. This can include testing for the entry of only positive or only negative numbers, or for some reasonable range of data. A date of sale that is greater (i.e., later) than the current date (system date) might be unreasonable and is probably incorrect. A very large or very small rate of pay could be flagged as an error. When testing for reasonableness, the user should be permitted to override the error message when necessary. For example, a retail store might want to flag a potential error if an order was entered for more than 1000 pianos. However, if someone really ordered 1001 pianos, the store would want to accept the order and override the programmed edit.

A set of values can be specified for a field within the DDS or the program. These values might be specific codes, rates, or any value that must conform to some set of rules. Since rules might change, hard-coding them into either the DDS or the program might not be a good solution. Fixed codes that will seldom change can be set up with fixed edit values. Changeable codes are easier to handle as separate files that can be maintained outside the program.

A common method for validating data from a screen is to check against a master file to determine whether a particular value really exists. Some examples of this method are the entry of part numbers and employee identification numbers.

Further quality assurance can be given by balancing totals of groups of data to a known total from some other system. For example, sales totals might be compared to bank deposits.

Many other edit capabilities are available using the combined functions of the DDS and the program itself. Together, these methods provide a set of tools for ensuring that data entering the computer is as error-free as possible for processing. Although few edits can completely prevent incorrect entries, the use of good edit procedures will help to avoid many problems.

Data editing within an RPG program has been discussed in earlier chapters that covered batch processing. Similar methods can be used to validate data being entered interactively. In addition, much of the data editing for an interactive application can be incorporated into the Data Description Specification.

CODING THE DATA DESCRIPTION SPECIFICATION ■

In Chapter 15, the basic entries for creating a Data Description Specification were outlined. The DDS also provides some excellent methods for editing data being entered and for controlling the screens associated with these edits.

In this chapter, some of the more complex entries will be defined. Examples of events that can be controlled on the DDS include the following:

1. Specifying special field functions such as underlining or highlighting a field and displaying a field in reverse image or in blinking mode on the screen.
2. Specifying validity checking for data entered. This includes error checking for blank fields, detecting a completely filled field, detecting incorrect data types, checking for specific ranges of values, checking data for a specific entry, or performing check digit verification.
3. Screen management functions such as erasing, overlaying, or retaining fields when new data is displayed.
4. Editing fields to be displayed on the screens.

There are more details on the subject of Data Description Specifications than can be adequately covered here. Only a few of the more commonly used features will be briefly explained.

Key Words (DDS)

Many key word entries are available in DDS for editing or for providing special effects for a screen. Key words are entered on the same line as the field being described or on the lines following the entry. Only a few of the key words will be presented here.

DSPATR

Special field attributes can be defined in the DDS by using the key word DSPATR in columns 45–50. Attributes for a display field or constant may be specified singly or in groups within parentheses. It is often necessary to specify more than one display attribute for a field. For example, you might want a field to be highlighted and to blink at the same time (HI BL). You might also want to position the cursor at that field so that the user can correct the entry (HI BL PC).

DSPATR can be used for the following functions:

BL — Blinking field
CS — Column separators
HI — High intensity
ND — Nondisplay; hidden field (will not display on the screen)
PC — Position cursor
RI — Reverse image field
UL — Underline field

Figure 16.5 shows some examples of the DSPATR key word.

FIGURE 16.5 The DSPATR Key Word

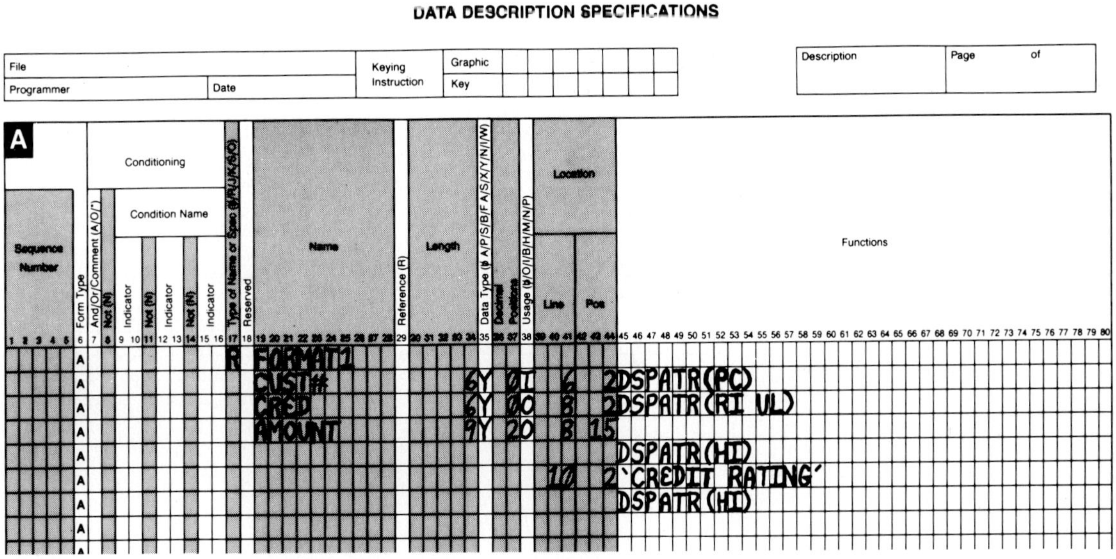

EDTCDE and EDTWRD

Edit codes (EDTCDE) and edit words (EDTWRD) are used on the DDS to display a field with edit features similar to those used to enhance fields on printed reports.

Edit codes for screens are the same as those used for printed output. Edit codes are specified by entering the key word EDTCDE in columns 45–50 of the DDS, followed by the desired edit code in parentheses. (See earlier chapters on printed output for more complete coverage of edit codes.) Figure 16.6 shows some edit codes and their meanings.

An edit word is similar to the edit word used for printed report editing. The desired editing is enclosed in parentheses following the key word EDTWRD. Figure 16.7 shows some possible edit words for fields.

ERRMSG

The key word ERRMSG causes a message to be displayed on the screen when an associated indicator is set on in the RPG program. The message is enclosed within parentheses and single quotation marks. The related indicators are entered in columns 9–17 on the DDS. Figure 16.8 shows the format for defining an error message.

FIGURE 16.6 Edit Codes Key Word

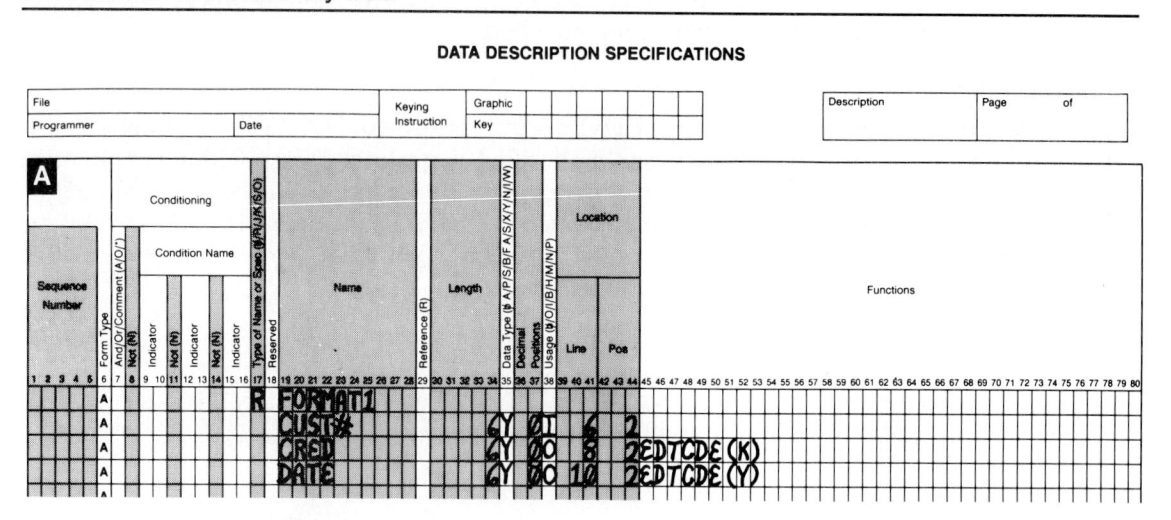

FIGURE 16.7 Edit Words Key Word

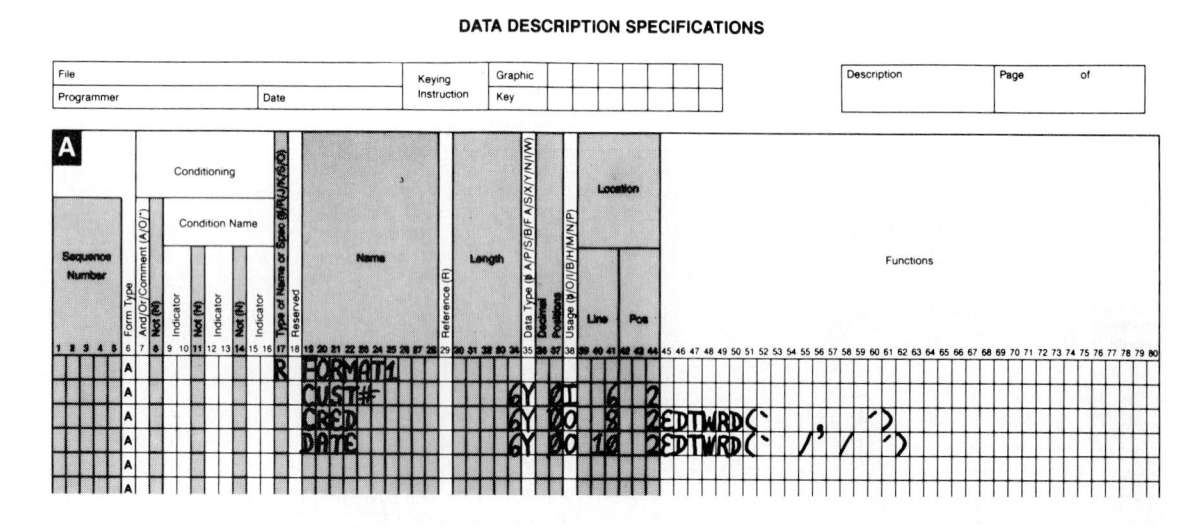

FIGURE 16.8 Format for Defining an Error Message

[DDS form showing:
R FORMAT1
CUST# 6Y 0I 6 2
71 ERRMSG('CUSTOMER# NOT FOUND' 71)
CRED 6Y 0O 8 2
65 ERRMSG('CREDIT LIMIT EXCEEDED' 65)]

PRINT

Though less important to the functioning of a program, the key word PRINT can be a convenience to the user and a useful tool in researching program problems. When this key word is included in the DDS, striking a PRINT key causes the contents of the screen to be moved to a print file to be printed, providing a permanent record of the contents of the screen at that moment. The PRINT key word can be followed by the name of the printer on which printing should occur. If no name is entered, the output will go to the default printer. Figure 16.9 shows how the PRINT key word is used.

RANGE

Validity checking for data entered can be specified with the use of key words such as RANGE. The RANGE key word is useful for defining a range of values for edit purposes. The upper and lower limits of the range are enclosed in parentheses and separated with a space. Figure 16.10 shows the format for this key word. In this example, values that do not fall within the range 20,000–50,000 will be rejected. The screen will be inhibited until a correct value is entered.

FIGURE 16.9 PRINT Key Word

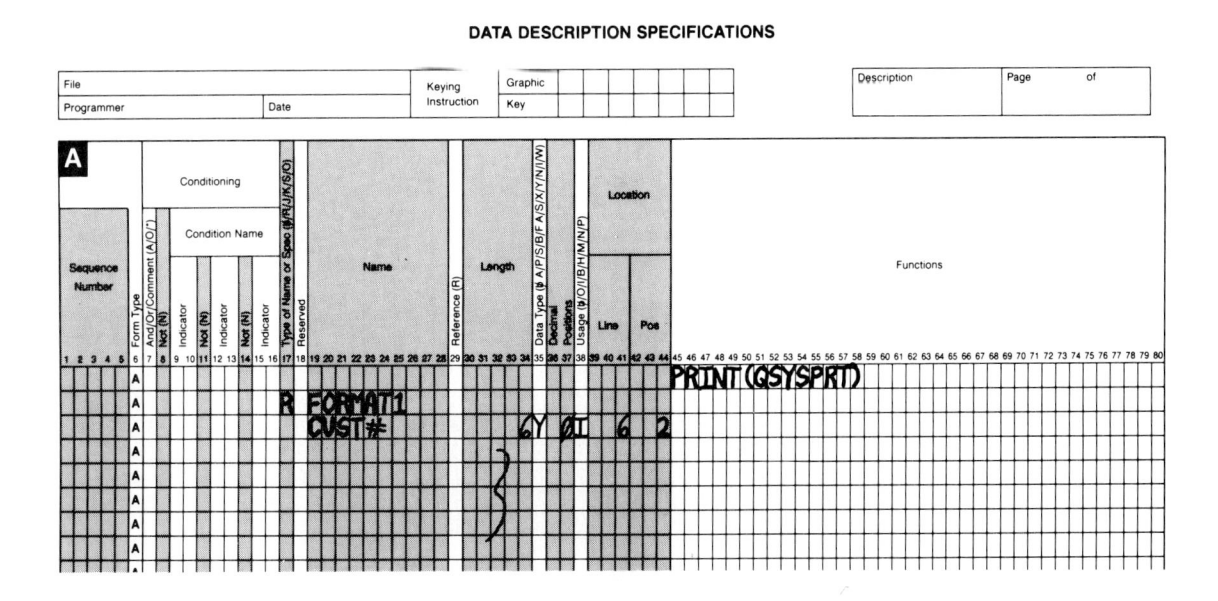

[DDS form showing:
PRINT(QSYSPRT)
R FORMAT1
CUST# 6Y 0I 6 2]

FIGURE 16.10 RANGE Key Word

```
     R FORMAT02
       PART#              15Y 0I   7 3RANGE(20000 50000)
```

REF

The key word REF is used when the attributes of fields are not contained within the DDS. The attributes of each field are compiled in a separate data dictionary, which has been defined in its own DDS. Figure 16.11 describes this relationship.

It may be difficult for the student to recognize a use for this key word since it is so easy to key the attributes for each field into the file in which the field resides. In a very large company, however, with a large programming staff (and staff turnover) managing a large inventory of programs, standardization becomes very difficult. Large software companies often encounter the problem of maintaining multiple versions of very large software packages consistently for their many customers. When a change is made in one program in a complex system, it may have a domino effect that can destroy the consistency of many other related programs. Maintaining a single reference file for making global changes gives some assurance that the changes will be applied in a consistent manner.

FIGURE 16.11 Relationship of Field Reference File and Screen DDS, Using REF

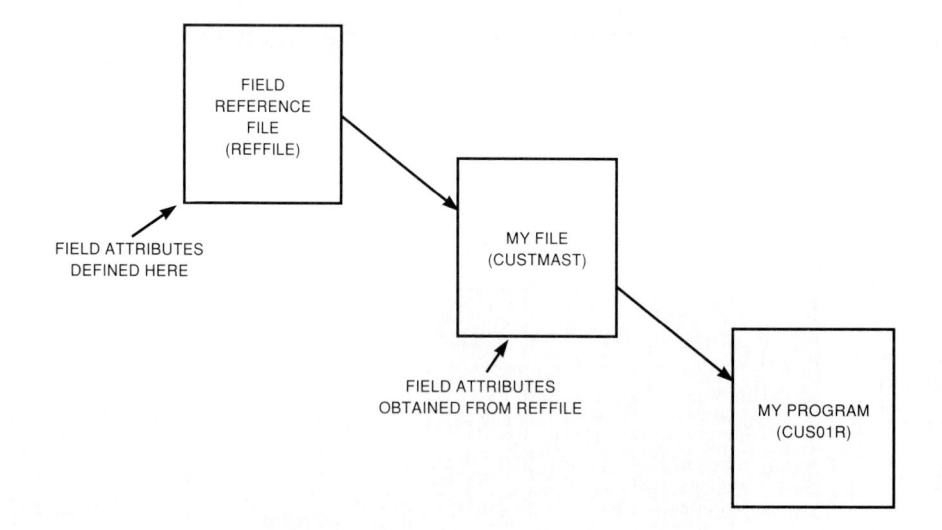

REFFLD

The key word REFFLD is used with the key word REF. The REFFLD defines which field attributes in the reference file are to be associated with the field identified on the DDS. Figures 16.12(a) and 16.12(b) show that the fields ORDDAT, DUEDAT, SHPDAT, and INVDAT will all carry the attributes of a field called DATE in the field reference file. This means that all four dates will always be six positions in length with zero decimal positions.

TEXT

TEXT is a commonly used key word. It performs no function in the display file. It is purely a documentation function, providing comments to assist future programmers in understanding the contents of each field. The comment is enclosed within parentheses and single quotation marks. Figure 16.13 shows some of the kinds of comments that are useful in a DDS.

FIGURE 16.12(a) DDS for Field Reference File

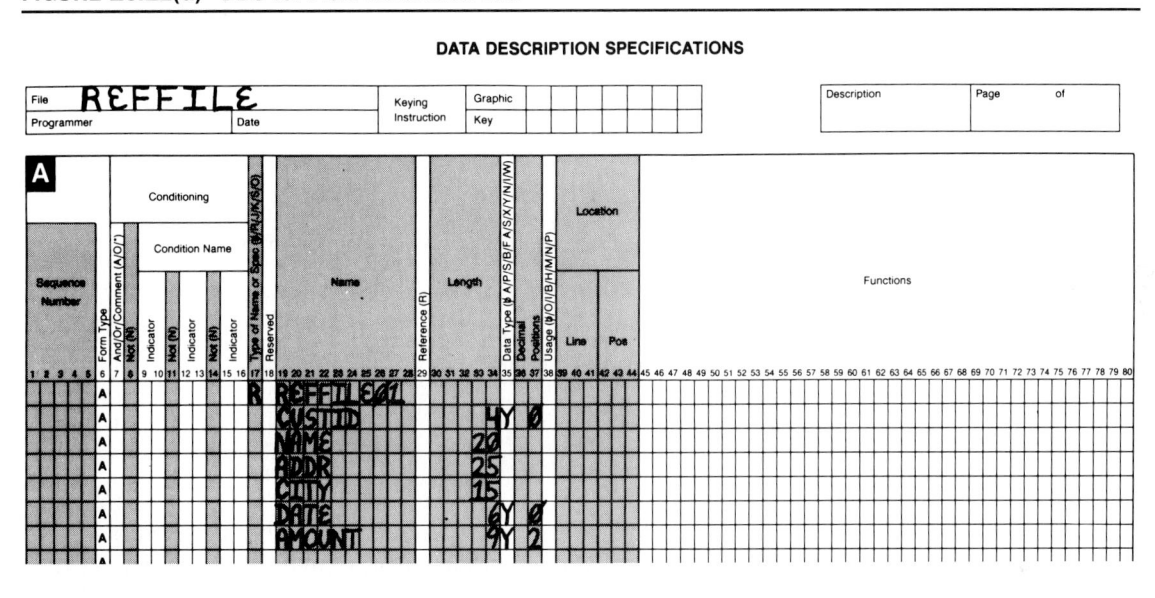

File: REFFILE

Form Type	Name	Reference	Length	Data Type	Decimal Positions	Functions
A	R REFFILE@1L					
A	CUSTID		4	Y	0	
A	NAME		20			
A	ADDR		25			
A	CITY		15			
A	DATE		6	Y	0	
A	AMOUNT		9	Y	2	

FIGURE 16.12(b) DDS for CUSTMAST File Using REF and REFFLD

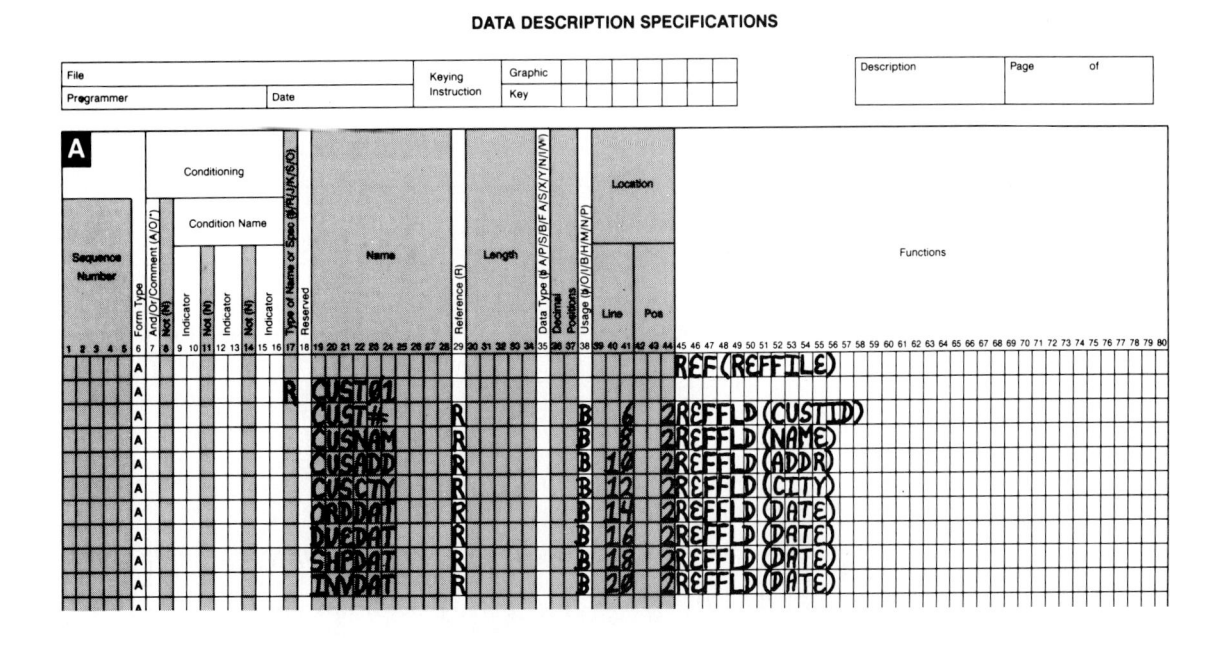

Form Type	Name	Reference	Length	Data Type	Decimal Positions	Usage	Line	Pos	Functions
A									REF(REFFILE)
A	R CUST@1								
A	CUST#	R		B			6	2	REFFLD(CUSTID)
A	CUSNAM	R		B			8	2	REFFLD(NAME)
A	CUSADD	R		B			10	2	REFFLD(ADDR)
A	CUSCTY	R		B			12	2	REFFLD(CITY)
A	ORDDAT	R		B			14	2	REFFLD(DATE)
A	DUEDAT	R		B			16	2	REFFLD(DATE)
A	SHPDAT	R		B			18	2	REFFLD(DATE)
A	INVDAT	R		B			20	2	REFFLD(DATE)

FIGURE 16.13 DDS Comments (TEXT Key Word)

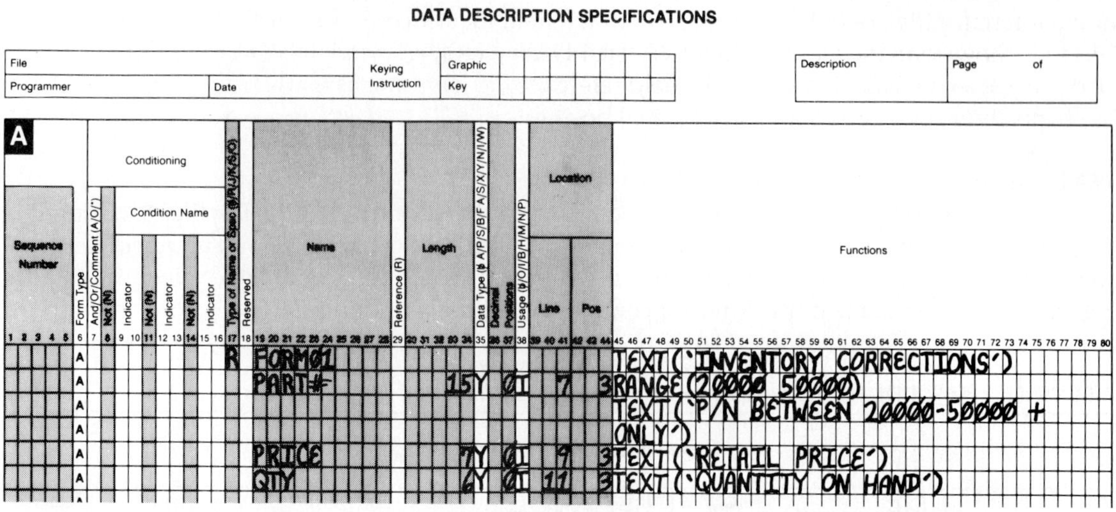

[Data Description Specifications form showing:
- R FORM01 — TEXT('INVENTORY CORRECTIONS')
- PART# 15Y 0I 7 3 RANGE(20000 50000)
- TEXT('P/N BETWEEN 20000-50000 ONLY')
- PRICE 7Y 0I 9 3 TEXT('RETAIL PRICE')
- QTY 6Y 0I 11 3 TEXT('QUANTITY ON HAND')]

VALUES

The key word VALUES identifies specific values for edit purposes. Figure 16.14 shows the format for VALUES. In the example, only the values A, B, C, and V will be accepted as valid.

Other Key Words

Many more key words are available for use in the Data Description Specifications. These can be studied in the DDS manual (usually available in mid-range computer centers).

Command Keys (Function Keys)

In the previous chapter, a command key was defined in the DDS to allow the user to escape from the screen. Command keys can be useful for many functions needed with on-line applications. Two general types of command key functions can be defined in the DDS: command attention (CA) keys and command function (CF) keys.

When the user presses a function key that has been defined in the DDS as a command attention key, the RPG program will receive the information that the key has been pressed, but no data will be transferred. When the user presses a function key that has been defined in the DDS as a command function key, the RPG program will receive the information that the key has been pressed and a data record may be passed along with that information.

FIGURE 16.14 VALUES Key Word

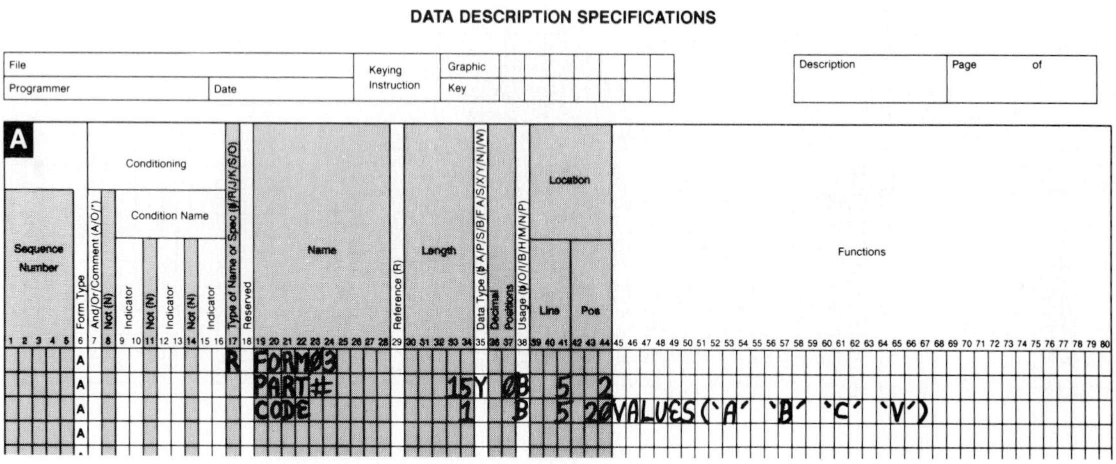

[Data Description Specifications form showing:
- R FORM03
- PART# 15Y 0B 5 2
- CODE 1 B 5 20 VALUES('A' 'B' 'C' 'V')]

410   RPG: A Programming Language for Today

Command keys are directly related to indicators within the RPG program. These indicators are KA through KY and are related to command keys 1 through 24 (KO is not used). If the command key CA01 is specified in the DDS, as shown in Figure 16.15, indicator KA will be set on in the related RPG program any time command key 01 is pressed.

A second indicator may be attached to a command key, as shown in Figure 16.16. In this example, both indicator KA and 65 can be used in the RPG program. When command key 1 is pressed, both indicator KA and indicator 65 will be turned on in the RPG program. The words within the single quotation marks are merely text comments.

Uses for command keys include the following:

- Escape from the program with no update of files.
- Return to a previous screen.
- Call another program.
- Submit a job to be run in batch mode.
- Request HELP text information.
- Process the update function.
- Request more information from other files.
- Delete a record.

FIGURE 16.15 DDS with Command Key CA01 Specified

(Data Description Specifications form showing: CA01 in Functions area; R EMPFMT record format; ID# field 6Y 0B 7 8; NAME field 20 B 12 8)

FIGURE 16.16 Attaching a Second Indicator to a Command Key

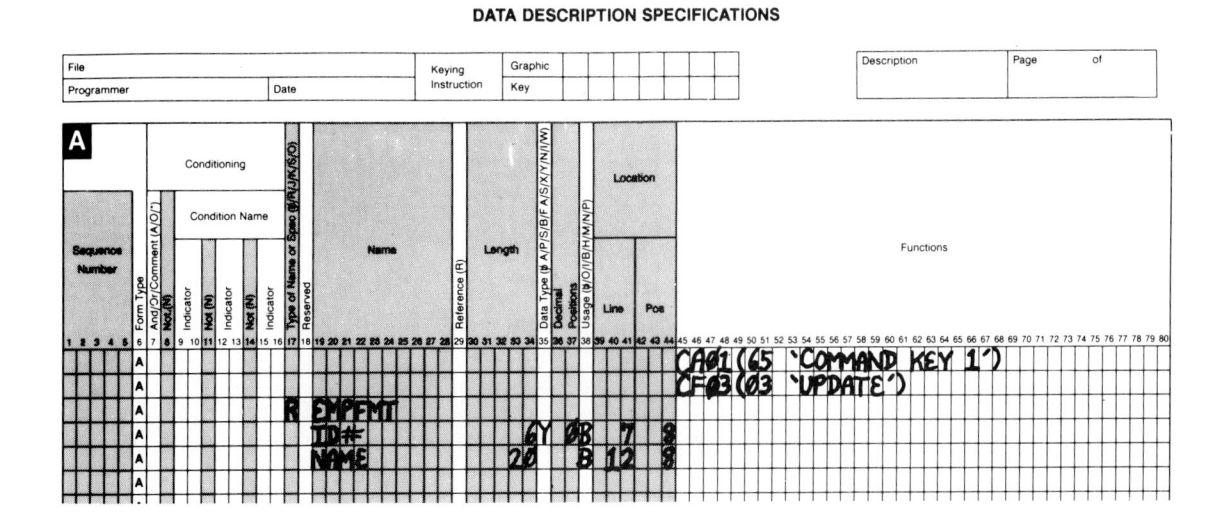

(Data Description Specifications form showing: CA01(65 'COMMAND KEY 1') and CF03(03 'UPDATE') in Functions area; R EMPFMT record format; ID# field 6Y 0B 7 8; NAME field 20 B 12 8)

Chapter 16 On-Line Updates Using RPG III/400

SAMPLE PROGRAM SHOWING PROGRAMMING FOR ON-LINE FILE UPDATE ■

Details of the Data Description Specification could be discussed in greater depth; however, it will be more useful at this point to see how an update program is written using some of this information. Figures 16.17(a), 16.17(b), 16.17(c), 16.17(d), and 16.17(e) show the requirements for a program that allows the user to input data from a screen and update a customer file.

Two screen formats are used. The first screen allows the user to enter the requested customer number and transaction code. The second screen displays the fields required in the customer master file and allows for the addition of records, update of fields in existing records, and review of records that are to be deleted.

In addition to the customer master file that is to be updated, there will be a transaction file to keep an audit trail of every activity. This is particularly important in an interactive environment. One reason for using a transaction file is to ensure that there is a way to determine who made changes to a file and when those changes were made. If any errors occur, it is possible to trace back to determine the cause. A second reason for a transaction file is to provide a backup file. The file updates could be rerun from the transaction file if some disaster caused the loss of the current copy of the CUSTMAST file.

FIGURE 16.17(a)   Customer File Update Program: Flowchart

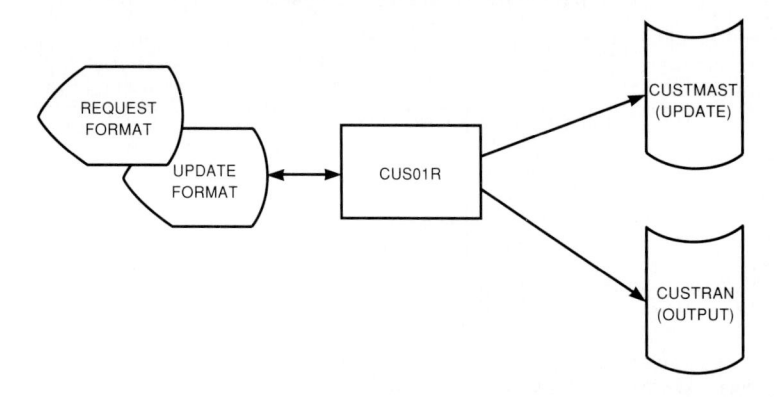

FIGURE 16.17(b)   Customer File Update Program: CUSTMAST Record Layout

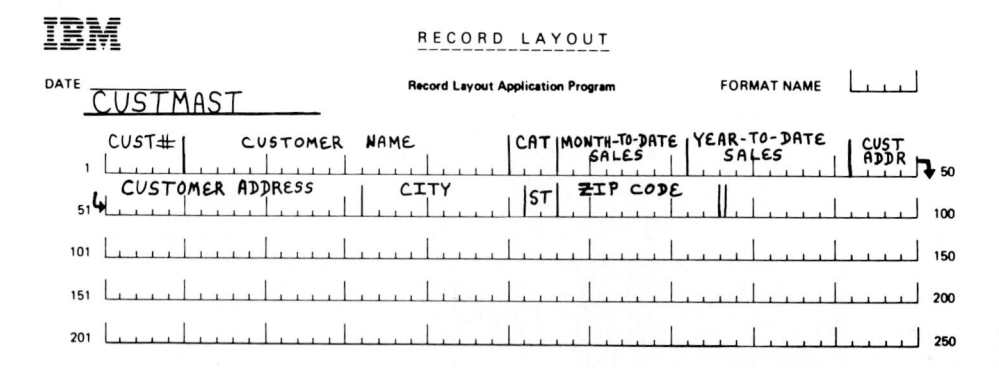

FIGURE 16.17(c) Customer File Update Program: Transaction Record Layout

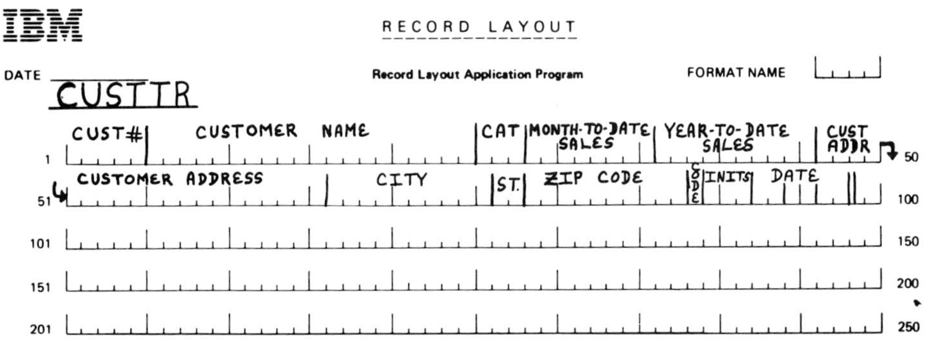

```
IBM                           RECORD LAYOUT
DATE                  Record Layout Application Program    FORMAT NAME
     CUSTTR
      CUST#|  CUSTOMER   NAME      |CAT|MONTH-TO-DATE|YEAR-TO-DATE| CUST
                                        SALES         SALES        ADDR
   1                                                                       50
      CUSTOMER ADDRESS       | CITY    |ST.| ZIP CODE |S|INITS| DATE
  51                                                  D                   100
                                                      E
 101                                                                      150
 151                                                                      200
 201                                                                      250
```

FIGURE 16.17(d) Customer File Update Program: Sample Screen 1

```
    ILL1617                CUSTOMER MASTER UPDATE




        ENTER THE CUSTOMER #
        CUST#


        ENTRY CODE (A, C, OR D)



        ENTER YOUR INITIALS




                                          CF-01 TO EXIT
```

FIGURE 16.17(e) Customer File Update Program: Sample Screen 2

```
    ILL1617                CUSTOMER MASTER UPDATE




        CUST#           00032
        CUSTOMER NAME        SAMS PLACE
        STREET ADDRESS       23 PRODUCE LANE
        CITY/STATE           CENTRAL       WA
        ZIP CODE             98325
        CATEGORY             VX





        CF-01 TO EXIT    CF-05 TO ADD, UPDATE OR DELETE
```

Describing the Screen Format

The Data Description Specifications for the sample screen and for the files are shown in Figures 16.18(a), 16.18(b), and 16.18(c). This is how the Data Description appears in the computer when the file is created. This sample takes advantage of some of the features available in DDS for editing and describing the input data.

The first screen format (IL16171) allows the user to enter a customer number and a code A, C, or D. The code indicates that the customer record is to be added, changed, or deleted. On line 1500 of the DDS, values of A, C, or D are the only codes allowed for the field SCCODE. Command key 1 will permit escape from the screen with no further action. Error messages will be displayed if a change or deletion is requested for a record that does not exist or if an existing record is to be added.

The second screen format (IL16172) displays the customer record, if it exists. Blank lines will be displayed for data entry if a record is to be added. Command key 1 will permit return to the first screen with no update to the record. Command key 5 will update the record. Pressing the ENTER key will redisplay the screen and show any errors. If invalid data were entered into any of the fields, an error message would be displayed. The entries would be redisplayed with the invalid field highlighted, and no update would take place. For simplicity in this example, we have done no editing.

The field names used for the screen display describing the customer master file are *not* the same names as those used in the physical file. This gives the programmer better control over which value is being placed in each field before it is updated. After a record has been updated, the program returns to the first screen display to accept more entries.

FIGURE 16.18(a)   DDS for Display File

```
FILE NAME    -    ILL1617F.HOLD         TYPE OF FILE -    DISPLAY
SOURCE FILE  -    QDDSSRC.CABLE         MEMBER       -    ILL1617F      02/24/92
TYPE OF DATA -    *DATA
OPTIONS      -    *SRC   *LIST
GENLVL       -    20
AUTHORITY    -    *ALL
TEXT         -    ILLUS FOR 16.17
COMPILER     -    IBM SYSTEM/38 DATA DESCRIPTION PROCESSOR

                                        DATA DESCRIPTION SOURCE

SEQNBR  *... ... 1 ... ... 2 ... ... 3 ... ... 4 ... ... 5 ... ... 6 ... ... 7 ...
  100       A* TITLE: UPDATE CUSTOMER MATER   (ILLUS. 16.17 & 18)
  200       A* DATE:  7/1             AUTHOR:
  300       A***************************************************
  400       A                                        PRINT
  500       A                                        CA01(01 'END OF PROGRAM')
  600       A                                        CA05(05 'UPDATE RECORD')
  700       A           R IL16171
  800       A                                     2 25'CUSTOMER MASTER UPDATE'
  900       A                                     2  2'ILL1617'
 1000       A                                     7  2'ENTER THE CUSTOMER #'
 1100       A                                     8  2'CUST#'
 1200       A             SCCUST       5  B       8 25
 1300       A                                    11  2'ENTRY CODE (A, C, OR D)'
 1400       A             SCCODE       1  B      11 26VALUES('A' 'C' 'D')
 1500       A             SCMSG1      30  O      12  2
 1600       A             SCMSG2      30  O      13  2
 1700       A             SCMSG3      30  O      14  2
 1800       A             SCMSG4      30  O      15  2
 1900       A                                    16  2'ENTER YOUR INITIALS'
 2000       A             SCINIT       3  B      16 25
 2100       A             SCMSG5      30  O      17  2
 2200       A                                    22 40 'CF-01 TO EXIT'
 2300       A*
 2400       A           R IL16172
 2500       A                                        OVERLAY
 2600       A                                     2 25'CUSTOMER MASTER UPDATE'
 2700       A                                     2  2'ILL1617'
 2800       A                                     8  2'CUST#'
 2900       A             SCCUST       5  B       8 15
 3000       A                                     9  2'CUSTOMER NAME'
```

FIGURE 16.18(a) *Continued*

```
3100         A              SCNAME       20    O  9 25
3200         A                                 10  2'STREET ADDRESS'
3300         A              SCADDR       20    B 10 25
3400         A                                 11  2'CITY/STATE'
3500         A              SCCITY       10    B 11 25
3600         A              SCST          2    B 11 37
3700         A                                 12  2'ZIP CODE'
3800         A              SCZIP         9    B 12 25
3900         A                                 13  2'CATEGORY'
4000         A              SCCAT         3    B 13 25
4100         A              SCMSG5       30    O 16  2
4200         A              SCMSG6       30    O 17  2
4300         A                                 22  2 'CF-01 TO EXIT'
4400         A                                 22 20 'CF-05 TO ADD, UPDATE OR DELETE'
```

FIGURE 16.18(b) DDS for CUSTMAST File

```
                         DATA DESCRIPTION SOURCE

SEQNBR  *... ... 1 ... ... 2 ... ... 3 ... ... 4 ... ... 5 ... ... 6 ... ... 7 ...

  100    A* TITLE: CUSTMAST
  200    A* DATE:  7/8        AUTHOR: CABLE
  300    A********************************************************
  400    A              R CUST01
  500    A                CUSNUM       5              TEXT('CUSTOMER NUMBER')
  600    A                CUSNAM      20              TEXT('CUSTOMER NAME')
  700    A                CUSCAT       3              TEXT('CATEGORY')
  800    A                CUSMTD       8S             TEXT('MONTH-TO-DATE +
  900    A                                             SALES')
 1000    A                CUSYTD      10S             TEXT('YEAR-TO-DATE SALE')
 1100    A                CUSADR      20              TEXT('STREET ADDRESS')
 1200    A                CUSCTY      10              TEXT('CITY')
 1300    A                CUSST        2              TEXT('STATE')
 1400    A                CUSZIP       9              TEXT('ZIP CODE')
 1500    A              K CUSNUM

                  * * * * *  E N D   O F   S O U R C E  * * * * *
```

FIGURE 16.18(c) DDS for CUSTTR File

```
FILE NAME    -   CUSTTR.HOLD           TYPE OF FILE -   PHYSICAL
SOURCE FILE  -   QDDSSRC.CABLE         MEMBER       -   CUSTTR         02/24/92
TYPE OF DATA -   *DATA
OPTIONS      -   *SRC    *LIST
GENLVL       -   20
AUTHORITY    -   *ALL
TEXT         -   TRANSACTION OUTPUT FOR ILLUS. 16.17 & 18
COMPILER     -   IBM SYSTEM/38 DATA DESCRIPTION PROCESSOR

                         DATA DESCRIPTION SOURCE

SEQNBR  *... ... 1 ... ... 2 ... ... 3 ... ... 4 ... ... 5 ... ... 6 ... ... 7 ...

  100    A* TITLE: CUSTTR (TRANSACTION OUTPUT FROM ILL16.17 & 18)
  200    A* DATE:  7/7        AUTHOR:
  300    A********************************************************
  400    A              R CUSTR01
  500    A                TRNNUM       5              TEXT('CUST NUMBER')
  600    A                TRNNAM      20              TEXT('CUST NAME')
  700    A                TRNCAT       3              TEXT('CATEGORY')
  800    A                TRNMTD       8S             TEXT('MTD SALES')
  900    A                TRNYTD      10S             TEXT('YTD SALES')
 1000    A                TRNADR      20              TEXT('STREET ADDRESS')
 1100    A                TRNCTY      10              TEXT('CITY')
 1200    A                TRNST        2              TEXT('STATE')
 1300    A                TRNZIP       9              TEXT('ZIP CODE')
 1400    A                TRNACT       1              TEXT('TRANSACTION CODE +
 1500    A                                             A = ADD, C = CHANGE +
 1600    A                                             D = DELETE')
 1700    A                INITS        3              TEXT('USER INITIALS')
 1800    A                TRNDAT       6S 0           TEXT('TRANSACTION DATE')
 1900    A              K TRNNUM

                  * * * * *  E N D   O F   S O U R C E  * * * * *
```

Accessing the Screen File in the RPG Program

Programming should always be done using a structured format. This is even more important for programming on-line applications. The flowchart in Figure 16.19 shows the logic to be used for programming an on-line interactive file update application.

Figure 16.20 shows the File Description Specifications for the sample program. There are three files: the workstation file, the customer master file, and the transaction file. The workstation file is coded CF in columns 15–16 (C for combined file and F for full functional file, which will not be processed by the RPG cycle). The physical files, CUSTMAST and CUSTTR, are both update files (U in column 15). They are keyed files (K in column 31), and both require the A in column 66 since both may have records added. All are externally defined (E in column 19).

The main section of the program is a loop. This loop will be repeated until the user presses the command key to end the processing. Separate subroutines are used to edit for add, change, and delete functions. As shown in Figure 16.21, the first screen is displayed using the EXFMT operation. The test for command key 1 is made to determine whether the user wants to escape from the screen immediately.

When an entry is received from the first screen, the codes are validated by the DDS key word entry VALUES. No special action is required in the RPG program to perform this edit. The program, however, must provide the coding for validating the customer number. The program must check whether the customer number exists. This is done by using the SETLL and READE operations. If the number does not exist, an error is detected based on the combination of the code entered and the condition of the indicator for the READE, and the appropriate error message will be displayed.

FIGURE 16.19 Structured Approach to On-line Programming—Hierarchy Chart

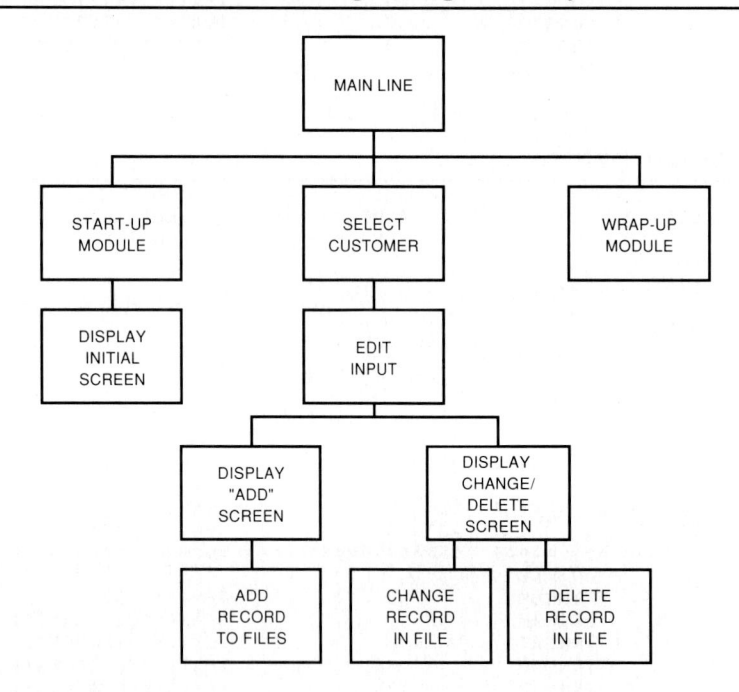

FIGURE 16.20 File Specifications for an On-line Program for Updating Files

RPG CONTROL AND FILE DESCRIPTION SPECIFICATIONS

```
F TL1624FA CF  E                    WORKSTN
F
F CUSTMAST UF E        K             DISK                    A
F CUSTTR   UF E        K             DISK                    A
```

FIGURE 16.21 Calculation Specification for Structured Update Program

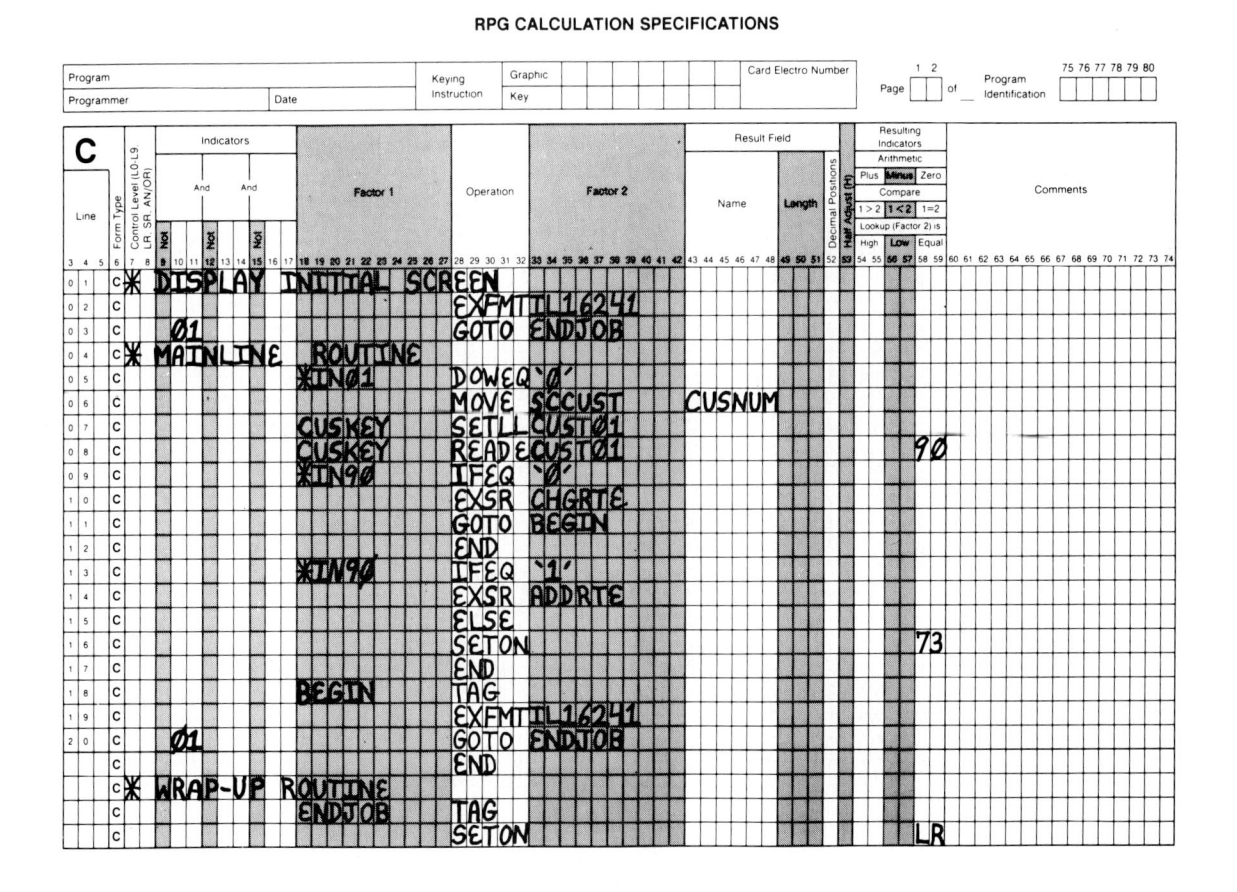

RPG CALCULATION SPECIFICATIONS

```
C* DISPLAY INITIAL SCREEN
C                    EXFMT TL16241
C   01               GOTO  ENDJOB
C* MAINLINE ROUTINE
C        *IN01       DOWEQ '0'
C                    MOVE  SCCUST    CUSNUM
C        CUSKEY      SETLL CUST01
C        CUSKEY      READE CUST01                        90
C        *IN90       IFEQ  '0'
C                    EXSR  CHGRTE
C                    GOTO  BEGIN
C                    END
C        *IN90       IFEQ  '1'
C                    EXSR  ADDRTE
C                    ELSE
C                    SETON                                73
C                    END
C        BEGIN       TAG
C                    EXFMT TL16241
C        01          GOTO  ENDJOB
C                    END
C* WRAP-UP ROUTINE
C        ENDJOB      TAG
C                    SETON                                LR
```

417

For a change transaction (code C), the CHGRTE subroutine is performed as shown in the coding in Figures 16.22(a) and 16.22(b). The coding for a deletion (code D) is also included in the CHGRTE subroutine.

If the request is to add a record (code A), the ADDRTE subroutine will be executed. The ADDRTE coding is shown in Figures 16.23(a) and 16.23(b).

When one of the subroutines is performed, the second screen format is displayed using the EXFMT operation, and further edits can be performed. The methods for editing data are the same as those used in batch processing. Only the method for displaying the errors and allowing corrections is different. When an error is found, processing returns to the beginning of the subroutine and the screen format is redisplayed with the appropriate error message. The indicator associated with the error causes the invalid field to blink because the DDS for this defined the indicator with the key word DSPATR(BL).

When the data is found to be correct and command key 5 is pressed, the appropriate data is moved from the screen fields to the fields in the CUSTMAST and CUSTTR records and the update operation is performed. The CUSTMAST record is updated (or added or deleted) and a copy of the transaction is added to the CUSTTR file.

Control then returns to the mainline of the program. The logic returns to the beginning of the main loop and the first screen is redisplayed. If command key 1 is pressed, the LR indicator is turned on and processing ends. Figure 16.24 shows the coding for the entire RPG program.

In this example, two display formats were used. Only one format was displayed on the screen at any time. In complex applications, it may be necessary to display multiple formats simultaneously.

FIGURE 16.22(a) Subroutine for Changing Records

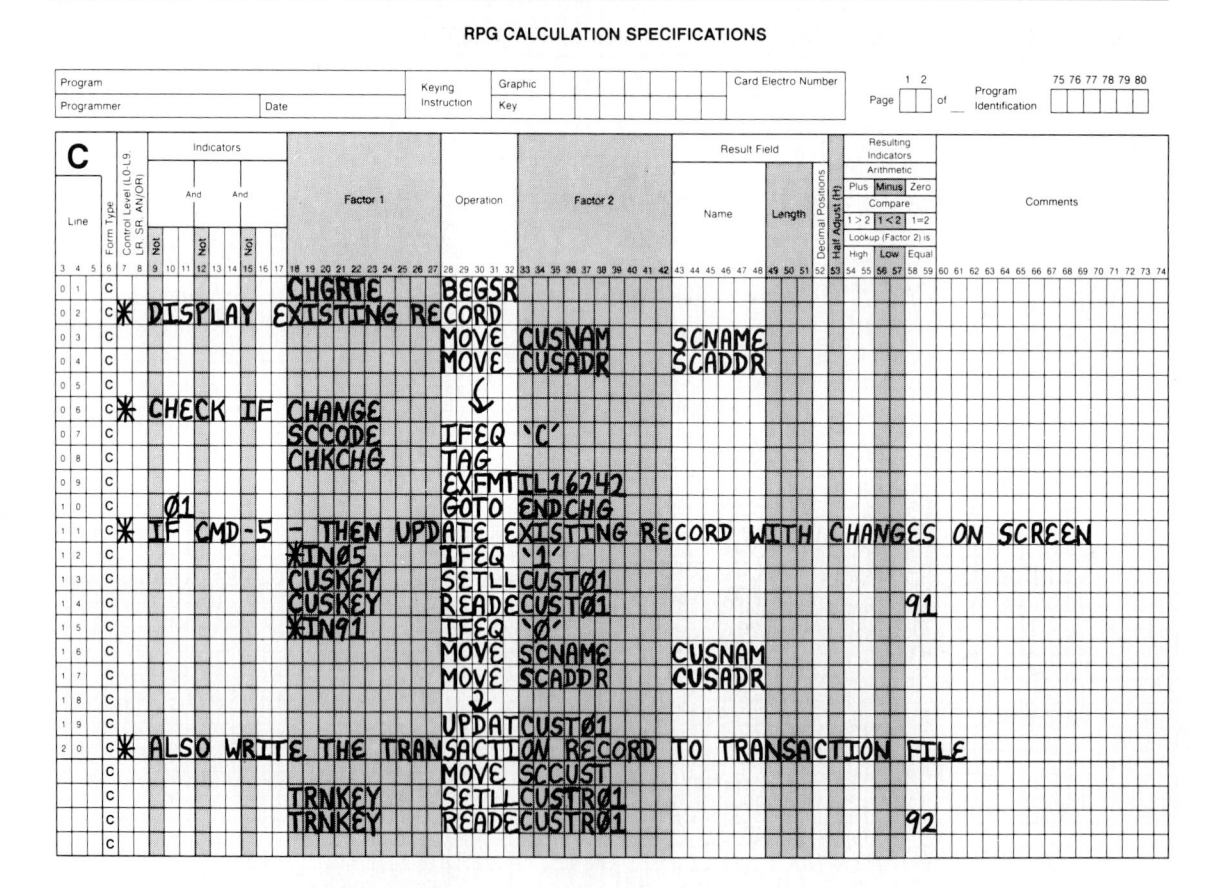

RPG CALCULATION SPECIFICATIONS

```
Line  Indicators   Factor 1    Operation   Factor 2    Result Field  Length  Resulting Indicators
01  C              CHGRTE      BEGSR
02  C* DISPLAY EXISTING RECORD
03  C                          MOVE        CUSNAM      SCNAME
04  C                          MOVE        CUSADR      SCADDR
05  C
06  C* CHECK IF CHANGE
07  C              SCCODE      IFEQ        'C'
08  C              CHKCHG      TAG
09  C                          EXFMTIL16242
10  C     01                   GOTO        ENDCHG
11  C* IF CMD-5 - THEN UPDATE EXISTING RECORD WITH CHANGES ON SCREEN
12  C              *IN05       IFEQ        '1'
13  C              CUSKEY      SETLL       CUST01
14  C              CUSKEY      READE       CUST01                            91
15  C              *IN91       IFEQ        '0'
16  C                          MOVE        SCNAME      CUSNAM
17  C                          MOVE        SCADDR      CUSADR
18  C
19  C                          UPDAT       CUST01
20  C* ALSO WRITE THE TRANSACTION RECORD TO TRANSACTION FILE
    C                          MOVE        SCCUST
    C              TRNKEY      SETLL       CUSTR01
    C              TRNKEY      READE       CUSTR01                           92
    C
```

FIGURE 16.22(b) Subroutine for Changing Records

RPG CALCULATION SPECIFICATIONS

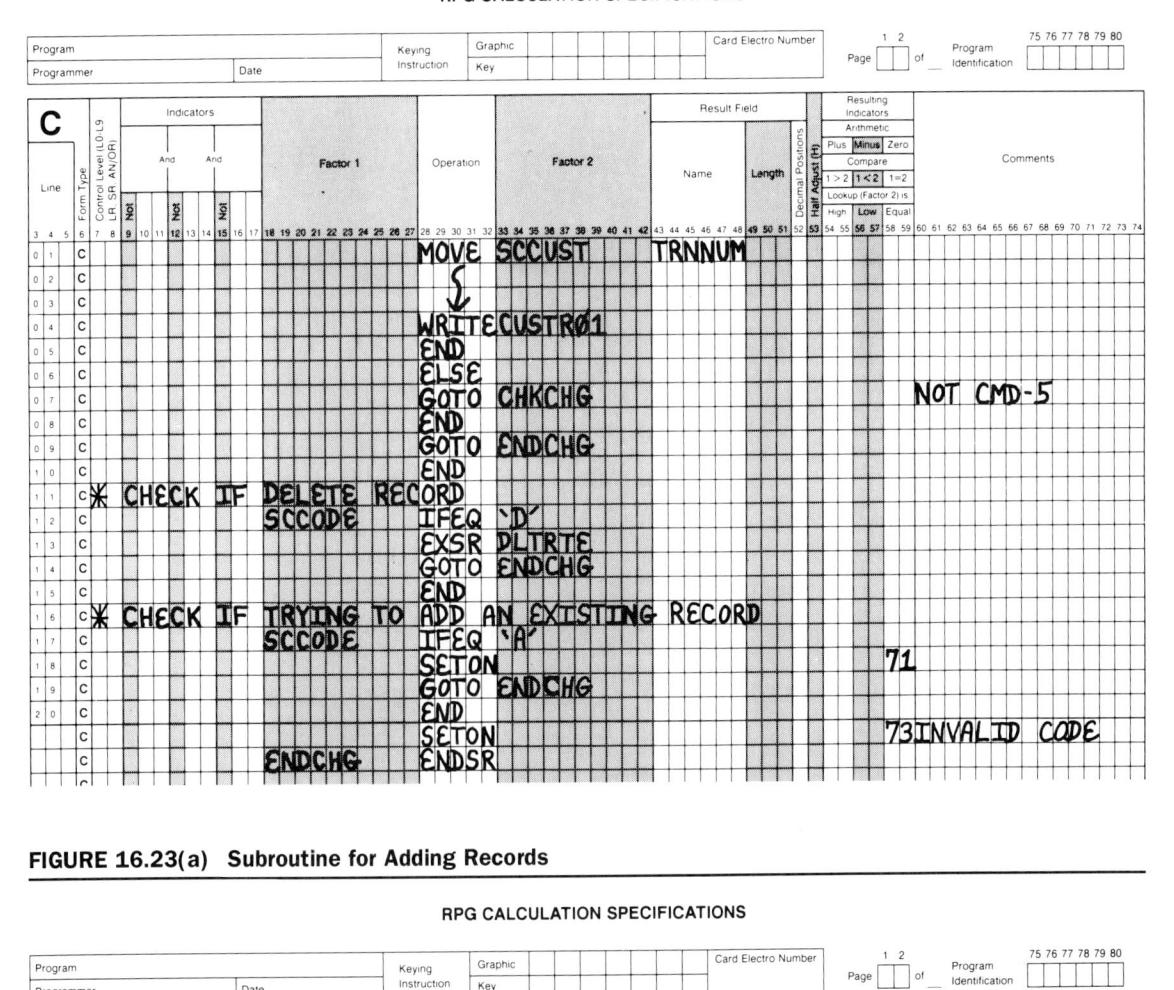

```
Line  Factor 1        Operation  Factor 2     Result   Len  Comments
01 C                  MOVE       SCCUST       TRNNUM
02 C                   ↓
03 C
04 C                  WRITE      CUSTR01
05 C                  END
06 C                  ELSE
07 C                  GOTO       CHKCHG                     NOT CMD-5
08 C                  END
09 C                  GOTO       ENDCHG
10 C                  END
11 C* CHECK IF DELETE RECORD
12 C   SCCODE         IFEQ       'D'
13 C                  EXSR       DLTRTE
14 C                  GOTO       ENDCHG
15 C                  END
16 C* CHECK IF TRYING TO ADD AN EXISTING RECORD
17 C   SCCODE         IFEQ       'A'
18 C                  SETON                                71
19 C                  GOTO       ENDCHG
20 C                  END
   C                  SETON                                73 INVALID CODE
   C   ENDCHG         ENDSR
```

FIGURE 16.23(a) Subroutine for Adding Records

RPG CALCULATION SPECIFICATIONS

```
Line  Factor 1        Operation  Factor 2     Result   Len  Comments
01 C   ADDRTE         BEGSR
02 C* DISPLAY BLANK LINES READY FOR INPUT
03 C                  MOVE       *BLANKS      SCNAME
04 C                   ↓
05 C
06 C* ADD A NEW RECORD
07 C   SCCODE         IFEQ       'A'
08 C   CHKADD         TAG
09 C                  EXFMT      TIL1624Z
10 C 01               GOTO       ENDADD
11 C* IF CMD-5 THEN ADD A NEW RECORD
12 C   *IN05          IFEQ       '1'
13 C   CUSKEY         SETLL      CUST01
14 C   CUSKEY         READE      CUST01                  91
15 C   *IN91          IFEQ       '1'
16 C                  MOVE       SCNAME       CUSNAM
17 C                   ↓
18 C
19 C                  WRITE      CUST01
20 C* WRITE THE TRANSACTION RECORD ALSO
   C   TRNKEY         SETLL      CUSTR01
   C   TRNKEY         READE      CUSTR01                 92
   C                  MOVE       SCCUST       TRNNUM
```

FIGURE 16.23(b) Subroutine for Adding Records

RPG CALCULATION SPECIFICATIONS

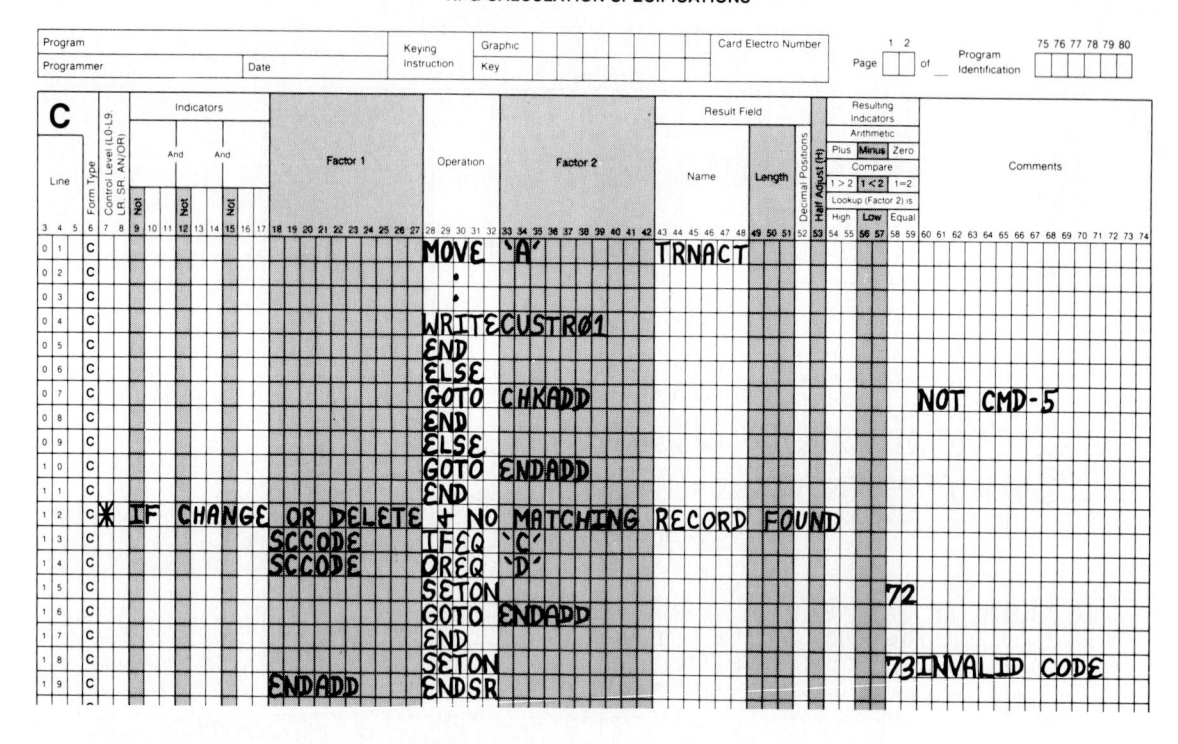

Line	Form Type	Indicators	Factor 1	Operation	Factor 2	Result Field Name	Length	Resulting Indicators	Comments
01	C			MOVE	'A'	TRNACT			
02	C								
03	C								
04	C			WRITE	CUSTR01				
05	C			END					
06	C			ELSE					
07	C			GOTO	CHKADD				NOT CMD-5
08	C			END					
09	C			ELSE					
10	C			GOTO	ENDADD				
11	C			END					
12	C	* IF CHANGE OR DELETE + NO MATCHING RECORD FOUND							
13	C		SCCODE	IFEQ	'C'				
14	C		SCCODE	OREQ	'D'				
15	C			SETON				72	
16	C			GOTO	ENDADD				
17	C			END					
18	C			SETON				73	INVALID CODE
19	C		ENDADD	ENDSR					

FIGURE 16.24 Compiled Program for On-line Update

```
SEQUENCE       1         2         3         4         5         6         7
NUMBER    67890123456789012345678901234567890123456789012345678901234


        100  F* TITLE: ILLUS FOR 16.24 (UPDATE CUSTMAST & OUTPUT CUSTTR)
        200  F* DATE:  7/14         AUTHOR: D.CABLE
        300  F***********************************************************

NAME OF PROGRAM WILL BE ILL1624B IN LIBRARY CABLE

             H
* 1019              ALL DECIMAL DATA ERRORS IGNORED
        400  FIL1624FACF  E                    WORKSTN
             RECORD FORMAT(S):   FILE IL1624FA LIB CABLE
                       EXTERNAL FORMAT IL16241 RPG NAME IL16241
                       EXTERNAL FORMAT IL16242 RPG NAME IL16242

        500  FCUSTMASTUF  E              K     DISK                        A
             RECORD FORMAT(S):   FILE CUSTMAST LIB CABLE
                       EXTERNAL FORMAT CUST01 RPG NAME CUST01

        600  FCUSTTR   UF E              K     DISK                        A
        700  F***********************************************************

        800  C* START-UP ROUTINE
             RECORD FORMAT(S):   FILE CUSTTR LIB CABLE
                       EXTERNAL FORMAT CUSTR01 RPG NAME CUSTR01
   A000000       INPUT  FIELDS FOR RECORD IL16241 FILE IL1624FA FORMAT IL16241
   A000001                                            1    1 *IN01
   A000002                                            2    2 *IN05
   A000003                                            3    7 SCCUST
   A000004                                            8    8 SCCODE
   A000005                                            9   11 SCINIT
   B000000       INPUT  FIELDS FOR RECORD IL16242 FILE IL1624FA FORMAT IL16242
   B000001                                            1    1 *IN01
   B000002                                            2    2 *IN05
```

FIGURE 16.24 *Continued*

```
B000003                                               3    7 SCCUST
B000004                                               8   27 SCADDR
B000005                                              28   37 SCCITY
B000006                                              38   39 SCST
B000007                                              40   48 SCZIP
B000008                                              49   51 SCCAT
C000000      INPUT   FIELDS FOR RECORD CUST01 FILE CUSTMAST FORMAT CUST01
C000001                                               1    5 CUSNUM
C000002                                               6   25 CUSNAM
C000003                                              26   28 CUSCAT
C000004                                              29   36 0CUSMTD
C000005                                              37   46 0CUSYTD
C000006                                              47   66 CUSADR
C000007                                              67   76 CUSCTY
C000008                                              77   78 CUSST
C000009                                              79   87 CUSZIP
D000000      INPUT   FIELDS FOR RECORD CUSTR01 FILE CUSTTR FORMAT CUSTR01
D000001                                               1    5 TRNNUM
D000002                                               6   25 TRNNAM
D000003                                              26   28 TRNCAT
D000004                                              29   36 0TRNMTD
D000005                                              37   46 0TRNYTD
D000006                                              47   66 TRNADR
D000007                                              67   76 TRNCTY
D000008                                              77   78 TRNST
D000009                                              79   87 TRNZIP
D000010                                              88   88 TRNACT
D000011                                              89   91 INITS
D000012                                              92   97 0TRNDAT
     900  C            CUSKEY     KLIST
    1000  C                       KFLD              CUSNUM
    1100  C            TRNKEY     KLIST
    1200  C                       KFLD              TRNNUM
    1300  C*
    1400  C* DISPLAY INITIAL SCREEN
    1500  C                       EXFMTIL16241
    1600  C    01                 GOTO ENDJOB
    1700  C* MAINLINE ROUTINE
    1800  C            *IN01      DOWEQ'0'
    1900  C                       SETOF                            717273
    2000  C                       MOVE SCCUST       CUSNUM
    2100  C            CUSKEY     SETLLCUST01
    2200  C            CUSKEY     READECUST01                          90
    2300  C* CHECK FOR CHANGE/DELETE
    2400  C            *IN90      IFEQ '0'
    2500  C                       EXSR CHGRTE
    2600  C                       GOTO BEGIN
    2700  C                       END
    2800  C            *IN90      IFEQ '1'
    2900  C                       EXSR ADDRTE
    3000  C                       GOTO BEGIN
    3100  C                       ELSE
    3200  C                       SETON                                73
    3300  C                       END
    3400  C            BEGIN      TAG
    3500  C                       EXFMTIL16241
    3600  C    01                 GOTO ENDJOB
    3700  C                       END
    3800  C* WRAP-UP ROUTINE
    3900  C            ENDJOB     TAG
    4000  C                       SETON                                LR
    4100  C                       RETRN
    4200  C***************************************************************
    4300  C            CHGRTE     BEGSR
    4400  C* DISPLAY EXISTING RECORD
    4500  C                       MOVE CUSNAM       SCNAME
    4600  C                       MOVE CUSADR       SCADDR
    4700  C                       MOVE CUSCTY       SCCITY
    4800  C                       MOVE CUSST        SCST
    4900  C                       MOVE CUSZIP       SCZIP
    5000  C                       MOVE CUSCAT       SCCAT
    5100  C* CHECK IF CHANGE
```

FIGURE 16.24 *Continued*

```
SEQUENCE       1         2         3         4         5         6         7
NUMBER    678901234567890123456789012345678901234567890123456789012345678901234
     5200 C            SCCODE    IFEQ 'C'
     5300 C            CHKCHG    TAG
     5400 C                      EXFMTIL16242
     5500 C     01               GOTO ENDCHG
     5600 C* IF CMD 5 - THEN UPDATE EXISTING RECORD
     5700 C            *IN05     IFEQ '1'
     5800 C            CUSKEY    SETLLCUST01
     5900 C            CUSKEY    READECUST01                    91
     6000 C            *IN91     IFEQ '0'
     6100 C* NOTE THAT THE KEY & DOLLAR AMTS WILL NOT BE UPDATED
     6200 C                      MOVE SCNAME   CUSNAM
     6300 C                      MOVE SCADDR   CUSADR
     6400 C                      MOVE SCCITY   CUSCTY
     6500 C                      MOVE SCST     CUSST
     6600 C                      MOVE SCZIP    CUSZIP
     6700 C                      MOVE SCCAT    CUSCAT
     6800 C                      UPDATCUST01
     6900 C* WRITE THE TRANSACTION RECORD
     7000 C                      MOVE SCCUST   TRNNUM
     7100 C            TRNKEY    SETLLCUSTR01
     7200 C            TRNKEY    READECUSTR01                   92
     7300 C* NOTE THAT THE CUST# IS NEEDED IN THE TRAN RECORD
     7400 C                      MOVE SCCUST   TRNNUM
     7500 C                      MOVE SCNAME   TRNNAM
     7600 C                      MOVE SCADDR   TRNADR
     7700 C                      MOVE SCCITY   TRNCTY
     7800 C                      MOVE SCST     TRNST
     7900 C                      MOVE SCZIP    TRNZIP
     8000 C                      MOVE SCCAT    TRNCAT
     8100 C                      MOVE 'C'      TRNACT
     8200 C                      MOVE SCINIT   INITS
     8300 C                      MOVE UDATE    TRNDAT
     8400 C                      WRITECUSTR01
     8500 C                      END
     8600 C                      ELSE
     8700 C                      GOTO CHKCHG
     8800 C                      END
     8900 C                      GOTO ENDCHG
     9000 C                      END
     9100 C* CHECK IF DELETE RECORD
     9200 C            SCCODE    IFEQ 'D'
     9300 C                      EXSR DLTRTE
     9400 C                      GOTO ENDCHG
     9500 C                      END
     9600 C* CHECK IF TRYING TO ADD AN EXISTING RECORD
     9700 C            SCCODE    IFEQ 'A'
     9800 C                      SETON                          71
     9900 C                      GOTO ENDCHG
    10000 C                      END
    10100 C                      SETON                          73
    10200 C            ENDCHG    ENDSR
    10300 C*********************************************************************
    10400 C            ADDRTE    BEGSR
    10500 C* DISPLAY BLANK LINES READY FOR ADDITION
    10600 C                      MOVE *BLANKS  SCNAME
    10700 C                      MOVE *BLANKS  SCADDR
    10800 C                      MOVE *BLANKS  SCCITY
    10900 C                      MOVE *BLANKS  SCST
    11000 C                      MOVE *BLANKS  SCZIP
    11100 C                      MOVE *BLANKS  SCCAT
    11200 C* ADD A NEW RECORD
    11300 C            SCCODE    IFEQ 'A'
    11400 C            CHKADD    TAG
    11500 C                      EXFMTIL16242
    11600 C     01               GOTO ENDADD
    11700 C* IF CMD 5 THEN ADD NEW RECORD
    11800 C            *IN05     IFEQ '1'
    11900 C            CUSKEY    SETLLCUST01
    12000 C            CUSKEY    READECUST01                    91
    12100 C            *IN91     IFEQ '1'
    12200 C                      MOVE SCNAME   CUSNAM
```

FIGURE 16.24 *Continued*

```
12300  C                         MOVE  *ZEROS     CUSMTD
12400  C                         MOVE  *ZEROS     CUSYTD
12500  C                         MOVE  SCADDR     CUSADR
12600  C                         MOVE  SCCITY     CUSCTY
12700  C                         MOVE  SCST       CUSST
12800  C                         MOVE  SCZIP      CUSZIP
12900  C                         MOVE  SCCAT      CUSCAT
13000  C                         WRITECUST01
13100  C           TRNKEY        SETLLCUSTR01
13200  C           TRNKEY        READECUSTR01                    92
13300  C                         MOVE  SCCUST     TRNNUM
13400  C                         MOVE  SCNAME     TRNNAM
13500  C                         MOVE  *ZEROS     TRNMTD
13600  C                         MOVE  *ZEROS     TRNYTD
13700  C                         MOVE  SCADDR     TRNADR
13800  C                         MOVE  SCCITY     TRNCTY
13900  C                         MOVE  SCST       TRNST
14000  C                         MOVE  SCZIP      TRNZIP
14100  C                         MOVE  SCCAT      TRNCAT
14200  C                         MOVE  'A'        TRNACT
14300  C                         MOVE  SCINIT     INITS
14400  C                         MOVE  UDATE      TRNDAT
14500  C                         WRITECUSTR01
14600  C                         END
14700  C                         ELSE
14800  C                         GOTO  CHKADD
14900  C                         END
15000  C                         GOTO  ENDADD
15100  C                         END
15200  C* CHANGE OR DELETE AND NO MATCHING RECORD FOUND
15300  C           SCCODE        IFEQ  'C'
15400  C           SCCODE        OREQ  'D'
15500  C                         SETON                           72
15600  C                         GOTO  ENDADD
15700  C                         END
15800  C                         SETON                           73
15900  C           ENDADD        ENDSR
16000  C***********************************************************
16100  C           DLTRTE        BEGSR
16200  C* DISPLAY EXISTING RECORD
16300  C           CHKDLT        TAG
16400  C                         EXFMTIL16242
16500  C    01                   GOTO  ENDDLT
16600  C* DELETE A RECORD
16700  C* IF CMD 5 - THEN DELETE EXISTING RECORD
16800  C           *IN05         IFEQ  '1'
16900  C           CUSKEY        SETLLCUST01
17000  C           CUSKEY        READECUST01                     91
17100  C           *IN91         IFEQ  '0'
17200  C                         DELETCUST01
17300  C* WRITE A TRANSACTION RECORD
17400  C                         MOVE  SCCUST     TRNNUM
17500  C           TRNKEY        SETLLCUSTR01
17600  C           TRNKEY        READECUSTR01                    92
17700  C* NOTE THAT THE CUST# IS NEEDED IN THE TRAN RECORD
17800  C                         MOVE  SCCUST     TRNNUM
17900  C                         MOVE  SCNAME     TRNNAM
18000  C                         MOVE  SCADDR     TRNADR
18100  C                         MOVE  SCCITY     TRNCTY
18200  C                         MOVE  SCST       TRNST
18300  C                         MOVE  SCZIP      TRNZIP
18400  C                         MOVE  SCCAT      TRNCAT
18500  C                         MOVE  'D'        TRNACT
18600  C                         MOVE  SCINIT     INITS
18700  C                         MOVE  UDATE      TRNDAT
18800  C                         WRITECUSTR01
18900  C                         END
19000  C                         ELSE
19100  C                         GOTO  CHKDLT
19200  C                         END
19300  C           ENDDLT        ENDSR
E000000     OUTPUT  FIELDS FOR RECORD IL16241 FILE IL1624FA FORMAT IL16241
E000001                          *IN71      1  CHAR   1
E000002                          *IN72      2  CHAR   1
E000003                          SCCUST     7  CHAR   5
```

FIGURE 16.24 *Continued*

```
E000004                             SCCODE     8  CHAR    1
E000005                             SCMSG2    39  CHAR   30
E000006                             SCMSG3    68  CHAR   30
E000007                             SCMSG4    98  CHAR   30
E000008                             SCINIT   101  CHAR    3
E000009                             SCMSG5   131  CHAR   30
F000000        OUTPUT FIELDS FOR RECORD IL16242 FILE IL1624FA FORMAT IL16242
F000001                             SCCUST     5  CHAR    5
F000002                             SCNAME    25  CHAR   20
F000003                             SCADDR    45  CHAR   20
F000004                             SCCITY    55  CHAR   10
F000005                             SCST      57  CHAR    2
F000006                             SCZIP     66  CHAR    9
F000007                             SCCAT     69  CHAR    3
F000008                             SCMSG5    99  CHAR   30
F000009                             SCMSG6   129  CHAR   30
G000000        OUTPUT FIELDS FOR RECORD CUSTO1 FILE CUSTMAST FORMAT CUSTO1
G000001                             CUSNUM     5  CHAR    5
G000002                             CUSNAM    25  CHAR   20
G000003                             CUSCAT    28  CHAR    3
G000004                             CUSMTD    36  ZONE   8,0
G000005                             CUSYTD    46  ZONE  10,0
G000006                             CUSADR    66  CHAR   20
G000007                             CUSCTY    76  CHAR   10
G000008                             CUSST     78  CHAR    2
G000009                             CUSZIP    87  CHAR    9
H000000        OUTPUT FIELDS FOR RECORD CUSTRO1 FILE CUSTTR FORMAT CUSTRO1
H000001                             TRNNUM     5  CHAR    5
H000002                             TRNNAM    25  CHAR   20
H000003                             TRNCAT    28  CHAR    3
H000004                             TRNMTD    36  ZONE   8,0
H000005                             TRNYTD    46  ZONE  10,0
H000006                             TRNADR    66  CHAR   20
H000007                             TRNCTY    76  CHAR   10
H000008                             TRNST     78  CHAR    2
H000009                             TRNZIP    87  CHAR    9
H000010                             TRNACT    88  CHAR    1
H000011                             INITS     91  CHAR    3
H000012                             TRNDAT    97  ZONE   6,0
* * * * * E N D   O F   S O U R C E * * * *
```

KEY FIELD INFORMATION

FILE/RCD	PHYSICAL FIELD	LOGICAL FIELD	ATTRIBUTES
02 CUSTMAST			
CUSTO1			
	CUSNUM		CHAR 5
03 CUSTTR			
CUSTRO1			
	TRNNUM		CHAR 5

CROSS-REFERENCE LISTING

FILE/RCD   DEV/RCD   REFERENCES (D=DEFINED)

DEFINING MULTIPLE SCREEN FORMATS ■

Some programs require many different formats to be displayed. Before entering an order, for example, an order entry clerk might need to look up some of the following information:

- The customer number from an alphabetic view of the customer master file
- The shipping address from a ship-to file
- The part number of the item requested from an item master file
- The availability of the item in the local warehouse file
- The price of the item in a price master file
- Substitution part numbers (if the item happens to be out of stock)
- A list of possible terms codes from a terms code file
- A date of availability in the open purchase order file

The list could be much longer depending on the type of company and variety of needs. The clerk will need to be able to display any of eight different screens from any of the other screens. In addition to these look-up files, there might be an order entry function that could require a dozen different entry screen displays. Information from one screen may need to be transferred to fields in one of the order entry screens to minimize the keying requirements.

Each of the screens can be displayed as it is needed. As screen replaces screen, the data in every screen must be retained and redisplayed when requested.

We will not attempt to describe this very complex program here. The programmer must be aware that requirements for such complexity are commonplace in business programming. Figures 16.25(a), 16.25(b), 16.25(c), and 16.25(d) show sample screens and a complete program that accesses more than one screen.

FIGURE 16.25(a) Sample Screen 1 for Order Entry Program

```
     ILL1625                 ORDER ENTRY SELECTION



                         ENTER ORDER#

                              1








                                                       CF-01 TO EXIT
```

FIGURE 16.25(b) Sample Screen 2 for Order Entry Program

```
     ILL1625                 ORDER HEADER INFORMATION
     ORDER#        00001

     CUST#         02345              SHIP-TO NUMBER   00312
     CUSTOMER NAME BULLFROG INC.      SHIP-TO NAME     OAK PLAZA
     ADDRESS       ROSE AVE.          SHIP-TO ADDRESS  67 OAK STREET
     CITY/STATE    LODI        CA     CITY/STATE       OAKVILLE      IN
     ZIP CODE      90608              SHIP-TO ZIP CODE



          CF-01 TO EXIT
```

FIGURE 16.25(c) Sample Screen 3 for Order Entry Program

```
            ILL1625                ORDER DETAIL INFORMATION


            SKU#         000585
            ITEM#        081351685-02
            DESCRIPTION         OAK THINGS
            QUANTITY            1
            UNIT PRICE        135.50




                    CF-01 TO EXIT
```

FIGURE 16.25(d) Complete Program for Order Entry Program

```
SEQUENCE      1         2         3         4         5         6         7
NUMBER    67890123456789012345678901234567890123456789012345678901234



    100   F* TITLE: ILLUS 16.26 ORDER ENTRY ILLUS (MULTIPLE SCREENS)
    200   F* DATE:   7/13         AUTHOR: D.CABLE
    300   F* DESCRIPTION:
    400   F************************************************************


NAME OF PROGRAM WILL BE ILL1626 IN LIBRARY CABLE

              H
* 1019            ALL DECIMAL DATA ERRORS IGNORED
    500   FIL1626FMCF  E                  WORKSTN
          RECORD FORMAT(S):  FILE IL1626FM LIB CABLE
                  EXTERNAL FORMAT IL162601 RPG NAME IL162601
                  EXTERNAL FORMAT IL162602 RPG NAME IL162602
                  EXTERNAL FORMAT IL162603 RPG NAME IL162603

    600   FORDERS  IF  E           K        DISK
          RECORD FORMAT(S):  FILE ORDERS LIB CABLE
                  EXTERNAL FORMAT ORDER01 RPG NAME ORDER01

    700   FCUSTMASTIF  E           K        DISK
          RECORD FORMAT(S):  FILE CUSTMAST LIB CABLE
                  EXTERNAL FORMAT CUST01 RPG NAME CUST01

    800   FSHIPTO  IF  E           K        DISK
    900   F************************************************************
          RECORD FORMAT(S):  FILE SHIPTO LIB CABLE
                  EXTERNAL FORMAT SHP01 RPG NAME SHP01


   1000   E                       MSG     1   3 30
   1100   E************************************************************


   1200   C* START-UP ROUTINE
A000000   INPUT  FIELDS FOR RECORD IL162601 FILE IL1626FM FORMAT IL162601
A000001                                       1    1 *IN01
A000002                                       2   60SCORD#
B000000   INPUT  FIELDS FOR RECORD IL162602 FILE IL1626FM FORMAT IL162602
B000001                                       1    1 *IN01
C000000   INPUT  FIELDS FOR RECORD IL162603 FILE IL1626FM FORMAT IL162603
C000001                                       1    1 *IN01
D000000   INPUT  FIELDS FOR RECORD ORDER01 FILE ORDERS FORMAT ORDER01
D000001                                            1    60ORDNUM
D000002                                            7   11 ORDCUS
D000003                                           12   160ORDSHP
D000004                                           17   220ORDPNO
D000005                                           23   37 ORDITM
D000006                                           38   52 ORDDES
```

FIGURE 16.25(d) *Continued*

```
D000007                                          53   580ORDQTY
D000008                                          59   652ORDPRC
D000009                                          66   710ORDDTE
E000000        INPUT   FIELDS FOR RECORD CUST01 FILE CUSTMAST FORMAT CUST01
E000001                                           1     5 CUSNUM
E000002                                           6    25 CUSNAM
E000003                                          26    28 CUSCAT
E000004                                          29   360CUSMTD
E000005                                          37   460CUSYTD
E000006                                          47    66 CUSADR
E000007                                          67    76 CUSCTY
E000008                                          77    78 CUSST
E000009                                          79    87 CUSZIP
F000000        INPUT   FIELDS FOR RECORD SHP01 FILE SHIPTO  FORMAT SHP01
F000001                                           1    50SHPNUM
F000002                                           6    25 SHPNAM
F000003                                          26    45 SHPADR
F000004                                          46    55 SHPCTY
F000005                                          56    57 SHPST
F000006                                          58    66 SHPZIP
 1300   C               ORDKEY     KLIST
 1400   C                          KFLD           ORDNUM
 1500   C               CUSKEY     KLIST
 1600   C                          KFLD           CUSNUM
 1700   C               SHPKEY     KLIST
 1800   C                          KFLD           SHPNUM
 1900   C                          EXFMTIL162601
 2000   C     01                   GOTO ENDJOB
 2100   C*
 2200   C* MAINLINE ROUTINE
 2300   C               *IN01      DOWEQ'0'
 2400   C               SCORD#     IFEQ *ZEROS
 2500   C* ORDER# CANNOT BE BLANK
 2600   C                          MOVE MSG,1     SCMSG1
 2700   C                          GOTO BEGIN
 2800   C                          END
 2900   C*
 3000   C                          MOVE SCORD#    ORDNUM
 3100   C               ORDKEY     SETLLORDER01
 3200   C               ORDKEY     READEORDER01                     90
 3300   C               *IN90      IFEQ '0'
 3400   C                          EXSR GETCUS
 3500   C                          EXSR GETSHP
 3600   C                          MOVE ORDPNO    SCSKU#
 3700   C                          MOVE ORDITM    SCITM#
 3800   C                          MOVE ORDDES    SCDESC
 3900   C                          MOVE ORDQTY    SCQTY
 4000   C                          MOVE ORDPRC    SCPRC#
 4100   C                          WRITEIL162602
 4200   C                          WRITEIL162603
 4300   C                          READ IL162603                    45
 4400   C     01                   GOTO BEGIN
 4500   C                          END
 4600   C               BEGIN      TAG
 4700   C                          EXFMTIL162601
 4800   C     01                   GOTO ENDJOB
 4900   C                          END
 5000   C               ENDJOB     TAG
 5100   C* WRAP-UP ROUTINE
 5200   C                          SETON                            LR
 5300   C**********************************************************
 5400   C               GETCUS     BEGSR
 5500   C* GET CUSTOMER NAME & ADDRESS
 5600   C                          MOVE ORDCUS    CUSNUM
 5700   C               CUSKEY     SETLLCUST01
 5800   C               CUSKEY     READECUST01                      92
 5900   C               *IN92      IFEQ '1'
 6000   C* CAN'T FIND THE CUSTOMER
 6100   C                          MOVE MSG,2     SCMSG2
 6200   C                          GOTO ENDCUS
 6300   C                          END
 6400   C                          MOVE CUSNUM    SCCUST
 6500   C                          MOVE CUSNAM    SCNAME
 6600   C                          MOVE CUSADR    SCADDR
```

FIGURE 16.25(d) **Continued**

```
6700 C                   MOVE CUSCTY    SCCITY
6800 C                   MOVE CUSST     SCST
6900 C                   MOVE CUSZIP    SCZIP
7000 C         ENDCUS    ENDSR
7100 C***************************************************************
7200 C         GETSHP    BEGSR
7300 C* GET SHIP-TO ADDRESS
7400 C                   MOVE ORDSHP    SHPNUM
7500 C         SHPKEY    SETLLSHPO1
7600 C         SHPKEY    READESHPO1                    79
7700 C*
7800 C         *IN79     IFEQ '1'
7900 C* CAN'T FIND THE SHIP-TO ADDRESS
8000 C                   MOVE MSG,3     SCMSG3
8100 C                   GOTO ENDSHP
8200 C                   END
8300 C                   MOVE SHPNUM    SCSHP#
8400 C                   MOVE SHPNAM    SCSNAM
8500 C                   MOVE SHPADR    SCSADR
8600 C                   MOVE SHPCTY    SCSCTY
8700 C                   MOVE SHPST     SCSSTE
8800 C                   MOVE SHPZIP    SCSZIP
8900 C         ENDSHP    ENDSR
9000 C***************************************************************
G000000   OUTPUT  FIELDS FOR RECORD IL162601 FILE IL1626FM FORMAT IL162601
G000001                        SCORD#     5   ZONE   5,0
G000002                        SCMSG1    35   CHAR    30
H000000   OUTPUT  FIELDS FOR RECORD IL162602 FILE IL1626FM FORMAT IL162602
H000001                        SCORD#     5   ZONE   5,0
H000002                        SCCUST    10   ZONE   5,0
H000003                        SCNAME    30   CHAR    20
H000004                        SCADDR    50   CHAR    20
H000005                        SCCITY    60   CHAR    10
H000006                        SCST      62   CHAR     2
H000007                        SCZIP     71   CHAR     9
H000008                        SCSHP#    76   ZONE   5,0
H000009                        SCSNAM    96   CHAR    20
H000010                        SCSADR   116   CHAR    20
H000011                        SCSCTY   126   CHAR    10
H000012                        SCSSTE   128   CHAR     2
H000013                        SCSZIP   137   CHAR     9
I000000   OUTPUT  FIELDS FOR RECORD IL162603 FILE IL1626FM FORMAT IL162603
I000001                        SCSKU#     6   ZONE   6,0
I000002                        SCITM#    21   CHAR    15
I000003                        SCDESC    41   CHAR    20
I000004                        SCQTY     48   ZONE   7,0
I000005                        SCPRC#    55   ZONE   7,2
I000006                        SCMSG2    85   CHAR    30
I000007                        SCMSG3   115   CHAR    30
* * * * * E N D  O F  S O U R C E * * * * *

         TABLE/ARRAY ------- MSG
    9200  RECORD NOT FOUND
    9300  CUSTOMER NOT FOUND
    9400  SHIP-TO ADDRESS NOT FOUND

    KEY FIELD INFORMATION

                      PHYSICAL    LOGICAL
         FILE/RCD     FIELD       FIELD       ATTRIBUTES
    02   ORDERS
           ORDERO1
                      ORDNUM                  ZONE  6,0  SIGNED
    03   CUSTMAST
           CUSTO1
                      CUSNUM                  CHAR    5
    04   SHIPTO
           SHPO1
                      SHPNUM                  ZONE  5,0  SIGNED

    CROSS-REFERENCE LISTING

         FILE/RCD     DEV/RCD     REFERENCES (D=DEFINED)

    03   CUSTMAST     DISK        700D
           CUSTO1                 700D E000000    5700       5800
    01   IL1626FM     WORKSTN     500D
```

WRITE/READ OPERATIONS ■

The program examples in these chapters have used the EXFMT operation for displaying screens. This works well for displaying a single format and retrieving data from the screen. When multiple formats are used, however, it may be necessary to place several different formats on the same screen. One format may display at the top of the screen, another on the bottom of the screen, and a third in the center. These may differ depending on the options requested.

When multiple formats are to be displayed, separate WRITE and READ operations are used. A WRITE displays data to the screen but retrieves no data. A READ operation retrieves information from any input-capable fields on the screen.

Figures 16.26(a), 16.26(b), and 16.26(c) show sample screens and an example of a program that uses WRITE and READ operations to display several screens. The last operation is an EXFMT to permit retrieval of data.

Notice that a WRITE operation must precede a READ. Something must be displayed to a screen before anything can be retrieved.

FIGURE 16.26(a) Sample Screen 1

```
    ILL1626                    ORDER ENTRY SELECTION



                             ENTER ORDER#

                                   1




                                                         CF-01 TO EXIT
```

FIGURE 16.26(b) Sample Screen 2

```
    ILL1626                 ORDER INFORMATION

    ORDER#          00001

    CUST#           02345              SHIP-TO NUMBER   00312
    CUSTOMER NAME   BULLFROG INC.      SHIP-TO NAME     OAK PLAZA
    ADDRESS         ROSE AVE.          SHIP-TO ADDRESS  67 OAK STREET
    CITY/STATE      LODI       CA      CITY/STATE       OAKVILLE      IN
    ZIP CODE        90608              SHIP-TO ZIP CODE


    SKU#        ITEM#         DESCRIPTION      QUANTITY      UNIT PRICE

    000585   081351685-02     OAK THINGS          1            135.50



         CF-01 TO EXIT
```

FIGURE 16.26(c) Complete Program

```
SEQUENCE      1         2         3         4         5         6         7
NUMBER    67890123456789012345678901234567890123456789012345678901234567890123




    100  F* TITLE: ILLUS 16.25 ORDER ENTRY ILLUS (MULTIPLE SCREENS)
    200  F* DATE:  7/13         AUTHOR: D.CABLE
    300  F* DESCRIPTION:
    400  F*****************************************************
```

FIGURE 16.26(c) *Continued*

```
NAME OF PROGRAM WILL BE ILL1625 IN LIBRARY CABLE

                H
 * 1019                  ALL DECIMAL DATA ERRORS IGNORED
     500    FIL1625FMCF  E                    WORKSTN
            RECORD FORMAT(S):   FILE IL1625FM LIB CABLE
                    EXTERNAL FORMAT IL162501 RPG NAME IL162501
                    EXTERNAL FORMAT IL162502 RPG NAME IL162502
                    EXTERNAL FORMAT IL162503 RPG NAME IL162503

     600    FORDERS  IF  E         K          DISK
            RECORD FORMAT(S):   FILE ORDERS LIB CABLE
                    EXTERNAL FORMAT ORDER01 RPG NAME ORDER01

     700    FCUSTMASTIF  E         K          DISK
            RECORD FORMAT(S):   FILE CUSTMAST LIB CABLE
                    EXTERNAL FORMAT CUST01 RPG NAME CUST01

     800    FSHIPTO  IF  E         K          DISK
     900    F*********************************************************
            RECORD FORMAT(S):   FILE SHIPTO LIB CABLE
                    EXTERNAL FORMAT SHP01 RPG NAME SHP01


    1000    E                     MSG     1   3 30
    1100    E*********************************************************


    1200    C* START-UP ROUTINE
 A000000    INPUT   FIELDS FOR RECORD IL162501 FILE IL1625FM FORMAT IL162501
 A000001                                            1    1 *IN01
 A000002                                            2   60SCORD#
 B000000    INPUT   FIELDS FOR RECORD IL162502 FILE IL1625FM FORMAT IL162502
 B000001                                            1    1 *IN01
 C000000    INPUT   FIELDS FOR RECORD IL162503 FILE IL1625FM FORMAT IL162503
 C000001                                            1    1 *IN01
 D000000    INPUT   FIELDS FOR RECORD ORDER01 FILE ORDERS FORMAT ORDER01
 D000001                                            1   60ORDNUM
 D000002                                            7   11 ORDCUS
 D000003                                           12   16 ORDSHP
 D000004                                           17   220ORDPNO
 D000005                                           23   37 ORDITM
 D000006                                           38   52 ORDDES
 D000007                                           53   580ORDQTY
 D000008                                           59   652ORDPRC
 D000009                                           66   710ORDDTE
 E000000    INPUT   FIELDS FOR RECORD CUST01 FILE CUSTMAST FORMAT CUST01
 E000001                                            1    5 CUSNUM
 E000002                                            6   25 CUSNAM
 E000003                                           26   28 CUSCAT
 E000004                                           29   360CUSMTD
 E000005                                           37   460CUSYTD
 E000006                                           47   66 CUSADR
 E000007                                           67   76 CUSCTY
 E000008                                           77   78 CUSST
 E000009                                           79   87 CUSZIP
 F000000    INPUT   FIELDS FOR RECORD SHP01 FILE SHIPTO FORMAT SHP01
 F000001                                            1    50SHPNUM
 F000002                                            6   25 SHPNAM
 F000003                                           26   45 SHPADR
 F000004                                           46   55 SHPCTY
 F000005                                           56   57 SHPST
 F000006                                           58   66 SHPZIP
    1300    C           ORDKEY    KLIST
    1400    C                     KFLD           ORDNUM
    1500    C           CUSKEY    KLIST
    1600    C                     KFLD           CUSNUM
    1700    C           SHPKEY    KLIST
    1800    C                     KFLD           SHPNUM
    1900    C                     EXFMTIL162501
    2000    C     01              GOTO ENDJOB
    2100    C*
    2200    C* MAINLINE ROUTINE
    2300    C           *IN01     DOWEQ'0'
    2400    C           SCORD#    IFEQ *ZEROS
```

FIGURE 16.26(c) *Continued*

```
2500 C* ORDER# CANNOT BE BLANK
2600 C                       MOVE MSG,1       SCMSG1
2700 C                       GOTO BEGIN
2800 C                       END
2900 C*
3000 C                       MOVE SCORD#      ORDNUM
3100 C           ORDKEY      SETLLORDER01
3200 C           ORDKEY      READEORDER01                       90
3300 C           *IN90       IFEQ '0'
3400 C                       EXSR GETCUS
3500 C                       EXSR GETSHP
3600 C                       MOVE ORDPNO      SCSKU#
3700 C                       MOVE ORDITM      SCITM#
3800 C                       MOVE ORDDES      SCDESC
3900 C                       MOVE ORDQTY      SCQTY
4000 C                       MOVE ORDPRC      SCPRC#
4100 C                       EXFMTIL162502
4200 C    01                 GOTO BEGIN
4300 C                       EXFMTIL162503
4400 C    01                 GOTO BEGIN
4500 C                       END
4600 C           BEGIN       TAG
4700 C                       EXFMTIL162501
4800 C    01                 GOTO ENDJOB
4900 C                       END
5000 C           ENDJOB      TAG
5100 C* WRAP-UP ROUTINE
5200 C                       SETON                              LR
5300 C********************************************************************
5400 C           GETCUS      BEGSR
5500 C* GET CUSTOMER NAME & ADDRESS
5600 C                       MOVE ORDCUS      CUSNUM
5700 C           CUSKEY      SETLLCUST01
5800 C           CUSKEY      READECUST01                        92
5900 C           *IN92       IFEQ '1'
6000 C* CAN'T FIND THE CUSTOMER
6100 C                       MOVE MSG,2       SCMSG2
6200 C                       GOTO ENDCUS
6300 C                       END
6400 C                       MOVE CUSNUM      SCCUST
6500 C                       MOVE CUSNAM      SCNAME
6600 C                       MOVE CUSADR      SCADDR
6700 C                       MOVE CUSCTY      SCCITY
6800 C                       MOVE CUSST       SCST
6900 C                       MOVE CUSZIP      SCZIP
7000 C           ENDCUS      ENDSR
7100 C********************************************************************
7200 C           GETSHP      BEGSR
7300 C* GET SHIP-TO ADDRESS
7400 C                       MOVE ORDSHP      SHPNUM
7500 C           SHPKEY      SETLLSHP01
7600 C           SHPKEY      READESHP01                         79
7700 C*
7800 C           *IN79       IFEQ '1'
7900 C* CAN'T FIND THE SHIP-TO ADDRESS
8000 C                       MOVE MSG,3       SCMSG3
8100 C                       GOTO ENDSHP
8200 C                       END
8300 C                       MOVE SHPNUM      SCSHP#
8400 C                       MOVE SHPNAM      SCSNAM
8500 C                       MOVE SHPADR      SCSADR
8600 C                       MOVE SHPCTY      SCSCTY
8700 C                       MOVE SHPST       SCSSTE
8800 C                       MOVE SHPZIP      SCSZIP
8900 C           ENDSHP      ENDSR
9000 C********************************************************************
G000000    OUTPUT  FIELDS FOR RECORD IL162501 FILE IL1625FM FORMAT IL162501
G000001                             SCORD#      5  ZONE  5,0
G000002                             SCMSG1     35  CHAR  30
H000000    OUTPUT  FIELDS FOR RECORD IL162502 FILE IL1625FM FORMAT IL162502
H000001                             SCORD#      5  ZONE  5,0
H000002                             SCCUST     10  ZONE  5,0
H000003                             SCNAME     30  CHAR  20
H000004                             SCADDR     50  CHAR  20
H000005                             SCCITY     60  CHAR  10
H000006                             SCST       62  CHAR   2
H000007                             SCZIP      71  CHAR   9
H000008                             SCSHP#     76  ZONE  5,0
H000009                             SCSNAM     96  CHAR  20
```

FIGURE 16.26(c) Continued

```
        H000010                              SCSADR   116  CHAR    20
        H000011                              SCSCTY   126  CHAR    10
        H000012                              SCSSTE   128  CHAR     2
        H000013                              SCSZIP   137  CHAR     9
        H000014                              SCMSG2   167  CHAR    30
        H000015                              SCMSG3   197  CHAR    30
        I000000      OUTPUT  FIELDS FOR RECORD IL162503 FILE IL1625FM FORMAT IL162503
        I000001                              SCSKU#     6  ZONE   6,0
        I000002                              SCITM#    21  CHAR    15
        I000003                              SCDESC    41  CHAR    20
        I000004                              SCQTY     48  ZONE   7,0
        I000005                              SCPRC#    55  ZONE   7,2
        * * * * * E N D  O F  S O U R C E * * * * *

                TABLE/ARRAY -------- MSG
          9200   RECORD NOT FOUND
          9300   CUSTOMER NOT FOUND
          9400   SHIP-TO ADDRESS NOT FOUND


        KEY FIELD INFORMATION


                              PHYSICAL      LOGICAL
                FILE/RCD      FIELD         FIELD         ATTRIBUTES


          02   ORDERS
                 ORDER01
                              ORDNUM                      ZONE   6,0   SIGNED
          03   CUSTMAST
                 CUST01
                              CUSNUM                      CHAR    5
          04   SHIPTO
                 SHP01
                              SHPNUM                      ZONE   5,0   SIGNED


        CROSS-REFERENCE LISTING


                FILE/RCD      DEV/RCD       REFERENCES (D=DEFINED)

          03   CUSTMAST       DISK          700D
                 CUST01                     700D E000000    5700      5800
          01   IL1625FM       WORKSTN       500D
```

SUMMARY ■

In this chapter, you have learned that developing on-line applications is more complex than writing programs that read a file and print a report. It is necessary to plan and design display screens that are easy to use. The screens must be self-sufficient to guide the user through prompts to make the appropriate entries on the screen.

You have learned that the Data Description Specification (DDS) makes programming for on-line update applications simpler. The DDS permits many editing and special functions for display screen processing. You have also seen more in-depth examples of the use of key words and command keys in the Data Description Specifications.

Finally, you have learned about two methods used to display screens and retrieve data at the same time. One of the methods involves the use of the EXFMT operation. The second method uses separate WRITE and READ operations to better control management of the screen functions.

REVIEW QUESTIONS ■

1. What are some of the edits that should be performed on input data?
2. What are some of the items for which editing can be performed based on coding in the DDS?
3. What are some of the functions that can be specified for the DSPATR key word on the DDS?
4. How can a field be underlined on a display screen?
5. How can a field be highlighted on a display screen?
6. How can a range value be entered on a DDS for validity checking?
7. How can an error message be specified in the DDS?
8. What is the function of the key word PRINT?
9. Explain the coding on the DDS for command keys.
10. When should the key word TEXT be used in the DDS?
11. In a program for updating a file, why should the field names on the DDS for the display file be different from the names of the fields in the physical file to be updated?
12. Why is it useful to enter in the updated file the current date and the name or initials of the person making changes to that file?
13. Why is it a good idea to retain a copy of every transaction as well as the updated version of the file?
14. What is the benefit of using several different screen formats in a program?
15. What is the function of a WRITE operation? A READ operation?
16. How does the EXFMT operation differ from the WRITE and READ operations?
17. When writing a program using a display file, why must a WRITE operation precede a READ operation?
18. Why is it necessary to provide an escape function in every program using a display screen?
19. Why is it necessary to set on the LR indicator when the escape function is performed?

DEBUGGING EXERCISES

Instructions

The following RPG programs contain an error or errors. Some of these errors are indicated by the RPG compiler on the program listing. A list of syntax errors is given at the end of the program listing. Other types of errors may occur which will not be shown. These are called logic errors.

Study each program and its syntax errors. Locate each error (including logic errors) and on a separate coding form make the correct entry for the line(s) in error.

Explain each error and how it should be corrected.

```
       100   F* TITLE: DEBUG PROJECT 16-A
       200   F* DATE:  6/30          AUTHOR: D.CABLE
       300   F* DESCRIPTION:
       400   F**********************************************

NAME OF PROGRAM WILL BE PJ016A IN LIBRARY CABLE

             H
* 1019             ALL DECIMAL DATA ERRORS IGNORED
       500   FIM330TFMCF  E                    WORKSTN
             RECORD FORMAT(S):  FILE IM330TFM LIB NEWMOD
                   EXTERNAL FORMAT IM330T01 RPG NAME IM330T01
                   EXTERNAL FORMAT IM330T91 RPG NAME IM330T91

       600   FIBODTLFLIF  E          K         DISK
       700   F**********************************************

       800   C* START-UP ROUTINE
             RECORD FORMAT(S):  FILE IBODTLFL LIB MOMS
                   EXTERNAL FORMAT IBODTL10 RPG NAME IBODTL10
    A000000      INPUT  FIELDS FOR RECORD IM330T01 FILE IM330TFM FORMAT IM330T01
    A000001                                           2   2 *IN76
    A000002                                           1   1 *IN79
    A000003                                           3    110SCORD#
    A000004                                          12   12 SCPRNT
    A000005                                          13   13 SCUPDT
    B000000      INPUT  FIELDS FOR RECORD IM330T91 FILE IM330TFM FORMAT IM330T91
    B000001                                           1   1 *IN79
    C000000      INPUT  FIELDS FOR RECORD IBODTL10 FILE IBODTLFL FORMAT IBODTL10
    C000001                                           1   2 BDCMP#
    C000002                                     P     3  40BDLOC#
    C000003                                     P     5  90BDORD#
    C000004                                     P    10 110BDSEQ#
    C000005                                     P    12 150BDODTE
    C000006                                     P    16 190BDOQTY
    C000007                                          20  32 BDITM#
    C000008                                     P    33 373BDPRCE
    C000009                                     P    38 402BDDISC
    C000010                                          41  45 BDUNIT
    C000011                                     P    46 500BDACT#
    C000012                                     P    51 540BDSQTY
    C000013                                     P    55 560BDFEET
    C000014                                          57  62 BDLCTN
    C000015                                          63  63 BDTAXI
    C000016                                     P    64 683BDCOST
    C000017                                     P    69 710BDDEPT
    C000018                                          72  84 BDCATL
    C000019                                     P    85 870BDPPD#
    C000020                                     P    88 900BDSET#
    C000021                                     P    91 942BDSHCG
```

```
C000022                                              95   96 BDRSNC
C000023                                         P    97   99 BDJINV
C000024                                         P   100 104 BDSQT1
C000025                                         P   105 109 BDSQT2
C000026                                         P   110 111 BDSLC1
C000027                                         P   112 113 BDSLC2
C000028                                             114 114 BDDRPS
C000029                                         P   115 117 BDPRCG
C000030                                             118 118 BDRSTK
C000031                                         P   119 121 BDCMRT
C000032                                         P   122 126 BDMKDN
     900   C                    MOVE SALOC#    SCLOC#  20
    1000   C* MAINLINE ROUTINE
    1100   C                    READ TAG
    1200   C                    MOVE SCORD#    SAORD#   9
    1300   C                    EXFMTIM330T10
* 5154                               5154-**********
    1400   C         *INKA      IFEQ '1'
    1500   C                    SETON                                 LR
    1600   C                    RETRN
    1700   C                    END
    1800   C                    MOVE SCCMP#    IBCMP#
    1900   C                    MOVE SCLOC#    IBLOC#
    2000   C         KEY        SETLL IBODTL10
    2100   C         KEY        READE IBODTL10                        33
    2200   C         *IN33      IFEQ '1'
    2300   C                    MOVE SCQTY     IBQTY
    2400   C                    UPDAT IBODTL10
* 5198                               5198-*****
    2500   C                    ELSE
    2600   C                    WRITEIBODTL10
* 5197                               5197-*****
    2700   C                    END
    2800   C                    GOTO READ
    2900   C                    RETRN
    3000   C************************************************************
D000000     OUTPUT   FIELDS FOR RECORD IBODTL10 FILE IBODTLFL FORMAT IBODTL10
D000001                              BDCMP#     2 CHAR     2
D000002                              BDLOC#     4P PACK   2,0
D000003                              BDORD#     9P PACK   9,0
D000004                              BDSEQ#    11P PACK   3,0
D000005                              BDODTE    15P PACK   6,0
D000006                              BDOQTY    19P PACK   7,0
D000007                              BDITM#    32 CHAR    13
D000008                              BDPRCE    37P PACK   9,3
D000009                              BDDISC    40P PACK   4,2
D000010                              BDUNIT    45 CHAR     5
D000011                              BDACT#    50P PACK   9,0
D000012                              BDSQTY    54P PACK   7,0
D000013                              BDFEET    56P PACK   2,0
D000014                              BDLCTN    62 CHAR     6
D000015                              BDTAXI    63 CHAR     1
D000016                              BDCOST    68P PACK   9,3
D000017                              BDDEPT    71P PACK   4,0
D000018                              BDCATL    84 CHAR    13
D000019                              BDPPD#    87P PACK   5,0
D000020                              BDSET#    90P PACK   5,0
D000021                              BDSHCG    94P PACK   7,2
D000022                              BDRSNC    95 CHAR     2
D000023                              BDJINV    99P PACK   5,0
D000024                              BDSQT1   104P PACK   9,0
D000025                              BDSQT2   109P PACK   9,0
D000026                              BDSLC1   111P PACK   2,0
D000027                              BDSLC2   113P PACK   2,0
D000028                              BDDRPS   114 CHAR     1
D000029                              BDPRCG   117P PACK   5,0
D000030                              BDRSTK   118 CHAR     1
D000031                              BDCMRT   121P PACK   4,2
D000032                              BDMKDN   126P PACK   9,2
* * * * * E N D   O F   S O U R C E * * * * *
```

```
* 7024        500    IM330TFM FILE NAME HAS NO CALC REFERENCE TO INPUT RECORDS
* 7064        500    IM330TFM FILE NOT REFERENCED FOR OUTPUT
* 7078       2000    FACTOR 1 LENGTH IS    4 BUT LENGTH OF KEY FIELD IN FILE IS    2.
* 7078       2100    FACTOR 1 LENGTH IS    4 BUT LENGTH OF KEY FIELD IN FILE IS    2.
```

KEY FIELD INFORMATION

```
                        PHYSICAL     LOGICAL
          FILE/RCD      FIELD        FIELD        ATTRIBUTES


     02   IBODTLFL
               IBODTL10
                        BDCMP#                    CHAR   2
                        BDLOC#                    PACK   2,0   SIGNED
                        BDORD#                    PACK   9,0   SIGNED
                        BDSEQ#                    PACK   3,0   SIGNED
```

CROSS-REFERENCE LISTING

```
          FILE/RCD      DEV/RCD      REFERENCES  (D=DEFINED)


     02   IBODTLFL      DISK         600D
               IBODTL10              600D C000000   2000   2100   2400
                                    2600  D000000
     01   IM330TFM      WORKSTN      500D
               IM330T01              500D A000000
               IM330T91              500D B000000


          FIELD         ATTR         REFERENCES  (M=MODIFIED  D=DEFINED)

          *INKA         A(1)         1400
          *IN33         A(1)         2200
* 7031    *IN76         A(1)         A000001
* 7031    *IN79         A(1)         A000002  B000001
          BDACT#        P(9,0)       C000011D D000011D
          BDCATL        A(13)        C000018D D000018D
          BDCMP#        A(2)         C000001D D000001D
          BDCMRT        P(4,2)       C000031D D000031D
          BDCOST        P(9,3)       C000016D D000016D
          BDDEPT        P(4,0)       C000017D D000017D
          BDDISC        P(4,2)       C000009D D000009D
          BDDRPS        A(1)         C000028D D000028D
          BDFEET        P(2,0)       C000013D D000013D
          BDITM#        A(13)        C000007D D000007D
          BDJINV        P(5,0)       C000023D D000023D
          BDLCTN        A(6)         C000014D D000014D
          BDLOC#        P(2,0)       C000002D D000002D
          BDMKDN        P(9,2)       C000032D D000032D
          BDODTE        P(6,0)       C000005D D000005D
          BDOQTY        P(7,0)       C000006D D000006D
          BDORD#        P(9,0)       C000003D D000003D
          BDPPD#        P(5,0)       C000019D D000019D
          BDPRCE        P(9,3)       C000008D D000008D
          BDPRCG        P(5,0)       C000029D D000029D
          BDRSNC        A(2)         C000022D D000022D
          BDRSTK        A(1)         C000030D D000030D
          BDSEQ#        P(3,0)       C000004D D000004D
          BDSET#        P(5,0)       C000020D D000020D
          BDSHCG        P(7,2)       C000021D D000021D
          BDSLC1        P(2,0)       C000026D D000026D
          BDSLC2        P(2,0)       C000027D D000027D
          BDSQTY        P(7,0)       C000012D D000012D
          BDSQT1        P(9,0)       C000024D D000024D
          BDSQT2        P(9,0)       C000025D D000025D
          BDTAXI        A(1)         C000015D D000015D
          BDUNIT        A(5)         C000010D D000010D
```

```
* 7030   IBCMP#      A(4)      1800M
* 7030   IBLOC#      A(4)      1900M
* 7030   IBQTY       A(4)      2300M
* 7030   KEY         A(4)      2000       2100
         READ        TAG      11000       2800
* 7030   SALOC#      A(4)       900
         SAORD#      A(9)      1200J
* 7030   SCCMP#      A(4)      1800
         SCLOC#      P(2,0)     900J                      1900
         SCORD#      P(9,0)   A0000030     1200
* 7031   SLPRNT      A(1)     A0000040
* 7030   SCQTY       A(4)      2300
* 7031   SCUPDT      A(1)     A0000050
         '1'         LITERAL   1400       2200


         INDICATOR REFERENCES (M=MODIFIED D=DEFINED)
         *IN        A000001  A000002  B000001   2200
         KA          1400
         LR          1500M
         33          2100M    2200
* 7031   76         A000001
* 7031   79         A000002  B000001


MESSAGES

MSGID      SEV  NUMBER  TEXT

* QRG1019   00    1    IGNDECERR(*YES) SPECIFIED ON COMMAND. NO DECIMAL DATA ERRORS
* QRG5154   30    1    RECORD FORMAT NAME IN FACTOR 2 (POSITIONS 33-42) NOT DEFINED
                       IGNORED.
* QRG5197   30    1    WRITE OPERATION NOT VALID FOR THIS FILE. SPECIFICATION IGNORE
* QRG5198   30    1    UPDAT/DELET OPERATION NOT VALID. SPECIFICATION IGNORED
* QRG7024   20    1    INPUT RECORD NOT REFERENCED BY CALCULATION OPERATIONS.
* QRG7030   30    7    FIELD OR INDICATOR NOT DEFINED.
* QRG7031   00    6    NAME OR INDICATOR NOT REFERENCED.
* QRG7064   40    1    PROGRAM FILE NOT REFERENCED. FILE IGNORED
* QRG7078   30    2    FACTOR 1 (POS 18-27) LENGTH NOT SAME AS FIRST KEY FIELD IN F
                       IGNORED.


MESSAGE SUMMARY

TOTAL    00    10    20    30    40    50
  21      7     0     1    12     1     0

   30 RECORDS READ FROM SOURCE FILE
SOURCE RECORDS INCLUDE    22 SPECIFICATIONS,    0 TABLE RECORDS, AND    8 COMMENTS

QRG0008 COMPILE TERMINATED. SEVERITY 40 ERRORS FOUND IN PROGRAM

* * * * * E N D   O F   C O M P I L A T I O N * * * * *
* QRG1020              ERROR OCCURRED CREATING OR UPDATING DATA AREA RETURNCODE. COMPII
```

```
100  F* TITLE: DEBUG PROJECT 16-B
200  F* DATE:  7/1         AUTHOR: D.CABLE
300  F* DESCRIPTION:
400  F***************************************************
```

NAME OF PROGRAM WILL BE PJ016B IN LIBRARY CABLE

Chapter 16 On-Line Updates Using RPG III/400

```
                       H              ALL DECIMAL DATA ERRORS IGNORED
* 1019
          500    FIM330TFMCF   E                    WORKSTN
                   RECORD FORMAT(S):   FILE IM330TFM LIB NEWMOD
                            EXTERNAL FORMAT IM330T01 RPG NAME IM330T01
                            EXTERNAL FORMAT IM330T91 RPG NAME IM330T91

          600    FIBOHDGFLIF  E           K         DISK
          700    F***********************************************************


          800    C* MAINLINE ROUTINE
                   RECORD FORMAT(S):   FILE IBOHDGFL LIB MOMS
                            EXTERNAL FORMAT IBOHDG10 RPG NAME IBOHDG10
A000000          INPUT   FIELDS FOR RECORD IM330T01 FILE IM330TFM FORMAT IM330T01
A000001                                                2   2 *IN76
A000002                                                1   1 *IN79
A000003                                                3  110SCORD#
A000004                                               12  12 SCPRNT
A000005                                               13  13 SCUPDT
B000000          INPUT   FIELDS FOR RECORD IM330T91 FILE IM330TFM FORMAT IM330T91
B000001                                                1   1 *IN79
C000000          INPUT   FIELDS FOR RECORD IBOHDG10 FILE IBOHDGFL FORMAT IBOHDG10
C000001                                                1   2 BHCMP#
C000002                                         P      3   40BHLOC#
C000003                                         P      5   90BHACT#
C000004                                         P     10  140BHORD#
C000005                                               15  16 BHSTTS
C000006                                         P     17  200BHTIME
C000007                                         P     21  240BHSTDT
C000008                                         P     25  292BHOAMT
C000009                                         P     30  322BHODSC
C000010                                         P     33  360BHODTE
C000011                                         P     37  400BHSDTE
C000012                                               41  55 BHOPO#
C000013                                               56  60 BHORDG
C000014                                         P     61  640BHSHP3
C000015                                               65  94 BHINST
C000016                                         P     95  960BHSHWT
C000017                                               97  97 BHSHCD
C000018                                         P     98 1012BHSHCG
C000019                                         P    102 1052BHSHIN
C000020                                              106 106 BHNSHP
C000021                                         P    107 1080BHPYDS
C000022                                         P    109 1120BHINVD
C000023                                              113 113 BHPPAY
C000024                                         P    114 1182BHPPAM
C000025                                         P    119 1222BHSLTX
C000026                                              123 123 BHSPEC
C000027                                         P    124 1260BHREP#
C000028                                              127 128 BHRSNC
C000029                                              129 134 BHINIT
C000030                                              135 144 BHWSTN
C000031                                              145 146 BHTERM
C000032                                         P    147 1490BHJOB#
C000033                                              150 153 BHTXCD
C000034                                         P    154 1560BHIREP
C000035                                         P    157 1580BHOLOC
C000036                                         P    159 1622BHSHCM
C000037                                         P    163 1662BHSPCG
C000038                                              167 196 BHSPCD
C000039                                         P    197 1992BHCOD$
C000040                                         P    200 2032BHRSTK
C000041                                              204 204 BHTYPE
C000042                                              205 224 BHAUTH
C000043                                         P    225 2270BHJINV
C000044                                              228 248 BHCCD#
C000045                                         P    249 2510BHCEXD
C000046                                              252 257 BHMKEY
C000047                                              258 258 BHHDLC
C000048                                              259 259 BHSLTN
C000049                                              260 260 BHBTYP
C000050                                         P    261 2620BHBCH#
C000051                                         P    263 2670BHREF#
C000052                                              268 268 BHPPY2
C000053                                         P    269 2732BHPP$2
C000054                                              274 274 BHPPY3
C000055                                         P    275 2792BHPP$3
C000056                                              280 280 BHRTYP
C000057                                         P    281 2850BHRCK#
```

```
C000058                                         286 286 BHRUSH
C000059                                         287 288 BHHELD
C000060                                       P 289 2920BHDTRL
C000061                                       P 293 2940BHPRTY
C000062                                         295 298 BHSHPM
C000063                                       P 299 3020BHSHPD
C000064                                         303 317 BHINS#
C000065                                       P 318 3180BHSPLS
C000066                                       P 319 3222BHSCG1
C000067                                       P 323 3262BHSCG2
C000068                                       P 327 3280BHSLC1
C000069                                       P 329 3300BHSLC2
C000070                                         331 331 BHSST1
C000071                                         332 332 BHSST2
C000072                                       P 333 3362BHSCM1
C000073                                       P 337 3402BHSCM2
C000074                                       P 341 3420BH#CHG
C000075                                         343 343 BHIFCC
        900   C            BEGIN      TAG
       1000   C                       EXFMTIM330T10
 * 5154                                5154-**********
       1100   C            *IN02      IFEQ '1'
       1200   C                       SETON                        LR
       1300   C                       RETRN
       1400   C                       END
       1500   C                       MOVE SCCMP#     IHCMP#
       1600   C                       MOVE SCLOC#     IHLOC#
       1700   C            KEY        SETLLIBOHDG10
       1800   C            KEY        READEIBOHDG10                  40
       1900   C            *IN40      IFEQ '1'
       2000   C                       MOVE SCQTY      IHQTY
       2100   C                       UPDATIBOHDG10
 * 5198                                5198-*****
       2200   C                       ELSE
       2300   C                       MOVE SCCMP#     IHCMP#
       2400   C                       MOVE SCLOC#     IHLOC#
       2500   C                       MOVE SCORD#     IHORD#
       2600   C                       MOVE SCQTY      IHQTY
       2700   C                       MOVE SCPRC      IHPRCE
       2800   C                       WRITEIBOHDG10
 * 5197                                5197-*****
       2900   C                       END
       3000   C                       GOTO BEGIN
       3100   C                       RETRN
       3200   C            KEY        KLIST
       3300   C                       KFLD            IHCMP#
       3400   C                       KFLD            IHLOC#
       3500   C                       KFLD            IHORD#
       3600   C******************************************************************
D000000        OUTPUT  FIELDS FOR RECORD IBOHDG10 FILE IBOHDGFL FORMAT IBOHDG10
D000001                              BHCMP#     2  CHAR    2
D000002                              BHLOC#     4P PACK   2,0
D000003                              BHACT#     9P PACK   9,0
D000004                              BHORD#    14P PACK   9,0
D000005                              BHSTTS    16  CHAR    2
D000006                              BHTIME    20P PACK   6,0
D000007                              BHSTDT    24P PACK   6,0
D000008                              BHOAMT    29P PACK   9,2
D000009                              BHODSC    32P PACK   4,2
D000010                              BHODTE    36P PACK   6,0
D000011                              BHSDTE    40P PACK   6,0
D000012                              BHOPO#    55  CHAR   15
D000013                              BHORDG    60  CHAR    5
D000014                              BHSHPB    64P PACK   6,0
D000015                              BHINST    94  CHAR   30
D000016                              BHSHWT    96P PACK   2,0
D000017                              BHSHCD    97  CHAR    1
D000018                              BHSHCG   101P PACK   7,2
D000019                              BHSHIN   105P PACK   7,2
D000020                              BHNSHP   106  CHAR    1
D000021                              BHPYDS   108P PACK   3,0
D000022                              BHINVD   112P PACK   6,0
D000023                              BHPPAY   113  CHAR    1
D000024                              BHPPAM   118P PACK   9,2
D000025                              BHSLTX   122P PACK   7,2
```

```
D000026                              BHSPEC    123  CHAR     1
D000027                              BHREP#    126P PACK    5,0
D000028                              BHRSNC    128  CHAR     2
D000029                              BHINIT    134  CHAR     6
D000030                              BHWSTN    144  CHAR    10
D000031                              BHTERM    146  CHAR     2
D000032                              BHJOB#    149P PACK    5,0
D000033                              BHTXCD    153  CHAR     4
D000034                              BHIREP    156P PACK    5,0
D000035                              BHOLOC    158P PACK    2,0
D000036                              BHSHCM    162P PACK    7,2
D000037                              BHSPCG    166P PACK    7,2
D000038                              BHSPCD    196  CHAR    30
D000039                              BHCOD$    199P PACK    4,2
D000040                              BHRSTK    203P PACK    7,2
D000041                              BHTYPE    204  CHAR     1
D000042                              BHAUTH    224  CHAR    20
D000043                              BHJINV    227P PACK    5,0
D000044                              BHCCD#    248  CHAR    21
D000045                              BHCEXD    251P PACK    4,0
D000046                              BHMKEY    257  CHAR     6
D000047                              BHHDLC    258  CHAR     1
D000048                              BHSLTN    259  CHAR     1
D000049                              BHBTYP    260  CHAR     1
D000050                              BHBCH#    262P PACK    3,0
D000051                              BHREF#    267P PACK    9,0
D000052                              BHPPY2    268  CHAR     1
D000053                              BHPP$2    273P PACK    9,2
D000054                              BHPPY3    274  CHAR     1
D000055                              BHPP$3    279P PACK    9,2
D000056                              BHRTYP    280  CHAR     1
D000057                              BHRCK#    285P PACK    9,0
D000058                              BHRUSH    286  CHAR     1
D000059                              BHHELD    288  CHAR     2
D000060                              BHDTRL    292P PACK    6,0
D000061                              BHPRTY    294P PACK    2,0
D000062                              BHSHPM    298  CHAR     4
D000063                              BHSHPD    302P PACK    6,0
D000064                              BHINS#    317  CHAR    15
D000065                              BHSPLS    318P PACK    1,0
D000066                              BHSCG1    322P PACK    7,2
D000067                              BHSCG2    326P PACK    7,2
D000068                              BHSLC1    328P PACK    2,0
D000069                              BHSLC2    330P PACK    2,0
D000070                              BHSST1    331  CHAR     1
D000071                              BHSST2    332  CHAR     1
D000072                              BHSCM1    336P PACK    7,2
D000073                              BHSCM2    340P PACK    7,2
D000074                              BH#CHG    342P PACK    2,0
D000075                              BHIFCC    343  CHAR     1
* * * * * E N D  O F  S O U R C E * * * * *

*  7024       500    IM330TFM FILE NAME HAS NO CALC REFERENCE TO INPUT RECORDS
*  7064       500    IM330TFM FILE NOT REFERENCED FOR OUTPUT
*  7073      1700    KFLD AT SEQ NBR    3300 HAS LENGTH OF    4 BUT KEY FIELD HAS
*  7072      1700    KFLD AT SEQ NBR    3400 IS CHAR BUT KEY FIELD IS PACK.
*  7072      1700    KFLD AT SEQ NBR    3500 IS CHAR BUT KEY FIELD IS PACK.
*  7073      1800    KFLD AT SEQ NBR    3300 HAS LENGTH OF    4 BUT KEY FIELD HAS
*  7072      1800    KFLD AT SEQ NBR    3400 IS CHAR BUT KEY FIELD IS PACK.
*  7072      1800    KFLD AT SEQ NBR    3500 IS CHAR BUT KEY FIELD IS PACK.
```

KEY FIELD INFORMATION

```
                 PHYSICAL    LOGICAL
    FILE/RCD     FIELD       FIELD         ATTRIBUTES


    02  IB0HDGFL
            IB0HDG10
                 BHCMP#                    CHAR   2
                 BHLOC#                    PACK   2,0  SIGNED
                 BHACT#                    PACK   9,0  SIGNED
                 BHORD#                    PACK   9,0  SIGNED
```

CROSS-REFERENCE LISTING

```
         FILE/RCD    DEV/RCD      REFERENCES (D=DEFINED)

     02  IBOHDGFL    DISK         600D
         IBOHDG10                 600D C000000    1700     1800     2100
                                 2800  D000000
     01  IM330TFM    WORKSTN      500D
         IM330T01                 500D A000000
         IM330T91                 500D B000000


         FIELD       ATTR         REFERENCES (M=MODIFIED D=DEFINED)

         *IN02       A(1)         1100
         *IN40       A(1)         1900
* 7031   *IN76       A(1)         A000001
* 7031   *IN79       A(1)         A000002   B000001
         BEGIN       TAG          900D      3000
         BH#CHG      P(2,0)       C000074D  D000074D
         BHACT#      P(9,0)       C000003D  D000003D
         BHAUTH      A(20)        C000042D  D000042D
         BHBCH#      P(3,0)       C000050D  D000050D
         BHBTYP      A(1)         C000049D  D000049D
         BHCCD#      A(21)        C000044D  D000044D
         BHCEXD      P(4,0)       C000045D  D000045D
         BHCMP#      A(2)         C000001D  D000001D
         BHCOD$      P(4,2)       C000039D  D000039D
         BHDTRL      P(6,0)       C000060D  D000060D
         BHHDLC      A(1)         C000047D  D000047D
         BHHELD      A(2)         C000059D  D000059D
         BHIFCC      A(1)         C000075D  D000075D
         BHINIT      A(6)         C000029D  D000029D
         BHINS#      A(15)        C000064D  D000064D
         BHINST      A(30)        C000015D  D000015D
         BHINVD      P(6,0)       C000022D  D000022D
         BHIREP      P(5,0)       C000034D  D000034D
         BHJINV      P(5,0)       C000043D  D000043D
         BHJOB#      P(5,0)       C000032D  D000032D
         BHLOC#      P(2,0)       C000002D  D000002D
         BHMKEY      A(6)         C000046D  D000046D
         BHNSHP      A(1)         C000020D  D000020D
         BHOAMT      P(9,2)       C000008D  D000008D
         BHODSC      P(4,2)       C000009D  D000009D
         BHODTE      P(6,0)       C000010D  D000010D
         BHOLOC      P(2,0)       C000035D  D000035D
         BHOPO#      A(15)        C000012D  D000012D
         BHORD#      P(9,0)       C000004D  D000004D
         BHORDG      A(5)         C000013D  D000013D
         BHPP$2      P(9,2)       C000053D  D000053D
         BHPP$3      P(9,2)       C000055D  D000055D
         BHPPAM      P(9,2)       C000024D  D000024D
         BHPPAY      A(1)         C000023D  D000023D
         BHPPY2      A(1)         C000052D  D000052D
         BHPPY3      A(1)         C000054D  D000054D
         BHPRTY      P(2,0)       C000061D  D000061D
         BHPYDS      P(3,0)       C000021D  D000021D
         BHRCK#      P(9,0)       C000057D  D000057D
         BHREF#      P(9,0)       C000051D  D000051D
         BHREP#      P(5,0)       C000027D  D000027D
         BHRSNC      A(2)         C000028D  D000028D
         BHRSTK      P(7,2)       C000040D  D000040D
         BHRTYP      A(1)         C000056D  D000056D
         BHRUSH      A(1)         C000058D  D000058D
         BHSCG1      P(7,2)       C000066D  D000066D
         BHSCG2      P(7,2)       C000067D  D000067D
         BHSCM1      P(7,2)       C000072D  D000072D
         BHSCM2      P(7,2)       C000073D  D000073D
         BHSDTE      P(6,0)       C000011D  D000011D
         BHSHCD      A(1)         C000017D  D000017D
         BHSHCG      P(7,2)       C000018D  D000018D
         BHSHCM      P(7,2)       C000036D  D000036D
         BHSHIN      P(7,2)       C000019D  D000019D
         BHSHPB      P(6,0)       C000014D  D000014D
         BHSHPD      P(6,0)       C000063D  D000063D
```

```
            BHSHPM       A(4)       C000062D  D000062D
            BHSHWT       P(2,0)     C000016D  D000016D
            BHSLC1       P(2,0)     C000068D  D000068D
            BHSLC2       P(2,0)     C000069D  D000069D
            BHSLTN       A(1)       C000048D  D000048D
            BHSLTX       P(7,2)     C000025D  D000025D
            BHSPCD       A(30)      C000038D  D000038D
            BHSPCG       P(7,2)     C000037D  D000037D
            BHSPEC       A(1)       C000026D  D000026D
            BHSPLS       P(1,0)     C000065D  D000065D
            BHSST1       A(1)       C000070D  D000070D
            BHSST2       A(1)       C000071D  D000071D
            BHSTDT       P(6,0)     C000007D  D000007D
            BHSTTS       A(2)       C000005D  D000005D
            BHTERM       A(2)       C000031D  D000031D
            BHTIME       P(6,0)     C000006D  D000006D
            BHTXCD       A(4)       C000033D  D000033D
            BHTYPE       A(1)       C000041D  D000041D
            BHWSTN       A(10)      C000030D  D000030D
*  7030     IHCMP#       A(4)          1500M     2300M     3300
*  7030     IHLOC#       A(4)          1600M     2400M     3400
*  7030     IHORD#       A(4)          2500M     3500
*  7030     IHPRCE       A(4)          2700M
*  7030     IHQTY        A(4)          2000M     2600M
            KEY          KLIST         1700      1800      3200D
*  7030     SCCMP#       A(4)          1500      2300
*  7030     SCLOC#       A(4)          1600      2400
            SCORD#       P(9,0)     A000003D     2500
*  7030     SCPRC        A(4)          2700
*  7031     SCPRNT       A(1)       A000004D
*  7030     SCQTY        A(4)          2000      2600
*  7031     SCUPDT       A(1)       A000005D
            '1'          LITERAL       1100      1900


            INDICATOR  REFERENCES (M=MODIFIED D=DEFINED)

            *IN          A000001   A000002   B000001    1100      1900
            LR              1200M
*  7030     02              1100
            40              1800M       1900
*  7031     76           A000001
*  7031     79           A000002   B000001



     MESSAGES

       MSGID    SEV    NUMBER    TEXT

*  QRG1019     00        1      IGNDECERR(*YES) SPECIFIED ON COMMAND. NO DECIMAL DATA ERRORS
*  QRG5154     30        1      RECORD FORMAT NAME IN FACTOR 2 (POSITIONS 33-42) NOT DEFINED
                                IGNORED.

*  QRG5197     30        1      WRITE OPERATION NOT VALID FOR THIS FILE. SPECIFICATION IGNORE
*  QRG5198     30        1      UPDAT/DELET OPERATION NOT VALID. SPECIFICATION IGNORED
*  QRG7024     20        1      INPUT RECORD NOT REFERENCED BY CALCULATION OPERATIONS.
*  QRG7030     30       10      FIELD OR INDICATOR NOT DEFINED.
*  QRG7031     00        6      NAME OR INDICATOR NOT REFERENCED.
*  QRG7064     40        1      PROGRAM FILE NOT REFERENCED. FILE IGNORED
*  QRG7072     30        4      KFLD TYPE NOT SAME AS CORRESPONDING KEY FIELD IN FILE. SPECIF
*  QRG7073     30        2      LENGTH OF KFLD NOT SAME AS CORRESPONDING KEY FIELD IN FILE. S


     MESSAGE SUMMARY

       TOTAL    00     10     20     30     40     50
        28       7      0      1     19      1      0

       36 RECORDS READ FROM SOURCE FILE
       SOURCE RECORDS INCLUDE   29 SPECIFICATIONS,    0 TABLE RECORDS, AND    7 COMMENTS

     QRG0008 COMPILE TERMINATED. SEVERITY 40 ERRORS FOUND IN PROGRAM

              * * * * * E N D  O F  C O M P I L A T I O N * * * * *
*  QRG1020                    ERROR OCCURRED CREATING OR UPDATING DATA AREA RETURNCODE. COMPIL
```

PROGRAMMING PROJECT

Project Overview

An inventory master file is to be updated with new inventory data by means of transactions entered on a display screen. All transactions are edited for valid part number and valid transaction code. The master file is updated only if entries are valid.

Design and code the DDS to describe the screens, and then write the RPG program to allow a user to perform these updates. Sample data for this project can be found in Appendix D.

Input Format

The master file data for the project is found in a file called INVMAST in the sample data. The Record Layout for this file is shown in Figure 16.27.

Processing

The first screen allows the entry of a part number and a transaction code. If the transaction code is not A, C, or D, an error message is displayed and the first screen is redisplayed.

If the record is to be added (code A), the part number must not already exist in the INVMAST file. If it does exist, an error message is displayed. If it does not exist, a second screen is displayed showing the part number followed by blank spaces where the rest of the fields are to be entered. After the second screen has been filled in and the enter key has been pressed, the fields are moved to the INVMAST fields, the INVMAST is updated, the screen fields are returned to blanks, and the first screen is redisplayed. If a command key 1 is pressed, no record is added and the first screen is redisplayed.

If a record is to be changed (code C) the part number must exist in the INVMAST file. If it does not exist, an error message is displayed. If it does exist, the old record is displayed on the second screen. After the changes have been entered on the second screen and the enter key has been pressed, the fields are moved to the INVMAST fields, the INVMAST is updated, the screen fields are returned to blanks, and the first screen is redisplayed. If a command key 1 is pressed, no change takes place and the first screen is redisplayed.

If a record is to be deleted (code D), the part number must exist in the INVMAST file. The old record is displayed on the second screen before deletion. If the enter key is pressed, the record is deleted from the INVMAST file, the screen fields are returned to blanks, and the first screen is redisplayed. If a command key 1 is pressed, no deletion takes place and the first screen is redisplayed.

Output Format (Display Screen Layout)

The output format for the project is a screen with standard headings. The screen will show the part number, division number, part name, type, style, and warehouse. The screen layouts for this project are shown in Figure 16.28.

Examples of the screens are shown in Figures 16.29(a), 16.29(b), and 16.29(c).

FIGURE 16.27 Programming Project: Record Layout

```
IBM                         RECORD LAYOUT
DATE
FILE
NAME  INVMAST          Record Layout Application Program    FORMAT NAME

     DIV | PART # |    PART NAME    | TYPE | STYLE | WHSE | S
                                                            T
                                                            A
                                                            E
```

FIGURE 16.28 Programming Project: Screen Layouts

Display Screen 1 Layout Sheet

Row 02: PJX1629   INVENTORY UPDATE
Row 06:   ENTER TRAN CODE + PART#
Row 08:   X   XXXXXX
Rows 09–12: XXXXXXXXXXXXXXXXXXXXXXXXXXXXXX
Row 22:   CF-01 TO EXIT

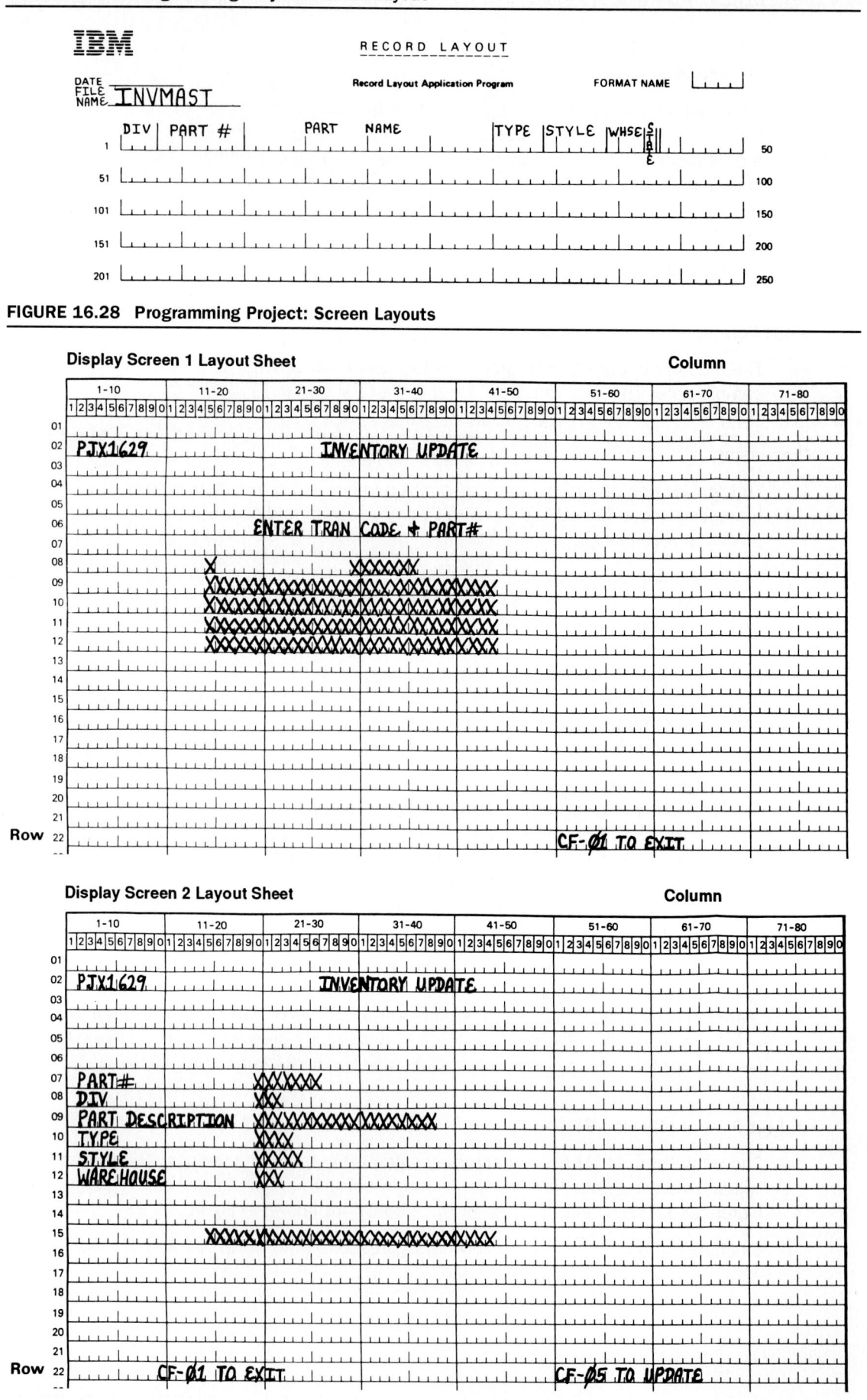

Display Screen 2 Layout Sheet

Row 02: PJX1629   INVENTORY UPDATE
Row 07: PART#   XXXXXX
Row 08: DIV   XX
Row 09: PART DESCRIPTION XXXXXXXXXXXXXXXXX
Row 10: TYPE   XXXX
Row 11: STYLE   XXXXX
Row 12: WAREHOUSE   XX
Row 15:   XXXXXXXXXXXXXXXXXXXXXXX
Row 22: CF-01 TO EXIT   CF-05 TO UPDATE

FIGURE 16.29(a)   Programming Project: Sample Screen 1

```
PJX1629                    INVENTORY UPDATE


                       ENTER TRAN CODE & PART#

















                                                        CF-01 TO EXIT
```

FIGURE 16.29(b)   Programming Project: Sample Screen 1

```
PJX1629                    INVENTORY UPDATE


                       ENTER TRAN CODE & PART#
                  A              00025













                                                        CF-01 TO EXIT
```

FIGURE 16.29(c)   Programming Project: Sample Screen 2

```
PJX1629                    INVENTORY UPDATE



       PART#            0000025
       DIV
       PART DESCRIPTION
       TYPE
       STYLE
       WAREHOUSE







            CF-01 TO EXIT                    CF-05 TO UPDATE
```

Chapter 17

Using Subfiles in RPG III/400

What you will learn in Chapter 17

Sample Inquiry Program Using Subfiles
  Defining a Subfile in the DDS
  Subfile Key Words
  Describing the Subfile in RPG III/400
  Loading the Subfile with Data

Clearing the Subfile
Displaying the Subfile
File Updates Using Subfiles (READC)
Managing Subfiles
  Subfile Key Words

Determining Subfile Size and Subfile Page Size
Accessing Specific Records in a Subfile
Using Multiple Subfiles
Exiting to Other Screens or Programs

There is often a need to display a group of records on the same screen. Figure 17.1 shows a screen that displays a list of employees. Each line on the screen represents one employee contained in one record in a data file. The display allows the user to scan more than one employee record at a time.

Displaying a group of similar data on a screen is done in RPG III/400 by gathering all the records to be displayed into a special group called a subfile, which is then displayed on the screen. A subfile is not a file in the conventional sense, such as files residing permanently on disk. It is a temporary file that is set up within a program and read from or written to a display screen.

In previous examples of on-line applications, only a single record was read or written to the screen at one time. There are many situations where this approach would be too slow. The following are examples of applications in which a group of records needs to be displayed on the same screen:

- The user needs to locate information for which the specific selection key is unknown.
- The user needs to select the correct record from a group of records for processing or to retrieve more detailed information.
- The user needs to see an entire group of records to determine which are in error and to correct the data where needed.
- A user is performing a data entry function in which rapid entry is needed.
- A user may need to see existing information before adding or modifying specific records. This screen would permit inquiry, adding records, and changing existing records.

Subfiles are valuable tools for displaying larger groups of information. Figure 17.2 shows the structure of a subfile.

FIGURE 17.1 Employee File Display

```
ILL171                    EMPLOYEE INQUIRY

EMPL#       EMPLOYEE NAME      ADDRESS              CITY/STATE
321         KEVIN BEHR         123 ACE BLVD         WHITEFIELD    MA
0542        KRYSTLE CLEAR      6582 BASS WAY        SEASIDE       CA
3258        MERRIDEE DANCER    9568 LOTUS BLVD      MAUI          HA
456         ASTRID LEON-TERRA  321 KAPOLANI AVE     HONOLULU      HA
2323        OWEN MOHR          222 ANY STREET       DULUTH        OH
9898        ANDY GAIN          835 LAKEWOOD BL      LODI          CA
```

FIGURE 17.2 Structure of a Subfile

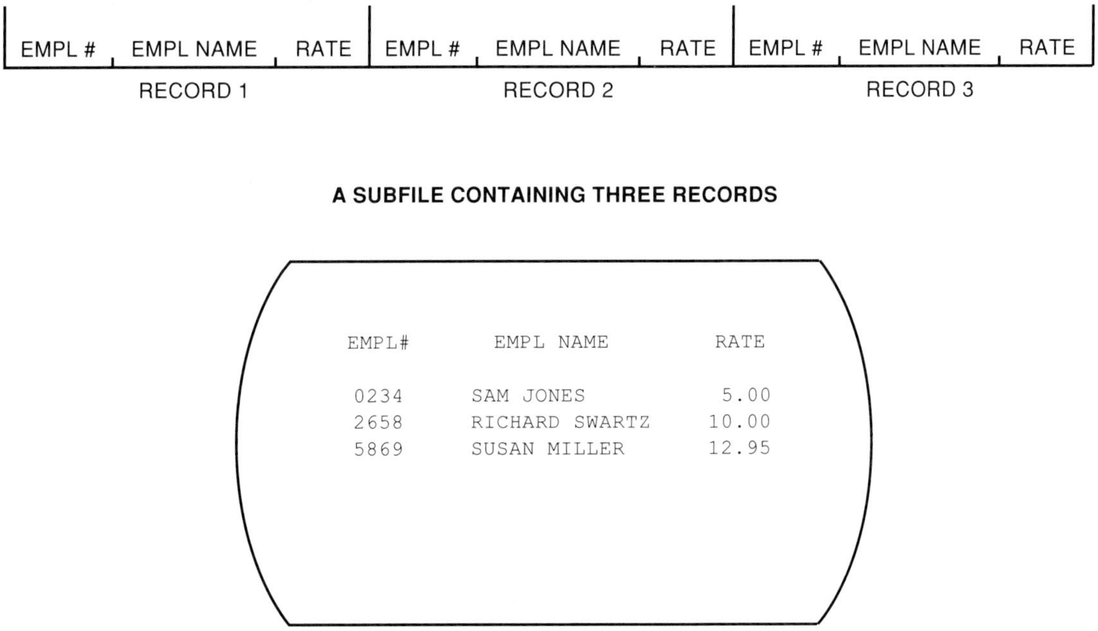

EMPL #	EMPL NAME	RATE	EMPL #	EMPL NAME	RATE	EMPL #	EMPL NAME	RATE
	RECORD 1			RECORD 2			RECORD 3	

A SUBFILE CONTAINING THREE RECORDS

```
    EMPL#       EMPL NAME         RATE

    0234        SAM JONES         5.00
    2658        RICHARD SWARTZ   10.00
    5869        SUSAN MILLER     12.95
```

The Data Description Specification (DDS) makes it possible to handle subfiles with relative ease in the RPG III/400 program. Subfiles have specific requirements for being handled in the DDS. It may be helpful to visualize a subfile as if it were simply a very large array, containing entire records instead of individual fields. Each data element is one record or block of information. Here the similarity ends, however, since subfiles are processed differently from simple arrays in RPG.

SAMPLE INQUIRY PROGRAM USING SUBFILES ■

To demonstrate the use of subfiles, a program will be described that will display a group of customer records on the screen. When the program is requested, the user will enter a customer number. The customer file will be searched for this customer number. A group of 80 records will be placed in a subfile and displayed on the screen in groups of 10 lines at a time. To see more of the file, the user will use the roll-up and roll-down keys to scan through the 80 records. Figure 17.3 shows the format of the screen.

Only ten lines of the subfile will be displayed at one time on the screen. This allows a few lines at the top of the screen for headings and at the bottom of the screen for messages or other information.

FIGURE 17.3 Customer Inquiry Screen

```
ILL1716                              CUSTOMER INQUIRY

CUST         CUSTOMER NAME      MONTH-TO-DATE    YEAR-TO-DATE
00032    SAMS PLACE                     1,893           1,893
00045    FRESH FOODS MARKET            32,000          96,000
00059    METHOD MARKETS                20,500         350,000
00078    OPEN MARKETS                  37,500         398,562
00128    OPEN MARKETS BRANCH           98,500         935,601
01023    VPMI INDUSTRIES            1,068,000       5,680,500
02345    BULLFROG INC.                  3,580         586,541
04568    FIRST CITY BANK            9,005,180       9,005,180
06892    DOLLAR INC.                  865,018      88,665,018
09871    BOOKS INC.                   459,080         956,172
```

Defining a Subfile in the DDS

Two record formats are needed in the Data Description Specification to describe a subfile. The first format, the description of the subfile record (called the subfile record format), is described like any other screen format. The second format (the subfile control record format) is the description of the attributes of the subfile, the search input field, the constants, and the command keys. The subfile control description must immediately follow the description of the subfile record.

The subfile record format contains the field information and its positions on the screen display. The format name for the subfile record format is entered in columns 19–26, as shown in Figure 17.4.

Subfile Key Words

The name of the subfile record format in this example is SUBCUS. The key word SFL is entered beginning in column 45. This identifies the record format as a subfile format. The other entries describe the placement of each field as it will appear on the screen. Since this will be an inquiry program, the fields are designated as output only. The line number indicates the line on which the first record of the subfile group is to appear. The position entries indicate the placement of each field on the line.

The subfile control record format causes the READ, WRITE, or any control operations of a subfile to take place. In the example in Figure 17.5, the format name for the subfile control record

FIGURE 17.4 DDS for Subfile Record Format

DATA DESCRIPTION SPECIFICATIONS

Seq	Type	Name	R	Length	Line	Pos	Functions
A							REF(MASTFILE)
A	R	SUBCUS					SFL
A		CUS#	R		5	2	
A		CUSNAM	R		5	9	
A		CUSMTD	R		5	31	EDTCDE(K)
A		CUSYTD	R		5	47	EDTCDE(K)

FIGURE 17.5 DDS for Subfile Control Record Format

```
                                    DATA DESCRIPTION SPECIFICATIONS

     A
                                              R CTLCUS                        SFLCTL (SUBCUS)
     A                                                                        SFLCLR
     A   60                                                                   SFLDSPCTL
     A  N60                                                                   SFLDSP
     A   65                                                                   SFLPAG(10)
     A                                                                        SFLSIZ(80)
     A  *
     A                                                                        OVERLAY
     A                                                                        ROLLUP(50 'ROLL TO NEXT SCREEN')
     A                                                                        PUTRETAIN
     A                                                                    2 32'CUSTOMER INQUIRY'
     A                                                                    4  2'CUST#'
     A                                                                    4 14'CUSTOMER NAME'
     A                                                                    4 32'MONTH-TO-DATE'
     A                                                                    4 48'YEAR-TO-DATE'
```

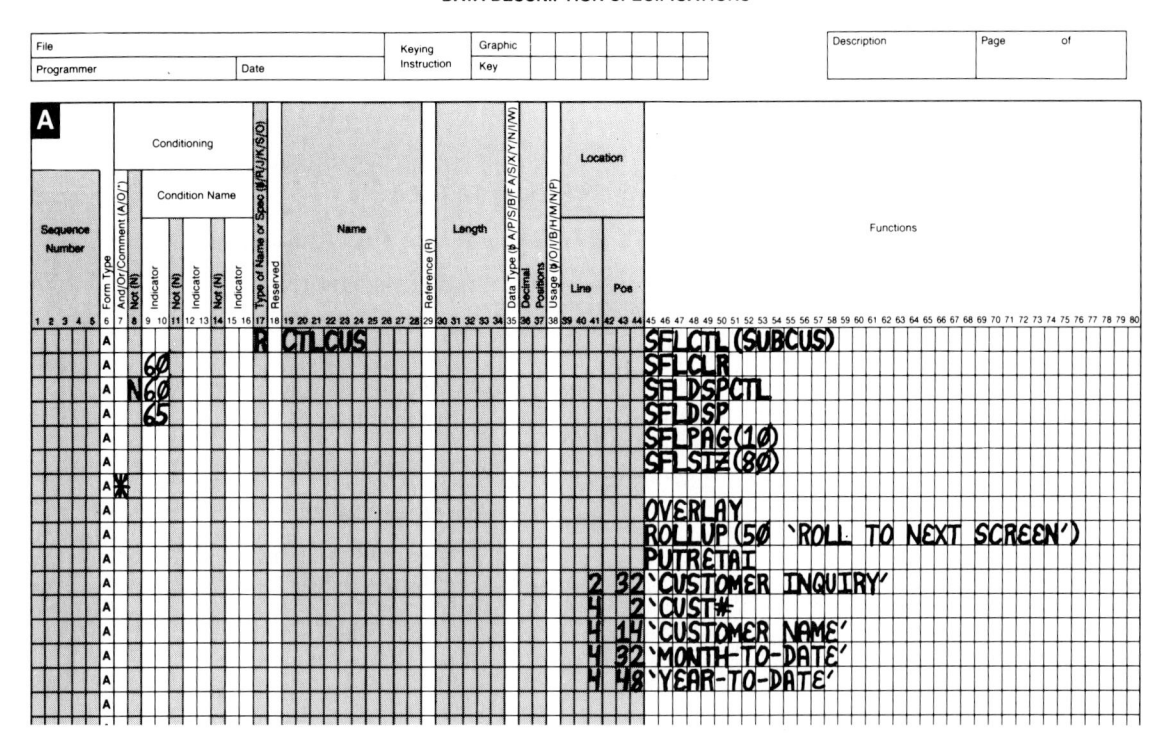

format, which is assigned by the programmer, is CTLCUS. The key word SFLCTL, beginning in column 45, is followed by the name of the associated subfile record format (SUBCUS) in parentheses. This defines the relationship between the subfile record format and the subfile control record.

The subfile control record contains several definitions that will control the activities of the subfile as follows.

- The SFLCLR key word is used for clearing the subfile. This will need to be done any time a new set of data is to be entered into the subfile. In this example, indicator 60 will control the clear function. When indicator 60 is on, the subfile will be cleared.
- The SFLDSPCTL key word indicates when to display the subfile control record. In this example, when indicator 60 is off, the control record will be displayed.
- The SFLDSP key word indicates when to display the subfile itself. In this example, when indicator 65 is on, the subfile will be displayed.
- The SFLPAG key word indicates the number of subfile records that will be displayed on a screen at one time. In this example, the number of records per page (or screen) is 10.
- The SFLSIZ key word indicates the total number of records that will be included in the subfile. In this example, the subfile size will be 80. The subfile size must be a multiple of the page size.
- The OVERLAY key word indicates that a new screen of data will replace or overlay the previous data displayed on the screen. This is used when the first screen is no longer needed.
- The ROLLUP key word indicates that indicator 50 will be set on in the program when the user presses the roll-up key.
- The PUTRETAIN key word indicates that the value in the requesting field (SCCUST) will not be blanked out or replaced when the subfile is displayed or rolled up.

The column headings and their locations on the screen are also defined on the subfile control record format.

The display file must be created before it can be used in the program. Figure 17.6 shows the entire DDS for the display file, including the subfile definition.

FIGURE 17.6 Complete DDS for Display File Using Subfile

```
FILE NAME -        IL1716FM.CABLE        TYPE OF FILE -      DISPLAY
SOURCE FILE -      QDDSSRC.CABLE         MEMBER -            IL1716FM       02/24/92
TYPE OF DATA -     *DATA
OPTIONS -          *SRC   *LIST
GENLVL -           20
AUTHORITY -        *ALL
TEXT -             DDS FOR ILLUS 17.16
COMPILER -         IBM SYSTEM/38 DATA DESCRIPTION PROCESSOR

                                    DATA DESCRIPTION SOURCE

     SEQNBR *... ... 1 ... ... 2 ... ... 3 ... ... 4 ... ... 5 ... ... 6 ... ... 7 ...

       100      A* TITLE: ENTER REQUEST SCREEN FOR INQUIRY (PROJECT 17.16)
       200      A* DATE:  7/13/91      AUTHOR:
       300      A* DESCRIPTION:  SUBFILES
       400      A***********************************************************
       500      A                                          PRINT
       600      A                                          CA01(01 'END OF PROGRAM')
       700      A                                          REF(CUSTMAST)
       800      A          R IL171601
       900      A                                        2 27'CUSTOMER MASTER INQUIRY'
      1000      A                                        2  2'ILL1716'
      1100      A                                        6 20'ENTER CUST#'
      1200      A            SCCUST         5  B         8 25
      1300      A  75                                          ERRMSG('RECORDS NOT FOUND')
      1400      A                                       22 51 'CF-01 TO EXIT'
      1500      A          R SUBCUS                           SFL
      1600      A            CUSNUM       R              5  2
      1700      A            CUSNAM       R              5  9
      1800      A            CUSMTD       R              5 31EDTCDE(K)
      1900      A            CUSYTD       R              5 47EDTCDE(K)
      2000      A*
      2100      A          R CTLCUS                           SFLCTL(SUBCUS)
      2200      A   60                                        SFLCLR
      2300      A  N60                                        SFLDSPCTL
      2400      A   65                                        SFLDSP
      2500      A                                             SFLPAG(10)
      2600      A                                             SFLSIZ(80)
      2700      A*
      2800      A                                             OVERLAY
      2900      A                                             ROLLUP(50 'ROLL TO NEXT SCREEN')
      3000      A                                             PUTRETAIN
      3100      A                                        2  2'ILL1716'
      3200      A                                        2 32'CUSTOMER INQUIRY'
      3300      A                                        4  2'CUST'
      3400      A                                        4 14'CUSTOMER NAME'
      3500      A                                        4 32'MONTH-TO-DATE'
      3600      A                                        4 48'YEAR-TO-DATE'

                   * * * * *  E N D   O F   S O U R C E  * * * * *
```

Describing the Subfile in RPG III/400

Processing a subfile requires that its entries be created within the program before the subfile can be displayed to the screen. Figure 17.7 shows the logic used in a program to load a subfile with data and display it. It also shows how data can be updated in the subfile.

Figure 17.8 shows the File Description Specifications describing the customer master file and a workstation file. The workstation file will use subfile processing.

The customer master file (CUSTMAST) is described as an input file since the program is an inquiry. The workstation file is described as a display file and is immediately followed by the subfile description entry.

In the subfile description entry, the name of the subfile record format, SUBCUS, is entered in columns 60–66. The entry K in column 53 identifies this as a continuation line. The entry SFILE in columns 54–59 identifies this as a subfile description. The entry RRN in columns 47–52 is the name of a field containing the relative record number used to locate each record in the subfile. All access to records in a subfile is controlled by the relative record number.

FIGURE 17.7 Diagram of Subfile Processing

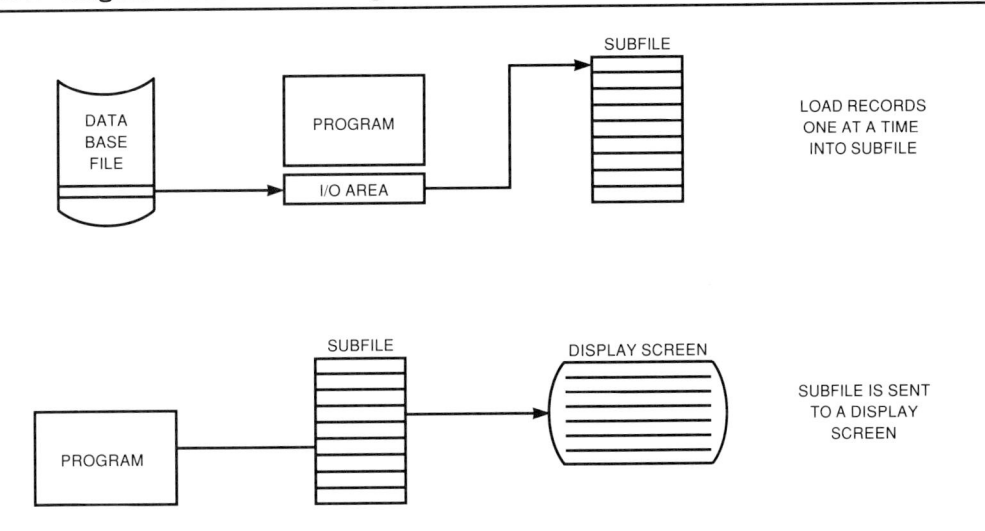

FIGURE 17.8 File Description Specification for Customer Master File and Workstation File

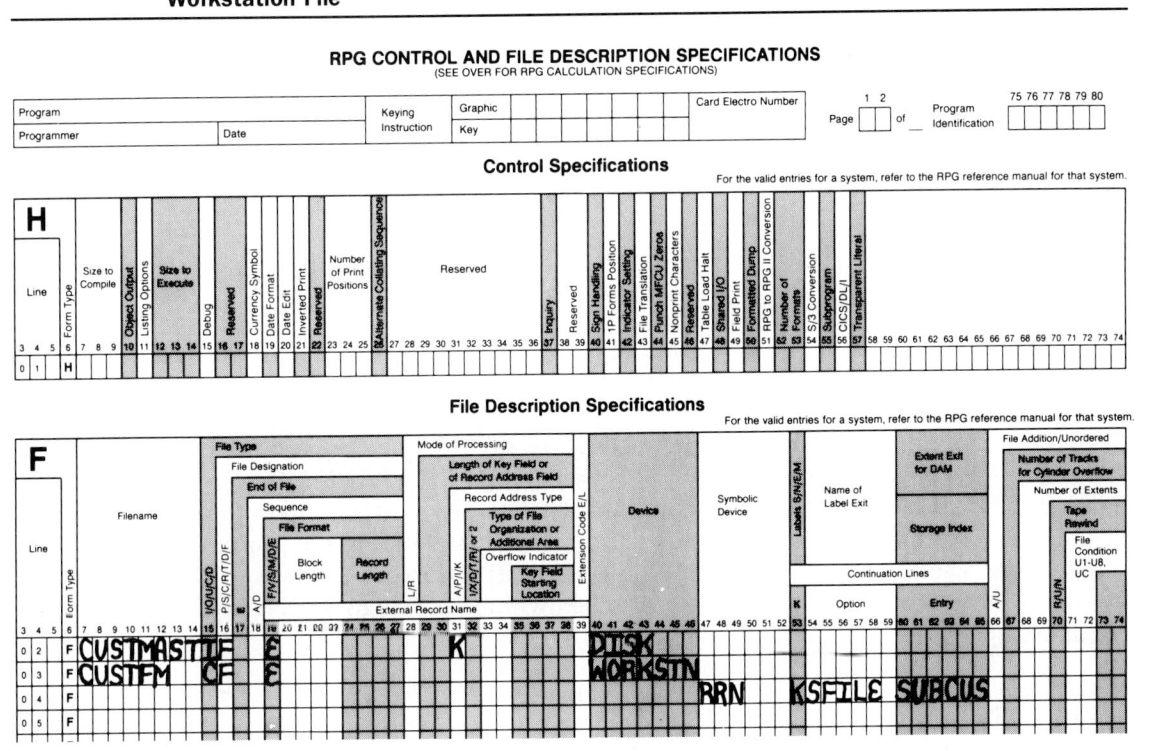

Loading the Subfile with Data

Before the subfile can be displayed on the screen, it will be necessary to create it. At the start of the program, all data resides in the CUSTMAST data file. When the initial prompt screen is displayed, as shown in Figure 17.9, the subfile contains all blank records.

Figure 17.10 shows the coding for displaying the initial prompt. If indicator KA is on, the user has requested escape from the screen. The LR indicator will be set on and the program will end. In this case, control is being returned to some other calling program or menu with the use of the RETRN operation.

Chapter 17 Using Subfiles in RPG III/400 **451**

FIGURE 17.9 Initial Prompt Screen

```
ILL1716                    CUSTOMER MASTER INQUIRY


                           ENTER CUST#
                              0003?


                                                       CF-01 TO EXIT
```

FIGURE 17.10 Calculation Specifications: Displaying the Initial Prompt

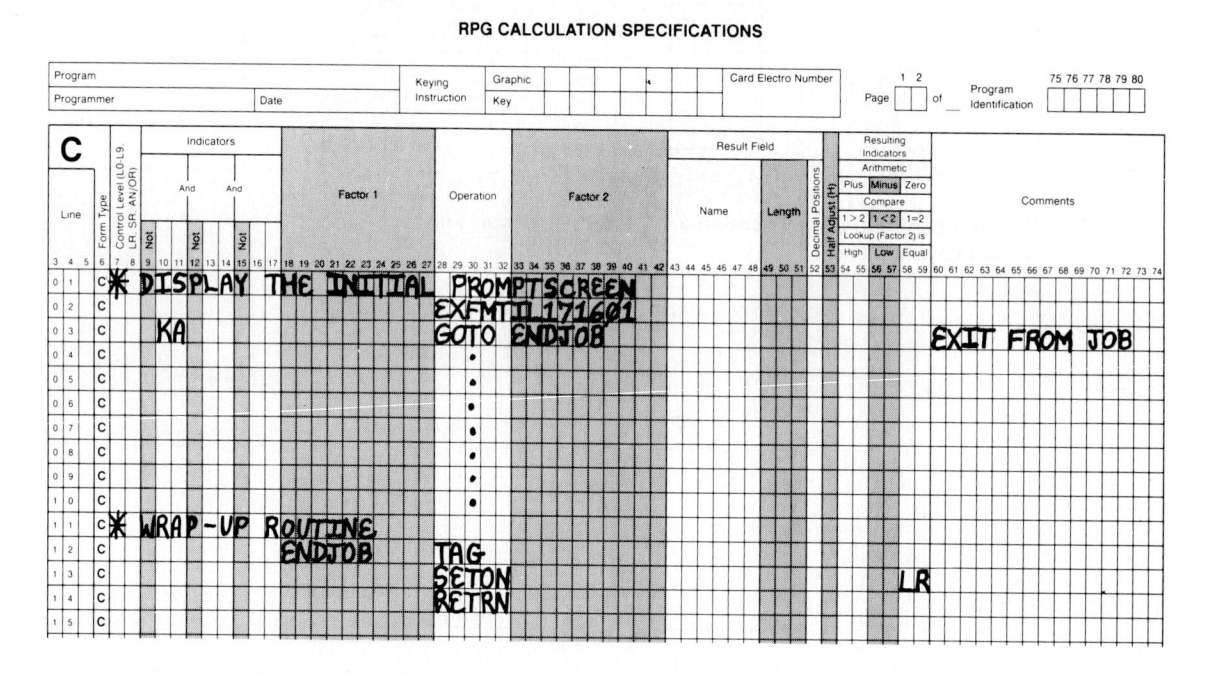

RPG CALCULATION SPECIFICATIONS

```
01 C* DISPLAY THE INITIAL PROMPT SCREEN
02 C                    EXFMT ILL171601
03 C  KA                GOTO  ENDJOB                              EXIT FROM JOB
04 C
05 C
06 C
07 C
08 C
09 C
10 C
11 C* WRAP-UP ROUTINE
12 C        ENDJOB      TAG
13 C                    SETON                                     LR
14 C                    RETRN
15 C
```

When the user enters a customer number at the prompt, the program searches the customer master file for a beginning point. This is done with a SETLL and READ. If no records are found, indicator 75 is set on. This means the requested number is beyond the end of the customer master file, and an error message is displayed. The program must return to the prompt and display the screen again. The coding in Figure 17.11 shows how this is done.

When the user enters a customer number within the range available, the program can continue.

Clearing the Subfile

If this is not the first time through the program, there will be data in the subfile that must be cleared before more records can be entered. The routine for clearing the subfile is shown in Figure 17.12. Refer back to Figure 17.5 and notice that indicator 60 was defined on the DDS to control the time at which the subfile is to be cleared or displayed. When indicator 60 is on, all records are cleared from the subfile and the subfile control record format is written.

Now the program can begin loading records into the subfile. Figure 17.13 shows the coding for loading the records. The field RRN must be defined as two positions of numeric data even though the field name was mentioned earlier in the File Description Specifications. The field RRN must be initialized to 1 to start the relative record number for the subfile at the correct position.

The first record read will be loaded as the first record in the subfile. Since the first requested record was read in the initialize module, the next WRITE operation in this routine will write a record to the subfile, SUBCUS. Notice that this is writing to the subfile record (SUBCUS), not to the

FIGURE 17.11 Error Message Will Display When Indicator 75 Is On

RPG CALCULATION SPECIFICATIONS

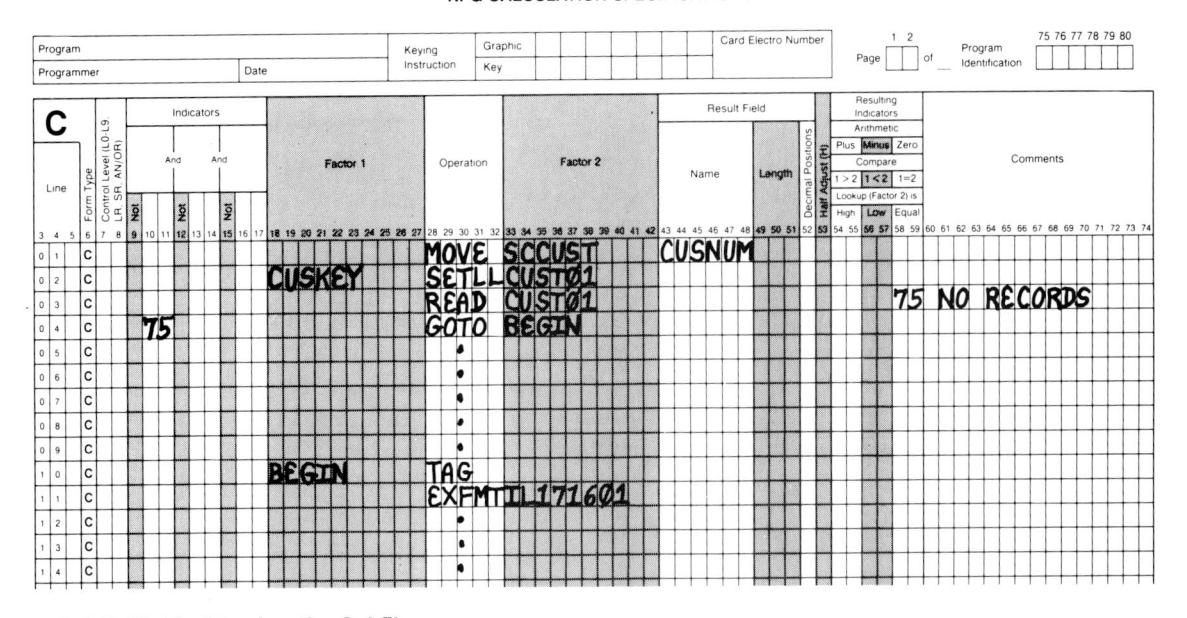

```
Line  Factor 1    Operation  Factor 2      Result    Len  Indicators
01 C              MOVE       SCCUST        CUSNUM
02 C  CUSKEY      SETLL      CUST01
03 C              READ       CUST01                       75 NO RECORDS
04 C  75          GOTO       BEGIN
05 C
06 C
07 C
08 C
09 C
10 C  BEGIN       TAG
11 C              EXFMTIL171601
12 C
13 C
14 C
```

FIGURE 17.12 Clearing the Subfile

RPG CALCULATION SPECIFICATIONS

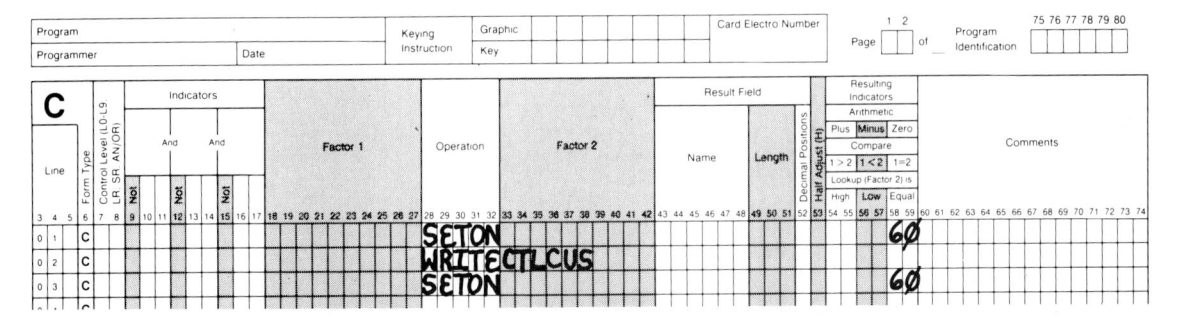

```
01 C   SETON                              60
02 C   WRITECTLCUS
03 C   SETON                              60
```

FIGURE 17.13 Loading the Records

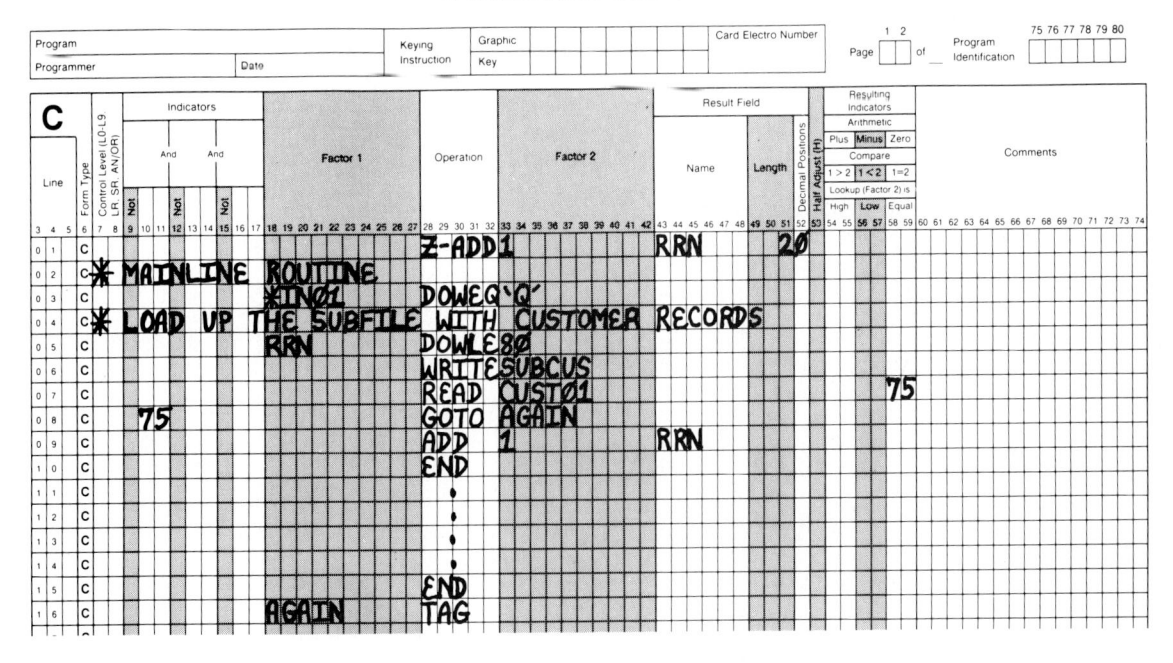

RPG CALCULATION SPECIFICATIONS

```
01 C                Z-ADD 1         RRN    20
02 C* MAINLINE ROUTINE
03 C       *IN01    DOWEQ 'Q'
04 C* LOAD UP THE SUBFILE WITH CUSTOMER RECORDS
05 C       RRN      DOWLE 80
06 C                WRITESUBCUS
07 C                READ  CUST01                  75
08 C       75       GOTO  AGAIN
09 C                ADD   1         RRN
10 C                END
11 C
12 C
13 C
14 C
15 C                END
16 C       AGAIN    TAG
```

subfile control record. The relative record number is incremented by 1 each time a record is added to the subfile. This routine will continue until the subfile is full (80 records) unless the customer master file reaches the end of the data, in which case indicator 75 will be set on. In either event, no more records will be stored in the subfile. The programmer must be careful that the relative record number (in this case, the field called RRN) never exceeds the size of the subfile. If this occurs, the program will fail when it attempts to reach the invalid number.

Since the field names in the subfile may not be the same as the field names in the customer master record, it may be necessary to move the CUSTMAST field names into the corresponding fields in the subfile. Figure 17.14 shows how this might be coded.

Displaying the Subfile

Once the subfile has been built, the program can send one page of the subfile to the screen in one WRITE operation. The coding is shown in Figure 17.15.

Notice that it is the subfile control record that is written to the screen. Writing the subfile control record causes a page of records in the subfile to be displayed. Figure 17.16 shows a compiled listing of the entire program for displaying a subfile.

FIGURE 17.14 Moving Data to Screen Output Fields

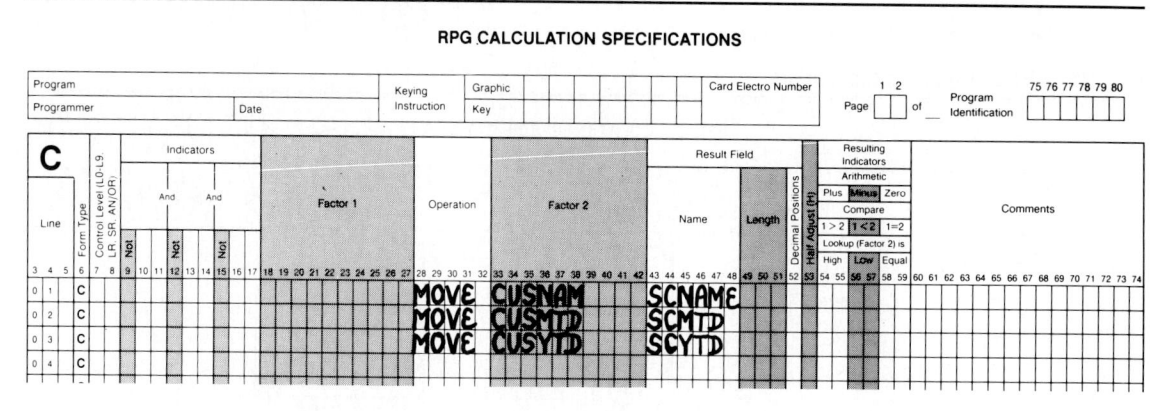

```
C           MOVE  CUSNAM    SCNAME
C           MOVE  CUSMTD    SCMTD
C           MOVE  CUSYTD    SCYTD
C
```

FIGURE 17.15 Displaying the Subfile

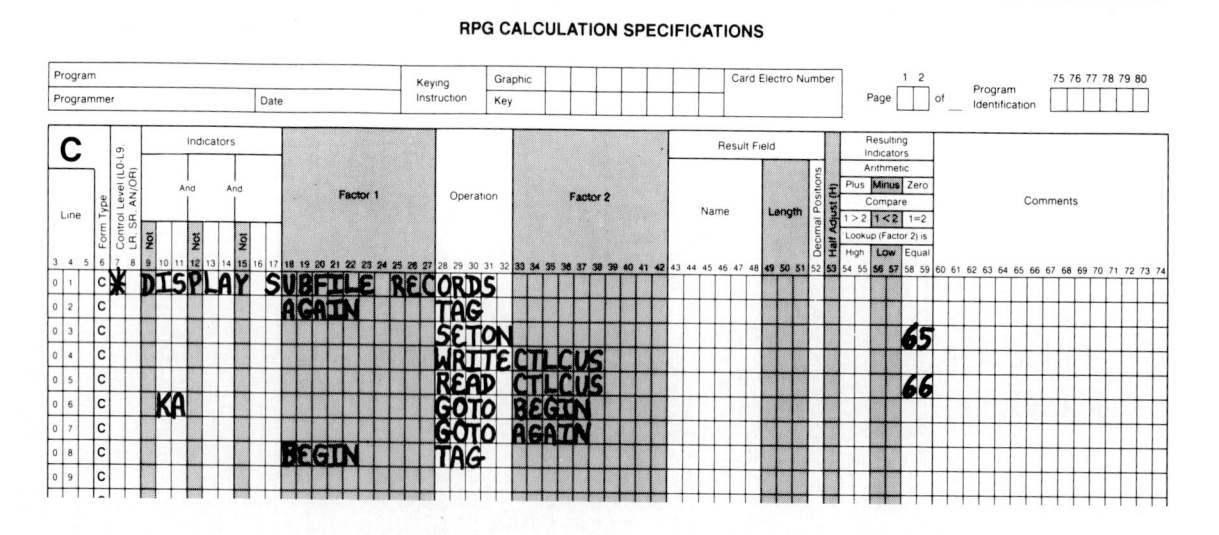

```
C* DISPLAY SUBFILE RECORDS
C     AGAIN   TAG
C             SETON                    65
C             WRITE CTLCUS
C             READ  CTLCUS             66
C   KA        GOTO  BEGIN
C             GOTO  AGAIN
C     BEGIN   TAG
C
```

FIGURE 17.16 Compiled Program for Displaying a Subfile

```
SEQUENCE       1         2         3         4         5         6         7
NUMBER    678901234567890123456789012345678901234567890123456789012345678901234


         100   F* TITLE: ILLUS 17.16 INQUIRY (WITH SUBFILES) CUSTMAST
         200   F* DATE:   7/14         AUTHOR: D.CABLE
         300   F* DESCRIPTION:
         400   F********************************************************

NAME OF PROGRAM WILL BE ILL1716 IN LIBRARY CABLE

               H
* 1019              ALL DECIMAL DATA ERRORS IGNORED
         500   FIL1716FMCF  E                    WORKSTN
         600   F                                       RRN     KSFILE SUBCUS
                 RECORD FORMAT(S):  FILE IL1716FM LIB CABLE
                         EXTERNAL FORMAT IL171601 RPG NAME IL171601
                         EXTERNAL FORMAT SUBCUS  RPG NAME SUBCUS
                         EXTERNAL FORMAT CTLCUS  RPG NAME CTLCUS

         700   FCUSTMASTIF  E            K        DISK
         800   F********************************************************


         900   C* START-UP ROUTINE
                 RECORD FORMAT(S):  FILE CUSTMAST LIB CABLE
                         EXTERNAL FORMAT CUST01 RPG NAME CUST01
A000000        INPUT   FIELDS FOR RECORD IL171601 FILE IL1716FM FORMAT IL171601
A000001                                               1   1 *IN01                END
A000002                                               2   6 SCCUST
B000000        INPUT   FIELDS FOR RECORD SUBCUS FILE IL1716FM FORMAT SUBCUS
B000001                                               1   1 *IN01                END
B000002                                               2   6 CUSNUM
B000003                                               7  26 CUSNAM
B000004                                              27  34 0CUSMTD
B000005                                              35  44 0CUSYTD
C000000        INPUT   FIELDS FOR RECORD CTLCUS FILE IL1716FM FORMAT CTLCUS
C000001                                               1   1 *IN01                END
C000002                                               2   2 *IN50                ROLL
D000000        INPUT   FIELDS FOR RECORD CUST01 FILE CUSTMAST FORMAT CUST01
D000001                                               1   5 CUSNUM
D000002                                               6  25 CUSNAM
D000003                                              26  28 CUSCAT
D000004                                              29  36 0CUSMTD
D000005                                              37  46 0CUSYTD
D000006                                              47  66 CUSADR
D000007                                              67  76 CUSCTY
D000008                                              77  78 CUSST
D000009                                              79  87 CUSZIP
        1000   C           CUSKEY    KLIST
        1100   C                     KFLD           CUSNUM
        1200   C                     EXFMTIL171601
        1300   C      KA             GOTO ENDJOB
        1400   C                     Z-ADD1         RRN
        1500   C                     MOVE SCCUST    CUSNUM
        1600   C           CUSKEY    SETLLCUST01
        1700   C                     READ CUST01                    75           3
        1800   C      75             GOTO BEGIN
        1900   C*
        2000   C* MAINLINE ROUTINE
        2100   C           *IN01     DOWEQ'0'
        2200   C* LOAD UP THE SUBFILE WITH CUSTOMER RECORDS
        2300   C           RRN       DOWLE90
        2400   C                     WRITESUBCUS
        2500   C                     READ CUST01                    75           3
        2600   C      75             GOTO AGAIN
        2700   C                     ADD  1         RRN        20
        2800   C                     END
        2900   C*
        3000   C* DISPLAY SUBFILE RECORDS
        3100   C           AGAIN     TAG
        3200   C                     SETON                          65           1
        3300   C                     WRITECTLCUS
```

FIGURE 17.16 Continued

```
       3400  C                         READ CTLCUS                  66                3
       3500  C     KA                  GOTO BEGIN
       3600  C                         GOTO AGAIN
       3700  C            BEGIN        TAG
       3800  C                         Z-ADD1          RRN
       3900  C                         MOVE *BLANKS    SCCUST
       4000  C                         SETON                        60              1
       4100  C                         WRITECTLCUS
       4200  C                         SETOF                        6065            1 2
       4300  C                         EXFMTIL17160L
       4400  C     KA                  GOTO ENDJOB
       4500  C                         MOVE SCCUST     CUSNUM
       4600  C            CUSKEY       SETLLCUSTO1
       4700  C                         END
       4800  C            ENDJOB       TAG
       4900  C* WRAP-UP ROUTINE
       5000  C                         SETON                        LR              1
       5100  C************************************************************
    E000000     OUTPUT  FIELDS FOR RECORD IL171601 FILE IL1716FM FORMAT IL171601
    E000001                               *IN75        1  CHAR      1
    E000002                               SCCUST       6  CHAR      5
    F000000     OUTPUT  FIELDS FOR RECORD SUBCUS FILE IL1716FM FORMAT SUBCUS
    F000001                               CUSNUM       5  CHAR      5
    F000002                               CUSNAM      25  CHAR     20
    F000003                               CUSMTD      33  ZONE      8,0
    F000004                               CUSYTD      43  ZONE     10,0
    G000000     OUTPUT  FIELDS FOR RECORD CTLCUS FILE IL1716FM FORMAT CTLCUS
    G000001                               *IN60        1  CHAR      1
    G000002                               *IN65        2  CHAR      1
    * * * * * E N D  O F  S O U R C E * * * * *
```

File Updates Using Subfiles (READC)

Update capability is often needed for subfiles. This can be done using the same program requirements as those just outlined. Only a few changes will be needed in the Data Description Specifications and in the program. Figure 17.17 shows the revised DDS permitting the fields in the subfile to accept data.

The CUSTMAST file will be defined as an update file. A transaction file will be added for audit purposes. This is shown in Figure 17.18.

The initializing and loading of the subfile will be exactly the same as for the inquiry program. The update function will begin after the subfile has been displayed. Since 10 records are displayed at a time, the user can make a change in one record or in all 10 records before pressing the enter key or the command key to perform the update.

FIGURE 17.17 DDS for Display File for Updating a Group of Records

```
FILE NAME -        IL1717FM.CABLE        TYPE OF FILE -   DISPLAY
SOURCE FILE -      QDDSSRC.CABLE         MEMBER -         IL1717FM       02/24/92
TYPE OF DATA -     *DATA
OPTIONS -          *SRC    *LIST
GENLVL -           20
AUTHORITY -        *ALL
TEXT -             DDS FOR ILLUS 17.17
COMPILER -         IBM SYSTEM/38 DATA DESCRIPTION PROCESSOR

                               DATA DESCRIPTION SOURCE

SEQNBR  *... ... 1 ... ... 2 ... ... 3 ... ... 4 ... ... 5 ... ... 6 ... ... 7 ...
   100       A* TITLE: ENTER REQUEST SCREEN FOR UPDATE (PROJECT 17.17)
   200       A* DATE:   7/20          AUTHOR:
   300       A* DESCRIPTION:  SUBFILES
   400       A***************************************************************
```

FIGURE 17.17 Continued

```
 500    A                                            PRINT
 600    A                                            CA01(01 'END OF PROGRAM')
 700    A              R IL171701
 800    A                                         2 27'CUSTOMER MASTER INQUIRY'
 900    A                                         2  2'ILL1717'
1000    A                                         6 20'ENTER CUST#'
1100    A                SCCUST       5   B       8 25
1200    A    75                                      ERRMSG('RECORDS NOT FOUND')
1300    A                                        22 51 'CF-01 TO EXIT'
1400    A              R SUBCUS                      SFL
1500    A                SCRNUM       5   0       5  2
1600    A                SCRNAM      20   B       5  9
1700    A                SCRMTD       8  0B       5 31EDTCDE(K)
1800    A                SCRYTD      10   0B      5 47EDTCDE(K)
1900    A*
2000    A              R CTLCUS                      SFLCTL(SUBCUS)
2100    A    60                                      SFLCLR
2200    A    N60                                     SFLDSPCTL
2300    A    65                                      SFLDSP
2400    A                                            SFLPAG(10)
2500    A                                            SFLSIZ(80)
2600    A*
2700    A                                            OVERLAY
2800    A                                            ROLLUP(50 'ROLL TO NEXT SCREEN')
2900    A                                            PUTRETAIN
3000    A                                         2  2'ILL1716'
3100    A                                         2 32'CUSTOMER INQUIRY'
3200    A                                         4  2'CUST'
3300    A                                         4 14'CUSTOMER NAME'
3400    A                                         4 32'MONTH-TO-DATE'
3500    A                                         4 48'YEAR-TO-DATE'

             * * * * *  E N D   O F   S O U R C E  * * * * *
```

FIGURE 17.18 File Description Specifications for Updating a Group of Records

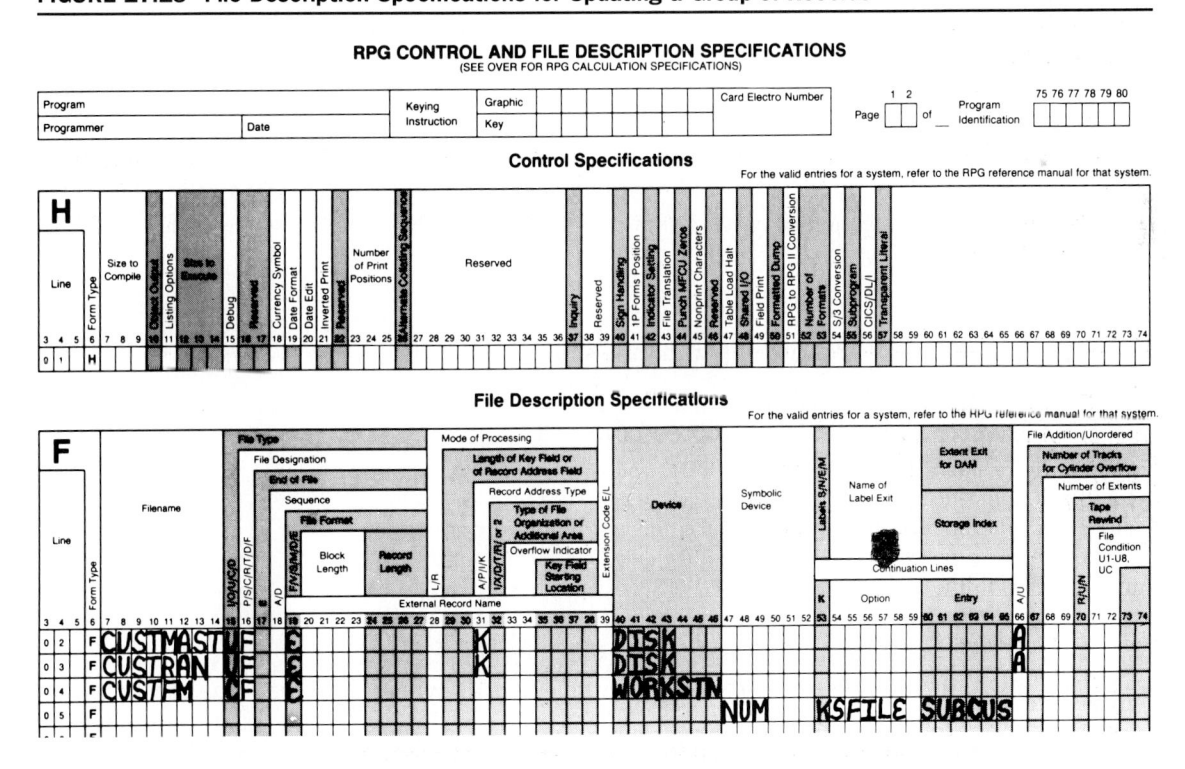

FIGURE 17.19 READC Operation

```
* UPDATES TO CUSTMAST FROM SUBFILE
C                    EXFMTCTLCUS
C                    READCSUBCUS                         38READ CHANGED
C       *IN38        DOWEQ'0'
C
C
C       PERFORM THE CUSTOMER FILE UPDATE ROUTINES MOVING DATA FROM SUBFILE TO CUSTMAST ETC.
C                    READCSUBCUS
C                    END
C                    GOTO BEGIN
```

The program must determine which record or records in the customer master file to update. This determination is made by the READC operation code. A READC represents "read next changed subfile record." Factor 2 of the READC operation holds the name of the subfile record format.

The READC operation requires an indicator in columns 58–59 of the Calculation Specifications. This indicator is set on when no changed records are found in the subfile. The coding in Figure 17.19 shows how a subfile is searched for records that have been changed.

The READC operation begins at the first record in the subfile. It searches for the first record to which a change has been made on the screen. When a changed subfile record is found, the programmer must perform any editing needed and execute the update routine for the data file. Processing of the subfile will continue until no more changed records are found in the subfile.

MANAGING SUBFILES ■

Subfiles provide complete flexibility for displaying groups of data for either inquiry or file updates.

Subfile Key Words

The following DDS key words are required for a subfile:

> SFL defines the subfile record format.
> SFLCTL defines the subfile control record format.
> SFLSIZ defines the size of the subfile.
> SFLPAG defines the size of the subfile page.
> SFLDSP identifies when to begin displaying records in a subfile.

Other DDS key words include the following:

> SFLCLR clears records out of a subfile.
> SFLDSPCTL indicates when to display the subfile control record.
> SFLLIN defines the number of spaces between records when more than one record is displayed on a line.
> SFLEND displays a plus sign (+) in the lower right corner of the screen when there are more records in the subfile than are shown on the screen. When the end of the subfile records has been reached, the + will be replaced by a blank.
> SFLINZ allows a subfile to be initialized.
> SFLMSG and SFLMSGID allow a message line to be written on the display screen.
> SFLDLT allows a subfile to be deleted.

Determining Subfile Size and Subfile Page Size

One of the first decisions to make when programming subfiles is how many records a subfile or a page should contain. Page size is determined by counting the number of lines being used for other purposes on the screen and allocating the remainder for the subfile.

Subfile size and subfile page size can be the same if the entire subfile can be displayed on one screen. Subfile size can also be greater than page size. When the subfile size exceeds the page size, the subfile size will be automatically extended to contain the larger number of records. The roll keys will cause the next (or previous) page of records to be displayed.

Although the maximum number of records allowed in a subfile is 9999, a smaller number is recommended because of the amount of time needed to build such a large subfile. A user would be waiting a long time before anything appeared on the screen.

ACCESSING SPECIFIC RECORDS IN A SUBFILE

A specific record in a subfile can be accessed if the programmer knows its relative record number. For example, if the record to be accessed is the first record in the subfile, it can be obtained by moving 1 into the relative record number field and chaining to the subfile, as shown in Figure 17.20.

Sometimes it is desirable to retrieve every record in the subfile. This might be done for a data entry application in which every record in the subfile would need to be added to a data file. Instead of using the READC operation, it would be possible to read each record and add it to the master file using the CHAIN operation. Figure 17.21 shows the coding for this type of program.

FIGURE 17.20 Accessing a Specific Subfile Record

```
C           1         CHAIN SUBCUS              33
```

FIGURE 17.21 Reading Each Record in a Subfile

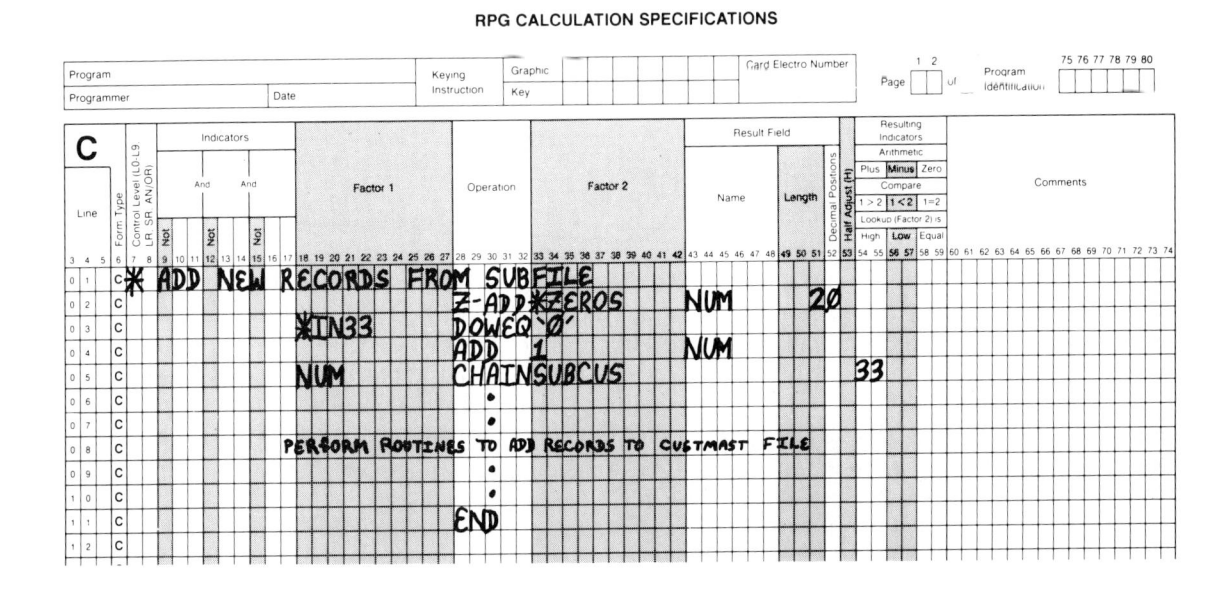

```
C* ADD NEW RECORDS FROM SUBFILE
C                    Z-ADD *ZEROS     NUM     20
C   *IN33            DOWEQ '0'
C                    ADD   1          NUM
C           NUM      CHAIN SUBCUS              33
C
C
C                    PERFORM ROUTINES TO ADD RECORDS TO CUSTMAST FILE
C
C
C
C                    END
```

FIGURE 17.22 Changing a Field in a Subfile

RPG CALCULATION SPECIFICATIONS

Line	Form Type	Control Level / Indicators	Factor 1	Operation	Factor 2	Result Field Name	Length	Decimal Positions	Resulting Indicators: Plus / High (54–55)	Minus / Low (56–57)	Zero / Equal (58–59)	Comments
01	C	* CHANEE FIELD										
02	C			Z-ADD	*ZEROS	NUM	2	Ø				
03	C		*IN33	DOWEQ	'Ø'							
04	C			READC	SUBCUS						35	
05	C		FLD1	CHAIN	MASTØ1				65			
06	C		*IN65	IFEQ	'Ø'							
07	C			MOVE	MSTFLD	FLD4						
08	C			UPDAT	SUBCUS							
09	C			END								
10	C			END								

There are many other situations in which retrieving a specific record in a subfile is useful. When loading a subfile, the WRITE operation is used to add records. When changes are made to the input fields in a subfile, it may be necessary to make corresponding changes to other fields on the screen. For example, when a code is entered, a description field might be retrieved from a master file and displayed on the screen to assure the user that the correct value was input. This is done by moving the master field into the corresponding field in the subfile record and executing the UPDAT operation. Figure 17.22 shows an example of such an application. The retrieved field must be updated in the correct subfile record.

USING MULTIPLE SUBFILES ■

The programmer will find many occasions for using more than one subfile in a program. The order entry example in Chapter 16, which displayed multiple screen formats in one program, will serve to show how several subfiles might be needed. Displaying a subfile in the order entry application can be useful to show:

- A list of customer names from which to select
- A list of several possible ship-to addresses
- A list of outstanding orders for a customer
- A list of items similar to the requested item
- A list of items available at other locations
- A list of substitution items
- A list of alternative prices
- A list of terms, codes, and descriptions
- A list of open purchase orders for the requested item with scheduled date

It would not be possible to display all of these subfiles on the screen simultaneously. However, it is often desirable to see more than one subfile for comparison purposes. It might be useful to see a list of the substitution items together with a price list, for example. Or a customer might want a comparison of merchandise available at remote warehouses and merchandise on purchase orders due to arrive soon.

RPG III/400 allows the use of as many as 512 subfiles in one program. Only 12 subfiles may be active in the program at one time. Up to 12 active subfiles can be displayed together.

The key word SFLDLT allows a subfile to be temporarily inactivated. By this means, the programmer can use up to 512 subfiles if necessary. The active subfiles can be created and displayed as needed, but when an inactive subfile is needed, one of the active subfiles will need to be deleted.

It is not always necessary to support multiple subfiles to retrieve other files or display other information. It is often simpler to exit from the program temporarily by calling another program.

EXITING TO OTHER SCREENS OR PROGRAMS

It is often useful to exit from one screen to retrieve another. Although this can be done using just one program that retrieves several screen display formats, it can also be done by calling a second (or third) program that displays some other formats. It could even be a combination of one program using multiple formats and calling multiple alternative programs that call their formats in turn. Figure 17.23 shows the complete program for displaying multiple screens and for calling another program. Data is passed from one program to another using the PARM operation.

Although the coding of subfiles is more complicated than most RPG coding structures, it is one of the most useful tools for executing applications for on-line interactive data retrieval. Once the basics of subfiles have been mastered, it is a simple matter to find combinations using the basic building blocks to design a modular program.

FIGURE 17.23 Complete Program for Displaying Multiple Screens and for Calling Another Program

```
SEQUENCE          1         2         3         4         5         6         7
NUMBER   67890123456789012345678901234567890123456789012345678901234

          100    F* TITLE: SCREEN
          200    F* DATE: 10/11/92        AUTHOR: D.CABLE
          300    F* DESCRIPTION:    XXXXXXXXXXXXXXXXXXXXXXXXXXXXXXXXXXXXXX
          400    F*************************************************************

NAME OF PROGRAM WILL BE IL1723 IN LIBRARY CABLE

                 H
  * 1019                      ALL DECIMAL DATA ERRORS IGNORED
          500    FIL1723FMCF  E                    WORKSTN
                   RECORD FORMAT(S):  FILE IL1723FM LIB CABLE
                         EXTERNAL FORMAT P005501 RPG NAME P005501
                         EXTERNAL FORMAT P005502 RPG NAME P005502

          600    FIIPOMSFLIF  E            K       DISK
          700    F*************************************************************
                   RECORD FORMAT(S):  FILE IIPOMSFL LIB MOMS
                         EXTERNAL FORMAT IIPOMS10 RPG NAME IIPOMS10

          800    E                    MSG    1    3 20
          900    E*************************************************************

         1000    C* STARTUP
       A000000   INPUT  FIELDS FOR RECORD P005501 FILE IL1723FM FORMAT P005501
       A000001                                      1    1  *IN01
       A000002                                      2    2  *IN02
       A000003                                      6    6  *IN05
       A000004                                      7    7  *IN09
       A000005                                      5    5  *IN79
       A000006                                      3    3  *IN80
       A000007                                      4    4  *IN81
       A000008                                      8    9  SCCMP#
       A000009                                     10  120SCLOC#
       A000010                                     13  190SCPONO
       A000011                                     20  282SCAMT
       B000000   INPUT  FIELDS FOR RECORD P005502 FILE IL1723FM FORMAT P005502
       B000001                                      1    1  *IN01
       B000002                                      2    2  *IN02
```

FIGURE 17.23 Continued

```
B000003                                             3    3 *IN80
B000004                                             4    4 *IN81
C000000     INPUT  FIELDS FOR RECORD IIPOMS10 FILE IIPOMSFL FORMAT IIPOMS10
C000001                                             1    2 IPCMP#
C000002                                         P   3    40IPLOC#
C000003                                         P   5    80IPPONO
C000004                                         P   9   110IPLNNO
C000005                                         P  12   150IPVND#
C000006                                            16    28 IPITM#
C000007                                         P  29   330IPUORD
C000008                                         P  34   383IPOPRC
C000009                                         P  39   410IPCSCT
C000010                                         P  42   450IPPODT
C000011                                            46    46 IPSTCD
C000012                                         P  47   500IPDLDT
C000013                                         P  51   550IPUTBO
C000014                                         P  56   590IPDUED
     1100  C           KEY       KLIST
     1200  C                     KFLD           IPCMP#
     1300  C                     KFLD           IPLOC#
     1400  C                     KFLD           IPPONO
     1500  C* MAINLINE
     1600  C           BEGIN     TAG
     1700  C                     EXFMTP005501
     1800  C    01               GOTO ENDJOB
     1900  C                     MOVE SCCMP#    IPCMP#
     2000  C                     MOVE SCLOC#    IPLOC#
     2100  C           KEY       SETLLIIPOMS10
     2200  C           KEY       READEIIPOMS10                 33
     2300  C    33               MOVELMSG,1     SCERR
     2400  C   N33     SCAMT     IFNE POAMT
     2500  C           POAMT     SUB  SCAMT     SCDIFF
     2600  C                     MOVELMSG,2     SCERR
     2700  C                     ELSE
     2800  C                     MOVELMSG,3     SCERR
     2900  C                     END
     3000  C                     EXFMTP005502
     3100  C    01               GOTO ENDJOB
     3200  C    02               CALL 'IL1724'
     3300  C                     PARM           IPCMP#
     3400  C                     PARM           IPLOC#
     3500  C                     PARM           IPPONO
     3600  C                     GOTO BEGIN
     3700  C* WRAP-UP
     3800  C           ENDJOB    TAG
     3900  C                     SETON                          LR
D000000     OUTPUT FIELDS FOR RECORD P005501 FILE IL1723FM FORMAT P005501
D000001                          SCCMP#     2  CHAR    2
D000002                          SCLOC#     5  ZONE    3,0
D000003                          SCPONO    12  ZONE    7,0
D000004                          SCAMT     21  ZONE    9,2
D000005                          POAMT     30  ZONE    9,2
D000006                          SCDIFF    39  ZONE    9,2
D000007                          SCERR     69  CHAR    30
E000000     OUTPUT FIELDS FOR RECORD P005502 FILE IL1723FM FORMAT P005502
* * * * * E N D  O F  S O U R C E * * * * *


          TABLE/ARRAY ------- MSG
     4100  P.O. NUMBER NOT FOUND
     4200  P.O. AMOUNT DOES NOT AGREE
     4300  P.O. AMOUNT IS CORRECT


                     PHYSICAL    LOGICAL
          FILE/RCD   FIELD       FIELD        ATTRIBUTES
```

FIGURE 17.23 *Continued*

```
   02  IIPOMSFL
           IIPOMS10
                  IPCMP#              CHAR  2
                  IPLOC#              PACK  2,0  SIGNED
                  IPPONO              PACK  7,0  SIGNED
                  IPLNNO              PACK  4,0  SIGNED


   CROSS-REFERENCE LISTING



           FILE/RCD    DEV/RCD    REFERENCES (D=DEFINED)
      02   IIPOMSFL    DISK       600D
           IIPOMS10               600D C000000    2100       2200
      01   IL1723FM    WORKSTN    500D
           P005501                500D A000000    1700  D000000
           P005502                500D B000000    3000  E000000



           FIELD       ATTR       REFERENCES (M=MODIFIED D=DEFINED)
           .PL001      PLIST      3200M     3200D
  * 7031   *IN01       A(1)       A000001   B000001
  * 7031   *IN02       A(1)       A000002   B000002
  * 7031   *IN05       A(1)       A000003
  * 7031   *IN09       A(1)       A000004
  * 7031   *IN79       A(1)       A000005
  * 7031   *IN80       A(1)       A000006   B000003
  * 7031   *IN81       A(1)       A000007   B000004
           BEGIN       TAG        1600D     3600
           ENDJOB      TAG        1800      3100      3800D
           IPCMP#      A(2)       C000001D  1200      1900M       3300
  * 7031   IPCSCT      P(5,0)     C000009D
  * 7031   IPDLDT      P(6,0)     C000012D
  * 7031   IPDUED      P(6,0)     C000014D
  * 7031   IPITM#      A(13)      C000006D
  * 7031   IPLNNO      P(4,0)     C000004D
           IPLOC#      P(2,0)     C000002D  1300      2000M       3400
  * 7031   IPOPRC      P(9,3)     C000008D
  * 7031   IPPODT      P(6,0)     C000010D
           IPPONO      P(7,0)     C000003D  1400      3500
  * 7031   IPSTCD      A(1)       C000011D
  * 7031   IPUORD      P(9,0)     C000007D
  * 7031   IPUTBO      P(9,0)     C000013D
  * 7031   IPVND#      P(6,0)     C000005D
           KEY         KLIST      1100D     2100      2200
           MSG(3)      A(20)      800D
           MSG,1                  2300
           MSG,2                  2600
           MSG,3                  2800
           PDAMT       P(9,2)     2400      2500      D000005D
           SCAMT       P(9,2)     A000011D  2400      2500  D000004D
           SCCMP#      A(2)       A000008D  1900      D000001D
           SCDIFF      P(9,2)     2500M     D000006D
           SCERR       A(30)      2300M     2600M     2800M D000007D
           SCLOC#      P(3,0)     A000009D  2000      D000002D
           SCPONO      P(7,0)     A000010D  D000003D
           'IL1724'    LITERAL    3200
           1           LITERAL    2300
           2           LITERAL    2600
           3           LITERAL    2800



           INDICATOR   REFERENCES (M=MODIFIED D=DEFINED)
           *IN         A000001  A000002  A000003  A000004  A000005  A000006
                       A000007  B000001  B000002  B000003  B000004
           LR          3900M
           01          A000001  B000001  1800     3100
```

FIGURE 17.23 Continued

```
            02           A000002  B000002    3200
 * 7031     05           A000003
 * 7031     09           A000004
            33                    2200M     2300       2400
 * 7031     79           A000005
 * 7031     80           A000006  B000003
 * 7031     81           A000007  B000004


    MESSAGES

     MSGID      SEV   NUMBER    TEXT

   * QRG1019     00      1      IGNDECERR(*YES) SPECIFIED ON COMMAND. NO DECIMAL DATA ERRORS
   * QRG7031     00     23      NAME OR INDICATOR NOT REFERENCED.


    MESSAGE SUMMARY

    TOTAL    00     10     20     30     40     50
     24      24      0      0      0      0      0

     43 RECORDS READ FROM SOURCE FILE
     SOURCE RECORDS INCLUDE    30 SPECIFICATIONS,     3 TABLE RECORDS, AND     9 COMMENTS

    PRM HAS BEEN CALLED

    QRG0003 PROGRAM IL1723 PLACED IN LIB CABLE. 00 HIGHEST SEVERITY FOUND

    * * * * * E N D   O F   C O M P I L A T I O N * * * * *
    * QRG1020              ERROR OCCURRED CREATING OR UPDATING DATA AREA RETURNCODE. COMPIL
```

SUMMARY ■

In this chapter we have briefly explored the methods for using subfiles to display groups of related records on the screen simultaneously. You have learned that a subfile is not a true file existing on auxiliary storage media. A subfile is a temporary file created in main memory for use in a specific program. The data for building the subfile is retrieved during the run time of the program, and data is obtained from some real data file or files. Some of the subfile data may be generated from within the program itself.

An empty subfile may be created and loaded with data from screen input. This input data may then be used as transactions from which a data file can be created or updated.

You have learned that subfiles permit a user to scroll through large volumes of data or to search for a specific entity. Subfiles are extremely useful for retrieving large amounts of information for display. Though they are more complicated to program, they are a very necessary part of the modern information processing system.

REVIEW QUESTIONS ■

1. Why is it sometimes necessary to display more than one record on a screen at a time?

2. How can a group of records displayed on a screen be more useful than one record when performing data entry functions?

3. Describe the function of a subfile.

4. What is the maximum number of lines that may be displayed on a screen when using a subfile format?

5. What are the two formats that must be coded on the DDS to completely describe a subfile?

6. What is contained in the subfile control description?

7. What is the function of the SFLCLR key word on the DDS when describing a subfile?

8. The subfile key word that indicates when to display the subfile control record is _____ .

9. The subfile key word that indicates when to display the subfile record itself is _____ .

10. The SFLPAG key word indicates the number of _____ that will be displayed on a _____ .

11. The SFLSIZ key word indicates the _____ number of _____ that will be contained in a _____ .

12. In what manner is the OVERLAY key word used with a subfile?

13. What is the function of the ROLLUP key word?

14. When is it necessary to use a continuation line with a File Description Specification?

15. Explain how a subfile is loaded with data.

16. How is relative record number used when building a subfile?

17. What may happen if the relative record number is advanced to a number larger than the total number of records in the subfile?

18. Explain how the subfile is displayed to the screen.

19. When using a subfile to perform updates to a file, the _____ operation is very useful.

20. What is the maximum number of records permitted in a subfile?

DEBUGGING EXERCISES

Instructions

The following RPG programs contain an error or errors. Some of these errors are indicated by the RPG compiler on the program listing. A list of syntax errors is given at the end of the program listing. Other types of errors may occur which will not be shown. These are called logic errors.

Study each program and its syntax errors. Locate each error (including logic errors) and on a separate coding form make the correct entry for the line(s) in error.

Explain each error and how it should be corrected.

```
     100   F* TITLE: DEBUG PROJECT 17-A
     200   F* DATE:  7/8            AUTHOR: D.CABLE
     300   F* DESCRIPTION:  SCREEN EXAMPLE
     400   F*************************************************

NAME OF PROGRAM WILL BE PJ017A IN LIBRARY CABLE

              H
* 1019              ALL DECIMAL DATA ERRORS IGNORED
     500   FENTPRDFMCF   E                     WORKSTN
     600   F                                   S1REC#KSFILE ENTPRDS1
              RECORD FORMAT(S):   FILE ENTPRDFM LIB CABLE
                  EXTERNAL  FORMAT  ENTPRD01  RPG  NAME  ENTPRD01
                  EXTERNAL  FORMAT  ENTPRDS1  RPG  NAME  ENTPRDS1
                  EXTERNAL  FORMAT  ENTPRDC1  RPG  NAME  ENTPRDC1
                  EXTERNAL  FORMAT  ENTPRD02  RPG  NAME  ENTPRD02
                  EXTERNAL  FORMAT  ENTPRD91  RPG  NAME  ENTPRD91

     700   E              MSG     1   6 40            ERR MSG
     800   E              LIB     1   8 10            LIBRARIES
     900   E*************************************************

    1000   C* START-UP ROUTINE
A000000      INPUT  FIELDS FOR RECORD ENTPRD01 FILE ENTPRDFM FORMAT ENTPRD01
A000001                                         1    1 *IN79
B000000      INPUT  FIELDS FOR RECORD ENTPRDS1 FILE ENTPRDFM FORMAT ENTPRDS1
B000001                                         1    1 *IN79
B000002                                         2   11 PGNAME
B000003                                        12   15 PGTYPE
B000004                                        16   25 PGLIB
B000005                                        26   26 PGDEL
C000000      INPUT  FIELDS FOR RECORD ENTPRDC1 FILE ENTPRDFM FORMAT ENTPRDC1
C000001                                         1    1 *IN79
D000000      INPUT  FIELDS FOR RECORD ENTPRD02 FILE ENTPRDFM FORMAT ENTPRD02
D000001                                         1    1 *IN79
E000000      INPUT  FIELDS FOR RECORD ENTPRD91 FILE ENTPRDFM FORMAT ENTPRD91
E000001                                         1    1 *IN79
    1100   C              *ENTRY    PLIST
    1200   C                        PARM         LIBL     10
    1300   C              KEY       KLIST
    1400   C                        KFLD         TYPE
    1500   C                        KFLD         NAME
    1600   C                        EXSR INIT
    1700   C*************************************************
    1800   C* MAINLINE ROUTINE
    1900   C* DISPLAY USER'S PROJECTS
    2000   C              TAG10     TAG
    2100   C                        MOVE *BLANKS  DESC
    2200   C                        SETON                        75
```

```
      2300  C                    WRITEENTPRDC1
      2400  C                    SETOF                         75
      2500  C                    MOVE *BLANKS   PGNAME
      2600  C                    MOVE *BLANKS   PGTYPE
      2700  C                    MOVE *BLANKS   PGLIB
      2800  C                    MOVE *BLANKS   PGDEL
      2900  C                    WRITEENTPRD01
      3000  C                    WRITEENTPRD02
      3100  C                    SETON                     30
      3200  C                    SETOF                            70
      3300  C*
      3400  C         TAG20      TAG
      3500  C   KA               SETON                               LR
      3600  C   KA               RETRN
      3700  C*
      3800  C************************************************************
F000000   OUTPUT  FIELDS FOR RECORD ENTPRD01 FILE ENTPRDFM FORMAT ENTPRD01
G000000   OUTPUT  FIELDS FOR RECORD ENTPRDC1 FILE ENTPRDFM FORMAT ENTPRDC1
G000001                          *IN75         1 CHAR    1
H000000   OUTPUT  FIELDS FOR RECORD ENTPRD02 FILE ENTPRDFM FORMAT ENTPRD02
* * * * * E N D  O F  S O U R C E * * * * *
```

```
* 7024      500    ENTPRDFM FILE NAME HAS NO CALC REFERENCE TO INPUT RECORDS
* 7003      500    RECNO FIELD NAME S1REC# NOT DEFINED OR USED IN PROGRAM
* 7018     1600    INIT FACTOR 2 OF EXSR NOT LABEL OF BEGSR
            TABLE/ARRAY ------- MSG
           4000    TYPE--MUST BE RPG, CLP, DSPF, PF OR LF
           4100    DUPLICATE ENTRY NOT ALLOWED
           4200    INVALID LIBRARY ENTERED
           4300    OBJECT NAME CANNOT BE BLANK
           4400    INVALID CODE- MUST BE D OR H
           4500    ALL REQUESTS HAVE BEEN ACCEPTED
* 8046      700    ARRAY NOT USED IN PROGRAM. ARRAY NOT CREATED
            TABLE/ARRAY ------- LIB
* 8046      800    ARRAY NOT USED IN PROGRAM. ARRAY NOT CREATED
* 8043      800    NO DATA PRESENT FOR TABLE/ARRAY. ZEROS/BLANKS ASSUMED
```

CROSS-REFERENCE LISTING

```
        FILE/RCD      DEV/RCD      REFERENCES (D=DEFINED)

    01  ENTPRDFM      WORKSTN      500D
        ENTPRDC1                   500D C000000      2300  G000000
        ENTPRDS1                   500D B000000
        ENTPRD01                   500D A000000      2900  F000000
        ENTPRD02                   500D D000000      3000  H000000
        ENTPRD91                   500D E000000


        FIELD         ATTR         REFERENCES (M=MODIFIED D=DEFINED)

* 7031  *ENTRY        PLIST        1100D
        *IN75         A(1)         G000001D
* 7031  *IN79         A(1)         A000001  B000001  C000001  D000001  E000001
* 7030  DESC          A(4)         2100M
* 7030  INIT          A(4)         1600
* 7031  KEY           KLIST        1300D
* 7031  LIB(8)        A(10)        800D
        LIBL          P(1,0)       1200D
* 7031  MSG(6)        A(40)        700D
* 7030  NAME          A(4)         1500
        PGDEL         A(1)         B000005D      2800M
        PGLIB         A(10)        B000004D      2700M
        PGNAME        A(10)        B000002D      2500M
        PGTYPE        A(4)         B000003D      2600M
        S1REC#(99)    A(1)         500
* 7031  TAG10         TAG          2000D
```

```
* 7031   TAG20      TAG         3400D
* 7030   TYPE       A(4)        1400
         *BLANKS    LITERAL     2100    2500    2600    2700    2800


         INDICATOR   REFERENCES  (M=MODIFIED D=DEFINED)

         *IN        A000001  B000001  C000001  D000001  E000001  G000001D
         KA         3500     3600
         LR         3500M
* 7031   30         3100M
* 7031   70         3200M
         75         2200M    2400M    G000001D
* 7031   79         A000001  B000001  C000001  D000001  E000001


     MESSAGES

     MSGID       SEV   NUMBER   TEXT

*  QRG1019      00      1      IGNDECERR(*YES) SPECIFIED ON COMMAND. NO DECIMAL DATA ERRORS
*  QRG7003      20      1      RECNO FIELD NAME NOT DEFINED OR NOT USED ELSEWHERE IN PROGRAM
*  QRG7018      30      1      FACTOR 2 OF EXSR DOES NOT SPECIFY LABEL OF BEGSR. EXSR SPECIF
*  QRG7024      20      1      INPUT RECORD NOT REFERENCED BY CALCULATION OPERATIONS.
*  QRG7030      30      4      FIELD OR INDICATOR NOT DEFINED.
*  QRG7031      00     10      NAME OR INDICATOR NOT REFERENCED.
*  QRG8043      10      1      NO SOURCE RECORDS PROVIDED TO INITIALIZE ARRAY/TABLE. ALPHAME
                               NUMERIC ELEMENTS ASSUMED ZERO
*  QRG8046      20      2      COMPILE TIME ARRAY/TABLE DEFINED BUT NOT REFERENCED


     MESSAGE SUMMARY

     TOTAL    00    10    20    30    40    50
      21      11     1     4     5     0     0

         45 RECORDS READ FROM SOURCE FILE
     SOURCE RECORDS INCLUDE   26 SPECIFICATIONS,    6 TABLE RECORDS, AND   12 COMMENTS

     QRG0008 COMPILE TERMINATED. SEVERITY 30 ERRORS FOUND IN PROGRAM

     * * * * * E N D  O F  C O M P I L A T I O N * * * * *
*  QRG1020              ERROR OCCURRED CREATING OR UPDATING DATA AREA RETURNCODE. COMPIL
_____

       100   F* TITLE: DEBUG PROJECT 17-B
       200   F* DATE:  7/8           AUTHOR: D.CABLE
       300   F* DESCRIPTION: SCREEN EXAMPLE
       400   F*****************************************************

     NAME OF PROGRAM WILL BE PJ017B IN LIBRARY CABLE

                 H
*  1019                   ALL DECIMAL DATA ERRORS IGNORED
       500   FIN020RFMCF  E                     WORKSTN
       600   F                                  RRN     KSFILE IN020S1
               RECORD FORMAT(S):  FILE IN020RFM LIB NEWMOD
                         EXTERNAL FORMAT IN020S1 RPG NAME IN020S1
                         EXTERNAL FORMAT IN020CTL RPG NAME IN020CTL
                         EXTERNAL FORMAT IN020F1 RPG NAME IN020F1

       700   FSUMMFL  IF  E            K        DISK
*  2120      700  DATA DESCRIPTIONS FOR FILE SUMMFL NOT FOUND
```

```
 800  E                          MSG     1   6 40                      ERR MSG
 900  E                          LIB     1   8 10                      LIBRARIES
1000  E************************************************************
      
1100  C* START-UP ROUTINE
A000000     INPUT  FIELDS FOR RECORD IN020S1 FILE IN020RFM FORMAT IN020S1
A000001                                              1    1 *IN01
A000002                                              2    2 *IN02
A000003                                              3    40SCYY
A000004                                              5    60SCMM
A000005                                              7   120SCBOH
A000006                                             13   180SCRCV
A000007                                             19   240SCPADJ
A000008                                             25   300SCADJ
A000009                                             31   360SCTOUT
A000010                                             37   420SCTIN
A000011                                             43   480SCSALE
A000012                                             49   540SCSLIN
A000013                                             55   600SCEOH
A000014                                             61   660SCOB
B000000     INPUT  FIELDS FOR RECORD IN020CTL FILE IN020RFM FORMAT IN020CTL
B000001                                              1    1 *IN01
B000002                                              2    2 *IN02
B000003                                              3    50RECNO
B000004                                              6    7 SCCMP#
B000005                                              8    9 SCLOC#
B000006                                             10   14 SCSKU
B000007                                             15   27 SCITM#
C000000     INPUT  FIELDS FOR RECORD IN020F1 FILE IN020RFM FORMAT IN020F1
C000001                                              1    1 *IN01
C000002                                              2    2 *IN02
1200  C           FSTSW     IFEQ ' '
1300  C                     EXSR INIT
1400  C                     END
1500  C************************************************************
1600  C* MAINLINE ROUTINE
1700  C           *IN01     IFEQ '1'
1800  C                     MOVE '1'       *INLR
1900  C                     RETRN
2000  C                     END
2100  C*
2200  C                     EXSR CLRFM                    CLEAR HEADER
2300  C*
2400  C           *IN02     DOWEQ'0'
2500  C                     WRITEIN020F1
2600  C                     EXFMTIN020CTL
2700  C           *IN01     IFEQ '1'
2800  C                     EXSR WRTSF
2900  C                     END
3000  C                     END
3100  C    KA              SETON                     LR
3200  C    KA              RETRN
3300  C*
3400  C************************************************************
3500  C           INIT      BEGSR
3600  C           *ENTRY    PLIST
3700  C                     PARM           LIBL    10
3800  C           KEY       KLIST
3900  C                     KFLD           TYPE
4000  C                     KFLD           NAME
4100  C                     MOVE '1'       FSTSW   1
4200  C                     ENDSR
4300  C************************************************************
4400  C           INIT      BEGSR
* 5110            5110-********
4500  C* CLEAR SUBFILE
4600  C                     MOVE '0'       *IN02
4700  C                     MOVE '0'       *IN02
4800  C                     WRITEIN020CTL
4900  C                     MOVE *BLANKS   SCCMP#
5000  C                     MOVE *BLANKS   SCLOC#
5100  C                     MOVE *BLANKS   SCDESC
5200  C                     MOVE *BLANKS   SCITM#
5300  C                     MOVE *BLANKS   SCSBCL
5400  C                     Z-ADD1         RRN
5500  C                     Z-ADD1         RECNO
```

Chapter 17 Using Subfiles in RPG III/400

```
  5600   C                    WRITEIN020S1
  5700   C                    ENDSR
D000000     OUTPUT  FIELDS FOR RECORD IN020S1 FILE IN020RFM FORMAT IN020S1
D000001                                SCYY    2    ZONE   2,0
D000002                                SCMM    4    ZONE   2,0
D000003                                SCBOH  10    ZONE   6,0
D000004                                SCRCV  16    ZONE   6,0
D000005                                SCPADJ 22    ZONE   6,0
D000006                                SCADJ  28    ZONE   6,0
D000007                                SCTOUT 34    ZONE   5,0
D000008                                SCTIN  40    ZONE   6,0
D000009                                SCSALE 46    ZONE   6,0
D000010                                SCSLIN 52    ZONE   6,0
D000011                                SCEOH  58    ZONE   6,0
D000012                                SCOB   64    ZONE   6,0
E000000     OUTPUT  FIELDS FOR RECORD IN020CTL FILE IN020RFM FORMAT IN020CTL
E000001                                *IN35   1    CHAR   1
E000002                                *IN80   2    CHAR   1
E000003                                *IN81   3    CHAR   1
E000004                                RECNO   6    ZONE   3,0
E000005                                SCUSER 12    CHAR   6
E000006                                SCCMP# 14    CHAR   2
E000007                                SCLOC# 16    CHAR   2
E000008                                SCSKU  21    CHAR   5
E000009                                SCITM# 34    CHAR  13
E000010                                SCAVUC 43    ZONE   9,3
E000011                                SCDESC 73    CHAR  30
E000012                                SCDEPT 77    ZONE   4,0
E000013                                SCCLAS 79    CHAR   2
E000014                                SCS3CL 82    ZONE   3,0
E000015                                SCVD#1 88    ZONE   6,0
F000000     OUTPUT  FIELDS FOR RECORD IN020F1 FILE IN020RFM FORMAT IN020F1
* * * * * E N D   O F   S O U R C E * * * * *


*  7004     500    RECNO FIELD NAME RRN NOT DEFINED
*  7064     700    SUMMFL FILE NOT REFERENCED FOR INPUT
*  7018    2200    CLRFM FACTOR 2 OF EXSR NOT LABEL OF BEGSR
*  7018    2800    WRTSF FACTOR 2 OF EXSR NOT LABEL OF BEGSR
           TABLE/ARRAY ------- MSG
*  8045     800    ARRAY NOT USED IN PROGRAM. ARRAY NOT CREATED
*  8043     800    NO DATA PRESENT FOR TABLE/ARRAY. ZEROS/BLANKS ASSUMED
           TABLE/ARRAY ------- LIB
*  8045     900    ARRAY NOT USED IN PROGRAM. ARRAY NOT CREATED
*  8043     900    NO DATA PRESENT FOR TABLE/ARRAY. ZEROS/BLANKS ASSUMED

      CROSS-REFERENCE LISTING

          FILE/RCD    DEV/RCD    REFERENCES (D=DEFINED)

      01  IN020RFM    WORKSTN    500D
          IN020CTL               500D B000000   2600      4800    E000000
          IN020F1                500D C000000   2500      F000000
          IN020S1                500D A000000   5600      D000000
      02  SUMMFL      DISK       700D

          FIELD       ATTR       REFERENCES (M=MODIFIED D=DEFINED)

*  7031  *ENTRY       PLIST      3600D
         *INLR        A(1)       1800M
         *IN01        A(1)       A000001   B000001   C000001   1700   2700
         *IN02        A(1)       A000002   B000002   C000002   2400   4600M
                                 4700M
         *IN35        A(1)       E000001D
         *IN80        A(1)       E000002D
         *IN81        A(1)       E000003D
*  7030  CLRFM        A(4)       2200
         FSTSW        A(1)       1200      4100D
         INIT         BEGSR      1300      3500D     4400D
*  7031  KEY          KLIST      3800D
*  7031  LIB(8)       A(10)      900D
         LIBL         P(1,0)     3700D
*  7031  MSG(6)       A(40)      800D
*  7030  NAME         A(4)       400D
         RECNO        P(3,0)     B000003D  5500M  E000004D
*  7030  RRN          P(9,0)     500       5400M
         SCADJ        P(6,0)     A000008D  D000006D
```

```
            SCAVUC        P(9,3)    E0000010
            SCBOH         P(6,0)    A0000050 00000030
            SCCLAS        A(2)      E0000013
            SCCMP#        A(2)      B0000040        4900M E0000060
            SCDEPT        P(4,0)    E0000012
            SCDESC        A(30)           5100M E0000011
            SCEOH         P(6,0)    A0000013 00000011
            SCITM#        A(13)     B0000070        5200M E0000009
            SCLOC#        A(2)      B0000050        5000M E0000007
            SCMM          P(2,0)    A0000040 00000020
            SCOB          P(6,0)    A0000014 00000012
            SCPADJ        P(6,0)    A0000070 00000050
            SCRCV         P(6,0)    A0000060 00000040
            SCSALE        P(6,0)    A0000011 00000009
            SCSBCL        P(3,0)          5300M E0000014
            SCSKU         A(5)      B0000060 E0000008
            SCSLIN        P(6,0)    A0000012 00000010
            SCTIN         P(6,0)    A0000010 00000008
            SCTOUT        P(6,0)    A0000009 00000007
            SCUSER        A(6)      E0000005
            SCVD#1        P(6,0)    E0000015
            SCYY          P(2,0)    A0000003 00000001
* 7030      TYPE          A(4)      3900
* 7030      WRTSF         A(4)      2800
            *BLANKS       LITERAL   4900   5000   5100   5200   5300
            ' '           LITERAL   1200
            '0'           LITERAL   2400   4600   4700
            '1'           LITERAL   1700   1800   2700   4100
            1             LITERAL   5400   5500

      INDICATOR  REFERENCES  (M=MODIFIED D=DEFINED)

            *IN           A000001  A000002  B000001  B000002  C000001  C000002
                          1700     2400     2700     4600M    4700M E0000010
                          E0000020 E0000030
            KA            3100     3200
            LR            1800M    3100M
            01            A000001  B000001  C000001  1700     2700
            02            A000002  B000002  C000002  2400     4600M    4700M
            35            E0000010
            80            E0000020
            81            E0000030

  MESSAGES

   MSGID    SEV  NUMBER   TEXT

 * QRG1019   00    1      IGNDECERR(*YES) SPECIFIED ON COMMAND. NO DECIMAL DATA ERRORS
 * QRG2120   40    1      EXTERNAL DESCRIPTION NOT FOUND FOR FILE SPECIFIED AS EXTERNAL
                          IGNORED.
 * QRG5110   40    1      SUBROUTINE NAME IN FACTOR 1 (POSITIONS 18-27) OF BEGSR OPERAT
                          LINES IGNORED UNTIL ENDSR FOUND
 * QRG7004   20    1      RECNO FIELD NAME NOT DEFINED. NUMERIC LENGTH OF 9 WITH ZERO D
 * QRG7018   30    2      FACTOR 2 OF EXSR DOES NOT SPECIFY LABEL OF BEGSR. EXSR SPECIF
 * QRG7030   30    5      FIELD OR INDICATOR NOT DEFINED.
 * QRG7031   00    4      NAME OR INDICATOR NOT REFERENCED.
 * QRG7064   40    1      PROGRAM FILE NOT REFERENCED. FILE IGNORED
 * QRG8043   10    2      NO SOURCE RECORDS PROVIDED TO INITIALIZE ARRAY/TABLE. ALPHAME
                          NUMERIC ELEMENTS ASSUMED ZERO
 * QRG8046   20    2      COMPILE TIME ARRAY/TABLE DEFINED BUT NOT REFERENCED


  MESSAGE SUMMARY

  TOTAL   00    10    20    30    40    50
    20     5     2     3     7     3     0

    57 RECORDS READ FROM SOURCE FILE
    SOURCE RECORDS INCLUDE    43 SPECIFICATIONS,    0 TABLE RECORDS, AND    14 COMMENTS

  QRG0008 COMPILE TERMINATED. SEVERITY 40 ERRORS FOUND IN PROGRAM

  * * * * *  E N D  O F  C O M P I L A T I O N * * * * *
  * QRG1020               ERROR OCCURRED CREATING OR UPDATING DATA AREA RETURNCODE. COMPILI
```

PROGRAMMING PROJECT

Project Overview

An inquiry program is needed that will display customer data from the customer master file. Instead of displaying one customer at a time, however, this screen will show ten customers.

When this program is requested, the first five customers in the customer master file will be displayed.

Create the screen (using DDS) and write the RPG program to produce this inquiry screen. Sample data for this project can be found in Appendix D.

Input Format

The input data for the project is found in a file called CUSTMAST in the sample data. The Record Layout for this file is shown in Figure 17.24.

Processing

When this program is called, the customer master file is accessed beginning at the first record, and a subfile is created containing the entire file. The first five records in the file are displayed on the screen. When the roll-up key is depressed, the next five records are displayed. A command 1 causes the program to end.

Output Format (Screen Layout Sheet)

The output format for the project is a screen with standard headings. The screen will show the customer number, name, address, city, state, and total year-to-date sales. The screen layout for this inquiry is shown in Figures 17.25(a) and 17.25(b).

An example of the finished screen display is shown in Figures 17.26(a) and 17.26(b).

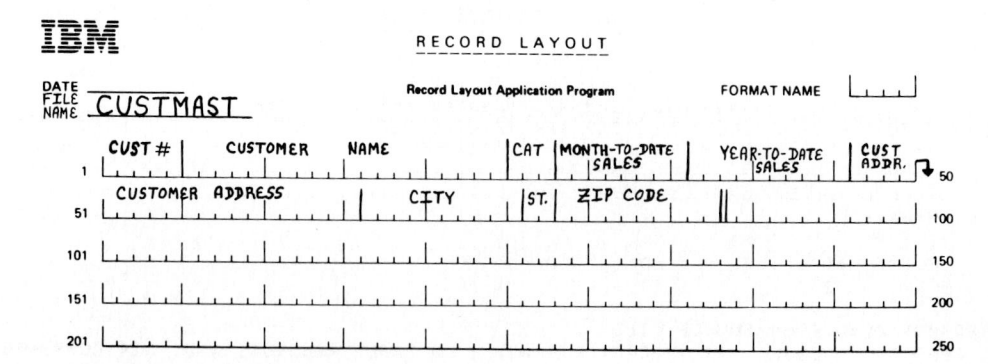

FIGURE 17.24 Programming Project: Record Layout

FIGURE 17.25(a) Programming Project: Screen 1 Layout

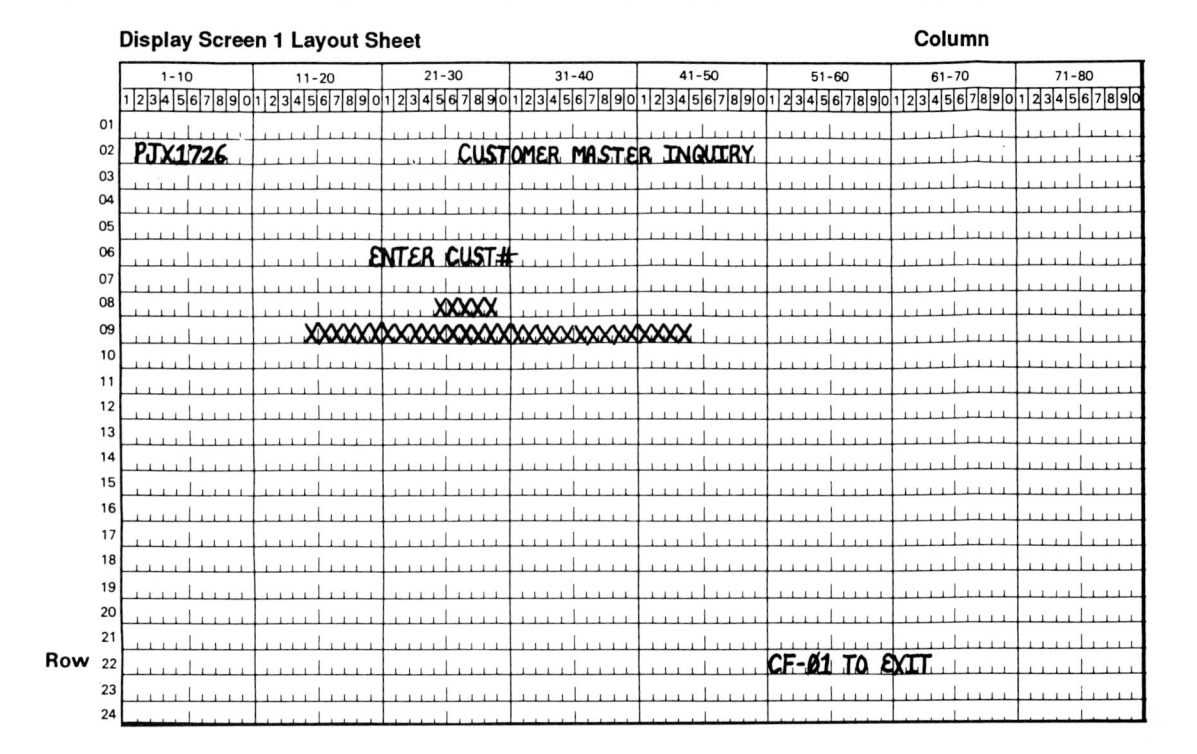

Display Screen 1 Layout Sheet

Row 02: PJX1726 ... CUSTOMER MASTER INQUIRY
Row 06: ENTER CUST#
Row 08: XXXXX
Row 09: XXXXXXXXXXXXXXXXXXXXXXXXXX
Row 22: CF-01 TO EXIT

FIGURE 17.25(b) Programming Project: Screen 2 Layout

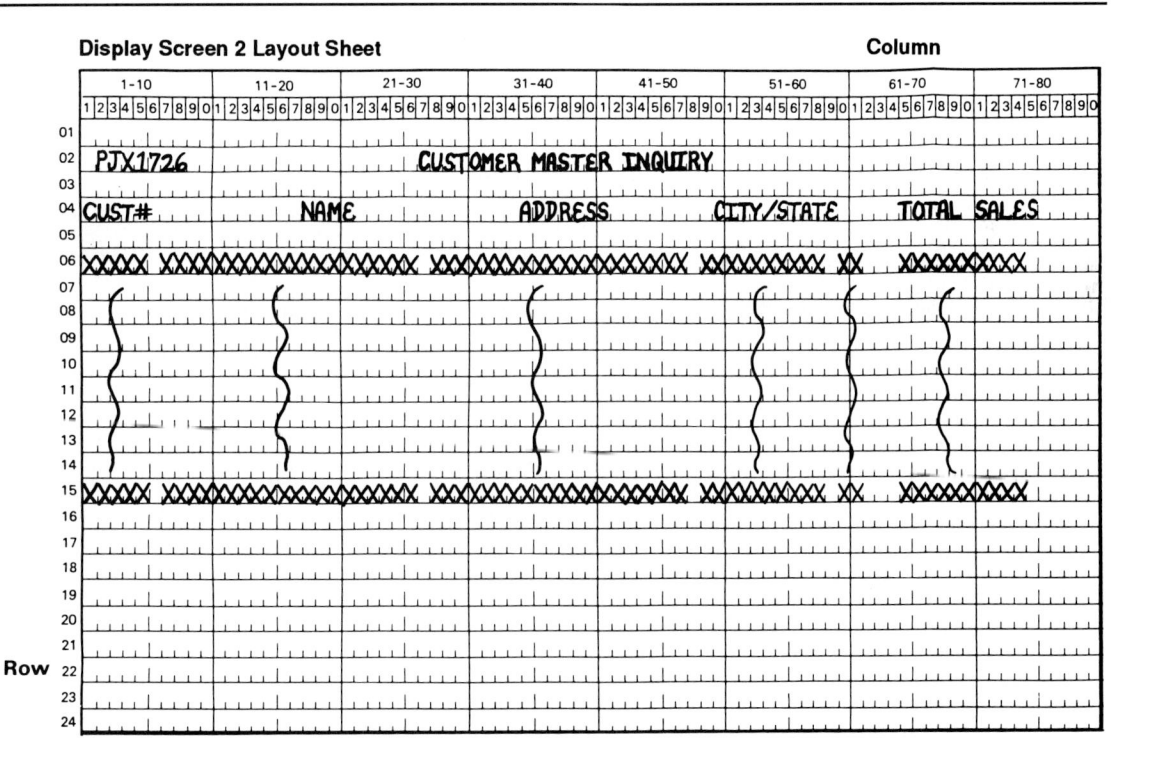

Display Screen 2 Layout Sheet

Row 02: PJX1726 ... CUSTOMER MASTER INQUIRY
Row 04: CUST#   NAME   ADDRESS   CITY/STATE   TOTAL SALES
Row 06: XXXX XXXXXXXXXXXXXXX XXXXXXXXXXXXXX XXXXXXXXX XX XXXXXXXXX
Row 15: XXXX XXXXXXXXXXXXXXX XXXXXXXXXXXXXX XXXXXXXXX XX XXXXXXXXX

FIGURE 17.26(a) Programming Project: Sample Screen 1

```
PJX1726                  CUSTOMER MASTER INQUIRY


                          ENTER CUST#

                             00032












                                                    CF-01 TO EXIT
```

FIGURE 17.26(b) Programming Project: Sample Screen 2

```
PJX1726                CUSTOMER MASTER INQUIRY
CUST#         NAME              ADDRESS           CITY/STATE
00032 SAMS PLACE             23 PRODUCE LANE      CENTRAL     WA
00045 FRESH FOODS MARKET     555 FARM-FRESH DR    SUN CITY    IA
00059 METHOD MARKETS         726 ALLEY LANE       GOLETA      CA
00078 OPEN MARKETS           777 LUCKY WAY        TUMBLEWEED  AZ
00128 OPEN MARKETS BRANCH    852 ARROYO GRANDE    FARMVILLE   NM
01023 VPMI INDUSTRIES        1045 WILDCAT WAY     VALENCIA    CA
02345 BULLFROG INC.          ROSE AVE.            LODI        CA
04568 FIRST CITY BANK        DIAMOND BLVD         LAGUNA      CA
06892 DOLLAR INC.            AVE OF THE STARS     HOLLYWOOD   FL
09871 BOOKS INC.             1000 FROZEN LANE     BLUEFIELD   MT
```

Chapter 18

Programming Efficiencies in RPG III/400

What you will learn in Chapter 18

File Sequence
   Physical Files (Sorted)
   Logical Files (Permanent or Temporary)
   Joined Files
   Open Query File (OPNQRYF)
   Array Sorts

Summarized Data
File Design
Special Data Structures
   Data Areas
   Multiple Occurrence Data Structure

File Information Data Structure (INFDS)
Program Status Data Structure
Structured Programming Methods
Tools for the Superprogrammer

Several factors contribute to the efficiency of a program. A discussion of two general areas will help to improve the execution efficiency for most programs:

1. The structure of the files
2. The design of the program

FILE SEQUENCE ■

The structure of the files used in a program can be as important as the program itself. A program can usually run faster and more efficiently if the files used are in the same sequence as that in the report or screen desired as output, but a surprising number of programs are not written this way. The run time for these programs can be very long because the program must search through the entire file to find the next record to be printed.

Several options are available to provide the correct sort sequence for a report or display:

1. Physical sort of the file
2. Logical views of the file
   a. Temporary logical files
   b. Permanent logical files
3. Logical view joining several files
4. OPNQRYF utility
5. Sort of data within the RPG program

Physical Files (Sorted)

Sorting a physical file and outputting a copy of it in a different sequence wastes both disk space and valuable execution time, unless the sorting is being done for some specific reason. If a physical file is being sorted to output a copy that will be transported to another computer requiring the data in some specific sequence, a sort might be justified. In normal daily operation for producing screens and reports, however, physical sorts are a somewhat obsolete means for sequencing files. Figures 18.1(a) and 18.1(b) show the sort parameters and the commands for executing the sort function.

Logical Files (Permanent or Temporary)

The use of logical files (sometimes called logical views) is a better method for accessing data in an alternate keyed sequence. It is more efficient to create logical files than to resequence a physical file every time a program is to be run. Logical views consume relatively little space on disk because the physical data is not included.

Creating a logical file does require execution time, and this can be significant if the physical file is very large. If sufficient disk space is available, logical files should be created once and retained permanently on disk. The more often a program is executed, the more reason there is to use a permanent logical file. If an application is run only once a year, it would not be wise to keep a permanent logical file in place on disk taking up valuable space. If a program is run every day, however, a permanent logical file would greatly improve run time and service to the users.

Although many logical files may be permanently attached to a physical file, wisdom dictates that disk space should be conserved. Create only the logical files that will be needed in normal operation and try to use the same logical sequence for several applications. The specifications for creating logical files have been discussed in earlier chapters. Figures 18.2(a) and 18.2(b) show the DDS for a logical file and the command for creating it.

FIGURE 18.1(a) Sort Parameters

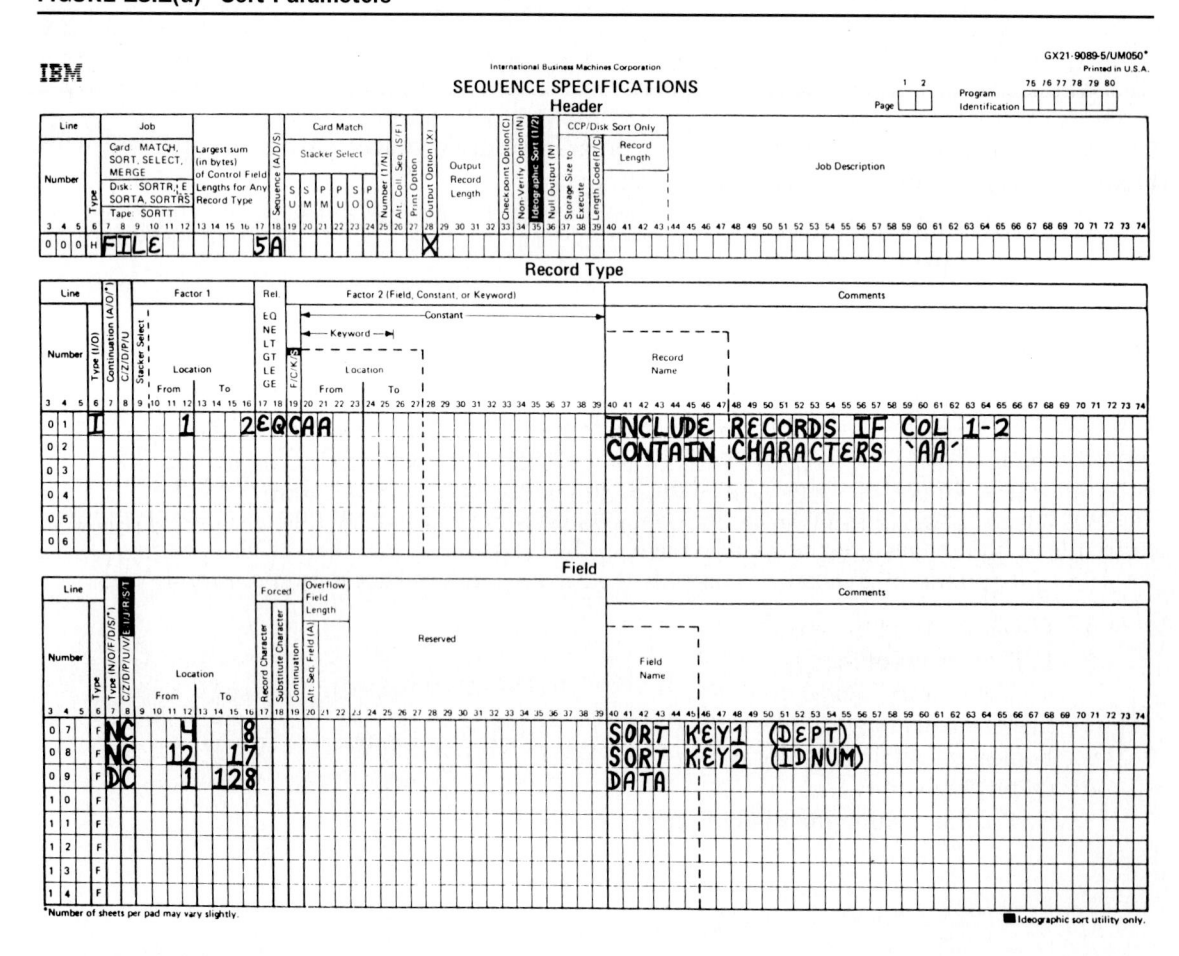

FIGURE 18.1(b) Commands for Executing Sort

FMTDTA INFILE(INPUTFILE.DATALIB) OUTFILE(SRTFILE.DATALIB)

SRCFILE(QTXTSRC.PROGLIB) SRCMBR(SORTIT)

OPTION(*NOPRT *NODUMP *NOCHK)

FIGURE 18.2(a) DDS for a Logical File

DATA DESCRIPTION SPECIFICATIONS

File		Keying Instruction	Graphic	Description	Page of
Programmer	Date		Key		

Sequence Number (1–5)	Form Type (6)	Type of Name or Spec (17)	Name (19–28)	Reference (R) (29)	Functions (45–80)
	A				REF(REFFLD)
	A	R	FMTØ1		
	A		CODE	R	TEXT('CODE AA')
	A		TRAN	R	TEXT('STATUS')
	A		DEPT	R	TEXT('DEPT WORKED')
	A		SUB#	R	TEXT('SUBSIDIARY #')
	A		IDNUM	R	TEXT('IDENTIFICATION #')
	A		NAME	R	TEXT('NAME')
	A		AMOUNT	R	TEXT('AMOUNT')
	A	K	DEPT		
	A	K	IDNUM		
	A				

FIGURE 18.2(b) Command for Creating a Logical File

CRTLF INPUTFILE.DATALIB QDDSSRC.PROGLIB

Joined Files

Joined files are a special type of logical file. They provide access to more than one physical file combined in one format within the logical view. Joined files can not only put the files in the desired sequence but also eliminate the need to access multiple files (and thereby reduce the amount of work to be done). Only one logical file will need to be accessed in the program.

The further benefit of a joined file is that the accessed physical files are combined based on definite relationships specified in the DDS for the logical file. Notice in Figure 18.3 that a common field exists in the two physical files. The relationship between the two files is based on the key field EMPID in the EMPLMAST file and EMPKEY in the EMPSKIL file.

The format name is entered in the DDS as it would be for any logical file. Instead of the PFILE key word, the key word JFILE is entered in columns 45–49. This is followed by the names of the physical files that are to be joined in this logical file. The first filename is the primary file, from which the join will begin. All other files are secondary files. In this example, the primary file is the employee master file, EMPMAST. The secondary file is a file containing skills possessed by each employee, EMPSKIL. Figure 18.4 shows the DDS for a joined logical file.

FIGURE 18.3 Physical File Record Layouts for Two Files

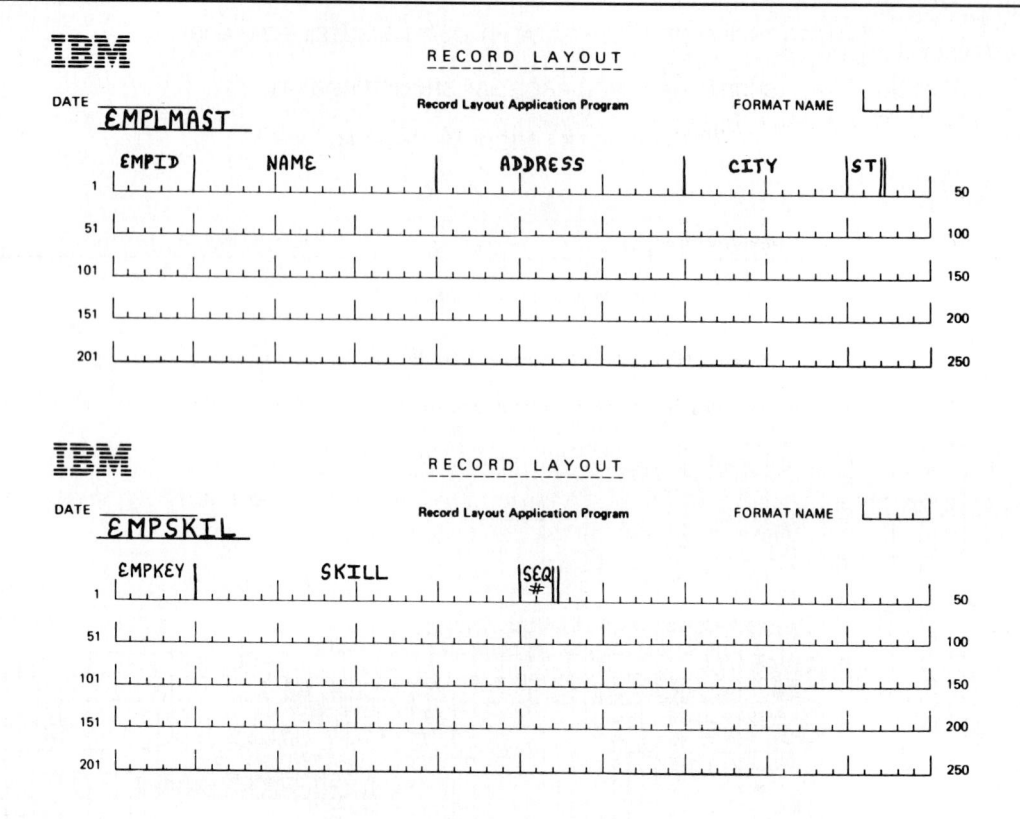

[IBM Record Layout form for EMPLMAST with fields: EMPID, NAME, ADDRESS, CITY, ST]

[IBM Record Layout form for EMPSKIL with fields: EMPKEY, SKILL, SEQ#]

FIGURE 18.4 DDS for a Joined Logical File Combining Two Files

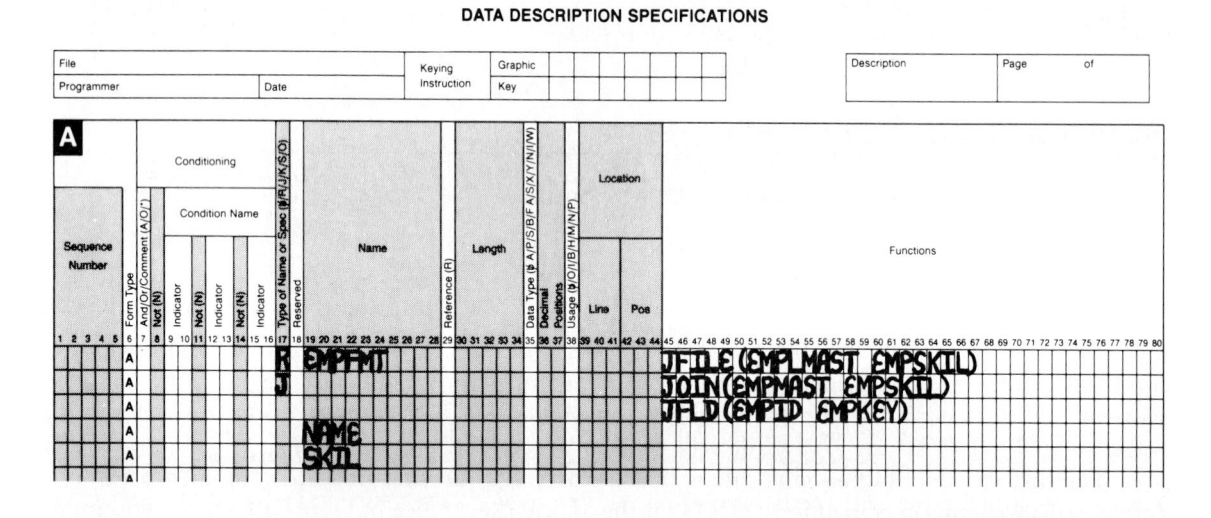

[Data Description Specifications form showing:]

```
A          R EMPFMT                      JFILE(EMPLMAST EMPSKIL)
A          J                             JOIN(EMPMAST EMPSKIL)
A                                        JFLD(EMPID EMPKEY)
A            NAME
A            SKIL
```

The key word JOIN defines the names of the files and the sequence in which they are to be joined. This is an optional entry when only two files are being joined, but is required for three or more files. The letter J is required in column 17. The key word JFLD defines the names of the fields that are common to the two files and are the fields upon which the connection will be based. EMPID and EMPKEY will contain an identification number for each employee.

In this example, the employee master file will control which records will appear in the joined logical file. This means that there will be a record in the logical file for every employee appearing in the EMPMAST physical file. Some employees, however, may have no record in the EMPSKIL file. Only the fields NAME and SKIL will be available in the joined logical file.

The joined logical file can provide faster response for inquiry programs. It is particularly valuable when three or more files must be accessed. The only requirement is that each pair of files must contain some common unit of information on which to base the connection.

Open Query File (OPNQRYF) ■

Open query file (OPNQRYF) is a command that allows the creation of a temporary version of a file within a procedure. This temporary file can be accessed from an RPG program, but it will not be retained on disk after the procedure has been executed.

Like a temporary logical file, a query file will occupy disk space only for the time needed to complete the requested processing. The OPNQRYF command will, however, require some execution time since it will be creating a new view of the file. Figure 18.5 shows the command for creating an open query file.

It is necessary to override the original physical file before beginning the processing. It is also necessary to open the file using the OPNQRYF command. After processing has been completed, it is necessary to close the file.

The OPNQRYF command provides many powerful methods for including or excluding selected data. It allows sequencing a file by fields that are not key fields, or even by portions of a field.

It is possible to perform an OPNQRYF function based on either a physical or a logical file. A logical file might be used when it fulfills only part of the requirements for performing some needed function. For example, a logical file might provide the correct file sequence, but a special selection criterion might be needed. Although the selection could be done within an RPG program, it might be faster to use the OPNQRYF function to eliminate unwanted records before processing. This method could also allow an existing RPG program to be used for processing under several alternative selection criteria. For example, a file might contain data for several different divisions of a company. The same RPG program could be used to print a separate report for each division, selecting the data for each in the OPNQRYF function.

Array Sorts

Sometimes the fastest and most effective method for producing the desired results is to arrange the data within the RPG program itself. Quite often, data sequencing is done by loading the data into an array and sorting the data using the SORTA operation. This can be rapid and effective for small amounts of data.

FIGURE 18.5 Creating an Open Query File

```
EDIT     US W:1    MBR: IL185CL           SCAN:
FMT **    ... ... 1 ... ... 2 ... ... 3 ... ... 4 ... ... 5 ... ... 6 ... ... 7
          ****BEGINNING OF DATA****
0001.00 /************************************************************/
0002.00 PGM
0003.00 /* OPEN QUERY FILE (IN SEQUENCE BY ZIP CODE, CATAGORY AND NAME) */
0004.00 OVRDBF CUSTMAST CUSTMAST SHARE(*YES)
0005.00            OPNQRYF    FILE((CUSTMAST)) KEYFLD((CUSZIP) +
0006.00                       (CUSCAT) (CUSNAM))
0007.00
0008.00 CALL PROG01
0009.00 CLOF OPNID(CUSTMAST)
0010.00 DLTOVR CUSTMAST
0011.00 ENDPGM
          ********END OF DATA********
```

Summarized Data

Another method for arranging data into a desired sequence is to read a large amount of data (in any sequence) and summarize it into a new file that has been created with some desired key. At last record (LR) time in the program the entire new file is printed and the created file is cleared. This method may work well when data sequence is determined by user selection and cannot be accurately predicted.

The programmer must determine which of these file structures fulfills the requirements of the application and the computer configuration on which it will run. Permanent logical files will provide the fastest access to data. If disk space is scarce, it may be necessary to sacrifice speed and create temporary logical, joined logical, or query files.

FILE DESIGN ■

In a large business environment, the programmer may not be able to choose the manner in which files are designed and structured. Small businesses that typically have mid-range computers using RPG, however, cannot afford the luxury of hiring a systems analyst. Under these conditions, the responsibility for file design is often left to the programmer.

File design has been studied for years and much has been written about it. IBM researcher Edgar Codd established some excellent principles for file design as early as 1969. Files structured in accordance with his principles are called normalized files. Briefly summarized, they provide the following advantages:

1. Data will not be redundant.
2. The flexibility and usability of the data will be maximized.
3. Add, delete, and update problems will be reduced.

The following example will illustrate these principles.

If all the information pertaining to some business function were placed in one record format, the resulting systems would be unnecessarily complex and very inflexible. For example, an inventory part record could carry the following information:

Part# (in-house part#)
Description (part description)
Quantity on hand
Warehouse# (warehouse where goods are stored)
Warehouse address
Shelf location (shelf where goods are stored)

Figure 18.6 shows what this file might look like.

FIGURE 18.6 Record Layout for Inventory Record Including All Related Fields

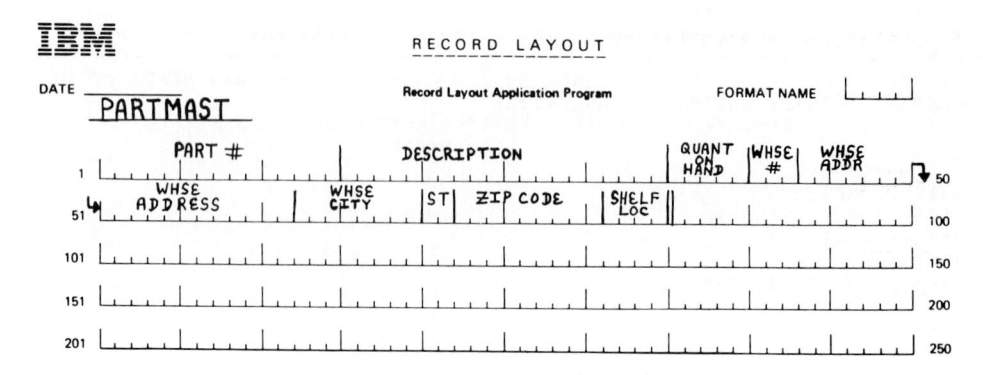

If all this information were carried in one record in one file, the programming would become more difficult. Some of the disadvantages of this structure are:

- A part record would need to contain multiple entries for warehouse and location information.
- Descriptions would be redundant, since many parts might exist at more than one warehouse.
- A new warehouse could not be added until a part that contained that information (i.e., was stored at that warehouse) existed.
- The integrity of the data would be put in doubt since the descriptive information would be repeated.

A better structure would separate the file into at least four different files:

1. A part master containing the following fields:
   Part#
   Description
2. A warehouse record containing the following fields:
   Part#
   Warehouse#
3. A warehouse address record containing the following fields:
   Warehouse#
   Warehouse address
4. A location detail record containing the following fields:
   Part#
   Warehouse#
   Shelf#
   Quantity on hand

Figures 18.7(a), 18.7(b), 18.7(c), and 18.7(d) show what this set of files might look like.

FIGURE 18.7(a) Part Master Record Layout

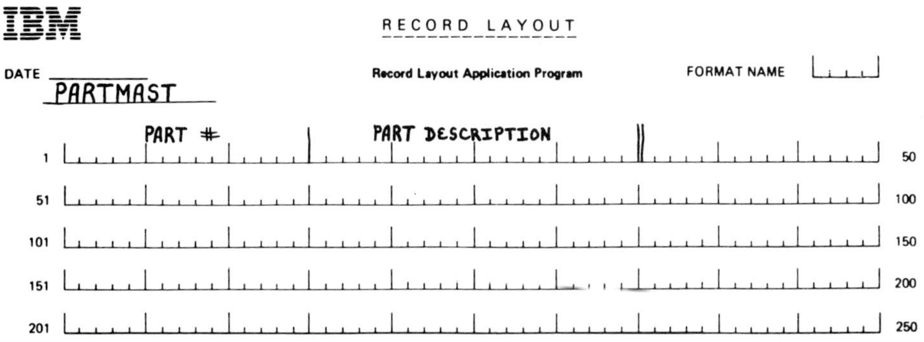

FIGURE 18.7(b) Warehouse Record Layout

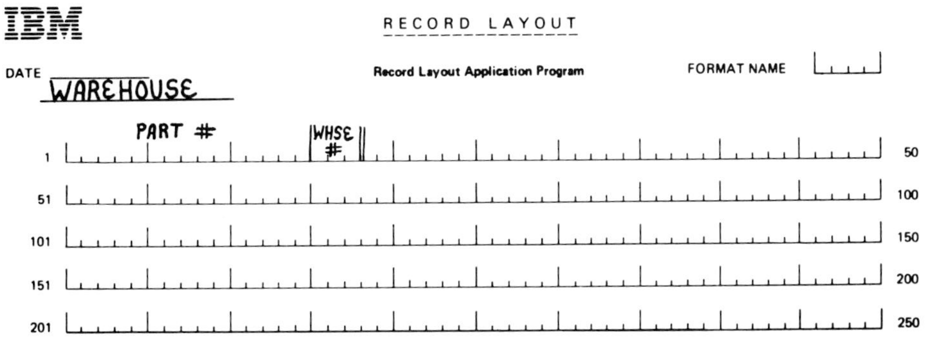

FIGURE 18.7(c) Warehouse Address Record Layout

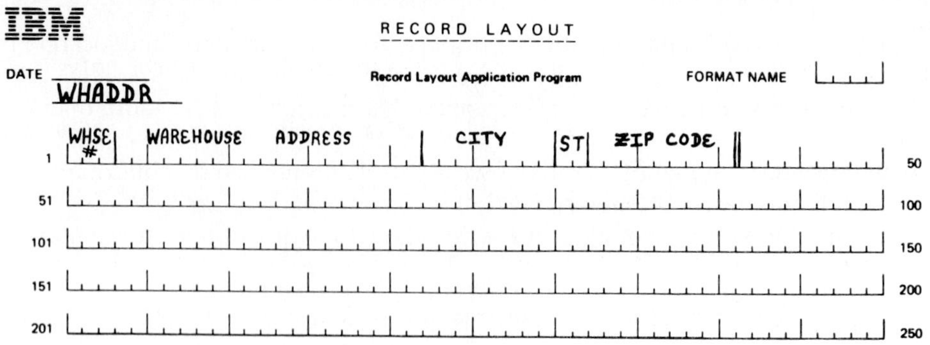

```
IBM                           RECORD LAYOUT
DATE  WHADDR        Record Layout Application Program    FORMAT NAME

   WHSE|  WAREHOUSE  ADDRESS      |  CITY  |ST| ZIP CODE
    #
```

FIGURE 18.7(d) Location Detail Record Layout

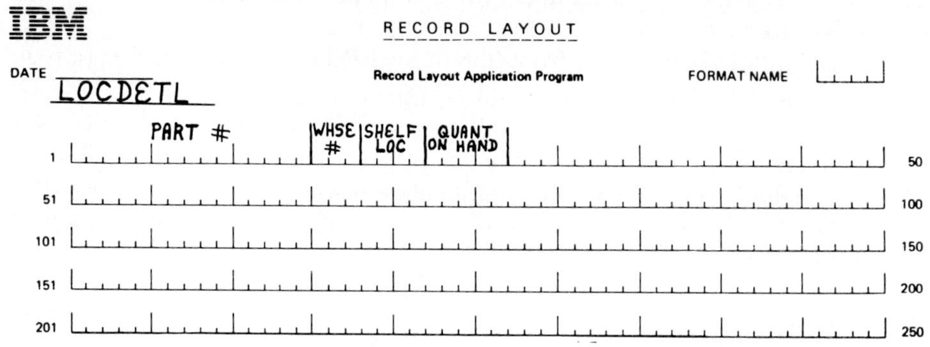

```
IBM                           RECORD LAYOUT
DATE  LOCDETL       Record Layout Application Program    FORMAT NAME

      PART #       |WHSE|SHELF|QUANT
                   | #  | LOC |ON HAND
```

This structure provides the following advantages:

1. Eliminates redundancy of descriptive fields such as warehouse address. This results in greater accuracy and reduces the amount of space needed for data storage.
2. Each part will have only one part master record.
3. Only the data needed for a report or screen will need to be accessed by a program.
4. Warehouses can be added as needed whether or not a part master exists. These warehouses can be accessed from other unrelated systems.
5. Descriptive fields can be changed in only one place and will affect all parts.

On the basis of this example, the principles of normalized file structure can now be spelled out as specific guidelines for the programmer:

1. Repeating groups of data should be placed in separate files. In the example, each part can exist at several warehouses and at multiple locations within each warehouse. Therefore, the warehouse and location data should be separated into independent files.
2. When there is a functional dependence between key fields and non-key fields, the non-key data should not be repeated unnecessarily. In the example, the warehouse address is a function of the warehouse number. It is not necessary to repeat the address for every part master record.
3. One fact should exist in only one place. In the example, the quantities on hand at each location can be added up to give the total quantity on hand at one warehouse. It is not necessary to keep a quantity figure in the warehouse record.

By structuring files into separate entities, less storage space will be needed and there will be much greater flexibility to make changes to the program when needed. It is seldom possible to predict future requirements. By providing a flexible database, the programmer will be able to respond to unexpected requests without rewriting an entire system.

SPECIAL DATA STRUCTURES ■

Data Areas

A data area is a special type of structure used to pass information between a procedure and a program or between jobs. It is not a true file and can contain only one record. This record contains only a small amount of data needed by the program. Data areas are useful for passing parameters such as a date, user name, or job description into a program.

There are two types of data area: the local data area (LDA), which has no specific name, and all other data areas, which are assigned names.

The LDA is available only within the program that accesses it, and only while the program is being executed. Debugging problems are more difficult in a program that is using an LDA.

The *named* data areas are accessible through commands and are available to multiple programs. A named data area can be created using the CRTDTAARA command. The data area is created as one field of data. A data area that is defined as numeric can be only 15 characters in length. A data area that is defined as alphanumeric can be as long as 2000 characters. Even though it must be defined as a single field in the data area, a large field can be broken up into subfields for use within an RPG program.

Data areas are handled differently from files in the RPG program. They do not require a File Description Specifications entry.

On the Input Specifications, a *U* is entered in position 18 followed by DS in positions 19–20. This defines it as a data structure. If no name is entered in columns 7–14, the local data area (LDA) will be assumed. If a name is entered, a specific data area will be accessed. The data area is broken up into separate fields in the data structure as needed. Figure 18.8 shows the coding for the Input Specifications data areas.

Three special calculation operations are used with data structures: IN, OUT, and UNLCK.

The IN operation retrieves a data area and allows it to be locked so it cannot be updated by another program while it is in use. Before the IN operation can be used, the data area must be defined with a *NAMVAR DEFN statement. Figure 18.9 illustrates the coding for locking a data area, making updates to it, and then unlocking it.

The result field of the DEFN statement contains the name of the data area. After the data area has been locked, the program may update the data area just as it would update any type of field. When the updates are complete, the data area can be unlocked using either the UNLCK or the OUT operation. In either case, factor 2 will contain the entry *NAMVAR.

FIGURE 18.8 Input Specifications for Data Areas

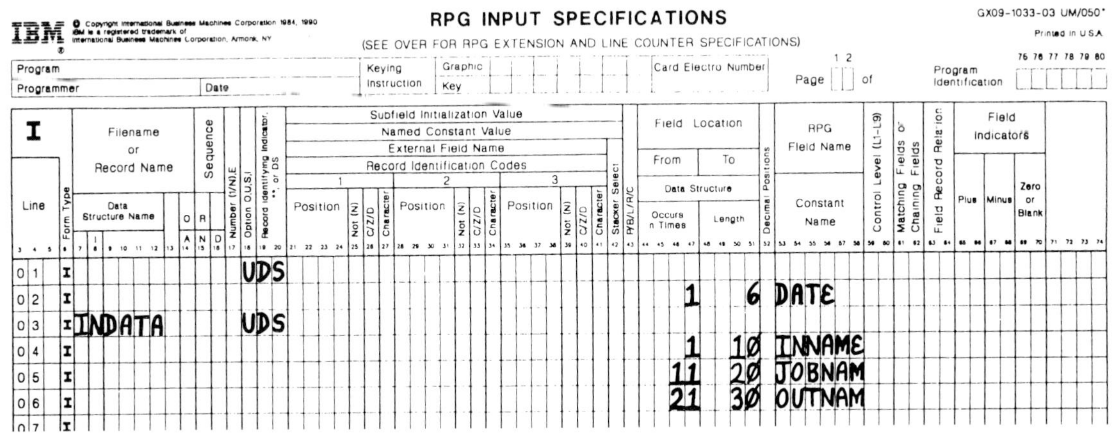

Line	Form Type	Filename or Record Name	Positions 18–20	From	To	RPG Field Name
01	I		UDS			
02	I			1	6	DATE
03	I	INDATA	UDS			
04	I			1	10	INNAME
05	I			11	20	JOBNAM
06	I			21	30	OUTNAM
07	I					

FIGURE 18.9 Locking, Updating, and Unlocking a Data Area

```
C  *NAMVAR   DEFN            *NAMVAR    INDATA
C  *LOCK     IN              *NAMVAR
C
C
C            MOVE  FLDA      INDATA
C
C
C LR         OUT             *NAMVAR
C
```

Multiple Occurrence Data Structure

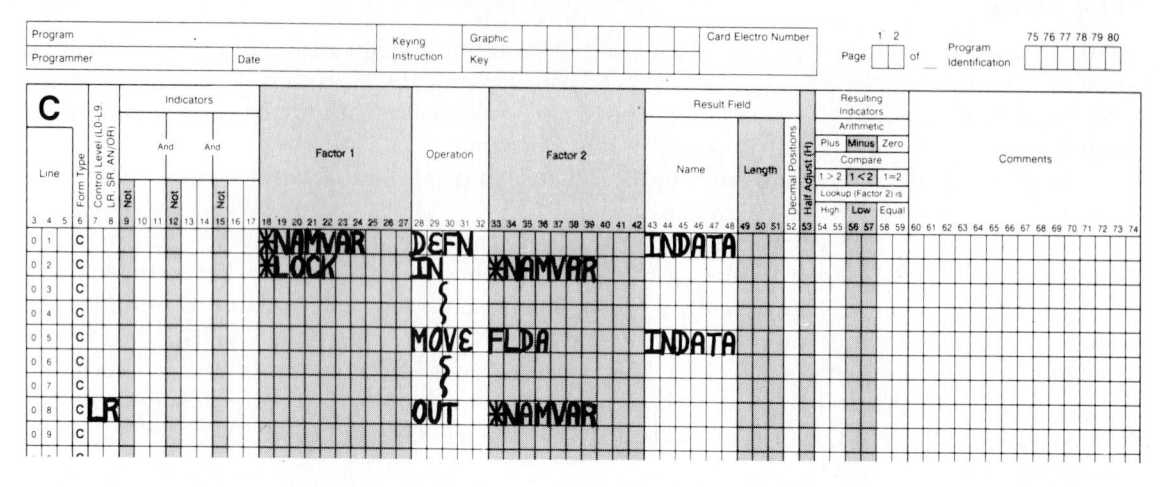

A multiple occurrence data structure is the same as any other type of data structure except that its definition may be repeated any number of times in a program. Thus, it forms a series of data structures with identical formats.

The number of occurrences of the data structure is entered in positions 44–47 of the Input Specifications, as shown in Figure 18.10.

All occurrences of a data structure have the same attributes and can be referred to individually. Only one data structure occurrence can be used at a time. The programmer can control the occurrence to be processed next by using the operation OCUR. The OCUR operation can be used only with multiple occurrence data structures. Factor 1 of the OCUR statement contains the value of the occurrence. If the first occurrence of the data structure is to be accessed, factor 1 should contain the value 1. Figure 18.11 demonstrates how the OCUR statement is used.

In this example, the occurrence is set at 5. This means that the fifth occurrence will be the next to be accessed and updated. Normal update operations are performed. The OCUR statement resets the occurrence to 6 for the next process. Factor 1 can be a literal or a data field containing the desired value. Factor 1 could even contain the name of another multiple data structure, in which case it would assume the occurrence value for the other data structure.

FIGURE 18.10 Input Specifications for Multiple Occurrences of the Data Structure

```
I  DS1        DS                              12
I                                   1  10  FLD1
I                                  11  20  FLD2
I                                  21  30  FLD3
I                                  31  40  FLD4
```

484   *RPG: A Programming Language for Today*

FIGURE 18.11 OCUR Statement

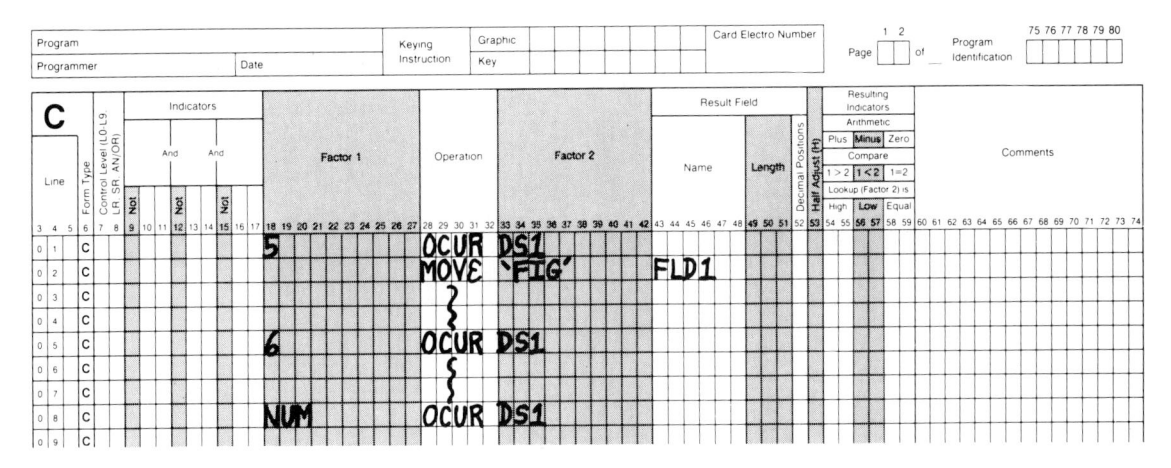

```
     5       OCUR DS1
             MOVE 'FIG'    FLD1
     ⋮
     6       OCUR DS1
     ⋮
     NUM     OCUR DS1
```

Factor 2 contains the name of the data structure on which the processing is being performed. The result field can contain the name to which the occurrence value will be transferred. An error indicator may be entered in positions 56–57. If the occurrence value is set at zero or to a value greater than that of the multiple occurrence data structure, the indicator will be set on and corrective action can be taken in the program.

File Information Data Structure (INFDS)

A file information data structure (INFDS) is a special data structure that can be defined to determine the nature of specific file exception errors in a program. The INFDS always contains predefined subfields as follows:

- The name of the file in which the error occurred
- The record being processed at the time of the error
- The last operation being performed
- The status code
- The RPG routine in which the error occurred

This is the same information available to the system when a program dump is received. The programmer is able to access this information by placing the INFDS in the program. Figures 18.12(a), 18.12(b), and 18.12(c) show the coding for the File Description, Input, and Calculation Specifications for using an INFDS data structure.

The field identified for the *STATUS will contain one of a series of error codes concerning files. This code can be used to identify the type of error being encountered.

Program Status Data Structure

The program status data structure is a tool for identifying the cause of errors in a program. Similar to the INFDS, this data structure has a specific format. The program status data structure requires no special entry on the File Description Specifications. It requires no name entry on the Input Specifications, since it is related to no specific file. It is identified as a particular type of data structure by entering an S in column 18 just before the DS entry. The subfields in the program status data structure are routine, status, parameters, and program name. The predefined subfields have field names assigned. The coding for the Input Specifications is shown in Figure 18.13.

FIGURE 18.12(a) Using an INFDS: File Specifications

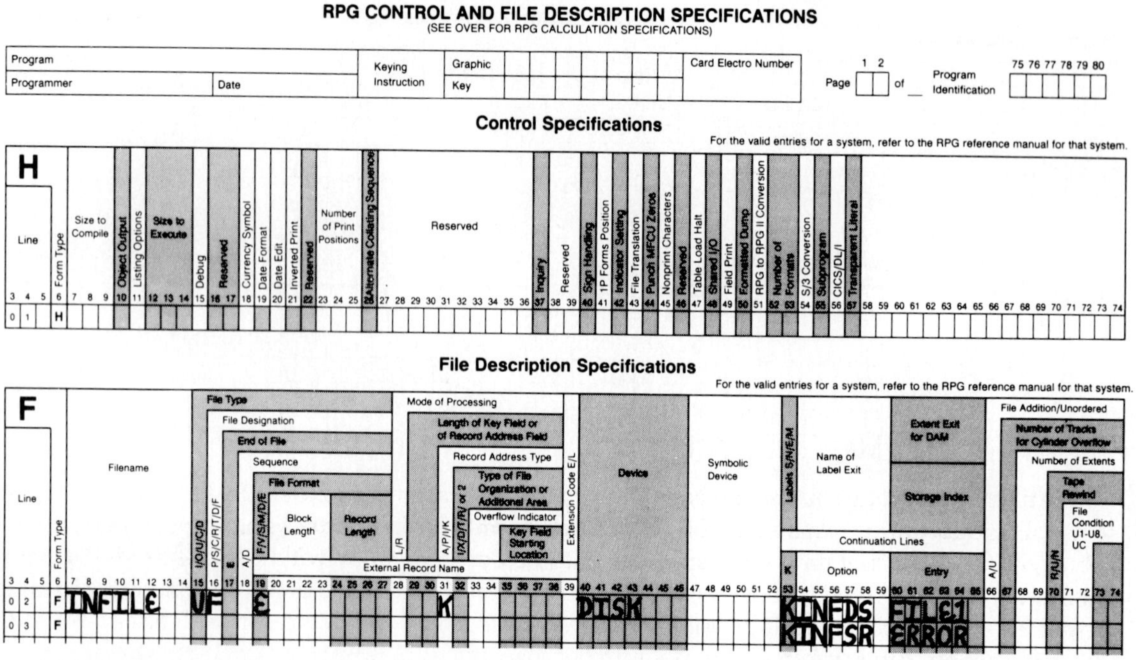

F-spec entries:
```
02 F INFILE  UF  E           K        DISK              KINFDS FILE1
03 F                                                    KINFSR ERROR
```

FIGURE 18.12(b) Using an INFDS: Input Specifications

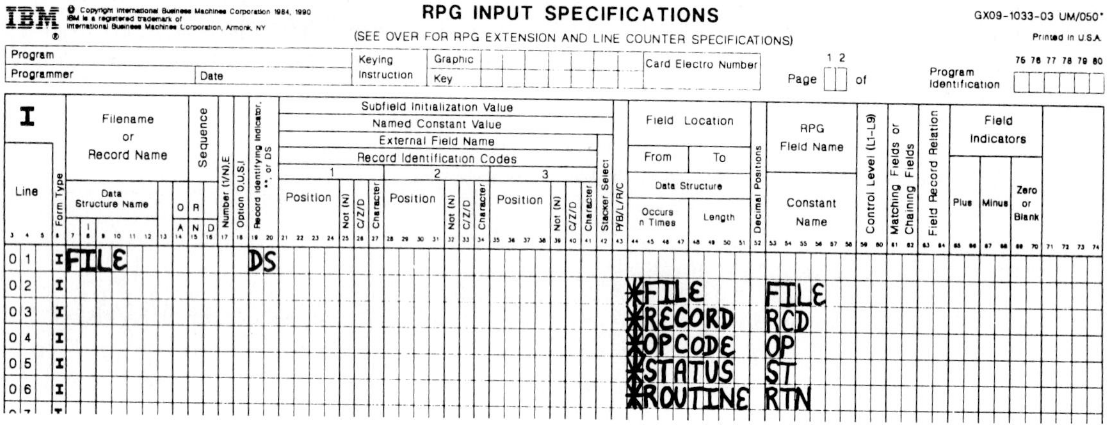

I-spec entries:
```
01 I FILE     DS
02 I
03 I                                   *FILE    FILE
04 I                                   *RECORD  RCD
05 I                                   *OPCODE  OP
06 I                                   *STATUS  ST
07 I                                   *ROUTINE RTN
```

FIGURE 18.12(c) Using an INFDS: Calculation Specifications

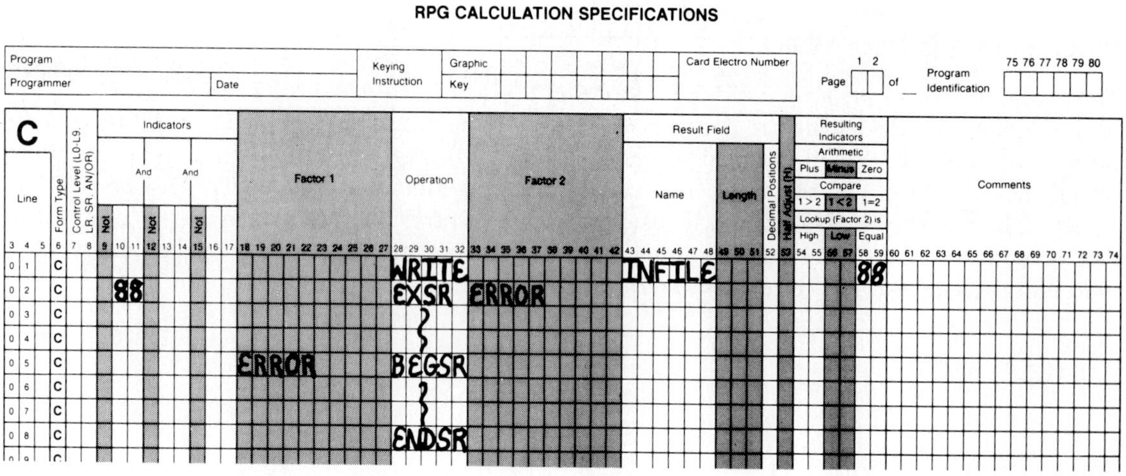

C-spec entries:
```
01 C                WRITE INFILE
02 C          88    EXSR  ERROR                  88
03 C
04 C
05 C       ERROR    BEGSR
06 C
07 C
08 C                ENDSR
```

FIGURE 18.13 Input Specifications for Program Status Data Structure

Line	I	Filename or Record Name / Data Structure Name	...	Subfield Initialization Value / Named Constant Value / External Field Name	Field Location From–To	RPG Field Name	Constant Name
01	I	SDS					
02	I					*ROUTINE	ROUT
03	I					*STATUS	STAT
04	I					*PARMS	PARM
05	I					*PROGRAM	PROG
06	I						

An error-handling routine can be written by the programmer and identified by the subroutine *PSSR. This subroutine can be called from within the program and used to handle any errors. The subroutine will execute any time a program error occurs in the program whether or not the subroutine has been explicitly called. Figure 18.14 shows an example of a subroutine for handling program errors.

The status code is compared to a specific error code. If this error is the one in the program, some specific action can be taken either to correct the problem or to notify the programmer about the event.

The subroutine can be coded to return to the program statement from which it came by moving the constant *DETC into a field identified as the destination. The subroutine can cancel the job by moving the constant *CANCL into the destination field. The destination field is then entered in factor 2 of the ENDSR statement.

FIGURE 18.14 Subroutine for Handling Program Errors

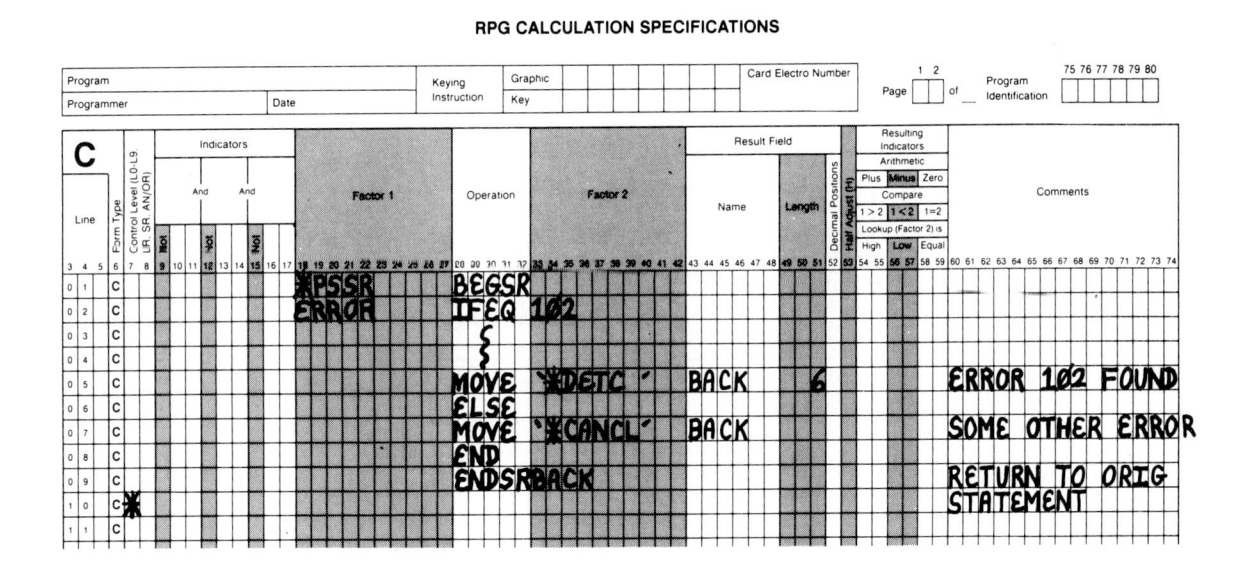

Line	C	Factor 1	Operation	Factor 2	Result Field Name	Length	Comments
01	C	*PSSR	BEGSR				
02	C	ERROR	IFEQ	102			
03	C						
04	C						
05	C		MOVE	'*DETC'	BACK	6	ERROR 102 FOUND
06	C		ELSE				
07	C		MOVE	'*CANCL'	BACK		SOME OTHER ERROR
08	C		END				
09	C		ENDSR	BACK			RETURN TO ORIG STATEMENT
10	C						
11	C						

Chapter 18 Programming Efficiencies in RPG III/400

STRUCTURED PROGRAMMING METHODS ■

Whole books have been written on the very important subject of structured programming. This section does not attempt to cover the subject in depth. It is hoped that the reader will have already studied structured programming and is aware of its concepts. This review covers structured programming as it is applied to the RPG language.

The top-down approach to program design is illustrated in the hierarchy chart in Figure 18.15. Structured programs are created as a series of separate modules that operate as independently as possible. In RPG these are called subroutines.

One of the goals of structured programming is the elimination of the use of the GOTO command. The use of a GOTO allows a programmer to branch anywhere within a program with no guarantee that good logic is being used or that the logic of the program will ever return to the point from which it came. The GOTO operation itself is not the problem. The problem lies in the logic that is used. Using a GOTO, a programmer is free to skip illogically back and forth and completely miss executing whole sections of code or execute a section more times than intended. This is how unending loops are created.

To avoid such problems, the GOTO logic can be replaced with Do Until or Do While logic that always returns the program to the next statement. This is done in RPG with the use of subroutines. This does not mean that the GOTO can *never* be used. It means that the GOTO should not be used indiscriminately. The EXSR and DOxxx operations should control the greater part of the logic.

A GOTO should never cause a return backwards through a program to an earlier statement. A GOTO should also not branch very far. It is preferable that it branch no more than 50 statements so that its destination is not difficult to find when debugging or maintenance is necessary.

The calculation section of an RPG program should follow the standard hierarchy chart. The main section of the Calculation Specifications should consist of a series of EXSR operations that

FIGURE 18.15 Hierarchy Chart

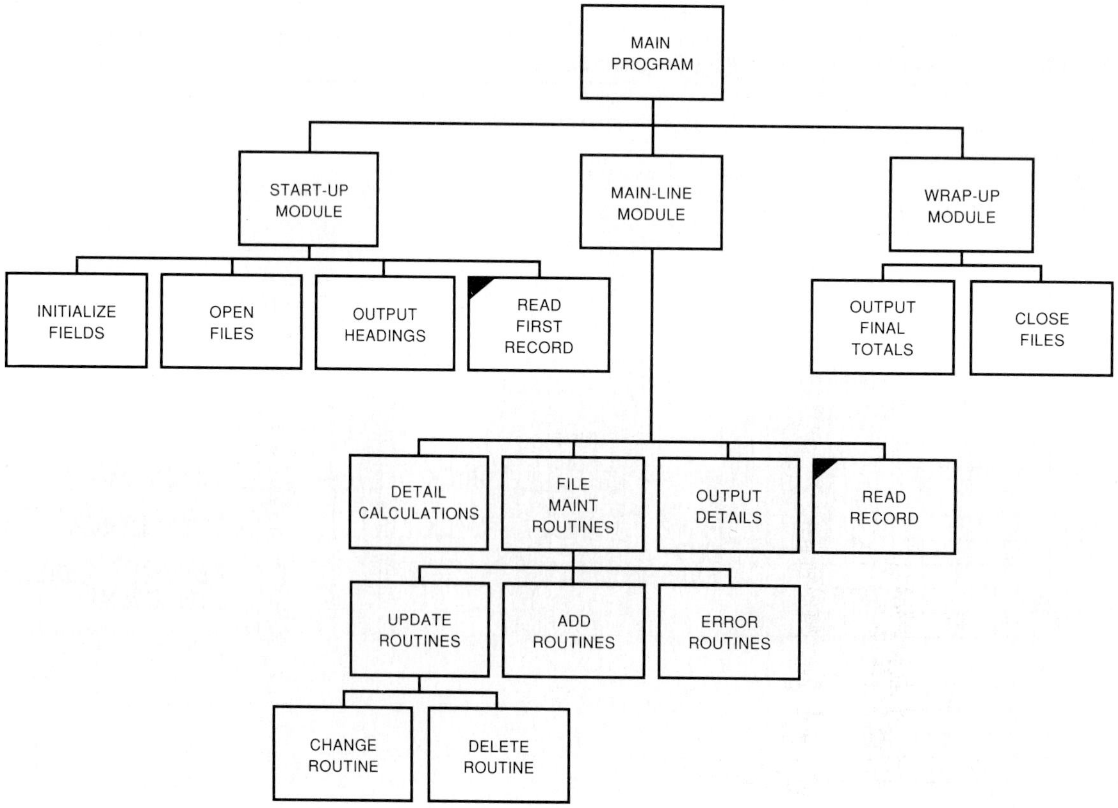

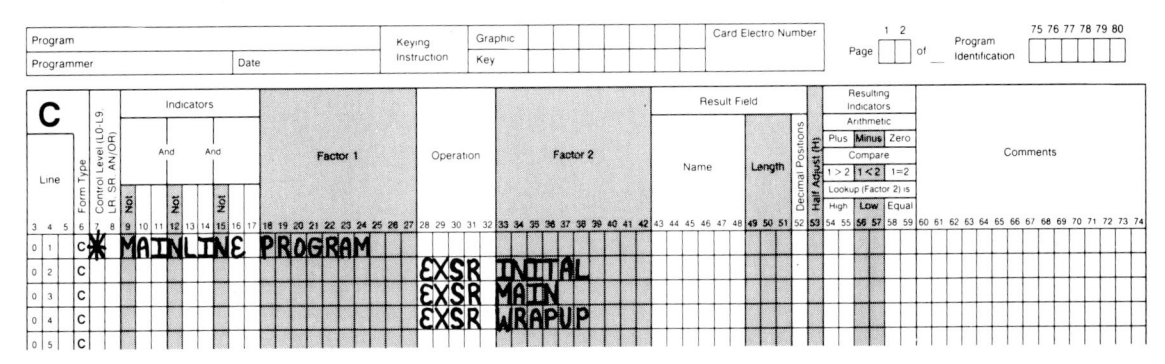

FIGURE 18.16 Calculation Specifications for Main Line of a Structured Program

```
* MAINLINE PROGRAM
C           EXSR INITAL
C           EXSR MAIN
C           EXSR WRAPUP
```

retrieve the appropriate subroutines. These may be optionally conditioned by events occurring within the preceding subroutines, but all the major work should be performed in the subroutines. Figure 18.16 shows the Calculation Specifications for the main line of a structured program.

The first subroutine to be performed is the initialization. All events that must be done before the beginning of processing should be contained within the initializing subroutine. Figure 18.17 shows some examples of the types of operations that might be placed in an initializing subroutine. Since it should be performed only once, the execution operation should be conditioned with an indicator (which must be off). That indicator must be set on in the subroutine itself. A truly structured program would not use the fixed RPG cycle for processing and therefore would not need to condition the initialize subroutine, since the program would never return to the beginning of the main line of the calculations.

The main processing section of the program consists of subroutines that call other subroutines and always return to the calling subroutine. Within these subroutines the coding consists of processing the full functional files using DO loops and READ operations in a structured manner. Note that the first SETLL and READ to the primary file was performed in the initialization module. As shown in Figure 18.18, this first record is processed in the main processing section, and the last event in the DO loop is the READ for the next record. The READ is placed at the end of the DO loop to eliminate the need for a GOTO operation.

FIGURE 18.17 Examples of Initializing Routine Operations

```
C     INITAL    BEGSR
C               TIME           TYME    60
C               MOVE *BLANKS   ERRFLD  1
C     DATE      MULT 10000.01  JDATE   60
C               SETON                         10
C               MOVE 35        KEYFLD
C     KEY       SETLL INFIL10
C               READ  INFIL10                    90
C     KEY       KLIST
C               KFLD           KEYFLD
C               ENDSR
```

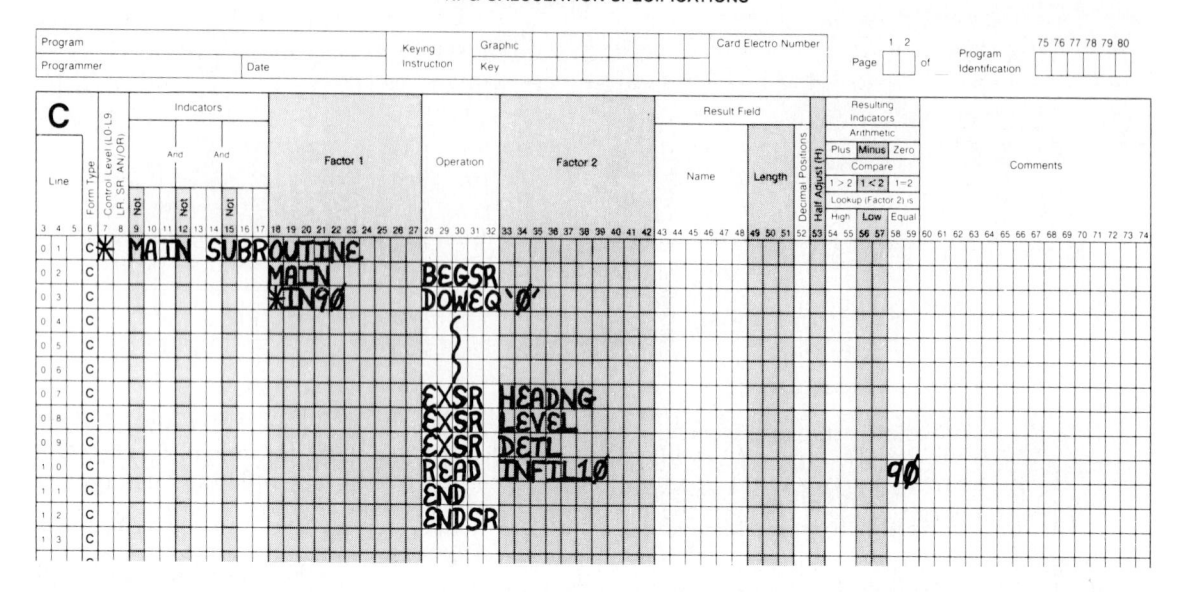

FIGURE 18.18 Example of Main Processing Routine

```
* MAIN SUBROUTINE
          MAIN      BEGSR
          *IN90     DOWEQ '0'
          {
                    EXSR HEADNG
                    EXSR LEVEL
                    EXSR DETL
                    READ INFIL10                    90
                    END
                    ENDSR
```

Indicators should be used only when required by RPG. RPG III/400 provides all the structures necessary for structured programming. These are the DOWxx, DOUxx, IFxx, and CASxx operation codes. These structures should eliminate nearly all need for indicators and should always be the preferred method for coding. The CABxx operation is not included in this group since it encourages the same faulty logic as a GOTO.

When all processing has been completed, a final wrap-up subroutine should be executed. This subroutine should include all final report totals or summaries required at last record time. Files are closed if necessary and the last record indicator is set on. Figure 18.19 shows a typical final subroutine.

FIGURE 18.19 Example of Wrap-Up Subroutine

```
* WRAP-UP ROUTINE
          WRAPUP    BEGSR
                    EXSR HEADNG
                    EXSR LEVEL
          {
                    EXSR FINTOT
                    ENDSR
```

TOOLS FOR THE SUPERPROGRAMMER

Efficiency in business data processing consists of such factors as the processing speed of the hardware, the speed with which programs execute, the amount of auxiliary storage required for the database, the ease of operation, the amount of time required to design, write, implement, and maintain the program, and of course the costs involved with all of these. It is impossible to achieve perfection in all of these factors at the same time since they pull in opposing directions.

However, it is the responsibility of the data processing professional to attempt to improve the efficiency of a system by achieving the best balance between the factors. The programmer may have little control over the selection of hardware or the amount of budget allocated to a project, but the other factors can be balanced to reach an optimal level of efficiency.

Some tips for obtaining that balance of efficiency follow:

- Never retain unnecessary or redundant data on disk. Although this appears obvious, there is often the temptation to create a quick file to respond to a sudden demand from users. This quick file may become a permanent file unless the programmer is careful to house-clean immediately. Although managing projects correctly often takes a little longer, a well-planned system should preclude the need for the quick fix. Unplanned emergency programs can cause problems that take more time to unravel than planning would have taken.
- Project planning should include file planning. Files should be designed to include all elements of data that will be needed by that system. Although predicting future needs is not easy, a good systems analyst will design the file with future goals in mind so that it will not be necessary to revise the file for every new application. This can prevent spending nonproductive hours in rewriting programs and systems.
- Normalized file structure provides greater flexibility for accommodating a variety of applications.
- If an entire file must be processed, the fastest method of processing will be sequentially. There is some debate whether using the RPG processing cycle is faster than using full procedural coding.
- If only a portion of a file is to be processed, the fastest method of processing will be to address it by key. Never process an entire file if only a part of it is needed.
- Use logical files with record selection when possible so that only the desired records will need to be examined in the program.
- Logical files that exclude unnecessary fields will process faster than logical files containing all fields.
- Chaining to a file (or files) repetitively in a program will cause it to run much more slowly. Run time may be reduced by creating JOIN files.
- However, maintaining many logical files will slow the processing of updates to the physical file. The number of logical files on a system should be kept to a minimum.
- When a file is used only briefly in a program, access it with an OPEN statement and then release it with a CLOSE statement as soon as it is no longer needed. This reduces the amount of memory needed to hold the file open during the entire program. It also releases the file sooner for use in other systems so that the other systems become more efficient as well.
- Never execute coding steps unnecessarily. The use of structured programming methods should help to avoid this. Steps that need to be performed only once in a program should be placed in a subroutine and performed only once. Avoid performing repetitive DO loops more times than needed.
- Use a field reference file (REF) for every field in every file. Although it requires an extra step in program development, REF has long-term benefits. It is valuable for establishing a single control point for all fields and their attributes. It is valuable for documentation and as a programming aid.
- Do not set up fields or indicators that are never used in a program. Every field and indicator has an associated cost in memory usage and processing time. Extraneous fields and indicators only serve to make the program less readable.

- Use the *LIKE DEFN operation to define the attributes of fields created in a program. This will help make future coding changes easier.
- On-line programs that access large files and load them into subfiles can take a long time to execute. The user could be staring at a blank screen for 20 minutes wondering what has happened. The programmer should avoid this by gathering the subfile data in smaller groups. The user is given only one group of records at a time with an option to continue to more data when needed.
- When subfiles for large amounts of data are created, the subfile size should be small (50–100 records). When the user requires data beyond the last record in the subfile, the program should contain the logic to load the next 50–100 records into the subfile automatically and display them on the screen. Using this method, the user will not have to wait for data and will have access to all the data required.
- Always document programs. A documentation section at the beginning of every program should explain the use of the program, the date created, the author, and any important information about the program. Some of the aspects that should be explained are:

    The use of external switches
    The meanings of all codes used
    Any special handling required
    Schedule on which program is to be run
    Dependence on other programs

- An entry should be made in the documentation section of a program every time a modification is made to that program. This entry should consist of the date, the name of the programmer, and an explanation of the nature of the change. Often it is useful to note the name of the user requesting the change. Entries should be made in this change log even when the change itself is minor.
- It is not necessary to be thrifty with documentation lines in a program. They have no effect on the speed of execution or the efficiency of the compiled program.
- Although documentation does not directly affect the efficiency of program execution, it can have a major impact on the overall efficiency of the data processing function.
- The programmer should always design programs that are easy to operate. Whenever possible, decisions and editing should be done by the program and not by the operator, data entry, or user. The fewer decisions that must be made by the people involved, the less opportunity there will be for errors to occur.
- A good program must anticipate errors and be prepared to deal with them. It is not good programming technique to allow the system to abort when an error is encountered. When the system cancels a program, it causes user frustration. The user may not understand what has happened or what to do about it. Aborting a program can destroy data or leave data in a half-updated condition that requires hours of programmer intervention. A system dump can hold up all the other users on the system until it completes. None of these is a desirable result. It is much better to try to predict what a user might inadvertently do to cause an error condition and write a few lines of code program to display a message. This gives the user an opportunity to take alternative action.

Efficiency includes the ease of maintenance of a program. Programming time is valuable and maintenance programming can be extremely time-consuming if the original program is poorly written. Structured code is easier to read and understand, so it will be easier to debug and maintain. By coding each separate function in a separate subroutine, the programmer can make changes to one function without affecting (or rewriting) the rest of the program.

Indicators should not be used in modern RPG programs. Some operations, such as the READ, require the use of resulting indicators, but these uses can be kept to a minimum. When a flag is needed, it is used in the format *INxx and used with the structured logic operations such as the DOWxx, DOUxx, IFxx, and CASxx. These structures improve the readability of a program and make the program easier to debug. These structures will execute more efficiently.

When a flag is needed, indicators should not be reused. Reusing indicators for different purposes does not improve efficiency—it only serves to make the program more confusing and probably will generate errors in the code.

The use of structured programming methods is in itself an efficiency. Writing structured code takes no more time than writing unstructured code. A programmer can produce a completed project more rapidly using structured code because the time for debugging and testing will be reduced.

Many other efficiencies could be considered. Each new application carries its own set of conditions that must be weighed by the programmer to determine the best solution. There is never enough time to create the perfect solution, even if one existed. Most programs are less than perfect.

It is the professional programmer's job to create programs that will execute without errors in the shortest possible time and with the least expenditure of resources and still produce the desired results.

SUMMARY ■

In this chapter you have learned about programming efficiencies. Many of the efficiencies in RPG III/400 are produced by good planning and system design. The fundamental structures that are true for other languages also apply to the RPG language.

Good file design can be a big factor in improving the overall efficiency of a system. When large files are used, design becomes of even greater importance in processing the data rapidly.

The choice of file structures may be a sorted physical file, a logical file, a JOIN file, or a file with which the OPNQRYF utility has been used. The file may be created as an array within an RPG program and sequenced with the use of the SORTA operation code. A file may be created and sequenced within an RPG program and output in the desired sequence using the logic itself. The choice of file structure is the responsibility of the programmer and is important to the success and usefulness of an application.

The analyst or programmer should know and use the best methods for building file structures. Normalized file structure is a method for ensuring that a system will have flexibility and design efficiency.

One type of data file that has not been discussed in earlier chapters is the data area. The data area is not a true file, but provides a convenient vehicle for carrying a small amount of data into or out of a program.

Besides the data structures discussed in earlier chapters for redefining files, there are several special data structures. Multiple occurrence arrays provide a method for using an array structure repetitively. The file information data structure (INFDS) and the program status data structure make system status information available to the RPG program. This information can be helpful in identifying program errors or other current status.

Structured programming methods are important in creating programs that are easy to debug and to modify when necessary.

The superprogrammer must keep all the efficiency factors in mind when designing and creating or modifying a computer system.

REVIEW QUESTIONS

1. What are some of the factors that contribute to greater efficiency in the execution of a program?

2. What are the methods by which a file can be manipulated to provide a desired sort sequence for use in a program?

3. When is it beneficial to perform a physical sort of a file?

4. When data is needed in a program in a sort sequence different from that of the physical file, a _____ file should be used.

5. When more than one physical file is combined to provide access to data, a _____ file can be created.

6. The OPNQRYF command not only provides a correct sort sequence for use in a program but also can be used to _____ records.

7. When the OPNQRYF command is used, the new version of the file is available until _____ .

8. Within an RPG program, data can be sorted into a desired sequence with the use of the _____ operation.

9. What are some of the benefits to be derived from the use of normalized file structure?

10. Explain the method for creating normalized file structures.

11. In what way does a data area differ from a physical file?

12. What are the two types of data area?

13. Name the three RPG operations that can be used with data areas.

14. Give some examples of applications in which a data area might be more advantageous than a physical file.

15. Explain the use of a multiple occurrence data structure.

16. The _____ operation is used to define the number of times a multiple occurrence data structure is to be used in a program.

17. What are some of the pieces of information that are available when the file information data structure (INFDS) is used in a program?

18. Explain the function of the *PSSR subroutine.

19. Give a brief explanation of the rules of structured programming.

PROGRAMMING PROJECT

Project Overview

A report is to be printed listing assets in sequence by acquisition date. A total of depreciated value should be printed at the end of each month. Write the commands and RPG program to produce this listing. Sample data for this project can be found in Appendix D.

Input Format

The input data for the project is found in a file called ASSETS in the sample data. The Record Layout for this file is shown in Figure 18.20.

Processing

Since the assets file is not in sequence by date, it will be necessary to find a method for producing the correct sequence. Write the OPNQRYF commands to put the assets file in the sequence required.

Using structured programming methods, read the file, print each line, and cause a level break to print totals after each month.

Output Format (Printer Spacing Chart)

The output format for the project is a report with standard headings. The report will show the asset number, description, date of acquisition, and depreciated value. The Printer Spacing Chart for this report is shown in Figure 18.21.

An example of the finished report is shown in Figure 18.22.

FIGURE 18.20 Programming Project: Record Layout

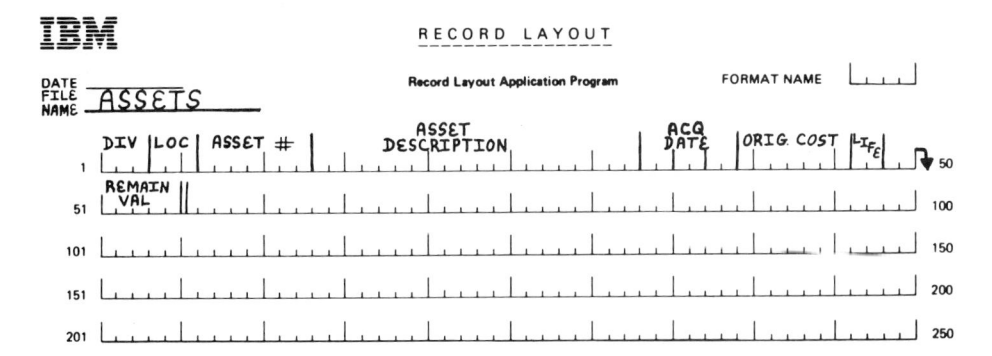

FIGURE 18.21 Programming Project: Printer Spacing Chart

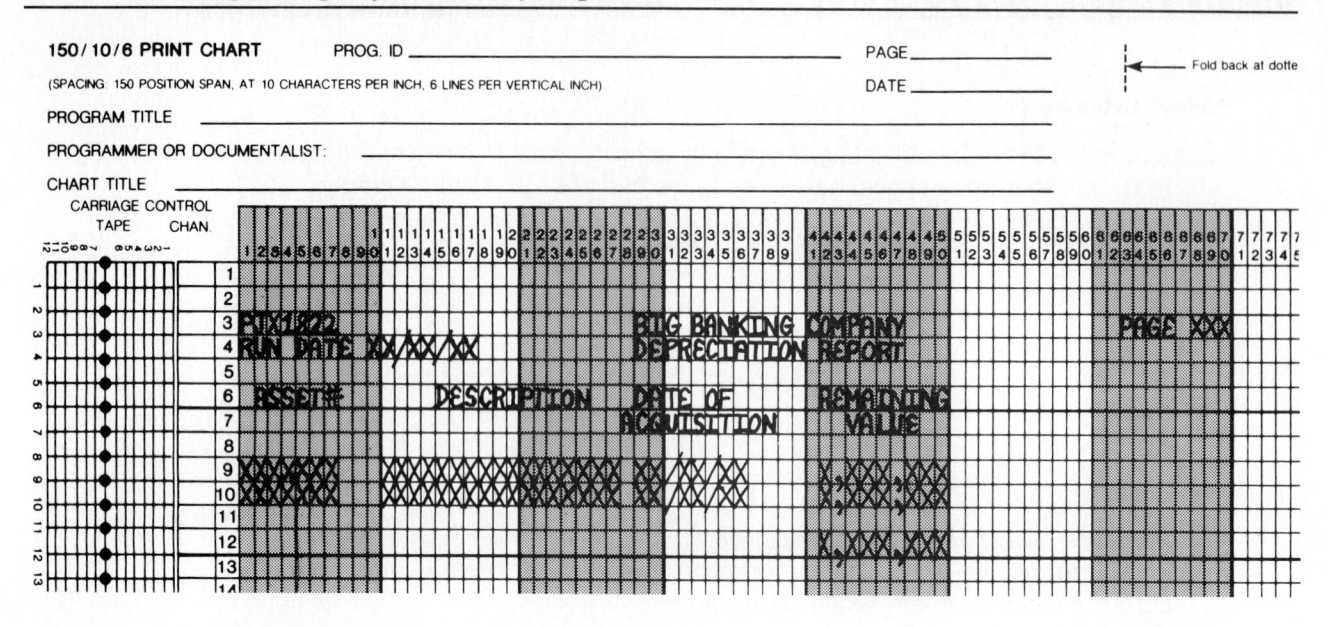

FIGURE 18.22 Programming Project: Finished Report

```
PJX1822                    BIG BANKING COMPANY              PAGE    1
RUN DATE  3/22/92          DEPRECIATION REPORT

    ASSET#      DESCRIPTION    DATE OF        REMAINING
                               ACQUISITION    VALUE

    12345       WRAPPING MACHINE    3/01/91    337,500

    25689       DISC MACHINE        4/01/91    166,930

    56987       GLITTER MACHINE     1/01/91     50,250

    48605       WANES-GAUGE         6/01/90

    58421       PAPER CUTTER        7/01/92     41,307

    73258       CODE GENERATOR      2/29/92     83,671

                                                684,658
```

496   *RPG: A Programming Language for Today*

Appendix A

Chart of Collating Sequences

ASCII	EBCDIC
blank	blank
!	.
"	(
#	+
$	&
%	!
&	$
'	*
(	)
)	;
*	-
+	/
,	,
-	%
/	>
0–9	?
:	:
;	#
<	@
=	'
>	=
?	"
@	A–Z
A–Z	0–9

Appendix B

Summary of Calculation Operation Codes

ARITHMETIC OPERATION CODES ■

ADD	Add
DIV	Divide
MULT	Multiply
MVR	Move remainder
SUB	Subtract
XFOOT	Cross-foot
Z-ADD	Zero and add
Z-SUB	Zero and subtract

LOGIC OPERATION CODES ■

CABxx	Compare and branch
CASxx	Case
COMP	Compare two fields or values
DO	Do
DOUxx	Do Until
DOWxx	Do While
ELSE	Else
END	End
IFxx	If statement

OTHER OPERATION CODES ■

BEGSR	Begin a subroutine
BITOF	Set a bit off
BITON	Set a bit on
CALL	Call another program
CHAIN	Access another file based on a key
CLOSE	Close a file
DEBUG	Identify problems in a program
DEFN	Define the attributes of a field
DELET	Delete a record from a file

DSPLY	Display a message
ENDSR	End a subroutine
EXCPT	Output a record
EXFMT	Execute a screen format on a screen; combined WRITE/READ
EXSR	Execute a subroutine
FEOD	Force end of data
FORCE	Force a file READ
GOTO	Branch to another line in a program
IN	Retrieve a data area
KFLD	Define a key field
KLIST	Name a key for a file
LOCK	Lock a data area
LOKUP	Look up a value in an array or table
MHHZO	Move high to high zone
MHLZO	Move high to low zone
MLHZO	Move low to high zone
MLLZO	Move low to low zone
MOVE	Copy a field or value (right-justified)
MOVEA	Copy a field or value to or from an array
MOVEL	Copy a field or value (left-justified)
OCUR	Define the occurrence of a data structure
OPEN	Open a file
OUT	Output a data area
PARM	List parameters
PLIST	Define the beginning of a group of parameters
READ	Read a record (or screen)
READC	Read changed records from a screen
READE	Read a record of similar key
READP	Read previous record
RETRN	Return to a previous program
SETGT	Set greater than
SETLL	Set lower limits
SETOF	Set indicator off
SETON	Set indicator on
SORTA	Sort array
TAG	Create a label
TESTB	Test a bit for on/off condition
TESTN	Test a bit for numeric values
TESTZ	Test a field for zone
TIME	Retrieve the system time for use in a program
UNLCK	Unlock a data area
UPDAT	Update a file
WRITE	Write to a file or screen

Appendix C

Card Processing Anomalies

Most card processing equipment is now obsolete and is seldom found attached to computer equipment. The RPG compiler, however, retains the options to handle card media.

FILE DESCRIPTION SPECIFICATIONS ■

The File Description Specifications will still accept READ05 or CARD as a device name (depending on hardware).

INPUT SPECIFICATIONS ■

The Input Specifications carries most of the antiquated options so a card reader device can be controlled. The following entries on the Input Specifications are used to direct the processing of cards only:

Sequence number   (columns 15–16)

A numeric entry is used to ensure that input cards are in sequence. Numeric entries must be in ascending order, starting with 01. The appropriate entries must also be made in columns 17 and 18.

Number   (column 17)

This entry is used in combination with the sequence number in columns 15–16.

1 — Only one record of this type can be present in the group.

N — One or more records of this type can be present in the group.

Option   (column 18)

This entry is used in combination with the sequence number in columns 15–16.

> Blank — The record type must be present.
>
> O — The record type is optional.

A card processing device usually is composed of two input hoppers and several output stackers. The stacker selection entry controls which stacker is to be used after they have been read.

Stacker selection   (column 42)

This entry determines which cards are to be dropped into which stacker after being processed. The default stacker is the first stacker. If several record types are being read as input, it might be desirable to separate them into separate stackers after they have been processed.

OUTPUT SPECIFICATIONS ■

A card processing device might be used as an output device to punch holes into blank card stock. To manage this there is an entry on the Output Specifications to control the stacker into which these output cards will be placed.

Stacker selection   (column 16)

A numeric entry (1 through 4) in column 16 will select the stack into which output cards will be placed. The default stacker will be stacker 1. For a combined input/output file, the stacker select code in the Output Specifications will override the stacker select code in the Input Specifications.

*PRINT   (columns 32–37)

*PRINT is a special word, specified in positions 32–37 (field name) of the Output Specifications. It causes all punched fields of a record type preceding the *PRINT specification line to be printed on the same card.

Appendix D

Physical File Descriptions for Files Available on Diskette

DATA DEFINITION ■

APOPEN (Project 4)

1–6	APOVEN	(6)	Vendor# (key)
7–26	APONAM	(20)	Vendor name
27–34	APOINV	(7)	Invoice#
35–40	APODUE	(6.0)	Due date xx-xx-xx (mm/dd/yy)
41–45	APOQTY	(5.0)	Quantity xxxxx
46–52	APOAMT	(7.2)	Amount xxxxx.xx
53–57	APODSC	(5.2)	Discount xxx.xx

ASSETS (Projects 14 and 18)

1–3	ASTDIV	(3.0)	Division
4–6	ASTLOC	(3.0)	Location
7–13	ASTNO	(7.0)	Asset# (key)
14–33	ASTDSC	(20)	Description
34–39	ASTDAT	(6.0)	Date of acquisition (yy-mm-dd)
40–46	ASTCST	(7.0)	Original cost
47–48	ASTLIF	(2)	Life (number of years)
49–55	ASTVAL	(7.0)	Remaining value

CUSTMAST (Projects 1, 2, 15, and 17)

1–5	CUSNUM	(5.0)	Customer# (key)
6–25	CUSNAM	(20)	Customer name
26–28	CUSCAT	(3)	Category
29–36	CUSMTD	(8.0)	Month-to-date sales
37–46	CUSYTD	(10.0)	Year-to-date sales
47–66	CUSADR	(20)	Customer address
67–76	CUSCTY	(10)	Customer city
77–78	CUSST	(2)	Customer state
79–87	CUSZIP	(9)	Customer zip code

INVDETL (Project 13)

1–3	DTLDIV	(3.0)	Division (Div 900 is a deleted record)
4–6	DTLWHS	(3)	Warehouse#
7–13	DTLPNO	(7.0)	Item part# (key)
14–32	DTLDSC	(19)	Part description
33–34	DTLUM	(2)	Unit of measure
35–39	DTLQOH	(5.0)	Quantity on hand
40–46	DTLAVG	(7.2)	Average cost xxxxx.xx
47–51	DTLBIN	(5)	Shelf/bin location
52–53	DTLTYP	(2)	Type of product
54–55	DTLCAT	(2)	Category code (AA, DD)
56–58	DTLDPT	(3)	Department

INVMAST (Project 16)

1–3	INVDIV	(3.0)	Division
4–10	INVPNO	(7.0)	Part# (key)
11–30	INVPNN	(20)	Part name
31–34	INVTYP	(4)	Type of product
35–39	INVSTY	(5)	Style
40–42	INVWHS	(3)	Warehouse (001 or 300 or 400)
43–43	INSTAT	(1)	Status (A=Active; D=Deleted)

INVTRAN (Projects 3 and 7)

1–1	TRNTYP	(1)	Transaction type (I,R,T,A)
2–8	TRNPNO	(7.0)	Part# (key)
9–14	TRNQTY	(6.0)	Quantity xxxxxx

LOANS (Project 6)

1–7	LNNUM	(7.0)	Loan# (key)
8–17	LNAMT	(10.2)	Amount of loan xxxxxxxx.xx
18–23	LNDUE	(6.0)	Date due

ORDMAST (Project 10)

1–6	ORDNUM	(6.0)	Order# (key)
7–12	ORDPNO	(6.0)	Part#
13–18	ORDQTY	(6.0)	Quantity ordered
19–24	ORDSHP	(6.0)	Quantity shipped
25–30	ORDDTE	(6.0)	Date ordered

ORDREQS (Project 10)

1–6	ORDREQ	(6.0)	Requested order#

SALES (Projects 5, 8, and 9)

1–3	SALCO#	(3.0)	Company#
4–6	SALLOC	(3.0)	Store location code (key 1)
7–12	SALDAT	(6.0)	Date of sale
13–13	SALDAY	(1.0)	Day of week (1=Monday, etc.)
14–21	SALITM	(8.0)	Item#
22–26	SALQTY	(5.0)	Quantity xxxxx
27–33	SALUPR	(7.2)	Unit price xxxxx.xx
34–38	SALREP	(5.0)	Sales representative# (key 2)
39–42	SALCM1	(4.2)	Commission rate 1 xx.xx
43–46	SALCM2	(4.2)	Commission rate 2 xx.xx

SALESUMM (Project 9) (Output record only)

1–8	SUMITM	(8)	Item# (key)
9–44	SUMQTY	(6.0)	Quantity array for 6 months
45–92	SUMAMT	(8.2)	Sales amount array for 6 months

FILE FORMATS FOR STUDENT FILES ■

(This file is to be created by the student.)

SALEHEAD (non-keyed file) (Project 12)

1–6	Sale date	Numeric
7–9	Store#	Numeric
10–13	Register#	Numeric
14–20	Transaction#	Numeric
21–25	Quantity	Zero decimals
26–32	Unit price	Two decimals
33–38	Discount amount	Two decimals
39–41	Salesperson	Numeric
42–42	Code	Alphanumeric
43–45	Transaction type	Alphanumeric

Index

Addition, 30
ADD operation, 30, 35
Alphabetic fields, 37
   comparing, 56–57
Alphameric fields. *See* Alphanumeric fields
Alphanumeric fields
   comparing, 56–57
   MOVE operation and, 138
Alternating tables, 164
   Calculation Specifications, 164–166
   Input Specifications, 164
   Output Specifications, 166
   sample program, 164–166
ANDxx operations, 327
Argument fields, 151
   defining, 153–154, 161
Argument table, 148
Arithmetic calculations, 29–36
   addition, 30
   division, 32–33
   multiplication, 31
   sample program, 36–46
   subtraction, 31
Arithmetic functions, 29–36
Arithmetic operations, 324
Arrays, 176, 181
   accessing, 181, 193–195
   Calculation Specifications, 192
   compile time arrays, 177–178, 183, 191
   constructing, 176
   cross-footing, 201
   examples, 177
   exception output, 193
   execution time arrays, 180, 184–189, 191
   Extension Specifications, 177
   indexes, 181, 193–195
   loading, 177–180
   LOKUP operation, 197–202
   MOVEA operation, 201–202, 205–207
   naming, 181
   operations for, 201–202
   pre-execution time arrays, 179, 184
   printing, 184
   searching, 197–202
   SORTA operation, 201–202
   sorts, 479
   XFOOT operation, 201, 203–205
ASCII format, 61
AS OF date, 111

Backup files, 219
Batch processing, 378–379
BEGSR operation, 68
Binary data, 270
BITOF operation, 274–275
BITON operation, 274–275
Bits, testing value of, 274–275
*BLANK, 324
Blank After, 84, 90, 107–109
Blank bucket, 139
Blanks, 57
   initializing fields to, 139
Blocking factor, 221–222
Blocking records, 221–222
Block length, 10, 221
Branching. *See also* GOTO operation
   within calculations, 67–69
   using subroutines, 68–69

CABxx operation, 334
Calculation lines, comments on, 39
Calculation operation codes summary, 498–499
Calculation Specifications, 38–40, 66, 82
   alternating tables, 164–166
   arrays, 192
   coding, 29–36
   exception output processing, 126–127
   external tables, 162
   internal tables, 156
   multiple level breaks, 100–102
Calculation Specifications form, 29–36
Called programs, 336–338
   passing parameters, 337
   receiving parameters, 337
   returning to calling program, 338
CALL operation, 336–338
Card processing anomalies, 500–501

Cards, 8
Case structure (CASxx), 334–335
CHAIN operation, 250–251
   versus READ operation, 355–356
Character (C), 64
Clearing fields, 84
CLOSE command, 365
Codd, Edgar, 480
Coding, 3–4
   Calculation Specifications, 29–36
   Data Description Specifications (DDS), 381–383
   formats, 6–8
   forms, 8
Collating sequence, 61
   chart, 497
Column headings, 42
Command keys, 380, 410–411
Command languages, 278
Comment field, 154, 161
Comments, 17–19, 409
   on calculation lines, 39
Compare and branch operation (CABxx), 334
Compare function, 54
Compare operation, 56–62
   alphabetic fields, 56–57
   alphanumeric fields, 56–57
   collating sequence, 61
   literals, 61–62
   numeric fields, 57–61
Compiler, 20
Compile time arrays, 177–178, 183, 191
Compile time tables. *See* Internal tables
Compiling, 15, 20–23
   table information, 155
Constants, 34–35
Control breaks. *See* Level breaks
Control level indicators, 80–84
Control program facility (CPF), 301, 304
Control Specifications, 6–9
COUNT field, 134
CPF (control program facility), 301, 304

Cross-footing, 201
Cross-reference tables, 148
Cumulative totals, 35
   methods for developing, 100–102
Cycle. *See* Fixed logic cycle
Cylinders, 244

DASD. *See* Direct access storage devices
Data areas, 483
Data Description Specifications (DDS), 303–304, 381, 404–411
   coding, 381–383
   command keys, 410
   externally defined files, 303–304
   key words, 405–410
   RPG III/400, 303–304
   updating on-line files, 404–411
Data editing, 404
Data file descriptions, file format names for, 309
Data operations, editing, 272–274
Data structures, 314–315, 483–487
   data areas, 483
   file information data structure (INFDS), 485
   multiple occurrence data structure, 484–485
   program status data structure, 485–487
DDS. *See* Data Description Specifications
Debugging, 284–286
   RPG III/400, 388–389
Decimal data, 270
Decimal positions, 59–61
DEFN operation, 339–340
DELET operation, 368
Detail amounts, printing, 188–189
Detail lines, 14, 42
Detail time, 84
Device, 10–11
Digit only (D), 64
Direct access storage devices (DASD), 242–246
   direct file organization, 246
   file organization on, 244–246
   indexed file organization, 245
   sequential file organization, 245
Direct file organization, 246
Disk access, 243–244
Disk packs, 243–244
Display files
   describing, 380
   file format names for, 311
Division, 32–33
DIV operation, 32
Documentation, xvii, 3, 17–19, 303, 492
Dollar signs, editing, 44–45

DO loops, 330–333, 488–489
DOUxx operation (Do Until), 330–332
DOWxx operation (Do While), 330–332
DSPATR key word, 405
DSPLY operation, 286–287

EBCDIC format, 61
Edit codes, 44, 113
Editing
   data, 404
   data operations, 272–274
   dollar signs, 44–45
   fields, 42–43
   on-screen data, 404
Edit words, 114–115
EDTCDE key word, 406
EDTWRD key word, 406
Efficiency. *See* Programming efficiency
ELSE operation, 326
End position, 15
ENDSR operation, 68
ERRMSG key word, 406
Error messages, 64, 402, 406
Errors, 64, 163–164, 485–487, 492
Exception output labels, 356
Exception output processing, 125–128
   arrays, 193
   Calculation Specifications, 126–127
   File Description Specifications, 125
   Input Specifications, 125
   labels, 356–357
   moving data, 135–139
   Output Specifications, 128
   page overflow, 128–134
Exception updating, 365
EXCPT operation, 125–128, 356–357
Execution time arrays, 180, 184–189, 191
   calculating level totals, 187–188
   defining and loading, 184–187
   printing detail amounts, 188–189
   printing level totals, 189
EXFMT operation, 384–386
EXIT operation, 280–281
EXSR operation, 68
Extension Specifications
   arrays, 177
   external tables, 161
   internal tables, 152–154
   table processing, 151
External indicators, 276–278, 280
Externally defined files
   changes in, 303
   Data Description Specifications (DDS), 303–304
   documentation, 303
   File Description Specifications, 305
   Input Specifications, 306
   naming conventions, 302

   programmer productivity, 302
External subroutines, 280–281
External switches, 276–278, 280
External tables, 151, 156
   Calculation Specifications, 162
   Extension Specifications, 161
   File Description Specifications, 160
   file maintenance, 162
   Input Specifications, 161
   Output Specifications, 162
   Record Layout, 158–161
   sample program, 158–162

Fetch overflow, 129
Field attributes, defining, 338–340
Field record relationship indicators, 64–65, 279
Fields, 8
   clearing, 84
   editing, 42–43
   initializing to blanks, 139
   location of, 13
   moving with MOVE, 136
   moving with MOVEL, 136–137
   names, 13–14, 290
   redefinition of, 313
   renaming, 365
   resetting to zero, 135–139
File descriptions, 17
File Description Specifications, 6–8, 11–12, 37, 81
   exception output processing, 125
   externally defined files, 305
   external tables, 160
   indexed files, 247
   sequential file processing, 226–227
File Description Specifications form, 9–11
   defining input file, 9
   defining output file, 11
   device, 10
   file designation, 10
   file format, 10
   file type, 10
   record length, 10
File design, 480–482
File format names
   data file descriptions, 309
   display file descriptions, 311
File formats
   File Description Specifications, 10
   indexed files, 246
File information data structure (INFDS), 485
File key, 351–353
File maintenance, 223–225
   external tables, 162
   indexed files, 252–253
File members, 311–312
Filenames, 9, 11–12, 14, 289

File organization, 313
Files. *See also* Externally defined files;
    File sequence; Subfiles
  on direct access storage devices,
    244–246
  normalized, 480–482
  in RPG III/400, 301
  types, 217–219
File sequence, 475–480
  array sorts, 479
  joined files, 477–479
  logical files, 476
  open query files, 479
  physical files, 476
  summarized data, 480
File type, 10–11
Final totals, 40
Fixed logic cycle, 15–17, 103–109,
    124–125
  effect on level breaks, 85–87
Flags. *See* Indicators
Flowcharts, 17
FORCE operation, 283
Formats
  renaming, 364–365
  for screens, 379–380
Form type, 11–12
From-to entries, 13
Full functional file processing, 349
Function field, 151
  defining, 154, 161
Function keys, 380, 410–411

GOTO operation, 67, 69, 126–127,
    488–490

Half-adjusting, 33–34
Halt indicators, 276, 280
Heading content, 41–42
Heading lines, 40
  line spacing for, 40
Headings. *See* Report headings
History files, 219
*HIVAL, 355

IBM AS/400, 299
IBM System/38, 299
If...then...else, 325–330
  ANDxx operations, 327
  IFxx operations, 326
  indicators with IFxx, 326
  nested IFxx statements, 329–330
  ORxx operations, 328
  selection with multiple alternative
    conditions, 328
  selection with multiple conditions,
    327
IFxx operations, 326
Indexed files, 181
  accessing multiple files, 287–288

adding records, 253
chaining to, 250–251
changing fields, 253
creating, 246–249
deleting records, 253
File Description Specifications, 247
file formats, 246
file maintenance, 252–253
Input Specifications, 247–248
inquiry programs, 249–253
multiple indexes, 309, 362–365
organization, 245
Output Specifications, 248–249
printed output from, 251
record address files, 258–261
Record Layout, 246
reorganizing files, 253
sequential retrieval, 258
updating, 253–256
Indexed sequential processing, 243
Indexes, 181, 193–195
Indicators, 39, 55, 333, 336, 490,
    492–493
  control level, 80–84
  external, 276–278, 280
  external switches, 276–278
  field record relationship, 64–65, 279
  halt indicators, 276, 280
  with IFxx, 326
  input, 62–64
  last record (LR), 280
  level, 80–84
  level break, 279
  matching record (MR), 228, 279
  output, 14, 41
  overflow, 37, 41, 279
  record identification, 12–13, 279
Indicator Summary form, 19
INFDS (file information data structure), 485
Initialization, 489
Initializing fields, 139
IN operation, 483
Input data, 36
Input devices, 10
Input files, 3
  defining, 9
Input format, 3
Input indicators, 62–64
Input Specifications, 6–8, 37–38, 81
  alternating tables, 164
  exception output processing, 125
  externally defined files, 306
  external tables, 161
  indexed files, 247–248
  multiple level breaks, 98–99
  sequential file processing, 227
Input Specifications Form, 11–13
  field location, 13
  field name, 13

filename, 11–12
form type, 11–12
from-to entries, 13
record identification indicator,
    12–13
sequence number option, 12
Inquiry programs, 380
  chaining to indexed file, 250–251
  indexed files, 249–253
  sample program, 250–253
Interactive applications, 383–384
Interactive programs, 378–380
Inter-block gap, 222
Intermediate level breaks, 99
Internal tables, 151–152
  Calculation Specifications, 156
  compiling table information, 155
  Extension Specifications, 152–154
  Record Layout, 154
  sample program, 152–156
Inter-record gap, 221
Invalid records, 64, 67

Joined files, 477–479

K edit code, 43
Keyed files, 308
Key field, 223, 245
Keypunched cards, 8
Key words
  Data Description Specifications
    (DDS), 405–410
  subfiles, 448–449, 458–459
KFLD operation, 351–353
KLIST statement, 351–353

Last record indicator (LR), 280
Level break indicators, 279
Level breaks
  control level indicators, 80–84
  effect of RPG cycle, 85–87
  methods for developing, 100–102
  in RPG III/400, 358
  sample program, 79–84
  sequence of input data, 79–80
  totals, 80
Level indicators, 80–84
Level totals, 187–189
Line Counter Specifications, 269–270
Line counting, 134
Line spacing, 40
Literals, 41–42
  comparing, 61–62
  moving, 138
Local data area (LDA), 483
Logical files, 306–309, 476. *See also*
    Joined files
Logical operations, 54
Logical views. *See* Logical files
Logic concepts, 54

Logic function, 54
LOKUP operation, 156
  arrays and, 197–202
Look-ahead feature, 282
Loops, 67, 126–127
  arrays and, 193–195
  DO loops, 330–333, 488–489
LR (last record indicator), 280

Major level breaks, 99
Master files, 218, 223–225
Matching record indicator (MR), 228, 279
Media, 9
Minor level breaks, 99
MOVEA operation, 201–202, 205–207
MOVEL operation, 135–139
  alphanumeric fields and, 138
  fields and, 136–137
  numeric fields and, 138
MOVE operation, 135–139
  alphanumeric fields and, 138
  fields and, 136
  numeric fields and, 138
Move zone operations, 272
Moving data, 135–139
  alphanumeric/numeric, 138
  exception output processing, 135–139
  fields, 136–137
  initializing field to blanks, 139
  literals, 138
  with MOVE, 136
  with MOVEL, 136–137
MR (matching record) indicator, 228, 279
Multiple indexes, 309, 362–365
  renaming fields, 365
  renaming formats, 364–365
Multiple level breaks, 98–103
  Calculation Specifications, 100–102
  Input Specifications, 98–99
  Output Specifications, 103
Multiple occurrence data structure, 484–485
Multiple output files, 89–90
Multiple record types, 62–66
Multiple screen formats, 425
Multiple subfiles, 460–461
Multiple tables, 166
Multiplication, 31
MULT operation, 31
MVR operation, 33

Named data areas, 483
Naming conventions, 289–290
  externally defined files, 302
  field names, 290
  file names, 289
  program names, 289

Negative values, 61
Nested IFxx statements, 329–330
Normalized files, 480–482
Numeric fields, 37
  comparing, 57–61
  MOVEL operation and, 138
  MOVE operation and, 138
  packed decimal format, 232–233

Object module, 15, 20
OCUR operation, 484–485
OF entry, 37
On-line file update. *See* Updating on-line files
On-line processing
  versus batch processing, 378–379
  concepts, 380
On-screen data editing, 404
OPEN command, 365
Open query files, 479
Operational instructions, 17
Operation codes, 29
OPNQRYF command, 479
ORxx operations, 328
OUT operation, 483
Output data, 36–37
Output files, 3
  defining, 11
  multiple, 89–90
  summarized, 87–89
Output indicators, 14, 41
Output report format, 3
Output Specifications, 6–8, 40–42, 83–84
  alternating tables, 166
  exception output processing, 128
  external tables, 162
  indexed files, 248–249
  multiple level breaks, 103
  sequential file processing, 229–231
Output Specifications form, 14–15
Output timing, 124–125
Overflow indicators, 37, 41, 279

Packed decimal data, 231–233, 270
Padding blanks, 57
PAGE field, 113
Page numbers, 111, 113
Page overflow, 41
  exception output processing, 128–134
  fetch overflow, 129
  internal control, 134
  sample program, 130–132
Parameters, called programs and, 337
PARM operation, 281, 337
Permanent logical files, 476
Physical file descriptions for files available on diskette, 502–504
Physical files, 306–309, 476

Positive values, 61
Pre-execution time arrays, 179, 184
Pre-execution time tables. *See* External tables
Primary file, 10
Printer layout charts, 17
Printer output, 9
Printer spacing, 4, 14–15, 40, 41
Printing
  arrays, 184
  detail amounts, 188–189
  from indexed files, 251
  level totals, 189
  tables, 166
PRINT key word, 407
Processing cycle, creating, 356
Program compilation, xiii–xiv
Program errors, 64, 485–487, 492
Program loops, 67, 126–127. *See also* DO loops
Programming, xi–xvii
Programming efficiency, 302
  data structures, 483–487
  file design, 480–482
  file sequence, 475–480
  programming tools, 491–493
  structured programming, 488–490
Programming languages, ix
Programming tools, 491–493
Program names, 8
  conventions, 289
Program narratives, 17
Programs
  compiling, 20–23
  processing steps, 4–5
Program status data structure, 485–487
Program testing, xiv–xv
Protective line, 64
Pseudocode, 17
Punched cards, 8

Quotation marks, 41

Random access processing, 242–246
Range cross-reference tables, 149
RANGE key word, 407
RA (record address) files, 258–261
READC operation, 456–458
READE operation, 355
READ operation, 284, 350, 353, 429
  versus CHAIN operation, 355–356
READP operation, 354–355
Read time, 84
Record address files, 258–261
Record blocking, 221–222
Record identification indicators, 12–13, 279

Record Layout, 13
   external tables, 158–161
   indexed files, 246
   internal tables, 154
   sequential file processing, 225–226
Record length, 10–11
Records
   adding to a file, 367
   blocking, 221–222
   deleting from a file, 368
   invalid, 64, 67
   multiple, 62–66
   updating, 223–225, 367
REFFLD key word, 409
REF key word, 408
Related tables, 148–149
Remainders, 32–33
Report dates, 111
Report detail, 42
Report format, standards for, 110–112
Report headings
   for columns, 112
   edit codes, 113
   edit words, 114–115
   page number, 113
   report identification, 112
   report title, 111–112
   sample program, 112–115
   standards for, 110–112
   system date, 113
   system time, 114–115
Report identification, 111, 112
Report time, 112
Report title, 41, 111–112
Report totals, 112
REQUEST format, 384–386
Reserved words, 29, 324
Resetting to zero, 84, 135–139
Resulting indicators, 279
RETRN operation, 338
Reversing signs, 274
Right justification, 10
RLABL operation, 281
Rolling totals, 101
Rounding, 33–34
RPG cycle, 103–109
   effect on level breaks, 85–87
   group indication, 104–106
   zeroing out a total field, 107–109
RPG overview, ix–xi
RPG III/400, 299–300
   accessing files, 353–356
   adding records, 367
   arithmetic operations, 324
   calculation enhancements, 323
   Data Description Specifications (DDS), 303–304
   data structures, 314–315
   debugging, 388–389
   deleting records, 368
   dynamic open and close of files, 365
   exception output labels, 356
   exception updating, 365
   externally defined files, 302–303, 305–306
   field attributes, 338–340
   field redefinition, 313
   file concepts, 301
   file format names, 309–311
   file members, 311–312
   full functional file processing, 349–353
   level breaks, 358
   logical files, 306–309
   multiple indexes, 362–365
   physical files, 306–309
   processing cycle, 356
   reserved words, 324
   retrieving records, 353–356
   structured programming, 325–340
   updating records, 367
RUN date, 111

SAA (system application architecture), 300
Screen design, 381, 400–402
Screen Design Aid (SDA), 381
Screen file, accessing, 384–386, 416–418
Screen formats, 379–380
   describing, 414
   multiple, 425
Sequence, 79–80, 154
   collating, 61
   sequential file processing, 228
Sequence number option, 12
Sequential files, 220–221
   File Description Specifications, 226–227
   Input Specifications, 227
   matching record indicator (MR), 228
   organization, 245
   Output Specifications, 229–231
   reading, using SETLL and READ, 350
   Record Layout, 225–226
   sample program, 225–231
   sequence checking, 228
   updating, 223–225
SETGT operation, 354–355
SETLL operation, 350, 353, 355
Signs, reversing, 274
Simple tables, 148
SORTA operation, 201–202
Sorts
   arrays, 479
   data, 79–80

   files, 476
Space entry, 14
Spacing, 14–15
Special characters, 61
Special words, 29
Specification forms, 3
Standardization, 300, 302
Storage devices. *See* Direct access storage devices
Structured iteration, 330–332
Structured programming, 68–69, 109, 488–490
   calling a program from within a program, 336–338
   case structure (CASxx), 334–335
   compare and branch operation (CABxx), 334
   Do While versus Do Until, 332
   field attributes, 338–340
   indicators, 333, 336
   setting flags, 336
   structured iteration (DO loops), 330–332
   structured selection (if...then...else), 325–330
Structured Query Language (SQL), 381
Structured selection, 325–330
Subfiles, 446–447, 492
   accessing specific records, 459–460
   clearing, 452–454
   defining in Data Description Specifications (DDS), 448
   describing, 450
   displaying, 454
   exiting to other screens or programs, 461
   file updates, 456–458
   key words, 448–449, 458–459
   loading with data, 451–452
   managing, 458–459
   multiple subfiles, 460–461
   page size, 459
   READC operation, 456–458
   record format, 448
   sample inquiry program, 447–458
   size of, 459
SUB operation, 31
Subroutines, 488–490
   branching with, 68–69
   external, 280–281
Subtraction, 31
Summarized data, 480
Summarized output files, 87–89
Summary reports, 87
Switches, external, 276–278, 280
System application architecture (SAA), 300
System date, 113
System time, 114–115

Table applications, 148–149
Table files, 218
    errors in, 163–164
    formats, 151
    maintenance, 162
    timing of, 163
Table processing
    benefits of, 149–150
    Extension Specifications, 151
Tables, 148–149. *See also* External tables; Internal tables
    alternating, 164
    compiling, 155
    multiple, 166
    printing, 166
    types, 151
TAG line, 67
Tape mark, 221
Tape media, 220–223
    processing master file, 223
    record blocking, 221–222
    sequential file processing, 220–221
Temporary logical files, 476
TESTB operation, 274–275
Test numeric operation, 273–274
Test zone operation, 272–273

TESTZ operation, 272–273
TEXT key word, 409
TIME operation, 114
Total field, zeroing out, 107–109
Total lines, 45–46
Totals, 80
Total time, 84
Transaction files, 218, 223–225
    matching record logic, 224–225
Truncation, 30
Two-table search, 164–166
TYME field name, 114
Type entry, 14

UDATE, 113
ULABL operation, 281
UNLCK operation, 483
Update programs, 380
Updating files, 223–225
    indexed files, 253–256
    sequential files, 223–225
    using exception updating, 365
Updating on-line files
    accessing screen file, 416–418
    Data Description Specifications (DDS), 404–411
    describing screen format, 414
    multiple screen formats, 425
    on-screen data editing, 404
    READ operation, 429
    sample program, 412–418
    screen design, 400–402
    WRITE operation, 429
UPDAT operation, 367
User manuals, 17

VALUES key word, 410

Workstation files, 450
WRITE operation, 367, 429

XFOOT operation, 201, 203–205

Z-ADD operation, 107–109, 138
*ZERO, 324
Zero, resetting to, 84, 135–139
Zeroing out a total field, 107–109
Zoned decimal format, 231
Zone only (Z), 64
Z-SUB operation code, 107